CHILDREN'S WORLD

CHILDREN'S WORLD

GROWING UP IN RUSSIA, 1890–1991

Catriona Kelly

YALE UNIVERSITY PRESS
NEW HAVEN AND LONDON

For information about this and other Yale University Press publications, please contact:

U.S. Office: sales.press@yale.edu   www.yalebooks.com
Europe Office: sales @yaleup.co.uk   www.yaleup.co.uk

Set in Caslon by Carnegie Book Production, Lancaster
Printed in Great Britain by TJ International, Padstow

Library of Congress Cataloging-in-Publication Data
Kelly, Catriona.
    Children's world: growing up in Russia, 1890–1991 / Catriona Kelly
       p. cm.
    Includes bibliographical references and index.
    ISBN 978–0–300–11226–9 (alk. paper)
    1. Children—Soviet Union—Social conditions.   2. Children—Russia—
    Social conditions.   I. Title.
    HQ792.S65K45 2007
    305.23094709'04—dc22
                                                              2007012118

A catalogue record for this book is available from the British Library

10 9 8 7 6 5 4 3 2 1

For Alex, Millie, and William

Contents

Illustrations

The material here comes from a variety of genres and could be the subject of a 'sources study' in its own right. Not simply the obviously artistic images, but also the apparently documentary materials have their own specific representational ambitions. For example, the photographs now held in the Central State Archive of Cinematic and Photographic Documents in St Petersburg were mostly originally taken by LenTass news agency photographers for Soviet newspapers (and hence show very little of the human tragedy of the Blockade). Even family photographs have obvious ritual and commemorative functions and do not simply record the everyday. Thus, photographs as well as drawings and paintings are part of ideology on the one hand, and also of the practices of memory captured by the oral history that I have used, as well as in written memoirs.

Chapter 2: Pioneers and Pet-Keepers, 1917–1935

Chapter 3: Thank You, Dear Comrade Stalin, for a Happy Childhood!', 1935–1953

Chapter 10: Nursery Days

Chapter 11: In Their Own Time

Chapter 12: Years of School

Conclusion: The End of Childhood?

Acknowledgements

This book has taken time to write – roughly as much as the actual process of raising a child to the age of starting school in the early Soviet era. Over the years that it took to research, I have been fortunate in the generous help that I have been given by individuals and by institutions. Not everyone can be listed here by name. The many informants who took part in the oral history project are, for reasons of professional ethics, necessarily anonymous, as are those of my Russian friends and indeed chance acquaintances who contributed, often spontaneously, fascinating details about their own childhood years. One does not always learn the names of people who ask questions or make comments at guest seminars, lectures, or conferences. I would like to thank all the many people who are not precisely identified very warmly, and assure them that my gratitude is just as great as it is to the people and institutions that are acknowledged directly. Of course, there is no sense in which anyone mentioned should be held responsible for any error of fact or recalcitrance of opinion remaining in the finished book; as the eminent bibliographer, John Simmons, was wont to say, 'there is always some mistake', and this (or these) ought always to be laid at the author's door.

The award of a research grant by the Leverhulme Trust (F/08736/A, 'Childhood in Russia: A Social and Cultural History', 2003–2006) – which supported the salary of a post-doctoral research assistant, the costs of interviewing in St Petersburg, Moscow, and elsewhere, and the organisation of a conference, Generations in Europe, held at New College, Oxford, in April 2005 – was essential to work on this book. Polly Jones, now Lecturer in Russian at the School of Slavonic and East European Studies, University College, London, who acted as my post-doctoral research assistant during the first year of the project, worked on an article about children and the Second World War cult, and also provided me with valuable material from *Pravda* and *Izvestiya* in the 1950s and early 1960s, as well as carrying out work in the State Archive of the Russian Federation (GARF) and in the archive of the United Nations in New York, and supplying some of the material from the Party and city archives in Sverdlovsk/Ekaterinburg (GASO and TsDOO SO) that is cited here. Andy Byford, who took over from Polly for the second and third years of the grant, searched the entire runs of *Nedelya* and *Ogonek* for the 1960s, provided some of the materials on Russian education, and contributed expertise from his own work on Russian child psychology in the early twentieth century. Polly and Andy also collaborated on the organisation of an international conference on Russian education, Study, Study, and Study! in May 2004, and Andy helped with running Generations in Europe. I am deeply grateful to them both for their hard work, enthusiasm, and good fellowship while the project was in progress.

The interviewing project in Russia drew on the time and effort of a large number of people, all of whom contributed greatly to its success. The interviewing work itself was carried out by Aleksandra Piir (in St Petersburg), Svetlana Sirotinina (in Perm'), Oksana Filicheva, Veronika Makarova, and Ekaterina Mel'nikova (in north-western Russian villages), Yuliya Rybina and Ekaterina Shumilina (in Moscow), and Yury Ryzhov and Lyubov' Terekhova (in Taganrog). I am particularly grateful to Aleksandra Piir, who was extraordinarily proactive in seeking out informants and suggesting lines to follow up; in collaboration with Elena Liarskaya, she also collected some of the material from the Central State Archive (TsGA) in St Peterburg that I have cited. In Moscow, Vitaly Bezrogov helped organise interviewing, and also generously shared materials from interviewing projects carried out by his home institution, and by colleagues in Nizhny-Novgorod. Al'bert Baiburin helped draft the questionnaires that were used for interviewing, as well as putting me in touch with interviewers, and provided much practical and intellectual help with work for the book generally, as well as criticism, friendship, and bracing injections of his inimitably sardonic humour. I owe him more than I can say.

Among institutions in Russia and elsewhere, I am grateful to the British Academy, which provided support through its Small Research Grant, Conference Grant, and Academic Exchange programmes; to the University of Oxford, which allocated moneys through the Ilchester Fund and Modern Language Faculty research grants; to New College, Oxford; and to the European University, St Petersburg, which has been a constant source of intellectual and practical support during my many research visits over the past years. A year's Special Leave, supported by the Humanities Division of the University of Oxford and the Higher Education Funding Council of England and Wales, was vital to the completion of the project. I would also like to thank my colleagues at New College and the University of Oxford for their help and encouragement, and Philip Bullock and Emily Lygo, who took over my teaching while I was on sabbatical. At the Taylor Institution Library, Oxford, gratitude goes in particular to Nick Hearn and Richard Ramage, and at the Bodleian Library, to Angelina Gibson. In Russia, unstinting help was given by the staffs of the many libraries and archives in which I worked: RAO NA, RGASPI, TsKhDMO and the Russian State Library in Moscow, RGIA, TsGA, TsGALI, TsGIA, TsAKFD and the Russian National Library in St Petersburg, and GASO and TsDOO SO in Ekaterinburg. My warm thanks also to the staff of the European University, St Petersburg, particularly the Rector, Nikolai Vakhtin, the Dean and Secretary of the Ethnology Faculty, Il'ya Utekhin and Elena Kokorina, and Alla Sokolova of the Centre for Jewish History.

Heartfelt thanks are offered to those who have read and commented on drafts of the book. At different stages, Steve Smith, Stephen Lovell, Gerry

Smith, Barbara Heldt, Al'bert Baiburin, and Nikolai Vakhtin read material that is incorporated here. Maria Khotimsky, Andy Byford, and Evgeny Dobrenko all read complete drafts; I would especially like to thank Evgeny for his enthusiastic but rigorous comments, which contributed a great deal to the coherence of the whole. I also had very valuable suggestions from different *kollektivy* with whom material was discussed: the audiences at the Russian History Workshop, University of Chicago; at a Slavic Department seminar, Northwestern University; and at seminars at the Davis Center, Harvard University; the Bakhtin Centre, University of Sheffield; the Russian Department, Bristol University; the Russian Department at my former workplace, the School of Slavonic Studies, University of London (now part of University College London); and a variety of different audiences at the annual conferences of the American Association for the Advancement of Slavic Studies. Valuable response of a 'virtual' kind was provided by participants in a written round-table discussion of my article "'The School Waltz'", published in *Antropologicheskii forum/Forum for Anthropology and Culture* in 2006. Among those who have made suggestions for lines to follow up, or loaned materials, or made gifts of books, or copies of manuscripts, I would particularly like to thank Mel Bach, Birgit Beumers, Konstantin Bogdanov, Ben Eklof, Karen Hewitt, Larry Holmes, the late Lindsey Hughes, David King, Mariya Osorina, David Ransel, Alim Sabitov, Maksim Shrayer, Nick Stargardt, Jurij Striedter, Polina Vakhtina, Aleksandr Zholkovsky, Irina Zorina, and, once again, Al'bert Baiburin, Vitaly Bezrogov, Evgeny Dobrenko, and Aleksandra Piir. Mikhail Leonovich Gasparov encouraged the idea of writing a history of childhood from the beginning, and presented me with a copy of his memoirs as a stimulus. It is a great sadness that he has not lived to see the finished book.

Some of the material that appears here was originally published in different form in a variety of journal articles and book chapters, including Simon Franklin and Emma Widdis, *National Identity in Russia* (Cambridge: Cambridge University Press, 2004); Polly Jones, Jan C. Behrends, and E. A. Rees (eds), *The Leader Cult in Communist Dictatorships* (Basingstoke: Palgrave, 2005); Eric Naiman and Christina Kiaer, *Everyday Life in Revolutionary Russia* (Indiana University Press, 2006); *Novoe literaturnoe obozrenie* (Moscow); *Antropologicheskii forum/Forum for Anthropology and Culture* (St Petersburg); the working paper series of the Program on Eastern European Cultures and Societies (NTNU, Trondheim); *Slavic and East European Journal*; and *Sotsial'naya istoriya: Ezhegodnik* (Moscow). The paragraphs on the Beilis case in Chapter 1 draw in part on Chapter 4 of my *Comrade Pavlik: The Rise and Fall of a Soviet Boy Hero* (London: Granta, 2005). My acknowledgements go to all the editors and publishers concerned, and also to everyone at Yale University Press, particularly Robert Baldock, for their interest in the idea and their expertise in putting the book through the production process.

I have also incurred many debts of a more personal kind, for help, hospitality, and friendship during my visits to Russia and elsewhere, and I would particularly like to thank Sheila Fitzpatrick and Andrew Wachtel in Chicago, Svetlana Boym, Stephanie Sandler, and Julie Buckler in Cambridge, MA, David Shepherd and Jeffrey Denton in Sheffield, György Péteri and Knut Grimstad in Norway, Katya and Oleg Borisovich Golynkin, and Sasha Zhuravlyov in London and St Petersburg, Mariya Alekshina, Sergei and Vadim Alekshin, and Nadezhda Borisovna Kudrevich in St Petersburg, the staff of the Norwegian University Center in St Petersburg, Al'bin Konechnyi and Ksana Kumpan in St Petersburg, Lidiya Sazonova and Mikhail Robinson, Natasha, Irina Mikhailovna and Lev Nikitych Pushkarev, Marlena Sergeevna Simonova, Natasha Dvortsina, and Veronika Arkad'evna Pankratova in Moscow, and Elena, Tamara Pavlovna, and Mikhail Efimovich Glavatsky in Ekaterinburg.

Given the subject of the book, it seems specially appropriate to end by thanking the different members of my own family, particularly my mother, Margaret Kelly, my husband, Ian Thompson, my sister and brother-in-law, Alison Moncrieff Kelly-Johnston, and my niece and nephews, Alexander and Camilla Davan Wetton and William Johnston, who, at fourteen, ten, and eleven are probably not old enough yet to read this book, but to whom it is dedicated, in the hope that one day they may.

Oxford, June 2006

Abbreviations and Conventions of Style

For the sake of convenience, journals which ran under a number of different titles at different periods are listed under just one title.

Alekseev	M. Alekseev, *Karyukha. Drachuny* (M., 1988).
BM	*Blagotvoritel'nost' i miloserdie: istoriko-dokumental'noe izdanie* (*Philanthropy and Charity: A Historical Anthology of Documents*, SPb., 2000).
BME (edn 2)	*Bol'shaya meditsinskaya entsiklopediya* (*Great Medical Encyclopaedia*, 36 vols; M., 1956–64).
BME (edn 3)	*Bol'shaya meditsinskaya entsiklopediya* (30 vols; M.: Sovetskaya entsiklopediya, 1974–81).
BNKP	*Byulleten' Narkomprosa* (*Bulletin of Narkompros*, M. 1920–30).
BNKZ	*Byulleten' Narkomzdrava* (*Bulletin of Narkomzdrav*, M., 1922–27).
BNKVD	*Byulleten' NKVD* (*Bulletin of the NKVD*, M., 1921–30).
BSE (edn 1)	*Bol'shaya sovetskaya entsiklopediya* (*Great Soviet Encyclopaedia*, 65 vols.; M., 1926–1946).
BSE (edn 2)	*Bol'shaya sovetskaya entsiklopediya* (51 vols; M., 1949–65).
BSE (edn 3)	*Bol'shaya sovetskaya entsiklopediya* (30 vols; M., 1969–81).
BURI	*Blagotvoritel'nye uchrezhdeniya Rossiiskoi Imperii* (*Philanthropic Institutions of the Russian Empire*, 2 vols; SPb., 1900).
BVR	*Blagotvoritel'nost' v Rossii* (*Philanthropy in Russia*, 3 vols; SPb., 1907).
CKI	Informal interviews (recorded in note form, not taped) carried out by Catriona Kelly. The identifier is followed by a place code, 'M.' for Moscow, and 'SPb.' for St Petersburg.
CKQ	Taped and transcribed interviews carried out by Catriona Kelly. The identifier is followed by a place code, 'E.' for Ekaterinburg, 'M.' for Moscow, 'Ox' for the UK, and 'SPb.' for St Petersburg.
DD	*Drug detei* (*Children's Friend*, M., 1925–33).
DG	S. S. Vilensky, A. I. Kokurin, G. V. Atmashkina, and I. Yu. Novichenko (eds.), *Deti GULaga, 1918–1956* (*Children of the Gulag* (M., 2002).
DoshV	*Doshkol'noe vospitanie* (*Pre-School Education*, Kiev, 1911–17).
DPF	A. N. Martynova (ed.), *Detskii poeticheskii fol'klor* (SPb., 1997).
DRE	L. Petrusheva (ed.), *Deti russkoi emigratsii* (M., 1997).

DSV	*Dekrety sovetskoi vlasti* (*Decrees of the Soviet Government*, M., 1957—).
DV	*Doshkol'noe vospitanie* (M.: 1928—).
Engel and Posadskaya-Vanderbeck	B. A. Engel and A. Posadskaya-Vanderbeck (eds), *A Revolution of their Own Views of Women in Soviet History* (Boulder, CO, 1998).
ENKP	*Ezhenedel'nik Narkomprosa* (*Narkompros Weekly*, M., 1922–48) (also ran in some years as *Byulleten' Narkomprosa*; *Narkompros: Prikazy i instruktsii*, etc.).
ES	*Entsiklopedicheskii slovar* (*Encyclopaedic Dictionary*, 41 plus 4 suppl. vols; SPb., 1890–1907).
GARF	Gosudarstvennyi arkhiv Rossiiskoi federatsii (State Archive of the Russian Federation), M.
GASO	Gosudarstvennyi arkhiv Sverdlovskoi oblasti (State Archive of Sverdlovsk province), Ekaterinburg.
IK	*Iskusstvo kino* (Cinema Art, M., 1936—).
KhSZUP	*Khronologicheskoe sobranie zakonov, ukazov Presidiuma Verkhovnogo Soveta i postanovlenii pravitel'stva RSFSR* (*Chronological Compendium of Laws, Decrees of the Presidium of the Supreme Soviet, and Decrees of the Government of the RSFSR*, 7 vols, M., 1958–59).
KP	*Komsomolskaya pravda* (*Komsomol Pravda*, 1918—)
KPBTsK	'Kopii postanovlenii Byuro Tsentral'nogo Komiteta VLKSM po rabote sredi pionerov i shkol'nikov (za 1919–1928, za 1929–1935, za 1936–1942, za 1943–1947, za 1948–1954, za 1955–1963)'. Typescript of regulations and decisions relating to the Pioneer movement passed by the Bureau of the Central Committee of the Komsomol held in the reading room of RGASPI-TsKhDMO.
KPSTsK	'Kopii postanovlenii Sekretariata Tsentral'nogo Komiteta VLKSM po shkol'noi i pionerskoi rabote (za 1919–1925, za 1926–1927, za 1928–1934, za 1935–1940, za 1941–1947, za 1948–1949, za 1950, za 1951, za 1952–1953). Typescript of regulations and decisions relating to the Pioneer movement passed by the Secretariat of the Central Committee of the Komsomol held in the reading room of RGASPI-TsKhDMO.
L.	Leningrad.
LI	*Leninskie iskry* (*Leninist Sparks*, L., 1925–91).
M.	Moscow.
Mariengof	A. Mariengof, *Moi vek, moi druz'ya i podrugi* (M., 1990).
MPDV	*Metodicheskie pis'ma o detskou vospitanii* (*Letters in Teaching Methods for Nursery Schools*, M., 1926–30).
MPV	*Moskva poslevoennaya: arkhivnye dokumenty i materialy*, ed. A. S. Kiselev, comp. M. M. Gorinov and A. N. Ponomarev, E. V. Taranov (*Post-War M.: Archival Documents and Materials* (M., 2000)).
NES	*Novyi entsiklopedicheskii slovar'* (*New Encyclopaedic Dictionary*, 29 vols, SPb., 1911–16).
NGPU	Interviews carried out by Nizhni-Novgorod Pedagogical Institution. A date code is also given.
NM	*Novyi Mir* (M., 1925–present)
Novak-Deker	N. K. Novak-Deker (ed.) *Soviet Youth: Twelve Komsomol Histories* (Munich, 1959).

NY	New York.
NZ	*Nashi dostizheniya* (M., 1929–41).
O	*Ogonek* (M., 1923—).
OMM	*Okhrana materinstva i mladenchestva* (*Protection of Mothers and Children*, Petrograd, 1916–18).
OND	*O nashikh detyakh* (*Our Children*, M., 1928–30).
OV	*Obshchestvennyi vrach* (*Public Health Physician*, M., 1895–1922).
Oxf/Lev	Interviews carried out with funding from the Leverhulme Trust, grant no. F/083736/A, 'Childhood in Russia: A Social and Cultural History, 1890–1991'. The code 'SPb.' refers to interviews conducted in St Petersburg, 'M.' to interviews carried out in Moscow, 'P' to Perm', 'T' to Taganrog, and 'V' to villages in Leningrad and Novgorod provinces. The place code is followed by a date code specifying the year in which the interview was conducted. For further information, see the project website, http://www.mod-langs.ox.ac.uk/russian/childhood/.
Oxf/Lev WQ	Written questionnaire version of the questionnaires for interviews used above, completed by two informants from St Petersburg and two from Nizhni-Novgorod.
PB	*Prizrenie i blagotvoritel'nost'* (*Welfare and Philanthropy*, SPb./Petrograd, 1912–17) (originally ran as *Obshchestvennaya i chastnaya blagotvoritel'nost' v Rossii*).
Pokrovsky, *FP*	E. A. Pokrovsky, *Fizicheskoe vospitanie detei u raznykh narodov, preimushchestvenno Rossii* (M., 1884).
PP	*Pionerskaya pravda* (*Pioneer Pravda*, M., 1925—)
PSS	*Polnoe sobranie sochinenii* (Complete Works).
PSZ	*Polnoe sobranie zakonov Rossiiskoi Imperii: sobranie tret'e* (*Complete Laws of the Russian Empire*, SPb., 1885–1916).
PZK	*Pervyi zhenskii kalendar'* (*First Women's Calendar*, SPb., 1899–1915).
RAO	Interviews carried out by students doing interview training at the Russian Academy of Education, Moscow; the identifier is followed by a place code (Nizhni-Novgorod, Moscow, etc.) and a date code.
RAO NA	Rossiiskaya Akademiya Obrazovaniya. Nauchnyi arkhiv (Russian Academy of Education. Scholarly Archive), M.
RGASPI	Rossiiskii gosudarstvennyi arkhiv sotsial'noi i politicheskoi istorii (Russian State Archive of Social and Political History), M.
RGASPI-TsKhDMO	Tsentr khraneniya dokumentov molodezhnykh organizatsii (Centre for Youth Organisation Documents), M., a department of RGASPI since 2000.
RGB OR	Rossiiskaya gosudarstvennaya biblioteka: Otdel rukopisei (Russian State LibraryManuscript Section).
RGIA	Rossiiskii gosudarstvenyi istoricheskii arkhiv (Russian State Historical Archive), SPb.
RS	*Russkaya shkola* (SPb., 1890–1917).
RSFSR	Rossiiskaya sotsialisticheskaya federatsiya sovetskikh respublik (Russian Socialist Federation of Soviet Republics), the title of the Russian Federation before 1991.
SemSh	*Sem'ya i shkola* (M., 1934—)
SemV	*Semeinoe vospitanie* (*Family Upbringing*, Astrakhan' 1911–14).

Shefner	Vadim Shefner, *Imya dlya ptitsy, ili Chaepitie na zheltoi verande*, in his *Lachuga dolzhnika* (SPb., 1995).
Siegelbaum and Sokolov	Lewis Siegelbaum and Andrei Sokolov, *Stalinism as a Way of Life: A Narrative in Documents* (New Haven, CT, 2000).
SK	*Sovetskoe kino* (1936–91).
SO	*Sotsial'noe obespechenie* (*Social Welfare*, M., 1926—: did not run 1942–55). (Ran as *Voprosy sotsial'nogo obespecheniya* 1926–1930).
SP	*Sovetskaya pedagogika* (*Soviet Pedagogy*, 1937–91).
SPb.	St Petersburg.
SPb-Pv–1903	*Sankt-Peterburg: Putevoditel' po stolitse s istoriko-statisticheskim ocherkom i opisaniem eya dostoprimechatel'nostei i uchrezhdenii* [SPb.: A Guide to the Capital with a Historico-Statistical Sketch and Description of the City's Sights] (SPb., 1903).
SPA	*Sovetskie pisateli: avtobiografii*, ed. B.Ya. Brainina and E. F. Nikitina (*Soviet Writers' Autobiographies*, 5 vols; M., 1959–88).
SS	*Sobranie sochinemi* (Collected Works).
Starzhinsky	Pavel Starzhinsky, *Moe vzrosloe detstvo* (M., 1982).
SURRKhP	*Sbornik uzakonenii i rasporyazhenii rabochego i krest'yanskogo pravitel'stva* (*Compendium of Laws and Regulations Issued by the Worker and Peasant Government*, 1919—).
SvoV	*Svobodnoe vospitanie* (*Free Education*, M., 1907–18).
SYu	*Sovetskaya yustitsiya* (*Soviet Justice*, 1930–41, 1957–93).
SZ	*Sotsialisticheskaya zakonnost'* (*Socialist Legality*, 1935–91).
SZRI	*Svod zakonov Rossiiskoi Imperii*, ed. D. Mordukhai-Boltovsky (*Code of Laws of the Russian Empire*, SPb., 1912–14).
T 7S PVIP	*Trudy sostoyashchikh pod Vysochaishim pokrovitel'stvom Sed'mogo s"ezda predstavitelei i vospitatelei ispravitel'nykh priyutov* (Papers of the Seventh Congress [...] of Directors and Supervisors of Educational Reform Shelters, Moscow, 1909).
T 8S PVIP	*Trudy sostoyashchikh pod Vysochaishim pokrovitel'stvom Vos'mogo s"ezda predstavitelei i vospitatelei ispravitel'nykh priyutov* (Papers of the Eighth Congress [...] of Directors and Supervisors of Educational Reform Shelters. Published as a supplement to the journal *Tyuremnyi vestnik* in 1912).
T	*Teatr* (1937—).
TsAODM	Tsentral'nyi arkhiv obshchestvennykh dvizhenii Moskvy (Central Archive of Public Associations of the City of Moscow; formerly the local Party archive).
TsDOO SO	Tsentr dokumentov obshchestvennykh organizatsii Sverdlovskoi oblasti (Centre of Documents relating to Public Associations, Sverdlovsk province), Ekaterinburg; formerly the Party archive.
TsGA-SPb	Tsentral'nyi gosudarstvennyi arkhiv (Central State Archive), SPb.
TsGAKFD-SPb.	Tsentral'nyi arkhiv kino-fotodokumentov (Central Archive of Cinematic and Photographic Documents), SPb.
TsGALI-SPb	Tsentral'nyi gosudarstvennyi arkhiv literatury i iskusstva Sankt-Peterburga (Central State Archive of Literature and Art, SPb.).
TsGIA-SPb	Tsentral'nyi gosudarstvennyi istoricheskii arkhiv-Sankt-Peterburga (Central State Historical Archive, SPb.).
TV	*Tyuremnyi vestnik* (*The Prison Herald*, SPb., 1874–1917).

TYuZ — Teatr yunykh zritelei (Theatre of Young Viewers, i.e. youth theatre).

VL — *Ves' Leningrad* (*All Leningrad:* street and business directory, 1924–27, 1931, 1935).

VM — *Vsya Moskva* (*All Moscow:* street and business directory, 1875–1917, 1923–36).

VO — Vospitanie i obuchenie (*Upbringing and Training*, St Petersburg, 1866–1917).

VP — *Ves' Peterburg* (*All St Petersburg*, street and business directory, 1894–1914; from 1915 to 1917 and in 1919, 1922, and 1923, published as *Ves' Petrograd* (*All Petrograd*)).

VV — *Vestnik vospitaniya* (M. 1890–1917).

ZMNP — *Zhurnal Ministerstva Narodnogo Prosveshcheniya* (SPb. 1834–1917).

ZYu — *Zhurmal Ministerstva Yustitsii* (SPb. 1890–1917).

Materials from archives are generally given in the following form: abbreviated name of the archive (GASO, RAO NA, etc.), followed by f. for 'fond' or collection number, 'op.' for opis or inventory number, 'd.' for delo or file number, and 'l.' for list or folio number. However, references to archive materials where the classification system is different (e.g. RGB OR) preserve that system.

Where more than one place of publication is given, books are listed under the first place of publication only. An exception is however made for the standard Soviet formula of the 1920s and early 1930s, 'M.–L.' (Moscow and Leningrad), which had institutional and propaganda significance: it was a point of honour for the 'central' presses to publish in both capitals. In the main text, the Russian titles of books, journals, films, articles etc. are normally translated into English, except in the cases of certain very well-known journals and newspapers (*Novyi Mir, Ogonek, Nedelya, Pravda, Izvestiya*). This practice has also generated some 'macaronic' forms – for instance, *Pioneer Pravda*.

Russian words and names are transliterated in a simplified version of British Standard. The soft sign ' is used only in the notes and bibliography, and names are given in their most familiar form (Sergei not Sergey, Dostoevsky not Dostoevskii). All translations into English are my own. The ellipsis [...] is used to signify omissions made by me.

References to 'digital version' are to the online version of this book accessible at www.mod-langs.ox.ac.uk/russian/childhood/. This includes fuller versions of the annotations (more sources are given, and more information about each source), a detailed multilingual bibliography, and a biographical list of the informants who are mentioned in my discussion. The site also includes extensive materials on subjects for which room could not be found between hard covers, e.g. the social and regional variations of childhood experience and children's role as witnesses of and participants in historical events (Part II) and specialist children's institutions and hospitals (Part III), as well as numerous tables of data, many additional illustrations, etc.

Introduction

Symbols of the Nation

A poster on display in Moscow during the 1999 election campaign showed a child of roughly 18 months old, looking outwards with what the slogan to the left of the image – I'M COUNTING ON YOU! – invited one to interpret as a wary yet trusting expression. The immediate message of the poster was that voting should be understood as a civic duty; the younger generation relied upon adults to protect them and to act as guarantors of their future. But, like any image, it might also be interpreted at deeper levels, raising the question of what it means to represent children, and to be a child, in the society where the image was produced and circulated.

It is not only in Russia that babies and small children act as the currency of politicians' integrity, and as symbols of the nation's future, in political propaganda. In 1999, the British press went into near-hysteria at the prospect of the forthcoming birth of a child to Tony Blair and Cherie Booth, an event that conveniently combined the 'statesman kisses baby' stereotype with a demonstration of middle-aged potency on the part of the father (the latter in its turn providing, one may suspect, a symbol of optimism for a 'middle-aged' nation full of anxiety about cultural decline). However, in the Soviet period, the context for the appearance of children in Russian propaganda was in some respects specific. Pictures of joyful small beings suggested not that Brand X or party politician Y would ensure children's happiness, but that such happiness was guaranteed by the state itself. The Soviet state placed children's affairs at the heart of its political legitimacy, emphasising that children were treated with greater care than they were anywhere else in the world. From 1936 especially, the notion that children owed their perfectly happy childhood to the Soviet leadership was to become one of the central tenets of propaganda, aimed both at the Soviet population and at potential supporters abroad. Intensive political indoctrination took place from nursery age, shaping the lives of millions of children; representations of children reflected prevailing views of ideal citizenship, from the politically engaged social activist of the 1920s or the Khrushchev thaw to the docile and grateful subject of the Stalin years. Childhood was also a central area for the modernising ambitions of the Soviet state, which sought to expand formal education, provide an all-encompassing network of institutional

1   I'm Counting on You. Election poster, central Moscow, 2000.

care, and intervene in the child-rearing practices of parents, especially where these were seen as 'backward' or 'failing'.

The presentation of children in propaganda as loving, docile beneficiaries of the leader had resonance with an underlying concept of adults as subjects and beneficiaries of the state, rather than as empowered citizens. In other European countries with large peasant populations and strong traditions of organicist politics, such as Italy and Ireland, there was also an established tradition of associating images of children with the state of the nation. But all over the 'West', including Italy and Ireland, the link between child symbolism and the nation was looser than it was under Soviet power, because of the pervasiveness of images of 'innocent childhood' in domains not under direct state control, such as commercial art, and the survival of private provision in the education system (which was also true of the Third Reich).

Yet the position of children under Soviet power was different in terms of degree, rather than intrinsically different, from their position in self-consciously 'modern' states more broadly. Both in Western Europe and in America, the twentieth century saw a growing involvement of state institutions in the regulation of childhood, and here, too, the idea that the proper treatment of children was a fundamental criterion of civilised existence was pervasive. The idea that the state was practically as well as symbolically responsible for children's lives was international. Hence the success of Soviet diplomats in gaining approval for international charters on children's rights at the United Nations. Across the 'West' (in the broadest sense, including Russia), the twentieth century saw childhood 'modernised', in the sense of shaped and transformed by governments that saw their own role as being to impose 'modern' values on the population, and to combat neglect and mistreatment of children within the family and within society at large.

There were significant continuities within national tradition as well as across national boundaries. From the 1890s, children began to acquire an unprecedented prominence in political discussions, legislation, medical discourse, the activities of philanthropic societies, and artistic representations within Tsarist Russia. Many of the conceptual changes that made themselves felt at this era – the shift towards an emphasis on 'free education' that was supposed to reflect child psychology more accurately, the emergence of a conviction that it was essential to protect from harm children who were in abusive or impoverished families, or had ended up orphaned or alone – had a profound effect on attitudes and policies in the new, Soviet, epoch too. It could be argued that the three decades between 1890 and 1917 saw more profound alterations in attitudes to children than the seven and a half decades of Soviet power, which (from the mid-1930s particularly) were characterised by a desperate striving for coherence and stability rather than 'the shock of the new'. In the years since the Soviet Union collapsed, there has been an upsurge of interest in perceptions of childhood that circulated among the Russian intelligentsia of the late Imperial era. This has had the piquant effect of making the distant pre-revolutionary past certainly more fashionable, and possibly also more topical, than the nearer Soviet heritage, though the latter is still massively important at the level of cultural inertia, if nothing else.

Living Childhood

Writing about childhood means more than analysing children's place in ideology and in cultural and social relations: it must also be an imaginative exercise. In his travelogue *From Heaven Lake*, Vikram Seth sets out an engaging conceit of how a language might best be learned: as a crash-course in growing up in a different culture:

As I doze off to the soporific drone of flies, I dream of being back at Stanford University. I have been crowned chairman of the Asian Languages department, and have inaugurated a six-month intensive course. Each week corresponds to a year in the life of the Chinese child. For the first week my students lie around on cots in the classroom, making various burbling noises while I and two other teachers talk in Chinese to each other. The students throw tantrums, but not as often as the American baby. They are wheeled about the campus in prams, and swathed in over-thick padded clothes, just as Chinese infants are: they always remind me of overheated dumplings. In my totalitarian scheme of things, my students are sung to sleep at regular intervals with lullabies. The second week, a few elementary words are taught to them: 'baba', 'mama', and so on. At mealtimes or when taken for a walk they are expected to display a proper curiosity for the names of objects. [...] Slowly, through the compressed years, the students come into contact with nursery rhymes, written characters, simple comic books, schoolchildren's slang and sneers, buying and selling vocabulary, the use of chopsticks, pen, brush and abacus. They now participate in adult conversation, read short stories, perform songs for visiting party dignitaries and foreign guests, drink endless cups of hot water from brightly-coloured thermos flasks, etc. As they rush through their adolescence and early adulthood, I introduce political thought, history, literature, bureaucracy, slogans and obscenities. By the end of the six-month course, in their twenty-sixth year, my students (all of whom are about to be married off and/or be sent off to the post that has been allocated to them) have some idea of the experience of their Chinese peers.[1]

Seth captures here some of the essential experiences of childhood, seen from within (ranging through the linguistic, symbolic, and material aspects of culture). His whimsical plan for language-learning also suggests the ways in which those experiences may differ from country to country – notably diet, games, clothes, language, table etiquette, and folklore. A similar induction course for Western students of Russian might include some of the same material as Seth's imaginary Chinese course: the experiences of being wrapped up like an 'overheated dumpling' to take the air, probably in the charge of a fierce babushka, and (up to the late 1990s) of being taught to use an abacus. But there would also be idiosyncratic experiences: eating special children's foods, such as 'milk kasha' (a sort of sweet, liquid, semolina pudding) or 'milk soup' (similar, only with macaroni); experiencing extremely early potty-training; learning to skate, toboggan, and, still more importantly, stay upright on icy pavements; participating in family leisure activities such as mushroom and berry-hunting; and watching the cartoons shown on the television programme *Good Night, Little Ones*, one of the few items of the schedule to survive the collapse of Soviet power practically unchanged. Those posing as Russian children would also learn to talk like children: to adopt wheedling and capricious intonations; to mispronounce certain consonants, saying *ts* for *ch* and *s* for *sh*; to use proper names and terms for body parts in the diminutive form.

A reconstruction of the world of Russian children must be sensitive to the way that childhood experience forms part of the elusive invisible network of assumptions and shared information understood by adult coevals 'from a half-word', as the Russian saying has it. Educated non-native speakers of a language are more likely to be in serious difficulties when talking to a three-year-old than when listening to a conference paper or taking part in a business discussion, or when reading a newspaper, historical essay, or even a modernist poem, and intelligent adults can imagine the life of an adult of comparable social background far more easily than they can that of a child.

Given that I am not Russian, this might seem a defeatist insight. If childhood is so nationally specific a phenomenon, how can an outsider even begin to explain it? One answer is that I did in fact go through an early induction into Russian culture like the one Seth describes, though the contact with a 'foreign' childhood was mostly virtual. Like a lot of British children, we had what we called a 'Russian doll', known properly as a *matreshka*, in our playroom: the inner layers soon got lost, but the intricacy of the design and the strangely vacant gaze of the doll on the front held our imagination for a while. Later, when I was about eight, a broadcast of *War and Peace* on the radio had the entire family riveted for weeks, and my sister and I rechristened all our dolls with mispronounced Russian names. Piano lessons often meant flying (in my sister's case) or staggering (in mine) through some dinky tune by Dmitry Kabalevsky. The Soviet-published textbook used for beginners' Russian at my school in London during the 1970s was designed for non-Russian child learners in the Soviet Union, and grammar

2   Tobogganing, 1936. Children were, and still are, often represented in Russian sources engaging in winter pastimes such as this.

learning was accompanied by material related to children's experience. In laborious Cyrillic copperplate, we wrote out sentences such as 'The children are gathering berries and mushrooms', 'The boys are playing snowballs', and 'I want to be a cosmonaut'.

Admittedly, as would-be sophisticated 14-year olds, we, unlike Seth's putative students, found being treated like 7-year olds irritating rather than inspiring. Nor did it go down well with a class of surly British students when, five years later, we were coerced into singing 'Unfortunately, Birthdays Come Just Once a Year', from the hugely popular children's cartoon, *Cheburashka and Gena the Crocodile*, as part of language practice on a Russian course in Leningrad. It would seem that one needs to be either under 10 or over 30 (or a writer) to find immersion in another kind of childhood a charming fantasy, rather than a recipe for tedium. However, these early experiences have left their traces: there is something familiar in Russian childhood, a sense that I never had with German (where early reading consisted of *Deutsches Leben*, about a two-up two-down family in the Third Reich whose teenage daughter was obsessed with making 'water waves' in her hair). I recently had a moment of delighted recognition when it turned out that I and a Russian friend had both learned the same first sentence (to me, wonderfully inconsequential) in our reading primers: 'The sun shines, but does not warm.' Shared memories, it would seem, really can create emotional solidarity, even if the material circulates in a very different context on each side.

In any case, there are, of course, universals in childhood experience. Vikram Seth, while concentrating on the particularity of infancy in China, also points to some of the ways in which this phase of life does not vary in different places. The use of lullabies to send children to sleep is a cultural universal, just as are the expectation that they will 'display a proper curiosity over the names of objects', and the acquisition of 'buying and selling vocabulary' (or, to be more accurate, the vocabulary associated with exchanges of goods). Exposure to 'written characters' of some kind is inevitable in any literate culture.

Even where culturally specific experiences are concerned, though, the foreign commentator need not necessarily despair. The particularities of growing up in culture A are likely to be more immediately evident to a person brought up in culture B. External observers are often less likely to generalise from personal experience, to elevate what is historically and socially specific to the level of a universal. Conversely, an external observer may find it easier to identify historical patterns, to sense continuities or discontinuities across generations.

The difficulty of seeing children's culture accurately 'from within' is perhaps particularly sharp in recent Russian culture. In the Soviet era, the sense that the state – and, from the mid-1930s, the leader, Stalin himself – was responsible for children's happiness meant that silence engulfed children whose experience of childhood did not fit the stereotypes of 'happy childhood'. Children in young offender institutions, or the children of social pariahs such as kulaks and prisoners in labour camps, vanished from view. While secret reports were compiled about abuses of these children and about bad treatment of children in orphanages, it was impossible to discuss such matters in print, since to admit that Soviet power

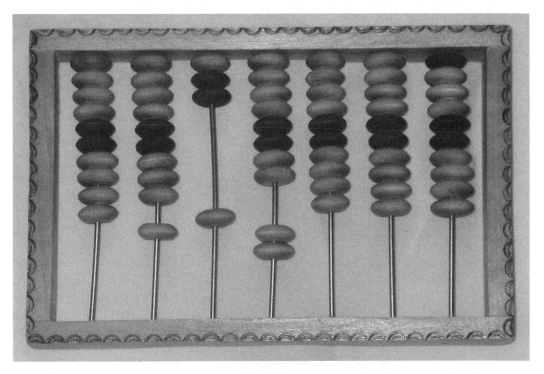

3   Toy abacus, 1985. Such items were still widely sold as educational toys in the late Soviet era, since calculators only began appearing in the early 1990s.

had done nothing to end the suffering of small children would have undermined one of the most important strands of the regime's propaganda – that the state had unique care for its little ones. The myth that childhood was the happiest time of one's life made any less than perfect childhoods seem aberrant. Hence the tendency of many memoirists and writers (especially those writing for children) to play down childhood trauma.

If the myth of happy childhood worked to 'censor out' experiences of childhood that did not fit the stereotype, it did not necessarily preclude such experiences in reality. A man brought up in the north-western Russian countryside during the 1930s and 1940s has piquantly recalled just how hollow schoolroom slogans about prosperity rang when you always went hungry and in rags:

> They'd tell us first off that we was living better than anyone, and we was better off than everyone, and so on and so on. Eh-eh-eh … As for us, of course, we couldn't get our heads round that, and specially not in class one. Well, how was we supposed to understand, living better than everyone … better … and better-off? When we, excuse me for being so crude, was sitting there with bare bottoms, and all …[2]

Of course, such recollections themselves are the products of stereotyped perceptions: almost everyone taking part in our interviewing in Russian villages began their memories with a phrase such as 'What kind of a childhood did I have? No kind of a childhood!' – pointing to an ethos of deprivation as a standard element in self-portrayal for anyone who grew up before the 1960s.[3] Equally, the denial that the informant experienced 'childhood' is at some level a recognition of the official myth: 'if "childhood" is what we were told about in our alphabet books and reading primers, then I never experienced anything like that', runs this line of thinking. But such perceptions represent not only an alternative view of reality, but also an alternative *reality* – a point that should be recognised if one does not want to perpetuate the censorship of 'abnormal' experience that was characteristic of official and intelligentsia evocations of childhood in Soviet times.

The official insistence that children were due, and generally received, loving concern from adults did not just lead to adjustment of personal recollections. It could lead to tolerance of what might, in other cultural contexts, have seemed abusive behaviour. For instance, in 1967, a 29-year-old Kaliningrad man caught and chained to the spot a 13-year-old boy because the latter had been picking flowers from a communal bed that he tended with loving care. The man was tried for 'vicious hooliganism' – in itself a decisive response. But in the liberal Soviet press, the decision attracted criticism as totally out of proportion to the man's crime. The possible anxiety and humiliation caused to the boy himself did not come into the discussion.[4] The lack of open discussion of failures and needs meant that Soviet administrators' concern for children often reached the level of lip service only. A Party boss in the provinces might know in theory that he had to allocate 38,293 roubles to the local orphanage network, but the knowledge that adjustments to budgetary levels might well remain secret made it all too tempting simply to siphon off funds to other areas where failure to comply was much more likely to result in public denunciation and career catastrophe.

There are some ways, then, in which the Soviet myth of happiness for children could act against the interests of children themselves. Yet one should be wary about too great an emphasis on dismal and tragic experience. There is no reason to doubt the sincerity of many memoirists from the cultural elite who claim to have experienced happy childhoods, or to suspect them (as a Freudian might) of using nostalgia as a retreat from the unbearable present.[5] Memory is, after all, dependent not only upon what one does experience, but upon what one is told one should experience. In a culture where accounts of early childhood as a time of perfect joy have often been read in childhood, adult myth easily became part of childhood reality.[6]

What is more, there were some practical reasons for happiness. During much of the twentieth century, Russian facilities in areas such as medical treatment, education, and leisure for children were (at their best) as good as, or better than, those in much more affluent countries, such as Britain, France, Germany, or the United States. Striking, too, in a country where physical violence among and towards adults was often regarded with equanimity, was the intolerance of the institutionalised physical punishment of children in most Russian schools after 1874. Over the century depicted here, foreign visitors often remarked the tolerant or indulgent treatment of babies and young children. While observations of this kind give at best a partial view of behaviour in Russian society, they are useful in recording behaviour within the circles and institutions to which foreigners customarily had access, and may be contrasted with earlier opinions about the coarseness of family relations among Russians belonging to precisely this social group.

Yet the experience of Russian children varied hugely. Above all, it depended upon the place of a child's parents in the social hierarchy. In the late Imperial era, many working-class and peasant children endured conditions ranging from hardship to open deprivation; educational opportunity was also severely restricted. Even in the supposedly egalitarian Soviet Union, conditions for these groups remained tough. Living accommodation was often dreadful, and, though formal restrictions on access to secondary education had disappeared, it was significantly harder for children to remain in high-quality formal education for ten or eleven years if their parents were factory or collective farm workers than if their parents belonged to the urban intelligentsia.

The blanket term 'Russian' covered many regional and indeed ethnic differences as well. The character of a village childhood was strongly dependent on the character of the landscape and the economic resources of the locality; and in this imperial culture, the term 'Russian' in the sense of 'citizen of the Russian Empire' did not necessarily mean 'ethnically Russian'. It could also apply to other people – for instance, the term *russkii inorodets*, literally 'Russian of other birth' (which in the strict legal sense was used for nomadic populations, such as those of the Russian north and north-east), was loosely applied before 1917 to ethnic minorities living within the boundaries of European Russia, such as Tatars.

After 1917, the term 'Soviet' replaced 'Russian' as the denomination of state affiliation (in Russian, 'citizenship'; in English, 'nationality'), and 'Russian' was applied, by intention, to those of Russian descent (in English, of Russian 'race', or, in modern parlance, 'ethnic origin'; in Russian, those 'Russian by nationality'). However, 'Sovietisation' (which in practice primarily signified Russification) meant that populations living within the Russian Federation, whatever their ethnic origins, were more and more likely, over the course of time, to be bilingual in Russian, or indeed to speak Russian as their only language. Intermarriage also produced a substantial population of mixed Russian–non-Russian composition. Members of this group had the right to assign themselves to either 'nationality': while the nationality chosen was traditionally the father's, fear of discrimination, and dislike of being perceived as different, made 'Russian' a preference, particularly among those of Russian-Jewish descent.

At the same time, 'passport nationality' did not elide cultural difference. Children brought up as 'Russian', but with a non-Russian parent, were likely to have some 'exotic' background factors in terms of diet, family relationships, private celebrations, and perhaps also attitudes to religion and to moral values. Conversely, intellectuals from other East Slavonic groups, such as Ukrainians and Belorussians, might have a fierce sense of national distinctiveness, yet live a strongly Russified existence as to language and cultural practices. Some of the most prominent contributors to the 'Russian' tradition of thinking about child care and pedagogy (Anton Makarenko, V. A. Sukhomlinsky) were ethnic Ukrainians, but ethnic background was not a factor that was raised in their work, or in the reception of this work during the years of Soviet power. Equally, while the formation of the myth of 'happy childhood' on the one hand and the creation of the Soviet welfare system for children on the other owed a great deal to writers, journalists, paediatricians, and pedagogues who happened to be of Jewish origin, the mental and practical structures and norms that resulted were used to regulate Soviet Russian society in the broadest sense. As with the signifiers of national identity used by other European imperial cultures ('French', 'British'), 'Russian' was a polyvalent term.

Experience was mutable from generation to generation as well. Changes that may be subjected to quantification include a decline in infanticide and infant mortality and a rise in abortion; a decline in family break-up through death (whether of parents or of siblings) and a rise in family atomisation through marital breakdown; a replacement of work-related activities in the family by formal education and supervision; a decrease in family size; a move away from traditional games to reading and, later, the watching of films and television; the improvement of housing and increased provision of private space for even quite small children. More elusive and subjective shifts include a link between the decline of family size and the development of child-centred living.

The development of the 'child-centred family' was not a straightforward process. With the decline of the extended family, upbringing became more susceptible to ideological control, as new parents looked to brochures and professionals rather than (or as well as) to older relations for support and guidance. In Soviet Russia, such political supervision of private life was provided in abundance. In the 1920s, the state initiated a full-scale campaign to alter traditional patterns of upbringing, particularly in the villages, working through institutions such as the Party Women's Sections, but also through formal education and through organisations recruiting children themselves, above all the Pioneer groups (founded in 1922). The provision of universal, state-sponsored child care became a vital ideological objective, albeit one that was realised only slowly. Even in the mid-1930s, when the nuclear family again began to be seen as an essential element in social stability, there was no attempt to reprivatise child care: instead, the family was represented in ideology as the primary 'cell' of political and social existence. And the rise in the numbers of working women, plus the continuing inadequacies of child care, perpetuated ties between family members across generations (grandmothers, aunts, and other female relatives were likely to find themselves drawn into an unofficial baby-sitting network). Compared with Western urban families, Soviet urban families of the mid-twentieth century manifested a rather greater stress on vertical ties (parents/ grandparents to children) and a rather lesser one on horizontal ties (between spouses and – as family sizes shrank and numbers of only children proliferated, and as age gaps between children increased – between siblings).

As public life became increasingly stressful and alienating, an appreciation of the family home as a refuge from public life developed. The apartment, even if this was only a single room of a communal flat, was a place where the door could be shut on the outside world and clandestine conversations held. And continuing emphasis upon the role of parents in inculcating discipline and morality meant that parents in practice exercised a good deal of authority, and enjoyed a considerable degree of autonomy.

Through Children's Eyes

All these general processes form the background to the discussion here, which shows more minute changes: how the understanding of childhood and the experience of childhood shifted from decade to decade. The discussion begins in the 1890s, the time when many of the Russian Modernists who later made such a huge impact on the representation of childhood (see Chapters 1 and 2) were themselves children; it concludes with the collapse of the Soviet Union in 1991. The century between those two dates saw some of the most momentous upheavals to hit Russia at any historical era. Aleksandr Herzen began his classic nineteenth-century memoir, *My Past and Thoughts*, with a reminiscence of his evacuation, as a baby, from French-occupied Moscow in 1812. Many of his twentieth-century successors had still more extraordinary early experiences: the toppling of political leaders, the horrors of collectivisation, and the catastrophes of war and revolution, which rendered millions homeless and precipitated child abandonment on a scale perhaps unmatched anywhere in history. Children were wrenched from their homes as refugees fled war zones, sometimes becoming separated from their families in the process; often the primary casualties of social horrors, they died as victims of bombardment, starvation, and epidemics; they were pressed into work roles at an early age, and into family duties such as queuing for food. They did not experience these cataclysms merely as victims: during the First World War, boys rushed to join the Russian Army at the Front (so many arrived that housing them became a serious social problem), and, in the Russian Civil War, children fought on both sides, where they, like their counterparts in wars before and since, often proved ruthless, unpredictable, and trigger-happy. Children caught up in the Leningrad Blockade suffered directly and at second hand, dying of emaciation and watching their relations die; they also fought to survive, stealing food and wangling themselves places in orphanages by lying about their age. Whether experienced from the point of view of the perpetrator or the sufferer, such violent historical events dominated the consciousness of all individuals whose childhood they overshadowed (or brought to an end). They also had a whole range of intermediate consequences: the fragmentary, haphazard, and volatile character of school education between 1918 and 1925, and 1941 and 1945, or the material deprivation endured by children growing up in the period of 'post-war reconstruction'.[7]

It is impossible to understand the specificities of growing up in Russia if the resonance of particular events is ignored. But this book is not meant primarily as a discussion of the cataclysms of twentieth-century Russian history as experienced by children.[8] Nor is it, in the first place, a history of institutions such as schools,

4 A crocodile of schoolchildren negotiates the bomb-blasted Suvorovsky prospekt, Leningrad, 1942.

children's organisations, publishing houses for children, and the like. Rather, it is a history of daily life as experienced by Russian children over the course of the twentieth century. It is concerned with the effects of institutions on children, not with the rationale for their creation or the way they were managed from the top: with the school curriculum rather than with professional conferences on pedagogy; with the rules and rituals of the Pioneer movement rather than the top-level organisation of that movement; with what children wore, where they slept, and what they ate, rather than with Soviet factories' output of children's clothing, cot-blankets, and dried milk. In discussing the 'cult of personality' during the Stalin years, I concentrate on propaganda directly aimed at children (posters in nurseries and schools, alphabets and reading books); in writing about play, I am less concerned with the place of games and pastimes in psychological writing than with reconstructing the sorts of amusements that children enjoyed out in the street and in the courtyard during the 'long twentieth century'.

Yet children's perceptions are shaped by adult direction in fundamental ways, particularly in the case of younger children: adults control the spaces that children may occupy and regulate the course of their daily routine, and children learn from adults how they ought to perceive the world. Hence, the book begins with a series of chapters that are intended as evocations of the 'boxes' or 'envelopes' in which childhood was lived. The four chapters in Part I 'Imagining Childhood' provide a history of representations of children in art, propaganda, child psychology, pedagogy, legislation, and journalism over the course of a century. The aim is to capture certain key points in the development of attitudes to children, such as the 'discovery' of children's art in the 1900s and 1910s or the emergence of Soviet ruler cults directly aimed at children in the mid-1930s, and to capture the contribution made by certain key figures to the evolution of ideas about children, including political leaders such as Lenin and Stalin; composers of influential literary and artistic representations of children and childhood such as Maxim Gorky, Viktor Shklovsky, or Andrei Tarkovsky; artists working for children such as Kornei Chukovsky and Samuil Marshak; the authors of normative guides on upbringing and popular works on child psychology; and the constructors of legislation. The chronological boundaries here reflect not just major national events (the 1917 Revolution, the death of Stalin), but also events of particular importance to children's lives – 1935 might be described as the Soviet 'year of the child', witnessing as it did major legislative changes (the reimposition of full criminal responsibility for certain crimes committed by juveniles, a crackdown on waifdom), an upsurge of propaganda for and about children, much of it related to the rising Stalin cult, and major changes of policy in schools and children's institutions.

Discourse analysis and institutional history alone do not get one very far in understanding childhood. A book that relied exclusively on these would be a history of adult aspirations for children, rather than of childhood as such; of categories and constructs, rather than mentality on the ground. Parts II and III shift from the general forces shaping childhood over time to the course of childhood as a linear progression from birth to adolescence. 'Children on

Their Own' considers the experience of being orphaned or abandoned, on the one hand, and, on the other, the effects of two representative types of 'total institution' for children – the orphanage and the young offender 'colony'. Part III deals with the lives of 'family children', an endangered and fragile, but still substantial, majority of Russia's children over the 'long twentieth century'. Different chapters deal with infancy; with early childhood (the 'pre-school' years); with the transition to independence and expansion of horizons in terms of imaginative experience, through leisure activities such as play and reading; and, finally, with school education, the start of which came as a huge shock to many Russian children and was often interpreted as the 'beginning of the end' of childhood. Within each chapter, I also consider how certain fundamental age thresholds might be crossed in different ways at different eras, and how shaping a given phase of development could alter. The 'modernisation' of childhood, with which this book is fundamentally concerned, accordingly emerges as a complex and ramified process, affecting babyhood more than schooling, for example, and unevenly present across space as well as across time.

Precedents and Sources

Researching childhood, it turns out, is far from easy, once one gets past the level of representations and legislation (which is to say, texts in the public domain). Both before and after 1917, children's affairs were dealt with by a variety of ministries and agencies, which sometimes had specialist sections, but sometimes grouped children's affairs under non-age-specific social categories ('the disabled'; 'labour legislation'). Material is therefore atomised; it is also in many respects imperfect. Statistics were published selectively – whether for patriotic reasons, or, conversely, because they were used to support a lamentatory narrative about Russian 'backwardness' compared with standards in the 'civilised world' (as happened in the 1900s, in the late 1920s, and in the era of *perestroika*). They were also collected haphazardly. For example, reports on the work of zemstvo hospitals and foundling homes were written by individual doctors according to their own ideas of what was important. Therefore, the rubrics for information contained might alter from year to year, making it difficult to track even basic figures, such as fluctuations in the numbers of admissions over a ten-year period. Alongside lack of system, a further cause for defects in statistics-keeping was prudent self-protection on the part of child-care professionals: in circumstances where recording high levels of dysentery in a crèche or escapes by prisoners in a reformatory was likely to lead to disciplinary action by higher authorities, the figures were usually quietly altered to comply with reasonable norms.

Written sources, including archival material, have significant flaws in other respects as well. They offer an elite perspective, concentrating either on the work of institutions and departments (in the case of policy documents, reports, etc.), or on the lives of literate historical subjects, often from privileged backgrounds (in the case of memoirs, 'mothers' diaries', and so on). What is more, their availability is subject to a significant time-lag. Material on children's institutions for the 1960s and onwards is accessible only haphazardly, sometimes because declassification of archives has not yet occurred, at other times because the material has yet to be committed to an archive in the first place. Where medical records are concerned, the ban on access to 'personal secrets' can be invoked to deny the researcher material even from the 1940s. For different reasons, autobiographical literature covering childhood from the 1950s onwards is sparse: few subjects under the age of 50 – unless they belong to the socially unrepresentative group of professional writers – are likely to sit down and write their memoirs.

All this makes oral history a crucial source, for the post-war period in particular. It is also an essential resource for obtaining information about child-rearing practices and childhood experiences among factory and collective farm workers, subjects that are very poorly documented in published literature. It provides precious material about the day-to-day life of institutions – schools, orphanages, nurseries, and so on – which was not collected in official sources. Accordingly, I draw on a large-scale interviewing project carried out in Moscow, St Petersburg, Perm' (a large provincial town), Taganrog (a small provincial town), villages in Leningrad and Novgorod provinces, and among *émigré* Russians domiciled in the United Kingdom (at the time of completing this manuscript, we had about 300 hours of tape on file, documenting work with over 150 informants). Informants were asked about their life history or (in the case of former child-care professionals) their experience of work with children; the interviews were 'semi-structured', in that a questionnaire was used, but with a very general opening question ('What is your most vivid memory of childhood?' 'How did you end up working with children?') that allowed a good deal of improvisation on the part of the informant.[9]

Obviously, oral history shares with published memoirs the problem of retrospection. As they develop, people revisit key experiences, perceive them differently, may even reshape and reinterpret them in fundamental ways, often depending on their perception of the immediate audience. Such reshaping is particularly likely in cultures which have undergone profound political transformation. When recollecting pre-revolutionary childhoods, Soviet citizens might spontaneously refer to 'Leningrad', and in post-Soviet Russia I have myself heard an informant refer to the second capital as 'St Petersburg' when talking of events in the early 1930s.

These are simple examples: more sophisticated changes concern the space in their lives that people remember as being occupied by ruler cult, Soviet patriotism, and so on. Informants rarely distort deliberately, but may misremember elements of their lives that were once of importance, and no longer are. All this makes it essential to supplement recollection with contemporary documents – life histories written by children as a school exercise in the early 1900s, or as part of the work done for classes in orphanages during the 1920s; children's drawings; diaries and letters. Private documents of the last kind are rare and tend to have been produced by atypical individuals, for example the future poet David Samoilov, by any standards an exceptionally intelligent and introverted 15-year-old, or Georgy Efron ('Moor'), the son of the poet Marina Tsvetaeva. But they have their own contribution to make to the history of childhood; as do the letters written by 'Pioneers and schoolchildren' to Party leaders, which alongside assurances of ideological probity sometimes contained personal testaments and autobiographical summaries, or requests for urgently needed practical help. Thus children learned their place in the political system, not just as loyal subjects, but as participants in the culture of lobbying, patronage, and making do.

The Boundaries of Childhood

The requirement for inclusivity at the level of sources has to be offset by compression in other respects. To begin with, 'childhood' is held here to apply up to the age of 13 or 14. The later teenage years are not analysed in detail. Breaking off just as children enter adolescence is in many respects artificial – after all, puberty occurs at different times in different individuals, and puberty as a 'cultural fact' need not necessarily coincide with the onset of puberty in a biological sense. And children of course associate with each other across the divide: particularly when one is writing about peer-group association, the distinction often has relatively little meaning. Equally, in traditional peasant and working-class families, advancing age meant the imposition of successively more demanding work tasks, up to ploughing (for boys) at the age of 10 or so; 12 was often the age at which children left, or dropped out of, school; it is hard to see 13 or 14 as a once-and-for-all break. There is some intellectual loss, then, in including adolescents 'by default' (in discussion of school life, or life in the Russian courtyard), but not addressing them in depth as a distinct group. Yet there are some important cultural reasons for making a break at this point. Modern Russian distinguishes between *rebenok* (a child, plural *deti*) and *podrostok* (a young person of roughly 14 years old or over), and applies different terms to pre-pubescent boys and girls and to post-pubescent ones (*devochka* and *mal'chik* versus *devushka* and *yunosha/molodoi chelovek* respectively). Before 1917, these thresholds were officially enshrined: article 213 of the 1900 Civil Code, invoking legislation that went back to 1785, set the three ages of childhood at 0–14, 14–17, and 18–20.[10] Puberty – as a cultural phenomenon, which may or may not coincide with the actual onset of sexual maturation in a biological sense – was thus widely seen as a crucial boundary, and associated with important threshold rituals and beliefs about psychological alteration. The conclusion, 'The End of Childhood?', considers some of these, in particular the transition to sexual activity, which, given the public puritanism that governed Russian culture at most periods between 1890 and 1991, was often a difficult and sometimes even traumatic experience for young people.

Alongside adolescents, another age group largely excluded from view is children before birth. This might on the face of it seem obvious, but in fact the whole question of when a child starts to be regarded as human is neither straightforward nor fixed. In traditional peasant culture, as will be described in Chapter 9, infants were regarded as strange and sinister beings who needed to be *made* human by the performance of certain rituals. Hence the practice of infanticide did not necessarily attract outrage, and was not severely punished in law. During the course of the twentieth century attitudes to abortion fluctuated. It was forbidden until 1917, but permitted during the 1920s and early 1930s, before being forbidden again in 1936, as an act that 'annihilates human life in its very beginnings, and assails the normal growth of population in our motherland'. Finally, after another policy U-turn, it was permitted once more from 1955. All this points to continuing uncertainty about whether abortion was to be understood as a form of child murder, or as the disposal of some part of the human body, not in essence distinct from the ordinary waste products of the menstrual cycle.

Selective in chronological terms, the book is also constricted in other ways. More space is, for example, given to variation in child-care practices in terms of social status than to possible regional variations. The focus throughout is European Russia – including both the lives of ethnic Russians and the two most culturally dominant ethnic minorities west of the Urals, and the lives of ethnic Russians and other Russified migrants to the territories east of that mountain range. Among ethnic minorities dwelling in European Russia and Siberia, specific discussion is limited to Jews and Tatars, the largest and most prominent groups, particularly in the urban context. These two groups represent intriguingly different case histories of minority cultures. Before 1917, Jews suffered explicit discrimination, and at times officially condoned persecution, incomparably more severe than anything visited on other groups of *russkie inorodtsy*, or 'non-Russian Russians', the term loosely applied to the Empire's non-Christian populations. Yet their participation in education at all levels was, even by 1917, much higher than that of all other ethnic groups, a differential that increased significantly in the post-revolutionary era. Even before 1917, there was a strong drive to assimilation (as represented in the illustration here of a rabbi's family from the Pale), a drive that considerably increased after 1917, when religious practice steeply declined, as did the use of Yiddish, despite early Soviet policies encouraging the teaching of minority languages in schools.[11] Among Tatars, institutionalised discrimination was less harsh, but negative stereotypes just as common, with reading books branding them as ignorant and simple-minded. The following story, printed in the famous pedagogue K. D. Ushinsky's reader *Native Tongue*, is typical:

A Tatar dreamt one night of a bowl of kissel, but there was no spoon, so the next night he went to sleep clutching a spoon. However, the kissel didn't reappear.[12]

Equally, readers of an impeccably liberal reading book first published in 1910, which remained in print till 1922, could read that the Bashkirs were like the Tatars, also of Islamic beliefs, and also, by implication, feckless and lazy: 'The free nomadic life has not got them used to hard peasant work. If a Bashkir has a pinch of tea and a handful of flour, he'll not move from the spot.'[13] The 'Russification' of Tatars took a good deal longer, hampered by poverty and prejudice: however, by the 1960s this community contained large numbers of highly educated and strongly assimilated individuals dwelling in Russian cities, whose contact with the

5 Family of a rabbi, Ostrog, Volynya province, 1910s. Note the completely assimilated appearance.

Tatar language was likely to be limited to speaking to elderly relations. As the paradoxical term 'non-Russian Russians' suggests, educated members of these two groups *were* to all intents and purposes Russian, marked as 'different' by prejudice rather than by objective factors. They therefore make excellent illustrations of the homogenising effects of state policy both before and after 1917, though the discussion has lost a good deal through the exclusion of other groups, for example the 'small peoples' of the Russian far north and east, that did not converge as quickly and effectively with mainstream values.

Discussion of religious minorities is equally selective. Some attention is given to Old Believers, but none to Russian Catholics, Russian Baptists, or to non-Christian populations beyond the world of monotheism (for instance Buddhists and animists). Equally, since covering all the multiplicitous areas of children's experience in equal depth would be impossible, the focus is on 'typical' experiences in the sense of widespread, average. Hence the chapter on schools concentrates on ordinary primary and secondary schools rather than the specialist hothouses (maths, music, and sports schools) that have often attracted Western attention in the past; the observations on children's literature and film highlight particularly widely read and popular texts that were familiar to most children at a given era; and the discussion of child-rearing and upbringing grapples with the practices adopted in run-of-the-mill intelligentsia, working-class, and peasant families, rather than families which self-consciously tried to be innovative in their approach to rearing children.

What Does Childhood Mean?

One more point should be emphasised firmly at the beginning. My purpose here has nothing to do with the exercise attempted repeatedly in the past by Western observers looking at Russia, who have been inclined to attribute the oddity of the place, as they saw it, to the supposed peculiarities of Russian upbringing. An egregious example was an article by Geoffrey Gorer hypothesising that certain significant elements in the Russian character might be traceable to the practice of swaddling. Since this could only be 'made tolerable' by periods of unwrapping the infant to be 'fed, petted and looked after', it generated an 'alternation of restraint without gratifications and complete gratifications without restraint [...] throughout the first nine months of life'.[14] Psychoanalytical analyses, with their assumption that Soviet (and more broadly Russian) upbringing was deviant because it did not endorse the emotional values current in the late twentieth-century West, are scarcely more helpful.[15]

It is vital to see the Soviet past in terms of possibilities available at the time, rather than those available in the twenty-first century. The suffering of children during the chaos and famine generated by the programmes of 'socialist construction' – in particular collectivisation, but also forced industrialisation – should be recognised as an appalling waste of human life. Human loss during the war years, too, was exacerbated by mismanagement. But the Soviet adults who lived through catastrophe often did their best to mitigate children's suffering, and, where they made bad decisions, did not necessarily make them in larger quantities than their contemporaries elsewhere.

It is instructive to consider the following appalling story from 1920, when the Volga area was gripped by famine:

[We] had not funds enough to provide food for all the children in the area where [we] worked. As it was, therefore, necessary to choose some of them for the receipt of rations, and to let the others die, the healthier children were those who were saved. Thus in the case of one family it was felt that the little girl who was already ill must be allowed to perish, while her younger brother, who had a stronger physique, was fed. He was not, however, old enough to be able to come to the central kitchen for his meals, neither was it possible to arrange for him to be taken there. An exception to the ordinary rule was, therefore, made in sending his food to his home. This home consisted of one small room – and there his sister lay dying. Day by day her strength ebbed lower through starvation; by putting out her hand she could have reached the shelf where her brother's food was kept, and yet she never attempted to take it. She understood the circumstances and uncomplainingly resigned herself to death. Only once, when the end was approaching, there was a moment in her gathering weakness when she forgot to maintain her self-control. She stretched out her hand towards the food, then she remembered that she must not have it; she drew back her hand and died.[16]

This anecdote, recording as it does an unpleasant exercise in social Darwinism,

6 Two child victims of the Leningrad Blockade, June 1942. A rare press photograph to give a hint of the prevailing horrors of starvation and disease.

the dispassionate choice of some, 'healthier', children who deserved to survive, at the expense of others (expressing an implicit preference in gender terms withal), reads like the sort of material that is cited in order to establish the 'totalitarian' credentials of Bolshevism, its inalienable inhumanity. But the perpetrators of the incident were not Soviet: they were British activists working for Save the Children. Faced with appalling deprivation, citizens of political systems where personal autonomy and the integrity of human life were accorded a high place acted in ways that they certainly would not have acted, given any choice.[17] Just so, 'rational upbringing', as visited on Russian children in the Soviet era, had its counterparts in other cultures. The degradation to which Soviet power reduced its human subjects is not to be underestimated. But in a system where most were treated badly, children were often treated better than most. There was nothing extraordinary in this – it was after all sheer common sense to ensure the survival of the new generation. But making children symbolise the iniquities of Soviet history is no more helpful to the understanding of that history than making them figureheads of the Soviet system's achievements.

I have also tried to avoid 'wisdom after the event' of another kind: placing too great an emphasis on the adults that the children described in the book later turned into. Certainly, there are broad ways in which one can trace a correlation between changing patterns of upbringing and changing patterns of adult identity. Brutalised children can change into brutalising adults; fear works more effectively on adults who have been socialised by resort to fear. But one needs always to maintain an awareness of serendipity and contrariness, of the capacity of human 'crooked timber' to defy its shapers. The products of children's institutions and of rough proletarian homes included intellectuals and poets, soberly self-educating workers, and happily married parents, as well as thugs, drunks, petty tyrants, and social deviants; many a nicely brought-up young lady from a genteel pre-revolutionary home, or a well-groomed young cadet, became a hard-working member of Soviet, or *émigré*, society after 1917. Not every abused child turns into a dictator or a domestic tyrant; some become thoughtful members of intellectual society, or indeed writers. Some members of generations where self-assertion is taught from an early age become reformist leaders (for example Khrushchev); others react against their upbringing and do everything they can not to implement its principles. The most that upbringing perhaps achieves is to make certain outcomes more predictable if one can assume some degree of continuity between the circumstances in which a person grows up and those they experience for all or part of their adulthood – which continuity, given the frightening instability of Russian political history during the twentieth century, often in fact eluded the human subjects who figure in these pages.

PART I

IMAGINING CHILDHOOD

Chapter 1

Free Spirits and Prodigies, 1890–1917

I'm sure you, like me, love only your own childhood:
what existed back then in the past.[1]
(Marina Tsvetaeva, letter to Anna Tesková, 22 April 1935)

In April and May of 1910, a large-scale exhibition of nursery education, Children and Work, was organised in the Ukrainian capital of Kiev, one of the centres of the pre-revolutionary kindergarten movement. At a speech to mark the opening, the director of the Kiev Froebel Society, N. D. Lubenets, made large claims for the significance of the event, which, she stated, was not just a one-off occasion, but a manifestation of rising interest in childhood:

> Children and schoolchildren are attracting more and more attention on the part of society, the state, and the nation at large. A kind of cult of childhood has come into existence; it is the glory and the distinguishing characteristic of our age. It has many different forms; it has made its way into legislation, inspired philanthropical endeavours, brought about vast changes in pedagogy, and created totally new branches of anthropology and psychology.[2]

By underlining the link between the new understanding of childhood and modernity ('the glory and distinguishing characteristic of our age'), statements of this kind not only bore witness to, but also asserted, the importance of the 'cult of childhood'. They initiated an association between the appropriate treatment of children and civilised values. In the words of the author of an essay about children's art published in 1910, 'A society where there is no love for children, where intense interest in the lives of these little neighbours of ours is lacking – such a society is still very crude, blind, and self-satisfied; and it will not step forward for a long time.'[3] The allegation that the enemy was ill-treating children started to be a staple of Russian patriotic propaganda during the First World War, as it had not been in earlier conflicts, such as the Crimean War, or the Balkan Crisis of 1878.[4] It followed that a society where children were treated properly had the right to be considered progressive and far-sighted.

Such statements tended not to be based on detailed comparative reflection (how children had actually lived before the modern age); often, too, consideration of the problem of where children's best interests lay was highly superficial. They were not historical or sociological formulations, but crusading banners whose primary purpose was to advertise the righteousness of a particular interpretation of children's welfare and to convert others to the cause.

Nevertheless, the organisers of the exhibition were entirely right to argue that their era had witnessed an explosion of interest in childhood, and that this phenomenon had had impact in a large number of areas. Alongside the ones they themselves chose to mention (legislation, philanthropy, anthropology, and psychology), one could add child welfare, children's literature, pedagogy, and the representation of children in the arts. In practical terms, change was limited by the conservatism of the Russian government, but discussions were lively, and all of them engaged with – even if not directly setting out – concepts of childhood that were (in the Russian context) radically new. Even if they had difficulty in achieving what they wished, pro-child activists had coherent ideals that were in many cases more imaginative than those which shaped policy later on.

Children and the Law

Prior to 1917, children had a limited status as juridical subjects. The concept of 'children's rights' as the term is often now understood – to signify freedom of self-expression and other aspects of personal autonomy[5] – was not a subject of general discussion. Lawyers were preoccupied with 'rights' in another sense: with a child's entitlement to sustenance, nurture, and protection from adults, and with the need to enshrine and defend this in law. The crucial phrase was *zashchita prav detei*, 'defence/protection of the rights of children', used interchangeably with *zashchita detei*, 'defence/protection of children'.[6] Issues that particularly preoccupied jurists at the time included the regulation of child labour and the institution of sanctions against poor employers, and the prosecution of parents who failed in their duty of care.[7]

The interpretation of 'children's rights' to mean primarily the protection of children was the international norm of the day too. Such an attitude was expressed in two British statutes, the Prevention of Cruelty to Children Act passed in 1904, and the Children Act of 1908, seen by Russian jurists of the day as a model.[8] Indeed, the first international convention on this topic, the 1924 League of Nations Declaration on the Rights of the Child, also legislated in this vein.[9] It was not until the 1970s that children's rights in another sense – the right to self-expression and to self-determination – began to be the subject of intensive discussion, even in Western cultures with a long history of debate on personal rights.[10] In economically deprived and strife-ridden societies into the twenty-first century, the personal liberty of children was of far less interest than was the concern to protect. The emphasis lay not on children's 'right to work', but on protecting them from exploitation in the labour market, and not on children's right to sexual self-expression, but on the need to stamp out child prostitution.[11]

The rudimentary nature of the debate on 'children's rights', in the sense of personal liberties, in Russia had another context too: the lack of legislation in an overall sense relating to children. Family law still enshrined the patriarch as mini-tsar in his own household, with his wife and progeny perceived as dependants.[12] In the phrasing of the 1900 Civil Code, parental power extended to children no matter what their age.[13] To be sure, 'power' on the parental side was tempered by 'responsibilities' or 'duties', which meant that, for instance, desertion of children attracted a prison sentence, and child murder was deemed a crime within the family as well as outside it. It was also compulsory to provide children with food, clothing, moral guidance, and, if the child were born into an Orthodox family, to bring him or her up as an Orthodox believer.[14] But the control of parents over children was none the less absolute, in the sense that it was not subject to challenge from the junior side.[15] Parents were entitled not only to 'make use of domestic methods of correction' if their children should be 'obstreperous and disobedient', but also to have them committed to prison if they should fail to respond to these methods.[16] As in medieval and Enlightenment tradition, parents were seen above all as stern guardians of morality. They themselves were legally responsible for their children's crimes and misdemeanours if these could be held to have occurred because the parents had been insufficiently vigilant, and they were also responsible for disciplining their children in cases where the misdemeanours were too insignificant to merit a prison sentence (or where the children were too young to qualify for one).[17]

Children were regarded not just as the raw material of their parents' moral endeavours, but as legal dependants in other respects. Those under 14 had limited property rights (a more or less universal situation in legal systems, of course, and one that at least had the virtue of inhibiting exploitation of those who were unlikely to have a full comprehension of complex documentation to do with deeds of title, say, as well as of economic realities).[18] Considerably more oppressive was the fact that children were precluded from engaging in litigation against their parents in cases of 'personal injury [*lichnaya obida*] or insult [*oskorblenie*]' (though they were permitted to denounce parents for serious crimes against other persons). Obviously, such a prohibition could only act as an inhibition to the reporting and identification of parental abuse. And, while the law deemed that a child under 14 could not exercise legal authority even through an intermediary, it also deemed that children between 10 and 14 were capable of criminal actions, for which they might be tried and punished in a court of law.[19]

But if all this is typical of the archaic and repressive character of Imperial Russian legislation with regard to roles within the family in general, the legal situation of children was also typical in another way. By the end of the nineteenth century, it had become the focus of lively discussion among liberal jurists and officials,[20] which occasionally made its way into actual legal change. In particular, two important pieces of legislation, dating from 1891 and 1902, significantly improved the legal status of children born outside wedlock.[21] The 1891 law introduced a process of legitimation for certain categories of children, notably those who were the fruit of pre-marital or extra-marital liaisons, but whose parents married at some point after their birth. The 1902 law granted automatic legitimacy to children in these categories, and allowed full legal rights to children of a marriage later pronounced null and void (who had been legitimable by petitioning to the sovereign from 1891, and illegitimate from the moment the marriage was dissolved prior to that). It also regulated procedure in the case of children born to single mothers (who were allowed to take their mother's surname and their godfather's patronymic, if no father was registered on the birth certificate, and who were entitled to maintenance payments from their natural father, provided his identity could be established). And it laid down custody arrangements in the case of divorced parents: children were to stay with whichever parent the divorcing couple agreed was best, with access rights (*pravo svidaniya*) allowed to the other, who was also required to contribute to the costs of raising the child. Though the category of illegitimacy remained in place, the changes, particularly those of 1902, constituted a significant liberalisation of Russian civil law.[22]

The main thrust of legal reform none the less was towards child protection, particularly outside the family. Legislation regulating child labour had a pedigree of some decades by the end of the nineteenth century. An important law, passed on 1 June 1882, forbade factory work for children under 12 and night work for any under 15, and limited those aged between 12 and 15 to a maximum of eight hours per day; it also regulated philanthropic and educational institutions.[23] An article of this law also required factory owners to open schools on the premises.[24]

By the late nineteenth century, child protection within the family had also come within the purview of jurists. For example, article 361 of the draft Criminal Code of 1895 imposed a prison sentence for cruelty to a person under 17; for forced marriage, where the person concerned was under 21; for forcing a minor into mendicancy; and for forcing a minor into sexual vice (*nepotrebstvo*).[25] The draft Civil Code of 1902 contained an article dealing with the termination of parental power, where a parent, adoptive parent, or guardian had lost their civil rights (*prava sostoyaniya*), or had been guilty of prostituting a child or abusing their authority over it. Incapable parents (who were under age, mad, disabled, habitually drunk, or otherwise incapacitated) could have their parental power removed on a temporary basis.[26]

Yet the inalienable association between parental authority and the authority of the state impeded large-scale reform. The early twentieth century saw the foundation of several pressure groups concerned with the effects of bad parenting. A Society for the Protection of Children from Cruel Treatment (Obshchestvo zashchity detei ot zhestokogo obrashcheniya) was set up in 1903, with Grand Duchess Ol'ga Aleksandrovna as its patron; in 1911 it had 93 children in its care.[27] However, it was only in 1914 that a society with a specifically legal remit, the Society for the Legal Protection of Minors, began its operation and the issue of affording abused children statutory protection – as opposed to providing for them in a philanthropic sense – started to receive specialist discussion. At its first meeting, members of the society expressed frustration at the difficulty of getting children removed from abusive parents (the major agents of abuse in the cases that had come to the attention of the Society for the Protection of Children from Cruel Treatment), but specific reforms were not suggested.[28] Change on a large scale had to wait until 1917, and the foundation of a legal order of a very different kind.

'Free Education'

A similar tension between the archaic status quo and pressure for change, often driven by a sense that Russia was falling behind Western Europe, was felt in the world of Russian education. On the one hand, Tsarist educational provision still, on the eve of the twentieth century, maintained the close relationship between schooling and social estate inherent in the educational reforms of Catherine II nearly a century and a half earlier. Indeed, this relationship was intensified by the so-called 'cooks' children' circular, a notorious and originally secret Ministry of Education document of 18 June 1887, which decreed that certain types of secondary school should cease admitting children who came from the peasantry and the *meshchanstvo* (urban lower classes).[29] Entry to the most prestigious boys' schools, such as the Alexander Lyceum in St Petersburg (formerly Tsarskoe Selo), the College of Jurisprudence, and the Corps des Pages, also in the capital, had in any case always been limited by statute to those with noble ancestry. The same applied to the Institutes for Daughters of the Nobility, the chief among which was the Smol'nyi Institute in St Petersburg, but which also included establishments in Moscow and in many provincial cities. The primary relevance of the 'cooks' children' circular was therefore to the most privileged types of urban day schools. First among these was the *gimnaziya* (classical high school), which had a curriculum including compulsory Latin and, until 1902, also Greek, and attendance at which was the single officially acceptable track to a university education. The *gimnaziya* was primarily intended to cater for city-dwelling members of the nobility and for the children of the service classes, although the presence of children whose parents belonged to the merchant class (a tax rank, rather than an estate) was tolerated (and there was no official limit on their numbers). A slightly broader social role was envisaged for the *real'noe uchilishche*, which, like the German *Realschule*, offered a larger range of scientific and practical subjects and was supposed to lead to some form of vocational tertiary education (a polytechnic or forestry institute, for instance). But it was other types of secondary school that were supposed to be the primary destination for the plebeian (including the offspring of merchant families): the so-called 'commercial colleges', offering training in bookkeeping and other business-oriented skills alongside the academic syllabus, the various 'trade' and 'craft' schools (*remeslennye uchilishcha*), where pupils studied for three to four years, the colleges and 'seminaries' for teachers, and the 'higher primary schools' (*vysshie nachal'nye uchilishcha*), which offered a four-year secondary course intended to complement the education offered in city primary schools.

The 'cooks' children' circular never achieved its stated aim of barring the way to secondary education for those who, as the minister responsible for drafting the document argued, would get ideas above their station if they received it. The base position, up to 1917, remained that *gimnazii* were open to all, regardless of social standing.[30] But the circular did make studying in elite secondary schools more difficult. The official supposition in the late Imperial era was that children from the peasantry and working class would have access to, at the most ambitious, a truncated course of secondary education with a strong vocational colouring. The majority of them would go through the primary system and no more.

Even this supposition, of course, pointed to changing social attitudes in the Russian establishment, in which fears that education for the masses would generate educational instability were starting to be outweighed by the belief that improved education was essential to the Russian Empire's economic competitiveness, military might, and status as a civilised nation. By the late 1890s, at least three years of primary education was compulsory in most European countries, including Romania, Portugal, Italy, and Spain, as well as the major industrial nations, and also in Turkey and the majority of American states.[31] In this period, the Tsarist government had not yet committed itself to the introduction of compulsory primary education. Only in 1907, during the reforming period initiated by the uprisings of 1905, did the first legislation in this area start to be drawn up.[32] But the late nineteenth century witnessed a huge expansion in the elementary school network run by the Ministry of Enlightenment. Between 1905 and 1911 alone, the numbers of such schools rose by 37 per cent, and the pupils in them by 47 per cent.[33] An even more significant rise took place in the number of schools run by the Russian Church, which increased more than eightfold between 1884 and 1903.[34]

From some points of view, the Russian primary school system represented organisational chaos – more than twenty types of institution were in existence, funded by a large number of bodies, including, alongside the Ministry of Enlightenment and the Church, local administrative units such as the zemstva and the City dumas, as well as private initiative.[35] But there was increasing conviction about the need to move towards state-controlled, systematically regulated, primary education. Even material published in the Ministry of Enlightenment's own journal represented the system of education by social estate as outdated and saw the introduction of a nationwide system of primary education as an essential step towards social justice and the establishment of national consensus. The prolific educationalist V. I. Farmakovsky called in 1905 for an integrated primary syllabus that would provide children from all social groups with an education that could be autonomous (for those not continuing with education after this first stage) while also offering appropriate preparation for the secondary school.[36]

Criticism was also starting to be aimed at what one commentator termed the 'bookishness, dryness and abstraction' of the state primary programme, alongside its 'limited horizons' in an intellectual sense. The fact that the school provided no proper tuition in manual labour was seen as a disadvantage to its peasant graduates: ideally, such an institution should not only provide tuition in 'craft skills', but train peasants 'how to prepare the mostly simple implements and objects required around the household and on the farm'.[37]

Certainly, the reformist debate in ministerial circles remained cautious. There was still a commitment to an estate-led educational system at secondary level. V. I. Farmakovsky, addressing the new model of the 'comprehensive school' which was becoming familiar to Russian educationalists from discussions in Germany, argued that integration at this level was undesirable. Different children had different needs at secondary level (some would end up at university, others disappear into employment at a much earlier stage), and parental choice would be adversely affected if educational differentials were to vanish.[38] These arguments were standard at the time. Given that there was an important constituency at the heart of Tsarist government (including Nicholas II) which was opposed on principle to the retrenchment of estate-based privilege, the introduction of the 'comprehensive school' did not seem even a remote possibility. At the same time, there was some re-examination of secondary-school provision from a different point of view – that of the academic demands made on pupils by the secondary syllabus, particularly the one current in the *gimnaziya*, which included, alongside classical and foreign languages, mathematics, physics, history and geography, Russian language and literature, and religious knowledge, and allowed almost no time to non-academic subjects such as physical or art education.[39]

Already in 1900, a commission set up by the then Minister of Education, N. P. Bogdanov, had proposed reforming the *gimnaziya* programme by setting up an eight-year secondary-school course in two stages (*stupeni*). The first five years were to be devoted to a broad programme of general education covering Russian, foreign languages, mathematics, history, geography, physics, chemistry, and nature study, with plenty of time for non-academic subjects such as physical education, drawing, singing, and handcraft. At this time, teaching was supposed to adopt a concrete, hands-on approach, and, in the words of a later commentator, 'not to do violence to the intellectual bent of the child's mind by unleashing a premature torrent of abstract ideas'.[40] Only the final three years were to introduce a more explicitly academic programme, serving as a bridge between school and university and introducing subjects such as classical languages. While, in the event, the reform came to nothing, it testified to a tentative recognition of 'child-centred' principles even in the educational administration.

In the 1900s and 1910s also, increasing public scrutiny was accorded to pedagogical techniques. It was widely recognised that the teaching of Greek and Latin, in particular, was deficient in signal respects. Even classicists admitted that teachers often showed 'a monotonous preoccupation with grammar', and were markedly unsuccessful in giving pupils the ability to understand Greek and Latin texts, let alone a love of the classics.[41] Ministry of Education commentators were, however, timid in comparison with many voices raised in this period, which saw an astonishing flowering of liberal pedagogy in the broadest sense. New educational forums, such as the Khar'kov Literacy Society, sprang up in the major towns of the Russian Empire; a specialist pedagogical press came into being, as manifested in a number of important journals, such as *Russian School*, *Education and Training*, the *Educational Herald*, and *Free Education*; and there was a series of landmark educational congresses, such as the All-Zemstvo Congress on Education (Moscow, 1911) and the All-Russian Congress on Public Education (held at the end of 1913 in St Petersburg).

The regimentation and intellectual narrowness of traditional education had, by the late nineteenth century, become the focus of widespread criticism. In the words of an article published by the *Educational Herald* in 1900, 'Among the countless faults of the modern school, the fact that all pupils in it are subjected to a single level of moral and intellectual stereotyping has a particularly fateful character.'[42] Criticism was supported by hygienists and psychologists, who emphasised the excessiveness of the demands made on schoolchildren, and the pernicious consequences of these in terms of physical and mental strain. Much was written on the 'exhaustion' from which children, especially secondary school children, suffered, and on the contribution made by this to rising suicide rates among young people: L. Prozorov, writing in 1914, pointed to a cluster of suicides in early summer and linked them with the fact that this was the season when pupils sat examinations and the issue of whether they might or might not go up a class was resolved.[43] Critics of this kind were often inspired, at one level or another, by the educational ideas of Tolstoy, and also by the experimental educational projects being set up overseas.[44]

Opponents of the status quo often spoke in positive as well as negative terms, advocating a transition to the 'free upbringing' movement whose roots lay in the writings of Western theorists such as Montessori and Froebel, as well as in the work of Russian writers on pedagogy such as Ushinsky and Tolstoy.[45] According to the programmatic statement by M. Gorbunov-Posadov in the first issue of the journal *Free Education* (1907):

> In the new school there will be no place for compulsion of any kind, for any violent assault on the soul of the child. [...] The basic form of human labour, physical labour, productive manual labour, will not be held in scorn and contempt. [...] Children will be given every means to satisfy the desire felt by every normal human being to discover a form of labour that best suits him. [...] We [the adults] are not teachers, but learners; we are not moral authorities, but searchers after truth.[46]

Even more conservative commentators were starting to take a direct interest in alternative forms of conveying information, such as taking the pupils on excursions into the surrounding environment rather than simply keeping them sitting in classrooms staring at the blackboard.[47] In the words of a modern historian of education, 'Russian educational theory was remarkably "child-centred" [in this period]. It focused on non-coercive motivation, fostering self-esteem and initiative, "discovery learning", and the mastering of learning skills and strategies. This is a major paradox: the existence – at least on paper – of a child-centred curriculum in a coercive, hierarchical, authoritarian society. In the jargon of historians of education, schools did not *replicate* society: this would suggest that they played a major role in transforming it.'[48]

This argument, however, cannot be pushed too far. Concepts such as 'non-coercive motivation' were certainly deeply entrenched in the work of 'free schools', such as 'The House of the Free Child' in Moscow, organised by a group of enthusiasts in the 1910s. This school was so keen not to encroach upon pupils' autonomy that there was no formal timetable: instead, pupils occupied themselves as they wished at a given point, though compulsory attendance had to be introduced for staff after the first few months had passed, in order that they could be around to provide tuition as required by the pupils. The staff made every effort not to impose their own wishes and opinions on the pupils, problematic as this might be when an individual became disruptive: the accepted technique was simply to abandon troublesome children to their own devices until they calmed down.[49] Similar work was carried on by the so-called 'village *gimnaziya*' outside St Petersburg.[50] Such schools, however, were private institutions with a very small intake, often (as with the House of the Free Child) exclusively of children from the intelligentsia; and they tended to wither away once the children concerned had got to an age where their parents began worrying about educational qualifications, at which point they reluctantly packed them off to the usual kind of school.[51]

For its part, the state school curriculum was 'child-centred' only in a restricted sense before 1917. At secondary level, the subordination of secondary schools to rigorous inspection by Ministry of Education officials (who could impose heavy disciplinary penalties on teachers, right up to dismissal), alongside the commitment of many individual teachers to academic values, were constraints to change. Complications were also generated by the revolutionary upheavals of 1905, which saw schoolchildren all over the Russian Empire participating in strikes and protests, evoking reactions ranging from amused condescension (as in a story by Nadezhda Teffi published in the St Petersburg satirical magazine *Satirikon*, which showed small boys lisping out their demands for 'fweedom' and 'fwee love') to alarm verging on panic.[52]

For liberal educationalists, the prevalence of strikes and political agitation in the schoolroom demonstrated how pointless it was to attempt to keep children ignorant of current affairs and democratic procedures. 'The worn-out phrases about how politics has no place in the school are precisely phrases, and no more,' wrote one such commentator in the conclusion to his survey of pupil unrest all over the Russian provinces.[53] The Ministry of Education, however, took precisely the opposite view, making repeated declarations that pupil organisations in schools would not be tolerated.[54] Reactions to political activity on the part of schoolchildren were decisive: in Ekaterinoslav, six *gimnaziya* pupils were expelled from the city on 18 December 1905 and another imprisoned at the beginning of the following year. Stavropol' pupils were warned in September 1906 by the local provincial governor that 'anyone who does not wish to continue his education and thus obstructs the majority will be invited to leave the *gimnaziya* immediately or will be regarded as responsible for the unrest taking place in the institution and expelled beyond the boundaries of our province or imprisoned'. He continued, 'Pedagogical personnel who fail to take action will be relieved by me of their positions.'[55]

Yet child-centred views of education were not entirely thrust from view, even at this point. For example, in response to the 1905–6 school unrest, measures were set in place to lighten school discipline. The wearing of school uniform was made voluntary, and school libraries were permitted to acquire books not on the 'recommended' lists issued by the Ministry of Education. Attempts were also made to involve parents more actively in the life of the school (parent associations were tolerated from November 1905).[56]

In the 1910s, 'free education', albeit in the most diluted sense, started to make an impact upon the secondary system. In 1915, Count P. N. Ignat'ev, the last Minister of Education under the Tsars, set up a large-scale commission whose remit was to work out in detail the syllabus for a new type of secondary school that would be 'national, autonomous, i.e. providing a general education in its own right and not simply a preparation for tertiary education, and with a course of seven years arranged as a first stage of 3 years and a second stage of 4 years'. What this meant in practice was that all secondary schools would henceforth be called *gimnazii*, and would have an identical programme in their first four years. Only in the top three classes would the syllabus diverge, with the 'Classics and Humanities *Gimnaziya*' concentrating on classical languages, the 'Modern Humanities *Gimnaziya*' on modern languages, and the 'Real *Gimnaziya*' (i.e. *Realschule*) on maths and sciences. Apart from giving the old 'Real Schools' the status of *gimnaziya* and introducing a new type of 'modern' secondary school, the effect of the proposals was a significant lightening of the academic load that had formerly been imposed on *gimnaziya* pupils. The first three years of the course now offered a 'general education' of exactly the kind that had been proposed in 1900, though here with 'physics' and 'chemistry' replaced by the more hands-on 'practical scientific study'. Once again, drawing, singing, and physical education (though not handcraft) were mentioned as central parts of the programme. In the second part of the course, academic subjects occupied a greater proportion of the timetable than in stage 1, but a significantly reduced place compared with the traditional *gimnaziya* timetable of the past. A total of 23–26 hours was to be devoted to academic subjects, and 4–5 hours per week to non-academic subjects, as opposed to the 27–29 hours on academic subjects, and none on non-academic subjects, envisaged by the status quo. In terms of balance, pupils would end up doing rather less maths, history, and geography, and significantly less Latin, than they had.

Syllabus content was also altered. The literary part of the programme, for instance, envisaged a drastic paring-down of pre-1800 Russian texts, along with the admission to the syllabus of the kind of 'ethically difficult' recent texts that officials had formerly been keen to see avoided – Dostoevsky's *Crime and Punishment*, say, or Tolstoy's *Anna Karenina*. The wide-ranging selection of poetry for compulsory study included such political 'hot potatoes' as Lermontov's 'Death of a Poet' (his assault on the official persecutors of Pushkin) and Pushkin's own 'The Village' and 'To the Sea'. 'Aesthetic education' was not only given an important place in its own right (in the form of drawing, the study of works of art, etc.), but also contributed much to the choice of literary texts for study. An earlier reform of the syllabus in 1905 had (to fierce objections from some, particularly university teachers of literature) attempted to slim down the historicist drive in the school literature programme, to select works on the basis of their 'poetic' value, and to place more emphasis on 'immanent reading'. The 1915 reform promised to go much further.[57]

Yet even these 1915 reforms (which were, in the event, frustrated by the collapse of the Tsarist government) should not be seen simply as a belated victory for 'child-centred' learning. Certainly, they had some remarkable features – such as the assignation of relevant children's classics to younger pupils learning a foreign language. In English, for example, reading was to include *Little Lord Fauntleroy*, extracts from *Gulliver's Travels*, Kingsley's *The Water Babies*, and Talbot Baines Reed's *The Fifth Form at St Dominic's*.[58] But the proposals also embodied other motifs that had been prominent in the 1900s and 1910s, and which were less to do with liberalisation than with increasing control over the school system. So far as the literature syllabus was concerned, the schedule of specified texts was set out with unprecedented precision. The 1905 syllabus had identified general areas for study (for example, 'Pushkin's Lyceum Years') but had left the selection of some individual texts (for instance, the lyric poems to be studied) to individual teachers.[59] Now, however, the exact material to be covered was regulated from the centre, not just the arrangement of it (which remained, as before, chronological, by date of a work's composition). To increased control over the syllabus was added increased emphasis on self-control, and on 'education for citizenship', in the treatment of pupils.

Throughout the nineteenth and early twentieth centuries, the main instrument of disciplinary control in Russian schools had been an adult with pastoral authority – the *klassnyi nastavnik* 'class supervisor' for boys, the *klassnaya dama* ('class lady', a translation of the French *dame de classe*) for girls. From the early 1900s, though, Russian educationalists had been looking with interest at what they saw as a different and potentially more effective system; what one enthusiast called 'the moral education of the English gentleman', or horizontal surveillance by prefects, accompanied by a strong emphasis on team sports as a focus of institutional patriotism, and by self-regulation on the part of individual pupils.[60] This interest was made concrete in official policy for the first time in the 1915 programme, which proposed introducing Scout troops – on a strictly voluntary basis – into the secondary school system (Scout drill would become part of the PE syllabus for participating institutions). The purpose of this would be, in the words of the programme itself: 'to inculcate in Russian youths between twelve and eighteen love for and fidelity to the motherland, the love of helping and habit of helping one's neighbour, and an independent, tough-minded character, which would be obvious in every action and be expressed in the fervent execution of everything demanded by one's sense of duty both in large matters and in small'.[61] In other words, a system of external control was to be replaced by one of internal control: the reformed school would not so much furnish its graduates with autonomy as tutor them in rational, willed techniques of self-subordination.

Model Nursery Schools

'Free education', then, was at best a marginal trend in secondary education, with 'moral education', 'education for citizenship' and, above all, academic education remaining the central values in the curriculum. The effects of the new 'child-centred' approach were limited even in the state primary system, though pioneering work was done by some staff in the government and zemstvo system.[62] It was accordingly private primary, and especially nursery, schools where radical pedagogical ideas could be enacted (as had, indeed, been true since the educational experiments of Vladimir Odoevsky and Leo Tolstoy in the first half of the nineteenth century).

By the early twentieth century, formal pre-school education was the subject of increasingly frequent discussion in print. The term *detskii sad*, a calque of 'kindergarten', had come into use during the 1860s, when some Russian disciples of Froebel began working with children in St Petersburg. With the close of the decade, however, most of these endeavours withered away, though one private kindergarten, run by Evgeniya Aristova, opened in 1873, and acting as a training centre, as well as a facility for children, survived to celebrate its twenty-fifth anniversary in 1898.[63] In some early discussions of the 'kindergarten', up to and including the turn of the twentieth century, the term was applied widely, to encompass a programme of liberal education for all children of below *gimnaziya* age.[64] However, in the early twentieth century, interest grew precisely in work with children below the age of eight, who were seen as particularly impressionable, and hence good material for early socialisation.[65]

As with other areas of work with children, a stimulating factor was awareness of work that was being done abroad. One article published in 1896 lamented that, while municipal kindergartens in Berlin were providing 4,500 children with a pre-school education that cost their parents next to nothing, a mere 260 children attended pre-school facilities in Moscow.[66] Some discussions of pre-school education concentrated on the likely benefits to children who came from deprived homes, or indeed had been deserted by their parents, but the 'custodial' view was by no means the only one in operation. Numerous articles emphasised the gains to all children from attending such institutions. It was argued that kindergartens should not be places that submitted children to intellectual drilling; their contribution to the development of co-ordination and imaginative thinking was stressed, and there were often claims that they had huge benefits from a social point of view as well, since children learned to get on with each other and learned from each other.[67]

The 1905 Revolution, which marked a general upsurge of enthusiasm for public work among the Russian intelligentsia, also saw the nursery school movement began to develop more widely. Parent associations sprang up in different parts of the Russian Empire to support kindergarten development, fostered by new legislation of 1908 which, for the first time, recognised nursery education as a specific area and set down rules for its operation.[68] There was a rise of interest in the theory of nursery education too. The work of Maria Montessori was translated into Russian in the 1910s, and educational journals (for example *Education and Training* and the *Educational Herald* as well as *Free Education*) frequently carried items about it. Numerous advice pamphlets, including practical guides for parents and teachers as well as discussions of child psychology in the abstract, paid tribute to the virtues of 'free education'.[69] A landmark was the founding in 1911 of the Kiev journal *Pre-School Education*, run by the Society of People's Kindergartens, which continued running till the October Revolution of 1917. The journal, which in its first issue looked forward to a time 'when the science of character education will be set in place and the "country of our children" discovered', campaigned energetically in favour of nursery education for all. Rebutting arguments that founding kindergartens destroyed the family or made children unfit for school, the journal's participants drew hair-raising pictures of the spoiled, petulant products of ordinary upbringing, and emphasised that only through nursery education could modern mothers cope with their load.[70]

Discussions of nursery education had become more prominent and expressed a greater confidence than before. They had also changed in character. There was increasing emphasis on the virtues of the nursery school as an instrument of instilling rational collectivism in children. According to one prospectus published in 1907, 'The company of other children of the same age is essential if a child is to develop harmoniously. [...] The worst punishment for a child is excluding him from communal work.'[71] Practical skills (a junior version of 'education through labour') were stressed. The recommended curriculum consisted almost entirely of educational games (work with alphabet cards, building blocks, and abacuses), of creative activities such as drawing, modelling, and handcraft, and of physical activities such as singing, dancing, and 'active games'; and of nature study.[72]

The Mind of the Child

New writing on pedagogy was, in a sense, the practical spin-off from the 'advances in psychology' referred to by the organisers of the 1910 Children and Work exhibition. But in fact the general direction of historical evolution in Russia went the other way. A new image of the child broke through in liberationist pedagogy (in the writings of Tolstoy or Ushinsky) well before anything resembling child psychology was in circulation. Indeed, some writings on the nature of childhood continued to be of a thoroughly conventional kind as late as the turn of the century. For example, P. Lesgaft's much-reprinted volume, *Family Upbringing and its Meaning*, revived the centuries-old Hippocratic or Galenic theory of the humours (sanguine, melancholy, choleric, and phlegmatic) in order to sketch the 'inborn' material that parents needed to shape.[73] Equally, while the Kiev organisers had also spoken of 'advances in ethnography', a good few writings on childhood remained of a traditionally nationalist, 'aetiology of the Russian people', variety, dwelling on the customs and practices considered specific to the individual culture.[74]

However, the established taste, among members of the intelligentsia, for anti-traditional writings on pedagogy generated interest in child psychology once this had begun to emerge in the West. The 1900s and 1910s, in particular, saw extensive publication of a whole range of translated material. Binet and Simon's study of how to test for intellectual ability (a forerunner of the later genre of 'IQ tests') first appeared in Russian in 1909, and Freud's writings on early childhood were published in the general edition of his works that began to appear in the 1910s.[75] But the most influential body of Western writings was probably that composed by members of the so-called 'child study movement', also known as 'paidology' – such as the American Stanley Hall, or the Briton James Sully.[76] Sully's *Studies of Childhood*, published in 1895, was translated into Russian in 1909 and was to have a lengthy influence on Russian writings about childhood. The book – lively, and still very readable more than a century later – took what was essentially a universalist-ethnographical approach to childhood. Drawing on close observation, Sully underlined the specificities of the juvenile psyche, its 'otherness' in terms of adult perceptions: 'At the cradle we are watching the beginnings of things, the first tentative thrustings forward into life.'[77] Like the 'primitive' cultures studied by contemporary ethnography, childhood was 'other' because it preserved perceptions going back to the 'beginnings of things', to the dawn of human culture. The dread mingled with incomprehension that was inspired in children by death was an illustration of this. Yet, paradoxically, Sully emphasised children's capacity for innovation, citing instances where they had rebelled against the moral and theological system imposed upon them by adults. A three-year-old girl who had been told of God's 'ever-spying eye' had responded, he related, by insisting, 'I will not be so tagged'.[78] He expanded in particular on children's capacity for linguistic invention, hazarding that they would develop 'the rudiments of a vocal language' even if they had no adult models, and suggesting that in some areas (for example, the articulation of consonants) their performance was often superior to that of adults.[79]

Russians were also well aware of Darwin's biological rather than ethnographical study of child psychology, in the diaries that he had written about his infant son's acquisition of movement, emotions, and language, and of the 1876 essay about language development in a small girl by Hippolyte Taine, which had inspired Darwin to publish these diaries.[80] Familiar, too, was the work of German scholars who had applied themselves to the close observation of children, such as Preyer; Preyer's work was used abundantly in the courses run by the pioneering Paedological Institute set up by V. M. Bekhterev at his Psycho-Neurological Institute in St Petersburg in 1907. And the late 1900s and 1910s saw the emergence of a number of original (in the sense of 'not translated') works by Russian pioneers of child psychology. *The Soul of the Child* (1909), by Ivan Sikorsky, the first Russian translator of Preyer, began with a lengthy and rather laborious discussion of the physiology of foetal, infant, and child development in its relationship to the evolution of species – the child's progression from frogspawn through lower mammals up to full human being, as it were. But it also contained a section on psychological development after birth which emphasised the idiosyncrasies of human nature – the child's capacity for language, for instance, or the importance of associations in the evolution of its mental world: '*The development of basic associations is therefore the most important event in the life of early childhood.*[81] Sikorsky stressed characteristics such as the capacity for 'inward attention', or rapt concentation on one's own mental world and on the nuances of emotion: anger was the earliest feeling manifested in a child, followed by fear and shame, but later children became able to sense more complex emotions, such as tenderness, aesthetic and intellectual feelings, and so on. Like Darwin and Taine, Sikorsky illustrated his book with examples from his observation of children, some taken from the behaviour of his own children – such as his 4-year-old son's exclamation, on seeing his father in the bath, 'Heavens, he's got shoulders!' (introduced as a case of how children judged the nature of the body from what they could see on the surface: here, the child was witnessing his father without clothes for the first time and realising there was 'something inside').[82]

It was in fact in the vein less of theorisation than of empirically based description that Russian adherents to the 'child study' movement of this generation were to make their most important contributions. One pioneer in the field was G. I. Rossolimo, a neurologist who became interested in child psychology from the late 1900s. Rossolimo, who presided over the Institute of Child Neurology and Psychology in Moscow from 1911 to 1917, invented his own forms of psychological profiling, with emphasis on attention span and on emotional characteristics, as well as on numerical, verbal, and spatial skills – a kind of fusion of the interests of Binet–Simon and of Hall and Sully. Rossolimo's main heuristic instrument was an elaborate questionnaire for the psychologically holistic investigation of the child, 'The Plan for the Study of the Child's Soul', as he termed it, which gathered information about parental background and living conditions, daily regime, moral education and other aspects of upbringing, and a whole range of psychological characteristics, including memory, aesthetic sense, taste for particular types of food and leisure activity, the condition of the 'will', physical constitution, and so on. The complete template for questions stretched to nearly forty pages, and an interview based on it would have taken the best part of a day.[83]

Rossolimo's template for the physician or other medical professional was not the only method of recording information on the early development of children available at the time. The 1910s saw a significant flowering of the genre of 'mother's' or 'father's' diary, the meticulous record of day-by-day observations on an infant and small child's development. Some such texts included practical detail – the process of weaning the child and teaching it to control its bowels, for instance.[84] But others were more or less exclusively records of psychological change. A. Levonevsky's *My Child* (1914) chronicled the writer's son's reactions to visual stimuli and to changes in his environment, his increasing ability to remember details, and his first attempts to articulate meaningful sounds, and later his capacity for flights of fantasy ('if you like we'll fwy on a pwane over that way, over that way, high-high-up') – all without reference to the details of child management.[85] In similar vein, Yuliya Ladunskaya contributed a small-scale study to the journal, *Family Upbringing*, in 1913 about the development of her son's capacity to conceptualise quantities. At one year and nine months, he referred to a thermometer as 'a warm', but at the same age he was starting to use some numbers, albeit in the progression 'theven, ten, lots'.[86] Like James Sully, such writers emphasised above all the dynamism of childhood and the child's capacity for spontaneous joy: in the definition of Sikorsky, a 'normal' childhood constituted not only steady intellectual progression but also 'cheerfulness', 'joy in life', love of play, 'lively mobility', and independence of mind.[87] In other words, the model of childhood in operation was close to the established model of the creative genius or artistic talent – which led in turn to an assertion of childhood as a quintessentially creative phase of life, and to a view of the child artist as the ideal artist.

Young Geniuses

The early twentieth century saw a widespread recognition of 'children's art' as a specific form of artistic activity, with its own rules of composition and methods of perception. Here, as in 'free education' and the development of child psychology, influence from the West played a significant role. Certainly, as early as 1872, the composer Modest Musorgsky had gone some way towards producing work filtered through the consciousness of a child. His outstandingly original song cycle 'The Nursery' evoked the persona of a mischievous but also imaginative and nervous child; in the words of Caryl Emerson, these were 'the sort of song[s] that children themselves might compose about their experiences', and they were rapturously received by children from the moment they were written.[88] However, Musorgsky's work did not immediately initiate a new tradition among Russian composers. For his successors, 'children's music' tended to mean 'music for children', and particularly technically straightforward pieces that could be mastered at an early stage of learning an instrument, as in the case of Tchaikovsky's *Album pour enfants* of 1878. This 'pedagogical direction' continued to dominate later on as well: so far as 'songs children might compose about their experience' (or more generally, 'music') were concerned, the line of musical development could be said to run from Musorgsky to Ravel (in *L'Enfant et les sortilèges*), and then back into Russian tradition through Prokofiev's works of the 1930s, most famously, *Peter and the Wolf* (1936).

In the visual arts, influence from the West was the primary stimulus. The inclusion of children's drawings in the Izdebsky Salon of 1909–10, or Yakov Tugendkhol'd's pioneering article on child art in 1916, came more than twenty years after such landmarks as Ruskin's praise for children's 'innocence of eye' in *The Elements of Drawing*, or the publication of Alfred Lichtwark's *Die Kunst in der Schule* in 1887, or the initiation of *Kind und Kunst* journal in 1890. Franz Cižek had started free (in the sense of liberated) art classes for children in 1897 in Vienna, and the Wiener Kunstschau had mounted an exhibition of children's art in 1908.[89] Once established, the drive to collect, exhibit, and imitate children's art flourished in Russia as vigorously as anywhere. As early as 1908, Benois was showing his daughter's drawings alongside his own; in 1916, the first dedicated exhibition of artistic work by children, presented as art, opened in Moscow; and in the same year a journal by children for children, *Our Magazine*, was started in Petrograd.[90]

Yakov Tugendkhol'd's belief that 'there is something divine in children's drawings – something capricious and elemental; although not all children are born equally talented, of course, it is possible to assert that all children are geniuses in an immanent sense',[91] was widely shared. Among a number of notable artists who collected children's drawings was Mikhail Larionov. His own *The Officer's Barber* (1909–10), in its 'deliberately "uncontrolled" description of anatomy, its flatness and perspective distortion, the reduction of the space into the two planes of foreground and background, the inconsistencies of scale (as in the enlarged scissors), and the limitation of the palette to a domination of brilliant red, blue and brown', represented a direct attempt to capture the peculiarities of children's work.[92] Other 'childlike' works included *Dog on a Chain*, with its use of dark outlining and boxy rendering of the creature's muzzle, or a set of panels of the seasons, in which naïve drawings were accompanied by poems imitating the orthographic and stylistic oddities of small children.[93] A similar fusion of verbal and visual arts drawing on the style of young children was Elena Guro's collection *The Little Camels of the Sky* (1914), where poems of studied alogicality and childlike simplicity of lexicon were set alongside bold and striking pen-and-ink drawings representing stylised animal forms.

The production by adults of such texts went hand in hand with a cultivation of work by children that matched the primitivist aesthetic of Russian Modernist groups such as the Cubo-Futurists and the Donkey's Tail. In 1914, Aleksei Kruchenykh, a contributor to manifestos and collections such as *A Slap in the Face of Public Taste* (1912), and the author of the important treatises on poetic language, *The Word as Such* and *The Letter as Such*, published an anthology of ugly, bold children's drawings, executed in thick dark crayon, which strongly resembled the work of modernist artists such as Olga Rozanova, Nataliya Goncharova, and the Burlyuk brothers. Both here and in the stories and poems that Kruchenykh also included, magic themes predominated: the drawing *The Queen of the Firs*, for example, showed a wild-haired, bulging-nosed androgynous figure lifting a potted twig to the top of a fir tree, eyeballed the while by a formidably grumpy-looking bird. *They Skwobelled* (Pasorilisya) showed the result of the squabble in question: two beaked creatures in human dress, one cannibalistically affecting a large hat with ostrich feathers, stood back to back, heads aloft in high dudgeon.[94]

It was entirely logical that the interest among modernist artists in children's art should have fed into the composition of works of art for children that revolutionised the character and quality of material on offer to young readers and viewers. Landmarks in the history of the illustrated book were Ivan Bilibin's editions of works by Pushkin, including *Mariya Morevna* (1899) and the *skazki* (fairy tales in verse), *The Tale of Tsar Saltan* (1905) and *The Golden Cockerel* (1910). All of these were sumptuously got up, with colour plates of outstanding quality (nine to a book of 20 pages, in the case of *The Tale of Tsar Saltan*) and in-text black and white vignettes. Less ambitious, but equally captivating, was *Old Mother Chatterbox's Tales about Animals*, with illustrations by S. M. Dudin and N. I. Tkachenko, published in about 1910.[95] Equally, the contribution made by modernist writers as authors of children's poetry (not only well-known specialists

7 The Queen of the Firs. Anonymous child's drawing from Aleksei Kruchenykh, *Children's Own Stories and Drawings* (1914).

8 Ivan Bilibin, *The Tale of Tsar Saltan* (1910). A particularly lavishly produced picture-book for the well-off nursery.

9 'The Fox and the Hen', by N. I. Tkachenko, from *Old Mother Chatterbox's Tales about Animals* (*c.* 1910), showing the widely popular folk motifs of the day.

such as Sasha Chernyi, Poliksena Solov'eva, Kornei Chukovsky, and Mariya Moravskaya, but also 'moonlighting' major poets such as Valery Bryusov, Sergei Gorodetsky, and Zinaida Gippius) completely transformed a genre previously (with some noble exceptions, such as the children's poems of Vasily Zhukovsky) characterised by hack-work versification and turgid moralisation.[96] New attitudes to children's art also, of course, influenced the teaching of art to children: the principles of 'free education' were extensively developed in commentaries which insisted that children should not be over-corrected (which had a terrible effect on their creative proclivities), and should be tutored in observation rather than in technical skills. Since 'inspiration always involves liberating oneself from life in general', teaching children to observe convention could only be stifling to their artistic powers.[97]

'The First Golden Dreams of Life'

Another point not mentioned in the Kiev organisers' thumbnail sketch of the 'cult of childhood' in the early 1900s was the development of a consumer culture aimed at children and, more particularly, parents. On offer were not just cultural goods such as books, but clothes, nursery furniture, and toys. The name Children's World was already in use before the Revolution for a specialist store in St Petersburg offering a vast range of books and goods, and with a mail-order service.[98] An equally impressive selection of items could be purchased at Child-Raising (Detskoe vospitanie) (in Leont'evsky pereulok, with a branch in Neglinnaya). The catalogue for 1899 has pages of perambulators, cradles, baby-changing tables, layettes, dolls, and games, with a spread of prices (for example long dresses in white piqué for small babies ranged in price from 6 to 8 roubles 'and upwards').[99]

A further significant development in this period was the evolution of special children's festivals. Chief among these was the Christmas tree party, *elka*, with its paraphernalia of wrapped presents and decorations, alongside, of course, the beribboned and candle-studded tree itself. This occasion was not native to Russia any more than it was to Britain, but, as in Britain, the 'invented tradition' was well established by the late nineteenth century. Moneyed families organised their own Christmas tree parties; institutions, such as orphanages, provided similar celebrations, complete with presents, for poor children.[100] Even some atheist revolutionary families did not feel it incumbent on them to ban trees from their households.[101] When the journal *Family Education* organised a reader poll on the *elka* in 1913, 42 out of 44 respondents were in favour of the custom, on the grounds that children enjoyed it, and that it developed aesthetic thinking and self-reliance.[102]

The move to a child-centred environment in terms of reorganising domestic space is another point recorded by autobiographers of the late nineteenth century. During the 1870s, for example, the parents of Prince Evgeny Trubetskoi blocked up the beautiful neo-classical colonnade of their inherited country mansion with plywood in order to expand the amount of space available for family use.[103] By the late nineteenth century, the recommendation in normative sources such as domestic manuals was that the 'biggest, most cheerful and sunniest room in the house, with a view of a garden or of green trees if possible' should be selected for the nursery, and that the room should be kitted out with a range of child-sized furniture (not only cots or beds, but desks, chairs, and tables). The special status of the nursery within the parental dwelling was the subject of sentimental eulogy:

> The place where the children of the family experience the first golden dreams of life, in which the young human saplings grow slowly into new trees, is, in its own way, a holy place. Strictly speaking, only those should be allowed to enter here whose relationship with the children is warm and loving, who are always ready to sacrifice at the very least the more trivial needs of their own ego for the good and well-being of the children at any time. [...] A joyful childhood casts its roseate glow on a person's whole life, no matter what storms have to be endured later on.[104]

A 'roseate glow' hung over not only written texts, but paintings. A typical example was a portrait by a minor woman painter, Emiliya Yakovlevna Shanks (1857–1936), *The Lesson* (1887). Though the medium was oil, the piece had the quality of a pastel, and its studiedly pretty subject was a small girl in a pink dress and blonde curls standing next to a vase of flowers and pointing out to her dolly a mezzotint of stern papa or grandpapa in his suit and stiff collar.[105] As here, the adored, indulged child became the subject of celebration. Portraits of round-cheeked tots with ribbons or Little Lord Fauntleroy suits abounded, and were not by any means limited to the *oeuvre* of minor painters such as Shanks. The portraits of Valentin Serov included several charming, but decidedly sentimental, studies (of Mika Morozov, son of the entrepreneur and patron of the arts, and of Serov's own sons Sasha and Yura), showing the subjects in androgynous mode (mops of curls, clothes in pastel hues) and as remote from the adult viewer, lost in an alternative world of mysterious, but always benign, dreaminess. Official photographs of the royal children often showed them posed informally and in

10 Valentin Serov, *Portrait of Mika Morozov.*

45

11   Vasily Rozanov, 'Portrait of the Author's Children', *Fallen Leaves.*

costumes and settings that underlined their status as children (in pinafores and sailor suits, looking with alertness and interest at the camera). And literature for children burst out into rampant cuteness: favourite subjects included, apart from the ever-present and always angelic mummy, puppies, kittens, Christmas trees, songbirds, and religious pieces about Little Baby Jesus.[106] This side of writing for children was summed up in a piece with the title 'Children's World' (1909) by A. A. Korinfsky:

> Children's world! No thunder and no snowstorms!
> Here a sun of purest beauty glows,
> As in a garden never wrapped in mist,
> Wondrous flowers bloom.[107]

Just as in the case of idealised portraiture, some very important artists contributed to the literary eulogisation of the 'children's world'. Among these was the thinker and journalist Vasily Rozanov, whose famous collection of fragments and aphorisms, *Fallen Leaves* (1913–15), was as eulogistic of family life with 'mummy' (his second wife) and his daughters as it was sardonic about intellectual idols ('the last mongrel run over by a tram' was worth more than the philosophy of Tolstoy or Solovyov). The collection was shot through with anecdotes and inconsequential reminiscences and interleaved with family photographs remarkable for their sheer lack of remarkability, their air of quotidian beauty.[108] A still more remarkable collection of photographs was created by the writer Leonid Andreev, a talented amateur photographer who preferred to shoot in colour. During the 1910s he obsessively commemorated family life at his big dacha on the Gulf of Finland, with special attention to the younger members of the family. The soft-focus shots of his beautiful son Vadim inside the family house with its 'Karelian' furniture, as shown on the front cover, could serve as icons of the intelligentsia culture of the period.

An equally significant instance of a prominent intellectual celebrating a childhood experience that might objectively be described as bourgeois was Marina Tsvetaeva. Tsvetaeva's two first collections, *The Evening Album* and *The Magic Lantern*, not only evoked children from the outside (for instance through 'the little golden eyes/of a sweet little girl, leaning against the window' in 'Watercolour'), but also spoke directly of the emotions of small children:

> It's scary in the salon: witches and devils
> Appear there every evening.
> Daddy's ill, mummy's playing at a concert …
> Time for bed![109]

Revolting Infants

The obsession with kindness to children and with children's innocence, sweetness, and frailty was not universal. The very ubiquity of the cult of childhood – added to the not entirely misplaced apprehension that there was something 'bourgeois' in the constant celebration of child happiness, the evocation of a 'children's world' hermetically sealed off from the adult one – generated sarcastic cynicism in some members of the Russian intelligentsia.[110] To be sure, the Western modernist representation of the pre-pubescent child as cultural vandal and sexual terrorist (as in, say, Wedekind's *Frühlings Erwachen*, or, later, Cocteau's *Les Enfants terribles*) had few equivalents in Russia – a rare exception being Lidiya Zinov'eva-Annibal's *The Tragic Menagerie*, whose heroine is, from her first moments of reason, a cold-eyed transgressor and existential adventuress.[111] On the whole, so far as the Russian *fin de siècle* imagination was concerned, children were sexual victims, not predators: this applied just as much to literary people such as Fedor Sologub (whose novel *The Low-Grade Demon* had at its centre a debauched young woman's attempted seduction of a schoolboy) as it did to the lawyers, philanthropists, psychologists, and pedagogues campaigning against the sexual abuse of children and child prostitution. As a specialist historian of sexuality at the turn of the century has pointed out, even members of the judiciary who were in other respects hostile to 'the arbitrary intrusion of the police and other authorities into the privacy of family life' were prepared to override this principle when the issue of the defence of minors was at stake.[112] Among writers too, the assumption that children were, or at the very least should be, innocent made representations of active childhood sexuality legitimate only in the quite specific context of autobio-graphical or quasi-autobiographical writings by 'exceptional' individuals.[113]

Yet if the subject of sex and violence perpetrated by children remained taboo, violence against children was sometimes invoked as a method of 'shocking the bourgeoisie' (as in Mayakovsky's sadistic line 'I love watching children die' from his cycle *I Love*). Excessive devotion to children could be seen by intellectuals as a characteristic of *meshchanstvo*: for instance, in Chekhov's play *Three Sisters* (1901), disgust at Natasha's egotistical maternity spilled over into dislike of its object (not for nothing did Natasha's first-born's name, Bobik, resemble the name of Dostoevsky's demon, Bobok).

It was particularly babies (formless, threatening creatures) who were seen as intimations of the monstrous. But not all representations of older children were sweet, whimsical fantasies. Some authors – for example Chekhov, or Nadezhda Teffi – depicted children who felt a wide range of emotions, not all of them reassuring or edifying. In Chekhov's 'The Children' (1886),[114] four children, along with the cook's small son Andrei, make use of their parents' absence in order to turn the apartment into a gambling den. Eventually the persistent squabbling over cheating turns into an actual fight; even before then, the children have displayed a range of unaimiable traits, ranging from greed to egotism, ambition, pride, and cantankerousness. In Teffi's story 'Nowhere', children waiting while the adults decorated the Christmas tree speculated on their presents: 'Let's hope they give me something nice and not any old rubbish.'[115]

If these stories treated self-assertion by children satirically, there were also texts that actively sought to encourage defiant behaviour. A landmark from the immediate pre-revolutionary era was *Crocodile* (1916), by Kornei Chukovsky, about a beast who after his arrival tyrannised the whole of St Petersburg, but whose reign of terror was ended when a local boy chose to stand up to him:

> They're all trembling with fear,
> They're all squealing with fear,
>> Only a single
>> Citizen
>> Wasn't squealing
>> Or trembling –
> The valorous Vasya Vasil'chikov.
>
>> He's a warrior,
>> A brave,
>> A hero,
>> No zero,
> See him walking alone – without Nanny.[116]

In the final part of the poem, Vanya foils an attack by all the wild animals, led in a revenge assault on humanity by the Crocodile, and initiates an era anticipated in the biblical vision of lions lying down with lambs and weaned children playing with asses, as youngsters and animals joyfully embrace each other, freed from the absurd tyranny of the 'raging viper'. A children's revolution (or counter-revolution – the poem is ambiguous) has brought peace and harmony to all the world.

With a diminished sense that respect for moral imperatives was inevitable or likely in children went an enhanced impatience with moralising children's literature. The introduction to Chekhov's parodistic 'Anthology for Children' (1883) addressed children not as benighted inferiors, but as reasonable equals: 'You should obey adults not only because you'll get birch soup if you don't, but also because it's only fair.'[117] More disturbing, from the point of view of convinced moralists, is 'The Little Boys', where the protagonist, Volodya, has his cosy sense of family life unsettled by the visit of Chechevitsyn, a school-friend with grand ambitions to escape to America. The story works like a nursery version of *Fathers and Sons*, with Chechevitsyn as nihilist Bazarov to his friend's Arkady. However, the effect of the story is not to make Bazarov ridiculous by suggesting that he is nothing more than a fantasising schoolboy. Rather, the story introduces a note of insecurity into what had previously been the unproblematic domestic harmony of Volodya's home – when the children's plan is discovered, and Chechevitsyn has been sent home, Volodya suffers what in an adult would be termed a nervous breakdown.[118]

Often, the assault on simplistic didacticism was accompanied by a stress on the importance of children's imaginative worlds. In Teffi's ironically named 'The Criminal',[119] five-year-old Vovka was a thief who had to be taken in hand by a friend of his mother's. Her warning of the dire penalties of being found out proved suitably corrective. Yet the story was more preoccupied with Vovka's fascination with the beautiful red pencils that were his first illicit booty, and with their radiant appeal in the dreary grey classroom where he was studying. Teffi's stories, like Chekhov's, could not be straightforwardly categorised as either 'adult' or 'child' literature: their insistence on the importance and vividness of childhood experience was directed both to actual children and to adults who associated well-meant adult interference with the aesthetic stultification of the young.

The boundaries of acceptable emotion were also (though less often) stretched in writing for younger children. Aleksandr Benois's outstandingly beautiful *Picture Alphabet* of 1904[120] was shot through with nostalgia for the world of pre-Emancipation Russian country life, with *Dacha*, for example, illustrated by an elegant mansion in the French style, set in a formal garden, rather than by the oxblood-coloured nightmare hunting lodges that were actually in fashion among the moneyed classes when the book was published. Plates such as *Khan – Khalat* were in a delicate orientalising style that took child readers into a fairy-tale version of the Russian Empire's further reaches. But there were also some more unsettling images. *Baba-Yaga* revealed two children cowering in the forest as the ferocious witch sailed by, riding her pestle and mortar. *Bai-bai* (Lullaby) showed a bedtime scene, set in an eerie half-light, in which a Russian nanny bearing more than a passing resemblance to Baba Yaga stood by her charge's white cot, putting her to bed. Besides hints of delicious horror of this kind, the book contained other imaginative delights. The curious child was able to search for 'hidden' objects and people – those beginning with the governing letters in an image, but not mentioned in the captions at the top. At the bottom of *Bai–bai*, for example, sat a small devil (*bes*); the image entitled *Gorod* (City) showed boys with soldiers and girls with nurses and doctors (to which the words *general* and *gospital'* could be applied). The pinnacle was reached in the image for Dandy (*Shchegol'*), which contained no fewer than eight brushes (*shchetki*) being assiduously applied to the supericilious central figure by lackeys. Prompts of this kind were sometimes multilingual. The *Baba-Yaga* image also suggested the English words 'Babes in the Wood' and 'Berries' (which the children were collecting); in the picture illustrating *Pishcha* (food), two pussies look greedily at a parrot. And among the books decorating the borders of a 'Cowboys and Indian' scene illustrating *Napadenie* (Attack) were copies of works by 'Main Reed' (*sic*) and 'F. Cooper'.

A governing theme, even in relatively conventional sources such as literature for working teachers, was the need to develop the child's imagination. Great emphasis was placed on the function of non-representational literature in educating children, particularly those in the pre-school age group. A vital instrument in this was held to be the *skazka*, a term applied alike to traditional folk tales (such as 'Ivan Tsarevich and the Grey Wolf'), to literary texts with subjects drawn from, or akin to, those in traditional folklore (such as Pushkin's verse *skazka*, *The Golden Cockerel*) and to texts where the supernatural or the magical was of importance (Chirikov's 'The Old House' bore the subtitle 'The Fairy Tale'). 'The reading aloud to children of *skazki*, stories, and poems provides rich material for the development of the child's imagination,' an activist in the child welfare movement asserted in 1914.[121] The practical correlative of this widely held opinion was that *skazki* were ubiquitous in readers produced for nursery and primary schools, and that children were encouraged to write their own *skazki* and to draw and paint subjects of this kind as well. While there were certainly some dissenting voices, the pre-revolutionary years were a time when surprising numbers of Russian intellectuals discarded the rationalistic views of child development that had been widespread since the 1760s and took a more positive attitude to the role of fiction in child development than had been traditional in their culture.

One should not exaggerate the emotional and imaginative demands placed on juvenile readers. Work by children themselves pointed to a considerable tolerance for sad events: a story by a 10-year-old girl in Kruchenykh's collection, 'The Orphan', finishes quite deadpan with the death of the central figure and the decoration of her corpse with flowers by a small boy.[122] But adults' narratives for children tended not to end like this. Chekhov's 'The Little Boys' is exceptional in the bleakness of its resolution: in most other cases, some talisman against fear and dread was provided. Equally, moments of rebellion or bad behaviour were usually short-lived. Chekhov's *The Children* ended with all five children worn out by their misdemeanours and sleeping soundly on the parental bed. If Russian authors were in tune with late nineteenth- and early twentieth-century British writers in terms of their impatience with moralising, they were also kindred spirits in the light-handedness with which they represented rebellion.[123] Historical stylisation, intertextuality, punning and sound play underlined the ludic spirit of subversion: like all kinds of carnival upheaval, this had conservative undertones, more poking one's tongue out at nanny (or saying boo to the governess) than burning down the nursery.

Admiration for subversion represented only one, highly innovative, trend in the late nineteenth and early twentieth centuries. There were plenty of writers who saw indulgent attitudes towards children primarily as a manifestation of adult selfishness. As early as the late 1880s, the figure of the spoilt darling whose main purpose in life was to augment the status of his or her parents (the 'designer baby', as late twentieth-century English would have called it) began to figure in tracts and behaviour books.[124] If some children's magazines, such as The Path, edited by the talented poet and translator Poliksena Solov'eva, gave space to new writers and new attitudes, others, notably the Cordial Word, were more obviously in the spirit of nineteenth-century didactic fiction. The prevalence of the skazka reflected concern with national tradition, as well as the view that children had a special relationship with the magical; reading primers and books for small children underlined moral, religious, and patriotic values. Conversely, children were taught about other nationalities according to a set of easily assimilated stereotypes. An essay written by an eight-year-old girl at a 'free kindergarten' in 1911, for example, summed up life in Turkey thus:

Трамъ, тамъ, тамъ, эй, смѣлѣй,
Барабанъ бей звончѣй.
Побѣдимъ
И опять

Новыхъ войнъ
Будемъ ждать.
Трамъ, тамъ, тамъ, эй, смѣлѣй,
Барабанъ бей звончѣй.

12 Georgy Narbut, 'Toy Soldiers', from V. Diks, Toys (1911).

Turks love smoking tobacco, and Turkish women love drinking coffee. On the street, Turkish women do not show their faces. Every day, the priest [*sic*] calls five times from the tower of the mosque to summon all the Turks to say their prayers. Turks wear red hats with black tassels.[125]

During the First World War, patriotism reached an all-time high. At a girls' gymnasium in Arkhangel'sk, pupils posted parcels to soldiers at the Front, helped with preparing first aid supplies, and took part in a tableau at the local theatre, with each allied country represented by a schoolgirl in national costume.[126] Even children in Froebel kindergartens in Kiev were encouraged to sit down and write letters to the 'dear little soldiers' serving at the Front, speaking admiringly of their bravery and belittling their own discomfort by comparison. 'I get cold going to school but I think: how must it be for our dear brother soldiers, I'd rather they were warm and me cold,' one child wrote from Kiev in January 1915. At the same time, when compared with the pro forma letters written by Soviet children a decade later, let alone with those penned in the 1930s, the letters were refreshingly personal: the children were encouraged to write individually, not as a group, and spoke frankly of their anxieties for friends and family. 'My uncle's the only one who's fought, he's in the army on active service, not long ago he came to Kiev and said he couldn't sleep for two days [...] he felt he was in heaven.' And in fact children did not have to be encouraged to take a direct interest in the war. Just as they spontaneously played games of 'Austrians and Russians', so they turned almost every topic in art lessons into an excuse to paint war scenes. A child who was asked to draw a wheel and then some object upon wheels immediately threw off a sketch of a gun-carriage standing in the middle of a battlefield, while the theme, 'The Christmas Tree', met the response of a Christmas scene in a military hospital.[127]

13   'A Gold Farthing is Little, But It's Worth a Lot'. Patriotic postcard, 1914.

Child Prodigies

The suspicion that admiration of childhood might not be compatible with the modernist objective of writing challenging art led writers and artists (where they were not celebrating their own 'inner child') to celebrate an idiosyncratic manifestation of childhood – the adult in miniature or 'infant grown old before its time'.[128] One significant result of this was the surge of interest in infant prodigiousness that became evident in Russia during the early twentieth century.

The child prodigy was of course not invented in the modern era. The term *Wunderkind* in the sense of premature artistic talent goes back to the early eighteenth century, and came into common use in the late eighteenth. In the musical world, Mozart and Beethoven were only the best known of an international pleiad that included one or two Russians, for instance Maksim Berezovsky (1745–77), who made his début in an operatic role at the age of 14. As one would expect, Russian child prodigies increased in number after Romanticism made its impact on the country, with Anton Rubinstein (whose concert tour to Germany aged 12, in 1841, was a critical and popular sensation), and Rimsky-Korsakov, who began composing in his teens, examples of the type whose fame persisted into adulthood.

For all that, though, the late nineteenth and early twentieth centuries did see a real explosion of musical *vunderkindy* from the Russian Empire (including Poland and the Ukraine). As the musical historian Gerd-Heinz Stevens has put it, whole 'shoals' of miraculously gifted children, mostly boys (the cellist Raya Garbusova, born in 1908, was a rare exception) descended upon Western Europe and America at this time. During the three decades between 1880 and 1912 alone, more than forty child superstars from the Russian Empire made their way on to the concert platforms of Russia and the rest of the world (by contrast, the preceding century had seen not more than a dozen or so enjoy international fame).

A strikingly large number of the performers came from Jewish families in multi-cultural and emancipated cities such as Warsaw and Odessa. Typical were the pianist Benno Moiseiwitsch, who won the Rubinstein Prize in Odessa in 1899, aged nine, Yasha Heifetz, also from Odessa, who began studying at the Imperial Music School in Vienna in 1906, aged a mere five, and who gave his first public performance of the Mendelssohn E Minor Violin Concerto a year later, Shura Cherkassky, who conducted the Odessa Symphony Orchestra for the first time in 1920, at the age of nine, a year after completing a five-act opera, and the Chernyavsky brothers, who gave their début trio recital in Reval in 1904 (they were then aged between 11 and 14).[129] Obviously, it was not only public interest in brilliant children that lay behind such success stories, but also the discriminatory legislation and institutionalised prejudice that cut off so many other paths of social advancement to Jews, added to the fierce ambition of parents who had themselves been denied a means of expression for their talents.[130] But children from well-off Russian families were not necessarily treated more indulgently. Rachmaninov's teacher Nikolai Zverev, who taught him in Moscow during the 1880s, preferred his pupils to have the minimum of contact with their families, and awed his small charges by his habit of throwing things across the room and even making free with his fists when he was displeased with their work.[131]

Yet child prodigies should not necessarily be seen as the wretched victims of monomaniacal parents, or circus freaks exploited by callous teachers and Svengalian entrepreneurs. Rachmaninov was grateful to Zverev for introducing some discipline into the life of the spoiled and lazy small boy he remembered himself as being, and the parents of both Benno Moiseiwitsch and Artur Rubinstein avoided pushing their exceptional offspring into premature concert careers. Sergei Prokofiev's mother, for her part, did everything she could to make her son's early education child-centred, according to the appreciations of the day: technical grind was avoided and the boy encouraged to enjoy playing through as much music as possible, rather than bothering to master each piece carefully.[132]

It was not just parents who were able to behave with tact. Some music teachers were already beginning to specialise in talented children, and the younger and livelier among them were often far more adept in dealing with their occasionally assertive and difficult charges than the old school of knuckle-rappers had been.[133] The sheer number of prodigies in early twentieth-century Russia meant that any single one of them was less likely to feel an isolated *monstre sacré* than he or she might have done in Britain or France in the same period.[134]

The cult of infant prodigiousness stretched into other arts as well, though none seems to have been as rich a field as music. A pioneer prodigy in the visual arts was the painter Valentin Serov, son of two well-known St Petersburg composers, who had begun studying with Il'ya Repin at the age of nine, in 1874, and who had his first pictures put into an exhibition by Repin when he was in his teens.[135] Still more important, since her reputation spanned two fields, the visual arts and literature, was Mariya Bashkirtseva, whose journal, chronicling the emergence of precocious genius, was to inspire generations of memoirists to insist on their own early creativity.[136] In such autobiographies the point was not (as in Romantic texts such as Wordsworth's *The Prelude*) to see the early development of the personality as foreshadowing later genius, but to insist on the emergence of genius fully-fledged at an astonishingly early age. Tatiana Shchepkina-Kupernik's 1949 memoir 'My Literary Path', for example, described how the writer taught herself to read at the age of four, and how some of her 12-year-old juvenilia were greeted warmly by Tchaikovsky, who even planned to set her one-act play *Eternity in a Moment* as an opera.[137] So common had the phenomenon become by the early twentieth century that Leo Tolstoy responded jadedly when V. V. Stasov was eager to show off his particular pet prodigy, the young Samuil Marshak: 'Oh, those *vunderkindy*! I've met so many of them and I've been disappointed so often. For the most part, they just flash past: they're as wasteful and useless as fireworks.'[138]

Extended Childhood versus Accelerated Adulthood

The split between the view of children as budding adults, needing constant nudging and pushing in the right direction, and of child genius as an end in itself, best not interfered with by adults, was only one manifestation of a wider-ranging distinction: between a view of the child as 'father to the man', and a stress upon the child as a unique form of human individual, whose specificity should be preserved as long as it could be. In its essence, of course, this division was far from novel: it went back to the mid-eighteenth century, when the early

Enlightenment understanding (as set out by Locke and Fénelon, for instance) of the child as a being capable of reasonable thought, if properly directed, began to give way to, or to be challenged by, Rousseau's representation, in *Emile*, of the child as a creature whose intellectual and moral freedom was not to be inhibited by any such direction. However, the 'quarrel of the rationalists and the sentimentalists' was newer and more significant in Russian culture than might be supposed, given that one of the things which the Romantic movement did not immediately bring with it to Russia was a Romantic cult of the child. The Romantic genre of the childhood autobiography reached Russia only in the 1850s, more than fifty years after it had become established in Western Europe.[139] There was an equivalent time-lag in the dissemination of novel approaches to child care. The single edition of Pestalozzi, and the one version of *Emile* published in the early nineteenth century, contrast rather strikingly with the popularity of, say, Madame Lambert, Fénelon, Locke, or Madame Genlis, all of whom saw the child essentially in terms of its potential for adulthood, and who were concerned with upbringing from the age of seven and upwards, regarding the early years as a sort of pedagogical blank space, a phase of development that could safely be left in the hands of a nurse.[140]

By the late nineteenth century, a huge increase in the influence of the 'sentimentalist' view had taken place. Championed since the 1850s by Tolstoy, it began to make serious inroads as the cultural authority of Tolstoy himself increased during the late 1880s, and as elite Russian families moved towards a more child-centred culture and a greater sense of dissatisfaction with institutionalised education.[141] An important part was played, too, by psychological studies emphasising the significance of the child's early imaginative development, and of play as 'the free and central expression of those interior things that need to be outwardly expressed',[142] rather than as a form of activity to be tolerated exclusively because it provided training in skills useful for adult existence.

But acceptance of the need for 'free upbringing' was not universal in the Russian intelligentsia. Aleksandr Bogdanov's utopian novel *Red Star* represented rather a different ethos. The 'House of Children' in which the little Martians were brought up certainly had a health and efficiency slant (premises surrounded by gardens and playgrounds, utilitarian, unisex clothes), but the emphasis was on 'upbringing for society' (with large shared dormitories, older children directing the younger ones, didactic lectures on history), not on self-development.[143]

So far as the representation of children from outside the cultural elite was concerned, rationalistic appreciations also predominated. Sometimes they were shown as young hooligans, unsettling society with their sinister presence as they lived rough on the streets, preying on passers-by. The late nineteenth century was to see the invention of the category of 'waif' (*besprizornyi*), a type of child that threatened civilised values. Yet the attitude increasingly was that such children needed support and re-education rather than punishment. They came to be understood as victims, as the actual or metaphorical carriers of 'disease' that could be cured, rather than as wilful or evil.[144] Naturalist fiction and poetry of the 1890s, such as Ekaterina Letkova's 'Lushka' or Chekhov's 'Sleepy', dwelt on children who were forced to do work of which they were not capable (caring for younger children), and on child abuse (Chekhov's 'In the Ravine' showed a baby becoming the object of vicious domestic revenge). Journalism and ethnography harped on sensational subjects such as *snokhachestvo* (the custom whereby a pre-pubescent male was married off to a nubile female, who was then impregnated by the boy's father in order to maintain household property within the same bloodline), teenage marriage, and child prostitution.[145]

14   Nikolai Bogdanov-Bel'sky, *At the School Door* (1897).

Where not seen as victims, such children were usually depicted as *vydvizhentsy*, symbols of social mobility through education, destined to lead the oppressed class from which they came into a new dawn. A typical painting by Nikolai Bogdanov-Belsky dating from 1892 depicts a lad in traditional clothing crossing the threshold of a classroom, his eyes alight with expectation. This stereotype was maintained in autobiographies by writers of lower-class origin, which – both before and after the Revolution – adopted a 'darkness into light' narrative structure. The title of Maxim Gorky's *Childhood* (1913) was meant to be provocative, evoking Tolstoy's lyrical memoir of a gentry childhood published in 1854. Where Tolstoy had emphasised the transition from childhood to later years as in most respects a loss, however, bringing with it an erotic fall from grace that stood in contrast to the harmonious and innocent mother–child relations of the early years, for Gorky, childhood was associated with disempowerment, terror, and indeed actual physical abuse.[146] This was the reverse side of the 'happy childhood' stereotype, in which transition to adulthood was unambiguously interpreted as a progress to enlightenment, and childhood itself as a form of fortunately temporary imprisonment.

Attitudes to nursery education were, in the words of one commentator, polarised between the different views of Froebel and of Montessori: 'In the Froebel system the kindergarten teacher leads the child; in the Montessori one she follows after the child.'[147] The sheer fact of chronology made Froebel's ideas more popular in early twentieth-century Russia than Montessori's (his work was better known because it had been around for longer). But there was considerable openness to her work as well, with even the resolutely Froebelian *Pre-School Education*, of Kiev, finding room for discussions of the Casa dei Bambini.[148]

Russian pedagogical discussions did more than regurgitate Western ones, however: they scrutinised them critically. After a visit to the Montessori schools in Rome, the St Petersburg specialist in nursery education Elizaveta Tikheeva returned deeply disillusioned with what she now saw as barely a method of 'free education' at all. The organisation of the classrooms was oppressive, the regime stereotyped, the children cowed and deferential. Performances in which the children fulsomely thanked the party of visitors in which Tikheeva had been included, and expressed their gratitude to the school director, struck her as revolting: 'A six year old publicly expressing his love for his school director, and calling him signore and inspector as well! And in front of people he's never set eyes on before! [...] Love in general, and most particularly the love of a child, is not direct in this way: it's silent and reserved.'[149] The children's handwriting was suspiciously perfect, the lack of noise almost sinister. In condemning the Montessori schools that she had seen as unnatural, Tikheeva also set out her own ideal of nursery education: one which would afford the child 'complete freedom' and 'natural development without compulsion', would allow plenty of movement and dynamism, and, while quite unsentimental (the fact that a French visitor had wept at a Montessori school illustrated that there was something unpleasantly morbid afoot there), would also allow space for 'fairy stories, the child's favourite'.[150]

Slaughtered Saints

By the 1890s, representations of the child were diversifying rapidly, running from 'free upbringing' and the collection/imitation of children's art, to the growth of a consumerist dimension of childhood; from concern for children's autonomy within the family to representations of children's rebellion against parental authority; from ironic treatments of moralism to moralism offered 'straight'. What most of these very different interpretations of the 'children's world' had in common was a sense that children's needs and psychic world were different from those of adults, and a conviction that they deserved at least a degree of freedom and autonomy from adult interference. For many, perhaps most, Russian adults who were aged 50 or under at the turn of the century, and who had themselves had a more 'child-centred' upbringing than earlier generations,[151] childhood was an imaginative space where the oppressive realities of the society in which they lived could be escaped. Though poor children were seen as the quintessential victims of an unjust society, there was an optimistic sense that their problems might be dealt with more easily than those of adults (they were more malleable, easier to lift from the slough of poverty). Notable, too, in a society where adult life was characterised by a near-obsession with social status, was the understanding of the 'children's world' as a place beyond class.[152] Though a sailor suit would never have been worn by a child from the peasantry or working class (children from this group were dressed in miniature versions of their parents' clothes), it seemed a democratic garment in the context of bourgeois and aristocratic culture. (Tsarevich Alexis was photographed wearing one, but it was also the customary

15 Photo-portrait of the
Tsesarevich Alexis in a sailor
suit, *c.* 1914.

garb of quite ordinary middle-class children.) Though the joys of work might
not be very obvious to a 12-year-old working night shifts in a glass factory, the
campaign for free education saw work-based education as an egalitarian measure,
as well as a contribution to personal development and the good of society at last.
And, while the philanthropic movement was partly fuelled by a conviction that
the children of the underclasses must be kept off the streets and subjected to moral
indoctrination if they were not to become a social menace, the pronouncements
spoke in terms of protection of the children concerned, rather than of protecting
the public.[153]

Child protection was becoming a central issue not only in its own right,
but also as a topic that was understood to reflect the state of society at large,
and hence a topic of considerable political sensitivity. An especially sensational
instance was a notorious child murder case of the 1910s. In 1913, Mendel Beilis, a
small craftsman from Kiev, stood trial for the murder of a 13-year-old schoolboy,
Andrei Yushchinsky, who had been discovered in a cave in the Luk'yanovka
district of the city half naked, and with multiple stab wounds. The local police
had originally treated the Yushchinsky murder as a routine affair, concluding
that the likely perpetrator was a person or persons involved with the mother of
a friend of Yushchinsky's, Zhenya Cheberyak, who was the hostess of a low-life
drinking den much favoured by local criminals. However, after the appearance by
members of extreme nationalist groups at Yushchinsky's funeral, the affair came
to the attention of chauvinist members of the central Tsarist administration and
a search was launched for a more politically expedient guilty party. A scapegoat

was located in the person of Mendel Beilis, a Jew living in the Podol' district of Kiev; his trial became a *cause célèbre* throughout the Russian Empire.[154]

Beilis's trial is generally remembered – quite rightly – as a high-water mark of late Imperial Russian anti-semitism, on the one hand, and a triumph for liberal legal values, on the other. But this was also the trial of an alleged child murderer, and the statements both inside and outside the courtroom made it clear that Yushchinsky's status as a child was crucial. Already at Yushchinsky's funeral, leaflets circulated by the chauvinist 'Black Hundreds' group had exhorted participants: 'Russian people! If you love your children, beat the Jews! Beat them till not a single one is left in Russia! Pity your children! Avenge the suffering innocents!'[155] At the trial itself, A. S. Shmakov, a member of the prosecuting team, had referred to Yushchinsky's 'martyr's death', and called the boy a 'gentle, innocent martyr for the Christian faith'.[156] At the same time, though, Yushchinsky was represented as a person who was not admirable in the ordinary sense: 'The boy grew up in abnormal family circumstances, subject to no control.'[157] The defence hit back by presenting Yushchinsky as a hero of quite a different kind: a monument of civic virtue, a boy slaughtered by bandits because of his distaste for the activities carried on at the Zherebyak thieves' den. 'If he had been a member of that clutch of thieves, then he would not have died a martyr's death,' P. Karabchevsky asserted.[158] For his part, Mendel Beilis himself concluded his brief final speech in his own defence with a touching appeal to the jury: 'I beg you to clear my name so that I will once more be able to see my unhappy children, who have been waiting for me these past two and a half years.'[159]

Every side involved in the trial attempted to establish probity by appeal to an idealised image of childhood. For the prosecution, Yushchinsky was a sacred martyr, albeit also a child who had been brought up rather badly; for the defence, he was a secular martyr and a hero of civic virtue, and the scion of a poverty-stricken, but essentially respectable, working-class family (despite evidence that the boy had in fact been ill-treated at home, and the local police's probably not unfounded suspicions that his murder was likely to be what the British police call 'a domestic'). Beilis pleaded his status as an ideal family man and loving father. The fact that an unsolved child murder committed in the early nineteenth century would not have received the same level of attention from the political elite of the day is related not only to changing attitudes towards Jews. The Beilis case was a landmark in attitudes to children as well, and reactions to it expressed an assumption that became still more prevalent during the first decades of Soviet power – that the health of a society is manifested by its humane treatment of its children, so that cruel treatment to children is a sign of a sick society.

The late nineteenth and early twentieth centuries saw crucial shifts in attitudes to children. As new areas of scholarly investigation, such as child psychology, developed, and as Russian professionals, from teachers to lawyers to doctors, became aware of work being done abroad, an increasingly critical view of the status quo in the Russian Empire began to emerge, and with it pressures for reform in law codes, school syllabuses, teaching methods, and upbringing generally. As children's affairs became of greater importance to adults, so children were more widely admitted to the public domain as individuals, whether as young performers at concerts or as participants in political meetings. Alongside 'free professionals', artists, composers, and writers took a growing interest in children, producing a wide variety of representations that were at times sentimentally sweet, at times collusive (taking an approving attitude to mischief and disruption), and at times positively hostile. Whether they celebrated childhood or treated it ironically, however, these artists and writers recognised the importance of this phase of life as a theme. There was not one major figure of the period who did not, at some point in his or her career, address the subject of childhood, whether in a personal sense (through autobiography), or with reference to society more broadly.

The variety of interests and images, the plethora of plans, was held together by some other assumptions as well. In particular, it was taken for granted that a 'normal' childhood was a phase of life that was, and should be, distinct from adulthood. Children should be living in safety, steeping themselves in imaginative experience, and gaining an education. The correlative was a conviction that it was not 'normal' for a child to be at work, or undertaking family responsibilities. This made the life of children from the working class and the peasantry seem aberrant, since such children were expected to contribute to the family economy from their early years. The would-be reformers of social attitudes to children were convinced that every child should enjoy equality before the law and equality of opportunity, but they imagined 'equality' in ways that had an unacknowledged social resonance, that were the expression of views of children which could only have emerged among educated, economically secure social groups, for whom children's rights to leisure and imaginative self-expression were as important as their rights to material welfare. The years after 1917 were to see this set of appreciations condemned as 'bourgeois', yet at the same time perpetuated in state policy and propaganda, as well as in private views of the child.

Chapter 2

Pioneers and Pet-Keepers, 1917–1935

Soon after the Bolsheviks took power in 1917, propaganda began to insist that children were treated uniquely well in the Soviet state (supposedly the most progressive in the world from all other points of view too). 'Only here does the state consider itself the higher guardian of the entire child population and act, where children's and adults' interests are in conflict, invariably on the side of the former,' asserted a book on child crime published in 1923.[1] Claims that children enjoyed better conditions than they did anywhere else in the world rapidly became a genre requirement of any text setting out information about children's affairs in the Soviet Union. In 1932, for example, a guide to protective labour legislation stated that the 1926 Criminal Code 'affords to minors far greater protection than is offered in any other country in the world'.[2] Children's exceptional status became a prop not only for the regime's national standing, but also for its international standing – as manifested by Soviet sponsorship of children's festivals (such as International Children's Week, first celebrated in Germany in 1921), and by the fact that visits to carefully selected, 'model' children's institutions were a fixture on the itinerary of every Soviet official visitor and of many humbler tourists, such as delegations of workers and students.[3]

Parades of superiority were not usually backed up by scrutiny of what was offered to children in the way of medical care, labour protection, anti-cruelty legislation, or welfare support in other countries. The standard mode of representation was one in which the life of the fortunate, well-loved Soviet child was contrasted with the grim exploitation to which children 'abroad' (that is, in the capitalist West, and the West's colonial dependencies) were subject.[4] Another important strategy was the 'then and now' contrast, whereby adults and children were hectored on the dreadfulness of conditions for children from outside the privileged classes before 1917. *Then* children had toiled in factories before coming home for scant meals of bread and water; *now* workers' children lived in modest luxury, and even had piano lessons.[5] Such propaganda contrasts not only vastly oversimplified the situation outside the Soviet Union and in pre-1917 Russia, but also ignored continuing hardship and inequity within the country itself.

Yet the new era did indeed bring fundamental changes in terms of the prominence of children's issues, in the nature of the issues under discussion, and in the prevailing understanding of what children's place in political culture and society should be. Many of the reforms built on the work of activists and pedagogues who had been campaigning for change before 1917, but change went much further than many of these individuals had been able to imagine. At the same time, support from the state also signified control by the state. Some areas of work with children were banned altogether (the most significant example is religious education, prohibited from 1918). All others were subject to regulation by Soviet agencies, whose policy was dictated less by concern for child welfare in the abstract than by the larger political concerns of the day. Thus, once the New Economic Policy was set in place, central funding was withdrawn from welfare institutions, leaving them struggling to find support from local administrations and from their own resources; when state planning was set in place in 1928, children's institutions (hospitals, schools, orphanages) were funded on the so-called 'left-over principle' (*ostatochnyi printsip*), meaning that budget levels were subject to variation depending on other calls upon funding. Children's needs were of high importance, but not of supreme importance: at the centre of the Soviet system lay productive labour, and children's contribution to productive labour could be at best restricted. At times of crisis, their needs would have to be sacrificed. The situation was captured allegorically in Gladkov's production novel *Cement* (1925), where the death of a baby was represented as a tragic but essential sacrifice in the great cause of building the new society.

Children might be unproductive at present; they were, however, essential to building the future. From the first, therefore, the leaders of the new regime targeted them not just as the recipients of nurture, but as an audience for political ideas. The first years of Soviet power were an era of relative *laissez-faire*: during the Civil War, the main task of the new leaders was to create a base of popular support to begin with. Much political activity went on in schools and in private children's clubs, but often of a disorganised, carnivalesque kind. In 1922, however, began a period of more intensive regulation, as marked by the creation of the 'Young Pioneer' organisation that year, a branch of the Komsomol (Communist Youth Movement) for children aged 10 to 15, followed by the banning of the Scout organisation. In its early years, the Pioneers (known from 1924 also as 'Young Leninists') was an eminently serious political organisation, and its members were represented as fiery young activists and models for what were officially known as 'unorganised children'. The following years were to see tightening central control in every other area of work with children as well, from literature and arts to education.

Subjects and Citizens

The most dramatic changes to thinking about children took place at the levels of the system which were most remote from everyday life: legislation and political debate. For a decade or so after 1918, the concept of children's rights was enshrined in legislation to an extent not matched before or since in Russian history. Certainly, while Soviet law had a Codex on Marriage and the Family, it never developed a Codex of Children's Rights: legislation was scattered in family law codes, labour protection codes, and civil and criminal codes. And children continued to figure to a restricted degree in legislation: for instance, in the Civil Code of 1923, they were invoked primarily as the inheritors of property; in the Criminal Code of 1926, their main presence was as the victims of sexual crimes (articles 151 and 152), and of desertion.[6]

But in family law, particularly, the changes under Soviet power were dramatic. The first move was relatively modest: a regularisation of the rights of legitimate and illegitimate children, such as liberal jurists had campaigned for well before the Revolution in any case.[7] Later came more fundamental measures, curtailing 'parental power' while imposing upon parents the *duty* to provide for their children. Now, parents were legally obliged to bring up their children properly, but only *entitled* to bring them up at all if they did so adequately. In the words of a 1925 guide to family legislation, 'The state protects children from every form of oppression (*posyagatel'stvo*), and provides them with a normal upbringing. Parents and guardians are reserved certain rights, with whose help they carry out the duties laid upon them.'[8] This principle was articulated directly in the Code on Marriage and the Family of 1926, article 33 of which stipulated, 'Parental rights are to be enacted entirely in the interests of children, and if they are not so enacted the courts may deprive parents of their rights.' At the same time, article 43 of the code conferred upon parents the obligation of providing for their dependent children, an obligation that (according to article 51) remained with them even if they had been deprived of their parental rights after being declared unfit parents.[9]

Thus, Soviet law partly inverted the central principle of Tsarist legislation on the family – the subordination of children to parents. Legal commentators spoke proudly of the 'emancipation of children from serfdom'.[10] Liberal treatment of ordinary children went with liberal treatment of children who transgressed. In 1918, the hopes of pre-revolutionary penal reformers came to fulfilment with the enactment of legislation raising the age of criminal responsibility to 18. While measures of 1920 and 1923 reduced this age to 16, and diluted the rehabilitationist spirit of the 1918 law, the essential principle – that children's misdemeanours should be scrutinised by specialist commissions, the so-called *komsonesy* or Committees on the Affairs of Minors – remained sancrosanct.[11]

The most radical sectors of Soviet society, such as Proletkult groups, went still further in their assertion of children's rights. The Moscow Proletkult group, for instance, put together a 'Declaration of Children's Rights', guaranteeing to children the right to leave their parents if they so wished.[12] For his part, the physician Fedor Orlov-Skomorovsky, extrapolating from his own appalling childhood to construct a case about the evils of family life full stop, declared ringingly, 'The hour of the children's rebellion against their parents in every family has come. And this is not a frightful time: it is a wonderful, long-awaited time.' He looked forward to a 'Spartan' society where children would be raised collectively (but coeducationally and without militarism, as they had not been in Sparta itself), and where they would be liberated from those 'low executioners' their parents, and from those 'gendarmes and torturers' their teachers, and would be free to take their place in civic life from the first. 'My parents had no right to bring me into life,' Orlov-Skomorovsky declared: it followed that they had no 'rights' of any other kind over their children either.[13]

Some of this new spirit found its way into policy discussions in the first days of Soviet power. At the First All-Russian Congress of Child Protection Activists in 1919, delegates argued that the centre of 'social education' should be the children's home, which would reach out to the rest of the community and point the way to go. 'We will influence children being raised in families, and set an example for all the circles that are not reached directly by the Communist Socialist Society,' one delegate declared.[14] The buzz-word of the day, for children's institutions of all kinds, was 'self-government'. All institutions, from nursery schools upwards, were supposed to organise discussion bodies (normally referred to as 'soviets') specifically for pupils, and to have pupil representation on their management committees ('teacher soviets', etc.). Through these, children were meant to be involved in management and decision-making, as well as in discussing topical political issues of the day.[15]

16   Children present a 'living newspaper', a common agitational genre of the day (mid-1920s).

On the whole, though, official policy-*making* was significantly more conservative than speeches and statements would suggest. For instance, though some government officials in the first three or four years of Soviet power assumed that orphanages would now be the basic method of caring for children, this assumption was often justified in reactive terms, as a response to the 'accelerating collapse of the family and its decline as a source of the principles of moral education'.[16] Voices were found, even at this stage, to defend the family as the 'basic unit of production' in society.[17] Discussion of children's rights had a limited impact upon actual legislation, which defined children's rights more or less exclusively within the family. There was no official charter of rights covering such matters as political representation, property ownership, or educational opportunity. Indeed, a good many rights – for example, the choice of nationality in cases where a child was of mixed descent – were explicitly reserved until the legal subject reached majority.[18]

Equally, utopian 'total institutions' remained thin on the ground. Certainly some existed: the Institute for the Care of Mothers and Children in Leningrad had 'a maternity hospital, after-care department, orphanage, birth-control clinic, abortion clinic, hospital for tubercular children, research institute for experiments on animals, and so on' under one roof.[19] Another case in point was Children's Town in Moscow, one of the education ministry Narkompros's 'model experimental' institutions. This combined an expert reception and diagnostic centre (*kollektor*), where children were disinfected and given a medical and psychological assessment, with seven orphanages. Three catered for 'normal' (including 'proletarian normal') children, and one each for children of school age, difficult children, gifted children, and children who needed specialist health care. Though plans for an on-site school ran into difficulties, the 'town' also had, in its early years, a kindergarten: the intention was to create as complete an environment for the children housed there as possible.[20] But on the whole, Soviet institutions were designed to service particular needs in the short term, rather than to provide a nurturing environment over long periods of time. The sole institution to which the majority of children who had institutional contact at all were exposed remained the school; and here, too, early radicalism was soon tempered, with instrumental views of education making a growing impact from the mid-1920s.

'Schools of Labour'

Before 1917, 'progressive education' had no more than a toehold on the school system, which continued to enforce the differentials of social estate. The new Ministry of Enlightenment set up by the Provisional Government in February 1917 did not succeed, during its short existence, in evolving a coherent policy for schools, let alone in imposing this on the institutions under its control. Such top-level reforms as were set out nibbled at the edges of the old system rather than altering it completely. In August 1917, it was decreed that those who had completed four classes of higher primary schools (i.e. had had a full seven years of education) might now progress without further formalities into *gimnazii* and *real'nye uchilishcha*; a month later, the Ministry announced the expansion of the network of four-year *gimnazii* and *real'nye uchilishcha*, that is, of schools offering a course specifically targeted at graduates of higher primary schools.[21] In themselves, these were important changes, intended to efface the automatic discrimination against working-class children that had formerly been underwritten by the system of selection for elite secondary schools. But by starting by improving opportunities for a group of pupils – primary school graduates – which was already (by the standards of mass education in late Imperial Russia) an educational elite, the Ministry of Enlightenment ignored more pressing problems, such as the need to expand elementary education in the first place. In this way, as well as in their preoccupation with minor reforms of the pedagogical colleges, the Minister of Enlightenment, Professor A. A. Manuilov, formerly Rector of Moscow University, and his colleagues manifested the remote attitudes to education at the grass roots that might have been expected of metropolitan academics. And policy statements by the new administration were characteristically academic in their cautious hesitancy. An announcement of the orthographical reform planned for January 1918 spoke of the need to 'avoid any imposing any *force* over the desires of the pupils themselves' when giving tuition in the new spellings required; but this was the only public pronouncement by the new administration that had the colour of 'free education', an approach never explicitly endorsed at the highest level.[22]

The Provisional Government's school policy only partly enacted the egalitarianism which, alongside freedom of speech, print, and association, was stated to be a central principle of the new order.[23] The Bolshevik regime, on the other hand, had from the first the ambition to introduce absolute parity in education. A statement made on 11 November 1917 by the Commissar of Enlightenment, Anatoly Lunacharsky, specified the central aims of the new order as being 'the achievement of *general literacy* in the shortest time possible', and 'the organisation of a *comprehensive school system that is totally secular in character*'.[24] By early 1918, it had been decided that every secondary school under Soviet power should be a 'unified school of labour', providing its pupils not only with the straightforward ability to read and write, but also with a reasonable level of political literacy, knowledge of the rules of hygiene and physical fitness, an awareness of the importance of self-discipline, and a sense of artistic appreciation and respect for the natural world. Schools should be relevant to the outside world; they should prepare children for a life of productive labour and of useful citizenship, but should nurture them without recourse to excessive force.[25]

There was a striking continuity between early Soviet rhetoric and that of pre-revolutionary reformers (not surprisingly, given the heavy representation in Narkompros of those associated prior to 1917 with the advocacy of 'free upbringing').[26] The 'Regulation on the Comprehensive Labour-Oriented School' of 30 September 1918, was, in phrasing, very close to the editorial manifesto for *Free Education* quoted in Chapter 1:

1. The principle of labour will become a powerful pedagogical weapon if labour in schools is creative and joyful, free of any violent assault on the personality [rather than the soul!] of the pupil and at the same time well-planned and socially organised. In this last sense, the school will be a form of educational commune, linked closely and organically with the surrounding world. 2. The old form of discipline, which fettered the entire life of the school and the free development of the child, can have no place in the school of labour. But the very processes of labour will teach the child the inner discipline without which rationally ordered collective labour is impossible. [...] In short, collective productive labour and the organisation of school life generally must bring about the upbringing of the future citizens of the Soviet Republic.[27]

Many early statements on nursery education manifested a similar continuity with those of pre-revolutionary pioneers. In the words of a slim brochure produced by Narkompros in 1921: 'By following the ideal of free, harmonious development for the human personality in the conditions of a communal life of labour, pre-school education will put into practice not only pedagogical ideals, but also general humanist ideals.'[28] At this stage, the educational commissariat was prepared to dictate general principles, rather than to supervise teachers' work in detail: in the first years of Soviet power there was no integrated central curriculum at all, and management of the classroom was carried out by the issuing of decrees that recommended to teachers the use of 'advanced' methods such as the 'Dalton system', whereby teaching took place according to broad themes that linked traditional subjects, and the 'project method', where children worked collaboratively on wide-ranging assignments rather than submitting individual pieces of work for which they received individual marks.[29]

Yet educational administrators were firmly convinced that education should be a way of inculcating a child into specific adult roles. As with Proletkult's views on legal codes, it was marginal idealists who voiced opinions such as, 'An ideal form of pedagogy [...] *must be totally free of any ulterior objectives lying beyond the child.*'[30] The regime was committed to a view of society as a rational, politically literate, hygienically aware, 'cultured' collective, and education was expected to teach rational collectivism from the beginning.

In line with the understanding of education as preparation for 'future citizenship' in a 'Communist society', visions of schooling marched in step with broader campaigns to transform the Soviet masses. From 1923–4, as the struggle began to generate *novyi byt* (a new kind of daily life of a Soviet kind), schools propagandised values identical to those set out in conduct treatises for adults (for instance Pavel Kerzhentsev's *How to be Organised*), and disseminated in the agitational campaigns organised by the Party and the Komsomol in cities and in villages. Growing emphasis on 'work discipline' in factories went with enhanced stress on discipline in schools. By 1927, the author of an article in a pedagogical journal was openly stating, 'The Soviet school is not the school of free education', and suggesting that compulsion was sometimes necessary in the schoolroom, even if the response to disruption should always be 'moral education rather than punishment'.[31]

17 *The Aeroplane Fund of the Red Army Soldier and Partisan*, poster advertising a fund-raising drive for Young Pioneers, *c.* 1924.

The flagships of new pedagogical method were the First, Second, and Third Experimental Stations of Narkompros, set up in 1919 to run model institutions in which new methodology could be pioneered. The major moving spirit in the stations was Stanislav Shatsky, who before 1917 had been using non-interventionist pedagogy in his work with 'difficult' children. From the mid-1920s, the First Experimental Station, directed by Shatsky, came under increasing pressure to make its work relevant to current political concerns; in the primary schools run by the station, the essay topics set for children began to shift from general themes about nature and rural life to much more openly ideological topics relating to industrialisation and other elements of 'socialist construction'.[32] As Wladimir Bérelowich has argued, the tide had turned once and for all against 'Tolstoyan naturalism' and in favour of 'scientific perfectionism', as manifested in paedological theory, with its emphasis on suppressing instincts rather than following them, and its view of education's purpose as 'guaranteeing correct development'.[33]

In some respects, the transformation was rather less straightforward than this neat description might suggest. For one thing, 'paedology' was applied in a variety of different ways. Just as before 1917, it sometimes signified the Russian variation on what was known in the West as 'paidology'. But, from the mid-1920s, the term *pedologiya* increasingly meant what in the Anglophone West would have been referred to as developmental psychology – the use of intellectual tests in order to establish a child's mental capacities and the appropriate treatment of these in cases of 'abnormality'.[34] While this direction in *pedologiya* might appear more obviously to merit the term 'scientific perfectionism', generating as it did a fever of diagnostic analyses, attitudes among paedologists to the *results* of monitoring in fact varied quite widely. One important discrepancy, for instance, lay between those such as Lev Vygotsky, who believed that 'abnormal' children were best educated in mainstream educational establishments, and those such as Adriyan Griboedov, who believed in separate provision not only for 'normal' and 'abnormal' children, but for every sub-category of the 'abnormal'.[35] And, in any case, professional child psychologists had at best a rather marginal status within Narkompros, where top-level policy decisions were on the whole taken by individuals with a background in pedagogy of a more traditional kind (Krupskaya, for instance), rather than by individuals with a first-hand knowledge of Binet-Simon testing, or the writings of Freud or Piaget.[36]

Rising strictness in education was not, in any case, the product of intellectual changes. Rather, it was brought about by political *force majeure*. The growing intolerance of 'chaos', 'elementalism', and 'voluntarism' in cultural development that characterised Soviet official society generally brought with it, in the educational world, a gradual reversion to central control over syllabus content and teaching methodology, of the kind that had been exercised by the Ministry of Enlightenment before 1917.[37] A landmark in this process was the introduction of a core syllabus (*kontsentr*) in 1925. Though much emphasis was still placed on integrated learning (the so-called 'complex' or 'laboratory' system) and on project work, and though there was still quite a lot of stress on 'creative' activities such as 'expressive reading aloud', teachers were firmly reminded that emphasis on personal initiative should not come at the expense of inculcation into collective life, and were provided with specific suggestions about material to be covered in the various areas of the programme.[38]

By 1927 guidance had become stricter, with material now divided into 'compulsory' and 'optional' sections.[39] In 1929, there was a brief interruption to the specialising trend, with a reassertion of project work under the radically inclined education minister Sergei Bubnov (who had now replaced the old-intelligentsia Anatoly Lunacharsky). Learning of all subjects was now supposed to be grouped round a single politicised theme, such as 'The Cultural Revolution' or 'The First Five-Year Plan'. But this move was in its turn soon reversed. A further publication of school programmes in 1930 spoke of 'a precisely defined sphere of systematic knowledge' as the object of school education, and exact subject timetables were supplied, a change that sidelined the 'complex system'.[40] In August 1931, the Party passed a resolution highlighting the need for 'carefully worked out programmes and study plans' in mathematics, chemistry, and physics, and in 1932, the 'laboratory-brigade method' (i.e. project work) was axed altogether.[41]

For about fifteen years, commitment to educational experiment within the Soviet administration was far greater than anywhere else in the world at the time. Western reforming pedagogues, such as John Dewey and Beatrice King, considered the new state a model for educators everywhere: here was a system that sought to achieve for all children what was being achieved for only some fortunate individuals in the West. However, before long, the tradition of top-down control and minute regulation of classroom practice reasserted itself, this time at the service of a different set of ideological requirements.

New Model Nurseries

A similar process of homogenisation and centralisation was evident in the area of nursery education. Here, the principles of free education were controversial right from the beginning of Soviet power. The resolutions of the First All-Russian Congress on Nursery Education (1919) not only emphasised that children were future citizens, but also saw them as performing an important instrumental role in transforming society. 'Pre-school education, which is imbued with the spirit of collectivism, and carries into the life of the child the inspirational principles of social life, of creative, free labour, must be a mighty factor in the re-education not only of children, but of the environment in which they live.'[42] Children, then, were to be guided by right-thinking adults in order to become ancillaries of Soviet power, participants in its civilising mission. The correct treatment of children thereby became an indicator of 'cultural growth' (that is, a phenomenon that pointed to Russia's capacity for successful modernisation),[43] but also a way of ensuring the viability of the Soviet experiment. Because children were the guarantors of the 'bright future', the state's concern with them at one and the same time underlined the humanitarian values of the new order, and provided a model of Soviet identity which emphasised the importance of *vospitanie*, or 'moral education', to the life of all citizens.

By the time of the Second All-Russian Congress on Pre-School Education, held in 1921, the theme of 'education for citizenship' had become insistent. In the turgid phrasing of a resolution passed at the Congress, 'Considering pre-school education to be one of the most important phases in the development of the personality of future builders [of socialism] and fighters for the realisation of the communist ideal, [this congress] makes the foundation of pre-school work the creation of forms of education which have as their basis universal Marxist concepts and which reflect the nature of the child in this revolutionary era.' The ideal of 'natural childhood' had been replaced by a more restrictive notion, that of the 'revolutionary child'. Often, this notion – in line with the dominant early Soviet ideology of 'class war' – had social overtones. In the words of N. Al'medingen-Tumim, writing in 1925, 'To the bourgeois slogan, "The child is central!" (Vom Kinde aus!) proletarian pedagogy adds the words, "Class is central!"'[44] The effect of all this was to reinforce a Lockian model of childhood, according to which any 'childish silliness' that distracted from the child's potential as future adult was meant to be strongly discouraged. Official objections to the Scout movement at the time when this was closed down and the Pioneer organisation set up, in 1922, included not only the fact that the movement was 'bourgeois' and 'imperialist', but that it set too much store by 'the playing of games'.[45] In the words of a resolution at the Third Congress on Pre-School Education in 1924, 'Play is not a biological end in itself.'[46]

In accordance with these ideological changes, manuals aimed at nursery teachers acquired a more earnest tone as time went by. A *Handbook of Nursery Education*, produced by Narkompros in 1919, was almost indistinguishable from pre-revolutionary publications. The children were supposed to have a wide range of toys, including not only work-related ones, but also dolls, *matreshki* (Russian stacking dolls), and a croquet set. The teacher was to sing to them in order to encourage their sensory development, and they were to be read large numbers of *skazki* – for example *The Wolf and the Goats*, and *Goldilocks and the Three Bears* for the youngest.[47] In similar vein, M.Ya. Morozova and E. I.Tikheeva's *Pre-School Education and Kindergartens*, published in 1920, described nursery education as 'the harmonious development of all the capacities of the soul', and warned: 'In the nursery school, there should be no attempt to teach drawing or modelling. Children are to draw and model because their soul has an insuppressible need to do this.'[48] Excursions, festivals, reading aloud, and games were the core of the suggested curriculum.

As early as 1922, however, there were signs of a greater emphasis upon education for work and collective socialisation. In a collection of essays published in that year, some contributors kept aloft the banner of 'free education'. Elizaveta Tikheeva, for instance, gave a gripping account of how sensitive handling by a nursery teacher was able to stimulate a normally taciturn and unhappy small boy into a stream of reminiscences about his granny: she had made him milk kasha and given him sugared bread, and he had sat beside her warm stove while he ironed, playing with his toy soldier, and his trumpet that really blew, and his ball.[49] But contrasting contributions came from E. Al'medingen-Tumim, who insisted that 'man is made for social life', while Yu. Fausek (going in the opposite direction from Tikheeva in 1915) praised the Montessori system for its contribution to the training of the will and the instilment of self-control.[50]

By 1924, with the construction of the first integrated pre-school curriculum for children, the more repressive interpretation of the purpose of nursery education had become dominant.[51] It was further institutionalised in 1926, when Narkompros began issuing its 'Letters on Teaching Methods', official instructions to nursery teachers. Wooden bricks were useful because they encouraged an interest in building (a concept with a metaphorical, as well as practical, resonance in a country committed to 'socialist construction').[52] Dolls, on the other hand, were not, most particularly not baby dolls, which fostered vanity in girls.[53] There was much emphasis upon normative educational targets and group participation. Teachers were told, for instance, that, while children might have their own flower and vegetable beds in the nursery's garden, gardening should be largely a collective project.[54]

As integration of the curriculum increased, so did political control. Already in 1921, the Second Congress on Pre-School Education had pointed to the need for organisation, especially of teacher training, as a riposte to the 'petty-bourgeois elementalism' brought by NEP. The 'chaotic growth' of nursery education since the First Congress in 1919 was described as a 'defect'.[55] In 1924, at the Third Congress, the watchwords of nursery education were stated to be 'collectivism, dialectical materialism, organisation', and the need for a link between nursery education and the Pioneer movement was underlined.[56] There was increasing stress on preliminary planning and on record-keeping (the composition of official reports, *otchety*).

For all their sympathy with the pre-revolutionary 'free upbringing' movement, and despite the continuing influence of theorists such as Montessori and Froebel, early Soviet pedagogues placed considerable emphasis upon the importance of the child's conformity to standard physiological and psychological patterns. Instruction manuals produced by educational theorists told researchers that they should record, in strictly quantified form, not only physical data about the child (its age, height, weight, and state of health, including evidence of any hereditary diseases and information on sleeping patterns), and information about parental standards of living and education, but information on levels of hygiene and taste, and on the adequacy of the upbringing being meted out to the child, and the suitability of the child's choice of friends. All of this was to be graded according to a 5-point scale. Clothing, for example, was ranked from 5 (well-constructed and fit for the season and purpose, tasteful and elegant) via 4 (adequately constructed and suitable, but not elegant), down to 1 (unsuitable, uncomfortable and untidy). A top mark for upbringing signified that this was well organised, with suitable attention given to intellectual targets (the child had plenty of books to read and writing materials to use, and also had its own room, its own table, etc.) The bottom mark signified that the child was either left totally to itself or treated with undue strictness (expected to work unduly hard, punished severely, nagged constantly).[57]

To be sure, collectivised child care was not always understood as a process of incessant monitoring. Sometimes it was seen as offering the opportunity for freedom of expression by children, and for child self-government. The children at the Pioneer Commune for Orphans attached to the Hammer and Sickle Metalwork Factory in Moscow, for instance, to all intents and purposes ran their own institution, carrying out domestic work in rotation and organising meetings to decide on rules and procedures, and on disciplinary measures for those who had offended against the collective norms.[58] But, by and large, collectivisation of child care was a substitution of one kind of adult power – that of professional pedagogues – for another – that of parents. Not only nurseries but other institutions, too, did their best to mitigate the supposedly pernicious influence of parents on their charges and to effect integration of the child into the collective.

The Regulation of Interior Life

Attitudes to moral development and to the exercise of imagination by children on the part of educationalists became – at least in some circles – more repressive than before the Revolution. Lenin's wife and key Narkompros administrator Nadezhda Krupskaya, for instance, moved from seeing the retelling of *skazki* by children of nursery-school age to their fellows as an example of 'free upbringing' in action, to a marked hostility towards the tales.[59] In 1923, Ershov's famous children's poem *Little Hunchback Horse* was denounced by a censorship official on the grounds of its lack of ideological soundness ('it's completely reactionary and anti-pedagogical, it's the tsar [...] and the boyars that are the measure of everything. It goes without saying that people do nothing but cross themselves the whole time').[60] GUS (the Learned Council, the body of Narkompros responsible for secondary censorship of school textbooks and, from 1927, of all literature aimed at children) maintained a full-scale war on *skazki* from the early 1920s.[61] From 1925, the Komsomol authorities added to the pressure by keeping a sharp eye on the ideological rectitude of children's books and journals, condemning those that failed to measure up to due standards of political awareness. In early 1925, for example, *New Robinson* was attacked for its 'excessively childish tone', a criticism to which the magazine responded by vastly increasing the amount of space given to agitational material.[62] For its part, *Pioneer*, the magazine of the Communist children's movement, found very little space for fiction of any kind alongside its advice columns and reportage on political events, public meetings, etc.; such stories as were published were usually mythologised accounts of children's participation in the Revolution and Civil War.[63] Favourite heroes of the 1920s, apart from Red Partisans, included the streetwise ex-waif, reformed by his stay in a Soviet orphanage but retaining the sharp-wittedness, independence, and cheeky humour that were sentimentally supposed to characterise children living rough on the streets.[64]

Not all heroes were children, of course. From the early days of Soviet power, in line with the saying 'a holy place cannot be left empty', the new regime sought to replace the sacred political and religious symbols of the past – the Trinity, the Mother of God, the saints, the royal family – with new, Communist, equivalents. School textbooks and decoration, and the trappings of the Communist children's movement, all played their part in conveying the magnificence of Lenin. In August 1923, for example, the Women Workers' Section of the Krasnaya Presnya District Committee of the Communist Party presented a newly formed local Pioneer troop with a photograph of the leader.[65] After Lenin's death in January 1924, the cult started to take off in a big way. Lenin anniversaries were marked by regular 'meetings of mourning and commemoration' (*traurnye zasedaniya*) organised by Party and Komsomol cells, at which children were also present.[66] In February 1924, the Secretariat of the Central Committee of the Komsomol produced an exemplary plan for a 'Lenin corner' to be set up in schools and Pioneer clubs: such a 'corner' was supposed to contain, among other things, a portrait, extracts from Lenin's speeches, details of his final illness, memoirs by acquaintances, and information about what Lenin had done for children. It was also to include a biography written by the children themselves, and a photo-spread of Lenin's life.[67] Children were plunged, like the rest of Russia, into mourning for the leader: they were encouraged to brood on Lenin's demise and on his legacy, to design mausoleums and monuments to commemorate him, and to compose songs in his honour.[68]

Even children of under seven were supposed to have 'a real appreciation of Lenin's personality (Lenin is the leader and teacher of the working class in their struggle with the bourgeois. He cared for the workers and their affairs. When he died he was buried in the mausoleum).'[69] The protagonist of Sofiya Zak's poem *How Pasha Spent the First of May* (1926), having encountered the Lenin Mausoleum while attending the First of May parade with his nursery school, was seized with eagerness to become old enough to join the Octobrists (the children's movement for 7–10-year olds): 'Oh I'm bored with being so small/But soon an Octobrist I'll be, after all.'[70]

It followed that the *skazka* was suspect even for this age group. In the words of one of the 'letters on method' addressed to nursery school teachers: 'There is nothing to justify cats dressed up in hats or dogs baking pies; these fairground images add nothing positive to a child's emotions, nor do they inculcate clear ideas about animal behaviour; in any case, one can show much more interesting things about animals than in representations of this kind.'[71]

With such a chorus of powerful voices condemning anthropomorphism, there were only two ways in which Soviet writers might uncontroversially represent animals. The first was fictionalised nature study, preferably with an agitational flavour, as in the case of Vitaly Bianki's *Forest Newspaper*, which chronicled seasonal events in the natural world in the style of Soviet journalism of the day ('City News' 'THE ROOKS HAVE ARRIVED', and so on).[72] The second was political allegory, as in this poem by Dmitry Tsenzor, published in 1923 alongside an illustration of an overweight and snarling family of cats:

> From behind the pulled blind
> The new moon peeps,
> The kitten is having a name-day party,
> The kitten is having a feast.
>
> All the family is at table,
> For the party: dad and gramps,
> In mummy's arms is mewling
> Youngest bruv, a picky type.
>
> The kitten feeds his face.
> The dishes are amazing:
> Greasy piglet with stuffing,
> Milk and sausage.

Presents for the kitten too:
Books, a rat, a bird, a ball,
The cats duff up the mice:
What a lovely day!

But in the cellar sadly weep
In solidarity the poor little mice:
Grumbling angrily at the soft life
Those damn cats lead.[73]

In a much better-known example of the same genre, Samuil Marshak and Elizaveta Vasil'eva's verse playlet *The Cat's House* (1922), a selfish puss, dressed in a 1,000-rouble dress and ear-rings as well as the traditional boots, refuses to allow into her dwelling some poor relations, and is duly punished by a terrible fire and destitution. Fortunately, the despised nephews and nieces turn out more charitable than she is, and the play ends with all the characters helping to rebuild the house for all of them to live in. But the basic analogy between pet cats and petit-bourgeois values remained intact.[74]

Not for nothing is Tsenzor's poem about a name-day party: celebrations of this kind were a major target for reformers. Birthday parties attracted the opprobrium of Krupskaya, who considered that they had no didactic function (a child did not in any case realise what it was to become older), and that they were likely to have pernicious effects because they emphasised the child's individuality.[75] It was inevitable that Christmas, a religious festival as well as an 'individualist' and 'bourgeois family' event, and one that also involved the 'waste' of ecological resources, should attract still stronger hostility. Accordingly, in 1928, the purchase and decoration of Christmas trees was forbidden by decree.

As even this was not enough to deter some Russians from what had now become a much-loved tradition, winter sports festivals were organised by activists with the aim of establishing an alternative amusement for the holiday. Propaganda carried by children's magazines exhorted the young to display leadership in the family, lambasted parents who attempted to find a cunning way out by decorating pot-plants instead of actual trees, and recorded parades by Pioneers carrying 'Down with the Christmas Tree' placards, to the horror of passing old ladies.[76] Children were taught agitational *chastushkas* (rhyming ditties) about the evils of cutting down a tree:

Don't chop down trees without need,
Show respect for the woods.
Instead of showing your greed
Plant a sapling, and do some good.[77]

Ecologically aware, collectively minded, and setting their faces against 'superstition', the children who campaigned against Christmas trees encapsulated the spirit of the new age.

Juvenile Activists

The governing image of 'Soviet childhood' over the first decade and a half of the country's existence was rationalistic, anti-bourgeois, and often pro-child and anti-adult (or at least hostile to private adult authority as represented by parental power, which was seen as shoring up the undesirable social attitudes of the past). It was also steeped in the 'class struggle' politics and gender prejudices of the day. The preferred model for children was a politically conscious male child of proletarian origins. David Moor's poster I'M AN ATHEIST, for example, showed a smiling young boy of 11 or 12 dressed in an oversized greatcoat and Budyonny forage-cap, the size of the clothing emphasising his impatience to grow into a militaristic adult role.[78] Still more eager to rush through childhood as quickly as possible was the baby in Samuil Adlivankin's *A Visit to the Tank Drivers* (1932), held head-high by his tank-driver father and beaming out from under his outsize Budyonovka.[79] The same point about accelerated development was made more subtly in Aleksandr Rodchenko's famous trilogy of Pioneer photographs from 1930. Here, all three children were shot from below, which rendered their faces monumentally vast; their chins are tilted and their eyes fixed upwards, staring towards the bright future.[80]

The emphasis on children's precocity was not a question of images alone. Children were actively encouraged to participate directly in the political process,

18   *There is No Knowledge Without the Book, No Communism Without Knowledge!*. Poster, *c.* 1930.
A child marches in step with adults in the fight against illiteracy.

handing out election leaflets, making speeches at meetings, and organising agitational work.[81] They were also given a role in the Communist International, whose ancillary organisation was known as the Communist Youth International (KIM). The most prominent KIM activities involved young people rather than children, but International Children's Week (abbreviated to MDN), promoted in the Soviet Union from 1924, allowed younger members of Soviet society to make their contribution to international solidarity. A brochure setting out model plans for the ninth such week, held in 1929, indicated the ambitious levels at which children were supposed to participate in the celebrations. They were to organise a special exhibition, or 'corner', for the week, in which would be a poster, a letter to the foreign children's organisation which came under their supervision, information about how much money they had managed to collect to support it, and a map showing the town, district, and country where it was located. A slogan in a foreign language was also to be displayed.[82]

Also in the late 1920s, the Pioneer wing of the Communist International began to hold its own, separate, congresses: the First International Communist Congress of Proletarian Children, held in 1929, involved 200 delegates, 60 of them from 'the capitalist countries of Europe, America, and Asia', who discussed a wide-ranging series of issues and, according to a contemporary source, 'laid the foundations of a children's communist international'.[83] In the late 1920s and early 1930s the international movement was more widely publicised in children's magazines and newspapers than the collectivisation campaign, even in the provincial press: the occasional article would focus on the work of 'agit-battalions' in the villages, but International Children's Week was given copious coverage, as was a comparable event, International Youth Day, usually held in the autumn.[84]

More localised junior sections of adult organisations included the 'child correspondent' movement, a miniaturised version of the 'worker correspondent' movement, aimed at setting up a network of unpaid journalists to supply copy from the factory floor for the Soviet press: the 'child correspondent' movement was particularly closely allied with the collective farm and village magazine *Friendly Lads*.[85] Many other organisations – for instance the philanthropic society 'Children's Friend', or the Osaviakhim movement – had sections for child activists. The Pioneer organisation itself was involved in every important campaign of the day, from the 'culture drive' of 1928–9 to the 'intelligence agents of industry' network of 1931–2, and the 'Let's Catch Up the American Chicken' attempt to make the Soviet poultry industry competitive in 1932–3.[86]

Throughout the 1920s, and most particularly during the 'cultural revolution' of 1928–32, children, above all Pioneers, were exhorted not only to take an active part in campaigning but to exercise leadership of 'backward' adults, even those senior to them in the family, such as parents. A brochure on *Social Work and the School* published in 1925 set out a staggering agenda for outreach work, including help with surveying the locality, road-surfacing, and bridge-building, as well as the more predictable areas of propaganda for hygiene, fire prevention, and ancillary work in crèches.[87] Even relationships with powerful adults were conducted on a footing of something like equality. In a letter addressed to Joseph Stalin in 1925,

19 Children at an election meeting, 1929 (*Our Achievements* magazine).

Pioneers from the small town of Mozyr' made a whole list of demands – they wanted Pioneer uniforms, exercise books, pencils.[88]

This model of the assertive child who could hardly wait to grow up was accompanied, quite logically, by a denigration of the 'golden childhood' model of appropriate juvenile existence, now associated with the class-ridden hypocrisy of pre-revolutionary Russia. The poet Dem'yan Bednyi would repeat Tolstoy's phrase, 'Oh unforgettable time, my golden childhood', in tones of caustic sarcasm.[89] With equal sardonicism, Viktor Kin (Surovikin) commented: 'My parents made a decision to bring me up carefully: they thrashed me at least three or four times a year. But that's enough about my childhood: it's not only boring for most readers, it's boring for me too.'[90]

Early Soviet culture reversed the gender asymmetry that had been current before 1917. Then, feminine, beribboned children had been celebrated in conventional works of art. But femininity was associated, in Soviet propaganda and ideology generally, with a 'backward' attachment to the cultural past (religion, home, private relationships).[91] Therefore, it was inevitable that girls (where seen positively) were often represented as boys in all but primary sexual characteristics – what the children's theatre director Nataliya Sats was later to call 'Petyas renamed as Nyuras'.[92] Where girls manifested traditional feminine behaviour, this tended to have negative connotations. In Lidiya Seifullina's orphanage novella *The Lawbreakers* (1922), the girl characters were sentimental cry-babies who had to be bullied by the adult supervisor into adopting a properly courageous attitude to sport and outdoor activity. The Young Pioneer girl activists celebrated in *Pioneer Pravda*, or portrayed by Rodchenko, on the other hand, were almost indistinguishable, with their cropped hair, plain shirts, and black knickers or short baggy skirts, from their male counterparts.

The culmination of this cult of self-assertive, politically aware, intellectually autonomous children came in 1932, as the Pioneer organisation celebrated its tenth anniversary. It began with a brutal child murder on the Urals–Siberian borders: Pavel Morozov, along with his little brother Fedor, had been repeatedly stabbed and dumped in the forest near their home village of Gerasimovka. On the basis of almost no evidence, the press – starting with the local paper – asserted that the two had been the victims of kulaks, 'wealthy peasants' who opposed collectivisation. From this it was a short step to portraying the boys themselves as revolutionary martyrs. Just over a month after the death of the Morozovs, *Pioneer Pravda* ran a splash article about the case. It reported that Pavel (renamed Pavlik), a fervent Pioneer, had been so devoted to the cause that he had not hesitated to denounce his father, the chairman of the local village soviet, to the authorities, when it turned out that the man had been issuing false identity papers to peasants expelled from their home villages because of their opposition to collectivisation. The boy had even been prepared to stand up in court and make his declaration. *Pioneer Pravda* quoted his alleged exact words: 'Uncle judge, I am acting not as a son, but as a Pioneer!' The article concluded with a clarion call for 'class vigilance' and implacable hostility to 'class enemies'; in surrounding materials, schoolchildren demanded that the criminals suffer 'the highest measure of punishment' (namely, execution by shooting), while 140 signatories from Pioneer groups across the Soviet Union vowed to continue the struggle that the boy's murder had tragically cut short.[93]

Over the next three years, Pavlik became a national hero. There were detailed reports in the Pioneer press describing the trial of his supposed murderers, members of his own family, led by his grandfather, and his two 'kulak' uncles by marriage. The affair turned into something of a modern Beilis case, with descriptions dwelling on the cruelty with which the Morozov boys had been treated and on the number of their stab wounds. Unlike the accused in the earlier trial, though, four out of five of those in the Morozov case were convicted, and duly sentenced to the execution by shooting that the pre-trial petitions had demanded.

As Pavlik became more famous (his younger brother more or less dropped out of the picture), the list of those he was said to have denounced became longer and longer. In 1933, the first life of the boy appeared, written by Pavel Solomein, a journalist in the Urals; it portrayed Pavlik's life as a 'conversion narrative', in which a boy from a backward village struggled to transform his community and himself, travelling from ignorance and darkness into knowledge and light.[94] When the book came to the attention of Maxim Gorky, Pavlik's cult was significantly boosted. Gorky was so struck by the story that he referred to it repeatedly in print and in speeches, and co-ordinated a push for a memorial to Pavlik. In 1935, the Politburo passed a motion endorsing the construction of such a monument on Red Square, next to the Historical Museum and the Museum of the Revolution.[95]

Needless to say, the legend that grew up around Pavlik bore little relation to reality. In fact, it seems most likely that the murder happened by chance. There is no concrete evidence that the denunciation ever took place (the source usually quoted for the story was Pavlik's mother, who admitted herself that she 'did not get on with' her husband and his family).[96] But whatever the factual foundation of his story, Pavlik was a figure for his time. He was one of a cluster of defiant child heroes who emerged in 1931–2. These also included Veronika, the heroine of a narrative poem by Eduard Bagritsky, 'Death of a Pioneer Girl' (also based on a real-life story), who refused on her deathbed to make the sign of the cross, and instead raised her frail hand in a Pioneer salute; Mustapha, the central character in Nikolai Ekk's film *Road into Life*, a former street child and petty criminal transformed by his stay in an enlightened orphanage into a model member of the collective, who submitted to murder by a former associate rather than betray the cause; and Mal'chish, the protagonist of the story-within-a-story in Arkady Gaidar's tale *The War Secret*, who died the death of the brave in a war against the faceless 'Boorjooey' (a corruption of 'bourgeois'). Resolute to the point of fanaticism, such children were models, for adults as well as their own contemporaries, for their revolutionary piety. Not coincidentally, all of them were more or less exactly 'coevals of the Revolution', a title that was to be used honorifically about a whole generation that was supposed to offer help for the future. At the same time, it is worth noting – even at this stage – a degree of ambivalence in the representation of such fervent children. After all, these most striking representatives of political commitment all paid for their actions with their lives. This gave them the function less of models for imitation (except in the abstract sense: self-sacrifice was a good thing), than of revolutionary ancestors, figures in the aetiology of Soviet power.

Among commentators who were coolly disposed to Soviet reality, or who maintained a belief in the sacredness of childhood, or both, the early Soviet model for childhood – assertive, politicised, masculine – inspired disquiet and suspicion. Evgeny Zamiatin, in an essay written not long after his emigration to France in 1930, evoked the typical Soviet child as 'an eight-year-old grown man', turned into an automaton by the political indoctrination imposed on him in schools. For Zamiatin, the fact that 'the influence of the family loses the battle with the influence of the school' was both obvious and tragic.[97] But one did not have to be a political dissident to find child activism problematic. Even in the Pioneer movement, there was a good deal of heart-searching about the extent to which children should be involved in serious politics.[98] And in satirical fiction published in the Soviet Union itself, the precocious activist was a standard figure of fun. The narrator of Mikhail Zoshchenko's ironically titled story 'Happy Childhood' (1925), enjoying a break in the Tauride Garden in Petrograd, spies a small boy whom he sentimentally invites to sit on his knee. He is shocked to be greeted with a hostile and ungrammatical tirade: 'Ain't got no time to waste humping up and down on your lap, I ain't. Your lap's a load of crap, I say, and you're a blinking fool too.' But at this point a standard satirical theme of the day, the fact that children had become the new adults, was given an idiosyncratic twist. Provoked by the narrator's surprise that a child could possibly have 'no time' to do what he wanted, the boy launched into a long complaint about the 'commissions and the Übercommissions, the speeches and the meetings', and his classmates nagging him when he does go out for fresh air. The narrator suddenly recognised the resemblance between the boy's situation and his own – over-stressed, perpetually hounded onwards to the next duty. Rather than being seen as a travesty of childhood, the boy's over-taxing schedule was used to suggest that helplessness, confusion, and victimisation by those larger and stronger than oneself were essential aspects of human existence more generally. It was the narrator's belief in happy childhood, rather than the boy's sense of being overburdened, which was out of kilter with the real world.[99]

In practical terms, the representatives of state authority were not always keen to encourage unilateral activity by children. An entertaining demonstration of this occurred in October 1924, when a group of Pioneers decided that they wanted to engage in an act of revolutionary refashioning, discarding their 'religious' first names and adopting politicised new ones, such as RKP (Workers' and Peasants' Party) and KIM. The response to this from Pioneer and Komsomol leaders was anything but rapturous: the children, instead of being congratulated, were expelled from the Pioneer organisation.[100] A famous play by Sergei Tret'yakov goes under the title, *I Want a Child!* and portrays a young Soviet woman worker's determination to conceive and rear her offspring in the approved emotionally detached and rational style.[101] There was, however, no text under the title *I Want to Be Born!* – even in utopian fiction, let alone the 'literature of fact' espoused by Tret'yakov. Just as in his play, it was adults who determined children's right to exist, and adults who regulated their existence once they came into the world. And from 1932, as target-directed learning and discipline started to be restored in the schoolroom, the assertive model of childhood began to lose dominance: now children were exhorted to get their heads down and study. At this point also, a campaign began to introduce children of all social backgrounds – but most particularly from the working classes – to what was known as the 'cultured life': the Pioneer organisation, for example, introduced a badge with the title, 'ART INTO THE LIVES OF PROLETARIAN CHILDREN', which was widely advertised in the Pioneer press.[102]

Children's Language, Children's Art

Even in the 1920s, the child who was politically active, or at the very least passionately interested in the world of work as opposed to the world of fantasy, was not the only model of positively valued behaviour, although this was certainly the dominant model. During the period of the New Economic Policy (1921–8), a number of energetic private presses, notably Raduga (Rainbow) of Leningrad, maintained something approaching a counter-tradition of children's books. Work published by private presses usually had higher production values than the editions brought out by the state houses; often, too, it displayed more continuity with pre-revolutionary tradition (for better or worse) than the writing showcased by official presses. 'Cats dressed up in hats or dogs baking pies' were not unknown: a famous 1924 poem of Kornei Chukovsky, for example, dealt with the wedding of a talking fly.[103] As this case showed – the Fly was liberated from her tormentor the Spider by a (male) Mosquito, who then claimed her hand in marriage – the conventional gender roles assailed in Soviet pedagogy were also quite often in evidence. In Vera Inber's poem 'The Centipedes' (1925), also published by Raduga, daddy centipede (literally 'Forty Legs') worked in an office, while mummy centipede minded their forty children and did the washing – forty times forty pairs of socks, etc.[104]

In addition, a lively alternative tradition of writing about (as opposed to for) children continued, often expressing views at odds with rationalistic emphasis on the teleology of socialisation. Where official campaigns sought to stamp out 'uncultured' childhood pastimes such as playing on rubbish heaps and mounted assaults on the use of slang,[105] ethnographers devoted their attention precisely to such practices. Elizaveta Shabad, the author of *The Living Language of Children* (1925), described as 'unfortunate' the efforts of kindergarten supervisors to get children in the age group 3–4, which for her was the most interesting in linguistic terms, to speak 'correctly'. Her study revelled in children's use of invented terms (such as *gynga-gynga-gynga*), and their penchant for what adults would see as non sequiturs; her citations of children's talk made some attempt to reproduce the phonetics of the original. 'Valya went out walking and Mummy did too and so did Auntie Nina and dere on the window was a lickle birdie, and flap flap off she flew and mummy has nice warm boots on and she bought a lovely fuwwy hat.' Without any moralising commentary, Shabad quoted instances of boasting, teasing, and bloodthirsty talk of violence:

20   S. Fedorchenko, P. Pastukhov, *Fairy Tale* (1925). An example of the high imaginative and technical levels of children's illustrated books in the 1920s.

I won't let you in, I'll bweak your house down.
I'll bweak *your* house down.
I've got a thooter at home, I'll thoot you.
I've got a gun that fires cowks, I'll kill you.
You'll use cowks, but I'll go bang bang with my thooter, then you'll die.
God died in our church and now he's cwying.
Lots of people died near where I live.
Well, *we've* got a wolf living in our summer camp.[106]

More systematic in analytical terms, but similar in its underlying attitude to childhood as subversive of adult norms, were Georgy Vinogradov's remarkable studies of children's language and folklore. *Children's Secret Languages* of 1926 was a pioneering catalogue of the morphology of the languages invented by children in the 12–13 age group, recording not only simpler variants (where a suffix or prefix was added, as in 'She-to saw-to me-to go-to past-to yester-to day-to'), but also complex variants which required consonant shifts and vowel harmony. *Children's Satirical Verse* (1925) was a rich inventory of scabrous taunts and rhymes, many including words that could not be printed for Vinogradov's adult public at the time when he wrote.[107] Such works built on the scholarly interest in children's language that had just begun showing itself before the Revolution;[108] their tenor also owed something (in Vinogradov's case) to the populist preference for authentic folklore, and (in Shabad's) to the enthusiasm for children's culture as subversive, that characterised the Russian Futurists.

The specificities of children's language were also highlighted in the second edition of Kruchenykh's anthology of work by children, published in 1923, which excluded the drawings printed in the first edition (probably for technical reasons), but included much more poetry and fiction. Like Shabad, Kruchenykh used loosely phonetic transcription, so that, for instance, a 2-year old's little poem was turned into an incantatory chant in *zaum'* (transrational language):

> Black night come,
> Oon come out,
> Clock ding-ding,
> Tie to eep …
> Day come – tie to wise.

There were also some examples of youthful surrealism:

> In her dream Lyalya spied
> An ass giving Papa a ride.
> Lyalya says Ho-Ho
> And she wants a go.[109]

The main way in which modernist writers adopted the notion of the 'revolutionary child', then, was in the sense of 'the child as an iconoclast of

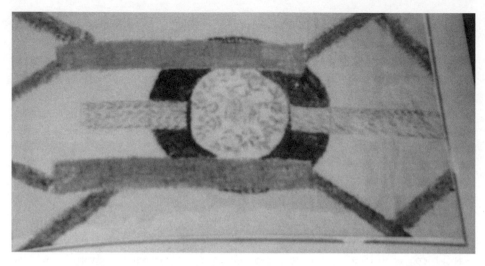

21 'My Garden'. Drawing by a child attending a village school run by the First
Experimental Station of Narkompros. Mid-1920s.

language'. Andrei Belyi's *Kotik Letaev*, in particular, was an absolute *tour de force*
of early linguistic experience, showing the way in which the sound and shape of
words were primary to the child's consciousness, with words acquiring resonance
long before they were properly understood.[110] Hearing through children's ears and
seeing through their eyes was one way in which modernist writers could 'make the
world strange', to adopt the term made famous by the Formalist theorist Viktor
Shklovsky. In Shklovsky's own fictionalised memoir, *The Third Factory* (1926), for
example, the narrator's son's red rubber elephant becomes a means by which the
narrator himself can revert to the wonder of childhood:

> All rubber toys have to squeak, or else how would the air get out? [...]
> My son is laughing.
> He laughed the first time he saw a horse: he thought that it meant its four
> legs and long muzzle as a joke.
> We're all moulded in different ways, but we have just one voice if you
> squeeze us.
> Move out of the way, red elephant: I want to see life without any jokes
> and to tell it things without using my squeaker.[111]

Despite the command to the red elephant to 'move out of the way', the rubber
toy in fact did provide the 'voice' for the narrator in the first part of Shklovsky's
memoir – a means for conveying the inescapable jokiness and scatological
obsessions of early childhood, and for retrieving the 'voice' lost when memory is
filtered through adult consciousness. Similarly, Boris Pasternak's poem 'So They
Begin. At Two Years Old' was an extraordinary combination of poetic credo and
evocation of childhood, where the the early years of *any* human subject were seen

as the time of a supremely creative alienation from the world through language and imagination:

> So they begin to understand,
> And in the roar of the started turbine
> It seems that mother is not mother,
> That you are not you, that home is somewhere else.
>
> What is the horror and the beauty
> Of the lilac perching on the bench
> To do, other than snatch away children?
> And that is how suspicions start.[112]

Pasternak's poem appeared in 1922, three years after the publication of Freud's essay on the uncanny, and his view of childhood here is similar, though it is not clear whether he knew the essay.[113] In the case of other writers – for example Eisenstein, whose writings on his childhood emphasised 'virtuous' childhood as

22 Vera Pestel', *Girl on a Divan* (1922). An example of the withdrawn and mysterious visions of childhood sometimes evoked in the early Soviet period.

a time of silent preparation for adult transgression – the progress from reading psychoanalytical literature to representation can easily be traced.[114]

In post-revolutionary memoirs, the world of the nursery has often become a darker and bleaker place, closer to the nightmare milieu imagined by Freud. Both in Belyi's *Kotik Letaev* (1920) and in the memoir-essays written by Tsvetaeva in Paris (notably *The House at Old Pimen*, 1934), the inspiration of the future artist was seen to proceed as much out of fear and trauma as out of the spellbinding sensual wonder of early experience.[115] (Zoshchenko's agonised psychoanalytical memoir *Before Sunrise* (1943), searching for the psychic wound in ever earlier layers of the memory, is a belated exercise in the same vein.)

The sense that childhood did not have to be conventionally happy, or indeed conventional in any other way, was a moving force in records of more humdrum forms of misery (as in Akhmatova's 'Northern Elegies' – 'And I had no kind of rose-pink childhood') or of emotionally unclassifiable experience (see particularly the memoirs of Russian-Jewish writers, such as Osip Mandelstam's *The Noise of Time*, or Anna Prismanova's autobiographical cycle *Sand*).[116] Sometimes, too, the casual sadism of the indulged small child came to seem monstrous in retrospect: Anatoly Mariengof was especially agonised, half a century later, by the memory of how he contrived the sacking of his devoted nanny when she refused to humour his 4-year-old caprice by grubbing under a sofa to fetch his ball.[117] At the very least, the child was seen as an observer whose faculties were not crusted over by life as the mature adult's were, and who could respond with immediacy to any experience, however everyday. For Aleksandr Pasternak, even a banal, snakes-and-ladders-style game called Polar Explorers became a dream world of adventure, while seeing a dray-horse beaten was so distressing as to be unbearable. Trifles such as a 'disgustingly' pink horse-hoof or a garish woollen monkey from the fair evoked extreme reactions: the child was as helpless before emotion as it was powerless in the face of cruelty.[118]

Though the writers of these memoirs were professional artists, many of them sought to speak for all children. In Soviet Russia during the 1920s, the capacity for artistry in all children was a widely and passionately held belief. Zlata Lilina, wife of Zinoviev, insisted to the All-Russian Congress for the Protection of Childhood in 1919: 'Every person can be an artist, a composer in his work.' The task of education should be to develop this multi-talented capacity in every child.[119] Vkhutemas, the Higher Art Studio in Moscow, a centre of avant-garde practices, had its own studio of children's drawings; there was also a special museum of children's art in the capital. And the article on children's art published in the first edition of the *Great Soviet Encyclopaedia* was illustrated with a plate of a child's drawing (published anonymously to suggest its universal import) which was at once orthodox in political terms (it showed an honest toiler on the new collective farm, a red-scarfed milkmaid) and avant-garde in style (the proportions of the figure were incorrect in neo-classical terms, and the colours were searingly bright). The article itself referred approvingly to the influence of children's art on painters such as Matisse, Larionov, Lebedev, and Kupreyanov.[120] It was common in the late 1920s and early 1930s for adult Soviet painters to model themselves on children's art. An example is Georgy Rublev's *A Factory Party Meeting* (1932), where the bright pure tones in shades of lemon, sea-green, pink, white, scarlet, and orange are applied unevenly, like dabs of watercolour. Faces are schematically rendered, sometimes with curlicues for mouth and eyes, and sometimes simply as pink blobs, and the exaggerated use of semantic perspective makes the background figures loom over a small stick-person tuning a radio in the foreground.[121]

Where children's art was seen as a model for adult art in its exhilarating boldness, it was inevitable that the figure of the child prodigy as a miniature adult artist should seem strange and ludicrous. The *vunderkindy* analysed in a collection of essays on neurology and psychology published in 1925 were of the kind that would now be named *idiots savants*, individuals whose extraordinary early genius in the sphere of music was accompanied by emotional and development abnormality – inability to react to others in some cases or, conversely, excessive suggestibility.[122] Isaak Babel's short story 'Awakening', from his collection *The History of My Dovecote*, offered a narrative about a failed child prodigy in which black farce was the predominating mood. Babel sardonically equated performance and commercial exploitation: the prompting for the child's disastrous excursions into the world of music came from his father's dream of fantastic wealth. 'Little Jascha Heifetz' was getting 800 roubles a performance: 'So how much for fifteen concerts a month? You can do the sums yourself.' The narrator, Babel's *alter ego*, 'was long past the Wunderkind age (I was then about fourteen, but so small and skinny I could have passed for eight. Hopes were pinned on that).' His playing was painfully awful: 'Sounds were stripped off my violin strings like iron filings.' Nevertheless, he was sent for lessons to a fashionable teacher, and forced to queue outside the music room with rows of 'hysterically overwrought' mothers 'holding clamped to their knees fiddles that far outsized the children about to give concerts upon them in Buckingham Palace'. According to a general trajectory in Babel's quasi-autobiographical prose, the civilising drive ended in failure. Just as education did not produce the desired results ('I was always lying as a boy. It was the result of reading a lot'), so music lessons simply enhanced the Babel-double's obsession with swimming, while his fiddle met its end 'sinking into the sand by a breakwater'.[123]

This kind of pressure was definitely not the way to encourage children's artistic abilities, it was clear. Instead, parents were meant to work by constantly expressing warm enthusiasm about any creation that was placed before them. A set of instructions for parents, 'How to React to Children's Drawings', issued in the mid-1920s, warned parents that they were on no account to scold children for drawings they thought were bad, that they absolutely must not offer corrections or draw anything for the child themselves, let alone suggest that it copy anything. Instead, they must do everything possible to make the child value what he or she drew.[124]

Some of the accounts by mothers recorded at the offices of the paedological movement in the 1920s show parents making efforts to record every manifestation of artistic genius in their children. In her *Mother's Diary*, for instance, Z. I. Stanchinskaya noted that her small son loved making up poems (each of

which she carefully recorded). An example composed when the child was four
and a quarter went like this:

> Pussy goes round the garden,
> And froggy walks after him,
> Croak, croak, croak.
> I'm a little croakerette,
> I'll eat up grass stems,
> And drink home-brewed beer.[125]

On the face of it, Stanchinskaya's exultation in pieces of this kind might seem
simply fond maternal piety, along the lines of keeping a ready-made album with a
compartment for 'baby's first curl'. But the recording was made in a context where
the aesthetics of the Russian avant-garde had made children's early linguistic
utterances seem important for artistic as well as sentimental reasons. Kornei
Chukovsky's famous and extremely influential study of children's language, *From
Two till Five*, drew on diaries such as Stanchinskaya's for evidence of children's
linguistic creativity, and used these, in turn, as the legitimising material for a
defence of his own linguistic strategies in his writing for children.[126] Thus, the
process of circular reinforcement reached its conclusion. The child was exposed
to literature that was designed to be in harmony with its assumed psychological
needs, and creative efforts based on such material were then received with
delight because they bore out the congruence between the original literature
and the psyche of the child. By extension, where the genius of *every* child was
championed, the genius of individual children faded into the background.[127]

The World of Wonder

The universalist views of 'child genius' bore fruit in the output of state presses
themselves. The Children's Literature Section of the State Publishing House
(Gosizdat), set up in 1924, which was directed by one of the most talented
children's writers in the Soviet Union, Samuil Marshak, was an especially
important haven for imaginative work, both verbal and visual. Among the writers
who worked for it were two members of the OBERIU group of absurdist writers
in Leningrad, the poets Daniil Kharms and Aleksandr Vvedensky, and two other
major poets from the city, Nikolai Oleinikov and Osip Mandelstam, as well as
the dramatist Evgeny Shvarts. Artists included Petr Sokolov (1892–1938), a pupil
of Kuz'ma Petrov-Vodkin, Sergei Makletsov (b. 1892), and Vladimir Lebedev
(1891–1967). The journals produced by the house – particularly the *Hedgehog* and
the *Siskin*, founded in 1928 and 1930 respectively – maintained high standards,
both in aesthetic and in technical terms, despite political pressure. Even explicitly
political texts produced by the Leningrad section and its counterpart in Moscow
were usually composed and presented with a strong sense of the need to appeal to
the imagination of children. Zak's *How Pasha Spent the First of May*, for example,
was made lively not only by the punchy verse, but also by the magnificently

trenchant illustrations by T. Kachkachev, which overcame the technical obstacles of three-colour printing by using vivid, poster-like blocks of black, scarlet, and royal blue.[128]

Soviet books for children did give space and weight to issues and slogans of the day, as is shown by the publication of titles such as *We Will Catch Up and Overtake the American Chicken!* (1930).[129] But, striking as such titles are, they cannot be seen as representative of state publishing for children as a whole. Generally, it is fair to say that the sense of guidance towards didactic objectives was not necessarily more evident in official children's books than it was in the work showcased by the private presses.[130] Chukovsky's own work, for instance, was didactic not only in its drive to develop children's imaginative capacities, but in its moral undertow. *The Huge Cockroach*, in which a kangaroo took the role of the small boy in 'The Emperor's New Clothes' and pointed out to the animals that the ruler they so dreaded was nothing more than an ordinary cockroach, offered an important lesson in standing up to bullying (a central theme in *The Crocodile* as well). *Washtobits*, whose small boy hero was pressurised into washing through a rebellion on the part of all the objects in the flat where he lived, afforded instruction on the importance of hygiene.[131]

Conversely, many books published by state presses espoused pedagogical ends that were in no sense specifically 'Soviet', but typical of twentieth-century children's literature in other cultures as well: kindness to animals, health and hygiene, technological progress, and so on. Sofiya Zak's *Borya at the Clinic* (1928), for example, issued a rhymed warning about the dangers of contaminated food, such as bought ice-cream ('Can it really be a treat/To eat ice-cream from the street?') and attempted to set children's minds at rest about visiting the doctor (who turned out to be a nice kind man, contrary to Borya's anxious expectations).[132] Other texts explored the theme of 'getting to know the world' in a more general sense (as set out in Dr Seuss's American classic *Are You My Mother?*). Vitaly Bianki's *The Bog* (1931), illustrated with beautiful, vigorous, wax-crayon illustrations by Yu. Vasnetsov, dealt with a child's adventures when getting to know the fauna at the site in question, from owls to newts, tadpoles, leeches, and beetles.[133] In a different, more urban vein was Sergei Rozanov's *The Adventures of Travka*, which used the occasion of a small boy getting separated from his father on the way to a ski camp to introduce child readers to a variety of technological phenomena, from the means of transmitting telegrams to the functioning of trams (while incidentally imparting to children exactly what they should do if they got lost).[134] Samuil Marshak's delightful *Luggage* was

23 Samuil Marshak and Vladimir Lebedev, *Baggage* (1927, reprinted 1936).

constructed as a mnemonic list of objects that a lady had unwisely consigned to travel by freight (on the pattern of traditional children's games such as 'Ma mère est allée au marché et elle a acheté …'). But the objects chosen had a splendid arbitrariness:

> A lady sent off by rail
> A divan,
> A suitcase,
> A vanity case,
> A picture,
> A basket,
> A cardboard box,
> And a weeny little doggy.[135]

The Absent-Minded Professor from Basseinaya Street, also by Marshak, had, unlike *Washtobits*, no pro-hygiene and pro-organisation payoff: instead, the absent-minded protagonist was left dozing quietly in a carriage at a main-line station, convinced that he had been travelling round in circles for 48 hours.

As far as writing for older children went, it was, if anything, the state presses that published more innovative work. Aleksandr Neverov's novella *Tashkent the Abundant*, published in 1923, enjoyed enormous popularity with child (and indeed adult) readers in the late 1920s and early 1930s – understandably, given the raw power of this tale of a small boy's journey across the Russian Empire for food to save his starving mother and brothers. Neverov's depictions are unforgettable: teeming railway junctions filled with desperate travellers struggling through the chaotic aftermath of the Civil War, refugee encampments with soup tents standing next to ditches running with raw sewage, and the boy Mitka's own constant brushes with disaster (ticket inspectors, thieves, con-men, as well as the humiliation of having to find somewhere to urinate in a packed cattle wagon). Though the end of the story showed Mitka's quest at least semi-successful (he was able to save his mother, though not his two brothers, who had died before he reached home), by far the most memorable moment was when Mitka overcame the final obstacles and arrived in the town he had seen as a paradise of abundance, a metropolis of flower gardens and orchards:

> Men and women were lying round all over the station: they were naked or nearly so, turned black by Tashkent's fierce sun: they were sick, they were dying. Mishka gazed at them from a distance, then came closer, then stood still.
> 'Surely there can't be hunger here as well?' he thought.[136]

Equally grim was Bianki's animal story *Karabash* (1929). Though the basic situation – the relationship between a young girl and her dog – sounds cosy enough, the story is in fact unremittingly stark. The heroine, Taika's, dog (a stray taken in by her when he was a puppy) is thrown out by her mother after he attacks some neighbours' chickens. He ends up living the marginal and dangerous existence of a street dog. Then she and her mother lose their home, the mother dies, and the girl ends up on the streets. Though eventually adopted by Karabash and his dog family, Taika does not (contrary to the Mowgli stereotype) find the experience particularly satisfying – she feels lonely and misses human company. Because of a rabies outbreak in the town where the girl and dog originally lived, the two have had to take refuge in the steppe, which seems a very hostile and empty environment. The *coup de grâce* comes when Karabash, who has saved his young human friend from being attacked by a rabid dog, his own former enemy, himself gets infected and, inevitably, dies of rabies. Even for an adult, this story makes harrowing reading: it comes close to breaking Alison Lurie's rule that total despair is not a tolerable quality in writing for children. A coda in which Taika finds joy and serenity in a Soviet orphanage with Karabash's son is realised in too perfunctory a way to soften the bleakness of the main narrative.[137]

If 1920s literature for young children was graphic and colourful in the manner of Soviet posters, work for older children tended to use the 'cinematic' effects current in adult prose of the day. Boris Zhitkov's very popular sea story *Dzharylgach* (1928), for instance, used short paragraphs to suggest the rapid inter-cutting of scenes; upper-case captions (THE BUCKET) at the openings of the brief chapters worked like inter-titles.[138] Less adventurous in compositional terms, but skilfully narrated and displaying a real ear for dialogue, was *Mariya and Mary* (1929), the tale of a catastrophe at sea in which almost the entire crew of a Russian boat, except for the cabin-boy hero, were drowned as the result of a collision with a vessel manned by British sailors.

If Chukovsky exaggerated his exceptionality as an imaginative writer, he was equally wrong to insist on his peculiarity as an advocate of the *skazka*. The quarrel between him and Krupskaya was merely the latest round in a battle over the permissibility of fairy tales that stretched back to the Enlightenment,[139] and which entered another acute phase in the years after the Revolution. At this point, N. N. Evergetov, writing in 1922, had eloquently argued for the specificity and wondrousness of the child's world. It was absurd to condemn anthropomorphism, given the fact that, for the child, everything was alive; hence the love of children for *skazki*. A child was even passionately interested in its own shoes. Play was vital, not only in boosting learning but in staving off boredom.[140] Even in the second half of the 1920s, there were other voices to speak up for the importance of the genre. A psychoanalytical defence was mounted, for instance, by M. V. Vul'f in 1926: he argued that 'the language of the *skazka* is the child's only language, and the world of the *skazka* is a reflection of the child's inner psychic world'.[141] Georgy Vinogradov, also writing in 1926, attacked the view that frightening *skazki* were pernicious as 'pedagogical sentimentality'.[142] Equally, while Chukovsky was later to brand 'the paedologists' as implacable opponents, two of the most prominent figures associated with the movement, A. R. Luria and Lev Vygotsky, respectfully and uncritically cited examples taken from *Little Children* (which they described as 'an interesting book') in an essay on child development from the early 1930s.[143] Thus, Chukovsky was not so much the solitary voice of common sense (as he liked to argue in later years) as the most prominent representative of a quite widespread trend in early Soviet Russian culture.

There were also, at the edges of Soviet Russian culture, some strikingly conventional representations of children. While agitational genres such as the poster concentrated on child activists, commercial art such as sweet-wrappings showed children in less politically significant roles; wrestling with a pet over a chocolate bar, for example. And the Lomonosov Porcelain Factory in Leningrad was, during the 1920s and early 1930s, issuing not only the plates with revolutionary vignettes and slogans for which it is now most famous, but also china statuettes showing plump, smiling children whose ideological props – a copy of the *Woman Delegate* magazine, say – made them look charming and amiable, rather than a threat to adult authority.

In official children's literature, too, sentimentality of a traditional kind was sometimes tolerated. In Sofiya Zaks's picture-book *The Pilot and his Cat*, the animal in question appeared not as a sign of bourgeois sympathies, but as a new Soviet citizen in its own right, 'the first cat-pilot in the world!' Thus, beyond the world of Narkompros and its 'experimental stations', attitudes to children and the family retained a degree of stability: the new society inherited not just pre-revolutionary strivings to set children free but also the established view that they should be nurtured, protected, and allowed to remain children as long as possible. This second set of attitudes was to become all the more important in the next phase of Soviet history.

24   *The Girl Delegate*, Lomonosov Porcelain
Factory, early 1920s.

Chapter 3

'Thank You, Dear Comrade Stalin, for a Happy Childhood!', 1935–1953

Where else, tell me, on earth
Is there a country like ours,
Where the constitution gives children the right
To live for ever and ever?
(Song from a carnival scenario, 1940)[1]

In the first decade and a half of Soviet power, contradictory attitudes to children emerged. There was widespread talk of 'children's rights' and of 'self-government'; children were encouraged to participate in political activity and in 'socially useful work'. Yet education was also seen as an instrument of political control, a way of supplying the new state with technically and politically literate subjects. Children were at once citizens and subjects, assertive yet docile. Equally, while much emphasis was placed on the importance of self-expression and creativity, excursions into the world of the imagination were mistrusted. Sentimental visions of childhood persisted, alongside attachment to the *skazka* as a way of shaping children's fantasies and developing their creative powers.

From the mid-1930s onwards, attitudes to children became much more consistent. All commitment to children's autonomy was abandoned: the model child was now without question one who was obedient, and grateful to adults for their guidance. Dziga Vertov's 1937 film *Cradle Song*, a film as characteristic of Stalinist culture as Leni Riefenstahl's *Der Triumph des Willens* was to the mentality of the Third Reich,[2] portrayed children as one of two stable points (the other was Stalin himself) in a country where frenetic motion ruled. Trains rushed across the Soviet empire; aeroplanes penetrated the frozen north; troops charged across Spain, fighting the good fight against Fascism. But all this material was inter-cut with shots of devoted mothers kissing and rocking their babies, and icons showing Stalin surrounded by devoted juvenile acolytes, and by footage of Stalin himself at the Eighteenth Congress of the Communist Party, where Young Pioneers added their voices to the hymns of praise.[3]

Thus children became models for adult behaviour in their utter devotion to the Soviet dictator. But, in many respects, patterns for children were subordinated

25 Viktor Govorkov, *Thank You, Beloved Stalin, for a Happy Childhood!* Poster, 1936.

to the governing ideals for adults. The discrepant emphasis on 'discipline' and on 'cheeriness' that was to be found in propaganda for adults had its counterpart in propaganda for and about children. The ideal was now a boy or girl who got top marks at school, but who, having safely completed his or her homework, and perhaps attended a Pioneer meeting too, then dashed off to the ice rink, spent some time playing on the swings in the local Park of Culture, or indeed helped him- or herself to a few 'Tales of Pushkin' chocolates. 'Happiness', traditionally understood as a state of fortuitous delight descending on a person unexpectedly, by act of God as it were,[4] now became the just desert of all Soviet citizens, but above all children. But 'happiness' still had to be earned; pleasure was the reward for subordination of the self. This essential insight lies behind what at first seems a paradox – that the era of high Stalinism witnessed a rehabilitation both of academic education and disciplinary control and of imaginative literature for children.

Celebrating Outstanding Pupils

The abolition of the 'brigade method' in 1932 was accompanied, quite logically, by a shift of emphasis from group achievement to personal achievement. Pupils were now formally assigned homework, on which they were marked individually rather than collectively; the pedagogical press began giving in-depth coverage to the issue of assignment.[5] Loads of homework were heavy, particularly as schooling advanced: official norms of October 1936 dictated up to an hour for the first two classes, and an hour and a half for Classes 3 and 4, two hours for Classes 5 and 6, three for Classes 7 and 8, and up to four hours per day for the top two classes of the school.[6]

Schools remained comprehensive in their intake and in teaching strategies. Pupils who displayed greater than average competence in German or mathematics might be encouraged by individual teachers, and – from the mid-1930s – rewarded with a school prize, but they were not corralled off into a 'set' by themselves, allowed to sit examinations early, or otherwise granted distinctions. However, there was now assiduous celebration, in the Pioneer press and in schools themselves, of pupils who consistently did well – known from 1932 by the title of 'shock pupils', a miniature version of the 'shock workers' who were currently being honoured in factories. While children of this kind ideally also had a role as outstanding political activists, their capacity to study well was of at least equal importance.[7]

Unlike 'shock workers', 'shock pupils' were rarely, if ever, given credit for star performances in woodwork or factory skills. Their achievements were of an academic kind – a point that went alongside the reassertion of academic values in education. Labour education was assigned a more and more marginal place in the timetable, until it was abolished altogether in 1937. It became the province of separate trade schools, and a new educational hierarchy was created, ranging from ten-year schools, feeders for universities, at the top, to village schools, stressing practical knowledge, at the bottom. With emphasis on academic values went emphasis on discipline. From 1932, schools had the right to expel disruptive pupils, and orderly conduct, as well as the systematic execution of homework by individual pupils, became a preoccupation of Soviet pedagogical literature.[8] And, in 1935, an elaborate Disciplinary Code, compulsory for all school pupils, was introduced.[9] 'Self-government' was phased out, and the Pioneer organisation – firmly integrated into the school network in 1932 – became an instrument of disciplinary supervision. From the mid-1930s, it was the norm for pupils to belong to the Pioneers, unless there were some pressing reason why not (usually that they did not deserve to), and a pupil who was disruptive could be punished within the Pioneer organisation as well as within the school.[10]

Alongside this process of tightening control went an increase in central authority over pedagogical discussion, as manifested, for instance, in the reorganisation of institutes working in the area of educational psychology. In 1931, one of these was closed (the Scientific Pedagogical Institute of Marxist-Leninist Pedagogy), and another (the Research Institute of Scientific Pedagogy at the Second Moscow State University) was reorganised as two departments within Narkompros itself. After 1932, the atmosphere became increasingly hostile to 'paedology' in academic institutions, with course loads reduced and prominent specialists in the discipline under assault.[11] On 4 July 1936, a decree of the Central Committee of the Communist Party virulently denounced 'paedological perversions in the Narkompros system'. The decree put an end to adventurous theoretical work in favour of the production of generalising textbooks on 'Soviet pedagogy' (an early example being a volume by Kairov, published in 1939). In 1938, the Higher Communist Institute of Enlightenment was also absorbed into Narkompros, and a wide-ranging reorganisation of Narkompros's own institutions took place, with the State Scientific Research Institute of Schools set up as the central authority on pedagogical education (previously, primary and secondary education had had Narkompros departments to themselves). Finally, in 1943, came the founding of the Academy of Pedagogical Sciences, which was to co-ordinate all research into the subject of education throughout the remainder of the Soviet period.[12]

Pedagogy itself now took on a new tone, emphasising the themes of discipline and subordination. Anton Makarenko's articles for schoolteachers, such as 'The Problems of Soviet Moral Education in Schools', underlined the need for mutual courtesy, but also the importance of refusing to tolerate 'the penetration into the collective of alien, indolently loafing elements'. Teachers were supposed to be smartly dressed, and pupils to conduct themselves with dignity – the distinction between 'self-criticism' (i.e. identification of problems in the collective) and 'whingeing' had to be clearly understood.[13] Makarenko's strictures accompanied a nationwide upsurge of rules and codes of all kinds: 1935 saw the imposition of uniform conduct regulations and achievement targets not just on Soviet schools, but on Soviet orphanages.[14]

'Young Talents'

The emphasis on rigid training extended to early education in the arts. The 1930s saw not only a recrudescence of traditional academic teaching, but also a restoration of the cult of the *vunderkind*. As early as 1932, a special group was set up at the Moscow Conservatoire, allowing fifteen talented children to study regularly with professors at the institution.[15] A more significant watershed, though, was the 'Competition for Young Talents' organised in Leningrad in 1933–4 (the original initiative was later said to have come from the Leningrad Party leader Sergei Kirov, murdered at the end of 1934). Forty-three thousand young artists from all over the country – musicians, writers, and painters – took part, by invitation, in this lavishly bankrolled contest. Prizewinners performed at gala concerts in Leningrad and Moscow (the former event was the subject of an appropriately bombastic canvas by a master of academic socialist realism, while the latter took place in the presence of Stalin himself). They were sent on extensive tours round the Soviet Union, taking part in readings and in concerts and enjoying treats and banquets along the way. The writers, for instance, visited Khar'kov and Zaporozh'e in 1935. They spent the New Year holidays of 1935–6 at a hotel in the elegant, if faded, resort of New Peterhof, where they enjoyed sleigh rides, gramophone concerts, and poetry readings. In the summer of 1936, they took part in an elaborate river cruise, progressing down the Volga before returning to Moscow. Here the education commissar, Sergei Bubnov, hosted a banquet whose splendours had not faded for the participants decades later. The delicacies set before the children included unheard-of treats such as lampreys, sturgeon, pressed caviare, tinned crab, strawberries with whipped cream, pineapples, bananas, and the most expensive brands of Soviet chocolates. Unable to contain himself, one boy filled his pockets with 'Northern Bear' sweets, which he bore off for furtive consumption later in the hotel where the children were staying.[16]

A more serious and permanent reward for participants was the nurturing of their 'young talents' that took place afterwards. Musician winners were sent for tuition to the conservatoire, artists to the Academy of Arts, where they were put through an extremely intensive programme of education, requiring many hours of practice a day. Certainly, there was still some room for Dalcroze eurhythmics and other forms of 'free' arts education in some places, such as the Gnesin Institute.[17] And – unlike, say, the metallic-sounding studies of Czerny, traditionally used to inculcate swift finger-work in young pianists – the compositions of pedagogically oriented Soviet composers such as Dmitry Kabalevsky were designed to engage young imaginations with narrative motifs, cheerful tunes, and bright harmonies.[18] But the nineteenth-century tradition of intensive technical preparation and assimilation, as early as possible, to adult standards drove the educational process.

Child prodigies were miniature versions of Stakhanovite record-breaking workers, favoured with publicity and rewards depending on their seriousness of purpose and their commitment to the Soviet cause. Occasionally, there were whispers of anxiety about the over-strain that might go with too early an exposure to intensive training, but more often the emphasis was on the advantages gained from early development of outstanding talent.[19] What is more, the 'prodigy' had a lower-level counterpart in the shape of the 'outstanding pupil' in the school, whose prowess might be rewarded not just by praise and prizes at the local level (within the school itself), but also by wider publicity and more prestigious rewards. In 1935, the Ukrainian Party leader Pavel Postyshev staged a party for 'outstanding pupils' in Khar'kov, accompanied by all kinds of displays and speeches of congratulation; in the following years, a number of Moscow 'prize pupils' were to have the honour of meeting Stalin himself.[20] As recently as 1932, Nadezhda Krupskaya had expressed her hostility to prize-giving, which she felt had an invidious flavour of individualism.[21] But this view – though occasionally still voiced in print[22] – was becoming a minority opinion. Now, Pioneer heroes of the activist kind ceded the stage to heroes of a quite different variety – those who could play Tchaikovsky's first piano concerto note-perfect at the age of 11, or those who only ever got top marks at school.

The Triumph of the *Skazka*

From the mid-1930s, 'children's creativity' increasingly signified expert assimilation to the artistic canons of the adult world. However, this did not mean that children were supposed to consume only artistic works that were primarily intended for adults. The period also saw the rehabilitation of a highly specific understanding of children's literature as a genre concerned primarily with fantasy and wonder. Krupskaya's attack on Chukovsky did not, as supporters of rigidly rationalist attitudes to upbringing must have hoped, usher in the final death throes of the *skazka*. To be sure, a Party decree of July 1928 ominously referred to the need 'to concentrate on producing a type of book that would facilitate the education of children in a spirit of collectivism'.[23] Whilst *Washtobits*, Chukovsky's humorous poem about a boy who is forced to wash when all the objects in the flat rebel against his slovenliness, was enough in tune with the hygienic side of 'education in a spirit of collectivism' to be reprinted in 1930, the more fantastical of Chukovsky's other *skazki* (*The Fly's Wedding*, *The Cockroach*) were placed 'on ice' after 1929.[24]

But the embargo on fantasy subjects was to prove of relatively short duration. In December 1931, a Party decree pronounced that it was vital to stamp out, not fantasy and political deviationism, but such 'defects of current children's literature' as 'the failure to pay attention to children's specific requirements [as readers], dryness and tediousness in the narrative style'. It also stipulated that

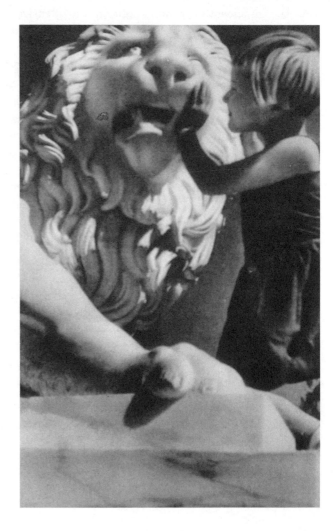

26   M. Shcheglov, *Getting to Know Each Other*, *Our Achievements*, 1936. A small girl makes free with the symbol of Tsarist might; no doubt the image also plays on the Biblical prophecy of the 'lion lying down with the lamb'.

'fellow travelling' writers (i.e. those without an explicit Party affiliation) should be treated 'gently'.[25] This last stipulation could have raised only hollow laughter in the members of the Children's Section of the State Publishing House in Leningrad, who, not long after the decree was issued, were subjected to a police investigation, leading to the arrest of Daniil Kharms and Aleksandr Vvedensky.[26] Yet the December 1931 decree did in fact presage a change of line in children's literature. Kharms and Vvedensky were released shortly after their arrest, and continued working as children's writers; when the Children's Section of the State Publishing House was re-formed as the State Publishing House of Children's Literature in 1933, titles by Chukovsky were among the first books on its list.

When the First Congress of Soviet Writers was held in 1934, Chukovsky and Marshak (another writer who had previously been accused of anthropomorphism, but had, for the meantime, consolidated his institutional position as the head of Detizdat in Leningrad) gave addresses on the future of Soviet children's literature. Marshak, who had the uniquely prestigious role of 'co-speaker', addressing the forum immediately after Gorky's opening speech, was allowed to argue the case for imaginative literature at enormous length (around 15,000 words, or about ten times the standard length of a scripted paper). Children's books must be handsomely produced and look inviting, and their contents must not be 'dry and dreary, like the reports of some political meeting'. 'It is essential not only to register things,' Marshak insisted, 'but to invent and imagine them.' 'Petty pedagogical demands of a utilitarian kind' were the bane of properly inventive writing. The crucial genre in children's writing was the *skazka*, defined by Marshak as 'a poetic-fantastic narrative', albeit also one that 'endorsed new ideas and facts', and that manifested 'an epic respect for its own time'.

From this point on, Chukovsky and Marshak were to play central roles in the articulation of official policy relating to children's literature and associated areas (for example the teaching of literature in schools and the training of talented young writers). The 1936 decree condemning 'paedological perversions', though signifying a move back towards conservatism in the field of educational policy, routed their main enemies in Narkompros.[27] By completely discrediting child psychologists, it gave unchallenged authority to other experts – teachers, children's writers – as commentators on the minds and needs of children.

The position of both Chukovsky and Marshak was always precarious. In children's literature, as in any other area of Stalinist culture, those elevated by the Party leadership were in constant danger of being cast down by it. Marshak narrowly survived the Great Purges: in 1937, as a new wave of assaults was launched against the Leningrad branch of the state children's publishers, now named Detgiz, he was forced to remove himself to Moscow. Two years later, the publishing house he had created in Leningrad endured a blow from which it never recovered. In February 1939, the Komsomol Central Committee denounced 'wreckerdom' (i.e. politically motivated sabotage) at Detgiz.[28] Oleinikov was arrested in that year, Kharms and Vvedensky in 1941; all three were to die in prison. Like Marshak, Chukovsky survived the Purges, but suffered badly one generation removed, this time in a personal rather than professional sense: his son-in-law, the physicist Matvei Bronshtein, was arrested and executed in 1937. Yet Chukovsky and Marshak remained the two most famous children's writers in the Soviet Union. Their books, in particular Marshak's, were published in large print runs and repeatedly reissued, and they were constantly invited to pontificate about the special place of children's literature and of the child in Soviet culture, and were canvassed for their views on education and morality.

One reason for the rise to prominence of Chukovsky and Marshak in 1934 was the patronage of Gorky, who from 1932 until his death in June 1936 was the most powerful writer in the Soviet Union (and one of the nation's premier political figures). Marshak had been lamenting the over-politicised condition of Soviet children's literature to him since the late 1920s, and the laments had not fallen on deaf ears. The mid-1930s also marked a rehabilitation, in all Soviet art and artefacts aimed at children, of *skazka* themes. Such themes were used to decorate the ceilings of the new 'Pioneer Palaces', spectacular clubs for children providing access to a range of leisure facilities and hobby 'circles'. The first of these, in Khar'kov, had a whole room dedicated to the *skazka*, whose oval, rather than oblong, shape marked a shift from 'machine-made' to 'organic' aesthetics.[29] In similar vein, the Moscow House of Pioneers, opened in 1936, had a whole series of rooms decorated with *skazka* topics, from the fables of Krylov to Chukovsky's popular story *Dr Aibolit*.[30]

Fantasy motifs of this kind also appeared in Soviet art for children. Prokofiev's musical fantasy *Peter and the Wolf*, for instance, took a child activist character (in the original scenario he was called 'Petya the Pioneer'), and confronted him not with kulaks or 'enemies of the people', but with a traditional animal bugbear from folk life. However, in conformity with the emphasis on kindness to animals that was taught to children by the Pioneer movement and in schools (which were all supposed to have their 'living corners' of plants, geological samples, white mice in cages, and so on), the wolf escaped slaughter and was placed at the centre of a joyful procession celebrating peace and social harmony.

Another authoritative version of the new fairy tale was Aleksei Tolstoy's *The Little Golden Key*, first published serially in *Pioneer Pravda* during 1935. The hero of this fantasy adventure novel, Burattino, was based in some respects on the Italian nursery favourite, Pinocchio (he had been carved by a peasant from a speaking log, and had round cheeks, bright eyes, and a very long nose, as well as an unruly character). However, the adventures Burattino lives through are quite different. Eluding the wicked puppetmaster Carabas-Barabas and a whole gaggle of his acolytes (among them a self-serving cat and sly vixen, both based on traditional characters from Russian folklore), Burattino and his puppet friends Malvina and Pierrot, and his kind owner Papa Carlo, find their way, at the end of the story, to an extraordinary wonderland graced by a mechanical theatre. The contrast between the emphasis here on beauty, comfort, joy, and magic, and the hollow disappointment that is the final insight of the characters in *Karabash* and *Tashkent the Abundant* could not be greater.

Some aspects of Tolstoy's story integrated it with rising themes in Stalinist propaganda and propaganda literature for adults: the emphasis on a benighted past versus a brilliant present and, more especially, versus a brilliant future (the negative or ambiguous characters in *The Little Golden Key* are almost all old). Equally, the plot archetypes of the *skazka* (transition through ordeals to a land of light and beauty) began to dominate literature for adults in the mid-1930s as well (as, for example, in the famous production novel *How the Steel was Tempered*). But Party ideologues purveyed the *skazka* as a model much less assiduously to writers for adults than they did to children's writers, and Socialist Realist novelists writing for adults would not have got away with portraying winged horses, animated puppets, or golden fish in their work.[31] An outcome of the promotion of the *skazka* was that children's literature became, after 1934, the sole, though constantly endangered, refuge of writers who wished to publish work on non-realist themes, including the Leningrad absurdists Daniil Kharms and Aleksandr Vvedensky.[32]

A Soviet Fairyland

The first dedicated department store for Soviet children, with the pre-revolutionary name Children's World, opened in Leningrad in August 1936. The store was meant as a leisure venue as much as, or more than, a place where purchases could be made: it contained a hairdresser and a café as well as various departments for clothes, games, and toys, and was planned to have rooms where children could try out games, photographic equipment, and musical instruments alongside the facilities for sale.[33] The emphasis on secondary facilities was just as well, given that the contents of the store (as with other Soviet department stores) comprised a strictly limited selection of shoddily crafted items.[34] But the point was that this was supposed to be a paradisiacal venue, one where the perfect happiness of Soviet childhood was demonstrated and enacted. A publicity shot of the opening, which showed 'Pioneer activists' from the nearby palace staring admiringly at a window display containing no more than statues and flower arrangements, set the tone: mere acquisition was the very least of the store's functions.[35]

Nevertheless, acquisition by children of material goods was considered licit, particularly if these arrived in the form of gifts, as at the ritual of the 'New Year Tree'. In 1935, the ban on trees was suddenly overturned (it is generally thought that Pavel Postyshev was behind this reform, as he was with parties for prize pupils). Traditional Christmas festivities were renamed 'New Year' festivities, and brought forward from 6 January to New Year's Day. Towering firs were obtained by institutions such as work collectives and trade unions, as well as Pioneer palaces, where the tree formed the centrepiece of children's parties attended by adults dressed up as Grandfather Frost (a suitably secular version of St Nicholas) and his glamorous female companion the Snow Maiden.[36] No longer the accoutrement of an individual family festival, the festive tree was now the ornament of collective celebration.

At some real-life parties, children would be given 'practical toys', such as miniature telephones, that were considered to offer training for their future careers. But the main point of the festivals was still to allow the children to enjoy themselves. Even at 'model' parties run by exemplary nursery teachers, trees were usually decorated with sweet-boxes, toy cottages, holly berries and the like, and the children themselves were usually costumed as snowflakes and bunnies, not as Red Army soldiers or Stakhanovite factory workers. Any remaining Bolshevik sensitivity about political symbolism was quickly shed: in December 1935, officials visiting a nursery school had objected to paper chains as 'emblems of slavery', but by 1937 these decorations had become *de rigueur*.[37]

Along with the arrangement of these new facilities and festivals, insistence that the Soviet Union was the *best* place in the world for children became ever more shrill. 'In not a single country of the world is there such enormous concern for children, a concern felt by the broadest strata of the labouring people,' claimed a leading article in *Soviet Justice*, published in mid-1935.[38] The apogee of this myth was reached in Aleksandrov's enormously popular film *Circus*, whose heroine, played by the glamorous Lyubov' Orlova, was an American star driven to the Soviet Union because her parentage of a mixed-race son had made her the target of racist calumny. The culminating scene showed the small child passed from hand to hand among spectators who had just watched Orlova's daredevil act as a human cannonball, singing as they did so the film's number one hit song, 'Broad Is My Motherland'.[39]

As the case of *Circus* indicates, *skazka* was an ambiguous term: it could also be applied to the 'fairy-tale reality' that supposedly characterised Soviet existence. And *skazka* was not only, or even mainly, a genre marked out by obviously fantastical events, even when the intended audience was children. *The Little Golden Key* was in fact rather unusual in its unabashed evocation of a fantasy otherworld. In most respects, children's literature was a version of Socialist Realism writ small. It, too, was supposed to deal (in a manner suited to the child's mentality) with the themes of socialist production, revolutionary history, and scientific progress. Among the possible *skazka* subjects mentioned by Marshak were the real-life stories of gooseherds who ended up as test pilots.[40]

While Soviet children's magazines might contain more material on hobbies than previously, and less about activism, they bulged with educational matter – popularising articles on science, pieces on geography, articles imparting general knowledge about the Soviet Union.[41] And the hobby activities that were encouraged were often work-related: a good illustration was the Children's Railway network, where children spent their free days running proper miniature stations and lines with locomotives and carriages, and taking paying passengers out for rides.[42]

Good Children, Bad Children

Stalinist children were not only rewarded; they were also punished. The shift towards stricter governance in schools was matched by the instigation of a harder line on juvenile crime. A law passed on 7 April 1935 reduced the age of full criminal responsibility in cases of 'theft, causing violence, bodily injury, mutilation and murder' to 12; in November 1935, reduced sentences for children were forbidden. To be sure, professional lawyers (whom the changes, almost certainly made on Stalin's personal initiative, had taken by surprise) did all they could to mitigate the severity with which children were treated.[43] However, this was a question of legal professionals attempting to frustrate the intentions behind top-level policy, not of a rethink at the top.

The assertion of the authority of teachers and police officials in no sense represented a realisation of the utopian visions of collective upbringing that had been popular in some quarters during the 1920s. The 'nationalisation' of childhood at this level was accompanied by the reinforcement of parental authority at another. Propaganda now hymned the achievements of exemplary parents (concentrating upon skilled workers as a model for less 'cultured' members of the working class), and castigated the signal failures of those who did not realise that 'if a person brings up his children properly, he is a good Communist'.[44] Parents were supposed to be the primary line of governance within the quasi-autonomous 'social cell' of the family. As an article in *Soviet Justice* put it in 1937, family life was 'a profoundly intimate sphere'.[45]

In line with the shift in attitudes towards parents, official versions of Pavlik Morozov's life underwent change. Now, there was stress on the heart-searching that Pavlik's action had cost him. Rather than making his confession with relish in public, Pavlik tormentedly blurted it out in private, requiring assurance from another adult – the local teacher in some versions, the local representative of the secret police in others – that his action against his father was legitimate.[46] Scenes of this kind not only stressed that inter-generational rebellion was permissible only in exceptional circumstances, but also engaged a compensation mechanism whereby the patriarchal authority of the representatives of the state replaced the patriarchal authority of the child's real father and of his blood relations more generally. In the words of a story published by *Our Achievements* magazine in 1936: 'The family should not be comprised merely of blood ties. We will pay for such blood ties in blood.'[47] In other words, the family was to be encouraged where it was a force for social harmony, but controlled where it appeared to threaten the collective ideal.

As the Pavlik Morozov story revealed – even in this reworked version – the new emphasis on parental authority did not grant *carte blanche* for parental will. The rights of parents were endorsed only in so far as these suited the central purpose of legislative change, to make the family the instrument of social control. Parents were held to blame if children went to the bad (since the caring Soviet state, which had provided every resource for infant welfare, was clearly not culpable in this respect). The mid-1930s saw a hardening of attitudes to 'neglectful' mothers. There were calls in the legal press for longer sentences to be handed out to women convicted of infanticide and of child abandonment.[48] The most famous family reform of the 1930s, the 28 June 1936 decree 'On the Protection of Motherhood and Infancy', not only presented a package of welfare measures (improved arrangements for maternity support, promises of huge expansion in child-care facilities), but also outlawed abortion, which was now seen as a dereliction of maternal duty. In 1937, divorce arrangements were tightened up, in the interest of 'combating frivolous attitudes to the family and to family responsibilities': now, it was essential for both partners to turn up at the registry office for the dissolution of marriage to take place.[49]

Errant fathers were pursued with fervour. Legal literature repeatedly exhorted that they be called to order in child abandonment cases, and that they be made to pay for their misdemeanours. A man 'unmasked' by a female plaintiff as the absconding father of her children (whether a deserting husband or a one-time lover) was, by 1937, almost certain to have an alimony order (at a cost of up to one third of his salary) made against him.[50] In the words of one commentator on the alimony issue, this was a 'fight for children's welfare', but the punitive intonation of most articles on the subject indicated that it was also an attempt to bring feckless parents to book.[51] The underlying construct of the family was a traditional, 'Victorian' one: fathers were supposed to be the providers, and mothers the carers. It was extremely rare for a child to be placed with the male parent after divorce. Indeed, even in a case where there was cogent evidence that a mother had regularly sent one of her two children out to buy vodka (as well as entertaining male company at home), the courts at first decided to award custody of her younger son to her (the elder one was placed with his father), though this decision was later overturned by the Supreme Court on the basis that the father 'had a much better understanding of how to rear the growing generation'.[52]

If families were seen as ideal mini-collectives, replicating proper social order on a small scale, the fundamental purpose of 'rational upbringing' was to integrate the child into a broader collective, that of Soviet society at large. In 1940, an open letter addressed by the 'parents' assembly' of the Soviet textile industry to 'all manual and white-collar workers' defined 'Communist moral education' in the following terms:

> Raising children in the Communist spirit means developing in them a sense of sincerity and truthfulness, self-abnegation and heroism, love of work and fidelity to their socialist motherland, to the Communist Party and to our great wise leader Comrade Stalin.[53]

Childhood, that is, was to be preparation for a life of disinterested labour and submissive existence as a co-operative subject of Soviet power. Parents were supposed to treat their own children much in the manner of a kindly supervisor of a children's home (as Makarenko himself was), or an enlightened schoolteacher.

'Thank You, Dear Comrade Stalin, for a Happy Childhood!'

Another factor harmonising the two apparently contradictory elements in the Soviet cult of childhood – authoritarianism and the sanctity of childhood happiness – was the theme of child protection, now insistently heard in Soviet propaganda. 'The rights of children' were no longer understood to mean autonomy, even in the most limited sense. It is indicative that the Soviet Constitution of 1936 carried no statement at all about children's rights (even if the promise of a right to education was clearly relevant to this sector of society above all). And later editions of the *Great Soviet Encyclopaedia* dropped the article on 'Children's Rights' in the first edition: instead, the general article on 'Children' carried a statement to the following effect:

> In the Soviet state children are surrounded by the care of the entire nation. The socialist society, the party of Lenin and Stalin are concerned that the younger generation should grow up healthy and physically strong, cheerful and full of joy in life, educated and cultured, in order that it is able to continue with the project that has been successfully begun by the older generation of builders of Communism.[54]

From 'revolutionary soldiers' and the vanguard of the Revolution, children had become the quintessential beneficiaries, and petitioners, of the Soviet state, which could, like a stern parent, choose to withhold rewards and mete out punishment if it so chose. In the first two weeks of April 1935, *Pravda* ran a succession of items that perfectly embodied these polarities. To one side lay articles about the children's cinema, the production of special lines of animal-shaped chocolates, and sweets in boxes ornamented with pictures of shock workers, along with photographs of well-scrubbed children making paper planes at their model-building club. To the other lay a lead article announcing the stark new measures on juvenile crime, which came in response, the article argued, to children's erroneous sense of 'their right to dissipation, caprice, and to the impunity of every sort of action'.[55]

The ultimate embodiment and facilitator of both discipline and happiness was of course Joseph Stalin. There was a special branch of the 'cult of personality' directed at children, which followed much the same path chronologically as the branches of the cult directed as adults. Occasional portraits of the leader began to appear in the children's press in the early 1930s,[56] but it was not until the end of 1933 or beginning of 1934 that the full impact of Stalin-worship began to be felt. In February 1934, however, schoolteachers being advised on coverage of the forthcoming plenary session of the Central Committee were instructed: 'Pupils must be left with a strong and wonderful feeling about those grandiose deeds which have been carried out under the supervision of the Communist Party over the time surveyed, and of the great changes that stand before the Land of the Soviets. Against the background of the struggle for socialism must be shown the guiding role of the Leninist party and of the great leader of the international proletariat, Comrade Stalin.'[57]

In 1935–36, *Pravda* began to carry material belonging to a genre that was to become one of the most significant in 'cult of personality' propaganda over the next seventeen years: the portrait of the ruler with devoted child acolyte. In July 1935, the newspaper printed a story, 'I gave a bouquet to Stalin!' in which pioneer Nina Zdrogova excitedly recounted how she had been thanked for her tribute with a kiss and 'We're going to be friends, you and I', as well as chocolates and a bag that turned out to contain cherries ('I checked later'); in August, a picture

27   Stalin with Gelya Markizova.

of the leader with his own daughter Svetlana appeared in the paper.[58] On 29 June 1936, 'Happy Childhood Day', a photograph of Stalin embracing a small girl with the resonant name of Engel'sina Markizova (known as Gelya for short), who had presented him with a bouquet when a delegation from the Burat-Mongolian Autonomous Republic visited the Kremlin, was published on the front page of *Pravda*.[59] The photograph was later, in its poster version, to become one of the most famous images of the Stalin era, with copies pinned up in schools, pioneer camps, clubs, and other children's institutions.[60]

This genre was not invented by or for Stalin. Occasional representations of Lenin with children had begun appearing after the leader's death in 1924 (such as a group portrait by the modernist painter Pavel Kuznetsov). However, the status of such images was relatively marginal (Kuznetsov's painting received much adverse criticism, as a result of which he destroyed the canvas),[61] and it was not until the 1960s that 'Lenin and children' images became a mainstream genre. Unlike the cult of Lenin, too, the Stalin cult presented the leader as the patron and guide of children, rather than a model for their emulation. There was a genre of Stalin biographies for children, but far more prominent were images in which he was shown embracing them and patting them on the head, or protecting them from harm. Stalin's help was available when that of ordinary (one might say, mortal) parents failed, as in the case of the boy narrator of the Yiddish writer Lev Kvitko's poem 'Cradle-Song', a poem sung by the boy to his mother. The boy tells how, when walking in the woods, he has been attacked by various wild creatures, most of which he was able to chase away himself. But then, along comes a more threatening foe, a pack of wolves:

> Once more I leaned against the green pine.
> And suddenly grey wolves crept up to me:
> They opened their great teeth –
> Now they'd tear me to pieces!
> For sheer terror I couldn't stir ...!
> Mum, mum, mummy, my sweetheart, come here!
> But Stalin found out that I was in the wood,
> And Stalin spied, heard I was in deadly danger,
> So he sent a tank out for me,
> And I rolled off down the forest path.[62]

Stalin was by no means the only Soviet leader to make his appearance in children's literature, propaganda images, and ceremonials. Other members of his inner circle, notably Molotov and Voroshilov, also figured routinely. (It was Molotov who was considered the patron of Artek, the most famous Pioneer camp, and fulsomely thanked for allowing an extension of the camp's territory in the late 1930s. It was Voroshilov to whom propaganda Soviet boys vowed their resolution to grow up fast and fight for the motherland.) However, just as in real-life politics, the leader's prominence was always underlined. An anthology *Happy Childhood* published in 1939 (the year of Stalin's sixtieth birthday celebrations) showed an indicative sense of proportion: of thirty-one pieces, seven contained tributes to Stalin, while Molotov and Voroshilov clocked just one paean each.[63]

Children were left in no doubt that their special relationship with Stalin was a result of the ruler's munificence, and not something to which they were automatically entitled. Hence the ubiquitous phrase, 'Thank You Dear Comrade Stalin for a Happy Childhood!' emblazoned over the doorways of nurseries and schools, pinned up on walls, printed on book and magazine covers, and chanted by children at festivals.[64]

In the 1920s, children's letters to leaders had emphasised that children were the coming generation, who styled themselves upon adults in order to perfect themselves in the performance of their ideological duties. Letters of the Stalin era, on the other hand, portrayed children as the protégés of their wise leader, who was seen offering help and advice not only in the context of politics, but in the context of most other areas of human existence, and as taking a direct personal interest in their activities. Busya Goldstein, for instance, remembered that the leader had told him he was better than the violinist who had played before, and had explained in detail why. Later, the family had received a large flat, with a separate music and work room for Busya: this enormous privilege, too, was interpreted in a directly personal way, since Busya had previously been worrying how he might receive Stalin in suitable style if the leader chose to pay his family a visit.[65]

In the 1920s children had been encouraged to treat important political leaders as human beings, albeit powerful ones: they might address them on a footing approaching equality (using the second person singular, for example), and recall humorous details of the encounter. In 1925, one small boy remembered Lenin as small and sturdy, rather than the gigantic figure that he had expected, and humorously recorded the leader's eagerness to leave the room and get on with something more important once he had welcomed the group of children.[66] It is impossible to imagine a memoirist in the late 1930s or the 1940s risking such *lèse-majesté*: by then, children who met the leaders were expected to regard them as super-human entities. Rather than bonhomously addressing the leader in the informal second person, children now expressed a sense of honour that *he* should have used the formal mode of address to them.[67] The leader was never referred to in the USSR itself by the facetious title 'Uncle Joe' (which would translate perfectly easily as Dyadya Osya),[68] but almost always as 'Comrade Stalin' ('Comrade' was always given in full, rather than abbreviated to 'Com.', as was standard for lesser mortals). Less frequently, his name and patronymic ('Iosif Vissarionovich'), or the honorific appellation 'father' (*otets*) might be used; unlike Lenin, he was never known affectionately by his patronymic alone. The requirement that all, even the youngest citizens, address Stalin formally placed a respectful distance between children and the Party leader.

Like any other members of Soviet society, too, children were subject to regulation by official censorship. No representation of the leader that might appear disrespectful was to be allowed in public. Thus, children's artwork was carefully managed so that the assurance of due dignity could be guaranteed. The issue of *Young Artist* published for Stalin's sixtieth birthday in 1939 included no artwork by juvenile enthusiasts celebrating the leader, but only reproductions of work by professional artists; participants in celebratory concerts were carefully selected not only in Moscow and Leningrad, but also in the provincial capitals.[69]

Keeping a Watchful Eye

Of course, children were not expected simply to bask in the reflected glory of Stalin. Initiative was still expected from them in some ways. They were constantly reminded that the security in which they lived was under threat, that the price of their 'happiness' was ceaseless 'vigilance' towards the enemies of the state. Even by the early 1930s, poison gas training – in case of future invasion – had become a staple part of children's indoctrination.[70] Articles in the Soviet press in 1935 and 1936 praised the achievements of Pioneers who had spied suspicious figures lurking in border areas, or brought law-breakers to the attention of the Soviet police.[71] The theme of 'the enemy without' (who was especially dangerous when he was also 'the enemy within') began to resound with particular urgency during the years of the Great Purges. In Agniya Barto's long poem *At the Border Post* (1937), a boy was rewarded with the gift of an Alsatian puppy for alerting guards to a marauder.[72] And Sergei Mikhalkov's 'The Enemy' (also known as 'The Spy') depicted a still more dangerous enemy: one who had ingratiated himself into the very bosom of a Soviet family:

28 Boy with two border guards and their Alsatian dog, Agniya Barto, *At the Border Post* (1937).

He slept next to us at night,
And, like a thief, concealed
That he was opening our drawers
And then closing them again.

And suddenly that same year
We had floods in our mines,
And the chemical factory burned down,
And the electricity system burned out.[73]

In situations such as this, where an 'evil serpent/Crawled into the bosom of an honourable family', to quote two more lines in the poem, children could help by being alert and discreet. Like adults, children took part in military parades and sang bellicose songs ('Don't touch us and we won't touch you/But if you do/We'll fight for all we're worth ...').[74] It is a notable fact that much more effort was put into advising children of the dangers posed by suspicious foreigners than into teaching them about road safety, despite the fact that traffic accidents and mishaps at home certainly constituted a larger threat to life and limb, even in the decades before the Second World War.

But at the same time as being exhorted to do their patriotic duty, children were also constantly reminded that it was adults – parents, police, politicians, and Soviet border guards – on whom security finally depended. Brave children might bring spies to the attention of professionals, but they did not tackle enemies themselves. Unlike the heroes of Civil War narratives, children of the late 1930s had a strictly ancillary function even where they did partake in activities with a political coloration. In Barto's *At the Border Post*, the boy vigilante was not even allowed to accompany the head border guard when the latter rode off to shoot down the perfidious invader of Soviet territory. Military preparedness was encouraged in children – keep-fit exercises, even learning to shoot – but unauthorised employment of these skills was definitely not approved.[75] Children were supposed to *play* at being secret service agents, and to help the valiant defenders of the motherland by training guard dogs for border detachments; they were not supposed to go on investigative expeditions or patrol with Alsatians themselves.[76] Pint-sized 'Voroshilov marksmen' might play a central part in children's carnivals, but they were always armed with cardboard rifles.[77]

Models for Adults

The elevation of the child revolutionary and the feisty young proletarian had been in tune with the militaristic mood of the Soviet regime in the 1920s and early 1930s, and with a particular interpretation of service to the nation which held that all right-thinking adults must contribute to social work and to public discourse. From the mid-1930s, the figure of the good and docile child rewarded for hard work and for obedience by all the gifts at the disposal of the paternalist state reflected a very different ideal of Soviet citizenship. Adults were also now expected to adopt a filial role in relation to the Party leadership and to brim over with gratitude to those in power, most particularly, of course, Stalin himself. In the same way children thanked Stalin for a happy childhood, choruses of adults, as ventriloquised by Soviet propaganda, thanked him for the benefits they allegedly enjoyed: modern cities, well-run civic institutions, and abundant supplies of food and consumer goods.[78] Adults were now supposed to be docile spectators of 'festivals' rather than assertive participants in 'meetings'.[79]

Children were still the ultimate model citizens of the Soviet state, more perfectly grateful than any adult could be, and the shift in preferred representations of them was an indication of how expectations of citizenship itself had changed. They basked at the warm heart of the Soviet state, enjoying its *zabota i vnimanie*, 'care and attention'. Here, the state's capacity for care and the state's capacity for surveillance were united. Enjoying the first meant also submitting to the latter. In everyday speech, the word *opeka* can suggest charitable concern, combined with a desire to regulate the behaviour of its recipient for his or her own good. But in the Stalin era this word acquired a derogatory resonance, as in the phrase, *melkaya opeka*, busybodying. In contrast to this manifestation of unacceptable concern, *zabota i vnimanie* came to mean benevolent surveillance, 'looking out for' others. Yet at the same time, the association of the phrase primarily with benevolence to children foreshadowed the loss of autonomy that was implied in accepting such charity. In Stalinist society, control was impossible without care; but, equally, care was impossible without control.[80]

The humane treatment of children, like the liberation of women and the support of the proletariat for the regime, was seen as proof of the Soviet Union's status as a progressive society. Of the three, it was the humane treatment of children that did most to popularise the Soviet order among intellectuals. Even those who had serious reservations about Soviet policy in other ways – for example, Fedor Sologub – used the position of children as a proof to themselves that the system was not all bad.[81] Children's welfare was often cited in letters and protests composed by working-class or peasant Russians. An anonymous letter to *Izvestiya*, sent from the North Caucasus Territory in 1932, asserted that the children of collective farmers were being fed adulterated bread. 'Let there be at least some good white bread for babes in arms,' the writer pleaded.[82] Thus, the regime's standing with the two social groups its own ideology saw as pivotal to its support rested, at least in part, upon the appropriate treatment of children. Inevitably (and particularly once children's welfare had become directly associated with Stalin's personal prestige), the myth of 'happy childhood' became still more of a fixture in official propaganda than the myth of the absolute equality of men and women or the myth of the Soviet Union as 'worker paradise'. From the mid-1930s, the mainstream Soviet press generally reported stories about the ill-treatment of children only if they involved cases from benighted Western countries, such as America, Britain, or the Third Reich,[83] or if they portrayed the dreadful lives led by children in Russia before 1917. The result was that many Soviet citizens absorbed the insistent propaganda message and genuinely believed that there was nowhere in the world where children lived so well as they did in the Soviet Union. This was a culture where enormous efforts were expended on protecting 'good' children from painful experiences, sometimes at appallingly high cost to adults, a number of whom, like the father in Roberto Benigni's sentimental celluloid portrayal of the Holocaust, *Life is Beautiful* (1999), risked life and sanity in order to create a 'normal' world for their dependants.

The Paradoxes of Perfection

Yet official policy did not always work in exactly the manner that had been anticipated. A specific case in point was the festive tree. Official versions of this in public buildings, as noted earlier, were intended as a demonstration of official largesse to children, but were in practice accessible to a fairly narrow layer of the privileged.[84] However, once it became possible to celebrate New Year without a legal penalty, the festival was 'reprivatised', and Soviet families began to hold their own, individual, New Year parties. Of course, a tree as such was beyond the means of most, but a single fir bough might be purchased and decorated; no professional Grandfather Frost would be present, but a member of the family or a friend was likely to dress up as the New Year master of ceremonies and arrive with a number of small gifts. Private festivals of this kind were pretty well free of political content, and even the finger-wagging, moralistic traits of Grandfather Frost were turned into a joke, rather than being the occasion for teaching children a lesson.[85] Official New Year tree ceremonies were in part a way of tutoring the offspring of the Soviet elite in new roles (hence the use of telephones as gifts: the Soviet official's progress up the status ladder was marked by the acquisition of increasing numbers of telephones, culminating in object of desire number one, the scarlet 'government telephone' on the desk of the bureaucratic inner circle).[86] Family ones, on the other hand, reinforced different values: intimacy, affection, and even, to a certain extent, self-indulgence. To be sure, the fact that New Year was an officially approved occasion (not a clandestine one, like Easter), a day celebrated by all upright Soviet families, made it a force for social bonding. But what most children remembered later was New Year's Day in *their* family: confecting home-made decorations, eating special food, and dressing up in their best to await the visit from Grandfather Frost.[87]

The effect of official policy was thus sometimes to foster a kind of protective individualism that would certainly not have been considered desirable. There was a second and allied paradox. As institutionalised education insisted, with ever-growing vehemence, upon the idea of the child as future adult and subject of the state, so an alternative tradition, given leeway by the state's emphasis on the sanctity of the 'children's world' and supported by domestic practices, celebrated a sentimental idea of childhood as a space – perhaps the only space in Soviet culture – that lay beyond politics. On the one hand, this meant that it was no longer possible to argue from issues of children's welfare to issues of welfare in a broader sense: no Russian jurist of the 1930s would have dared to argue, as jurists in the 1910s openly did, that the fair and considerate treatment of child defendants in the juvenile court made it 'the harbinger of just such a court for adults'.[88] And children were no longer seen as a prime audience for myths in which tyranny was successfully confronted: it is instructive to contrast Chukovsky's *Crocodile* with Nikolai Zabolotsky's 1933 tale 'How the Mice Made War on the Cat', in which the mice fail to win their battle against a voracious feline who finds them more delicious to eat than even chocolate.[89]

But, at the same time, the depoliticisation of childhood safeguarded children from the full tyranny that the Soviet state was capable of unleashing upon its subjects. Despite the emphasis on 'discipline' in propaganda, subversive behaviour by children was not regarded as harshly as it might have been had the perpetrators been adults. Even during the Great Terror, activities that might well have caused adults to be tried under article 58 of the Criminal Code were treated with relative leniency. In 1936, 12-year-old Aleksei Dudkin, the son of a Party official in Leningrad, organised a game that he called 'counter-revolutionary Trotskyite-Zinovievite band'. 'This was a kind of cops and robbers game in which Dudkin himself played the part of Zinoviev, while other children took the roles of Trotsky, Kirov, Kamenev, Nikolaev (Kirov's killer) and an NKVD official. The first part of the game re-enacted the murder of Kirov. The scenario for the second [...] was to have been the murder of Stalin by the same terrorist gang of counterrevolutionary terrorists.' Given the extreme suspicion of all deviance that characterised Soviet society at the time, it is not surprising that the authorities should have taken this seriously and launched an investigation. What is more unexpected is that Dudkin himself seems to have escaped official punishment, though his father was reprimanded for his failures in proper parenting.[90]

Again and again, it was adults responsible for children – educators, supervisors of children's homes, children's writers and editors in publishing houses – who were blamed for perceived deficiencies in provision and for ideological error, rather than punishment being meted out directly to the children themselves. Even in a period when adult 'enemies of the people' were subject to extremely brutal (and widely publicised) repressive measures, corporal punishment remained taboo, both in families and in state-run institutions. In 1937, no less, Anton Makarenko attacked the beating of children as inhumane in his *Book for Parents*. Beating was 'a tragedy of pain and humiliation, or a tragedy of learned indifference and cruel endurance on the part of the child': it was also counter-productive, in that it lowered the authority of the parent and encouraged, rather than combating, child caprice.[91] Just a year earlier, a publication commemorating the tenth anniversary of the death of the founder of the Soviet secret police, Feliks Dzerzhinsky, had quoted at length from 'Iron Felix's' correspondence to his sister, in which he vehemently exhorted her to avoid harsh punishment: 'Use of the rod and severe treatment will teach them hypocrisy and falsehood.'[92] Traces of the central tenet of Soviet paedology of the 1920s – that any child was reformable if sympathetic treatment was given – remained visible in the changed ideological world of late 1930s Stalinism.

Licence was extended in particular to younger children, above all those below school age. Though the 1936 attack on 'paedological perversions' was ostensibly as relevant to nursery school practices as it was to school-teaching more generally, and though the authors of manuals felt it incumbent upon them to denounce 'bourgeois' theorists such as Froebel and Montessori, nursery education retained a Froebelian tone long after academic values and rigid discipline had been restored in schools. It is notable that Krupskaya continued to voice (albeit in a diluted form) the ideals of *svobodnoe vospitanie* (free education) in statements about *detskie sady* (nursery schools) at a time when the voicing of such ideals with regard to ordinary schools would have been most unwelcome.[93] And in 1941, five years after 'labour education' had vanished from the mainstream school programme, a nursery school teacher was still able to advocate it passionately to her colleagues at a professional conference.[94] Equally notable is nursery schools' role as a last refuge of mixed-gender education in cities after 1943, when single-sex education was restored to schools catering for children of seven and above in major urban centres.

Even primary schools were supposed to be less rigid and regimented than those for children of the top four classes. In 1932, for instance, when discipline and academic achievement had become official requirements of secondary schools, teachers in primary schools were instructed that they should teach basic mathematics with tact and consideration for their audience: 'Not a single rule, not a single proposition should be proclaimed dogmatically.' The skills to be taught were observation, questioning, measuring, weighing, deduction, and generalisation.[95]

Children's books for the pre-school age group and for the age group known as 'younger schoolchildren' (8–11-year-olds) were also a good deal less politically conscious than those aimed at older ones. Arkady Gaidar's timeless, lively, good-humoured story 'Chuk and Gek' (1939) was quite different in tone to his more moralistic tales for older children, *Timur and his Team* and *Military Secret*. It began with a mock-epic description of a fight between the two boys over their treasure box, and continued by depicting their tremendous journey with their mother to visit their geologist father in Siberia. Ideology impinged on the story only indirectly (through the theme of civilising the northern wastes, and through patriotic tributes to 'that far-off great city, the finest in the world', with 'red stars glittering day and night on its towers: Moscow, of course').[96] Likewise, Sergei Mikhalkov's work for children included not only solemn exhortations to vigilance and backbone, but also jollier pieces. 'Uncle Styopa' (1936), for example, had a hero who was not only a model of *kul'turnost'* (always remembering to wash and clean his teeth), but who was also a figure from Soviet fairy tale: an amiable giant delighted to lift children up so they could get a better view of military parades.

29 V. Kanevsky, illustration to Sergei Mikhalkov's *Uncle Styopa* (1936). The gentle giant lies down to sleep with his foot on a stool.

Спать ложился дядя Степа —
ноги клал на табурет.

There was particular tolerance on the part of Soviet adults of the fact that younger children (especially boys) might find absorbing decorum tiresome and frustrating. No less a personage than Gorky was the author of a poem comically sympathising with children's determination to stamp their own egos on social circumstances:

> Oh you poor children,
> What a frightful time you do have;
> Fathers and mothers everywhere,
> So disobedient and stubborn ...[97]

For the first decade or so of their lives, then, children were generally not subject to the strict treatment that older children had to expect, and there were occasions of tolerance even for indiscipline on the part of the latter, provided this could be seen as a manifestation of harmless mischief, rather than of social subversion. And in this country where the censorship bodies rigidly controlled all other forms of printed expression, books for small children were not required to undergo preliminary censorship at all.[98] As they grew older, children had to become more self-disciplined and more responsible, but it was not until 14 or 15, the age for entering the Komsomol, when anything approaching an 'adult' degree of self-awareness and self-control began to be expected. In the meantime, even children who were occasionally mischievous or silly could enjoy the largesse of the Soviet state with impunity.

Victims and Warriors

The myth that all Soviet children lived in peace and prosperity was perfected only five years before the invasion of the Soviet Union by Germany in 1941 plunged this myth, like the underlying myth of 'happy existence', into near-fatal crisis. The invasion caught the Soviet Union in a state of disastrous military unpreparedness, and the regime's legitimacy was severely threatened by the invaders' success in gaining territory, and by the defeat and disarray of the Red Army. At the same time, the Soviet propaganda machine, at least, worked effectively from the start. Unlike their new allies in Britain, and later America, the Soviet government did not have to set up special institutions to disseminate consciousness-raising material to the masses, or make efforts to recruit well-known artists and writers to work in these new institutions. And many of the stereotypes of propaganda could easily be reworked to serve the new situation. Now that the diversion of resources to military production had brought the manufacture of consumer goods almost to a standstill, images of serenity and plenty were redundant; but the established figure of the perfectly camouflaged foreign agent ready to pounce on any unwary Soviet citizen and exploit indiscretions had an obvious and immediate relevance – indeed, it had come to seem, in retrospect, nothing less than prescient.

The established importance of the child as symbol for the Soviet nation inevitably made children significant actors in wartime propaganda as well,

30　Children looking at a wartime wall newspaper. Press photograph, Leningrad, 1943. The child activist ideal transformed into real life.

though in rather contradictory ways. On the one hand, the war years saw a revival of the stereotype of the child activist, in abeyance since the early 1930s. For example, Evgeny Katsman's painting *From the Sovinformbyuro* (1944) shows two children posting flyers on a wall in a bombarded city. Both are girls, but thoroughly boyish in appearance. The girl actually fastening up the flyer is dressed in an outfit of trunks, braces, and shorts that calls to mind 'rational dress'; her companion, a bobbed blonde, eyes the viewer fiercely, without a trace of collusion or apology. These children are tough, resilient, and resourceful (they have pressed chunks of fallen masonry into service in order to reach up to the right height for posting the flyer effectively). Its lurid colouring and literalist rendition apart, the picture represents a direct reversion to 1920s iconography.[99] Soviet propaganda also celebrated young people who had taken a more active role in the war effort. The outstanding example of this was 'Partisan Tanya', hanged by the Germans in 1942. 'Tanya' – later identified as the Muscovite Komsomol girl Zoya Kosmodem'yanskaya, then aged 17 – had volunteered for active service with a Partisan unit, where she had behaved with exemplary fortitude and resolution. Profiles dwelt on 'Tanya's' refusal to surrender her patriotic duty and personal dignity in the face of torture (including the amputation of her breasts) and impending execution. Later, after the war, she was to be the subject of a hagiography jointly authored by her mother and the teacher and pedagogical writer Frida Vigdorova. Right up to the collapse of

Soviet power, and indeed afterwards, her cult was honoured by the building of monuments, by displays in schools, and by regular anniversary commemorations. But 'Tanya'/Zoya was not the only example of pre-adult patriotism on show during the war itself. The group of young partisans in Poltava later to be celebrated in Fadeev's novel *The Young Guard* also showed teenagers risking – and in some cases losing – their lives in defence of the motherland. Children had a leading role in the celebration of victory as well: at the gathering on Red Square held to mark 9 May 1945, a child declaimed a stirring patriotic poem to the assembled crowds.[100] Retrospective images also paid tribute to children's resourcefulness and courage: for example, Ivan Aristov's *The Saving of the Banner* (1950) portrayed a small boy defiantly clutching a Komsomol or Pioneer standard that he had removed to the relative safety of his family's room, while German soldiers paraded outside.[101]

Yet children were not always seen as empowered. The Soviet authorities, like all twentieth-century nations under dire threat, recognised and exploited the propaganda value of victimised children for the patriotic cause. The most assiduously promoted 'military' heroes, such as Zoya Kosmodem'yanskaya, were those who had been martyred by the Germans, rather than those who had successfully carried out feats of 'unchildish' bravery. Pavel Antokol'sky's poem 'The Ballad of the Unknown Boy' (1942) hedged its bets, since the fate of the boy who avenged the deaths of his mother and sister by blowing up an SS officer's Mercedes with his car remained indeterminate, just as his age did:

31   Digging for victory. Press photograph, Leningrad, 1943.

Is he fifteen, or is he ten, or is he even younger? [...]
Was he blown up? I do not know. The bloody trace is silent.[102]

The harshness of the image of the boy with the grenade was softened by the notion that he might have been killed in the act of punishing his tormentors.[103]

Another prevalent motif was the loss of childhood through suffering. In Agniya Barto's poem 'The Little Girl', a child whose mother had been snatched from her by the Germans was left not just 'severe' but 'weary'.[104] And children might be seen as victims first and foremost, as in Aleksei Pakhomov's drawings of the Leningrad Blockade, or as in news photographs of the time.[105] Agniya Barto's poem 'In Spring' evoked child suffering in the occupied zone, juxtaposing the stereotypical Socialist Realist spring – blossom, opening buds, and a political parade – to the spring of wartime: rubble in the streets, scorched trees, and in the park a dead child. (The gallows humour lent by the jingling rhymes was certainly not intentional):

A slaughtered little girlie
In the park had made her bed:
Her hair all gold and curly,
And a bullet through her head.[106]

Revenge was certainly anticipated in return for these atrocities, but it was adults who were supposed to take it. Aleksandr Surkov's poem 'He Killed the Children and Burned the House' (1942) depicted a Fascist invader who was tossed on to a bonfire for these crimes by six women.[107]

Whether they were spies, couriers, bill-posters, or under-age partisans, there was a strong sense that children could and should participate in the war effort in some way. In a modulation of the traditional emphasis on 'vigilance', children were made aware that they could help the Soviet cause by keeping a sharp eye out for troop movements and by doing their best to unmask suspicious strangers. In this vein, Pavel Antokol'sky's poem 'Katya Kozlova' depicted a resourceful young girl who managed not only to evade the unwelcome interest of 'a German boss, a Gestapo chief, or something', but also, with the partisans' help, to poison her sexual harasser with cyanide dripped into a glass of wine.[108]

Leisure reading was of course not the only way in which children were infused with patriotic spirit. As in any country at time of war, school education also stressed martial themes. Boys were supposed to have a compulsory grounding in military education, including subjects such as map-reading and orienteering, and girls underwent complementary studies in subjects such as first aid.[109] All of this was part of an ever-increasing emphasis on gender difference, which was expressed in the reimposition of single-sex education, made compulsory for city secondary schools in 1943. The girls' schools were now not only separate from the boys' institutions in a physical sense, but also had alternative curricula, including subjects not taught at all in the boys' schools (pedagogy, domestic science, needlework, and child care). In some schools, girls got a daily lesson on good manners as well as all the other training in 'womanly' skills.[110] Pioneer groups, too, started to be divided along gender lines, and the specifications of the hobby circles reflected a strong emphasis on gender-appropriate activities, such as embroidery.[111]

Children of the Motherland

With victory came a fundamental change in representation of the war. Zinovy Tolkachev's series of drawings, 'The Children of Auschwitz' (1945), highly praised by Soviet critics when first made, received a critical pasting when shown at the Ukrainian Art Exhibition in 1947.[112] Literature for children and young people was every bit as reticent about the real costs of military action. Post-war classics with which every child reader was supposed to be familiar included Boris Polevoi's *Tale of a Real Person* (1947), the story of a brave Soviet airman who refused to be invalided out when he lost both legs, and who by dint of sheer effort of will turned himself into an ace pilot again, and Pavel Zhurba's life of Aleksandr Matrosov, who had used his own body to block a gun embrasure, and fought till the last drop of his blood was spent. But even these tales seemed reasonably gritty when compared with Aleksandr Fadeev's novel *The Young Guard* (1945, revised 1951), the technicolour portrait of a group of resolute Komsomol partisans and undercover Soviet agents in the Ukrainian provinces, going defiant to their deaths at the hands of the Nazis. Most particularly in its second redaction (Fadeev rewrote the book in response to accusations that he had underplayed the significance of the contribution made by the local Party administration to resistance), *The Young Guard* was a wartime comic strip of noble, handsome, resourceful Soviets versus perfidious, brutal Fritzes: alongside it, propaganda representations of the Civil War (such as Sholokhov's *Tales of the Don* or Serafimovich's *The Iron Flood*) seemed models of sophistication.[113]

The significant reversals of the first months after the German invasion were now forgotten; instead, an airbrushed version of the war had the Red Army ruthlessly repelling the invader, and then thrusting deep into Western Europe. In Sergei Mikhalkov's 'The Map', a 'warrior' (*sic*) saves a map hanging on a classroom wall from the Fascist invader, and then returns it to the same town after the war. It is brought into the classroom and the children rehearse, from a safe distance, the road to Berlin:

> It was torn by a shrapnel piece
> From Oryol to the Dnepr banks,
> And a dark spot lay next to Oryol.
> Yes! It was a Red Army soldier's blood.
>
> And the pupils found the map a place
> And every day, with understandable impatience,
> They switched round the little red flags,
> For the advance to the West, the invasion.[114]

During most of the war and after it, the heroes whom children were invited to admire were those caught up in the conflict, rather than activists. Volodya Dubinin was given a place in the general tomb of the valorous dead in Kerch'; some of his personal effects were transferred to the town museum, and the street where he had once lived was named after him.[115] But no monument to the boy was put up in Moscow, and it was not until the 1960s that a Pioneer hero was to be granted an honour of this kind; in fact, it was 1964 before Dubinin got a monument of his own even in Kerch'. In terms of the honour accorded them, then, child heroes were placed several steps down from adult ones.

The shift away from child autonomy extended into the creative sphere. The late 1940s saw ever-tightening control over branches of the arts directed at children: statements invariably harped on the centrality of patriotic themes, and attacked texts and artefacts seen as likely to undermine the task of inculcating 'Soviet patriotism' from an early age. In an article published prominently in *Pravda* on 29 August 1946, 'Communist education' and 'patriotic education' were said to be manifested particularly strongly in Samuil Marshak's 'Ballad about a Monument', a poem that would 'make even the smallest heart tremble with an enormous sense of love for its own, Soviet fatherland'. On the other hand, Nikolai Chukovsky's *The Silver Island* was condemned as being far too close in style to a Western detective novel. The greatest quantity of bile, though, was reserved for the Leningrad children's magazine *Murzilka*, and in particular Chukovsky's fantastic poem *Bibigon*, about a capricious dwarf, published in the magazine earlier that year. This character was deemed totally unsuitable as a model for children. He was boastful and a liar, and from the wrong class background too: 'even though he's knee-high to a sparrow and is some kind of a freak from another planet, he has to be a count!' 'There is no fantasy in this story, only pretentious drivel,'[116] the critic, Aleksandr Krushinsky, asserted, before turning to another text that he considered equally absurd, Aleksandr Ivich's story 'Balls and Galoshes', which tried to teach children the value of rubber by inviting them to imagine a world without it.[117]

Krushinsky's article brought to an end a period in which the composition of a *skazka*, provided it was aimed at a child audience, gave an author some protection from official censure. The late 1940s saw no equivalents to Tolstoy's *Little Golden Key* being published, let alone to the early work of Chukovsky and Marshak. Even for smaller children, the preferred form of the *skazka* was now a tale on a traditional subject, for instance an animal story such as 'The Fox and the Vixen'.

The foundations of patriotism were supposed to be laid long before a child graduated to Lermontov's 'Borodino' or to the edited highlights of *War and Peace*. A poem for tots written by Agniya Barto, 'Mashen'ka Gets Bigger', evoked the schoolchild's formative experience of contact with the first words in its reading primer:

> In the street is a red house,
> Three-storeyed, built of stone,
> Here Masha, Mummy's little girl,
> Will read through lesson one.

> In her primer she'll read the words:
> Stalin. Motherland. Moscow.[118]

Even very small children were now taught that their security depended upon constant vigilance, and border guards became the heroes of lullabies as well as of adventure stories and newspaper reports:

> Your life is protected
> And your home and motherland,
> By your friends in every region:
> There are more of them each day.

> They bar the way
> To war, world-wide;
> The best friend of little children leads them,
> And he lives in the Kremlin.[119]

Stalin was now not only the chief warrior, but the chief border guard as well.

'Patriotic education' could take on more active forms than this. Teachers in every subject were expected to press home the patriotic theme. A model lesson on the Dnepr Electrification Scheme instructed the teacher 'to emphasise, during the final discussion, how under the supervision of the Communist Party and the leader of the working people, Comrade Stalin, nature is being conquered and transformed to the benefit of the socialist motherland'.[120] Pupils learned by heart a variety of formulations about their country: 'Our country is the Union of Soviet Socialist Republics. Our country is the largest country in the world. There are no capitalists and landowners in the USSR: everyone works for himself and to the general good. The Soviet Union is a fraternal union of nations; in no other country is such a friendship of nations to be found.' They were also told that Soviet people loved their country because there was no exploitation there, and children had a special place: 'In the Soviet land children are surrounded by special love and concern. Soviet children warmly love their motherland, their nation, and great Stalin.'[121]

Patriotic education was *de rigueur* in secondary schools. Military education continued to be a compulsory part of the curriculum long after hostilities with Germany ceased (though from 1946 it was restricted to the higher classes of secondary schools).[122] More importantly, patriotism was – by design – a crucial part of teaching on all other subjects as well. Inspectors from the Academy of Pedagogical Sciences, touring Moscow schools in 1948, observed with concern that 'some teachers do not devote sufficient attention to the issue of educating pupils in the spirit of Soviet patriotism'. In contrast to this dereliction of duty was the shining example of School No. 175 in the Sverdlovsk district, where a history lesson on industrialisation had shown how things should be done. 'The entire lesson was suffused with Bolshevik party spirit and inspired in the pupils love and devotion to the Party and to her leaders, a feeling of pride in our Motherland.

[...] From the point of view of ideological and political education, very valuable was the fact that quotations from Lenin and Stalin were used in order to resolve the key questions of the lesson.'[123]

It was not just in ordinary schools that patriotic motifs were emphasised. In 1944, military and naval cadet schools – decried during the early Soviet period as anti-humanitarian institutions redolent of *ancien régime* values – were refounded as 'Suvorov Colleges' (for the army) and 'Nakhimov Colleges' (for the navy), admitting boys from as young as 13. Thereafter, the 'Suvorov cadet' began to be promoted as the model for all right-thinking Soviet boys, a particularly prestigious embodiment of patriotic values.[124]

Representations of this kind, though, mark a less significant change than the proliferation of 'patriotic' images of very small children. Where the ideal nursery school teacher of Narkompros propaganda during the 1920s had played down the role of militaristic games and toys,[125] representations of kindergartens dating

32   *Thank You, Comrade Stalin, for a Happy Childhood.* Poster, late 1940s.

33   Boris Vladimirsky, *In a Soviet Kindergarten* (late 1940s).

from the late 1940s placed such activities and items at the centre. A painting of a nursery school by Boris Vladimirsky (1878–1950), for example, placed a girl playing with a doll far into the margins and out of focus; pride of place was occupied by two squat, crew-cut small boys, who had bricks, a teddy bear, and a celluloid duck before them on the table but were lovingly fingering the toys that were clearly their favourites, a model rifle and a miniature machine-gun. In the background, a model tank squatted on top of the piano, and what looks at a careless glance like a vase of cheerful toy flags turns out to be a garland of miniature pennants decorated with the face of Stalin.[126]

But the post-war era was not associated only with ideological education of an explicit kind. Even in moralising representations, children were allowed ducks, dolls, and bears, as well as bricks and guns. A 1948 *Pravda* review of an exhibition of children's paintings began, as one might expect, by emphasising themes that were also canonical in adult Socialist Realism of the time (official celebrations and ceremonial occasions, such as 'A Concert at the Collective Farm'; Soviet labour; Socialist construction). However, it also insisted, 'Children are children, and they love *skazki* and magic.' In this vein, a special 'children's issues' number of *Krokodil*, published in February 1952 and focusing above all on literature, recommended to its readers not only Arkady Gaidar's tale of Pioneer do-gooding, *Timur and his Team*, and Lev Kassil's biography of the Kerch' war hero Volodya Dubinin, *The Street of the Younger Son*, but Kataev's expansive and lyrical novel *A White Sail Gleams*, and Yury Sotik's *The Invisible Bird*.[127]

Some elements of the 'children will be children' ethos still survived, then, alongside the new emphasis on discipline. In the same way, Stalin's image was divided. On the one hand – as in his 'warrior' or 'border guard' manifestation – he was all-seeing, and vengeful as the Old Testament God. Images in the Pioneer press usually featured him in marshal's uniform, and the poetic tributes printed increasingly converged with tributes written by adults (indeed, on some occasions the Pioneer press simply reprinted material by adults, rather than venturing to publish any work by juvenile readers). Meetings with him often now took a mediated form: children would have contact not directly, in a meeting at the Kremlin, but via a letter of congratulation or an icon (in one text of the late 1940s, the daughters of a carpet weaver took a ride across the Soviet Union on a carpet woven by their mother and emblazoned with an icon of the country's all-seeing leader).[128]

But there was also emphasis on another persona of Stalin, one indulgent of 'little children' in the manner of the New Testament Christ. Though his own daughter was now adult, he continued to be represented in fond scenes with small children (usually girls). In order to mark the celebrations for 1 May 1952, *Pravda* carried a front-page photograph of Stalin embracing seven-year-old Vera Kondakova, watched by a smiling Malenkov and Bulganin.[129] Children continued to express their devotion and thankfulness to him for their 'happy childhood'. One children's festival in June 1946 began in the usual style with a model Pioneer reading out a letter of gratitude to Stalin, followed by a grand parade of Pioneers and an aerial bombardment of balloons and flowers from planes flying over; it was rounded off with bicycle races and a football match.[130] Also in this mode, Fedor Reshetnikov's *Dear Stalin* (1950) showed a beaming and avuncular Stalin absorbed in a letter from a small male admirer.[131]

The older the children, however, the more serious the stress on discipline (with carnivals such as the 'children's festivals' allowed as an occasional breathing space). The 1940s saw a good deal of anxiety about indiscipline among adolescents in particular, which was linked with a further move towards rigidity in pedagogy. This was associated, in turn, with an increased respect for the traditions of pre-revolutionary educational institutions, including not just the cadet school, but also the *gimnaziya*.[132] The Soviet authorities also experienced a short-lived enthusiasm for the traditional English boarding-school as a mechanism for generating well-disciplined, self-reliant individuals. This was manifested by an intriguing event in the literary world: the publication in 1946 of a translation of Talbot Baines Reed's didactic boarding-school novel, *The Willoughby Captains*. To be sure, only a year later, the publication was viciously denounced, with the book described as a portrait of a mindless educational establishment where the only values were sport and fighting. What exactly, the reviewers wondered, could Children's Literature have meant by placing on its list this fearful book, and giving leeway to such an obvious instrument of bourgeois moral values?[133] But this denunciation is a good deal less odd than the fact that a book hymning the English prefect system was considered suitable for Soviet publication in the first place.

The Soviet school story – also of a thoroughly didactic type – was one of the boom genres of the era. An example of the trend was V. Oseeva's *Vasyok Trubachov and his Friends* (1949), in which the hero – a boy of essentially sound moral character – finds himself at odds with the school establishment and has to be reintegrated, through public 'self-criticism', into the collective at large. Vasyok is like a flawed version of Gaidar's Timur, who needes to be taught his place in the patriarchal order. While Oseeva's story was unusually lively and entertaining, the theme of self-assertion brought low was canonical: in another school-based piece of the era, this time meant for an older audience, A. B. Geraskina's play *Matriculation Certificate* (1948), a gifted but idiosyncratic boy was brought to a realisation of his faults by temporary expulsion from the Komsomol and by a narrow failure to achieve the all-round top marks necessary to secure him the gold medal he had been confidently predicted.[134]

Stress on discipline in texts for children was mirrored in texts for teachers. The resurgence of nationalism in pedagogy was marked by the rediscovery of K. D. Ushinsky, whose writings on subjects such as 'Nationality in Social and Moral Education' (1857) and 'The Moral Element in Russian Education' (1860) were repeatedly republished in the 1940s. The emphasis was not only on Ushinsky's importance in a historical sense, but on his relevance to the present day. 'Only in our socialist society can [Ushinsky's ideas] be fully realised,' Mikhail Kalinin proclaimed in 1941, words cited approvingly in a 1945 collection of the pedagogue's writings.[135] Though Ushinsky was, inevitably, represented as a thoroughly progressive writer, the essays reprinted included not only his strictures on the importance of music and movement (once genuinely pioneering, in the Russian context), or his introduction to his primer *Native Tongue*, a path-breaking book when published in 1864, but also his Slavophile excursions on the unique warmth of the Slav family and the importance of patriotic education, and his cautious defence of corporal punishment as 'a way of helping the child's weak will to develop'.[136] Reissues from the pre-revolutionary era also included various works by P. Lesgaft, whose opinions on the importance of 'temperament' were recapitulated – without acknowledgement – in a 1950 manual for Soviet primary school teachers. And the writings of Makarenko continued to be widely published, and presented as authoritative, in magazines for teachers and parents.[137]

Not only the duties of children but the 'rights and obligations' of parents, as they were officially termed, were defined and policed even more strictly in the post-war era. A new law on marriage and the family promulgated on 8 July 1944 put an end to divorce by mutual consent in families where children were present, and reintroduced the distinction between children born inside and outside wedlock.[138] Certainly, 'the interests of children' were still a primary objective in family law. Yet – as in the late 1930s – this principle was often evoked in a spirit of irritation with 'irresponsible' parents rather than of neutral concern for children's welfare. An item in *Socialist Legality* in 1946 made it clear that mothers who had had the temerity to desert their children need not expect that they would later be able successfully to apply for custody.[139] The principle of 'rejection of a child' as permanent was to apply till the end of Soviet power.

Quite logically, in this broader context, representations of the ideal family harped still more relentlessly on social duty than they had in the 1930s. In the words of the canonical late Stalinist baby book, the raising of children was never merely an individual matter; it was a national one, with parents looking forward to the 'sight of sons or daughters who have become worthy citizens of their great Motherland'.[140] Articles about model parents in the journal *Family and School* underlined that parents who took this great duty seriously would make sure their children were far too busy to have any time for frivolity. Rather, after homework had been carefully and rigorously supervised, leisure time was spent in useful and purposive activities – with father reading aloud, say, and mother sewing, while the children listened or perhaps played quietly in a corner. Everything, from meals to socially useful work, was organised according to a strict daily timetable, and words like 'fun' were simply not used.[141]

34   Aleksandr Reshetnikov, *Bad Marks Again* (1952).

Just as in the 1920s and 1930s, it was juvenile males whom propaganda identified as most likely to chafe against discipline. But now the last residue of the 1920s tolerance, or even approval, of male rebelliousness had vanished. Now the idea was that boys should settle down and begin behaving responsibly. Didactic fiction repeatedly represented the conversion of book-hating small boys to model pupils. In Nikolai Nosov's *Vitya Mamleev at School and at Home* (1951), Vitya was transformed from a carefree scaramouch heedless of his teacher's exhortations to catch up on maths during the summer holidays to a responsible member of society able to convert a malingering friend to good citizenship: in the process of cataloguing his conversion, Vitya recorded his efforts to battle with 'weak will', which even extended to refusing a cake his mother had just baked in order to prove he was able to resist it.[142]

The conversion through shame of the reluctant schoolboy became a theme in official art of this period as well. The most famous representation of the subject was in a painting by Fedor Reshetnikov, *Bad Marks Again!*, exhibited at the All-Union exhibition in the year it was painted, 1952, to a warm critical reception.[143] A rackety-looking small boy has struggled reluctantly home from school with his battered briefcase, and presented his mother with a predictably awful report. His Pioneer sister looks fiercely down from her pile of homework at the table; his mother gives him a look of despair and outrage. The room in which all this takes place is carefully contrived to indicate that the family is quite well-off. A glass partition door suggests this must be a separate flat, not a room in a communal one; the miscreant's younger brother, to the right, is astride a bicycle; a toy boat is stored in a rack to the right of the handsome-looking tea-table. As a review in 1953 put it, a pair of skates mounts 'clear evidence against the boy getting the bad marks'.[144] Obviously, his problem is lack of motivation rather than lack of opportunity or bad family background, a point reinforced by the exemplary behaviour of his older sister. In Adol'f Gugel' and Raisa Kudrevich's two-handed work *A Big Surprise*, also shown at the 1952 All-Union exhibition, a slightly older boy indulges in even more reprehensible behaviour: his mother comes back to find him puffing away on a cigarette, while his much younger sister, teddy bear in hand, stands to the right, a picture of innocent consternation.[145] Notable in both these paintings of small boys gone wrong is the absence of a male authority figure, a patent indication of misrule. Conversely, in Sergei Grigor'ev's painting of a courtyard football match, *The Goalkeeper* (1949), an adult male among the spectators acts as the guarantee of the legitimacy and probity of the game (though he sits so close to the action that, were the scene taking place in real life, he would be in danger of being knocked out by the ball).[146]

Images like this, along with the moral stories in which fathers and teachers put small boys back on the right track, pointed to a vacuum at the heart of Soviet society. The family was still held to stand or fall by the effectiveness, or otherwise, of the father as the instrument of social discipline. Soviet child-care literature did not give advice to mothers on managing boys alone. Yet, in practice, fathers were often absent, deficient, or indeed dead. Rather than offering a practical solution to the real social problems posed by disruptive small boys, propaganda images harped on a solution that was simply not realisable (intervention of the father). The risk was, of course, that they would inadvertently perpetuate the problems they sought to resolve.

Given that the control of daughters *was* supposed to be within the competence of mothers, even single ones, it followed that there was much less emphasis on the problems of dealing with female bad behaviour.[147] It is notable that the naughty boys in the Reshetnikov and the Gugel' and Kudrevich paintings all have positive female counterparts; in the Grigor'ev football painting, the girls all sit primly on the bench next to the adult 'referee', looking positively Victorian in their ribbons and woollen bonnets.[148] Where girls were seen as socially disruptive, the stereotyping was quite different – the emphasis was on egotism and materialism, rather than on actual transgression. In a 1952 collection of stories by Valentina Oseeva, for instance, unacceptable behaviour by female pupils was at the level of selfish refusal to share possessions, and a snobbish, unhelpful attitude to others, rather than insufficient effort in class; boys, on the other hand, were represented as careless, slapdash, but basically good-hearted.[149]

At the same time, boys predominated not only among negative role models, but among positive role models. In contradistinction to the situation in the 1920s, this was a sign less of society's 'masculine' preoccupations than of the fact that pedagogues felt that boys were in greater need of instruction. A hagiographical study of Mayakovsky's childhood, written by his mother and published in 1953, assiduously made the early years of the poet's life relevant to the modern Soviet child by the insertion of anachronistic detail – the claim that 'New Year' (rather than Christmas) had been a time for family celebrations with a tree, or that little Volodya and his father had celebrated their 'birthdays' (rather than the more accurate 'name days') on the same day. From the first sentence of the book, Volodya's life was represented as an ideal pattern for imitation: 'Volodya fell in love with books at the age of four and was always begging me to read to him [...] *skazki* at first, and then Krylov's fables, verse by Pushkin, Nekrasov, Lermontov and others.' Like the ideal Soviet child, Volodya loved animals, was tidy, worked hard at his lessons and obtained good marks in all subjects (with the exception of the obviously dreary and irrelevant religious knowledge). While 'unfortunately' unable to join the Pioneers, which had not existed in his youth (even high-Stalinist tall tales for children had some factual constraints), he was politically active and committed to the revolutionary cause. By the age of 13, in fact, 'he was thoroughly grown-up, independent, and did not need special attention from me'.[150]

All in all, the 1940s and early 1950s were a time when the principles of the late 1930s, called into question by the exigencies of the war, were once again reimposed, and indeed intensified. Now, once more, children were shown as the beneficiaries of state largesse, provided they behaved in the ways the rulers of the state deemed appropriate. Indeed, attitudes to discipline became still more repressive, as manifested in the tightening of control over children's literature, in the flourishing of the school story as a genre, and in the deeper entrenchment of academic values in education. To be sure, there was a persistence (in muted form) of the idea that younger children had special needs, which they must be allowed to realise in play. But attitudes to older children were strict or indeed severe: even the long-established hostility to corporal punishment became somewhat muted.

The years between 1935 and 1953 saw a full-scale assault on the vestiges of 'free education', as embraced, in official rhetoric, by the abusive term 'paedology'; this era also witnessed a curbing of child activism, accompanied by a resurrection of the ideal of the docile, obedient small child, often represented in propaganda as a girl. Good children would be rewarded for their efforts, bad children suitably punished; the figure of Joseph Stalin – the wise yet stern father – was celebrated everywhere as the living embodiment of this double role of paternity. The 'care and attention', or mixture of concern and surveillance, exercised by the state, and the abject gratitude that was the Soviet subject's appropriate response to this, was symbolised in the figure of the leader embracing a beaming small girl. While child activism was briefly rehabilitated during the Great Patriotic War (an era that also saw the emergence of a new kind of child hero, stoical unto the grave), in the post-war years there was a revival of 'ruler and child' imagery, a downplaying of Partisan heroes and an emphasis on children's role as the quintessential victims of the aggressor, as well as on the need for discipline and self-control. While some elements of this vision of childhood – for example the central role of Stalin as manifestation and instrument of state authority – were to be transformed during the next phase of Soviet history, others (such as the idea that children ought to be the recipients of tender concern) were to prove much more enduring.

Chapter 4

'Let There Always Be Sunshine',
1953–1991

The death of the Generalissimus, Comrade Stalin, did not mark an immediate shift in attitudes to the young. At the outset, even the dead leader's cult continued its existence unscathed. Children were prominent in reportage about the mourners at Stalin's funeral. The photo-coverage in *Pravda* on 9 March 1953 included a special section, 'Children Bid Farewell to the Leader', showing the usual beribboned small girls paying their respects to the corpse. In similar vein, the magazine *Family and School* carried a photo-spread in its April issue with the caption 'Children in the Days of National Mourning', where a group of children – who once again, according to established propaganda convention, were almost all girls – recalled their reactions when they heard of the leader's death. Emotional states were predictable – 'I wept terribly', 'Tears choked my throat', 'My mother and I read Mikhail Sholokhov's "Farewell, Father" and wept' – and so was the determination to derive some didactic benefit from the tragedy. Grief should inspire survivors to do more school-work: 'Stalin was happy when he saw pupils getting good marks. Stalin was sad when they got bad ones,' remarked one 8-year old.[1]

Such reactions were not inventions of the central Soviet press. In the Russian capitals and provinces, teachers and kindergarten supervisors strove to impress the solemnity of this moment upon their charges. As a woman brought up in Taganrog, who was six when the leader died, recalled:

> I remember how one of the supervisors was crying her eyes out in the kindergarten head's office, the door was open, and we children all went to have a look, very scared, something had happened, and then they pinned a portrait of Stalin in this red lace circle, this frame, on our left sides …[2]

For a year or so, propaganda management continued to preserve the imagery and rituals that had obtained in Stalin's lifetime. The first anniversary of his death, in March 1954, was commemorated respectfully in children's magazines and in family newspapers such as *Family and School*. An official manual for nursery school teachers that also appeared in 1954 stated that teaching 'love of the Soviet motherland, for the Soviet people, for the great leaders Lenin and Stalin' was an official part of the syllabus.

'Grandpa Lenin'

The central importance of political indoctrination as such persisted right up to the end of Soviet power. To be sure, Stalin himself rapidly ceased to dominate the world of Soviet children. In 1954, an important change was made to the Pioneer oath: members of the organisation now promised 'in the presence of their comrades' to 'be true to the testaments of Lenin' – the post-1942 reference to 'Great Stalin' was dropped.[3] While Khrushchev's anti-Stalin speech of 1956 was not discussed in the schoolroom or the children's press, after 1961, posters, statues, and murals of Stalin in all child-centred sites began to disappear. As with other 'purges' of imagery, the precise process is difficult to trace, but it is interesting to note that the building of the new Pioneer palace in Moscow, begun in 1958 and completed in 1962, coincided neatly with the height of post-Stalin iconoclasm. Where the old 'House of Pioneers' in the centre of the city had made images of Stalin the centre of its decorative scheme, the new palace employed a range of strikingly ideology-free images – characters from folk tales and from children's literature, portraits of national types.[4] In 1962, the House of Children's Literature in Leningrad expended over 300 roubles on the 'liquidation' of Stalin portraits in the building.[5]

Yet though Stalin had vanished, the symbolic vacuum created by his disappearance was quickly filled. Of course, none of his successors was associated with a personal cult on the same scale, though occasionally the new leaders would receive an honourable mention. For example, the tireless Sergei Mikhalkov's 'Be Prepared!' cited the astronaut Titov as an adult example of the Pioneer motto put into action. When Titov returned from orbit, a telegram was sent to the leader without delay:

> And as for Khrushchev,
> He's absolutely delighted.[6]

Press coverage of the era gave large amounts of space to pictures of Khrushchev with small children, usually of the established 'Stalinist' beribboned and bouquet-clutching kind.[7] After Khrushchev's fall from grace in 1964, 'cults of personality' directed at the living were treated more cautiously. Rare indeed were items describing contact with the leaders, and those that did appear described occasions stripped of tradition and ritual.[8] Though Brezhnev's memoirs were compulsory reading in schools, items about his childhood in the general press were few and far between, and placed more emphasis on the hair-raising poverty that his family had lived through than on his own exceptional characteristics.[9]

But, in compensation, there was now an all-out expansion of the Lenin cult, and one embracing, in particular, images aimed at a young audience.[10] This involved, to begin with, further proliferation of the traditional 'childhood of Lenin' material, with a range of new texts appearing for children's consumption, and the construction of cultic objects in schools. As an American visitor who was taken on an official tour of a kindergarten in Moscow recalled:

> On the front wall [of the room for four-year-olds] hung a portrait of Lenin as a small boy, with plants and bouquets of flowers placed beneath it by the children. Each room had a similar altar to Lenin[,] who grew older as the age group advanced.[11]

Lenin was promoted to the 'avuncular' status formerly occupied by Stalin. Pioneer camps, nurseries, and kindergartens, for example, were decorated with a regulation image of 'Il'ich' leaning slightly forward (as though making concessions to child height), his face crinkled into an indulgent smile, and his hand raised in a friendly wave.[12] Certainly, the Lenin cult was still something to be taken very seriously. Pioneer initiation rites tended to take place on Red Square, in the Museum of the Revolution, or, for those not within travelling distance of Moscow, by the local Lenin statue or monument.[13] But the icons to which children were exposed in schools and other institutions captured a softer, more 'domestic' side of the dead leader.

Cosmonauts and War Heroes

A rather livelier kind of personality cult was disseminated in publicity about space travel. Children's magazines and newspapers documented in detail the successes of the country's various ventures into space, especially Yury Gagarin's first manned fight into the cosmos (1961). Space travel was not represented as only, or even mainly, a scientific phenomenon and a technological breakthrough. Depictions of it drew on tropes associated with representations of travel into unknown lands going back to classical times, highlighting the strangeness of the destination yet its familiarity (that is, its similarity to destinations familiar from existing literature). Articles about actual space journeys blurred into invented narratives belonging to the increasingly popular genre of science fiction, which was widely represented in children's magazines and books in the post-Stalin era.[14]

Optimistic visions of an ever-expanding Soviet Union, where planets might turn into attendant 'republics', were not the only representations of the nation presented to Soviet children of this era. There was also a return to the Second World War as an ordeal – albeit one survived with heroic dignity and fortitude – rather than as a triumph. The early 1960s saw a huge proliferation in the number of war heroes that the juvenile Soviet public was supposed to honour. The already famous Volodya Dubinin and Zoya Kosmodem'yanskaya were joined by a pleiad of figures, including Valya Kotik, Adik Neverko (who fought with the Partisans in Minsk province and received the 'For Valour' medal), Lyonya Golikov, and many others.[15] *Sputnik*, a pull-out supplement to the magazine *Pioneer Leader*, published a series of model biographies of such heroes in 1961 which were meant to be collected and stored for instructive reading in the 'Pioneer room' of Soviet schools; statues were erected to commemorate them, notably of Lyonya Golikov and Valya Kotik at the All-Soviet Exhibition of Economic Achievements in Moscow (the monuments were unveiled on 1 June 1960).[16] Often these heroes had taken a more active part in the war than the Pioneers presented by fiction

35   Boris Lebedev, *Pavlik Morozov*, illustration to V. Gubarev's life of the hero (1958 edition).

and reportage in the immediate post-war era. Trofim Prushinsky, for example, had been bayoneted by the Germans for leading them astray during a search for the Soviet side, while Lida Matveeva had been hanged after she was caught signalling to Soviet tanks in Rostov to warn them of a German ambush. For his part, Lyonya Golikov, posthumously named Hero of the Soviet Union for his exceptional valour, had died in battle, aged only 13.[17]

Yet children were still not taught about the effects of the Holocaust on the Soviet Union, or indeed about the mass murders of the inhabitants of entire villages, including their child populations, in the war. The taboo on such material started to be breached only at the end of the Soviet era, and then only in texts aimed at an adult audience, such as Elem Klimov's film *Come and See* (1985). On the other hand, there was now more emphasis on the real suffering endured by children during the Leningrad Blockade. The diary of little Tanya Savicheva, aged nine, who had watched her entire family succumb to starvation and left a seven-line litany of their deaths, was turned into a key exhibit in the memorial museum at Piskarevskoe cemetery, opened on Victory Day (9 May) and featured in the monument to the 'young heroes of Leningrad' raised in 1968.[18]

Heroic stories of this kind served not just to remind children of the sacrifices that had been made on their behalf (though this was a very important function).

They also served as models of self-sacrifice, discipline, and devotion to the common cause. These virtues continued to be propounded to children relentlessly in the post-Stalin era. The writings of Makarenko retained their authority as representations of the ideal of the rational collective, with its demands for conformity and loyalty from individual members.[19] Vasily Sukhomlinsky, a successor to Makarenko from a later generation, though giving greater importance to 'spiritual' values and to individual traits in different children, also stressed the need for dutiful self-abnegation in the face of social demands.[20] Indeed, there was in some respects a move towards still greater emphasis on the need for discipline: for instance, much was now written on the importance of good manners and decorum in children.[21] In many texts, 'collective spirit' still remained the ultimate value, and 'communist education' the manner of generating this.[22] 'Children's rights' was still a term that signified children's claims to protection: the specific 'rights' of children were absent from the new constitution of 1976, just as they had been from its 1936 predecessor.

'Let There Always Be Sunshine'

As in the Stalin era, the complement to the notion of the child, especially the older child, was often the sentimental vision of a small person lost in a special world of wonder and magic. For example, in an address to a plenary session of the Board of the Union of Writers in December 1960, Kornei Chukovsky attacked 'dreary and non-poetic' and 'haemorrhoidal' writing for children. Once again, he urged that children's own writing should be a model for professional adult authors and quoted several examples of the kind of children's writing that he had in mind. These included two poems by tiny children in celebratory mode:

> Let there always be sunshine,
> Let there always be blue sky,
> Let there always be mummy,
> Let there always be me.
>
> Thank you, sun, for being!
> Thank you, dear river, for flowing!
> Thank you, dear flowers, for growing!
> Thank you, bushes and trees![23]

Yet the choice of these particular texts as exempla of juvenile literary production also captured some of the contradictions of the Thaw era. Had one word been changed in each poem ('Let there always be Stalin!' and 'Thank you Stalin, for being!'), either of these efforts would have been received with rapture by any Soviet magazine in 1936 or 1948.

Inevitably, alongside celebration of childhood innocence and gratitude went celebration of the Soviet state as a place where these qualities were specially valued and rewarded. A cartoon sent in by a reader to *Ogonek* in 1957 caught this idea in rather an individual way. Captioned 'What my son imagined when he was reading his history textbook', it showed a child trying to comprehend the unfamiliar past by reference to the world that he knew. A reference to 'His Highness' conjured up the gangly children's hero Uncle Styopa, and 'court society' meant the caretaker chasing children with his broom; the term *rostovshchik* (usurer) was taken to refer to Uncle Vova from Rostov. The cartoon marked a shift in attitude to the national past. In the 1920s, 1930s, and 1940s, children had been constantly reminded that they were fortunate compared with their parents' generation, and that pre-revolutionary Russia had been a dreadful place. Now, the past was sometimes understood as a place that had no relevance to their experience of the world at all. In the words of the then Party leader, Leonid Brezhnev, speaking in the early 1970s: 'Childhood is a vast country without a past, but with a present that reaches into the future.'[24]

With the children of propaganda now living in an even simpler version of mythic time than they had in the first decades of Soviet power (the present plus the future minus the past, rather than versus the past), it was inevitable that the *skazka* should retain its grip as a central genre. According to a 1967 manual for parents, the *skazka* was 'the child's best friend, a fount of joyful experiences from the earliest years of its life'.[25] In Soviet children's culture generally, *skazka* motifs proliferated. They dominated the decoration of public buildings, such as the magnificent new Pioneer palace opened in Moscow during 1962, and they dominated entertainments for children. Children's theatres and puppet theatres staged *skazka* plays, and there was wholesale promotion of animal acts involving costumed and trained animals, both in the circus and in zoos.[26] And the *skazka* poems of Kornei Chukovsky were now the backbone of juvenile poetry lists. Though *Moidodyr* and *Tarakanishche* retained their place as favourites with publishers (between 1953 and 1991, the former poem was reprinted 57 times in book form alone, not counting editions in collected works and anthologies, and the latter appeared no fewer than 39 times), works that had once been under a cloud, such as *Mukha-Tsokhotukha*, *Barmalei*, and *Bibigon* also had numerous new editions.[27]

36 'We'll Grow!' Greetings card, 1957.

The work of Chukovsky's contemporary and comrade-in-arms Marshak was also extensively republished. In the post-Stalin era, both these writers rose to an unassailable authority as 'founding fathers' of Russian children's literature.[28] In the late Stalin era, Marshak had been far more prominent than his friend and rival. No doubt because of this, Chukovsky now became the primary member of the duo. Indicative of changed trends was a collection of essays on children's literature by the famous Formalist critic and political weather vane Viktor Shklovsky, published in 1966. The appearance of this book was all the more striking in that Shklovsky had in fact been one of the last voices to articulate a 'Krupskian' suspicion of Chukovsky's tales. In 1936, he had published an article in *Pravda,* ironically wondering why Soviet children's literature was so thickly peopled with giraffes and hippopotamuses, and so thinly strewn with collective farms and city apartment blocks. Chukovsky's Dr Aibolit (the Sovietisation of Dr Dolittle) had, as Shklovsky sarcastically put it, 'too large a private practice'.[29] But now, thirty years later, Shklovsky demonstratively abandoned his earlier doubts and launched into a fulsome celebration of Chukovsky's work. Where in 1936 he had asserted that children were just as fascinated by the everyday as by the magical (for example, for them it was wonderful and mysterious that horses did not have horns), he now championed Chukovsky's books as 'written for children, not parents', and as a challenge to dreary moralism in their perpetration of cheerful mischief.[30]

New Worlds

The perpetuation, in children's literature, of established aesthetic standards has caused one historian to argue that the Thaw was less obvious in literature for children than it was in writing for adults, and that 'many poets devoted their efforts to summing up their writing'.[31] Certainly, competence and liveliness were more widespread in post-1954 literary production than genuine originality. Tat'yana Makarova's narrative poem *The Tale of an Ant called Ant* (1973), whose eponymous hero had to leave his home, but then found a fine new abode for self and family in a discarded tin that had once contained prepared stew, and held a house-warming (tin-warming?) party to celebrate, was very like a new version of Chukovsky's famous poem *Mukha-Tsokhotukha,* though Makarova's verse-writing lacked the dynamism of Chukovsky's.[32] Meanwhile, Sergei Mikhalkov and Agniya Barto, classic Soviet writers of the second rank, continued to work in their established vein, with further groups of disciples clustered round them. In the world of poetry in particular, it is hard to name an epoch-breaking publication from the post-Soviet era. Younger writers who did innovative work felt constantly frustrated by the restrictive canons of the children's publishing houses and by the extent of Mikhalkov's influence on editorial choices.[33] The floodgates were not to open until the late 1980s.

Yet the analysis that little changed after 1953 is, on balance, unfair. To begin with, as in other areas of Soviet culture, the late 1950s and 1960s, in particular, witnessed a search for an alternative, pre-Stalinist, Soviet history. The most explicit aspect of this was the selective rehabilitation of famous children's books that had been out of print, or infrequently reprinted, since the early 1930s. Significantly, the grittiest, least 'childish' classics, such as Neverov's *Tashkent the Abundant,* were not among those rediscovered for young audiences, nor was there a sudden rush to reprint the ideologically declarative fiction that had come out in *Pioneer* at the time.[34] Instead, it was lyrical, imaginative works evoking the charm of worlds far from the present, such as Lev Kassil's *The Conduct Book and Shvambraniya*, or Aleksandr Grin's novel of idealistic young love, *Scarlet Sails*, that were preferred.

The recuperation of the imaginative past is one reason why one could argue that children's literature went through a much longer and more fundamental 'thaw' than adult literature. It is a striking point, for instance, that the work for children by Kharms, Oleinikov, and Vvedensky was 'rehabilitated' much earlier than their work for adults. And such new editions were influential. The characteristic mood of stories and poems, if not exactly like that of these earlier writers, was often zany and skittish. Sergei Baruzdin's *Tell Me!* (1962), illustrated with charming stick-figure drawings by V. Statsinsky, was typical of the day, containing as it did little verses about a man who was so fond of his cat that he lost touch with human company altogether, and another man whose tongue was 'longer/than the Moscow River Bridge,/Longer, than the Moscow river itself/Plus the Oka'.[35]

37 Chapter title from Yu. Tomin, *A Wizard Walked Round Town*, one of the popular hits with child readers of the 1960s.

Equally, the tiny sketches of Viktor Golyavkin were sometimes quite conventional in their emphasis on the importance of honesty, hard work, bravery, and so on. But occasionally they reached delightful heights of humorous surrealism, as in the tale of some small boys who sneaked, ticketless, into the parachute jump ride at Gorky Park, and realised too late that they had no desire at all to jump. Consumed by guilt about having got a free jump, they then bought tickets, only to find themselves having to go through the process all over again.[36]

The move back towards adventure stories of the kind that had been popular in the 1920s and 1930s was accompanied by another characteristic trend in Thaw literature for children: a downplaying of moralism. Nikolai Nosov's hugely popular Ignoramus (Neznaika) was a person totally lacking the virtues of truthfulness, politeness, tidiness, and love of hard work considered requisite in the Soviet child. Ignoramus himself was a strikingly new phenomenon in children's literature, a kind of beetle-sized Khlestakov who could not stop lying, even when perpetually found out, but also a character capable of a range of emotions, not all of them predictable: misery at parting from a friend, distress at his fellow Infants' cruel teasing. Alongside Nosov's rare ability to portray characters in more than one dimension went a considerable capacity for whimsical invention – reed-stalk plumbing in the girls' settlement, Greentown, and a 'pistachio-cooled' eight-wheel, large-engine car in the boys' town, Snakesville. While occasional motifs recalled the literature of the 1940s (especially the emphasis on rigid gender distinctions in dress and behaviour), the narrative drive was quite different. In this world of questionable objectives, the determination to maintain sex-role exclusivity seemed not so much to emanate from a 'natural' complementarity of roles as to embody adult foolishness in another key.[37]

The relative permissiveness of Nosov's stories was typical of the day. Certainly, 'forbidden themes' still existed – for example death, sex, politics other than a small range of canonical subjects (the life of Lenin, the Pioneer movement), characters who withstood moral conversion, 'nasty' and 'cruel' subjects. And publishing plans continued to be used as a means of manipulating literary production: established authors would be approached to produce work on subjects considered appropriate, and there was pressure on editors not to take too much from the 'slush pile'. Editorial conferences and 'round tables', at which extant publications were favourably or unfavourably reviewed by outside experts as well as by internal staff, were used to steer the work of individual editors, and lectures by pedagogical specialists arranged so that the broader issues of social and moral education could be raised.

Yet editors had some leeway: they could build up their own relationships with favourite writers, bring on new talents, and manipulate the 'internal review' system to torpedo work they did not like, so that working with uncongenial authors or typescripts was relatively rare. Editors also had some say at the editorial college level – and quality came into this (it was hard for any one person, even the director, to argue successfully for the publication of a patently inferior book). Again, the perceived political 'innocence' of children's literature was a help;

to become involved in a squabble about whether some book about a talking bear, say, got published or not would have struck the average Party bureaucrat as demeaning, and so authors who went up the line to try and appeal to get publishers' decisions changed normally failed. Intervention rarely went beyond a cursory check to see whether the publishers had fulfilled their legal requirement to process a manuscript within a certain period of time.[38]

One result was that, once more, children's books became, as they had been in the late 1920s and early 1930s, a refuge for talented people who could not express their anti-realist aesthetic sensibilities in adult art – illustrators as well as writers. Certainly, people working in this area did not have *carte blanche*. The illustrator Vitaly Statsinsky, editor of the children's magazines *Jolly Pictures* and *The Cottage Loaf* (1956–64 and 1967–72 respectively), recalled how 'every month they [the censors] carpeted us and wanted to know why we had hardly any Young Pioneers in the paper, and lots of silly bunnies and ponies and so on'.[39] But artists such as Statsinsky continued to draw their 'bunnies and ponies', sometimes in the form of delicate wood engravings or pen-and-ink sketches, sometimes in a more robust, folk-inspired style, and sometimes according to the emerging canons of post-modernism. Grigory Pavlishin's very brightly coloured and psychedelic illustrations to Makarova's *Tale of an Ant called Ant*, for example, were a good deal fresher than the poem itself. Prominent illustrators of the 1960s and 1970s displayed a wide range of talents, from the broad-brush style of Lev Tokmakov, whose robust figures looked like the decorations on painted ceramics, to the elegantly wayward gouaches and watercolours of the Traugot brothers or the emphatic designs of Mai Miturich, whose work for *The Tales of Uncle Kornei* (1972) included a sketch of a raging, scarlet-bearded ancient, his chest bearing, Tiresias style, two mud-pie-shaped, puce-coloured bosoms.[40]

Interestingly, as in the 1930s, some of the most original talents were involved in work for children under duress. Genrikh Sapgir, who published no fewer than twenty children's books between 1960 and 1970, confided in a friend that he had become involved in writing for young readers at the suggestion of the poet Boris Slutsky, and had only ever done it 'for the money'. The only children's book he had published which gave him any sense of personal achievement was his illustrated alphabet.[41] But the achievements of such reluctant writers still reached significantly higher flights of fancy than those of some adult writers who willingly worked for children, and indeed of some full-time professional children's writers.[42]

Some material published in the post-Stalin era was imaginative by any standards. The view of the *skazka* as a 'safe' children's genre accorded a certain freedom of manoeuvre to some very talented artists and writers. A short novel by Yury Koval', for example, began with the narrator watching black swans swim in central Moscow, and continued with the tale of a boy trying to buy a pig and ending up with a 'tatty-looking ginger dog', which dog in time led the boy and the police to some bee-keeping villains.[43] On the whole, though, the post-Stalinist *skazka* worked to celebrate precisely the familiar and the domestic. In Eduard Uspensky's humorous and entertaining story, *Uncle Fedor, the Dog and the Cat*

(1974), the family took delivery of a special 'home sun', a sort of 'privatised' natural resource meant to fill the house with warmth and light all day.[44] In children's literature of this kind, stress was kept determinedly at bay: a house fire, for example, was likely to threaten little more than the scorching of an omelette.[45]

The Child Artist Rediscovered

A non-instrumental, utopian view of all children's natural potential for creation – along the lines of the ideas circulating in the 1910s and 1920s – also became a major theme during the early 1960s. In pedagogy, this was usually quite timidly expressed. For example, an article on the value of play to effective learning published in 1956 cautiously informed nursery teachers that children were themselves capable of inventing roles to act out, though it might be better if teachers did not allow them to do this.[46] In 1962, two prominent official painters introduced an anthology of children's paintings rather apologetically: despite its technical weaknesses, children's art did have the right to be considered real art, and, while interfering too strictly with a child's efforts was not a good idea, over-praise was equally pernicious – children must be carefully guided so that they could improve their work. Yet the anthology itself displayed an enormous range of highly coloured and lively children's drawings, with just as much space given to the schematic and non-naturalistic work of the under-nines (where animals, including dressed-up ones, were the most dominant subject) as to the more naturalistic pictures of 9–14-year-olds.[47] More surprisingly, perhaps, the impeccably conservative, mass-market journal *Ogonek* also chose material of this 'primitive' kind – colourful, schematic, and asymmetrical – for a spread on children's art that appeared a few years earlier, in 1958.[48]

In the area of children's writing there was also some diversity, with amateurs often considerably more adventurous in their revision of past dogma than were professional pedagogues. In his introduction to *Children Write Poems* (1964), the writer Vladimir Glotser explicitly alluded to the 'free education' theories denounced as 'Formalist' in the 1930s. He cited Tolstoy's exhortation to adults not to pester children unduly about handwriting and spelling, and ridiculed teachers who thought that love poems were 'petit bourgeois' and who held that children should be writing pieces about plenary sessions of the Central Committee. He stressed that children often wrote poems in non-traditional verse forms, and without using recognisable metres. One of the pieces he chose to illustrate his thesis was a light-hearted and witty poem about the Soviet space programme written by a 12-year-old in 1957, in which the lyric hero wryly described having to give up his place in a rocket to a dog.[49] Ten years earlier, this ironical reaction to a major state achievement would probably have caused a political scandal.

Glotser's book was very much in tune with the general mood of the Russian creative intelligentsia during the late 1950s and early 1960s. But it would be a mistake to see it as in any way 'dissident': *Children Write Poems* was recommended to parents by thoroughly official sources, such as a manual on 'education in the family' published under the imprint of the Academy of Pedagogical Sciences.[50]

38   Poster for the performance of a play, School No. 330, Moscow, 1958.

And 'self-generated artistic creativity' was one of the themes stressed in the leisure work carried out by the Pioneer organisation. A discussion document of 1960, for example, praised a Komsomol worker with Pioneers in Brest province, who had declared 'we should not do anything on children's behalf, but help them out'. A report of the same date gave an enthusiastic write-up to a school where the children themselves had organised an exhibition of arts and crafts and chaired a parents' meeting at which this was presented.[51]

The link between children's perception and innate creativity was, of all 1920s values, perhaps the one that was most completely rehabilitated in early Soviet culture, at any rate among the cultural intelligentsia. The rediscovery of children's art went alongside the rediscovery of modernist painting and sculpture, and of 'primitive' art, from African sculpture and pre-Columbian pottery to traditional Russian forms of popular art, such as the *lubok* (folk print) and the peasant wood-carving. As in the 1920s, it followed that children's art was often assimilated to 'primitive' tradition.

The revived sense of a link between children's perception and creation and primitive art was suggested in Mikhail Bakhtin's famous study of carnival culture, *François Rabelais and his World*, published in 1965 though begun thirty years earlier, in the Stalinist 'Year of the Child' (1936). Certainly, no direct parallels were drawn between children's view of the world and the medieval world-view, between ontogeny and phylogeny; equally certainly, Bakhtin's construct of the carnival subject, fixated on the lower half of the body, unpredictably violent, and exuberantly ribald, was as far out of step with the ideal child of late 1930s myth as his celebration of the physical was at variance with the neo-classical canons for representing the body asserted by Socialist Realism. Yet there is a striking similarity between Bakhtin's representation of carnival – visceral, dynamic, revelling in puns, rhymes, and verbal teases – and the modernist understanding of children's perceptions and language that had been expressed by early twentieth-century writers such as Georgy Vinogradov, Kornei Chukovsky, Viktor Shklovsky, and Daniil Kharms. In a sense, *François Rabelais and his World* can be understood as a kind of oblique memoir of childhood, a flashback to the days when every adult body, seen from below, seemed distorted, swollen, grossly dispropor-tionate, grotesquely ungainly, and when physical processes such as urination and defecation seemed wondrous events.

Bakhtin's fatalistic emphasis on the *boundaries* of carnival rebellion – the fact that its wild celebration and inversion of reality must inevitably give way to a sober and well-regulated status quo – can also be read against the post-Stalinist acceptance that childhood could be granted infinite tolerance if its exuberance were kept between careful limits. In the 1920s, ideal children could hardly be too rebellious and revolutionary; in the 1930s and 1940s, only innocent mischief was tolerated, and then only from the smallest children. By the 1960s something of a middle ground had been reached – children were seen as creative, dynamic, imaginative, and idiosyncratic in their perceptions; but at the same time childhood was understood as a stage to be lived through: less a vision of the 'bright future' than a golden age set in the past. This view persisted through the rest of the Soviet era. As Fazil' Iskander put it in his cycle of stories *The Childhood of Chik* (1971–88): 'Childhood dreams that all this will last for ever: mama, the sun, the world, and a favourite teacher'. But the illusion was easily disrupted: with the disappearance of a favourite teacher, the sense of eternity was already tarnished. With this sense of childhood as an *episode* went an altered use of children's language. In Iskander's cycle, Chik's voice, leaking into the main narrative, was used to suggest the boy's quaint naïvety rather than his energetic capacity for 'seeing the world otherwise'.[52]

Consumers and Young Communists

The post-Stalin years thus saw the tension between 'disciplinary' and 'indulgent' models of childhood become still more pronounced. As in the Stalin years, this was expressed in attitudes to self-control versus the right to consumption. The Soviet government of the post-Stalin years continued to proclaim 'Communist morality' as an essential goal for both adults and children. The Twenty-Second Congress of Soviets in 1961 was notable for the promulgation of the 'Moral Code of the Builders of Communism', stressing the continuing importance of collective values and patriotic commitment. Its eighth point stipulated that 'mutual respect within the family, concern for the proper upbringing of children' were essential.[53] Similarly, the resolutions of the Twenty-Third Congress of Soviets in 1966 spoke of the need for 'conscious discipline and cultured behaviour', and named the production of didactic films and plays, and the dissemination of pedagogical material for parents on radio and television, as important targets of the next five-year plan.[54] Yet at the same time an explicit commitment was made, at the Twenty-Second Congress and later, to enhanced production of consumer goods. Normative literature started to encourage acquisition; state-sponsored advertising made Soviet citizens aware of new 'wonder goods' (supposedly soon to become available in their local stores); mass-market magazines started to run consumer columns.[55] As during an earlier pro-consumer drive in the mid-1930s, goods for children were among the items highlighted. Splashes on the covers of *Ogonek* from the late 1950s featured, for example, a 'children's corner', with bookshelves and toys, and selections of children's clothes; *Nedelya* regularly ran items on clothes, furniture, and play items for juveniles. And numerous books were published that promoted the state's commitment to manufacturing special furniture and garments for children, and to providing a range of attractive, safe, and imaginative toys.[56]

The rise of consumer-directed production did not just affect items from daily life. The post-Stalin era also saw an expansion in the manufacture of 'presentation editions' for children that was part of a general post-Thaw transformation of books into commodities.[57] Traditionally, the quality of book production for children had been regulated strictly, but on utilitarian grounds. There were norms regulating the size of print (13 to 16 point) and the colour of paper (white letters on black paper were strongly discouraged, for instance), since legibility was considered a primary value. The technical editor, responsible for overall design, and the book illustrator had a reasonable amount of choice in determining the broader issues of layout etc., but there were significant economic constraints: books had to be published in high print runs and at low prices, so that expensive paper and colour separation printing would have taxed resources to or beyond the limit. In the 1960s, however, a drive began to produce high-quality illustrated books on shiny paper, a development helped by technological progress in the colour printing industry.[58] The handsome, well-produced volumes that resulted used attractive typefaces and had multi-coloured illustrations and glossy dust-wrappers. Though the number of titles involved remained small (the Leningrad branch of Children's Literature would reckon to produce not more than twenty-five in a year), the books had an extremely high profile – they were exhibited at national and international book fairs, for instance – and soon acquired a reputation as desirable and precious objects. As a result, they were almost impossible to get hold of, never appearing in ordinary shops. One former editor remembered that friends would be moved practically to tears by gifts of such 'presentation editions'; in the late 1970s and early 1980s, the only places where they were legally on sale were the Beryozka hard currency shops for foreigners.[59]

The paradox of enhanced choice in material terms versus continuing ideological regimentation was summed up in the founding of Children's World, the flagship children's department store, on Dzerzhinsky Square in Moscow. The Dzerzhinsky Square department store was reasonably plain in appearance (in keeping with the return to architectural asceticism that had been set in train by the ministerial decree of 1955 banning 'excesses' in building plans). Here were none of the sculpture galleries, bas-reliefs, fountains, mosaics, or coloured intaglios that had characterised the grandest public buildings of the Stalin era. Now, there were streamlined galleries divided into small counters of different items, many of them functional – pens, writing equipment, and bags, as well as toys, clothes, and nursery equipment. The main concession to opulence was a large internal roundabout, complete with coloured lights and curlicued gilding, at the centre of the U-shaped central hall. There was no real sense here of shopping as a 'total leisure experience', though some drink and food stalls were provided in order to make a visit slightly more than a mere exchange of money for goods. But the sheer size of the facility, alongside the fact of the creation of a purpose-built space for children's goods in the first place, and the range of goods available, made the opening of Children's World a significant event.

The site of the new store conveyed more than commercial prestige, though it was in central Moscow, and opposite the end of Kuznetsky most, historically the capital's most elegant shopping street. Children's World also faced directly on to the headquarters of the KGB. The public was thus reminded of 'Iron Felix' Dzerzhinsky's legendary love of children, at a stage when the government was doing its utmost to revive the cults of child-loving dead leaders (Kirov in Leningrad was another example) in preparation for the disappearance from the scene of 'Grandpa Stalin'. At the same time, the pairing of the treasure house of treats for children and the headquarters of the secret police dramatically confronted children with the alternatives to which the two extremes of possible behaviour – obedience and deliquency – might lead. Sergei Mikhalkov's poem 'Uncle Styopa the Policeman' spelled out this juxtaposition of the temple of indulgence and the reformatory. Uncle Styopa the law-enforcer showed his love for *good* children by meting out well-deserved punishment to school bullies. And he enacted the officially sanctioned policy of punishment for *bad* children by pursuing and bringing to justice a hooligan who had been damaging goods in – where else – Children's World.[60]

Alongside its portrayal of an important symbolic conglomeration of the time, the poem also articulated a fashionable commitment to cementing ties of friendship and co-operation between small children and the Soviet police while the former were still at a suitably impressionable stage. Political crimes were not at issue now. Uncle Styopa, despite apparently operating out of the Lubyanka itself, turned his punitive energies to petty crime, not international espionage or political subversion. No longer were Soviet border guards and modern-day Chekists the heroes of children's literature (even if popular culture for adults sometimes took Civil War Chekists as protagonists).[61] Rather, tutelage in law and order emphasised non-political crime, and most particularly hooliganism, as the evil to be combated.[62]

Н. Храброва. ЭДЖЕКЕ • Рассказ Е. Носова «ТЫСЯЧА ВЕРСТ» • ЗВЕЗДЫ ПЕРСЕЯ • Журналы в апреле •

СЛАВА НАШЕЙ ПИОНЕРИИ!

ОГОНЁК

39 Cover of *Ogonek* magazine commemorating the sixtieth anniversary of the Pioneer movement, 1982.

Despite the studied idealisation of the 1920s in many areas of Soviet culture, the child activist was never restored to the centrality he had occupied in the first decade and a half of Soviet power. Just as in the 1930s and 1940s, assertive children inspired disquiet rather than awe. In Lyudmila Razumovskaya's play *Dear Elena Sergeevna* (1980), the vicious persecution by a group of schoolchildren of their teacher – they arrive with birthday presents in order to gain entry to her flat, and force her to hand over the key of the school safe so that they can substitute a fresh set of answers to their maths examination – was used to symbolise the cynicism of late Soviet society generally. 'My dad says that if someone doesn't take what you offer, then you've offered too little,' one of the boys observed, while another, more philosophically, remarked that 'What a limited person sees as bad doesn't raise any objections in someone with a broader mind, isn't that right?'[63]

In alternative literature, representations of childhood and children worked according to similar preconceptions. The *enfant terrible* in the established Western modernist sense – the standard-bearer of an avant-garde assault on bourgeois morality – was still an unknown phenomenon in Russian literature. In the unofficial samizdat and tamizdat Russian literature that began to emerge once censorship clamped down again in the late 1960s, rebellious children were seen as representing social malaise.[64] Children continued to be presented primarily as victims and innocents. For example, the culminating image in Joseph Brodsky's poem 'The Bust of Tiberius' was the cruel emperor clutching tinies under his cloak ('swarms of infants babbling at your ripe/stiff sausage'), in a grotesque parody of the 'Happy Childhood' murals of the Stalin era. Here, the meaning of the ruler icon was stood on its head: rather than suggesting the state's capacity for endless nurture, it implied its capacity for abuse masquerading as paternal concern.[65]

'Little Workers' and Gifted Children

The educational policy and pedagogical theory of the day was equally contradictory. The Central Committee decree of 25 December 1958, 'On the Strengthening of the Link of the School with Life', brought back into the school programme an emphasis on 'labour education' that had vanished by the mid-1930s. Further, the passing of the decree was accompanied by public debate of a kind not seen since the discussions surrounding the prohibition of abortion in 1936. Certainly, the debate was carefully stage-managed, and its conclusions were in some respects irrelevant: the text of the final decree was in most important ways identical to the preliminary 'theses' that had been published in *Pravda* five weeks earlier.[66] But some of the opinions expressed – for example, those of prominent scientists insisting that specialised maths and science education were essential in order to produce qualified entrants to universities and institutes – were to have weight in the long term, if not in the short term.[67] Educational reform, which for more than two decades had been presented to the Soviet public *post factum*, in the form of top-level decrees advertised after they were passed, was now transformed into a topic that might legitimately be the subject of differing views.

But top-level educational policy of the post-Stalin era did not represent an unconditional return to 1920s thinking. There was no move back to project work or the 'brigade system': the rationale behind the reintroduction of 'education for labour' during the Khrushchev era was not making education more interesting for children, but producing better-balanced school graduates who would be happier about proceeding into manual employment, and more effective when they got there.[68] Much the same instrumental drive lay behind the enhanced commitment to 'total institutions' for children, such as the boarding-school, at this point.[69]

In any case, government policy soon swung back towards the 'academic values' that had driven Soviet education since the mid-1930s. The 1958 restoration to the curriculum of labour education – along with ancillary measures of 1957 and 1958, which accorded preference at university entrance to applicants who had spent time in employment, and abolished the privileged status of pupils awarded the gold and silver medals for outstanding performance in school examinations – proved extremely unpopular with influential sectors of public opinion, headed by representatives of universities and research institutes. Those working in higher education were firmly of the belief that emphasis on work education had come at the cost of falling standards in intellectual subjects; moreover, they resented the attempt to dictate selection of applicants (an area of their activity not previously subject to state interference of this wholesale kind).[70]

Once 'work education' lost its most powerful sponsor with the fall from power of Khrushchev, the pressures from the pro-academic lobby rapidly attained their ends. From autumn 1964, the quota for working applicants was abolished, medal-holders regained some of their former privileges, and universities were once again allowed to make their own decisions about applicants' suitability.[71] Significantly, the more lasting reforms of the Khrushchev era generally had to do with the reinforcement of educational differentials than with any reassertion of the egalitarian inclusiveness of the 1920s. On the one hand, the network of technical schools and colleges underwent expansion, so that far more working-class Soviet citizens now had access to specialised secondary education, and (in a limited sense) tertiary education, than before. On the other hand, from the early 1960s greater attention was given to the special needs of 'gifted children', a category that it was now increasingly felt should have their talents fostered from an early stage.

Already in 1961 an article on Soviet pedagogy was giving a reasonably neutral account of programmes for gifted children in the US.[72] This *rapprochement* in theoretical terms was soon matched by expansion of provision at the practical level. Numbers of full-time specialist music and arts schools increased significantly: by the late 1960s, there were 50 specialist art schools across the Soviet Union, and, by 1973, 36 music schools. While the number of specialist sports schools also grew, expansion here (reaching 25 by 1976) never reached the same level.[73] A still more obvious drive was towards specialisation in academic education. The most notorious aspect of this for Western observers was to be the creation of maths and physics hothouses, for example the Novosibirsk Maths and Physics Boarding-School (with a timetable of 36–8 hours per week for the two-year course in the top forms).[74] But far more significant in terms of its broad impact was the institution of an extensive network of 'special schools', both schools with a separate curriculum from entry to graduation (*spetsshkoly*), and schools with a considerable degree of specialisation in the higher classes (known in Russian as *profil'nye shkoly* or *shkoly s uklonom*). Additionally, from 1967–8 schools were allowed to devote a small amount of time in the higher classes to specialist courses (*fakul'tativnye kursy*), selected by the pupils themselves.[75]

The most significant group, numerically speaking, of the 'special schools' proper were the language-teaching schools (schools that taught a foreign language from entry at age seven and offered some teaching of mainstream subjects in foreign languages) in the major cities. By 1961, criticism of existing provision in Soviet schools had become quite extensive. Not enough hours were allocated to foreign languages, and teaching concentrated far too much on reading and writing, at the expense of oral communication; the selection of languages offered (French, German, and English) was still mired in pre-revolutionary tradition; language-learning was begun too late; classes were too large, and teachers not properly qualified. It was, commentators said, time to take the small number of extremely popular schools instituted in the late 1940s, where languages were properly established in the programme, as a model for the Soviet education system in a broader sense.[76]

The Soviet authorities remained committed to this type of special school for the next thirty years. The Twenty-Third Congress of the Communist Party (held between 29 March and 8 April 1966) endorsed the 'further development of the higher and middle special school', which it linked with the 'growth of culture and of technical literacy'.[77] By 1967, there were already 700 language schools across the Soviet Union.[78] Equally rapid was the development of the 'profiled schools', those with a larger number of hours devoted to maths or sciences in the top classes. There were 536 schools of this kind across the Soviet Union in 1963, catering for about 1.2 per cent of the population of ten-year schools.[79] A decree passed on 10 November 1966 on the one hand emphasised labour and vocational education, but on the other endorsed the principle of 'in-depth teaching' of academic subjects – humanities as well as science and mathematics – and thus fostered the further development of 'profiling'.[80] However, the next important reform, in 1984, pushed in the other direction, increasing targets of pupils who were supposed to go into vocational schools at 15, and pressing for more practical and less ambitious methods of teaching academic subjects in mainstream schools.[81]

The post-Stalin era, then, saw educational policy at first move back towards the egalitarian ideals of the 1920s, with their emphasis on across-the-board exposure to training in manual skills, and then reassert the academic values of the 1930s, according to which high-level intellectual training was to be provided – but only to some Soviet children – before finally moving a little way towards vocationalism again. Official commitment to equality of opportunity remained strong in the 1970s and early 1980s as well: discussions in the educational press were widely opposed to routine streaming.[82] Special provision for children who had a talent in some particular area was one thing; selection of the generally academically gifted quite another. Post-Stalinist educational policy, then, was at once committed to equality of opportunity and to differential provision, a contradiction that pointed to an underlying contradiction between an understanding of ability as innate, and a view that any child could do as well as any other, if given the right opportunities.

Discussions of educational methodology were just as contradictory, though for rather different reasons. To begin with, the Khrushchev thaw witnessed some quite bold reassessments of the old emphasis on discipline and obedience. A particularly outspoken articulation of anti-disciplinarian views came in an article by the writer Aleksandr Sharov, published in 1965.[83] As well as a plea for sensitivity and clemency, and for imaginative teaching, the article was a vehement defence of the importance of play:

> It is in schools, courtyards, fights and noble actions, tears and laughter, in play – but especially in play – where the future world is made by children. The more a child plays, the richer his play is, the more happiness there will be in

the future. [...] Children aren't engaged in 'unproductive mischief' when they play. They are constructing the moral co-ordinates of the future.

The common obsession with school-work was simply foolish: 'Basing everything on study is the same as trying to box up the spring wind.'[84]

In critiques of this kind, excessive discipline was seen not only as inhumane in a general sense, but as contrary to children's essential nature, and hence counter-productive. Discipline-driven teaching was perceived as fatally dry and stultifying. The 1960s also saw formula-dominated instruction become the subject of criticism, or at times even open mockery. Kornei Chukovsky, for example, took to task the role-model-centred literature teaching that had been imposed on teachers in the second half of the 1930s, ridiculing the way that it led to stereotypical and banal assessments of the work of great writers:

Every single one, every single one of the classic writers is always described as follows: 1) he loves his motherland; 2) he loves his nation and people; 3) he expostulates against the social abuses of his time; he (like every other classic writer) is 4) a humanist, 5) a realist, 6) an optimist, 7) has no faults and all in all no distinguishing features whatsoever.[85]

It is notable, however, that none of these discussions was led by a professional pedagogue, or even a working teacher, or was published in a mainstream educational journal. To be sure, such individuals and journals did begin a partial reassessment of the issue of teacher-led versus child-centred learning. A de-Stalinising editorial published in *Soviet Pedagogy* in 1956 criticised not only the dead leader's evil influence on pedagogical writings, but also the dry academicism of the genre itself: it was time to concentrate less on 'how to teach' and more on 'how children learn'.[86] In its turn, the interest in the learning process brought educational psychology to the centre of intellectual life for the first time since the assault on 'paedological perversions' in 1936. Educational discussions in the West started to be reported without the note of sarcasm that had been obligatory during the late 1930s, 1940s, and early 1950s, and there was a muted, but perceptible, process of rehabilitating long-unmentionable home-bred authorities such as Lev Vygotsky. Characteristic too was the revival, in a restricted and timid way, of educational sociology, which brought with it the redeployment of an instrument that had been left to rot since the early 1930s.[87] As in the 1920s, empirical methods were often used to underline conceptual innovation: it was common for surveys to be cited in support of the argument that children learned more effectively if their interest was kept alive.[88]

Though discipline remained the ideal, there was a small-scale reassessment of the best ways of achieving good order in practical terms. Despite its forbidding title and some ritualised nods in the direction of Makarenko, an editorial on 'Strengthening Discipline and Order in Schools' published in *Soviet Pedagogy* in November 1955 actually spoke out against excessively harsh control, and pointed out that dull teaching was often a contributory factor to poor discipline.[89] This emphasis on the need for 'interesting' educational work was typical of the times:

while teachers who revived the 'extreme' methods of the 1920s, such as project work, were likely to find themselves the target of sharp criticism from officially empowered sources, the need to foster 'active learning' became a ubiquitous discussion topic of the day.[90] And attention was given to the importance of teaching non-academic subjects, such as music and art, as a way of varying the timetable and aiding concentration.[91]

But none of this constituted an endorsement, in a major sense, of the ethos of 'free education'. Just as in literature for parents, so in literature for teachers, the main authorities were still nineteenth-century Russian, and particularly Soviet, pedagogical theorists. The standard pedagogical textbooks of the era were lightly revised versions of Stalinist originals, and a formal ban was never placed on pre-1953 methodological materials, which made it possible or even likely that these would continue to be used where new materials were hard to come by.[92] And the leading pedagogical authorities remained nineteenth-century Russian writers, more particularly, Soviet writers such as Makarenko and Sukhomlinsky. The latter was in signal respects less authoritarian than Makarenko: for example, he asserted that 'Every child is an artist', and he stressed the importance of creative education in the broadest sense – including the organisation of school festivals – as a method of developing a rounded personality.[93] However, his pedagogy remained thoroughly teacher-centred, and in this sense could not be described as libertarian, by comparison either with the practices current in experimental schools in the 1920s or with the practices that were coming into favour in America and Western Europe in the 1960s. Notable, too, was the fact that Vygotsky's works, say, appeared in a small edition (30,000 copies) published in six volumes by the Academy of Pedagogical Sciences – in other words, an academic publication aimed, in the first place, at the libraries of pedagogical institutes, rather than for use as a textbook for training teachers themselves.[94] And the re-emergence of this one thinker, only loosely associated with the paedological movement to begin with, in no respect signalled a rehabilitation of 'paedology' as such, which remained a problematic concept up to the end of Soviet power.

Equally, the academic priorities of the past still remained in place, with subjects such as maths, sciences, history, and literature the core of the programme.[95] Pupils were still expected to cope with a large workload. The legal requirements for the setting of homework (which, it should be noted, established norms rather than maximums), ranged from one hour per day in Class 1 (for 7-year olds) up to four hours per day in Class 8 (for 15-year-olds). This was on top of a school day that ran from 24 hours per week for the lowest forms up to 30 hours a week for Classes 5–9 (and 32 hours per week for the top class). At the end of every school year, pupils underwent quite a formidable programme of examinations, especially those in Years 8 and 10 (who were sitting a national qualification).[96] And 'patriotic education' remained central to the programme. The 10 November 1966 decree 'On the Further Improvement of the General Secondary School' placed 'the formation of an elevated Communist consciousness' second only to 'furnishing pupils with the elements of learning' among the purposes of Soviet education. While concrete achievement targets in terms of 'learning' were not specified, it was stated that pupils were to leave school with a grasp of 'the laws of social development', 'the revolutionary and labouring traditions of the Soviet people', and with 'an elevated sense of Soviet patriotism' and of 'readiness to defend the socialist Motherland'. Similarly, the 1970 Statute of the Soviet School stated that the school should not only provide pupils with a 'general secondary education' and foster their 'all-round development', but also build a 'Marxist-Leninist world view' and a love of the motherland and of the Communist Party.[97]

As in the Stalin era, the subjects particularly affected by the emphasis on 'patriotic education' were history and Russian literature. Into the late Soviet period, the teaching of both subjects continued to be extremely rigid. A 1975 article telling teachers how to use Gaidar's story *Military Secret* for the 'patriotic education' of Class 4 (11-year-olds) suggested asking the children in the group to complete the following questionnaire:

1. What do you know about the writer A. Gaidar?
2. Which books by Gaidar have you read?
3. Of those you have read, which have you particularly liked, and why?
4. Which illustrations from *Military Secret* can you remember?
5. Which heroes made the biggest impression on you?
6. What *was* the 'military secret' that the enemies couldn't guess?
7. Did you understand everything in the book?[98]

40 Pioneer rally to celebrate the movement's sixtieth anniversary, Leningrad, 1982. The woman standing on the right of the tribunal is Valentina Matvienko, Governor of St Petersburg from 2003.

The focus on role models (indicated here by the question, 'Which heroes made the biggest impression on you?') was absolutely routine: even in the late 1970s, when a greater emphasis on imagination had become permissible, it was still possible for a critic to comment that a certain author's stories, while perhaps a touch over-moralistic, had at the same time the virtue of 'teaching young readers about nobility in human behaviour'.[99] Thus the underlying values of Soviet pedagogy remained consistent, with pressure for change limited to details of methodology.[100] It was not until the very end of the Soviet era that traditional pedagogy started to be openly questioned, a process initiated by a swingeing attack on the Academy of Pedagogical Sciences at the February 1988 plenum of the Communist Party, and continued by a wholesale restructuring of the Academy as the 'Russian Academy of Education' in the early 1990s.[101]

'No Children, Only Cactuses'

Sentimental or control-centred views of childhood were not ubiquitous. By the 1980s, a significant section of the Russian cultural intelligentsia had begun to see childhood as an undesirable state of dependency and malleability. Interpreted in this sense, 'childhood' became an allegory for the subordinate position of the adult Soviet citizen, constantly patronised and deceived by his or her mentors. In the words of a 1987 sketch by the satirical comedian Mikhail Zhvanetsky: 'This isn't a country, it's a kindergarten. Radio and television announcers talk to us all as though we were feeble-minded, or children.'[102]

The sense that childhood might be an oppressive or distasteful condition was at least distantly allied with another anti-child orientation of the post-Stalin years: a revival of the modernist mistrust of producing children in the first place. Rather than being asserted with defiant self-confidence, as in the early twentieth century, distaste for children was now articulated with guilt and fear. In a poem by Boris Slutsky, for example, the Russian intelligentsia's accumulation of 'cultured' possessions and knowledge and its 'procreatophobia' were self-ironisingly contrasted:

> Real people have children. We only have cactuses
> standing silent and frigid. [...]
> The more books, the fewer babies,
> The more ideas, the fewer children.[103]

In terms of government policy, the 1970s and 1980s saw a concerted effort to encourage child-bearing in the face of what was described as 'the demographic crisis' – the declining birth rate in the Russian Federation (as opposed to the Central Asian republics of the Soviet Union). Newspaper articles presented the Russian public with stark statistics of low population replacement in the west of the Soviet Union and outlined the economic threat posed by an ageing population.[104] Sentimental images of young children had the obvious function of sustaining this campaign. But, on the other hand, they could only contribute to the inverse relationship between 'ideas' and 'babies' in a context where some sections of the intelligentsia were becoming increasingly impatient with the celebration of childhood to begin with.

At the same time as acquiring an increasing solidity and dominance, children were beginning to vanish from view altogether. In the early Soviet era, the child had represented a confident national identity, whether symbolising the internationalist ambitions of the USSR and the possibilities of mass participation in politics (in the first fifteen years of Soviet power), or multiplicitous but harmonious national populism, under Stalin's wise governance (as during the next two decades). By the late 1980s, the sense that even children were disillusioned and cynical had taken hold, bringing in its wake the feeling that the times were profoundly out of joint, now that those traditionally associated with hope for the future had also lost their ideals.[105] For the first time in a hundred years, children had – temporarily at least – become associated primarily with pain and suffering, as a traumatic reassessment of the actual achievements of the Soviet regime with regard to ensuring children's happiness began, and as children also came to be seen as the quintessential victims of marketisation and of social collapse, at threat from everyone, even the crews of invading UFOs.[106] In the despairing words of one young woman watching the tanks in the street in August 1991, 'Why did I give birth?'[107]

The decades after 1953 saw a partial – but only a partial – reversion to the ideals of independent, assertive childhood that had dominated Soviet society during the 1920s. There was an upsurge of interest in genres such as the adventure story, with its focus on young male protagonists. With the demise of the Stalin cult, the beribboned small girls who had formerly been represented as the ideal subjects of the Soviet ruler faded into the background; girls of this kind still occasionally figured in photographs of Khrushchev and Brezhnev, but such images no longer had the canonical status of the pictures of Gelya or Mamlakat that had been disseminated in their thousands in the 1930s and 1940s. The revived tolerance of assertiveness was reflected in the stirrings of liberalism in pedagogy, in the resurgence of an interest in 'children's art' as a phenomenon distinct from adult creativity, and in reforms in the handling of juvenile delinquency within the criminal justice system. Once more, work in art forms directed at children – illustrated books, cartoon films, literature for children – became a recourse for artists whose aims to do innovative work were hampered by the continuing hegemony of Socialist Realism in art forms aimed at adults.

Nevertheless, as in the child's poem 'Let There Always Be Sunshine', made famous by Kornei Chukovsky, the old stereotypes of children – particularly young children – as perpetually joyful, innocent, and docile persisted. In children's literature, the canons established by Chukovsky himself, by Samuil Marshak, and by other long-established writers such as Agniya Barto and Sergei Mikhalkov still held sway. Indeed, the repression to which Chukovsky, in particular, had been subjected on several occasions between 1917 and 1953 gave his poetry, including works reprinted throughout the Stalin years as well as the long-invisible *From Two to Five*, a kind of counter-cultural lustre for the Russian intelligentsia. Espousing the myth of 'happy childhood' came to seem a respectable position for a Soviet intellectual who was coolly disposed to Soviet power, as well as for an enthusiastic supporter of the regime.

Yet there were also some sceptical voices. By the 1970s, a satirical view of the Soviet Union as a 'paradise for children' in the sense of a place that reduced adults to infantile status as well had begun to make an impact, and there was increasing anxiety about bringing children into a world that was so little equipped to provide them with a perfectly happy childhood. The scene was now set for the agonising debates about the effectiveness of child welfare provision, particularly in total institutions, that accompanied the collapse of Soviet power, and with it the collapse of the myth of 'happy childhood' that had sustained the authority of the Soviet leadership for seven decades and more.[108]

PART II

CHILDREN ON THEIR OWN: STREET WAIFS, ORPHANAGE INMATES

Chapter 5

The Kindness of Strangers, 1890–1917

O dear Ma,
Don't go early to your grave:
You know yourself,
An orphan's life is no life.[1]

Throughout the twentieth century, professionals, politicians, ideologues, and members of the public at large assumed that 'normal' existence for children meant being brought up by their natural parents. At the same time, increasing awareness that some children might have to endure abuse and neglect from their parents, along with rising rates of child abandonment, made the provision of alternative care a crucial ideological concern and practical necessity. Because successive Russian political regimes remained attached to an ideal of the rational institution as a utopia of human transformation and a crucible for new social forms, such 'alternative care', throughout the 'long twentieth century', was almost always provided in orphanages – known as 'orphan houses' or 'houses of moral education', or, in the term that came to be preferred after 1917, 'children's homes'. This chapter traces both the history of the processes by which children ended up in need of such alternative care and the evolution, over time, of the facilities that were provided for them.

Children in Need

Where families were pressed by want, children suffered commensurately. If supporting them became an impossible burden on the household, parents had few alternatives. Certainly, it might be possible to find a childless family that was prepared to take the child in: in some areas, informal fostering of this sort was customary, and an adopted child was likely to end up with full inheritance rights.[2] There were even places where fostering was formalised through the custom of 'selling' the child to the fostering couple.[3] A traditional form of welfare support at village level was 'the rota system' (*po ocheredi/po cheredu*), according to which needy persons (orphans, the old, the homeless) were parcelled out house to house, a day here, a day there. Communal forms of charity such as this have sometimes been romanticised in retrospect, but zemstvo workers who encountered them face to face in the late nineteenth and early twentieth centuries tended to report that compassion was thin on the ground: it was hard to get villagers to contribute to food handouts or to collections to fund charitable institutions. In the circumstances, those forcibly billeted on their neighbours could often expect a thin time.[4]

If fostering could not be arranged, a child whose family could not support it and who could not find work was likely to find itself fending for a living through begging. A survey of welfare arrangements across the Russian Empire in the first years of the twentieth century recorded that children and the old made up a significant proportion of mendicants in some areas (for example, Smolensk and Yaroslavl' provinces).[5] Orphans were likely to join this group: according to traditional custom, they were entitled to inherit movable property, but not their parents' share in the communal land allocation.[6] Many traditional songs lamented the plight of *siroty* (a term that could be applied to any person without family, including widows or widowers, not just children), but pity was not necessarily forthcoming from the community at large. In the words of one early twentieth-century commentator in Yaroslavl', orphans sensed the 'hostility of their fellow-villagers', and hence 'their hearts grew tough and maliciously inclined towards society'. The path towards mendicancy was hard to escape.[7]

Illegitimate children – deemed the living embodiment of their parents' sin – were another category of despised and marginal juvenile. They were at serious risk of ill treatment: a full 23 per cent of the cruelty cases scrutinised by the Society for the Legal Protection of Minors in 1900–14 involved children born outside marriage.[8] And they were subject to the opprobrium of the entire community. As Kornei Chukovsky, born to an unmarried laundress in St Petersburg, remembered: 'I was so terribly ashamed of saying that I was "illegitimate". We used to use the awful word *baistruk* (bastard).'[9] Chukovsky felt so sensitive about his family origins that he was, in middle age, to destroy letters he had written as a young man addressing the topic, and refer to it only in his private diaries.

Both orphans and illegitimate children might find themselves packed off directly to an institution, such as the Imperial Foundling Homes in St Petersburg and Moscow, instituted in the reign of Catherine II. These enormous institutions absorbed 5,000–10,000 children a year, and had as many as 30,000 foundlings on their books at one time, including those who were farmed out in villages; children born outside wedlock made up the overwhelming proportion (over 90 per cent) of their population.[10] The picture was different in other orphanages, since the Imperial Foundling Homes' traditional policy of anonymous admissions made these a favoured destination for unmarried mothers, but even so, the proportion of illegitimate children was unrepresentatively large, compared with the proportion of such children among live births: in 1904, such children comprised nearly 40 per cent of the 'clientele' of the institutions run by the Empress Maria Department, responsible for the Imperial Foundling Homes and a bewildering range of other children's institutions (31,535 of a total figure of 80,000).[11]

But institutionalisation from infancy was not the only possible fate. A bastard child might grow up with its mother for at least the first few years; equally, an orphan might lose its parents at any stage during childhood. And once 'rootless' children were mobile, social alienation often brought, as a next step, migration to the city – where begging was likely to be more lucrative, and possibilities of occasional earning (through criminal activity if nothing else) were richer. Here such children flowed into the tide of abandoned and orphaned children – a volatile and extremely varied group drawn from orphans and abandoned children, runaway apprentices, abused children fleeing their parents, and mentally disturbed youngsters. Once again, 'bastards' were strongly represented. A survey of 803 beggars in Basmannyi district of Moscow in 1898 established that around 12 per cent were illegitimate.[12] But they were not necessarily the most psychologically damaged category of street child: according to a welfare worker who dealt with girl criminals, and who reported to the First Congress on Family Upbringing in 1913, all 600 of those she had helped over the previous three years had ended up in trouble as the result of a family conflict.[13]

Lone children growing up in cities – whether they had moved in from the villages, or been born in the town – had little in the way of support to rely on. There were no reception centres or individual inspectors deputed to look out for them and transfer them to institutionalised care. Most ended up, sooner or later, living on the streets. Since living on one's own offered scant chances of survival, children forgathered in groups, pooling knowledge about where to find a night's shelter (adult dosshouses, or shelters aimed specifically at children), or a tolerable night's sleep outdoors (by perching on hot-water pipes, for instance).[14]

The two capitals, Moscow and St Petersburg, had areas which were notorious for the prevalence of abandoned children. These included Khitrov market in Moscow (a haunt of socially marginal and criminal adults as well), and Smolenskaya Square, a scarcely more savoury area of the city centre on the east bank of the Moscow River opposite the Kiev Station.[15] In St Petersburg, favoured places included the Uprava area of Nevsky Prospekt, as well as the Vyazemsky warehouses abutting on the Haymarket (Sennaya ploshchad') in St Petersburg. Depending on their 'home patch', gangs of children would gravitate towards particular areas in pursuit of crime. The Uprava pickpockets found lucrative pickings on Nevsky Prospekt or around the Nikolaevsky (later Moscow) station, and the 'technologists' (those living in the region of the Technological Institute on Zabalkansky Prospekt) swarmed along that prospekt and its side roads. For their part, the 'Haymarket Gang' (*senniki*) prospected around a particularly poor area with a notorious flea market that was the setting for scenes in Dostoevsky's *Crime and Punishment*, and a gathering-place for adult tramps and thieves.

Here, according to contemporary descriptions, the children banded together in groups and lived rough, camping out in any shelter they could find, which might include rubbish dumps (a good source of heat and of salvageable materials). They survived from hand to mouth, bingeing (if the takings from thefts allowed) on tobacco and alcohol. Some took jobs, with newspaper-selling being an especially popular occupation; others turned to crime in order to scrape a living, and

41 Children at a city market,
W. Barnes Steveni, *Things Seen in
Russia* (1913).

particularly to theft.[16] A. A. Bakhtiarov's *Belly of St Petersburg* portrayed a street
boy selling new books, seasonal goods such as flowers in spring, or Christmas tree
ornaments in winter – and starting to pilfer when all else failed.[17] Criminological
studies of the 1900s indicated that pickpocketing and other forms of robbery were
rife in central areas of Moscow and St Petersburg within easy reach of areas where
abandoned children found shelter, with most of the offenders (if figures for arrest
are anything to go by) being boys.[18]

Girls, on the other hand, predominated among those involved in another form
of criminal activity, prostitution. Around 10 per cent of adult prostitutes in the
early twentieth century had first become involved in the activity when they were
under 15 years old; just under 10 per cent of girls summonsed to the St Petersburg
juvenile court in its first year of operation had been working as prostitutes.[19] The
extremely high rates that clients with sexual purposes in mind were prepared to
pay for access to pre-pubescent girls were certainly a factor: one early twentieth-
century source states that the charge for access to such a child in the specialist
brothels of Moscow was then at least 100 roubles a time, more than three times
the monthly wages earned by a housemaid.[20] There was also a small number of

cases involving sexually disturbed children for whom prostitution seems to have been a path to the streets, rather than vice versa. A 9-year-old girl recovered in the centre of the city by the Moscow House of Charity in the 1900s had begun to offer herself to passers-by for money despite her mother's disapproval, expressed in the form of beatings. Once in the safe house, the girl had to be kept on her own, as she constantly swore, beat her head on the wall, attempted to bite anyone within reach, and offered herself for sex to any other inmate of the facility, male or female.[21]

Street children often became involved in consensual sexual activity at an age that struck observers as shockingly young.[22] Other widespread leisure activities included drinking (after prohibition had been imposed in 1915, eau-de-Cologne and illegally distilled *kharzha* were more likely tipples than the traditional vodka), gambling, fighting, and the singing of songs about street life:

> My father he pegged out in clink,
> Locked up and wrapped in chains:
> My mam bore me that very night
> In a ditch beside a fence.
>
> When I grew up, the people all
> Would yell as past I went:
> 'You're just a bum who has no dad,
> Born underneath a fence!'[23]

The appearance and behaviour of street children – dirty, foul-mouthed, rapacious, and violent – perturbed and distressed their elders still more than did the sight of indigent adults. The sight of these unfortunates cruelly undermined the preferred understanding of childhood as joyful and innocent. Popularly known as 'nobody's children' (*nich'i deti*), they were referred to by educated observers as 'unsupervised children' (*besprizornye*), a neologism that came into use during the 1880s.[24]

The solution to *besprizornost'* was seen to lie in the provision of the 'care' and 'supervision' that children were held to lack. Articles by welfare workers and jurists assumed that life on the streets spelled legal and moral catastrophe: parental neglect and juvenile crime were two sides of the same phenomenon. In the homes of alcoholic parents, particularly, were bred children like the boy recorded by the criminologist D. A. Dril' in 1908, who 'smokes, thieves, swears, masturbates, and blackens the name of his own mother'.[25] Unsupervised children were a threat not just to themselves or their victims, but to society at large, 'infecting' other children in the locality with the bacilli of immorality.[26] Moreover, the 'infection' threatened to become an epidemic especially after the onset of the First World War. In this context commentators could cite a 284 per cent rise, between 1910 and 1916, in crimes perpetrated by minors across the Russian Empire and in figures from the juvenile courts in Moscow and Petrograd, indicating sharp rises in misdemeanours that reached trial in those two cities.[27]

Ever present though the figure of the *besprizornyi* was in discussions of 'modern life', especially after 1910, the protection and control of 'unsupervised' children was only one of many child welfare issues preoccupying the minds of educated Russians in the late Imperial era. Others included infant mortality; poor nutrition; the exploitation of young workers; child prostitution; abuse and neglect on the part of parents; and the plight of what in another time and place would be termed 'latchkey children', or juveniles who had to fend for themselves while their parents were at work. It was widely argued that such problems were especially prominent in Russia, as opposed to Western Europe and America, and that facilities for combating them were inadequate.

In a historical sense, these accusations were in some respects unjust. It was only in the mid-nineteenth century that a serious gulf opened up between welfare provision in Russia and in the West, and not until the 1900s that state provision in the latter started to develop apace. There was more weight behind the accusations of lack of direction and co-ordination in Russian government welfare policy. The structure of state support varied considerably from place to place, as was evident in different policies for dealing with orphans. Where zemstva existed, they might run their own orphanages, 'farm out' infants to private individuals, subsidise charitable initiatives, devolve duties to zemstva at local level, or play no part in supporting homeless and orphaned children at all (as in the cities of St Petersburg, Moscow, and Novgorod at the end of the nineteenth century, where the only orphanage facilities were government-run).[28] State provision as such was just as confused. Figures from 1899 indicate that around twenty different government departments were responsible for overseeing charitable institutions of one kind or another. The major specialised authority was the Empress Maria Department. In 1909, figures stood at 26 orphanages in Moscow, 28 in St Petersburg, and nearly 250 in the provinces, 24 institutes for blind children, 25 for the deaf and dumb, seven 'village shelters', 10 hospitals, two orphanage-hospitals, one reception centre for homeless children, the Imperial Clinical Gynaecological Institute for Poor Women, maternity homes in Moscow and St Petersburg, three children's hospitals in St Petersburg and one in Moscow, and a children's library.[29] But philanthropic work was also overseen by offices in ministries with a quite different remit (such as the Transport Ministry, with seven charitable institutions).[30] Additionally, some government departments had, at best, a 'semi-state' character: they acted not as sources of finance for institutions, but as regulators for private initiatives (publishing model statutes, organising inspections). This applied not just to the Ministry of Internal Affairs, which was explicitly responsible for supervising voluntary societies, but also to the Imperial Philanthropic Society and the Empress Maria Department. Certainly, there was generous support for individual institutions, particularly the Imperial Foundling Homes, which were receiving funding to the tune of 1.5 million roubles in 1914.[31] But other institutions had a much less privileged position: shortage of funds was the object of lamentation in almost every publication about welfare issues issued in Russia during the late nineteenth and early twentieth centuries.

Equally striking was the erratic spread of funding and of charitable work.

The reforms of the 1860s had ostensibly delegated the supervision of welfare and primary medicine to the zemstva, elected local administrative bodies at district (*uezd*) and provincial (*guberniya*) level. But not all areas of the Russian Empire had zemstva in operation; even in provinces that did, provision was erratic, depending a great deal on the priorities of the local administrators in allocating their always scant resources. The same was true of local administrations in towns and cities. In 1901, 209 towns in European Russia and 16 in Siberia spent nothing at all on welfare.[32] A voluntary scheme was established in 1899, allowing and encouraging cities across Russia to adopt the Moscow system of voluntary 'guardianships' supervising social support in individual urban districts. But only forty cities signed up for the scheme in the first ten years of its operation.[33] Private charity was equally erratic. An inspector who visited dozens of provincial orphanages on behalf of the Empress Maria Department called at an orphanage in a rich village where the keeper's wife was dressed in St Petersburg fashions and gold jewellery, and the children had better-appointed metal bedsteads than would have been found in most city orphanages. But this was exceptional: it was commoner for homes to have good food, but no washrooms (as in Ekaterinburg), or to be clean and tidy, but in need of repairs (Irbit). And there was also a proportion of places were conditions were worryingly bad – as in Ufa, where the children were fed soggy bread and cold soup that had fermented, or Chistopol', where the kitchen and bath-house were filthy, and the vegetable garden overgrown. In his summing-up, the inspector praised the dedication of staff, which was evident also in the descriptions of the best homes, and emphasised that under-funding was the main cause of practical problems.[34]

It was often hard to secure even small amounts of money to underwrite measures that would have had an immediate and beneficial impact on children's lives. For example, in 1913 the St Petersburg zemstvo turned down a proposal to provide hot lunches to children in city schools on the grounds that this would be 'too expensive', despite evidence that nearly a quarter of children in primary schools were undernourished.[35] Setting up institutions such as orphanages was considerably more costly; not surprisingly, therefore, institutional coverage remained thin. In 1902, even Moscow and St Petersburg had a distribution of only 14–16 charitable institutions per 100,000 population; distribution in provincial Russia was somewhere between four and eight institutions per 100,000, with Siberia falling off the scale at less than one institution per 200,000 inhabitants.[36] Institutional provision for children was no better than it was for other categories of the population. As late as 1916, the total number of orphans of peasant origin holding places in closed institutions across European Russia was only 36,905, and the budget for them 4,946,396 roubles. In the whole of Siberia, only just over 2,000 orphans were in institutional care, and in the Baltic provinces and north-western Russia, around 1,200.[37]

While remaining convinced of the superiority of institutional care, then, the Tsarist government (unlike its Soviet successor) was largely prepared to leave the provision of such care to individual initiative. The era of the Great Reforms was accompanied by a very significant expansion in the number of charitable societies and institutions across Russia. At the start of the 1860s, there were only 92 charities across Russia, and 249 institutions. By 1871, these figures had risen to 798 and 809, and by 1899 to 3,504 and 2,875.[38] Charitable efforts directed at children followed the same general pattern. Between 1801 and 1860, 198 new institutions offering full-time care to children came into existence; between 1861 and 1899, the number founded was 1,010.[39]

Of major importance was the Society for the Guardianship of Poor and Sick Children (also known as the Blue Cross), which was running about thirty children's institutions by as early as 1898, including a 260-place crèche, three hostels, and a canteen serving free or nearly free meals to 180 children a day. The society also organised an inspection network (through its Section for the Defence of Children from Cruel Treatment) to check on the conditions of apprentices throughout the capital, and provided shelter to children who needed to be removed from abusive employers (there were around 100 on the books in 1898).[40] The society had branches in provincial cities as well as in the capitals. The Kazan' branch, for instance, organised a Refuge for Homeless Children, opened in 1890, which was catering for 135 children by 1910, and a children's hospital, which was completed in 1899 and which handled 460 in-patients and 2,516 out-patients in its eleventh year of operation.[41] Among smaller charities, notable was Children's Aid, set up in 1885, whose journal of the same name reported on energetic activities in a range of areas, including the prevention of cruelty to children, support to needy schoolchildren, and the organisation of facilities for the blind, alongside sentimental poems about street waifs and children 'saved' from death by charitable endeavour.[42] In 1897, the Society for the Guardianship of Homeless Children began operating, with a hostel sheltering about sixty such individuals.[43] Activity increased still further in the early twentieth century, and especially after 1905, when founding voluntary associations of all kinds became more straightforward. Children's charities that emerged in the 1900s and 1910s included the Society for the Defence of Children from Cruel Treatment, set up in 1903, whose patron was Grand Duchess Olga Aleksandrovna, the Society for the Care of Crippled and Idiot Children (set up in 1912), Aid to Mothers (set up in 1911), the League for the Defence of Children (set up in Kiev in spring 1914), and the Society for the Legal Protection of Minors (set up in 1914).[44]

The foundation of children's charities appealed to philanthropists for several reasons. More radically inclined activists saw them as a way of reforming society 'from below' by targeting 'future citizens', and as a way of addressing human-rights issues that were otherwise considered taboo. For conservatives, separate work with children was a method of protecting these vulnerable individuals from the threat of corruption by badly behaved adults.[45] There were also general private charities that offered support to children: one example was the Society for the Guardianship of Wounded Soldiers, Cripples, and Abandoned Children, run by a group of philanthropists in St Petersburg.[46]

But, while voluntary work became the backbone of welfare provision by default, the Tsarist government's ingrained suspicion of associationism on the grounds that it might be politically subversive hampered the development of the voluntary sector. As one survey of charities remarked in 1907, many existed in an extra-legal limbo: had the law been enforced, they would have ceased to exist. No wonder that the work of such charities was characterised by 'atomisation and disorganisation', and a lack of focus in targeting specific welfare issues.[47]

The dedicated children's charities varied considerably in the extent to which they had a focus and a set of discrete objectives. Some were specialised – there was, for example, a number of groups concerned particularly with pre-natal and infant care.[48] The Society for the Legal Protection of Minors (founded in 1914) occupied itself with lobbying for more stringent legislation to combat the abuse of children, especially within the family.[49] Child labour was the province of the Guardianship of Minors Existing by the Fruits of their own Labours, a St Petersburg organisation which ran subsidised hostels for young workers, while the Children's Town (Detskii gorodok) in St Petersburg set up 'summer playgrounds' to offer 'rational leisure' to poor children in cities.[50]

The majority of organisations, however, were not so specific in their aims. The St Petersburg Guardianship of Poor and Sick Children, founded by Anna Balitskaya in 1882, had, by the 1910s, 12 sections in different parts of St Petersburg, and 38 different institutions under its care. The society's efforts stretched into every area of welfare endeavour: hostels for young workers; grants of clothes and footwear to children attending trade schools; clinics; maternity hospitals;

42 Soup kitchen, Nizhni Novgorod province, 1892.

cheap canteens; 'summer colonies' to allow city children to spend time in the Russian countryside; orphanages; free kindergartens for working women; and a special low-cost hostel for working women, provided with child-care facilities. The variety of initiatives was not necessarily detrimental: the society had a high profile and prominent supporters, and its Blue Flower Day was successful in raising funds.[51] With some of the smaller societies, though, dispersal of energies seems to have been more of a problem. In 1912, a new St Petersburg society, Children's World, published its constitution, stating the intention to organise educational facilities such as evening classes and preparatory schools, libraries and reading rooms, public lectures, art classes, and children's festivals (including tree-planting sessions), excursions, games, sports and gymnasiums, alongside clinics, summer colonies, and sanatoria. However, the society then disappeared from view, having apparently failed to realise even part of its ambitious set of hygienic and educational objectives.[52]

But, if some societies had a remit so large that they failed to establish any kind of separate identity, others were so particularist that the term 'clique' might have been more appropriate. These included welfare organisations attached to specific schools and institutes, for example, or charities aimed at raising money for the children of professional groups. Some of this last group were quite rich relative to the size of the population group they represented. For example, the Society for the Welfare of Doctors' Orphaned Children (Obshchestvo popecheniya o sirotakh-detyakh vrachei) had an income of 19,444 roubles in 1910 and 34,063 roubles in 1911.[53]

From the start of the twentieth century, though, increasing efforts were made not only to organise individual initiatives, but to unify and rationalise charitable work as a whole. While the members of the Imperial Philanthropic Society were rebuffed when they tried to organise a co-ordinating drive of St Petersburg charity groups in the 1870s, and again in 1891, harmonisation at the level of specialised children's charities was to prove more successful after 1900. The Blue Cross managed to set up an umbrella group of fifty children's charities in 1902, known as the Union of Children's Aid Organisations (Soyuz uchrezhdenii detskoi pomoshchi); though the actual achievements of the Union were modest, being more or less limited to the issuing of guides and other circulation of information, the recognition of a common interest was none the less important.[54] And, when a national society of charitable organisations – the All-Russian Union of Societies, Organisations, and Activists in Public and Private Relief (Vserossiiskii Soyuz obshchestv, uchrezhdenii i deyatelei po obshchestvennomu i chastnomu prizreniyu) – was finally established in 1908, children's charities were drawn into the support network, and children's issues figured prominently in the first Russian National Congress on Charity, held in 1910.[55]

The changes in the late nineteenth and early twentieth centuries did not relate only to the practical world of 'small deeds', as philanthropic activities were contemptuously described by revolution-minded anti-gradualists of the day. There was also a wide-ranging, and dynamic, discussion of welfare policy, ranging from macroscopic issues (how to structure and rationalise provision) to microscopic ones (the nature of appropriate care within institutions or welfare structures).

To begin with the first: the late Imperial era saw growing consciousness, both within and outside the establishment, of the need for integrated policy at the highest level. In the words of an official history of Russian philanthropy, published in 1907:

> Only a totally rational organisation of public welfare and philanthropy, by which is meant the well-organised and co-ordinated interaction of all kinds of aid to those in need, can offer real aid to the unfortunate of all ages and all states of life. It stands to reason that aid to children has to be directed towards nurturing those deprived of parental care into physically and morally healthy young men and women, and providing them with knowledge and skills sufficient to allow them to fulfil their needs by earning their bread in the future.[56]

The emphasis on 'organisation' and 'co-ordination' is striking. Gone were the days when piecemeal effort was considered enough. Equally striking is the requirement for provision of care to those from 'all states in life', alongside the provision of a social model that sets out specialist care on the basis of age rather than social status. In other words, care should be offered to all, and modulated in terms of universal characteristics, not class-specific ones.

The First World War, which added hugely to the burden on welfare institutions, provided a further galvanising force to the co-ordination of philanthropic activities. Above all, it generated a new preparedness on the part of the Tsarist regime to sponsor charitable endeavours. The Tatiana Committee, set up to handle the needs of refugees, took a particular interest in the welfare of children: efforts were made to reunite families and to provide displaced children with education in their own languages.[57]

Orphanages Old and New

The generous underwriting of charities dealing with doctors' daughters and the like reveals the persistence of status-consciousness as expressed in a sense of primary affinity to a social estate (*soslovie, sostoyanie*) and to the impact of this on welfare policy ('looking after one's own'). The earliest orphanages had been estate-specific: the Imperial Foundling Home for peasant and plebeian children, the Catherine Institute for female orphans of gentry rank, etc. These institutions continued to function, with their original remit, right up to the Revolution, as did other estate-specific institutions, such as those for plebeian townspeople (*meshchane*), or for the orphans of merchants (*kuptsy*)[58] – despite the fact that the vast majority of needy children came from peasant or working-class families. But sensitivity to the needs of non-gentry children improved in the late Imperial era. A new type of institution for peasant orphans was the Agricultural Shelter for Village Orphans set up under the Department of Empress Mariya Fedorovna in

1891,[59] and a survey of zemstvo-run orphanages as of 1 January 1914 established that around three-quarters of the 39,366 children living in such institutions across the Russian Empire were of peasant origin.[60]

Some institutions (including some new ones) might still be 'estate-led' in character, but others were committed by their constitutions to providing care for all the needy, no matter from what social group they came. The constitution of the Prince Oldenburg Shelter (Priyut Printsa Ol'denburgskogo), for example, founded in 1890, specifically stated the institution's aim to be 'the moral and intellectual education of children of both sexes, primarily orphans, *without distinction of [social] origin, standing, and religious confession*'. It specified quite a wide-ranging curriculum, particularly for girls, who were to receive tuition in languages and history, not just handcrafts and the three Rs.[61] Concern for the welfare of peasant children (whose presence in the population of the needy was commensurate with the overwhelming dominance of peasants in the Russian population overall: they made up almost three-quarters of the overall orphanage population on 1 January 1914) did not have to mean concern to tie peasant children to village life. A wide variety of institutions, including city and town hostels as well as workhouses, offered support to this sector of society, some alongside other social groups.[62]

Nevertheless, arrangements for children from 'inferior' social groups often reinforced status differentials. Emphasis was placed on providing training in manual labour: the 'workhouses' (*doma trudolyubiya*) in cities taught boys cobbling and carpentry, and girls sewing and housework, while the 'village refuges' provided a programme of agricultural work. The explicit function of these refuges was indeed to provide a bulwark against the perceived 'decay' of village life by means of an infusion of industrious, well-trained, morally sound, and pious young people, enriched by a sense of God's goodness and of religious principle.[63] The model charters for such institutions were decisive about the arrangements for moral education, specifying the need to have on the staff a supervisor (*smotritel'*), 'a person renowned for his or her impeccable character', as well as a tutor in religious knowledge. They were considerably vaguer about the arrangements for ensuring hygiene and comfort, though a medical examination was stipulated for each child upon arrival.[64]

While the tone of 'village refuge' publicity material was particularly strident, the motif of 'social correction' was extremely widespread. The 1885 charter of the Moscow Children's Aid society stated that its purpose was to 'ensure the welfare of orphans and the children of poor parents of all estates, working for the religious and moral education of these and the provision for them of tuition in handcrafts and trades'.[65] In 1910, the inmates of the Refuge for Homeless Children run by the Society of the Guardianship of Poor and Sick Children in Kazan' would rise at six, 'carry out their simple toilette', and, after twenty minutes of prayers, and a breakfast consisting of tea and bread (with milk only on non-fast days), would proceed to the workshops, where they spent most of the day. Leisure activities – walks, boat trips, and so on – were organised, but only on holidays, and 'free play' was not built into the programme. Time not spent on work was expected to be dedicated to useful activities: making the inmates' clothes in the case of girls, book-binding, shoe-mending, stocking-knitting and reading for boys.[66]

Campaigners for working-class children in cities tended to highlight the function of charity in curbing social danger. The 1898 prospectus for the Children's Workhouse in Vyazemsky Palace, on the Fontanka, set up in an area of St Petersburg with extremely large numbers of children (and adults) living rough, clearly represented this missionary drive. The home's purpose was to give aid to the children living locally, who were described as ragged, shoeless, filthy, often orphaned and usually without birth certificates, 'lacking any conception of religion and morality, and undergoing neither intellectual training nor character education'.[67] One notes the order of the abstract nouns specified – religion, morality, education – and the way in which this locates moral principle above practical aid. Priorities in government regulation were similar: a survey of orphanages in St Petersburg province from 1911 included records of illness and of the inmates' further destinations after leaving, but also records of the children's 'most significant misdemeanours', and of the types of punishment administered (detention, deprivation of sweet things or of treats, a ban on visits from relatives).[68]

Publicity materials for charitable institutions likewise stressed the centrality of morals. It was pointed out that orphanages and shelters had their own chapels, that the day opened and closed with prayers, and that religious and moral instruction was an important part of the educational syllabus.[69] The collections of photographs of institutional activities that were produced for fund-raising purposes always included shots of the chapel, alongside pictures of the institute Christmas tree, well-scrubbed groups of children playing outside, spotless dormitories, and so on.[70] Yet the rationale for this was practical as well as ideological: devout religious believers were the most likely to reach into their pockets. Even in the last decades before the Revolution, the Orthodox Church was one of the most efficient co-ordinators of welfare activity in the Russian Empire. In 1899, 2,148 of the 7,349 charitable institutions in the Russian Empire came under the Department of the Orthodox Confession, and in 1914–15, 15 of the 141 new institutions for children were organised by this department.[71] The involvement of the military in looking after its own is notable also: the 317 institutions for poor children boasted by St Petersburg in 1907 included two special homes for soldiers' children, among them the esoteric 'Shelter for the Children of Lower Ranks of the General Staff', on the Fontanka.[72]

Once again, it is important to keep a sense of historical proportion. The concept of orphanages as primarily corrective institutions, responsible above all for moral instruction, was routine in Western Europe of the day as well.[73] Given the torpor of the Tsarist government with regard to welfare issues, and the chronic under-funding of the zemstva, the Russian Orthodox Church's extensive involvement in philanthropy was vital.[74] Besides, not all Orthodox believers were necessarily social conservatives: while some lamented the decline of personal alms-giving in favour of coldly 'Western' charitable organisations, others enthusiastically espoused the impersonality and egalitarianism of the new ethos of 'scientific charity'.[75]

In any case, a novel feature of the early twentieth century was the founding – albeit in small numbers, and sometimes in the teeth of government resistance – of self-consciously secular institutions. These included, for example, the children's clubs and 'summer colonies' run by Stanislav Shatsky, The Settlement and Children's Rest and Work. The Settlement group of clubs was founded in the Sushchevsky district of northern central Moscow in 1905. Over 75 per cent of the district's inhabitants came from the lower classes, and the literacy rate was around 61 per cent in the over-twenties (though in the range of 77–87 per cent among 8–19-year olds): the clubs' membership was entirely drawn from this group.[76] The purpose of the clubs – based on American and British models – was to foster self-reliance and self-government among children. Small groups of children (twelve boys in the first year the scheme was run, larger groups including both girls and boys later on, but never exceeding a few dozen) were taken out to summer at a dacha near Moscow, where a strict regime of 'self-help' was in operation. The children proved difficult to deal with ('At first the children were left to themselves, and during that week or couple of weeks, they were like a very herd of humans, like a flock of animals let out for the summer') being given to smoking, swearing, and lying through their teeth, and having a hostile attitude to adults that Shatsky and his colleagues – probably rightly – attributed to beatings and ill-treatment in the past.[77] But gradually their trust was won, using the method of general public assemblies (*skhodki*), where problems were discussed, disruptive elements isolated, social conflicts resolved (for example the mutual contempt and aggression of girls and boys), and policy negotiated.[78] The all-year clubs that were opened later in the city itself operated similar policies, devoting as much time to general assemblies as to leisure activities, such as excursions or outings to the ice rink.[79] In other words, as the organisers emphasised, the clubs were a 'cultural centre' and a place for 'people from different social situations to meet on a foundation of shared interests and activities and to find a means to draw together that is without the dissonances inherent to philanthropy in the traditional sense'.[80]

Shatsky and his group divided philanthropic work into 'social', 'cultural', and 'moral':[81] their own orientation was clearly towards the first of these three. But in fact the division was in a final sense artificial, given that their own work clearly had a strongly ethical dimension (as expressed in the fostering of co-operation and group solidarity as ends in themselves), as well as a socio-political concern with creating 'the workers of the future' and 'future citizens'.

Conversely, in mainstream institutions, the recommended regime usually, by the turn of the century, placed emphasis on health and hygiene as well as on moral improvement. By the early 1900s, children in the Moscow Provincial Zemstvo were spending the day according to the following model timetable:

7.00 a.m. Reveille
7.30 Breakfast, followed by tidying, housework for those on duty and walks for the others
9.00 Lessons
12.00 Lunch, followed by break

13.00   Lessons

14.00   (or 15.00 for older children) Handcrafts, prep, recreation

16.00   Tea, followed by more handcrafts, prep, recreation

19.00   Supper, followed by bed for younger children

21.00   Bed for older children.[81]

Later timetables were worked out more precisely, as is shown by the following, evolved by the Society for the Protection of Homeless Children in 1917:

Reveille 6.00 a.m. (6.30 a.m. in winter)

6.00/6.30–7.30   Washing, dressing (older children to help the younger)

7.30   Prayers

8.00   Breakfast (barley coffee and milk)

9.00   Sanitary inspection, tidiness check; older children (7–8-year-olds) to help with housework

10.00   Milk for smallest children, lessons for older ones

12.00   Lunch

14.00   Exercise: walk for older children, games for younger ones

17.30   Supper for younger children, sanitary inspection, prayers, and wash

19.30   Supper for older children, followed by bed.[82]

43   Christmas party in children's shelter, 1910s.

While regime regulation was not so punctilious in the 'village shelters', model designs for accommodation concealed, behind their *style russe* wooden façades, modern, well-founded premises, including cloakrooms, meeting rooms, storage and cellarage, and indoor lavatory facilities. The buildings were supposed to be set in grounds that included a separate playground as well as domestic buildings, utilities, and a school block.[83]

It was not just the disposal of time, but other aspects of orphanage life that were starting to be controlled. In the Moscow Provincial Zemstvo orphanage, extremely detailed records were kept of inmates' background medical histories, and (if an official publication about the place is to be believed), a diet that was in tune with contemporary peasant eating habits, but more varied and nutritious. Meat soup was served daily for dinner, followed by some meatless dish, such as vegetable pie and salad; much the same appeared at supper; and there was kasha with milk or butter for lunch, and milk with bread for tea. On Sundays and holidays, roast meat would make an appearance, and on special occasions a pudding such as *kissel'*; fast days were not kept very strictly. With about sixty or seventy children in the orphanage, the consumption rate reached around 80 kilos of veal and veal bones a year, and four or five hams; soups were made with about 7–8 kilos of meat, a bucket of vegetables, and two buckets of potatoes.[84] The managers of private shelters were also increasingly aware of nutritional and hygiene issues. At the shelter which the Bobrinsky family ran on their estate during the famine of 1891–2, the children were at first given a farinaceous diet largely based on more 'digestible' refined flour; as they recovered, they began to be fed foods that were closer to traditional peasant dishes, so that readjustment would not be so difficult. On arrival, the 'starvelings' were thoroughly washed in carbolic and water, which ensured that they were well scrubbed before they settled down with the other children.[85]

The Limits of Good Care

The case of Children's Aid, whose activities are copiously documented in its annual reports, gives a sense of the considerable energy and imagination invested by private philanthropists in work with poor children at this period. Its founder, Nadezhda Stasova, was inspired to set up the group after visiting the West in 1887, where she had been especially impressed by the Children's Palace (Palazzo dei bambini) in Naples. The society began in a modest way, with twenty members and a day nursery for fifteen children. In spring 1896, it opened a temporary hostel for homeless children; later developments included a second day-care centre in 1901.[86] By 1902, the society had sixty members and had succeeded in raising useful sponsorship from local businesses, for example donations of medicines from the Shaikol'sky pharmacy, gifts of clothing and food, and even free bathing facilities at the neighbouring *banya*.[87] The annual report for 1908 indicated ever-rising numbers of visits to the day-care centre (14,006, as opposed to 10,988 in 1907); a cheap canteen had been opened during this year, and an Easter festival, with traditional foods such as paskha and kulich and presents of clothes, had been organised.[88] But the real expansion in its activities and membership came in the 1910s. By 1915, there were no fewer than 212 members, 57 of whom had joined in 1910 or later, and who included such influential figures as Sof'ya Panina and the prominent feminist Praskov'ya Ariyan, editor of the First Women's Calendar, and several ladies of title: the level of privilege among the membership is indicated by the fact that many had their own telephones. The facilities now catered for up to 100 children at any one time, and fund-raising had become significantly more lucrative than before.[89]

At the same time, provision remained well below what was required in order to deal with the numbers of needy children in Russian cities and villages. The 327 children's institutions of St Petersburg in 1899 provided between them just short of 8,000 places, in a city whose population was already over a million.[90] Specialist provision for poor children in public institutions – as suggested by a 1903 guide to the city – was decidedly thin. Only seven of eleven publicly funded orphanages (including those under the Empress Maria Department) were accessible to such children, with a total of around 450 targeted places. The additional provision was made by charitable institutions, most operating on a small scale. The institutions run by the Society for the Protection of Poor and Sick Children had 165 places in hostels for homeless children, and 85 in hostels for victims of cruelty. The Society for the Protection of Homeless Children had a hostel with 103 inmates, and the House of Charity had 53 girls 'rescued from vice' in its section for minors.[91] Provision by the provincial zemstva was equally small-scale. In Smolensk, for example – a province whose population had reached over 1.5 million by 1904 – the central provincial hospital had a ward accommodating just a few dozen children at a time, with a mere 200–300 passing through the facility every year.[92]

The advantage of small numbers could be that there was some chance, in the better homes, of individual attention. The miserable record of infant mortality in the Imperial Foundling Homes, with their many thousands of inmates – records from the 1900s indicated that only about a quarter of those admitted survived to their twenty-second birthday – are testimony to the drawbacks of mass provision.[93] On the other hand, the Demolenovskaya school for orphans in Luga, south of St Petersburg was a family-style home where the inmates lived in small individual houses and were given a good practical education; photographs record well-appointed premises with green space, and with contented, well-fed-looking children.[94]

But the quality of care provided was, more often, in doubt. Mortality among infants was extremely high, even compared with the rates for the population generally. Figures published in 1901 indicated a death rate, across the zemstva, in the 30–40 per cent range.[95] This is more than borne out by reports from individual zemstva, such as Voronezh, where the average rate of demise over the years 1892–1900 was in the range 56.6–76.4 per cent.[96] The 1901 figures indicate that only 14 per cent of children placed in orphanages as babies were still alive by the age of 14.[97]

There were some signs of improvement – at least in the handling of small children – by the early twentieth century. By then, Russian institutions were beginning to take interest in a measure that was coming into favour in Western Europe, the so-called 'open placement system' or *otkrytyi priem*. Rather than surrender their children on an anonymous basis, mothers were encouraged to maintain contact by being paid a subsidy to breast-feed after the children had been placed. This measure – in at least some Russian orphanages – could be a disappointment from the perspective of encouraging permanent mother–child relations: there were cases where mothers disappeared as soon as the subsidy did, simply delaying the moment when full-time care had to be provided.[98] However, it had a favourable effect on the survival rates of children in homes. In 1898, the mortality rate among children being fed by their mothers at the Moscow Foundling Home was 23.8 per cent; among other children, it was more than twice as high (56 per cent).[99]

Orphanage work was helped by the higher profile of children's issues in society at large. As philanthropic efforts with the young became 'fashionable', so the supply of private money increased, funding not just separate facilities but also badly needed improvements to public ones. In Voronezh, for example, the zemstvo foundling home was transformed by a donation made by the Vigel' family, who turned over a well-built, sensibly planned, and centrally heated building on their estate not far from the provincial capital. The home moved into its new facility in 1901, an event that was followed by a dramatic drop in the overall death rate. By 1902, this was down to 12.4 per cent, and by 1904, to 10.5 per cent.[100] Figures from the First Congress of Russian Children's Doctors in 1912 indicated that the maintenance of aseptic conditions produced very dramatic increases in survival rates, lowering the death rate from 27.6 to 7.5 per cent in one place, from 78.6 to 40.7 per cent in another, and so on.[101]

Improvements, however, tended to be transient. A sudden influx of babies needing care, as the result of an epidemic, severe food shortage, or other such crisis put the premises and staff under pressure. In 1905, when the Smolensk zemstvo hospital facility dealt with over a hundred more children than in 1900, each wet-nurse in the home had no fewer than three babies to feed. 'There is constant yelling day and night,' an observer noted.[102] Another unpredictable stress factor came from haphazard funding, particularly for those running zemstvo foundling homes. In the words of a weary Voronezh zemstvo doctor in 1903, the authorities tended to inject cash only when rumours started going round 'that the infants are being tormented, or actually starving'.[103] Having achieved a turn-around in the death rates at the Voronezh home, the staff there were then subjected to a funding cut, which affected, in the first place, the quality of diet.

Between 1902 and 1909, the annual cost of feeding an inmate fell from 343 to 251 roubles: this was accompanied by an increase in the mortality rate from 12.4 to 24.1 per cent.[104] In Smolensk in 1911, zemstvo activists recorded that a recent cut in support for mothers feeding their own children had meant that fewer mothers were now prepared to feed their children, with the result that more children had to be taken into permanent care, causing overcrowding.[105] Like Russian doctors more generally, those attending to foundling home patients remained convinced that human milk was essential to the survival of babies.[106] But homes could not compete with private employers in the wet-nurse market. Wet-nurses left as soon as they could get better employment, leaving behind only those whom no respectable home would consider.[107] The result was endemic shortages of staff, and hence distressed and ailing infants.

As well as feeding, housing could be a problem. Government orphanages had purpose-built accommodation that was solid and spacious, but – in the case of the main homes in the capitals, such as the Catherine Institute for orphaned girls from the gentry and nobility in St Petersburg – dated from an era before warmth, light, and ventilation had been perceived as essential to the health of small children. To be sure, some private charities were very well equipped. The 160-place hostel run by the Society for the Guardianship of Wounded Soldiers, Cripples, and Abandoned Children was described by an inspector sent by the city authorities as housed in a 'spacious mansion, with plenty of light and air'.[108] Less privileged institutions had to make do with what they could find. The Vigel' estate house where the Voronezh orphanage was housed from 1901 might have central heating on paper, but unfortunately the circulation of warmth worked badly. The temperature frequently dropped to below 10 degrees Celsius on cold days, while on warm ones the influx of fresh air was very small.[109] Such problems were exacerbated during the First World War, which caused child homelessness on a mass scale. For instance, the shelters for homeless children set up in Kiev during the war were shoddily built and equipped, and undersupplied with food: staff had to beg for extra edibles from the traders in local bazaars.[110] Even before this, overcrowding, squalor, and neglect were far from unknown.[111] At best, facilities in orphanages tended to be spartan: for instance, the children in Vyazemsky Palace Workhouse slept on straw mattresses and made their own clothes, footwear, and stockings.[112]

Children in Care

The ascetic character of orphanages was not necessarily only a money-saving measure. It could, by intention at least, be a way of making working-class children feel at home. But how far this worked is open to question. There were certainly some cases of children who responded well to the care they received in the orphanages, becoming less introverted, settling down and finishing school, finding themselves honest employment. However, at other times, children's better promptings had a hard struggle with the lure of the street. 'I'm not really hoping to turn out an honest person, it's so hard to break with theft, and your mates, and that kind of life,' a 16-year-old told the staff in the St Petersburg juvenile court in 1910. Visiting the People's Palace (a temperance hall of the day) and reading adventure stories had been a high point of this boy's life, and he was sentimentally devoted to his mother; but she had decided he was 'beyond help', and it was not clear what other support he would get.[113] In the Vyazemsky Palace Workhouse, the disappearance of inmates – sometimes encouraged by their mothers, who had previously used them to run errands – was common.[114] Many of these children had previously lived rough, with no adult supervision at all: it was likely to take more than an ethos of self-denial and the dignity of labour to win them over. Records from the St Petersburg juvenile court indicate that tough, streetwise young teenagers often had a high opinion of themselves: brushes with authority could easily generate a sense of triumph.[115] And children from peasant backgrounds, at least, were likely to feel wretched in orphanages. A boy from Volynya, who ended up in Kiev in 1916 having fled his home as a result of the war, bitterly remembered how the orphanage servants had treated him with mocking contempt while they were cleaning him in the *banya*; the supervisors had been abusive. Rare excursions out of doors simply reinforced the sense of alienation from 'normal' people enjoying themselves in parks. The boy traced his own 'going wrong' (he ended up committing a minor offence) to this, and to the deep nostalgia that he felt for village life: he remembered 'two old huts with a broken-down porch, and everything so dear'. His testimony broke off in lamentation:

> I ended up in the orphanage and now I must weep and wail, wondering why I ended up in the orphanage. I ended up in the orphanage because I was deceived by wicked people.[116]

The obsessive circling of the syntax conveyed the boy's extreme distress. Of course, this account was composed after he had ended up in trouble with the police and arrived in the Kiev juvenile court: it was no doubt shaped by a desire to impress his 'innocence' upon the court and therefore mitigate his punishment. But the sense of hurt and grief he expressed was undoubtedly genuine. Comparably wretched was Anna Karelina, who detested the foundling home in which she grew up and saw life there as a round of unpleasantness and humiliation.[117]

Even where well-intentioned, staff were not necessarily competent. The most consistent problem identified by Empress Maria Department inspectors in the 1900s was poor-quality teaching, both of work skills and more particularly of intellectual subjects. A cooking school in a Perm' orphanage, for example, brought little benefit to inmates because it was run so badly they learned next to nothing; similar problems were recorded in Ufa, Chistopol', and Vyatka. In some cases, the difficulties may well have been the result of overcrowding – one supervisor might have to deal with as many as fifty inmates.[118]

The late nineteenth and early twentieth centuries saw two diametrically opposed responses to situations of this kind. The first was criticism of institutional care as a fundamental principle, combined with a search for alternatives. The setting up of the Guardianship of the Poor by the Moscow Duma in 1887, modelled on the welfare arrangements obtaining in Elberfeld, Germany, marked the advent of a new type of support, concentrating on out-relief (handouts of food, clothes, and cash) rather than on the provision of institutional care. In 1899, a model set of regulations was introduced allowing for the formation of comparable guardianships, with boards of local volunteers, in cities all over the

Russian Empire. The take-up was limited: municipal bodies in some smaller cities felt that their provision for the poor was already satisfactory, while municipal bodies in others worried that the institution of a guardianship would commit them to spending they could not afford.[119] However, by 1909 forty cities did have their own guardianships; in Moscow and St Petersburg, districts had their own branches as well. The volunteers were under terrible stress, working long hours for unpredictable amounts of money, and often in unsatisfactory conditions. But the very existence of the guardianships constituted a significant break with the past.[120]

Fostering and 'Farming Out'

Weight was also given to another possible alternative to institutional care: fostering. In essence, this was nothing new – the Imperial Foundling Homes had traditionally boarded out inmates, sometimes from infancy, in peasant families, and some zemstva had also used this method of care (for instance Chernigov, Poltava, Penza, Simbirsk, Kaluga, Perm', and others). However, these had been commercial arrangements, with families taking in a child in return for a cash payment from the orphanage.[121] The type of fosterage now preferred was one where an orphan was placed in a family long-term, what was often referred to as 'the Scottish system', from its prevalence in that country. Families might well be paid a cash subsidy – a small-scale scheme run by the Empress Maria Department was paying out 4 roubles a month for children under 10 – but were expected to treat their wards like their own children.[122] The Society for the Protection of Poor and Sick Children had sixty children in fosterage of this kind by 1903.[123]

On the whole, however, as with out-relief, the attitude taken was that this system, while no doubt excellent abroad, would not work in Russia. Anxieties were raised about the difficulty of regulating the system (as with the already widespread practice whereby mothers would make a private arrangement to have a child looked after in another family).[124] Sometimes, too, commentators on fostering and adoption voiced fears that the motives of those taking children into their families might well be 'selfish'.[125] These fears were by no means fantastic. It was indeed very difficult for orphanage staff – already at their wits' end about how to provide care for 'in-patients' – to take an interest in the welfare of those living at a distance. In many cases, little to no regulation took place.[126] And in circumstances where peasants expected their own children to provide a significant input into farm work, a child who was an outsider could indeed easily be the target of exploitation and the object of neglect. Rates of survival among children being farmed out were comparable to, or indeed worse than, they were for children in orphanages.[127] A system under the aegis of the Empress Maria Department, where country priests were used to recommend appropriate families, made sense on paper, but in practice it turned out to be difficult to persuade priests – unlike German pastors – to co-operate.[128]

There do seem to have been some cases, though, where fostering was more successful. In Voronezh province, zemstvo staff did not manage much regulation of babies farmed out in villages till the early twentieth century, but after this, more effort was made to keep track of what was going on. In 1903, the zemstvo foundling home introduced detailed record cards for inmates, on which was set out information about where the child had been found, their physique and appearance on arrival, their weight, illnesses survived in the home, vaccinations endured, and so on. Equally detailed information was given about the process of fostering, including whether any nursing infants in the family – whether those in care or the family's own – had died, their background in terms of fostering, and so on. The cards also contained space for records of inspections. At this stage, the home also acquired an official set of regulations setting out its aims and general practices.[129] Even before regulation was tightened up, fostering did not necessarily present a uniform picture. A. V. Kvyatkovskaya recorded in 1900 that some families became deeply attached to the children whom they had taken in, and were even prepared to go through the complicated and costly process of formal adoption. Others went about the process informally, signing up for 'permanent care' (*vsegdashnee popechenie*), or declaring the children 'their own' (*prinimaya v deti*). Certainly, neglect was sometimes to be observed, and at times children had to be returned to the home. The low rate of pay offered to families for boarding also meant that the arrangement was most attractive to those who were poorest, so that children might end up with adults who did not have the resources to care for them properly. Kvyatkovskaya cited a case of a small boy she had observed whose mother had been forced to loan out her cow because she could not afford the fodder: the child looked thin and was in rags. Neighbours pressed round, complaining that the woman was dirt poor and did not look after him properly, 'she teaches him nothing but swear words'. But the doctor also noted that the prospect of separation threw both child and foster mother into extreme distress: they clung together, resisting the idea of being broken up. She decided in the event that 'depriving him of a family and mother-love' would be a worse crime than allowing him to remain in circumstances which were, in material and intellectual terms, less than ideal.[130]

The obvious practical lesson from this incident – that foster mothers needed more financial help – was absorbed by the Voronezh zemstvo. By 1903, support to families had risen to a more generous 4 roubles a month. This measure had ambiguous effects: on the one hand, a doctor commented, it had proved attractive to opportunists, and hence actually generated a number of cases of neglect. But it was also deepening the pool of people interested in fostering, including those who came from rather better-off families. Hence, on balance, the results had been positive, since the zemstvo orphanage had a wider choice of people with whom it could place infants.[131]

Fostering, then, was a social institution with a mixed character, as is suggested also by memoirs of those who survived it. Despite the worries about 'selfishness' and exploitation on the part of adults who took in orphaned children, or children whose parents could not afford to keep them, accounts of fosterage tend to be more positive than those of life in the orphanage. Anna Balashova, taken in by a childless elderly couple in the 1900s, was treated with consideration and affection;

her mother, who lived locally, was often able to visit, and the arrangement worked well from all sides.[132] Valya Dement'eva, born in 1912, was boarded, after her father's death in 1914, with a widow in her parents' village, whom she adored.[133] These cases, of course, were informal, private fostering arrangements, rather than institutional ones, but some positive comments on the latter are also recorded. Vasily Gerasimov, who spent time in an orphanage and with a family, was not unduly hostile about the former. But he expressed warm gratitude to the Finnish family who fostered him.[134] That said, Gerasimov's childhood fell in an earlier period than the one under consideration here – he was born in the middle of the nineteenth century – and it is possible that his recollections might have been less glowing had they related to the economically stressful period stretching from the 1891 famine till the end of the First World War.

Reforming Institutional Care

Whatever their thoughts about alternatives to institutional care, commentators were generally agreed that the nature of provision needed to be changed. At government level, this meant tightening control over children's institutions – harmonising regulations and increasing surveillance of on-the-ground practices.[135] Among individual activists, it could also mean trying to provide children with a greater degree of sympathy and understanding. In the eighteenth century, institutional care had sometimes been advocated precisely because it was emotionally neutral and rational and thus offered a real alternative to the wayward life of the family. Parents were encouraged to bring children up in similarly rational ways.[136] In contrast, by the late nineteenth century, life in homes tended to be seen as mechanical and aseptic, as an artificial form of upbringing that cramped natural development. This attitude had also reached the government officials pushing forward politically conservative types of institution such as 'village refuges', who now argued that 'all the supervisory personnel in the home should be imbued with the spirit of loving parental attitudes to children'.[137]

Of course, these fine sentiments stood in sharp contrast to the demanding regime envisaged for inmates in 'village refuges', which required them to rise at 5 a.m. in winter and 4 a.m. in summer for a day of work and lessons, with very few breaks for rest and play, lasting until 8 p.m. – on the assumption that inmates who were being trained for a life as agricultural labourers had best grow up with a routine that bore some relation to what would have been expected of comparably aged children in a Russian village. This assumption also governed the character of the living spaces, which were supposed to offer spartan, but practical accommodation (in practice, they were essentially barracks dressed up in a 'cottage' style).[138] But the 'family' sentiments in some other types of institution were carried through more forcefully into day-to-day life. Children's Aid in St Petersburg, for instance, had a doctor on the books from the beginning, and aimed to treat the children like 'members of one big family'.[139] A city official who inspected the home run by the Society for the Guardianship of Wounded Soldiers, Cripples, and Abandoned Children in 1913 reported enthusiastically, 'At every step and in every detail one can see love for children, the very tenderest concern for them, and competence with regard to the matter in hand.'[140] And a model for the future that gained warm support in some places was the 'artificial family', or small-scale home in which several children were placed under the care of so-called 'parents' (as pioneered in Sheffield). This pattern, its advocates claimed, was preferable to the attempt to break down large homes into smaller units under the care of a 'house mother' or 'house father', since it was less artificial and allowed inmates more contact with ordinary life.[141]

Another development was the growth of a sense that inmates needed support after they left institutions. By the first decade of the twentieth century, a full fifty-five committees attached to Empress Maria homes offered support to former inmates after they left.[142] Efforts were also being made to stop up an especially unfortunate gap in provision, between the upper age limit of many orphanages (12) and the lowest age at which children might legally enter employment (14). The plan was to set up 'trade sections' in orphanages and other such institutions in order that children might carry out a properly supervised and non-exploitative apprenticeship.[143] Once again, Children's Aid in St Petersburg worked energetically in this respect: former pupils of its day-care centres were encouraged to remain in touch, and were often helped with personal problems when they did: in 1915, for example, the charity's governing body obtained a passport for one former pupil and a sewing-machine for another.

Altogether, a shift was taking place in attitudes to abandoned children, and more broadly poor children. Rather than being seen simply as a social threat to be disciplined, they were beginning to be considered as needy individuals requiring care that took into account their individual background and circumstances. 'Unsupervised' children, whatever their faults, were still children, who required reintegration into society rather than isolation and punishment. An allied conviction that rehabilitation was not only possible, but essential, where children were concerned, was ubiquitous in discussion of the appropriate juridical handling of juvenile crime, though it had sadly little influence on day-to-day practice in the courts and penal institutions.

Children on Trial

Late Imperial Russian attitudes to crime generally were by no means uniformly rehabilitationist. Theories of crime as a 'physiological' phenomenon, innate from birth, had a considerable hold. In his influential compendium *Juvenile Criminals*, published in 1884, D. A. Dril' referred with respect to the work of Krafft-Ebing, Lombroso, Charcot, and others, and cited numerous case studies of murderers who came from families with a history of epilepsy and suicide, hysteria, insanity, and violence.[144] However, even adherents to endogenous explanations of criminal activity were usually prepared to concede some role to the environment when it came to young offenders. Dril' himself was, by the 1900s, placing as much emphasis on the role of family alcoholism as on 'bad heredity', and his attitude was typical of the time.[145] It followed that there was a broad consensus that punitive solutions

– long-term incarceration, for example – were less desirable than programmes of re-education and training for work. As one jurist wrote in 1917, citing a slogan from a 1913 congress on child upbringing held in Washington: 'One can always say with certainty: there is no such thing as an incorrigible case.'[146] Acceptance that policy on children should seek to rehabilitate, not chastise, the offender was broad enough to make discussion of juvenile delinquency the spearhead of liberal attitudes to penal policy more generally. The jurist P. Lebedinsky commented in 1913: 'The modern and increasingly widespread campaign to combat juvenile crime is perhaps the most vivid and striking reflection of the sea-change in attitudes towards the aims and purposes of state penal policy that is so characteristic of our times.'[147]

The widespread support for rehabilitationist solutions, however, had limited effects on the realities of the Tsarist legal system. In this area, as in most other areas of welfare work with children, the state was usually inert where it was not actually obstructive. In the late eighteenth and early nineteenth centuries, the Tsarist regime had been abreast of initiatives all over Europe, but the Nikolaevan era had seen stagnation in this area, as in other areas of social welfare policy. The pioneering reforms in the reign of Catherine II, introducing a reduced tariff of penalties for 10–17-year-olds and abolishing the legal answerability of the under-10s, had undergone little change in the first half of the nineteenth century, and the broadly based legal reforms of the 1860s had not seen alterations to the manner in which juvenile offenders were tried and convicted. At the end of the last decade of the nineteenth century, however, pressure from liberal jurists, who were keenly aware of Western reforms to the law on crimes committed by minors,[148] had results. A new law of 2 June 1897 reformed the provisions in the 1885 Punishment Code, articles 137–9, 356, and 416, and made changes to the procedures for cases involving minors. The law did not alter the established age threshold of 10 at which children became liable to juridical punishment in the first place, but it did introduce a distinction in punishment tariffs depending upon whether the child was deemed to have committed the alleged offence with or without understanding (*razumenie*) of its actions. Moreover, it required the court investigator to take steps to investigate the issue of whether the child had or had not understood; in the latter case, the trial could be stopped and a supervision order made. Now it was also made incumbent upon the court to inform parents about the case, and to call them into the court if it was felt their presence would be helpful. Doctors, teachers, guardians, and other responsible persons could also be presented with a court summons. The accused him- or herself was not required to be present throughout the case, but was called to 'give explanations' as needed.[149]

Although dissatisfied with what they saw as the still excessively punitive nature of the law,[150] liberal jurists did their best to test its ramifications to the limit. A 1912 commentary by one such jurist, Kh. Charykov, emphasised that the law had brought real potential for change in at least four ways: the capacity to involve parents in cases where minors were undergoing investigation and trial; the recognition of 'social supervision' orders as a possible response to child crime; the introduction of separate processing for cases involving minors; and the obligatory provision of minors with a defence lawyer. Of these four changes, particularly important, in Charykov's view, had been the introduction of 'social supervision' orders and of separate processing. The presence of parents was something whose efficacy he felt to be questionable, given that they were often at least partly responsible for the child's drift into crime in the first place. The mandatory legal defence – something which he supported in principle – did not apply in the lower courts, and, though children were supposed at the very least to have the services of an 'intermediary', even this was usually problematic in the case of those who had no fixed address. But the introduction of 'supervision orders' had had a fundamental effect on sentencing policy, as had the last of the reforms, separate processing for cases involving minors.[151]

And indeed, there is evidence that, by the 1910s, both these principles had been widely accepted, at least in the major cities. A survey of the Moscow courts in 1908 established that referral of convicted young offenders to 'responsible persons' (not necessarily parents) for supervision, and the use of suspended sentences, was becoming quite prevalent.[152] Separate processing was formalised on 22 January 1910, with the opening of the first-ever separate juvenile court in the Russian Empire, presided over by N. A. Okunev, a former magistrate (*mirovoi sud'ya*) with twenty years experience, who had undertaken study visits to juvenile courts in Western Europe.[153] A month later, the Moscow juvenile court was given permission to begin business by the Minister of Justice, and by 1915 there were functioning juvenile courts in Khar'kov, Kiev, Odessa, Ekaterinoslav, and Nikolaev as well.[154]

Reformatories for the Young

The institutions to which young offenders were referred after conviction were starting to come under closer legal scrutiny. Already on 5 December 1866, a new statute had constructed an alternative, for offenders under the age of 17, to incarceration in a prison or a labour camp alongside adults. Now, young offenders could be referred by the courts to a 'corrective shelter' (*ispravitel'nyi priyut*) instead of an institution of a more punitive character. Shelters could be set up by zemstva, 'societies' (such as charitable organisations) and religious groups as well as by the Directorate of Prisons. But the development of such 'shelters' was slow – only thirteen had been set up by 1881 – and regulation of their structure and function was lax. The 5 December 1866 statute was skeletal in character: it decreed that key members of staff should be qualified (the director was supposed to be a person with a teaching certificate, as well as with impeccable moral credentials), and it established a syllabus (the three Rs and religious knowledge). It also laid down one or two points about the punishment scheme obtaining in the shelters: for instance, escapees could be held for up to a month (but no more) on strict regime (i.e. in a *kartser*, or punishment cell) if they attempted escape.[155] But nothing was done to ensure the enforcement of these regulations: no inspection scheme was set up, nor was there an attempt to harmonise the institutional structures set up by the different organisations envisaged by the statute as service providers (zemstva, charities, private individuals), or even to establish a coherent funding mechanism.[156] In the words of a commentator writing in 1911, provision was 'different in every different place', and 'things went along in their own sweet way' (*delo nalazhivalos', kak Bog na dushu klal*). Given a dearth of official regulation, or indeed of published guidance, it was essentially the exchange of information among those actively working in reformatories – the congresses of 'representatives of Russian corrective institutions', held at roughly three-year intervals from 1881 – which acted as a force for convergence.[157]

The materials from such congresses also made clear how considerable diversity was. By the early twentieth century, the term 'corrective shelter' was beginning to be challenged by another term, 'educational shelter', with the terminological distinction pointing to key discrepancies in character. An important example of a shelter of the early type was the Rukavishnikov shelter in Moscow. When founded in 1864, the shelter had been pioneering: after various vicissitudes (especially the death of the first director in 1875), it was taken over by the Moscow municipality (with a donation of 130,000 roubles from the Rukavishnikov family) in 1878. At this point, discipline was to some extent relaxed, with more free time being allowed; in 1903, a summer colony was set up for the under-16s.[158] However, the character of the shelter still remained 'corrective' much more than 'educational'. In 1908, the director of the shelter, speaking at the Seventh Congress of Educational-Corrective Shelter Representatives and Supervisors, declared his hostility to 'lovey-dovey stuff' (*igra v lyubov'*), and insisted that 'strict order and strict discipline', as well as a commitment to 'moral education', were essential to a successful 'educational-corrective institution'. When the inmates were guilty of violence, or had been found using weapons, the staff had no hesitation in using corporal punishment.[159]

Day-to-day reports kept by supervisors in 1906 and 1908 confirm that the Rukavishnikov shelter was a place of harsh, military discipline. What was seen as malingering (as in a case where an inmate refused to work because he said his hand was hurting) was punished by transfer to a bread and water diet, or no food at all; inmates who delayed in getting into bed might have their mattresses removed; smoking and refusal to work were punished by a stint in solitary confinement; swearing was countered by a 'severe reprimand'.[160] Violence was met with violence: an inmate who wounded the director in the shoulder with a knife and then went for the deputy director with his fingernails got 20 lashes and a spell in solitary; an inmate who tried to stab another inmate in the lavatories got 10 lashes.[161] At the same time, it should be noted that the very fact that supervisors had to record punishments and account for them meant that their behaviour, as well as that of the inmates, was subject to regulation. And by the early twentieth century, the attitude taken to supervision sometimes had liberal elements: for example, a talk given to supervisors in 1908 described searches of the parcels sent to inmates by their relatives as 'a sad necessity', since such parcels often contained tobacco and vodka.[162] By 1900, it was customary to use incentives – such as badges and prizes – when inmates did what they were supposed to, as well as punishments when they did not.[163]

By the 1900s, though, the Rukavishnikov shelter – described by one concerned commentator in 1917 as a 'barracks': a large, soulless, alienating institution that did more to turn any inexperienced young offenders within its portals into hardened criminals than it achieved in the way of reform[164] – was widely seen as a retrograde, indeed pernicious, institution. Already at the 1908 Congress, the director's comments on 'order', 'discipline', and the use of corporal punishment were received with hostility: a questioner from the floor demanded whether the use of corporal punishment had been cleared with a psychiatrist (here the director equivocated, saying that the shelter did have 'a doctor' in attendance).[165] And a report on the Fifth All-Russian Congress of Workers in Houses of Correction, held in 1900, revealed widespread dissent about other methods of punishment as well. Some directors vehemently opposed the use of the lock-up for disruptive inmates, while others swore by it; some felt that depriving inmates who broke the rules of food was inhumane, others, that it was an essential corrective measure. In the Vladimir youth colony, corporal punishment was explicitly forbidden, while the Tver colony pioneered behaviour regulation by 'peer surveillance' (disruptive inmates would be ostracised till they broke down and started to co-operate).[166]

By the end of the 1900s, the tide was starting to turn in favour of a less punitive attitude to shelter inmates. At the 1908 Congress, for instance, the director of the Kiev shelter described his institution simply as 'educational', the word 'corrective' having fallen by the wayside.[167] Three years later, in 1911, a fair few directors emphasised their commitment to new ways. Many institutions now used older inmates as mentors, guides, and regulators of younger ones, or rewarded good behaviour by the assignation of responsibilities (in the Yakovlevsky girls' shelter, for instance, trusted inmates might be asked to undertake tours of duty in the library). Much emphasis was placed on the use of rewards – periods of home leave, or extended periods of home leave, permission to take independent walks, excursions to the theatre – as well as, or rather than, the use of punishments. Punishments, where meted out at all, might well now take the form of an oral reprimand, or depriving a young person of a treat, or of leave, rather than confining him or her to the lock-up. Staff now put considerable effort into ensuring young people's future, taking pride in the achievement of 'graduates' who had moved on to worthy employment or further training (work in a shop, perhaps, or handicraft courses). In some places, the 'family' model attracting interest among orphanage workers was also beginning to be adopted: in the words of the Vladikavkaz director, 'the regime is, as far as possible, of a "family" kind'.[168]

More control was starting to be exercised over inmates' requirements in terms of healthy living. In the late nineteenth and early twentieth centuries, the day-to-day regime was not regulated from the centre. Much time was devoted at the 1900 Congress of Reformatory Staff to an argument about whether official norms of sleep provision should be set, but the discussion was inconclusive.[169] Later congresses, however, established broad norms for rest (2–3 hours) and sleep (8–10 hours), while stressing the importance of considering inmates' needs on an individual basis, particularly if they already had health problems. Increasing emphasis was placed on the role of psychologists and psychiatrists in collaborating with reformatory staff.[170] And by the 1910s, the regimes of at least some shelters were, if anything, less demanding than those of orphanages of the normal kind. The Vyatsk shelter, for example, required a 6.30 a.m. reveille and four hours' labour a day in the workshops, plus three and a half hours of school; but inmates also had about two and a half hours' free time (after lunch and supper) built into the timetable, including time for outdoor exercise in the form of a 'walk'.[171]

Changes of this kind were the result less of the influence of the 'free education' movement than of official awareness of how young offenders were treated outside Russia. The official journal of the Chief Prisons Directorate, the *Prison Herald*, does not appear to have publicised Stanislav Shatsky's work with 'difficult' children in Moscow, but it regularly carried reports on foreign reformatories, and foreign observers attended the Eighth Congress of Educational and Corrective Shelter Representatives in 1911. As in every other area of policy on children, the authority of the medical establishment – and especially of current ideas about hygiene – was crucial.

This combination of influences affected not only ideas among reformatory staff, but policy in government offices, which was beginning to accommodate a different attitude to the 'discipline versus rehabilitation' model. A new law dating from 19 April 1909 officially banned corporal punishment in all reformatories, and endorsed a new type of 'shelter', a 'corrective and educational institution' (*vospitatel'no-ispravitel'noe zavedenie*) for criminals aged between 10 and 18. Young criminals were now supposed to be given training in manual skills, alongside elementary intellectual procedures (a grounding in the three Rs equivalent to that offered by the first class of a primary school), and religious education. There was now greater emphasis on the need for professional standards among the staff, who were supposed, for example, to inform themselves about new ideas concerning penal policy by regular attendance at specialist conferences.[172] And increasing numbers of 'shelters' were functioning as agricultural 'colonies' – both because this was helpful in terms of income (making them eligible for subsidies from the agricultural ministry, and allowing funds to be raised from the sale of produce), and because it ensured the provision of skills training and a 'healthy life' in the fresh air.

The 19 April 1909 law did represent an incomplete reconciliation with rehabilitationist, rather than punitive, policy. The constitution of the new institutions retained the old emphasis on the 'moral correction' of inmates as well as on 'the preparation of them for an honest and hard-working life'. Attendance at conferences for supervisors was no substitute for in-depth training, a matter about which the new statute was silent. But, at the very least, this law constituted an attempt to guarantee even the most disadvantaged and socially threatening children the education that had now begun to be considered the prerequisite of any normal childhood. And the constitutions of individual shelters, by the 1910s, were focusing on qualities valued in the contemporary education system generally, such as self-reliance. In the words of the *Constitution of the Smolensk Provincial Zemstvo Educational-Corrective Colony-Shelter*, 'In general, the regime of the colony-shelter, without subjecting the personality of the inmate to repression of any kind, encourages his natural inclination to virtue and industry, and gradually subordinates him to the inner discipline which in the final form of its development is expressed in a sense of duty.'[173]

At a practical level, however, there remained stubborn problems in dealing with young offenders, both in the courts and after sentencing. In the courts, a central difficulty was that almost all judges lacked expertise in child psychology, yet were able to request referrals to medical professionals only in a small number of instances, such as to establish whether a defendant was mentally normal or, as the language of the day had it, 'imbecile'.[174] On the whole, judges decided cases idiosyncratically and 'on the hoof': practices varied from court to court, even within one city.[175] Even specialist justices sometimes took a punitive line with defendants. V. M. Levitsky, a judge in the juvenile court in Kiev, for instance, saw child crime as in part a reflection of enhanced economic opportunity for children:

> The newspaper boy's large earnings effect a wholesale emancipation of him from parental power. [...] Left to themselves, planted in unpropitious conditions, exposed to the life of the street and to unpredictable fluctuations in earnings, newspaper-sellers quickly become tired of living at home, with its fixed timetable, and start sleeping at a friend's place or at dens of vice and places of 'ill repute' (*sumestnye kvartiry*).[176]

Levitsky passionately advocated the principle of 'nothing granted without work being done' for street children generally; as a reference to 'proper work' elsewhere in his article suggested, this meant manual labour, such as had traditionally been expected in labour camps and 'houses of correction'.

Legal professionals' hands were also tied by the deficiencies of the system in a broader sense, and particularly by the sheer number of cases they had to deal with. Juveniles were assigned special 'guardians' to watch over their interests, but they were hideously overworked, compared with their counterparts elsewhere, as an article published in 1914 revealed. To be handling twelve cases simultaneously was considered an unacceptably high figure in the German system: in Russia, however, a guardian could expect to have to deal with around 100.[177] A 1917 article by E. Ginzburg gave an outline of the guardian's role as it ideally should be that was both sensible and imaginative. The guardian should investigate each individual case thoroughly, with sensitivity to the likely stresses on a young offender (the possibility of brutalisation in the past, the pressure to enhance status by boasting in the present). They should try to press for a non-custodial solution: ideally, fosterage in a decent working-class family, or accommodation in a hostel in the country, or correction by means of 'labour aid' (assignation of the young person to a job of some kind). But at the same time Ginzburg managed to convey the formidable obstacles that stood in the way of even the most industrious and well-intentioned guardian. The young offender was likely to be suspicious and frightened, and might well have been beaten up by the police while in custody. There were serious problems about what to do when he or she was on remand: referral back to the parents was possible (but unsatisfactory if they had contributed to the child's involvement in crime in the first place), and so was placement in a hostel (however, as other sources convey, places in hostels were desperately short). Fosterage or transfer to a country hostel were ideal, but hard to arrange; it was likely the young offender would end up with a custodial sentence. The Russian guardians could not rely, as their American equivalents could, on support from the police and from the education system, in order to ensure a viable alternative.[178]

Judicial practice was not the only problem. Problems also persisted in the reformatory network, one of the most under-funded sectors of the welfare system. An article published in 1916 pointed out that in some parts of Western Europe such institutions could rely on 75 per cent funding from central government, and also received support from local communities; in Russia, on the other hand, state funding was next to non-existent.[179] Formally, responsibility was delegated to the zemstva, but money was very tight here too: in 1900, the colonies received a total of only 29,700 roubles from zemstva funds (as opposed to 512,000 allocated to orphanages more generally).[180] Equally, this was not an area that the voluntary sector considered attractive, a point that held back expansion with private money.[181] Space in dedicated institutions was extremely limited.

Certainly, things did improve in the late nineteenth and early twentieth centuries. If there had been only 13 reformatories in existence right across the Russian Empire in 1881; by 1914, the number had risen to 59. But even after expansion, the number of places was decidedly inadequate. In 1914, 7,843 children across the Russian Empire were convicted of crimes deemed to warrant a custodial sentence, but there were just 2,500 dedicated places available in the colonies. Capacity was better than in 1900, when only 17 per cent of convicted young offenders had a chance of getting a place in a colony, but it was still far from adequate.[182] Such colonies as existed often struggled along financially. Particular difficulties were suffered by the Poltava colony, which suffered a cash crisis in 1905 and could not expand to take further inmates in 1910 because the zemstvo would not increase its subsidy.[183] For its part, the Vladimir colony was running a budget deficit of over 6,000 roubles in 1910.[184] Even solvent colonies had to piece their funding together from a variety of sources. In 1896, the girls' reformatory run by the St Petersburg Ladies' Prison Philanthropy Committee financed itself by a 4,000-rouble grant from the State Treasury, 1,000 roubles from the City Duma, 1,495 roubles from the Advocates' Council, 282 roubles 85 kopecks in donations, 148 roubles from investment income, a payment of 51 roubles 31 kopecks from the Directorate of Prisons, 649 roubles 59 kopecks from charity and church collections, and 383 roubles 14 kopecks from selling milk, ice, and crafts made by the inmates.[185]

All of this suggests that the pious talk of 'incentives' and 'family atmosphere' at conferences may not always have spilled over into reality. Certainly, there is some evidence of malaise even in the generally upbeat public statements by shelter administrators at conferences. Escapes by inmates were low in some reformatories (the Yakovlevsky shelter recorded only two in 1909, and none at all in 1908, 1910, and 1911), but significantly higher in others (at the Rukavishnikov shelter, there were escapes on a 'mass scale' in 1910).[186] Riots were not infrequently recorded, and not just in the 'revolution year' of 1905, when most juvenile facilities were gripped by the unrest spreading through Russian society at large.[187] For instance, major upheavals gripped the Odessa reformatory in the summer of June 1911. The problems began on 11 June, when a group of particularly tough inmates, left out of a theatre excursion because of alleged bad behaviour, attacked a *dyad'ka* (untrained auxiliary supervisor), leaving him to make a hasty and only just successful escape. The inmates then wrote on a wall in blood, 'This is the blood that the *dyad'ki* drink, our blood.' The authorities beyond the reformatory at first took a sympathetic view: they responded to complaints of ill-treatment on the part of the staff by sacking the director, and placed the police in charge as an interim measure. On 12 June, however, the inmates rioted again, this time arming themselves with metal bars from their bedsteads, setting fire to mattresses, and making wide-ranging demands for changes to the reformatory regime – a lifting of the ban on smoking, better access to leave, a less demanding timetable. By the end of June, when the board of guardians took charge directly, more than half the inmates had run away, and structural as well as cosmetic repairs – the rebuilding of some storehouses on the site, for instance – had to be undertaken. Despite this further change of administration, unrest continued well into the summer.[188]

In the Odessa reformatory, a similar disciplinary regime to that adopted in the Rukavishnikov shelter had been in operation.[189] What this meant in reality can be sensed by reading between the lines of a comically defensive report presented by the director of the board of guardians at the Seventh Congress of Reformatory Staff in 1912. The local inspectors had over-reacted, he claimed, and completely misrepresented the situation. An overflowing latrine found in one of the punishment cells had simply been forgotten: it did not represent the normal state of affairs in a well-run and sanitary shelter. Equally, the ill-treatment of which inmates complained had been exaggerated:

> As for a naked inmate being found in the lock-up, this person had been put there in that condition for the first time, and although such a measure cannot, of course, be considered anything other than unsuccessful, and the director was duly rebuked for it, in all justice it must be said that the inmate in question was, in every sense of the word, the terror of the instutition, boasting exceptional physical strength. The reason that he was naked was that there had already been a case when an inmate placed in the lock-up had hanged himself, and on this occasion the inmate in question threatened that he would do the same. In addition it must be observed that the measure placed the inmate in no danger, given that the weather on 5 June in Odessa was exceptionally hot.[190]

The effect of this self-justifying statement is not too far from the comic denials of abuse articulated by the mayor in Gogol's play *The Government Inspector*: 'The complainant flogged herself.' But staff in reformatories were faced with genuine problems. The inmates of their institutions covered a wide range, including not only some children referred by their parents for 'correction' or dispatched because they were temporarily on the streets, but also a significant proportion of convicted offenders, including repeat offenders (in 1899, for example, 17 per cent of 'corrective shelter' inmates were 'doing time' on the second or subsequent occasion).[191] Individuals of this kind had probably endured abuse and neglect, and might regard considerate treatment as a manifestation of weakness. Others found it hard to get out of old habits, as with a 14-year-old lock-breaker placed by his colony in art school, who thieved from the school but was readmitted when he promised to return the money, and then ended up dropping out again after a quarrel with the school's director.[192] Children ranged in age, too, with some in the lower teens or even as young as ten, but others considerably older, with the latter, obviously, representing much more of a problem in terms of control and guidance. The idealistic staff at the Egorov shelter in St Petersburg found themselves at first facing serious difficulties with the inmates, many of whom had recently been disgorged from police custody and had been hardened by their experience there and on the streets. The name 'arrestee' was regarded by such tough lads as a 'badge of honour'; the staff found to their horror that inmates' behaviour was quite unpredictable, and might veer unpredictably from apparent co-operation to the cynical performance of some 'nasty act'. Only gradually did the inmates come to realise that the set of values dominating their environment was now quite different; while they adjusted, conflict was unavoidable.[193]

Altering the behaviour of brutalised children and adolescents took time and patience. In 1912, the director of the St Petersburg 'education and correction shelter' reported that the escape rate was running at 11 per cent – disturbingly high, considering the liberal way in which the inmates were treated. This home remained committed to 'education through labour', but those wanting quick results were likely to feel a strong pull towards the 'order' and 'discipline' recommended by the director of the Rukavishnikov shelter.[194] Under-staffing and under-provision naturally decreased the likelihood of imaginative work with children. In a practical sense, the situation got even worse after 1914, since the juvenile prison population expanded considerably. In 1915, for example, the Petrograd reformatory, meant to hold 80 inmates, was in fact housing 120, with children sleeping two to a bed.[195] No wonder that a concerned observer, writing in 1917, described the whole system as unsatisfactory from top to bottom: the colonies were badly run, and escape from them was frequent.[196]

Penal reformers had clear ideas about what should be done. Alternatives to detention in reformatories (such as supervised fosterage in approved homes, or trade education) should be used more widely and there should be a diversity of types of custodial institution. Mentally abnormal young offenders should be held separately from others, and the 'normal' population divided according to age and experience, with only the oldest and toughest offenders subjected to anything resembling a penitential regime. Transfer between different types of institution should be possible, so that good behaviour could be rewarded and bad corrected.[197] And there should be a significant expansion of the remand system, which was under huge pressure, especially once young offenders started to be arrested in larger numbers from the start of the First World War. There were dedicated remand facilities solely in places with juvenile courts, and these could take only some of the juveniles those courts were currently processing. For instance, in 1913 the remand centre in St Petersburg was able to acccommodate only 400 boys a year, less than a third of those who came up before the courts in that year.[198]

However, the continuing paucity of funds from central and local government and the unattractiveness to the general public of the young offenders' case tended to vitiate the bravest hopes for reform. To be sure, the colonies did (if publications by their staffs are to be believed) bring about some successful transformations, as in the case of a boy who stood up to recite a poem of praise to the Tsar ('Great glory to the Builder/That God's mercy sent him to us,/And infused young hearts/With sacred love for the Patron').[199] But, by and large, experience of life in reformatories appears to have inspired less enthusiastic feelings than this. 'Regimes', even in the places committed to humane treatment, were quite severe: the St Petersburg boys' reformatory, for instance, worked its inmates for most of the day, with two hours of school before lunch and seven hours of manual work in the afternoon and evening, as well as an hour of housework before any of this started. A mere half-hour was allocated for leisure, in a 14-hour day.[200]

There were worse fates, though, than to end up in even a badly run colony: above all, being consigned to the adult penal system. As early as the 1890s, the presence of children in general cells, spending time 'among adults and hardened criminals', was causing disquiet, and there was insistence on the need to give better information to local magistrates about alternatives to prison sentences.[201] But, with limited places in colonies, the practice of incarcerating children among adults continued. In 1908, 7.25 per cent of convicted offenders were receiving prison sentences even in Moscow, a city relatively well supplied with houses of correction.[202] Also notable was the high proportion of young offenders sent by the courts into police custody (*politseiskii dom*, 28.18 per cent, *uchastok*, 16.48 per cent).[203] The figures for magistrates' courts across the Russian Empire in 1915 were even more depressing: here, over two-thirds of offenders aged 11–18 received prison sentences (though the proportion was smaller, 20 per cent, among children aged 11–13).[204]

According to regulations published in 1903, 'minors' (10–14-year-olds) and 'juveniles' (14–17) who did find their way into ordinary prisons and camps were supposed to be housed in separate accommodation.[205] Here, they were meant to live their days according to a regime much like the one obtaining in the 'houses of education and correction': two hours' schooling a day was sandwiched between stints in the prison workshop, accompanied walks and drill for exercise, morning and evening prayers, and two-hour chapel services on public holidays. But such sections existed only in Moscow and St Petersburg, and were – according to the warders running them – fraught with disciplinary problems.[206] Figures dating from 1905–8 indicated that a good many of the 8,000 or so children incarcerated in adult institutions shared accommodation with adults, especially children who were older. The majority of 10–14-year olds of this period were in separate cells (though in 1908 'the majority' signified under 60 per cent). However, less than half those in the 14 and over age group were placed in such cells; what is more, a significant proportion of inmates (100–200 of the 10–14-year-olds, depending on the year in question, and 1,000–1,300 of over-14s) received no school education at all while locked up.[207]

Children imprisoned in such circumstances were at serious risk. According to contemporary campaigners for legal reform, they were likely to receive an expert training in criminal techniques, emerging after their sentence as fully-fledged desperadoes. They were – also going by contemporary reminiscences – often subject to brutal abuse from both warders and inmates. Certainly, prisoners were no longer shackled, as they had been in the early nineteenth century, but homosexual rape was common, and there were recognised terms for boy catamites (*margaritki*, 'daisies', for instance, or *plashkety*, perhaps from *plashmya*, 'to lie flat on one's face'). Boys also curried favour with older men by doing all they could to act tough: a relatively innocent example was witnessed by a professional jurist who visited a prison in the 1900s and saw a boy in solitary confinement lean out of a window and entertain the adult prisoners exercising in the yard with a virtuoso display of foul language.[208] A young inmate's poem in the traditional vein of the 'arrestee's song' lamented the fate of the confined:

> In my prison cot I am lying,
> With a dusty old mattress beneath;
> I'm rotting away with consumption,
> And soon I will slide into death.[209]

All in all, the treatment of young offenders was, despite reformers' best intentions, even less satisfactory than the treatment of young people in orphanages. Personal testimony of those who survived the colony system is even harder to find than personal testimony of former inmates in pre-revolutionary orphanages, but some of the evidence – the extent of disciplinary problems, for example – speaks of malaise. Certainly, though – as in institutions more broadly – reactions partly depended on a child's age and background. A child hardened by years of ill-treatment and by life on the street might adjust to the repressive atmosphere of a 'corrective shelter' more easily than one who had taken a 'turn for the worse'; conversely, a child who had spent most of its time on the streets, and perhaps never even attended school, might find an 'educative' institution bewildering. Much depended, too, on the attitudes of individual directors and staff. In the worst circumstances – such as in badly run reformatories, or adult prisons – there is every reason to suppose that penal facilities did more to reinforce the criminal propensities of their inmates than to prepare these for a lifetime of honest labour.

Not all the children who ended up incarcerated with adults had committed an offence to begin with. S. K. Gogel', a prominent campaigner in the penal reform movement, estimated in 1901 that there might be as many as 3,500 children held in provincial and district-centre jails across Russia, assuming that there were between five and ten in each such prison. Spot checks suggested that these estimates were on the low side: in Ryazan' in 1898, for instance, there had turned out to be 73 children in the towns' two prisons, and, in the same town in 1899, 55. Odessa's jails held 20 children, including a boy of 12 who had remained locked up for seven months after the death of his mother. Gogel' pointed out that some efforts were being made to provide special accommodation for such children in the penal system: for instance, the women's section of the Moscow House of Correction operated a crèche for the children of prisoners, while the prison in Tomsk had a special hostel for older children, which was shortly to be expanded to 192 places.[210] Alongside such provision within the prison system itself, private initiatives also expended energy on the fate of arrestees' children. One such was a shelter set up for the children of prisoners at the labour camp in Nerchinsk, whose organisers painted a distressing picture of their target group. Housed in earth dugouts, they were 'dirty and undernourished', and, what was more, 'remote from any supervision [nadzor] [...] undergoing a complete course of lectures on how to be a successful criminal.'[211] As with 'unprotected' children generally, the sense that such children were 'innocent' and had not deserved their fate vied with the sense that they presented, if left to themselves, a threat to the stability of society: the contrasting interpretations worked together to make the 'rescue' of such children seem a task of central social importance.

The years after 1890 witnessed a huge upsurge in charitable initiatives of all kinds, including charitable work with children. Efforts flowed both into 'out work', such as the provision of soup kitchens, and more particularly into the support of model institutions, including orphanages, reformatories, hospitals, and homes for 'defective' and 'backward' children. Perceptions of need were often still dominated by ideas about social status, with working-class children, especially street children, perceived as a threat to the broader community. All of this could impede efforts by the crusading professionals who sought to better the lives of orphans and of sick and mentally impaired children. But by far the largest problem lay in the parsimonious attitude of the Russian government to welfare provision, and its suspicion of voluntary initiative as a potential source of social subversion. While tolerance of charities, as of other kinds of association, increased after 1905, financial support still did not expand to the requisite levels. Nevertheless, some important changes had taken place by the 1910s: the foundation of specialist juvenile courts, for example, the institution of an informal network of children's charities, and reforms to the regimes of orphanages and of reformatories. Critically, activists on behalf of children, working on the basis of comparisons with Western Europe, had developed strong ideas about what should be done for children – ideas that would be realised in the next phase of Russian history.

Chapter 6

Orphan Heroes, 1917–1935

The Russian Revolution and Civil War saw the problems of child abandonment, already severe in the early years of the First World War, spiral to unprecedented heights, along with the numbers of children needing institutional care. In early 1917 there were 30,000 children in orphanages; a year later, numbers had more than doubled, to 75,000; by 1919, they had reached 125,000. The dreadful famine and war conditions of 1920–1 provoked a still more dramatic increase: to 400,000 in 1920, and 540,000 in 1921.[1]

Numbers rose out of all proportion when famine struck along the Volga in 1921–2, reducing at least 4 million children to total destitution and want. In some aid centres in small towns, 300–400 children a day were arriving in severe need. It has been estimated that the 1.5 million children receiving food aid constituted barely a tenth of those actually requiring help.[2] As F. A. Mackenzie, an eyewitness from Britain who visited the area in 1922, recalled, even where children got aid, it was not necessarily effective. Children (like famine victims always and everywhere) wanted only the food they were used to, such as bean soup and tea; the cocoa and chocolate on offer were brusquely refused. The supplies, which would have been stretched to breaking point in any case, were rendered inadequate by the constant pilfering of local aid workers: children received thin, watery soup rather than the thick broth that was supposed to be served. In one home Mackenzie visited, the death rate was running at 50 per cent per week.[3] According to figures from official reception centres alone, 2 million children had been abandoned across the Russian Federation by 1923, the numbers reaching 37,500 in Vyatka province, 37,300 in Perm' province, 46,800 in Simbirsk province, and a staggering 61,600 in Samara province.[4]

Not all the orphans stayed put. In the words of a 1919 report to the Executive Committee of the Children's Protection House, Petrograd, 'Anticipating the famine to come, the entire population of the district has literally taken to its heels, hoping to avoid a painful death.'[5] Flight was encouraged by official policy: according to figures published in 1928, 50,000 left the afflicted provinces of their own accord, but a full 100,000 were evacuated through official programmes.[6] Once the crisis was over, efforts began to resettle displaced children in their families, but these were hampered by the low number of families (only just over 12,000) that came forward to take children back. Official bureaux (the 'address offices') placed relatively small numbers, with requests for their services reaching a peak of 1880 in 1924.[7] Apart from the two capitals, places with especially large clusters of orphaned or deserted children included Rostov and the western provinces of Soviet Russia (the centre of severe fighting during the Civil War), and the Urals, an area often sought out by homeless children themselves.[8]

Figures for desertions were still running at 35,000 children a year in 1925, and in 1926 there were about 300,000 abandoned children in total, of which more than half were still living on the streets.[9] Two years later, forced industrialisation, followed rapidly by collectivisation, added to the numbers of deserted and needy children. Figures from an anthology of secret police documents compiled by Alexis Berelowitch and Vladimir Danilov indicate that 2.5 million people were forcibly displaced from their homes in 1930–1 alone; up to 40 per cent of individuals in some transports were children.[10] Children suffered worst in the famines and epidemics of the day; in extreme cases, they might become victims of cannibalism, but even the most loving parents were likely to place them in an orphanage, at least temporarily, as a respite measure at a time of extreme desperation.[11] A report from Western Siberia filed on 16 May 1932 stated that there were currently about 2,500 destitute children in the region, 90 per cent of whom came from areas of the countryside where the harvest had failed, or from the families of low-paid workers.[12] It was not until the mid-1930s that demand

44 'Children's Friends, Return the Abandoned Child to the Ranks of the Labouring People'. Poster, 1920s.

started to tail off, at which point the Soviet government itself increased demand by instituting a 'clean up the streets' policy that further boosted orphanage numbers. Thus, though both the Provisional Government and the Bolsheviks were committed to state support of children's institutions, in practice, financing and regulating institutions was to prove extremely problematic; yet the first decade and a half after the Revolution saw not just a history of failure (exacerbated by government dictate), but of human heroism on the part of child activists, of brave dreams, and of mixed experience on the part of children.

Regulating Welfare

The ways in which broader involvement by the state could help ensure the effectiveness of institutional provision for children were starting to be recognised by the Tsarist government in the early years of the twentieth century. The First World War was a watershed in terms of public support for orphanages, in particular. But it was not until the February Revolution of 1917, and the formation of the Provisional Government, that fundamental changes in institutional provision began. On 5 May 1917, the Ministry of State Welfare, with Prince D. I. Shakhovskoi as minister and Countess S. V. Panina as his deputy, was founded. Work immediately began – using the traditional method of setting up commissions of inquiry – on how welfare provision was to be improved. This included a Conference on Questions of Social Aid to Children, embracing four committees: Motherhood and Infancy, Social Aid to Normal Children of All Ages, Defective Children, and Child Offenders.

The committees in turn drew up lengthy schedules of desiderata (for example, children's clubs, legislation on labour protection for children). Notable in their work was a strong emphasis on the principles of 'free education'. The Second Section, for example (dealing with Social Aid to Normal Children) stated that the current type of children's institution was too formal. Support to needy children was better directed through 'open door' institutions, on the model of the British Barnardo homes, and through drop-in centres offering food aid; all kinds of support must bear in mind children's spiritual interests and the need to develop independence and self-reliance in them. The Third Section (Defective Children) firmly asserted the rights of all children to a normal education, which was to be offered in parallel institutions covering the full range of different levels, from crèches to seven-year schools, which were offered in the mainstream school network. There were to be separate institutions for separate types of 'defectives', whether physical, intellectual, or 'moral' (in other words, 'difficult' or 'delinquent' children), and there was to be supervision of children when they left such institutions, to ensure that they could become fully integrated into society. For their part, young criminals were to be educated, not punished, and the juvenile court network was to undergo expansion in order to ensure referral to the appropriate type of institution.[13]

The Provisional Government did not enjoy sufficient time in office to begin serious work on these ambitious plans, but they are of interest because of their close similarity to policy under the Bolshevik regime during its early years. There were, however, some major practical differences. The Bolsheviks' hostility to 'bourgeois philanthropy' and 'voluntarism' precluded reliance on private charity, which had been the primary method of response to social distress before the Revolution, and which had also been allowed a significant role, alongside state endeavours, under the Provisional Government's plans for welfare reform.[14] Certainly, some place was given to volunteer work during the first fifteen years of Soviet power, partly because the withdrawal of central state funding in 1918 left catastrophic gaps in provision for children.[15] The League of Rescue for Children, led by E. D. Kuskova and set up in autumn 1918, was a particularly active organisation: in the first year of its existence it settled 3,500 children in impromptu communes, where they built their own huts and tended their own allotments.[16] From 1923, the Children's Friend acted as an umbrella group of local societies, which raised funds to help children in need and publicised their problems in journals and newsletters. By 1931, the organisation had 1.8 million members all over the Soviet Union.[17]

Yet the Soviet government's tolerance of charitable initiatives (which were felt to be a threat to state control) was limited even in the early days after the Revolution. Reliance on 'voluntarism' was tolerated as a short-term, emergency measure. During the Volga famine, the Soviet government was even prepared to accept help from foreign charities such as the American Relief Association (which supported nearly 60 per cent of the 254,179 children receiving aid in 1921) and the Save the Children Fund, which concentrated resources in Saratov, where more than 120 million children's meals were served in 1921.[18] But aid was most certainly not an acceptable solution in the long term. Already in 1920, the League of Rescue for children had fallen into disfavour (apparently because some tactless questioning by foreign visitors had alerted the Soviet authorities that children cared for by the League were allowed to have crosses above their beds if they so wished), and in January 1921 the organisation was absorbed into the Moscow Education Office (MONO), itself a sub-department of Narkompros.[19] For its part, the Children's Friend, as a wholly Soviet organisation, was tolerated until the early 1930s, but then began to come under unjust attack as feeble and ineffective (for which read, ideologically unacceptable).[20] The Children's Friend never regained its importance or its autonomy. Its journal was wound up in 1933, and the organisation itself shut down on 1 July 1935.[21]

Ideological hostility to voluntary organisations did not aid the provision of efficient help to children: such organisations were specialised in a way that official provision was not. From 1918, the overseeing of children's institutions was divided between three different commissariats – Narkompros (the Education Commissariat), Narkomzdrav (the Commissariat of Health), and Narkomsotsbes (the Social Welfare Commissariat). Narkomzdrav was responsible for infants under the age of three and physically handicapped children, and Narkompros dealt with 'normal' orphanages for the 3–14 age group, for 'mentally defective' children, and also for 'difficult' and 'law-breaking' children.[22] For its part, Narkomsotsbes ran a variety of welfare facilities. In some respects, the division of responsibility seems to have originated in ministerial tradition, rather than in operational logic, with Narkomsotsbes taking over facilities formerly run by private charities, while the other ministries absorbed those set up by the state.

Alongside these multi-ministry arrangements, the founder of the Soviet secret police, Feliks Dzerzhinsky, campaigned for more involvement on the part of his organisation, which culminated, in January 1921, in the formation of the so-called Children's Commission (Detkomissiya, known in the Ukraine as TsKPomDet, or the Central Committee of Children's Aid).[23] From then on, the Cheka and its parent commissariat, the NKVD (People's Commissariat of Internal Affairs), played an increasingly significant role in the assessment, referral, and institutional care of children. In June 1927, the Commission (renamed the Commission for the Improvement of Children's Lives) was given the status of an all-Soviet organisation and department of the Party's Central Committee.[24] The justice commissariat, Narkomyust, was also involved in child welfare in that the initial processing of juvenile delinquency cases came under its remit.[25]

This assignation of institution types to separate ministries was further complicated by the assignation to separate ministries of duties *within* different types of institution. A decree of 15 September 1921 gave jurisdiction over sanitation and hygiene in all children's institutions, including those administered by Narkompros, to the commissariat of health.[26] In 1922, Narkomzdrav rammed home its authority in such matters, stipulating that no children's institutions were to be opened until the plans (choice of site, premises, etc.) had been vetted by its representatives.[27] A further decree of 1923 imposed twice-annual sanitary inspections of inmates and premises on all institutions.[28] Though homes for 'moral defectives' were generally the responsibility of the education ministry, in 1922 Narkomzdrav assigned itself the right to open 'curative educational colonies' for 'morally defective' children if they also happened to suffer from a physical ailment of some kind.[29] And in 1919, the social welfare commissariat was operating a wide range of institutions in Petrograd province: three labour colonies, one orphanage, eight children's health colonies, and one colony of unknown purpose in Syas'ko Radkovskaya.[30]

It was equally common for commissariats to claim that some area did not fall within their jurisdiction. Narkompros, for example, was constantly emphasising in the 1920s that sick and 'idiot' children should be the clients of Narkomzdrav.[31] At the same time, some areas of welfare did not fall into the responsibility of any ministry involved in child welfare. This applied, for instance, to the provision of leisure facilities in cities. To some extent, this gap was filled by the Komsomol and Pioneer organisations, which had a welfare remit of sorts. However, the primary function of these bodies was – especially in the 1920s and early 1930s – political education, and they in no way acted as a universal safety net for the system's failures.[32]

Ministerial conflict could be exploited by acute directors of institutions in order to achieve their ends – a case in point being Anton Makarenko, who appealed to the NKVD when Narkompros would not let him set up a Komsomol group in his model reformatory.[33] But by and large, those doing practical work with children tended to find the situation irritating rather than conducive to autonomy. 'It's hard to imagine now how things were organised,' one woman who worked in the orphanage system just after the Revolution remembered. 'The social welfare ministry [*sic*] "made the space available", the education ministry supplied the food and the personnel to deal with it; the ministry of culture provided the supervisors. These three authorities had nothing whatever to do with each other and there was no chain of command. The housekeeper and I could not dictate anything to each other, and neither of us could do anything at all to try and arrange life in a normal way.'[34]

'The Way to Calvary'

Before children reached institutions, they had to be identified as needy in the first place. From 1922, the Children's Social Inspectorate was supposed to act as a task force in every district, identifying cases where children were being exploited at home or in their place of employment. Inspectors were meant to visit all places of employment, and had the right to call on families where children were not being properly cared for. If neglect was observed, inspectors had to file a report, and might, at their discretion, remove children into the state care system (consign them to an orphanage reception centre).[35] A Narkompros directive of August 1926 affirmed the role of the Inspectorate and instructed that its members should liaise with local authorities and voluntary organisations, including the Children's Friend, and refer cases of abuse or neglect to the latter. In 1932, the force (renamed the Child Protection Inspectorate) was assigned not only strictly protective tasks (the prevention of cruelty), but regulatory tasks. Officers employed by the society were to be posted in public places (stations, bus stations, cinemas, harbours, markets, tram stops, squares, gardens, and ice rinks were all mentioned specifically), and were supposed to curb 'anti-social behaviour' by minors – 'riding on tram-buffers, fighting, street-trading, gambling, and pointless loitering in markets and shops, outside cinemas and clubs, and on stations'.[36]

The intentions behind the inspectorates were good. A 1923 guide set out an ambitious programme for training courses, involving four months of study in such subjects as law and comparative law (for example how Western countries responded to child abandonment), child psychology, psychopathology, criminology, hygiene, first aid, and practical work with abandoned and delinquent children.[37] But how effective the inspectorates were is questionable. The 1926 directive suggested staffing norms of two in every 'large population centre', particularly provincial capitals, and one in smaller towns.[38] Caseloads this high (potentially, many thousands per inspector) would hardly have allowed even part of the child protection brief to be carried out. In practice, the first line of response to street children was usually beat policemen, who – going by survivor memoirs – often treated street children suspected of an offence brusquely, or indeed roughly.[39] Equally, memoirs indicate that children were – once 'processed' in this primitive way – frequently dumped in the nearest jail or 'deported' as quickly as possible from the area where they had come to police attention, rather than transferred to one of the reception centres run by the NKVD.[40]

When or if a child reached a reception centre, the treatment it received was not certain to be in tune with current ideas about best paediatric or pedagogical (paedological) practice. Once again, parallelism was partly to blame. In the early Soviet years, 'reception points' or 'sorting shelters' were run by the social services and health commissariats as well as by Narkompros and the NKVD, and the set-up in each case was slightly different.[41] Some types of such 'points' or 'shelters' were visualised as multi-skilled diagnostic and re-educational centres. The 1918 instructions for those run by the social welfare ministry included the statement, 'The general style of life should have a completely family character, which precludes regulating times rigidly.' They also stipulated that staff should work with inmates on an individual basis, seeking to develop their particular traits and to prevent them from encouraging each other's criminal propensities.[42] A guide to child welfare published in 1922 provided quite a complex template for psychological assessment in reception centres, with a choice of forty-seven adjectives to describe character, from 'cheerful' and 'curious', via 'flaccid', to 'quarrelsome'. Personal characteristics were supposed to be investigated, including grasp of hygiene, occupational background, and abilities, and the child had to undergo a questionnaire ('What is the most noble profession? What are you going to do to provide for your old age?')[43] Other centres worked more like orphanages or communes, laying on broad programmes of 'arts education' and attempting to initiate the process of rehabilitation by democratic participation.[44] Others again were merely holding centres, with all the hygiene and supervision problems that

45 Children's Home, Moscow, early 1920s.

went with the role.[45] In the best of circumstances, the main pressure on reception points was to clear new arrivals quickly. In the early 1920s, for instance, staff were supposed to make referrals to a home within three days.[46] The impact of any expertise available could be at best limited.

Of course, expertise was not necessarily essential. More important, perhaps, was a sympathetic and understanding attitude to the new arrivals. In the first post-revolutionary years, the cultivation of such an attitude was encouraged by official policy. No abandoned child, it was held, was beyond help. 'In [Communist society] there must be no deprived children, no children "belonging to no one",' declared a delegate to the First Congress of Child Protection Activists in 1919.[47] There was a strong tendency to romanticise abandoned children. In the words of an orphanage worker, writing in 1928: 'Our homeless child is not at all like his pre-revolutionary equivalent, weak, cowed, knocked about, pathetic. He is often bold, free, with plenty of initiative, and inventive.'[48] Grigory Belykh and Leonid Panteleev's famous novel, *The Republic of Shkid* (1926), was a lively exposition of this view of waifs. Adapted from the two writers' personal experience, the book depicted the early years of a home for young offenders, most of them former street children. The essential trajectory of the book was summed up in a song sung by the inhabitants of Shkid:

> Our path is long, our path is hard,
> We'll need to labour every hour
> To win through in the end,
> To win through in the end.[49]

But Belykh and Panteleev's plot did not move along this 'path' relentlessly. Those relegated to the 'republic of Shkid' included characters resistant to the institution's rehabilitationist magic, for example Siver Dolgoruky, an experienced thief who ended up corrupting several of his fellows rather than being reformed. Even pupils who were not such tough nuts took time to be softened up – Belykh and Panteleev's *alter egos* 'Yankel" and 'Lenya' found themselves in trouble for making a scurrilous film-strip based on trashy American Western movies, while 'mucking about' (*buza*) was the favourite activity of most of the school. A sense of enjoyable but not always harmless mischief came through, as well as a picture of street children's specific culture, their street slang and songs, not to speak of their pilfering skills.

Similar motifs appeared in Nikolai Ekk's highly entertaining film *Road into Life* (1931), famous, among other things, as the first sound film ever made in Russia. Once again, this was a text with an upbeat ending, showing the orphans welded into a new collective, under the wise care of their supervisor, and celebrating the opening of a stretch of railway line built by their own hands. But it also suggested the romance and adventure of street life: an amusing piece of inter-cutting juxtaposed a vignette of a shoemaking lesson with a scene in which young thieves snip out the pocket of a lady's astrakhan coat, leaving her bloomers on view. While the rationale for this montage was to show skills learned on the street converted to good use, the lure of misdemeanours came across strongly as well. This was no doubt one reason why the film was so popular, grossing 2.8 million roubles, far ahead of any other title of the time.[50]

Crumbling Palaces, Open Doors

In real life, of course, both the waifs themselves and the institutions mandated to receive them were very different from the model homes eulogised by Ekk, Panteleev, and Belykh. Life on the streets was less a question of romantic social defiance than a desperate struggle for survival. Just as before 1917, street children congregated in particular areas of cities (especially round major stations), and sought out places where they could sleep rough in relative comfort and safety; for instance, close to asphalt boilers or next to rubbish dumps. They took any employment they could find; otherwise, they lived on their wits, often by petty crime and by parasitic activities such as begging and busking. Children tended to mass in groups, with older children caring for younger siblings; within groups, a strict hierarchy obtained, with bullying, exploitation, and even rape of younger, 'undefended' children likely. In turn, street children easily became victims of unscrupulous adults, both as sex workers and as ancillaries in theft and other types of crime – the attitude being that a child was fair game, since a child was not subject to the same penalties as adults.[51]

The shelter offered to children by the Soviet state bore little resemblance to the model homes in propaganda and works of art, or indeed to the optimistic statements in congress resolutions and guides for orphanage workers. In the terrible post-revolutionary years, Soviet baby homes had a record that was as bad as, or worse than, the 'angel factories' of Tsarist Russia. In some Ukrainian homes, mortality stood at 100 per cent in 1921–2. While figures from Kursk in 1923 were better (64 per cent mortality), they were still very poor compared with what the better homes had achieved in the 1910s.[52] As with the homes of the pre-revolutionary era, figures improved significantly if mothers could be induced to stay with their babies and feed them. One sub-type of baby home, the mother and child home, was specifically organised in order to cater for this possibility, offering pre-natal care, supervised delivery, and shelter and support after the birth.[53] The 1926 figures indicated that the rate of mortality in these was 7–10 per cent on average, as opposed to 32.4 per cent in the ordinary type of baby home. But the network of mother and child homes was significantly smaller than the network of baby homes (alternatively known at this period as Infant Homes): in 1925, there were 287 of the latter across the Russian Federation, but only 96 of the former.[54] Efforts to provide care for vulnerable children somewhere other than in 'angel factories' were concentrated on the crèche system: already by 1922, commentators in the health service had realised that proper support at this level led to a lowered rate of child abandonment, and hence to decreased strain on the network of 'closed institutions'.[55]

So far as older children were concerned, in the first years after the Revolution, emphasis was placed on orphanages and homes as ideal social institutions, operating in a cloud of co-operation and enthusiasm. At the First Congress of

Child Welfare Activists held in Moscow in February 1919, for example, discussion focused on the moral and psychological side: the power of self-government to reform children who seemed recalcitrant; the therapeutic role played by art, literature, and theatre; the importance of running homes of the 'family type', which adopted the 'open door' principle.[56] The centrality of 'open door' policies and of 'self-government' for inmates continued to be underlined in the 1920s as well. In this vein, a section on the 'open children's home' in a guide to child welfare issues published in 1922 declared: 'It is difficult to define in concrete terms the characteristics of work in such homes. The ability to create a cosy corner that children like, to get them interested in the home, so that they drop in every day, if only for a short time, has to be the start.'[57] Issues to do with the practical day-to-day running of institutions took second place to assertion of their utopian function as training schools for young minds. Supervision of hygiene in homes would, it was assumed, be the responsibility of institution doctors, who would carry out weekly inspections of children, provide inoculations, check that the premises were in a sanitary condition and take special measures during epidemics.[58] It was not until 1923 that even the health commissariat drew up a procedural guide for inspections. Visits to check hygienic conditions and to examine inmates were stipulated, at regular, but also lengthy, intervals (six months).[59] In the early years, inspections tended to rely on paper evidence, requiring from orphanage administrations a stream of reports about what they were doing – a system that was, clearly, wide open to abuse.[60]

Material conditions were also very difficult. In the early days of Soviet power it was common to turn over elite buildings such as former palaces, monasteries, and country manors for use as orphanages and shelters. This practice, however striking in symbolic terms, was often a nightmare in practical terms. Such buildings were poorly adapted to institutional use in the best of situations, since they lacked specialised equipment or furnishings; the depredations of war and revolution had often made conditions in them totally squalid. Elizaveta Tikheeva, writing in 1922, painted a dismal picture of a nationalised Petrograd mansion: 'There is nothing on the walls but filthy torn wallpaper, the floors are covered with refuse, there are crippled pieces of once luxurious furniture shoved without sense or system into the corners of rooms, the cupboards and storage areas are a mess, and so are the tables, and in the middle of all this sit filthy children with shaven dirty heads in filthy hand-me-down clothes, with their stockings falling down and their noses dripping.'[61] A similar report was made to the Krasnaya Presnya Communist Party women delegates' meeting in March 1923. In Orphanage No. 19, the bedding was soiled, the children had to drink out of rusty unwashed tin mugs, the store-rooms contained an unholy mixture of medicine and salt herring all in one place, and no one had bothered to fumigate the rooms after a scarlatina outbreak. Understandably, nearly half the inmates played truant some or most of the time.[62]

Abuses were reported *ad hoc* to the local Party authorities, which took them extremely seriously.[63] But there were also failures of care that went unrecorded. Vadim Shefner, who lived in children's homes for several years in the mid 1920s while his mother was working there as a supervisor, endured a serious scalding in one home at dinner time, when boiling water was being poured into the children's mugs for tea. The incident (which could perfectly well have been blamed on poor supervision by the staff) attracted no fuss whatever: it was simply regarded by all concerned (including the child himself) as an accident.[64]

The 'hands off' regulation of institutions could encourage imaginative behaviour. In August 1919, there were plans to set up a special facility for bed-wetters in Petrograd, so that these children could be saved from the humiliation and stress of life in ordinary orphanages, and be offered specialist treatment and care.[65] And dedicated staff did their best to ameliorate chaos and decay. A bath might be made out of an old horse trough, and hot water boiled on a heating stove, or the supervisors (meant to be responsible for the moral and intellectual side of the children's welfare) might roll up their sleeves and build the bath-house that was so badly needed.[66] Care for the non-material aspects of the children's existence could be equally assiduous. For instance, in Novgorod province orphanage in the early 1920s children were delighted by a Christmas tree.[67] In the flagship Narkompros home located in the former Znamensky Monastery, Moscow, teachers, while acknowledging that their charges were difficult and demanding, watched keenly for signs of their better nature. 'They were as restrained today as they were boisterous yesterday,' one woman teacher recorded in 1923. She also delightedly remarked that her charges became lively and responsive if the right subject-matter were chosen. They had particularly enjoyed a visit to the zoo with commentaries about the animals, and a story about the adventures of a feisty little orphan. The desire to inspire enthusiasm and establish rapport with the children precluded ideological rigidity: as well as talking about heroic role models, supervisors might read aloud fairy tales, get children writing their own autobiographies, or talk to them about the countryside and the beauties of nature.[68]

In many cases, supervisors were extremely conscious of children as individuals, or at least as members of diverse categories. Alongside the 'harmonious natures' who had survived abandonment more or less unscathed (about 15 per cent of the group), one commentator wrote, one might find 'weak types susceptible to bad influences' (7–8 per cent), disruptive older children who were better off learning a trade than being kept in the schoolroom (10 per cent), thieves and sensualists who might be transformed by work (7–8 per cent), retrainable beggars (no proportion given), children with nervous problems or mental handicaps (7–8 per cent), and around 50–60 per cent of just 'middling' children. The personalities of each needed to be carefully studied so that the right approach could be taken and the 're-education', which was so necessary, achieved.[69] In many institutions, 're-education' might remain a pious fiction, but the better homes achieved much in the way of 're-educating' their charges, and of generating self-discipline and responsibility by the use of persuasion. The House of the Child, a model orphanage in Odessa, deliberately set its face from the outset against 'barrack-like organisation', preferring to allow the children to express themselves gradually through physical exercise and play. Reportedly, the results were extremely successful. From sullen silence and misanthropy, the children gradually progressed not only into more confident self-expression, but into self-reliance. Eighteen months after the House had opened, the adults in charge could, they reported, happily leave the children to take care of themselves while they went off to visit a conference, and be certain that an unsupervised meal would not turn into 'pandemonium', as it had at the beginning, but be conducted in a cheerful but orderly fashion.[70]

This particular orphanage was special in a number of ways. Unlike most, it had a homogeneous intake in terms of age (the children were all in the kindergarten phase); it was also a small institution run by enthusiasts who had a background in child psychology and in child care. The same was true of the home for Latvian children in a former mansion in St Petersburg, which genuinely did provide the happy family atmosphere spoken of at the conferences of the day.[71] But there were simply not the resources to allow slow, careful treatment, with psychological input, of all the many thousands of orphaned and abandoned children. A thumbnail sketch of the size of the problem is given by figures for Leningrad Central District in 1924. Only 28.5 per cent of the child population was embraced by institutions (and this included kindergartens and crèches as well as residential facilities). Even so, the number of orphanage inmates on the books in just this one district was not far short of 6,000.[72]

46 Reception hall, Mother and Child Care Point, Leningrad. This facility, located in a former mansion, exemplifies the practice of converting palatial dwellings into children's institutions.

From September 1924, a means-tested scale of charges for parents who wished to place their children in homes was introduced.[73] But this dealt with only one, numerically insignificant, category of orphanage inmate. Other attempts to make children's homes self-sufficient in economic terms – decrees of 1921–2 that they were to have their own vegetable patches and to teach useful skills, and, in 1924, that children capable of going into employment were to be found jobs[74] – had little impact. In some homes during the early 1920s, judging by personal recollections, rations were limited to a pound of oat bread a day, or – still more inadequately – 250 grams of bread.[75] Personal stories of this kind are confirmed by official records, which reveal that staff in some orphanages had no idea what the inmates were up to, that plans for organising day-to-day life were often rudimentary at best, that conditions in orphanages verged from the desperate to the absolutely unspeakable (particularly during the immediate post-revolutionary years), and that abuses on the part of staff were rife.[76] Not all adults working in orphanages were the selfless, committed individuals represented in Soviet literature. So far from generating a new revolutionary consciousness in children, or providing a haven for them, many homes could not provide adequate care even to the low proportion of abandoned children who actually reached them; at the same time, the cost of this inadequate level of provision swallowed no less than 27.5 per cent of the entire education budget.[77]

Damaged Souls

Orphaned or abandoned children themselves were often very different from the feisty but co-operative heroes of rehabilitationist legend. To begin with, they were very often unhealthy in a physical sense. Figures from a Moscow reception centre in early 1919 indicated that only 11 out of 128 children admitted in that year had been fully fit: of the remaining 91 per cent, 5 per cent were suffering from rickets, 7 per cent from scrofula, 3 per cent from mange, 2 per cent from ringworm, 2 per cent from TB; nearly half the group had trichomoniasis, and more than a third were deaf and dumb.[78] The psychological profile of the intake was no more encouraging. A record of the inmates of the House of the Child in Odessa at play indicates that abandonment had not left these unscathed: favourite games included Zoo Animals Escaping from their Cages, and Mother, in which a cruel parent beat, scolded, and tormented her offspring.[79]

Orphanage workers inspired by the ethos of 'free education' found their idealism called into question by early encounters with charges who were confrontational, uncooperative, and possibly even violent. In February 1923, an anonymous orphanage worker in Moscow recorded how stressful it could be to try and get such children even to remain in the classroom, let alone to do any work:

19 February 1923 After ages spent trying to get the children to come to lessons, four eventually did come and sit down. The others insisted that they did not want to study. They run and hide in the classroom cupboard, or under the desks; some take themselves off for a walk without bothering to ask permission. The dormitories are usually kept locked, but since the stoves have to be fed, every now and then the doors get opened. The children seize their chance and go and hide under the beds. I have to spend all my time urging them to come and learn.[80]

The 'open door' policy underestimated the sheer allure of thieving, drug-taking, drinking, and prostitution for children who had spent any length of time on the street. Such activities were not only responses to immediate economic deprivation, but gestures of social identity. A gang ethos was pervasive among children living rough, and a rigid hierarchy obtained, with 'family children', those new to the street, regarded with contempt by the more experienced. The commission of a crime, or the sharing of alcohol, drugs, or sex with other gang members were ways in which a neophyte could raise his or her status in the gang.[81] And, while petty theft was by far the commonest misdemeanour committed by minors throughout early Soviet history, followed by crimes against public order, there was also a small hard core of children involved in crimes against the person, as well as in prostitution.[82]

Children themselves romanticised the lure of transgression. Waif folklore abounded in celebrations of murder, cruelty, violence, and transgressive behaviour generally. In the 1920s, the waifs were among the main purveyors of the so-called 'cruel romances', street ballads of unhappy love and violent death:

> Though we forget, our children will not
> The story that I'm going to tell you about.
> In brief, to cut the details short,
> A husband's killing of his wife I report.
> On a street in the middle of Leningrad city
> A workman lived with his wife and his kiddy,
> His little daughter who was so sweet,
> He had a good job and life was a treat.
> Until one windy and rainy day
> The sister of his wife came to stay. [...]
> What must be, must be, as you know:
> He got the hots for the sister, so,
> Like any beast so ravening wild,
> He decided to skewer his wife and child.[83]

For abandoned children, the street – whatever its dangers – signified freedom, excitement, and power, and the orphanage incarceration:

> We ain't got no toys,
> What you give – we'll take,
> We'll spend what we get
> On cards – as a stake.[84]

The obvious risk of a non-interventionist care policy – and in particular one combined with sentimental idealisation of the 'active', 'lively' older boys who were most likely to be inveterate thieves and bullies[85] – was that it would do nothing to combat the values ruling the streets. And it does indeed seem that escapes were frequent, and that there were orphanages and reformatories where abuse of the most vulnerable children and defensive metamorphosis of 'family kids' into thieves and rowdies were a good deal more common than the conversion of street children into model members of the collective.[86] Orphanages run under a liberal regime did not necessarily provide safe havens for the frail and timid. Even if such children avoided serious violence, they had to endure teasing that could sometimes be vicious. Vadim Shefner remembered that the children in his home were adept in thinking up cruel nicknames for each other (Shefner's was Cross-Eyed Git, because of his squint; other inmates were known as Toothless Viper and Stinkboots). The only defence against taunts was to become an expert fighter: Shefner himself gained a degree of respect and acceptance by learning to lash out viciously with his feet.[87]

'The Fight with Child Homelessness'

From the mid-1920s, policy increasingly swung against the 'open door' and towards coercion of children into official institutions. A 1926 decree of the Council of People's Commissars of the RSFSR with the unwieldy title, 'In Confirmation of

Some Measures in the Fight with Child Homelessness in the RSFSR', set out a variety of 'tracks' along which homeless children might be sent, including direct referral to hospitals or clinics, penal colonies, reception centres, closed children's institutions, or (in the cases of small children) maternal protection organisations.[88] The following year, the Child Protection Commission instituted a 'three-year plan' aimed at the 'eradication' of child homelessness. It had two components: an effort to round up and institutionalise children living rough, and a drive to reduce the extant orphanage population by 68,000 in order to find space for the street children.[89] In other words, children were now to be forced to enter institutions, whether they happened to want to or not.

Attitudes towards the regime operating in orphanages had also altered. During the late 1920s, Anton Makarenko's methods – which involved a good deal of military-style drilling, a heavy emphasis on manual work, and the dressing-down of disruptive inmates at meetings of the full 'collective' of the orphanage, i.e. in front of all the inmates and the staff – began to suit the tenor of the times.[90] Such strategies were not new inventions: they revived the practice of the more liberal juvenile reformatories of the 1900s and 1910s. But this heritage was not acknowledged: Makarenko represented himself as the spokesman of a fundamentally new, 'Soviet', commitment to order and self-discipline, imposed from the top (by the orphanage director), but willingly accepted and affirmed by the collective as a whole.

As well as a growing stress on discipline, there was growing emphasis on hygiene in children's institutions. An article of 1928 expressing concern about the very high rates of disease among orphanage inmates linked this with problems in the running of the homes. Space was short, exposure to fresh air was not built into the timetable, and supplies of clothes had only just reached tolerable levels. While 'self-help' was a good idea, loading inmates with heavy physical work was not. The article made a range of recommendations incorporating the hygienic principles of the day: an open and healthy site for the building itself; better food, prepared by expert staff; better living space; light and bright furniture that was fit for the purpose; an allowance of at least six buckets of water per person per day; and a rational timetable, with at least two hours' outdoor exercise, half an hour's PE and 8–9 hours' sleep per day. It also recommended that proper records be kept of the inmates' requirements.[91] In 1929, hygiene modules were introduced to staff training courses, and in 1932 'sanitary minimums', requiring regular airing and swabbing down with disinfectant, were imposed.[92]

The practical effects of these changes were rather muted – a pattern that would occur again and again in the history of Soviet children's institutions. In the short term, the 1926 decree and 1927 plan do seem to have had a significant effect on the visibility, if nothing else, of child abandonment in major Russian cities.[93] The 1932 measures, on the other hand, were defeated by the ever-expanding numbers of 'unsupervised' children. Besides the victims of the collectivisation campaign in 1929–32, these included the flotsam of mass industrialisation during the First and Second Five Year Plans, as new migrants to the cities flooded into factory jobs: with the real value of wages falling by half between 1928 and 1932, women as well as men rushed into employment, leaving children who could be considered half-way capable of looking after themselves unattended outside school hours.[94] On to the streets also floated the jetsam of the new disciplinary procedures in Soviet schools. School exclusions, permitted from 1932, simply ensured that the most difficult pupils became a general social, rather than a specifically educational, problem. Two years after the practice was first allowed, in 1934, 40 per cent of young offenders in Moscow turned out, in the course of police investigations, to be pupils on school exclusions. In professional journals, if not in mainstream newspapers, Soviet jurists admitted that expulsion from the Pioneers and from school could be the top of a slippery slope down which children slid inexorably into waifdom and then into crime.[95]

While the restrictions on private trading that followed the end of NEP allowed campaigners for children's welfare to step up their time-honoured campaign to stop children from carrying out 'degrading' activities such as newspaper-selling and boot-blacking, restrictions on the means by which children in need might legally support themselves increased, rather than ameliorating, the likelihood that minors would find themselves on the wrong side of the law. In Sverdlovsk province, during the third quarter of 1932 as compared with the second quarter, the numbers of minors arrested went up by more than 50 per cent.[96]

The task of reducing orphanage numbers also proved problematic. To begin with, the crackdown on child homelessness had made institutions the main dumping ground for any stray children. Child protection officers were explicitly instructed that they should (having duly made a written record of the anti-social behaviour at stake) convey a child they had caught behaving badly back to its family, or else to an orphanage or an official reception centre.[97] In practice, officers and police officials often did not bother to check whether the child even had a home, but simply took it straight to the nearest orphanage or reception centre, or indeed to the police station, if this was the most expedient method of extricating themselves from further responsibility for the child concerned.[98] Between 1931 and 1933, the orphanage population across the RSFSR increased by around 130 per cent, from 105,561 to 241,744, and 570 extra orphanages were opened. However, comparison of numbers of orphanages and numbers of inmates indicates that the average number of children per orphanage rose from around 75 to over 120.[99] In September 1933, a report recorded that Ukrainian orphanages were packed to more than double capacity, with over 128,000 children instead of the normal maximum of 60,000. Conditions at the same time in the Danilov Monastery in Moscow, the city's main reception centre, were, according to an observer from the Children's Commission, simply 'inhumane', with 1,250 children held there, yet there were also 3,000 children still on the streets awaiting placements in institutions.[100] Desperate officials, caught between instructions to clean up the streets and instructions to reduce orphanage populations, would try to force children to leave their town. Aleksandr Saranin, originally from the Urals, was at first unable to persuade workers in the Vladivostok reception centre to take him in, securing admission eventually through personal connections.[101]

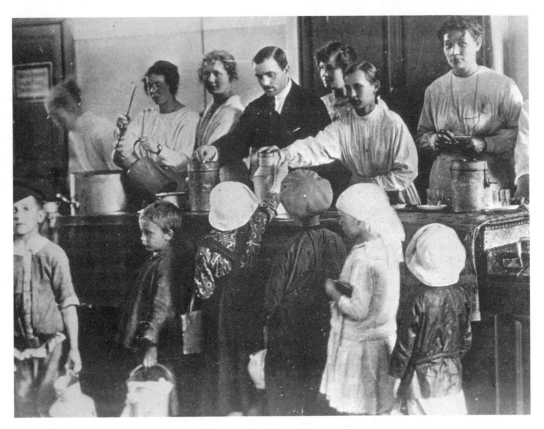

47   Soup kitchen, Moscow, early 1920s.

Inevitably, given the overcrowding, talk of improved hygiene often went no further than talk, especially since supervisors were often inadequately trained. Reports from the late 1920s indicate that conditions were, at least in the worst orphanages, just as bad as they had been in the chaotic first years of Soviet power. According to a sketch written by a supervisor at the Young Republic children's commune in Moscow province in 1928, the hygienic regime existed only as a grotesque parody of itself:

A cracked bell sounds, and a tousled orphanage inmate leaps from his lopsided bed. His head aches from the fusty air, his side twinges from the lumpiness of the bed. He wants to go straight back to sleep – last night the doors were squeaking and banging till very late and keeping him awake.

He runs his fingers through his hair to tidy it, and pulls his trousers out from under his pillow, hauls them on and rushes to the washstand. There's a queue there though. Fierce swearing hangs in the air. A quarrel is in progress. What's the problem? The boy on duty never brought the water – someone took the bucket to the kitchen yesterday and it got left there, and then it ended up in the canteen being used for milk.[102]

There were model orphanages, however. One such was a home for about forty inmates out in the countryside around Moscow, with its own farm and agricultural land, working like a self-sufficiency commune. In the circumstances, the boast that there had never been an attempt to run away seems perfectly plausible.[103]

Reception centres likewise ran the gamut. At one end was No. 3 centre in Moscow, which, in 1930, was acting more like a college of petty crime than the first stage of state rehabilitation, with flick-knife-wielding and lock-picking as rife as smoking, and escapes by inmates (including a case where the absconders made off with a pile of coats) frequent. At the other was the centre where Sof'ya Tyumina worked, where reasonable methods were in operation, such as refusing to deal with the children until they adopted more civilised modes of behaviour, and also using story-telling sessions to entertain them.[104] Whatever the overall success of the 'open door' policy, descriptions by supervisors in the better institutions presented an attractive picture. In 1928, for example, a report in the magazine the *Children's Friend* enthusiastically portrayed the 'Open Doors' reception centre in Moscow. Inmates who had previously smoked, abused alcohol, wet their beds, and been uncontrollably rude and excitable, were, the report said, transformed by their stay here, and especially by exposure to 'serious work'. The author concluded: 'Our experience indicated that the temptation to set up "cheap shelters" should be resisted, and that institutions for abandoned children should be reformed.'[105] The central problem with this suggestion was, predictably, financial: so long as numbers remained high, the provision of 'cheap shelters' was a fact of life.

As for the children themselves, they remained as they had been in the first years of Soviet power – traumatised or street-hardened on arrival, and often physically sick as well. A large-scale survey of 1928 indicated that nearly 70 per cent of new admissions to orphanages were suffering from an organic disease of some kind, often malnutrition-related (anaemia, hypertrophy, lung problems). Experience of famine was also likely, especially among boys, around 70 per cent of whom would have gone hungry before reaching the orphanage.[106] According to a smaller-scale, but probably representative, survey done in Moscow in 1928, around 20 per cent of inmates came from broken and/or abusive homes.[107] Naturally, the orphanage populations were often difficult to manage. Sof'ya Tyumina, who worked at a reception centre in the early 1930s, remembered tangible hostility when she first arrived: she was greeted in the dining room by shouts of 'Eh, you, woman!', swearing, and spoon-banging.[108] For such children, and for many working-class and peasant teenagers and pre-teens as well, confinement in an orphanage was an affront to their dignity. Many continued, therefore, to use the orphanage as though an 'open door' policy applied, visiting occasionally to tide them over during bad times, such as the dreadful famine years of 1932–33, and returning to street life and petty crime when the situation was more propitious.[109]

The late 1920s and early 1930s saw the rise of a 'culture of blame' according to which supervisors themselves were held accountable for difficulties in homes. Typical was a 1928 article contrasting three different homes: a place in Tersk district, so filthy the dormitories had to be entered in galoshes; a model establishment with children in clean clothes; and a 'satisfactory' place with large workshops and tidy surroundings and inmates.[110] But the fact was that force of numbers and shortages of equipment put staff under tremendous pressure. The combination of stress, poor institutional support, low pay, inadequate training, and low prestige was too much for many. Staff shortages were endemic. In 1932, each doctor responsible for the welfare of orphanage inmates in Moscow would have, at best, around 400 patients in his or her care, and, at worst, up to 850.[111] It is perhaps no wonder that some staff resorted to brutality to deal with their difficult charges. As 'Nicholas Voinov' recalled of the Third International Home in 1931, 'The rules of the home dictated that every child wash once a day, and every day the supervisors herded us here with the help of sticks, blows and shouts. No matter what kind of order was issued by the Home, it was received with curses, protests and shouts, and everybody considered it his duty to resist.'[112]

'Homes in Worker Families'

One apparently obvious solution to the problems of overcrowding and mismanagement would have been to make arrangements for children outside the institutional system, by assigning them to new families. In the first years of Soviet power, however, when some observers considered that even children with two parents were best removed from the clutches of the family, fostering and adoption were problematic in ideological terms. Adoption was explicitly banned in article 183 of the 1918 Code on Marriage and the Family, and participants in discussions about homeless children regularly expressed disquiet about placing children outside institutions.[113] In-family solutions were at first resorted to reluctantly, and in a reactive way – by *refusing* space to children who could conceivably be billeted with a member of their own family. In 1921–2, children with living parents began to be turned away from orphanages, and in 1924 children with relations of any kind began to be discharged from institutions.[114]

The obvious snag in this narrowly conceived policy was that abandoned children tended to come from families that could not afford to raise children (hence the abandonment): around 85 per cent of them were the offspring of peasants or labourers.[115] In the mid-1920s, therefore, a rethink on fostering and adoption was well under way among child-care activists, particularly doctors, as opposed to educationalists. Some were starting to argue that keeping infants in homes was costly and offered poor results in terms of survival. Lack of space was another factor prompting a rethink. By 1923, a small-scale fostering scheme had been piloted in Moscow. The experiment was a success, and Mossovet, the city authority, permitted an expansion in 1925.[116] The same year saw an alteration, at national level, to the ban on adoption, which was now permitted as a 'temporary measure' in urban families. In 1926, the decree On the Confirmation of Some Measures in the Fight with Child Homelessness also allowed peasant families to adopt a child, with a maximum of one to each household, or *dvor*.[117] While there were problems with finding urban families who even wished to adopt, in the villages things were different: 19,000 children, or one-tenth of the orphanage population, were transferred out of institutions in 1926.[118]

Of course, both adoption and fostering remained controversial. Narkompros was bitterly criticised in 1930 by an activist from the Children's Friend movement in Moscow, who dismissed the whole fostering drive as 'a waste of money'.[119] But at the same time as this assault took place, another activist from the movement, herself from a working-class background, was carrying out a campaign to give abandoned children homes in worker families; by April 1932, this had led to the placing of 712 individuals.[120] Fosterage was being widely used in some places: in 1933, for example, 96,000 children were being fostered in the Ukraine, a figure only just below the 96,507 children then in orphanages.[121]

The early Soviet era, then, saw attitudes to child care move from disapproval of fostering and adoption to a reluctant accommodation of these practices. However, this did not necessarily represent an unambiguous improvement in children's situation. There genuinely was the danger that children 'out-housed' in less privileged families might be exploited as cheap labour rather than welcomed as additional members of the family, especially in the absence of detailed regulation.[122] Cases were reported where children were forced to eat scraps and to sleep in sheds and workshops.[123] The proliferation of orders relating to fosterage from the late 1920s and early 1930s – calling for proper supervision and for the placement of properly vetted foster children only (in good health and physically suited to agricultural work, if they were going to villages), and for the regular payment of subsidies to foster parents – indicates not only the extent of official concern but the extent to which sensible procedures were ignored.[124] Another difficulty with the system was finding foster or adoptive families in the first place, given that many parents had to use orphanage care to help their own children survive. Inevitably, the main attraction was often the subsidy that such children brought into the family, with the result that some host parents simply dumped their charges if cash payments were held up or suspended.[125]

Yet there could be positive experiences for foster children too. In some regions, foster parents came forward readily, and treated their charges with care and attention. A 1928 report on the Moscow fostering scheme by V. Pavlovsky indicated that mortality had dropped to 8.9 per cent once infants were removed from institutions. The significant discrepancy between 'foundling home' infants and 'family infants' that was recorded daily in child-care clinics evened out once children had been in foster families for a few months. Pavlovsky attributed this not just to better diet, but also to the greater opportunities for social contact: fosterage assigned children 'substitute mothers, and in some cases very good ones'.[126] In this area too, commitment on the part of dedicated people could overcome lack of support from officialdom, and from society more broadly. There were also cases where the foster children concerned, though treated in ways that would not have been approved by contemporary advocates of children's rights, were grateful enough for the care that was provided. 'How did they treat me? It's cold there in Siberia. They'd wake me at four to light the stove. So that it'd be warm when they got up. That was my duty. And peeling the potatoes,' one woman recalled of the Poles who fostered her in the mid-1930s, when she was six. She was not allowed out to play with other children and had no toys, and had to sleep wherever she could find somewhere to lie down. But she also recalled being well fed, and being allowed to attend school. Compared with the attitude of her own relations, who had thrown her out in the street wearing a sack and carrying a handful of rusks, this was sheer heaven.[127]

'Young Law-Breakers'

Before the Revolution, street children had been seen automatically as a social threat. After 1917, the pendulum at first swung the other way. There was no child, however 'socially neglected', who did not deserve public pity and concern. Rehabilitation in the collective was open to what would previously have been described as 'juvenile criminals' (the preferred term was now 'law-breakers') just as to other categories of 'unsupervised children'. Representations of orphans often did not distinguish between young offenders and others. Indeed, the governing image of the orphan (as in Seifullina's *The Lawbreakers*, or *The Republic of Shkid*, or *Road into Life*) was of the orphan as young offender. Attitudes of this kind fed into social policy. For the first fifteen years after the Revolution, majority opinion among jurists, pedagogues, and social workers, as well as among propagandists, was solidly behind rehabilitation. A prevailing trope saw 'law-breakers' as the hosts of 'infections' – in other words, as the victims of morbid conditions that were beyond their control; penitential institutions were useless, since therapy, not punishment, was required.[128] According to another way of putting it, delinquent children were 'objectively' speaking not guilty (their faults were the faults of society), though their condition required treatment because it was harmful in a 'subjective' sense (i.e. to the children themselves).[129]

This attitude was not a matter merely for oracular statements: it was enshrined in the Decree on Commissions for Minors of 9/22 January 1918, a triumph of rehabilitationist penal policy. The decree abolished prison sentences and court trials for minors, and set up instead special three-person commissions (Commissions on the Affairs of Minors: *komsonesy*), composed of a medical practitioner as well as representatives of the People's Commissariats of Justice and of Enlightenment, to examine cases. It stipulated that young offenders were to be referred to therapeutic-pedagogical 'shelters' rather than to penal institutions.[130] Associated with the *komsonesy* were 'brothers and sisters of social help', an updated version of the court guardians who had operated before 1917: these were supposed to arrange home visits, to talk rationally to the children about the progress of the case, to arrange health checks, and to foster love of the arts; in other words, to provide a whole programme of culture and civilisation.[131]

All of this was in tune with expert criminological opinion at the time. V. I. Kufaev, writing in 1924, insisted that the 'crimes' committed by under-14s could not be classified as such. Young offenders could not help themselves, and committed prohibited actions on impulse (he gave the instance of a Tatar boy who arrived in Moscow on 19 February 1923, having lost both parents in the famine epidemic of 1921, and who stole a primus, intending to sell it and buy food, only to be caught on his very first offence).[132] While analysts of young offenders tended to accept without question the need to place this category of child in institutional care rather than impose non-custodial arrangements such as supervision orders (because they often shared the mistrust of parents current among radical child-welfare activists), they firmly believed that institutional care should be of a non-punitive kind and expressed revulsion against the regime obtaining in pre-revolutionary corrective institutions, with their barred windows and their strict regimes. The dominant belief was now that all children, whatever their 'moral defectiveness', should go to a children's home.[133]

Yet even in the early 1920s there were some dissident voices; and, ominously, these were located at the pinnacle of Soviet power. As early as 4 March 1920, the Decree on Socially Dangerous Acts by Minors reduced the age at which children could be tried in the courts to 14 from 16, and redefined the hostels as 'institutions of healing and moral education' rather than 'ancillary institutions of healing': these points were established by personal corrections made by Lenin to the draft text of the decree. The decree also allowed the *komsonesy* to refer older offenders to the courts if they decided that 'medical and pedagogical' measures were insufficient (as in the case of 'hardened recidivists').[134] In 1923 came a move to allow 'particularly dangerous' minors to be processed by the criminal courts, and the Penal Code of 1924 and the Code on Punishment of the same year adopted a more repressive attitude to juvenile criminals than their predecessors.[135] A secret order of 1925 permitted *komsonesy* to shut up minors in houses of correction (*trudovye doma*) if they deemed this appropriate.[136]

As so often with Soviet treatment of children, too, on-the-ground practice deviated from pious ideals. At the early stages of their contact with authority, law-breakers suffered what one might call 'parity of disesteem' with orphans and street children of all kinds. All waifs tended to be suspected by the police of law-breaking whatever happened, and simply rounded up. If they reached reception centres, they went through the same process of cleansing, fumigation, medical and other assessments as everyone else – or, alternatively, they were passed straight through the courts and further on (as could also happen to children who had committed no crime). The 'children's commissions' were thinly spread, outside the major cities, and often lacked the range of expertise that was prescribed in statute: in the late 1920s, there were only 100 'social assistants' across the whole of the USSR.[137] Their work was often painfully slow – in Petrograd in 1920, for example, they dealt with only thirty cases a day, though more than a thousand young offenders a month were coming through the system.[138]

Yet the *komsonesy* did radically change legal processing. In 1924, only 10 per cent of the cases that came before them terminated in an order for institutionalisation: around 30 per cent of offenders were cautioned, 15 per cent simply released, and 15 per cent referred back to their parents for action to be taken. With a further 15 per cent of those appearing before the commissions assigned to an ordinary children's home or to the care of a social worker, the desire of these institutions to avoid punitive policies at all was clear.[139]

Institutional practices were also very different to those obtaining before 1917.

The homes for 'moral defectives' run by Narkompros and Narkomsotsbes were as liberal as, if not more liberal than, the orphanages of the day. New Life, a model home in Moscow province set up by Glavsotsvos (a sub-directorate of Narkompros) in early 1928, an 'institute of labour education for former girl prostitutes', was sited in parkland, with its own dairy farm, as well as the usual workshops and schoolrooms. It offered inmates a full day of schoolwork, training, and organised leisure (in the club facilities). Inmates were supposed to rise at 6 a.m., then spend 20–25 minutes tidying up their dormitories and washing (a strip-wash to the waist with cold water). Gymnastics and a general tidy of the orphanage premises were to follow, then there was to be coffee at 8 a.m., followed by sessions in the workshops, lunch at 11.30, followed by walks and more sessions in the workshops, dinner at 15.30, rest from 16.00 to 17.00, school homework from 17.00 to 20.00, then club activities, followed by another cold strip-wash and bed at 22.00. There was to be a still earlier start for those engaged in agricultural work, at 4 a.m.

The exposure of inmates to a cold strip-wash and daily exercises sounds on the face of it punitive, but this was approved by hygienic practice of the day in a broad sense. Despite having to deal with tough characters (three inmates in the early intake had been expelled by a dozen orphanages before reaching New Life), the staff remained optimistic and tolerant. The description of getting to work on the girls is less mythic than Makarenko's depiction of his work with his inmates (see Chapter 2). At first, certainly, the staff had their problems:

> The elections to committees were especially stormy. The highly developed egotism and desire to stand out that were generally evident meant that none of the inmates could understand why someone else had been chosen, and not herself. She would suggest the assembly elect her and threaten disruption if it didn't, or say she'd refuse to do anything and refuse to recognise the school council. Sometimes a girl would threaten to bash everyone 'on the mug' if she didn't get elected.

Soon, however, the staff's resolutely coercive treatment was having the necessary effects. The director was allegedly so popular among the girls that demonstratively ignoring an offender was an effective punishment. 'The main thing that we achieve in each individual case is that a person who has committed some culpable action should acknowledge that they have done this,' a worker at the home claimed, propounding a softer and less melodramatic version of Makarenko's strategy of control through conscience.[140]

In well-run penal colonies, success stories of this kind were no doubt possible or even likely. But, as with orphanages, some on-the-ground information, both from the period when Makarenko was running his colony and from when Matrosov was growing up in his, gives a much bleaker picture. A report from Klin district, to the south of Moscow, filed on 24 April 1920, registered a range of problems, from epidemics that had felled staff and inmates, to vandalism, added to a high turnover of officials in the local education administration so that there was no continuity of management.[141] In similar vein, a report from Tula dated 24 March 1924 recorded that inmates of a home for 'morally defective' children there were sleeping on the bare steel frames of their beds, or else on filthy mattresses, with ragged blankets as their sole covering; the workshops supposed to be used for labour education lacked equipment of any kind.[142] The Code on Labour Reformatories of 1924 made an attempt to standardise conditions in the juvenile colonies, but in a very general and abstract way: children were to remain under observation upon arrival for no more than one month; different categories of inmate (i.e. those serving time for more or less severe offences) were to be housed separately; no visits from 'harmful people' were to be allowed, but inmates who had served more than six months of their sentence might be allowed occasional leave.[143] The effect was a curious mixture of rigid control and liberal emphasis on self-monitoring: reform, it was assumed, could only take place if inmates were isolated from their normal surroundings, but they were also be trusted to return to the colony once their period of leave had concluded.

Certainly, the code did nothing to improve conditions in the worst establishments. In the late 1920s and early 1930s, filth, vermin infestations, abuse of inmates, and manifestations of psychological collapse ranging from 'neurasthenia' to self-mutilation and suicide, were all recorded in NKVD documents for restricted circulation.[144] The eyewitness account of Lev Razgon, who visited one of the most notorious detention centres for young criminals, the former Danilov Monastery in Moscow, when he was working as a journalist in 1925, shows that conditions were psychologically oppressive even when the practicalities were well managed. 'There was no cold, no hunger in that prison, and there were wall newspapers, and a cinema; even the sheets on the metal-framed beds were quite clean,' Razgon conceded. All this he had dutifully recorded in an article for *Komsomol Pravda*, but much else he had suppressed. 'I never mentioned how the children trembled when the supervisors yelled at them, how the older ones beat up the younger ones, or the prison hierarchy, where the smallest and weakest came off worst. I never said a word about how the little children were used as catamites by the older half-bandits, who were in turn used by the prison administration to run the prison.'[145] Again and again, in the course of the twentieth century, prison administrations would rely on 'trusties' to keep order, reinforcing systems of brutal exploitation within camps and jails, which, before 1917 as after, were less instruments of rehabilitation than training schools in degradation and crime. The demands that staff faced, and the stereotypical reactions that these could provoke, are clear in a 1918 inventory of children in a home for morally defective children, where the children are described not just as 'damaged' and 'embittered', but also as recalcitrant: 'insolent', 'persistent and pushy', 'apathetic'.[146]

Yet even persistent runaways sometimes absorbed elements of the socialisation in homes and colonies. A notable case was a group of boys who ran away in 1924 from a home set up in the former Rukavishnikov shelter in Moscow. After ten days, they asked permission to return. 'You needn't think we've gone to the bad, we keep everything clean. We've made a nice clean corner in a tumbledown house, with piles of clean straw, we don't let strangers in. We still have someone on cleaning duty, just like in the colony. Every day we go to the river and have a wash.'[147] As with orphanages more generally, much depended on the authority of the staff, and on their capacity for patience. The 'open door' system could bring about change, but its effects were extremely gradual. As time went on, administrators became increasingly unready to sit out the wait.

'Oh How Happy We Were!'

It remains an open question how children reacted to their experience in early Soviet orphanages. There is some evidence for despair or indignation inspired by bad conditions, as in the case of a former street child writing in 1924, 'The administration didn't look after the children and all they [the children] did was sniff cocaine and play cards. I waited a whole winter for them to send me to school. I waited and waited, but there was no good in it, and all you'd turn into in that place was an expert thief. That's what the administration was like.'[148] Another child recalled an appalling case of physical neglect in a Siberian reception centre in 1921: 'They put sleeveless print dresses on us, and it was minus four in the room.'[149] Yet this kind of recollection is not the only story. Survivors in the post-Soviet period (which is to say, after official pressure to articulate one's memories in a manner flattering to state policy had ceased) are often surprisingly positive about their experiences. For Mariya Belkina and her sisters, orphanage life seemed paradisaical after the horror of 'de-kulakisation' and begging on the streets. 'Finally we were allowed into the orphanage. Oh how happy we were! They liked little Ira and me, and we loved them, too, with all our hearts.'[150] On the other hand, Natal'ya Noskova and her younger sister, the daughters

48 Collecting milk from a children's food point, early 1930s.

of 'de-kulakised' peasants, had to endure, during 1932, not only deprivation and squalor, but violence. The elder sister was later to remember her sibling's anguished pleas, 'Nanny, please don't beat me, I've hardly anything to eat as it is.' Survival was only possible because the children treated each other with exquisite consideration in order to make up for the behaviour of the adults.[151]

Inevitably, in bad homes, inmates learned little apart from the values of the street. But contemporary writings of institution inmates themselves confirm the sense of gratitude and of loyalty to the staff and to the Soviet state for the chance to escape destitution that well-run institutions generated. 'Narkompros sent me to the Zachat'evsky [Monastery of the Conception] Reception Centre,' wrote one 16-year-old boy in 1923. 'As soon as I arrived, everything felt quite different and I started trying as hard as I could to turn out a good person.' 'I will always be grateful to the people that took care of us. I'll never refuse to risk my own life to defend the motherland and the Soviet government,' wrote another of the same age.[152]

Whether good or bad, children's homes offered inmates a quite specific form of existence – one where the child was never alone; where, on the one hand, the regime was likely to be predictable to the point of monotony, while, on the other, material conditions and the make-up of the community around might well be very unstable. Like their pre-revolutionary predecessors, the administrators of Soviet orphanages were deeply concerned with what would happen to their charges once they were old enough to be discharged (in the early Soviet period, pressure on space meant that this happened by the age of 14 or 15 at the latest). Already in the 1920s, official regulations had made provision for their departure: on 10 April 1925, a Narkompros order stipulated that orphans were to get privileged access to professional secondary education, and to employment on the factory floor.[153]

The reverse side of this paternalism was that, just as before the Revolution, manual labour remained the likeliest destination for orphanage graduates. Despite utopian statements about developing inmates' individual interests and providing them with teaching in the arts and literature, the children's homes often disgorged their former inmates into a life of unskilled labour, especially if they were girls. Figures from 1928 indicate that 60 per cent of the girls ended up in the textile industry, and that the figure for those who found work in craft professions such as carpentry, tailoring, or boot-making was a total of 10 per cent. Boys' graduation destinations were rather more evenly spread, with the majority (nearly 75 per cent) taking up jobs as metalworkers, tailors, and carpenters, and the remaining 19 per cent who found employment divided between boot-making and book-binding.[154]

Certainly, there were some remarkable success stories among orphanage children. These were celebrated in the model biographies published in official sources. In the late 1920s and early 1930s, *The Children's Friend* enthusiastically reported on former orphanage inmates who were now hostel managers or proletarian poets; in 1960, *The Great Medical Encyclopedia* claimed, 'Many former inmates of orphanages have become academics, artists, musicians, doctors, agronomists, pedagogues and technicians.'[155] But the majority of orphans went on to have much humbler lives – as manual workers in factories, or as employees of collective and state farms. Often, too, skills taught in the orphanage provided at best rather general introductions to working life. According to the memories of a woman born in 1908 and brought up in an orphanage in Leningrad, whose first job was in the Skorokhod shoe factory, 'They asked me, "Can you use a sewing machine?" and I said, "Yes," so then they sat me down and showed me how to use it [i.e. a machine for making shoes].'[156]

Yet the 'pre-programming' of orphanage children has to be seen in context. In early Soviet society, everyone was supposed to do his or her 'duty' where it suited administrators – whether he or she was a peasant graduate of a pedagogical college sent to work in an orphanage rather than back to the village, an engineer dispatched to Magadan rather than Moscow, or an inmate kept busy with boot-making when he or she would have preferred reading or playing the piano. Equally, conditions in orphanages were not necessarily worse than in other living accommodation – factory barracks, boarding-school dormitories, or, for that matter, kindergartens and crèches. Indeed, orphans were sometimes better off, at least materially, than ordinary children. One denizen of an orphanage in the mid-1930s recalled that the snack meals his orphanage provided for him were the envy of other children at his school, and his bad behaviour (right up to drawing a beard and glasses on a Stalin picture in his classroom) seems to have been treated more tolerantly than might have been the case had he been a 'family kid'.[157]

The sheer physical deprivation – not to speak of the mortality rates – characterising Soviet children's homes in the worst periods of political upheaval and food shortage was something most of Western Europe had not seen since the mid-nineteenth century. In the terrible years immediately after the Revolution, even morgues had to be pressed into service to act as temporary shelter for abandoned children.[158] But the cruelty and abuse endured by children committed to institutions in more affluent societies could be as bad as, or even worse than, that found in the worst homes in Russia.[159] Institutional care everywhere during the first half of the twentieth century was characterised by regimentation of child inmates and exposure to ideological indoctrination (chapel-going in the West matched political meetings in the Soviet Union).[160] Unusual, in the wider historical context, was the attempted liberalisation of the 1920s, rather than the formality of later decades. Additionally, the pervasiveness of *bezalabershchina* (sloppiness, not being bothered) could create space for human relations of a sort that did not emerge in more aseptic, 'better regulated' institutional cultures. While designed as the instrument of collectivism, the early Soviet orphanage depended – like many another Soviet institution – on individual initiative as much as, or more than, overall government policy. The struggles of committed individuals, who genuinely loved and respected children, to do their best in difficult circumstances are as much part of the history of institutions in the first three and a half decades of Soviet power as are the failures and abuses that took place.

In the first decade and a half of Soviet power many of the features that would characterise welfare policy throughout the country's history were set in place. These included state control, accompanied by intolerance of 'voluntarist' initiative, division of responsibilities between ministries, and an emphasis on institutional solutions to problems. Yet there were many specific features of this era as well, above all the sheer magnitude of the social problems that welfare officials had to struggle to deal with. Revolution and civil war, epidemics and famines, and the man-made catastrophe of collectivisation left hundreds of thousands of abandoned and sick children, yet the institutional infrastructure (particularly during and immediately after the Civil War era) was in a parlous condition. These strains on the system, added to the psychologically and physically damaged state of most inmates in children's homes, meant that the entirely laudable aim of using methods based on 'free education' in 'total institutions' was exceptionally difficult to realise in practice. Indeed, as time went on, the requirement to provide 'just about all right' care to the many rather than 'excellent' care for the few (since excellence on a mass scale was unachievable given budget constraints and staffing shortages) started to drive welfare policy. In the next phase of Soviet history this requirement was to become still more overriding, leading to a disappearance of most of the 'model' institutions, orienting themselves by Western 'best practice', which had been so proudly marshalled in the 1920s.

Chapter 7

Children of the State, 1935–1953

The mid-1930s saw fundamental changes to institutional provision for children. For young offenders, these to all intents and purposes reversed the liberal reforms of the early Soviet era, placing those who had committed misdemeanours back into the mainstream penal system, which was itself, under the pressure of the Stalinist obsession with discipline and of political purges, growing increasingly crowded and inhumane. There was also a crackdown on child homelessness: now, the place for a child under 14 that had no parents, or whose parents were neglecting it, was assumed to be an institution, whether the child personally wanted to be there or not. In the area of provision for handicapped children there were also reversals: the discrediting of 'paedology' led to a dismantling of professional diagnostic facilities for children who did not fit into the mainstream school system, and to a reintegration of thousands back into 'general education'. In some respects, facilities for sick children represented an exception to the general rule of contraction and enhanced rigidity, but it was only in major cities that significant improvements took place. The reforms were not uniformly harmful to children's welfare: in at least the better institutions, more emphasis on skills training, a greater degree of autonomy for institution directors, and improved clarity in institutional profile (so that 'difficult' and 'normal' children were less likely to be housed together) could work to the benefit of staff and children alike. But the overall effects were to curb many of the best intentions of earlier policies, while leaving some underlying structural problems – in particular, the absence of a central children's welfare agency or liaison body – in place.

The principle of shared responsibility for welfare was affirmed by a decree of the Council of People's Commissariats of 14 June 1935, which placed no fewer than four ministries in charge of children's institutions. Handicapped children were assigned to Narkomsotsbes, and jurisdiction over law-breakers was granted to the NKVD exclusively, while the commissariats of health and education had responsibility for a reduced range of homes: for the under-threes, and for sick children in the case of Narkomzdrav, and for 'normal' and 'difficult' children (who had no criminal convictions) in the case of Narkompros. Each ministry was mandated to evolve its own set of standards for the homes and regulations for their internal administration.[1] This division of duties remained in place until the end of the era of Soviet power (and indeed beyond), with the commissariats' successors (the Ministry of Enlightenment, later Education, the Ministry of

Internal Affairs, the Ministry of Health, and the Ministry of Social Welfare) inheriting the briefs that were set out in 1935.

In some respects, the boundaries of responsibility were now clearer, but there were still areas of possible overlap. 'Difficult children' were supposed to be in the care of Narkompros unless they had committed an offence, but the issue of whether a child actually went through the penal system was fortuitous – a practised young offender who had not fallen into the hands of the police would still end up in an ordinary orphanage. Not unnaturally, 'turf wars' continued to rage. In 1940, Narkompros irritably reminded the NKVD that the provision of employment for 'graduates' of penal colonies was the NKVD's responsibility.[2] Practical problems in the harmonisation of ministerial work were endemic. It might turn out that orphanages for the over-threes had insufficient places for the babies being cared for in Narkomzdrav baby homes, a problem that would come to light when the transfer was supposed to take place.[3] The compartmentalisation of different types of child led to inflexible attitudes: a child assigned to one commissariat (and later ministry) was very likely to stay in that ministry's homes until it reached post-institutional age (with the obvious exception of 'graduates' from health ministry baby homes). Transfers – for instance of 'reformed' law-breakers to ordinary orphanages – were supposed to be possible, but the mechanisms for them were vague and, it seems, ineffective.[4] In practice, the only way out of a particular type of home seems to have been down the hierarchical scale: it was a good deal more likely that a child in a 'normal' home who created difficulties would end up in a home for 'invalids' or for 'difficult' children, or indeed in a penal colony, than that the reverse process would take place (indeed, the threat of such 'downward' movement was built into official disciplinary procedures).[5]

Where the clarification of ministerial responsibility in the mid-1930s did end diversity was in the organisation of reception centres. With the NKVD put in charge and paedology discredited, the emphasis shifted once and for all to the hygienic and bureaucratic processing of children. After registration, a medical inspection was supposed to follow immediately, and then the child would be referred for treatment if needed. Then followed cleaning and fumigation (*sanobrabotka*), accompanied by a thorough wash, by shaving of the hair and the issuing of 'new' (or rather, second-hand but washed and sterilised) clothes. Finally, children's further destination would be determined: homes for the normal, the defective, for 'difficult' and 'dangerous' children, and so on, or employment (and after 1940, the labour reserves) if they were over 14.[6]

While administratively expedient, the reception centre reorganisation led to a 'de-skilling' of the diagnosis system. To be sure, staff in reception centres included a number with special training, such as doctors and teachers. But the extent to which their expertise could actually be deployed varied, given that directors were selected from NKVD career staff, and might well be unimaginatively authoritarian, and unsympathetic to the child welfare side of the reception centre.[7] An innovation of 1935 was children's rooms, attached to major police stations in cities and at railway stations, with staff who were specially trained to deal with children in trouble. However, the rooms, like the child inspectors, had a limited impact: in practice, a child's first contact was still likely to be with a completely untrained member of the ordinary police force, who, as before, would wish to get an abandoned child off his patch as quickly as possible, without worrying about the child's likely destination.

Once the Children's Friend had been closed down in 1934 and the Children's Commission of the Central Committee in 1935, there were no longer any official children's lobby organisations to help smooth over the cracks in the badly integrated system. But, as before, the unpaid help of citizens, mostly women, heeding the call to perform 'socially useful work' and to enact their civic duty, remained crucial. In 1936, the so-called Obshchestvennitsa (literally, Woman Social Activist) movement, a volunteer organisation made up of wives of factory managers, engineers, and skilled workers, took over many of the activities (crèche organisation, outside-school supervision) latterly assigned to the Children's Friend.[8] In the 1940s, the more broadly based Women's Soviets (an organisation not dissimilar to a Soviet Russian version of the British Women's Royal Voluntary Service) placed the Social Activist movement on a permanent footing, continuing to perform well-regulated volunteer work till the end of Soviet power.[9] Despite distrust of voluntarism, tolerance of what in other countries would have been described as charity work continued, espoused by the ladies of the Soviet elite among others – for instance, Klimenty Voroshilov's wife Ekaterina was, in the post-war years, a member of the governing council of Children's Home No. 35, a prestigious orphanage in Moscow.[10] But the work that volunteers of this kind could do was constricted: they could organise fund-raising for an individual orphanage or hospital, or lobby the local Party organisation to improve conditions, but they could not campaign openly for change to regimes or for de-instutionalisation at a national level, since this would have been interpreted as an act of political subversion and would have been highly dangerous. At best, such volunteers had a peripheral impact, making life easier locally but doing little to ameliorate the structural faults and deficiencies of financial support that were built in from above.

'Making the Streets Bolshevik'

The emphasis on discipline that characterised Soviet policy generally from the mid-1930s had especially sharp effects on the treatment of abandoned children. A sign of the times was a Narkompros directive of November 1934 criticising dramatic representations of the abandoned child that brandished 'impure language' (by which was meant expressions such as *plevaya baba*, roughly speaking 'rackety broad'). It called for censorship of existing dramas and more careful commissioning of new ones. As it turned out, *Road into Life* was not just the first, but also the last, waif movie to reach the screen.[11] By far the most influential waif narrative of this generation was Anton Makarenko's *Pedagogical Poem* (1933–6), which, unlike the orphanage narratives of the 1920s, was narrated entirely from the pedagogue's point of view and lacked the kind of folkloric detail that had enlivened, say, *The Republic of Shkid*. The only songs sung by the children in this book were hymns to the bright Soviet future:

What will we have in five years?
A city soviet, my dears,
A new workshop will be revealed,
A new orchard in the field,
And among other things,
Or so we hope, some electric swings.[12]

The fictionalised portrayal of orphanage life in *Pedagogical Poem* interwove the crucial Stalinist theme of discipline with the equally crucial Stalinist theme of celebration and jollity. But the outcome of the narrative was wholly serious: the transformation of these former dregs of Soviet society (Makarenko drily remarked that the 'special creativity which is supposed to make children's psychology close to that of scientists and scholars' could not be glimpsed in his charges when they were admitted to the reformatory) into useful Soviet citizens – 'engineers, doctors, historians, geologists, pilots, shipbuilders, radio operators, pedagogues, musicians, actors, and singers'.[13] An impudent boy was still described by the author as 'the best type', but his function was different to the cheerful subversives portrayed a decade earlier. He and his fellows were 'colonials' in more than one sense: the denizens of a penal colony, but also Soviet counterparts to the morally ambiguous but entrepreneurial outlaws of American Wild West stories. At first, Makarenko stated, the villagers nearby had looked askance at the *kolonisty* on their doorstep, some of whom had even taken to highway robbery on the local main road; but by the time they had been reshaped by Makarenko they were respected by all the neighbours, who gazed with wonder at the colony's model pigsty, while the local village girls cast admiring sideways glances at the tall, trim, soldierly reformatory youths.[14]

The 31 May 1935 decree 'On the Liquidation of Child Homelessness and Child Neglect'[15] sought to place the entire population of abandoned children under benevolent surveillance of this kind. This wide-ranging piece of legislation was aimed in several directions at once. First, it was intended to purge the streets of waifs and unruly children by tightening up measures against child vagrancy and juvenile disorder. The chairmen of town and village soviets were now made responsible for the welfare of orphans, and were liable for criminal charges if they did not do their job properly. Subsidies to needy parents were ordained, so that they would not be tempted into abandoning children in the first place. The fight against street hooliganism (the offences mentioned were fighting, riding on tram-buffers, and shouting abuse at passers-by) was to be stepped up. Second, a reordering of institutional structures, mainly intended to relax the hold of the Commissariat of Enlightenment on the orphanage system (and thereby to loosen the link between the children's homes and education in a broader sense), and to consolidate the influence of the NKVD, was set in train.[16] Finally, the decree made important changes to the regime operating inside children's homes themselves. Some were philanthropic in character: there was now to be a standard norm regulating diet in the homes, each one was to have its own vegetable garden, penalties were to be instituted against staff who thieved food, equipment, and so on, and a supervisory council (soviet) was to oversee the work of each home. Others, by contrast, were aimed at stiffening the programme of 'labour education' in the homes. Just at the time when the principle of labour education was being diluted in mainstream education, it was being enforced in Soviet orphanages. All the homes were to have a labour regime and a set of rules and regulations, and strictly defined paths were laid out for those over 14. Their sole route to further education was the factory or state farm school (FZU, *sovkhozuch*): otherwise, they were to go straight to the factory floor, into a mechanical training institute (MTS) (which offered courses in basic skills, such as tractor-driving), or into some other form of employment.

The practical implications of all this were various. To begin with, there was now much more rigidity in attitudes to different types of abandoned children: law-breakers versus others. Second, the last vestiges of 1920s romanticism about the admirable feistiness of street children had now disappeared: they had begun to be considered offensive to public order, to be removed from view as quickly as possible, as part of what a March 1935 article in *Pravda* about organised leisure for children called 'making the streets Bolshevik'.[17] Third, a forceful teleology had now been imposed on the rehabilitation orphanages inmates were supposed to undergo. 'Graduates' of orphanages were essentially now regarded as a pool of cheap labour; they might, for example, be dispatched to work on collective farms. An article in *Soviet Justice* spoke unctuously about how the children were to be provided with 'a family atmosphere' to live in as well as 'tolerable living conditions'.[18] They were probably lucky if they ended up with the latter.

Not everything about the changed atmosphere of the mid-1930s was bad. In 1934, the practice of tying orphanages to 'patron' (*shefnye*) enterprises, normally factories (which could help out with food supplies and material goods), was assigned a surveillance function as well (patron enterprises were instructed to send along inspectors to the orphanages under their protection).[19] In a system where official supply lines and regulatory practices worked very badly, this sort of personal association could make all the difference to an institution's chances of day-to-day survival. Equally, the rehabilitation of the family taking place in the mid-1930s prompted greater tolerance of non-institutional solutions. In 1934, adopting a child became legal even where both birth parents were living, provided they gave their consent (or indeed without their consent, if they had been 'deprived of their parental rights' for unfitness in parenting).[20] Subsequently, a decree of 1 April 1936 also regulated fostering in a form not too dissimilar from the baby-farming that had been practised by children's institutions in Tsarist times. Orphaned children between the ages of five months and 14 years might be placed in a foster home, where they were supposed to remain until the age of 16. The mutual aid offices attached to village soviets, and the health and educational administrations in towns, were meant to oversee the arrangement and make sure that the children were settled in appropriate conditions (abuse was punishable under article 158 (1) of the Criminal Code). A cash subsidy of 25 roubles per month was paid to help with each child's keep, and kolkhoz dwellers were also eligible for grants to improve their homes and to buy livestock.[21] This measure bowed to the inevitable: once the children of the 'special exiles' displaced during collectivisation began to be returned to their native regions, orphanages became utterly incapacitated, and fosterage was the only way of even trying to cope. According to a report from Sverdlovsk region made in May 1935, 7,916 of these children were placed in foster homes in 1934, and a further 6,844 returned to their relations.[22]

To be sure, it is not clear how effective these supervision arrangements were. Given the lack of recourse to law for the adopted and fostered children themselves, and the inadequacy of the child inspectorate network, fostering no doubt continued to be a way of providing an extra pair of hands in some peasant families after 1936, as traditionally it had been before 1917. Whichever way, even in the 1930s adoption and fostering remained marginal approaches to dealing with abandoned or orphaned children. The 1926 figure of 19,000 orphanage children placed in foster homes, which represented somewhere around 14 per cent of the orphanage population at the time, can perhaps be taken as a benchmark for the proportion of children involved later on.[23] Support to parents (through counselling, say) in order that vulnerable families could be kept together was also limited: the child inspectorates tended to intervene and impose care orders in extreme cases, rather than offer aid in marginal ones. The 1936 assault on the paedological movement – which had operated well-regarded and well-used consultation and diagnostic facilities in some major cities – put paid to the pioneering counselling facilities that had begun to develop in the 1920s. The 1930s saw the supportive care network slowly expand in Britain, France, and America; in Russia, on the other hand, it suddenly contracted.[24] Mass institutionalisation remained the primary response to child abandonment throughout the Soviet period, both in practical and in ideological terms.[25]

With regard to institutional care itself, a major change brought by the 31 May 1935 decree was the inauguration at the highest level of integrated provisions on hygiene and equipment. In a further toughening of the 'culture of blame', sanctions were promised against staff in whose establishments abuses were found to have occurred. The next few years saw a stream of further regulations at state and local level urging institutions to conform to general standards. In Leningrad, for example, orphanages – as well as schools, nursery schools, and indeed all manner of children's facilities including cinemas, theatres, libraries, skating rinks and summer playgrounds – were by the late 1930s part of an inspectorate system working to norms evolved by the Regional Research Institute for the Protection of the Health of Children and Adolescents. According to its stipulations, orphanages were supposed to have at least one lavatory for every 30 children and one urinal for every 40 boys (and one lavatory for every 20 children of pre-school age). Each child was to have its own bed, and bedlinen was to be changed every ten days (personal linen every six days). The dormitories and other premises were to be kept thoroughly aired, and the ventilation and heating monitored carefully. The children were to wash their hands before all meals, and facilities such as bathrooms, lavatories, kitchens, as well as the windowsills, etc. of other premises, were to be scrubbed down with bleach every day. On being admitted to the orphanage, children were to undergo a medical inspection, fumigation, and wash, and be placed in quarantine for twelve days. All children in the orphanage were to be inspected every ten days, and a fresh fumigation and wash, and isolation, ordained if necessary. The cleaning staff were to have functional equipment, and were themselves to be cleanly and neatly dressed.[26]

These provisions on hygiene were not in themselves new. Many were found in normative literature of the 1920s, including the model charter for children's homes drawn up as early as 1921.[27] But novel (though entirely typical of the times) was the insistence, in the May 1935 decree, that abuses would be punished. It may be doubted how much the threat of such sanctions did to improve poor work by orphanage staff. They may even have made conditions worse in some places by inducing a sense of fear in workers who would previously have been prepared to improvise and to take personal initiative.[28] In any case, there were large numbers of staff who probably knew little about the regulations: as late as 1940, more than a third of staff taking part in a survey of twenty-two provinces had not extended their education beyond primary level.[29] Certainly, a stream of bad reports over the next decades indicated that problems could not always be cleared up by bureaucratic reorganisation and increased sanctions alone.

Newspaper reports of abuses began to dwindle in the late 1930s, but this was largely because the myth of Soviet childhood as uniquely happy pushed lives that did not fit the myth from view. Even fictional treatments were subject to strict regulation. The 31 May 1935 decree explicitly instructed the organs of Soviet censorship to 'exercise enhanced supervision of children's literature and films, and not to allow any literature and films which might have a pernicious influence on children, such as those representing the adventures of criminals etc.'[30] Among texts that vanished from circulation was *The Republic of Shkid* (not reprinted till 1961). Invisible in public printed culture (with the exception of journals in specialist fields, such as the law), 'abnormal' children were barely visible even in private discussions inside Party institutions. Records of life in institutions held in archives – those of the Central Committee of the Komsomol, for example – are patchy and incomplete. In this obsessively centralising country, much was left in the hands of local officials, and individual cases reached central authorities only when some scandal too horrible to be kept silent broke out.

Enough, though, did get published and recorded, and remembered in survivor memoirs, to make it clear that orphanage conditions continued to range, by and large, from the spartan to the dreadful. At the 'dreadful' end of the range came an orphanage in the Ivanovo region singled out for action by the Komsomol authorities in March 1936 after the suicide of a Komsomol member there. The children were poorly fed and inadequately clothed, kitchen utensils were covered in grime and maggots, and there was no heating and no bath-house (and presumably little in the way of other washing facilities either). Not surprisingly, a medical inspection in February 1936 established that forty-two children at the home were suffering from illness or infections of some kind. The mental and emotional side of the children's existence was just as badly served as the practical side. There was no school and no club; worse, several of the supervisors had meted out 'systematic beatings' to the inmates.[31] Equally appalling, according to the testimony of one former orphan, was Home No. 3 in Moscow, run, during the 1930s, by Semen Karabanov, a former associate of Makarenko's, but also 'a monster in human shape, who beat the inmates horribly'.[32]

At the other end of the range (spartan but tolerable) was the orphanage experienced by Misha Nikolaev in the late 1930s and early 1940s, where supervisors were brusque, the diet unappealing, and the education provided rudimentary, but where the children at least escaped physical abuse, filth, and parasite infestation.[33] Somewhere in the middle came an orphanage in a small town in Kalinin province, north of Moscow, where two brothers running the home workshops exploited the inmates as unpaid child labour in order to run a clandestine private business, the housekeeper had beaten the children with wet towels, ideological education had been non-existent, but the living conditions were not sufficiently dreadful to merit official comment.[34]

The authorities might crack down on crying abuses of this kind, yet the governing concept of 'tough love' may have acted as legitimation for them. Anton Makarenko's *Pedagogical Poem*, now held to represent the ideal of reformatory treatment, made light of an incident when Makarenko himself had slapped a troublesome inmate on the face with a poker. ('Having clean pedagogical hands was a secondary matter compared with the task before me. I firmly resolved that I would be a dictator if I had no other method available.')[35] Comparably, a 1949 article lauded an orphanage director for handling a rebellion in his orphanage using 'pindown' methods (to employ the term that would have been used in Britain or America five decades later). After the boys in the home he ran had broken into a barrel of lime during his absence, the director had pushed their ringleader up against a wall, forcing him into an agreement to call off the rioting. The article then switched from sketching this crisis point to a picture of the reformed orphanage. Before there had been 13 Pioneers, now there were 76 (out of 96 children); now the children had plenty of access to talks about the biographies of the leaders, and some were able to follow up their interest in the arts. The article finished with an encomium to Stalin and to the Soviet children that were growing up healthy and devoted to the leader.[36]

Tales about directors who sorted difficulties out by means of an act of aggression went some way towards undermining the frequently articulated view that corporal punishment was intolerable. It is only too easy to imagine that brutal supervisors might take this as licence for lashing out far more frequently than Makarenko recorded himself as doing. Equally, Makarenko's military-style methods, in the hands of less intelligent and socially tactful individuals, could turn into mere drill-ground bullying. Wolfgang Leonhard, the son of German Communists who spent some years in Soviet orphanages, had grim memories of the children's home that he entered in 1937. The iron bedsteads, crammed into rooms so small that there was almost no space between them, and the bad food were depressing enough, but what made the place almost unbearable was the crass regimentation meted out by the staff. The boys were constantly shouted at, made to line up for roll-calls; no trust whatever was extended to them. Every day passed in a constant round of filling in forms to request permission to leave the home (these were required even when the boys went out for a walk or round the corner for a bag of sweets).[37]

Orphanages were not necessarily better-run places once tighter regulation had been introduced in the late 1920s than they had been at the start of the decade. The enhancement of control from the centre that took place in the late 1920s and 1930s was a phenomenon with its own logic, influenced not just by day-to-day practicalities but by the considerations of high politics. The pros and cons of 'self-government' were never openly discussed: they were taken for granted in the 1920s and silently abandoned in the 1930s, when the open-door children's home also disappeared from the scene. Yet recollections of survivors suggest that the restoration of 'discipline' could be beneficial to orphanage inmates, giving them a genuine sense of security, provided the rules were applied with tact and humour. Nicholas Voinov, who returned to the former Third International Home in 1937, eight years after his first contact with the place, found it transformed. The dormitories were freshly whitewashed and hung with political slogans and portraits of the leaders (which in the old days would instantly have been defaced or torn down); there were training sessions aimed at 'each child's inclinations and talents'; and sponsorship had been secured from a local factory. Most remarkable of all was the new attitude of the orphanage staff, who radiated competence and a firm commitment to transforming their charges mentally. Their use of reasonable argument had, Voinov argued, a profound influence on him. He managed to complete school and was planning to go to art college when war broke out. Though encouraged by a friend to evade enlistment, he decided that he was determined to 'serve the motherland' and joined up as required.[38]

Some positive recollections of children's homes, imbued with feelings of gratitude to the state, seem compromised in advance because they were drawn from adults who later worked in education (or the Pioneer movement); in other words, whose adult lives were intimately connected with the circumstances in which they had been raised. But Voinov's account comes from a witness who had every reason to loathe the Soviet system, and hence seems more likely to reflect his view of things at the time. There were cases where the *dirigiste* dogma voiced by the *Children's Friend* in 1933 – 'A good orphanage director means a good orphanage' (set in stone by a measure of 1 September 1935 stating that directors governed on the basis of 'sole authority') – allowed dedicated directors greater room to manoeuvre than the militant utopianism of Narkompros in the 1920s would have done.[39]

It helped children's chances of reasonable treatment that the idealisation of the orphan was not just a literary and propaganda fiction, but a practical reality. Street children might inspire fear, but parentless children as such were usually the object of pity. A boy whose father was shot in 1934, and who escaped institutionalisation (his mother evaded arrest by moving illegally to Moscow) remembered that he was positively spoilt by his mother's friends, who showered him with toys and sweets, and that the neighbours in the communal flat 'encircled me with love and attention'.[40] In orphanages, of course, indulgence of this kind was less likely, but for some staff, at least, kindness was an ideal that they strove to realise as best they could. On the other hand, the fate of children who got sucked into the criminal justice system after the passing of the 7 April 1935 decree lowering the age of criminal responsibility was far less heartening.

'Juvenile Criminals'

In the 1920s, even hardened child thieves had been widely regarded as essentially innocent. From 1935 onwards, all homeless children began to be handled as though they were potential criminals. Certainly, it was sometimes argued that orphans were entitled to the 'happy childhood' that was the birthright of every Soviet child. Even hardliners on the question of juvenile delinquency considered it disgraceful that only 20 per cent of orphanage inmates were involved in the Pioneer movement by as late as 1935.[41] On the other hand, at least some orphans were the offspring of parents whom the regime considered politically suspect: those who had failed to look after them properly, those who belonged to a contemptible social group (dispossessed kulaks, for instance), or, worst of all, those who had actually been convicted and imprisoned for some crime.

The decree of 7 April 1935, extending full adult penalties to juvenile perpetrators of 'theft, violence, actual bodily harm, mutilation, and murder', was given the widest possible publicity, and in terms that left no doubt about the demise of rehabilitationism for good and all. A front-page splash in *Pravda* carried the headline 'AN END TO CHILD CRIME AND ITS FACILITATORS!' and the lead article below it was an overt assault on the institutions that had sought to challenge the concept of 'child crime' in the first place. There was to be no more 'pussy-footing around' (*mindal'nichan'e*) with minors; the allegedly totally impotent Commissions on the Affairs of Minors were to be abolished; and both the 'irresponsibility and impunity' of juvenile criminals, and the evil acts of those who lured them into crime in the first place, were to attract severe penalties. Though the article concluded with a sentence or two emphasising the continuing need for 'educative work', no doubt was left that this was now considered peripheral – an implication formalised in May 1935, when 'labour colonies' as well as reception points were placed under the jurisdiction of the NKVD.[42]

The 7 April 1935 decree did not, contrary to the boastful publicity surrounding it, in fact succeed in putting an end to anti-social behaviour by young people. Memoirs and crime statistics alike make it clear that a flourishing underworld culture still existed in the late 1930s.[43] Indeed, a report by Lavrenty Beria to Stalin and Molotov in February 1940 indicated that, while the numbers of homeless children in the cities had dropped between 1935 and 1939, the numbers of crimes committed by children had risen steeply, from 6,725 per annum in 1935 to 15,031 in 1936, 17,234 in 1937, reaching a peak of 20,166 in 1938 before declining once more to 13,286 in 1939. Furthermore, arrests of 'unsupervised' children with parents had also been at high levels: 156,000 in 1936, 159,000 in 1937, and 175,000 in 1938. Theft was rife, including among the under-12s, who were responsible for fully 25 per cent of thefts in Leningrad, for instance, but who could not be held criminally responsible even under the revised legislation. Sexual offences were also common, ranging from attempts by schoolboys to force schoolgirls into sexual relations to gang rapes, of which 'many' had been recorded in the recent past. To what extent the figures reflected increasing police vigilance, leading to higher rates of recording for misdemeanours, or indeed 'moral panic' about juvenile misdemeanours, is unclear. At all events, Beria's report was not concerned to discuss the niceties of diagnosis. Instead, it cut straight to proposed solutions to the assumed surge in child crime, such as opening orphanages where children could be boarded at their parents' expense, increasing the numbers of homes for 'difficult' children, and boosting the moral education component of school education and extra-curricular work with parents.[44]

Whatever the practical failings of the 1935 law in some respects, it did 'clean up the streets' in a superficial sense (by removing from view street children who lived in the open). It also put an end to public comment on the waifdom problem. In the late 1930s, journalists discussing crime by minors were aware of the delicacy of their situation: they were dealing with a subject that officially ought not to have existed. It became customary, even in specialist legal literature, to describe the existence of juvenile delinquency as 'an anomaly', and one that was in the process of dwindling to nothing. 'In contrast to the ever-rising rate of juvenile crime in capitalist countries, most Soviet regions, provinces and republics have seen crime drop markedly. We have achieved something of which no other country in the world is capable,' boasted an article in *Soviet Justice* in 1937.[45] Since, allegedly, Soviet welfare and educational reform had eradicated the environmental causes of misdemeanours by minors, the only possible explanation for the persistence of such misdemeanours had to be the recalcitrance of the criminals themselves. Accordingly, response to persisting crime should be severe: 'The organs of justice must realise that a liberal attitude to a defendant simply because he is a minor is quite impermissible,' wrote S. Potravnov in *Soviet Justice* in 1938.[46] And, in May 1941, yet another decree extended full criminal responsibility to every offence committed by a minor, not just the offences mentioned in the 7 April 1935 decree.[47]

A recent historian has argued that, to the Soviet regime, the colonies seemed 'an inexpensive institution with a seemingly limitless capacity for homeless children and juvenile delinquents'.[48] Well founded as this accusation of cynical expediency on the Soviet government's part may be, it should also be borne in mind that the general public, by and large, had at best a limited sympathy for homeless children. The low numbers of people prepared to adopt orphanage inmates, and the difficulty of finding them jobs, are testimony to this.[49] City-dwellers felt threatened by the gangs of potentially rapacious waifs roaming the streets, while villagers domiciled in the vicinity of labour colonies were unenthusiastic about their proximity to groups of individuals they still recalcitrantly termed 'young criminals' rather than 'social defectives'.[50] The crimes for which juveniles were responsible were mostly low-level – wallet-snatching, small-scale burglary – but the phenomenon was both persistent and highly visible. Also, as the ideology of 'happy childhood' spread, an increasing percentage of the population strongly endorsed the official view that street life was a travesty of proper childhood.

Finding Loopholes

A group whose mood was a partial exception to the general hostility or indifference was professional jurists. Even during the late 1930s, conviction of the need for sensitivity and special expertise in cases involving children persisted. Articles published in *Soviet Justice* and other such professional legal journals carried bitingly critical commentaries on deficiencies of procedure – excessive haste in processing juvenile offences, or, conversely, excessive slowness. They emphasised the need to arrange hearings in premises that were not grim and intimidating and to avoid tactless and harsh interrogation, and praised courts that had adopted special procedures, such as setting up separate juvenile chambers.[51] After the promulgation of the 7 April 1935 law, some cities (Moscow, Leningrad, Saratov, and Khar'kov) had competent juvenile courts, and some other places tried juvenile cases at special 'conferences', rather than in the main chambers.[52] As can be the case in any country when professional jurists get to grips with penalty systems set up by politicians, the draconian nature of the tariff sometimes rebounded. It was not uncommon for courts to make use of suspended sentences and supervision orders for children above the age of official criminal responsibility. In 1936, around a third of juveniles convicted of theft were receiving suspended sentences, just over half were sent to penal colonies.[53]

Yet the amount of latitude available to jurists was never very large, and it was considerably lessened after 1938, when juvenile chambers stopped operating (they were reintroduced only in 1943).[54] As Peter Solomon has calculated, the proportion of juveniles receiving non-custodial sentences was around half of the proportion that had received such sentences before the 1935 law went through (about 30 per cent as opposed to about 60 per cent). In fact, the numbers of young offenders sent to prison were now roughly comparable with the numbers sent there by Tsarist courts before 1917, and most of these young convicts were serving longer sentences than had been the norm before 1917.[55] Whatever manoeuvres of detail were made, the law of 7 April 1935 represented a real and significant change.

Moreover, jurists had, of course, no control over what happened to the juveniles who did get convicted and assigned to the mercy of what was, by the international standards of the day, a particularly inhumane prison system. Even before the April and May 1935 laws were passed, there had been a tendency to use the NKVD institutions as a dustbin. 'The People's Education departments take the path of least resistance. They try to foist all the children that they can't cope with, the difficult ones, on our institutions. I don't think you can just send all the homeless children there are to prison,' protested a female NKVD representative at the Third All-Russian Congress of Child Protection in May 1930.[56] Whilst, even after 1935, homeless children did not inevitably find their way into the penal system, disturbingly large numbers of those who passed through it

– 86,579 of the 155,506 children incarcerated in colonies between 7 April 1935 and 1 March 1940 – had never been processed by the courts, indicating the extent to which colonies were now the preferred catch-all for hard cases.[57] The result was a system that was bursting at the seams, with an average number of 500 inmates per colony managed by about 25 full-time supervisors.[58] Even if the supervisors were not callous, depressed, or drunk, they would have had their work cut out to ensure adequate care; many were all of these things and more. Secret reports laid bare squalor, neglect, and outright cruelty. In December 1937, for instance, the colony in Lenin's home town of Ul'yanovsk was recorded as having foully insanitary conditions, with lice infestations and epidemics; the inmates were being bullied and intimidated; the school was hardly functioning, and there was no training for work at all; funds were disappearing in mysterious ways, and so were many of the inmates.[59] It is small wonder that boredom, frustration, and unhappiness sometimes provoked open unrest, as in early 1939, when the inmates of the Ostashkovskaya, Valuiskaya, and Chepetskaya colonies rioted and wrecked furniture, equipment, and decorations in rooms, workshops, warehouses, and shops, causing damage amounting to tens of thousands of roubles.[60]

The authorities' reactions to incidents like this usually pulled in two directions. On the one hand (for instance, in the case just mentioned), they gave some recognition to the practical grievances that caused unrest, demanding improvements in the inmates' diet, the provision of adequate supplies of bedlinen, and a fundamental revamping of the education and leisure programmes. On the other hand, they came at the problem from the disciplinary angle, attempting to toughen up the regimes in the penal colonies still further. The set of regulations for the colonies in force from 29 July 1935 was relatively rudimentary. It divided inmates into 'full members' (those who 'carry out work tasks as assigned to them and are exemplary in terms of their general behaviour, and take an active part in the social and political life of the colony') and 'candidate members'. But the main thrust of the regulations was to emphasise the requirement that inmates engage in productive labour.[61]

Later sets of regulations, on the other hand, such as those introduced on 5 September 1938, spoke explicitly of the colonies' purpose as being 'the education, under conditions of a labour regime and strict discipline, of under-age offenders, the inculcation in them of work skills, professional education, so that honest citizens, devoted to their socialist motherland, can be delivered back into society'. The regulations were now also considerably more detailed in their articulation of expected, permitted, and forbidden activities. Inmates were assigned a 'production minimum', or work quota, for which they received token wages as an incentive. They were expected to participate in organising the daily life of the colony through membership of various committees, with remits ranging from food or sanitation to education and physical culture, and to treat colony property in a respectful manner. And they were expressly prohibited from leaving the colonies on their own, from 'card games and other forms of gambling', from drinking and the use of narcotics, and from 'keeping forbidden objects such as knives and razors'.[62]

In itself, the toughening of discipline did little to stamp out disorder. From 1939, therefore, another strategy was adopted: the setting up of special facilities so that trouble-makers (runaways and 'malicious disrupters of the regime of the labour colonies who have proved impervious to all the disciplinary measures available in the open colonies') could be isolated, along with young offenders who had been sentenced directly by the courts to incarceration in 'closed type' institutions. Every facility was to have six general groups and one 'special group' for unusually hard cases, each housed separately, with its own dormitory, classroom, and sanitary facilities; the workshops were to be used by no more than two groups at a time. Except between 10 p.m. and 8 a.m., each group was to be under constant supervision by two members of staff. Like all penal colonies, the 'isolator camps' had internal sanctions against the disruptive in the form of punishment cells, but they also had an extensively developed system of penalties and rewards more generally (running from reprimands to lengthening of sentence on the one hand, and from prizes to lightening of sentence on the other, with treats such as extra meetings, letters, parcels, cigarettes, and film showings coming in between). These were supposed to act as additional correctives to bad behaviour and incentives to good.[63] In 1940, further regulations deepened the penal character of the camp, with mandatory morning and evening roll-call, and a toughening of the punishment cell routine: mattresses were now not allowed during the daytime, and only 75 per cent of normal rations might be given.[64] At the best of times, the punishment regime was grim, with a ban on 'smoking, singing, noise, knocking [from cell to cell]' and only short periods of exercise (20 minutes) per day.[65]

Yet some consideration was shown, at least in ordinary colonies, for the age of the offenders. Guards manning the camp defences were officially forbidden to shoot at under-18s, having to fire into the air instead of at their bodies.[66] And the official denominator, 'corrective-educational', was not entirely misleading. Children's institutions were supposed to provide inmates with both a general and a political education (the latter being seen as an honour); institutions which failed to do this were regularly criticised in inspectors' reports.[67]

Children in the Gulag

A still more dismal fate than being dispatched to a colony was to end up in an adult prison or labour camp. There were numerous ways in which this might happen to under-18s. Space in dedicated reception facilities and colonies might be lacking; the police, or court officials, might be slack about establishing a juvenile offender's true date of birth; or officials might simply decide that the child 'deserved' severe punishment. In April 1921, at the height of rehabilitationism, the Children's Commission had to issue an order that children must not be kept in ordinary adult penitentiaries[68] – an indication that incarceration in an adult prison remained an inescapable first phase in the penitential system for large numbers of children. This situation persisted through the 1920s and 1930s, and was formalised in June 1935, when a directive issued by the NKVD stipulated

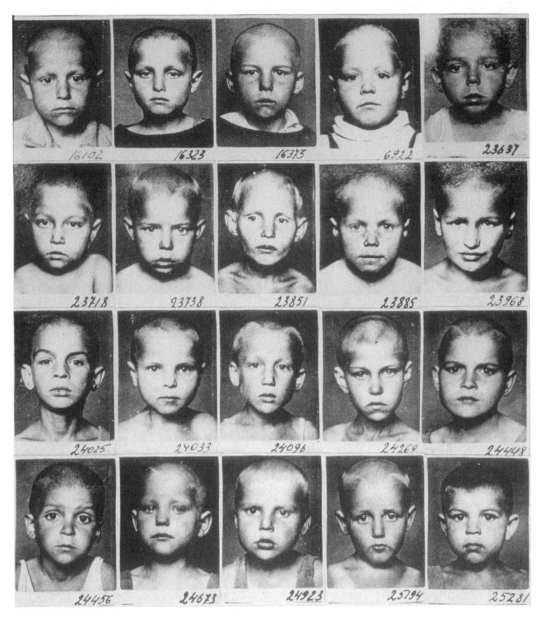

49 'Family Members of Traitors to the Motherland', identity photographs from an OGPU home, late 1930s.

that 'remand isolation facilities' in the normal prison system (OMZ) might be used for juveniles.[69] Conditions in such facilities were often appalling: a report of 19 February 1941 recorded desperate overcrowding in one KPZ (preliminary investigation prison), with one cell of 8.7 square metres shared by 25 children and another of 20 square metres housing 38. Not surprisingly, conditions were not only squalid but also dangerous: proper supervision was impossible, so that theft, violence, and sexual assaults, alongside the inevitable gambling, went on unchecked.[70]

Use of adult facilities did not stop with the remand phase. Under-18s who had committed crimes the administration deemed particularly serious (for example, political ones) were at considerable risk of finding themselves in a labour camp well before the 7 April 1935 law was passed. For example, in 1929, a group of five 16-year-olds from Leningrad who had been convicted under articles 58.10 and 58.11 of the Criminal Code ('propaganda or agitation, containing a call to overthrow, subvert, or weaken the Soviet regime', and 'any form of organised activity with the end of preparing for, or committing, one of the crimes listed in the present section of the Criminal Code') were swiftly dispatched to Solovki, despite the fact that they had been no more than 13 years old when the alleged offences were committed.[71] There are also records of harsh treatment of this kind dating from after the 1935 watershed. In 1938, Vladimir Moroz, a 17-year-old inmate of a children's home who had written a letter to Stalin complaining about conditions there, and who had also been keeping a private diary in which he indiscreetly questioned the likely guilt of Bulgarin, Pyatnitsky, and other victims of the Purges, was arrested (also under article 58.10). At first he stoutly denied the charge of 'counter-revolutionary activity', but then (no doubt after torture) made a full confession of guilt, and was sentenced to three years in a labour camp.[72] According to memoirs, the Moroz case was no aberration. Indeed, the prisoners in adult labour camps, to go by survivor testimony, sometimes included children as young as seven or eight.[73] Though regulations stipulated that juveniles should be confined apart from adult prisoners, these were frequently broken.[74]

Yet, as with children's experiences of armed combat and of revolution, camp life did not equate simply with victimisation of the children involved. In terms of the official rationing system, children did reasonably well. According to a table compiled by former prisoner Jacques Rossi and recording the procedures obtaining in the camps where he was held from 1937 to 1958, a 'child' ration was 27g sugar, 50g kasha, 33g fish, 33g meat, 400g vegetables, 400g milk, 17g fish oil, 17g veg. oil and 28g flour per day; the ration for 'minors' was 450g bread, 25g sugar, 100g kasha, 170g fish, 50g meat, 500g veg., 66g fish oil, 20g veg. oil, and 200g flour per day. Calibrated for average body-weight, these rations are considerably more generous than the 'basic' adult ration of 450g bread, 7g sugar, 80g kasha, 132g fish, 21g meat, 500g veg., 9g veg. oil and 6g flour per day.[75]

Better fed than the bulk of the camp population, children were also often better treated. 'Juveniles enjoyed certain unwritten privileges', one eyewitness, Lev Razgon, recalled. 'For instance, the guards knew they mustn't kill them.' The result of this relative impunity was to make the youngest camp prisoners into the most frightening and violent section of the camp population. The boys could be hired as contract killers by a payment of the standard camp currency, bread; the girls were equally ready to prostitute themselves. Their barracks, set at a distance from those of the other prisoners, was a no-go area for everyone, guards included.[76] Adult prisoners who encountered minors in their own barracks were usually appalled at their hardness. E. A. Kersonovskaya, whose years in inter-war Romania had made her relatively insouciant about 'deviant' sexuality, was none the less flabbergasted by the 14- and 15-year-old thieves in her labour camp, who engaged openly and noisily in sexual relations with each other, and boasted, for all to hear, about what they had done for the cooks in order to get extra rations.[77]

'An Apple Never Falls Far from the Tree'

The kaleidoscopic juvenile population in the camps included a contingent who had ended up there not because of some crime they had supposedly committed, but because they were the offspring of an adult, or adults, in the camps (being a carer, or being pregnant, was not considered a mitigating factor in sentencing policy). Such children had a decidedly ambiguous status, officially speaking. On the one hand, laws relating to children's rights could be invoked with reference to them, as in the case of the chief doctor of a sanatorium in Evpatoria, who successfully argued in 1937 that one of his child patients should not be removed when her parents were arrested, because 'according to the Constitution children are not answerable for their parents'.[78] Yet on the other hand, from as early as 1919, the laws relating to political offences recognised the category of 'family member of a repressed person' (which in the mid-1930s was replaced by the category of 'family member of an enemy of the people', and in 1942 by the category 'family member of a traitor to the motherland'). Those adjudicated to belong to this group (which had in practice less to do with blood relationship than the closeness of the social association between a person and the accused, and the extent to which a dependant or associate was held to have been contaminated by this) were – if they were of criminally indictable age – liable to a sentence of at least five years in a camp. Additionally, article 7 of the 1926 Criminal Code, relating to 'socially dangerous elements', was sometimes invoked in order to round up members of a suspect's family.[79]

These laws applied in the first instance to adult (or late adolescent) dependants and associates of an arrestee, rather than to children below the age of criminal responsibility. But the question of what should be done with the children of arrestees in this second category began to exercise the Soviet administration in 1934–5. A 10 November 1934 Central Committee decree stipulated that an arrested single parent's children of over the age of two who had no close relative to look after them should be placed in state care, and that their fate was the responsibility of the local education authorities or village soviets. However, articles in the legal press over the next two years had regularly to remind the authorities of their obligations, indicating another gap between regulations and practice.[80] Informally, police officials often tolerated fostering, a practice affirmed by NKVD regulations of August 1937. These latter drew a distinction between children of over 15 (who were to be carefully vetted, and whose fate was to be decided on a case-by-case basis), and children of under 15. It was permissible to arrest and interrogate the former, but not – in theory at least – the latter. And under-15s and 'harmless' over-15s did not necessarily have to be taken into state care.[81]

Those wishing to foster children of 'enemies of the people' were not always able to keep them from being transferred to homes.[82] But there were many cases where the practice was allowed, and where such children were saved from committal to homes. Children might also remain in the outside world in a less organised way – because, for instance, they had been elsewhere when their parents were arrested. Some of these even managed to plead (though hardly ever successfully) for their parent's or parents' return.[83] Occasionally, too, children were able to mount a legal challenge to confiscation of the living space that they had formerly shared with a parent now imprisoned for a crime.[84]

Yet large numbers of children of those arrested for political reasons did end up in orphanages. Here their fates were sometimes even grimmer than those of ordinary orphanage inmates. Certainly, committal to an orphanage of arrestees' children was partly intended as a welfare measure (there was a real likelihood that children left without a parent would end up on the streets).[85] However, it also smacked of incarceration, and the desire to prevent potential subversives from 'contaminating' the rest of society. In turn, the stigmatising association of arrestees' children with 'enemies of the people' sanctioned staff who were neglectful or sadistic. In some homes, such children were routinely beaten, abused, under-fed, and kept in conditions of squalor; in many more, they had to endure sermons about their own likely capacity for social evil, larded by the folk saying, 'An apple never falls far away from the tree it grew on.'[86] At best, they were likely to be ordered to forget their parents and treated with chilly neutrality.[87] Whether sent to an orphanage specially for children of 'enemies of the people', or to one with a broader contingent of inmates, children of arrestees were always under official suspicion. Any violation of the rules, such as an attempt to escape, was interpreted as subversive and punished with severity.[88] Activities such as the founding of secret societies aroused still more alarm than they did under normal circumstances, since they were seen as incontestable proof of counter-revolutionary tendencies.[89] The suspicion of inherited criminality, or criminality so deeply ingrained in a child's socialisation that it could not easily be corrected, meant some arrestees' children were packed off to NKVD institutions for young offenders, where they were in particular danger of enduring bullying and abuse from staff and from inmates.[90]

But not every institution to which the children of 'enemies' were committed was an NKVD hell-hole, and not all were run by a Soviet Mr Squeers. Some staff manifested considerable humanity to their charges. As in more mainstream homes, the attitude of the director was crucial. In Emma Grabovskaya's home, the director was tough-minded, but treated the children fairly and allowed them to join the Komsomol (an important step in social rehabilitation). A special home for arrestees' children run by Mark Malyavko in Smolensk province maintained quite exemplary standards of care. The children were not only well fed, well housed, and well looked after in an ordinary sense (the home on one occasion won a prize as the best orphanage in the Russian Federation), but were treated with tactful consideration for their individual circumstances. The director helped them to doctor their identity papers so that their dubious origins were concealed, and attempts by the Pioneer and Komsomol staff to denigrate their parents were firmly curbed.[91]

Considerate treatment was, it should be said, more effective in restoring children to the Soviet fold than was severity and contempt. A fair number of the children consigned to orphanages in any case felt resentment against the system for what they and their parents had endured, and treating them like miniature 'enemies of the people' reinforced this feeling.[92] This point was tacitly recognised in a top secret NKVD order of 20 May 1938, which condemned some orphanage staffs for their open favouritism towards children of the repressed, but which was also aimed against ill-treatment. It decreed that from now on children were to be properly fed, and that mockery of them, and the attempt to foster resentment of them on the part of other orphanage inmates, were to cease forthwith.[93]

Children born to imprisoned parents who were serving sentences, or who ended up with their parents in prison, were generally treated harshly. Even when rehabilitationism was at its height, in May 1921, Evgeniya Ratner, imprisoned because of her membership of the Socialist Revolutionary Party, had to write to Feliks Dzerzhinsky in his dual capacity as head of the NKVD and head of the Children's Committee in order to protest at the conditions in which her 3-year-old son Shura was being held alongside her in Butyrki Prison. Despite his tender age, the boy was kept locked up all the time, except for a mere hour-a-day's exercise. In August of the same year, the inmates of the concentration camps set up for participants in the peasant rebellion in Tambov province included over a thousand children, despite an order to release minors that had been issued a month earlier.[94]

If the view that prison was not the right place for children could be suspended when it came to children from 'bad' political backgrounds, it was equally true that the exaltation of the family in official propaganda of the late 1930s was accompanied by the routine profanation of family relations in prisons and camps. To possess a family photograph was an offence punishable by confinement to an isolation cell, and prison guards routinely suppressed mail from prisoners' children.[95] The treatment of women during pregnancy and after parturition, as well as of their infants, was callous or even brutal. Sometimes labour took place in the cell without medical help.[96] During transit to the camps, mothers with infants were housed, like other prisoners, in cattle trucks without sanitary facilities or running water. Clothes could not be washed, and nappies had to be recycled by the primitive method of scraping off faeces with a stick and then part-drying the still half-filthy cloth against an adult's arm or leg before it was replaced on the infant's bottom. Worse, death by starvation or exposure was a constant threat.[97] While political prisoners did not necessarily suffer worse than those serving terms on criminal charges (treatment of all mothers was bad), they were excluded from the amnesties for pregnant women and for mothers with children under 7 declared on 18 January 1945 and 22 April 1949, along with certain categories of ordinary criminal, such as bandits, murderers, and recidivists.[98]

Facilities were worst in prisons, but they were little better in transit and in labour camps. Certainly, 1934 regulations stipulated that crèches or children's rooms must be organised at all 'places for persons deprived of freedom'. However, they also spoke of the requirement to organise 'baby homes' only 'if these are essential'.[99] Clearly, much was left to discretion. Where such places did exist, mothers were allowed access for a maximum of twelve months after birth (or six months from 1939), and at times strictly regulated by the administration. If the camp staff followed the rules, access was reasonably generous when the mother was breast-feeding: seven visits were allowed per day until the child was three months old; from then to five months, the number was reduced to six visits; and in the sixth month, to five. Thereafter, though, visiting opportunities were starkly reduced – to twice a month at maximum, for one hour at a time, and strictly on the sixth and twenty-fourth days of the month. Visits were supposed to be held in conditions regulated by the usual daunting rules: it obviously made sense to insist that a mother who had just come in from manual work washed her hands, breasts and nipples before beginning feeding, but the requirement that feeding be conducted in strict silence and last no more than thirty minutes clearly had a punitive, rather than utilitarian, character.[100]

Provision for nursing mothers in the camps, from the point of view of work breaks, was, in theory, at least as good as it was for Soviet mothers working in ordinary places of employment (such as factories).[101] An order of 23 October 1940 set in place the usual hygienic principles: light, airy premises, with lino floors and painted walls; hygienic toys (made of rubber, celluloid, etc.) that could be washed or sterilised; regular bathing for the infants. Crèches, it was specifically stated, should be equipped and run to the standard of the Narkomzdrav infant homes.[102] However, much of this was not properly implemented in practice, just as with 'civilian' institutions; and camp inmates had even less clout with administrators than ordinary Soviet citizens. There was no redress if a mother was denied preferential rations or adequate access to her child, since administrators could always argue that the denial had been made as a punishment for bad behaviour.

Equally, mothers had no control over the behaviour of the staff in the camp nursery itself. Unlike those in a public nursery, abuses in a camp nursery would never have been reported in the Soviet press; hence, like infringements of adult prisoners' rights (infraction of stipulations on diet, working conditions, etc.), neglect of camp children could flourish with impunity. The official ratio of seventeen infants to one supervisor was no worse than in many civilian crèches, and better than in some, but the staff offered children in their care far brusquer treatment than would have been likely in civilian kindergartens. As Khava Volovich, incarcerated in the camps from the late 1930s to the late 1940s, and who gave birth to a daughter in prison, remembered:

> [The nurse] had to sweep the ward, wash and dress the children, feed them, keep the stove going, and do all sorts of special 'voluntary' shifts in the camp; but her main responsibility was keeping the ward clean. In order to cut down on her workload and allow herself a bit of free time, she would 'rationalise' her jobs; that is, she would try to come up with ways in which she could reduce the amount of time she had to spend on the children.

'Rationalising' jobs meant, for instance, that the children were fed scalding hot food, never picked up and handled, and were left sitting on their potties till they got prolapse of the rectum. The quality of care was poor in material ways too: there were never enough blankets to go round, and the hygiene left much to be desired.[103]

According to Volovich, the result of the careless and indifferent treatment of children in camp nurseries was a horrendous death rate – 300 infants a year perished in the crèche facility at the camp where she herself was held. Similar high death rates and cruel treatment (reaching as far as the violation of dead infants by the morgue supervisor) characterised the camp where Nadezhda Ioffe served her sentence in the late 1930s.[104] Even internal NKVD reports sometimes admitted that all was not well. A document filed on 8 May 1939 from Karaganda camp, for example, reported that the premises for infants were unheated, equipment and vitamins were chronically short, and mothers were cooped up in cold damp barracks.[105]

But not all camp administrations were so inhumane. As in every area of institutional life, the personality of the director was crucial. In the camp where Fruma Treivas was held after she was arrested in the late 1930s, the director referred affectionately to 'my little women', and the facilities provided were limited but adequate – clean (though old) sheets, washtubs, even disinfectant. Mothers were allowed access to their infants until the end of breast-feeding, and were given jobs in the crèche so that they were in constant contact. Yet, even here, mortality was a problem – so much so that mothers successfully pressed the administrators to allow them to transfer their children to the care of relations, despite knowing that this often meant a move to a hopelessly overcrowded room in a communal flat.[106]

Determined camp doctors could also do something to alleviate conditions in the crèches (one qualified paediatrician even arranged a visit to Moscow to lobby a top official on behalf of the mothers and infants in her care).[107] And in cases where the nursery jobs were not snaffled by women from the criminal underworld (like other 'soft' forms of employment not involving hard manual work, the position of nursery supervisor was much sought after), and went to women who were themselves mothers, the staff became very attached to their charges and suffered distress when they had to be transferred to baby homes after the regulation year or eighteen months was over.[108]

In the best of circumstances, though, a child born in the camps might emerge fatally damaged physically or psychologically, or both. M. K. Sandratskaya's daughter, for instance, ended up severely disturbed and refusing to eat; she was eventually to die of weakness and malnutrition.[109] And 'survivors', if they did not grow up insane or, to use Volovich's words, 'feeble-minded', were likely to acquire 'the cunning and craftiness of old camp lags'.[110] Contact with adult prisoners reinforced criminal behaviour in the children, who formed gangs and ranged the camp, robbing and sometimes even killing those they encountered. The practice of confining children with women and infirm elderly people put the second two categories in danger of verbal and physical abuse. Children themselves were vulnerable to adult prisoners, with regular 'auctions' of newcomers allowing criminals their pick of minors as sexual favourites; and the children themselves soon grew tough and wild, and made use of the camp authorities' reluctance to punish or control them.[111] Schooling was rudimentary to non-existent, and the intellectual and moral education of the children was left to chance. Prior to the Revolution, philanthropic organisations had been allowed to concern themselves with children settled in or around labour camps; after 1935, the sole space left for efforts on such children's behalf was the gap between arrest and sentencing. The secrecy of the camp system was not the only factor in this; another was the perception of such children as a threat, as creatures existing beyond the boundaries of normal childhood, a perception reinforced in its turn by the violence and aggression of which such brutalised children soon became capable.

War Orphans

The outbreak of conflict in June 1941 reversed the effects of the 1935 legislation on homelessness in two respects. Soviet cities once more filled up with abandoned, homeless, and simply lost children. Between August 1941 and June 1942, as many as 18,000 solitary children were rounded up by child-care professionals in Leningrad.[112] In 1943, 1944, and 1945, the NKVD reception centres across

50 Amateur dramatics, Leningrad orphanage in evacuation, *c.* 1943.

the Soviet Union processed 842,144 children, of whom over 600,000 had been deserted for good and all (the others were 'unsupervised').[113] But on the other hand, the effects of the war softened attitudes towards such children as a class. It was widely recognised that war orphans were a special category, and one obviously deserving of sympathy and help. The softening of attitudes showed itself, among other things, at the level of propaganda representations. For the first time since the early 1930s, orphans made their way back into mainstream literature, including works intended for children. In Mikhail Zoshchenko's maudlin story *Poor Little Fedya* (1945), children in an orphanage who mocked a boy for not being able to read were soon silenced when they heard that the child was a victim of Fascist repression.[114] Equally indicative of new attitudes was Vera Panova's story 'Valya', also a portrait of war orphans. Separated from their parents and placed in a children's home well behind the front lines, Valya and her sister are trapped in the home when both parents are killed. Though the home (inevitably) is a model institution, with kind staff and hygienic conditions, and pleasant inmates, the two girls would rather return to their native Leningrad. Eventually they achieve this dream, when their former neighbours offer to take them in.

Despite its 'best of all possible worlds' flavour, Panova's narrative, at least, was far from implausible. Evacuated children who became separated from their parents were in fact almost certain to end up in an orphanage (though families were often billeted on other families, single children were not routinely sent to lodge with strange families, as evacuees were in Britain).[115] And fostering was treated with considerably more approval during the war than it had ever been in Soviet history. A decree of the Council of People's Commissars passed on 8 April 1943 commended adoption (*usynovlenie*), long-term fostering (*patronat*), and short-term fostering (*opeka*) as ways of keeping children from waifdom. Indeed, a person could only refuse nomination as guardian of a child (*opekun*) if he or she had some good reason (such as an existing commitment to look after a child under eight).[116] Full-scale adoption was sometimes discouraged in case a child's real parents turned up,[117] but long-term fostering was acceptable because it was not seen to raise problems about whom the child 'belonged' to. Propaganda represented sheltering orphans in a strongly positive light: now, the model workers who appeared in photo-spreads had often adopted or fostered a child.[118] After the war, adoption and fostering continued to be regarded positively, and these methods of care were promoted in the post-Stalin era too.[119] In addition, efforts were made to improve provision within institutions. A ministerial decree of 23 January 1942, 'On the Placement of Children Left without Parents', set up local committees attached to Party executive committees which were to have the responsibility of dealing with orphans. These committees were to help ensure that orphaned children between the ages of 3 and 15 were swiftly processed through NKVD reception centres, and that under-threes were dispatched without delay to Ministry of Health baby homes.[120]

Measures of a familiar kind were passed to improve conditions within orphanages. On 1 September 1943 it became compulsory for all homes to have a nurse on the staff, and for medical inspections to take place three times a week (in cities) and twice a month (in the countryside). On 29 August 1944 legal protection was given to the property of children placed in orphanages, which was now supposed to be carefully docketed so that it could be returned to them when they left for the outside world.[121] Educational establishments were also directed to accord favourable treatment to orphans. For example, the decree of 21 August 1943 which founded Suvorov military colleges gave priority in admissions to 'orphans from the former occupied regions' alongside the children of Red Army veterans and Partisans. The same decree also set up twenty-three special 'trade schools' (*remeslennye uchilishcha*) with 400 places in each, offering a four-year programme, and teaching skills such as electrical or radio engineering, metalwork, carpentry, and sewing. Alongside these institutions, ambitious targets were set for orphanage places: 16,300 in institutions for older children and 1,750 in orphanages for young children. There were also to be twenty-nine new reception centres, each catering for 2,000 people.[122] 'Positive discrimination' of this kind continued into the post-war period: in April 1947, there was expansion of the trade-school network to act as a path for orphans into skilled industrial jobs.[123]

It is difficult to say to what extent these targets (which in the case of the second law were not given in concrete terms) were realised. Some children who went through the orphanage system after the Second World War certainly had more attention paid to their individual needs and talents than in previous decades. The prestigious Committee of Artistic Affairs Choir School, opened in Moscow in 1944 as a continuation of the former Leningrad City Choir School, had large numbers of pupils who were orphaned or partially so. According to the minutes of a staff meeting held in 1947, 'No other school has so high a proportion of orphaned children, children who have lost one parent, and children from outside Moscow.'[124] It is hard to imagine that the same could have been said of any of the specialist art schools of the 1930s, whose star pupils tended to be the children of metropolitan intellectuals and Party high-flyers.[125] The sense that the war had created a pool of innocent victims for which the entire nation was responsible also gave an impetus to devolution of responsibility for orphans to the population in general – an example being the scheme to found orphanages at specific factories and other large enterprises, initiated in 1945.[126] And, while adults who had been caught up in zones occupied by the German invaders frequently came under suspicion of collaboration, their orphaned children were nurtured by the state: in 1944, for example, forty special kindergartens were opened for such children on the shores of the Azov Sea and in the Kuban'.[127]

The day-to-day treatment of orphanage inmates was supposed to be informed by a sense that children had suffered terrible experiences during the war. 'Three main decisions were adopted', one orphanage worker reported to the journal of the Anglo-Soviet Friendship Association in 1942: 'to make the children feel they had come to their own hearth and home here [...] but at the same time to observe the established regime; to ask the children no questions whatsoever, to protect them from recollections of what they had lived through, and finally, attentively to study the personality of each child.' In the case of this home, the emphasis on cosiness and tolerance took the edge off the Makarenkan system

51 Certificate awarded to an orphanage director for her work during the Blockade, 1943–4.

of tough discipline and mutual surveillance that had been considered *de rigueur* in the late 1930s. Certainly, the worker reported that a child who had filched sugar had ended up by returning it to the canteen because the other children had made their disapproval painfully evident. But the transformation of the child was shown to have occurred not at this point (in fact, he had then decided to run away), but when he discovered that the home owned an accordion. The boy had lost his own accordion, burnt to cinders during an air raid by the Germans. He was not encouraged to feel indignant about this: the trope espoused in the article was recuperation rather than the need for vengeance. All over the Soviet Union, it claimed, there were homes like this, with 'thousands of other children, whose wounds, inflicted by Nazism, are being healed with so much effort and fond love'.[128]

At least some normative literature published in the post-war period recognised the possibility of psychological trauma ('nervous-psychological disturbance') in orphanage inmates. A manual of 1953, for example, suggested various kinds of management – from drug therapy to hypnosis – for conditions such as nervous tics, bed-wetting, and night-time anxiety. Hysterical conditions were to be treated on an individual basis.[129]

During the years of the war, a great many people, mainly but not exclusively women, flung themselves with enthusiasm and total dedication into the task of looking after children. Many were young and had little previous experience; others had scant education. The demands of the work were colossal: in orphanages, for example, staff routinely had to work a 12-hour day and then be available for night duty, which often included waking children for an air raid.[130]

However, adults deputed to look after children did not always act selflessly. During the chaotic first month of war, some supervisors panicked and fled, abandoning their charges in the struggle to hold on to personal possessions.[131] There were orphanage supervisors who were more interested in the correct processing of pieces of paper than in humane treatment of their charges, and there were officials working for child-care agencies who saw eating at the orphanage table as a perk of the job.[132] And, in practice, it was hard for orphanages to live up to idyllic visions and high hopes. The sheer quantity of institutions was one problematic factor. Between 1941 and 1947, the number of ordinary orphanages alone across the RSFSR more than doubled, from 1,661 to 3,900, while the numbers of inmates rose by more than 120 per cent, from 187,780 to 422,600.[133] Over the same period, baby homes in the Ministry of Health system – which had fallen from 765 in 1922 to 397 in 1940 – increased in capacity as well. A decree of 8 July 1944 gave priority to provision in this area, and by 1946 the numbers of such homes had reached 551 (with nearly 40,000 places, a rise of more than 50 per cent compared with six years earlier), and, by 1948, 688 (with close to 50,000 places).[134] Alongside orphans and the children of arrestees, institutions had a mandate to deal with other categories of children at risk: those whose parents had been 'deprived of their parental rights' because of inadequate care, and the children of single mothers who could not cope on their own.[135]

Figures of this kind pointed to unbearable stresses throughout the system. But needs varied from place to place. As a junior education minister reported in 1947, wartime evacuation policies had created a bulge of orphanage inmates in the Urals and Siberia, with figures tripling in Kirov, Sverdlovsk, and Krasnoyarsk provinces, in the Altai region, and in the Tatar and Bashkir Republics.[136] Pressure here was exacerbated by the official policy of not allowing orphaned children back to major cities such as Moscow and Leningrad, a measure that caused acute distress among these children, abandoned thousands of miles from home, while their fellow inmates who had been 'claimed' by parents or relatives travelled back to the capitals along with the orphanage staff.[137] Alongside pressure of numbers, orphanages had to deal with the predictable wartime and post-war problems – depredations to the fabric of buildings, or housing in temporary, unsuitable premises; dearth of equipment; shortage of food. A secret NKVD report of 25 January 1944 recorded that 199 complaints emanating from orphanage inmates in the vicinity had been picked up by the war censorship post in Narym in the previous month alone. A typical account by an inmate read: 'Life is bad. They give us only 500 grams of bread a day, and two glasses of sweet tea for breakfast, and cabbage soup for lunch, and three little fish for supper and eight potatoes in their jackets. Our clothes are awful. Please let me come and live with you, they beat me here.'[138] In 1944, 119 out of 988 orphanage children undergoing medical inspections in Leningrad province turned out to have TB, and inspections of conditions in the Urals and Altai established that soap and even water were critically short in some places, that bed-sharing was rife, and that there was not enough furniture to go round.[139]

A ministerial decree of 1 September 1943 attempted to combat these problems by mandating better medical surveillance of children's homes.[140] Its success was at best limited. In 1946, the Ministry of Health recorded that the provisions of the decree were being widely ignored; many homes had no doctors or medical personnel, and such doctors as were available were carrying out their work in an uninterested way: infections – including scabies and TB – were going unreported.[141] A separate report listed hideous problems all over the RSFSR. 'Overcrowding, dirt, breaches of hygienic and sanitary regulations, insufficient heating, irregular washing of the children, their underwear and bedlinen, have contributed to an increase in infections among orphanage inmates, especially of scabies, and also influenza and pneumonia.'[142] Once again, the ministry attempted to improve the situation by fiat, ordering that medical inspections should take place and that TB sufferers should be hospitalised.[143] Once again, however, their commands had next to no effect, partly because of continuing heavy demand. At the start of 1946, the NKVD children's centres were running at well below capacity, with overcrowding only in Leningrad, Pskov, and to a lesser extent the Tatar Republic.[144] But in 1947 the situation changed: there were 79,519 new admissions to orphanages across the RSFSR, a number that exceeded the figure for discharges by nearly 40,000 and that was only narrowly below the statistic for 1943.[145] A microscopic picture of the situation is given by the infant homes of Stalingrad, where admissions rose by nearly a third in 1947 compared with 1946, and where the majority of children (123 of 202) had at least one parent living; thirty-three of these had consigned their children on a temporary basis, being unable to afford to keep them.[146]

Not surprisingly, conditions were generally dire. In May 1947, a ministerial report stated that few homes were actually able to carry out inspections, and that health problems – emaciation and weakness in particular – were persisting. Forty-four per cent of children undergoing medical inspections in Tula had tested positive for TB, and by no means all orphanages had laundries, or indeed baths.[147] A series of inspections of provincial orphanages and reception centres, commissioned by the Central Committee's Department of Agitation and Propaganda, also in 1947, revealed a devastating picture. In Stalingrad province, for example, 5,200 children were being housed in premises meant for 3,000. There was no bedlinen, no cooking equipment, no crockery and cutlery in some orphanages, and furniture was very scarce. Fourteen supervisor posts were vacant, as were four posts for paediatricians; no doubt because of such staff shortages, many orphanages were not bothering to do educational work with children or run hobby circles for them, or even making sure that the inmates kept up with schoolwork (14.5 per cent of orphanage children were behind at school, and around 4 per cent had not been attending school in the first place). Food shortages were rife, partly because staff took their salaries in food. Bullying and other types of indiscipline were pervasive, and supervision was poor in other respects as well: in some homes there had been outbreaks of ringworm, mange, and (among those in the punishment blocks) even frostbite. Conditions in the reception centres were equally grim.[148] Further reports from Chuvashia, Bashkiria, Kaluga province, Kalinin province, and Tyumen' province painted things in comparably murky colours – in one particularly vicious case from Tyumen', bullying had spilled over into murder when a group of inmates lured Vasily Shelkanov into the woods and slaughtered him as an act of revenge for his reporting their earlier misdeeds to the authorities.[149]

Hygiene and sanitation should, on the face of it, have been easier to ensure in the Ministry of Health baby homes, which were staffed by medical personnel. Staff guides set out stiff requirements in terms of environment, equipment, and diet for such homes, which were supposed to deliver care according to a meticulous regime alternating feeds at three-hourly intervals with rest, hygienic procedures (washing, etc.), and physical and intellectual stimulation (trips outside into the fresh air, stints in the playpen with toys).[150] Reports from some areas did suggest that the baby homes were in slightly better condition than the orphanages for older children, though shortages of milk were widespread in 1947 and facilities were often in unadapted premises.[151] And, in some baby homes, mortality figures reached 50 per cent in this period.[152] When even the official ratio of carers to children stood at 1:15[153] – in practice, ratios were no doubt often worse – staff were under terrible strain. It did not help that pay was awful, so that working one and a half shifts was essential in order to get by; in addition, the status of institutional child care was so low that staff were likely to come under pressure from partners, families, and friends to take another job if at all possible.[154]

Yet, in the best homes, staff made an effort. In one Leningrad home they organised puppet plays and New Year trees for the children, and attempted to make play the centre of the daily regimen. Failures in hygiene stemmed less from negligence than from deficiencies in the regulations themselves: the fact that staff were allowed to handle food supplies directly meant that contamination with microbes was a constant risk.[155] At the same time the emphasis of this 'work collective' on kind treatment put them at variance with the local authorities, who looked with suspicion on attempts to 'spoil' the children, prohibited the use of 'mama' as a form of address from children to staff, and subjected the children to such perfunctory and alienating assessment procedures when they were due for placements in post-three orphanages that many would be wrongly classified as subnormal when they were simply intimidated.[156]

Official reports suggest that the picture was varied in homes for older children too. Evacuation could mean that children ended up packed like sardines in unsuitable temporary accommodation, but orphanages ended up housed better, rather than worse, than before. Much depended on local conditions – for instance, whether the orphanage had its own farm or market garden – and on the level

52   Leningrad orphanage in evacuation, *c.* 1943.

of help given by the authorities and the resident population. In Omsk, one orphanage was moved into a building that had not been cleaned in the most elementary sense, and had piles of filth lying everywhere. But in some other places visitors were helped to settle down by members of the local community: experiences varied widely.[157]

One unifying factor, though, was the expectation that children should participate in manual labour from an early age – which meant not only doing stints of housework duty (*dezhurstvo*) within the home itself, but contributing to the war effort, and later to 'post-war reconstruction', by carrying out jobs that there were no adults around to complete. A woman from Pskov province who reached her orphanage in Karelia after a horrendous train journey across north-western Russia remembered that the children were put to work harvesting the crops sown by the original inhabitants, the Finns, before they took flight across the border. The children worked 12–13 hours daily without resting. When victory came, they were delighted. True, they did not understand what it meant politically; but they were, at long last, given a day off.[158]

However, children did not necessarily resent the situation they were in. Staff as well as children had to endure terrible conditions.[159] Shortages were endemic through the whole of Soviet society, so that there was no sense of particular deprivation, and a sense of patriotic duty could make the sacrifices seem worth while. Interestingly, recollections by former orphanage inmates of the war and post-war eras on the whole bear out the official understanding of the orphanage as a haven, rather than a hell. A typical story is that of Lyudmila, a woman born in Leningrad in 1937, who ended up in a children's home for victims of the Blockade at the age of five, and remained there until she was 16. Her orphanage, No. 58, was located in a handsome two-storey building with an oak-panelled ceremonial hall, lined with pictures and mirrors, though with modern furniture, on Lieutenant Schmidt Embankment next to the Church of the Dormition. Outside was an attractive grassed yard with flowerbeds, where the children were able to play. Material conditions were good. The diet included meat as well as kasha and macaroni dishes, washed down by cocoa, milky coffee, or tea; for holidays, there was white bread with butter and cheese. Though the children were assigned regulation clothes, these included not just school uniform, but outfits for wear around the children's home, which they were allowed to adapt with personal details such as sewn-on collars and cuffs, and little brooches. The hygiene regulations of the day were observed (cold washes above the waist every day, visits to the *banya* and a change of underwear once a week, and regular cleaning of the home, with which the children helped when on housework duty).

But the regime did not impose too heavily on the children in other ways. After the evening meal, they were able to sit round chatting desultorily with each other and with the children's home staff; a kind housekeeper was always ready to provide extra helpings or a dose of some treat such as condensed milk from the store; and the older inmates could come and go quite freely, even finding chances to flirt with sailors whose ships were docked on the embankment outside. Though 'a government institution is still a government institution', and the staff were quite heavily stretched when trying to give attention to over a hundred children, benevolence and warmth came through. 'The supervisors had lost their own children, their husbands and their family, and they treated us very humanely. We children had lost everything there was to lose, and we were like wolf-cubs, like anything you care to mention. And the supervisors were able to thaw us out, and they thawed out themselves while doing it.'

Ideology was marginal at best, with official rituals limited to the singing of political songs at occasional meetings, and time free from lessons mostly devoted to hobbies such as chess, draughts, amateur dramatics, and (in the summer when the orphanage relocated to a dacha at Siverskaya, outside Leningrad), sport. Children were allowed one or two toys of their own each, and local factories donated 'seconds' from their production lines (slightly wonky wind-up models, for instance) to the general toy pool. Birthdays were celebrated, and a blind eye was turned to minor breaches of the rules (Lyudmila even managed to adopt a kitten). Punishments were imposed more or less only for poor school performance, and were relatively light: a telling-off at one of the public meetings, for example, or

53   Mealtime, Leningrad orphanage in evacuation, *c.* 1943.

being set to sweep down the stairs while the other children were having a walk or were out on an excursion. With reasonable material conditions and kind treatment, the children, not surprisingly, felt warmth towards the home and each other: bullying was unknown, nicknames were used affectionately rather than tauntingly, and the older girls made efforts to be friendly to the younger ones, adopting a protégée whom they would take around and instruct in *savoir-vivre*. In sum, Lyudmila insisted, 'we were one big group, one big family'. And, as with children in loving, safe families, the only hazards were imaginary ones: in this particular case, the ghost rumoured to stalk the corridors of the mansion at night.[160]

Lyudmila's general sense of well-being was quite widely shared, going by memoirs and oral history by those who lived in orphanages during the war and immediate post-war years. A woman born in 1942 and brought up in a Nizhni-Novgorod orphanage remembered the staff as being 'just wonderful'; work over the summer had been enjoyable and light: 'we weren't forced into it', and excursions to the theatre were frequent.[161] But not everyone was so happy: other Nizhni-Novgorod women of the same generation recalled their experience with less enthusiasm. The food was good, but 'you were still hungry all the time [...] it was the strict regime'. And the staff could be intrusive, deciding that you ought not to join the hobby circle that you wanted to because you weren't getting on well enough at school, or regulating the children severely. 'The biggest mistake was keeping us too ground down', a woman born in 1939 remembered.[162]

Impressions varied in part because single child's experience of orphanage life might well include more than one institution, run to quite different standards in

54 Reading outdoors, Leningrad orphanage in evacuation, *c.* 1943.

55 Baby home children at the seaside, 1940s.

practical and human terms. A woman who was institutionalised in Perm' province from 1947 recalled that the first home she went to was a grim institution where the children were punished by being made to kneel on dried peas ('it hurt our feelings. But who could we complain to?'). The second was a genuinely warm and friendly place, even if it could not offer the children either tooth-cleaning equipment or underpants.[163] Another woman institutionalised slightly earlier had an appalling time in her first orphanage, where thuggish older boys held the other children in terror; the supervisors stood by even when a boy was murdered by drowning in the lavatory. The second orphanage was less grim, though there was a sadistic woman supervisor who used to make the girls exercise without tops on, even though boys were present and the girls were already beginning to develop breasts.[164]

Even if orphanage existence was more or less cloudless, adjusting to it was not always easy. For all her uniformly positive summary of orphanage life in retrospect, Lyudmila remembered that arrival in the reception unit had been traumatic. Unusually plump by the standards of Blockade childhood, she was cruelly teased by the strangers with 'here she is again, fat steam train', which reduced her to tears. 'I couldn't speak after that, and for a whole year I didn't say anything. And I started to stammer really badly after that shock, them taking me away from home to some kind of strange institution.'[165] Her reaction seems to have been reasonably common. Children in reception centres could be observed pleading with visitors to take them away: 'Auntie, please take us, we'll be as good as gold!'[166] At the same time, once children had got used to institutional life, they sometimes wanted to stick with the familiar: one boy who was rediscovered by his family after the war had little interest in going back, complaining, 'When no one needed me, I got thrown out. And now I'm big, and they had to start looking for me.'[167] A placement with a family was not necessarily an improvement if, say, it meant returning 'home' to an intolerant step-parent.[168]

Not all children by any means got a chance to try their luck. According to official Soviet histories of the war, adoptive and foster parents came forward readily, out of a combination of pity and patriotic duty. But this sentimentalised reality. Abandoned children were still often left to fend for themselves, hunting on rubbish tips, treated by passers-by as though they were all little thieves.[169] In the circumstances, orphanage life could – as in previous decades – provide a vital sense of shelter. Conversely, sometimes conditions inside institutions that would have struck an adult as appalling were coolly accepted. When a girl new to orphanage life removed a New Year's tree decoration late at night and retreated to bed with it, she was soundly beaten by the other children in her dormitory (the slang expression 'to fix a dark one', *ustroit' temnuyu*, was current for this sort of group discipline). The punishment seemed at once fierce and just. 'Maybe it was a bit cruel, but it burnt itself into me for the rest of my life.'[170]

In any case, by the early 1950s, the peculiar circumstances of the war years had come to an end. Now, relationships between staff and inmates altered. Lyudmila, for example, recollected: 'In 1953, we had a swap, of our supervisors that is, and all the rest of the staff. And we got a new set of people, people who hadn't

56 Children on the climbing frame, baby home, Leningrad, late 1940s.

seen much of the war maybe, and they weren't as attentive or as kind. And they treated us ... the attitude to us changed completely. And we didn't like it, we'd got used to more humane treatment.' One member of staff, nicknamed 'Mr Stick' (Palkin) by the children, even resorted to physical violence at times. But, even now, the inmates' leverage as war orphans counted for a good deal. 'We used to dwell on our rights: "What have we got to do with it, we're not to blame for having lost everything in the war."' [171] The abusive supervisor was duly sacked after they complained.

If treatment for orphans improved during and after the war, their career destinies also became more varied. Orphanage graduates were more likely than other adolescents in the 'labour reserves' to end up in the trade schools, where they made up around a quarter of the intake between 1950 and 1952. [172] There were also more exotic destinies. The orphanage in Taganrog, for instance, sent numerous 'graduates' into the Soviet cultural establishment – as music teachers, activists in the local place of culture, or sports trainers. [173] An outstanding success story was Igor' Zolotussky, who made his way through the orphanage mill after his parents were arrested in the Great Terror, and who later became a prominent literary critic.

But, as Zolotussky's story indicates, escaping the standard destiny of manual labour was not always straightforward. He himself hated the orphanage and, after it was evacuated once war broke out, ran away to Siberia. But he was recaptured and sent to work on a collective farm. Later he was released from this, but duly dispatched to a trade school. Only the help of a sympathetic teacher enabled him to transfer to a full-status secondary school in Kotlas. [174] In the words of one former inmate (born in 1931), 'The state looks after you, keeps you, and you're supposed to do your duty to the state. That means entering the working class. Now you're supposed to work for the state.' [175] Lyudmila likewise remembered that the education offered in her orphanage was adequate but basic: 'the orphanage couldn't give us much'. Inmates were meant to pay back their dues to the state by leaving as soon as they reached adolescence and joining a factory school or (an option for girls) a pedagogical college. Exposure to broader cultural horizons was fortuitous: she and her friends were lucky enough to be helped by friends of her mother's, who sought the children out and organised visits to the theatre, music lessons, and even language teaching for them. [176]

The Hard Line Continues

The less acceptable face of abandoned children in the war and post-war years was their association with criminality. Like Soviet citizens generally, children responded to shortages and to the relatively permissive atmosphere that reigned during the conflict not just with stoicism and self-denial, but with illegal trade, fare-dodging, vandalism, and theft.[177] The authorities monitored the situation and reacted with alarm to the figures – in 1946–7, according to secret official reports, crimes by juveniles were running at a rate of roughly 12,000 per year in Moscow, and around 13 per cent of juveniles arrested were homeless children, while 42 per cent were not working or studying anywhere.[178]

Crime statistics were, as in any society, a symptom of 'moral panic' as well as an objective record of human behaviour. In the post-war Soviet Union, they prompted a further toughening of the penal regime aimed at young people, which began soon after the war started. In December 1941, the then acting procurator of the USSR, G. N. Safonov, expressed his approval for the application of the death penalty to young people of 16 and over who were guilty of crimes such as spying, treachery, and acts of terrorism.[179] While it is not clear how often, or indeed whether, the death penalty was exacted on 16–18-year-olds, the war years saw stiffer penalties being meted out upon the perpetrators of lesser crimes. According to a ministerial decree of 15 June 1943, those convicted of hooliganism, or guilty of persistent disruption in ordinary orphanages, could now be dispatched to labour colonies. That this measure had concrete results is suggested by a further ministerial decree passed on 6 June 1944 calling for 10,000 more places in the labour-education colonies.[180] Some real-life juveniles who committed misdemeanours during the war received sentences as draconian as the hardest-line member of the Politburo could have wished. In October 1944, for instance, five youths in Taganka district were given custodial sentences of five years each for their involvement in fourteen robberies.[181] As the problems with high crime rates continued after the war, so, too, did high inmate numbers. In January 1946, there were over 28,000 young offenders held in 67 labour–education colonies and 27 labour colonies across the USSR; a year later, the numbers stood at over 35,000 in the two types of institution.[182] Pressure on places did not lead to a revision of policy. On 7 April 1947, a decree of the interior minister created a further 10,000 places in the labour colonies.[183]

To be sure, the punitive ideology so purely expressed in 1935 was not consistently maintained. In 1943 it was recognised that young offenders required special treatment during the assessment and sentencing process, and juvenile chambers were opened up again.[184] V. Tadevosyan, one of the most vociferous supporters of the post-1935 hard line, did some swift back-pedalling: in 1945, he commemorated the tenth anniversary of the 7 April 1935 decree in an article which, while including some predictable comments about the harmfulness of 'liberal love', also argued that it was improper to assign custodial sentences to small children for petty thefts.[185] This perception was formalised in February 1948, when the Supreme Soviet spelled out that minors were a special case under a decree prohibiting 'parasitism' that it had issued in June 1947. 'By their very age, [children of 12 to 16] have not yet entered employment, or are only just in the process of doing so, therefore isolated cases of theft cannot usually be regarded as an indication of parasitism or as an attempt to evade socially useful work. [...] It should be taken into consideration that cases of theft at this age are frequently not dictated by selfish motives; they are a curious form of childish mischief. This is so, for example, with thefts of fruit and vegetables from gardens.'[186] Sometimes, too, trained lawyers took the risk of pointing out legislative anomalies – for instance, an article published in 1950 considered the question of whether, if children over 14 were held fully accountable for their actions, it was also possible to penalise parents for damage caused by their dependent children, where the latter were over 14.[187]

In practice, however, sweet reason and sophisticated argument was seldom much in evidence: the main pressure was to clear the streets and get offenders out of the public eye. And so juveniles who could not be fitted into the ever-expanding colonies continued, according to eyewitness recollections, to be incarcerated in adult camps. One of the characters in Solzhenitsyn's *A Day in the Life of Ivan Denisovich* is only 16, and several memoirists incarcerated at different times in the 1930s and 1940s remember seeing juveniles, including a 14-year-old Western Ukrainian sent to Kolyma for twenty-five years because he had shot at a Stalin picture fixed to his kite, or two children aged 12 and 15, who were among a contingent of deportees from Bessarabia and who were left to make the journey on their own when their mother was removed.[188] Occasionally, those sent to prison camps at an early age set down their own recollections, as in the case of a man who was consigned to the system aged 17, and who worked in building and then in the molybdenum mines.[189]

Conditions in the colonies and camps, once children reached them, were tough. During the war itself, the inmates of these facilities, like the inmates of other Soviet institutions, endured privation: official levels of ration provision were cut in June 1942 and again in May 1943, and it was not until October 1945 that an approximation to pre-war norms was reached.[190] As food shortages during and after the war made themselves felt, the temptation for staff to pilfer sometimes became irresistible.[191] Naturally, other problems, such as shortages of equipment and rough, callous, or indifferent handling by staff, continued to bite, and dissatisfied inmates continued to take any possible opportunity to escape (between nine and ten inmates per colony managed to take to their heels in January 1944).[192] And officially sanctioned severity towards those serving sentences in colonies also persisted. An NKVD directive of 14 February 1946 affirmed the principle that disruptive inmates should be sent to a special regime institution – i.e. somewhere where discipline was even tougher.[193]

It goes without saying that these punitive policies did little or nothing to clear up disaffection in the colonies, which remained plagued by practical difficulties and low morale throughout the post-war era too. One quite approbatory report on a Leningrad 'labour education colony' for girls compiled in the late 1940s, for instance, revealed that, while the inmates were able to wash every ten days (a generous concession, in its view), no footwear of any kind was available. Almost no 'labour education' was in fact provided, and, for the most part, the only work done by the girls was helping with domestic work (preparing and serving food, etc.). With numbers now swelled to over 65,000 in the 134 labour and labour-education colonies, and the entire country suffering shortages of food and consumer goods, the situation was next to unmanageable. In the worst institutions, inhumanity was added to practical difficulties: inmates continued to be beaten, tormented, and sexually abused by the guards and by older prisoners, and solitary confinement was meted out on the slightest provocation. On emerging from the colonies, the 'reformed' prisoners had little hope of a rehabilitated existence: even the trade schools were reluctant to take them on.[194]

Between 1936 and 1953, no significant changes were made to the overall management of children's institutions, or to the regime within them. Rather, measures were constantly passed – to little obvious effect – attempting to make staff comply with existing regulations. Particularly during the war and post-war years, this was an uphill struggle: in conditions of extreme deprivation, it was often not possible to meet the legal dietary norms, or to ensure humane treatment. At the same time, the outbreak of the Second World War did allow the spotlight to be turned once more on to certain categories of suffering children. So far as social attitudes were concerned, war orphans were a different category from street children in the ordinary sense. Within homes, too, children could use their 'war orphan' status to manipulate the authorities into providing better facilities. This special status, added to the levelling effects of the war itself (the widespread idea that the whole Soviet nation was 'in it together') helps explain why memories of the orphanage at this period of history are often warmer than those of other times. Children of this generation felt grateful to the state not just for their upbringing, in a moral sense, but for their sheer physical survival.

Chapter 8

Freedom and Punishment,
1953–1991

Orphanages are like prisons – each one is different.[1]

Throughout the Stalin period, reports had reached the authorities of malaise in the orphanages and young offender colonies, prompting legislative and administrative action. On 8 April 1952, yet one more decree on the 'Liquidation of Child Homelessness' was passed, this time calling for more educational work and an end to rough treatment in orphanages; the reasons behind escapes were to be investigated, and regimes in individual orphanages were to be subject to regulation. Measures were set in place to help orphanage inmates once they left the institution: the factory schools (FZU) were directed to give priority to applicants from the orphanage network, and children leaving orphanages for an FZU were now supposed to get a cash handout and a set of clothes (inmates going straight into a job were presented only with a suit of clothes).[2] The reforms repeated changes made many times before, and similar reforms were to follow them. But, with the end of the Stalin era, there was an important change in the phrasing of reform measures. A decree on improvements in the orphanages passed on 21 October 1953 articulated not just a need for corrections at the practical level (for instance the importance of getting fosterage supplements paid on time), but also called for an end to the 'incursion on the rights' of inmates.[3] This return to the 1920s language of rights represented a radical shift in the rhetoric according to which discussion of children's institutions took place.

The effects, in practical terms, should not be overstated. The post-Stalin era did not see any review of the policy of institutionalisation for children in need as such. It was still accepted that the best place for orphans, and for children whose parents were deemed to be incapable – or who declared themselves incapable – of looking after them, was state care; large numbers of young offenders continued to be sent into detention. The multi-ministry system remained in place, with all the wasteful parallelism and rigidity that went with it. A child classed as 'imbecile' was still exceptionally unlikely to end up in a home for 'normal' or indeed 'backward' children – even if the original diagnosis was later negated by its behaviour. Even 'mildly backward' children were likely to stay where they were.[4] Equally, work with 'normal' children in baby homes was quite different from work in orphanages, so, in the best of circumstances, long-term denizens of the care system were likely to go through bewildering alterations of experience as they grew up.[5]

Part of the problem, as before, lay in the nature of reception facilities. Staffing levels in the child inspectorates were still very low: an entire city district, with a population of tens of thousands, was entitled to no more than one inspector. For much of the time, this person would be office-bound, handling strings of people arriving with problems or preparing cases on 'deprivation of parental rights' for court hearings.[6] As before, the ordinary police often made up the front line – and not necessarily trained personnel either. As late as the mid-1970s, an area of Moscow province with eighty-five population centres had only one children's inspector, and ten 'children's rooms'.[7] Sometimes, 'children's rooms' were used as dumping grounds for operatives who were unsatisfactory in other respects.[8] The general attitude is well conveyed by a character in Yury Miloslavsky's story 'Lyudmila Ivanovna's Son' who, reacting to a case where a teacher's son has been involved in a gang rape, exclaims:

> I'd have rammed those bastards' legs right through their arses – scuse my French – and broken all their legs. I've got Ol'ga Nikolaevna Maslova on the juvenile cases – she'd have wrenched their balls right off, pardon me! Can't keep your dick in your trousers, eh – well, you can put up with what you get![9]

On the other hand, there were some cases where a lighter touch was employed: a woman born in Perm' in 1958, for example, recalled that when she slapped another girl's face during a street fight aged 15 ('they laughed at me in this really provocative way and pointed, and I said, "What's your problem?" and then they had to start ... So I got up and gave one of them a really good thwack round the chops, I really let her have it'), the result was a fine, rather than the court case that might have been expected.[10] Perhaps gender (violence perpetrated by girls was simply 'not serious') had something to do with this.

Not surprisingly, given the caseload, police and inspectors still played little role in identifying abuse, which came to light by other means. A child might report cruelty to a teacher or Pioneer activist; an adult of this kind – or a doctor in a children's clinic – might notice that something was wrong.[11] But such individuals often found it difficult to achieve anything concrete: they could warn parents that their activity was likely to lead to legal action and make 'trouble' (*nepriyatnosti*) for them at their place of work, but actually taking the child away was a cumbersome process that was not within the jurisdiction of individual child-care professionals.[12] As before, Komsomol, trade union, and Party support networks, and volunteer organisations such as the Women's Soviets, gave some back-up (at the very least, neglectful parents could be sanctioned, a possibility that disappeared in the post-Soviet era). But there was, until the last days of the Soviet regime (and the creation of the Lenin Fund for Children in the late 1980s), still no coherent lobby group representing the needs of children, as opposed to the interests of the 'Soviet family' in general.

From 'Children's Homes' to 'Boarding-Schools'

In many ways, the nature of children's institutions remained similar too. Despite the promotion of the early Soviet period as a model in post-Stalinist culture generally, there was no reversion to the 'open door' policies of the 1920s. Administrators were still convinced that failures in children's institutions were traceable to weak central control: a decree of 30 January 1954 introduced a system of regular compulsory three-month inspections of orphanages.[13] Within institutions, too, control remained tight: 'self-government' continued to be of a Makarenkan collective discipline variety rather than a conduit for the expression of opinion on the part of inmates. A 14 September 1959 decree regulating 'self-help' in schools and orphanages stipulated that inmates should (in traditional style) help prepare and dole out food, clean dormitories, and repair furniture and clothes.[14]

Yet elements of institutional life were beginning to change. The regime became less punitive in certain respects. In September 1956, new food rations for orphanages increased the variety of foods regularly offered and upped the proportion of protein, as opposed to carbohydrate.[15] And the 14 September 1959 regulations contained an important warning against overload, at least among younger children, who were not to be asked to do floor-washing and were only to help with large pieces of laundry (as opposed to small items of clothing, etc.) if the institution had a machine.[16]

More diversity was starting to emerge in terms of the provision of full-time care. The Khrushchev era saw a considerable expansion of the network of boarding-schools, which had formerly been quite small. During the 1930s, such schools were the destination of small numbers of children from the pinnacle of the Party elite – for example, the children of foreign Comintern officials were housed in a magnificent establishment at Ivanovo-Voznesensk, which offered, according to one former pupil, 'a very privileged education. We had everything.'[17] The system had been widened in the immediate post-war years, during which time new categories had appeared, notably boarding-schools for certain types of war orphan, and boarding-schools serving outlying rural areas, with special establishments catering for children from ethnic minorities.[18] There is some evidence that there were also a few schools for the sons and daughters of Party officials, apparently founded because of Soviet leaders' admiration for the products of British public schools whom they had encountered during diplomatic negotiations in the war years and after. Some institutions of this kind continued to exist in later years as well. A woman who worked in one during the 1970s recalled that conditions there were quite unlike those in other facilities for children left permanent or temporary orphans. 'There were four beds to a dormitory and camel-hair blankets, and the floors were carpeted.'[19]

The purpose of the boarding-schools set up by the Twentieth Congress of the Communist Party in 1956 was different.[20] These were urban, rather than rural,

57   Hero of the Soviet Union Makhmut Safievich Aktuganov visiting the Pioneer group
at Orphanage No. 80, Leningrad, 1954.

schools, and were aimed at a broad spectrum of the young, especially those with
a working-class background. They were intended as 'model teaching institutions'
that would combine labour education and 'Communist education', turning
their graduates into well-balanced adults who could contribute fully to Soviet
society.[21] Alongside these utopian aims, there were practical ends in view. The
new boarding-schools were meant to provide the children of single parents, and

of working families where child care was a problem, with full-time institutional care, as a later stage of the 24-hour nurseries and kindergartens for younger children.[22] In some major cities, such as Sverdlovsk, provision was targeted at large plants, where hostels might be set up near existing schools to create a sleep-over facility.[23] The system increasingly came to be that orphaned and abandoned children would be housed in an institution called an 'orphanage' until they were of school age, and then transferred to an institution called a 'boarding-school' once they reached seven. By the 1970s, six of the eleven surviving orphanages in Sverdlovsk province had been converted into boarding-schools.[24] In principle, the fact that boarding-schools were not purely for orphaned or abandoned children could generate an element of de-segregation, as children of highly placed officials living abroad (as well as the children of single parents or overstretched workers) were housed together, wore the same uniform, ate the same food, and had the same lessons.[25]

As in previous eras, there continued to be a gulf between intentions and achievements. Child abandonment was not a pressing problem in the way it had been during and immediately after the Second World War. By the 1960s, orphanages were starting to close rather than open, as the children consigned in the 1940s reached maturity and moved on. Of the 155 orphanages founded in Sverdlovsk province between 1917 and 1969, only 3 were set up in the 1960s,

58 'Staroladozhskii' Orphanage No. 1, Leningrad province, Volkhovo district. Children from the 'Young Technicians' hobby circle doing designs for agricultural implements, 22 February, 1955.

as opposed to 138 between 1940 and 1949. And, by the 1970s, the total number of full-time institutions for children (including both orphanages and boarding-schools) across the province was 11, an enormous decline compared with three decades earlier.[26] Nevertheless, the number of new institutions set up was well below official state targets. In 1960, for example, only 600,000 boarding-school places, out of a planned one million, had in fact been made available.[27]

Detailed comment on conditions in orphanages and boarding-schools of the post-1953 era is difficult because much material has not yet been declassified or was not recorded to begin with. But available evidence from archives, interviews, and reportage by foreign visitors suggests that problems persisted. A report from Sverdlovsk in 1959, for example, remarked that, while 80 per cent of *internat* premises were sanitary, there were problems with food supply, so that the children did not get an adequate diet. The rate of drop-out was also worrying.[28] Two years earlier, boarding-school directors from rural areas taking part in a national conference admitted that it was often extremely difficult to keep children in touch with their birth families.[29] A Western visitor three decades later found the model orphanages she was taken round extremely well equipped (one pre-school home had a kiln and a darkroom, another a 'Russian cottage' with a stove). But even these 'respectable' homes often had dreary and impersonal public areas and dormitories, with a decidedly 'institutional' feel.[30] As in earlier generations, the patronage system could help in ensuring a better than average standard – but only provided that the patrons themselves put effort into helping out in material and practical ways.[31]

These bald observations are more than confirmed by the more detailed accounts accessible through oral history. One woman teacher who took employment in a Leningrad *internat* in the early stages – until the atmosphere there drove her out – remembered a bizarre combination of high-level provision in a material sense, down to expensive uniforms for the children, and emotional sterility. One of her fellow workers beat the children, but more pervasive was a general atmosphere of unconcern verging on neglect. This teacher found herself bringing sandwiches from home because some of her charges were hungry, and holding others in her arms at night so that they could cry themselves to sleep. In no way did the school fulfil its function as a refuge from society: few parents bothered to visit, and, when children were sent home, parents were quite capable of stripping off their school attire and selling it to pay for the next bottle of vodka.[32] A woman who began working in a boarding-school for orphaned and abandoned children in 1970 recalled that, prior to their arrival, some of the children had been treated in the orphanage not just neglectfully, but cruelly. 'Of course, they were disobedient, very wild, but no one had taken an interest in them, done anything about raising them [...] They told me that the supervisor would push two chairs together like that, and make the children stretch their legs out and then [she'd] sit down on their legs. They got beaten till they were blue.'[33]

Yet not all testimony is so grim. To be sure, life continued to be decidedly 'institutional'. As described by a woman who worked as a supervisor at a boarding-school in Leningrad from 1962:

Of course we had a strict order of the day, every day. [...] There was a fixed hour for getting up. The older children got up at seven, and the younger ones ... class 5 and up, I suppose, at half-past seven. So the supervisors would get to work by then. And when I was there, we had compulsory exercises, yes, exercises, every morning. [...] And when I arrived, I'd go straight to the dorms and say, 'Right. Blankets over the bedstead.' And we'd go and do our exercises. Then afterwards they had to make their beds. [...] Everything was supposed to be clean, neat, nice. There was a face-towel and a towel for your feet. [...] They'd be coming out and they'd know: they have to show me they've washed behind their ears, they'd show me their hands, they'd not just show me them, they'd lift them to my nose. [...] Then they'd go and tidy up, and then they had breakfast, the duty boys and girls would tidy up the dorms. [...] And then we'd go to schools for the lessons.[34]

Nevertheless, this record of regimentation makes clear that in this era, unlike earlier ones, the hygienic regulations stood some chance of being carried out. The exercise of sniffing the children's hands was made meaningful by the availability of 'strawberry-scented soap'.[35]

Certainly, provision was still not generous. Food was monotonous, and inmates tended to become obsessed with eating in compensation. One set of clothes was the norm even in reasonably well supplied schools.[36] Growing children had to make do with two pairs of cotton tights – of such poor quality they immediately ran into holes – every three years, and one coat every four years. Nylon tights were not supplied (they were almost impossible to find in Soviet shops at the time as well); less explicably (though this was probably to do with the fact that supply quotas did not keep in step with the norms of dress), adolescent girls had to do without bras. And everyone in the orphanage, or the boarding-school, wore exactly the same, allowing for the number of darns and patches, and for substitutions when some item of clothing had fallen apart and had to be replaced before its time.[37] Provision of equipment was also limited: a woman born in 1967 and sent to an orphanage and then a boarding-school, after her hard-drinking and hard-living mother was deprived of her parental rights, recalled that the home did have a television and a piano – but only because inmates and former inmates had clubbed together and raised the money for these items.[38]

Yet none of this bespeaks the devastation that characterised at least some homes in earlier generations. The fact of a clothes supply, however modest, rather than constant recycling of old clothes, was already a material change. It would appear that most post-Stalinist 'closed institutions' for children were reasonably well supplied with food and furnished to a level of basic adequacy, if not necessarily in a way that was welcoming and cosy. Staff continued to do what they could to improve life for their charges. To be sure, as one former supervisor recalled, 'Of course, you couldn't treat them affectionately. Because if you tried that, the other thirty, and you had thirty-five of them in a group, would start getting jealous, and then a fight would break out, and then you'd have a mêlée, and that would be it.'[39] But, on the whole, her memory was of reasonably harmonious work

59 'Staroladozhskii' Orphanage No. 1, Leningrad province, Volkhovo district. Children from the 'Young Technicians' hobby circle making and painting agricultural implements, 22 February, 1955.

circumstances, with children who still felt gratitude for the home and education they were getting from the state.

The sense of gratitude is independently attested by many former orphanage inmates from this generation.[40] They appear not to have experienced the same sense of frustration as did many of their counterparts among 'family' children during their exposure to another form of institutional contact – ordinary school education. Political education was much less likely to generate an ironic reaction: even heroes such as Pavlik Morozov inspired respect.[41] And the side-effects of social stratification seem to have been less marked here. In boarding-schools, where the children of officials and 'orphanage kids' were provided for together, the need to wear institutional clothes all the time was a leveller; and – according to the recollections of a former supervisor, at least – a sense of camaraderie was pervasive, with the more privileged children doing what they could to help the others in material and intellectual terms.[42] At the same time, there are also some less cosy stories: the girl who tried to kill herself by swallowing needles after being raped by a man who had offered to help her when she lost the money she was carrying; the pupils so intimidated they did not dare to correct teachers even when they knew they were wrong. Windows still had bars on them, 'like in the nick' (*kak v tyurage*), in one former inmate's recollection, and the atmosphere was sometimes not very different.[43]

In the circumstances, adoption might have seemed a relief; but in practice it, too, was subject to strict controls, which gave children little say in their destiny.

60   Children's Home No. 44, Leningrad. Picking cabbage in the vegetable garden, 1955.

61   Two children from Orphanage No. 49, Pushkin, Leningrad, with the medals they received at the All-Soviet Agricultural Exhibition, 1956.

A woman attending a Leningrad boarding-school in the mid-1960s was simply told that a couple that had visited were going to adopt her:

> And they called in one of the supervisors [...] and they called me in too. And they said, 'Here are your parents.' [...] I said, 'So why do I have to go there?' 'They've taken a liking to you, their little girl died and you're a bit like her, and you haven't got anyone, you're a positive-thinking type, and so go and live with them.' [...] When they came, they had a good look at me. They asked me something, I don't remember what. Well, sort of, 'So you'd come and live with us?' they asked. I said, 'I don't know.' [...] 'Well, you'll be fine,' they said in chorus, 'you'll be fine with us. We've got our own flat. You can go on attending this school. We'll replace your mummy and daddy.' Something like that.

Not surprisingly, the girl herself felt extremely unhappy about this precipitate offer; in the event, the adoption did not go through.[44]

Subjective impressions of institutional care continued to vary, then. Objectively speaking, the most crucial change to have overtaken such care was the reduction in the numbers of children needing to use it. With rising prosperity, mass desertion of children had – for a time – ceased to be a problem. During the 1960s, 1970s, and early 1980s, the orphanage system became the repository for children who were in one sense or another marginal, in particular sick and handicapped children; the children of sick, alcoholic, or otherwise incapable parents; and the offspring of single mothers, since the social stigma of birth outside marriage remained powerful. In the late Stalin era, such women had usually simply abandoned their babies, often in hospital, which meant that a number of infants had their first experiences of institutional care from staff who had little time to spare for them. They would arrive at baby homes in a dreadful condition: torpid, unresponsive, and given to compulsive hand-sucking and masturbation.[45] In the 1960s, by contrast, a system of formal 'refusal of one's child' was in operation, allowing a mother to request placement of the infant on a temporary or permanent basis in a state-run institution.[46] While this measure increased the likelihood that a child would get adequate care after birth, if anything it increased disapproval of abandoning mothers, too, since the act of placing the child in an institution now came across as one of calculation rather than desperation.[47] And the prevalence of children from 'socially oppressed' backgrounds in orphanages in turn enforced the traditional tendency to regard orphanage children as 'beyond the pale', which resurfaced with a vengeance in the early 1960s. Valeriya Mukhina, the author of a 'mother's diary' about her twin boys' childhood in the early 1960s, noted in 1966

62   Pioneer meeting at a rally of orphanage children, Razliv Lenin Museum, near Leningrad, 1959.

63 Group of pupils at the orphanage offering musical education sponsored by the Rimsky-Korsakov Musical Education Orphanage, Leningrad, 1982.

and 1967 that her children used the word *besprizornyi* as an insult, and referred to confinement in an orphanage as a dire threat ('you'll end up in an orphanage if you go on acting like that!')[48]

Sick and handicapped children continued, throughout the post-Stalin era, to be treated as categories requiring institutional care. But for children whose parents were for any reason deemed to be 'failing', there was a partial move away from compulsory institutionalisation. To be sure, the staff of children's institutions – schools, clinics, hospitals – were still expected to keep a watch out for neglected children so that they could be removed from their parents.[49] Institutionalisation had a coercive, 'all or nothing', character: a mother needing temporary support had to make a tough decision about whether to cope on her own or risk losing the child for good (two periods of six months were the longest that a child could be committed to an institution on a non-permanent basis).[50] But non-institutional options were now being developed. As early as 1960, the authorities in Sverdlovsk considered introducing a system whereby 'families in need' (described here as families 'not coping with the upbringing of their children') would be placed on a special register and assigned mentoring (*shefstvo*) in the shape of supervision by parents who were 'exemplary workers'.[51] Such mentoring systems reinforced the work that was being done, as in previous decades, by voluntary organisations such as the 'women's soviets', by the Party and Komsomol, and by trade unions. In addition, from the 1970s, there was the introduction – on a small scale – of family counselling and guidance facilities.[52]

Exploration of non-institutional solutions was also evident in a partial *rapprochement* with adoption and fostering, as shown, above all, by the recognition now given to the fact that this might be an acceptable type of long-term care. By the 1970s, approbatory material about fostering was starting to proliferate in Soviet journalism: a 1975 reader's letter to *Nedelya*, for example, contrasted the grim institutional life the writer had experienced (generating a 'violent need for spiritual warmth, for involvement, for human closeness') with the joy of being raised in a foster home. The writer insisted that life skills could be learned only in a family, and that proper happiness was only possible there.[53] Journalists painted rosy pictures of foster life – one, a family in Moldova who had adopted six children after bringing up two of their own, and whose ready-made family, housed in a spacious cottage willingly made available by the local collective farm, was multi-national (the USSR in miniature).[54] One reason for altering attitudes was greater confidence in the likely success of fostering arrangements. A large-scale inspection of 861 children carried out in Sverdlovsk during 1955 established that 691 were looked after to a 'satisfactory' standard, and 170 to a 'good' standard.[55] As families began to live more comfortably, it became more likely that decisions to adopt or foster would be undertaken on philanthropic grounds, rather than out of a desire to add to the household income.[56]

In the 1980s, positive assessments of adoption started to appear: it was now seen as a long-term solution, the once-and-for-all placement of a child with new parents, whom it should be brought up to regard as 'mummy' and 'daddy'.[57] Members of staff in the state orphanage system recall an upsurge in adoption placements from the 1960s.[58]

Yet these changes remained muted in effect. As a Western expert on child welfare has put it, the old pattern of 'support and control' remained in force (with more emphasis, one might add, on the latter).[59] Only in the mid-1980s was the grant assigned to fosterers raised to anything like a realistic level, and even then the money paid was less than the cost of an institutional place.[60] And, while state support to single mothers was instituted in 1970, followed by the introduction of a grant, in 1985, to tide over those who were not receiving alimony payments, the level of payout remained small – only 20 roubles per month, or about one-seventh of the officially declared average wage in 1980.[61] Taboos on illegitimate births remained: it was typical for unmarried young women, if they did not opt for an abortion, to be under great pressure to 'renounce their maternal rights' and give the child up for adoption.[62] There was heightened awareness that institutional solutions were costly, as well as potentially inhumane (according to an estimate of 1989, each inmate of a children's institution cost the state 3,000 roubles a year to maintain). But alternative solutions, such as paying child support to single mothers, developed slowly at best.[63]

The main drive was still to improve institutional provision. There was a revival of the interest that had been shown during the early twentieth century in 'Family Type Children's Homes', a system modelled on the Kinderdorf programme used in Austria, according to which the orphanage would be divided up into 'family units' of ten or so children, all sharing a pool of specialised facilities.[64] In 1988, the popular weekly newspaper *Nedelya* ran a competition for architectural designs for new children's homes, and gave publicity to orphanages that were taking individual initiative (for instance, encouraging children to design and make their own portable hi-fis).[65] And, with the move to 'self-accounting' or partial marketisation, begun under Gorbachev in 1987, and the new tolerance of 'informal' associations, it became possible for private charities to operate again. At first, the main activity was in the shape of donations to Russian institutions by Western and 'joint venture' companies, and organised whip-rounds on the part of individuals, but within a few years some home-run children's charities had taken off.[66]

64 Children from Home No. 53 using the computers donated by Honoured Artiste of the Russian Federation Edita P'ekha, Leningrad, December 1989.

It was not, though, until after 1991 that the full benefits (and hazards) of the withdrawal of state control and of state funding began to be evident. Before this, provision for orphans retained much of the character it had had before 1953. In the best of circumstances, children's homes still created a specific personality type that might adjust to life outside the home only with difficulty. Though state support of a material kind for inmates might be provided when children left their homes and boarding-schools,[67] help with the psychological adjustment required for leading an independent life was not usually forthcoming. For young people who never remembered sleeping anywhere but a dormitory, even having a room to oneself could be a shock, as many interviews record. Getting settled with a job, and adjusting to life in an emotional sense, was much tougher than practical adjustment. A typical case was a woman from Nizhni-Novgorod who, unusually, was able to complete full secondary education and to enter university, but who then dropped out – 'I started getting terrible headaches' – and took a job in a grenade factory. It took her some years to get a position that suited, in the personnel section. Unable to cope with the practicalities of life, she survived because of the director's personal kindness: he found her a job as a Pioneer leader which secured her free board and lodging in the orphanage itself. The standard institutional upbringing, where one did not talk about one's problems and was taught to respect high ideals, turned out to fit the rough-and-ready character of ordinary Soviet life rather badly, she thought.[68] Yet this woman, who ended up married, with a son, was better-off than another woman from a similar background, for whom the orphanage had essentially provided a training in misanthropy.[69]

Once press censorship relaxed in the late 1980s, these problems began to be highlighted: it was typical, a *Nedelya* article reported in 1989, for girls to end up working in heavy industry, getting, if they were lucky, a tiny room in a factory hostel, and ending up with a baby when they embarked on a love affair as a way out of isolation and loneliness. As this article pointed out, the basic problem lay in sending orphanage inmates out into the world when they were only 15.[70] During the 1960s and 1970s, the 'extended childhood' formerly experienced only by children of the social elite had begun to be the destiny of children of the working class and peasantry as well.[71] But policy in orphanages had not kept pace. By the late 1980s, a whole cluster of factors – not just shrinking state support and climbing rates of child abandonment, but the erosion of the early Soviet collective ideal, so that institutional life seemed aberrant in a way that it had not seemed before, not even thirty years earlier – had brought new malaise to children's 'total institutions'. But at the same time there was an openness to reform unseen since the measures to 'liquidate child homelessness' pushed through in the middle of 1935. In 1989, for example, a measure was passed stipulating that all children's institutions were to have a psychologist on the staff, a change which expressed recognition that child care was not just about hygienic regimen and moral education, but also about trying to develop the child's emotional capacities and social skills.[72] Yet, as at earlier stages of Russian history when liberal hopes had run high, the general context did much to frustrate the best intentions – a development that was to become all the clearer in the early 1990s, as marketisation brought food shortages and budget crises to homes just at the time when their services were more critically required than at any period since the Second World War.[73]

Rehabilitating Rehabilitation

Attitudes to social deviance generally during the Khrushchev era were a mass of inconsistencies and contradictions. Khrushchev's denunciation of Stalin in 1956 named the purges of political opponents as one of the former leader's major crimes; yet incarceration continued to be used for containing political opposition right up to the late 1980s. And while ordinary criminals might incidentally benefit from the political amnesties of the day, attitudes to crimes against property and against the person remained hard-line. The history of responses to crimes and misdemeanours by minors, on the other hand, was more complicated. Here the general trend – proceed slowly and painfully as it might – was towards greater leniency and understanding. From 25 December 1958, 14–16-year olds were liable for criminal prosecution only for especially serious crimes; courts tried not to impose criminal tariffs if they could avoid it. The revised Criminal Code of 1960, article 10, affirmed this situation, and issued a list of offences that had to be tried in the courts: murder and other crimes against the person such as rape and grievous bodily harm, armed robbery, 'vicious hooliganism', and serious offences against state or public property.[74] In November 1961, the Commissions on the Affairs of Minors, suspended in 1935, were revived, though their role was now to act as ancillary facilities to the courts: all cases that did not involve crimes against the person were referred to them, including cases (for example, robbery) which, officially speaking, should have ended up in the penal justice system, where they were first offences.[75]

Rehabilitationist practice was further formalised when the plenum of the Supreme Soviet underlined on 3 July 1963 that, 'with regard to [minors], the notion of punishment must up to a point be subordinated to the aim of correcting and re-educating the guilty person'. The preamble to the decree cited numerous instances of abuses of minors' rights – for example, not bothering to establish a child's exact age, slackness in processing cases so that motivation was not clarified, and failing to allow a defence lawyer to young defendants – and set in place measures to try and correct these. It was firm about the need to make sure that cases involving minors were sent to a single judge, so that someone in a particular 'people's court' could build up expertise relating to this area of juridical work.[76]

In similar vein, an article published in *Soviet Justice* in 1965 drew jurists' attention to the possibility of avoiding custodial sentences. Courts could impose programmes of character education themselves, or refer cases to the Commission for Minors if there was not enough evidence to proceed with a case, or if the case involved a crime that was not 'socially dangerous'. It was also possible to consign a young offender to supervision by the work collective or 'public organs' (i.e. the police – a form of binding over). Examples were given of rehabilitationist solutions that had been successful, as in the case of a 16-year-old boy who had taken to vagrancy and petty theft and who was now a model citizen after a stint on probation and at a special boarding-school.[77] The mid- to late 1960s saw an increase in the numbers of such 'special boarding-schools' (officially known as '*internaty* of the closed type'), which became the standard destination for under-16s convicted of minor offences (theft, hooliganism, etc.), or who were deemed unmanageable by their parents.[78]

Accompanying all this, the general trend in the Soviet press and in professional legal journals was to represent anti-social behaviour as a problem deriving from failures on the part of adults. In 1960, one article in *Nedelya* considered the case of Sasha, who had been causing serious difficulties at his school, his actions including verbal abuse of teachers, violence against fellow pupils, and theft. The article pointed out that the boy's father was an abusive drunk, and insisted on the need for more love and understanding rather than the course preferred by the school: expulsion.[79] In the late 1960s and 1970s there were repeated efforts to make the practice of the courts more child-friendly: in March 1968, a decree of the plenum of the Supreme Court made it possible to exclude parents from the courtroom if their presence was deemed distracting or threatening, and made it mandatory for courts to investigate whether alcohol abuse had been involved in the commission of a crime. The decree also suggested that specialist judges should be responsible for all cases involving children, including sex offences, inheritance rights, and the deprivation of parental rights.[80]

The return to the perception of crime as being the result of deficient upbringing and moral education had an impact also on measures for crime prevention. In December 1967 a law was passed setting up a new system of 'public educators', volunteer workers appointed by the courts to work with minors deemed in need of this supervision (these volunteers were supposed to be educated adults with experience of working with children or of 'socially useful' activities of other kinds, and they were to report to the local education authorities and Committees on the Affairs of Minors). They had a cautionary function (to alert the agencies to which they were tied if the minor did not seem to be responding properly to 're-education'), but were also supposed to act as advocates for the child's welfare, reporting back to the authorities if the level of care exercised by parents and school-teachers seemed to be deficient, and articulating demands for better conditions at school or work if these were needed.[81]

There was a good deal of discussion too about the requirement for the courts to be fully professional when adjudicating offences by minors. Some passing remarks about the deficiencies of 'bourgeois criminality' notwithstanding, a 1967 account by a Soviet jurist describing a fact-finding trip to the English juvenile courts was for the most part neutral in tone. The failure to condemn the practices, as opposed to the preconceptions, of English justice left the distinct impression that the Soviet legal system might have something to learn from the use of specialised courtrooms abroad.[82] In the meantime, Soviet courts were encouraged to do the best they could with the resources at their disposal. The Sverdlovsk District Court in Moscow was cited as exemplary because juvenile cases were always referred to one particular judge who had acquired a good deal of experience in dealing with these and took care to brief herself thoroughly. The need to explore issues of motivation and possible mitigating factors was underlined, 'in order that the harsh lesson [taught by the courts] should be a real warning for the future'. In other words, a punitive attitude was deficient in utilitarian terms as much as it was inhumane.[83] Further Supreme Court measures in 1972 and 1976 returned to the need to investigate causes properly, and in particular to make sure that adults who had condoned or encouraged bad behaviour by children got due punishment.[84]

At the same time, commitment to rehabilitation remained less than wholehearted. Young offenders continued to be dealt with by the criminal justice system, even if they were spared its full punitive force; complete decriminalisation of offences by minors was simply not raised as an issue. And statements about the need for understanding were always balanced by criticism of 'excessive liberalism' in dealing with minors.[85] Such criticism was in part a masking device, meant to deflect attention from what was actually a significant shift in penal policy. But policy on the ground, no doubt in part because of the differing signals 'from above', also tended to lurch between punitive and rehabilitationist models, as can be seen from the scattered information available in local archives for Sverdlovsk province in the 1950s and early 1960s. A great deal of anxiety was still expended on 'juvenile crime' – including relatively low-level incidents, such as a case where some boys crawled into a station flowerbed, pulled up plants, and swore at staff.[86] The vast majority of incidents involving minors were petty thefts: these stood at 480 of 595 named crimes in 1959, for example.[87]

There were, of course, some extremely unpleasant cases involving juveniles, in particular rapes of younger children. In 1962, a group of youths gang-raped a 15-year-old girl after a drinking bout; in 1965, a 17-year-old stabbed to death a passer-by who had refused a light for his cigarette. The recorded crimes in 1959 included 93 serious assaults and 12 murders.[88] But the number of such crimes was small, in any given year, and fluctuated unpredictably. In 1965, for example, there were as many as sixteen murders, but the previous year, only two.[89] In the first ten months of 1962, '100 per cent of all rapes and 100 per cent of all serious assaults' were committed by juveniles; but the relevant gross statistics stood at three rapes and six assaults.[90] And the monitoring of crime statistics was as revealing about 'moral panic' as it was about rising levels of crime. Between 1952 and 1955, crimes committed by juveniles rose by around 17 per cent, but, over the same period, cases where legal action was taken against the perpetrators rose by nearly 60 per cent. In 1955, 100 per cent of crimes where juveniles were involved resulted in legal action of one kind or another, and a full 381 of 449 accused were dispatched to colonies for minors.[91] Figures for legal action taken and numbers sent to the colonies from 1955 onwards are not so clearly presented in the archives. But fragmentary information suggests some continuation of the hard line, at the level of primary action, at any rate. In 1961, for example, a full 250 juveniles were processed by the 'children's rooms' at Sverdlovsk's various police stations.[92]

Yet some changes were visible from the late 1950s onwards. Certainly, the first reaction to 'unsupervised' children was still to see them as a threat to public order, with the police, assisted by popular militias, as the primary instrument for repressing this threat. However, there was now a greater emphasis on the need for such people to have special training.[93] By 1956, only one police precinct in Sverdlovsk city was without a special 'children's room'.[94] Numbers of children sent to the colonies appear to have got significantly smaller. Of 110 juveniles who stood trial in 1959, only 30 were convicted; and, while 79 juveniles were dispatched to the colonies in 1958, just seven went down this route in 1959.[95]

The cautiously rehabilitationist spirit is also evident in the painstaking reviews of individual case files carried out by the Sverdlovsk Procuracy's Juvenile Affairs Department in the early 1960s. On 27 February 1964, the Department reported on the case of one 15-year-old boy who had run away from Chelyabinsk educational colony. The administration had taken no steps to recover him; the boy had duly returned home and was helping his family financially. A supervision order at the Ural Footwear factory was the recommended step. Similarly, later in 1964, a 15-year-old boy who was a hardened thief, as well as a drinker and smoker, was spared the colonies because he had a heart condition. The few cases where decisive action was recommended concerned individuals who were, in the Soviet jargon of the time, 'recidivists', and whose case files revealed nothing that would have been perceived by the commissions as mitigatory – as in the case of a boy of 15 who had already served time for theft in the colonies and who had committed repeated offences since being released (the theft of money and food from shops and kiosks, the theft of five tennis rackets and a tennis net from a sports club), as well as acting as an evil influence on his peers ('he gathers groups of teenagers together and teaches them how to steal').[96]

The work of the Commissions on the Affairs of Minors was controversial within the agencies of law and order. They were, for example, sharply criticised in 1964 for overturning sentences of committal to the colonies: this was said to be questionable in terms of the rules in operation, and foolish in practical terms (offenders inevitably reoffended).[97] The police, in particular, tended to hold to the repressive line: in 1960 the head of the Sverdlovsk city militia proposed that parents who did not stop their children from becoming a social nuisance should be punished.[98] Declining figures for those sent to the colonies did not necessarily correlate with rising figures for children let off with a caution or given a supervision order: other custodial options, such as consignment to a 'strict regime' orphanage, come up on an individual basis in the files.[99] But leniency was becoming more characteristic, even at the 'front line' between police and law-breakers. For example, in 1964, the police in Krasnoural'sk decided not to proceed with action against three boys who had stolen sweets and other items from a children's crèche. In one case, the point may have been that the child involved was very young – only seven years old. But the other two boys were 13 and 14, a perfectly normal age for more serious action. However, because all three had 'honestly admitted their guilt' when rounded up, it was decided to go no further.[100]

The tenor of the times generally was moving against punitive action. By March 1955, the numbers of inmates in colonies had already diminished significantly, compared with numbers from the late 1940s.[101] The emphasis had now switched to crime prevention. On 15 December 1958, the government took the eminently sensible – and long overdue – step of banning the sale of alcohol to children.[102] The Komsomol was exhorted to intervene, and to exercise 'mentoring' (*shefstvo*) of parents to make sure that they kept their children on the straight and narrow. There were also attempts to recruit children themselves as participants in the crusade for law and order. As noted in Chapter 4, a revitalisation of the cult of the 'Pioneer activist' (especially Pavlik Morozov) formed part of this, but there were also some new-style initiatives. Whilst children were not involved in the key law and order movement of the 1960s, the popular militias or *druzhiny* (which drew their members from those of Komsomol age or above), there were attempts to promote a positive attitude among them to the Soviet police. Sergei Mikhalkov's sequel to his popular 'Uncle Styopa' verse tale finishes with a passage in which the hero hymns the virtues of the Soviet police to a crowd of little children:

> No wonder people shun
> The militia post
> And are afraid of militia men
> When their conscience isn't clean.[103]

The profile of the police was raised by 'agitation' as well as propaganda. In the early 1960s came the foundation of a special organisation in Kursk, 'The Young Friends of the Soviet Militia'. The children were meant to act as ancillary workers in the crackdown on activities by 'unsupervised' peers in the town. The groups, which soon spread to other parts of the Soviet Union, were juvenile equivalents of the popular militias that were intended to clean up street drunkenness and disorderly behaviour and had been enthusiastically developed by the Soviet state in the late 1950s.[104]

The success of such prophylactic initiatives was, in the event, rather uneven. The ban on selling alcohol, for instance, had limited effects: many adults, whether out of ignorance or out of a refusal to take the ban seriously, continued to purchase alcohol for young people, or indeed to sell it to them. An undercover investigation in Rostov-on-Don in the early 1960s discovered that under-age customers were able to buy drink in no fewer than seventeen shops in the city centre, and that the managers of these shops took no real measures against the assistants who had broken the law. As a result, further legislation of 3 July 1965 criminalised 'enticing minors to drunkenness',[105] but with limited deterrent effect. It was not until the mid-1980s, as a result of Mikhail Gorbachev's crackdown on excess drinking generally, that child alcoholism began to be recognised as a serious problem.[106] Equally, there is no evidence that the 'friendship' organisations did much to improve the profile of the Soviet beat police force, which continued to inspire a mixture of dislike and contempt from most citizens, however law-abiding.[107] An ambitious young person from a non-intelligentsia background might think seriously about joining the secret police, which was the route to a good salary, job security, premium living conditions, power, and the tempting possibility of travel abroad. But the ordinary police was seen as a career destination for those whose school marks were too low to get them into other kinds of white-collar profession. Naturally, collaborating with such individuals did not seem particularly prestigious or heroic.

The 'softly softly' attitude to juvenile misdemeanours also faced difficulties. The processing of cases by the Commissions on the Affairs of Minors' was desperately inefficient. A report published in the legal press in 1965 established that only 16 per cent of new cases over the previous year had been dealt with by the Commissions by the end of the year and some from 1963 had been carried forward beyond the end of 1964.[108] All of this could only boost the case of those in the administration convinced that treating offenders with understanding was a waste of time, and that a 'short sharp shock' was all that such individuals needed. Certainly, the few youth crime cases that reached the Soviet press before glasnost culminated in stiff punishment. In 1984, *Nedelya* printed a story about a first-year student from the Chuvash State University who had been set upon and beaten and kicked to death by a seven-strong band of 15- and 16-year-olds from his former school. The members of the band received sentences ranging from three and a half years to ten years of youth custody, and their parents – blamed for the 'unbridled' behaviour of the youngsters – were subjected to disciplinary measures at work.[109] In the long run, though, rehabilitationism slowly made its impact.

In 1985, no less a figure than the director of the All-Soviet Crime Prevention Institute at the USSR State Procuracy blamed unruliness among young people on incompetent upbringing – too much laying down the law, and not enough reasoning and tolerance.[110]

Once censorship was relaxed in the late 1980s, a stream of articles in the Soviet press highlighted disciplinary problems in cities. In Kazan', it was claimed during 1988, 'gang war' was raging unchecked.[111] In 1989, *Nedelya* reported on the case of a desperado 8-year old who had committed a stream of thefts in the Karelian capital of Petrozavodsk. The article observed that the boy concerned was below the age where he could be sent to a colony; he would have to be placed in a special-regime home.[112] But the surge of 'true crime' stories did not lead to pressure – among journalists at least – for stepping up punishments and widening criminal responsibility. Rather, arguments in favour of understanding and re-education dominated public discussions. Typical was a 1989 article by Irina Ovchinnikova, a senior journalist dealing with social affairs at *Nedelya*, arguing that young offenders, like single mothers, deserved help rather than condemnation, or a reference in 1987 to the typical young offender as 'an adolescent deprived of family warmth, embittered, hardened, neglected'.[113] And this despite the citation of statistics indicating that crime rates were rising – in 1989, for example, as many as 900,000 juveniles went through the courts across the Soviet Union.[114]

Policy also altered, during the post-Stalin era, towards the children who did reach colonies and special orphanages, particularly in the latter case. Makarenko remained the touchstone of good practice, but (as also happened in the area of child-care advice more generally) what was associated with his name did not necessarily remain stable. One 1963 study, of a special orphanage in Nizhnii Tagil', laid as much emphasis on *self*-monitoring by inmates as upon regulation of behaviour by means of collective pressures. Pupils were assigned individual plans of self-improvement, from 'I will always keep my hands clean' to 'I will do everything the group elder tells me without argument', to 'I will make sure my mentee B. studies well and goes round looking clean and tidy'. They were encouraged to reflect critically on their own behaviour: 'I hate the way I always lose my temper about things.' The training in the orphanage, while still heavily oriented towards vocational education (learning to use lathes, etc.) gave some weight to non-work pursuits as well: pupils were encouraged to write poetry for the wall newspaper and to participate in song and dance evenings and in amateur dramatics. Clearly, this was an exceptional institution (and testimony from a current and a former inmate confirms that much of the home's success was due, once again, to the influence of individual members of staff). At the same time, the fact that this relatively sympathetic regime was being put forward as a success story ripe for emulation elsewhere illustrates how much the Ministry of Education's policy towards such children's homes had changed.[115]

Some at least of the special boarding-schools conformed to a similar type. One, for miscreant boys in the Leningrad area which opened in 1967, enjoyed exceptionally well equipped premises (in its earlier incarnation, the place had been a prestige boarding-school). It had excellent workshops, and the inmates were provided not just with one uniform, but with several, depending on activities (track suits for morning jogs included). Discipline depended more on loss of the privileges that came with good behaviour – home visits, parcels, parental visits to the home – than on punishment as such, though inmates who tried to escape were humiliated by having their heads shaved and having to wear pastel-coloured pyjamas right through the day. Much emphasis was placed on self-regulation: 'days of self-control' were held at quite frequent intervals, minor misdemeanours would be tried by 'comradely court', and inmates would be invited to reflect on their own behaviour. Especially admirable efforts were rewarded with badges and a place on the board of honour. A certain amount of trust was extended to the boys, especially on summer camps, where the opportunity to run away would have been more obvious. All of this, again, sounded like revived Makarenko, though the staff themselves were, when interviewed in 2004, keener to associate their work with Sukhomlinsky. Certainly, the militaristic style of the regime (modelled on a cadet corps) was closer to Makarenko, as was the adherence to universal surveillance techniques: inmates were allowed no privacy, even in the dormitories. But the antecedents of the regime were certainly of less interest to the inmates than the fact that they were allowed some room for self-assertion.[116]

Nevertheless, life in the school was no utopia. The boys came from tough, difficult backgrounds; many arrived with as much as three or four years missing from their school education; some were mentally handicapped, others psychologically disturbed. Staff turnover was high, with many attracted to work there in the first place less by dedication than by the fact that employment would secure them a Leningrad residence permit. Not all were suitable for work with children, and sexual relationships between staff and inmates were not unknown (one member of staff had to be sacked after it turned out he had made a habit of seducing the boys in his charge). Though a major problem in the boys' lives was often the lack of male role models of a positive kind, the majority of the staff were female, which perpetuated the gender conflicts obtaining at home. At the best of times, the values being put forward were at a huge distance from those the boys had absorbed at home, and closer to those operating in the institution next door – an adult prison, whose inmates would often express their love of children by tossing packets of cigarettes over the fence to the youngsters. And the inmates in the school, like those elsewhere, sometimes ill-treated each other (up to the level of rape). Not surprisingly, long-term members of staff, among the men at least, tended to take a tough line, voicing liberal sentiments in a tone that brooked no argument and that enforced subordination to authority as a primary value. No wonder also that, despite the staff's pride in 'rescuing' some boys from a life of crime, the majority of them – as much as 70 per cent – 'graduated' straight into the prison system.[117]

Children in Prison

Inevitably, in colonies, the toughest level of custodial institution for children, change was still more muted. To be sure, there were some reforms. On 5 October

1955 there was an increase in the overall numbers of colonies, not, this time, in order to accommodate larger overall numbers of inmates, but so that the size of each colony could be reduced.[118] Rules that came into force in 1956 emphasised the educational element in detention. Every colony was now to have a 'methodology room' where supervisors could read up on relevant literature. There was to be an end to 'bald administration' (a term that meant bullying by those at the top of the hierarchy), to 'capricious authoritarianism' (*proizvol*), and to the practice of allowing selected inmates to tyrannise others. In a throwback to the philanthropic nineteenth century, every institution was to have its own 'board of guardians', including representatives of local Party and trade union bodies. However, there was still to be a strict regime, with punishments and rewards of the old kind, and 'commanders' (group leaders) were still to be appointed from among the inmates. But the reintroduction of 1920s-style representative bodies (the 'soviet of inmates', for instance) was evidently intended as a corrective to all-out domination by those nominated to positions of authority.[119]

By the late 1980s there was open talk about the need for reform, and especially for more humane treatment of inmates, partly because rising crime rates made clear that, in their present form, colonies acted neither as a force for change, nor even as a deterrent.[120] Coverage emphasised the good results of creative work. In 1987, a *Nedelya* article presented as a model a colony in Armenia where there were regular concerts and where the inmates were encouraged to become involved in hobby circles.[121]

The extent to which all this influenced day-to-day life in most colonies is questionable. Central files for the period are still classified, but some information can be gained from material in provincial cities. Material on the Verkhotur'e Children's Labour Colony in Sverdlovsk province during 1959–60, for instance, indicates – on the positive side – that the vast majority of inmates were aged 16 and over (92 of 99 new arrivals in 1959, and 26 of 236 new arrivals in 1960). But it also points to the fact that large numbers of first offenders were also being banged up: 48 out of 99 admissions in 1959, and 170 of 236 admissions in 1960, came into this category. Even the bald and uninformative official report shows that some of the old malaise still lingered. Four inmates, all new arrivals, had run away in 1959; six had been injured at work. The size of this colony was dauntingly large: 520 inmates on average. Not surprisingly, discipline was hard to enforce, particularly since the adults employed on the site (as workmen, for example) proved a bad influence. Children would join these adults in drinking bouts and sometimes cross-generational 'scandalous acts' would be performed.[122]

Forward projections from the late 1950s indicate that it was planned to reduce the size of individual colonies to around 350 inmates.[123] But it is not clear whether these reductions in size were actually achieved; and, in any case, even in colonies of 300 or so, juveniles were likely to be left to their own devices. The evidence suggests that, by and large, colonies remained grim places. Oral history reveals that regimentation – censorship of mail, intensive regulation of the inmates' day – continued, and that facilities were large and anonymous (it was standard for the camp population to be divided into 'troops' housed fifty to a barracks dormitory). Solitary confinement was the standard recourse if inmates needed to be disciplined. Only after the collapse of Soviet power did the rules ease up slightly: for instance, the length of parental visits was increased from three days to a week, religious observance began to be allowed, and consenting homosexual relations were no longer prohibited. But these improvements were offset by a steep decline in living conditions, as inmate numbers rose and the food supply worsened sharply, making it hard to comply with the official dietary norms.[124]

Even staff working in the best facilities, where skills training and leisure activities were provided for inmates, were often not specially trained, and regarded their main role as preventing serious disruption. An informant, 'T', who worked in a particularly well-run strict regime penal colony in the Urals from the mid-1980s to the early 1990s, gave a full and balanced picture of the system's achievements and problems.[125] This institution was provided with a sports ground, a cinema, a library, and a folk band, and there were extensive workshops, where inmates received 50 per cent pay for the jobs they did. The director categorically forbade corporal punishment, asking staff straight out, 'Would you hit your own children?' Guards were never allowed to get into situations where they were one to one with inmates, which thus reduced the likelihood of confrontations, and a strict watch was kept on the different divisions of the camp to check that bullying did not take place. For similar reasons, inmates were not allowed to take food parcels into their barracks, but had to consume the food in a special room.

Yet, at the same time, T. indicated the stress points in the colony's work. Staff were not necessarily specially trained; the appeal of the job was simply that it was relatively well paid. Most of the inmates came from deprived backgrounds, and some were seriously psychologically disturbed – as in the case of a 16-year-old murderer who stated, dead-eyed, 'It's no harder to kill a person than a blowfly.' With a different director, the regime would have been less humane: the person in charge was always referred to as 'the boss of the zone', and many such individuals spent their formative years running logging camps in the wilds, which they were able to treat as personal fiefdoms; they then applied the same 'might is right' principle to the children's camps. The potential for disruption was always present: a serious riot in 1976 culminated in the rape of a middle-aged nurse in the sick bay, and the informant's own time working in the colony saw one murder (of a 15-year-old with a home-made knife, *zatochka*) and a suicide. And always below the surface bubbled the social tensions of the group itself, divided into *bugry* and *muzhiki* ('toughs' and 'ordinaries') – a division which the staff simply accepted. They themselves relied on amenable 'toughs' and on informer networks in order to maintain control.

Seen from the perspective of child convicts themselves, this was a world of 'dog eat dog'. Internet discussions of Leonid Gabyshev's 1989 novel *Odlyan*, which describes life in a youth colony during the 1970s, confirm the plausibility of the grim picture of life he sets out. A former inmate commented that some of the supervisors had been all right in some places ('many of them were women, who treated you affectionately, like children'), but that some had not. Survival was largely a matter of being tough. 'Local connections count for a lot in prison, but what matters most is what kind of person you are. How much spirit there is in you, as they say. How good you are at standing up for yourself. How much of a human being you are, and not an arsehole. Though actually, things are tougher in juvenile camps, even now. It isn't so much being a human being that gets respect, it's being a wolf...'[126]

A study by Ekaterina Efimova, published in 2004, confirms that detention continued to provide the traditional socialisation in 'the law' in a criminal sense – the rules of 'thieves' honour' and the gang hierarchy. Right up to the 1990s, newcomers were often met with some test they were likely to fail, such as being asked to do dirty work (if they agreed to this, they would immediately drop to the status of 'injured', *obizhennye*, i.e. pariahs), or being told a riddle about prison life, and being thrashed when they gave the wrong answer. Essentially the hierarchy worked in the same way as in adult prisons, with the most desperate and 'hooliganish' at the top, a system reinforced by the Makarenko system of encouraging leadership among the inmates. Each dormitory block in the youth colony (colloquially known as *khata*, or village hut) was run by an 'overseer' (*smotryashchii*) and his 'brothers' (*bratva*), who had the right to call on other inmates to service their practical needs – the *shnyri*. Pariah prisoners would also be made to do jobs, but only the dirtiest and most unpleasant ones. Leisure time was spent playing cards, cobbling clothes, footwear, and tools together, singing prison songs, and writing 'prison albums' – collections of aphorisms, prayers, drawings, and song texts, decorated with motifs of barbed wire and guard dogs, and in carving crude tattoos, usually carrying hierarchical names and symbols, on one's own body or that of another inmate.[127]

Colonies had their own superstitions – hearing a warder's keys drop was a good omen, promising early release – and their own emotional world. Toughness was all, but sentiment towards women, particularly one's mother, was allowed. The repertoire of songs and other folklore testified to these traditions: as an aphorism had it, 'Only your mother is worth your love/she'll wait for you till you're out of jug.' A favourite theme of songs was the boy who went wrong after an unhappy love affair, though others paid tribute to the cult of hooliganism.

Less information is available on youth custody for girls, but it seems that the conditions here resembled those in women's prisons. Relations between inmates were less brutal, with a cult of love replacing the cult of strength (adult women prisoners carved on themselves devices such as TOMSK, spelling out in Russian 'Only You Have Touched My Heart', or TOBOL – 'I Am Sick For You With a Cooling Love'). Hierarchies were less strongly reinforced; though they did exist, with dominant groups excluding other prisoners, or occasionally stooping to allow them temporarily into the inner circle. But some young women in the colonies were badly damaged in a psychological sense: this was expressed less in violence against others (though there were cases where newcomers were beaten), than in self-harm (in a colony visited by a *Nedelya* journalist in 1989, 10 per cent of the inmates were considered 'at risk' of escape, self-mutilation, or suicide).[128]

The first serious ethnographical studies of life in prisons and colonies only started appearing in the post-Soviet period. However, it is reasonable to project quite a lot of the everyday life, rituals, and folklore back through the decades. Records from the 1990s include some obvious novelties (pictures of bundles of dollars in albums, religious imagery), but songs of the 1920s remained in the repertoire (sometimes marked as such by archaic vocabulary, for instance the word *nagan* for a revolver). Prison folklore, slang, rituals and beliefs, and prison attitudes – the rigid power hierarchies, the sentimentalisation of life and love on the streets – were to a large extent stable over the generations.[129]

Thus, the superficial liberalisation of the post-Stalin era did little to transform young offender institutions into efficient instruments of rehabilitation. Many inmates, exactly in line with the nature of the education that they had received, graduated not to 'socially useful work', but to adult labour camps, whether they were immediately transferred there[130] or ended up there at a later stage, having drifted back once more into the life that was most familiar to them. Part of the problem still lay in the fact that supervisors had to collude in the system of exploitation if they were to maintain order: 'class leaders' would be picked from the dominant social group, the adult hoping that they would manage to pick 'a tough in the decent sense' rather than a tough through and through.[131]

Children who were incarcerated 'in their own right' were not the only group of minors who might end up in penal custody. The state prison and camp system continued to handle the offspring of adults who had been sentenced to 'do time' in one or other institution. The idea of a common interest between 'enemies of the people' and their descendants continued to be an obstacle to child welfare in this era. Certainly, the situation had improved, both because the era of mass political purges had come to an end, reducing the size of the prison and camp population and hence the numbers of children processed by the system, and because treatment of prisoners had grown more humane in this respect, as in most others. For instance, according to the Penal Code of 1970, mothers were now allowed access to their children for two years rather than one.[132] Yet the mother–child relationship, where prisoners were involved, was still understood as a privilege rather than a right, to be withdrawn if the mother was deemed not to deserve it: the code allowed mothers to give birth outside the camp (i.e. to have access to specialised obstetric care) only if they had displayed a 'conscientious' attitude to work.[133]

With declining numbers in Russian prisons overall, however, the number of prisoners' children also declined. But, as in previous generations, there was still a significant population of children consigned to adult penal institutions because space was not available in the colonies. Such children often ended up in cells with adult prisoners, who encouraged habits such as drug abuse, and their interests in crime flourished in the atmosphere of licence and corruption. Just as in the past, prisons had a negative, rather than a positive effect. Yet specialist youth institutions also had, at best, a limited impact on children's interest in crime: in 1984, 11.4 per cent of the population of girls' colonies were repeat offenders, and, in 1987, this had risen to over 20 per cent.[134] Generation after generation, the treatment of children in the penal system was both inhumane and, from a utilitarian point of view, pernicious, serving simply to reinforce the anti-social and criminal tendencies of those committed. By the late 1980s this was beginning to be recognised, yet figures for incarcerated juveniles remained very high: 40,000 at the start of the twenty-first century, the overwhelming majority of whom (38,000) were boys. A collection of life histories of such children published in 2001 revealed familiar tales of distress: broken families in early childhood, and often domestic violence, followed by a turn to crime, and then incarceration. As always, this was recalled in a mournful spirit:

> The worst thing in prison is the loneliness. There's no one to share the pain of your loneliness. There's no joy, no triumphant laughter. Even though the girls try very hard to make things better. And we don't think much of what *they* [the supervisors] do for us.
>
> When we behaved ourselves in a way 'not befitting', the prison bosses started laying into us minors. They'd do it when we weren't saying anything, for instance, when we didn't want to own up to why we wouldn't do what we were told.
>
> They think they've got the right to hurt us. Although you'd think they should recognise we're children who've never seen any joy.[135]

Yet judges continued to dole out stiff sentences: theft, the crime for which around half of juveniles were 'doing time', could attract three years even for a first offence. Charities working with juvenile offenders still had an uphill struggle to persuade the general public that this group – consisting of some of the most deprived children in the Russian Federation – was worthy of sympathy.[136]

By the late 1980s, many of the central assumptions of Soviet policy relating to children were in tatters. Institutional care – the flagship of rational child management for seventy years – was increasingly criticised, not just for its incidental failures, but in itself, as a fundamentally wrong-headed system. The 'onward and upward' trajectory adopted by the history of orphanages, young offender centres, and hospitals – which in Soviet days had been claimed to provide ever-increasing access to ever-improving facilities – had been brought to an abrupt halt by reports of top-to-bottom under-funding, under-staffing, and indeed dishonesty. While these reports did not necessarily demonstrate that malaise was significantly worse than it had been in previous decades, their effect on a public denied access to negative reporting about children's lives was electric. As a doctor wrote in 1989: 'For decades we have placed the adjective "happy" next to the word "children", and insisted that "the only privileged class in our country is children". These slogans gradually drove out of our head any concern for children in real life.'[137]

As a matter of fact, this assessment was a polemical exaggeration. The view of 'happy childhood' as an ideal had also had some positive impact on Soviet institutional planning, which was – whatever criticisms one might make of it

– far more effective than institutional planning prior to 1917. And the problems that beset children's homes, colonies, and other 'total institutions' (child abuse, embezzlement, unintentional mistreatment by poorly trained and overworked staff) were not unique to the USSR. During the post-Stalin era, particularly, there were significant improvements to most areas of institutional provision, and some liberalisation as well. The establishments of the 1960s, 1970s, and 1980s were not world-leading utopias, as some of the institutions of the 1920s were; on average they were a great deal better than all but the premier establishments of this era, and indeed of the 1930s, 1940s, and early 1950s.

Yet even the best-run post-Stalinist institutions, such as boarding-schools, often fell below the standards celebrated in propaganda; while the worst institutions (including the colonies for young offenders) subjected children to conditions where the worst phenomena of street life – bullying, theft, sexual abuse, gang infighting – often flourished unchecked.

Where standards were high, they were often high in spite of the official mechanisms of control, rather than because of these. Certainly, the introduction of explicit rules and targets was, in itself, no bad thing. Equally certainly, Party and ministerial administrations could be called upon to settle incidental problems – staff could demand that a late delivery be chased up or insist that overdue repairs be carried out. But there was no recourse if overall budgeting figures were insufficient or if regulations proved unworkable. One message comes over again and again from the history of Soviet institutions: the need for extraordinary levels of self-reliance and initiative in a system that did much to discourage the manifestation of exactly these qualities. In the words of a doctor working in Leningrad in the 1970s: 'We had only ourselves to rely on, so to speak – our own senses, our own knowledge.'[138] This could stand as an epitaph to the better elements of the entire system of institutional provision for children not just in this era, but throughout the seven decades of Soviet power, and before 1917 as well.

PART III

'FAMILY CHILDREN'

Chapter 9

Babyhood

God takes care of drunks and little children.[1]

It is not uncommon for Russian memoirists to claim that they recall exactly how they were born. The Soviet writer Ivan Paderin gave a detailed description of his entry into the world in the family *banya* and insisted that, ever since, the smell of Siberian pine planks like those used to construct the walls had remained a favourite with him.[2] The claim to such a memory smacks of poetic licence (along the lines of Andrei Bely's insistence he could clearly recall life as a foetus).[3] But the bath-house did remain the traditional place, in some parts of Russia, for a woman's confinement, well into the twentieth century. The reasons for this were both practical and ritualistic. A bath-house was easy to heat and clean; it could be flushed down with buckets after the birth had taken place. It was also a liminal space, between the main dwelling and the forest, where the woman giving birth might be protected from harm, and at the same time prevented from ritually polluting the rest of the household.[4]

Well before the birth, the expectant mother would have been advised by knowledgeable associates to avoid all sorts of unpropitious activity, from stepping over a tub of water (which could lead her to bring forth a hunchback) to kicking the dog or cat (which might give her an illness such as distemper). Even before conception certain precautions were taken, such as the eating of particular foods, while intercourse might take place in special positions so that the conception of a boy or girl was ensured. During the birth itself, both medical and ritual measures ensured the swift and safe passage of the infant into mortal existence: herbal draughts and movement about the room were pressed on the mother to ease labour, the birth position of the child was corrected, windows and doors were flung open to work sympathetic magic, and charms and prayers were recited (St Solomonida, the Orthodox equivalent of St Rita in Italy, was considered the patron saint of women in labour). The woman's hair might be unloosed, and knots undone, to help release the child, and her stomach might be massaged with the holy oil from an icon lamp.[5]

Once the birth was safely completed, equal care was taken with the next procedures. The umbilical cord would be cut through on an object of ritual significance, such as an axe (for a boy) or a spindle (for a girl). It would then often be hidden away in the icon corner. The afterbirth would also be disposed of with ceremony: it was often placed in a wicker basket and buried in a ritually sacred spot – under the threshold, behind the stove, or in the floor below the icon corner.[6]

The baby would then be washed – a procedure that had both hygienic and ritualistic significance – and dressed. The first garment was, traditionally, an old shirt belonging to either the mother or the father, depending on the sex of the infant itself (though the father's shirt might also be used for girls as a way of ensuring the next child was a boy, if the birth of a girl was considered a disappointment). This shirt had purely ritual meaning, being wrapped round the child, rather than put on it. The everyday infant dress was made up of layers of linen strips (traditionally old linen was used for this, as new or freshly laundered clothes were considered unpropitious). The accepted method was to use a bottom layer made of three separate cloths (*pelenki*), one covering the head, a second, folded triangle-wise, over the infant's crotch and buttocks (the *podguznik*, or 'bottom-cover'), and a third round the abdomen. On top of all this came the swaddling proper, the *svival'nik*, a single long thin strip of linen, wound round the child criss-cross fashion or (if it was a very long piece) arranged as many overlapping rings. Swaddling was held to have many advantages: protecting the child from accidental knocks, or from damage if dropped on the floor; making it feel secure and comfortable, and hence quiet and easy to manage; and shaping its limbs and head properly. Speaking less matter-of-factly, it was part of a tangle of ritualistic practices whose central purpose was the moulding of the 'soft' and vulnerable infant during its first year into a tough, 'hard' individual capable of greater resistance and endurance. A similar sense of the infant's defencelessness generated a prohibition on cutting the child's nails and hair during the first year of its life.[7]

Despite the dangers that birth posed to the purity of others, a mother was not expected to pass through the experience alone. An experienced relation might come along to help, or the procedures might be supervised by a woman known for her expertise in the locality generally, called a *povival'naya babka* or *povitukha* ('swaddling woman'). It was traditional for the midwife to refuse at first to help with the delivery, and to give way only when the future mother had knelt and begged for her aid; traditional gifts in return for this included a *karavai* (large rye loaf), a bundle of flax, and a length of linen cloth.[8] The company of a person who had the authority of experience was some comfort on its own; besides, though traditional midwives were unable to help in case of serious complications (a woman undergoing a breech birth was likely to endure extensive tearing as the infant was ripped from her body; and, if the mother had a narrow pelvis, both mother and child were almost certain to expire), they were skilled in helping women undergoing labour to relax, and in applying warmth and massage in order to ease pain during and after delivery.[9]

Like the procedures for birthing, those employed for care in early infancy combined ritual and practical considerations. The standard method of feeding was by the breast, often till quite late (12–24 months: the proverbial expression was 'three to six fasts', counting Advent, Lent, and the fast before the feast of the Dormition in August), though infants always had solid food as well, which was believed to make them stronger.[10] The transition to full weaning was accompanied by special traditions. It was customary to attend church and then, on returning, to place the child on the dining table and give it a little bread and salt. A prayer was then said to protect both mother and child from *toska* (grieving). Preferred days for all this to happen included Clean Thursday (Maundy Thursday), and the Sunday before Shrovetide.[11] As the integration of weaning into the church calendar suggested, for pious Russians the question of whether babies should also fast (i.e. be deprived of milk) on milkless days was a ticklish question. It was also sometimes considered ritually necessary to keep a child from the breast till it was christened, or even till the churching of the mother.[12] Not just feeding, but care of the body was often out of step with modern appreciations of hygiene: for the majority of children, though, deprivation of mother's milk less often happened for religious reasons than because feeding had to be fitted into the mother's ordinary work routine. This – as well as the belief that the practice was 'strengthening' – led to the practice of integrating solid food into the diet from early on and to the use of home-made dummies (*soski*), such as rags dipped in milk or something sweet, or plugs of chewed bread.

According to Christian tradition (like that of all other religions), 'man does not live by bread alone'. Equally, babies were not supposed to survive on milk and water alone. Assuming everything went well, a celebration of the child's arrival that also marked its reception into the community would take place shortly after birth. In Russian villages, the *krestiny* (christening proper) was preceded by a number of important secular rituals that welcomed the child into the world and the community. These included, besides the cutting and burial of the umbilical cord and the burial of the placenta, the assignation of a name (traditionally, the midwife would visit the local priest so that he could say a prayer on the child's behalf and suggest a name). A 'birthing party' (*rodiny*) with ritual foods would also be held for close family and friends.[13]

None of this effaced the importance of the baptism itself. A child was considered only partly human, and indeed even a threat, until christening took place ('unchristened' babies belonged partly to the demonic world: hence the custom, found in many other places in Christian Europe as well, of burying them in unconsecrated ground).[14] The name itself was also important: without a name a child was formless, not human (hence also the custom of conferring the name of an ancestor).[15] However, if the child's life was not in danger, the ceremony often did not take place directly after the birth (Old Believer communities tended to have children baptised particularly late). At least eight days seems to have been the norm.[16] The prayers and rites were those universal in the Christian Church – public renunciation of Satan and recitation of vows alongside a dip in holy water and an anointing with sanctified oil – though a tiny baby, unless it was very sickly indeed, would undergo total immersion in the font, as Orthodox tradition required (only in the case of emergency baptism of infants close to death was the head-splashing, customary in the Western Church, employed). In villages, it was believed that screaming was a good omen, but if the child lost control of its bladder this meant bad luck.[17] After the ducking, a small cross (gold if this could be afforded) was hung by the priest round the child's neck, where it was supposed to remain throughout his or her life as an outward token of Christian faith. A special meal following the ceremony was an essential part of the christening, wherever it was held. In villages, the food prescribed by tradition was kasha (porridge, with the swollen grain symbolising new birth), and eating was preceded by a form of grace in which the midwife asked God's blessing on the child as well as on the food; festival foods and vodka were also consumed in quantity. At this ceremony, the midwife would be generously rewarded for her trouble.[18] And, as everywhere in the Christian world, christening involved the official conferral of the child's name – selected less to underline the new arrival's individuality than to emphasise his or her links with family tradition. A child might be named for its father, mother, or a more distant ancestor; it was also perfectly acceptable practice, in very large families, for several children to be called by the same name and distinguished from each other only by adjectives: 'big Masha' and 'little Masha', 'fat Vanya' and 'thin Vanya'.[19] Thus the naming became yet another way of absorbing the child's threatening strangeness, of making him or her (in various senses) *familiar*.

The mixture of joy and fear inspired by infants, and the syncretic nature of the rites surrounding them, reflected the 'double-faith', or more accurately 'multi-

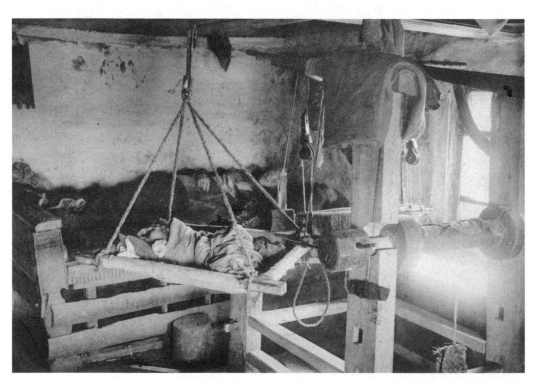

65 Hanging cradle, Nizhni Novgorod province, 1892.

faith', world-view of peasant culture, which was also evident in the rituals and practices surrounding the christening. Besides acting as mentors to, and protectors of, the child and providing it with gifts, the godparents played an important role in bridging the divide between secular and sacred worlds (and between different kinds of sacredness as well). They 'purchased' the child from the midwife (a device to ensure separation from the demonic sphere), accompanied it on the (according to tradition, hazardous) journey to the church, and held the child during the christening service (a girl would be held by her godmother and a boy by his godfather). They then processed back from the church to the child's home, handing it back ceremonially to the mother, who would be located at one of the ritual centres of the household – the stove or the icon corner. Naturally, they also took an obligatory part in the christening feast, alongside the midwife.[20]

In a world where the forces of good and bad were in perpetual conflict, rituals were engaged in from the moment of a child's birth to protect it from harm. The wicker or wooden cradle (*kolybel'*, *lyul'ka*) in which the infant lay was often suspended from the ceiling, both to keep it out of the way and because traditional beliefs suggested that a child placed on the ground was more easily subject to contamination by demons. Before a child was laid in it for the first time, a cat might be put there so that any evil spirits were diverted.[21] The *pestushki*, songs sung to accompany activities such as swadding or bathing, often had the flavour of spells:

> Water runs off the goldeneye,
> Vova's illness runs away,
> Sweet dreams, sleep tight,
> Good health to the boy.[22]

Traditional lullabies sought to keep at bay bugbears and bogeys, such as Buka, to invoke the help of traditional protectors – for example, friendly animals – and to create for the infant a future of peace and prosperity.[23]

Lullabies, of course, also had a practical function, that of sending the child to sleep. Whether the cradle stood on the floor or hung from the ceiling, the rocking motion was used to produce a soporific effect as the singing went on. Hush words such as *bayu-bai* or *lyali-lyuli* were employed to encourage a feeling of peace and security. Many traditional texts placed the child in a world of comfort and plenty, a cradle land of Cockaigne where hangings were soft and luxurious, and food plentiful. In the words of a text collected in the twentieth century:

> O lulla lulla lulla bye,
> Biscuits at your head,
> Apples by your arms,
> At your feet gingerbread,
> Sweeties by your hands,
> Raisins and almonds.[24]

Going Wrong

The ideal template for traditional infant care sought to provide warmth, affection, and sustenance, while shielding against metaphysical threats and ensuring the child's normal development as it grew. Occasionally, these aims came into conflict. For instance, the idea that the child should be protected from cold and strong light could mean that its shirt would be left on when it had a severe rash or was ill. Used nappies might be hung up to dry, rather than washed; if a mother had to leave the house to work in the fields, a baby was likely to be left tied in its cradle, to wallow in its own mess all day.[25] When a child did fall ill, little might be done to aid it: a fatalistic attitude was taken to an infant that was felt to be doomed, *ne zhilets* (a phrase best translated perhaps as 'not long for this world').[26]

In addition, poverty and deprivation could easily interfere with 'best practices'. Those peasant women who could make use of a traditional midwife and give birth in the relatively comfortable circumstances of a bath-house or other such building were, by the standards of Russian rural culture, relatively privileged. In communities where women had to work right through pregnancy, elaborate preparation was ruled out for many, and it was fairly common for women to go through labour unaided, in a field or by a road.[27] As one Soviet obstetrician was to comment, a pregnant woman could expect less considerate treatment than a draught horse.[28] In such situations, one may assume, the ritual procedures of birthing were delayed or truncated, and the infant arrived in life uncelebrated and unwelcomed.

If the mother were unmarried, preparations would be furtive, given the likelihood of social disgrace, were the birth to come to light. A woman from the elite could take steps to avoid shame by pretending to 'adopt' her own offspring, or by having it farmed out to relations; by the late nineteenth century, women of all classes could make use of the discreet facilities available in a 'maternity shelter'.[29] But infanticide was not an uncommon event in the countryside, a situation the Church may have encouraged by placing greater emphasis on the inadmissibility of certain sexual acts than upon child slaughter. One confessional manual of the eighteenth century decreed a penance of twenty years for infanticide in the womb (induced abortion) or for child abandonment, as compared with a penance of forty years for masturbation or for attending church in an impure condition.[30] Infanticide cases that reached the civil courts were dealt with relatively leniently: if a woman did not get off (as more than 60 per cent of defendants did in some years), she might end up sentenced to no more than a few days or weeks in police custody. Sometimes mothers' reactions were simply panic-stricken and contained no element of calculation, as with a 20-year-old peasant girl who killed her child after a swift and painful labour, alone in a wood.[31] But there were also women in poor villages for whom children represented an intolerable burden, and who deliberately helped them into another world. 'These women have no pity, no fear of the Lord, no faith, no respect for the law, nothing but dark enmity', wrote a shocked medical worker from Moscow province in 1916.[32] The British journalist

William Barnes Steveni even claimed – with what accuracy it is hard to say – that desperate parents sometimes sold children for use in magic rituals. He gave the example of a miller in southern Russia who had purchased a child from a poor family for six roubles and drowned it in the millstream because the mill was not working properly.[33]

A child from a deprived household was under threat in early infancy as well: an undernourished mother was unlikely to be able to sustain her infant, and in such households her labour could not easily be spared while the child was small (in richer ones, there was a chance that extra help would be hired to release her from work). The child might be left in the care of an older sibling, with a young hired nanny, or indeed on its own altogether. This practice could provoke fatal accidents: a brother or sister who was still a small child might drop an infant on the head or shake it violently, in a rage, when it was crying; unsupervised infants might choke on their dummies, or strangle themselves with the strings of their hanging cradles.[34]

Neglect extended to low-level infections. Oral thrush was considered inevitable ('I thought all babies had "flowers" in the mouth, just like meadows have grass in,' one woman marvelled, when shown by a health worker how to deal with the problem). Conjunctivitis and rashes would simply be left to themselves. If a child did not die, it might end up with serious physical problems: hernias, scarring, even blindness.[35] In the circumstances, it was only thoroughly healthy children who stood a good chance of surviving, and then only if no catastrophe such as a food shortage or an epidemic afflicted the locality.

The Battle with 'Backwardness'

By the late nineteenth century there was a mounting sense, among the educated public, that traditional child care was in many respects pernicious and that an enlightenment campaign was urgently required. Among the practices regarded as a manifestation of 'uncultured' and 'uncivilised' conditions was swaddling – as had been the case in Britain during the eighteenth century too.[36] Still more animus was directed at the work of traditional midwives and at the use of home-made dummies, which offended the rising emphasis on infants' sensitivity to bacterial contamination. Birth in Russian villages was usually a kind of 'martyrdom', wrote M. A. Novosil'tseva in 1916, with an ignorant folk midwife in attendance:

> One has to shudder at this thought, especially when one sees the kinds of measures she resorts to. I have no room to give all the grisly details, but suffice it to say that women giving birth are regularly heaved up and down, passed under horse-collars, forced to straddle barrels, steamed in Russian bath-houses till they are practically comatose, dragged round the house till they collapse. And on top of that there is the filth of the midwife herself, her dirty hands, the lack of any antiseptic – one can only wonder that the percentage of deaths should not be higher.[37]

Reactions of this kind were driven by the rates of infant mortality, which were felt to be out of line with those acceptable in a civilised country.[38] In 1913, the death rate among newborns in European Russia was running at 28 per cent, or 283 per 1,000. Of all deaths that occurred 61.6 per cent fell in the 0–1 age group, and the average death rate for this age was 26.5 per cent. In some districts of central Russia, the rate of infant death was significantly higher. In Novgorod, Saratov, Kaluga, Smolensk, Olonetsk, Vologda, Moscow, Kostroma, Nizhni-Novgorod and Perm' provinces, the death rate for those under the age of one was between 34 and 38.6 per cent. In industrial areas, 54 per cent of children died before their third birthday. According to some estimates, around 84 per cent of children were undernourished. Conditions were worse in Moscow than in St Petersburg. The discrepancy between these rates and those in some European countries – 13.9 in Britain, 16.7 in France, 19.9 in Germany, and 21.3 in Austro-Hungary – was regularly cited in order to point to Russia's backwardness and to the need for change.[39]

In attempting to evaluate reactions of this kind, one should be wary of too much Foucauldian or post-feminist scepticism about the hegemonic aims of the medical profession and of that profession's alliance with the state as an intrusive force. It is true that late Imperial Russian attempts to medicalise child care in the countryside were faulty in more than one respect. To begin with, institutional development was slow, with much – particularly before the 1910s – left to private initiative. Second, the dissemination of superior obstetric and infant care practices was often wanting in terms of the human and emotional side of birth and child-rearing that traditional practices, at their best, supported. Third, the view of traditional child care that was conveyed in health propaganda – as a self-reinforcing system of neglect and superstition – was reductive. Not all traditional practices were life-threatening. Some could even be beneficial: for instance, putting children inside a solid-fuel stove, seen by health workers as barbarous, in fact provided them with essential warmth, with the stove acting as a primitive incubator.

Even where it was detrimental, traditional care often 'killed with kindness' rather than expressing neglect or indifference. Feeding solids early came from the conviction that 'milk isn't a real food'.[40] Enormous efforts were expended to protect children, though in the first instance from malevolent spirits and the 'evil eye' rather than from infections or microbes. Nor were peasant attitudes to sick children always characterised by indifference. It was certainly true that mothers who lost children would be exhorted not to grieve for them too deeply – as in the popular saying, 'It is sinful for a mother to weep for children, since every infant that dies is another candle lit in God's presence.'[41] But the attitude to childhood sickness was not necessarily quiescent. Children might not be taken to a doctor (this depended on whether one was available and felt to be trustworthy), but they might well be taken to a healer, even if the parents were desperately poor.[42] Or other strategies might be adopted: for instance, Konstantin Trenev's mother 'sold' him as a small baby to a rich neighbour because the Ukrainian belief was that saving the child justified such an act.[43] (It is not hard to imagine how this custom would have looked to an outsider unaware of its significance.) The reminiscence of being a baby which 'nearly died' recurs again and again in memoirs: while this point should be treated with caution, since the the idea of being snatched from the jaws of death smacks of autobiographical legend (the exceptional person who is singled out by fate for survival), it is clear that some parents did make every effort they could to save small children. And if children did die, they were laid out in the traditional manner, with a candle placed in their hands, and given a Christian funeral and burial if possible.[44] Equally, proverbs and sayings about children expressed not only cynical sentiments, but also a sense of joy ('Children are the grace of God'), or at the very least ambivalence: 'Children are joy for some, grief for others.' The fate of an unloved child was proverbially dreadful, as suggested by the saying, 'An unloved child doesn't even have a death to itself', but this of course recognised that a loved child could expect very different treatment.[45]

Yet the extent of infant mortality was a very real problem. The overall rate of death among the under-ones in European Russia in 1913 was only slightly better than the death rate for the same age group in the second half of the sixteenth century in England, which then stood at 27 per cent.[46] The human distress caused by the phenomenon is not to be underestimated: in parts of Kaluga province in the 1910s, the average woman would, by the age of 45, have given birth to 14 children and lost 12 of these.[47] Memoirs give some idea of how statistical abstractions translated into actual human experience. Ostap Vishnya, born in the rich farming country of Ukraine in 1889, witnessed a full 12 of his 17 siblings survive. Mikhail Isakovsky, born in Smolensk in 1900, was more typical, being one of 13 children, only five of whom lived beyond infancy. The rate of survival in Anna Dubova's family, also from Smolensk, a decade later, was not much better (only seven children of 14 managed to make it to adulthood).[48] Sometimes it could seem that the mourning never stopped. As the film director Aleksandr Dovzhenko, one of just two surviving children out of 14, recalled: 'Whenever I remember my childhood and the hut I was brought up in, the immediate association is wailing and funerals. The first telegram we ever received was one announcing the death of my brother, a docker in Rostov. [...] My mother spent her life saying goodbye to people: she wept her life away.'[49] While the main grief remembered here is the mother's, children brought up surrounded by dying siblings suffered referred pain as well.

Infant mortality, then, was a tragedy for everyone; and there is some incontrovertible evidence for the link between death rates and traditional child-rearing practices. The main cause of the deaths of very small children, apart from epidemics, was gastro-enteritic infection, a type of ailment that might be the result of bad water supplies, but was equally likely to result from inappropriate diet or bacterial contamination.[50] Rates of infant survival in some ethnic minority communities – for example, among Jews and Tatars – were significantly better than in the majority Russian population. Infants in these two groups were weaned later and were less likely to be fed on a mixed diet from the early stages of life, because the Russian belief that solid food was 'better' for babies than milk on its own was absent.[51] Russian physicians were understandably impressed by evidence

66 Children with the midwife who brought them into the world, Jewish Pale, 1910s.

from Western Europe that showed a significant drop in infant deaths and a spread in the understanding of hygienic practices, once medical consultations for mothers had been set up.[52] In the Russian countryside, however, educational work of this kind largely remained a pipe dream: activists fantasised about the possibilities of acting on mothers by getting trained nurses to work with them, or by setting up institutions for children that would also work as centres for the dissemination of information to parents, but could do little to bring such fantasies to life.[53]

City Mothers

In the city, the medicalisation of medical care was more rapid, and traditions vanished more quickly. Though traditional midwives had worked in at least some city bath-houses during the early nineteenth century,[54] by mid-century elite Russian women would not have dreamed of making use of a bath-house, or of an untrained midwife. If they gave birth at home, a specialist obstetrician would be in attendance (as happens both with Anna and with Kitty in Tolstoy's novel

Anna Karenina, set in the 1870s); otherwise, they were delivered in a lying-in hospital (*rodil'nyi dom*). The second type of delivery, in a specialised clinic, was still considered something of an eccentricity in the 1870s (again, *Anna Karenina* provides evidence of this, through Lyovin's ironic wonder at Vronsky's decision to build a lying-in hospital for the peasants on his estate). However, in the early twentieth century it became increasingly common, for urban women at least, to use such a facility. By 1913, Moscow had ten lying-in hospitals with a total of 565 beds; even two years earlier, as many as 64 per cent of the city's births had taken place in the hospital sector. The proportion of hospital births in St Petersburg was slightly lower, at just over 60 per cent in 1914, but in some provincial cities a significant majority of women were giving birth in institutions by the 1910s: 67 per cent in Ivanovo-Voznesensk by 1912 and 75 per cent in Ryazan' by 1914. Even women from the social elite, of the kind who would previously have expected a physician to attend at home, were using the new facilities.[55]

Looking after babies was also transformed by the work of medical experts. The year 1901, for instance, saw the opening of the first ever incubator for premature children, in the City Shelter for Premature Children, which treated 37 children in its first year of operation (33 of whom survived). In 1903, the shelter moved into more capacious accommodation on the Fontanka, and by the 1910s was catering for 200–300 children at a time, including not only premature babies but also sickly infants and the children of the wet-nurses employed to feed the shelter's patients. While the death rate was higher than the impressive figures for the first year suggested (it ran to 20–25 per cent, not counting children who died in the first days after admission), the opening of the facility – which was for some years afterwards the only one in the country – represented a significant step forward.[56]

Infant care was highlighted as a key issue at the First All-Russian Conference of Paediatricians in 1913, which also drew attention to the work of Georgy Speransky at the First Infirmary for Nurslings in Moscow.[57] This facility, set up in 1910, was the first dedicated hospital for infants in Russia, and consisted of an out-patients section, with special isolated cubicles to be used by visiting mothers so that contact between sick children was avoided, and an upper floor for use by in-patients. Since the hospital was a private initiative, fees had to be charged, but a charitable society attached to it provided subsidies to needy mothers who would not otherwise have been able to afford treatment.[58] The 1910s saw the foundation of a number of other specialist infant-care institutes, including the Institute for the Protection of Maternity on Kamennoostrovsky Prospekt in St Petersburg, and a clinic under the direction of A. A. Russov in Kiev.[59] Specialist conferences also proliferated, for example a Congress on the Care of Children held from 11 to 16 May 1914. At these events, and in the professional medical press during the 1910s, emphasis was placed on the need for increased support to mothers, both of an institutional kind (maternity hospital facilities, access to crèches) and of an economic kind.[60] Similar ideas were set out in pamphlets produced by women in the Social Democratic movement, most famously Aleksandra Kollontai. A stimulus to utopian planning in these areas was the development of the welfare sector in the West, particularly France, Germany, and Britain; as with welfare facilities more broadly, the need for Russia to 'catch up' was repeatedly stressed.[61]

The early twentieth century also saw the creation of a number of specialist societies that attempted to circulate information about work in the field of infant care, and to lobby for improvements to the provision available. In 1904, N. A. Russkikh, a zemstvo physician from Ekaterinburg who had drawn doctors' attention to the importance of infant care at the Pirogov Congress in 1898, set up the Union for the Struggle with Infant Mortality.[62] This initiative remained relatively small-scale, with a budget of no more than a few thousand roubles – though it did have representation in several major Russian and Ukrainian cities, organising, for example, 'Drop of Milk' groups, modelled on a French precedent, which sponsored the distribution of milk substitutes to needy mothers. In Saratov, the 'Drop of Milk' facility was catering for about 60–100 children a month by 1915.[63]

Another relatively small-scale enterprise was Aid to Mothers (founded in 1911), which organised consultations for new mothers and the distribution of brochures promoting hygienic child care in St Petersburg.[64] But another association, also founded in 1911, represented a real step forward in terms of the public profile of maternal and infant care. This was the All-Russian Guardianship for the Protection of Mothers and Infants, initiated by Karl Andreevich Raukhfus, a physician and social activist, and the director of the Prince Oldenburg Hospital for Children in St Petersburg. The society's incorporation by statute as a guardianship, under the patronage of Empress Alexandra, indicated that the highest authorities in the Russian Empire were now taking seriously arguments about the threat posed by infant mortality and poor health during infancy to Russia's competitiveness as an economic power.[65]

The activities of such societies gave a boost to practical initiatives. By the 1910s, several major Russian cities had 'shelters for mothers' offering guidance on how to look after small children, dispensing facilities, drop-in mother and baby clinics, and sometimes free food for small children. The Guardianship for the Protection of Mothers and Infants, for instance, had, by 1917, five shelters for mothers, all of which also acted as information centres.[66] In Moscow, the Protection of Motherhood society, founded in January 1908, later that year set up a small hostel in a five-room flat with running water on Dolgorukovskaya Street. Uncertain support caused the society to go into abeyance shortly afterwards, but it restarted in April 1914, and, like other charitable efforts, was given a boost by the First World War, attracting commercial sponsorship, a number of generous legacies, and – in late 1915 – a subsidy from the Tatiana Committee. By 1916 it was operating two reception centres, several ante-natal and post-natal shelters, an administrative centre with laundry, and a mother and child home, combining ante-natal and post-natal accommodation. Between 1914 and 1915, the society's income rose from around 11,000 roubles per annum to over 34,000, a significant improvement on the 1,741 roubles received in the first year of its operation, 1908, even allowing for wartime inflation.[67] In suburban St Petersburg, noteworthy was the work of the Society for the Protection of Mothers and Nurslings in Tsarskoe Selo, set up in 1914 and offering maternal guidance, free layettes for the needy, and a milk distribution service.[68]

The ambition of those organising mother and child welfare was to provide an integrated package of medical care, including medical assessments and programmes for rational home care, which might be disseminated through the distribution of leaflets, through visits by a district nurse (*patronazhnaya sestra*), or both.[69] Russian experts also took a considerable interest in strategies for monitoring the target population, for example the keeping of elaborate record cards, with details of family environment as well as of the child's physical and psychological characteristics.[70] The intention was that every mother – most particularly from those sections of the population blighted by 'ignorance' and 'superstition' – should be under the benevolent and omniscient supervision of physicians before, during, and after birth took place.

In fact, however, many charitable initiatives in the area of infant care – like other such excursions into welfare – reached small fractions of the needy population. The Tsarskoe Selo society processed 147 patients in its first year of operation; the Moscow Protection of Motherhood society had, even after its 1915–16 expansion, space for only about 65 women and 80 children.[71] By contrast, the 'Drop of Milk' facilities in St Petersburg reached an impressive 300 mothers a day by 1912, but the set-up was plagued by financial irregularities that tarnished its reputation among charity workers in the capital.[72] Ambitious in a different way were the achievements of a 'shelter' on Vasilievsky Island in St Petersburg, which sent an impressive number of patients – over 2,000 – through its mother and baby clinic the year that this opened, 1915. However, only 74 women attended a newly opened ante-natal clinic in 1917, while a district nurse system set up in 1915 organised visits to no more than 70 new mothers. Even those mothers who were reached by the shelter's work did not necessarily prove malleable: a substantial proportion simply ignored what they were told by the experts.[73]

Breast is (Not?) Best

What the experts themselves said varied, particularly where educated women were concerned. A case in point was breast-feeding. 'Skilled breast-feeding' was the order of the day in advice directed at working women,[74] but, with better-off mothers, other approaches to diet were entertained. Artificial milk substitutes, for instance, were starting to come into use by the 1900s. To be sure, the attitude to these among much of the medical profession in Russia was suspicious. One critic of 'artificial feeding' commented in 1905 that the method had become distressingly popular. Nestlé milk was 'beloved by doctors', and their support for it caused mothers to be misled: 'Praise of this kind only causes confusion and anxiety in intellectual society, which – like those who advise it – soon learns to kow-tow to foreign products and respond to every stimulus in this direction.'[75]

Wet-nursing was the subject of similarly conflicting advice. On the one hand, it was regularly denounced in normative literature and expert commentaries.[76]

67 Sterilising
equipment, Zhuk,
Mother and Child
(1911).

But many experts accepted that the practice was going to continue, whatever they said about it, and directed their efforts into considering how it might best be regulated. It was suggested that a minimum age to be attained by a woman's own child before she started selling her services should be set by law, that the profession should be legally regulated, and that employers should be compelled to accept a nurse's own child in the house where she was working.[77] Still more energy went into considering how infants might be protected from the lurking dangers of the unhygienic plebeians called into service as wet-nurses. Medical journals regularly ran articles about the risks posed by wet-nurses who were syphilitics or alcoholics, and it was emphasised to mothers that they should do all they could to vet the person who was performing this service to their infants.[78] For mothers who could afford it, there were medical institutions that would certificate a nurse. The Imperial Philanthropic Society had an Office for the Certification of Wet-Nurses (which had come into existence as early as the 1800s); the St Petersburg Private Lying-In Hospital (Sankt-Peterburgskii chastnyi rodil'nyi dom), and the Wet-Nurse Hostel, also in the capital, both ran services which vetted wet-nurses on health grounds and brought them together with parents (at the cost of a fairly substantial fee paid by the latter).[79] From 1881, the Myasnitskaya Hospital in Moscow ran a thorough Bureau for the Inspection of Wet-Nurses, which subjected women to a detailed medical examination involving pretty well every part of the body, including genitals and rectum as well as breasts, arms, shoulders, and legs.[80]

Advice on how to breast-feed (as opposed to why to do this) less often came up in printed sources aimed at the social elite. However, there was apparently some market by the 1910s for Laktagol, a nutritional supplement for nursing mothers which was advertised, for instance, in a leading feminist publication, *The First Women's Calendar*.[81] Baby-care books aimed at educated women had started, by the late nineteenth century, to emphasise not only the importance of breast feeding, but also the importance of adopting the correct techniques when nursing the child. Later editions of V. N. Zhuk's immensely influential *Mother and Child*, reprinted ten times between 1881 and 1916, had a section instructing mothers that they must not stand up, as many nurses and mothers were inclined to do, or lie down, but must sit upright with the child held on their knees; Zhuk also gave information on how to put the child to the breast. Zhuk's book included a section on choosing wet-nurses, and another giving information about types of teat that could be purchased for a feeding-bottle.[82]

The mixed messages about how to behave were reflected in the real-life behaviour of the Russian social elite, as was the tendency of the privileged, in any society where choice is available, to exercise choice. Lev Kassil' recalled that his mother breast-fed him at first, but that he then had a wet-nurse, and after that, again, a bottle (which he got so attached to that he later purloined his brother's).[83] And wet-nurses enjoyed a privileged, as well as heavily controlled, place in society, much as they had in the early nineteenth century. It was standard for a nurse to be given a significant lump sum in cash, as well as her opulent traditional costume (coloured sarafan, strings of coral, false pearls, and beads, and high embroidered *kokoshnik*, or tall curved head-dress). She was treated like cut glass in the household because of a belief that her milk would curdle if she were crossed. But at the same time she was expected to use the servants' entrance, and (by the early twentieth century) given a thorough scrubbing and disinfection to make sure that she was clean enough to be released on genteel babies. There was seldom any attempt, from either side, to prolong contact once the period of nursing (usually six months) was concluded. One girl brought up in a large St Petersburg family recalled that only one of the wet-nurses employed for the six children became genuinely attached to the infant she looked after, a development that had rather sad consequences, because her visits, though tolerated by the other servants, made no impression whatever on her former charge.[84] Modernisation of the institution often went no further than using one of the vetting services, or checking over a wet-nurse oneself; in the case of the family just mentioned, the method adopted was to employ one of the nurses certificated by the Lying-In Hospital in St Petersburg.[85]

Temples of Hygiene

Some aspects of early twentieth-century infant-rearing, as propounded and as lived, were studiedly modern. Treatment in the leading lying-in hospitals and maternity homes was – like treatment in comparable institutions in Western Europe – centred on hygiene and regularity. In Moscow in the 1910s, for example, once the umbilical cord had been cut, a newborn would be carefully labelled with its mother's hospital number in a bracelet or a locket, and would be wiped down with Vaseline or liquid paraffin in order to remove the layers of primal slime. Depending on the institution, a further cleaning in the shape of a bath might then take place before the infant was carried off to a separate ward and placed with the other babies. Feeding took place strictly according to the clock, at precisely spaced intervals, and before each feed the mother's breasts would be sponged down with a solution of bromide as a disinfection measure. When nappies needed to be changed, this was done in a separate room kept only for the purpose. In the reports on the facility published during the 1910s, figures were cited to prove that measures of this kind, and careful supervision of the infants, had reduced mortality from 7.5 per cent in the early 1900s to around 3–4 per cent. The hospitals also had an intensive educational programme for mothers, beginning with advice provided in the hospital itself, and continuing with regular consultations at which the baby would be weighed and measured and looked over by a doctor, and the mother would be closely questioned about the kind of care she was giving. It was claimed that, by 1913, 84 per cent of the mothers attending were breast-feeding exclusively, with a further 11 per cent providing a mixed diet.[86]

Advice for mothers – in the form of brochures and books, as well as of free leaflets given out at clinics – emphasised the 'hygiene and regularity' themes. There was a widespread assumption that infants were essentially inert at the intellectual level, with development taking the form of evolution of the sense organs and emotional impulses.[87] It was care at the physiological level that was required, and specialists in physiology who were qualified to provide it.

Experts presented their views in simplified form by means of a new genre, the brochure or pamphlet aimed at women of little education. Numerous publications of this kind were issued by charitable societies, by zemstva, and by philanthropic individuals; they were also given out to mothers in baby and child clinics. The standard format was to intersperse strictures against the deficiencies of traditional practices – giving birth standing up led to prolapses and tearing of the perineum, the use of bread chaws and other home-made dummies was insanitary and dangerous (in the words of E. A. Pokrovsky, chief doctor at the Moscow Children's Hospital, 'the chaw has killed more people than plague, cholera and all other illnesses combined') – with insistence on the need for hygiene and elaborately detailed descriptions of bathing, breast-feeding (at regular intervals, of course), dressing the infant, and so on. The tone of such publications brooked no argument: 'If a mother is healthy, she is obliged to feed her child. This is a law passed down to mothers by God Himself.' Mothers were assured of the advanced competence of expert care: any sick child must immediately be taken to the doctor, and public crèches were an ideal method of providing care for children while their mothers were occupied, say during the harvest. 'The children in them are not left alone; they are placed in the care of attentive, sensible, carefully selected "nannies" who have been approved by the entire *mir* [peasant commune], who will not let the child sit round hungry, cold, and dirty, tormented by insects and animals.'[88]

The tone of those addressing themselves to mothers of the educated class was rather less stentorian, but the basic attitude was that 'the expert is always right'. The doyen of advisers at this level was Vladimir Zhuk, who regularly updated his *Mother and Child* to include material on the latest advances in obstetrics and child care, as well as comments – not always approbatory – on new products, such as Jaeger clothing for mothers or different types of walking-frame for toddlers.[89] His book was unique, so far as Russia was concerned, in its colossal dimensions – getting on for a thousand pages – and in its detail: mothers were told not only what to do, but what the reasons behind the instructions were in clinical terms.[90] The discussion everywhere set its face against accepted belief not sustained by science – Zhuk condemned swaddling without qualification, told mothers that they should not be worried about such traditional 'bugbears' as infant chills and teething, and commented, with regard to expectations that wet-nurses should be morally upright as well as healthy, 'Evidently, people have always been inclined to demand in others qualities that they themselves lack.'[91] If this lighter than usual touch probably helps explain Zhuk's popularity, the general effect of the book was utterly serious. Mothers were repeatedly informed that cleanliness was vital, ordered to supervise gains and losses in weight with the aid of elaborate charts, instructed that they should dress their children exclusively in warm, light clothes allowing plenty of freedom of movement, and urged to avoid rocking the child, which might cause injury to the brain. Close monitoring was expected, with later editions including height and weight charts to set out 'normal' rates of progress. Nursery furniture was to be of washable, tough materials such as metal and enamel (a metal cot was preferred to the traditional cradle). Most importantly, the house was to give priority to providing appropriate accommodation to children: 'The room intended for the child, contrary to established beliefs, must be the largest, the lightest, the most cheerful – in a word, the best room in the entire flat.'[92]

No other child-care writer of the late Imperial era was as widely published as Zhuk, but there were a few alternatives to his book, including *The Physiology and Illness of the Child* (1909) by G. N. Speransky (later to become the number one guru of Soviet infant care, but then a young doctor at the Moscow Children's Clinic), which offered very similar advice. For instance, Speransky told mothers that they should have a spacious nursery (at least 5 cubic metres in area) heated to 18–20 degrees Celsius, with fittings in metal, enamel, or wood painted in bright colours. Children should have a daily bath and be taught to rinse their mouth after meals; rocking was 'without question harmful', and so was swaddling, given that children had a need for constant freedom of movement. A dummy was not recommended, and if one was used it should be boiled at regular intervals. A regime should be introduced early, as getting children used to a correct one later on was troublesome. This involved, in particular, regular feeding – at set times, not less than two to two and a half hours apart – and the child's weight should be monitored routinely in order to check that the rational system was having rational results.[93] Speransky, in other words, was in tune with the Western child-care experts of the time. In Britain by the 1880s, for example, 'orphanage discipline' had become the model for advanced parenting; feeding times were supposed to be ordered by the clock, rather than by infant need; and practices such as kissing children and rocking them were severely discouraged.[94]

The extent to which these model arrangements were observed in real life is, of course, open to question. An album produced by V. N. Zhuk, in which mothers could record their conformity with the hygienic requirements set out in his baby book and track the infant's progress in terms of weight targets and so on, did not enjoy the popularity of the original book, suggesting that parents were still less than obsessive about following the directions in manuals.[95] Zhuk himself sadly observed that 'even in Germany', let alone Russia, the requirements of hygiene were often considered laughable.[96] An amateur pioneer of urban ethnography observed in 1892 that St Petersburg bedrooms and nurseries were 'often unsatisfactory from a hygienic point of view', as the inhabitants of flats reserved the best and lightest rooms, on the street side, for receiving guests.[97] In addition, there were many members of the cultural elite who simply did not have the resources to comply with hygienic ideals, however much they wanted to. Even if parents were lucky enough to inhabit several rooms – the case with only just over 50 per cent of the population in St Petersburg, for example – providing a 'sunny' room might be difficult, as many less prestigious dwellings overlooked an internal courtyard ('well') or an enclosed yard, into which light penetrated only feebly.[98]

Fixtures and fittings were just as likely to depart from hygienic norms. To be sure, pre-revolutionary specialist shops could provide a formidable array of baby-goods to the well-off: for instance, Caring for Little Children, with branches in St Petersburg and Moscow, was, by 1899, able to supply, among other things, best-quality linen nappies, baby jackets, cardigans, caps, and swaddling wrappers (made of print, piqué, embroidered nansook, etc.), as well as dresses, skirts, blouses, bodices, and outer-wear for older babies. The total cost of a layette (assuming that the baby needed twenty nappies and ten of everything else) would have been somewhere between 25 and 100 roubles (around one to four times the cost of a housemaid or nursemaid's monthly wages). To this had to be added the cost of a pram or pushchair (9–80 roubles), of a cot and bedding (about 40–60 roubles), and of a tub (about 20 roubles). Concerned parents who had the economic resources could also invest in a special table for changing nappies at around 15–50 roubles, a bath-table for 4–7 roubles, and a 'chamber pot with hermetically sealed lid' for 3 roubles.[99] Obviously, an outlay of hundreds of roubles on baby goods was not an option for many families. Large numbers – one may assume – improvised, or recycled clothes and equipment from and to friends and relations. In any case, many of the expensive baby items were not so much 'hygienic' as ostentatious – covered in frills, lace, pin-tucks, and ruffles. Between parents who could not afford goods of the kind recommended by experts, and parents who preferred to dress their children like little dolls, there was a good deal of room for practices of which medical specialists would have disapproved.

Yet there were, by the 1910s, at least some well-off mothers who took the hygienic code very seriously. M. P. Stakhorskaya, who published her 'mother's diary' in 1916, was one of these. She took care to breast-feed her son Lev, affectionately known as Masik (born in 1907); she dressed him entirely in loose clothes of linen and cotton, and never covered him with more than a cotton sheet when he was lying down: at certain times of day, he would be left half naked so as to allow free passage of air, and his bottom was never kept covered. She fastened him with ribbons to the mattress so that he could move his hands, but without risk of scratching his eyes, and suspended 'Froebel's first gift' – a blue and red ball – above his cot so that he could look at it while resting. At the same time, 'spoiling' was avoided; though she carried him round for the first month, after that he was left to sleep alone.[100]

Elena Krichevskaya, a comparable mother, graphically described how she resisted the temptation to comfort her small daughter when the latter was crying in her cot:

> I bend over her cot and she turns her little face, all distorted with crying, towards me and stretches her puffy little hands towards my face, and I can see pleading in her face, and trust that I will do what she wants, and I can guess that Marusya wants me to take her in my arms. And oh, the need to pick her up! Of course one should, one should squeeze her tight and cover her with kisses, carry her round the room – one's heart is beating so loudly – 'but it's not a good idea,' reason whispers quietly, but firmly.[101]

Thus mothers – their own feelings notwithstanding – paid tribute to the cult of 'emotional hygiene' perpetuated by child-rearing books. But a contemporary, N. I. Gavrilova, whose son was born four years later, in 1911, raised him rather differently. Levik was fed on sugar water for the first four days of his life as his mother's milk was thought to be insufficient, then given artificial formula, before, finally, a wet-nurse was got in; he was fed by this method until weaning, which took place at the age of 11 months. Gavrilova took no particular interest in his attire, and played only traditional children's games with him, such as *ladushka* (clap-clap handies).[102]

Hanging Cradles

Working-class mothers, of course, had a far more restricted range of options at every stage of infancy, from birth to feeding, accommodation, and clothing. Some did take advantage of the lying-in hospitals that had become available by the early twentieth century. Between 1900 and 1906, servants, traders, and other working women made up 40 per cent of patients in such hospitals in St Petersburg.[103] But the extent of these was not adequate to need. If a woman who did not find a place in such hospitals was lucky, she had a home birth with a midwife attending; if she was less lucky, she might simply give birth next to the machine that she operated in the factory. In St Petersburg, where a survey carried out in the early 1910s indicated that over 70 per cent of mothers worked right up to the moment of birth, labour on the shop floor was a very real possibility.[104] Infant care was equally hand to mouth. The very idea of a 'nursery', in circumstances where an entire family had to share one room, or indeed more than one family one room, was out of the question. The space allocated to the baby would consist exclusively of the place in which it slept, probably a traditional hanging cradle suspended above the parental bed. Assuming that the mother had not come into contact with health workers, or that she had ignored what they said, a chaw was likely to be used to pacify the child, and it would certainly be swaddled in the traditional manner. Weaning would be completed by 6–9 months at the latest. In other words, the ways in which infants were looked after were close to those current in villages; indeed, it was not uncommon for women to farm out children with relations back home rather than keep the child in the city, and survival rates were on average better if this was done than if the child remained with its mother. The average survival rate for children under three in rural areas stood at around 50 per cent in the early twentieth century; in the Pirogov Factory, where there were unusually good conditions for pregnant and nursing mothers, only 38 per cent of babies could expect to see their third birthday.[105]

The reasons for this were not usually to do with women's indifference or hostility to their children. Most working-class mothers, like mothers in villages, wanted the best for their babies and treated them with as much solicitude and affection as they could. They would feed the child in the best way they knew (even if this meant early solid food – 7.5 per cent of mothers in St Petersburg in the 1910s began feeding solids from the moment of birth).[106] They would sing lullabies, play with it, tell it stories, and generally provide for the non-material side of its life.[107] The problem was that women's income was essential to many working-class families, particularly in the poorest sector of society – among St Petersburg workers with family earnings of 20 roubles per month or less, nearly 60 per cent of mothers were in paid employment.[108] Hence, child care had to be delegated from an early stage. By and large, this meant to a non-professional person. In St Petersburg in the 1910s, for instance, over 65 per cent of working-class mothers left their babies with a relative, the child's older siblings, or a landlady. Nearly a third of this group depended on older children in order to keep the child looked after.[109] This method posed the same risk of accident as in the countryside; in fact, it was possibly more risky, because the environment in places like worker barracks was less child-friendly (the baby might topple down the stairs, or be dropped on a hard floor or from an upper window; if it was taken out for air, there were outdoor hazards such as building sites and traffic).

There was, though, a group of mothers who did come into contact with health information, which could be significant at the local level. In Odessa, for example, nearly 3,000 children passed through the mother and child clinic set up by A. O. Gershenzon between its opening in May 1908 and 1 December 1912. Those attending included a proportion of intellectual mothers who wanted to learn how to do things properly, but 80 per cent of the public came from the lower classes – workers, craftspeople, small traders. Not all patients made repeat visits: mothers who were already breast-feeding tended to come once or twice at most, but women who were feeding artificially turned up more frequently for information, and, as time passed, there was a move towards longer consultation periods on the part of patients more generally. Gershenzon himself felt that the facility was a huge success. 'You should see the huge interest – one could even say, heartfelt interest – with which [mothers] watch their children being weighed, how distressed they become if the child's weight has dropped and how delighted they are if he or she is putting on weight well and the doctor has praised them for giving good care and feeding the child properly.' As well as praise from the doctor, another important pedagogical tool was peer pressure: consultations were held in one big reception room so that everyone present could hear a mother's conversation with the doctor, which, Gershenzon felt, led to useful dissemination of information and inspired a spirit of 'competition' in the mothers. He himself proudly recorded that there had been a significant rise in levels of women solely breast-feeding their infants – from 15 per cent in 1908 to 27.5 per cent in 1912.[110]

There is a notable deficiency in the evidence about many aspects of child-rearing outside the elite. E. A. Pokrovsky's monumental ethnographical study, *The Physical Education of Children among Various Peoples, particularly of the Russian Empire* (1884), provided a wealth of detail on traditional birth practices and infant care among Russians and 'Russians of other birth'. But Pokrovsky was a physician, working on the basis of 'know your enemy', and he was not concerned with the mental and spiritual side of infant care. For their part, mainstream Russian ethnographers did collect material about, say, protecting children from the evil eye, but focused on ritual rather than on socialisation, and worked much more assiduously in the countryside than they did in cities. Hence, records of how Russian city women of the lower classes looked after their babies at the emotional level are thin. But the material available suggests that, while traditional lullabies and infant games persisted, traditional rituals did not. The celebratory side of birth and early infancy seems to have been left to the rites sanctioned by official religion. For instance, it was customary for city-dwelling women of the Russian Orthodox faith to attend church to give thanks for their safe delivery once they were fully recovered from giving birth.[111] The ceremonies ushering the infant into the spiritual world also had an explicitly Christian character. Though there are some indications that religious observation was declining in the working population of Russian cities by the early twentieth century, particularly among men, the practice of baptism was still pretty well universal among those belonging to the Orthodox faith.[112]

Naming Children

Christenings in urban families, like those in villages, were at once religious and social occasions. The two traditional days for baptism, in cities as well as the countryside, were the eighth day after birth and the fortieth day after birth (the latter coincided with the 'churching' of the mother).[113] Cases of later christening were unusual, and mainly occurred in intelligentsia families of at least vaguely oppositional ideas. For instance, M. P. Stakhorskaya's son was christened as late as at 5 years old (in naming him 'Lev' (Leo), after Lev Tolstoy, his mother suggested her guarded relationship with the Orthodox Church, which had recently excommunicated her hero, as well as her liberal views).[114] The christening ceremony took the same form as in the village, but without the serving of ritual food. Surviving traditions were generally to do with sociability and conspicuous consumption. It was customary for the child's godparents to make a significant financial outlay. The godfather paid the priest for the ceremony and gave the child its baptismal cross, and the godmother presented the priest with a handkerchief, and the child itself with a robe and a bonnet.[115] Indeed, by the late nineteenth century, christening had, in well-off circles, become a ceremony that was not only opulent but also private: it was held in a family's domestic chapel, if they had such a thing, or, failing that, in a church which was small enough to have the atmosphere of a private oratory.[116] Wealthy peasants in the countryside also liked to have the priest round to their homes. In less well-off families, on the other hand, christening would take place in an ordinary church. It was customary for the rite to take place just before Mass, so that the child could be given communion immediately, and it seems likely that, where costs needed to be kept low, parents would have opted for a place in a collective ceremony, rather than a separate one.[117]

As well as initiating the child into membership of the Orthodox Church, baptism was a form of welcome into the community more broadly. The central element of this, the naming rite, worked rather differently in cities than in the village, acting less as a way of 'bringing the infant into the fold' than of emphasising its individuality. In Elisaveta Fen's words, by the early twentieth century, educated families 'chose their children's names freely'.[118] Admittedly, Orthodox parents were required to choose a name listed in the church calendar. But the practice of naming the child according to the saint's day on which it was born, or according to the name of a near ancestor, was falling out of use, and some exotic choices were now made alongside the familiar Mariyas, Aleksandras, and Nataliyas. Calling a child Olimpiya or Kleopatra, names quite popular in the merchant classes, would have seemed vulgar and provincial to a university professor and his wife, but the artistic intelligentsia was happy to give its daughters names such as Mirra and Ariadna.[119] Literary precedent made acceptable the bestowing of names that had been rare before famous books made them canonical: Tatiana (after Pushkin's heroine), popular from the mid-nineteenth century, was now joined by Tamara, from Lermontov's *The Demon*.

An explicit sense of social status also played its part. In the late eighteenth and early nineteenth centuries, both a country gentleman's daughter and her maid might have been called Paraskeva, shortened to Parasha, or Avdot'ya, shortened to Dunya. By the late nineteenth century, the former name had fallen out of favour with the educated classes (and where used at all, was abbreviated to the genteel Polina); the latter name had been replaced by the pedantically correct alternative Evdokiya. In some traditional gentry families, as well as in the upper echelons of the aristocracy and the royal family, naming patterns were usually conservative: Kseniya, Anastasiya, Zinaida remained in frequent use, as they had in the early nineteenth century. In peasant circles, Kseniya and Anastasiya were also widely used, but here alongside names that would not now have been favoured higher up the social scale, such as Malan'ya, Avdot'ya, or Pelageya. Where given names were universal, diminutives varied: a middle- or upper-class Anna would be known familiarly as Anechka or Annen'ka, a peasant or working-class one was likely to go under the names Annushka, Anyuta, An'ka, or Nyura.[120]

Children from other Christian denominations would also undergo baptism, in most cases also in infancy (the Baptists represented an obvious exception). Among non-Christians, different kinds of naming ritual were observed. In the case of Jewish babies, the *shames* (synagogue reader) would announce the birth from the pulpit, and eight days after birth the child would be circumcised (if male), and assigned a name (in the case of both sexes).[121] In strict Orthodox families, this would be a version of a Hebrew name – Moshe, Abram, Esfir', Revekka – but assimilated Jewish families were beginning to avoid such names, opting either for names of Hebrew origin that were not exclusively in use among Jews (Osip, Mikhail, David, Sarra, Yakov), or for non-Hebrew names that did not have over-obvious Christian associations (Evgeny, Sof'ya, Boris, Aleksandra). Westernised names (Oskar, Vil'yam, Rozaliya, Ida, Emma) were particularly popular.[122]

Among Tatars who were Muslim (as most were), both sexes went through a naming rite, known in this case as the *isem kumu*, *ai salu*, *atatu*, or *azan*, at which the local mullah recited prayers and then called aloud the child's name repeatedly.[123] Before 1917, the names used were usually Turkic forms of Arabic religious names – Khasan, Zafir, Zeinap – or Turkic compounds with a religious meaning, for instance Gubaidulla, 'the slave of Allah'. An interesting peculiarity was that, unlike Russian families, Tatars strove *not* to give a child a name that was already in use: statistics from 1897 indicate that the 64 males and 54 females in one village had as many as 97 different names between them.[124] At the time of the naming ritual, small boys were also circumcised (a rite known in Tatar as the *sonnet*).[125]

In religious minorities, too, the secular celebrations surrounding the naming ceremony would depend on the wealth of the family into which a child was born; so would the relationship between recognition of the child's birth within the community and the recognition of the birth on the part of the state. In Jewish families resident in the Pale of Settlement, it was fairly common for parents, in the early nineteenth century, not to bother to register their child's birth because the act was felt to be unnecessary, and because official registration exposed sons to compulsory military service, anathema to Orthodox Jews.[126] The extent to which evasion persisted during the late nineteenth and early twentieth centuries is unclear, but there was still a separation between reception on the part of the state and of the community, since religious ministers who were not Orthodox Christians, unlike Orthodox priests, did not act also as officers of the state.

In various other ways, traditional child-rearing in Tatar and in Jewish families differed from child-rearing in Orthodox families. Not only did breast-feeding tend to continue longer, but supplementation with solid food was less common. The cradle into which an infant was put, and the way it was dressed, might also be different, though generalisation is difficult, given that Jewish and Tatar communities were spread across a wide geographical range and in some cases assimilated to local practices, so that what was characteristic of a non-Russian community in one place might not be characteristic of such a community in another. Whether a Tatar child was swaddled, for instance, depended on the region (as it also did with Russian babies: in some parts of northern Russia infants were either not swaddled at all, or swaddled only briefly).[127] Equally, clothes and diet among Tatars, as among Jews and Russians, varied considerably from place to place.

A few general tendencies can be identified, though. Typically, Jewish children were put into a standing cradle, or one on rockers, rather than in a hanging cradle, and were clad in padded jackets over the top of a simple shirt in order to keep them warm. In some places, though, the child might be left naked for the first few days, or indeed until circumcision (for climatic reasons, this practice was more characteristic of south-eastern areas of the Russian Empire).[128] Tatar cradles varied by region – in the Erevan area, a hammock-like affair known as a *tchoch*, as used by the Armenians themselves, was preferred, but elsewhere hanging or standing cribs might be used. But clothing was more consistent, almost always consisting of a shirt and a padded jacket, known in this case as a *yermolka*.[129] Characteristic of Tatars also was the fact that the child was frequently washed. While this was no doubt an echo of the centrality of washing in Islamic religious practice, it had folk overtones in some places: for example, in the Crimea and in Siberia, the child might be given rinses in salt water, or salted water, which were believed to 'harden the skin'. And, while solid food might not be given to Tatar babies on a regular basis, in some places a ritual meal of oil and honey was given to an infant on the day of its birth.[130] In this group too, the pervasiveness of beliefs about the evil eye's possible influence on the baby meant that, for the first forty days after birth, the new arrival would be closely watched.[131]

Practices among non-Russians were, of course, just as subject to change in line with shifts in status and educational threshold as were practices amongst ethnic Russians. While it was (according to ethnographical observers) traditional for Jews not to wash their infants very frequently – in some places, a child would not be washed until after the circumcision had been performed – educated Jews living in the big cities were among the most passionate proponents of hygienic practices (they were widely represented amongst the pioneers of 'mother and child care' in Russia).[132] The late nineteenth and early twentieth centuries, then, witnessed not just a drive by medical experts to exercise influence over child-care practices, but a spread of such influence in real terms.

There were alterations not only in the way that children were treated but in the way that parents thought about this. Attitudes to child care became much more self-conscious. Adults became convinced that professional advice was essential to children's well-being, and that intervention was essential if symptoms deviated from the norm. This could mean, for instance, that an unfortunate child whose stools did not seem to be exactly as described in the books was subjected to an almost daily process of enemas, to restore order.[133] And it now emerged that keeping meticulous written records was a prerequisite to looking after the infant. The ritual of weighing the child regularly had more than a practical function: it produced a simulacrum of the child's changing daily identity, tabulated in figures and with the imprimatur of science. Parents themselves obediently followed the instructions to record the minutiae of their infants' daily lives, setting down moments in the evolution of perception, movement, and cognition as they were commanded by articles in the family press.[134] Spared the anxieties created by traditional beliefs about child development, they were mired in another set of anxieties, this time with origins in medicine. Perception of teething was one example. Specialists such as Vladimir Zhuk assured mothers that any dread of the process was quite unfounded, but also provided normative guidelines about what teeth broke through when which were bound to generate fears in mothers whose children were out of synchrony with the supposedly standard timetable. Equally, the emphasis on 'moral education from the cradle' meant mothers were now exhorted to be vigilant about policing bad habits in the tiniest children: a child who tried sucking its finger (the Russian equivalent of sucking its thumb) must have the offending digit painted with wormwood or kvas (a yeast compound) starter so that the child gave up the habit in disgust.[135]

The Limits of Enlightenment

There were still some barriers to the onslaught of 'modern' child-rearing practices, however. Large sectors of the population – especially in the countryside – were outside the reach of up-to-date advice on obstetrics and child-rearing. Manuals were of no use to the illiterate; pregnancy and child-care consultations had little impact outside the cities. At best, a peasant woman might get attention from an overworked zemstvo doctor or nurse. A priest who talked to E. A. Pokrovsky in the early 1880s remembered only one visit by a professional midwife to his village in twelve years.[136] Coverage was sparse in later years as well. The commitment of zemstvo physicians to dealing with medical emergencies – epidemics of infectious disease in particular – pushed obstetrics to the margins. 'The zemstvo cannot put the organisation of help with giving birth to the foreground, or spend significant sums on this; it must devote much more attention to such more serious scourges of health among the people, such as infectious diseases and syphilis,' declared K. G. Khrushchov, a doctor from Voronezh province, in 1900. He himself thought that normal births required little in the way of medical help, and that the main purpose of a doctor's involvement was to provide general health guidance and counteract the 'heap of daft superstitions and prejudices' that surrounded early infant care.[137]

Khrushchov's views attracted adverse comment from some of his colleagues, but he seems to have articulated a calculation that was being made silently in the province where he was working. According to figures that he cited himself, of the 146,000 births in Voronezh province in 1898, no more than 2,748, or 1.88 per cent, had medical personnel in attendance. This figure was below the average figure for zemstvo provinces, which then stood at 2–5 per cent.[138] To be sure, some expansion took place in the early twentieth century: by 1902, 4,069 births across the province were taking place with assistance.[139] Figures for births in the provincial zemstvo maternity facility in Voronezh town itself (not included in the cross-*guberniya* totals, which related to provision at district level) also went up: in 1897, 918 births took place here, and, in 1902, 1,346.[140] But out in the country medical attention was still very thinly spread. In Bogucharskii and Bobrovskii districts of Voronezh province, with populations, in 1908, of 360,000 and 271,000 respectively, figures for attended births remained in the low hundreds throughout the early 1900s, and had reached only 778 and 553 by 1910.[141]

Figures for some parts of Smolensk province were still smaller. The provincial centre, Smolensk itself, showed marked rises in hospitalised births during the late nineteenth and early twentieth centuries, from 58 per annum in 1880 to 1,017 in 1915.[142] But out in the country things were different. In Krasninsky district in 1905 – where the population stood at over 100,000, and where, going by 1900 figures, live births must have reached over 5,000 – just 105 women received medical attention when in labour.[143] And in the enormous Perm' province, with a population, in the late 1890s, of nearly 3 million, which a vast influx of settlers from elsewhere in Russia had raised to 3.7 million by 1911, a mere 7,054 births were attended in 1900.[144]

A significant proportion of attended births were cases where something had gone wrong. For instance, of the 419 births in Bogucharskii district in 1902, 61 were abnormal, and in a further 49 cases the 'birth' attended was in fact a spontaneous abortion.[145] Damage limitation, then, was a central object of medical treatment. Where dire need was the main criterion for intervention, back-up after the birth was thin to non-existent: doctors might complain about the evil influence of 'superstition' and 'prejudice', but they did not have the resources to run baby-management classes for new mothers. Midwives were equally overloaded; what is more, they sometimes – if reports by doctors are to be believed – had sloppy attitudes to hygiene, neglecting to wash their own hands before touching patients.[146] Their competence to advise patients about 'scientific baby care' was definitely in question. In any case, there was suspicion in country areas of outsiders who sought to direct behaviour, particularly if they were women.[147] Both obstetric provision and advice for young mothers, then, were patchy, reaching city populations – and then only selectively – rather than the rural majority.

'The Hands of the Anti-Christ'

Professional baby care as offered by institutions such as the crèche was by and large absent from the Russian environment before 1917. The first crèches in France went back to the 1840s, and a number had been founded in Germany in the 1850s. In Russia, on the other hand, development was belated and relatively slow. Once again, this was not a question of lack of goodwill: it was widely held that the expansion of the crèche network was essential, both to relieve women of burdens and to provide them with information about proper infant care.[148] But lack of state support, and reliance on private initiative, were impediments in this area, as in the development of the institutional infrastructure generally.

Certainly, by the late nineteenth century some of the larger factories offered facilities to women workers. At places like the Savva Morozov factory in Moscow and the St Petersburg rubber factory there were model nurseries, with doctors on duty, clean clothes provided for children on arrival, mugs of sterilised milk, and Froebel games.[149] A similar service was provided in the nurseries run by charitable institutions in the cities.[150] But the numbers of such nurseries were very small: at the start of the twentieth century, only about forty factories in Russia had facilities, while charitable foundations catered for a maximum of 900 children in the Russian capital.[151] Working-class women in towns were generally thrown on their own resources when it came to infant care. According to a survey of St Petersburg workers carried out in the 1910s, only 0.7 per cent of women entrusted their children to nurseries, with the remaining 99.03 per cent making *ad hoc* arrangements with relations and neighbours.[152]

Progress in villages – in terms of provision of seasonal facilities – was a little more rapid. Such nurseries cost significantly less to organise than urban facilities: N. A. Russkikh, writing in 1913, quoted figures of 4.3 kopecks per day in the country versus a minimum of 12.8 and a maximum of 40 kopecks a day in cities.[153] They were also widely recognised as an important instrument in the struggle with infant mortality: once mothers witnessed their children flourishing as a result of rational management, it was held, they would alter the way they looked after them at home.[154] However, state support in this area was non-existent, and facilities developed haphazardly. Typical was the situation in Bobrovskii district, Voronezh province, with an adult population of nearly 300,000 in the early 1900s, where even temporary crèches could be counted on the fingers of one hand. In 1900, there were two in the entire district; expansion over the next two years saw the number rise to five.[155] Perm' province – with a population of over 1.5 million – could boast eleven crèches in the 1900s, provision that commentators felt was comparatively generous.[156]

In some zemstvo provinces, though, the crèche network was more extensively developed. Samara province, for example, had 90 kindergartens by as early as 1899, while in Vologda province 174 were opened between 1902 and 1907.[157] Crucial here was the goodwill of the local zemstvo doctor, who might or might not feel that there was time and energy to spare for co-ordinating the organisation of a crèche and regulating its activities. In some places, doctors were too overloaded to contemplate helping out. As a report dating from 1908 lamented, 'With every passing year, fewer and fewer doctors are found who want to run [crèches].' The problem lay partly in the fact that the doctor might well have to travel a few versts to reach the site (which in rough conditions could take several hours for a return visit), and partly in the fact that the facilities were usually extremely simple, consisting of an infant dormitory and feeding facilities (a 'trough', in the disparaging Russian term), rather than the sort of life-changing 'pedagogical-medical' facility that might have carried prestige.[158]

Yet some doctors were still prepared to take this task on, especially where philanthropists could be found to help out with raising finances and with the organisational work.[159] Increasingly, organisations other than the zemstvo became involved in this area, in some cases to more marked effect. By 1912, 4,806 children, or more than a third of those in children's institutions under the Empress Maria Department, were infants and small children accommodated in village crèches.[160] In 1916, the Guardianship for the Protection of Mothers and Infants had over 25,000 children attending village crèches in its care.[161] Facilities in some localities expanded rapidly: in 1913, for instance, Cherdyn' district, in a relatively remote corner of Perm' province, had ten temporary harvest crèches.[162]

Even at its largest, the seasonal crèche network could make hardly any impact on the children of rural Russia in proportionate terms. And initial reactions to institutionalised child care were often hostile. As the philanthropist Anna Pomeryantseva noted, in some places crèche organisers were even suspected of witchcraft or Satanism, with mothers exclaiming indignantly, 'I'd rather the Lord took them himself than they fall straight into the hands of the Antichrist!'[163] According to a study carried out by the Guardianship for the Protection of Mothers and Infants, crèches appealed particularly to the socially marginal, above all poor mothers living in isolation from traditional families. Around a quarter of the mothers who took part in the survey cited 'poverty' as a reason for sending their children there, while nearly three-quarters mentioned the fact that there was no other care available to them.[164]

But attitudes could depend – just as the existence of crèches in the first place did – on purely local features. In Penza province, the take-up of infant care was particularly enthusiastic among the Tatar population (for the idiosyncratic reason that a local mullah was himself a strong supporter of the crèche).[165] In a Russian village where a well-liked priest or doctor was behind the scheme, acceptance would also have been assured. As Anna Pomeryantseva pointed out, it was also important for staff themselves to prepare the ground and to explain carefully what the crèche was going to do: a communicable or 'friendly' carer would certainly achieve good results.[166] Other commentators recorded that peasants' fears of putting their children in crèches were perfectly rational – they feared that they would be ill treated, or that swingeing charges would be exacted. Once these anxieties were alleviated, local opinion usually turned favourable.[167]

Reformers had high hopes of the civilising effects of the time children spent in organised care. According to Alina Gibsh, a doctor from Odessa, 'No matter how short a time children spend in a crèche, the principles instilled give a boost to their development and do not pass without trace for their future life.'[168] This claim is probably exaggerated, given the simplicity and hand-to-mouth character of crèche facilities, in villages particularly. Overstretched district doctors might – at best – drop in a couple of times a week to check that all was well, and the level of facilities offered varied considerably from place to place, depending on the generosity of the zemstvo and the enthusiasm of volunteers. Sometimes, beds, drinking and eating vessels, clean clothes and so on were provided for children directly; in other places, parents were expected to bring all these things along themselves. Whichever way, the crèche building was likely to be a rough log cabin at best, perhaps with an awning to throw a little shade in hot weather.[169]

But even if crèches were simply furnished, they might have a missionary function: in one facility in Kaluga province, the children were placed to sleep in baskets, but hygiene rules were strict: bottles used for feeding were sterilised, and needy mothers who were paid to act as wet-nurses were warned about the need to observe a strict diet. A woman who broke the rules about not feeding solid food was summarily expelled.[170] No doubt contact with this kind of regulation did provide a counterweight to traditional practices. And, by reducing the number of infants who had to be left completely by themselves when their mothers' labour was needed elsewhere, crèches made some contribution to reducing levels of infant mortality: among babies attending the crèches operating in Simbirsk province during the 1910s, for instance, the death rate stood at 11.4 per cent, rather than the general average of 42 per cent.[171]

In cities, too, crèches could have a beneficial impact. The meals that were doled out were of benefit to infants and children who might otherwise be getting a diet that was not simply 'incorrect', but deficient in vital nutrients. In 1896, for instance, children in the Children's Aid Society crèches and hostel were fed a rather stodgy diet, with no fresh fruit or vegetables, but with meat twice a day; the standard dishes were meatballs, kashas, soups, macaroni, liver, and *kisel'*.[172] Monotonous as it must have been, the diet was at least filling and protein-rich. So far as the few children who attended them were concerned, then, crèches probably had more positive than negative effects, at any rate on their physical health. Given that numbers were small, and care in the hands of enthusiasts, it is fair to assume also that the likelihood of psychological neglect and emotional damage was relatively small.

Protecting Mothers and Children

As with other areas of children's lives, 1917 marked a watershed in official policy on childbirth and infant care. Where the Tsarist administration had left the development of crèches and lying-in hospitals largely to voluntary effort, from February 1917 the evolution of these facilities became a state priority. The new Ministry of Public Welfare included a Mother and Child section, and the subject was extensively discussed at the All-Russian Conference on Child Welfare held from 10 to 14 August 1917. At the conference, P. Medovikov stressed the importance of setting up 'a network of exemplary institutions in major cities', while another speaker portrayed mother and child hostels as an effective and humane way of limiting the population consigned to institutional care, a social phenomenon that was now regarded as, at best, a necessary evil.[173] For her part, Z. O. Michnik highlighted the need for the kind of educational activity that her own clinic on Vasilievsky Island had been specialising in for several years, asserting that mother and child consultations and outreach through district nurses were a great deal more important than free milk distribution.[174]

Once the Bolshevik coup had taken place, mother and child work, like work in the area of total institutions for children, in many ways remained on the same track. Obstetrics, post-natal care, and day care were brought under state control, and granted state support and state funding. The institutional base for these areas – in keeping with the extant tradition of seeing infancy as above all the domain of hygienic expertise – was the People's Commissariat of Health, which presided over state crèches as well as over maternity hospitals, clinics, and consultancies. The emphasis on prophylactic work was unchanged: the early Soviet period saw the launch of an all-out, state-sponsored propaganda campaign, accompanied

68 Babies 'campaigning' for better treatment from their parents (fresh air, breast feeding, healthy parents, trained midwives, dry clean nappies etc.).

by posters, brochures, and direct agitation, to promote the medicalisation of childbirth and infant care. Women were exhorted to consult *akusherki* (trained midwives) rather than traditional midwives, to discard home-made dummies, and to feed by the breast and only by the breast.[175] Material of this kind was disseminated through the state mother and child consultancies, which were hung with posters and slogans, and where doctors adopted the same assertive tone as they had before 1917.[176]

The central problem in realising rationalistic ambitions was that the Soviet mother and infant care programme was starting, like the orphanage system, from a very low base. According to Soviet figures from 1937, there were no more than nine mother and child consultancies across the Russian Empire in 1914, offering no more than 1,395 places.[177] A specialist study of 1950 estimated the number of maternity beds in 1914 at 5,513, reduced by war and revolution to 4,696 in 1918.[178] An additional difficulty was the devolution of financial responsibility from central government to local administrations in 1922–3, which generated a fall in health commissariat beds by around two-thirds (from 8,315 to 2,750).[179] Typically, children's institutions of all kinds – crèches as well as consultancies – had to make good a considerable shortfall in funding. In Vyatka, for instance, they were allocated only 3 per cent of the health budget, which paid around 40 per cent of institutional costs.[180] But, as time went on, local administrations began to be more generous, and other divisions of the state system – the industrial sector, the trade unions – started to contribute a share of costs.[181] Overall figures for expansion were impressive. By 1925, 372 consultancies were in operation, and, by 1928, 2,148. By 1937, consultancy numbers had more than doubled, at 4,384, and by 1941 they had reached 5,803.[182] Maternity beds had risen to 23,433 in 1931, 33,387 by 1936, and 41,600 by 1937.[183]

An instructive case study of developments at a local level is Vasilievsky Island in St Petersburg, where the former 'shelter for mothers', integrated into the state system as Point No. 15 of the Mother and Child Care Department of Narkomzdrav, expanded its timetable (from 31 'receiving days' for the mother and infant clinic in 1917 to 248 in 1924), and catered for ever larger numbers of patients. The mother and infant clinic, for example, dealt with over 10,000 visits in 1924 (up from 74 in 1917), while the district nurses had more than 2,000 on the books in 1924, a huge increase from 70 in 1915. To be sure, the impressive overall figures here came at the price of strain within the system: if the average number of patients per district nurse in 1915 was 138, this average hovered around the 400–500 mark between 1916 and 1924. But the provision for patients was both more generous in terms of numbers accommodated and significantly more ambitious in range: sections added in the immediate post-revolutionary years included a legal advice centre, courses for paediatric nurses and for nursery nurses, a sexually transmitted diseases clinic, a 'quartz crystal centre' (providing a form of electric current therapy), a home for abandoned babies, and a laboratory.[184] In Leningrad, 90 per cent of nursing infants were on the books of a consultancy by as early as 1924.[185]

Expansion was, inevitably, less impressive in the countryside. Here, under-staffing and the lack of infrastructure were the rule. The number of consultancies did expand more than sixteen times in 1923–4 (from 4 to 69), but even the latter figure was, obviously, pathetically out of kilter with the size of the rural population.[186] During the 1920s, the primary mother and child care worker – where one existed – was a village nurse, who might take round 'portable exhibitions' to provide mothers with information about equipment and techniques, and distribute brochures, as well as visiting homes to spread the hygiene gospel.[187] As late as 1930, 90 per cent of peasant women still gave birth without the help of a trained midwife, a statistic attributable to the shortage of midwives as much as to the inclinations of peasant women themselves.[188] In 1936, less than half the existing mother and infant clinics were located in the countryside, catering for no more than an eighth of the total number of patients across the Russian Federation.[189] The 27 June 1936 decree on 'Motherhood and Infancy' promised not only to create 11,000 more maternity beds in general hospitals by 1939, but 14,400 more midwife posts in villages, with staff recruitment of 5,000. Some progress was made: between 1936 and 1938, according to official figures, the number of maternity facilities in villages almost doubled.[190] But expansion continued to fall short of what would have been required to medicalise child care effectively (if one believes official figures at their most optimistic, not more than a quarter of mothers can have come within the system).

Into the 1950s, official medical provision, at least in remoter parts of the countryside, remained desperately inadequate; in the countryside particularly, many women simply did not have recourse to ante-natal consultations or to post-natal clinics, and births continued to be attended by *babki*. 'Of course the *babka* helped with the baby', one woman from the eastern side of Tavda province recalled of her experiences in the late 1940s. A neighbour whose memories related to the early 1950s confirmed the information, and recalled that the standard ways of looking after children had been entirely traditional: either an old woman living locally had been got in to sit with them, or they had been taken out to the field and left lying there while their mothers got on with the work. Both these women also remembered that they had got no maternity leave when giving birth.[191] As these cases show, it was one thing to pass 'mother and child care' decrees – in the Labour Codex of 1929, Soviet women had been granted leave of eight weeks, to cover the period before and after birth, and the length of the post-natal period had been raised from 63 to 77 days in the Mother and Child Protection statute of 9 July 1944 – and quite another to get them enacted where local administrators were working without supervision.[192] Even where leave was offered, there were ways of cutting corners: a woman in Novgorod province who became pregnant in the early 1950s remembered that, when her medical certificate of pregnancy was stolen, she was treated as though she were not pregnant, and lost her leave allocation.[193]

Like Soviet rural hospitals generally, many maternity facilities were under-equipped, and their personnel often poorly trained, or at the very least callous and brusque. Dirt and mismanagement were pervasive. 'I gave birth but the afterbirth did not come out, and [the doctor] said, "I am not going to stay here sitting beside you," and she rode off,' one woman from a rural district recalled of her experience in 1941.[194] Given that traditional midwives generally had superior social skills, if not medical ones, it is little wonder that those peasant women who could still find a *babka* generally preferred to rely on her, even if an alternative was available – though in some regions traditional practitioners had been regulated out of existence by the end of the 1930s.[195] The work of such practitioners kept non-medical beliefs alive: in 1933, one wise woman told the family of a newborn girl that she would certainly die soon (the reason for this stark diagnosis was nothing more serious than an umbilical hernia).[196]

The transition to medicalisation was achieved more quickly in cities, which already had a much more extensive network of medical facilities before 1917. Among middle-class mothers at least, changes involved less medical intervention as such than a shift away from assisted home births and towards universal hospitalisation. During the First World War and the Revolution, admissions to maternity hospitals throughout Russia in general dropped by almost 50 per cent, but in major urban areas such as Petrograd the vast majority of pregnant women continued to be hospitalised for births, and medicalisation continued apace in the 1920s. By the end of the decade, 90 per cent of births in Moscow were in hospitals, and 100 per cent of births in some provincial towns.[197] Figures from 1940 indicate that Moscow had nearly 5,000 beds in specialist maternity hospitals alone, and that there were 256 centres offering pre-natal consultations.[198] As Elizabeth Waters has argued, attitudes changed not only because of improved access, but also because of living conditions. The overcrowded and unhygienic barracks and tenements that many working-class families inhabited were an uncongenial environment for the delivery of a baby, and women living in cities were less likely to have access to a female support network. In the circumstances, 'maternity shelters and homes provided an alternative that, if far from attractive, represented the lesser of two evils'.[199] On the whole, it seems to have been the better-off mothers who preferred to give birth at home. Inna Shikhaeva-Gaister, the daughter of a highly placed Party official, remembered that her mother had all her older children (born in the late 1920s and early 1930s) at home, though, when the last of them was due in 1936, 'Professor Arkhangel'sky had grown too old', so she reluctantly had to settle for a hospital birth.[200] Home births do not seem to have resurfaced, even among the most privileged, until the late Soviet period, when a woman might come to an extra-legal (*blatnoi*) agreement with a doctor to attend her at home.[201]

A woman enjoying this kind of social status probably had no cause for worry. The superlative (by Soviet standards) medical facilities enjoyed by the Kremlin elite included a specialised maternity unit, in operation since the early 1920s. A woman from the outer circle of the Party elite who gave birth there in 1962 remembered that it had 'the best equipment available, and the best doctors – the only shortage was of patients'.[202] While the last observation would not have been true during the first three decades of the clinic's existence, when the Party elite was less superannuated than in the post-Stalin era, the first two certainly were.[203]

Needless to say, the quality of maternity hospitals was not generally at the level enjoyed by this narrow metropolitan elite. But some model homes existed. One of these was the Krupskaya Maternity Hospital – known before the Revolution as the Abrikosova Lying-In Hospital from the name of the merchant benefactress whose donation had allowed it to be founded and already a flagship of Russian obstetric practice when it was set up.[204] Continuity of excellence was helped by the fact that obstetrics was an area – like other branches of medicine – where 'bourgeois specialists' were tolerated from the first.[205] As with other types of institutional care for children, professionalism and determination were sometimes able to triumph over dreadful material conditions. Anna Kuznetsova-Budanova, one of the specialists, recalled that no incubators were produced by Soviet factories until the 1930s, but a sense of solidarity helped the staff make do: an incubator was built by the in-house workman.[206]

'Keep Your Mouth Shut!'

However, not all medical personnel were so adept at dealing with difficult conditions. Well into the second half of the twentieth century, some maternity homes were in a positively dire condition. Official reports detailed horror stories of filth (faeces on lavatory walls, blood on the floor of delivery rooms), infections, and iatrogenic accidents such as the breaking of babies' bones during delivery by incompetent obstetricians and midwives.[207] Even in Leningrad, it was common for midwives to take the wrong course of action, or none, when confronted with complications such as breech births.[208] Personal reminiscences confirm the picture, recalling filth, neglect by staff, and appalling facilities for patients – beds crammed together in tiny rooms, no soap of any kind available.[209] Conditions were particularly bad during the war and the post-war years, when heating shortages threatened the lives of premature babies, staff and equipment were hard to find, and the baby boom of the day filled hospitals to overflowing.[210] But they were less than ideal at most times.

In the circumstances, it is scarcely surprising that the more delicate elements of patient care were almost always neglected. Women were usually left to struggle to hospital by themselves, which tended to increase the stress brought by the onset of labour. According to a typical story from Leningrad in the 1930s: 'Well, I got myself home, but there was no one around, and my waters had broken. What should I do? No idea. So I went and got a neighbour.'[211] Admission to a maternity hospital then had to be sought, which was not straightforward unless the woman had personal connections, or the money for a bribe, or both.[212] Officially, maternity hospitals were required to admit emergency cases – a situation that could provoke women who wanted the best available treatment to defer application to the last minute, then land on the doorstep of a prestigious maternity home.[213] In the case of the Leningrad woman just mentioned, though, the duty doctor in the first home that she applied to happened to be drunk, and refused admission; she eventually found a bed at the Snegiryov home, fortunately before the baby had arrived.[214]

The staff dealing with patients were not necessarily any more considerate. Pain and anxiety were shrugged off: there were no painkillers, but anyone who cried out was likely to be dubbed *prichitalka*, 'a wailer'. 'Much of the time, I was all alone in the delivery room,' one woman recalled of her delivery in June 1941.[215] Not only in the 1930s and 1940s, but throughout the second half of the twentieth century, women who encountered problems in delivery sometimes experienced a level of treatment that had improved little, if at all, since the early 1900s. Even if the diagnosis of a problem was accurate (by no means a certainty), correct treatment might not be forthcoming, and humane relations were decidedly the exception rather than the rule.[216] Some staff were disengaged, others brusque, and some actually sadistic, as an interviewing project conducted in the 1990s made vividly clear:

'[They said]: "It doesn't hurt when you're screwing your husband, does it, but now you're having a baby and you say it hurts!" They yelled things like, "Keep your mouth shut, no messing, no fussing!" All in all, they treated us quite badly.'
(Woman b. 1966, gave birth Moscow 1985 and 1995).

'And the midwife said: "You're a bad mother – you've gone and suffocated your baby!" Of course, it made the most nightmarish impression on me. I felt like a real criminal.'
(Woman b. 1936, gave birth 1963, 1968).[217]

The informants in the project had had children over a wide time range (1946–94). The consistency of experience through almost half a century is striking, and is borne out by other oral history. Even in major cities such as Leningrad, it was rare for delivering mothers to be given painkillers.[218] Infants would be removed as soon as they arrived, and would then spend up to a day and a half in separate premises, sometimes next to the ward, so that their cries were clearly audible to the mothers. Babies might well end up being released from hospital, after about a week usually, with a lower weight than their birthweight.[219] Conditions got still worse in the late 1980s and early 1990s, because maternity home capacity had not kept pace with rising populations in urban areas, and because the shift to individual budgeting had worsened shortages of equipment.[220] But the brusqueness and apparent lack of concern among staff were jarring factors long before this. 'Nobody treats you kindly: the conditions are too tough,' a woman who gave birth in Odessa in the 1970s recalled, while also emphasising her gratitude to the doctors: 'They saved [my daughter's] life, and they saved mine.'[221] Freda Utley, who gave birth in the mid-1930s, recalled a similarly alienating experience. She lay in labour for around 36 hours, till, after a change of shift, the incoming doctor decided that there was a risk of foetal heart failure if birth were not induced. She was then given an injection, and an ordeal followed:

> He and another doctor threw themselves upon my chest and abdomen. Meanwhile a third doctor cut me a little, and at last my son was born.
>
> I lay and watched my screaming baby being cleaned and dressed, and then a ticket with his number was tied around my wrist.

It took another six hours for Utley to be stitched up, though in this high-prestige maternity hospital she spent them in a clean, quiet ward with only eight other people, and with a bed to herself.[222]

Rough treatment did not stop at upbraiding women in the delivery room, where there was perhaps a mistaken belief that 'one pain drives out another', in other words that women who were yelled at would find it easier to cope with the contractions. It extended to the general treatment of mothers on the ward. Admission involved not only the shaving of pubes, strip-wash, and forcible enema also customary in many Western hospitals until the late twentieth century, but also the removal of all personal items, ostensibly on the grounds that they might pose a hygiene risk.[223] This process has been explained by an ethnologist as ritual humiliation and 'profanation of the sacred', marking off the birth as a unique cultural event.[224] Given, though, that patients in many other kinds of Soviet hospital were often treated in a similarly inconsiderate way, it perhaps also stemmed from the disempowerment of laypeople within a medical system where 'abjection displacement' – the callous treatment of patients by professionals who themselves felt undervalued and over-stressed – was endemic.

A bad maternity hospital bore more resemblance to a barracks than to a clinic. Those not wearing hospital clothing would be yelled at, and anyone under suspicion of being a single mother would be treated with outright contempt. What was more, though the staff might throw their weight around when it came to making patients miserable, they sometimes failed to offer basic advice: women might not be shown how to quiet their babies, how to put on a nappy, or even how to breast-feed.[225] Of course, some mothers in well-run clinics were treated with far more consideration.[226] But the practice of separating mother and newborn was universal.[227] Mothers accepted this as routine, superficially at least, but the frequent rumours that there might be mix-ups in children's identity are probably testimony to a degree of subconscious anxiety and distress.[228]

One of the problems of expanding medical care was that it elided aspects of childbirth (for instance psychological and emotional issues) that could not be adequately addressed by the medical orthodoxies of the day.[229] The pioneering Soviet obstetricians of the 1920s and early 1930, like their counterparts in Western Europe and America, did their utmost to underline the separateness of the medical world from everyday life through the creation of an aseptic environment and the imposition of strict rules, including an absolute ban on visitors.[230] This tradition continued into the late Soviet era. Where the most 'advanced' British and American hospitals had, by the late 1950s, started admitting fathers and other relations to an area inside the hospital where babies might be inspected through glass, and a decade or so later were allowing visitors as far as the mother's bed, into the 1990s, Russians who wanted to catch a glimpse of a new baby still had to gather in the courtyard below a maternity home and wait for the mother to sneak her offspring to the windows. However, the most alienating experience was often the sheer filth of the facilities. In the words of a woman who gave birth in 1980: 'The conditions were dreadful. It was dirty, in the toilet, for instance, there was a queue, dirt, cockroaches crawling everywhere. I'm not exaggerating. And I even ... I [thought], I'm not going there again [...] I'm not ever giving birth again.'[231]

Hospital experience varied, depending not just on the quality of care (which could at its best be high), but also on levels of expectation. Some women whose birth experiences took place in 'average' homes were grateful for the care they received and felt that the doctors, nurses, and midwives were doing their best in trying circumstances.[232] As always, the personal factor was important – one woman whose first birth had been agony (no pain relief, extensive tearing to her vagina) had a transformed experience the second time, thanks to a kind and competent anaesthetist.[233] Increased hospitalisation, along with the provision of ante-natal advice and consultations to pregnant women, and the institution of statutory entitlement to maternity leave, did ensure a certain *minimum* standard of medical aid to large numbers of Soviet women. This was reflected in levels of maternal mortality. Statistics relating to this area were not kept systematically, but the limited information suggests that they fell noticeably over the course of the 1920s, before rising in the war years, but dropping again by the late 1940s.[234] Perinatal death also seems to have improved. In late 1940s Leningrad, the figure for maternity hospitals stood at around 2 per cent.[235] Figures for 1951 are similar.[236] Figures from the early 1960s indicate that such deaths had reached under 1 per cent across the USSR as a whole, with higher than average rates recorded only in non-Russian parts of the Union (Armenia, Azerbaijan, Turkmenistan).[237]

Levels of mortality among the under-ones also declined over the century. By 1926 they had already dropped by a third, compared with 1905 – moving Russia, in terms of European parallels, from the sixteenth century into the twentieth (the rate for the Soviet Union as a whole, at around 16 per cent, was close to that for France in the 1910s). The death rate improved still more noticeably in some of the bigger cities: in Moscow it halved between 1911 and 1925.[238] As with other areas of child health, forced industrialisation and collectivisation saw some reversal of these gains: figures for the small town of Serpukhovo, near Moscow, for example, saw the average rise from 12.7 in 1928 to 13.0 in 1929, with figures for individual factories rising as high as 16.5 in 1927–30, as opposed to a high of 9.8 in 1925–6. However, by the 1930–2 period, levels in some places were back down to the 6.7–8.7 range.[239] Inevitably, another 'demographic trough' was entered during the war, when babies and small children were one of the most vulnerable categories of the population. Post-war famine also hit hard. Available figures suggest that in 1946 deaths among the under-ones stood at 44 per cent higher than in 1945, and in 1947 they had risen again by 70–80 per cent in some areas, such as the Krasnodar region and the Bashkir Republic.[240] From 1948, however, the numbers began to decline again. By 1957, the overall rate for the RSFSR had fallen to 4.5 per cent, by 1960, to 3.5 per cent, and by 1962, to 3.3 per cent. Certainly, there were still discrepancies according to location. Moscow led the way in this period as well: deaths here were already down to around 2.5 per cent by 1957.[241] There were other areas of the Russian Federation – the rural hinterlands above all – where things did not look so rosy. But even here the death rate improved significantly in the early 1960s, and improvements continued into the 1970s. In 1970, the rate reached 2.6 per cent, and in 1985, 2.1 per cent.[242]

All the same, the suffering of the remaining mothers who lost children should not be underestimated.[243] Mortality rates remained worse than in some other parts of the industrialised world, as was clear even from certain official figures.[244] High rates of trauma-induced deaths among infants in 1951 indicate that there was a significant proportion of cases where mortality could have been avoided.[245]

What was more, there were also increasing pressures against improvement. Rising rates of alcohol consumption among women of child-bearing age were reflected by increases in the rate of defective births.[246] By the late 1980s, it was starting to be admitted that the state of things in the Soviet Union was far from encouraging. A report of 1989 pointed out that the mortality rate of 2.5–2.6 per cent among under-ones was actually around 500 times higher than the rate in Japan.[247] Yet, seen in its own terms (as an index of improvement in a large, regionally diverse, economically challenged, nation-state, rather than by comparison with a small, prosperous, and relatively culturally homogeneous one), the late Soviet infant mortality rate represented at least a reasonable achievement.

Looking after Infants

The improvement in survival rates under the age of 12 months reflects the fact that post-natal care was also undergoing a process of medicalisation. Overall figures for clinics, according to a Soviet history of the mother and child care movement, stood at 2,148 in 1928, 3,265 in 1932, 4,384 in 1937, and 5,803 in 1941.[248] In bigger cities, the numbers of such clinics grew particularly fast: in Moscow, for example, the number of women taking their children to clinics increased almost ten times between 1920 and 1927, by which date over 80 per cent of mothers were attending.[249] Administered by the Motherhood and Infancy Protection Department, set up as part of the Commissariat for Social Welfare in 1918, but transferred to the Commissariat of Health in 1920, the clinics offered a range of services to mothers, including, from 1938, the provision of legal advice and practical support to do with issues of living space.[250] But their main purpose was to act as 'schools for mothers', in the slogan of the day, providing both 'in-house training' through inspections by doctors and nurses, and 'guided homework' in the form of visits by district nurses three or four times during the first month, and at monthly intervals later on.[251] They were at the centre of a network of institutional resources aimed at transforming women's behaviour and drawing on both propaganda (in the form of brochures, of which millions were being printed by the end of the 1920s) and agitation (didactic dramas, outreach lectures, magic lantern shows, seminars).[252] They disseminated a model of 'modern motherhood' which was consciously intended to imitate Western teachings about hygienic care, and which had a closely similar content (it also perpetuated the ideals set out in Russian infant-care literature before 1917, but this point was not highlighted in Soviet propaganda).

According to the standard advice, a child was to have a 'sunny, dry and warm room' to sleep in, without soft furnishings, rugs, or hangings, and was to be provided with its own bed, lying on a horsehair or straw mattress. If a dedicated nursery was not available (a situation whose likelihood even the authors of advice literature, a uniformly utopian genre, could not ignore completely), the child should at the very least be in its own special corner, the *detskii ugolok*. 'A child is allocated the most light-filled, warmest, and driest corner of the room,' pronounced a manual of 1937.[253] Bathing was to take place daily in clean water, and boiled water was to be used for some purposes, for instance bathing a girl's genitals.[254] Other essentials included fresh air (with cot clothes kept to a minimum so that air could circulate, and the child taken outside for up to four hours a day).[255] Toys must be made of hygienic materials, such as rubber, and everything around the child must be kept spotlessly clean.[256] The propaganda explicitly sought to assault and undermine traditional practices, which were condemned as 'superstitious' and 'backward'. 'The infant is bundled up tightly and put in a hanging cradle covered with a filthy, dusty cloth, hung high up in some dark corner. The infant never sees light or sun; he finds it hard to breathe under his heavy cloth. Flies torment him, and sometimes bed-bugs and fleas as well,' claimed a manual of 1928. In such circumstances it was inevitable that babies, recently arrived from warmth and freedom in the womb, should be forever crying.[257]

69   Mothers, Don't Kiss Your Babies on the Lips and Don't Let Anyone Else Kiss Them!
Poster, early 1920s.

The posters hung in clinics and nurseries, the pamphlets handed out to mothers there, and baby-care books all emphasised not just hygiene, but system. It was vital to maintain a strict regime from the first. Feeding, for example, was supposed to happen at regular intervals: according to one source, every three to three and a half hours, but never at night.[258] Not only was sleeping and eating organised according to a regular pattern, but the child was supposed to be encouraged into orderly habits with a moral resonance as early as possible. This included coaxing it into sitting up as early as this was feasible, and – once solid food had been introduced – encouraging it to be as tidy as possible during feeds.[259] Soviet baby books often systematised this preparation of the child for a life of discipline and self-restraint according to the collection of techniques and procedures known as 'tempering' (*zakalivanie*), which involved bathing with cold water and exposure to fresh air – including cold air. Speransky's *The Care of the Young Child* (1929), for instance, advised that this process could hardly start too early.[260]

'Tempering' was not unique to the Soviet Union: it was paralleled in the contemporary German cult of *Abhärtung*, 'hardening', which also involved building up physical endurance as a way of 'educating the will'.[261] A still more rigid sense of 'regime' was propounded by the leading Anglophone guru of the 1920s, Truby King, whose books suggested a positively hair-raising degree of regimentation. King, a New Zealand medical practitioner, had derived his ideas about child care from a successful time spent as an intensive stock-breeder. This left him with not only a pioneering formula for artificial infant feeding, but also with dogmatic ideas about the importance of strict regime and absence of fuss. As his daughter proclaimed in 1934, 'A Truby King baby has as much fresh air and sunlight as possible, and his right amount of sleep. His education begins right from the very first week, good habits being established which remain throughout his life. [...] Not treated as a plaything [...] he is the happiest thing alive.'[262] What this euphemistic description concealed was extreme rigidity in treatment of infants, who were supposed to be given no more than five feeds over 24 hours, spaced at regular intervals during the day (night feeding was considered improper). Apart from over-feeding or irregular feeding, prohibitions included rocking baby to sleep, placing it in the parental bed, letting it have a dummy or suck its thumb, and failing to ensure that it defecated regularly first thing in the morning. Truby King's books contained photographs showing the super-babies that could be produced by his patent methods: two squat toddlers in summer dresses, for example, were captioned 'Healthy, happy little girls, ages two and nearly four years old. Good jaws and sound teeth. Nursed four-hourly from birth – never more than five times in twenty-four hours; plenty of fresh air and exercise – never any coddling.'[263] In France, Britain, Germany, and America, professionals sought to contest the dominance of parents: in the words of Maurice Crubellier, 'The well-being of the child underpinned the power of those in the know – physicians, psychologists, and pedagogues – *over those who were ignorant*.'[264] Even a book explicitly aimed at 'a thoroughly literate reader', Speransky's *Infant and Baby Care*, was careful to warn mothers that their judgement was fallible.

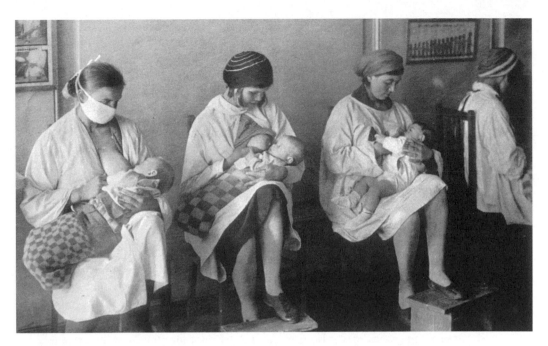

70   Hygienic breast feeding, *c.* 1930.

'Often a mother thinks that her baby is perfectly healthy, but the experienced gaze of the doctor notices deviations from the correct path of development.'[265] As in the West, clinics operated incentive schemes, rewarding 'model' mothers, and there was a medically sanctioned version of the 'beautiful baby' contest, with prizes offered to the 'healthiest baby'.[266]

Given the high degree of resemblance between the Soviet campaign to 'modernise' motherhood and those in other countries, it is interesting to note a couple of slightly eccentric features in Soviet baby-rearing propaganda. One relates to the question of how best to feed infants. Exhortation to mothers to breast-feed was ubiquitous throughout the early 1920s, and continued in the late 1920s, and indeed through the entire Soviet period, even when puritanism about discussing 'physiology' had set in. *Mother and Child*, a manual published in 1925, devoted almost a quarter of its space to breast-feeding, optimistically insisting that it was one area of child care that even new mothers would have no problems with, 'because nature herself takes good care of the process'. As well as gaining immunity to disease, breast-fed children did not suffer problems with vomiting or diarrhoea, and the only reason for removing a child from the breast was if the mother had TB. Artificial feeding was tolerable only if the mother was dead, and then only if proper human milk was unavailable.[267] In the words of Speransky, writing in 1929: 'The departure from the path of nature is immediately evident in the form of a whole range of illnesses, digestive problems, etc.'[268] Mothers were advised to continue breast-feeding to quite a late age: up to 18 months, at least to the level of two feeds a day.[269]

To be sure, there were hints of hostility to breast-feeding in Makarenko, who chose a scene of a woman encouraging her capricious child to drink a mug of milk to illustrate an argument that natural motherhood was intrinsically egotistical: 'Where life is directed by instinct, a mother's only aim in life is to feed her child.'[270] Proper human motherhood, on the other hand, ought to be concerned with spiritual values, such as order and discipline. But the fact that Makarenko used a child past breast-feeding age, and a portion of cow's milk, to illustrate his point softened the impact of his assault on 'natural' motherhood: the faint hint that breast-feeding might be a still more disgusting manifestation of instinctive behaviour was not articulated into a specific message. 'Breast is best' was the general message among Western experts too: in the words of Truby King, 'It is desirable to state emphatically that no system of bottle-feeding can ever give to either mother or child the advantages which both derive from suckling.' But *Feeding and Care of Baby* contained a substantial section on artificial feeding: King was prepared to tolerate the practice if the mother was in poor health or unable to produce sufficient quantities of milk. And at least some early twentieth-century Western baby books represented artificial feeding as more hygienic and more 'modern'. In Jules Sevrette's *La Jeune ménagère*, for instance (reprinted repeatedly between 1904 and 1925), Louise the model mother does not breast-feed, but Madame Perrin, wife of a drunken workman, does.[271]

By contrast, in Soviet hospitals even mothers who were in poor physical condition after delivery were expected to breast-feed their infants. One woman who contracted puerperal fever and lay at death's door for days after the birth was expected to nurse every three hours 'when I was at least semi-conscious'.[272] The causes of this overriding commitment to nursing were practical as well as ideological: the production of effective breast milk substitutes was expensive, compared with reliance on the natural product. Given the problems of production that beset every area of the Soviet food industry from the state's first years until its collapse in 1991, providing sufficient quantities of dried milk substitute for significant proportions of the population would have been problematic; production started on a small scale only in the mid-1950s.[273] Milk was not routinely pasteurised in the Soviet Union until the late 1980s, even in cities, so the anxieties of advice literature authors about the hygienic risks of cows' milk seem well founded.[274] So human milk continued to be preferred, including as a way of feeding orphaned babies, or babies whose mothers were unable to nourish them properly because of illness. These children were catered for officially in centres where women deposited surplus breast-milk, which operated from the 1920s. A Western visitor who observed these centres in operation in 1930 recorded that milk was not given away, but sold, though on a strictly non-profit basis: a mother would be paid 40 kopecks per litre of milk, and those purchasing milk – which was allowed on production of a doctor's certificate only – were asked to pay 50 kopecks. This observer also noted that the sale of milk could constitute an important supplement to the household budget for working-class women whose milk yield was high.[275] This marketing of breast-milk – on however controlled a basis – was an intriguingly aberrant phenomenon in a country where 'voluntary' (in actual

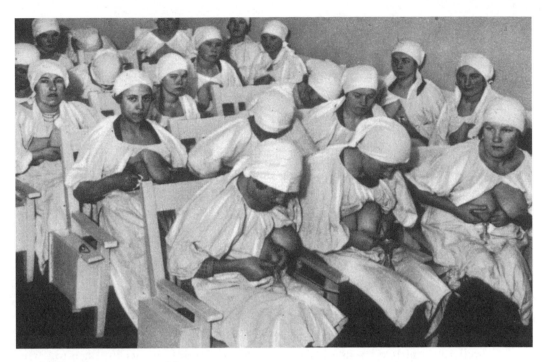

71   Milk expressing station, Moscow, *c.* 1930.

fact unpaid, but compulsory) social participation was the characteristic method of meeting shortfalls in state provision. It essentially represented the nationalisation of the wet-nurse system, tolerable to Soviet sensibilities, one may assume, both because it was strictly regulated from a hygienic point of view, and because the state acted as mediator between providers and consumers, thus dissolving the link between wet-nursing and domestic service that had traditionally existed.[276]

At the same time, resorting to wet-nurses on a private basis did not suddenly end in 1917. Some mothers from the cultural elite still attempted to make such arrangements, at least in the first years after the Revolution, though it had now become much more difficult to find suppliers.[277] But on the whole the commoner pattern, even in this social group, was breast-feeding by the mother herself.[278] As opposed to the post-1936 campaign stigmatising abortion as 'unnatural', breast-feeding was a case where official strictures and popular opinion were largely in harmony. The prohibition of abortion was covertly ignored by many Soviet women: even in villages, where large families had traditionally been seen as a blessing, economic deprivation drove many to terminate their pregnancies, often by hazardous and unhygienic methods born of desperation, such as the use of syringes full of boiling water.[279] Breast-feeding, on the other hand, was uniformly seen as 'better' and 'more natural'. Despite this, women from the peasantry, and indeed working class, continued to believe that breast-milk needed supplementation by solid food. While Soviet baby experts disapproved of dummy use just as fiercely as their pre-revolutionary counterparts, the *soska* continued in use well into the 1940s.[280] And when a child did need artificial feeding, traditional methods might be used, such as a cow's teat attached to the end of a cow's horn that had been filled with milk.[281]

Swaddling was a case where expert opinion in Russia diverged more sharply from views in the West. To be sure, reservations were expressed about tight swaddling.[282] But if baby books advised against the traditional *svival'nik* (swaddling cloths), they often also advised mothers to wrap the baby 'quite tightly' – advice that continued in force well into the 1950s.[283] It was the practice in government crèches to wrap babies up in closely folded blankets. Staff questioned by Western visitors denied that this was in fact 'swaddling'; indeed, the term used in normative guides was not *svivanie* (swaddling), but *pelenanie* (wrapping).[284] However, in practice the effects on the child were comparable. And swaddling of the traditional kind continued in some working-class families until the end of the 1930s.[285]

In rural areas and small towns, it was not until the 1960s that there was any kind of a move away from swaddling, a change that occurred as a result of widening access to medical care and to shop-bought baby goods. Certainly, during the 1940s and 1950s, babies were usually wrapped in a way that allowed them greater freedom of movement.[286] But some mothers remained conservative well into the late twentieth century: two of our informants in Taganrog who had their children in the 1990s stated that they had 'wrapped tightly', and one even produced her own version of the traditional rationalisation of this practice: 'I wrapped him in nappies for six months, when all the children his age were being dressed in rompers and so on, I was sure you should do it so his legs would be straight, not crooked.'[287] Use of the chaw (bread dummy) was frowned on, though still found in some places;[288] swaddling or tight wrapping, on the other hand, had some medical sanction.

Conformity, or otherwise, to the hygiene ethos more broadly was heavily dependent on social status, which in its turn was linked with educational opportunity. Educated mothers were likely to be more susceptible to pressures on the part of baby-care professionals, since there was a much greater likelihood they would be familiar with these in the first place. One author of a 'mother's diary' in 1918–21 was so deferential to the authority of child-care books that she was in a constant state of anxiety about whether or not her child conformed to the supposed norm. Measuring him at the age of a year and a day, she discovered that he was 2 centimetres longer than one authority had laid down a child should be, but 4 centimetres shorter than another authority had dictated was appropriate. Rather than draw the conclusion that the child fell comfortably into the 'average' range, she began to worry that he might be defective.[289] A decade or so later, another mother from the 'anxious child-care professional' class subjected her baby to 'tempering' (i.e. hot and cold 'hardening' exercises) from the age of two weeks – with the unfortunate result that he went down with sunstroke after being exposed to too much light and fresh air on her windowsill.[290]

But mothers of this over-conscientious kind constituted a highly specific and small group. It is questionable how much most women even knew about hygienic stipulations of this kind, given that the district nurse system and the tutorials for mothers did not achieve anything like universal coverage. And advice was not always adopted wholesale. A clinic operating in Leningrad in the early 1920s claimed very high absorption rates for the infant-care techniques that it propounded, with the vast majority of mothers trusting health-care professionals and prepared to absorb what they were told by them.[291] But this may have been partly because women quickly learned what to do and say when in the presence of a health-care professional. Oral history gives a rather different picture, particularly in the case of Russian villages, where traditional and modern practices were intertwined and where the authority of the doctor was challenged by that of older women living locally.[292]

Another important barrier to implementing 'modern' recommendations was formed by the circumstances in which families lived. Surveys of the early 1920s revealed a strong link between literacy levels and quality of care, but a still stronger one between socio-economic status and quality of care.[293] Obviously, children could not be found a sunny, dry, and warm room if all the family had was a dank room facing into an internal courtyard, and mothers in the poorest families were likely to play a larger role in supporting the family budget by work, and hence to have less time and energy to attend to the needs of a small baby. Washing babies punctiliously and drying nappies was difficult enough in communal flats, where the sink would be under pressure for different uses, and where neighbours might object when they saw lines of washing in a public space. But such problems multiplied in a barracks or hostel, where one kitchen was shared between twenty to sixty families, rather than three or four, or even ten, as in most communal flats. Crucial, too, was access to running water, which was far from universal even in cities before the 1960s.

In the countryside, bathing continued to be done only once a week (twice for infants), hanging cradles were still in use, and the laundering of baby clothes was infrequent.[294] There was simply no access to cots, prams, factory-made nappies, and so on. In cities, the new-building drives of the late 1920s and 1930s provided some parents with better conditions in which to raise children, but washing and laundering remained problematic for those in communal flats. Acquiring consumer goods was possible, but far from easy. Vasily Pochitalov's painting *Motherhood* (1939), which shows a child sleeping in a 'four-poster' cot with gauze curtains, implies the day-dream status of such appointments by placing alongside the image a richly decorated New Year tree, and, to the right of the cot, an elegantly dressed, glamorous young mother stitching sweetly at an item from the child's layette. If this is the world of 'happy childhood' imagined in official propaganda, Lev Zevin's painting *Bathing Their Son* (1938) is considerably more plausible. Here, mother and grandmother bathe a baby in a tin washtub placed on top of a small table. Though the painting gives a sense of fairly generous space, by Soviet standards, it is clear that the child is being looked after in a room for general family use, and not one piece of special equipment is in sight (even the towel is adult-sized).[295] Memoirs confirm that at this stage the baby's 'cradle' might well be just a box or conveniently sized trunk.[296] The 'children's corner', if it existed, was mostly just a tiny cupboard-like space behind a curtain or a plywood partition.

That said, early Soviet propaganda saw restraint in consumption as inevitable and laudable: this was *willed* poverty, associated with an ethos of self-control and self-denial. And, just as in the West, the ethos of physical hygiene spilled over into the 'hygiene of emotions'. Excessive pampering was considered harmful. There was to be no rocking, and mothers were strongly discouraged from kissing their children.[297] Remembering infant care in the late 1930s, one woman recalled that the district nurse 'told me never to pick the baby up when she cried, once I had determined that she was dry and nothing was hurting her. Otherwise, she said, I'd become a slave to her.'[298] Breast-feeding was to be carried out according to a strict regime: smaller infants were to be given the breast at 6, 10, 1.30, 5.30, and 8, and older ones could be limited to fewer feeds than that.[299] Time-keeping was not so much a question of rationalising parents' lives as of starting to train children in the punctuality and discipline requisite to their role as responsible future members of society. In the words of Georgy Speransky, 'Character education [*vospitanie*] should begin from the first days of a child's life.'[300]

Naming the Newborn

Another aspect of rational child-rearing was that it was supposed to be atheistic. The early Soviet era saw an intense campaign against christening and other forms of religious naming ceremony, and against religious upbringing more generally. This was not purely negative: from the early 1920s, Komsomol and Pioneer groups organised an alternative ceremony, the *oktyabriny*, or 'October baby naming' or 'Red christening'. At one such ceremony in 1925, for example, children were given the suitably revolutionary names Vladimir (after Lenin), Kim (from the initials of the Communist Youth Organisation), and Metallina.[301] Apart from the naming ceremony itself, 'October baby namings' were likely to include the presentation of linen and clothes for the new baby (functional stockings and rompers, rather than a lace robe), the pinning of a red star on its outer garment as a token of its 'induction into the Octobrist organisation', and a speech on some suitable topic such as 'the new forms of domestic life'.[302]

In the mid-1930s, the symbolism of these ceremonies modulated in line with the de-activisation of childhood experience generally. A painting by Aleksandr Bubnov, *Naming the Newborn* (1936), suggests that the infants are being received into 'happy childhood', rather than signed up to the Octobrists: the most noticeable members of the congregation are themselves children, some dressed in frills and ribbons, and a beaming small girl turns towards the viewer, inviting him or her to partake directly in the ceremony.[303]

How many such celebrations actually took place is not clear: the infrequent reporting of them in the Pioneer press, even during the 1920s, would suggest they were rare. The standard way of naming children was for some relative to go along to the local registry office (ZAGS) and have the birth recorded, with the intricacies of the ceremony limited to the fact that the recording relation might hit on some

72   Red Christening, 1920s.

name that was not the parental choice, or that the official might refuse to register a name that he or she considered bizarre.[304] But if the propaganda campaign against christening did not necessarily work well in a positive sense, official disapproval of religious ceremonies, added to the increasing difficulty of gaining access to a priest who could perform them, as churches closed and clerics were driven into exile, does seem to have had an effect. In her 1928 study of Moscow working-class families, Kabo suggested that the numbers having their child baptised had already dropped by nearly a third since 1917.[305] As churches closed in the countryside in the late 1920s, it became harder for parents to arrange baptisms: in some places, a layperson would be brought in to perform the ceremony, while in others children might be christened months or years after they were born.[306]

By the 1930s it was older generations as much as parents that kept the tradition going, as was indicated by a 14 February 1935 ruling that it was a crime to christen children against the wishes of their parents, even if 'other relatives' wanted the rite to take place.[307] The sole reminder of the ceremony was now often secular: parents who did not have their children christened might still select a 'godmother and godfather' for the child, though not necessarily on the basis of religious principles (the custom was to choose a man and woman who were close friends and had acted as witnesses at the wedding, whatever religion they did or did not belong to).[308]

The loosening of ties with the Church also loosened customary practices in relation to given names. As Zoshchenko's comic story 'Roza-Mariya' suggests, with its priest who refuses to name a baby by the 'Jewish' name of Roza, clerics might still impose the authority of the calendar of saints upon their congregations.[309] But, increasingly, they were not consulted. In the 1920s, a village school-teacher who called his son Leonard (after Leonardo da Vinci) was something of a prodigy. But distaste for 'backward' names such as Savva or Kuz'ma (for boys) or Avdot'ya and Paraskeva (for girls) began to spread during the next decade, as parents educated in the Soviet system made choices for their own children; by the 1940s, Irinas and Ol'gas were probably as common in the countryside as they were in cities.[310] In fact, the middle of the twentieth century saw a good deal of standardisation of naming patterns: the most popular names among all social groups were Aleksandr, Vladimir, and Sergei for boys, and Irina, Nataliya, Tatiana, and Ol'ga for girls. This began to be disrupted only in the post-Stalin era, which witnessed, for instance, a fashion for 'Old Russian' names such as Yaroslav, and a mild revival, among city-dwelling intellectuals, of such 'old-fashioned' favourites as Mariya, Sof'ya, Stepan, or Semen. In any case, children would rarely be named because their birth fell near a saint's day.[311] What relatives were called still had weight, but, as relatives themselves went by more standard names, so the pool of names dwindled further.[312]

The same process of 'Sovietisation' took place among members of minority faiths as well. By the 1930s it was extremely unusual for Russian Jews to be given religious names, with the preferences of some parents inclining more to sobriquets with a political resonance ('Arlen' from 'Armiya Lenina', for example). There was also the possibility of compromise – such as calling a girl Maiya, which was understood, in the Soviet context, to refer to the First of May holiday, but could

Уголок ребенка.

73 Design for a child's corner in the peasant hut, Z. Michnik, *The Child's Corner in the Peasant Hut* (1928).

obviously have a secret meaning for the parents who chose it. Another direction was the choice of Russianised forms of Western European names – Nelli, Robert – or of established Russian names that were derived from Greek ones: Arkady, Anatoly. But, in the long run, most Russian-Jewish parents tended to prefer invisibility, selecting widely used first names such as Nataliya or Irina for girls, and Vladimir, Aleksandr, or Andrei for boys. Such names were not only more 'normal' but easier to pronounce than, say, Khanna or Moishe.[313] This tendency was reinforced by the 'anti-cosmopolitan' campaigns of the late 1940s, during which some Soviet Jews renamed themselves and Russianised their surnames – Kuznetsov from Goldschmied, Kruzhkov from Kreisler, Olenin from Hirsch – or opted for the camouflage of a widespread surname such as Ivanov or Nikolaev.

Partial Russification also happened, though more slowly, among Tatars. In villages at least, religious naming ceremonies and circumcisions remained fairly widespread until the 1950s, but began to vanish rapidly at that point.[314] In cities, practices of this kind died out well before the Second World War. Here, too, the decline of religious practice went with marked shifts in naming patterns. After a brief heyday for Soviet names (of the 'Arlen', etc., type) in the 1920s, the most characteristic pattern, among socially ambitious parents, was the selection of a 'Western' name: Al'fred, Emiliya, or, in the case of one of the most famous Soviet Tatars, Rudol'f Nureyev. Some such names had mythological, historical, or literary associations: Mars or Marat, for instance. It was not until the 1970s and 1980s that there was a revival of traditional-style Turkic names. The main persistence of tradition lay in the preference for variety, with invented names (Al'fiya, for instance) widely used alongside exotic ones, and a relatively low incidence of 'mainstream' Russian names.[315] At the same time, children whose parents had made 'unpronounceable' or offbeat choices were likely to find themselves assigned standard diminutives at school, so that Al'fiya might become Alya, or Khalida, Lida.[316]

Negotiating Change

As material conditions improved further during the post-war decades, there was more chance that popular and official ideas about child care would converge. The modern *izbas* constructed from the 1940s onwards were easier to keep clean than old ones, even if there was still no piped water or drainage in most of them; as piped water and gas networks spread in Russian cities, mothers had more chance of complying with medical advice. Improvement in the social infrastructure also made its mark. By the late 1950s, around 97–8 per cent of mothers in major cities were being visited by a nurse in at least the first month of the baby's life, making pedagogical input almost universal. The main category of mothers excluded from the catchment was those living illegally, without residence permits, in a given city, who were denied access to anything other than emergency medical treatment.[317] Overall rates of attendance at pre-natal consultations, however, were only 68 per cent across the USSR in 1970, pointing to a significantly lower average in rural areas. But by now 91.5 per cent of babies would be seen by a nurse during their first month of life.[318] The standard of care provided might not always be very high – in some cases, staff were overworked and expectant mothers might be inspected in five or ten minutes;[319] by the 1970s, pre-natal facilities were beginning to fall behind international levels, since ultrasound scans and other machine-assisted inspections were not on offer. However, the majority of mothers had some contact at least with medical aid.

Customs also changed in line with the eagerness of parents themselves to do the 'right thing', the product not just of education and health activism, but of the psychological dynamics characteristic of all modernising cultures, according to which people admire new things and practices for their own sake, and eagerly abandon the old. It would appear, for instance, that traditional forms of dummy had fallen out of use by the early 1950s in cities,[320] and the last references to 'swaddling' of the traditional kind among urban informants go back to the 1930s. Concern to keep babies clean had reached almost obsessive levels with some mothers by the 1970s.[321]

In villages, many of these changes were delayed. Reliance on older women as advisers – in the absence of mother and baby clinics – naturally perpetuated tradition: in the 1950s and early 1960s, a grandmother was likely to swaddle her daughter's new baby in the traditional way.[322] But, as health care improved, more women came within reach of 'modern' ideas. A significant factor was the introduction of incentive schemes aimed at inducing a higher level of co-operation with state-sponsored maternity care. In the mid-1960s, collective farm workers became eligible for maternity pay, for the first time in Soviet history, but only so long as they obtained certification for attendance at the 'consultations' offered by ante-natal clinics. It was also becoming increasingly common for women wholly educated under the Soviet system to see traditional births as 'insanitary' and 'backward', and hospital treatment as superior: in the words of a woman born in 1933 who gave birth in the 1950s, 'the *babka* was no help at all'.[323] In the 1970s, 'feeding regimes that were fully medically directed' started to be in evidence.[324]

Equally significant was the growing availability of consumer goods, including baby goods as well as factory-made furniture and clothes. By the 1960s, rubber dummies were taking over from plugs of bread and other traditional methods of quieting a baby, and mothers were beginning to wrap their children less tightly and to use shop-bought nappies. More infant goods were becoming available, even in relatively remote areas, a development that in turn had an impact on child-rearing. An informant who gave birth to a son in Leningrad province in 1961 remembered that children would still be swaddled ('You'd wrap them tight-tight down the seams, so their arms wouldn't turn out crooked'), but then recalled: 'I think we just swaddled them the first few months, then, those all-in-one romper suits had started to come in then, you put those on and he's ... it's nice and warm, he can sleep all spread out. I think we swaddled them tight for a couple of months, so.'[325] By the start of the twenty-first century, young women – much to the disgust of their elders – had even begun using disposable nappies.[326]

Over several decades, then, Russian mothers became more familiar with medical guidance and more rigorous in applying it. One might also suppose that infanticide declined, given more intensive surveillance by health professionals, rising prosperity, and access to abortion, which was legal from 1918 to 1936, and again from 1955. The problem in making an assessment, however, is the lack of visibility of the topic. From the mid-1930s, references to this kind of child-killing, as to other varieties, were more or less precluded by the Soviet censorship, and before that references are scanty.[327] Despite their general concern with infant welfare, Russian physicians took no interest in explaining sudden death, other than establishing whether it was due to an infection. But there are occasional hints in archival sources that unlawful killing did not completely stop. For example, in 1955 a four-month-old baby at a Leningrad crèche was referred to hospital for double-sided pneumonia, and prescribed penicillin. He was then allowed back home, where he shortly afterwards died. The diagnosis given was 'asphyxia of unknown origin'.[328] The parents had perhaps seen fit to relieve a suffering child from his misery.

Coercing mothers into following instructions was not straightforward, and progress did not run smoothly in all areas. There seems, for example, to have been a move away from breast-feeding in the post-Stalin era. In 1956, health authorities in Sverdlovsk raised the alarm about the number of mothers who were failing to feed their infants for a sufficiently long period: 'A large contingent of children are transferred to mixed diets and artificial diets at an early stage.'[329] Similarly, David Ransel's research on women in rural Russia suggested that, by the 1970s, many were shortening the length of time that babies were fed, from over a year to six or seven months. There was even the occasional case of milk substitute use.[330] Official opinion – in the case of the Sverdlovsk results – saw the cause of the situation in the fact that district nurses and post-natal clinics were not doing enough to foster breast-feeding among new mothers.[331] There were perhaps other factors involved as well. In cities, the state network of 'milk kitchens', despite expansion, was insufficient to requirements and some of the facilities were antiquated, which meant that they worked inefficiently.[332] And milk substitutes were now becoming more readily available, as was made-up baby food. This, combined with the pressure on crèche places and the increasing numbers of women who worked, pulled in the opposite direction from the growing eagerness of new mothers to do as they were told by medical professionals. There were some cases of very long feeding at this period, but, it would seem, only with mothers who did not work.[333]

Parents had difficulties in complying with their 'duties' because of the besetting shortages of goods, at any rate in the later post-Stalinist era.[334] As Terry Bushell, a British journalist married to a Russian, recalled of his experiences in the 1970s: 'We had no problem with a pram and a plastic bath. Everything else was acquired with difficulty or from foreigners or not at all. [...] Even nappies were a problem.' Where they could, the couple stockpiled disposable nappies; otherwise they laundered traditional terry ones in a semi-functional washing-machine. More rarefied items, such as playpens and high chairs, were available only in the flagship store, Children's World, where they were delivered once a week and were instantly sold to the queue of expectant customers.[335] This problem appears to have been acute in Moscow: oral history from provincial cities does not suggest that cots, nappies, and other baby goods were in particularly short supply. Nor was there any scarcity of the sort of ready-made meals that were used for weaning children,

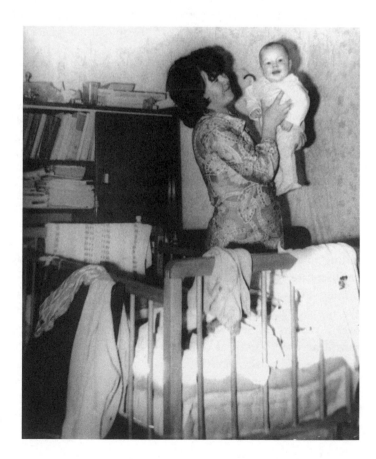

74 Cot, working-class family
     flat, Leningrad, 1970s.

though finding the most popular varieties (buckwheat, for instance) sometimes required effort. On the other hand, families did rely on relations living in the country, or with vegetable gardens, to supply the fruit and vegetables that were now thought essential for weaned infants and small children.[336]

As with Soviet everyday life more generally, increased availability (in theory) of material goods went with a greater desire to purchase such goods, an expectation sustained by propaganda of the day. Advice literature and popular magazines such as *Ogonek* and *Nedelya* celebrated the new consumer goods that had become available; the new generation of Socialist Realist painters also portrayed such items. As early as 1955, Valentina Shebasheva's painting, *At Home*, represented parents bathing their child in circumstances that were quite luxuriously appointed: a special baby-bath (albeit one made of tin rather than the plastic that would have been considered 'modern' in a Western home), a real cot, and plenty of wraps for the child. Even a plastic duck could be glimpsed among the accoutrements of modern babyhood. It is interesting to compare the painting with Zevin's 1938 scene: apart from the proliferation of material objects, what is notable is the involvement of the child's father in the domestic idyll, a detail that, in a society still devastated by the aftermath of war losses and asymmetry in the male/female populations, was just as far out of reach of many families as the battery of special child-rearing equipment.[337] (That said, it was in this generation that many fathers genuinely did begin taking an active part in the care of their infant children, perhaps encouraged by normative texts that placed greater emphasis on paternal responsibility.)[338] The 'perfect Soviet family', like the pot of gold at the end of the rainbow, receded from view even as it became apparently more accessible: growing prosperity generated higher standards and, in turn, a sense of failure among parents who might have felt that they were doing very well in earlier decades, when providing even basic care was a problem.

The End of 'Emotional Hygiene'

Another, equally important shift in ideals of the nursery was represented by the anxious, nurturing air exuded by both parents in Shebasheva's domestic scene. By now, 'emotional hygiene' was a vanished ethos. Arkady Plastov's *Spring* (1954) was considered a landmark at the time when it was painted because of its informally posed nude. Now it seems equally remarkable for the contrast between the naked woman, posed outside a traditional wooden Russian *banya*, and the tightly swaddled bundle of the toddler standing beside her, round which she is just wrapping yet another layer.[339] 'From the first day of his life the baby enters an atmosphere of love and concern,' said the *Dictionary for Parents*, published in 1967, while also cautioning against excessive indulgence of small children.[340]

It should be said that, even in the early Soviet era, real-life parents had proved very reluctant to treat babies with the recommended degree of detachment. Certainly, some educated mothers were punctilious in their efforts to accommodate the psychological recommendations of advice literature. Rybnikova-Shilova, for instance, avoided kissing and cuddling on 'hygienic' grounds, and gave enemas at regular intervals; Raisa Orlova made herself and her baby wretched by sticking to a schedule that ruled out night feeds.[341] But even 'rational mothers' sometimes broke the rules, reflecting in their diaries emotions such as pride, irritation, affection, and anxiety over their small children – and suffering all over again when they realised that the children were themselves in turn picking up such uncontrolled moods.[342]

An important factor in undermining 'rational upbringing' throughout the post-revolutionary era was that mothers from the social strata that would have been most inclined to espouse an ethos of 'emotional hygiene' – the educated middle classes – were far more likely to be in direct, intimate contact with their infants than before 1917. Pressure on living space in the cities, combined with the Soviet authorities' determination to improve conditions for working-class families, generated the policy euphemistically described as 'compression' (*uplotnenie*), which required those living in large flats to allocate sections of their living space to tenants on the housing list.[343] A family that had originally inhabited a six- to ten-room flat might find itself crammed into one, or at best two, rooms, sharing kitchen, bathroom, and hall with the other inhabitants of the improvised commune. Instead of being down the far end of a corridor close to the kitchen and servants' quarters, infants were now placed in cradles right next to the parental bed. The resulting investment of emotional energy can be sensed in Soviet depictions of parent–infant relations. Mothers' diaries show women worrying constantly about what to feed their babies (fussing when a small child would not eat an omelette, for example), and poring anxiously over excreta as a guide to how well the diet was working.[344] And, while such documents anxiously recorded a child's progress towards the great goal of intellectual development, they also enthused sentimentally over moments that did not fit into the cognitive teleology, taking pride, for instance, in the fact that their baby was inconsolable when they were not around.[345]

'Emotional hygiene' does not seem to have been much more successful outside the elite. Working-class and peasant parents tended to be quite strict with older children, but, with babies, they were often indulgent. As Alice Field recorded in the early 1920s, 'I noticed that the Russians are always kissing their children' (and this even when sitting in the waiting rooms of clinics decked with posters instructing them not to!).[346] Naturally, in later decades, when professional advice about handling babies had become less stern, physical contact was still less inhibited. From infancy, a child was likely to be wrapped in what one foreign observer called a 'pampering feminine cocoon', with strangers on the street also nagging amiably about the need to keep the child well wrapped up and so on.[347]

Collectivising Child Care

The relationship between professional advice and family relations on the ground was never straightforward. The ethos of hygiene was slow to impose itself; the ethos of 'emotional hygiene' had limited impact even on women from the intelligentsia. But, even if mothers often failed to care for children in the manner that experts felt they should, most experts continued to expect that mothers would be their infants' primary carers. To be sure, some of the utopian plans from the 1920s envisaged collective child-rearing for this age group too. Well before the Revolution, as noted in Chapter 1, utopian socialists such as Konstantin Tsiolkovsky and Aleksandr Bogdanov had given public nurseries a place in their futuristic visions of ideal modern cities. After the Revolution, kindred spirits, such as V. Dyushen, the main mover behind the Moscow 'Children's Town', a network of homes and settlements with a strong emphasis on inmate self-government, saw their chance to turn poetic fantasy into practice.[348] Throughout the 1920s, model nurseries occupied an important niche in propaganda visions of the soon-to-be-achieved future. Constructivist designers produced prototypes for feeding-bottles; photographs in prestigious journals showed purpose-built, sleekly modern blocks; foreign visitors were trooped round the establishments considered to be at the cutting edge of 'Soviet everyday life'. Nurseries continued to make regular appearances in propaganda both for internal and external consumption right to the end of the Soviet era.[349] Also highlighted were special facilities such as 'mother and child rooms' at major stations, where women with babies and small children could take naps, get changed, and where medical and catering facilities were available.[350]

75   Collective farm crèche, early 1930s.

How effective such provision was in reality is difficult to assess. Certainly, nurseries were a good deal less dominant in practice than they were in fantasy. Even in the last decades of Soviet power, the state nurtured only a fraction of the infant population. In Sverdlovsk, a relatively wealthy and privileged industrial town, the under-ones, a population amounting to around 45 per cent of the target age group, represented less than 10 per cent of the population of children in state crèches during the 1960s. At the time of the baby boom of the late 1940s, the proportion of under-ones in Leningrad nurseries peaked at one fifth of the total roll for crèches, which in its turn represented only a fraction of the entire under-one population in the city.[351] Not only did Soviet crèches not extend their care to all, or even the majority of, infants: their contribution to 'rational care' was flawed in other respects as well. Beyond the relentless optimistic images of utopian propaganda lay an everyday reality of compromise, struggle, and material deprivation, where 'rational living' often carried little, if any, weight – just as in orphanages, prisons, or other types of children's institution.

Nevertheless, the organisation of crèches had more logic than the organisation of the orphanage system: there was not the same atomisation of effort between different ministries and agencies. However, crèches were, until 1960, under a different administration from nursery schools (the health ministry, rather than the education ministry), which meant that children who entered the child-care system before the age of two or three had to be transferred to a different institution once they reached the age of three or four.[352] Parents, having fussed round to collect a pile of documents to register a child at around one, then had to repeat the exercise a couple of years later when it reached nursery-school age.[353] Fragmentation of educational principles resulted: as an official report commented retrospectively in 1965, 'The finicking divisions of institution types led to children being transferred too often from one institution to another, which confronted them with different systems of upbringing, and disrupted their normal development.'[354] On the other hand, a major problem, once crèches and nursery schools were amalgamated, was finding staff in the latter who were also competent to work with infants.[355]

But the biggest problem with day care was a more basic one: providing enough places. Only a proportion of infants under one were in the system (in the 1960s, some crèches explicitly excluded children below five months old).[356] Yet there was still a substantial mismatch between available space and demand. Certainly, provision started to expand significantly once the Bolsheviks took power. Figures from 1925 indicated that there were already 534 factory nurseries by 1925, up from 447 in 1923.[357] In 1928, *yasli* places in the RSFSR had reached 31,955; by the end of 1930, they stood at 59,940, and by 1 January 1934 at 202,000.[358] But such figures remained well below the size of the target population. In 1925, Moscow region, then with a total population of around 2 million (and hence an under-three population of perhaps 200,000), had only 90 crèches with 5,145 places. Over the next few years the numbers of places rose (in 1926–7 they stood at 5,503, and in 1928–29, at 6,471), but they remained well below the numbers of children in the target age group.[359] Closer case studies confirmed shortages of places even in major industrial centres – in Ivanovo in 1928, for example, the 185 nurseries with 9,943 places compared with an estimate of 71,779 children in the target age group (leaving over 85 per cent of children outside the system).[360] A study of several important Leningrad factories published in 1935 indicated that there was an average of 8.2 places available per 100 women workers, which meant that only just over a quarter of the target age group were attending nurseries.[361]

For all the determinedly upbeat tone of late 1930s press reports and their proud boasts about achievement, they often laid bare the continuing mismatch between available places and need. An article published in *Pravda* in July 1936 hymned the case of the Sulinsk metalworks, which was just setting up its own 120-place nursery; this facility could have catered to only a fraction of the infants born to workers employed at the plant. In October 1936, another such report celebrated the superb crèche at the Tula gun cartridge factory, where the infants had their own 'magnificent home': once again, the number of places was just 120, though over 500 births had occurred to women workers at the plant in the first seven months of 1936 alone.[362]

Yet provision for women working for major enterprises was considerably better than it was for the urban population in general. With the switch to all-out industrialisation during the First Five-Year Plan, the main drive behind the nursery movement was to provide women in factories with back-up so that they could work long shifts.[363] Access to nursery facilities for other sectors of the urban population was a secondary consideration. Even women from the political elite were relatively badly served. The purpose-built crèche included in the design for the Narkomfin block in Moscow was never in fact erected, though a makeshift space for day care was eventually fixed up in the gymnasium, rest area, and summer dining room.[364] The spirit of the times was that parents should themselves participate in the work of the crèche: in 1926, for example, the regional soviet of Moscow *volost* peasant women's organisations moved that parents should be got to provide food and make cots; and from 1924, parents were encouraged to buckle down and organise care facilities in their co-operative dwelling houses, just as the Narkomfin inhabitants later did.[365]

Official figures from 1936 claimed a staggering rise in crèche places, from 257,000 places across the Soviet Union in 1928 to 5,143,400 places in 1934.[366] But the overwhelming proportion was in temporary summer supervised playgroups, or indeed makeshift facilities where the babies were stored in mobile plywood wagons in serried ranks, like wasp larvae in a nest.[367] Expansion in this sector was fast, but not fast enough to satisfy demand. In 1924, a survey of 31 provinces indicated there were now 483 village nurseries across these, as opposed to 230 in the previous year.[368] In this period, the network had hardly begun to function: indeed, even the 1934 figures were way below what was needed.

The 28 June 1936 Decree on the Protection of Mothers and Infants sought to resolve this situation. It called for a 100 per cent rise in crèche places by 1939, comprising a growth of 500,000 regular all-day places and of 4 million summer playgroup places. But, in practice, the stipulations of this decree were to prove no more realisable than the ambitious projections of the 1920s. Officials working in Leningrad province in 1940 had problems even keeping track of the number of places available, though they did know that the provision of new places was 80 per cent behind what had been planned.[369] In 1941, the addition of new all-day places was running at less than half the target that should have been reached two years earlier (213,577 places had been added over five years), and growth in summer playgroup places seems to have been at least as far behind target. In some places, for example Leningrad province, the number of day-care places in the countryside actually declined between 1935 and 1939, perhaps in order to boost the modest enhancement of city crèche space that occurred in the same period.[370]

As with other types of children's institution, the war years halted expansion. True, it was reported in 1944 that no waiting lists existed.[371] But this was because of targeting of resources on major cities, not because of growing provision overall, which had reached only 36.6 per cent across the Russian Federation as a whole, and a microscopic 2.9 per cent in the countryside.[372] In addition, the official upper limit on group size was raised, so that ratios of 35 to 40 children to one supervisor were tolerated in theory (in practice the groups were no doubt even larger).[373] And if things were manageable during the war, in the late 1940s the combination of war damage to nursery premises and a rising birth rate started to put the system under terrible pressure. In Leningrad, for example, places rose from 14,279 in 1945 to 15,030 in 1946, 19,715 in 1949, and 20,635 in 1951. But these relatively small increases – kept low by the fact that in some years gains had to be offset against losses when unsuitable premises were closed down – were quite insufficient to meet demand. In 1949, it was reported that the supply of places was equivalent to 13.2 per cent of the target age group across the city, and 8 per cent in the city centre, where queues for admission were extremely lengthy. A report of 1951 placed a concrete figure on the size of the queue: 8,176, of which 1,792 were classified as 'extremely needy'. Despite the fact that many nurseries were critically overcrowded, they could not cope with demand.[374]

By the mid-1950s, the situation appears to have levelled out in some parts of Leningrad: for example, Kalinin district was reporting no queues by 1955.[375] Across the country, though, undersupply was still creating problems. To be sure, provision of places had risen: by 1958, there were 733,900 children in permanent crèches across the Russian Federation, as opposed to 408,700 in 1950 (and 514,400 in 1940).[376] In the early 1960s, a drive began to increase capacity in rural nurseries and kindergartens.[377] But this was still insufficient compared with potential demand. In 1959, only 12 per cent of the target age group was catered for nationwide, and, in 1962, 16 per cent. This figure had risen to 21 per cent by 1965, but waiting lists were not getting any shorter. In 1963, 517,300 parents were recorded as on the queue, and, in 1969, 500,000. In the same year, just 28.4 per cent of those wanting places managed to arrange them (and 10.4 per cent in the countryside).[378]

Later information about numbers is hard to find (many files from the period are still classified). But figures in published sources, when compared with age-group numbers, indicate a continuing shortfall. For instance, in Moscow by 1976 there were just over 380,000 places in every kind of child care, 54,800 in autonomous crèches, and 325,600 in combined crèches and kindergartens. While

76   Crèche in the Kirov Factory, Leningrad, 1950s.

this is a significant improvement on the 1940 figure of just over 125,000 child-care places of all kinds, it still did not represent complete coverage.[379] In the circumstances, nurseries found themselves making difficult decisions about which of the many waiting parents should be allowed priority. The usual procedure was to review applications in committee, which was obviously cumbersome in terms of staff time, as well as distressing to petitioners.[380]

Child-care provision, then, was never universal; it also departed from the utopian ideals of the early Soviet planners in another respect: it had to be paid for. Charges, introduced as a 'temporary measure' in 1924,[381] remained in force throughout the Soviet period, though dues were lowered or waived for particularly poor families and for especially large ones. In 1948, for example, the basic charges stood at 45 roubles a month in towns and 30 roubles a month in the countryside, with 25 per cent extra for the extended programme (12–14 hours a day) and 50 per cent extra for the 24-hour programme.[382] But the charges for child-care do not seem to have constituted an obstacle to participation in the crèche system. A study of Leningrad factory workers published in 1935 suggested that only 8.8 per cent of mothers did not have their children in nurseries because of the cost. Lack of place availability was a much more significant deterrent, at 24.3 per cent.[383] While surveys of this kind ceased being carried out from the late 1930s onwards, the raw data on crèche provision indicate that the picture remained similar. In cities, the fees were likely to be within reach of many manual workers, though a family of kolkhoz workers paid in kind rather than cash might in principle have had problems footing the bill.

'Sitting with Baby'[384]

Throughout the Soviet era, large numbers of mothers still had to rely on *ad hoc* arrangements. The better-off employed the Soviet equivalent of servants, *domrabotnitsy* or 'home workers' (compare the British euphemism for a maid, 'home help'), who officially were supposed to be registered with a trade union, paid fixed rates, and assigned work to a standard contract.[385] The less well off – if they employed anyone at all – would pay small amounts to a teenage *nyan'ka*, or assign a pittance to a neighbour in their factory or hostel or flat so that she would 'sit with the baby'.[386] A child's older siblings might be pressed into service, sometimes with tragic results: one Leningrad woman was to be haunted for a lifetime by the death of her infant brother, whom she had let slip while carrying him up the stairs. The child shortly afterwards developed meningitis and passed away.[387] But juvenile child-minders were not necessarily better qualified if they were paid. A woman born in 1921 recalled that, when an infant, she nearly died as a result of her young nanny's attempts to calm her.

> She didn't want to mind me, so she stuffed my mouth full of wheat ears. [...] And when my mother came back from the field, she gives me the breast, But I'm suffocating, suffocating, because my mouth's packed full of wheat ears and all. Pins, maybe, God knows what it all was. But my dad knew what was going on [...] he saw that his little girl had something in her mouth, she was suffocating. Well then. So they grabbed hold of me and started shaking me .... There were no doctors then, nothing. They dealt with everything themselves. And I've got ears of wheat in there. So they sent that nanny straight to hell. That's what nannies were like, back then.[388]

Fewer risks were posed by calling on an adult relation or friend for baby care: a childless woman, or one with grown children, might happily agree to such an arrangement. One of the few ways in which post-war Socialist Realist novels, such as Anna Karavaeva's *Motherland*, or Galina Nikolaeva's *The Harvest*, engage with reality is in suggesting that arrangements of this kind were common.

Some mothers, in fact, preferred to negotiate child care informally. It was common in the early Soviet period for women from outside the elite to feel worry or shame about placing their children in care.[389] A full 38.2 per cent of Leningrad women workers in 1935 kept their babies out of factory crèches because they had someone around at home who could look after them.[390] Among some, it was considered shameful to put one's children in day care; 'as bad as it is today [the 1990s] to put your baby in an orphanage', one woman remembered.[391] The standard narrative in official propaganda showed such resistance (always represented in any case as a characteristic of 'backward' women, such as village-dwellers) as quickly and effortlessly overcome once mothers had seen the benefits of nursery care for themselves.[392] But this oversimplified the situation. Under-provision of nursery care could be a cause of resentment in working-class women with factory jobs.[393] Conversely, middle-class women were often reluctant to take up crèche places. In the words of one woman looking back to the 1930s: 'In my day mothers [...] weren't in such a big hurry to put their babies in nurseries and dump them into the hands of strangers; they brought them up themselves.'[394] The woman in question was the wife of a professor of engineering, which is to say, a member of the affluent Soviet middle classes. But less privileged members of the intelligentsia, for example, journalists and translators in Moscow, sometimes had similar feelings. The point was not so much the unfamiliarity of institutionalised child care as a concept, as its deficiencies as a reality.

To begin with, crèche staff were often under-qualified. In the 1920s, the universal suspicion of 'bourgeois specialists' extended even to the employees of these humble institutions. Party membership was considered a more important qualification than pedagogical or medical training: one trained paediatrician remembered having to stage a tantrum in the local Narkompros office before she could gain a placement anywhere in a crèche, and afterwards having her life plagued by the half-educated but dogmatic Communist who ran the institution where she obtained it.[395] In the early 1930s, the situation changed: specialist training was now considered important, but pressure to expand facilities meant that nurseries had to take on unqualified staff if they were to operate at all. As late as 1951, 17 per cent of the staff at crèches even in Leningrad had no specialist training of any kind, while 28 per cent had received training in the form of a short, high-speed course.[396] But where staff shortages were persistent, administrators really had no option other than to run the risk.[397] This could mean that individuals who were not only incompetent, but dishonest, ended up on the books: at times of food crisis, crèches were as vulnerable as other institutions to pilfering by the unscrupulous.[398]

Under-funding and under-qualification generated a predictable set of problems: official reports on crèches indicated that levels of hygiene and standards of care were sometimes disturbingly low, as even the Stalinist press sometimes recognised. An August 1935 *Pravda* article, for instance, drew attention to a range of problems in different parts of the Soviet Union. Food in many places was dreary and equipment short, the most bizarre case of under-equipment being a shortage of potties at the Emal'nosud crèche in Rostov – when Emal'nosud factory happened actually to manufacture potties.[399] Inevitably, the stress of the war led to still further problems: even far beyond the front line, in the Urals, where many nurseries had been evacuated, there were constant hitches in the food supply lines. Food and heating supplies were also short in Gorky (Nizhni Novgorod) province; in Penza, there was only one doctor to see to 1,200 children. A report on Leningrad in 1945 was more positive, but it did note shortages of eating vessels and a dearth of fresh vegetables at meals.[400]

Hygiene problems persisted well into the post-war era. Report after report filed with the health ministry painted a negative picture. Crowding was one problem; another was that crèches sometimes had no gardens, verandas, or balconies, precluding the 'air baths' and 'sun baths' that were supposed to be part of the programme. Or sometimes staff themselves ignored this requirement, giving children no exposure to 'tempering' techniques at all.[401] The detailed reports available on Leningrad for the late 1940s and early 1950s substantiate these points. Only 38.4 per cent of institutions were housed in purpose-built accommodation, and, of the buildings that had been adapted for nurseries, some were thoroughly unsatisfactory from a hygienic point of view. They might not only lack outdoor space, but also have accommodation scattered over several floors or be without 'basic sanitary and hygienic facilities' (running water and sanitation). Often, rooms that were prescribed in official guidelines, such as a place for washing children's potties, were simply non-existent. Overcrowding, decay to the fabric, and equipment shortages were rife. Not surprisingly, staff found it difficult to cope. In just one district of Leningrad, Smol'nyi, twenty doctors left and eighteen arrived over the course of 1950; in Leningrad as a whole, there were 99 departures and 108 arrivals. In the words of the report's authors, 'This turnover on the part of medical personnel is often dependent on poorly thought out assignations of doctors to the crèche system, and it in turn has a detrimental effect on the work of the crèches themselves.' The instability of the supervisory network was no doubt one reason – alongside poor facilities and sanitation – for the worryingly high level of infectious disease, with seven nurseries reporting large-scale outbreaks of dysentery in 1951.[402]

The report concluded with a list of changes that needed to be made. These – apart from an opening salvo on the need to pay more attention to the theories of Ivan Pavlov – were soberly practical in character: more staff training, more training for mothers in infant care, and more effective dissemination of best practice through the creation of model nurseries in a variety of districts all over the city. The report yet again stressed the importance to children's health of breast-milk, which was stored in the crèches, for use when mothers could not get back during the day.[403] But a report produced five years later, in 1955, revealed that some of the problems identified earlier had persisted. For instance, levels of infectious disease were high; in many areas, almost all the children had been ill during the year, some more than once. In particular, almost all districts reported cases of dysentery, some running into hundreds (while the dysentery rate stood at 82 in the prestigious Kuibyshev district in the centre of Leningrad, it was 282 in the Kirov district, a part of the city where heavy industry was concentrated, and a massive 309 in the Kalinin district. In all cases, the number of children who had used crèches during the year was around 2,000). The spread of the infection on this scale was certainly related to sloppy hygienic practices.[404]

The one area of official policy that did get widely implemented, in the early Soviet period at least, was 'emotional hygiene' – less for systematic reasons, no doubt, than because of low staff to infant ratios. As an American visitor recalled of her observations in the mid-1920s, 'When a child does cry they do not try to stop it by pampering.'[405] Ethel Mannin, who visited a nursery and kindergarten in 1934, had similar remarks to make:

> I was shocked by the pallor of the children, by the fact that there wasn't a single window open in the place, by the lack of heating – it not being yet the fifteenth of October when – and not till then – heating is turned on; by the

sight of babies sleeping indoors in sealed rooms instead of outside in the air, and by a plate of bread with flies wandering over it, by the condition of the infants' eyes and noses.[406]

Mannin was otherwise so eager to be impressed with everything she saw in the Soviet Union that these remarks have the ring of authenticity, especially coming from someone who had seen public infant care at work abroad.

The background to what Mannin saw was, of course, the huge pressure to provide child-care facilities of any kind, however makeshift, and however deadening to the infants involved. The industrialisation drive meant that women needed to be got into the factory, and child care had to be provided to get them there. Infants and small children would therefore be consigned to the crèche for long hours, sometimes, indeed, round the clock. In 1944, for instance, 26 per cent of all crèche places were in 24-hour facilities.[407] Such support was aimed particularly at single mothers, who tended to make use of it because they had no alternative. Standard hours in crèches were always long: 12 hours or more, with many factory facilities operating a night shift as well as a day shift so that women could work late or overnight.[408]

'Hospitalisation', in the sense of institutionalised psychological trauma and emotional deprivation, must have been widespread among many 'graduates' of such crèches. Not all facilities, however, were bad. Internal Ministry of Health reports also did single out some places for glowing commendation, such as the 140-place state farm crèche in Gorky province visited during 1968 as part of an all-Soviet tour of rural nurseries. In a well-appointed building with verandah, this crèche also had a PE hall and a garden. There was plenty of bedlinen, which was frequently changed; the food was abundant and nutritious; and the menu had been designed by a paediatric nurse.[409] Herschel and Edith Alt, who visited a metropolitan nursery in the late 1950s, found this in very good order relative to US or Western Europe, though it was eerie to hear the children wake up 'without sound': 'Never had we seen a group of healthy children awaken after afternoon naps in this fashion.'[410]

Among the good effects of the crèche system, too, was that it allowed the opportunity to children who lived in polluted industrial cities, and whose parents were not in the dacha-owning stratum of Soviet society, to spend some time in resort areas, or the countryside, during the summer. In 1955, for example, one third to two-thirds of the children in Leningrad crèches were taken away for some part of the summer.[411] If nurseries exposed children to additional risk in terms of infectious disease, they also provided centres where vaccination programmes could be carried out, providing some protection against illness as well.[412] In any case, the real choice was often not between inferior institutional care and better care at home, but between a crèche and unqualified child-minding, or even just having to dump the child on its own. A woman whose children were born in Novgorod province in the late 1940s recalled: 'Who was supposed to look after them? Later, we lived … somewhere else, not here … my mother-in-law wasn't around, we didn't get on, something like that. I was allocated a room there. I

77 Crèche at its summer dacha, Leningrad, 1950s.

was working next door, and the room was right there, so I'd leave them and then come running back – and she'd be all covered in wee and poo. I'd wipe her down again and run back to work. I'd be there all day, I was sort of like taking toilet breaks. Oh, it was dreadful!' While this woman's memories of the crèche were not cloudless – her daughter had picked up a stomach infection and become very ill – she recorded that the crèche doctor had given the child excellent treatment.[413]

Treatment of children varied from institution to institution as well. A 1964 British visitor to nurseries in Moscow noted that the hospital atmosphere was superficial: the staff might wear white coats, but their relationships with the children were usually quite relaxed. Soviet jargon often gave a misleadingly formal impression: 'a music lesson with the pedagogue' turned out to consist of a smiling young woman simply singing to a group of babies. Staff spent a great deal of time playing with children and keeping them entertained, and there was plenty of stimulation from climbing frames, jingly toys, and so on.[414]

So far as mental stimulation of children went, the situation seems to have improved from the beginning of the 1960s, with the amalgamation of the crèche and nursery school network. The primary purpose of the 1959 Central Committee and Council of Ministers decree, 'On the Further Development of Children's Pre-School Institutions, and the Improvement of Education and of Medical Provision', which brought crèches and nursery schools together, was to harmonise regimes in the institutions: it was absurd, a leading article in the journal *Pre-School Education* argued, when children who had been used to sleeping twelve to twelve and a half hours in crèches were suddenly expected to sleep fourteen hours in the nursery school. But policy now aimed to move away from the purely 'biological approach' that had traditionally been adopted in crèches, and to offer a greater level of mental stimulation. 'From the first day that a child of crèche age arrives in the pre-school institution, much attention must be paid to the development of his sight and hearing,' the leader article went on. Kindergartens were supposed to build on the paediatric knowledge that had been accumulated in the crèche network; in reverse, crèches were supposed to draw on the pedagogical experience of the kindergartens.[415]

Individual from Birth

Institutional reform was only one change at this stage. By the late Soviet period, there were some signs of opposition to the institutionalisation of infants and very small children in the first place, as exemplified by the decree of 22 January 1981 allowing mothers who had an employment history of a year or more up to a year's maternity leave on reduced pay.[416] Instead of trying to increase participation in the state system among the under-ones, administrators now assumed that such children would stay with their mothers. Another Western visitor, this time in the early 1970s, recalled that there were 'very few' children under 18 months in the nurseries that she visited; and official Soviet report of the period showed that a large proportion of those using these facilities were unskilled workers (i.e. those whose status, in socio-economic terms, was low).[417] One can compare the situation with *internaty*: the state was moving from a model where *all* children were to be provided for in the institutional system to one where only children of needy parents (or needy children) were to be provided for.

Nursery care was no longer the sole model for successful nurture, it seemed. In parallel, mothers were taking a more robust and independent attitude to child-rearing advice. For instance, Valeriya Mukhina, the author of a diary recording the first six years of life of her boy twins, was, like earlier exponents of the 'mother's diary' genre, a trained pedagogue, and might accordingly have been expected to be quite rule-bound in her attitude to child care. This attitude did not persist very long, however. In the first few months of the twins' life she certainly paid much attention to 'physical culture' and 'tempering', trying to develop their reflexes and seeing they got plenty of fresh air. But when the two contracted pneumonia, and were additionally found to be mildly anaemic, at seven months, her faith in the system wavered. Rather than decide, as a 1920s mother might have done, that she had been lax in carrying out the instructions, she blamed the system: 'None of it, not the air, the sun-baths, the daily PE, has done any good.'[418]

Mukhina was also determined to treat each child, from the first, as an autonomous being, one not precisely resembling any other individual. Her twins were dressed identically (not only as babies, but as small children too), but she began to draw fine distinctions on the psychological level immediately after their birth. One, Andrei, had more definite features and was more active in a physical sense, while Kirill was more delicate-looking and quieter.

Feingefühl of this kind eventually generated anxieties about whether collective recipes suited one's own precious and individual children. Equally, the spread of hygienic ideas could make parents feel righteous in terms of the Soviet system: adults who came closer to measuring up to the ideals in state propaganda could afford to be assertive about what provision was made for their children. Certainly, anxieties did not necessarily impact directly: the problem for many parents remained getting a crèche place to begin with, which often required leverage with the staff (for instance membership of a useful profession or trade, such as plumbing or dressmaking).[419] But in time, the growing capacity to criticise what was on offer, accompanied by increasingly bad publicity about standards in state-run institutions, would precipitate a collapse of trust in the nursery system altogether. Child-care professionals were starting to be more critical as well. A woman who worked as a district paediatrician in Leningrad in the early 1980s recalled that she soon became convinced that the system of sending children of nursery age out to the countryside for the summer was a bad idea. The level of infectious disease among such children was high, which meant stuffing them with antibiotics; separation from the family caused psychological distress. Her personal campaign against the procedure, however, made her unpopular not only with local administrators, who measured their prestige in terms of the number of children dispatched to recuperate at nursery dachas, but with parents, who were convinced that anything that was scarce (as such places were) must be worth having.[420] Yet, as the all-family holiday became more widespread in working-class families too, the sense that babies should be dispatched on their own was bound to come under scrutiny.

From the late 1980s, newspapers started to do what earlier had been unthinkable: to question the quality of state care for infants in the broad sense, rather than simply picking on incidental abuses. In 1987, *Pravda* stated openly that commitment to institutional care had been a mistake.[421] Like staff in other state institutions, supervisors in crèches came under suspicion of neglecting and abusing children – despite years of propaganda warning against corporal punishment, one's daughter might come back with the unmistakable mark of a slap on her body.[422] Increasingly, normative literature of the 1980s asserted that experience in the first three years of life was fundamental in shaping character, and warned against the likely harmful long-term effects of leaving children to cry unattended.[423] In this context, the hygienic regimen of the traditional crèche, with its emphasis on efficient, impersonal service to maximum numbers, came to seem inhumane even if explicit abuses were not taking place.

But looking after children within the family was becoming ever more difficult. As the premises of 'milk kitchens' aged, and staff came under increasing pressure, standards of hygiene fell. By now, it was widely felt that the use of powdered milk was preferable, but the supply of this was subject to constant, unexplained shortages.[424] By 1989, supplies of milk were running at 60 per cent of demand,

and supplies of other types of infant food were even less adequate – 50 per cent in the case of fruit and vegetable mixes, 30 per cent in the case of meat, and 10 to 12 per cent with pasta and starch products.[425] Retrospectively, the crisis of the late 1980s and early 1990s looks trivial by the appalling standards of Russian history: there was no mass starvation, and in 1993 the supply situation began to right itself again, at least where the better-off members of society were concerned.[426] But it caused deep malaise and distress while it lasted. Notable, too, is the fact that reminiscences of nursery life by former inmates from the post-Stalin generation are often negative. A woman from Perm' born in 1958 conceded that there was no physical abuse, but remembered having caught hepatitis in her *yasli* and having found the rest hour stressful and boring.[427] Such recollections are not so much objective records of what went on in the crèches as indications that the new generations of children were becoming more sensitive to their surroundings, because the new home-centred culture sometimes made nurseries seem potentially threatening.

Over the 'long twentieth century', care for infants developed in ways that were often contradictory and haphazard. One tendency was the admission of ever larger numbers of infants to institutions – day nurseries and sometimes even day-and-night nurseries. Here, it was argued, they would receive care that was superior to that which even enlightened mothers could offer. At the same time, the provision of infant care was driven by external concerns – the point was to maximise the numbers of women available for paid work, particularly in factories and in the agricultural sector. The aim of providing large numbers of children with basic care at minimum cost, on a sort of 'hygienic baby farm' basis, proved incompatible with the quality imperative.

Certainly, Soviet clinics and nurseries – like Soviet maternity homes – fulfilled some of the ambitions of early twentieth-century reformers. Maternal and infant mortality declined significantly; general health among small children improved. Change made itself felt in the area of home care as well. Among all social strata – at different rates – baby care was 'modernised', with tight swaddling abandoned in favour of less restrictive methods of wrapping children, bread dummies replaced by rubber ones, and educated mothers, at least, uniformly breast-feeding children. Yet, as with medical facilities more generally, infant care could not correct certain underlying social problems – poor diet, alcoholism, the effects of industrial pollution. And the difficulties of developing an advanced network of care facilities across vast distances and inhospitable terrain made the process of reaching children in outlying areas of the countryside slow and unpredictable. Much the same was true, as we shall see, of the care and upbringing of older children.

Chapter 10

Nursery Days

A happy childhood casts its rosy glow over a person's
entire life, no matter what storms brew up later on.
(Mariya Redelin, *The Home and House Management*,
1900).

Learning to Walk, Learning to Speak

The shift between 'infancy' and 'childhood' is conventionally seen in terms of a
number of key changes, above all the transition to independent movement (first
crawling, later walking); the acquisition of speech, and the absorption of the
elements of self-control, particularly the ability to regulate bladder and bowel
function. In all cultures, the normal child is required to pass through these
different stages of development, but the symbolic importance given to each, and
the ways in which parents or other carers are expected to participate in the process
of the child's development, are likely to vary. The treatment of the different phases
of life is also subject to evolution within a culture, over the course of time.

In Russian traditional culture, regulation of bladder and bowel function was
usually more or less taken for granted. Children old enough to walk were dressed
in clothing that allowed excretory needs to be satisfied without special attention
(boys had leggings with an open gusset, girls, dresses worn without knickers).[1] No
doubt such children learned to moderate their habits by observing adult behaviour,
and by learning, in time, to visit the places customarily used for excretion by
adults – for example, barns, dung heaps, and (in the most sophisticated dwellings)
outside privies; no doubt also, encouragement or coercion by parents or older
siblings taught them to be 'tidy' fairly quickly. But the process was not considered
worthy of special anxiety or attention. 'Accidents' appear to have been greeted
calmly, without a sense that they hindered the child's likely development towards
civilisation. In the words of a woman from the Urals when her grandson came
back from school soiled in 1928, 'As long as humans wear pants, they'll wet them
occasionally.'[2]

What might inaccurately be described as 'potty training' (because no one used
a potty) was mundane. Walking and talking, on the other hand, had resonance

354

in the symbolic universe. In order to help the child to walk, a special ritual of 'freeing' the child's legs was customary. A long thread would be spun on the spindle and wound round the child's body. It would then be sliced between the child's legs in order to sever the invisible chains that were held to immobilise it and prevent it from walking. Or a child might be led through a stream or over a heap of pebbles as a 'hardening' process.[3] The place of linguistic acquisition was still more ramified: because of an association between hair and mental processes, there was a prohibition on cutting the child's hair until it could speak, while a special rite of 'unknotting' (in which the child was required to try and smooth out the umbilical cord, knotted after birth, or to untangle locks of its own hair) was used to 'open up' and release mental powers. In popular religion, the appearance of speech, however, also signified a fall from grace: tiny children were considered to be fluent in the 'language of angels', knowledge of which they lost when they started to speak ordinary human words.[4]

This did not of course mean that children were brought into the world of movement and language exclusively through ritual. Walking-frames, whether curved wooden structures that the child could lean on as it stumbled along, or wheeled trolley affairs to encourage it to stroll as it pushed, were widely used in peasant households; before it reached this stage, a child might be put in a 'sitter' that kept it from slumping sideways when in a seated position.[5] Language was also helped along in all kinds of practical ways. As in any society in the world, objects would be named when the child began asking about them. Children who were too young to play independently would be kept amused with games that combined gestures with texts. With very tiny children, the texts were usually brief: for example, a mother might call out 'Handies, handies, give us your handies!', before

78   Baby walker, V. Zhuk, *Mother and Child* (1911).

reaching for the child and lifting it out of the cradle. A chant of 'Flap-flap the owl!' went with a gesture waving the child's arms like wings, and 'Here comes the moon!' with sideways sweeps of the child's hands.[6] As the child grew older, texts got more elaborate, turning into little humorous narratives. Mothers would, for example, take hold of a small child's legs and recite the following chant:

> We're riding, we're riding to see gran and grandad,
> On a pony, wearing our red hat.
> Roly-poly – BUMP![7]

Such games helped young children discover the outlines and capacities of their own body, and the features of their environment.[8] But they were also, of course, an expression of affection and physical intimacy between the mother (or other adult) and the child, a way of prompting children to match text and action, and an initiation into language. Not that physical interaction was always purely harmonious: like adults in other countries, Russian parents were irritated by finger-sucking (the equivalent of thumb-sucking in Britain or America), and a child caught doing this might well get a slap.[9]

Adults taught children traditional nursery rhymes, many of international types. One common type was the Russian equivalent of 'Ladybird, ladybird, fly away home':

> Ladybird, fly,
> Back to the sky,
> Your little children
> Are buying cakes and pies.
> Reading books by the ton,
> But they want you back home.[10]

Rhymes of this kind, alongside their linguistic and imaginative functions, familiarised children with the idea of absence, offering some psychological preparation for a stage of life when mothers would not be so readily available as in the earliest years.

Linguistic acquisition took pride of place in turn-of-the-century educated parents' observation of their children's development, though in a quite different way: these observers were highly self-conscious, and their views of the centrality of language had been influenced by recent pedagogical writings on children's language. The writings of Pestalozzi on 'mother tongue', though translated into Russian in the early nineteenth century, had left no important traces on the culture of the time; now, though, the works of Sully, Hall, Dix, Preyer, Perez, and later Piaget, Vygotsky, and above all Chukovsky, were widely read, and fed directly into the day-to-day experiences of parents.[11] Parents monitored their offspring's linguistic progress: the many 'mothers' diaries' of the day proudly recorded tots' lisping efforts to say difficult words, and their later capacities for striking metaphor – 'what's that big typewriter?' when seeing granny's piano for the first time.[12] They might also play special vocabulary-building games: a popular example in the late twentieth century was one where the trick lay in making oral lists of nouns starting with the same letter ('bricks', 'bread', 'bacon', and so on), which continued until the imagination of the players was exhausted.[13] A child from this sort of background, or indeed one from any background who happened to have a strongly verbal bent, was likely to recall word-learning at least as vividly as its first encounters with the physical world.[14]

The moment when a child started to be able to stand and move about independently was recorded excitedly in parents' diaries. 'And then one day (at one year, one month and 15 days), Dima's nanny put down in front of him an empty scent bottle (one of his favourite toys at the time), and started to ask him to come and get it. The tempting bottle overcame Dima's usual hesitancy: he suddenly made several steps one after the other and was soon walking independently,' A. Levonevsky recorded in the 1910s, after having described in detail Dima's earlier flailing attempts to move about on his own two legs.[15] A child was not necessarily completely left to itself: machines to help might be purchased, whether of the traditional 'Zimmer frame' variety, or some more modern kind.[16] But the question of how to get a child to walk does not seem to have generated any particular philosophical anxiety, and, if anything, urban parents were *less* preoccupied with it than were adults in traditional Russian villages. Interestingly, too, for all the concerns about protecting children from dangers in microbe form, little effort was expended on anxieties about safety in another sense – avoiding the sort of accidents that became likely once mobile small children first came in contact with the domestic environment. Judging by memoirs, a major cause of trauma and indeed death was scalding when small children cannoned into samovars full of boiling water, but no child-care manuals offered advice on such incidents, nor did diaries show parents 'child-proofing' the house, in the way that was routinely done by parents in the late twentieth century.[17]

By the early twentieth century, though, bowel regulation was seen as a subject in which a model parent ought to be interested. A. L. Pavlova, the author of a 'mother's diary' composed in the late 1910s, devoted a considerable amount of space to the training of her small boy, Adik, born in 1915. By the age of two, the boy was regularly being placed on a pot: his first complete sentence, uttered at two and a half, was 'Mama, Adya do pee-pee past potty a bit.' By three, he was expected to be dry in bed at night. After a series of episodes in which he wet and fouled the sheets, Pavlova punished the boy by refusing to speak to or touch him, an act of rejection that, understandably, made him very upset: 'Mama, Adya won't do pee-pee no more, not petit or gros.' At this point his mother consoled him by being nice to him all day, though at the

79 Baby walker, G. Speransky, *Advice to Mothers*, 1952.

same time she warned him he would be punished once more if he failed to control himself in the future. With that, the immediate problem apparently cleared up.[18] Striking here, apart from Pavlova's concern to get the child through the process of training as quickly as possible (typical not just of the era, but of later eras as well), was her tolerance of discussion of the subject, so long as this was veiled in baby-talk and in euphemisms borrowed from foreign languages. More customary nursery euphemisms were *pisat'* and *kakat'* for urination and defecation, and, or alternatively, *delat'*, or *khodit' po-malen'komu/po-bol'shomu* (to go for a big or a little one), both of which remained in use throughout the twentieth century.[19]

Euphemism was only one sub-domain of the special language used by adults with children, in exchanges that began before the child was able to speak, and continued as it gave its first replies. Many elements of this language used with children were, like euphemisms for physical phenomena and processes, those present in many other European languages as well: simplified grammar and syntax, and the use of special lexis and an indulgent intonation.[20] Russian baby-talk, however, also abundantly employed the rich range of diminutives present in the language, giving an emotional coloration to everyday processes, such as dressing, eating, or dealing with parts of the body:

MOTHER: Are you going to wash your own hair [dim.] Sveta?
SVETA: Yes. [...]
MOTHER: Let's get on, Sveta, or you'll be getting tired. Let me turn
the water [dim.] on. There [puts the shower in the child's hand]
There you are, nice and warm [dim.] Is that nice for you, nice
water?[21]

The affectionate, wheedling nature of the address to the child is easy to capture in English at some points (*na, teplen'kaya* – 'nice and warm'). But the diminutives in the Russian express this tone much more consistently. Given that such diminutives are routinely used about parts of the child's own body (here, the literal equivalent of 'hair' is 'little head', *golovka*), an association between cuteness and smallness is established. Emphasising this too strongly would be misplaced: since diminutives are pervasive in the language used to children, a child is likely to use them about adults' body parts and attributes. In the same way, a child learning to speak may use adult-speak, referring to itself by given name and 'you'. Diminutives may therefore not appear to say anything specific to very small children about their own bodies and status at all. However, as children grow, they rapidly – in Russian culture as in any other – acquire an independent attitude to the language, based not simply on imitation and repetition, but on the capacity to work by analogy and to vary set models.[22] In addition, adults begin to talk differently to them, in a more 'adult' way. Thus, as alternatives become available, the use of diminutives starts to be coloured by the particularly close relations that obtained in the nursery; and so they acquire – retrospectively at least – a function of marking off early childhood as a special era.

Rational Parenting

The conversations just cited were recorded in the late 1960s and early 1970s, but socialisation of the emotions through language use happened in this way considerably earlier.[23] The difference, in earlier eras, especially before 1917, was that, in prosperous middle-class households such as these, the person employing diminutives might have been a nursemaid or nanny.[24] However, even if nurses were employed, the responsible mother was supposed – unlike her counterpart in many eighteenth-century manuals, who began to direct upbringing only when the child had reached a state where intellectual and moral education could begin – to supervise the details of the child's daily life meticulously.[25]

As with babies, the first of the 'modern mother's' duties was to create a suitably hygienic environment. Like infants, older children were meant to have specially decorated and meticulously arranged nurseries, with furniture scaled down to suit and fittings organised so that dust and dirt did not collect. They, too, were supposed to have special diets and a well-regulated, repetitive regime. Part of this was the cult of *zakal*, or 'tempering', which observers regarded as a Russian offshoot of the contemporary English obsession with cold-water washing as a route to mental resolution and psychological toughness. A book published by Speransky in 1910 described the practice as 'physical gymnastics' for the human organism. Unlike Soviet baby books, Speransky's did not recommend that all this started in infancy: instead the author specified 10–15 as a sensible age range to begin with the practice. But the combination of exposure to cold air and 'cold rubs' that he recommended was exactly the same.[26]

So far as the link between physical hygiene and emotional hygiene went, many writers were not as repressive about small children as they were about babies. The emphasis was, rather, on self-discovery and development of the imagination. In the words of A. Dernova-Yarmolenko, editor of the journal *Family Upbringing*, writing in 1911, 'A careful, tidy child is not a child at all, just as a child with no imagination is not a child, or is a mutilated child.'[27] Petr Lesgaft's *Family Upbringing and its Significance*, first published in the 1880s, offered readers a range of pathetic individuals created by mistaken kinds of upbringing. There was Mr Hypocrite, a revolting little creep who abased himself before his school-teachers while enjoying the hearty contempt of his fellows, whose little treasures he coolly pilfered. There was also Mr Ambition, an arrogant monster created by adulation in the family, and there were the equally sad types manufactured by parental tyranny: Mr Timid-Underdog, Mr Vicious-Underdog, and Mr Totally-Degraded. Only kind, moderate, and rational behaviour could create the ideal type, Mr Kindheart, though Lesgaft did acknowledge the contribution made by what he termed 'temperament' (that is, innate 'humours' of the type identified by Hippocrates and Galen).[28]

Lesgaft's book was, in fact, rather less liberal than those of some other writers of the time, who stressed the importance of creating 'character' (in the Victorian sense: 'Character is what one may term the demonstration of a person's will, where founded on real truths').[29] Even in *Family Upbringing*, opposition to tyranny was matched by opposition to indulgence: A. N. Filippov, for example, warned readers against mollycoddling of a kind that stuffed children with rich food and prevented them from getting any exercise, and hence created fat little couch potatoes.[30] But on the whole the journal preached the Tolstoyan message of peace and goodwill to all men. Parents were counselled not to buy their children war toys, warned that children who were harshly treated were likely to behave cruelly towards others (their little sisters, animals, and in due course other adults and themselves), and instructed that punishment could have adverse physical as well as mental effects. This applied not just to beatings, which inflicted wounds and might inspire precocious sexual feeling, but also to standing a child in the corner, which might damage its posture and the circulation of the blood.[31]

The accumulation of material possessions was supposed to proceed along rational lines. It was accepted that children should have toys, which were regarded as a valuable aid to developing the imagination. But ready-made toys were regarded with suspicion, being unduly mechanical in various ways. An article by Vladimir Ladunsky published in 1914 condemned expensive dolls that were only good for dressing and undressing (boring), fairground games such as 'Japanese Bi-Ba-Bo' (stupid), Froebel's geometric objects (stupid), and caricatures of fat men or miserable Pierrots (vulgar).[32] Equally rationalistic was the attitude to gender education. The contributors to *Family Education* were vehemently in favour of egalitarian treatment of the sexes, and of coeducation as a way of attaining this. Girls and boys were equal, wrote N. E. Rumyantsev in 1912, and girls should be educated in exactly the same way that boys were.[33]

As with the new advice on babies, some parents took counsel on small children very seriously. The vogue among progressive parents for the theories of Froebel and Tolstoy is attested by mothers' diaries of the early twentieth century. It was customary for children to be presented with one of the Froebel 'gifts' (developmentally graded sets of geometrical shapes) at an early stage, and for much effort to be expended on diet and on clothing.[34] Underwear, for instance, might take a form then becoming popular all over Europe – the liberty bodice, an undergarment that gave the child some protection against feared anatomical disorders such as curvature of the spine, and provided a way of attaching the stockings in which all respectable children were dressed, but which did not curtail movement as severely as the corsets that had once been used for children.[35] 'Modern' dress for children minimised, so far as possible, gender distinctions between boys and girls. Small girls were expected to take exercise and were dressed in variants of their brothers' clothes (for example, versions of the massively popular 'sailor suit'). Hair was combed out rather than being set in ringlets; sometimes it was trimmed to shoulder length. An example is shown in Mikhail Nesterov's beautiful portrait of his daughter Natasha, dating from 1914. The child, then aged 11, wears a bright blue dress like a miniature painter's smock, its skirt short enough to show almost the full extent of her bony, coltish legs; her hair is uncombed and hanging loose, her feet pushed into flat, strapped walking sandals.[36]

The Limits of Reason

In their attempts to select an appropriate, child-centred regime for their children, some parents went to extraordinary lengths. The wife of one high-ranking St Petersburg officer tried out on her son Swiss, German, and English methods in turn, switching from muesli to meat and milk-heavy dishes, before finally settling on porridge and cold rubs.[37] But, even within the cultural elite, parents like this constituted a minority. Anxieties about the national tradition of producing 'superfluous men' with an inclination to 'dreaminess' (*mechtatel'nost'*), along with alarm about the high suicide rate among young people, created a ready audience for the Victorian cult of 'manliness', 'character', 'resolution', and 'backbone' (qualities supposed to be inculcated from early childhood). The regime to which Paul Ignat'ev, raised in the 1890s, was submitted included 'Bible lessons with his mother, lean food, cold baths, riding, fencing, and cold winter walks in the streets of Petersburg to build up the legs and the lungs'.[38]

There were also parents who took very little interest in raising their children. For working-class and peasant mothers, 'upbringing' essentially meant seeing a child safely through its most vulnerable years. Once able to walk, talk, and (in the most basic sense) look after itself, the child would be left to the supervision of older siblings, or perhaps without supervision at all; in many areas it was hard for casual observers to tell the difference between children with parents, and children who had no parents.[39] Even if moral guidance was offered – as might be the case – no effort would be made to give the child a special diet, or to provide it with 'rational dress': food would simply be provided at the family table, and dress would consist of miniature versions of adult clothes. Close contact between child and mother was limited to the early years (by the time children became toddlers, another infant had almost certainly arrived to take their place, so that prolongation of the relationship would have been difficult in practical terms, even if it had been considered desirable).[40] But, though parental non-intervention was associated in social commentaries with parents from the working class and peasantry, there were also well-off and well-educated parents who did precious little to supervise their children. The writer Dmitry Tsenzor, for instance, recalled: 'Nobody brought me up. I led the life of a street-boy.'[41] At times, neglect could shade into abuse, a phenomenon that was less recognised in children from well-off families, but by no means unknown.[42]

Among parents who did take an active part in upbringing, large numbers seem to have maintained an attachment to established patterns. Children often seem to have been dressed in more restrictive, and more heavily decorated, garments than the latest advice literature anticipated. The tradition of treating boys the same as girls in their first few years, though declining, was still quite prevalent. Anatoly Mariengof remembered being dressed 'by my parents in the most offensive way: I'm not put in trousers, as a proper male should be, but in little dresses – blue and pink. And my hair's long as well – to below my shoulders.'[43] Once boys had graduated beyond the dress stage, middle-class and upper-class parents of the day often dressed them in adaptations of adult male attire – such as knickerbocker suits[44] – rather than in 'rational' childswear, such as knitted tops and trunks, or short-sleeved shirts and shorts.

Small girls from moneyed households could also expect to be dressed elaborately. A catalogue produced by a prestigious shop in St Petersburg in the 1900s contained a large number of stiff and frilly outfits for girls: every top was decorated with lace, embroidery, and often braiding.[45] A photograph of Tamara Abel'son, daughter of a timber merchant in St Petersburg, shows the boys in sailor suits, but Tamara in a frilly white muslin dress.[46] Parents who went for this kind of look might also have their children painted by fashionable portraitists in 'chocolate-box' style, or parade them in the beauty contests by correspondence that had started to be organised in women's magazines. During 1914, *Woman* published a whole series of photographs from such a contest, showing large-eyed, ethereal children gazing soulfully into the camera.[47]

Indulgence in a material sense did not necessarily go with indulgence in other senses, however. In the Abelson household, the children were treated relatively strictly, at least in public. 'Children were expected to eat the food served them and, once they had started to eat a slice of bread, were forbidden to leave even a scrap, because bread, we were told, was produced at the sweat of a peasant's brow.'[48] Attitudes of this kind prevailed in many traditional gentry households as well. In the words of the dancer Tamara Karsavina: 'Mother often said her love for her children was "rational". I remember her stern at times and never foolish or tender.'[49] There were still families in the 1900s and 1910s where children were expected to address their parents formally, using the second-person plural (the equivalent of *vous* in French).[50] Such usage was apparently commoner towards fathers than mothers; at the same time, real fathers, unlike those in books, were at times rather more indulgent than the child's female parent, especially if the child was a girl.[51]

Strictness of demeanour was often accompanied by severity in administering punishment, where this was felt to be necessary. Corporal punishment was by no means unknown in Russian middle- and upper-class families before 1917. Disobedience, speaking 'out of turn', and being late for meals could all provoke a thrashing.[52] Another popular strategy was locking children in a dark room until they came to their senses – a treatment that Olga Forsh, for instance, recalled enduring in the early 1880s.[53] Alternatively, a 'token slap on the hand' might be administered along with a lecture on good behaviour. As Elisaveta Fen recorded, sententious assessments of conduct were routine. Children would be told that their activities were *nekrasivo* ('unattractive', the rough equivalent of 'bad manners'), or *nekhorosho* ('bad', in the sense of 'immoral', a more important rebuke). To be told your behaviour was *nekhorosho* 'made you feel really uncomfortable, not merely ashamed but guilty and condemned'.[54]

In traditional gentry families, there was a firm expectation that children would learn good manners, especially table manners, at an early stage. Nadezhda Teffi's recollection of pre-revolutionary norms in her story 'Upbringing' (1937) began with a sardonic sketch of harassed parents severely, but ineptly, trying to teach their children how to behave at table. A father who bawled, 'Elbows off the table, you little son of a bitch!' represented absurdity of one kind; a teacher in a pension who told her charges, 'The Apostles never put their elbows on the table, only Judas', another:

> Yes, the trials that any child of self-respecting parents has to go through are sore ones indeed. Don't eat off your knife, don't blow in your cup, don't dunk your biscuit in your tea, don't swing your legs, don't speak till you're spoken to. But on the other hand, there's nothing to beat the delight of the moment when your upbringing finally comes to an end and you can exercise your right to put your feet, let alone your elbows, on the table, and to pick up lamb bones in all five fingers and gnaw them.[55]

By the early twentieth century, however, strictness of this kind was beginning to seem rather old-fashioned to some (including, judging by her ironic tone, Teffi herself). Youngsters were now sometimes allowed to behave, even at table, in a manner their grandparents might well not have tolerated from their children, sitting in relaxed positions and with their elbows pointing outwards rather than clamped to their sides.[56] Indulgence was also expressed in the development of a genre new to Russian culture – the anecdote centred on some unintentionally comical observation made by a small child. When Anatoly Mariengof, bored by a concert, asked of a violinist, 'Will he soon stop sawing his box in half?' his parents, rather than telling him not to be so silly, soon spread the story round the entire town.[57]

Religion and Morality

Just as had been the case for earlier generations of Russian children, nannies often provided a counterweight to 'rational upbringing' (especially when this was of the chilly variety). As Tamara Talbot-Rice remembered, 'My beloved nurse, Anna, was the one member of the household who never found fault with me. Her constant love and devotion, her unshakeable conviction that I could do no wrong, enveloped me in a cocoon of security grievously dented by her departure when I was six years old.'[58] It was nurses, rather than parents, who were often responsible for a child's first religious upbringing, which tended to emphasise love of God (*krotkii Bozhen'ka*, or, literally, 'gentle little God').

This is not to say that parents exercised no religious influence. The writer L. Panteleev (pseudonym of Aleksei Eremin) was profoundly shaped by his mother's faith, 'lively, active, effective, and happy into the bargain – she considered any form of low spirits a sin'. Morality was inculcated less through dreary sermons than in the form of humorous anecdotes, such as the tale of a young woman so absurdly refined that she was embarrassed to stop and pick up money she had dropped.[59] Such conscious attempts to make religion accessible to children were characteristic of the early twentieth century: the 'gentle Jesus' cult of Victorian England made its way into some elite Russian households, with Vladimir Nabokov, for example, being taught to recite a prayer to this vision of the deity.[60]

Observant households introduced the child to a whole set of moral values. The virtues that Panteleev remembered being taught by example – hard work, consideration for others, and tolerance – were typical of those inculcated in Orthodox families generally. But just as important, in the child's growing consciousness of faith, were the ritual practices and the calendar of Orthodoxy. Fasts were often mitigated for children: fish was substituted for meat, almond milk for cow's, and there might even be special Lenten delicacies, such as potato dumplings with mushroom sauce, or sweetmeats. If even Lent could be so pleasurable, it is not surprising that, for many small children, religious festivals were associated as much as anything else with worldly pleasures. Rather than celebrating birthdays, most Russian children celebrated the feast day of the saint that they were named after (the *imeniny*, or name day). But the nature of the revelry was much the same as on a birthday: gifts, a party, and cakes by the dozen, which in Moscow meant especially the prized chocolate cakes from von Einem, Sue, or Abrikosov.[61]

Of course, part of the deeper meaning of festivals sometimes sank into children's consciousness too. It might seem tempting to slide along the polished wood floors during Lent, when the carpets had been taken up to 'impoverish' the house according to custom, but children trying out games of this kind knew they would be rebuked with the awful words, 'Fancy behaving like that in Lent! Try that again and you're sure to break your leg!'[62] Influential in a spiritual sense was the beauty of the church services, more attractive to the perceptions of many children than the starkness of Lutheran or non-conformist rites.

> The gold of the iconostasis has a round, plump shine. The brocade altar-curtain shines scarlet and crimson behind it. I feel happy, touched, delighted all at the same time. And the ringing, sonorous singing of the deacon, with the choir's surging responses of 'Lord, have mercy!' and 'Lord, be with us!', and the thin but somehow exhilarating cry of a baby being christened, and the smells of aromatic oil, incense, burning candles, warm human bodies packed together... And above all the prayers, and the sense of wanting to pray within oneself.[63]

At the same time, religion was not always so meaningful: a boy growing up in an observant household might wonder why his father, having begged forgiveness of a servant on 'Forgiveness Day', could yell at the same man for drunkenness just 24 hours later.[64] Observation of religious festivals and supervision of the religious guidance given to children were often perfunctory. Families might attend church only on major festivals, and children end up knowing – at best – the texts of a few prayers, such as the Lord's Prayer and the Hail Mary.[65] The presence of Orthodoxy in the household might be limited to a few nationally coloured traditions: the maintenance of an 'icon corner', the serving of special foods during Lent and other major fasts, or at Easter and Christmas, and possibly grace before meals.

In working-class, and more particularly peasant, families, on the other hand, religious ritual was likely to be more central to a child's everyday experience. This did not necessarily mean Orthodoxy in a formal sense; it could be contact with the popular or local cult of a saint, or with rites for sanctifying a new house, protecting farm animals, or seeing off an older male relative into the army.[66] Church fasts were taken extremely seriously in most households. Milk products were likely to be denied throughout major fasts: when the children in the writer Konstantin Trenev's family asked for some milk one spring, their grandmother pointed to a jug hanging on a tree and told them it would remain there till the end of Lent.[67] Old Believer households represented an extreme version of Orthodox tradition: a rigidly ordered life. It was expected that children would learn prayers from their early youth, say them at frequent intervals during the day, and wear not only a cross, but also the belt that the priest had placed over their christening robe, at all times when they were dressed. Extremely proper behaviour was expected at table, and rigid observance of the codes of purity was required. Fasts were strictly observed: a prohibition was placed not only on the eating of forbidden foods, but also upon the enjoyment of foods and on pleasure and merry-making of any kind.[68]

In peasant families, insistence on the need for children to observe religious prescription was underpinned by the shortage economy in which such families lived. In the winter months when Advent and Lent fell, milk and eggs were likely to be scarce in any case. Still more importantly, it reflected the generally demanding and stern attitude to children. Children over the age of two, unless direly sick, would be fed the same as everyone else, and expression of caprice in

80   Izba interior, Smolensk province, 1890s.

eating preferences was out of the question. When food was served, children came at the bottom of the hierarchy, which was headed by the senior adult male; once he had picked out the best bits, everyone else took 'pot luck' in the communal dish. At the end of the meal, the children thanked the head of household for what they had received.[69]

Generally, the attitude to children, once they had reached the age of seven, was strict. Misdemeanours were punished by beatings or by sharp scoldings; disobedience was not tolerated.[70] On the whole, children did what their parents said, and obediently helped out in the household from an early age. 'I knew nothing but potties, nappies, and washing clothes,' recalled a woman born in Ryazan' province in 1897, who was put to work looking after her younger siblings once she was through three years of parish school.[71]

In working-class families, much the same practices obtained. Children ate at the general family table, were expected to do what their parents told them without argument, and had to muck in and help out from an early age. Beating was not uncommon: in the words of one woman born in 1898, her mother (a loom operator in a textile factory) 'beat me till I was half-dead'.[72] Yet severity did not represent the full story. Parents could also be indulgent, where circumstances allowed. 'Mother spoiled me – after all, I was the only daughter,' recalled a woman born in a Moscow province village in 1900, who later moved into the city for work. Another woman recalled her father – a stoker at the Prokhorov factory – as strict-looking, 'but very kind'. It tended to be in families under pressure, such as those with single mothers or large collections of foster children, that expectations were harshest: 'The kids with mothers and fathers were always running around outside, but we worked from when we were tots,' a woman born in Orel province in 1912 remembered.[73]

Religious attitudes also varied: even in pious families, belief was not always presented in a punitive fashion. Poorer families kept the fasts more strictly than those with money in hand, but when festivals arrived, those above the breadline also arranged a good spread of home-made delicacies: thick meat soup and pies with different kinds of filling. At Easter, Anna Kuznetsova-Budanova remembered, there were so many hard-boiled eggs that the children got sick of eating them. Just as memorable were the traditional entertainments, especially during the twelve days of Christmas (svyatki): songs to the accordion, games, visits from mummers in masks and fancy dress, fortune-telling.[74] Feast days were not the only treats for children in religious families: the poet Sergei Esenin was to recall a pilgrimage with his grandmother as a particularly exciting experience.[75]

Rather the same mixture of sternness and celebration was characteristic of religious upbringing in other communities of faith. Outside the moneyed elite, Jewish parents were not always indulgent: in many artisanal households, children would be expected to contribute to the household economy once they reached their early teens.[76] Religious festivals were family-centred, and children, especially the eldest son, had an important place in them. In Tatar households, children were also strictly treated, and self-restraint was expected in front of one's elders, above all one's father – but, from babyhood up, children were integrated into rituals and festivals, with even babies, in some areas, fed special treats of honey soon after they were born.[77]

A significant minority of Russians – mainly, but not exclusively, from the upper and middle classes – espoused a secular 'religion'. Associates of the different branches of radicalism, in particular, led an explicitly and determinedly humanist way of life. Christening children was unavoidable, since a birth could not be registered unless the service was performed. But church attendance would be eschewed, religious festivals ignored, and instruction in Orthodox (or other) belief avoided. Families of this kind would offer a counterweight to religious teaching in school. When Vadim Andreev responded to a mark of two (a failing grade) in religious knowledge by grunting like a pig during prayers, he was bawled out by the school director and sent home in disgrace. His stepmother considered the fuss ridiculous, and told him he had done exactly the right thing.[78]

Even in these circles, though, children might encounter believers close at hand. Nannies, for instance – one among many conduits of piety in religious families – could offer, in non-religious ones, a unique means of contact with religious practices and tenets. This no doubt contributed to an increasing sense, in the early twentieth century, that placing a child with an untrained nanny might not be the most appropriate form of child care, and that more systematic solutions should be found. The linguistic purity ensured by contact with a real Russian peasant nanny was a cliché of drawing-room conversation. But, as a satirical story by Nadezhda Teffi showed, there was increasing concern in some quarters that the types of Russian usage children in fact picked up from modern-day servants were thoroughly urban, and – to invoke the snobbish register – vulgar. The story showed a mother boasting about her nanny's credentials as a representative of 'true Russian' values, but severely deflated when the nanny was overheard telling a decidedly modern folk tale, with a princess dressed in 'corduroy' rather than swansdown, brocade, or velvet.[79]

'Professionalising' Child Care

One way in which well-off parents who felt uneasy about the cultural resources of nannies might attempt to provide a child with a better start in life was by the time-honoured method of engaging a French, English, or German nurse or governess. Vladimir Nabokov had a procession of English, French, and Swiss attendants; Russian-Jewish princess Tamara Abelson had no fewer than three governesses at once, one English, one French, and one German (her mother had been educated by only one governess, a strict Englishwoman by the name of Miss Rate, but had decided on 'a sounder education' for her own children).[80]

Increasingly, though, formal pre-school education was beginning to be considered as an option, especially for children in the 4–7 age group. The prompting for this was not only concern that children should have trained supervision, but a conviction of the virtues of collective education. The view expressed in the prospectus of one Moscow nursery school published in 1907, 'The company of other children of the same age is essential if a child is to develop harmoniously',[81] was widely shared by progressively inclined parents. Indeed, it was such parents who were the main moving force behind the early development of the kindergarten movement, with 'parents' societies', after 1905, setting up small-scale 'family' kindergartens in both capitals and in many provincial cities.

In 1903, St Petersburg had a very small number of model kindergartens. For example, the Women's Patriotic Society had two, while the Children's Aid Society ran a kindergarten alongside its drop-in crèche for working mothers.[82] But after the Society for the Furtherance of Nursery Education began to function in the autumn of 1906, kindergartens were opened rapidly. By the end of the year there were sixteen 'home kindergartens' in the city, and by the start of 1907 the society had over 150 members. Alongside the kindergartens as such, it organised parents' groups, libraries, and a summer 'colony' where children could be boarded in the countryside.[83] The society had 500 members by 1911, and playgroups, excursions, propaganda, and publishing initiatives were now among its activities.[84] By the 1910s, several dozen institutions in St Petersburg were offering pre-school education, a few with a specialist slant (for example Russo-French and Russo-German establishments, with conversation in the respective foreign languages as part of the nursery day; there was even a Jewish kindergarten offering instruction in Hebrew).[85] In Moscow, the Circle of Collective Education for Children was the main dynamo, opening a People's Kindergarten in November 1909 alongside its other activities.[86] By 1916–17, Moscow had some forty kindergartens, which supported around 2 per cent of the relevant age group. Whatever the inadequacy of this coverage in the absolute sense, it represented impressive growth in proportionate terms, especially given that initiatives depended entirely on voluntary work.[87] Hours were sometimes surprisingly generous: several places specialising in caring for the children of 'intelligentsia mothers' advertised 9, 10, or even 13-hour days.[88] And one flagship facility, the Universal Kindergarten in Memory of O. N. Kal'ina, was housed in a magnificent modernist building on Bol'shaya Tsaritsinskaya (now Bol'shaya Pirogovskaya), and combining a child-care centre with a children's library, club-room, concert rooms, and so on.[89]

A Kiev society for the furtherance of nursery education was founded in 1907. By 1913, the city had eleven kindergartens catering for 800 children, including two special nurseries for Jewish children.[90] Other major cities in the Russian Empire where child care was developing included Odessa, with four kindergartens by the 1890s, Tiflis, with one in the same period, and Chelyabinsk, where a parents' society along the same lines as in Moscow and St Petersburg was set up in 1910.[91] Saratov acquired a kindergarten in 1913, as did Tomsk; in the latter case, the population of 'the northern Athens' was chided by *Pre-School Education* for having left things so long.[92] Many smaller towns, including Astrakhan and even Yeisk, a port on the Sea of Azov, had parents' groups as well.[93]

The majority of facilities were 'private' not only in the sense that they had no state or local government funding, but also in that they charged fees. For example, the Poltava kindergarten levied the quite hefty sum of 7 roubles a month when it opened in 1911, a sum dictated by the small number of children who entered at that time.[94] But by no means all nurseries imposed payment. By the 1910s, five kindergartens in Kiev offered free tuition, including one at the Froebel Institute in the city (founded in 1909) and the Tsarevich Alexis People's Kindergarten (founded in 1905).[95] Most 'people's kindergartens' – which also existed in Astrakhan (1913), Poltava (1914), and Taganrog (1914), among other places – were run by individuals, charitable societies, or religious bodies.[96] But there was also a tentative movement to set up municipal kindergartens. Moscow, for instance, had two of these by 1911, and St Petersburg three by 1912.[97]

As with crèches, factory managements and zemstva played some role in developing child care. Indeed, the word 'crèche' was frequently used for a facility that housed small children as well as babies. An example was the child-care centre at the famous 'Trekhgorka' (in full, Trekhgornaya manufaktura), an enormous textile works in the heart of the Presnya district of western Moscow, set up in 1906, which by 1908 was catering for 170 children.[98] Another type of initiative was represented by a nursery at the Railway Engine factory in Khar'kov, where a kindergarten for the children of white-collar workers and skilled workers was set up in September 1911, with a running subsidy from the factory management. Demand was such that a second nursery soon had to be started; by 1912, there were 270 children being cared for, in a programme that included hot breakfasts and magic lantern shows as well as 'learning through play'.[99]

Yet overall numbers remained small. In 1911 there were only 100 kindergartens in operation across Russia, a figure that was strikingly low compared with the figures for France (5,863), the US (4,363), or Austro-Hungary (3,150). The number of places provided in individual kindergartens was also small – a good percentage of those recorded as operating consisted of small groups organised on an *ad hoc* basis in private houses.[100] Unlike other European administrations of the period, the administration of the Russian Empire took a minimal interest in nursery education. But even this was starting to change by the 1910s. In 1909, for the first time in history, the Ministry of Enlightenment paid out a subsidy for the nursery education of poor children. As the editors of *Pre-School Education* pointed out three years later, the amount granted – 20,000 roubles (roughly comparable with six or seven professors' annual salaries at the time) – was enough to fund each child in need of pre-school education to the tune of about one kopeck.[101] However, the very fact that ministerial notice had been taken of the nursery school network – both in granting the subsidy and in setting up norms for the operation of kindergartens – represented an important breakthrough.

The start of the First World War brought much greater readiness to commit money from the public purse, primarily for the children of conscripts. By 1915, Petrograd had eleven day shelters and seven round-the-clock shelters, six 'children's refuges', two kindergartens, two clubs, and two special schools for children of men in the reserves.[102] Other places with special facilities for this last category included Tomsk.[103] And, in 1916, the Ministry of Enlightenment was moved by the plight of conscripts' children into providing more generous subsidies. The nursery school activists of Volchanskaya district, for example, were granted 22,000 roubles in two tranches as help towards the running of kindergartens in their locality: they were now able to run as many as 103 summer kindergartens, catering for over 16,000 children during the harvest season.[104]

Activists were determined that poor children should have the best available care. According to a eulogistic report in *Pre-School Education*, the Poltava People's Kindergarten was light, bright, and warm, with a full five rooms (including a toy room, 'library', sick bay, and games room) for its thirty children; the walls were decorated with pictures of animals.[105] Corners were not meant to be cut on nursery teaching. A 1900 guide put out by the Empress Maria Department for 'people's kindergartens' recommended a fair degree of regimentation: the day was to begin with a hygienic inspection of those attending, followed by words of praise or blame to the parents depending on how clean they turned out to be. Children who were persistently untidy were to be made to wear a black apron; the day was to begin with prayers, and include a session on the catechism. Training was to be steered by rewards and punishments: among the former, it was suggested that boys might have their names put on a board, while girls, as befitting their humbler role in life, might be encouraged to make gifts for some loved one. But even this relatively tightly ordered schedule included activities such as singing, reading, and free play, while basic educational skills were supposed to be taught in a light-hearted way – counting in the form of games and chants during a walk, for instance. As the guide summed up, the mode of life was to be 'as in a poor, but well-conducted family', and activities were to be kept varied, short, interesting, and helpful to the children's intellectual and physical development.[106]

If even programmes for 'people's kindergartens' had a child-centred orientation, kindergartens for the children of the more fortunate were usually wellsprings of 'free education', with a decided Froebelian and Montessorian tone. The training consisted (refinements such as foreign languages aside) of a mixture of training in basic literacy and numeracy skills (work with words and letters, games with building blocks and abacuses), creative activities such as drawing, modelling, and handicraft, physical activities such as singing, dancing, 'active games', and an introduction to nature study.[107] Teachers were encouraged to combine the activities thematically. For example, they would organise a discussion about the habits and features of some animal, beginning with tame ones ('Almost all the children are likely to have a cat at home'), and continuing with wild ones. Having got the children to participate in a directed conversation ('Which animal that we all know and love does a wolf resemble? [...] A she-wolf is a very affectionate mother'), they would then get them to make pictures, cut-outs, and models of wolves; there would be readings aloud of Russian folk tales which had wolves as characters; and the children would sing wolf-related songs and play wolf-related games.[108] As this material suggests, tuition often emphasised material of national origin – which included, alongside folk tales, folk songs and traditional games, such as blind man's buff or hide-and-seek (adapted for playing indoors and preceded by little improvisations in which children were selected for teams on strictly egalitarian principles).[109] But internationalist work also went on: in one St Petersburg free nursery school, for example, children learned geography by dressing up in national costume (absorbing the teaching about ethnic difference so enthusiastically that they would adopt roles on a cross-gender basis rather than act out a nationality they did not resemble). They also drew pictures of life in different countries and wrote little stories about what people got up to: 'In Sweden you sometimes get waterfalls. Swedes have very nice national costumes. In winter Swedes often ski.'[110]

What evidence there is suggests that children enjoyed their activities at nursery school. Ol'ga Volosistova, born in 1912, nostalgically remembered her days at the Trekhgorka kindergarten: 'We had a nice time there. I remember, there was a piano, we used to do dances and go on excursions.'[111] Even where the day was essentially organised as a holding operation, the 'culture and hygiene' ethos of the nursery education movement had the potential to make an impact. Certainly, the organisers of child-care facilities for working-class children – unlike their Soviet counterparts – made efforts to provide a diet that was familiar to children, on the grounds that otherwise readjustment to home life might be problematic. But they were insistent on the importance of organising children's time thoroughly, and of providing exemplary nursery accommodation, with light, air, space, and specialised equipment such as low tables and chairs.[112] For a child who had come from an overcrowded basement or attic apartment, such an environment must have seemed like another world.

Even the few working-class children attending kindergartens were unlikely to experience this as their exclusive method of non-parental child care, however, given the compressed opening times of most of the few kindergartens that did exist. It was unusual for a nursery school to be open more than eight hours in the day (for example, the Tsarevich Aleksei City People's Kindergarten in Kiev, founded in 1905, had a timetable running from 9 to 4.30).[113] Since manual workers commonly worked at least 10-hour shifts, the kindergartens were at best a partial stopgap; in the early evening there had to be reliance on older children, or on neighbours, for at least some child-minding. All in all, the nursery school movement – like the crèche movement – was important less for what it achieved in percentage terms than because the ambitions and educational values of the nursery school planners were to shape educational policy for pre-schoolers after 1917 as well, particularly during the first decade or so of Soviet power.

Reason and 'Regime'

Before the Revolution, the dissemination of propaganda for 'rational upbringing', and the organisation of model institutions where it could be seen in action, were, like other areas of the effort to 'modernise childhood', left more or less entirely to private initiative. After the Revolution, this situation changed. The flood of educational material put out by state-run publishing houses included not only advice on how to look after babies, but counsel on dealing with older children. A key part of what such material contained was information about what to avoid, as with the long-running campaigns against corporal punishment, and against 'superstition', by which was meant both traditional beliefs in the supernatural, and the dissemination of the tenets of religious faith. The second motif became particularly important after the 8 April 1929 decree banning the organisation of 'special meetings for children, young people, women, whether for prayer or for any other purposes'.[114]

Equal emphasis was placed on the patterns that parents were supposed to cultivate: cleanliness, tidiness, and reliability, the centrality of which was best manifested in a regular, strongly ordered daily regime. The development of linguistic and intellectual facilities was left to specialist commentators, such as Lev Vygotsky. Guides for the mass market were more concerned with disciplining the body. Baby books continued to recommend brisk socialisation in 'personal habits'. As well as instructing mothers that they should not allow their child's crying to run their lives, N. P. Eiges, writing in 1948, advised that potty training should begin at around 5–7 months and be completed by the age of two at the latest.[115]

Potty training was – implicitly rather than explicitly – part of the larger subject of 'regime': the organisation of the child's day into an ordered pattern, with leisure, meals, and rest occurring at regular intervals. This was to apply to older children just as to younger ones.[116] Physical discipline of this kind was supposed to go with mental and moral discipline, the child learning to conform to patterns that were those of society in general. This was one part of the process of educating the child for his or her future role in the collective – at the microscopic level of school classes, and, later, the work environment, and at the larger level of public life in general.[117] The motif – present in writings on education before 1917 – had now made its way into material for mothers as well. Soviet books, even in the first decade of the regime's existence, still often acknowledged the superiority of mother-care: 'The child's own mother is the best educator for the child in its first years of life, and the home the best environment,' wrote A. N. Antonov in 1925.[118] But – as with babies – much effort was put into exhorting mothers to care for children to the same level as in children's institutions (or rather, to the same level as it was imagined such institutions cared for children). The ideal model for the mother was the concerned, nurturing kindergarten supervisor.

Excessive severity was seen as irrational; but so, too, was excessive indulgence. Admittedly, some child-care books published in the 1920s did urge parents to allow children as much freedom as possible, sometimes evoking as a norm a child that was assertive to the point of obstreperousness. In *How to Organise Your Children's Leisure* (1929), A. Babina argued that a tractable child was an 'abnormal' child:

> Parents want to have the sort of child that is quiet, obedient, silent, and so on, but they have no idea that quiet, obedient, silent children are, in essence simply abnormal, sick children. Parents who have children like that should, instead of feeling joy and delight in them, consult a good doctor as soon as possible in order to find out how to cure them of their morbid condition.[119]

But a contrary strand emphasised the need for order and discipline: 'We should raise the child so that he is an "easy", "nice", "quiet" fellow-resident in our cramped apartments.'[120]

Despite the obsession, in the public sphere, with child activists, the ideal that persisted in the private sphere was the well-disciplined, docile child. Anton Makarenko's *Conversations with Parents* ordered readers to carry on a 'battle with idleness' by giving children a host of little jobs (for instance logging travel and telephone calls made by members of the family). They were to insist on obedience and to be inflexible in meting out punishments. Upbringing had to be first and foremost an education for citizenship: good parents set their child an example through 'work, character, behaviour', while bad ones displayed a range of weaknesses, including unduly repressive attitudes, irresponsibility (consigning the child to a grandmother 'or even a *domrabotnitsa*'), authoritarianism, too much love, too much kindness, treating the child as a friend, or attempting to bribe it ('the most immoral kind of authority').[121]

Another book by Makarenko, *The Book for Parents* (1937), pursued a similar line, illustrated by cheery case studies of good and bad parenting. The ideal parent here was calm, detached, 'the senior executive member of a collective'; significantly, too, he was a father rather than a mother. In the best regulated of Makarenko's families, mothers tended to be soft-hearted and short-sighted, and it was fathers who exercised the enlightened discipline essential to the running of the family collective, a group analogous to the factory brigade (and, by implication, to the military unit).[122] Even a child's playroom was represented as a kind of well-regulated police state in miniature. Little Vasya, the model boy in a narrative from *The Book for Parents*, is shown checking up on the arrangements in his 'toy kingdom', where a system of universal surveillance such as might have delighted the heart of Foucault obtains. 'During the night, no one had run away, no one had hurt or offended his neighbour, no one had squabbled. This was because colourful wooden Van'ka-Vstan'ka, the gonk, had been on guard duty all through the night.'[123]

Makarenko also maintained a steady campaign against a tendency that he felt to be widespread: placing children before anything else. Two separate narratives in *The Book for Parents* exposed the terrible consequences of such behaviour. In one, a librarian who ran her life round her son and daughter ended up with adolescents who never helped round the house and spent their time complaining that they wanted even more in the way of material goods than they already had. In another, two parents ensured that their little Viktor grew up with every possible educational advantage (lessons in German from early childhood, Schiller in the original from 12), and tiptoed round the home while he did his school-work, but found themselves with an adult son who would not even agree to call in at a pharmacy on his way out for the evening to fetch medicine for his sick father.[124] A lack of sufficient strictness, according to Makarenko, could only end by producing cuckoos in the nest.

Makarenko's attitude to 'spoiling' was typical of the Stalin era, as expressed also in the caricatures of over-indulgent parents and their spoilt and uppity children carried by the humorous magazine *Krokodil*.[125] Hard and fast judgements were made about the causes of this undesirable social phenomenon. Invariably, the spoiling parents were shown as prosperous members of the new Soviet middle class, such as 'responsible officials', engineers, factory managers, or top-ranked skilled workers (the father of Makarenko's priggish little Viktor was a high-level official in a central department of Narkomzem, the agriculture commissariat). Another universal claim was that spoiling was much more likely in small families, especially where there was only one child. Viktor, according to Makarenko, was 'one of those sad stories with an only son, a little emperor, as hero'.[126]

The assault on 'spoiling' was, of course, a correlative to the growing insistence on the importance of discipline that ran right through Soviet culture in the 1930s, a topic also abundantly represented in child-rearing literature. Beatings might be taboo, but parents who tried to reason with their children, instead of laying down the law, were favourite satirical targets. One of Makarenko's figures of fun was a 'professor of pedagogy' who tried to punish his son's rudeness at the family table by telling him he was banned from eating at home in future, and must take his meals in cafés. The result was a son who revelled in eating out, and, when his daily allowance did not pay for all he wanted, took to theft to fund his meals more generously.[127]

A stereotyped division between a nurturing mother and a disciplinary father was standard in Soviet normative sources from the mid-1930s. Prior to this, occasional books, at least, had attempted to go for a more egalitarian representation – though often, even at this point, rather conventional assumptions about gender roles emerged between the lines. For example, Nikolai Al'tgauzen's *Father and Child* (1929) emphasised the leading role of the male parent in contraception, in organising the trip to the maternity hospital (lest his partner become dizzy with pain), and in regarding the child as 'a person and a citizen'. Certainly, the book insisted that girls and boys should be received with equal joy, now that there was equality of the sexes, and that the father should help out with child care (washing, supervising feeding, etc.), but the essential model was one of fatherhood as male-to-male relations, detached 'comradeliness'.[128]

Yet the ideal of gender egalitarianism – in bringing girls up like boys – persisted throughout the early Soviet period. For example, beauty contests for babies and children, which had started to be quite popular in Russian women's magazines in the late Imperial era, disappeared after 1917. To be sure, children portrayed in newspapers, posters, films, and so on were always conventionally good-looking. But competitions for 'the most beautiful baby' and the like were definitely taboo. Egalitarian, too, was the treatment of children's fears: both boys and girls were encouraged to overcome these and to shape 'character' and 'will' in order to take their rightful place in the collective.[129]

'Good Enough' Parents

The priority for most parents during the first four decades of Soviet power was to ensure that their children got a sufficiency of food of any kind. It was only a child from the top end of society whose early memories could include spitting out the hated kasha that was supposed to be 'good for you'.[130] Not only would most families not have tolerated the waste, but few of them lived in circumstances where they could afford to consider a separate diet for children. Indeed, in the post-war years, even children of the Soviet elite usually had to make do with a very basic diet: the daughter of a highly placed official from the trade ministry recollected that her dream, as a young girl, was to become a baker so that she would be able to eat white bread. A soya bean cutlet seemed the height of luxury and sophistication.[131] Equally, when living in a communal flat, parents from the intelligentsia might not be able to provide children with a 'children's corner', let alone with a separate room, though furniture might be arranged to divide off at least part of shared living space, and children in middle-class households were likely to have a bed of their own, as well as the individual toothbrush, towel, underwear, and linen recommended by the manuals.

Yet considerable effort was made by many, perhaps most, parents in the Soviet intelligentsia to put into practice the tenets in child-care books relating to intellectual education. Parents might not be able to obtain educational toys, but they made every effort to ensure that their children were provided with books. And the moral patterns associated with 'rational education' were extremely influential. Diaries by mothers published under the aegis of the paedological movement, for instance, dutifully agonised over the success and failure of their efforts to raise their offspring rationally. Instead of scrutinising children's propensity for creative eccentricity or conscientious objection to the status quo, as diary-writing mothers before 1917 had done, they tended to weigh up the children's potential to become members of the new collective. V. A. Rybnikova-Shilova did all she could to ensure that the aspects of upbringing that did lie in her powers were regulated as the books suggested. Kissing and cuddling were avoided on 'hygienic' grounds, and enemas regularly given. She became extremely concerned when her child was not fully potty-trained at 16 months. Her expectations of intellectual and moral development were just as rigid. She was less concerned to record language acquisition than to fret about whether the child was speaking correctly, and childhood waywardness brought about severe heart-searching. 'I terribly want to encourage patience and self-control in the boy,' she wrote soon after he turned two; at 2 years and 11 months she was pleased to discover 'a sense of application' (*usidchivost'*) in him.[132]

This was not a unique case. 'He's so uneven in temperament,' a contemporary of Shilova's complained of her son, who had reached the grand age of 3 years 10 months at the time. On the other hand, at least the boy measured up to the 1920s ideal of 'rational upbringing' in some ways: a month short of four, he had disliked magic *skazki*, preferring to these the more 'realist' genre of animal tales.[133]

In the 1930s and 1940s, too, real parents (not just the characters in photo-spreads in magazines) sometimes honestly attempted to implement the dictates of the behaviour literature which they had read, and to raise their children in the spirit of collective solidarity, sacrifice of self to the common cause, and determination to become cultured. One woman remembered detesting her trips to the family dacha in the 1940s. This was not just because the trains were always so crowded and the streets often horribly muddy, but because it was here that the process of active 'character education' bore down on her the most:

It was precisely at the dacha that my parents tried to 'accustom me to socially useful work'. In town, I had hardly any duties: just my homework and tidying up my toys. But the dacha offered great opportunities for character education. 'We can't have a girl growing up without wanting to get her hands dirty!' my mother used to say. [...] There was no washing-up liquid in those days, and you had to save water – the well was some distance away and the water had to be boiled up on a paraffin heater every time. 'So you've had enough of washing the dishes?' my mother would ask. 'But you haven't had enough of eating, have you?' What could a nine-year-old martyr say to that?[134]

The 'Soviet' flavour of this emphasis on 'discipline' should not be exaggerated. A 'modern' pre-revolutionary mother might equally well have voiced such views, and one finds them also in writings by *émigré* Russian mothers (as in the case of Princess Mariya Obolenskaya, comparing governesses and observing that Miss Clegg, while manifesting 'attention to the child's physical needs', 'was much less effective than Mrs Stokes in character-building').[135] What was more specific to Soviet Russia was the uniformity with which educated parents subscribed to the view that children should not be corrected in a physical sense. Oral history and memoirs alike almost always insist that such punishment was never resorted to.[136] Instead, preferred methods of persuading a child – if reasoning with it did not work – included (as before 1917), shutting it up in a dark room or cupboard, making it stand in a corner, or giving it a moral dressing-down.[137]

Resisting Norms

This is not to say that official standards of appropriate upbringing were necessarily accepted without conflict. For at least some educated parents, the fact that a rational Soviet upbringing was supposed to be atheist was a major point of divergence, and religious instruction continued to be provided at home on a clandestine basis. Regular attendance at services was problematic. Large numbers of religious buildings were closed down in 1929–30; though some Orthodox churches – but by no means the majority – were reopened during the Second World War, the Khrushchev years saw another assault on religious practice, and with it, a further wave of church closures. But some parents were determined that their children should learn at least the elements of faith. For example, a Leningrad lawyer and his wife, observant Jews who moved to the city in 1930, followed kosher dietary law as far as they could, where possible celebrated the Sabbath and major Jewish festivals, attended secret prayer meetings, and even sent their son to a *heder* when the family was living in wartime evacuation in Samarkand (during this era in Central Asia, the authorities made little attempt to control religious practices in a detailed way).[138]

Yet many parents were themselves indifferent, or positively hostile, to religion. In families with Christian connections, it was often not parents, but other adults – a child-minder or nanny, a grandparent, particularly a grandmother, a neighbour in the communal flat – who provided the primary point of contact with religious practices. A child might occasionally be taken along to church (an elderly person was less likely to attract interference by the authorities), and possibly even christened, whether with, or, as in many cases, without, its parents' knowledge. Naturally, early contact of this kind did not result in a sophisticated grasp of Christian doctrine, though it might generate a vague sense of belief.[139] Piety of this type was likely to be combined with outward conformity, which the authorities did all they could to enforce by means of rational collectivism. 'If anyone saw you'd gone to church, a Pioneer or whatever, it would come up at a meeting straight away,' a woman from Novgorod province (born in 1928) remembered.[140]

Much the same was true in Jewish families. The majority of city-dwelling Jews brought up their children in a thoroughly rationalistic way, without even the diluted sense of Judaic tradition (festivals and special foods) to be found in some assimilated Jewish families before 1917. In the twenty-one years between the abolition of internal passports in 1917 and the institution of point no. 5, 'nationality', on the Soviet passport (revived in 1932), Russian Jews were at last allowed to live without being constantly reminded of their nationality. The past of legal restrictions and 'backward' custom was the last thing many wished to remember. A man who grew up in one of the rare observant families during the 1930s and 1940s has claimed that there were no more than 500 or so other families across Russia who lived as his did.[141]

But traditions sometimes prevailed. Once secular humanism became the orthodoxy – from the early 1930s – children of religious families grew up with the sense of belonging to an endangered minority, catacombed in Soviet reality like the Christians and Jews in the pagan world of ancient Rome. Conflict with parental values was, for the average child from such a family, simply unthinkable: religion was the only belief system that counted, even if one had to pay lip service to Communist rhetoric at school.[142] As late as the 1950s, there were parents from rural areas who refused to let their children join the 'godless' Pioneers;[143] equally staunch, despite mounting state persecution as their numbers increased, were non-Orthodox Christians from sects such as the Baptists.

For children whose parents were not religious believers, on the other hand, there was a strong likelihood that observance might seem at best a colourful and exotic irrelevance. Lev Kopelev, from a Jewish family in Kiev, savoured his grandmother's delicious family feasts, especially at Passover; but, siding with his mother, who used 'synagogue' and '*heder*' as terms of abuse (roughly synonymous with 'mess' and 'chaos'), he found other elements of traditional behaviour absurd and embarrassing. He refused point-blank to learn Hebrew, would not go through the bar mitzvah (even though his grandfather offered him the gift of a bicycle as a reward), and was offended by relations who kept their hats on at table almost as much as he was by the shtetl boys who lectured him about the evils of eating pork.[144] Among Muslims, too, religious conviction in a strong sense often failed to be transmitted across generations. For the Tatar writer Gumer Bashirovich, growing up in the 1910s, the landscape of the Koran seemed alien: 'We children from the central belt of Russia, where almost every village has its abundant river and there are streams everywhere, a lake glimmering wherever you look, couldn't imagine why we had to learn the strict rites of how to wash with sand, in case you "suddenly" ended up in the waterless Sahara.' In the circumstances, what appealed was secular literature, in this case Tatar (for children in later generations, it might well have been the Russian classics).[145]

Some children from once Christian families felt an equally strong sense of alienation from the customs and rituals with which relations put them in touch. According to a Muscovite woman born in 1936, whose grandparents, but not parents, were religious believers: 'When we were living in Gorky [Nizhni Novgorod] I got taken to church, but to be honest, it put me off for life. They lined up all the children in the front row and there was this huge priest looming over me all dressed up in his kit, and with this long black beard, very scary, I thought, and singing in a deep bass voice. And I took fright very badly and really didn't want to go to church again after that.'[146] Although peasant nannies often had the offspring of 'godless' parents (Jewish, Communist, non-believer, etc.) christened, such efforts rarely, if ever, planted long-term Christian convictions in the young.[147] Children were among the most vehement supporters of militant atheism during the Cultural Revolution, participating in icon-burning sessions and making anti-religious speeches. School and Pioneer work was crucial. In 1929, *Our Children* magazine triumphantly reported that a group of Tatar children who had been fasting for Ramadan had been persuaded to change their minds by a pep-talk from the school doctor.[148]

Of course, the home background could have unexpected long-term effects as well. Some of those who had contact with religion in childhood were to return to religious belief much later, as adults.[149] Yet overall, the characteristic process that took place under Soviet power was the secularisation of childhood experience. The metaphysical dimension was not stamped out altogether, but was increasingly given a highly specific place – in literature and the arts, where it could be conveniently labelled as fantasy. Even those who encouraged small children to soak up fairy tales and to take part in New Year revelry led by 'Father Frost' emphasised that this was *just* a case of make-believe. The result of this in children who were brought up to believe Soviet ideology implicitly and uncritically – in other words, to believe, rather than to be sceptical – was often what one could call a metaphysical subjunctive. In the words of a five-year-old boy who had just returned from a New Year party in 1966, 'Actually Father Frost doesn't really exist. It's just a real person dressed up as him. But that's exactly what he would look like if he did exist.'[150]

If asserting religious values remained a minority occupation, there were also more mainstream ways of departing from official norms. An instance – at least in the 1920s – was gender socialisation. Certainly, there were model mothers of the day who strove to instil egalitarianism and comradeliness in boys and girls from the toddler stage. A. I. Pavlova took pride in the fact that her son 'had no shame' about his relationships with girls, 'and I've never made any attempt to encourage him to. The feeling will come by itself in due course.'[151] However, a majority of parents still clung to traditional ideas about sex roles. Among some, compartmentalisation turned into watchfulness for difference and a desire to encourage this. One 'rational mother' of the early 1920s proudly noted that her son was already (at 16 months!) beginning to show 'boyish interests', e.g. in hammering and sawing, watching horses and carriages, and that he wanted to wear caps not hats, and to have a belt like the one his father wore.[152] A decade later, Irina Klyuchareva, widowed when her son was five, felt acute anxiety about the likelihood of his turning out well: 'Can I, without a father, without male influence, manage to raise the boy to be brave, courageous, strong in mind and body, and devoted to the Motherland?' Her response was to place great emphasis on self-reliance, sending the boy off to the bakery alone when he was as young as six, or leaving him to get to school on his own, and to return from there in the dark unaided. Fortunately, Klyuchareva's model of manliness did not extend to total emotional severity: she encouraged Andrei to treat his younger sister 'tenderly', and was delighted when she observed him doing this.[153]

Inevitably, strong emphasis on gender roles tended to be reflected in children's behaviour. The children at A. I. Pavlova's son's school included a small girl who refused to help Adya put on his coat, appealing to her mother: 'I'm ashamed to, mummy, I'm a girl and he's a boy.'[154] But if mother and daughter were in collusion here, there were occasions when children asserted themselves (or the values of their school and their coevals) against parental pressure. In the early 1930s, Yuliya Drunina was appalled when her parents attempted to make her wear a bow, the epitome of 'bourgeois taste' from the point of view of her school-friends: when they refused to let her take it off, she cut it off herself, complete with the lock of hair it was attached to.[155] A study of primary school pupils from 1926 pointed out that, while there were some gender differences between boys and girls (the latter being much more inclined to make models for the entire group, the former for themselves), there was also some convergence of interests: boys were more interested in mechanical things, by and large, but a group of girls had made a cardboard aeroplane and an air balloon alongside their doll's house furniture.[156]

Once official norms had swung back towards a greater degree of gender differentiation, not all parents immediately fell into line. Even in the late 1930s, many girls in urban families were still kitted out in the short dress and bobbed hair look that had been considered 'modern' in middle-class families since the 1900s.[157] Material conditions were crucial: in circumstances where hand-me-downs, and remade versions of adult clothes, were in common use, changes in fashion made themselves felt slowly, if at all. During and immediately after the war, the culture-wide emphasis on asceticism and streamlining made itself felt in this area too, as did the extreme shortages of clothes, including essentials such as coats and shoes.

The late 1940s, a time of elaboration in dress and decoration generally, on the other hand, does seem to have witnessed the triumph of gender-determined dress even for tiny children – for instance frilly dresses, and huge gauze ribbons (*bantiki*) for little girls. However, there were some class variations here. Model girls in posters, magazine photographs, and paintings always had their *bantiki*. So, too, did a lot of their real-life counterparts.[158] But among some members of the Russian intelligentsia, fluffy ribbons were despised and regarded as 'petit bourgeois'. The mothers and fathers of this generation were, after all, those who had come up through the Soviet schoolroom in the 1920s and 1930s.

At the same time, many aspects of 'the child's world' were strictly denominated by gender irrespective of parents' class. Girls were expected to play with dolls, while boys were not; socialising with other children was generally encouraged on a gender basis; and the extent to which children were expected to help with household tasks varied according to sex. Not surprisingly, some small girls resented the discrepancies. Irena Donskaya, brought up in Komsomol'sk-on-Amur in the late 1940s and early 1950s, remembered constant shouts of 'How could you, you're a girl!' whenever she did something reprehensible, such as urinating in the bushes instead of using the earth closet in the yard. Boys were bought toy cars: she was fobbed off with a celluloid doll's head for which her mother provided a home-made torso and legs. Her father's mockery when she asked him to make a wooden pistol like the one he had just made for the neighbour's son made her feel resentful for years (even though she got the gun in the end).[159] And girls from traditional families were quite capable of holding their own among their peers when it came to boisterous behaviour – playing pranks and even brawling.[160] However, children's own day-to-day life enforced gender distinctions: when playing in the street or yard, for example, they usually associated on gender lines, and chose different types of games depending on their sex.[161] A girl who did not conform to norms was likely to be branded *patsanka* (ladette) or *ataman*, a boy taunted about being 'a girl'.[162]

'Spoiling'

Another area where attitudes differed from what was recommended was the extent to which children were indulged. The insistence on the spoiling theme in Stalinist propaganda and caricature is testimony to the reluctance of many parents to treat their children with the cool detachment characteristic of what Makarenko termed 'senior executive members of the collective'. Average family size shrank during the early Soviet period: the shortage of accommodation, the fall in the real value of wages for those in white-collar professions, added to the increasing numbers of women entering employment, unsupported by a properly functioning child-care system, meant that few parents had the resources to provide for more than two children.[163] Over the same period, one-child families became significantly commoner than they had been before 1917. Recalling his experiences as a small boy in the 1890s, the dramatist Evgeny Shvarts thought it worthy of remark that he had been an only child, and hence indulged.[164] By the mid-twentieth century, this comment would have seemed too obvious to be worth making.

Of course, not all only children were indulged, nor was the presence of only one child in the family the sole cause of indulgence, where this occurred. The greater closeness between parents and children that was the result of smaller living space also played a role – especially with the well-educated parents who had formerly been most attached to strictness and 'character-building'. Many parents of the early Soviet era were genuinely more attached to their offspring than their predecessors before 1917 had been.[165] As well as enforcing intimacy, the sharing of space blurred the old hierarchical distinctions between 'bedroom' and 'nursery', and lowered barriers between the generations. Some of this is captured in the work of Vera Pestel', whose canvases portray new-style children, particularly girls with cropped hair, sitting, self-contained and meditative, in barely furnished family rooms.

It was not just constricted space that encouraged warmth between parents and children. Those with access to privacy of any kind (a separate family room, if not a flat) frequently perceived this as a place of refuge from the militaristic and authoritarian character of the Soviet workplace. To be sure, children themselves could pick up the aggressive atmosphere of Soviet social intercourse generally and transfer this to interchanges at home – as in one example cited in a pamphlet on upbringing from 1954, where a small boy is reported saying to his mother, when she asked whether he was in a bad mood, 'Why should I waste my time dealing with you, idiot?'[166] But this was unusual. More often, family life was constructed so that it would be quite different from broader social relations. Middle-class parents were eager to spare their children the abrasive and abusive treatment that they themselves regularly encountered from superiors at work, while children took refuge in the home from the pressure to behave well that was imposed upon them at school.

Indulgence could also be an impulsive response to family pressures on the part of overstretched 'responsible officials' who were too overloaded and preoccupied to have much time for their children.[167] To begin with, such parents often had to depend heavily on the services of secondary carers – grandparents, for instance, or nannies – who were unlikely to subscribe to the tenets of 'rational upbringing'. When parents dealt with children directly, they might avoid confrontation, as a form of apology for not being around very much. Single mothers, whose time was extremely limited, were vulnerable to feelings of guilt, which might well be exploited. Where a mother's presence was limited to fleeting sensory impressions – the sound of a typewriter clattering late into the night – children tried to impose their emotional needs in any way that they could. An obvious way of gaining attention was a languorous collapse into temporary invalid status. According to one woman born in 1940, being ill was 'sheer bliss. It meant fever and feeling a bit dizzy. An anxious and caring mother who didn't go to work and made you jelly and put mustard poultices on your back. Being ill meant that they read to you and when your temperature went down they'd let you have books, pencils and drawing-paper in bed. Being ill meant having a nice sweet cough mixture prescribed by the excellent district children's doctor.'[168]

In any case, messages from official sources about how to treat children were mixed. Behaviour books might talk of 'strictness', but they also created a model of family life where children occupied the primary place. Divorce was to be avoided because it was injurious to children's interests; parents must always exercise understanding; family life must be full of 'cheerfulness and *joie de vivre*'; a child's will was not to be 'crushed'.[169] And the move away from punishments inevitably meant that parents who could afford to do so began using what manuals described as 'encouragement' as a way of managing children – which in practice sometimes meant material incentives (gifts in return for good behaviour).

Indulgence of children took more than material forms, though. It became common for adults – including parents, but not only them – to lavish praise on children. Typical was a father from the Leningrad military elite who considered his daughter's prowess in learning Chukovsky's children's poems by heart prodigious, and frequently observed so in her presence.[170] Children who had any developing talent were encouraged to show this off at family gatherings.[171] By underlining kindness to children as an absolute ideological good, and denying most adults access to any other context where affection and warmth to others might be expressed, the state was creating the conditions for the very 'spoiling' that normative literature condemned as 'un-Soviet', a way of rearing 'enemies to the Soviet system'.[172]

That said, the effects of the rise of the child-centred family should not be exaggerated. Many demands were still made on children. Progress at school was closely monitored; sons and daughters were expected to be obedient, and to keep their clothes and other personal possessions tidy. Older children in particular had to help with housework, and often shopping as well. Even formal table manners were a point of considerable interest.[173] Yet the general trend in educated families was nevertheless towards closer, more child-centred, relations. The growing importance of family festivals was one sign of change. Revelry for the new Soviet special occasions – the anniversary of the October Revolution on 7 November, May Day, International Women's Day – included taking children along to the demonstrations; children also participated in the celebration meals, even if sometimes sitting at a separate table.[174] Though the introduction of state atheism had precipitated the demise of the name-day party, this was replaced by birthday celebrations, often attended not just by other small children, as in Britain, but also by a child's parents and their friends, who duly drank toasts to the hero of the day and plied him or her with compliments.[175]

Educated parents absorbed many of the tenets of Soviet behaviour books (the stress on the need for discipline imposed by reason, rather than physical force, the necessity of imposing an orderly style of life, and of dressing and housing the child in a 'rational' manner) and enacted these as far as they could. The prevalence of 'spoiling', or the persistence of alternative gender values, was attributable less to a conscious desire to subvert, or to deviate from, official dictates, than to contradictory messages in these dictates themselves, and to the pressures of Soviet everyday life.

Making Do

Soviet mothers from outside the elite remained to a large extent beyond the reach of propaganda for 'rational upbringing'. In peasant households, the old ways went on until at least the Second World War. Policing of children's bodies was – from the point of view of hygiene experts – deficient. Bowel control was still left to the child itself to regulate.[176] Among older children, self-monitoring was the rule: 'When you'd worn yourself out hanging round, you took yourself to bed,' a woman born in 1938 remembered. Everyone went to the bath-house once a week, but no fuss was made about washing in between: once again, children looked after themselves.[177] Children were fed from the general family table, on a grain-heavy diet that was unlikely to include much meat or dairy products and might well be short on vegetables, even pickled ones.[178] Traditional dress was still ubiquitous, even in relatively 'Sovietised' areas: trousers (or a skirt, for girls) with a jacket cut to a simple outline and made of homespun linen. This basic attire of shirt and skirt or trousers was worn in a single layer (without underwear) throughout the year, with extra layers added or subtracted as the temperature demanded. A coat (probably confected from tatters of sheepskin, or cut down from an adult jacket) would be put over the top in cold weather, when children would also adopt a miniature version of the standard adult footwear, strips of rag used as puttees (*portyanki*) under bast shoes. In dry weather, children, like adults, went without a covering and barefoot.[179]

Conditions inside many working-class households were, from the perspective of an educated observer, quite insanitary: shared beds, no separate towels, underwear changed insufficiently often. But material conditions meant that they could not be altered. The minutes of parent–teacher meetings held at the First Experimental Station's Central Nursery School in Moscow reveal a rather tragic confrontation between the idealistic expectations of the teachers and the intractable circumstances in which families lived. One mother observed that she would gladly give her children separate beds, but she simply had not the space and the money to do this. Another protested that to divide the children up during the winter would have meant that one of them would have to sleep without a blanket.[180] Well into the 1930s, both the reality in which working-class children lived and the aspirations of their parents remained extremely simple. The height of luxury was represented by a Leningrad mother who wrote to her husband at the Finnish front in 1939, 'Vova's got nice clean warm clothes I bought him a few new things'.[181]

Yet faint signs of change were beginning to show, even in the countryside. Before 1917, returning migrants, with their city clothes, had inspired envy and a desire for emulation among younger people in the villages; in some areas, manufactured clothes had almost entirely forced out homespun even by the 1890s.[182] While the impoverishment that set in after 1917 restricted opportunities to make such purchases, any factory-made items that did arrive in villages were – as in the past – often considered superior. Mikhail Alekseev, awarded a pair of sateen trunks and a white blouse for outstanding achievements as a Pioneer activist, wistfully recalled how light and accommodating the garments seemed after the stiff resistance of his usual linen wear.[183] Soviet children who attended kindergartens, and later schools, were confronted with images of children wearing 'normal' (i.e. city) clothes, which might lead to embarrassment about their own lack of shoes and factory-made jackets. At the same time, garments of this kind were the objects of fantasy until well after the Second World War. Men and women brought up in a Urals village in the early Soviet era recalled, during an interview in 2003, that 'homespun' was routine throughout their childhood and youth.[184]

Gender norms also tended to be enforced in traditional ways. In cities, certainly, 'unisex' wear made some inroads, to judge by 1920s and 1930s photographs of working-class kindergarten classes and Pioneer troops showing girls with short hair and wearing 'rational dress'. Conversely, when a 'frillier' ethos started to become fashionable, means did not always allow working-class mothers to espouse it. It was not until well after the Second World War that puffed skirts, embroidery, and flamboyant ribbons began to be dispersed among this public – at which point they became even more popular than among white-collar workers, let alone intellectuals. But in the countryside, distinctions between boys and girls were firmly enforced in terms of clothing: for example, girls never wore trousers. Equally, work assignments were linked to gender. Girls were expected to take on jobs such as tidying the house and minding younger siblings, while boys worked in the fields, or sometimes avoided doing work of any kind.[185] Similar divisions of labour seem to have applied in working-class families.[186] Yet, as before 1917, girls might be expected to help out with non-traditional work, such as ploughing, when circumstances demanded it, or boys to baby-sit younger children or to help with household tasks.[187]

Reliance on older children to supervise younger more or less ruled out any possibility that child-care would comply with the norms set down in books. The situation was vividly described by an elderly woman from Novgorod province who began looking after younger children in the mid-1920s, when she was 10. 'They'd run in and see me if they felt like it. "Baba Nyura's coming." I'd feed them all. Give them something to drink. [...] Those wee brats [*vyblyadki*] were all brought up by me. [...] I'd peel the potatoes and do the "eenie meenie" [*taty-baty*] with them. [...] "Nyunya, eep," they'd say. Well, I'd let them sleep. Lay them down. Then get them dressed and give them some milk, Some watery kasha. Something to eat and drink. "Eeep" – and I'd lay them down.'[188] Hard-pressed parents from the peasantry and proletariat also kept to an ethos of 'make do' where shaping the child's perceptions in a moral or intellectual sense was concerned. Damage limitation rather than active regulation was the rule. In the words of Antonina Koptyaeva: 'Upbringing? I don't remember anyone bothering with it.' Her own mother, a widow, had far too many other things to do to think scientifically about raising the children. 'The main thing was to get a hot meal on the table, even if it had to be one without meat or dairy products. Then there was washing and ironing our clothes, and if there was a peep out of us she'd thrash us with a bunch of twigs or even a stick.'[189] Though this account goes back to the first years of Soviet power, it can be matched decades later. Rather than being carefully supervised, offspring grew up living 'as they pleased', according to a woman who grew up in the north-west Russian countryside during the 1930s. Parents were affectionate, but had hardly any time for their children, a contemporary from a similar background agreed.[190] A woman born in Perm' in 1936 recalled, '"Being friendly" meant living with your relatives. [...] There were no [close] relationships between any of the fathers and the children. [...] It wasn't customary for fathers to have warm personal relations. [...] I had no sense at all my parents were "bringing me up", whether from my father's side or my mother's. I don't think it was characteristic of that social stratum at all.'[191]

Direction, where it occurred, was sometimes largely by means of corporal punishment. One mother on a collective farm in the 1940s, maddened by her young daughter's refusal to get up at dawn and start preparing breakfast for the younger children, picked up a ladle and gave the girl a great dunt on the side of the face, scarring her permanently.[192] Yet there were also parents from working-class and peasant families who preferred not to use corporal punishment, stopping at a thorough scolding.[193] And, while the offering of incentives was not as common as it was in middle-class households, this method of moral direction was adopted by parents who could afford it.[194] Generally, working-class and peasant parents treated their children as considerately as circumstances would allow. Elena Kabo's close study of working-class families in the late 1920s indicates both the pressures that these parents were under and the efforts they made to do the best by their children. The time that parents had free to spend with children was severely constrained, not only because working hours were long, but because extra activities (such as feeding animals, gardening, looking after lodgers) had to be taken on to help out the family budget. On average, mothers and fathers spent less time 'educating children' (25 minutes a day) than they did 'caring for animals' (37 minutes). But, especially in families where parents were literate, effort was often made to buy toys, maintain separate beds, and supervise children's play. Even in the humblest families, beating was not universal, and parents might well treat children affectionately.[195]

The concern of working-class parents to do the best by their offspring is borne out by notes on the family circumstances of children attending the Central Kindergarten in the early 1920s. The Luk'yanovs, for instance, inhabited a typical wooden house in a north Moscow courtyard: the family shared three cramped rooms, one of which doubled as a workshop for the father (who was a cobbler). The only sanitation was a row of earth closets in the courtyard; however, the children were allowed to use a pot in the house rather than visit this. Though the mother had traditional ideas about discipline (she would hit the children with a belt and box their ears when they were naughty), the father made them wooden cubes and benches to play with, and the samovar would be put on specially when the children got back from school.[196] A similar account is given by a memoirist who grew up in a working-class area of Leningrad, Krestovsky Island. Here, there was no sanitation or electricity until the early 1930s, buildings were uniformly low and wooden, and the inhabitants lived like peasant farmers, with their own chickens and even farm animals. But, although keeping the children clothed was a struggle, their mother made sure they had toys to play with, crafting them rag dolls herself out of any spare pieces of fabric.[197]

Parent Blame

Whatever the good intentions of working-class and peasant parents, their ideas about upbringing were often out of harmony with the 'modern' methods propounded by child-care professionals. Ignoring the central problem – lack of resources – Soviet child-care propaganda of the 1920s and 1930s concentrated on trying to persuade parents to change their ways. Disruption by children in the classroom was routinely seen as resulting from a defective home environment, as in the case of 'Volodya Zh.', aged 11, the son of a drunken father and an invalid mother, who shunned his home as much as he could, or 'Boris S.', whose difficulties at school were said to come from his mother's religious, anti-Komsomol stance.[198]

Attitudes hardened further in the mid-1930s, when it began to be emphasised that it was not socio-economic circumstances, but selfishness, that caused parents to make mistakes. An example came in the 'Geta' case, the much-publicised show trial in April–May 1935 of a factory worker and a technician for the ill-treatment of their daughter, who had been abandoned in central Moscow because neither of her two natural parents (who had been divorced after her birth) was prepared to be responsible for her care.[199] Attitudes to neglectful parents were now punitive: a measure of June 1935 made the living parents of children placed in orphanages financially liable for their upkeep, on the grounds that such individuals could only have deserted their children out of recalcitrance.[200]

Rebukes to parents ignored the realities of the family in the years after the Revolution, the era of the 'disappearing parent', as revolution, political purges, war, starvation and epidemics annihilated millions of adults, as well as children. Even in more ordinary times, stress and deprivation made it hard for families to keep together. In Moscow in the mid-1920s half of all registered marriages ended in divorce, and, by the end of the decade, the divorce rate was running at almost 80 per cent of registered marriages.[201] Given that unregistered marriages were common (and equally unstable), the experience of spending one's entire childhood with both birth parents was the exception rather than the rule. The tightening of divorce legislation in 1936 and 1944 created some impediments for the most enthusiastic serial monogamists (it was rarer now for a man or woman in their mid twenties to have notched up half a dozen broken relationships and several children alongside),[202] but could not hold collapsing households together. Particularly after the Second World War, huge numbers of children grew up fatherless: at Pioneer camps in the late 1940s and early 1950s, the open days for families, the so-called 'Parents' Days', were in fact usually more like 'Mother and Grandmother Days'.[203] While the late 1950s saw some normalisation of the ratio of adult men to adult women through population replacement, marital stability did not improve: throughout the late Soviet era, divorce rates in Russian cities were equal to, or higher than, those in comparable metropolitan centres in Western Europe and America.[204]

Mixed Messages

The family guidance of the 1960s and 1970s continued the established tradition of speaking in moral, rather than practical, terms. Advice literature recognised the problem of marital break-up by emphasising the father's role in the family (i.e. by suggesting that marital break-up should not happen), rather than by giving advice on how to bring up children as a single mother.[205] In the 1980s, commentary on divorce started to become more widespread, but it was still, often, a moralistic kind. Broken marriages were frequently represented as the 'fault' of the couple whose relationship had come to grief.[206] However, some articles were now starting to deal in a more matter-of-fact way with the aftermath of marital break-up, stressing the need for conciliatory behaviour on the part of the former wife and husband, and the possibility of satisfactory relations once new partners had come into the frame.[207]

This contradiction – between sententiousness and pragmatism – was typical of child-care literature of the era, which, as with propaganda generally, represented an uneasy accommodation between Stalinist and pre-Stalinist values. On the one hand, there was a return to a 'pure', 1920s-style, model of hygienic living, with the streamlined look coming back strongly for furniture and clothes in particular. Frilly styles were now reserved for special occasions and outfits with trousers were occasionally recommended for small girls. The emphasis was on practicality. 'One can often see on the Moscow boulevards small girls playing in the sand wearing nylon dresses. Their flowing hair and the large bows on their heads are not at all in keeping with this activity, of course. [...] What sort of clothing is a girl to wear on [holidays], if she has a nylon dress every day of the week?' enquired a 1963 article in *Pre-School Education*.[208] 'The chief point in designing children's clothes is hygiene,' another article of the same year stated.[209] Combination garments, such as dungarees, were favoured for both sexes, with decorative elements mostly confined to bright colour combinations and simple patterns.[210]

'Rational' patterns continued in force at the level of intellectual and moral education as well. Guides to child care advocated 'discipline' – which should be inculcated from an early stage – and underlined the pernicious nature of 'spoiling'. 'Children who are spoilt are those who are most often disobedient. [...] In these circumstances, an undisciplined, disobedient child will emerge, an egoist who respects no one and pays no heed to anyone.' The 'capricious and stubborn' child must be made to obey.[211]

Yet the disciplinary ethos was no longer quite so dominant. For instance, the old style of stern fathering was coming to be seen as suspect. One 1967 manual expressed disquiet over the 'curious division of labour' that had mothers nurturing their children on a full-time basis, and thoroughly indulging them as well, with the father called in as a punitive force when things got out of hand.[212] Sergei Mikhalkov's play *Someone Else's Role* (1973) satirised conventional gender stereotypes too. The mother at the centre of the drama would not be stern with her child even when he was behaving badly, because she was anxious that the child would be 'traumatised' by punishment. The offending child's father, on the other hand, exclaimed irritably, 'He should have his trousers taken down and his hide tanned!'[213]

A different attitude was sometimes now taken to 'spoiling' as well. A series of articles published in the weekly newspaper *Nedelya* in the early 1970s asserted that so-called 'spoilt' children often turned out better than ones who were treated more severely. As toddlers and small children they might be difficult, but by their teenage years they were self-confident and independent. This line proved controversial with some of *Nedelya*'s readers, but was warmly defended by the newspaper's staff.[214] Indeed, *Nedelya* generally took a rather liberal attitude to upbringing, underlining the need for understanding, tolerance, and a respect for children's initiative. The paper's leading child-care guru was Simon Soloveichik, who published many articles during the 1970s and 1980s, and who insisted that children should not be guided too obviously: the main point was to inculcate desirable characteristics, such as generosity, by example and by reward of good motives as they were shown.[215]

Another significant sign of change was the increasing interest being taken in upbringing outside the Soviet Russian world. For instance, Soviet magazines might carry laudatory articles about extended families in Central Asia where everyone respected one another and no one ever seemed to argue. Once again, understanding and the capacity to reason with children came across as more important than laying down the law.[216] Room was even found for new ideas from the West: in the early 1970s, 'neurosis therapy' began to be available for difficult children and adolescents in Leningrad.[217] If innovations of this kind reached only handfuls of families, far more were reached by the articles in the Soviet press dealing with Western behaviour guidance, and by translations of normative literature. Among these, as in the world of infant care, Dr Benjamin Spock's advice manual was particularly influential. Spock's book itself reached a limited audience – its print run was not large, considering the size of the Soviet population – but extracts from his work published in newspapers had a larger circulation.[218] 'Advanced' material of this kind was significant because it reached precisely the group of conscientious middle-class parents who had been the key readers of, say, Makarenko – thus reshaping attitudes among those who had formerly been most in tune with 'Soviet' ideas about rational upbringing.

At the same time, other influences remained in play. Much publicity was given to the views of Vasily Sukhomlinsky, who placed more emphasis on encouragement and on emotional sensitivity than Makarenko had, but still insisted on firm values and strict control.[219] Many publications harped on the fact that 'good manners' were essential for children; indeed, this theme had become more dominant than in the 1930s and 1940s. Writing in *Nedelya*, one Pioneer even suggested that it was time that 'good manners hobby circles' were set up, to foster correct behaviour among his contemporaries.[220] On the other hand, the early 1960s saw a reassertion of 'self-tempering' and 'education of the will' in child-care literature, in line with the revival of early Soviet values that was evident more generally.[221] In the late 1970s, a couple called Lena and Boris Nikitin became national celebrities. According to the enthusiastic stories about them, the two had brought up a houseful of healthy children by encouraging baby gymnastics from the earliest possible moment. Photo-spreads of the family showed a nosegay of beaming, muscular juveniles happily hanging on their trapezes and practising their body-building exercises.[222]

In the area of upbringing, then, a degree of 'cognitive dissonance' was now in evidence, and this affected gender socialisation as well. On the one hand, there was a revival of the 1920s propaganda emphasising equality and 'comradeliness'. In *Nedelya* in the late 1960s and early 1970s a discussion of whether boys should help with the housework resulted in a majority of readers stating that they should.[223] But a good deal of material celebrating gender difference was published, too, with famous writers and other prominent figures remembering their boyish mischief back in the past, and large numbers of articles harping on boys' capacity for self-assertion and the need to foster this in upbringing by means of physical exercise programmes and so on.[224] And, if the 1960s cult of feisty boyhood allowed some leeway to 'tomboy' images of girls, as in the 1920s, by the early 1970s anxieties over the rising divorce rate and declining birth rate fostered an official campaign to promote complementary gender roles as a preparation for harmonious family life.[225]

Varied Results

Child-care practices in reality were still more diverse, and in some cases contradictory, than the ideal images of the day. Parents who reasoned with their children did exist outside the pages of conduct books, as did fathers who were committed to doing more than laying down a tough line when children became unmanageable. But so did parents who punished children for reasons that the latter could not fathom, and who had hair-trigger tempers, as well as fathers whose contribution to home life was to slump in front of the television, or to disappear for days on end, while the child's mother struggled single-handedly with minding the baby.[226]

Yet one element in Soviet 'rational education' did become thoroughly entrenched during the post-Stalin years. It was now very unusual for formal religion to play any role in childhood experience. Children born from the mid-1950s onwards had parents (and perhaps even grandparents) who had been wholly educated in the Soviet system, and who – unless they came from a family of determined believers – were likely to see religious observance both as risky and as stemming from ignorance or 'backwardness'. Children might be christened – this was still common in families with rural connections – and the family might have an icon somewhere, but prayers would not be said, nor would the tenets of the faith be discussed.[227] Whilst the era saw a rise in conversions to evangelical Protestant denominations, such as the Baptists, despite persecution by the authorities, the proportions of such believers seem to have been as small as their fervour was warm; certainly, our interviewing has turned up not even one case of such a family in quite a large and regionally diverse sample group. Not until the era of glasnost, when official control over the Church relaxed, did a larger-scale religious revival take place, generated in part by children themselves, who might now express a wish to be christened or suggest to their parents that they would like to wear a cross.[228]

On the other hand, vehement atheism was also very unusual. It was quite common to make traditional Easter foods, such as *kulich* (the Easter loaf), or coloured eggs, some time in late April or early May, but mostly such practices were seen as ways of celebrating the onset of spring.[229] Typically, attitudes to religion were uncomprehending, rather than explicitly hostile: in the words of a woman born in 1975, 'My upbringing wasn't atheist, it was just ordinary: no one in my friends' families celebrated religious holidays or went to church. If anything like that had gone on, it would have been laughed at.'[230]

But not everything about child-rearing had been so effectively Sovietised. Other types of parenting were widespread as well. Just as in other eras, it was not unknown for parents – even otherwise indulgent ones – to administer a smack or even a thrashing when they felt this was necessary.[231] Corporal punishment was, by all accounts, used almost universally in working-class and peasant families.[232] Strict control was still exercised in some families over how children behaved at table, and over the way they acted in the presence of visitors – interrupting and clamouring for attention were definitely not allowed.[233] A standard method of behaviour regulation was the withdrawal of love: 'I don't have a granddaughter any more,' as a visiting grandmother said to her Leningrad granddaughter in 1960.[234] This method was endorsed by normative literature: in the words of a house management manual published in 1965, it was necessary to 'manifest coldness to the schoolchild until his behaviour improves. [...] After one makes a critical observation, one should not immediately treat children affectionately.'[235]

The limited evidence available suggests that, as in the early Soviet era, intelligentsia parents were often more indulgent than working-class ones. In recordings of family interactions dating from the late 1960s and early 1970s carried out for a manual on Russian conversational usage, the small son of some university teachers expresses himself with a good deal of caprice. While grumbling at him ineffectually, his grandmother resorts to persuasion and collusion, not confrontation:

> [ALESHA]: Don't wannoo. [i.e. to get out of bed after his afternoon rest]
> [GRANDMOTHER 1]: Why should I care whether you do or don't?
> [ALESHA]: I'm not going. How many times do I have to tell you?
> [GRANDMOTHER 2]: Just listen to him! Phew!
> [ALESHA]: Gran? Eh?
> [GRANDMOTHER 1]: Why don't you get up and have some ice-cream?
> [ALESHA]: What?
> [GRANDMOTHER 1]: There's some ice-cream! Get up and you can have some.
> [ALESHA]: Have a look what's on TV.
> [GRANDMOTHER 1]: Don't you talk to me like that. Don't be so uppity.
> [ALESHA]: Go on, have a look.

[GRANDMOTHER 1]: OK. [Looks] There's nothing on.
[ALESHA]: What, not even on Channel Three?[236]

A child displaying this level of self-assertion and petulance in a working-class household would probably have had to endure at the very least a telling-off, as in the case of a man born in 1960 who vividly described his home life as 'somewhere you sleep, watch television, and hear "nag nag nag" all the time'.[237] 'Nagging' represented only the lowest level of the disciplinary scale: in the same informant's description of a typical situation, 'You get a smack on the bum, you stand in the corner, and *then* you have to ask forgiveness for not eating some revolting meatballs?'[238] But, on the other hand, there were intelligentsia households where discipline was very firmly enforced, if not necessarily by 'a smack on the bum'. An example is a mother from Sverdlovsk who, when she discovered her small son had innocently helped himself to a drink when a delivery man's back was turned, forced him not only to return the purloined item, but also to apologise for his behaviour to the workman concerned.[239] In a good many families there was a whole range of rules and prohibitions, relating both to moral matters and to other areas of behaviour. Examples given by a Russian mother who brought up children in the 1980s and 1990s, and whose mind had been focused by time spent abroad, included forcing children to dress warmly when they went out during the winter, prohibiting them from playing in puddles or doing anything that might mean getting wet, not tolerating interruptions when adults were talking, and absolutely never allowing a child to make a scene in public.[240] The participation of grandparents in upbringing, and the phenomenon of 'late onset parenthood' (especially fatherhood) among adults who had postponed child-bearing until after the years of 'socialist construction' and war, sometimes meant that children were treated with greater indulgence, but it could also foster a self-conscious desire to avoid 'spoiling' and emphasise discipline and self-control.[241]

Attitudes to gender socialisation were also very varied. Dress became more feminised, even among parents who believed in 'rational upbringing'. Frilly hair ribbons were still considered 'petit-bourgeois' by many intellectuals, but pretty dresses were customary wear for small girls on smart occasions, and skirts were on the whole preferred, though trousers or leggings might be resorted to in cold weather or for leisure activities, or for spending time outside at the dacha. Girls were still given dolls; boys, guns and cars. Girls were more likely than boys to be expected to learn to help out around the house, though the latter might be given 'out' jobs such as fetching bread or carrying out the rubbish. Children who deviated from traditional gender roles were still likely to be rebuked: 'stop behaving like a boy!' (or, alternatively, 'like a girl').[242] But the idea that children should all be indulged could take the edge off gender distinctions. In the words of a woman to her daughter in the late 1950s: 'When you grow up, you'll have to work all the time, so now I'm going to wait on you hand and foot.'[243] Equally, while boys might be told that it was 'manly' to help with loads, let women first through doors, help them with their coats, and so on, the expectation of toughness and independence was mitigated by the idea that childhood was precious and should be preserved.[244] Children themselves continued to react in quite diverse ways to gender socialisation. While many girls felt no conflicts at all, some engaged in 'tomboyish' behaviour, an example being a Moscow woman born in 1966 who referred to herself in childhood as 'Yanka' (roughly, 'Jake'). Such behaviour was perhaps less a symptom of serious gender conflict than a legitimising device: by pretending to be a boy, a small girl gave herself the chance of taking part in livelier, more daring games than would usually have been the case. Identification with an elder brother could be another factor.[245]

All in all, the post-Stalin era by no means uniformly saw a move towards greater permissiveness, whether in official norms or in real practices. Indeed, by international standards, if experiments in social psychology are to be believed, parents showed a more than average inclination to intervene and to engage in strictures with errant children.[246] While the greater availability of one-family flats might take the pressure off family relations in some ways, it forced parents and children in upon themselves to a greater extent than before, without neighbours to act as a source of support or a focus of irritation, and without neighbours' children to provide constant companionship. When things did go wrong in parent–child relationships, the atmosphere could rapidly become poisonous.[247]

'Everything for the Children'

It is difficult to see the second half of the twentieth century in terms of progress towards 'enlightened' parenting, or – as was often the point of view of working-class and peasant grandparents – away from the sort of discipline and high expectations that they had sought to instil in their own children.[248] A safer generalisation might be to say that the *material* side of upbringing changed significantly at this point. This was prefigured in normative literature, which

81   Selection of party cakes. This 'festival selection' was a favourite choice for children's birthday celebrations in the 1970s.

began to stress that consumer goods – furniture, clothes, shoes, etc. – should be attractive as well as hygienic and practical.[249] Sometimes Western items (in one case, Italian-made plastic laminated nursery furniture) were held up as models for Soviet design; on other occasions, 'cutting edge' Soviet items were featured.[250] The coverage included things that might have been described as luxuries – most egregiously, perhaps, a special children's umbrella with a handle shaped like a flower, designed by a team of psychologists, sociologists, artists, and engineers.[251] At other times, a touch more realism was displayed – as in the case of designs for girls' dresses that could be adjusted to fit as the girl grew taller.[252] But whichever way, there was unprecedented attention to the fact that children needed large numbers of special things – from lace jabots to fancy hairdos.[253] As well as ensuring that the child's environment was pleasant from this point of view, Soviet normative literature had started to insist that children be made the centre of attention in other ways: for example, there should be elaborate parties for children's birthdays, or the home should be decorated for New Year.[254]

Accommodating expanded expectations of what a child needed was far from easy. While the post-Stalin era did not – until the beginning of the 1990s, at any rate – see a repetition of the severe food shortages of the post-war era, providing children with the recommended amounts of nourishing foods, particularly milk, fresh vegetables, and fruit, demanded much time spent queuing, and often also large amounts of luck, or, more likely, as the system of *blat* (personal pull) took hold, connections with shop staff or with well-placed friends. Food purchases could also be made at the semi-private collective farm markets, but here prices were high: a single lemon or orange might cost up to 5 per cent of an average monthly wage. Children's clothes were scarce, as were toys, games, and various types of sporting equipment; purchasing such items on the black market was prohibitive. And there was no official state allocation here, as there was for baby clothes.

Nevertheless, the rise in the value of wages, in real terms, added to the increasing availability of consumer goods – one might have to scrabble to get them, but in principle they did exist – was beginning to make a difference. Children brought up during the 1960s and 1970s on average lived in considerably greater comfort than their parents had two or three decades earlier.[255] As early as 1958, the ethnographers describing Viryatino village concluded that there had been a marked change in attitude to children's needs in the recent past. In the words of one of the ethnographers involved in the study, 'Parents will usually put their children's interests before their own.' By now, special clothes and utensils for children (plates, baby baths), and even children's books (though books in general were rarely purchased) had become valued items. Alongside these changes, the study claimed, the general attitude to upbringing had softened, and though children were still expected to obey directions without argument, harsh punishment had become rare.[256] Again, one needs to remember that Viryatino was an exceptional village, but oral history points in the same direction. Informants recall that, even in relatively modest families, there was now an ethos of 'everything for the children'.[257]

This ethos was put under severe pressure when the state monopoly on the sale of goods was lifted in the late 1980s. A flood of foreign-produced goods overwhelmed Soviet stores, and these goods were also assiduously publicised in the Soviet press.[258] In the 1960s, 1970s, and 1980s, material about consumption had retained some elements of sobriety, with advice embracing how to get items mended, or how to make them oneself, as well as how to acquire new ones.[259] Now, publicity concentrated exclusively on what was shiny, new, and expensive. Yet precisely at this point, the real value of wages declined precipitately (and, as state support retrenched, employees in government-run factories, enterprises, and institutions would often receive salary cheques month in arrears). The belief that children should be bought whatever they wanted clashed painfully with the sheer impossibility of purchasing the sort of expensive items a child was likely to ask for, from Barbie dolls to foreign sweets such as Mars Bars and Snickers. 'There were too many tempting things around, and it was all very tough, especially for parents,' one woman who brought up a daughter at this time remembered.[260] Indeed, even acquiring basics could cause terrible stress: as prices spiralled during the early months of 1991, Children's World department store in Moscow was besieged by parents desperate to acquire clothes and other goods while they could still afford them. After a month during which customers bought anything they could get their hands on after queuing for hours, the store was left with sufficient stock to cater only for a couple more weeks of trading.[261]

Even before 'savage capitalism' overtook Russian culture, the rising expectations of what was essential for children's well-being meant that many parents could

82   Interior of a flat belonging to a working-class family in Leningrad, 1970s.

83   A day off in a working-class Leningrad family, 1970s.

not contemplate attending to the needs of more than two children at most. Accordingly, birth rates continued to fall, despite increased prosperity.[262] Numbers of children per family also declined. By 1960, 86 per cent of worker families in cities had two children or less; by 1978, 88 per cent. In villages, the birth rate held up for longer – 25 per cent of families had three or more children in 1960 – but were still significantly lower than in the past. By the 1970s, family size in rural areas of the Russian Federation was at most slightly higher, and in some places lower, than in urban areas.[263]

Both the officially tolerated, but socially critical, literary genre of 'village prose', stories of rural decline in the Soviet countryside, and studies of rural families by official Soviet painters done at this period pick up on the 'small family' theme. In canvases such as Andrei Tubanov's *A Fisherman and his Son* (1964), showing a father turned away from the viewer and looking towards his pale ginger-haired child on the bed, or Yury Kagach's *In the Family: First Steps* (1969), where adults watch a child wobble hesitantly across the floor, there is a sense that all interest is tensely focused on the children of the household.[264] The practicalities of Soviet life meant that 'everything for the children' often translated in reality as 'everything for one precious child'.

'Serial Only Children'

One-child families were not the only characteristic type of this period. The social pressures that made parents hesitate about considering a second child – lack of living space, the importance of the mother's income to the family budget, so that long absences from employment were problematic, difficulties with child care – meant that those couples which did opt to enlarge their family often did so a considerable length of time after their first child was born. Parents did not feel that they had the space or resources to care for two children who were close together in age without external support, yet they could rarely rely on such support. A statistic from the early 1960s indicated that 27.6 per cent of women who had abortions gave the lack of a crèche place for an already existing child as a reason for their decision.[265] Certainly, maternity leave was generous, and became more so during the 1980s. However, the level of subsidy – a one-off payment of 50 or 100 roubles depending on how many children the mother already had, and an entitlement to take leave on full pay immediately before and after the birth, followed by a longer period on a fixed state grant – still meant a drop in wages for most, and a significant drop for the better-paid.[266] A mother who became pregnant too quickly after giving birth to her first child might also end up in a downward spiral of failing to achieve the *stazh* (length of time at work needed to qualify for benefits) and being driven into part-time work, and hence becoming vulnerable to losing work altogether.[267]

Accordingly, gaps of 8–10 years between children were not unusual, rather than the 2–3 years characteristic of the average two-child British or American family. Of 69 informants consulted by Ekaterina Belousova for her survey of birthing experiences in the late Soviet and post-Soviet eras, more than two-thirds (48) had only one child. Of the other 21 informants, 14 had two children spaced between 5 and 11 years apart; only five had children less than five years apart (the other two cases were a family with twins, and a family of nine children, both of which are for different reasons exceptions).[268] In other words, a standard family situation, in cities at any rate,[269] was of 'serial only children', upon each of whom love and attention could be lavished. Contraceptives might be elusive, but the free availability of abortion meant that family planning was achievable by other means.

The situation of a 'serial only child' was quite specific in various ways. To begin with, association with another person who also occupied the role of 'child' in the family structure, but essentially belonged to a different generation, created very particular relationships.[270] Jealousy did not work in the same way with such a large age difference: the older child's insecurity about being replaced in its parents' affection was more likely to be verbalised, and a child of this kind of age was more likely to feel glad about having a younger sibling, and protective of its frail and dependent companion. At the same time, relationships were often more distant than they might have been between children who were close in age: the children might well not fight, but they were also unlikely to play together (since the older child was customarily expected to act as child-minder to the younger, rather than as a companion in the ordinary sense). The older child would often be seen as a kind of surrogate parent – an extra mother, in particular.[271]

To be sure, sibling rivalry was by no means unknown, to judge by oral history. However, parents reacted to it without shock or condemnation, reassuring the older child that it was still loved, and trying to persuade it to accept and love the new arrival.[272] In any case, tensions seem to have arisen less around the existence and person of the sibling in itself than because of secondary factors – above all, the expectation that the older child would baby-sit, and act as example for, its younger brother or sister, with the younger child as an annoying impediment to their own social life.[273]

Important as parental, and more generally family, influence might be, it was often only part of children's pre-school experience. Though nursery education was never available for all Soviet children, it had begun to cater for a majority nationwide by the late 1950s; by the 1980s, up to 80 per cent of the target age group in some major cities (Moscow, Leningrad) were going through the system. The pre-school years cannot therefore be understood without a glance at what was going on in Soviet kindergartens.

Nurseries of Citizenship

The foundations of an integrated system of state-run kindergartens were laid in the very month of the Bolshevik Revolution. In October 1917, a Pre-School Education Section (PES) was set up as part of the education ministry, Narkompros, and this was followed by the opening, in 1918, of 'pre-school political sections' in all branches of Narkompros at *guberniya* and city level. Like crèches, kindergartens were considered important by the Soviet authorities because institutionalised child care was a requirement for recruiting women into the labour force. But they were also seen as crucibles of 'new *byt*' (everyday life), of modern, rational methods of bringing up children. 'The decoration and furnishings must be simple, attractive, and cosy. [...] There must not be anything fussy, excessively elegant, or luxurious in the kindergarten,' proclaimed a manual of 1919.[274] If the early manuals generally concentrated on aesthetic education (as in the example just cited), and on the atmosphere of the ideal kindergarten with its samples from the natural world and its drawing equipment, from the mid-1920s there was considerable emphasis, too, on sanitary procedures. The cursory health check-up on arrival suggested in the early manuals had been supplemented by a much more insistent hygienic regime, with regular hand-washing sessions punctuating sessions of eating, handicraft, nature study and play and supervisors told to check that children wiped their bottoms thoroughly when they had finished using the lavatory (before, of course, making them wash their hands yet again). Gradually, too, more and more attention was devoted to what was termed *zakal*, a toughening regime in which children were exposed to longer and longer periods of fresh air and to brisk rub-

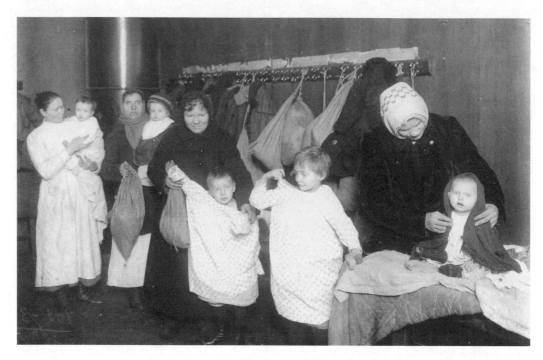

84   Undressing children at a day shelter in Petrograd, *c.* 1920.

downs with cold water. While the frenetic policing of fingernails and bottoms that had been characteristic of the 1920s appears to have abated somewhat in later years (or perhaps was now taken for granted), prophylactic washing was now the subject of vehement emphasis.[275] Rules of 1932 also laid down hygienic standards for the building itself, which was to have parquet floors washed with hot water and soap daily, toilets placed at a distance from the rest of the facilities and kept scrupulously clean (and cleared at regular intervals if they were earth closets). Potties were to be washed out after every use, and there was to be a monthly 'sanitary day' on which the entire premises was cleaned and spruced up.[276]

One function of the 'garden' with which kindergartens were supposed to be surrounded was the exposure of children to the healing elements, air and sun, the nectar and ambrosia of contemporary medicine. However, even if actual kindergartens had an external facility (which many did not – see p. 406 below), this might well be in a polluted urban district. A solution that Soviet nurseries took over from pre-revolutionary children's institutions was the relocation of nurseries to the countryside or green spaces during the summer. This was supposed to be an alternative environment, a special hygienic world. Kindergartens were not simply educational establishments: they were also centres of 'cultured behaviour' in the broadest sense, inculcating everything from love of reading and a respect for the arts to a concern for the integrity of the natural world and good manners.[277]

In retrospective commentary by critics of the Soviet regime, it was customary to stress, above all, the way in which kindergartens had acted as places of political indoctrination. Vladimir Voinovich's satire, *Moscow 2042*, represented them as places where 'children learn, in a relaxed and cheerful atmosphere, to spy on one another and to denounce one another and their parents to their supervisors, and to denounce their supervisors to the director of the kindergarten'.[278] It is certainly true that Soviet kindergartens – like other children's institutions – were meant to give due weight to politics and to 'patriotic education'. Nursery schools were supposed to organise public meetings devoted to issues of the day, and learning targets included basic political information (knowing about the meaning of 1 May, about Lenin's biography). Games also often had political ends: a manual of scenarios for the nursery school published in 1925 suggested, for instance, that children might play Aeroplanes (in which paper darts were landed in 'Germany', followed by a joyous Soviet conquest and the establishment of children's communes), Trotsky and Lenin (enacting a meeting in the Kremlin), or the self-explanatory Lenin's Funeral.[279]

In the Stalin era, Soviet festivals became occasions not only for dancing, singing, playing, and the distribution of small gifts to children, but also for reminding children of the benevolent dictator to whom they supposedly owed all this largesse. In the model nursery at the Trekhgorka factory in Moscow, children celebrated 7 November and other revolutionary festivals by parading round the school hall in 'bright, picturesque costumes' representing the different nationalities of the Soviet empire. As they marched, they sang a song of tribute to the Soviet leader:

> We sing to praise a country
> That's the most wonderful of all,
> We sing of battles, victory, and joy,
> About our nation's glory,
> About our free motherland,
> About dear Stalin.[280]

Celebration of the regime was not limited to high days and, such as the 7 November or the anniversary of Lenin's death. It permeated teaching on every day of the year as well. When children were acquainted with Soviet geography, for instance, they were informed at length about Georgia, since this was Stalin's birthplace; preparatory sessions for the transition to primary school included material about Stalin's concern for the school-building programme; and excursions around the local town or city were likely to include a session when the nursery teacher pointed out a prominent local monument ('Look, children, what a big sculpture of comrade Stalin!') and explained its mythic connection with the place where it stood (Stalin had personally founded that particular factory, and so on).[281]

Nursery schools also disseminated Russo-Soviet patriotism of a more general kind. Just as before 1917, folklore and proverbs, and trips to the forest, remained fixtures in the programme.[282] But the 'upbringing' offered was about more than this. Nursery schools were supposed to be as concerned with the correct use of the handkerchief as they were with the right reaction when the Soviet flag was raised. They provided basic tuition in physical exercise, in music and art appreciation, and in nature study, and tried to inculcate a love of animals. They also exposed children to the moral values considered essential in the Soviet collective – above all, the development of 'will and character', and the ability to combine particular friendships with general amiability, so that the solidarity of the collective was not endangered, and so that children could disseminate the new morality outside the kindergarten too.[283]

This understanding of the nursery school had in its turn effects on what was known as 'the mutual interaction of family and school'. Kindergartens were supposed to propagandise appropriate practices in upbringing among parents who were, by implication, failing in this regard. Parents were meant to attend advisory meetings organised by kindergartens, to read didactic brochures made available in the kindergarten libraries, and to reinforce the kindergarten practices at home.[284] The long Russian intelligentsia tradition of engaging in well-meant but somewhat condescending *missions civilisatrices* to supposedly backward peasants and workers militated against the assumption of a relationship of equality between staff and parents.[285]

Regime and Self-Reliance

The civilising objectives of the Soviet kindergarten were aided by the extension of the programme beyond what had been customary before 1917. By the late 1920s, even the so-called 'general kindergarten' (*obshchegrazhdanskii detskii sad*) had a programme of six hours (as opposed to the standard four-hour programme of middle-class pre-revolutionary kindergartens), while the 'factory shelter' (*fabrichnyi ochag*) and the village kindergarten had a programme of anything between 12 and 24 hours.[286] This gave ample opportunity for the staff to organise a hygienic regimen of the kind approved for small children as well as babies in the 'advanced' pedagogy of the day. A typical schedule began with the children's arrival and the removal of coats and outerwear (brochures for staff advised them to make sure the children were not too heavily dressed). A thorough wash and teeth-cleaning was supposed to follow, combined with delousing and a check for infectious diseases. The children were then marched off to the dining room, where they would help to lay the table for 'tea' (in fact a breakfast of bread and milk, kasha, or some other such nursery dish). Then followed an orderly routine of (in order): clearing up; games or excursions; sun-baths or water-bathing; lunch (meat soup then mashed potatoes, or vegetable soup with butter followed by noodles); an hour and a half's rest; a snack of milk or milk and water along with bread sprinkled with sugar; then more games or excursions, followed by, finally, setting the table for supper, supper (to a menu like the lunch one), more games and story-telling, and home. The patterns set out in this early model regime were followed later on as well.[287]

By means of this routine, children were supposed to progress smoothly and unproblematically towards a whole series of intellectual and hygienic targets.

85   Dinner at the nursery, early 1920s.

By the age of two to three, children in model Narkompros kindergartens were meant to know the names of various domestic animals, the different duties of the professionals in the kindergarten, their own age and sex, the names of various parts of the body (polite ones, no doubt), and the terms for clothes, furnishings, and buildings. They were expected to ask when they wanted to relieve themselves, to sit on the pot spontaneously, and to button themselves up afterwards (with help). Three- to four-year-olds were supposed to be familiar with some birds as well as domestic animals, to perform simple drills such as walking in line correctly, and to use the lavatory on their own, neatly and without wasting time.[288]

Teachers were instructed to keep detailed notes of children's successes, or failures, in meeting their targets, along the lines 'Zhenya and Lida got the tune right after one singing, after a second everyone except Volodya and Vasya could sing it'.[289] Records of this kind were meticulously kept in the nursery schools and *ploshchadki* (temporary crèches) organised by Narkompros's own First Experimental Station, in the villages of Velkino, Dobroe, and Krivskoe in the Moscow area. Three-year-old Vasya Kondrash'ev was recorded as knowing his own name, though not his sex, of being 'dry at night provided he is put on the pot regularly', of being 'capable of standing in a queue for a short while', and of washing his hands before meals. He refrained from eating off others' plates, and was happy to sit quietly till the meal was over.[290]

The standard Soviet kindergarten programme made much of the fact that everyone was supposed to do everything at the same time, and to stop performing an activity on command. The amorphous character of 'free education' had been replaced by a clear-cut progression through the day, in stages. But group homogeneity was not necessarily accompanied by communality. In contradistinction to procedures in crèches, both methodology and propaganda highlighted the cosy, 'family' atmosphere of the kindergarten. A 1921 Narkompros pamphlet on running nursery schools instructed supervisors that they should form mixed-age groups so that children played as they might in a family.[291] The child's individual needs were also a matter of concern. For example, a brochure of 1929 specified a separate cup, plate, and spoon for everyone, and preferably a fork as well; each child was to have its own towel, and its own peg to hang things on.[292] The same point was made by Sofiya Zak in a 1930 poem intended for reading aloud in nursery schools:

> As many pegs
> as there are kids,
> As many coats
> as there are kids.[293]

In the 1930s also, though the ideal baby-care facility might be one in which infants were shown being hosed down by white-coated nurses or lined up in

86 Setting the table in the nursery school, 1932.

identical sterile cots, the propaganda kindergarten was associated with rather a different set of conventions. In official photographs, plump tots were shown surrounded by toys and by other entertaining devices, such as aquariums, and dressed very much as well-cared-for bourgeois children would have been before 1917; verbal texts emphasised the 'joyful days' that were spent by them under the benevolent care of the state.[294] The kindergarten was still seen as a place for 'individual' development in a 'family' atmosphere. One propaganda tract for foreign readers gushed: 'Here the child has his own bed, his own cupboard, his own tiny household.' Indeed, in some ways this 'second home' was better than the child's first home, since it offered more space, and energetic, noisy play was tolerated: 'What child would be permitted to cause such commotion at home?'[295] The official perception of the kindergarten, then, was rather more multi-faceted than the official view of the crèche: it was supposed not only to service children's physical requirements or to mould them ideologically, but also to cater to their emotional and intellectual needs.[296]

Ruptured Dreams

The reality of nursery school provision, like that of crèche provision, often differed significantly from the ambitious and contradictory ideals. Even setting up an adequate institutional network faced constant practical setbacks. The immediate objectives which the PES of Narkompros set itself at the First Russian Conference on Pre-School Education in spring 1919 were modest – necessarily so, given the very large numbers of children potentially eligible for pre-school places (8 million across Soviet Russia) and the tiny numbers of extant institutions (in the low hundreds). A maximum of 2.5 per cent of children in the target group were to be catered for in the next few years, which would require the foundation of 3,000 new institutions and the training of 8,000 supervisors (each of whom was supposed to be responsible for 15–20 children).[297]

Even this projection, let alone the conference's longer-term aim, the provision of nursery places for all children of pre-school age by 1939, proved over-optimistic. To begin with, the capping of public spending that marked the onset of NEP not only impeded further improvement but precipitated a decline. In autumn 1919, the proportion of nursery places to the target age group was still well below 2.5 per cent even in some major towns (in Samara, for example, there were no kindergartens at all). But the threshold had been met or crossed in several cities or indeed provinces (for example Moscow, where 10 per cent of 3–7-year-olds, five times the number served in 1916–17, were placed in kindergartens, or Novgorod province, where 7.2 per cent of this group were already in nursery education). In 22 out of 31 reporting provinces, it was possible to compute the magic average of 2.5 per cent.[298] In 1926, the proportion of children in the target group placed in nursery schools was officially stated to be only 1.8 per cent. By 1928, again going by official declarations, it had dropped to 1 per cent.[299]

The numbers of children in nursery schools began to increase once the First Five-Year Plan had started: in 1928–9 they stood at 129,257, and, in 1930–1, at

336,236; by 1932–3, the number had reached 1,145,800. But, thereafter, growth once more slowed down. The grand promises of the June 1936 Maternity Protection Decree came no closer to fulfilment than they did in the area of infant care. In 1940, there were still fewer than 2 million kindergarten places across the Soviet Union as a whole (catering for at most 15 per cent of the target age group).[300] Coverage was especially patchy in the countryside, where (though the collective farms of propaganda might have model kindergartens),[301] many children, like many infants, were likely to have access, at most, to a temporary nursery open during harvest time.[302]

The central problem remained that the state's ideological commitment to nursery education was not underwritten by the financial support necessary to provide proper facilities on the scale required. Here, as everywhere, the 'leftover principle' obtained. In 1928, the share of the education budget allocated to pre-school institutions was only just over 9 per cent, and by 1932 this had fallen to a still more miserly level, just over 5 per cent.[303] The state's response was to try and squeeze extra funding from industrial concerns, but this proved difficult. In 1934, it was made compulsory for enterprises with 200 or more female employees to devote a sum equivalent to 25 per cent of the payroll to subsidising the plant's own crèche and kindergarten or to block-purchasing places in kindergartens located in workers' home districts; however, managers had to be reminded again and again of their legal duty to contribute to child-care provision.[304] Much the same obstructionism applied to other institutions, such as residential co-operatives, whose directorates were also likely to find 'more pressing' needs on which to disburse funds.[305] No doubt there were equal problems with getting collective farms to observe the much more vaguely phrased stipulation of 1935 that they were to use their autonomous funds (*natural'nye fondy*) and money reserves (*denezhnye sredstva*) to fund crèches and temporary nurseries.[306]

There were also difficulties emanating from poor central planning. The razzmatazz surrounding the promise of universal child care in the 1936 'mother and child' decree was followed by an admission in January 1937 that the building programme was lagging behind the levels needed to expand the network as envisaged: even architectural templates for model nurseries had still to be drawn up.[307] The establishment of new kindergartens in Novgorod district was running as much as 80 per cent behind plan.[308] Numbers of places were inadequate in another sense too: kindergartens accepted only children aged six or less, yet the starting age for schools was eight. Therefore, in the time between their seventh and eighth birthdays, children fell into a kind of administrative black hole. If both parents were at work, they were likely to be left unsupervised, and to stray into the very 'waifdom' that the Soviet state dreaded and was attempting to combat through the work of children's institutions.[309]

The nursery school/school mismatch was dealt with in 1943, by the lowering of the primary school start age to seven, but expansion of nursery places inevitably received a severe setback during the Second World War. During the war itself, enormous efforts were made to provide sufficient places to allow working mothers to hold down factory jobs, and the huge drop in the birth rate also led to a contraction of queues. But, in 1950, numbers of kindergartens and places – 45,200 and 1,788,000 – had actually fallen *vis-à-vis* 1940 (46,000 and 1,953,000).[310] This figure included seasonal nurseries and crèches: numbers of kindergarten facilities alone looked healthier on the basis of a ten-year comparison, standing at 23,999 in 1940 and 25,624 in 1950 across the USSR, and 14,409 and 17,755 across the Russian Federation. While numbers of places dropped slightly across the USSR over the decade (1.171 million to 1.169 million), they rose in the Russian Federation (751, 900 to 829,800).[311] Yet this was still far short of the figures for the target population, which ran into many millions.[312] By 1947, there were 715 nursery schools in Moscow, as compared with 535 schools; however, the latter catered for 560,000 pupils while the former accommodated only 50,000.[313] Once the products of the post-war baby boom reached nursery age (from 1949 onwards), the system became overloaded to breaking point.

The insufficiency of places was not the only problem with kindergarten provision. Despite the hopes of reformers in the 1920s, free day care for older as well as younger children remained a chimera. As with crèches, charges introduced as a 'temporary measure' in 1924[314] remained in force throughout the Soviet period, though parents did not pay the entire cost of a place. During the latter years of NEP, parents whose children attended the Kaluga province nursery schools run by the First Experimental Station contributed 6–7 roubles of the 8–9 roubles that it cost to fund a place; they were also expected to supply bedding and sheets.[315] Once full state control was restored, parental contributions dropped. In 1935, for instance, the parameters were set at 25–35 per cent of the actual cost.[316] In 1948, the costs were 60 roubles per month in towns, 50 roubles per month in the country, with a surcharge of 25 per cent for kindergartens with a so-called 'all-day' programme (i.e. 12–14 hours), and of 50 per cent more for kindergartens with a 24-hour programme.[317] In the late 1950s (after the currency reform), the charge stood at 12 roubles a month, or about 10 per cent of a skilled factory worker's wages.[318]

Few can have been kept out of the child-care network by economics, then. All the same, finding a kindergarten place was – especially in the early Soviet era – much easier for parents who were, in one sense or another, privileged: because they lived in a major city and worked in an industrial enterprise considered to be of primary importance, say, or were employed in a model collective farm or prize-winning state farm, or because they belonged to the Party elite.

Yet, though institutionalised care for toddlers was 'exclusive' in the sense that it was scarce, it was not necessarily of high quality. The propaganda kindergarten was a purpose-built structure, with clean lines, in the high modernist style associated with the Russian Constructivists.[319] A crystal palace outside, inside it was warm, light, clean, and generously equipped with functional items. There were some model kindergartens that came somewhere near these standards. Among them was the famous Moscow Trekhgorka cloth factory kindergarten network, which had already expanded to three different premises by 1919, and which had its own exurban facilities, trained teachers, and full sanitary facilities by the late 1930s.[320] But the fact that this kindergarten was a fixture on the itineraries of visiting foreign dignitaries revealed its exemplary status. Most kindergartens were far more modestly appointed. Even access to gardens was in short supply. In Leningrad in 1924, 62 per cent of *detskie sady* (day nurseries) were in houses, but 67 per cent of *ochagi*, or nurseries with an extended programme, were accommodated in ordinary apartments. Equipment was often scarce: almost two-thirds (again, going by the figures for Leningrad in 1924) lacked furniture of the appropriate size for small children.[321] Though the crash programme of building begun in 1936 meant that more children were housed in purpose-built blocks, even at this stage conversions of old buildings were common.

In some kindergartens, as in some orphanages and *yasli*, dedicated staff did their best to struggle with dilapidation, under-funding, and inadequate equipment. A British diplomat who visited Elizaveta Tikheeva's model kindergarten in 1932 recorded that 'the entrance is filthy and smells of cats and defective sanitation', but also noted that 'the school itself, which is on the first floor, is fairly clean'. Even in this famine year, some kind of a meal was provided for the children, as was entertainment: they were 'rehearsing for a show to celebrate the anniversary of the Red Army'.[322] But not every kindergarten operated on this relatively high level. Ethel Mannin, who visited a Soviet nursery under what should have been less trying circumstances, in 1934, found it just as bleak as the model crèche in the same building. Mannin was disturbed by 'the joylessness of the toddlers staggering about the play-rooms'. In part, this was a result of problems with equipment:

> The games facilities provided for the children seemed to me inadequate. There was a miniature sand-pit, with a slide above it, but though this was the only really useful – from the child's point of view – games-material provided, there were no children utilizing it. [...] There were no children playing with clay or plasticine or any such thing. There were a number of children standing about crying; there were others 'mooning' about; there was one jigging about and holding itself with a frantic expression on its ugly little face.

The only toys were rough and ready wooden animals, which Mannin felt were of little interest to the children ('what can one *do* with a wooden animal?')[323]

Attempts to expand the kindergarten network left little in the way of resources to consolidate existing kindergartens. By the early 1930s, even former model kindergartens and child-care centres were beginning to show the effects of a decade or so of dilapidation through constant use. However, in circumstances where the entire monthly wages bill for running a facility cost significantly less than new furniture, linen, and eating utensils, and where numbers of new kindergartens had to be equipped from scratch, renewal of the inventory at an established institution was not going to come high up the list of priorities.[324] Even as late as the early 1950s, the model village of Viryatino's kindergarten had only a few toys, all hewn from wood by a local carpenter, and mothers had to provide bedding and bedlinen themselves.[325]

Yet the under-equipment of kindergartens generally attracted little criticism and comment. It was not until the post-Stalin era that such matters, along with poor hygienic conditions, began to arouse official interest on a large scale. Certainly, there had been attempts to 'legislate' for hygienic norms in kindergartens since the 1920s.[326] But inspection reports, even in the late Stalin era, were primarily concerned with details of educational methodology: too low a proportion of the staff had been properly trained, too many of them were elderly or else totally inexperienced, patriotic education was going well (or badly), music teaching was incompetent, and so on.[327]

Finding properly qualified personnel was indeed a problem, particularly in the countryside, since both the conditions and the pay were unattractive to anyone who had trained in a city institution. In practice, institutions were prepared to accept untrained staff, even at the level of director of the kindergarten, a situation formalised on 3 May 1937 when a decree of the Soviet of People's Commissars permitted the employment of such people subject to agreement from the local representatives of Narkompros, as well as from the organisation (collective farm, factory, etc.) to which the kindergarten was attached.[328]

Even if staff were adequately trained, they were likely to be seriously overstretched by the high child–supervisor ratios. The target norm of 15–20 children per supervisor set out at the 1919 Congress contrasts rather strikingly with a figure quoted by a participant from Kursk province, citing ratios of 30–40 children per supervisor as a norm. The 1929 Resolutions of the Fourth Russian Congress on Pre-School Education adjusted even the target maximum up to 30 children per group.[329] According to official rules of 1935, a supervisor in a rural nursery could expect to have 'at least' 25–30 children in her care.[330]

Supervisors in cities also had a tough life. As members of an occupational group that had low prestige – unlike factory workers or even teachers – they earned low wages and had little leverage with regard to supplies. Discomfort was a high risk, and poverty always a threat.[331] And of course the thinness of supervision had its effects on children too. Overstretched staff were likely to impose regimentation, simply for reasons of expediency, but could not check in detail that children were actually carrying out their orders. For example, a group of children at a village kindergarten in the 1930s who objected to enforced afternoon rest were able simply to absent themselves, because the supervisor did not notice that five or six of the fifty or more children in her care had gone.[332]

Official sources admitted that standards in nursery schools were variable. In 1951, a report singled out Moscow, Leningrad, Voronezh, Ivanovo, and Sverdlovsk for praise, and Amur, Kurgan, Vologda, Northern Ossetia, and Dagestan for criticism.[333] In the best institutions, staff worked with extraordinary dedication, and the relatively liberal pedagogy characterising nursery schools in the early twentieth century persisted not only in theory, but in practice. An anthology published in 1950 comprised large numbers of cheerful, lively, and largely ideology-free games that had been invented by nursery school supervisors in the course of their duties. One teacher had made up a song to turn washing into a game, and another had invented a game in which all the children held little batons and struck a triangle when they received a cue in rhyme, in order to introduce the children to the principles of rhythm.[334] In humbler institutions, though, equipment was rudimentary: toys might be limited to a concrete rocking-horse and a few toy cars; worse, conditions were likely to be uncongenial, with staff unable to combat bullying by individual small children because they were too hard pressed to notice.[335]

Child Minding

Many children were not exposed to the system at all, good or bad. In the early Soviet era, those attending nursery schools were a minority; a tiny minority in the countryside.[336] For the most part, working-class and peasant mothers who could not place their children in a kindergarten were forced to make the same kind of private arrangements that they made for babies – rely on help from the child's siblings or from other relatives, employ a teenage nanny, or come to some arrangement with a neighbour. If they could not do this, the children would have to run round unsupervised, with the same dangers of possible accidents as in pre-revolutionary days.

Middle-class mothers often fell back on *domrabotnitsy*, just as they did in the case of infants. In the early Soviet era, some women working in this role were former nannies. In whatever case, the relationship between a *domrabotnitsy* and a child tended to be similar to that between children and traditional nannies: when parents were unavailable most of the time, the nanny became an important source of warmth and companionship.[337] Another, rather different, type was the former upper servant, who tended to act as a substitute 'rational mother', providing advice and guidance which the mother was too preoccupied to supply.[338]

But domestic help was not the only solution adopted by those left beyond the state system. Placing the child in a private playgroup (*progulochnaya gruppa* or *detskaya gruppa*) was another way of coping for working women who did not have access to the state kindergarten network. During the late 1920s and early 1930s, such arrangements were positively encouraged: guides appeared informing potential organisers of what was required in the way of premises and equipment, and praising mothers who had set up playgroups on their own initiative in co-operative dwelling houses. A guide published in 1935 claimed that there were 158 improvised kindergartens of this kind in Moscow, as well as 21 nurseries, catering in total for over 10,000 children.[339] In the prestigious Narkomfin building, where the planned communal kindergarten proved even more elusive than the planned crèche, a former *domrabotnitsa* successfully ran a private kindergarten for some years.[340] But, once housing co-operatives were abolished in 1938, official encouragement of semi-private initiatives of this kind also dissipated. Though some survived on a semi-legal basis, development slowed down.[341] This increased the tendency to make *ad hoc* arrangements or to keep child care within the family. There were in any case parents who feared that a nurse might be 'backward', and were reluctant to commit a very young child to institutionalised care, and for them a relation, above all a grandmother, was usually the preferred solution.[342]

But, as with everything in the Stalin years, decisions about child care were only partly the result of personal choice. Even a parent who was in a favourable position, materially speaking, might give up the option that they would have preferred, all things being equal, in the belief that the alternative was a patriotic duty. Valentina Bogdan, a well-paid, high-profile standards engineer who could afford a nanny, and who had managed to find a person her daughter was thoroughly happy with, still felt she ought to send her daughter to the factory kindergarten both in order that the girl (an only child) could go through some group socialisation, and because the organisers of the kindergarten were convinced the standard would improve if more demanding, educated mothers sent their children there.[343]

Pre-School Education for All?

The post-Stalin era saw, as with crèches, an attempt both to widen and to improve provision of care for older children. A decree of the Central Committee and Council of Ministers passed in 1959, 'On the Further Development of Children's Pre-School Institutions, and the Improvement of Education and of Medical Provision', planned for 70 or 80 per cent participation in the pre-school system by 1965.[344] In March 1965, a government directive stipulated that all new buildings were to make space for kindergartens on the ground floor, and that the directors of enterprises were to make over 20 per cent of their accommodation to child-minding facilities; collective farms were to underwrite such facilities on their territories; and employees whose children could not be accommodated in the workplace were to be given a cash grant in recompense.[345]

These measures did have a decided impact on provision. The raw data for increases in places are impressive. The number of nursery places more than doubled between 1960 and 1970, and rose by around 25 per cent in the five years after that.[346] On the other hand, if one compares available places with the size of the target age group, it is clear that provision still fell significantly short, amounting to about 12 per cent in 1958, roughly 20 per cent in 1960, and just under 50 per cent in 1970.[347] Waiting lists were not as bad as for crèches – they stood at 100,000 in 1957, for instance[348] – but this was no doubt because many desperate parents had given up by the time their children reached three or four. Overall provision reached an all-time high of 68.5 per cent of the target age group in 1985.[349] But this still meant a significant shortfall in places. 'If you only knew how hard it had been to get you a place in a kindergarten, you'd never cry [when you went there],' one fictional Soviet father rebuked his daughter in Vasily Belov's 1978 story 'An Upbringing à la Dr Spock'.[350]

Belov's story was set in Moscow, where provision was, as with nurseries, better than it was everywhere else. By the mid-1960s there were already more than 2,000 combined nursery schools and crèches in the capital, accommodating over 280,000 children.[351] Big cities generally were relatively well provided. In 1970, it was announced that 66 new kindergartens had opened in Gorky between 1965 and 1970; interestingly, the majority (56) outside the car factory system, where provision had evidently always been fairly generous.[352] Rural areas, on the other hand, presented a different picture. Of the 1.4 million children in the system across the RSFSR in 1957, only 213,000 came from the countryside; figures for the late 1950s from Bashkiria, Tatarstan, and Urdmurtia indicated that three times as many urban children as rural children were in nursery education.[353] A leader article in *Pre-School Education* in March 1961 openly admitted that there were hardly any pre-school institutions in some (by which one should probably understand, 'most') rural areas. In the fertile Altai region, for instance, there were facilities in 108 out of 161 state farms, but in only 7 out of 530 collective farms. In Vladimir province, just 2 collective farms had kindergartens out of 279 in total, and in Kirov province, only 8 out of 340. Some encouraging examples were cited: 18 collective farms had acquired kindergartens in Sverdlovsk province in 1960, and 49 state farms; in Rostov province, a full 40 kindergartens had opened their doors in the same year.[354] But some rural areas still had no government facilities at all, right through the 1960s.[355]

As with nurseries, it was lack of place availability, rather than the cost of nursery education, that was the problem. In Gorky (Nizhni-Novgorod) during the early 1970s, the standard charge was 12 roubles 50 kopecks per child per month, less than 6 per cent of the official average family wage at the time.[356] While even this would have been beyond the poorest families, free places were available. But, like many sought-after commodities and services in Soviet society, pre-school education was, for many, accessible only in theory, access to it being controlled by perceived need (a factory worker ranked higher than a publisher's editor, say), rather than by cost.

As for another part of the 1959 decree's remit – improving the quality of nursery education – here, too, the authorities were beginning from a low base. The view that pre-school institutions should now fuse pedagogical and medical objectives affected the traditional concept of the kindergarten as a centre of 'enlightenment', just as it affected the original concept of the crèche as above all a hygienic institution. Already in the early years of the post-Stalin era, inspections had detected signs of malaise in some provincial institutions. A survey of 1953–4 had uncovered serious problems of overcrowding in Rostov, as well as tatty furniture. In 1954, a similar tour of inspection laid bare food and equipment shortages in Leningrad, Irkutsk, and other places. In 1957, a general report on collective farm nurseries (such as existed) indicated that all was not well here either: it was common for kindergartens to be housed in ordinary *izby* (village houses), with no attempt to customise the facilities. Sessions of play took place directly on the street, with no supervision; and towels and sheets were scarce to non-existent. Certainly, there were places where dedicated staff maintained 'exemplary cleanliness in the harshest of conditions', but this was far from universal.[357]

An intensive inspection by the newly formed Scientific Research Institute of Pre-School Education of the Academy of Pedagogical Sciences in 1960 confirmed this impression. A kindergarten in Ryazan' province – at a large cloth factory, rather than right out in the countryside – had no running water or sanitation; lighting was poor. In Oryol province, the kindergartens inspected were cluttered, and one had no toys of any kind. In Orenburg province, one facility seen by the inspectors had dirty linen and no specialist staff, and no work at all was done on teaching methodology. As with crèches, outbreaks of infectious disease were a hazard; detailed nursery-by-nursery reports made clear why this should be, recording dirt spattered on walls, overcrowding, and lack of ventilation. Even in Moscow, where sanitary conditions were fine, some points attracted criticism: the games provided had been monotonous. The sample dialogues in the report (transcribed from real sessions) did indeed suggest stodginess in the teaching, as well as in the food. For example, a lesson on measurements in Rostov went like this:

SUPERVISOR: What object am I holding in my hand?
TOLYA: You are holding an exercise book in your hand.
SUPERVISOR: And what object is this?
SASHA: You are holding a book in your hand.
SUPERVISOR: Tell me, children, what size is the book, and what size
   is the exercise book?
KOLYA: The book is quite big, and the exercise book is smaller.
SUPERVISOR: And what other differences do you see?
OLYA: The exercise book has no drawing on it, but the book has a boy
   drawn on it, and a steam-boat and a trolley-bus.[358]

Early education experts did what they could to try and improve the situation. From the mid-1950s, strong interest had been shown by Soviet architects in learning lessons from best practice abroad: a manual published in 1957, for example, admiringly cited the light, spacious buildings constructed for kindergarten use in contemporary Switzerland, Germany, and America, and declared that Soviet building was now moving away from the 'Empire style' and 'classicism' of the late 1940s, with its excessive use of decoration, towards a plainer, more functional style.[359] In the early 1960s, *Pre-School Education* ran dozens of articles on the proper internal organisation of facilities, carrying photographs of Scandinavian-style streamlined room layouts, with glass-fronted cabinets, low chairs and tables, geometrical toy-boxes, and shelf units bearing pot plants, clay ornaments, and sturdy wooden toys.[360] The magazine also exhorted its readers in the direction of best pedagogical practice, with articles about exemplary nursery schools as well as advice of a direct kind.[361]

Pedagogy during the 1960s underwent no really dramatic changes. The third edition of A. I. Sorokina's standard manual, *Pre-School Pedagogy* (1961), continued to emphasise 'education for citizenship' and collective values. Nursery regimes remained as they had been; the material on work-related activities such as role-playing games had not been altered (even the photographs from 1951 were recycled). Teachers were made aware that they should do their bit to propagandise the Lenin cult: stories about Lenin's childhood and about the Lenin museums were to be part of the daily routine.[362] 'Atheistic education' was another ideological element foregrounded at this time, in line with the resurgence of anti-religious propaganda that characterised the Khrushchev era.[363] And many topics favoured in the past – love of the motherland, the achievements of the Pioneer movement – stayed on the official programme.[364]

Yet kindergarten education had never been all about ideology; still less was it now, when ideology was generally losing some of its hold on Soviet culture. The softening of attitudes to 'discipline' that made itself felt in advice literature generally was also evident in material directed at nursery teachers. In the words of the director of a Moscow kindergarten, N. F. Boyarskaya, writing in 1961: 'Children should not just be respected: they should also be loved – in a rational way, of course, but also in such a way that the child is secure in his sense of the rational and just love being extended to him, and always seeks help and protection from us.' Fear of 'spoiling' was less significant than the conviction that children should be treated with consideration.

By all accounts, material conditions in state kindergartens had become considerably better by the 1970s than they were even in the 1960s, let alone the 1940s or the 1920s. There were now not only more kindergartens, but also increasing numbers of purpose-built kindergartens. Since construction of educational buildings of this kind continued to follow centrally approved patterns, the new hygienic preoccupations could be translated directly into practice. A model kindergarten at Novye Cheremushki, in south-western Moscow, for example, had a bright, open site, with a range of low, large-windowed buildings facing a well laid out garden, with covered recreational facilities that were accessible in bad weather.[365] However, the eccentricities of centralised planning made themselves felt. Facilities were usually situated reasonably conveniently in terms of access, and were generally placed away from obvious hazards such as major roads, even if curious decisions were sometimes made in terms of other aspects of location: for example, a top-floor kindergarten in one Moscow building happened to be without a lift.[366]

87   Playtime, nursery school, Sverdlovsk, 1970s.

The human resources needed for running effective kindergartens naturally continued to present problems. Difficulties in finding qualified staff persisted into the 1960s and 1970s, so that children were often placed in the hands of unskilled young women, or, still more undesirably, of pensioners too elderly and unfit to supervise twenty or thirty small children in any other way than by dragooning them into submissive inertia, or by meting out physical punishment. In the worst institutions, supervisors and nannies, whether out of overload or indifference, took next to no interest in the children. One boy had to be removed from a Leningrad kindergarten in the early 1980s because, in the words of his elder sister, 'he had snot hanging down (excuse me for saying so) practically to his belly-button'.[367] This informant's analysis, 'everything depends on the supervisor', sums the situation up. According to an astute, Russian-speaking Western visitor, the American journalist Susan Jacoby, at least some kindergartens were able to create a very attractive environment for their charges. Bright, plant-filled rooms with plenty of toys, and staff who treated the children with open affection – 'it is difficult to fake the warm relationships observed in many Soviet day-care centres' – were characteristic of at least the better places.[368]

Whatever the flaws of the Soviet pre-school system in the late 1950s, 1960s, and 1970s, it did provide an increasing number of children with care that was at least of adequate quality. This appears to have been recognised and valued by most parents. To be sure, they were not usually consulted directly. So far as the authorities were concerned, their principal role continued to be as recipients of advice about how to bring their children up to the standards laid down in the nursery school (untidiness and egotism should not be tolerated).[369] But at the point when some consultation did take place – during the large-scale inspection of kindergartens that followed the 1959 decree – parents often expressed satisfaction with the education their children were getting. Typical was the father who expressed pleasure in the fact that his daughter was learning lots of poems and stories by heart and making friends with other children. Criticisms were generally of small problems that the parents evidently hoped would be put right – not enough fruit; mess in the kindergarten yard.[370]

Disillusion

The 1960s and 1970s marked a high point not only in terms of access to the kindergarten network, but also in satisfaction with the care provided. By the 1980s, attitudes had started to change. Those adults with access to Western radio stations, such as Voice of America, could hear adverse reports of the sanitary conditions in children's institutions; unofficial Soviet literature also often contained explicit criticism of these.[371] Once Mikhail Gorbachev's campaign of glasnost opened up conditions in children's institutions to public discussion, criticism of the kindergarten network started to be heard in open discussion as well. According to figures published in 1989, about a third of kindergarten buildings were defective.[372] The statistic in itself did not point to a collapse of standards (in earlier decades of Soviet power, the proportion of defective buildings was undoubtedly higher). However, its publication had a shock effect on a society used to believing that children were always given the best possible treatment. Equally, groups in nursery schools had always been large, but now people were becoming aware that, in Western countries, this was no longer considered good practice: rather than planning for 25 children to a supervisor (and tolerating up to 40), education authorities abroad ordained groups of more like 10–15 per person.[373] Even more conservative figures, such as the deputy president of the Committee of Soviet Women, admitted that much in the present system had to be put right.[374] As in other institutions, a 'family atmosphere' had now become the ideal. As an extension of this view, voices started to raise the question – sheer heresy in earlier eras – of whether children would not be better off at home than in institutional care.[375] By 1991, the proportion of children attending kindergartens had declined by more than four percentage points (to 63.9 per cent).[376] The downward trend was to continue for the rest of the decade, exacerbated by rising charges, as state subsidies were retracted, combined with falling wages.[377] But the reaction against the kindergarten was started by bad publicity.

Attitudes to the kindergarten, then, followed a pattern that comes up again and again in Soviet history: rather than criticism being a reflection of falling standards, rising standards brought rising expectations and criticism as a knock-on effect of these expectations. Indeed, long before the publicity about problems with hygiene came to the surface, some parents had begun to regard with disquiet the indoctrination offered in nursery schools. Valeriya Mukhina, a 1960s contributor to the genre of 'mother's diary', for instance, levelled explicit criticism of a 7 November festival at her sons' kindergarten:

> You got the feeling that the whole festival hadn't been arranged for children's benefit at all, it had been arranged for adults to gush over. The children looked very serious and well disciplined, but there was no sense of real joy and life about them at all. I think it ought to be possible to have vitality *and* discipline. All in all, watching that celebration just made me feel sad.[378]

Apart from the political didacticism that she identified during the festival, Mukhina was also irritated by other things – such as the habit of giving the children marks for their drawings, about which she actually raised a protest, only to find that the supervisor had responded to this by giving marks to all the others, and not to the twins, upsetting the latter considerably.[379] Earlier mothers' diaries had taken the opinions of professionals entirely on trust. Now, professional opinion was viewed more critically. As ambitions among parents rose, expectations of kindergarten education rose likewise. By the post-Soviet era, parents were starting to expect that kindergartens would offer training in maths and foreign languages – ignoring, as one supervisor wearily pointed out, the fact that their children were at an age when they still needed to be taught to hold a spoon.[380]

This criticism was in signal respects a phenomenon independent of the life of kindergartens. Conditions in them were improving, in a material sense, by and large – though the rise of corruption in the late Soviet era did make an impact on this sphere of life as well.[381] The day-to-day routine remained very much as it had been in earlier generations,[382] and indoctrination had certainly not got more intensive. Actually, what Mukhina's children seem to have been learning from the kindergarten was more at the level of general moral *sententiae*, and not worthy of remark. If they came home saying things about Lenin, or even about the Soviet Union, Mukhina did not notice.[383] Certainly, at least some kindergartens – such as the KGB 24-hour facility in Moscow – continued to have their 'Lenin corners', but by and large teaching about politics – child heroes, for example – was kept for the school programme.[384]

As kindergartens improved, resistance to them increased. For instance, more and more facilities were starting to have the chance to give children a spell in the country during the summer – but this was no longer seen as an unambiguously good thing, because the attitude was that children should be with their parents.[385] Rather than spearheading social change – as had been the aim in the early twentieth century – nurseries remained at the mercy of it. And so, even when numbers peaked, the state never achieved its aim of bringing all children into the network of 'institutions of moral education': as institutionalisation expanded, so too did the hold of the family on the Soviet child.

There were practical reasons for this as well. Even in the post-Stalin era, parents continued to rely on informal child-care arrangements. To be sure, nannies had become less common, now that a second crash industrialisation drive had absorbed migrants from villages who might once have been searching for domestic employment. But child-minding by members of the family or neighbours continued, as did the placing of children in unofficial playgroups.[386] By the 1960s, this situation was coming to be recognised by the Soviet press, with articles on the one hand criticising the persistent shortages of nursery places, and, on the other, writing warmly of alternative solutions: praising a 'nanny service', or child-care agency, set up in Riga, suggesting that working as a child-minder might well suit active pensioners, or emphasising that state child-care facilities would only be able to cope if parents and grandparents helped – say, by acting as assistant to overworked supervisors.[387]

From another point of view, though, the persistence of 'informal' methods of child-care showed the persistence of child-rearing practices that experts considered backward or misdirected, and generated social tensions of another kind: frustration at the demands imposed by a 'second shift' of parental responsibilities. Letters and articles in the Soviet press of the day gave abundant voice to these concerns, with grandparents suggesting they would like to lead their own lives, free of 'second shift' child-care burdens, and child-care experts suggesting that grandparents' socialisation methods might well be old-fashioned and unpopular with their charges.[388] Yet, at the same time, the failures of state child care – both in terms of coverage and of quality – meant that *ad hoc* arrangements not only persisted, but in fact became more entrenched, during the decades after the death of Stalin, with the proportion of children in day care reverting, at the end of the twentieth century, to the levels reached three decades earlier.

Conclusion: Being Brought Up

Before 1917, patterns of looking after small children, just like the patterns of looking after babies, were strongly dependent on the social status of the family concerned. But the first two decades after the Revolution witnessed a significant *uranilovka*, 'levelling out', as formerly comfortably off middle-class parents found themselves, whether scattered abroad or remaining in their homeland, living far more impoverished lives than before 1917. From the early 1950s, on the other hand, prosperity started to grow, as did access to manufactured goods, though shortages of items for children were just as endemic as shortages of everything else. Another dynamic was that of the widening access to institutional education, so that nursery school education formed part of the experience of more and more children. Through much of the Soviet era, though, it was only a minority of children who experienced a full, formal, pre-school education. But, equally, it was only a minority who were entirely looked after by their mothers. Prior to 1917, better-off women uniformly employed nannies, while peasant and working-class mothers had to rely on any child-care support they could get in order to balance work and child-care duties. After 1917, mothers who could not find places for children in the state child-care system, or did not wish to place their children there, used much the same kind of *ad hoc* arrangements, as well as (if their financial resources allowed) having recourse to domestic servants or to informal child-minding groups, which were technically illegal in some periods but still continued to function undercover.

It is harder to generalise about the intellectual and moral sides of upbringing than about the practical sides, whether for a given generation or across generations. Before the Revolution, social status, once again, was crucial, with 'intellectual' and 'moral' education of an explicit kind being to a large extent the concern of the educated classes, though children from the peasantry and working classes who were given a religious upbringing would have absorbed ethical values from it. After the Revolution, codes of 'rational upbringing' were supposed to be absorbed nationwide, but reality proved more complicated than the intentions of politicians, administrators, and professional educators. There was confusion in parents' minds even on topics where official propaganda throughout the Soviet period remained fairly consistent, such as the importance of social responsibility and of dedication to collective values. 'Sovietisation' was quite marked in the first four decades after the Revolution, but in a fairly narrow stratum of society – partly because the material basis for 'rational upbringing' was not accessible to many. On the other hand, as a greater degree of homogeneity spread in material terms in the post-Stalin era, a wider range of child-rearing models emerged. The cramped conditions in which the overwhelming majority of families lived brought adults and children together: as awareness of the code of 'rational upbringing' spread, so did parents' reluctance to treat their children with the emotional detachment that this code required.

As for how children reacted to all this, much depended on individual circumstances. This is true even of institutionalised upbringing in nursery schools, where one is talking about exposure to a relatively coherent set of values: the child's home background, as preparation for its reactions, was still crucial. Some were jangled by the spartan and even sleazy nature of the material conditions. Elena Bonner, for instance, was left with a horror of public conveniences all her life after encountering the stinking lavatory in her kindergarten.[389] But not all children would have been so struck by this experience. As a child from a privileged background, Bonner was probably at a better than average kindergarten; however, such children could also expect better conditions at home, which perhaps made the institutional experience more disgusting to them than to children from factory dormitories. In the late Soviet decades, as more families acquired private flats, first experiences of institutional lavatories evoked more widespread revulsion.[390]

Much the same – variation within a given era by child, but growing dissatisfaction over time – was true of attitudes to kindergarten diet. In the early decades of Soviet power, the repetitive soups and milk puddings would have been unlikely to appeal to a child whose family could afford dishes such as steak, salad, and ice-cream;[391] but such families were very rare. For children from poorer families in cities, the kindergarten menus were at least as good as what they could expect to eat at home. And in the countryside, children in institutionalised child care sometimes ate so much better than anyone else around that measures had to be taken to prevent them surreptitiously removing food to take home. It was only in the post-Stalin era – when standards of living had risen – that the nastiness of nursery food began to be a more frequent complaint.[392]

The picture is also complicated with regard to psychological or emotional reactions. Certainly, the fact that nursery school was *different* from home could be alienating. But it could also be invigorating, as for a boy whose interest in Leningrad history began with his time at a kindergarten in the Yusupov palace.[393] What children more often found traumatic in nursery school was being plunged into a new set of social relations. For some, contact with large numbers of other children was the problem (obviously, only children, or children with just one sibling, were likely to be particularly affected by this side of kindergarten life). Annoyance about no longer being the centre of attention was a possible reaction.[394] But a sense of victimisation could also emerge. Vadim Shefner, for instance, remembered being subjected to merciless teasing on his first day at a kindergarten (in 1918 or 1919) because he was the only boy not in shorts, and wearing just a shirt. The other boys shouted, 'A woman's dress! a woman's dress! the new boy's got a woman's dress!', while the girls greeted him with an insulting ditty usually applied to inappropriately dressed girls:

> Look at you!
> Knickers on view!
> Skirt short and sweet
> Like an orphan off the street.[395]

It took several days for Shefner to stop feeling acutely self-conscious; it could have been a good deal longer.

Obviously, a competent supervisor should have put a stop to behaviour like this, which quite clearly did not contribute to harmonious collective life. But supervisors and nannies were not necessarily fully familiar with the principles of liberal nursery education disseminated in Narkompros instructions. For instance, despite the early Soviet kindergarten's pretensions to rationalistic egalitarianism, a 'division of collective labour' tended to operate, with girls expected to take a larger share in the 'self-help' rituals of clearing up after meals.[396] In the post-war era, this kind of gender reinforcement became official policy anyway: girls would be encouraged to play 'mummy', while boys settled down to build a garage for their toy cars.[397]

This sort of stereotyping would not have been to the taste of small boys who happened to prefer dolls, or girls who would rather have played with cars. But such individuals were no doubt in the minority. More disturbing, in the general run of things, were supervisors' violations of codes of practice in other respects. In the hands of incompetent supervisors, the hygienic regime, which had the potential to give children a sense of security through repetition, easily transmuted into rigid and unimaginative drilling.[398] Most children understandably disliked contact with short-tempered, loud-voiced members of staff, who appear to have constituted a prominent minority.[399] And some suffered from sadism of an explicit kind. When Larissa Miller wet her bed in an overnight kindergarten, rather than use the bucket that had been put out for the children, she was severely punished: 'The teacher combed my hair, tied a big bow on my head, and seated me on the middle of the veranda for all to see. On a clothes-line behind my back, my wet sheet was hung out to dry. I sat there with the pretty bow on my head till lunch time and everybody came to have a sneer.'[400]

This incident had an unusual background: Miller's grandmother worked at the kindergarten concerned, where 'her obvious Jewishness and hot temper' had made her unpopular.[401] But it did not require chauvinism for staff to behave unkindly. Wrapping wet sheets round children was routine in one Leningrad kindergarten during the Blockade years, the staff's hearts not having been softened by the crisis.[402] A woman at nursery school in Odessa during the 1960s vividly recalled the inexplicable humiliation of having her knickers removed during the rest hour – apparently a punishment for not having gone to sleep on demand. 'I'll never forget it, it was so shameful, for a long time it was a trauma.'[403]

But many first-hand memories of former pupils are more positive. 'They read us books, and showed us those slide things, and we played games,' recalled one man from a working-class family in Leningrad who attended nursery school from the mid-1930s.[404] A woman who was at a village nursery school in the Urals at the end of the 1930s had similar memories: songs, games, and lots of fairy stories, 'when we lay down to sleep, they'd always tell us a story'.[405] Often, the fact that the nursery school was well stocked with toys could be an attraction;[406] or it could be exotica of other kinds, also not available at home, such as pets. Being able to act out different kinds of fantasy with large numbers of children was a plus: retrospectively, it is easy to mock the politicised 'role-playing games' that children were asked to take part in, but the feeling they provoked at the time was often excitement.[407]

Nursery school comes at too early a stage in people's lives for us to expect more detailed memories than this. Not surprisingly, what children were taught in terms of intellectual or political content tended to escape recollection. But the ideological side of early education did get through to at least some pupils at the time, as is clear from the memoirs set down by adults in the late 1930s and 1940s. Parents opposed to the Soviet regime were sometimes horrified to hear their children parroting sentiments along the lines, 'Mummy, Auntie Tanya told me we should love Stalin more than anyone.'[408] Yet the reason why indoctrination could be successful was partly that it was propounded in psychologically effective ways, by means of songs, poems, and celebrations. The fact that many supervisors shared in the official ideology of 'the sanctity of childhood' in turn secured their charges' affection, and made any moral guidance that they chose to give soak in. As Dora Shturman, who herself attended a nursery school in the 1920s, expressed it, pre-school children 'ingested the phraseology of Soviet Communism' if nothing else.[409] Attendance at nursery schools could affect attitudes in practical ways as well: for instance, children learned (for better or worse) how to behave in a group; they might also have eccentricities of pronunciation corrected, and might be weaned off the habit of doing things with their left, rather than their right, hand.[410]

But children not exposed to nursery school could equally well pick up orthodox ideas from books, posters, adult conversations, or the atmosphere at large. Andrei Sergeev remembered sitting at home in 1939 (he was then aged six) and 'copying pictures of Pushkin as a little boy and of Marshal Voroshilov into my Pushkin centenary exercise-book. Voroshilov was the best leader of all. Only Stalin was better than him. Stalin was the nicest, kindest, most reassuring person in the world – and an essential part of my childhood. THANK YOU STALIN FOR A HAPPY CHILDHOOD – this made me imagine a winter sunset with houses along a broad path, going up a gently rising slope, and people walking along, and children dragging their toboggans.'[411] And if left-handers were not trained out of their habits at nursery school, it would certainly happen in the schoolroom, and probably in a brusquer spirit as well.[412] There is no evidence that children who attended nursery school necessarily made more assiduous or obedient pupils. Possibly adjusting to institutional education at school was easier, but even this is not wholly clear, given the very great difference in style between pre-school and school teaching. In the words of one pedagogue writing in 1951: 'Children from kindergartens, who have got used to being treated affectionately, and in an encouraging rather than demanding way, sometimes get offended when they arrive in school and find that serious demands are being placed on them, that they're expected to carry out a given task accurately; they don't like their faults and weaknesses being pointed out.'[413] Certainly, the mismatch between what educational administrators hoped the pre-school system would achieve and what it actually achieved remained a major anxiety, harped on, for example, in the columns of *Pre-School Education*.[414]

Some children were miserable at nursery schools; but others were considerably more miserable at home. One major cause of misery, right through the twentieth century, was alcohol abuse. In a 1913 survey of 902 village schoolchildren's ideals and ambitions, only a small proportion of respondents (around 2 per cent) named their father as a person they looked up to, and the reason given by those few who did was, 'Because he's sober.'[415] Drink stimulated violence against other family members, including children. Dem'yan Bednyi's mother 'treated me like a dog and beat me unmercifully' when in her cups.[416] Children were acutely sensitive to the social shame brought on a family by a flamboyant drunk. When Dmitry Nabokov's beloved grandmother became alcoholic after the death of her husband, he would 'sit shaking' as she emerged, red-eyed and panting, to collapse on the wet ground, kerchief adrift, and begin talking loudly to her dead husband, lamenting him and rebuking him for having left her alone. 'People would stand by the well in silence, crossing themselves and not moving; it was not considered proper to interrupt a woman's conversation with her dead husband.'[417] The fears and stigmas of alcoholism continued through the next decades as well. Even if children were not caused physical damage by parents who drank, they were likely to suffer considerable mental distress. 'I'm not saying that he hurt us in a physical sense, it was just that all the swearing we heard had an impact, because there were families where they didn't say things like that and didn't drink [...] I wanted to write down all those nasty words, that's what the effect was. Because I kept hearing them, probably. [...] I wrote a few words down on a bit of paper, three or four words, and with mistakes in too – going by the sound. And so I got a thrashing,' remembered a woman from a small town in Perm' province, born in 1960.[418] A further danger was a copycat addiction, particularly in the late twentieth century (juvenile alcoholism expressed as a proportion of overall figures rose from almost zero in 1940 to 1.5 per cent in the 1950s, and 5 per cent by the early 1980s).[419]

Misery could be caused by poverty in itself. All the informants in our village interviews remembered being hungry at some point, particularly, but not only, during the war. Pockets of deprivation survived into the 1960s: A boy from southern Russia, one of three children, whose mother was unwell and could not work, remembered that food was perpetually short; he began smoking by the age of eight as a way of coming to terms with the hunger.[420] Similar was the case of a Leningrad schoolgirl who, in reply to a school assignment of the early 1960s, 'What I wish most of all in the world is ...' began, '... that I could sit down and eat till I feel full'.[421] While deprivation at this level does not seem to have persisted into the 1970s, there were still cases of families in relative need. A Leningrad boy brought up on his mother's wage of 80 roubles a month (half the official average) in the late 1970s remembered that, though he had tasted condensed milk, the family couldn't afford to buy it, and he always had hand-me down shoes (and felt lucky because he was near the beginning of the chain of their users).[422]

Parents who could hardly afford to feed their children were obviously unlikely to bother about the niceties of moral education. 'Now people bring children up, but all we knew was dragging water and feeding the cattle,' a woman born in Kaluga province in 1882 recalled.[423] Violence from parents was deeply resented. One of the children in Rybnikov's survey, explaining why she had named her mother as the most important person in her life, wrote down 'because she doesn't belt me'.[424]

It is not surprising that adults from this kind of background should, looking back, have scoffed at the idea of a 'happy childhood', or indeed a 'childhood' at all. Yet 'rational upbringing' could have a negative impact too. 'Soft' methods of correction, such as refusing to speak to a child, or talking severely to him or her, sometimes created almost as much distress as physical punishment.[425] Even thoroughly indulgent treatment could have drawbacks. It could be interpreted as manipulation – the purchase of goodwill in order to exercise pressure to behave in certain ways – or, conversely, as neglect (failing to correct a child because the parents could not be bothered).[426] Any case where the child *was* disciplined emerged as particularly unjust against the general background of *laissez-faire*.[427] Equally, where a child was (as not infrequently happened) the only person in the house whom everybody loved, it could find itself in the unenviable position of mediator at large, required to intercede in any situations of conflict: 'Tell your father it really *is* time he bought himself a new pair of winter shoes.'[428] But the investment of emotional energy in children did not necessarily overburden them, or make them demanding. Even in the most consumer-driven phases of the era – 1900–14, the late 1980s – children did not always expect that everything would land in their laps. The cherished daughters and sons of the Soviet middle classes often found themselves helping on the family vegetable patch in the thin years of the early 1990s, just as their counterparts in villages and worker settlements had traditionally done.[429]

It is equally difficult to generalise about the effects of negative emotional experiences, such as the death of a parent, or marital breakdown – a pervasive phenomenon after 1917 – on children's sense of well-being. No doubt there was some comfort in numbers: children who had lost one or both parents were likely to come across many others in the same position; equally, the sense of stigma that children endure in circumstances where divorce is considered shameful and abnormal was spared those living at a time and place where it was more or less the norm. Certainly, oral history and memoirs suggest that not all children felt traumatised by growing up in households that were, from the point of view of child-care literature, not 'normal'. 'Normal', for a child, often meant simply what it was used to. Change was often fiercely resisted, and so the arrival of a new partner was likely to be the occasion for a battle of wills, often conducted obliquely. Larisa Miller, resentful of her mother's pasty new admirer, took to sleepwalking at night: faced with this, and the fact that the man had been filching sugar saved for the child, her mother gave in and showed him the door.[430] But some children brought up from birth in unconventional households felt bewilderment or curiosity, rather than anxiety or distress. Elena Rzhevskaya, the product of a 1920s bohemian household where the mother spent her life veering between her husband, the children's father, and her ever-present admirer 'BN', recollected watching the overheated scenes dispassionately: since her father was always working and seldom around, and the children liked 'BN' in any case, they were not alarmed by, or even particularly interested in, the surges of adult emotion.[431]

Yet children could feel deprived by their lack of a father or a mother, emotions perhaps reinforced by the prevalence of 'normal' nuclear families in Soviet children's literature. Larisa Miller, whose father died at the Front in 1942, when she was two, spent her entire childhood with a sense of lack: 'I was waiting for him to come back, I searched for him everywhere, I composed stories about him. I missed him most acutely when quarrels broke out in the family, and also when mother was dismissed from *Red Army* newspaper, when she and I roamed the streets, reading "Help Wanted" notices, and when I was harassed by other children in the yard.'[432]

However, even if parents were absent or unsatisfactory, grandparents could offer compensation. Sometimes they fostered young children whom parents could not afford to look after.[433] More often, they were sources of indulgence and especially of entertainment, from traditional folk tales (*skazki*) to oral history to family lore.[434] Siblings too could be an important source of emotional sustenance. Roughness from siblings, or other children in the family, on the other hand, was seldom the cause of emotional heartache. The poet Esenin recalled being dumped by adolescent male relations on a semi-wild pony and thrown into water in order to give him a 'swimming lesson', but expressed no lasting resentment at this.[435]

As this chapter has shown, childhood experience depended on a great many variables, relating not only to social status, but to the nature of the individual family – how well a child's parents got on, how interested they were in upbringing, and how much their ideas about appropriate child-rearing and nurture coincided with the child's own feelings about how he or she should be treated. Indulgent treatment was by no means ubiquitous, even in the late twentieth century. Before 1917, there were many families, in the social elite as well as further down the scale, where strict discipline, including the use of corporal punishment, was common; right into the late twentieth century, some parents continued to thrash children who brought home bad school marks or were mischievous or disobedient. There were some families where father and mother anxiously pored over normative guides such as Makarenko, others where people had never heard of such things and consulted older members of the family, thus perpetuating behaviour patterns of a kind normative guides would have condemned; there were still others where parents were relaxed and simply did as they felt; there was also a minority of completely dysfunctional families where the parents were too drunk to care, or simply never around.

Yet the twentieth century did see a significant proportion of parents model themselves on 'rational upbringing' as propounded in the guides. It also, however, saw a more indulgent ethos of 'children first' spread to broader sections of the population, as families became smaller and began to inhabit more constricted living space; as parents themselves, rather than servants, became responsible for raising children;[436] and as the network of state-sponsored consultative facilities spread. By the 1960s, this ethos was arguably more influential than the ethos of 'rational upbringing' that had been advocated by normative guides between 1900 and 1950. Complying with the ideal of the ever-understanding and ever-loving parent, in circumstances where goods were short and living conditions hard, imposed considerable costs on adults. However, it did increase the likelihood that children would be treated with affection and consideration. In this period, too, the myth of 'happy childhood' was readily absorbed by children themselves. 'Maybe the only good thing in the Soviet Union was the sense of a safe, secure childhood,' recalled a woman brought up in an intelligentsia family during the 1970s and 1980s.[437] By no means all children had the opportunity to 'live the myth', but those who did came from the most influential sectors of Soviet society, in terms of public opinion, and thus their experience reinforced its dominance.

Even before this period, at least some historical subjects, by no means exclusively from the cultural elite, appear to have been happier than the adults who surrounded them. In the phrase of a woman brought up on a collective farm in the Urals in the 1940s, 'childhood is childhood' – by which she meant that childhood was the freedom to do as one liked, to play around occasionally rather than get on with the work, to do something forbidden and get away with it.[438] In her village, children shared the deprivation endured by their elders – food shortages, having no shoes to wear – but respite from the daily grind was more frequent.

Cynicism about the 'happy childhood' myth sometimes seems tempting, especially given that those eulogising childhood happiness were sometimes those doing most to ensure the wretchedness of other adults. In 1937, during the Great Purges, Vladimir Petrovich Stavsky, the alcoholic, self-serving, embittered Secretary of the Union of Soviet Writers, and the author of countless denunciations of his fellow writers, including Mandelstam, wrote an entry in his private diary hymning his early life with the following string of treacly cliches: 'And the moon the snow and the smoke the pale blue glow of the stars aroused an overwhelming feeling in me, my distant, irretrievable and eternally beloved childhood ...'[439] The fit of nostalgia seems even more out of place here than it does in Chekhov's Lyubov' Ranevskaya, reminded by her cherry orchard of her innocence (lost some decades before speaking). Yet mockery may obstruct adequate understanding. If one accepts Nancy Ries's hypothesis that one cause of adult Russians' misery in the 1980s was their tendency to talk about misery all the time (i.e. asking such rhetorical questions as 'Why is Russia so full of suffering and misfortune?' may 'help sustain the kind of social and cultural institutions which perpetuate that suffering'),[440] it would follow that thinking one ought to be happy in childhood might sometimes contribute to actually achieving this. By extension, one might move from seeing the idea of a 'fairy-tale childhood' as *invariably* associated with false consciousness and with a distortion of the proper path to maturity, and view it, rather, as a possible source of strength and survival in adults enduring pervasive wretchedness that they are not empowered to change.

Chapter 11

In Their Own Time

Managing the Future

When attempting to shape children's characters, adults are often primarily concerned with the adult that the child is going to turn into. Prohibitions and restraints that are irksome to children are justified by adults' assumption that their longer-term view makes them more conscious of children's welfare than children are themselves. But an equally important part of upbringing is what one might call its 'accidental' or unplanned side: what children observe when watching adults. Such 'eavesdropping' (in the broadest sense) is a vital part of growing up: for instance, a child's apparently inexplicable hostility towards a carer may be traceable to unconscious signs of intolerance that its parents are emitting.[1] In the early phases, this situation may occur when parents underestimate a child's capacity for comprehension – as when a Moscow girl intruded on the conversation between her great-grandmother and a woman who was visiting to consult about whether she should have an abortion or not:

> They were talking their grown-ups' talk, and then I suddenly said, You shouldn't do it, you'll soon be married and everything'll be fine. And she said, Well, I've got no one lined up. And my grandmother said, Where did you get all that from? And I said, I dreamed of Auntie Tanya with eight toes. That means she'll get married and have a child. She said, Where did you get that from, who am I supposed to get married to, do you mean the man I love will come back? I said, I don't know, but someone'll turn up, and you don't need to do anything. And after that, [my great-grandmother] talked to all her visitors with the doors closed.[2]

At a later stage of existence, eavesdropping may become a conscious part of a child's development, as shown in Il'ya Averbakh's film *Other People's Letters* (1976), which hinges on a tussle between an authoritarian new teacher and an obstinate girl in her class who turns spy to persecute the would-be mentor.

Children's observations and experience outside the family home are another area that adults have difficulty regulating, though they may make efforts to do so. Throughout the twentieth century, children from elite households were generally allowed out of doors only when accompanied. Before 1917, they might be sent to a park or garden with a nanny or nursemaid. The main parks in St Petersburg for children were the Aleksandrov Gardens on Admiralty Square, the Catherine Gardens on Nevsky Prospekt, by the Maly Theatre, the Solov'ev Gardens on Vasilievsky Island, and, above all, the Summer Gardens, where the statue of Krylov, decorated with figures from fables, was a specially favoured destination for walks.[3] In Moscow, a child might be walked along the 'boulevard ring', particularly the section near Tverskaya (Marina Tsvetaeva, for instance, was regularly taken in the late 1890s by her nurse 'to visit Pushkin', the writer's statue at the end of Strastnoi Boulevard).[4] By the late nineteenth century, an alternative destination – for a special treat – was the zoological garden: in Russia, these places included a whole range of entertainments, but it was still generally the menagerie that appealed most to juvenile visitors.[5]

After 1917, a similar range of destinations was likely, though now the accompanying adult might be a grandparent, rather than a parent or a child-minder.[6] In addition, the 'parks of culture and rest' set up in the 1920s and 1930s all included special facilities for children: in the early years, green space and 'cultured' leisure centres such as theatres and displays of plants and animals, and, in the late Soviet era, a section of 'attractions' (roundabouts, Ferris wheels, dodgems).[7] In all of these places, children would be carefully supervised: 'running wild' was not an option.

Even in more 'neutral' contexts from the point of view of public order, such as the streets and courtyards of major cities, unaccompanied children were not necessarily left in peace. Many adults not acting in an 'official' capacity would also attempt to correct any youngsters' behaviour that they found unacceptable, by verbal remonstration if nothing else, just as neighbours might in communal apartments.[8] This tendency was reinforced, in the Soviet era, by the large quantity of normative guides urging citizens to intervene if they witnessed disruptive or improper actions.[9] Intervention was particularly likely if the children were from the 'younger school-age' group, which is to say, 'old enough to know better', but not old enough to be seen as a threat by the remonstrator.[10]

If parents and adults could exercise a high degree of control outside the house, they were naturally likely to exercise still more control inside it. Middle-class parents who subscribed to the theories of 'rational upbringing' were especially prone to direct leisure tastes, purchasing educational toys and books to nudge their offspring in the right direction. Yet children still ended up with quite a lot of freedom to do what they liked, both in the house and outside it. To begin with, large numbers of adults were indifferent or permissive about what children got up to, provided it did not annoy them directly. The type of overstretched parent from the working class or peasantry who did not engage in active upbringing of any kind would certainly not be greatly troubled by what children did outside the house. Hence, despite official rules and regulations, and despite campaigns to get adults to see all children as 'theirs', a *laissez-faire* attitude often prevailed. Few children had problems about obtaining cigarettes, despite a legal prohibition on selling them: if the sales assistant in a shop was obstructive, another adult could usually be found to make the purchase on behalf of the under-age addicts;

the same was true about buying alcohol.[11] Equally, ordinary passers-by did little to curb activities such as riding on tram couplings – forbidden in the school rules of 1935, and provoking anxiety among road-safety watchdogs both before and after[12] – or fighting in streets and courtyards. Given that most adults did not intervene directly when children did things that were harmful to health and safety, they were extremely unlikely to exercise control over anything apparently innocuous.

Even where leisure activities took place within the home, or under the direct supervision of parents, children exercised a good deal of imaginative freedom. Adults might well make efforts to encourage children to take up 'educational' hobbies, and there were numerous children who did enjoy photography, radio-building, sewing, and especially reading.[13] But parents and teachers could not necessarily control the direction that children's interests took once they had become enthusiastic about such activities. Children were as likely to use their sewing skills to craft doll's outfits or dressing-up clothes as they were to employ them in darning socks; and what they read, and how they interpreted it, was in practice very varied. Hence, while 'the child's freedom to move from place to place and choose where to be outside the house is always limited and controlled by adults',[14] children's activities could run contrary to what was planned for them and considered acceptable.

From 'Little Pie' to *Lapta*

Play is a constant of childhood experience, present in all eras and societies; leisure, on the other hand, or the integration of play into broader patterns of learning and working, is both historically and culturally specific. In traditional peasant households, children were left to themselves for much of the time between the age when they could first toddle round by themselves (somewhere between one and eighteen months) and the age when they were considered old enough to begin light work (six or seven). Once a child had reached the second age boundary, tolerance of 'foolishness' rapidly decreased.[15] Sometimes it was only on festival

88   Cat and Mouse game,
E. A. Pokrovsky, *Children's Games, Mostly Russian* (1887).

Рис. 52. Кошка и мышка.

days that there was time to spare from work tasks such as digging, mowing, and looking after animals.[16] In working-class households, play was more likely to occupy time snatched from the round of household duties and husbandry (fetching water and fuel, clearing up, feeding chickens, working in the vegetable patch). But children themselves were able to treat work activities – for example, collecting berries, or nutting – as games rather than chores, and to treat time spent minding summer pasturage as adventure.[17] Even if there were few toys, there were often animals to knock about with: yard dogs, or occasionally even a cat.[18] Fortunately the Russian calendar was relatively abundantly provided with holidays, so children could find time not only for amusements such as climbing trees, fishing, thieving in cabbage patches and orchards, sledding or skating in winter, and collecting overlooked 'treasures' such as chips of glass, sweet-wrappers, fruit stones, and buttons,[19] but also for formal games.

Among organised games of this kind, particularly popular were the international favourites, hide-and-seek and 'catch'. Often, chasing games of this kind, rather than being played as plain 'it' or 'tig' (in Russian *salki*), were associated with mini-scenarios. Some of these involved animals. In Kite and Sitting Hen, for example, the former would try to catch the latter's 'chickens', who in their turn, of course, attempted to escape being caught. In Wolf, one child hid behind a tree and another, the 'wolf', approached. The first child asked, 'Who's that?' and the wolf replied, 'Me'. The second child said 'Click' and mimed someone unlocking the door, then ran as fast as it could in the opposite direction.[20] Other popular characters in chasing games (in common with the emphasis on eating in children's folklore generally) were kinds of food. In Karavai, Karavai, Come Pick the One You Love, the main character was a big rye loaf.[21] In Little Pie, one child acted as 'baker', a second as 'buyer', while the others lined up behind the baker, with the 'little pie' at the end. The buyer asked: 'Where's my little pie?' and the baker replied, 'Behind the stove.' The 'pie' had to run to where the baker was without being caught by the buyer; if s/he succeeded, s/he then took over as baker, while the baker became the pie. If the buyer caught the 'pie', s/he would take over as baker and the last in the row then became the 'pie'.[22]

A third variety of chasing involved characters from *skazki*. In the rough-and-tumble game of Snowman and Broom, two children would nominate themselves as the 'Snowman' and 'Baba-Yaga' (from the name of the famous witch). Baba-Yaga would arm herself with a stick and go and hide in a corner. The other children would roll the Snowman on the floor (as though making a real snow figure), then put him or her upright, pretend to mark his or her eyes and mouth, and push a 'broom' (i.e. a stick) under the Snowman's arm. They would then sing a taunting song to draw out the Baba-Yaga. As its last words were sung, the Baba-Yaga would rush out and try to push the Snowman over.[23] This last kind of catch blended into the contest of strength such as Stone Walls, recorded in Kursk province in the 1890s, in which most of the players formed two lines; a single player from one side would then attempt to burst through the opposite line. If successful, they would be allowed to take one player away, if not, they would themselves have to join the opposite line, and so on.[24]

Prevalent were contests of strength and skill: tug of war, for instance, or contests in which one group of children attempted to storm a 'fortress' guarded by a second group of children, or took turns in trying to burst through a chain of closely packed players on the opposition side.[25] Often such games involved the use of implements – less usually balls, in traditional villages or small towns, than short heavy sticks (*bitki*). In *gorodki*, a game resembling Aunt Sally, sticks were thrown in order to topple a pile of short cylindrical skittle-like pieces of wood (*churki*).[26] In *lapta*, a game analogous to cricket, baseball, or rounders, players flailed with a bat at a short heavy stick (in the original version) or at a regular ball (in the modernised one), before making a 'run' by sprinting as fast as possible toward a boundary line, trying to avoid being caught 'out' by the players on the other side.[27]

It tended to be boys who played these rougher and more energetic games, along with *chekharda* (leapfrog), or *shagardai* (a sort of tournament in which one team of players sprang on to the backs of the other team, lined up in a row like a long vaulting horse in a gym: if the members of the 'horse' team could not stand up to the pressure and collapsed, they had to endure the process again, until they did manage to stand firm, or until the entire band of players collapsed in a laughing, exhausted heap).[28] Boys alone played *mayalka*, in which an improvised ball of rags was kicked and made to fly as far as possible, with the winner the person who made it go furthest before landing.[29] In contradistinction to Britain, hopscotch (*klassy*) was also often a boys' game. And, as one man born in the 1930s recalled, 'girls weren't always allowed' to join in when boys were engaging in mock battles, such as Cossacks and Robbers.[30]

There were some games played more or less exclusively by girls: various kinds of skipping game (*skakalochka*), for instance, or dancing and mime games such as 'Mother, teach me how to pick flax'.[31] A number of games were attempted by both sexes: these included *pyatnashki* (a form of 'catch' in which the person pursuing tried to make a hit on those fleeing by throwing a ball at them), and *shtander*, where a player threw a ball hard at a wall to make it bounce off, and then called out the name of a person who was supposed to catch it, who then took over the throwing role if they did manage to trap the ball.[32] Such games (as in Britain) would always be preceded by a counting ritual determining who was to be the leader (*vodyashchii*, or 'it', in British children's slang), usually accompanied by grumbling on the part of those who had not managed to escape the role.[33]

Not only gender, but age, too, was important in determining what games were played: there were significant differences between the repertoires of older and of younger children. Counting games ('Angel-bangel three atroo fitzel faouse fee a foo an dan rigistan rigi rigi rops!', and other equivalents of 'Eenie, meenie, minie, mo'), and making mud- or sand-pies were, not surprisingly, amusements proper to younger ones.[34] Older children, on the other hand, used counting games instrumentally (when deciding who played which role in catch, for instance): verbal games played in their own right were more complex. Their games were also more active, indeed often rougher: quite harsh punishment was meted out to the losers in ball games, who were lined up against the wall and had to wait patiently

89   Boys on a seesaw, Jewish Pale, 1910s.

while the ball was thrown at them, hard, seven or eight times.[35] Older children would also consciously avoid playing games that they regarded as 'babyish', moving on to ones that were new and perceived as more challenging.[36]

Many of the games already described were found everywhere children played – school playgrounds as well as fields, streets, courtyards, and gardens. The same applies to another very popular kind of game, the mock battle. Here, as with the different variations of catch and contests of strength and endurance, there was quite a high degree of stability over time. The game of Cossacks and Robbers, for example, remained popular throughout the late nineteenth and early–mid-twentieth centuries.[37] Among boys, games of this kind sometimes spilled over into serious fighting, which was a ubiquitous pursuit in its own right, with confrontations becoming increasingly ritualised as children grew older. In cities, territories ran from yard to yard, or street to street; in the countryside, boys from one village would turn out to confront boys from another after attending school, or on holidays, a practice that continued right through the twentieth century.[38]

Rivalry was expressed in another kind of competitive activity too: the exchange of insults, which was just as common in streets and yards as it was in school playgrounds.[39] If the particular enemy was not around, fierce taunts would be scrawled on the walls of the courtyard holding him or her up to general ridicule: SASHA'S AN IDIOT and VANYA'S MENTAL.[40] A lower level of insult was represented by the use of joking nicknames, which might be fanciful derivations of a person's first name or last name – 'Molchok', or 'Silence', from Molchanov, 'Vorobei' (Sparrow) from Vorob'ev – animal names such as 'Duck' or 'Fox', or some label so abstruse that no one really knew what it was for.[41] Also extremely popular were various sorts of games of chance: *orlyanka* ('heads or tails'), in which small bets were placed on the spin of a coin, and card games such as *lopatka* (a kind of whist). There were also more esoteric types of gambling game: in Valentin Kataev's novel *A White Sail Gleams*, for example, the two boys at the centre of the story become obsessed with a kind of Aunt Sally game in which uniform buttons were placed on top of a makeshift shy, and short wooden sticks thrown at them: the player who succeeded in flipping a button over was entitled to keep both it and the wager his opponent had laid on the outcome.[42]

'Uncle Yakov' and the Lenin Mausoleum

Traditional types of collective game had various common features that made them unpopular with proponents of 'rational upbringing'. They were chaotic, noisy, and often depended on the display of behaviour traits (violence, avarice, competitiveness) which were deeply uncongenial to the pervasive romantic belief in children's natural innocence. Games of this kind became uncongenial to rational sensibilities when played in towns, and above all in public places close to living accommodation. By the late nineteenth century, the sight of groups of children 'loitering' in streets and courtyards had begun to suggest to philanthropists a frightful image of deprivation: lack of exposure to formal education plus induction into 'the law of the street', hooliganism and petty crime. In 1894, the physician and ethnographer E. A. Pokrovsky commented with concern on the 'pallid' children that he had seen in Moscow the previous year, and drew attention to the new practice, in England and other places, of setting up recreation grounds for city children.[43] An early example of a similar initiative in Russia was the opening, a year later, of a playground in the provincial city of Orenburg. Carefully sited on a steep river-bank, it was surrounded on the other sides by a moat and a ditch so that domestic animals were kept out, and used for supervised games led by teachers at the local *gimnaziya*.[44] In the 1910s, a drive began to set up children's playgrounds in the major cities; like many other areas of philanthropy, this was stimulated by the First World War. Before 1914, there was only one playground in St Petersburg, but by 1915 the number had risen to fifteen.[45] Playgrounds provided not only, or indeed mainly, space for games, but also, and more particularly, programmes of leisure activities, such as lectures and visits to museums.[46] Russian reformers passionately believed in every child's right to enjoy as long a childhood as possible, and aimed to maximise the amount of time that children had available for leisure. But, at the same time, they also sought to regulate every moment of the child's day, including the hours expended on play and entertainment.

After the Revolution, this emphasis on the regulation of play became still more pervasive, and the belief that play should be primarily an educational experience was turned into official pedagogical orthodoxy. In 1919, an editorial published in *Children's Proletkult* magazine, the organ of a Communist children's group in Tula, and written by 15-year-old Sergei Khaibulin, ringingly denounced unsuitable forms of play: 'Down with mischief-making [*shelopainichestvo*], playing "heads or tails", hooliganism and so on. This is no time to be messing around, it is time to be building a new, radiant Communist life.'[47]

This attitude to play persisted throughout the 1920s and early 1930s. Unsupervised play was usually seen as a manifestation of lack of supervision in a wider sense. During the discussions that led to the founding of the Pioneer movement in 1922, a member of the Bureau of the Central Committee of the Komsomol lamented that 'the market and the influence of the capitalist street are the only contributors to the moral education of our children'.[48] In similar vein, seven years later, Zlata Lilina's tract, *Parents, Learn How to Bring Your Children Up*, condemned the situation in a hostel housing workers at the Staro-Glukhovskaya factory on the Klyaz'ma River, not far from Moscow. While adults drank, 'strummed on the accordion', swore at each other, and fought, the corridor was left stinking and the children were abandoned to their own devices. They spent their time lying on the concrete floor while playing cards for money pilfered from the adults in the hostel, sneaking off to Harry Piel films, getting drunk and vandalising that temple of culture the 'red corner', roaming the streets till late, or infecting themselves with venereal disease.[49] In 1938, an article in *Soviet Justice* was to speak with pursed lips of 'the evil influence of the street, the market, and the courtyard'; all of these places, like stations, boulevards, and department stores, were magnets for children, and breeding grounds for juvenile crime.[50]

Campaigners for rational leisure drew no distinction between activities that really were harmful to health (such as drinking), or cruel (such as torturing birds or robbing their nests), or illegal (such as theft), and those which simply ran contrary to the aesthetic appreciations of hygienically inclined Soviet adults (for example playing card games, scribbling graffiti, or watching Western silent films). Equally, leisure spaces that, to children themselves, had very different symbolic resonances – courtyards, the public areas of communal flats or barracks, and streets in cities, fields and streets in villages – were rolled together into a single incubator of deviancy, the haunt of what a troop of Young Pioneers, writing to Stalin in October 1924, disdainfully classified as 'the ordinary childish life, one without any purpose'.[51]

Sententious interpretations became still commoner in the 1930s, when aesthetic distaste at 'uncultured' leisure pursuits began to be combined with paranoia about spontaneous games as an expression of political subversion. The cult of childhood innocence notwithstanding, Party and civic authorities took any games with the faintest political coloration in earnest. In 1937, for instance, the fact that children in a number of Soviet cities (including Moscow, Saratov, Penza, and Gorky) were playing games of 'Reds' versus 'Whites' was used as evidence for the existence of a single 'militarised children's organisation', with branches in all these places – despite the fact that games of this kind were an established tradition from the late nineteenth to the late twentieth century.[52]

At the same time, politically coloured 'mass games' were usually a standard feature on rational leisure programmes. In 1924, for example, Pioneers from the working-class district of Khamovniki, in Moscow, took part, wearing white hoods and robes, in The Fascists' Funeral, a sort of Communist *auto-da-fé* which used Ku Klux Klan costume (Klan members were known as 'American Fascists' in the Soviet press) to satirise Fascist rites.[53] A brochure published for International Children's Week in 1929 carried instructions for a complicated version of 'catch' called the Underground Meeting, in which 'Fascists' tried to arrest 'Pioneers' who were holding an illegal meeting, while a third force of 'Social Democrats' hedged their bets by attempting to interfere with the 'Pioneers', without, however, directly co-operating with the 'Fascists'.[54] And, in 1932, the peasant children's magazine *Friendly Lads* enthusiastically reported on an exemplary group of village children who had repudiated the traditional and 'boring' modelling of snowmen (more accurately, 'snow women', *snezhnye baby*) in favour of a more ambitious kind of construction: the Lenin Mausoleum, made out of compressed snow-blocks dyed red to resemble the original.[55]

The danger with this sort of organised play was of course that it threatened to increase the appetite for exactly the kind of politicised game that the authorities most feared – battles between Fascists and Communists with the former as the 'goodies', maybe, or a round of Let's Demolish the Lenin Mausoleum. However, this does not seem to have been an issue that was raised by campaigners for 'rational leisure' in the 1920s or the early 1930s, perhaps because of their tendency not to credit children with much capacity for autonomous invention. According to the standard pattern of representation, unsupervised juvenile leisure was characterised by absence: it was a cultural blank space. Children hung round courtyards out of boredom; when they ran out of songs to sing, or games to play (which happened very quickly), they could easily be inveigled into deviant activities by evil-minded adults. The safest strategy was to pre-empt temptation.

Playing on their Own

Whether unsupervised play was seen as 'destructively anti-social' or 'quirky and amusing', such play was always understood as being an intellectually and aesthetically constricted phenomenon. What children did on their own was naïve and silly and might annoy or amuse the observer depending on his or her taste. Such an understanding ignored children's astonishing adaptability and skill in making use of limited resources. One woman brought up in the Latvian seaside town of Libau (Liepaja) in the late nineteenth century remembered that the children in her family had made 'sandcastles' with the clean dry soil under a tree, not having a sand-pit available.[56] In the absence of toy guns and swords, branches and sticks – or, in winter, icicles – would be used by children as stand-ins.[57] Throughout the twentieth century, country children made do with next to nothing: toy guns could not be had for love or money, but very effective pea-shooters might be made out of the hollow stem of a shrub, and whistles could be crafted in a similar way.[58] Children of all social brackets, however poor or rich, sometimes got by with even less than this, turning their own bodies into the equipment for play. A woman who grew up in the early 1900s remembered playing a whole range of games that would have horrified campaigners for 'cultured living'. She and her friends held snorting, honking, and grunting contests; they competed over who could dribble the most, or blow bubbles in their own dribble. They stuffed peas up their nostrils and enjoyed the peculiar sound this made when they spoke, or tried to push feathers as far as possible up their noses as a test of stoicism. They waggled their ears, twanged rubber bands on their teeth, stuck their tongues out as far as possible or rolled them into tubelets; they gobbled down supposedly inedible substances such as chalk, or gum from cherry trees.[59]

What adults classed as 'hooliganism' might in fact be espoused for positive rather than negative reasons: not because children had nothing better to do, but because games that adults disliked seemed exciting and stimulating in their own right. With unusual realism, an article in *Pravda* in 1935 cited the case of a schoolboy in Stalingrad who had found organised games 'boring', preferring traditional pursuits such as skittles, running round the streets, watching icebreakers on the Volga or playing *chizhiki* (a stick and bat game like *lapta*).[60] Catch and hide-and-seek remained as popular after the Revolution as they had been before, being recorded in all eras from the 1920s to the 1990s, and the traditional elements of strife, jeering, and competition were also retained.

The persistence of traditional recreations is made clear by a lengthy blacklist of 'cruel', 'silly', and 'old-fashioned' games circulated by the Komsomol Central Committee in 1936. Pioneers and Octobrists were not to be allowed to play 'cruel' games such as Lame Vixen (a Russian equivalent of the British game Grandmother's Footsteps where the Vixen got revenge for the taunts lavished on her by pouncing on any children who were slow to run away), games involving boyars or princesses (described as 'old-fashioned'), or 'silly' games such as '*chek-chek pyatachok, vstavai Yasha durachok*' (a form of what in English would be known as Donkey).[61] Jeering at the pursuer remained a standard element of 'catch' games into the late twentieth century. A particularly extended example, Grey Cat Vas'ka, was recorded in Karelia in the 1950s:

> Vaska the cat is dark as night,
> Vaska's tail is so so white,
> Like a dart he flies.
> He shuts his eyes,
> He spreads his paws
> Flexes his claws,
> His teeth are sharp as knives.
> Vaska has a bushy tail,
> You'll hardly hear him crawl,
> But he won't catch us – RUN![62]

The authorities had an equally hard time stamping out types of play that, so far as they were concerned, lay well over the boundary-lines of tolerability. The frequent exhortations against gambling, fighting, and riding on tram-couplings in propaganda of the late 1920s and 1930s, and the presence of specific prohibitions on such activities in the school rules of 1935, indicate that small boys in cities were as prone to risky pursuits as they had been before the Revolution. This appreciation is confirmed by oral history: 'You'd see a car coming and hang on to the back and get a ride. And we'd get rides on them, what, trams, yes, "on the sausage" we called it,' a man brought up in late 1930s Leningrad recalled.[63] While riding on tram-couplings, and hitching rides on cars, seem to have become less common in the second half of the twentieth century (perhaps because of changes in sartorial practices: as Afanasy Salynsky remembered, it was easier and safer to jump off the back of a moving vehicle if you were wearing clogs, a traditional form of footwear that had more or less died out in large cities by the post-war era), fighting and gambling flourished unabated, as did under-age smoking and drinking. Children too young to ask adults to purchase tobacco on their behalf made do with 'cigarettes' of moss, leaves, or whatever other substance came to hand.[64]

90 Boy smoking, Jewish Pale, 1910s.

As well as a high degree of consistency across time in leisure practices, there was considerable consistency across space. In the far southern resort town of Sukhumi, a thoroughly multi-national city that was administratively in Abhazia, boys growing up in the 1930s also loved fighting, ball games, and gambling games such as Heads or Tails and Knockover, where a stack of piled coins was first of all used as the target for players to flick 5-kopeck pieces at; the player who got his 5-kopeck piece nearest the target had the chance to try and splat out the stack with an expertly aimed coin.[65]

But if play was in some respects stable (with genres such as catch, throwing games, and mock battles, as well as football, fighting, and gambling, retaining popularity for decades), it also, like any other form of popular culture, was subject to modulation over the course of time. The age of the children involved was enormously important. City children moved from first ventures into the sandpit or general exploration of their surroundings in early childhood to more elaborate games with scenarios (mock battles, different forms of catch and of ball games) in the pre-adolescent phase, and finally, over the borders of adolescence, into activities that often involved a high level of risk-taking. By 11 or 12, children had often begun to smoke, some of them would have started to experiment with alcohol, and − in the late Soviet era at least − sometimes with other kinds of intoxicating substance, such as glue. By 14 or 15, a boundary had been crossed, and by now the yards had become the disputed territory of mainly male gangs, who engaged in serious fighting with weapons such as bicycle chains, and among whom toughness − to the extent of possession of a criminal record − popularity with one's fellows, and capacity for hard drinking and smoking were paths to the role of gang 'king'.[66] In the countryside, age was also important, with smaller children playing chase, counting games, hide-and-seek, and hopscotch, while older ones were more likely to go for *lapta*, and eventually for the courting games that were a prelude to pairing off and eventually to marriage.[67]

Games also changed over time in a different sense − as a result of broader social shifts and the ways in which these impacted upon children's experience. School education generated new variants of archetypal games. A woman who grew up in the 1890s in Kursk province remembered that she and other children, all aged around 10 or 11, had played a complicated form of catch known as *Kalym* (Tatar Tribute Gold) (the title came from history lessons at school). Here the pursuer had imprisoned the 'Russians' in an old shed with a holey roof: since it was possible for the captives to escape, the pursuer had to concentrate not only on chasing the 'Russians', but also on guarding them once they were caught. 'We used to play this game with great enjoyment and for considerable lengths of time.'[68] An informant taking part in a study of children's games at the First Experimental Station of Narkompros in the mid-1920s recalled a game called Search and Requisition, played in a suburban Moscow courtyard during the first years after the Revolution. The boys would act as Red Army Soldiers and the girls (well padded out with cushions) as The Swindler and The Fat Bourgeois. Paper twists of salt and other provisions stolen from the kitchen stood in for the shop goods. The Red Army Soldiers burst their way into the premises, shouting and yelling abuse, and punching and kicking their victims (this was where the padding came in useful). They would then duly requisition the 'goods', and depart triumphantly with the words, 'Now we're off to Sukharevka' (the largest and most infamous flea market in Moscow).[69] A generation later, children responded to school education and radio coverage, and to the content of children's magazines, by playing Border Guards, Chelyuskin Pilots, Tractor Drivers, or Combine Harvesters; in the 1940s, 'Young Guard' games, based on Fadeev's novel, became popular in some places.[70]

With an altered social context, games could acquire a new significance. A time-honoured 'dare', going into the cemetery alone at night, acquired spurious topicality for boys in one village in Tver' province during the early 1930s: they liked to see it as a demonstration that they did not entertain absurd superstitions about ghosts and about life everlasting.[71] And war games preserved morphological similarities over time,[72] while altering in terms of naming patterns. Reds and Whites (played in the 1920s) was later replaced by anti-capitalist struggles, in which the Soviet Union was pitted against France, England, Italy, and America. In the decades after the war there were battles between 'Soviets' and 'Germans', or, more simply, 'war games'. In one Leningrad courtyard, factory scrap was commandeered to act as tanks and so on, while the defenders took up position in used kvas barrels, which were useful because their lids could be flipped down to provide protection against flying missiles such as snowballs.[73] Indeed, Second World War games were so widespread and popular that they even became the subject of sardonic 'sadistic rhymes' (of which more later).

Family circumstances also shaped activities. A favourite childhood game of Aleksandr Pasternak and his brother Boris, sons of a renowned academic artist in Moscow, was Exhibition-Private View.[74] Lidiya Libedinskaya remembered that in her courtyard, in the late 1920s and early 1930s, the preferred game for girls had been 'Decembrist wives', which had the participants retreating to 'Siberia' (a rooftop), to sit there by the hour with sacks of pebbles (symbolising provisions, presumably), and with toys standing in as children. The idea for the game came from Libedinskaya's grandmother's stories about the wives of the leaders of the 1825 rebellion following their husbands into exile.[75]

Role-playing games were not usually as esoteric as this, however. Far more popular were situation dramas that were closely connected to everyday life: shops, doctors and nurses, and above all Mummies and Daddies (known in Russia as Mothers and Daughters, since boys were always more reluctant to take part: if they refused, then this would be excused by some assumption along the lines, 'Daddy's at work', or 'Daddy's gone away'). Frequently, this game was associated with the emergence of family conflicts and their resolution – the participants would quarrel about who was to do what – and players were 'typecast' in relation not only to gender but also to age (the smallest children would play the 'youngest daughter', and so on).[76] In villages, role-playing games seem to have been particularly closely related to local life. Popular, for instance, were work songs, with gestures, such as 'We were sowing, sowing the millet'.[77] Children frequently built play-houses, which they would use for playing Mummies and Daughters, or sometimes for imitating local adult activities.[78] These were not necessarily domestic. Country children were less likely to play 'shops' than city children were (there might not necessarily be a retail outlet locally), but there are records of games like Dairy Farm, with the girls acting out the role of milkmaids.[79]

Play Spaces

Games changed not only as a reflection of topical issues, but because the spaces and equipment available for play altered. The provision of formal playground facilities could contribute to this process, but oral history suggests that the provision of facilities was usually at a very modest level – freezing over part of the territory of a yard to create an improvised skating rink, for instance, providing a couple of nets to mark out a pitch for basketball, or setting up a simple machine such as 'giant's footsteps', where ropes hung down from a frame allowing children to spin round, as though on an improvised swing.[80] But facilities of this kind were confined to urban areas, and even there were not elaborate: tarmac square swings and slides would stand alone beside metal garages, untidy thickets of saplings, and

91 Model railway, Kuzmin'ki Leisure Park, Moscow. Elaborate purpose-built facilities like this were to be found in city culture parks, but children used them occasionally only.

stretches of rough grass or, according to season, snow or mud. Specific facilities for older children were on the whole neglected. Even in the late twentieth century, therefore, courtyards and streets were the main place many children played in; up to the Second World War, they were the only play space for many.

The courtyard itself went through important historical changes over the course of the 'long twentieth century'. Before the Revolution, and during the years immediately after it, children often stuck to family groups. Such exclusivity was not limited to well-off families. The children from the working-class Luk'yanov family, who were sole occupiers of a small wooden house in north central Moscow in the early 1920s, generally played alone or in the company of just one other small girl, even though right next door was an apartment block inhabited by

92 Out in the courtyard. A high-Stalinist representation of a decorous ideal, rather than a documentary photograph. Still from *The Girl from Class One*.

437

large numbers of children who regularly needed to walk past the house on their way to school or to the canteen in the Monastery of the Sorrows next door.[81] From the late 1920s, on the other hand, city children overwhelmingly often played in groups denominated by location, gender, and age, rather than by blood relationship. Here, though some rules (contrary to the appreciations of critical adult outsiders) did operate, the dominant group members were often boys in early adolescence, increasing the likelihood of activities that parents might not approve. Boys in particular tended to engage in potentially dangerous behaviour, such as climbing, jumping from sill to sill across wide gaps at altitude, and fighting with others in the yard or from yards further along the street.[82] After the Second World War, occupations became especially risky. In one working-class area close to the Moscow River, boys not only delighted in traditional pastimes such as diving into the scummy water to fish out condoms (which they used as balloons), or hitching themselves to the back of trucks so they could 'ski' along the frozen streets, but also recycled, as home-made fireworks, powder from the spent shells then lying round everywhere. The louder the bangs and the blacker the smoke, the more they liked it.[83]

Apart from 'proletarianising' children's play, the emergence of the courtyard as the primary play space for town children also had other effects on the nature of leisure. Despite children's capacity to improvise, there were some ways in which the features of the play space could not be altered. Without sufficient room, there were certain kinds of active game that were simply impractical. As cities urbanised, the traditional garden-like courtyard was replaced (especially in central St Petersburg-Leningrad) by an asphalted 'well' without grass or trees and surrounded on four sides by rows of windows or by blank 'fire walls'. This background helps explain the disappearance of *kolodka* (a kind of rounders), or *lapta*, both played with sticks or hard balls that could do significant damage to windows, in favour of soccer (already the most popular kind of ball game for boys by the early twentieth century) and *gorelki* (catch, played with a rubber or rag ball).[84] It is more difficult to explain the decline of other traditional games, such as *lodyzhki* (knuckle-bones), which Nikolai Aseev remembered playing in the hemp-fields on the outskirts of the small town in Kursk province where he was brought up during the 1890s, or *gorodki* and *shashki* (types of skittles and Aunt Sally), but perhaps the difficulty of finding suitable equipment in the urban environment was the cause. The latter two games, at least, would not have worked well on uneven surfaces such as rutted asphalt.[85]

If the courtyard imposed restrictions, though, it also suggested possibilities. Popular among girls, for instance, were throwing and catching games where the constrictions of courtyard space were turned to positive advantage. In a typical game, the ball was thrown up and caught while a player shouted and performed a series of actions: '*tsokhi-tsokhi – boki-boki*' (the player hit herself on the side and span round), '*lady-lady*' (hands were clapped), '*syady-syady*' (the player sat down), '*koleno-koleno*' (the ball was thrown under the knee and caught), '*dver'-dver'*' (the player touched the door while catching), '*zver'-zver''* (the hands were clapped immediately before catching the ball), '*belka-belka*' (the player bent down and hit the ball on the floor before throwing it up), '*tarelka-tarelka*' (the player whirled round like a top).[86]

The courtyard's significant features – the cellars, the roof spaces, and the rubbish dump – could stimulate a variety of imaginative games as well. A story by a 10-year-old girl included in Aleksei Kruchenykh's 1914 anthology of children's writings and drawings told the sad tale of a child orphaned and lying alone in her 'dark bed', too weak to work. When spring came and the children came outside into the courtyard to play catch, tig, and 'witch games' (a variety of *pyatnashki* where those hit by the ball had to freeze to the spot), a small boy in blue trousers chased his pet cat out into the courtyard, where she ran into a cellar. 'Suddenly he saw the girl sitting there with her eyes wide wide open, then she slowly fell back on to her bed and lay quite still. The boy went up to her but she was dead. Then the boy picked flowers and laid them round the girl and went out and closed the door.'[87]

This ethereal narrative, with its representation of solitary play, is clearly the work of an early twentieth-century child from a middle-class background. After the Revolution, though, cellars were among the places that were most popular for collective games. They were used (as an old shed or barn, or bushes or trees, would have been in a less featureless environment) as a *shtab*, or 'den', meaning anything from a robber's lair to the headquarters of a spy network. Shefner remembered that he and other boys had turned a cellar in their courtyard into a 'robber cave', decorated with skulls, crossbones, coffins, and revolvers. Here they would gather to tell hair-raising ghost and robber stories.[88]

The rubbish heap (or its later replacement, the *bak*, a large metal refuse container) was the source of equally intense fascination. It was not only a place where children could satisfy their desire to destroy objects, but also somewhere where treasures such as used sweet wrappers (*fantiki*), bottle tops, and shards of coloured glass might be discovered, and then carried off to be stored in a child's 'treasure trove' (*tainik*) or 'secret place' (*sekret*: the former term was used by boys and the latter by girls, and while the former tended to prefer ready-made places, such as chinks in walls, the latter would often bury their treasures underground). If some games annoyed adults because they were dangerous, exploratory games were inflammatory for different reasons: in the course of them, children entered spaces that were considered dirty and abject, avoided at all costs by respectable people of mature years.

Small towns, right into the late twentieth century, were likely to have much more undeveloped open space, and so were industrialised settlements (*poselki*), or the satellite areas of a larger town (known before 1917 as *slobodki*, and in Soviet days as the *prigorod*). Yet games were often 'urban' (running down the embankment in a railway town, for instance), and territories, as in big cities, ran district to district, school to school, or courtyard to courtyard, rather than village to village, as in the countryside.[89] In villages, natural features – trees, ravines – would have to be used instead. Interestingly, too, in villages risk-taking seems to have been of a different order. On the one hand, children spent a lot of their time pushing at boundaries, as was manifested, for instance, in the common habit among boys of pilfering fruit.[90] Contact with real danger was less widespread, partly, no doubt, because children tended to be exposed to scary experiences in the course of everyday life. A child who was sent alone into the forest to take cows to pasture, or to check game snares or hives, had no need to stoke up fear artificially, when the thought of marauding bears and wolves, or indeed human predators such as bandits, lay constantly in the back of its mind.[91] By and large, games fell into a fairly narrow and stereotyped range, including hide-and-seek in various forms, blind man's buff, and different kinds of catch, some accompanied by insulting rhymes.[92]

For rather different reasons – to do with the less stressful conditions, and the greater opportunities for letting off steam in a non-aggressive way – city children transported to the country for the summer played less rough and intense games than they did at home. In dacha areas, fights and vertiginous climbing were less common than elaborate fantasy scenarios, for instance Cowboys and Indians with the 'Indians' wearing berry necklaces and bird-feathers in their hair, very much the kind of game that middle-class children had played before the Revolution.[93] Wherever they lived, though, children were capable of indulging in another kind of activity that did not fit the image of 'happy childhood': cruelty to insects and animals. This might involve tormenting local dogs and cats, hunting down birds, or torturing beetles or flies by slowly pulling them to pieces – often less out of an enjoyment of inflicted pain than out of sheer curiosity.[94]

Playing Indoors

Some outdoor games (though not those involving discarded rubbish) were transferable to interior spaces. Ball games, catch, or hide-and-seek could be played in the corridors of communal flats or barracks, which acted as undercover courtyards in foul weather.[95] Inside individual dwellings, a child could make a den of sorts using furniture. Nabokov remembered playing, at the age of four, 'cave games' in a space behind an old cretonne-covered divan in his mother's country house at Vyra. 'In a burst of delicious panic, on rapidly thudding hands and knees I would reach the tunnel's far end, push its cushion away, and be welcomed by a mesh of sunshine on the parquet under the canework of a Viennese chair and two gamesome flies settling by turns.'[96] Later, other children were to play similar games, though, given the limited resources of Soviet dwellings, it was usually a table that served as refuge. In some cases, this practice could serve as a way of gaining a degree of privacy when living space had to be shared with parents: one man who grew up in the 1970s remembered as a child getting so used to taking refuge under a table with a blanket or cloth thrown on top that he continued doing this even when the family had moved to a place where he had his own room.[97]

Furniture was used not only for making lairs, but also for more active games. The pretend train made on chairs by Anna Karenina's son Serezha had a real-life counterpart in some of the games played during the 1900s by one girl and her brother. A 'boat' would be constructed from a stool and the laundry basket propped up on chairs, with the sister and her dolls in the basket to act as passengers. Letting out ear-piercing squeals from a whistle, the brother would shout 'Danger, danger, shark to port!' and would bang away with his toy cannon. Often the game ended when the 'boat' collapsed and the children and dolls tumbled on to the floor.[98]

Children only really had a chance to play games like this last one when there were no adults around to fuss over possible injuries, not to speak of damage to the furniture. After the Revolution, when replacing broken chairs became difficult, if not impossible, and when adults and children shared a much smaller living space, tolerance of noisy and boisterous play inevitably decreased. When Zinaida Stanchinskaya's mother found her five-year-old grandson creating a den from the dining table, a curtain, and some chairs, she put a stop to his activities immediately.[99] Usually, when playing at home, children were expected to amuse themselves quietly and to cause the minimum of disruption. The irony was that the resources for children to play on their own were much less extensive after 1917.

Before the Revolution, children from the wealthiest families tended to have very large numbers of toys at their disposal. These included the fashionable educational cubes and cylinders, sold, for instance, at the Trinity Workshop in St Petersburg,[100] but also a range of rather less obviously improving items, in particular dolls. These did not always have to be of the ringleted and frilly variety: the young Elisaveta Fen, for instance, preferred her boy doll Yury in his Little Lord Fauntleroy outfit to Tamara the girl doll.[101] Popular also were dolls in national dress: the future painter Mstislav Dobuzhinsky remembered his wooden and much-loved peasant doll 'Akulina', in a traditional head-dress, and a Nutcracker with a hook nose in a Loden coat, as well as a variety of wind-up toys.[102]

Not everyone, of course, liked dolls. One mother recalled in the 1920s that her boy and girl, brought up in the 1900s, spurned human effigies of every kind, but had, instead, an enormous collection of porcelain animals, each one with its own name and fictional character, though to adults the creatures looked identical. As the children grew older, the games that they played became more elaborate. When the First State Duma was opened (in 1906), the animals were recast by their owners (then about 10 and 11 years old) as members of the Duma 'and pronounced thunderous speeches'. A year or so later, the boy made up a special opera, *How Richko Lost his Tail*, featuring the children's favourite animal, a china dog. After that, the creatures were allowed to go into honourable retirement.[103] Whilst these games were unusually elaborate (and imaginative), references to animal toys are common in memoirs and maternal diaries. When aged about five, M. V. Stakhorskaya's small son had a toy rabbit that he would insist on feeding at table, though, as she irritably observed, he knew perfectly well that the beast was not in fact alive.[104] By the 1910s, teddy bears (*mishki*) were starting to become popular in Russia, as well as in the West: well-off children were likely to have imported bears, from the Steiff factory for instance, but those from humbler families might have home-made ones, crafted perhaps from an old coat.[105]

The considerable influence of Tolstoi's writings on the Russian intelligentsia meant that some families tried to avoid traditional 'boys' toys', such as guns, military uniforms, or miniature soldiers.[106] But this was a marginal trend: plenty of small boys were still encouraged to play with such items, combining with brothers or school-friends to arrange elaborate mock-battles.[107] Other war toys included battleships, which could be used to enact exploration narratives *à la* Jules Verne as well.[108] Toy trains were perennially popular, and were an item that slightly older children (from 10 upwards) might save up to buy themselves.[109] Even children from relatively impecunious middle-class families, such as Tamara Karsavina, were likely to have at least a few attractive items: though Karsavina insisted 'there was no room for even small luxuries', she also remembered that 'we always had a Christmas tree', and that she owned 'a handsome set of doll's drawing-room furniture, a round table, sofa and chairs covered in red plush'.[110] The average child certainly had many more objects than its predecessors growing up in the early nineteenth century. S. M. Solov'ev, recalling his childhood in the 1830s, could recall no items of amusement of any kind apart from books.[111] Now, indulged children were often treated to quite opulent items as gifts: Sergei Prokofiev's father, for instance, gave him the materials (bricks, timbers, reed thatch) to build a miniature house in the garden, which, when finished, was furnished with special child-size tables and chairs.[112]

This sort of toy would never have swum into the ken of poorer children; nor would foreign-manufactured animals or dolls have been part of their childhood experience. By and large, village children had, at best, a few home-made items: rag dolls, in particular.[113] As far as the less fortunate children in cities went, the brightly coloured toys sold at market stalls and by street traders represented the height of likely aspirations. A photograph taken by a British traveller in the 1910s shows a pedlar, watched longingly by two young children of proletarian appearance, selling, alongside wooden ladles and feather dusters, a range of goods for playing with: miniature wooden horses on wheels, stiff-spined dolls dressed in primitive imitations of fashionable wear, carved wagons, tambourines, and coloured bricks.[114] Other items of this kind included brightly coloured clay horses and birds, and carved and painted wooden bears.

The more opulent hand-crafted items often found their way into well-off households as well, particularly when parents had an ideological interest in the cottage industry movement (whose productions were often on sale at charity bazaars run by ladies of the aristocracy). Among the toys owned by Nicholas II's children were not only Western-made toy ships and cars, dolls and dolls' furniture, such as a glamorous swan-shaped doll's pram, but painted wooden figures of the kind made in Sergiev-Posad.[115] Children from well-off homes delighted in buying cheap items themselves: 'Chinese shells' that opened in water to reveal strands of paper flowers,[116] or the items on sale at the Palm Week toy fairs. E. M. Almedingen remembered, alongside soap and different kinds of snack, such as halva and toasted bread, and Easter eggs of all sorts, 'oddly-coloured sweets, paper windmills, crudely painted wooden crocodiles, hot apples studded with cloves and poppy seeds and multi-coloured balloons.'[117] Other staples of this occasion were flashy, gadgety things of different sorts: 'American devils' with soaring mercury globules inside glass tubes, blow-up dolls that squealed 'Go away,

93 A toy pedlar, St Petersburg, 1910s.

94 Wooden horse and cart, 1910s. Toy Museum, Moscow, photographed 1926.

«Музей Игрушки».   Тройка резная из дерева. Владимирская губ.

go away!' (*uidi-uidi*) as they deflated, and clay whistles or wind-up balalaikas, good for tormenting parents and relations.[118] Among the very poorest children, even these toys were unlikely possessions, but loving parents doing their best to amuse a child might give a small boy a whistle cut from a reed, or a chip of wood rough-hewn into the semblance of a horse's head, or a small girl a 'doll' made from a log dressed in scraps of material to suggest a skirt and scarf.[119] Anna Kuznetsova-Budanova's father would bring back empty account books from the warehouse he worked in at a factory in southern Russia: the children were delighted by these, as they added realism to the games of Shopkeeper and Buyer with which they loved to entertain themselves.[120]

After the Revolution, the pedagogical suspicion of 'frivolous' items for the young, the bias of Soviet industry against consumer goods, and the material difficulties of many families combined to make it so that the vast majority of children, even from reasonably well-off families, had far fewer things to play with. Though displays of suitably hygienic and edifying toys (such as bricks and what one Soviet pedagogue described as 'the excellent Meccano') were a feature of pedagogical institutes and of the Toy Museum in Moscow, there was very little state manufacture of items for use by individual children.[121] During the NEP period, toys were available from private shops, and afterwards from special outlets for the socially privileged, but these items were inaccessible and expensive. It was mainly parents and grandparents who had once themselves had model menageries and so on who were prepared to indulge their children. Lidiya Libedinskaya, for instance, remembered being presented, in 1928, with a red flannel bear that she

95 Central Market toy, early 1920s. Wooden horse and cart, 1910s. Toy Museum, Moscow, photographed 1926.

had coveted, and eventually with a dress and shoes for the toy ursine, but she also remembered the sobering cost of the shoes: one rouble, or 50 per cent of her grandmother's pension, for the shoes (with the bear, the cost was less important than the fact that the only place where such a toy could be got was the special outlet for employees of the secret police).[122]

Inevitably, given the importance of artisanal production to the supply of cheaper goods before 1928, the end of NEP led to a slump in availability of toys.[123] By 1931, this situation had attracted the attention of the then Commissar of Enlightenment, Sergei Bubnov, who on 14 July 1931 issued a decree setting up a methodological centre attached to Narkompros that would investigate the production of properly 'Soviet' toys, relevant to socialist construction and to the industrialisation drive, rather than the dated and ideologically unsound items on the market at the time.[124] But it was only in the mid-1930s that Soviet administrators began making serious efforts to boost toy production (a move in line with the enhanced interest in consumer goods that characterised an era when 'life had become jollier').[125] In 1936, *Pravda* exploded into a positive plethora of articles criticising the poor quality of objects that were available, and the unimaginative choice of what to produce on the part of Soviet factories. The youngest children were fairly well served, but there was much less for older ones, and objects were often of poor quality. Smudgy and ungainly wooden figures passed for dolls, shaggy and savage-looking hairy lumps for toy animals; it was impossible to buy doll's tea-sets and other miniature furniture, and 'a real teddy bear is becoming a deficit creature'. There were no model metro trains or even model cars, even if it was now possible to buy a fairly adequate toy telephone. The Narkompros authorities spent more time engaging in idiotic efforts to censor perfectly innocent items than they did in encouraging factories to produce things that children might actually enjoy playing with. And there was still not a sniff of the 'excellent Meccano'.[126]

As with most discussions of Soviet consumer goods of the period, the exhortations to the toy industry were more effective in exposing problems than in setting them to rights. Toy manufacturers were often dependent on the supply of raw materials from elsewhere in Soviet industry (for instance, teddy bears were made of a knitted fabric called *trikotin*, which was itself critically short).[127] In any case, it is doubtful how many even of these fairly unattractive-sounding objects found their way into the average Soviet household. Certainly, items such as bicycles were far beyond the reach of most families, as is obliquely suggested by a reference in a speech made by the wife of a Stakhanovite worker in 1936, which described how just under a third of a 980-rouble bonus earned by the Stakhanovite himself had been set aside to buy a bicycle for the couple's son. (At the time, 300 roubles was only slightly lower than the average monthly wage for industrial workers.)[128]

It is not surprising that memories of growing up in the 1930s suggest that many children were expected to make do with at most one or two purpose-manufactured toys – a few miniature cars, a horse on rockers, alphabet blocks.[129] This included children of white-collar workers and intellectuals. Indeed, economic resources seem to have been more important than family status in dictating how many objects children had to play with. The only daughter of two factory workers, whose mother used to take her shopping every time she received her wage packet, and who had a large number of doting unmarried uncles, had an unusually rich collection, consisting not only of dolls, but of a much-prized orange glass doll's tea-set, a memorable birthday present.[130] By now, families in cities did not much go in for making toys (with the exception of ornaments for the Christmas or New Year tree).[131] But home manufacture continued to be the sole method by which toys were acquired in most rural families. The only bicycle in Pavel Starzhinsky's village was cobbled together from odds and ends, including the remains of an old spinning-wheel.[132] An indulgent father who was good at wood-turning might make a few figures for the children with his lathe.[133] Dolls were almost invariably of the rag variety, though the occasional lucky child with relations in a city not too far away might be given a shop-bought model; or sometimes a visiting trader would offer rubber balls and other cheap toys in exchange for old clothes.[134] Even in cities, the most opulent types of plaything were the prerogative of children from the Soviet elite – such as the daughter of a successful actress whose 'family' included a doll with eyes that actually shut, a celluloid baby doll, two teddy bears, a model tiger and a miniature bunny rabbit.[135] A fair number of individuals from less privileged circles who grew up at this time are certain that they never had any toys at all.[136]

The 'toy famine' naturally became significantly worse during the Second World War and its aftermath. In the words of one woman born in 1940, 'No, of course we didn't have toys: it wasn't the time to be worrying about things like that.'[137] However, on reflection, this person recalled a favourite doll that she had been given as a prize for good behaviour in the orphanage where she was brought up. In fact, children in orphanages were sometimes better off in this respect, during the post-war years, than were their fellows outside institutions. 'Patron' factories and other well-wishers might make donations of toys. No. 58 Orphanage in Leningrad was kept supplied by a local manufactory which offloaded slightly substandard versions of the wind-up tin playthings that it produced.[138] Even after the war had ended, the enormous capital demands of repairing the infrastructure in cities and in collective farms left little capacity for the production of consumer goods of any kind, and toys were not at the top of the list in any case. Well into the 1940s, children in villages and small towns continued to play with the traditional rag dolls and wood-chip animals, and children in bigger towns still had access to only a few poorly made yet prized toys.

By the early 1950s, there were some signs of a revival of interest in producing play items for children. But a good many games and toys that reached the shops were crudely designed and poorly produced. A spread in *Krokodil* in February 1952 denounced some quite attractive-looking objects for ideological reasons. A brightly coloured wooden boat was lambasted as 'having elements of Formalist art'; a merry red-cheeked clown in a baggy patchwork jumpsuit was considered an excessively 'naturalistic' illustration of 'the evil effects of heavy drinking'; a blow-out squeaker known by the traditional name of Mother-in-Law's Tongue was condemned merely on account of the name, and in the same way an appealing 'Oriental' looking figure was held reprehensible, probably because its name, the Thief of Baghdad, might have awakened interest in a life of crime. However, some of the criticism in the article was rather easier to understand. To judge by the photographs, three figures of rabbits really were, as the article suggested, approximate in their relation to any living creature, shoddily made, and unattractively presented. And the prices of several items – for example, over 40 roubles for the wooden boat – would undoubtedly have been well beyond the reach of most families at the time.[139]

In itself, though, it is doubtful whether the scarcity of toys spelled deprivation. Other pastimes, such as board games (draughts, snakes and ladders, spillikins,

96 Studio portrait of girl with teddy bear, Sverdlovsk, *c.* 1936. The bear in question was, as the subject of the photograph recalls, supplied by the photographer.

and so on), and paper games (writing joke poems or comic letters) were popular alternative ways of passing the time.[140] In any case, Russian children, like children in most other cultures, were often just as happy playing with everyday objects as with toys. Tamara Karsavina's collection included 'some fungus growth from beech trees', 'big plane leaves, dried in a book and beaten with a hairbrush till they became quite transparent and as made of lace', and tiny dolls that she would cut out of paper and place in rows on the windowsill in the nursery.[141] Andrei Sergeev, growing up in the late 1930s, had several hand-me-down treasures: an old tea tin dating from Tsarist times, the case from some Gillette razor blades, and a mother-of-pearl purse. His only bought toy was a set of toy soldiers bought in a shop not far from where he lived.[142] In a much humbler household, a peasant cottage out in Novgorod province, a woman born in 1927 turned an old washtub held together with wire into a magnificent bed for her dolls, lining it with cloth and improvising a pillow.[143] Shards of glass, old tin cans, rags, and other 'worthless' objects might get turned into treasures for play.[144]

Children could also derive a good deal of amusement from exploring the nooks and crannies of their environment. Even a child as indulged as Vladimir Nabokov found his visits to the lavatory as fascinating as any of his official toys (see p. 489 below); the surrounding environment was likely to evoke a still richer response in children with less to distract them in the way of official toys. Shortages of food and other types of consumer goods – clothes and shoes in particular – seem (judging by memoirs) to have been far more traumatic than scanty provision of objects to play with. Certainly, there were cases where toy ownership became an index of status among children. A Muscovite woman who took part in the film *The Girl from Year One* as an extra in the late 1940s remembered being mortified when her old doll was put to shame by other children's possessions (the children had been asked to bring along their own props for a group scene).[145] But it was only in very particular circles – here, the pupils of an elite Moscow school – that such an experience was likely.

In the post-Stalin era, however, things began to change, in line with the increasing availability of consumer goods more generally. Following the general interest in improving supplies of consumer goods, the press gave attention to this type of material object as well. Already by 1960, Children's World in Moscow had started to sell new lines of soft toy, such as furry white elephants, which (contrary to proverbial tradition) created a huge demand when first released to the Soviet public.[146] As with other kinds of possession, expectations of likely levels of ownership also expanded. By the mid-1960s, normative manuals assumed children would have quite a wide selection of things to play with. A 1967 publication, for instance, suggested not only items with an educational lustre, such as Konstruktor (a Soviet version of 'the excellent Meccano'), toy cranes, and a model collective farm, but also a miniature zoo and models of popular fictional characters such as Cipolino, Dr Aibolit, and even Chukovsky's Crocodile. By now, making home-made toys was envisaged as a way of keeping children busy during dull moments, rather than as a method of providing them with playthings in the first place.[147] In addition, some sources now suggested that children should be allowed to play with toys for longer – entry to school should not automatically mean the shelving of dolls, cars, mice, and furry bears.[148]

One might expect propaganda sources of this kind to err on the side of generosity. However, it does seem that some middle-class children had an enormous repertoire of playthings compared with what would have been available even a decade earlier. As toddlers, Valeriya Mukhina's sons, born in 1961, had about a dozen small animals (the classic toy bear – in this case, made of hygienic plastic – a horse, a goat, a wolf, a cat, a rubber duck, and, more exotically, a badger, a puss-in-boots, and a wooden zebra). Alongside 'educational' items, such as building bricks, toy berries and a large plastic key, they owned several rather less obviously improving possessions, such as a red plastic car, and some stacking Russian dolls (*matreshki*); later, they were given both a tricycle and a rocking-horse. At the dacha they not only had toys they brought from town, but also special items, such as stilts and a sand-p it. Small wonder that the other children from the settlement tended to congregate in the Mukhins' garden.[149]

This number of items was rather high, even by the standards of the middle classes during the post-Stalin era. Toys were quite expensive, so large-scale items, such as dolls, would be occasional gifts only, the source of joy and delight in their owners. In the early 1980s, one woman recalled, her mother would make efforts to buy her as birthday presents 'beautiful German dolls, ones with arms and legs that bent or that said "Waah" and "Mama", we had several beautiful blue-eyed blonde German dolls, and my friends and I would sew clothes for them and dress them up and make them look pretty'.[150] And it was not just children from professionals' families that had such items: a lorry driver's daughter born in 1969 remembered that her father would 'buy anything I pointed at' in the toy shop, and that her prized possession was a 'big, big doll that walked by itself and said "Mama".' 'Whenever he had money, he'd say, "Let's go to Children's World,"' and the large number of toys at home had included a crowd of toy animals.[151] Another man from a similar background (his father was a construction worker) recalled that his most prized birthday present was a version of Konstruktor that allowed him to make a working miniature traffic light, but that he also had quite a lot of toys, including a big collection of model aircraft augmented 'almost weekly' by his father, and various home-made items, also made by the latter.[152] In fact, social class was (as in other phases of Soviet history) less important in terms of 'toy power' than economic status: a child from a one-parent family was unlikely to end up with expensive items, and might well have only a few simple, favourite objects: home-made wooden toys, a doll with a stuffed cloth body, a plush teddy bear.[153]

Of course, proliferating numbers of toys helped boost the social differentiation that was becoming more obvious in other ways as well. Children now had very different ranges of playthings available to them, from the simplest Soviet-made coloured bricks up to foreign-produced train sets, or dolls with joints and closing eyes. All the same, the lack of brand names acted as some kind of counterweight to cupidity. A child could point imperiously at toys when taken to Children's World, but use of the phrase 'I want ...' was hindered by the elusiveness of objects of desire. Without ready availability of branded goods, such as Barbie, Lego, Action Man, Space-Hoppers, and so on, it was more difficult to articulate demands exactly. Even a child who did manage a specific request of the kind, 'I want a blonde German doll that says "Mama" like Liza's got' would soon learn that acquiring toys of this kind took time and effort. Many widespread types of toy remained extremely simple: these included the *pupsik*, a rudimentary kind of celluloid (or, later, plastic) baby doll that continued to be as popular in the 1960s as it was in the 1940s, or the *golysh*, a bare plastic girl doll with moving arms and legs meant for dressing by the proud purchaser.[154] In any case, many parents preferred toys that they considered 'educational'.[155] It was only at the very end of the Soviet era that obsession with brand names really took off, helped by newspaper reports exclaiming over the superiority of foreign-made toys and the wonders of items made by Fisher-Price, Lego, and other Western firms.[156] For most of

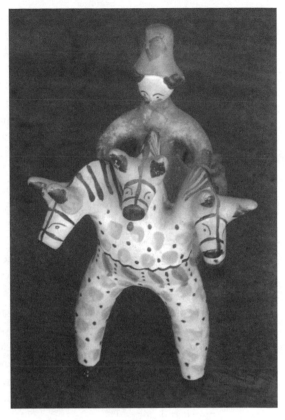

97 Clay toy in the traditional style, 1970s.

the late Soviet era, let alone the first decades of Soviet power, the best-off Russians lived significantly less opulently, in this respect as in so many others, than the best-off Russians had before 1917. Conversely, peasant and more particularly working-class children's access to manufactured toys altered significantly: by the 1960s, working-class children in big cities, at any rate, had become important participants, whether directly or through their parents, in the market for toys of all kinds.

The Magic World of Print

Though books, like toys, are consumer goods and require a financial outlay, book ownership and toy ownership occupy quite different locations in terms of social values. In Russia, books have by custom been regarded as intrinsically different from other purchasable objects, a tradition intimately associated with the conviction that reading is (at least potentially) an activity of peculiar virtue and civilising power. From the late nineteenth century, these two appreciations fused in the drive, among Russian intellectuals and philanthropically minded publishers, to provide working-class and peasant Russians with reading material

449

of high quality. Children were recognised as a crucial target group, and great effort was expended on the composition and publication of suitable materials for their consumption. Among the most famous activists working in this area were Nikolai Rubakin, a brilliant self-taught writer and pedagogue who was a passionate missionary for self-education, Maxim Gorky, and of course Leo Tolstoy, whose adaptations of folk tales for children were enriched by the sessions he spent working with peasant children and getting them to tell stories of their own. Such initiatives were continued and expanded in the Soviet era, with Party and Komsomol authorities declaring a determination to provide children with quality books at accessible prices.[157] Unlike the declarations about toy provision, these had at least some effect: print runs for children's books were large and their prices were indeed kept low.

There was some sense, then, in which reading was a cross-class activity for children in the way that, say, playing with train sets was not. To be sure, before the Revolution, better-off children had access to a wider variety of books; it was only they, for instance, who would have been able to enjoy the most opulently produced illustrated editions (such as the publications of Pushkin's verse tales illustrated by Bilibin, or Benois's *Alphabet in Pictures*). The only books with plates familiar to poorer children (apart from school primers) were popular editions aimed at adults: when these fell into the hands of young children, they tended to ignore the text and 'read' the pictures. This happened, for instance, to Aleksei Chapygin, born into a peasant family, who chanced on a copy of *Paradise Lost*: he found the work itself deadly boring but was spellbound by the pictures of 'angels and saints'.[158]

'Chancing on' was indeed the usual way in which child reading progressed in peasant and working-class households. Until a child reached school, he or she would probably not have encountered a special children's book (except, perhaps, for the textbook brought home by an older sibling), and parents would do little or nothing to direct their children's tastes. In time, the school programme (Pushkin, Krylov, Tolstoy, Lomonosov, and so on) had its effects, as did the contents of school libraries (which, like the content of educational programmes, were carefully regulated by the educational ministry). A survey conducted in 1916 indicated that the village children who named a literary figure as their personal hero (only 7 per cent of those participating in the survey) all picked someone from classic texts of the kind that would have been set reading in the schoolroom: Taras Bul'ba, Yury Miloslavsky, Gulliver, Uncle Tom.[159] But despite the efforts of educators to propagandise suitable reading and direct the interpretation of books along edifying paths, the children of uneducated parents consumed books with what a devoted pedagogue would have seen as a total lack of system. Aleksei Novikov-Priboi, growing up in the 1890s, devoured everything he could lay his hands on: supplements to popular magazines, books about astronomy, books about Jack the Ripper, religious books – even the *Criminal Code of the Russian Empire*.[160] For his part, Mikhail Svetlov sustained himself for some time on a random stack of books which his mother, a sunflower-seed seller in Ekaterinoslav, had been given to make paper twists for her wares.[161] Often, the act of reading itself was as important as the content. In the words of one lower-class boy who grew up in the early twentieth century: '[Books] took me out of my hard, poor and dark life into a blindingly bright world of fairy-tale.'[162] Adventure stories were a particularly popular way of effecting the escape. Working-class children gobbled down traditional *lubok* books (for example two eighteenth-century tales of bloodthirsty criminals, *The Frightful Bandit Churkin* and *Van'ka Kain*) alongside translations of books by such writers as Mayne Reid, Fenimore Cooper, Jules Verne, and Conan Doyle, and 'penny dreadful' thrillers such as the 'Nat Pinkerton' series of detective novels.[163] None of the memoirists who recalls reading such material remembers being encouraged or discouraged in their enthusiasm by adults.

Educated parents, on the other hand, were usually inclined to take an interest in their children's books. The standard menu began with adaptations of folk tales in the nursery (these would be read aloud to younger children).[164] Then followed 'quality' children's literature (as published, for instance, in the magazines the *Cordial Word* and the *Little Glow-Worm*), mixed with a selection of works by famous Russian writers that had become firmly established as suitable for children (Krylov's fables, Pushkin's verse tales, Zhukovsky's ballads, Gogol's *Evening at a Farm near Dikanka*, and the selected poems of Nekrasov), and with abridged (i.e. bowdlerised) editions of Western classics such as *Gulliver's Travels*, *Robinson Crusoe*, and *Don Quixote*.[165]

A particularly effective way of controlling material aimed at children (in the nicest possible way) was reading aloud. The fascination of hearing a parent read could mean that even books some adults might have found demanding had a child enraptured. The future painter Dobuzhinsky remembered, alongside the usual fairy stories, Gogol', Nathaniel Hawthorne's retellings of Greek myth and legend, and Gnedich's translation of Homer's the *Odyssey*.[166] Illustrated editions were another way of enticing children to read, or at any rate pick their way through, material that was not child-centred in an obvious way.[167]

By the early twentieth century, parents did not have to make choices about children's reading on their own: they could consult advisory bibliographies, such as I. V. Vladislavlev's *What to Read?* (1911). Here, Vladislavlev suggested that, up to the age of about 12, children's literature (provided it was of good quality) was perfectly acceptable reading, but after that, as children started to become interested in adult books, direction was required. The list of recommended reading that he supplied included a mixture of exemplary memoirs (for instance Vera Zhelikhovskaya's *What I Was Like as a Child*, 1891, and Sergei Aksakov's *Family Chronicle*), Russian classics (Pushkin, Lermontov, Gogol', Turgenev, and extracts from Dostoevsky, among others), and translations (often in abridged form) of foreign literature (for example Swift, Defoe). Mass-market literature by Russian authors was emphatically not included, though the equally 'trashy' writings of the British novelist Ouida were, presumably because they were lent snob value by their foreign origin.[168]

It would be misleading, though, to suggest that children from the social and cultural elite consumed exclusively 'quality' material, and those from the bottom end of the social scale nothing but 'garbage'. Books such as the moral tales of

Tolstoy, or of another great advocate of popular education, Nikolai Rubakin, had a profound effect on the readership at which they were aimed. Kornei Chukovsky was in later life to recall the pivotal part played by Rubakin's didactic fiction for children in his own struggle to 'become a person', as the language of the time put it.[169] Conversely, children from middle- and upper-class Russian homes displayed a formidable appetite for writing of a kind that would not have met the approval of parents and teachers. Jules Verne, Fenimore Cooper, and Mayne Reid were just as popular with the sons and daughters (particularly the sons) of university professors, lawyers, doctors, and insurance agents as they were with the children of peasants and workers.[170] The writer Pavel Lebedev-Polyansky, the son of a civil servant, remembered enjoying, alongside Mayne Reid, Jules Verne, and Chekhov's tongue-in-cheek sensationalist story *The Black Monk* (whose parodistic intent he probably did not appreciate), *The Frightful Bandit Churkin*, and Matvei Komarov's popular picaresque novel, *The English Milord and the Countess of Brandenburg*, which for half a century had been a byword among Russian radicals for literary vulgarity.[171] Well-bred girls seem to have had less of an appetite for adventure stories of this kind (though there was a female readership for Jules Verne).[172] However, a good many were addicted to the genteel romances and tales of boarding-school life written by Lidiya Charskaya, such as *Nina Dzhavakha* (1903), in which a Georgian princess who has been allowed to gallop round on a fiery steed with her pet eaglet on her wrist adjusts to life in a strict girls' boarding-school.[173]

In 1912, the critic (not yet children's writer) Kornei Chukovsky subjected Charskaya's work to an annihilating review, denouncing the nursery favourite for sentimentality, absurdity, and lapses of taste.[174] Chukovsky, though, missed the point. Charskaya was not writing for cynical adults who turned on her the full blast of their carefully cultivated literary judgement. Her writings might have seemed milksop by comparison with boys' adventure stories or the British boarding-school yarns of the day, but they expressed a mild defiance to the stultifying emphasis on gentility and propriety that was imposed in Russian girls' schools. Girls loved her work, fervently identifying with the heroines and imagining themselves acting out the romantic plots that these heroines found themselves caught up in, an identification facilitated by the first-person narratives that Charskaya loved to use.[175] In reviews by adults, Charskaya was slammed as an example of everything that was worst about feminine taste, yet instances of boys reading her – and even writing her fan letters – were fairly frequent.[176]

Just like children from the working class and peasantry, the children of educated parents read voraciously and eclectically. The future critic Yury Tynyanov relished a fairly independent selection of Pushkin – he loved 'The Song of Prescient Oleg' rather than the verse tales or the usual poems printed in anthologies for children – but also mass-market, abridged editions of *The Bride of Lammermoor* and the popular tale *Ermak Timofeevich*.[177] The same child was quite capable of reading both for entertainment and for instruction. Books that Elizaveta Fen, from a landowning family in Belorussia, remembered enjoying included the *Childhoods of Famous People* series, *Uncle Tom's Cabin*, *The Prince and the Pauper*, the Hans Andersen weepie 'The Little Mermaid', but also *Tom Sawyer* and *Huckleberry Finn*.[178] For her part, the future poet Poliksena Solov'eva read Andersen stories and Gogol' (standard enough fare for children), but also rather less obviously 'suitable' material such as the lyric poems of Fet and a selection of lives of the saints.[179] Equally, children were likely to read intellectually ambitious and well-produced journals bought by their parents (the *Footpath*, the *Cordial Word*, the *Young Reader*) alongside chapbooks produced by mass-market publishers such as Sytein.

Children's tastes were catholic in other ways too. Despite the efforts of teachers and of some parents to inculcate 'national' values from an early age, they did not discriminate between texts on the basis of their culture of origin. Stories by Grimm, Andersen, and Perrault were devoured alongside Russian nursery classics such as *The Tale of Ivan Tsarevich and the Grey Wolf*, and, later, Louisa Alcott and Frances Hodgson Burnett rivalled Charskaya as providers of girls' reading. No Russian author writing for boys was nearly as popular as Mayne Reid or Fenimore Cooper.[180] Many Russian children would have been astonished to learn that the perennially popular poem *Messy Styopka* was an adaptation of Heinrich Hoffmann's nursery classic *Struwwelpeter*. Booksellers' catalogues give an equally eclectic impression of nursery taste: editions of fairy tales by Andersen and of *skazki* by Pushkin appear alongside brochures of 'Russian folk tales'; Hodgson Burnett's *A Little Princess* (translated as *Sarah Crewe*) rubs shoulders with the the travels of N. M. Przheval'sky, the adventures of Jules Verne, and retellings of saints' lives.[181] Attempts by adults to discourage children from reading 'trash' sometimes backfired, resulting in subterfuge rather than obedience. On being set a school essay, 'My Favourite Book', one early twentieth-century schoolgirl decided to play safe by naming the popular, but respectable, poet Nadson, rather than telling the truth (Lidiya Charskaya and Lermontov). She received a good mark for her efforts (which would probably not have been the case if she had dared to mention Charskaya).[182]

It was no doubt partly recognition of the dangers of driving children's real tastes underground that led advocates of 'free education' to tolerate rather franker expressions of opinion by children about their favourite reading. In 1911, Musya V., a 10-year-old at Ol'ga Kaidanova's nursery and primary school in Moscow, compiled a list of the books that she had read recently, marking them on a scale of 1 to 6. Among her favourites were *Evgeny Onegin*, *Little Lord Fauntleroy*, *Little Women*, Nekrasov's poem *Russian Women*, and Gogol's *Old-World Landowners*. She was more lukewarm about the poetry of Nikitin and Kol'tsov (two mid-nineteenth-century peasant poets), *Tom Sawyer*, and *Little Men*, and did not like *The Golden Fish* (a retelling of a traditional Russian folk tale) or the children's magazine the *Little Glow-Worm* one bit.[183]

Even when they read 'the right books', children did not necessarily read in the way that adults of pedagogical inclinations might have deemed appropriate. Vadim Safonov, born in 1904, remembered, 'When I read Lermontov as a child I interpreted him as one of those entertaining writers of exotic travel books – a sort of Caucasian Mayne Reid, I suppose.'[184] Again, supporters of the free education movement seem to have tolerated such 'aberrations' more calmly, as the capacity of the 10-year-old girl just mentioned to disparage Kol'tsov and Nikitin, idols of the Russian populist movement, makes clear.

Permissive attitudes to reading, like most other aspects of 'free education', did not long outlast the Bolshevik Revolution. The library purge administered by Nadezhda Krupskaya in 1923–4 removed from the shelves many volumes specifically aimed at child readers, such as folk and fairy tales, the works of Lidiya Charskaya, and children's magazines, including the *Cordial Word*, henceforth to be a byword for sentimental vulgarity with Soviet commentators. It also hit at many of the categories of adult reading most eagerly devoured by juvenile readers: chapbooks such as *The Tale of Bova Korolevich*, and popular songbooks; crime novels; sensational historical novels; and romances, such as the novels of Anastasiya Verbitskaya.[185] Certainly, in the early days of Soviet power, there were attempts to provide Soviet alternatives to the sort of adventure stories that had been popular before the Revolution.[186] A contributor to a Soviet pedagogical journal, writing in 1924, quoted verbatim a child's story about robbers who hid in a peasant's trunk, were discovered by a pilgrim staying the night in the hut, and were then shot when the police came to round them up; he commented quite neutrally that it was in the vein of *Tarzan* and *Atlantis*.[187] But attitudes to adventure stories became considerably more repressive as time went on. As early as 1924, a 'librarian-pedagogue', E. Nelidova, condemned adventure stories, including Pavel Blyakhin's impeccably *bien pensant* Civil War thriller *Little Red Devils*, as unsuitable for child readers.[188] An official list for Pioneer leaders circulated in 1925 still included Mayne Reid and Stevenson's *Treasure Island* as recommended reading, but, by 1927, Land and Factory publishing house was being rebuked for having inexplicably decided to 'dig up' the latter from rightful oblivion, and in 1928 a Party decree expressly condemned 'elements of unhealthy adventure-storyism' in children's prose.[189]

This repressive attitude towards suspense fiction was only partly revised during the 1930s. Tarzan fortuitously escaped the library purges of 1932, and Jules Verne was specifically singled out for approval in another decree of 1933 (it was no doubt the 'scientific' flavour of Verne's books that rendered them acceptable).[190] But Mayne Reid, Fenimore Cooper, Conan Doyle, and the 'Nat Pinkerton' detective novels followed Charskaya into the 'forbidden' category. Reviews of adventure fiction almost always contained some negative remarks on the possible lack of pedagogical virtue in the genre, conveying that the authorities' accommodation with it was hard-won, reluctant, and might be revoked at any time.[191]

Teaching Children How to Read

The practice of reading was seen, throughout the Soviet period, as a crucial area of 'culturedness'. In the second half of the twentieth century, Soviet commentators began to boast of having 'a public that reads more than any other in the world', and that Soviet children had far better access to quality books than their counterparts elsewhere. A pronouncement by Lev Kassil' in 1964 is typical: 'One can say with absolute confidence that throughout the entire extent of our motherland there is not one single dwelling with even one child in it where there is not also at least one children's book.'[192] As a matter of national pride, reading was far too important an activity to be wasted on mere entertainment, as parents were often reminded. It might even be dangerous if too pleasurable: '"Binge-reading" that forces out other activities is not only harmful because it impairs a child's all-round activities, but because it can provoke feebleness, passivity, and morbid dreaminess,' thundered *Family and School* in 1953.[193] The well-brought-up child reader was one who selected only quality material: Soviet children's literature, and, later, suitable works by classic Russian and Soviet writers for adults; lives of outstanding individuals; popular science books; manuals of chess problems.

Attempts to regulate children's reading did not stop at *ex cathedra* statements. The state children's presses responded to Party and ministerial directives by promoting this or the other category of approved books; from the late 1940s, they also organised 'Houses of the Children's Book' in Moscow and Leningrad that did important outreach work, organising competitions for the best book review by a child, sending lecturers to conferences of librarians, co-ordinating meetings between writers and their juvenile audiences, and acting as a clearing-house for readers' letters.[194] Control was also exercised through libraries directly. Authors who attracted official disapproval were removed from public access, and librarians attempted to nudge readers towards appropriate choices. The procedures for doing this were described in a 1926 article about the library at School No. 1 in Moscow:

> Young readers (the schoolchildren of Moscow city) arrive in the library totally under the influence of the street and the cinema rather than the schoolroom, to judge by their requests. Boys want adventure books above all (Jules Verne, stuff of the Pinkerton kind), and girls want stories about the lives of children [this is probably code for Charskaya's school stories].
>
> The library takes into account children's interest in books with particular subjects, and attempts to 'switch over' that interest to books with educational value.[195]

By 'books with educational value', the authors of the article meant ones depicting socially relevant and politically correct heroes, or books with futuristic, utopian themes.

From the early 1930s, the dual method of proscription and prescription was further reinforced. More and more items disappeared from the so-called 'readers' catalogues' (those available for public consultation, as opposed to the 'general catalogues' for staff use, which were a more or less accurate record of the actual contents of the library). Readers' catalogues were used to direct readers to material that was considered edifying; card indexes recorded what children wanted and what they were in fact given.[196] As an educational activist wrote in 1928, 'At the present time, the children's library is not a mere book repository with the function of doling out loan volumes, but a living pedagogical institution.'[197] Only some privileged categories of reader, such as members of the Friends of the Book hobby circle, were allowed to borrow what they liked, and these children had enhanced borrowing rights in terms of number of books borrowed too.[198]

Schools played their part in manipulating children's choice of leisure reading. By 1927, attempts were being made to formalise control of pupils' extra-curricular reading: alongside 'compulsory' lists of material for study in class appeared 'optional' sections of additional volumes for independent reading.[199] The system was made explicit in 1930, when the list of works to be read in pupils' spare time included for Class 5 (12-year-olds), Mariya Ul'yanova's memoirs of Lenin, Panteleev and Belykh's *The Republic of Shkid*, works by Pushkin, Lermontov, and Tolstoy, a selection of stories by Chekhov, and children's editions of *Gulliver* and *Don Quixote*. By the age of 14, children were supposed to be reading such books as Gladkov's *Cement* and the novels of Zola and Jack London outside school.[200] According to the standard Soviet 'carrot and stick' system, teachers not only imposed these recommendations, but also carried out assaults on books that children were not supposed to be reading.[201] Moreover, the tuition given in literary analysis in classrooms (whether this emphasised 'class war', as in the 1920s, or patriotism, as in the late 1930s) was supposed to provide children with a template that they could apply to reading in the broadest sense. A final step in the regularisation of extra-curricular reading was taken when the 'class supervisors' introduced to Russian schools in 1947 were made responsible for regulating this. 'Class meetings', or indoctrination sessions, were supposed to include discussions of books read on a 'voluntary' basis, so that control over reception could be ensured.[202]

Just as before the Revolution, there were expectations that conscientious parents would support 'good reading' initiatives at home. Soviet women's magazines regularly ran reviews of suitable books for children, and libraries targeted parents through brochures and talks.[203] The use of multiple means of guidance aimed at children themselves – exhortation and direction by librarians, agitational events such as reader conferences, thematic work projects with assigned reading alongside – to direct children's book consumption continued right through the Soviet period.[204]

By the late 1960s, there was some criticism of excessively controlling behaviour on the part of librarians.[205] But regulation through recommendatory bibliographies, posters, and personal advice persisted. An article about children's reading of Pioneer newspapers published as late as 1983 still emphasised the need to develop 'political thinking' above all, and to teach children to read systematically; it advocated methods such as circulating a memo with a list of instructions ('Read every article carefully!', etc.), holding competitions and quizzes about the content of each issue, putting together a display board of related items, acting out the 'plots' of specific stories, and so on.[206]

Reading Practices

How effective, one might ask, was all of this? Gathering evidence is difficult, but it seems likely there was more pedagogical effect on reader tastes in the early

Soviet period. At this point in Soviet history, private libraries were still relatively rare, so the impact of public library holdings on children's reading is likely to have been considerable. Parents from the Soviet 'new intelligentsia' (people from working-class backgrounds who had acquired an education through personal effort, supported perhaps by attending one of the 'Sunday schools' organised by political radicals, or, after the Revolution, through the Party system of 'worker faculties') were likely to take a respectful view of recommendations on reading for children. Children from this kind of background were certain to be exposed to orthodox material, for instance Civil War classics such Furmanov's *Chapaev* (1923).[207] In the 1930s, a child from such a 'new intelligentsia' home was likely to cut his or her teeth on Chukovsky, Barto, Mikhalkov, and Marshak,[208] before moving on to material for older children and the classics of Socialist Realism. Afanasy Salynsky, brought up in the 1930s, remembered being 'overwhelmed' by *How the Steel is Tempered*; he read Neverov's *Tashkent the Abundant* (a set book for earlier generations) independently, and with pleasure.[209]

In all periods, too, reader guidance was extremely successful at the level of how children responded to questionnaires. Even in the late Soviet period, juvenile readers in a focus-group study of 100 14- to 17-year-olds identified preferred reading by genre (following the manner in which reader preferences were monitored by Russian libraries), and not by the titles of individual works. Lists of favourite authors were unimpeachably orthodox: Agniya Barto, Sergei Mikhalkov, A. N. Tolstoy, Gaidar, Chukovsky, Marshak, Eduard Uspensky's *Cheburashka and the Crocodile*, with few examples of non-Russian literature on show (Kipling's *The Jungle Book* was an exception). The dominance of material intended for children in the age group 4–10 suggests these teenage readers may have been chary about revealing the books which they actually liked at the time of responding to the questionnaire.

Even this fairly suspect and limited list of preferred reading identified some interesting priorities. Over half the readers stated that they had enjoyed reading folk tales more than anything else. The most popular 'literary' writer, Chukovsky, attracted only 21 votes, with the other writers lying in the range 5 (Kipling) up to 12 (Barto). The folk tales mentioned included not only 'national' Russian favourites such as 'Ivan the Fool', but also the international favourite 'Cinderella', which had been enjoyed by 37 children, and was stated by girls to be their favourite story of all.[210]

Children's desires to read particular books were sometimes frustrated by book shortages. In the early Soviet era, only two or three books might be taken out from a library at one time, and there was a long waiting list for popular titles.[211] Even official sources point to problems with some genres, for example songbooks and music in the early 1950s.[212] Yet the same shortages could foil librarians' and pedagogues' attempts to direct children's reading, leading children themselves to organise informal book exchanges to make up for the shortfall.

Certainly, in private, eclecticism continued. Some children (though this category was not recognised in any official commentaries) were not enthusiastic about reading at all. 'I read what I had to,' one girl from a working-class

Leningrad family recalled of her childhood in the 1970s and 1980s.[213] The statement, 'I did not read serious books – they were boring' summed up the attitude of many children after 1917 as well as before.[214] Conversely, children might avoid 'childish' material in favour of not just of adult fiction, but also of non-fiction. In the second half of the twentieth century, magazines such as *Young Technician, Young Naturalist,* or the *Model-Maker* were sometimes popular among the sort of children who were not keen on literary reading.[215]

Among children who did enjoy reading, and who did gravitate to fiction, tastes for fantasy material endured. Folk and fairy tales remained popular early reading throughout the Soviet era – the attacks on them in the 1920s had little impact.[216] Pre-teen tastes were dominated by 'unhealthy adventure-storyism'. Zadornov recollected that he was unusual among his school-mates in placing such a high emphasis on realism, and also that Jules Verne's books, especially *The Children of Captain Grant,* 'captivated' him and his brother.[217] While their brothers were busy with such material, girls often resorted in secret to Charskaya's novels, which had survived in private even as they became inaccessible in public libraries. Even in orphanages, girls managed to binge on this 'forbidden reading'.[218]

Trash Soviet fiction had its clandestine admirers too. Inna Shikhaeva-Gaister remembered a Soviet novel about boxers that did the rounds at her school in central Moscow; though it was 'complete rubbish', she and her classmates 'could not wait to get our hands on it'.[219] And significantly, the most popular modern children's writers were often those who, in one way or another, accommodated this taste for adventure and exotic incident. For example, whodunnit themes came through strongly in Kataev's *White Sail,* where the two boy heroes foil the efforts of a sinister Tsarist agent with a flamboyant moustache to track down and arrest a revolutionary sailor, Rodion Zhukov. Equally, when child readers turned to adult literature, they often sought out strongly plotted texts with vivid characters. Extremely popular from first publication into the post-Soviet era were Il'f and Petrov's comic novels *The Twelve Chairs* (1928) and *The Golden Calf* (1931) with their trickster hero Ostap Bender.

That said, the average Soviet childhood also involved consumption of literary classics. Those who had intellectual ambition were likely to read these in quantity, and might also read foreign works in translation. An especially popular non-Russian writer was Dumas, but those with access to large libraries might roam more widely: a well-read Kiev boy's childhood favourites included a translation of James Greenwood's 1866 weepie, *The History of a Little Ragamuffin*.[220] The abolition of enforced classical education had even made Greek and Latin literature seem more attractive than before 1917.[221] And juvenile taste embraced not just books for adults, adventure stories, clandestine favourites such as Charskaya, and books about boxers, but also children's literature as such. Early Soviet prose writers very often mentioned in memoirs and interviews include Arkady Gaidar, Nikolai Nosov, Panteleev, Vitaly Bianki, Boris Zhitkov, and (especially among women) Natal'ya Dan'ko; among late Soviet prose writers, Rady Pogodin, Eduard Uspensky, Vil'yam Kozlov, Viktor Dragunsky, and Yury Koval' were often cited with approval.

Child readers – especially younger ones – gravitated as strongly to poetry as to prose. Chukovsky and Marshak were perennially popular, and individual poems by Sergei Mikhalkov ('Uncle Styopa') and Agniya Barto ('The Chatterbox') were also read by generation after generation, even if some works by these two writers came across as 'wooden poems meant for learning in the classroom'.[222] Also enjoyed by many, once republished in the 1960s, were the works of Kharms, Oleinikov, and the other members of the avant-garde OBERIU movement who had diverted into writing for children. Few individual poets of later generations were to attain such a high profile – partly because, like parents in many other countries, Soviet mothers and fathers tended to encourage children to read books that they had themselves enjoyed in childhood.

There were, though, some changes in readers' tastes over time. According to surveys carried out by Children's Literature publishing house in Leningrad, role-model narratives about heroes such as Dzerzhinsky and Kirov became markedly less attractive to child readers in the late 1950s and early 1960s than they had been in the early 1950s. Conversely, adventure stories and science fiction were significantly more popular, as were foreign books.[223] Favourites of children of educated families in the post-Stalin era included Astrid Lindgren's *Pippi Longstocking*, Lewis Carroll, the stories of Hans Andersen, A. A. Milne's *Winnie the Pooh*, and, in later generations, Tolkien's *The Hobbit* (which Soviet children tended to interpret as an anti-totalitarian fable on the lines of Chukovsky's *Barmalei* or *The Big Cockroach*).[224]

Obviously, changing tastes were in part the result of shifting priorities in the children's publishing houses, which were now publishing much more in the way of fantasy and adventure.[225] But there were other factors in play as well. The post-Stalin era witnessed a marked growth in private libraries, including inherited treasures and discoveries from second-hand bookshops as well as Soviet-published books.[226] Such libraries might even include underground literature (*samizdat*) and Russian books published abroad (*tamizdat*), as well as sought-after and hard-to-find volumes by Russian authors published in small editions (for example Bulgakov, whose *Master and Margarita* became a cult book among Russian teenagers in the 1970s and 1980s), and translations of Western classics.[227] Naturally, the fact that such books were not on the school programme only added to their allure among young readers. And, in turn, the fact that substantial private libraries were found only in the more privileged sections of the intelligentsia meant that there was a status differential in terms of private reading as well.

Yet children themselves continued to read in ways untrammelled by intellectual snobbery, simply soaking up whatever came to hand. A man from a working-class Leningrad family born in 1960 remembered reading with enjoyment an eclectic mixture of foreign classics, Soviet classics, and no kinds of classics at all: Dumas, Kassil's *Shvambraniya*, Konstantin Paustovsky's *The Black Sea*, but also Vladimir Belyaev's *The Old Fortress*.[228] Anxiety about exactly this catholicity of reading comes through in 1960s and 1970s guides for parents, which approved lack of discrimination only where very tiny children were concerned – a child who could not yet read could be given *any* book to encourage interest in books generally.[229]

The pervasiveness of the fear of indiscriminate reading indicates the existence of the phenomenon that provoked the anxiety.

If children were reading the 'right' books, they were no more inclined to be reading them in the requisite way after 1917 than they had been before. Of course, some children did internalise adult values. Nikolai Zadornov remembered realising in the 1930s that Vladimir Arsen'ev's travelogue–adventure novel *In Usuriisk Region* (1921) was 'plausible' whereas 'battles between Indians or pirates with hundreds or even thousands of casualties', such as were to be found in Mayne Reid or Fenimore Cooper, were not.[230] Reactions of this kind were of course connected with the emphasis on verisimilitude in school-teaching. At the same time, there is something to be said for Kornei Chukovsky's view that the shift to an expectation of realism, from a fascination with *skazki* to suspicion of them on practical grounds – 'How can Baba Yaga fly along in a pestle and mortar when she hasn't got a propeller?' – is developmental, occurring in most children somewhere between the ages of 7 and 10;[231] to be followed, at least in some cases, by a move back to a less earthbound view of reality in the teenage years.

Expectations of 'plausibility' were perhaps not just the product of school-teaching, then. Conversely, private reading practices did not necessarily march in step with the educational system's insistence that books should be read as treatises about how to behave. Even in official surveys, children were quite capable of saying that their favourite characters in literature were Tatiana Larina *and* Gogol's loathsomely smug anti-hero Chichikov, or Anna Karenina, Ostap Bender, *and* Sherlock Holmes.[232]

The way that even 'proper' writers could inspire aberrant readings is clear in the specific case of Arkady Gaidar. Gaidar was relentlessly pushed to children as a 'great patriot' (by means of statues, museum displays, official biographies, and teaching in classes).[233] Naturally, part of this got absorbed. The answers to an official school questionnaire carried out in the 1960s indicated that children knew that Gaidar 'loved life and his Motherland very much'. They also said they liked the ideologically shaped bits of the narratives ('the heroic deeds the children got up to' in 'Military Secret', for instance). But when asked to recapitulate material from Gaidar, they adapted this in their own way. The Chief Burzhuin, Mal'chysh's adversary in 'Military Secret', for instance, got turned into a bogey straight out of a fairy tale. In one child's description, he had 'long legs like beanpoles and he was showing his big teeth and he wanted to take over the world'.[234] In other words, only part of children's response even to a story of this kind was concerned with the 'dominant patriotic theme'[235] that professional pedagogues saw as its main message.

Small wonder that Gaidar's other stories, which were less overtly 'patriotic' than 'Military Secret', tended to be read as straight adventures. *Timur and His Team* – itself an accurate reflection of games played by children in courtyards and streets – easily got absorbed back into the world that inspired it. 'When I was in class 4 [i.e. 11 years old], my schoolfriends and I organised a "Timur Team". We dug a wide, fairly shallow pit running along the railway line, and dragged along poles and plywood panels to make a roof. Then we'd buy a loaf of white bread and some lemonade and go and spend time there.'[236] Indeed, many Soviet children's favourites, such as *Timur*, survived the collapse of the system that inspired them and went on being read in the 1990s and beyond – partly, but not only, because of the 'parent choice' factor.[237]

Responses of this kind to 'official' literature are not surprising. Both in the late nineteenth and in the twentieth centuries, Russian children's literature often evoked the same archetypes as children's literature in other cultures. Notable, for instance, is the enduring international popularity of 'lost and found' stories, exemplified in Russian tradition by Chekhov's *Kashtanka* (1887), whose hero (a cross between a mongrel and a dachshund, Chekhov's own favourite breed) gets lost while out walking with her original owner, a joiner with a liking for a drop too many, and ends up renamed and working for a stage entertainer before returning to her original owner.[238] An associated, if not identical, theme, was travel – explored, for example, in Gaidar's merry story *Chuk and Gek*. These stories had an obvious didactic function – defining the identity of the child (or substitute child) protagonist, sketching his or her negotiations with the world, and sometimes also ramming home the message 'east west home's best'. But they encouraged imaginative exploration, and so had a considerably larger meaning than the apparent one. They were about 'being someone else' as well as 'being yourself'. Thus, they eased the burden of uncertainty endured by children in times of social upheaval, while also providing a sense of space and potential to those growing up in more settled eras, when security might be offset by a sense of restriction and claustrophobia.

Young Authors

Reading could act as an encouragement to be creative. The most obvious way in which this stimulus might take effect was when children produced writing of their own. Naturally, the literary practices current among adults were crucial – as in the fairly widespread habit, among children from pre-revolutionary intellectual families, of starting up literary journals. Aleksandr Blok and his cousins, for instance, had a home paper with the revealingly pompous title the *Herald*. This venture was begun in 1885, when Blok was all of five years old.[239] The literary efforts aired in forums of this kind tended to be equally pompous. Poliksena Solov'eva's first poem, written at the age of eight, would have done credit to a mediocre adult versifier of the day: 'The leaves they are a-flying; the nightingale's not heard; birds are no longer crying; the wolf stalks round the wood.' A philosophical work, 'A Treatise on the Afterlife', which she completed at the age of 10, was certainly just as derivative.[240] When Dmitry Tsenzor wrote his first 'real' poem in the early 1890s, this 12-year-old prodigy modelled himself meticulously on the style of Semen Nadson, the most popular sentimental poet of the day.[241] But the prize for callow pretension was taken by Anatoly Mariengof, who, as an early teenager in Nizhni-Novgorod, bought himself a skull to keep on his writing-table, in imitation of Hamlet, and at 17 or so produced an epic poem with the would-be classical title 'Hymn to a Hetaera'.[242]

Not all juvenile inventions were exercises in preciosity. As boys, Lev Kassil' and his brother Os'ka invented a private country, Shvambraniya, whose annals they transcribed over a number of years. Shvambraniya, an island surrounded by a marine entity called 'oshun', was shaped like a fat trident, with three jagged peninsulas; to the south of it lay 'Pilguinia, Land of Strangers', a smaller island. (Later, Shvambraniya also developed 'enemies within', when the boys assigned the southern ends of the island to two separate countries, Kaldonia and Balvonia, the former of which was a colony of Shvambraniya in all but name, but the latter of which was a threatening, although perpetually unsuccessful, foe of the Shvambranians.)[243]

Writing was just as popular after the Revolution as well. In the early years, creative writing was even included, for a while, in the school programme – though with a restricted range of permitted genres (the diary, the exercise in 'futurology' about the Soviet Union in fifty years' time, the ethnographic sketch). But children continued to produce work for themselves that was based on private reading, including the 'trash fiction' and tear-jerking poetry of the day. The writer Mikhail Svetlov's *magnum opus* as a boy was a two-and-a-half page novel in which the heroine died at the top of page 3.[244] In 1935, aged about 11, the future poet Yuliya Drunina dutifully penned poems about 'comradeliness' for consumption in the classroom, but worked for her own pleasure on a dreadful urban romance in the style of a lesser Symbolist:

> In the thick of tavern debauchery
> I found my true ideal:
> It was gypsy Mariula
> And a goblet filled with wine.[245]

Alongside the many works written by Soviet adults 'for the desk drawer', there was a comparable clandestine tradition for children (who also, of course, wrote a different kind of forbidden text – pithy and obscene – on the lids of their desks). Among girls, material of this kind might be transcribed into a private 'album' (what in the West would be called a scrapbook), a genre frowned on by school-teachers through the decades, but showing an astonishing survival capacity. 'Albums' contained a whole range of texts, not only or even mainly private writings, but also orally transmitted material, favourite sentimental poems from school textbooks and private reading, as well as cuttings, postcards, photographs, drawings and so on.[246] Boys were less inclined to keep 'albums' of this kind – outside certain specific contexts such as juvenile reformatories – but they might circulate their masterworks in manuscript form, or 'publish' them in an informal magazine or in the so-called 'wall newspaper', the agitational noticeboards that decorated the walls of Soviet classrooms.[247]

Not all children who tried their hand at fiction, drama, or poetry turned into professional writers later on, though such people were more likely to remember their early literary efforts, and perhaps also to preserve, over the decades, the first lopsided, straggling verses or histrionic, bloodthirsty melodrama. For the majority, writing was a phase to be lived through, flourishing most (the occasional instances of extreme precocity aside) between the ages of seven and fourteen. And in turn, the retreat from imaginative reality was often understood as marking departure from childhood itself and entry into a sterner and higher reality.[248]

The Curtain Goes Up

Of all 'cultured pastimes', as they were officially known, reading and writing were the most widely accessible, particularly in the Soviet period, when huge efforts were put into disseminating books through the provision of cheap editions for children and of accessible library facilities. Certainly, the system had its flaws. In the 1970s, only 10 per cent of children's book accessions to libraries ended up in the countryside, less than half the number recommended by the Ministry of Culture.[249] But children in a village were still more likely to come across a book by Mikhalkov than to attend a staging of one of his plays, and to read *A White Sail Gleams* than to see the cinematic adaptation of the book. Provincial towns as well as cities had their children's and youth theatres, but a child living in a small town or a village would be likely to visit these only once in a blue moon, perhaps when a school trip was organised. Outside 'cultural centres', the theatrical experience was associated with *khudozhestvennaya samodeyatel'nost'*, a term that could be roughly translated as 'artistic self-help' ('amateurism' suggests something too informal) – non-professional activities organised by local activists or Pioneer workers. In the 1920s, agitprop sketches prevailed; during the Stalin era and later, the standard fare was performances of theatrical classics and adaptations of famous novels.[250]

The Soviet children's theatre was 'egalitarian' in the sense that prices were low even in the most prestigious theatres, and also in the sense that most people had access to theatre of some kind at one or another point in their childhood. But the idea that the audience for professional children's theatres was representative in an overall sense – as claimed by Soviet theatre activists such as Nataliya Sats – is of the same order of simplification as the idea that the Soviet Union had the most enthusiastic reading public in the world. It was not until the era of television that professionally staged drama for children (and adults) really did come within reach of a mass audience.[251]

Before the Revolution, the gulf between mass audiences and the professional theatre was considerably wider. The first attempts by intellectuals to organise drama for a 'democratic' audience in the cities began only in the 1870s, and, for rural audiences, in the 1890s.[252] None of the theatre activists involved in what was called the 'people's theatre' movement was specifically interested in producing work for children, nor were the commercial theatres of the day much aware of juveniles as a discrete section of their audience. Early experiences of theatre therefore usually involved the adult repertoire. In outlying rural areas, this would have meant traditional shows such as *Tsar Maksimilian* or *Anika the Warrior* ('morality plays' in the tradition of *Everyman* or *King George and the Dragon*), and in the cities, fairground shows such as harlequinades, puppet shows, circus acts, variety shows, and melodramas, and perhaps also – by the late nineteenth century – a spectacle in one of the theatres organised by factory employers to keep workers sober and out of mischief.[253] Children might also find themselves caught up in performances of theatrical or quasi-theatrical events by non-professionals; for instance, they might take part in the mumming shows that were traditional in some parts of Russia (the west particularly) during the Christmas season, or in role-playing games such as 'Repka' ('The Beet', a tug-of-war where a group of players tried to haul another player 'out of the ground').[254] At the other end of the scale, a child from a well-off family in a city was likely, sooner or later, to be taken to a performance in the 'legitimate' theatre, perhaps to the matinée of a ballet or opera on a fairy-tale theme (*The Snow Maiden*, *The Sleeping Beauty*), but, just as probably, to the performance of a *style russe* spectacular such as the ballet *Roxana*, where Slavs were pitted against Turks, or Glinka's adaptation of Pushkin's *Ruslan and Ludmilla*.[255]

By the late nineteenth century, there were a few more signs of the development of a 'children's theatre' as such. In *A Few Words about the Children's Theatre*, which had reached a second edition by 1908, B. S. Glagolin drew Russian readers' attention to initiatives in the West, particularly the Paris children's theatre with its phantasmagorical and firework spectaculars. He argued for the need to build on children's love of drama and spectacle and create a special theatre for them, in the same way that there was a children's literature.[256] Occasional authors produced plays for a juvenile audience: V. F. Stel'skaya's *The Touch-Me-Not*, for example, was a Charskaya-like comic drama set in a girls' boarding-school, in which prickly new girl Valya gradually got accepted by her classmates with the help of popular Nina.[257] By contrast, Ada Chumachenko's play *Lully the Musician* was a more imaginative piece of work, a musical biography of the young Lully as a mischievous boy, saved from social disaster by his capacity to bewitch patrons with his music.[258]

While these were at best hesitant new beginnings, the mainstream theatre was also becoming more hospitable to work for children. The repertoires of the main academic theatres, particularly of opera and ballet, had started to include performances aimed at a young audience. Mostly, this consisted of 'folksy' work that had originally been intended for adults, such as Cesare Pugni's *The Little Hunchback Horse* (1864), an opera based on the versified folk tale by Petr Ershov. But it was also starting to include specialist material – a turning point here was the premiere of Tchaikovsky's last ballet *The Nutcracker* (1892), which rapidly became a classic of the juvenile repertoire all over the world.

Children's early theatrical experience was likely to include popular forms such as pantomime. As a didactic and socially engaged 'theatre for the people' movement developed, with a repertoire drawn from literary classics, staged in the realist manner, a suspicion of dramas of the kind traditionally staged in villages and fairgrounds had developed. Fantasy and spectacular had begun to seem 'childish': the result was that traditional entertainments began to be considered suitable fare for children and were adapted to make them acceptable to this audience. For instance, *Petrushka* (a knockabout glove puppet farce closely similar in plot to *Punch and Judy*) was discreetly purged of foul language, eroticism, and excessive violence for performances in front of children, or for amateur performance by children at home, or indeed for private reading.[259] The harlequinades, melodramas, and variety shows staged in fairground theatres with live actors were also enjoyed by some children, among them the future theatre director Vsevolod Meyerhold, here playing successor to enthusiasts from earlier generations such as the painter Alexandre Benois.

There was plenty of activity in the amateur theatre too. While it is scarcely fair to argue, as the Soviet director Nataliya Sats did at the First Congress of Soviet Writers, that 'there was no such thing as children's theatre' in an artistic sense before 1917, only 'a kind of cottage industry carried out by "nice" parents who had nothing better to do than put on shows for Christmas and Easter',[260] home shows were indeed starting to become popular by the 1910s. They were acquiring specially written guides, such as *How to Set Up a Children's Theatre*, published by the Vol'f press. In 1912, N.N. Bakhtin produced a list of more than a hundred plays suitable for children, including farces (*The Dangerous Pie*, adapted from the French), magic and fantasy dramas, and historical plays, such as Baden-Powell's *Pocohontas*. His introduction to the inventory ranged over a wide variety of possible themes and approaches, including shadow plays, fairy tales, Biblical stories (though here there might be problems with theatre censorship), and so on.[261]

Children's theatre, then, was not 'invented' after 1917. However, it is true that, like children's literature, the theatre started to get an unprecedented amount of institutionalised support, and input from talented people, in the Soviet period. To be sure, this had little impact on the repertoire of the mainstream theatres – the Bol'shoi, for example, continued to offer much the same fare as it had in the past: *The Nutcracker*, *The Sleeping Beauty*, *The Little Hunchback Horse*.[262] But, in terms of the founding of autonomous, permanent theatres with a specialist repertoire aimed at children and young people, the early Soviet period did mark a real watershed.

The new permanent theatres were of two main kinds. On the one hand, there were 'theatres of the young viewer' (TYuZy), or youth theatres, on the other, 'children's theatres' as such (*detskie teatry*). The youth theatres, which often had close links with the Komsomol, began to be founded soon after the Revolution. The Moscow *TyuZ* opened its doors in 1919, as did its Kiev equivalent; the Leningrad one began operating in 1922. Such theatres were primarily intended for older children, from the upper end of the school age group (13–16 or so), and for young people, as was a second type of youth auditorium, the 'Young Worker' theatres, many of which were set up in the late 1920s.[263] Their repertoire was close to the repertoire of mainstream adult theatres, which, in the 1920s, meant agitational pieces and 'living newspapers', alongside politically coloured full-length dramas such as adaptations of Gorky's famous novel of rising revolutionary consciousness, *Mother*.[264] This movement began reaching down to slightly younger children in the late 1920s and early 1930s, the key era for explicit political agitation directed at pre-teens. The Bauman district in Moscow, for instance, had a Theatre of Working-Class Children (founded in 1930), aimed at 12–13-year-olds from the Pioneer movement.[265]

By the 1930s, in line with a move that was being made across the Soviet theatre generally, much more emphasis was put on stage classics, though new Soviet work still sometimes found a place. For example, in the 1934–5 season, the Central *TYuZ*, now in a prestigious location just off Gorky Street, was staging, alongside Aleksandr Afinogenov's *Black Ravine*, Gogol's *Marriage*, Ostrovsky's *A Family Affair*, and Calderon's *El alcaide de sí mismo* (The Watchdog of Himself). On the other hand, some provincial and suburban theatres were faithful to 1920s traditions for longer. For instance, in 1934 the Moscow Provincial Theatre of Young Viewers, founded in 1927, was offering its public *We're Growing Up with October* by Agniya Barto.[266]

Slightly different in their didactic orientation were several theatres whose self-descriptions stated that they were concerned with 'the education of cadres of cultured spectators'. These included the Pioneer and Schoolchild Theatre at the Committee of Popular Education (KONO). In 1934, its repertoire included *We're the Children from the Alley*, but also a play by the early nineteenth-century dramatist and satirical poet Vasily Krylov.[267] A number of small touring theatres offered similar mixed programmes, though here often with a leaning to the agitational. These included, for instance, the Moscow District Puppet Theatre, founded in 1929, which had five brigades organising 'political campaigns, meetings, parties, revolutionary festivals and other such enterprises at factories, new apartment blocks, coal-fields, peat works, collective farms, state farms, schools and kindergartens'.[268] However, such efforts had little impact outside the big cities, and it was mostly in the form of amateur dramatics that the theatre reached children living even in relatively accessible villages.[269]

Early Soviet youth theatres sought to inculcate the political awareness that was expected from older Pioneers as well as from members of the Komsomol. Stagings were usually streamlined and functional, with emphasis placed on getting across the spoken word rather than on theatrics. In some cases – notably the Leningrad Theatre of Young Viewers, under the direction of A. A. Bryantsev – drama was part of a whole domain of political activism. This theatre had a 'spectator *aktiv*': 'delegates', young people acting as liaison officers between their school and the theatre, would distribute tickets to fellow pupils and attend 'delegate conferences' to discuss the repertoire, listen to talks by the management, and, in time, also by former 'delegates'.[270] Certainly, the Leningrad *TYuZ* shows did not consist of dry political readings – music and striking scenery were employed – but its agitational purpose was still unmistakable.

The special theatres for younger children, on the other hand (including the 'junior' department of the Leningrad *TYuZ*, which specialised in fairy tales and staged the premières of several plays by Evgeny Shvarts, one of the leading lights of the Soviet children's theatre in the Stalin era),[271] were rather more varied in repertoire and production techniques. Like writers for pre-school or first and second form children, playwrights, directors, and actors working for these age groups benefited from the assumption that children of 10 or 11 and under had their own world-view and psychology. Theatre for this age group displayed more continuity than theatre aimed at older children. As a critic writing for the journal *Teatr* pointed out in 1987, the youth dramatists of the 1920s, 1930s, and 1940s quickly vanished from the repertoire, but the short, pointed, and humorous plays for younger children written by such masters of the genre as Samuil Marshak and Elizaveta Dmitreva were still the backbone of Soviet theatrical tradition.[272] Very popular with this audience throughout Soviet power were puppet shows, which in the 1920s and early 1930s included agitational versions of *Petrushka*, with the hero turned into a mouthpiece of cultured values, but in later decades were more likely to have in their repertoire adaptations of folk tales and literary classics.

One of the children's theatre pioneers who flourished under the relatively liberal provision made for little children was Natal'ya Sats (1903–93), who founded her first theatre group at the age of only 15, in mid-1918. According to Sats's memoirs, this began as an informal touring group, bringing performances to children in districts that were cut off from the centre because of interruptions to the transport network. By 1919, despite obstruction from some local bureaucrats, who did not see theatre of any kind, let alone children's theatre, as a priority at a time of economic crisis – and a cool reception from some actors and theatre administrators, who felt that performances for children were beneath their dignity – Sats had managed to win backing at the highest level, from Anatoly Lunacharsky, the Commissar of Enlightenment. In October 1919, Lunacharsky gave the order conferring on Sats's theatre, formerly the Mossovet Theatre, the title of State Children's Theatre. The theatre was soon one of the best known in Moscow.

Overall, Sats's work lay somewhere between that of two famous directors for adult audiences at the time, Aleksandr Tairov and Vsevolod Meyerhold, although Sats's musical talents were all her own. Not a playwright in the first instance, though she co-operated in numerous adaptations and stagings, Sats was a director of huge energy, and an extremely effective entrepreneur. A kind of Diaghilev of the Soviet world, she was expert at nurturing talented playwrights, such as Evgeny Shvarts or Aleksandra Brushtein, and at persuading writers and other artists who had little experience of the children's theatre to take it seriously. Her most famous collaboration of the second kind was probably with Sergei Prokofiev, whose orchestral fairy tale, *Peter and the Wolf*, was written at Sats's suggestion and with her assistance.[273] The rapid rise of Sats's theatre to prominence, its frequent foreign tours, the appearances by Sats herself at all manner of conferences and meetings (most notably, the First Congress of Soviet Writers in 1934), and the elevation of the theatre to the status of Central Children's Theatre in February 1936 (an honour that was accompanied by the granting of one of the Moscow Arts Theatre buildings), all speak of the extraordinary regard in which Sats was held by the top level of the administration.

Yet Sats, who seems to have been remarkably tough and plain-spoken, for all her doe-eyed, gamine, slightly flapperish exterior, was prepared to do battle to defend her artistic vision. Though paying her political dues with shows such as *The Squealer* (about a juvenile whistle-blower), Sats was militantly hostile to preaching. 'When the author mentally glues a goatee beard to his face, or calls himself Mariya Ivanovna and starts moralising in mid-play, having completely forgotten the characteristics of the person he's supposed to be, that's not art at all, of course, and it's no use either.'[274] Though the theatre's very first production, *The Pearl of Adalmina*, played on a Cubist-style stage in the manner of Aleksandr Tairov's Moscow Chamber Theatre, was later branded in an official publication of Sats's own theatre as having 'marks of insufficient experience with children', its non-realist elements such as time travel and masks were used later as well, and characters included animals as well as orphans and factory workers.[275] Sats was also explicitly internationalist in her search for the best approach to children's theatre, praising, for instance, Erich Kästner as 'a master of the genre' at the First Congress of Soviet Writers,[276] and maintaining warm friendships with, among others, Erwin Piscator. Her great forte was manoeuvring within the permissible in order to produce work that was lively, original, and attractive to spectators. She immediately saw the potential of Aleksei Tolstoi's story *The Little Golden Key*, and commissioned the writer to work up a dramatisation that replaced the mechanical theatre in the final scene of the original book with a live version of the 'theatre within theatre' device, allowing the Central Children's Theatre to 'act' itself on the stage.[277]

Theatre flourished not just in the two capitals, but in the provinces. Some of the most successful plays of the 1920s, and indeed of all eras of Soviet history, were created by Samuil Marshak and Elizaveta Dmitrieva while working in Krasnodar between 1918 and 1922. As with Sats, a major vein of inspiration here was the *skazka*, described in the introduction to a collection of their plays published in 1922 as a source of 'ethical content' and a stimulus to the imagination. Imaginative work was done with theatrics: plays were furnished with prologues showing authors getting made up for their roles, or directors commissioning plays (which were supposed to encourage children to take up amateur dramatics themselves), and original music was commissioned for the performances.[278] There were good theatres in Kiev and in Khar'kov, and by 1930 many other major provincial towns had developed their own facilities.[279]

Puppet theatre was one of the key areas for innovation by talented theatre activists, and introduced many children to live performance. The figureheads from early days were the Moscow artist Nina Simonovich-Efimova, who had begun work as a marionette artist during the 1910s, Sergei Obraztsov, also from Moscow, and Evgeny Demmeni, whose Leningrad operation was set up in 1919. Of the three, Obraztsov was the individual whose style was most in tune with the times; he had begun his career staging agitprop plays in courtyards and on Moscow streets, and displayed his political nous by obtaining permission, at the start of the 1930s, to name his theatre after the education commissar from 1929, Sergei Bubnov. His early work included a staging of Marietta Shaginyan's parody thriller *Mess Mend* alongside more traditional shows, such as an adaptation of Chekhov's canine weepie, *Kashtanka*. In an autobiography written in the late 1980s, Obraztsov confirmed his enduring sense of political proprieties by boasting that the first anti-Nazi propaganda plays had been staged by his theatre the day after war was declared.[280]

Evgeny Demmeni's theatre, on the other hand, was rather more remote from the ideologies of the day. Certainly, in the special section taking theatre to the collective farms (the State and Collective Farm Puppet Theatres), socially relevant plays were preferred: choices for the 1934 season included *Virgin Soil Upturned*. But the main city theatre largely drew on traditional *skazka* topics, and on adaptations of the classics and of Soviet children's literature. In the 1920s, for instance, shows included a staging of Marshak's *Baggage* and of *The Wolf and Seven Kids*, as well as Gogol's *Tale of the Two Ivans*; in the 1930s, *The Jungle Book*, *Gulliver in the Land of the Lilliputians*, and *The Tale of Tsar Saltan* were among the plays on offer.[281]

All in all, the Soviet children's theatre offered a rich repertoire. But the total impact of the art form was generally less than the impact of reading. Taking children to the theatre was something that many adults – teachers and hobby circle organisers if not parents – felt that they ought to do; it was not something that children themselves passionately required. To judge by memoirs and oral history, trips of this sort made their impact: people can usually remember at least some of the plays and shows that they saw. But sources also confirm that visits to the theatre were not made all that often, and that many young viewers 'cut their teeth' on matinée performances of adult work rather than material specifically aimed at their age group.[282] It was often amateur activities – organising a puppet show at home, for instance – that provided children with their most memorable theatrical experiences.[283]

The golden age of Soviet children's theatre, like the golden age of Soviet children's literature, came to an end in the late 1930s. Natal'ya Sats was arrested in 1937, and, though released from prison camp in 1942, spent the next two decades leading a marginal existence. For some years she ran the Opera and Ballet Theatre in the Kazakh city of Alma-Ata; after the general rehabilitation of former political prisoners in 1956 she was able to return to Moscow, but was assigned to the State Touring Theatre rather than to the theatre that she had founded, the Central Children's Theatre, or to the Children's Opera Theatre that she longed to set up.[284] Only in 1965, when the Moscow State Children's Musical Theatre was founded, was she able to renew her original vocation. The theatre was housed in a large, well-appointed, and opulently decorated new building on Prospekt Vernadskogo, the avenue leading south from the centre towards Moscow State University, not far from the new Pioneer palace. Besides a full-size theatre with 1,110 seats, it had a studio theatre with 300 seats, a crèche, a buffet, and an interior ornamented with figures from fairy tales and children's literature.[285] It was, all in all, probably the most luxurious theatre in Moscow.

Like the Pioneer palace built nearby in 1962, the appointments of the theatre kept a delicate balance between political orthodoxy and fantasy. The sculptures included an image of Mariya Ul'yanova, Lenin's mother, playing the piano and surrounded by her children, but a whole range of characters from the fairy-tale operas of Rimsky-Korsakov and other non-realist texts also figured in the decoration. The repertoire of the theatre was, following the general trends of the post-Stalin era, definitely more escapist than engaged in character, with a strong emphasis on fairy tales rather than on agitational works.

During Sats's absence, the children's theatre generally had become much more conventional. Few new theatres were opened during the late 1930s and 1940s, figures who had become well known for imaginative work, such as Evgeny Demmeni, were subjected to personal attacks as 'ideologically unsound', and the repertoire stagnated, as even official sources were lamenting by 1950. Earnest school and family dramas dominated the scene, so far as older children were concerned; younger children were treated, for the most part, to sentimental and mundane adaptations of traditional folk tales.[286] Certainly, there were some brighter figures at work, notably Evgeny Shvarts, or indeed Sergei Mikhalkov, whose plays might be conventional in terms of the values expressed, but were neatly structured and humorously expressed. But, by and large, talented artists did not choose to go into the children's and youth theatres: as was pointed out at a national congress held in 1950, it was common for such theatres not to take up interesting new work until it had been staged in the mainstream theatre system.[287] Worse, there were signs that youth and children's theatre was not doing much to reach its target audience: a survey of 1954 established that the proportion of children who attended the theatre even once a year barely reached 12 per cent.[288]

At this point, it began to be widely admitted that the children's theatre had reached a crisis. One sign of the times was the mounting of high-profile attacks on didacticism and stodginess, which were accompanied by reviews praising work that was politically neutral, and dealt in a sensitive way with difficult topics such as the remarriage of a parent.[289] Another was the increasing amount of publicity given to stagings of a non-naturalist kind, as manifested by a revival of interest in the puppet theatre, which was the subject of special conferences in 1954 and 1957. By 1958, the number of full-time professional puppet theatres across the Soviet Union, which had stood at 40 in 1937, had climbed as high as 100.[290] During this period also, Soviet artists in all areas of the theatre became much more aware of work that was being done overseas, participating in international festivals and reading about foreign playwrights and directors in their professional journals.[291] Non-Russian classics – adaptations of Andersen, stagings of *Emil and the Detectives* – started to make their way on to the Soviet boards.[292] Alongside revivification of the repertoire went an enlivening of stage technique: reviews from the late 1950s indicate that showcase productions of this era had a far less fossilised feel than those put out a decade earlier.[293]

These trends continued into the 1960s and 1970s. Despite worsening international relations at the highest level, Soviet artists continued to take part in festivals and to study the achievements of theatre directors abroad – mainly in the 'brother nations' of Eastern Europe, but by no means exclusively so.[294] Further foreign classics made their way into the repertoire: by the late 1970s, Soviet theatres for the young were staging adaptations of work by Harper Lee, alongside more predictable children's fare, such as *Mary Poppins*, J. M. Barrie's *Peter Pan*, and Felix Salten's *Bambi* (known to an earlier generation of Soviet children from the Disney cartoon of 1945).[295] A great deal of indigenous talent and energy also came forward, and was showcased in national festivals such as the All-Soviet Children's Theatre Displays of 1958 and 1962.[296] As with children's literature, children's theatre could be, at its best, a refuge for talents unable to flourish in the artistic mainstream. Both Viktor Rozov and Mikhail Roshchin began their careers by writing for youth theatres; alongside these dramatists, refugees from other genres, such as the poet Genrikh Sapgir, sometimes made a contribution.[297] Some of the liveliest stagings around during the 1960s and 1970s were by directors working for the youth theatre, including Anatoly Efros at the Central Children's Theatre in Moscow and Lev Dodin at the Theatre for Young Viewers in Leningrad.[298] As in previous generations, puppet theatres remained havens for imaginative work – not just in Moscow and Leningrad, but all over the provinces as well.

The post-Stalin era saw a growth in institutional support for children's theatres. New youth theatres were founded in numerous important Soviet towns, including Perm' (1964), Krasnoyarsk (1964), Vologda (1975), and Orel (1976); the Irkutsk theatre, which had been homeless for some years, was reopened in the mid-1960s. A great deal of effort was put into designing special buildings that would provide child audiences with the necessary unimpeded sightlines, and into training staff so that the first experience of attending a theatre would be encouraging.[299] In 1963 a Ministry of Culture decree made it compulsory for all adult theatres to have in their repertories at least two plays for children. Achieving this target took a few years, but by 1967 every theatre in the Soviet Union was reported to be offering at least one matinée performance, and by 1969, 76 per cent of theatres had two or more children's plays on offer.[300] Contemporary reviews make clear that high-quality work went on in a variety of places: uniformly acclaimed was the Theatre of the Young Viewer in Riga, but interesting productions were also staged in Leningrad, in Ryazan', in Chelyabinsk, and in a good many puppet theatres, including the Moscow Province Puppet Theatre, the different puppet theatres of Leningrad, and in houses in Tallinn and Magnitogorsk.[301] Important 'outreach' work was also being done in some places, particularly in the provinces. At the children's theatre at the palace of culture attached to Metallurg, a big factory in Western Siberia, children themselves were involved in the productions, helping to make the puppets and going on tour performing with them.[302]

Yet some underlying problems continued. Children's theatre might provide a haven for the artistically ambitious, but it was a trap for them as well. The vast majority of material was aimed at younger children – 124 out of 164 plays in adult theatres during 1969 came into this category – and the traditional *skazka* type still held sway.[303] As a commentator writing for *Teatr* drily observed in 1966, there was only so much mileage an actor could get out of playing a wolf or a duck.[304] But it was not a lot more attractive to produce, or perform in, the 'problem' plays of the era: despite much talk about the need for 'teen dramas' exploring delicate issues such as family problems, such plays remained thin on the ground compared with, for instance, 'school story' material.[305]

An intrinsic problem was the authority exercised by elderly people whose work had once been innovative but who now represented the distant artistic past. By the late 1960s, the directors of the Theatre of Young Viewers in Irkutsk had been in post for forty years,[306] and this was by no means unusual. Nataliya

Sats continued to direct until she was in her eighties, as did Sergei Obraztsov. Inevitably, the directorial style of such individuals, practised as it was, had lost its power to surprise and inspire. Sats's gifts included an ability to seek out and nurture talented younger collaborators (in the last period of her life, she worked with the composers Khachaturyan and Kabalevsky).[307] With Obraztsov, a more egotistical and hands-on operator, artistic stagnation was more sharply felt. However, his Central Puppet Theatre continued to impress, if only as a 'living museum' of 1930s and 1940s theatrical traditions.

Senescence at the top was not the worst problem, as it could eventually be remedied by a change of director. The advancing age of actors themselves – particularly star actors who refused to be retired or even to contemplate switching from playing children into adults as they became older and more arthritic – could go a long way towards frustrating radical aims. Time-honoured traditions – for example the fact that small boys were always played by miniature women 'in drag' (*travesti*) – remained unassailed, despite increasing rumbles of discontent.[308]

At its best, Soviet children's theatre was the envy of the world; at its worst, as numerous commentaries from the 1960s, 1970s, and 1980s frankly admitted, it was absolutely awful. Moralising dramas, with caricature figures locked into preposterous plots, were crudely produced, carelessly staged, and hammed up to the nines by casts with pancake make-up over their wrinkles. Many theatres, whether youth or adult, took the attitude that children would be pleased enough to see anything – and regarded this 'captive audience' simply as a way of raising money at minimum effort.[309] Yet evidence suggested that children were, if anything, becoming more demanding, with shows that had originally gone down well with 11- and 12-year-olds now appealing only to the tinies.[310] By the 1980s, the prestige of the children's and youth theatre had declined to a level where staffing problems had set in: more than a third of Young Viewer theatres were unable to fill the position of artistic director.[311]

Despite all the institutional support lavished on this area of the Soviet theatre, then, the artistic decline noted in 1954 could not be fully arrested. Structural decline was equally difficult to deal with. Children's theatres were one of the few types of institution aimed at young people whose numbers actually contracted, rather than increased, in the post-war years. In 1940, Moscow had six children's theatres; by 1965, however, this number had fallen to four.[312] There were fewer 'live' children's theatres operating across the Soviet Union in 1970 (40) than there had been in 1941 (48). By 1986, this figure had declined again (to 33). And while the puppet theatre network had reached 102, this represented a growth of only 2 compared with the total attained by 1958.[313]

These statistics reflected the fact that the march of time was also moving against children's theatre in another way. In the face of increased competition from other kinds of entertainment, above all cinema and television, the potential audience was shrinking. By the early 1980s, the average child, even in Moscow, was visiting the theatre only once in three years.[314] As one commentator lamented in 1986, the problem was not just that children might well be diverted by 'low entertainment', such as cartoon films, from visiting the theatre in the first place, but that watching such material transformed tastes, making it difficult for them to accept the artistic values with which they were confronted when they arrived to watch a play.[315] By the 1980s, some educational authorities had recognised the problem and were offering 'theatre induction sessions' in schools, but this was by no means universal.[316] To be sure, the glasnost era ushered in a short-term revival, with a rise in the proportion of plays aimed at children being staged in major 'adult' theatres, a range of new appointments in the leading children's and youth houses, the creation of various new initiatives, such as Lyudmila Ul'yanova's 'home theatre', From Three to Seven, and a good deal of activity by children themselves, exploiting the new freedom from censorship for amateur and 'studio' troupes.[317] But by the mid-1990s the excitement had died down again, and audience figures and new productions and initiatives had once more gone into a decline.

In the context of the social and cultural institutions aimed at children, the history of theatre is a slightly offbeat phenomenon. With nurseries, kindergartens, or play facilities, the twentieth century saw institutional support increase, but never sufficiently to cope with public demand. In the case of the theatre, however, the improvements to infrastructure and state support during the 1960s and 1970s failed to halt declining public interest. There was more consistency in the development of the Soviet circus, a genre which was much more dependent on visual appeal and which therefore translated to television relatively easily.

Before the Revolution, circus acts were, with the exception of a small number of large permanent venues, such as the Cinizelli Circus in St Petersburg, generally offered by small-scale touring companies. However, after 1917, the circus, like the theatre, began to receive generous government support. By 1939 there were already 68 permanent troupes all over the Soviet Union, so that most major cities had their venue. Numbers were initially reduced during the war (only 18 were operating in 1942), but had risen again by 1945, aided by the promotion of this type of entertainment as a vehicle for wartime propaganda. By 1980, an outline history of the Soviet circus was able to claim that there were more permanent circuses in the country than in the rest of the world put together.[318]

The shows consisted of a mixture of acts featuring performing animals (the liberty horses of Italy or England were less favoured than bears, dogs, and so on doing tricks), daredevil acrobatics such as trapeze acts, human cannon spectacles or pyramid-building, and clown shows. This material was by no means exclusively aimed at children. Especially during the first decades of Soviet power, there was considerable emphasis on 'agitational' material, such as clown sketches in the 'class war' vein, or mass spectaculars staging the history of the Revolution and Civil War. However, even in this era lighter notes were often sounded by animal acts in which an elephant 'wiped its tears' when a sentimental song was played, or by bear-taming numbers performed in Russian costume or dances by liberty horses wearing garlands of roses.[319] The clown acts, with time, lost their satirical impetus; by the late Soviet era, they included material that was designed primarily for children.[320]

The general belief among parents and circus activists alike was that children 'loved' the circus and would be delighted to go along. For some children, this was definitely true. In the future theatre director Vsevolod Meyerhold, one such child, evenings in the Big Top awoke a lifetime interest in the physical theatre. Yet memoirs and oral history generally reveal moderate enthusiasm, in retrospect, with some informants saying frankly that they did not much like it, having little love for the sight of animals doing tricks.[321] Whichever way, the circus was always understood as a 'one-off' experience, to which the child might be taken once a year, say. It had a 'special' status, analogous to the Christmas pantomime in Britain. Theatre-going, on the other hand, was supposed to be a much more frequent practice, and the children's theatre was meant to prepare its audiences for a 'cultured' adulthood when they would see a play at least once a month. Yet the dramatic arts retained an exclusive flavour, despite the sincere efforts of those involved.[322] For different reasons, then, theatre and circus (presented live) remained relatively exclusive pursuits. The performance arts that were absorbed on a wider scale were those that could be disseminated more easily, beginning with the cinema, which, from the mid-1920s to the early 1960s, was, for most city children, the standard non-literary artistic experience.

At the Movies

Children's theatre, like children's literature, represented the application of an established art form to an audience whose supposed special needs had newly become prominent. Children's cinema likewise took time to develop: what children saw at the dawn of the medium was not made with them in mind. Whether a ticket was bought for them, they purchased one themselves, or sneaked in at the back, young members of the audience would simply watch what was on offer: newsreels, melodramas, comedies, historical films. The young Yury Tynyanov's early experiences included a reel about the French Revolution, pink with age and crackly.[323] Nikolai Zabolotsky remembered being dressed up as a girl so that he could, without shame to honour, be taken to see weepies acted by the number one stars of the day, Vera Kholodnaya and Ivan Mozzhukhin.[324] But early experiences could provoke disquiet or bewilderment rather than rapture. The figures might seem out of proportion, while the material veered between the mundane and the terrifying. In a 'rather dreary shed-like building with a big screen', one woman recalled, 'there suddenly appeared nature scenes ("exactly like real life") and suddenly – oh horror – a train, which rushed straight at us from the screen'.[325]

After the Revolution, too, dedicated children's cinemas were few in number. There was only a handful of them even in Moscow during the mid-1930s. Most of these were located in culture clubs, with only one autonomous institution, the Young Viewers' Cinema, in the centre. At this last, ticket prices, though about half those in other cinemas, were quite high by comparison with children's economic resources.[326] Just as before the Revolution, attending the cinema was often a clandestine activity: Afanasy Salynsky remembered that you had to sneak into films at the railway workers' club or the club at the artillery warehouse – sometimes the sentry turned a blind eye.[327]

However they got there, the cinema remained hugely popular with children. A survey of 3,000 children (aged 8–19) conducted in 1924 revealed that 41 per cent visited the cinema four times or more a month.[328] A survey of 244 pupils of Moscow School No. 7 carried out in 1929 indicated that 219 of them, or almost 90 per cent, had visited the cinema at least once in the previous month. (In contrast, only 50 per cent had visited a museum even once in their lives.) Attending the cinema was very much a peer-group activity. 'Parents get in your way when you're watching'; 'they're a millstone round your neck', some viewers commented. Eighty-eight per cent of children preferred to visit without them.[329]

One reason why parents might have 'got in the way' was that children tended to lap up fare that many adults would not have approved. There were films in the Soviet repertoire that were more or less 'suitable' and at the same time massively popular, notably the Georgian director Ivane Perestiani's adventure story *Little Red Devils* (1923), a 'Soviet internationalism' effort that was set in Ukraine, and with a partly Russian cast. It told the story of Misha, a *Komsomol*, and his sister Dunyasha, the children of an upright proletarian murdered by supporters of Makhno during the Civil War, who joined up with an American Black boy circus artiste, Tom, in order to do battle against the counter-revolution. The popularity of the film can be gauged from the fact that a whole series of sequels was made.[330] But children also enjoyed commercial Western films. In Arkhangel'sk in 1920, a group of pre-teens 'were shown the American classic *The Three Godfathers* and the mysterious *The Man in Grey*. [...] One might think that constant repetition would have killed all interest, but no, we savoured each well-known scene, each gesture, every tear, and when at times there were no volunteers to play the piano we replaced the music with our own vocal efforts.'[331] If given the chance, juveniles also watched with enthusiasm definitely 'unsuitable' films, for example erotic melodramas such as *The Abortion* and *The Prostitute*.[332]

The fact that cinemas were full of 'latchkey children', sometimes watching material that was (to put it mildly) rather racy, was one reason why Soviet commentators, subscribe though they might to Lenin's conviction of the didactic potential of film, displayed some uncertainty about whether it was a good idea for children to attend.[333] Many of the most popular of the silent films on show in the 1920s were Western-made, adding to these uncertainties. In 1929, the author of a brochure on 'Communist education' commented that there was no point in giving children lectures on the evils of selfishness and egotism in the abstract if they immediately went and saw those qualities exalted in the films of Harry Piehl and Douglas Fairbanks.[334] Star-struck schoolchildren who imagined glittering futures as Soviet versions of Fairbanks or his female counterpart Mary Pickford, neglected their school-work, and fell out with their parents were stock figures in propaganda of the late 1920s.[335] More sinister types were those in whom the cinema supposedly inspired the taste for a life of crime.[336] From the early 1930s, the sense that watching 'unsuitable' films was positively harmful became still more prevalent – here, as with children's literature, the closing in of cultural censorship and increasing emphasis on the need to control and discipline children became mutually reinforcing principles. The duties assigned to the Child

Protection Inspectorates included making sure that children were not allowed into late screenings, or into films that were prohibited viewing; the model school rules agreed by the Komsomol Central Committee in May 1935 instituted a ban on 'loitering round cinemas'.[337]

Yet with increasing control over the film repertoire, cinema also came to be accepted, in the 1930s, as a means of providing instructive entertainment for all the Soviet family. Solitary and unsupervised viewing was still frowned on, but attendance in company with responsible adults was positively encouraged. Parents were exhorted to monitor their children's viewing, but also assured that the cinema was didactically useful, provided the right films – as recommended by teachers and other experts – were watched.[338] By the late 1930s, there was widespread access to the cinema not just in cities but also in small towns, and – if only in the form of weekly showings at the local culture club – in many villages as well.[339]

In order to encourage parents to accompany children to the cinema, the repertoire filled up with movies that had appeal across a range of ages. Among these were action films, such as the Civil War pieces *Chapaev* (made by the Vasil'ev 'brothers' in 1934) and *We Are From Kronstadt* (Pavel Dzigan, 1936), and musicals, for example Grigory Aleksandrov's *The Circus* (1936), *The Merry Lads* (1934), and *Volga-Volga* (1938). Memoirs and oral history indicate that both these genres genuinely were popular with young audiences, who were prepared to watch favourite movies, particularly *Chapaev*, over and over again.[340] When performances were sold out – as often happened with *The Merry Lads* – they would use the old device of creeping in at the back.[341] Films like this were 'commercial' in terms of aesthetics and popular appeal, though made by state-sponsored studios; they did much to compensate for the disappearance of Hollywood set pieces from the Soviet repertoire (Western commercial films vanished from circulation with the end of the New Economic Policy).

Alongside the creation and distribution of 'family entertainment' went a drive to create cinema specifically aimed at children, such as might safely be watched by unaccompanied minors, or shown to school groups either in local cinemas or in the school building itself. From the early 1930s, Soviet newspapers tirelessly reminded film professionals that the children's cinema was an area where more activity was needed.[342] The *de facto* Year of the Child in 1935–6 was accompanied by resonant public statements about the need to provide more and better films for young audiences. The debate was opened by A. Kal'varskaya, who lamented that fewer than twenty films for children were in the Soviet repertoire, and pointed to a quality problem with these: studios were only too happy to dump their worst film stock and most junior directors on the juvenile repertoire. Praising one or two directors who were currently working, she also pointed to comedy as a gap: 'No one has such a strong right to joyful, cheery laughter as our young viewers.'[343] The same point was made in another article carried by the same issue of *Soviet Cinema*, which also emphasised that fantastical subjects were important in order to broaden children's imagination.[344] Later in 1935, the magazine reported that 25 per cent of Soviet film production was now to be devoted to children's film.[345]

A year later, Soyuzdetfil'm, the first dedicated studio, was set up. Between 1933 and 1940 more than one sixth of the entire production of Soviet film studios, measured by title, was devoted to young audiences; in the years of the Great Terror, 1937–8, almost the only films made were for children.[346] A favourite genre was the adaptation of a work of classic literature, not necessarily one originally intended for children, and not necessarily Soviet. Among the leading titles were Mark Donskoi's *écranisations* of Gorky's autobiographical trilogy, and a version of Stevenson's *Treasure Island*. Material in the books was adapted in line with the current Soviet aesthetic: for example, in *Treasure Island*, Jim Hawkins was recast as 'Jenny', a girl dressed up as a boy, providing the female character that Stevenson had omitted from his original novel.[347]

More ambitious, from a cinematographic point of view, was Aleksandr Ptushko's *New Gulliver* (1935), which used Swift's novel as the basis of a a mixture of live acting, puppetry, and animation.[348] This period also saw the beginnings of the Soviet animation industry in its own right. In the pioneering days of Wladisław Starewicz, who founded Russian animation in the 1910s, this genre had been aimed at adults, but now most output was for children. The inspiration came less from Starewicz than from Disney, whose themes were deemed unacceptable for Soviet consumption, but who was regarded as a model of technical perfection.[349] However, a good many of the most popular Soviet films for children, such as Aleksandr Razumnyi's *Timur and his Team* (1940) or Vladimir Vainshtok's *Children of Captain Grant* (1936), were not technically or pictorially particularly imaginative. This had no impact on their popularity – quite the reverse. There is an interesting divergence between the films that appealed most to adult critics and those recorded as favourites in memoirs and oral history.[350]

During the Great Patriotic War, little attention was given to children's cinema. Production did not pick up immediately after the war: these were years when the number of Soviet-made films of all kinds plummeted. Between 1945 and 1953, the total number of all titles, including shorts and filmed stage performances, reached only 183, as compared with 308 films in the strict sense made between 1933 and 1940.[351] Children and adults solaced themselves with 'trophy' films, in particular the wildly popular *Girl of My Dreams*, rather than watching the improving history dramas that were standard Soviet fare.[352] As in the late 1930s, the children's cinema actually looks quite healthy, measured by the general yardstick, especially given that the output included some films that displayed a measure of genuine cinematographic innovation, including, for instance, Evgeny Shapiro's *Cinderella* (1947), a lush black-and-white version of the fairy tale not too far in spirit from Cocteau's *La Belle et la bête*. Particularly striking was Aleksandr Ptushko's *Stone Flower* (1947), a pioneering colour production making use of 'trophy' Agfa film stock, which had a rather creaking plot about a Urals worker learning to make a perfect marble sculpture, but which created some unforgettable images, especially of landscape (birch trees turning autumnal at an accelerated tempo against a lake). Well loved at the time, these films remained popular in later generations too. Equally successful was a film made right at the end of the Stalin era, Ivan Lukinsky's cinematic adaptation of Gaidar's *Chuk and Gek* (1953).[353]

By the late 1950s, a genuine spirit of innovation and excitement had made itself felt in children's cinema, as in the cinema more generally. Indicative of the new spirit were lively, slightly subversive films such as Elem Klimov's *Welcome – and Keep Out!*, about children – mostly boys – doing their best to have independent fun at a Pioneer camp.[354]

Conditions had changed not just aesthetically, but also practically. Institutionally, cinema for children and young people was not the backwater it had once been. In 1959 the production centre for children's cinema was renamed again – it now became 'Youth' – and activity increased. From under a dozen children's films in 1957, production climbed to around forty films a year in the early 1960s.[355] Energy went into the making of cartoon films (*mul'tfil'my*), an activity in which some of the brightest Soviet talents were engaged. A high point of the repertoire was Yury Norshtein's *Tale of Tales* (1979), with a script by the writer Lyudmila Petrushevskaya. Animation was regularly publicised in the Soviet press, which brought to readers' attention, for example, A. Karanovich's *écranisation* of *The Adventures of Baron Munchausen* and V. Dezhin's *The Return Match*.[356] The humbler genre of film strip also enjoyed success: children might watch folk tales translated to the screen, but equally well the adventures of Sherlock Holmes and Dr Watson.[357] A wider selection of foreign films was being shown, particularly from the 'brother nations', including, for instance, Cuban cartoons and East German Westerns (should one perhaps say 'Sauerkraut Westerns'?), as well as art films.[358]

Yet there was no outright break with the past. Many films made for children were still well intentioned and dull, so 'unsuitable' material continued to be a draw. A 1962 study cited the (probably imaginary) case of one Lyonya, a boy in his early teens who, left to himself by his mother, had exploited his above-average height to see foreign thrillers and even Fellini's *The Nights of Cabiria*.[359]

The anxieties of these commentators were exaggerated: it was actually significantly harder for children of this generation to get into cinemas 'on the sly' than in the past.[360] But the portrait of the cinema-obsessed teenager was not altogether a caricature. Nevertheless, the absolute numbers attending cinema started to go down in the 1960s and 1970s (one cause for this must have been the falling birth rate, but another was certainly the arrival of television as a mass medium). A 1967 encyclopaedia for parents which recommended that children be 'taught' to like the cinema obliquely indicated that cultural missionaries were conscious of the cinema's diminishing appeal.[361] All the same, figures for cinema attendance remained higher than for theatre attendance in most places. A survey of 1969 revealed, for instance, that 91 per cent of children in two large provincial towns, Voronezh and Gorky (Nizhni-Novgorod) attended the cinema once a week, and 33 per cent several times a week. While figures from elsewhere (Sverdlovsk and Novosibirsk) indicated that 93 per cent attended the theatre 'regularly', the lack of precision suggests that in practice this probably signified 'several times a year' at most.[362] Similarly, 90 per cent of children taking part in a 1979 survey of 495 readers of the newspaper *Leninist Sparks* stated that they enjoyed going to films, as opposed to only 40 per cent who enjoyed reading, and a relatively insignificant 9 per cent who liked visiting the theatre.[363] The children's film magazine *Eralash*, founded in 1974, which carried scenarios and picture spreads publicising recent releases for the juvenile market, rapidly established itself as a favourite, and was one of the rare Soviet magazines that was able to keep running in the post-Soviet period.[364]

Oral history bears out the enduring love of the cinema, above all in small towns, where the cinema might well be the only entertainment generally available:

> Every evening they'd show a film, or two films at the weekend.
>
> Only mostly they'd keep showing the same films that were on television, the same kind of thing. But you should have seen what happened if they put on some Western-made film, specially if it was a comedy. All hell broke loose. Even if they were old ones, we'd go again and again . . .[365]

Other observers confirm the popularity of foreign films, ranging, in the early 1980s, from *King Kong* to *Space Invaders*.[366]

But Soviet films were watched with enthusiasm too. Cartoon films, for instance, were perennially popular. Post-Stalinist successes included the series *Just You Wait!*, a Tom and Jerryish effort featuring Little Rabbit, with Wolf, a hooligan and social nuisance, as the opposing baddie.[367] Extraordinarily popular was *Gena the Crocodile* (1970), scripted by the children's writer Eduard Uspensky. It starred Cheburashka, 'a little creature unknown to science' but resembling a large-eared bear, and recently arrived in a crate of oranges from an unspecified place abroad; he was now homeless and living in a telephone kiosk. His co-star was friendless Gena, who had nothing better to do than blow bubbles all day. The two, having met up, started work on building a House of Friendship, helped by a group of equally marginal and unloved individuals. Once the house was finished, the builders realised that they had all become friends, and settled down to live happily ever after. The film was remarkable not so much for its subject – though this was attractive enough – as for its cutesy characters, and because it became the focus of a marketing exercise not unlike a state-sponsored version of those organised by Disney or Warner Brothers at the same period. A spin-off book quickly followed the film; Soviet newspapers and magazines ran items featuring Cheburashka; and Cheburashka toys went on sale.[368] Thus, even in the television age, children's cinema managed to hold its own (indeed, as in the West, television was, if anything, a boost for the popularity of the cinema, since so much of children's favourite television – cartoons or *skazka* adaptations – consisted of material originally made for the cinema, or composed in cinematic genres).

Radio for the Children!

Unlike the cinema, radio was entirely an institution of the Soviet period, and one that took time to develop. Soviet ideologues immediately grasped the potential of cinema in a culture with widespread illiteracy, but took a while to see radio as a resource for reaching the masses. Part of the problem was technical: though the state was eager to associate itself with this dynamic new medium, the provision of radio sets created predictable problems. Sets started to make their way into homes only in the mid-1920s, and generally into households which were privileged.[369] The main drive from the top was to get the receivers into workplaces and public buildings, including schools.[370] By the late 1930s, though, private set ownership was more widespread, encouraged by the formation of radio-building hobby circles (at schools and Pioneer palaces, for example). Quite a number of families now had a *tarelka*, or dish-shaped radio receiver on their walls, though this might pick up a local network only. It took until the 1950s for radios to reach outlying rural areas, but families in cities and towns and the countryside lying round these were likely to be 'in tune' well before.[371]

Dedicated radio broadcasting for children began as early as April 1925, with a magazine programme, *The Radio Pioneer*. In 1929 the schedules began to offer a 'Listen with Mother'-type programme, *Sing and Play with Us!* Other regular items included pep-talks for parents on subjects such as the evils of corporal punishment, and programmes for village schoolchildren as well as for children of Pioneer age.[372] In 1930, the main Radio Committee acquired a children's section to oversee the content of specialist programmes.[373] But broadcasting for children at this point had a restricted function. Oral history suggests that family listening sessions, including plays, literary readings, speeches by Party leaders, and news, made more impact than children's programmes as such. In particular, the news from the Front during the Second World War, presented by Yury Levitan, was an unforgettable part of all wartime childhoods.[374]

After the war, the technology of the radio network developed more rapidly. Even provincial schools might now have their *radiouzel* – radio relay centre.[375] Family ownership of radios grew more widely too. And it was now that specialist programming really started to take off: by 1948, as much as three hours a day was being devoted to children's listening.[376] At this stage too, newspapers for children, such as *Pioneer Pravda*, began to carry the radio schedules (something that had not happened before the war).

The schedule of programmes comprised a complete strategy for organising children's time outside school. The day began at 7.45 a.m., with a rousing programme with the title *Pioneer Reveille*, which was at the centre of the morning schedule for decades. It comprised a mixture of 'hard news' Soviet-style – record-breaking statistics, state visits by Party leaders – with reports on Pioneer activities, and lighter items such as lost dogs who found their way back to their owners across Siberia, and so on, alongside marches, upbeat songs, and other musical interludes.[377] Later programmes were a mixture of straight informational items, often on scientific subjects (for instance, talks by academics about geology, astronomy, or biology, biographies of Beethoven), quiz programmes (for instance *Have a Guess*, first broadcast in 1944), musical recitals, and autobiographical talks by famous people. There were also various items of a mixed type, for instance, *The Riddle Concert*, where the titles of the pieces performed were announced only at the end, or *The Young Geographers' Correspondence Club*, which appears to have been a kind of scientific 'brains trust' session in which experts answered questions sent in by young listeners; or *The Young Captains' Club*, a monthly programme in which children competed to become one of twenty-five 'corresponding members' on the basis of a general knowledge contest. Other regular slots were occupied by a drama programme, *Theatre at the Microphone*, and what in modern Britain would be called 'classic serials', i.e. adaptations of famous books for reading aloud (these included children's books as well as texts by, say, Tolstoy and Pushkin). In other words, apart from *Pioneer Reveille* and a regular digest of items published in *Pioneer Pravda*, very little of the material was specifically 'Soviet' in character, and most of it could equally happily have found its way into the schedules of the BBC at precisely the same era.[378]

Radio programmes were extremely popular: presenters and producers received torrents of fan mail (encouraged, but not necessarily initiated, by the interactive nature of programmes such as *The Young Geographers' Correspondence Club*).[379] Often, the radio would be on constantly, as a background to meals, conversations, homework; but favourite programmes would command full attention. Dramatisations and readings were still tops, but the children's programmes of this generation were better able, judging by reminiscences, to establish a profile for themselves: among those remembered by informants are *Have a Guess!* and the folk tales read aloud by Maria Petrova.[380]

In the 1950s, 1960s, 1970s and 1980s, the radio schedules continued to observe much the same pattern. *Have a Guess!* remained very popular; book dramatisations and discussion programmes (for example *The Radio-Club of Interesting Meetings*) had a firm place in the schedules, alongside, of course, ideological programmes such as *Pioneer Reveille*, and sermonistic items such as *A Talk about Courage, Valour, and Glory*. The dramatic repertoire, similarly, included both plays about Lenin and adaptations of more obviously 'childish' material, such as the stories of Gianni Rodari, or readings of *A White Sail Gleams*.[381] The presentation of material remained much the same as well, with presenters emphasising the gulf between themselves and their young public. A survey of children's radio published in 1966 urged on broadcasters forms of address such as 'Dear children', 'Honoured schoolchildren', and 'Greetings, my dear little friend!'[382]

The radio, then, was not adapting to take account of new directions in youth culture, or indeed of the changing tastes of younger listeners generally. By the 1960s it had stopped being central to most children's lives, and specific memories of listening often relate to programmes that would be on for the whole family, such as choral medleys of patriotic music in the morning, *Workers' Lunchbreak* at noon, or *A Rendezvous with the Song* in the evenings.[383] But children might still catch special programmes at specific times of day, particularly after school, listening to broadcasts such as *For Kids about Little Animals* as they plodded through their homework.[384] And radio ownship continued to increase even after 1960, which suggested the importance of broadcasts as aural 'wallpaper' and general background noise, if nothing else.[385]

'Good Night, Little Ones!'

By the late twentieth century, television was probably children's most important leisure activity inside the home, but this situation took time to develop. As in other parts of Europe, sets were a rare luxury in the late 1940s and early 1950s, but official figures claim that ownership began to climb rapidly by the end of the decade – from 8 in 100 families in 1960 to 25 in 1965, 51 in 1970, and 77 in 1976.[386] Oral history also suggests that, in most families, television arrived some time between the late 1960s and the mid-1970s, with sets that could receive colour acquired perhaps in the early 1980s.[387] By 1960, the audience for television in the larger cities already outstripped the audience for cinema by seven to one.[388]

When television was still a novelty, the supposedly intellectually deleterious effects of the new medium on children provoked unease. As the satirical magazine *Krokodil* put it in 1952, 'If a schoolchild manifests excessive interest in television broadcasts, his level of schoolwork goes down.'[389] Soviet magazines printed advice for parents worried about the possibly damaging effects of the medium on their little ones, such as a 10-point quiz reproduced from *L'Humanité* that was supposed to establish whether the child was watching TV in a useful or harmful way.[390] However, once the Soviet authorities had become committed to TV as a force for spreading political orthodoxy and rational leisure, attitudes to its place in the life of children began to change. In 1963, the model family described in the standard school alphabet book had added television-watching to its schedule of cultured leisure activity – though only as an afterthought:

> Ours is a big family. We have our own flat. In the evenings we gather in the dining room. Father reads the newspaper. Mother and Grandmother listen to him. Brothers Kolya and Petya play draughts. Sister Sof'ya sews herself a dress.
>
> Sometimes we watch television.[391]

Once television had been recognised as an acceptable educational tool, there were steps to develop not only the repertoire for schools viewing, but also the schedule of programmes for viewing at home. The embryonic schedules of the early 1960s, when television broadcast for only a few hours a day, included quite a high proportion of child-directed material: cartoons for the tinies, feature films (such as an adaptation of Olesha's story *The Three Fat Men*) and information programmes (including ideological items related to the Pioneer movement and so on) for older children.[392]

As the schedules expanded over the next decade, children's television retained its place, with programmes grouped at particular stages of the day. A 'post-school and homework' viewing schedule began at 4.30–5 p.m., and was generally made up of feature films, television plays, cartoon films, and programmes about nature, great writers, and so on. There was also a morning slot, which included physical jerks (*Get Up and Do Your Exercises!*, at around 9 a.m.), cartoon shorts for the under-sevens who were not attending nursery school, and educational items such as children's choral concerts and magazines about the Pioneer movement. Regular features included *For Kids about Little Animals*, *Nature Tales*, and *The TV Hedgehog* (presumably a cartoon for small children).[393] In other words, the material represented an adaptation to the visual medium of the tried-and-tested formula used for children's radio; it altered little during the next twenty-five years.

If content was predictable to the point of fossilisation, timetabling was not. By and large, programmes were not shown at set times: a cartoon film might appear at 4.30 p.m. one day, but at 5.15 the next, perhaps pushed backwards by a feature film or the broadcast of a play or ballet. However, the centrepiece of the evening schedule was, from 1964, always an animation and fantasy special with the title *Good Night, Little Ones*, with a saccharine lullaby theme tune, 'Now the Tired Toys are Sleeping/And the Bears', broadcast nightly on weekdays just before the main evening news programme, *Time* (Vremya) on Channel One.[394]

In itself, *Good Night, Little Ones* was fairly similar in style to British children's programmes of the 1950s, 1960s and 1970s – puppet shows such as *Muffin the Mule*, *Andy Pandy*, and *Bill and Ben*, for instance. The difference lay in the timing: the British programmes were shown around midday, or alternatively, as in the case of *The Magic Roundabout*, broadcast during the late 1960s and 1970s, in the 'post-school' slot. Thus, *Good Night, Little Ones* was meant to be watched by children with their parents, not by children alone. Given the limited choice available to Soviet viewers, official programmers could be certain that the vast majority of Soviet families would indeed watch *Good Night, Little Ones*, followed by the news, and that this would in turn contribute to the dissemination of the kind of regular regimen considered so important for all Soviet citizens, and particularly for children. Supper at seven, *Good Night, Little Ones* at 8.30, bed for the tinies, and then news for the older children and adults: this was the routine anticipated by cultural planning, and one that was often followed, though in reality the youngest children might well stay up for the news as well.[395]

Watching television was thus meant to be a collective practice. And it usually was, in a way that would have been hard to visualise in an American family of the late twentieth century, where multiple set ownership meant that all members of the family were likely to be watching quite different programmes simultaneously. Constraints of space and access to consumer goods were such that Soviet families seldom, if ever, owned more than one television set. This would be a precious item – its brand name and specifications probably remembered for years afterwards.[396] It would be placed in a communal room such as the kitchen, or the main room used for meals and other gatherings (and usually used as the parental bedroom, or another bedroom, as well).[397] In communal flats, neighbours who owned a television often allowed at least the children from other families to come and watch in their room, and children would also sometimes get access to television at a friend's house.[398]

The fact that television was a social activity, in the way that listening to the radio, or reading (when reading aloud was still common), had been in earlier decades, meant not only that conversation and running commentaries were likely to accompany viewing, but also that programme choice was a matter for negotiation and even squabbling. Parents were quite likely to indulge children for some of the time, but not always. As Vladimir Irov, born in 1959, remembered, one evening, when he was aged about five, the television was, as usual, tuned to *Good Night, Little Ones* in order to humour him, the youngest of the family. However, Irov then decided, in a fit of toddler tyranny, that he wanted the television turned over to watch something else. (There probably was nothing else in which a child would have been interested: the point was purely to try and get his own way.) Despite the fact that the sole reason for watching had been to please the smallest child, Irov's parents stood their ground, explaining to him that everyone else wanted to watch the programme that was showing at the moment, and that they would only change channels when it was finished.[399] Of course, precisely the opposite reaction would have been likely in some families, with the child's every caprice willingly catered to by the adult public. Communal viewing did not simply signify children's programmes for all, though: it could also mean that quite small children might end up seeing 'adult' programmes, a point anticipated by programmers, who warned parents in 1962 that a television adaptation of Tolstoy's *Resurrection* was 'not recommended for children'.[400]

The extent to which any Soviet television programme was 'unsuitable for children' was, in fact, strictly limited: at weekends, even the late-night schedule might include items that could equally well have been watched by young viewers, such as popular Soviet films. But the items that were specifically aimed at children were among the most attractive in the viewing schedule. Confronted with a choice between *Do Some Industrial Gymnastics!* or *The Distribution of the Gross National Product under the Ninth Five-Year Plan* at 6.45 p.m. on a Tuesday evening, any sentient adult might well have decided to wait for a cartoon session or feature film an hour later, or turned over to watch *Cinderella* being danced on the other channel.[401]

Material aimed at children, during the evening schedule at least, was generally light on ideology. For instance, though the fiftieth anniversary of the Pioneer movement in 1972 was marked by a commemorative programme, on 3 September of the same year (the anniversary of the death of the Pioneer hero Pavlik Morozov), young audiences were invited to watch a film adaptation of Kipling's story 'Rikki-Tikki-Tavi' and a programme called *The Merry Roundabout*.[402] Largely, the schedule consisted of the ever-popular cartoons, including both original productions and adaptations of books, for example Nosov's *Neznaika*.[403] Among programmes for older children, especially successful was a quiz-cum-talent-contest-cum-variety show, *KVN, The Club for Cheerful and Inventive People*, first broadcast in 1961, in which teams of students and young workers competed against each other less to answer questions than to make the biggest impression. Typical was a dance contest in which the first participant came on stage and put on a thoroughly professional show, but the second brought the house down by dancing so badly that people could scarcely believe their eyes.[404] Watching television was by now often less a self-educating activity than exposure to pure entertainment.

Children themselves certainly found television highly enjoyable, savouring the fare as much as earlier generations had savoured what was offered to them on radio. While standard children's programmes such as folk-tale adaptations were lapped up, even news and informational programmes could seem novel and interesting to this audience. For instance, Valeriya Mukhina's twins, then about four and a half, glued themselves to a news broadcast about Nasser's Egypt in May 1966 ('Is Nasser a good person? Is he a tsar? Or is he like Lenin? What is he like then?').[405] And it was often 'all-family' programmes that ended up sinking into children's culture (as had earlier been the case with film). The favourite characters of playground anecdotes included not just cartoon characters such as Cheburashka, but also Stirlitz, the Soviet agent posing as a Nazi leader who was the hero of the TV thriller *Seventeen Moments of Spring*, not to speak of Sherlock Holmes and Dr Watson, transferred to Soviet television in the 1970s. And watching *KVN* was a highlight for younger children as well as for adolescents and adults. The show was such a landmark that it was even used as a date marker: 'We got our first [TV set] when *KVN* was on.'[406]

Healthy Hobbies

Among the most popular fare for children in the 'general' TV schedules was spectator sport in its different varieties: in the Soviet Union, mainly ice hockey, football, basketball, and ice-skating. As with children's exposure to the theatre and other types of spectacle, the process was at once age-old and characteristically 'Soviet'. Audiences for sport had included children well before 1917 – but it was in the 1930s and 1940s that taking them along 'to the stadium' became a widespread activity.

The Soviet era also witnessed a boom in participant sport for children, in the sense of varieties of game and physical activity that were also organised professionally to competitive ends. On the whole, the part played by school education was less significant here than it was, say, in Britain, where even academic schools were likely to consign their pupils to the sports ground three or four, or more, times a week. By contrast, PE had a marginal role in the school programme both before and after the Revolution, and in practice exposure might be even less than officially envisaged because of shortages of teachers (this was particularly the case in the early decades of Soviet power). The upper limit for sports lessons in the late 1950s and early 1960s, the time when 'physical culture' was most heavily represented, was 72 hours per year, or a maximum of two hours a week over the course of a normal school year. For the most part, PE in schools was a hole-in-corner affair, and few establishments had properly equipped sports centres or even gymnasiums; in the 1920s and 1930s, indeed, many lacked even the most basic equipment.[407]

Exceptional in the general meagreness of their provision were sports facilities for exceptionally talented children. During the first two decades of Soviet power there were no educational institutions of this kind (unless one counts the Moscow Circus and Variety School, founded in 1927). Sports activities were co-ordinated for everyone through the 'physical culture' movement (and, from 1932, the 'Be Fit for Labour and Defence' movement, which gave a more explicitly militaristic slant to sporting activities). But, in tune with the emphasis on rational rivalry that ran through the Stalin era generally, more support for competitive sport began to be offered in the mid-1930s. From 1934, after-school sports sessions, known as 'sports schools', for 10- to 16-year-olds, began to cater to this group. By 1940, 262 such schools had been established; development was interrupted by

98 Sports banner (trophy for victors in a school tournament), 1970s.

the war, but it proceeded rapidly after 1948. By 1958 there were more than 1,000 sports schools, by 1967, 2,772, and by 1975, 4,938. After 1966, the age range covered expanded to 7–18.[408] From 1962, a small, exclusive network of boarding-schools to train children to Olympic levels in sport were also developed: 25 such schools had opened by 1976, and by 1983 there were 35, with a target of 40 schools and 15,121 pupils across the USSR by 1986.[409]

Quite different were the 'sports schools', which were part-time facilities. These, opened in large numbers during the 1970s under the aegis of the transport ministry and the trade unions as well as the education ministry, catered for many thousands of pupils. Those attending were a select group; admission required not just permission from parents and the school director, but a letter of recommendation from the PE teacher at school. They provided an ambitious and wide-ranging programme for children aged from about 10 up to 18, with several hours of instruction a week even at a relatively young age. Though the official programme included such predictable abstractions as 'the moral image of the Soviet sportsman', the main stress was on practical instruction, which in a good many cases was highly successful and enjoyed by those who received it. Such facilities did much to compensate some children for the lack of PE training in ordinary schools; at the same time, their existence had a detrimental effect on the provision of sport in the mainstream, making sports lessons within 'general education' even more perfunctory than before.[410]

In the 1960s, the network of children's stadiums, summer camps, and sports facilities of all kinds was given an official boost. Articles about the virtues of sporting activity started to proliferate in the press.[411] There was a particular expansion of 'voluntarist' sports organisation, encouraged by official exhortations to housing co-operatives, collectives of residents, and factory managements to provide more facilities for children, by legislation to this effect, and by incentive campaigns such as national competitions (for example, 'Olympic Snowflake', a winter sports event organised across the RSFSR in 1964–5).[412] From the early 1960s, 'parent committees' were set up at big apartment blocks, so that local energy and expertise could be drawn upon to organise sports coaching, help with homework, and youth groups to keep children from mischief-making down in the infamous courtyard.[413] In this period also, sporting equipment, like toys, was highlighted as a priority in the production of consumer goods.[414]

Large numbers of children in the post-war generations played at least some sport; sometimes seriously and to high levels, more often just for fun. To be sure, oral history would suggest that the level of those engaged in sport that was organised by professionally competent adults outside the school network was way below the most optimistic estimates in propaganda sources (90 per cent). Hardly anyone remembers 'official' sporting activities in the countryside, and access to facilities in small towns and cities was also patchy, so estimates from PE teachers of 20–5 per cent seem closer to the mark.[415] But children did not necessarily take part in sports only on an official basis. It was natural for activities that were enjoyed passively to be imitated: children who played a game of ice hockey on the improvised rink outside the block where they lived might not be included in the statistics, but this level of 'sporting activity' was very widespread.

Well before 1917, spontaneous bouts of this kind were widely recorded, including not only traditional games, such as *lapta*, or children's favourites, such as catch, but also soccer. For Yury Smolich, later a successful writer, football and 'the law of the street' were more important during childhood than books (a rare confession indeed!).[416] His younger colleague Yury Nagibin, growing up in the Soviet period, was also obsessed with football – to the despair of his parents, who thought the career of engineer more suitable for their son.[417] The mania stretched across wide swathes of the Soviet Union, gripping boys in Abhazia, too, in the 1930s.[418] By the post-war era, football was being played in town and city courtyards everywhere.[419]

Football appealed because it could be played on an informal basis (in the tradition of what was known in Russia as 'wild football', *dikii futbol*). The other spectator sports, for example ice hockey, basketball, or volleyball, required additional equipment. But where that was available, or could be cobbled together by children themselves, these sports were played with enthusiasm too. An informant brought up in a worker settlement in Bryansk during the late 1940s and early 1950s remembered skating using home-made skates as well as football, and even sessions of gymnastics organised by the children themselves. A man of a similar age from a small town in Krasnodar region remembered being encouraged by his friend to have a go at running: some small-size spikes were borrowed from a girl they knew, and off the two went for their joint training sessions.[420]

Sport of a recognisable kind – unlike self-directed forms of exercise, such as scrambling up walls, exploring cellars, or riding on tram-buffers – was a type of leisure activity that was considered admirable in every way. It involved healthy exercise, teamwork (individual sports, such as tennis, received less encouragement), and 'socialist competition'. Card-playing, on the other hand, was the symbolic antithesis of sport: it was sedentary, furtive, and smacked of an unseemly interest in personal gain (the official perception seems to have been innocent of the intellectual stimulation offered to some by games such as bridge). Collecting was something of a grey area also, because of its links with acquisitiveness: though it was popular both before and after the Revolution on a private basis, the sole form of it to receive official approval after 1917 was stamp-collecting.[421] Other sedentary leisure activities that could be seen as disinterested and educational were in a different category. Chess, for example, had a long history of popularity in Russia anyway, but began to receive intensive official encouragement in the late 1930s, with the publication of chess-playing guides for amateurs and the foundation of chess 'circles' at countless Pioneer houses and palaces. Photography – considered a fusion of the scientific and the aesthetic, a way of encouraging interest in physics and chemistry as well as in the visual arts – was also strongly propagandised. Activities of this kind had a larger body of practitioners than in the West, and not just among the children of educated parents.[422] Strongly encouraged, too, were activities such as model-building, which were associated less with play as such than with juvenile excursions into the world of science and technology.[423]

Less popular, even before 1917, were nature-based activities, such as botanising, bird-watching, or butterfly-hunting. Vladimir Nabokov, a famous exception to the general rule, came from a family with strong Anglophile leanings whose taste in leisure activities (bicycling as well as nature study) lay outside the mainstream. Traditional contacts with the natural world among members of the Russian gentry took the form of hunting and shooting (though not often fishing). Russian village children might well have a spontaneous appreciation of the beauty of nature (as indeed emerges in many memoirs), and of course absorbed traditional beliefs about herbal cures, the behaviour of wild animals, and so on, but were unlikely to steep themselves in nature for the sake of it. And, among city children, it tended to be domestic animals that represented the natural world – above all dogs and cats, though sometimes also tame birds, or even rescued wild creatures.[424]

After the Revolution, there was some attempt to encourage nature study. Keeping pets was regarded as 'petit-bourgeois' – proprietorial and insanitary – and strongly discouraged. But the 'campaign for new life' within the Pioneer movement included a campaign against cruelty, particularly to birds. Pioneer troops were kept busy putting up bird-boxes and exhorting 'unorganised children' not to throw stones at their feathered friends. Another important drive was the foundation of 'young naturalist' circles, or 'Michurinite groups', which taught children to observe the natural world, often with a strong emphasis on social utility (absorption of Soviet theories on agricultural development was expected). The activities of such groups were regularly covered in the Pioneer press. Often, this kind of hobby would be encouraged by school circles, as was the case with a girl from Taganrog who made her own version of the 'Red Book' of endangered species early in the 1980s.[425] But, as before, the appreciation of nature in a formal sense required a certain degree of economic security. Fishing in a town or city might be a way of passing the time; in a village, it was much more likely to be valued as a means of adding to, and varying, a scanty and monotonous diet.[426]

In educated urban circles, approved hobbies represented the acceptable interface between childhood and adulthood. A child who completed its homework and got out the chessboard, or vanished into the darkroom, or fashioned some planks into a feeding-table for the local birds, was doing something obviously useful, and often, into the bargain, expecting adults to act in a tutorial and supervisory role. (The fact that children often treated hobbies as crazes, absorbing themselves deeply for a few months in an activity before abandoning it, did not impede the view that pastimes such as photography were educationally useful.)[427] But not all ways of passing the time that children enjoyed were so easily sanctioned. This applied not just to activities that were clearly 'against the rules' and morally or aesthetically pernicious, but also to ones that were not obviously useful. It is, indeed, here that tension between adults and children who were not rebellious in any premeditated sense often made itself felt.

'Wasting Time'

Many of children's leisure activities were, from the adult point of view, appropriate for their age. Reading, watching films or television, or listening to the radio were perfectly 'classifiable' in terms of the time budgets that were imposed on children, and slots would be timetabled to allow such activities to take place. Rather different, however, was the case of the child who appeared not to be doing anything (whether worthwhile or stupid) at all: who had vanished into its own thoughts, into the world of mute contemplation. Nabokov has given a description of this state with reference to visiting the lavatory, an activity that he, like many other young children with access to a relatively little-used facility, could prolong almost for ever:

> As a small child, however, I was assigned a more modest arrangement [than the 'sumptuous but gloomy' toilet he used later on], rather casually situated in a narrow recess between a wicker hamper and the door leading to the nursery bathroom. This door I liked to keep ajar; through it I drowsily looked at the shimmer of steam above the mahogany bath, at the fantastic flotilla of swans and skiffs, at myself with a harp in one of the boats, at a furry moth pinging against the reflector of the kerosene lamp, at the stained-glass window beyond, at its two halbordiers consisting of colored rectangles. Bending from my warm seat, I liked to press the middle of my brow, its ophryon to be precise, against the smooth comfortable edge of the door and then roll my head a little, so that the door would move to and fro while its edge remained all the time in soothing contact with my forehead. A dreamy rhythm would permeate my being. The recent 'Step, step, step,' would be taken up by a dripping faucet. And, fruitfully combining rhythmic pattern with rhythmic sound, I would unravel the labyrinthian frets on the linoleum, and find faces where a crack

or shadow afforded a *point de repère* for the eye. I appeal to parents: never, never say, 'Hurry up,' to a child.[428]

The point of the expostulation is that adults saying 'Hurry up!' to children represent a constant of socialisation, at home just as much as in the schoolroom. That said, teaching children concepts of time was one of the tasks allotted to the school syllabus in the Soviet era, and the structure of formal education itself introduced a child to the concept of a regularly ordered day. But clocks were, by the early twentieth century, quite widespread in urban society generally, and even a village home in European Russia might, by the 1920s, have its pendulum clock.[429] The appearance of clocks, and, more abstractly, the emergence of 'industrial' concepts of time, of Ford 'time and motion' studies and industrial charts, made teaching about rational time-keeping a still more important part of bringing children up, sharpening conflicts between children's capacities for consistent work and concentration, and adult demands for 'mature' and 'responsible' attitudes.

Children's imaginative experience could come under fire, then, not so much because it was dangerous or immoral (as with gambling or wall-climbing), as because it was futile and silly. Of course, its 'time-wasting' propensities did not mean that it was necessarily static. Children were very interested in action. Their own fictions – like those of children in many other cultures – tended to be event-driven. Typical was a tale told by one of Vera Mukhina's young twins, then aged nearly four:

> Once there were some partisans. They had a gun. They did battle and shot at each other. They were defending the Motherland. They used to kill nasty people. They all lived together. And then they went flying off in a plane. They started shooting from there. Then they all sat down on a bench to have a rest. They rested, they rested, and then they started shooting again. They shot and shot and then they went home. [...] And then a crocodile came up. He broke the window. Then he started eating the partisans and the negroes. But one person got away – he hid in the stove. And he shot the crocodile in the stomach ...[430]

Children responded with fierce enthusiasm to unusual events in real life as well: for example, coronations, when the street decorations, illuminations, and fireworks were the source of sharp delight; or, at a later stage, political demonstrations.[431]

Juveniles who appeared to be deriving entertainment from 'nothing at all' could be witnessing some mundane (from an adult point of view) occurrence and gaining excitement from a first-time contact with this. For one boy brought up in a provincial town in Tula province during the 1920s, for example, the breaking-up of the ice on the river in spring was something extraordinary and fascinating:

> It was a shattering sight. The river wasn't particularly wide: it was called the Fair Mech' – but when the ice was melting, it got all swollen, well, like any

river does, and watching that sight was ... I remember how struck I was when I saw it. So much that I came home and wrote a poem about it [...]:

> Just see our river, the Fair Mech', run,
> The time to look after the houses on the bank has begun.
> The river doesn't think this is funny,
> Anyone who arrives late will get punished.
> She'll pour water all over the fields,
> It'll reach as far as the wealds.
> The ice will gather by the bridge at the start,
> They'll have to use dynamite to blow it apart.[432]

Rivers, even in a less dramatic condition, were often the most interesting thing outside the home: on a major navigational river, for instance, watching boat traffic was a favourite occupation.[433] But children could also have their attention drawn by exotic visitors – exiled beggars, gypsies, madmen – or by other kinds of traffic, such as cars, planes, or, in the countryside, tractors.[434] In many of these cases, an adult might have paid little attention to the phenomenon in hand, and it was often offbeat everyday details that struck a child even when something unusual was happening. For Anatoly Mariengof, the most remarkable thing about a royal parade witnessed in childhood was the governor of Nizhni-Novgorod riding his horse 'back to front' – which is to say, facing its tail – so that he did not have to turn his back on the Tsar, riding in the carriage behind.[435]

The Black Hand

'Time-wasting' did not always involve pleasant impressions. Children also exercised a good deal of energy on anxieties, which adults often found just as paltry as their enthusiasms. Such fears were sometimes of a topical, locally specific, kind – as in the case of a woman brought up in a small town in the Moscow region, whose anxieties, like those of her peers, revolved around the local jail:

> I remember a thing called 'the black crow' [Black Maria, police wagon]. And we'd all [look] with horror ... it got passed on to us children, we'd point it out, 'Here's the black crow, there it is, it's coming over here!' We knew there was a courtroom on the corner ... of Gogolevskaya and Pisemsky streets, and that was where the court was. [...] Prisoners got taken there, arrestees, people being banged up. And sometimes I even heard, 'The black crow'll come and it'll take you away!' [...] But then someone would say, 'But they're enemies of the people!' And everyone would calm down.[436]

Imagination could also be provoked by notorious murders: for some children, Pavlik Morozov was less vivid as a picture of Communist virtue than as an example of a fragile person one's own age slaughtered by wicked enemies for reasons that were horribly difficult to understand.[437] In the 1970s and 1980s, a pressing fear was nuclear war – for a boy brought up in Perm', dreams were haunted by visions of American planes circling over the city, ready to drop their atom bombs on the population.[438]

But fears could also reflect enduring, transhistorical childhood anxieties: the dark, in particular, and the bogeys that might come out of it. Here, the pitch of emotion might also be raised by the habit among many adults of invoking such bogeys to keep children in order, or simply to tease them:

> Once my parents – and I believed whatever they told me – told me some dreadful story about a boy, a made-up story, and he went out one day, and someone ... Baba Yaga stole him away, and someone came after her too, and when I was about four this just sank right down, I remember it all to this day! [*Laughs*]. I was so afraid of the dark! And even if I had to go to the toilet at nights, I'd wake my mother ...[439]

Alongside Baba Yaga, other popular figures were 'devils', '*Buka*' (a kind of catch-all bogey figure), fierce creatures such as wolves, and members of ethnic minorities such as Tatars and gypsies. Traditional rhymes also evoked such creatures, who were not always driven away. They might also be invited in, as in a ubiquitous rhyme used to send small children to sleep:

> Lulla, lullaby,
> Bogey, go under the barn,
> Under the barn is a little wolf,
> He'll grab Nina by the side.[440]

At some level, also, children appear to have had a psychological need for such fears, as was expressed in the genre of *strashilka*, or horror story. These little spine-chillers, usually so short they could be narrated start to finish in a hectic whisper over about a minute, tended to take a stereotyped form: terror seeped into the domestic environment, usually overcoming a girl. Often, nemesis arrived in the form of a huge black hand:

> One day a girl arrived home. The Black Hand flew after her and chased her all the way back. The girl ran into the kitchen. The Black Hand ran after her. The girl ran into the living room. The Black Hand flew in there too. The girl ran into the little room. The Black Hand flew after her again. There was no way out of the little room. The girl hid under the bed. The Black Hand flew up and lay down on the bed. Then the Black Hand heard something scrabbling under the bed, flew down underneath and said, 'Give me my heart back!'[441]

In *strashilki*, horrors were presented baldly. Sometimes, a maternal prohibition was violated, but this was not essential: it was commoner for there to be a sense of absolute and inexplicable terror.

Childhood fears are a cultural universal, but the expression of them may vary. There are records of scary tales being told over quite a wide historical period. A man from a peasant family born in the late 1880s recalled a coeval coming out with a spine-chiller:

'One day my father was going past the cemetery at night. Suddenly a corpse came running towards him, wearing a white shroud. My father's hair stood on end. He gave his horse a whack with his whip, made the sign of the cross, and fell face-downwards in his sledge.' The boy wanted to go on, but we stopped him. We didn't like that story one bit.

Similarly, in the 1920s, an orphanage supervisor came across a small girl electrifying a group of children with a story about a train accident. The supervisor was soon shooed away, to hear, as she left, the audience ask anxiously, had the girl survived after the train ran over her?[442] Deliberate attempts to evoke fear seem to have been less common in the years of the Purges and of the Second World War, no doubt because so many real-life horror stories were in circulation. Once Soviet society became more settled and prosperous, though, horror stories started to become popular again, and from the early 1950s the *strashilka* began to emerge as a specific genre, narrated to a captive public in the school playground, or during what was sometimes appropriately known as the 'dead hour' (the period of compulsory rest) at a Pioneer camp.

The same period also saw the flowering of a comparable genre, that of 'sadistic verses'. Unlike *strashilki*, these tended to represent children carrying out horrors, rather than having these inflicted upon them, as in a popular type parodying the Second World War propaganda that was foisted on children in such quantities at school:

> The kids in the cellar were playing Gestapo:
> They tortured and murdered plumber Potapov.[443]

Thus the indoctrination in the horrors of the Second World War to which children were exposed at school, and often at home too (by parents or, as the generations passed, grandparents), was transformed into a genre which would definitely not have attracted the approval of most adults.

Whatever the nature of their contemplative life and the ways in which they chose to explore the world beyond the family, children were likely at one point or another to find themselves, through their early gestures of independence, the subject of conflict with adults. Inducting children into a sense of time economy seems to be a cultural universal, and one that more or less always provokes discord. The lack of tolerance of time-wasting felt by many peasant adults has already been mentioned, but educated adults could be equally repressive. To some extent, the material being published from the 1890s and 1900s about the importance of play in its own right acted as counterweight to such irritation, generating a widespread recognition of play as a legitimate subject of pedagogical, psychological, and ethnographical investigation. However, those devoting themselves to analysis of play as an 'end in itself' tended to adopt the view that children's psychological world was highly specific – that play was an activity peculiar to children, as well as one with its own particular character. This view was accompanied by a complementary shift towards seeing leisure activities that were not sanctioned by some goal of intellectual or moral self-improvement as devoid of serious purpose and unsuitable for consumption by adults – 'childish', in a word. Whatever type of 'school' they thought children should attend – 'free', or highly structured and academic – educated Russian adults were more or less uniformly persuaded that children should attend some sort of school. And the nature of the school itself, for most generations of children during the twentieth century, marked a very important boundary of psychological existence – in essence, the beginning of the end of childhood itself.

Chapter 12

Years of School

Stand up, all those who remember the non-leaking inkwells,
Pale wooden pencil-boxes, and all the rest on the list:
Chinese plimsolls for gym, and the t-shirts with little white hems [...]
Snow-white Finnish exercise books in their navy-blue covers,
And the day when they told us to bring along fountain pens.
(Marina Boroditskaya, 'Stand Up, All those who Remember')[1]

Children who reached the school entered a different world, with its own peculiar inventory of essential goods, a world where time was divided into regular stretches by bells, where rules had to be followed, and where older children were as vigilant as teachers in imposing norms of behaviour (though the norms of behaviour they imposed might well fly in the face of what teachers wanted). Schooling constituted a process of socialisation in a very broad sense: it combined intellectual training (*obrazovanie*), skills training (*obuchenie*), and moral and character education (*vospitanie*). It also introduced many children to a world of new rituals and practices, running from the public repetition of homework to the celebration of a whole range of festivals. For example, during the Soviet period, peasant and working-class children whose birthday was never celebrated at home might find themselves the centre of attention in the classroom on the day when it occurred, as the teacher invited the other pupils to congratulate them on this joyous occasion.[2] No wonder that early experience of school figures in most memories of childhood as a highly specific era, quite unlike the experiences lived through before it.

In taking a 'child's eye' view of school, this chapter says little about the institutional context of classroom experience. The content of the syllabus was – in state schools at most stages of Russian history (the years between 1918 and 1928 being a rare exception) – dictated from the centre, by the educational ministry. So, too, was the range of different school types (academic, practical, a mixture of both), and the nature of teaching methods used (whether child-centred and permissive or *dirigiste*). School inspections were intended to ensure that ministerial directives were carried out, and to harmonise the character of school-teaching at a microscopic level.[3] All of this should, in theory, have done much to curb regional and local variations. Yet in practice quite a lot of differences were found, depending not just upon the existence of widely varying types of institution (especially at the secondary level), but also upon funding levels and upon individual choices and beliefs. Teachers could adapt curricula and pedagogical directives from the educational ministries and commissariats; they could be more or less successful in maintaining order, and in getting their pupils enthusiastic about their subject. They might take official exhortations to give those who were falling behind extra coaching more or less seriously.[4] And the character of the director was, for many teachers and pupils, crucial to their experience of school life. Whether the director was flexible and humane, or rigid and authoritarian, and how he or she chose to interpret educational directives, made every difference to the nature of the institution in a broad sense.

99 Father teaching his son to read, 1910s.

In addition, teachers' work was affected fundamentally by relations within the teaching body at large: the nature of the *kollektiv*, to use the Soviet term.[5] An enemy within the ranks, particularly if this person held the powerful role of 'education manager' (*zavuch*), the director's deputy in the Soviet secondary school could create serious problems. While the structure of pre-revolutionary secondary schools, and of primary schools both before and after 1917, was slightly different (there was no equivalent of the *zavuch*), the significance of having a competent and understanding director, and decently inclined, open-minded colleagues, was equally great. In the sameway, teachers' commitment to the profession could be affected by all sorts of personal factors – notably adequate pay and access to respectable living conditions, both of which were denied many during the first decades of Soviet power.[6] The individual lives of teachers will be more or less invisible here, but need to be borne in mind as background all the time.

Invisible also – but equally important – were the educational activities of parents. A mother, father, or other relation was quite likely to teach a child to read, not necessarily with any great pedagogical skill. Often, an old reading-book would be used, and irritation or impatience were not unknown. A woman born in 1972 into a family one generation removed from the peasantry remembered that her mother's approach to tuition in reading was spectacularly unsuccessful:

> She got out the alphabet book and said, 'Read this, "Ma-ma". What does it say?' And I couldn't answer, I couldn't say what 'mama' said. She repeated ten times, '"Ma, ma". What does that say?' And I said, 'I dunno.' When she asked me that the tenth time, I burst into tears, I howled bitterly, I simply didn't understand what 'Ma-ma' said at all. And she said, 'Stop acting thick,' and grabbed the alphabet book and flung it at the wall. That's how good I was at reading![7]

The situation here was particularly vexed – the girl concerned got on badly with her mother to begin with, so that her inability to read 'ma-ma' was no doubt partly the result of a psychological block. Significantly, it was the girl's father who eventually taught her to read. But it is reasonable to assume that parental teaching of literacy did not always represent a stimulating and peaceable alternative to the drilling and the mechanical drawing of lines and hooks that was practised in the schoolroom.

Parents also exercised influence in other ways. They had little formal influence (parent–teacher associations were non-existent until 1905, and had a fairly marginal role after that), but a considerable degree of leverage at an informal level. In the eras before education was made compulsory, they decided whether the child would attend school in the first place, and how long he or she would stay there. Once the child had arrived, they might try to influence either the syllabus, loudly complaining that the child did not seem to be learning anything useful, or the marks system (by presenting bribes to the teacher, an activity that was especially common before 1917 and after 1970). As a man who attended school in Odessa during the 1970s remembered:

It was a classic case of back-scratching. A teacher would have a mum in the class who worked in a food shop, a dad who ran a pharmacy, a granny who was a doctor. And the same held in reverse: the granny would have her granddaughter's schoolteacher as a patient, and if anything went wrong at school, the teacher would see her right: she'd take the girl for private lessons, put her exam marks up, and so on. The pharmacist dad would 'get hold of' medicine that was short (and everything was back then, right down to aspirins). At exam time, the 'parents' committee' would step in. They'd organise a whip-round and buy some present for the teacher, a big crystal vase or whatever. When a three-hour written exam was going on, the teacher would 'just pop out for a moment'. Arranging the rest took no trouble at all.[8]

Odessa, it should be said, was an unusually rackety city. But almost everywhere there were at least some teachers who were prepared to be elastic. It was hard to survive in a material sense if one was not; and, with examination marks in the hands of individual schools until well after the collapse of the Soviet Union, there was little to stop 'adjustment' going on if the staff of a school wished it to happen.[9]

Parents had indirect effects on children's school lives too. Teachers sometimes operated informal systems of discrimination, treating the children of powerful officials or other prominent social figures more considerately than those from more humble backgrounds. This practice seems to have been common before 1917 and in the Brezhnev era, but was not unknown at other times. The complaint that you would not get anywhere at school if you were from a working-class family was often voiced by informants from working-class backgrounds in our oral history project, who could all cite chapter and verse for their claims. But, while teachers might pander to the sense of social status that operated in society more broadly, they might seek to correct this, ignoring parental background in their dealings with children, or operating a system of 'positive discrimination'. Before 1917, political radicals, such as the Populists, were well represented in the teaching profession. Whether they espoused such views or not, many teachers did all they could to encourage intellectually able, but financially disadvantaged, pupils, even sometimes paying fees themselves, or offering children accommodation, in order to help with studies. Mikhail Isakovsky, for instance, was the beneficiary of charitable donations from the teachers living locally when he needed the fees to attend secondary school.[10]

The tradition of charitable initiative by teachers hung on after 1917, and help could be extended to pupils who were suffering discrimination on political grounds, as well as to members of the peasantry and working classes.[11] Though teachers were an important conduit for state ideology, they sometimes protected pupils who belonged to socially abject categories, rather than orchestrating ostracism of them. Alex Saranin, from a kulak family with White Russian connections, remembered that, indoctrination about 'class war' notwithstanding, his teachers in a small town in the Urals were prepared to award him a book prize as best pupil in the first year, and to back his application for a scholarship to continue education after the three-year primary course was finished.[12] In the late Soviet era, teachers might strike blows against consumerism by forbidding pupils to wear anything that made them stand out – even wristwatches, in some schools.[13] The tradition that home and family were regarded as *separate* from school life, the pervasive understanding that the teacher should place the welfare of his or her pupils beyond anything else, and teachers' inherited status as quintessential representatives of the oppositional intelligentsia, all counterbalanced the fact that teachers – at any rate those in prestigious urban secondary schools – belonged to the traditionally loyal professional middle class.

Memoirs, oral history, and diaries all make it clear that many teachers did take their responsibilities seriously and that they were concerned for their pupils' welfare, both in terms of covering the curriculum and well beyond. Especially in the Soviet period, the organisation of informal out-of-school activities with children was common – indeed, it was one of the duties of the 'class supervisor', or form teacher. Some teachers, for instance, ran literary societies where pupils met and discussed books not on the syllabus; a group of children growing up in Odessa in the 1970s made their first acquaintance with Bulgakov's and Dostoevsky's novels in this way.[14] There was, to be sure, an element of danger in organising such clubs, whether under the Tsarist regime or the Soviet one: all manifestations of associationism not sanctioned by higher authority were likely to be seen as politically subversive. But many teachers were none the less prepared to take the risk of informal contacts with pupils, even in the Stalin era. One woman at a Moscow school in the 1940s recalled that her class teacher spent a good deal of her free time with some of the girls in her group, taking part in their games and trying to teach them to overcome their fear of the dark.[15] Extra-curricular contact of this kind positively flowered during the 1960s, when official encouragement was given to 'informal' activities with children, particularly if they involved sport and other forms of 'rational leisure'.[16] While official guides continued to stress teachers' function as a conduit for official values, and as regulators of discipline, in at least some cases contact was warmer and more personal than methodological prescription envisaged.[17]

This kind of informal contact was all the more valued in that teacher–pupil relations in the classroom itself were usually extremely formal. Indeed sometimes – depending on the personal dynamics – they verged on antagonism. Yet dedicated teachers were the major reason why school could seem a haven to some pupils from stressed and harried backgrounds. The school could seem 'another world' in a positive sense: somewhere one was not beaten, where reading was seen as a vital intellectual activity and not as a waste of time, where good marks and hard work got one approving recognition. But if the figure of the teacher in some ways transcended time, much else about school experience had strong temporal links – both in the sense that the socialisation of children at school was primarily concerned with giving them a sense of time and of time management, and in the sense that it was subject to alteration as the decades passed. The sense of specificity, both in time and in space, began from the moment children arrived at the school.

Another Time, Another Place

The first factor that established school life as profoundly different from home life was the nature of the building. Admittedly, this was not necessarily true in Russian villages, where, right up to the late twentieth century, a school might be located in a converted peasant hut. Not all such places were as bad as the parish school premises remembered by the writer Aleksandr Neverov, who attended lessons there in the 1890s: 'A low dark building with long desks, a filthy ceiling, partitioned off from a room used by the church caretaker.'[18] Few, though, were likely to offer children the light and space that made the acquisition of basic academic skills easier, and that was helpful if the class were engaged in non-academic activities such as dance or handicrafts. In towns as well, before 1917, smaller establishments, especially if privately run, might amount to no more than a couple of rooms. A St Petersburg school on the corner of the Fontanka and Voznesensky Prospekt operating in the 1890s, for example, consisted of two rooms in a three-roomed family flat, equipped with blackboards, desks and chairs for the tinies, a long table and chairs for the older children, a desk and chair for the teacher, and not a stick of furniture more.[19]

But not all schools, even before 1917, were hand-to-mouth conversions of existing buildings. Purpose-built primary schools began to be constructed in some numbers by the Ministry of Education during the 1890s. One of these, on Vasilievsky Island in St Petersburg, opened in 1897, had – according to an approving report in an official guide to the capital – twelve rooms, including a school hall, a church, 'bright cloakrooms', a separate janitor's room, a library, a surgery for the school doctor, and a laundry.[20] Such schools conformed to a 'model' pattern that had been in circulation since the 1880s.[21] By 1903, only twenty such schools had opened, including those in the Russian capital.[22] But they were a sign of burgeoning change; at worst, government buildings were functional, and provision of equipment in them was quite generous: each child was issued a slate and slate pencil as well as an ABC, though food had to be taken along (some mothers provided their children with hand-sewn print bags in which to carry this).[23]

Prior to the 1960s, which saw a concerted effort to amalgamate primary and secondary school facilities on one site, these types of school were more often separate. Secondary schools tended to have more architectural pretensions, especially before 1917, when this acted as a sign of the 'estate' character of education. Official prescription of appropriate styles went back to the Educational Institutions Statute of 1828, in the wake of which the architect A. F. Shchedrin had put together a number of model designs, including not only a very basic one-roomed parish school and a city school with a one-storey layout, but also a plan for a *gimnaziya* that had a two-storey range with twin staircases and a pillared entrance topped by pediment displaying the name of the school.[24] The most prestigious types of state secondary school would be among a provincial town's handful of most impressive buildings. Solidly built of brick or stone, not wood, their assertive, neo-classical style, with the façades painted in an officially

100 Assembly
hall of the former
Elizavetinskaya
gimnaziya, Moscow,
photographed in the
1910s.

approved colour such as butter yellow, brown or green, picked out with white, stamped on the viewer's mind the relationship between education and social power in a broader sense.[25] 'Commercial schools' and 'city schools' were likely to be more modestly appointed, but still offered serviceable facilities that were reasonably spacious and decently constructed.

Inside, most schools also had a markedly institional, 'government', character. Before the Revolution, this was conveyed by the length and breadth of the corridors and the pomp of the staircases in secondary schools, by the glamour of the assembly hall, and also by the decorations in the classroom, focusing upon portraits of the Tsar and other dignitaries. There was little attempt to introduce visual relief to the surroundings with paintings, plants, and so on, or to encourage children to contribute to the environment themselves.

Quite different were the schools operated by the 'free education' system, where there was a great deal more evidence of children's presence. A school run by Olga Kaidanova in Moscow during the 1910s, for example, was the image of happy chaos, with children crowded into a homely, cluttered space that served as workshop and meeting room as well as classroom, and that had numerous examples of artwork on the walls.[26] But tiny numbers of children were educated in such places – Kaidanova's catered for seventeen – and the ambience there was atypical. The vast majority of schools, whether state institutions or private ones, regimented their pupils in visual as well as intellectual terms. 'Peeling painted floors, like in cheaply furnished kitchens, dark ceilings with peeling plaster, grubby window-panes,' was how Anatoly Mariengof remembered his Penza *gimnaziya* in the 1910s.[27] Elizaveta Fen's more prestigious provincial Institute for Daughters of the Nobility was equally oppressive and gloomy: the dormitories had white paint on the lower panes of the windows, and 'white cotton blinds were always pulled

101 Corridor, Elizavetinskaya *gimnaziya*, Moscow, photographed in the 1910s.

half-way down', while the boarders' workroom, though lighter, was no more congenial. The entire building gave the sense of 'a place of confinement'.[28]

Reminiscences of this kind reflected the fact that the hygiene ethos was rather weakly entrenched in government educational policy before 1917. The 1893 Codex of Statutes on Scholarly Institutes and Educational Establishments, for instance, included no stipulations on acceptable classroom size, norms of construction and internal decoration, and equipment among its many thousands of provisions.[29] It was left to private individuals, often addressing themselves to the organisers of private schools, or those funded by the zemstva, to convince Russian teachers that attention to the physical environment of education was vital, and to list the necessary details of its organisation. The school should be built with a north–south orientation, so that the classrooms faced south, south-east, or south-west, the building materials should be dry, and close attention should be paid to ventilation. Equipment should be chosen with attention to the physique of the pupils and the need to avoid stress on their eyesight. The buildings should be kept clean, dry, and well aired at all times.[30]

By the 1900s, however, some zemstva were beginning to take an interest in school hygiene, though activities were often limited to recording just how unsatisfactory conditions were. In 1913, the medical-sanitary commission in Perm' province recorded serious overcrowding in some places, including one school with 115 pupils, but only 0.12 cubic metres of air for each, where desks were placed so close together that six pupils had to sit in a serried rank with no space between them at all.[31] As with all other areas of zemstvo activity, the level of organisation and control varied from province to province, and from district to district. In some places, guidance was issued to school management on the proper organisation of hygiene and sanitation, doctors co-operated energetically with educational administrators in picking out sites for new school buildings and inspected extant buildings, and school pupils, at regular intervals; in other places no guidance was issued, and inspections took place erratically or not at all.[32] Purpose-built modern schools represented an increasing proportion of educational accommodation, but only a proportion: in one district in Voronezh province, for example, nearly one-third of the buildings that were actually owned by the different educational administrations, as opposed to rented premises, dated from before 1890.[33]

The Decree on the Unified School of Labour saw the disappearance of private, church, and zemstvo-funded schools; from now on, the state was responsible for all school building, and acceptable standards were regulated from the centre. Yet styles of building remained varied. To begin with, many pre-revolutionary buildings continued in use; indeed, such buildings were listed as among the more spacious and better adapted school buildings in inspectors' reports from as late as the 1950s.[34] Later generations of buildings reflected educational fashion: the 'health and efficiency' ethos of the 1920s generated a fashion for streamlined, glass-rich buildings in a mass-market Constructivist style. Under the First Five-Year Plan, with its commitment to the expansion of education, construction of these took place not only in major cities but also in the provinces. The buildings were, inevitably, hymned in Soviet propaganda as world-beating, which might not

102   Late 1890s design for the façade of a primary school.

have meant a lot, but some appear to have been loved by those who worked there. A teacher who did her compulsory work stint (*raspredelenie*) in Krasnouralsk in the 1950s recalled the First Five-Year Plan school that she worked in as 'magnificent. Like a palace! And the collective was magnificent. Half of them were people who'd graduated from the school. They'd got qualified and then gone back to work in their own school.'[35]

The second half of the 1930s, by contrast, and more particularly the late 1940s, saw a return to a more traditional type of building, high rather than spacious, and with relatively restricted use of glass (though classrooms, at least, were still supposed to have wide, high windows). One-off projects were notably regressive in character: for instance, in Leningrad, prestige school buildings of the 1940s mostly adapted the neo-classical principles of the Tsarist era.[36] These buildings were strongly geared to the academic syllabus of the day, which created problems when the curriculum reforms of the late 1950s introduced activities requiring workshop space.[37] The enhancement of the 'labour' element in the 'unified school of labour' that went in step with these reforms, alongside renewed interest in non-academic subjects such as music, sport, and art, brought with it a return to a 'utopian modernist' approach, bolstered by influence from the West. A typical design included a large entrance lobby, off which stood an assembly hall and a gymnasium, with, at the rear, wide corridors that were also used as recreation rooms in bad weather, and a range of classrooms leading off these.[38]

But the vast majority of Soviet schools were not one-off projects. Like nurseries and kindergartens, they were pattern-book designs whose main virtue was supposed to be maximum capacity at low cost. Once the 'campaign for cultured life' started in the late 1920s, so too did pressure to harmonise school construction according to approved principles. The resolutions of the All-Russian Conference on School Construction, published in February 1929, sought to impose on schools a specific set of essential rooms, including a recreation hall, kitchen, cloakroom, lavatories, rooms for the teacher and for a janitor, and a wood-shed, as well as, of course, the classrooms.[39] Building of new schools to such plans was made compulsory in February 1931, and the plans were published to act as a pattern for construction.[40] Old buildings necessarily continued to be used – indeed, another directive, this time of September 1931, stipulated that houses confiscated from the victims of de-kulakisation should be turned over for educational use – but, gradually, the proportion of new buildings rose. By 1969, half of schools in some areas occupied such buildings, with concentrations greatest in the larger cities. Around 120 schools in Leningrad during the late 1960s and 1970s were constructed to just two designs, both of an unimaginatively boxy kind; alternative projects with a more experimental character ended up shelved for economic reasons.[41] Few buildings indeed had the impact of pre-revolutionary *gimnazii* – the most strenuous efforts in educational construction being reserved, at any rate after 1932, for university and institute buildings. Even the programme of boarding-school building embarked upon in the late 1950s generally produced identikit results, though the sports facilities and internal appointments might be rather more generous than in the average school.[42]

On the inside also, Soviet schools were – at best – sparely functional to the point of bleakness. Some relief to the eye was provided by political symbols – not only, or mainly, ruler icons, though portraits of Lenin and Stalin certainly did hang in prominent places, such as the main staircase.[43] Banners, noticeboards bearing announcements, competition results, and 'wall newspapers' lined the walls of corridors and classrooms, and, from 1932, every school was supposed to have (and most city schools did have) a 'Pioneer room', or organisational centre and reading room for the Pioneer movement. Otherwise, decoration was at best unremarkable. Despite the obsession with hygiene that characterised Russian culture of the 1920s and early 1930s, regulation of the school in this regard began fairly late. The first normative guides – issued on an advisory basis only – began appearing in the mid-1920s.[44] These early sets of hygiene instructions were not particularly detailed in terms of practical guidance. A 'sanitary passport' scheme was introduced in 1936 in Leningrad, but this was in the first instance a system of collecting information to facilitate inspections of the fabric of the building and of basic equipment.[45] Such 'passports' were made compulsory for all schools in 1941, but the information contained in them related to square footage and building structure and to basic information about plumbing and sanitation, rather than to the details of decoration.[46] By contrast, one notes the punctiliousness with which educational fashion was recorded in official pronouncements, with a directive of 5 September 1931 recommending that two-piece tables should replace the old-style Erisman desks (with bench attached) (the latter were once again to come back into style later in the 1930s), and another, of 1 August 1932, requiring that production of writing slates to the 'pre-war' (i.e. pre-revolutionary pattern) should be set in train.[47] Yet even here, enactment in practice remained haphazard: the reintroduction of desks with folding lids in August 1934 suffered a setback when it turned out that there were no hinges and screws to be had in many places.[48]

Inevitably, the Second World War brought an end to even these tentative efforts: the problems were now how to deal with war damage, and the wear and tear imposed by the fact that many schools not only operated a multi-shift system, but were used on a part-time basis by other institutions as well.[49] These problems survived into the post-war era, and school manuals of this period concentrated less on hygienic concerns than on the ritual appointments of the classroom, which were both easier to control and more in step with late Stalinism's obsession with decorum and symbolic authority. A 1950 manual for primary school teachers stated that heavy curtains should be avoided so that light could enter the windows freely, but otherwise dwelt on objects of ideological, rather than hygienic, resonance. 'If a small box for rubbish is placed in the classroom, this will teach the children how to be tidy,' it instructed; pot-plants might be placed on the sills as an aesthetic touch. Most importantly, though, 'on the walls of the classroom should be framed, glass-fronted portraits of the leaders and of famous writers. A wall newspaper will be on display, alongside a timetable and a list of the children in the class.' Another inner wall of the classroom was dominated by the clock.[50]

Far more detailed were the 'Rules for the Sanitary Administration of Schools with a Programme of General Education and Boarding Schools' that appeared a decade later, in 1962. The 'Rules' provided guidance on every detail of the building, from the colour of walls (the top two-thirds of which were to be whitewashed or treated with distemper in a pale shade, while the bottom third was painted in a darker shade of washable emulsion), to ceilings (white), to floors (concealed by a pale floor-covering), to woodwork (painted white) to desks (painted pale green or grey).[51] Meanwhile, the Soviet press reported excitedly on material innovations – specially designed furniture from Riga, for instance, or streamlined, 'modern', equipment – that were now being installed in the latest generation of school buildings.[52]

However, increased educational spending was often reflected in superficialities, such as the craze for technical gimmicks such as systems where pupils answered questions by pressing buzzers as though in a quiz show.[53] Basic equipment, such as exercise books, usually remained of low quality.[54] And the gamut of school buildings at this period might run from a newly built show project for a 'model school', designed by a named architect, down to a crumbling inner-city building, perhaps even with war damage. A team from the Academy of Pedagogical Sciences' Scientific Research Institute of Forms and Methods of Education, which visited Sverdlovsk in 1957 to check on the trial run for the new curriculum introduced nationwide in 1958, saw a range of ten 'typical' schools that included, among others, a pre-revolutionary former *gimnaziya* (spacious and well laid out), a brand new building, a six-year-old building, two pattern-book buildings of some age, only one of which was specified to be 'in good condition', and a building of unspecified age that was 'in need of repairs and modernisation'. The buildings ranged in height from one to four storeys, and in size from 11 to 35 rooms, and the provision of equipment was very variable, with many schools short of essential workshop and laboratory materials, and one school soldiering on with a solid fuel stove system rather than central heating.[55] The picture remained roughly similar up to the end of the Soviet era.

Shaping the Environment

Whatever its personal idiosyncrasies, and in whatever era, the school – unless located in an ordinary house – was likely to have higher ceilings than the child was used to, and bigger rooms (even if there were more people in them). It might also place him or her in an alien sense environment, exposing the nervous new pupil to painfully heightened noise, or indeed disgusting smells or tactile experiences. Vladimir Nabokov was to recall with a shudder the soggy towels and shared pink soap of his school lavatories.[56] In the Soviet era, lavatories could make some pupils reach breaking point: no doors were provided, so that seeing to one's biological needs brought gross loss of privacy. 'It was better to excuse yourself during class so there wasn't anyone around. But whichever way, toilets in kindergartens and at school were a complete nightmare. I taught myself never to use the toilet in the morning, though in an emergency I could always run home, since we lived right nearby,' one man recalled of his schooldays in the 1970s.[57]

For other pupils the ultimate threshold of horror was constituted by school food ('like the contents of a latrine', recalled one ungrateful consumer from the 1960s; pupils at nineteenth-century boarding-schools expressed themselves more delicately, but felt an equal sense of revulsion).[58] It was, of course, only relatively fortunate children who could have reacted so strongly. Most children in villages were not provided with school meals until well into the post-war era.[59] For urban children who were under-fed, or actually on the verge of starvation, as many children were in the early 1920s and during and immediately after the Second World War, school food could mean the difference between life and death.[60] Even later, the canteen fare could be a godsend for the under-fed. 'My dream was one of those four-kopeck pies,' a man from southern Russia recalled of his schooldays in the late 1950s.[61] Some pupils simply liked the food anyway: the pies were worth eating even if you weren't hungry, another informant recalled, 'because they really were tasty'.[62] For well-fed and fastidious pupils of this era, avoiding school food was easy enough: if reaching a shop during breaks was a problem, food could always be purchased on the way home. In the 1970s, one Leningrader and her friend used to spend the 32 kopecks doled out by their parents for school lunch on portions of ice-cream with syrup as a treat to mark the end of the school day.[63]

Other aspects of the school environment, such as the physical fabric, were likely to seem more alienating. Pupils had relatively little control over the decoration of their classrooms, though from the 1920s it was customary to compel them to engage with their surroundings by enforcing on them 'self-service' of the kind also required in orphanages: a *dezhurnyi*, or 'day orderly' would be appointed to help keep the classroom tidy, replenish the chalk, make sure the blackboard-rubber was in place, water the plants, and so on.[64] However, if it was difficult to alter the environment in a positive sense, it was easier to do this in a negative way – through vandalism. It is difficult to tell how frequent this was, but strictures against it in the school rules of various generations suggest that it constituted a persistent problem. A form of vandalism that was reported by alarmed members of authority in the early Soviet era was attacks on political cult objects, portraits of Soviet leaders in particular.[65] This may have happened at other times as well (certainly, Tsarist portraits suffered during the Revolution). There are also some records of lower-level forms of vandalism, such as defacement of desks.[66] The fact that the school was already shabby did not necessarily provoke greater outbursts of destructive instinct: children housed in a new building might treat it badly, while pupils at an apparently more modest school adopted a more protective or neutral attitude, perhaps because there was a feeling that damaged items might not be replaced.

Responses like this were of course risky: pupils might end up disciplined for 'hooliganism' or even, if attacks were made on objects of political significance, for counter-revolutionary activity. The likeliest form of rebellion against the school environment, therefore, was evasion. Pupils might, for instance, try and spend as much time as possible outside the school premises – unless the authorities had anticipated them by locking the outside doors, a strategy that was practised in some Soviet schools, especially in the Stalin era – or simply attempt to ignore their surroundings as best they could. Whichever way, they could do little to change things. In another area of material culture, however – their clothes – pupils had a little more leeway, which at times they gleefully exercised.

In the late Imperial era, pupils at primary schools were not expected to wear a uniform, but pupils at most types of secondary school were. The uniform current for boys at most types of state-supported urban day school was a miniature version of the service jacket (*mundir*) worn by adult civil servants, a Sam Browne belt, and a cap bearing the badge of their school. While the *mundir* was not, formally speaking, essential, individual headmasters sometimes unilaterally imposed it on all pupils.[67] For their part, girls, both in the 'institutes for daughters of the nobility' and in the state *gimnazii*, wore a costume based on the fashions of the early nineteenth century and consisting of a plain brown waisted dress and a frilly apron. 'Getting a uniform made' was the standard next step after a child had gained its place at secondary school, and wearing this dress seems to have carried a certain amount of pride, at least among pupils at the more prestigious kinds of secondary school (it was, after all, a badge of success). The uniform badges also successfully imparted a corporate identity, with pupils at the No. 1 *gimnaziya* in Kiev known as 'the pencils' because their caps bore emblems in roughly that shape (they were officially supposed to be olive branches).[68] For these reasons, no doubt, improvisation seems to have been limited to incidental details. Boys in some schools, for instance, took care to batter their uniform caps before they were ever worn, because, in the words of an old hand, 'only swots and creeps wear new ones'.[69] Girls' improvisation seems to have involved dressing up, rather than dressing down, such as setting one's hair in ringlets, a small form of individualism that was mercilessly curbed by school staff, who might take action even against pupils with naturally curly hair.[70] In both these cases, deviance was presumably tolerated by parents, but there were other cases where adults and home enforced the school line. Children detested the scratchy wool hoods that they were supposed to wear over their hats in the coldest weather, and open rebellion about pulling these up was 'a symptom of adolescence'.[71]

The early Soviet era saw uniform temporarily disappear as an area of disputation. Between 1918 and 1943 there was no centrally imposed, compulsory school uniform, though some ambitious city schools dictated the wearing of one on a local basis – for example, School No. 36 in Sverdlovsk had one modelled on the uniform once worn by the young ladies of Smol'nyi Institute for Daughters of the Nobility.[72] But insistence on special dress pointed to the prestige of a school's catchment, as well as to its educational prestige: the main problem for most pupils of this era, particularly in the countryside, was the struggle to find adequate clothes and footwear in which to attend school at all.

Problems of this kind continued past the official introduction of a formal national school uniform in 1943, modelled on the pre-revolutionary norm and consisting of hairy grey jackets, trousers, and a school cap for boys, and brown dresses and frilly aprons for girls. Clothing shortages no doubt lay behind the fact that, according to oral history, some pupils could get away with attending school in their own clothes, rather than in the prescribed attire.[73] Even in the most prestigious Moscow schools, most pupils made do with what their mothers could find; only the children of top officials were smartly turned out.[74] The white aprons used for high days and holidays were so scarce in one Leningrad school that pupils shared one between all of them, donning it only to have their photograph taken.[75] But while inadequacies caused by shortages might be tolerated, pupils who attempted to follow the burgeoning fashion interests of the day – the constant caricatures in the Pioneer press were some indication of how influential these were – could expect severe treatment. A woman brought up in Leningrad remembered being subjected to the punishment of being sent home to change her nylon stockings for humbler lisle or wool ones because the director objected to the former. 'The uniform was right out of date even then,' she complained.[76]

If battles of this kind between teachers and pupils were current even in the 1940s, they came to the fore in the post-Stalin era, when a general rise in the standard of living, and availability of more diverse clothing, including (on the black market) foreign makes, gave a further boost to the fashion ethos. In circumstances where, in the late 1960s, the ultimate status symbol was a pair of Western jeans,[77] uniform was widely disliked, particularly by older pupils. 'Market research' from this period indicates that uniform was unpopular on grounds of comfort as well: a survey in the late 1950s established that the stand-up collars worn by 82 per cent of older children were felt by half of those forced into them to be itchy and constrictive.[78] It was during this period that customisation really took off, though care was still required – teachers continued, as in former eras, to force pupils to correct their ways, say by yanking down the hem of an excessively short skirt, or shoving a girl's head under a tap in order to rid her of curls and make-up.[79] But minor modifications were attempted, which were at one and the same time tiny gestures of rebellion, and – for those who could afford them – parades of 'cultural capital' in terms of access to scarce, or indeed Western, goods. One former pupil at a sophisticated Leningrad school recalled that girls used to liven up the monotony with coloured tights (an item that came into the category of *defitsit*, almost impossible to buy); she herself got into a good deal of trouble for covering up her Komsomol badge with a Western badge bearing the name Jesus Christ Superstar.[80] A reform of the school uniform in the early 1970s attempted to bring the attire closer to modern tastes, but the synthetic jackets, skirts, and trousers that were introduced did not appeal any more than earlier versions. Teachers were, despite their duties as regulators of good order, sensitive to pupils' feelings: in 'extended day' schools (a type introduced in the mid-1970s that provided supervised homework sessions and leisure activities for pupils who had no one to care for them at home), uniform was not compulsory in the afternoons. Not surprisingly, regulation dress was one of the first casualties of educational liberalisation in the late 1980s.[81]

School pupils, like orphanage inmates, were exposed to a process of stripping of individual identity and the imposition of a corporate and collective spirit. For 'family' children, entering the doors of the school often brought the first contact with temporal regimentation. Few Russian children below the mid-teens had watches, even in the post-Stalin era; they would gauge time when they were playing, 'intuitively'.[82] In the school, however, they encountered a day marked out by bells, which might have a shock effect on those unused to it. As a man born in the 1880s who continued his education, after a village primary school, in the city, remembered: 'They sound the bell downstairs and I rush up to the person sounding it. But then what? It turns out that he isn't ringing for pupils to gather round him, but so they know it's time for bed.'[83]

Hygienic procedures might also convey the sense of a new world. Medical inspections, at which pupils were weighed, measured, and examined for parasitic infestations, could function not only as practical, neutral observation, but as forms of ritual disempowerment. 'You turn up with your head shaved to the bone and they check you over for lice and that,' one Leningrad man recalled of his schooldays after the Second World War.[84] Pupils after the war were treated in a rather less rough-and-ready fashion, but none the less the process was more reminiscent of a conveyor belt than anything else: 'They just wanted to tick the box and get you out,' one woman recalled of the 1970s and 1980s.[85] Remembered with uniform horror by all were inoculations and, most especially, visits to the dentist, which, like medical inspections, were compulsory and brusque: mass drilling and filling (without anaesthetic) was the order of the day.[86] Though evidence on the effects of medical inspections at earlier periods is elusive, it is fair to assume that those exposed to them reacted in much the same way as to contacts with the medical world more generally.

Many schoolchildren found at least some encounters with the school daunting. An entire folk tradition dealt with appropriate techniques for placating fate so that one would avoid disaster within the building – knotting handkerchiefs to avoid being asked difficult questions in class, always coming to school by the same route, wearing old clothes for examinations to bring good luck.[87] At the same time, seeing children as the inert victims of the school environment would be misleading. Medical inspections ensured a level of basic care for those whose parents failed to check up on cleanliness and well-being, and targeted cases of malnutrition. Uniforms provided acceptable clothing for families who could afford little for their younger members. And children themselves could get involved in the process of regimentation through environment and material culture. Some were just as assiduous as adults in imposing the hygiene and dress regulations that the school authorities required. For others, acting as a classroom orderly was enjoyable, rather than a chore: 'It was our home [zhilishche], and if we did anything to it, we did it properly, otherwise there was no point to begin with,' a Moscow woman who started school in 1978 remembered.[88] Promptings like this led young people to participate in the 'sanitary commissions' set up by decree on 25 March 1920,[89] and act as custodians of their peers.

In any case, school life was not meant simply to *deprive* and *repress*. It was meant to provide pupils with a positive sense of their own identity as pupils, a feeling of corporate solidarity, and a grasp of the way the school differed from the rest of the world on a higher level – a metaphysical level, one might almost say. This particular side of school life was captured through ritual and ceremonial, which was used both to bracket off the start and end of school time from time considered more broadly, and to mark specific high points within that school year.

Threshold Rituals

For more than fifty years under Soviet power (and indeed beyond – this occasion is one of the few Soviet festivals to have survived the collapse of the system that spawned it), children's official welcome to school took the form of the 'Day of Knowledge' or 'First Bell' festival held on the first of September every year. Not a public holiday in the sense that workplaces were closed, this was definitely a festive day. Children, and most particularly those entering Class I, arrived at their *alma mater* wearing party clothes and clutching bunches of flowers (gladioli were especially popular), accompanied by their parents, who often took commemorative photographs. The entire school would be lined up in some place suitable for ceremonial rallies: possibly the school yard or assembly hall, or, if room here were insufficient, some convenient local venue such as a cinema. Here a 'festive assembly' (*prazdnichnaya lineika*) would be held, at which the school director was likely to 'say something about our duty to study well and about the Party and the government'.[90]

103   1 September, Sverdlovsk, 1947.

The foundations for the holiday were laid in 1935, when legislation harmonised the dates of school vacations right across the Soviet Union.[91] Thereafter, children were allowed to register at new schools on other dates only in the most exceptional circumstances (such as when parents were forced to move to a new city for work reasons).[92] The First of September was from the start not just a bureaucratic boundary, but also a ritual occasion. Even before the harmonising law had time to take effect, in September 1935 an illustrated report appeared in *Pravda*, showing 'The First Lesson' at Karl Liebknecht School, Kropotkinskaya Street, Moscow.[93] The following year, considerably more extensive coverage appeared, with space given to several different 'human interest' stories from both Moscow and Leningrad.[94] Thereafter – with the obvious exception of the war years – stories about the start of the new year, with pictures of clean, well-dressed, beaming infants, were a fixture in the Soviet press around the start of September.[95] Samuil Marshak's poem, 'The First of September' (1935), a staple in anthologies intended for 'younger schoolchildren', rammed home the pan-Soviet resonance of the new festival:

> The First
>   of September!
> The First
>   of September!
> The First
>   of September –
> Is a date
>   To remember –
>
> Because on that day
> All the little girls
> And all the little boys
> In cities and towns
> And villages all around,
> Took their bags
> And their books
> And their lunches
> Under their arms,
> And rushed off as fast as they could
> For the first time to school!
>
> This happened in Barnaul,
> In Leningrad,
> In Torzhok,
> In Blagoveshchensk,
> And in Tula,
> On the Don,
> And on the Oka,
> In Cossack stanitsas,
> In Caucasian auls,
> And in Central Asian kishlaks.[96]

Geographical range was held together by temporal homogeneity. The perception was that schoolchildren all over the Soviet empire could be found doing the same thing at the same time. Time zones were not taken into consideration. Nor was the fact that many schools, right through the Soviet period, operated a shift system, according to which some children studied in the afternoon or indeed in the evening. In the late 1930s, for instance, 80 per cent of Soviet schools were

104 Still from *The Girl from Class One*, showing Marusya's first day at school.

still running at least a second shift. Loss of school stock during wartime, and the requisitioning of buildings for non-educational purposes,[97] made the situation much worse. During the 1930s and 1940s, schools not operating a shift system were rare and privileged: they included such flagship Moscow establishments as School No. 25 and School No. 175.[98] The multi-shift system persisted into the post-Stalin era too, though it seems to have become rare in the bigger cities.[99] A morning shift from 8 a.m. to 2 p.m. would be followed by an evening shift from 3 p.m. to 9 p.m.; where a third shift was in operation, this ran from 5 p.m. to 11 p.m., with the first and second shifts pushed forward to accommodate it.[100] Diligent pupils who did their homework in the morning were likely to be over-tired by the middle of the second shift; children left unsupervised while both parents worked could avoid homework altogether if they wished. In the words of a boy who studied on the second shift in the 1960s and 1970s, 'You can't get a thing done. In the mornings, you just want to sleep. By the time you've done this and that, and inspected your territory, and eaten an ice-cream ... it's nice to have an ice-cream now and again. You'd just get nothing at all done. Well, unless your parents were sitting over you, in which case you'd be boring the pants off yourself doing your lessons ...'[101]

Poor work discipline was not the worst hazard of the shift system. Schoolchildren coming back from the late shift, especially girls, could be in actual physical danger. In the Siberian city of Stalinsk (Novokuznetsk) in the autumn of 1937, a gang of seven youths, including two boys of school age, staked out School No. 25, and carried out a series of rapes and attempted rapes on girls returning from evening lessons. There were extremely serious assaults on two 17-year-olds, one of whom was attacked as she returned home at eleven in the evening, dragged into the cellar of a hostel, and multiply raped, and the second of whom was both raped and so severely beaten that she was hospitalised for ten days. The attacks, understandably, so terrified other girls that they began refusing to attend school at all, or taking evasive action by leaving before the end of classes and departing via the back door of the school.[102]

Inconvenient realities of this kind were ignored in representations of the First of September, though, where the welcome given to new pupils stood for the unity of the nation and the harmony of its temporal boundaries. Schooldays were reliably always the same, and in the safe monotony of their activities children provided an exemplum for adults.

The First of September was an integrated, national festival, a 'Day of Knowledge' bringing the entire educating and educated population together. Stalinist in its origins, it was consolidated and boosted in the 1960s, when a renewed anti-religious drive was accompanied by a propaganda campaign promoting non-religious social festivals – birthdays, weddings, ceremonies accompanying the issuing of the Soviet passport (national identity card), first day at work parties.[103] It was at once official and genuinely popular: for most mothers and fathers, accompanying one's nervous and excited seven-year-old to school was a major day, demanding advance preparation and commemoration in the family album.

Nothing on this scale had previously existed in Russian history. The sheer diversity of schools before 1917 ruled out a celebration of this integrational kind. However, institutions did mark the beginning of the school year in their own way, normally by holding some kind of religious ceremony. The most pompous celebrations were in secondary schools such as *gimnazii*, where prayers and a sermon would be accompanied by a speech from the director and probably from the school inspector as well.[104] Children who began attending school at the start of the educational year would find that their first day coincided with this occasion. After having their names recorded by the teacher in the school roll, the formal ceremony would start: 'Eventually the priest arrived and the prayers began. After they had finished, the priest blessed us, and told us to study well, to pray to God for success, and we went home, having been told lessons would begin the next day.'[105] Most new boys and girls would be carefully dressed by parents, either in their new uniforms or else in their best clothes.[106] But pupils at village primary schools often began attending at some quite different time of year, simply arriving in the classroom on an ordinary day. As Mikhail Kol'chenko recalled of his experience in the late 1890s: 'When we arrived, [my friend] took me into the classroom, where he showed me the various pictures hanging on the wall. I looked at them with great attention. About ten minutes later the reverend deacon arrived – we didn't have a teacher then, for some reason, and the deacon took classes instead. He saw me and said, 'So we've got a new boy, have we?' And then he asked me who had sent me along and so on, and I gave what answers I could.'[107]

This downbeat sort of experience continued into the 1920s, when children might still be signed on at more or less any time of the year. Even if children arrived on the official start date, there would be no ceremony. 'I started attending school in 1927, and the beginning of the year wasn't marked in any way. We just arrived, they took down our names, and lessons started right away. There were no festivals of any kind.'[108] A child's relations might dress it in new clothes, but the initial contact itself consisted of no more than enrolment and departure for a classroom. It was family and friends who were likely to feel that the day was special.[109]

The history of the rituals marking the other end of the school year, the beginning of the holidays, had, by contrast, more continuity. It was a legal requirement of the *gimnaziya* that each year should end with a formal assembly (*akt*), at which a report on the year's work would be read out, lists of those allowed to progress upwards to the next form would be announced, and prizes and matriculation certificates would be distributed.[110] This event was usually held in the autumn, so that candidates who had failed could resit their examinations before it took place. But there were also less formal ceremonies with which the school 'signed off'. The end of the school year inspired genuine joy in the vast majority of pupils, even if they had positive feelings about their studies – as a boy born in the late 1880s recalled, 'The most glorious day for us was the day we were let out for the summer holidays.'[111]

Unofficial celebrations of the end of the school year continued after 1917 too. Anna Grigorova's schoolgirl diary of 1928 records that the end of the year was marked by an evening of amateur dramatics, choral songs, and even a performance by a jazz band.[112] A few years later (to accompany the reintroduction of formal examinations), the occasion was given an official status. In May 1935, a Narkompros order was published decreeing that 'children's festivals' should be held to mark the end of the school year on 25 May, including a report by the school director on what had gone on during the year (to last not more than twenty minutes), presentation of prizes to the best pupils, and of school-leaving certificates, and a concert or other such performance.[113] On 1 June 1935, the graduation of the first cohort from the new ten-year schools was marked in Moscow by an elaborate meeting in the Hall of Columns of the Union Building, presided over by Sergei Bubnov, the Commissar of Education.[114] In the course of time, the occasion, known as 'The Last Bell', become associated with numerous other rituals. Like the First of September, it involved the participation of the whole school, but was particularly concentrated on one group of pupils, in this case those who had just completed their ten-year stint of education and were about to sit their examinations. An important part of the ceremony was the ringing of the last bell itself, which in some schools was done by the smallest female pupil, who was carried to the bell in the arms, or on the shoulder, of the tallest school-leaver.[115]

After the 'Last Bell' followed another, more pompous kind of celebration, the 'school-leavers' ball'. This, too, as a phenomenon on a national scale, was essentially a creation of the Stalin years. In 1936, the Flower Festival in Kiev, organised at the behest of Pavel Postyshev, the Secretary of the Ukrainian Communist Party as well as of the Central Committee itself, included a celebration of the end of the school year with boat trips, a sports festival, and a leavers' ball in the Pioneer

Palace.[116] However, the start of the new tradition was hampered by the outbreak of war,[117] and it was not until the late 1940s that the 'leavers' ball' appears to have become fully established. (Significantly, this was a time when ballroom dancing – in some cases accompanied by instructions to the participants that the opposite sexes should not speak to one another, or even that they should hold hands only through a handkerchief – became a popular leisure activity.)

The leavers' ball continued to be a fixture of the school calendar in the post-Stalin era. But, in a new cultural context, it had shifted in significance. In terms of official literature, this had now become an exercise in 'conspicuous consumption', with much advice being parcelled out on clothes and hairdos.[118] Obviously, this development impaired the ball's status as a show of corporate solidarity. In addition, the 'cognitive dissonance' of the era made itself felt here, as everywhere else. For some, it was still a special occasion: 'it was wonderful [...] they let us drink cider. I've got photos of myself in a dress, with flowers. And they gave out certificates and medals, and then there was a table laid in the school hall.'[119] But not everyone reacted with such enthusiasm: changing tastes made their mark. In many schools, a formal waltz was still an essential part of the occasion; yet, unlike their contemporaries in, say, Austria, Russian young people of the post-Stalin era were not taught ballroom dancing, and by the 1960s rock and pop would have been their preferred music anyway. For many, the whole evening was overshadowed by the imminent school-leaving exams, which took place in the weeks after 25 May. It was essential to get good marks in these, across a formidable range of subjects, to qualify for university entrance. Young men in particular were likely to be in a state of anxiety, since failing to gain a place at university meant that it was impossible to avoid conscription into the Soviet army. At the best of times, this fate was undesirable, since army life was physically demanding and psychologically brutal; after the Afghan war began in 1980, it meant risking death or disablement, and was to be avoided at all costs.[120]

If pupils did want to mark the end of school, the most memorable part of the proceedings was what happened after the official ceremonials were over: the informal celebrations with friends, including, by this stage, perhaps a boyfriend or girlfriend.[121] Independent parties would in any case have been going on for several years before the 'Last Bell' was heard. So far as the school administration was concerned, the end of Class 8 was of no particular significance: those going on to a *tekhnikum* or PTU 'left quietly and without any fuss'.[122] But, for the pupils actually moving on, it was obviously a significant occasion; and for those who stayed, the end of Class 8 brought not only separation from those leaving, but the completion of the first set of state exams. Not surprisingly, this is often remembered as a young person's first experience of drinking alcohol in quantity, possibly to excess, and first 'grown-up'-style party as well.

Registration and Entrance Tests

Though the First of September ceremony gave the impression that children had entered the school as if by magic (and it had that effect upon many of its participants), it was not the first occasion on which children would have visited the school building. Several weeks before the First of September, parents had to take a child along to the school, accompanied by a pile of identity papers and certificates, in order to get him or her formally registered. This, rather different, occasion represented most children's first contact (if they had never ended up in a hospital or an orphanage) with the formidable sifting apparatus of the Soviet bureaucracy, its capacity to reduce a person to a pile of paper (and to treat all on-paper irregularities with punitive disapprobation). From 1935, schools were required to keep a personal file on every pupil, and in this the documents, as well as a lengthy form completed by the child's parents, would duly be docketed.[123]

Registration had, of course, been necessary well before the First of September was instituted in 1935. Before 1917, however, it had simply involved turning up and signing on – not necessarily at the start of the school year. 'The time had come for me to go to school. It was 3 October 1894. My father took me to school in the morning, the teacher wrote my name down in the book, and there I was with my new companions in my new surroundings', Maksim Kotlyarov, from Tomsk province, recalled in the 1900s.[124] For a few years after 1917, even this formality was not officially required (though no doubt most schools kept their own records), but on 29 August 1923 preliminary registration was again stipulated, and official school record books (*dnevniki*) were reintroduced.[125] However, a precise date for registration – 20–5 August in villages, and 15–25 August in towns – was only set ten years later.[126]

During the early Soviet era, even if pupils did sign on as officially required, the procedure tended to introduce them to a salient, though from an official point of view shameful, characteristic of the Soviet system: its capacity for disorganisation, if not chaos. According to a report in *Leninist Sparks* from 1929:

> The first table you get to, they ask, 'Which street are you from?' 'Nizhegorodskaya Street.' 'Well, then you're in the wrong place. You should take your boy to School no. 162 on the Vyborg Side.' Slopping through the mud, Volodya has to drag all the way over to the reception point on Vyborg Side.

Poor information bedevilled the process: people were not informed that they must register at a reception centre in their own district, nor were they told that registration would not be performed unless a document certifying age was produced.[127] At the very least, the changes of the Stalin era made it more likely that parents would know where to take their package of documents, and what it should consist of; they could also have more confidence that the items would be properly filed once handed over.[128] Whichever way, the child might make contact for the first time with a new, official self: registration might be the first time that he or she had come across the concept of a surname. 'They asked me, "What's your surname?"', remembered a man from Novgorod province, born in 1925. '"How am I supposed to know what a surname is?" "Well, what's your dad's name?" "Gavrya." "Well, then you're Gavrilov."' Thus the boy ended up with what was not actually his surname but a back-formation from his father's forename.[129]

Initial contact with the school could also take another form: the sitting of a test or examination designed to assess a child's capabilities. This was the standard first experience of educational life for a good many secondary-school pupils in the Russian Empire. Indeed, even some rural primary teachers would carry out informal assessments, attempting to work out how much a child knew about reading, writing, and religion so as to get a grasp of his or her educational needs. Sometimes, children who already had some skills were placed immediately in the second form. As Mikhail Kol'chenko recalled of his first day at school in the 1890s: 'The teacher gently sat me at the desk, and the religious knowledge class started. There were only five pupils, and I was the sixth. I can still remember how I spent the first day. Before we got to learning letters, arithmetic and the other subjects, the teacher asked me, "How many gods are there?" But I wasn't foxed: my parents had told me a bit about God at home, so I said, "There is one God, but he has three persons." And then I got asked to recite prayers aloud and so on.'[130]

In this case, the assessment happened in a friendly spirit, but much more formidable tests had to be passed by those entering the state *gimnaziya*, consisting of dictation (laced with examples forcing the candidates to discriminate between *e* and *yat*, two vowels that sounded identical but looked utterly different), arithmetic, and oral tests in Russian, a foreign language, geography, history, and religious knowledge. To judge by memoirs, this was an occasion that children dreaded, the minute details of which stayed with them all their lives. 'My heart turned to an icicle, and my head filled up with a fug like the one in [a local pancake bar],' Anatoly Mariengof graphically remembered.[131] Even passing the examination might not end the ordeal: for Jewish pupils seeking entry to the state *gimnaziya*, it was essential to obtain outstanding marks if they were to force their way into the small quota of pupils allowed to attend this type of school, so the stress felt by these entrants was likely to be still higher. While lesser types of publicly-funded secondary school set less intimidating tests, they still represented a great hurdle. Often a sort of 'tie-breaker' system was in operation, and an apparently straightforward exercise had a hidden catch that children had to puzzle out. Fedor Panferov, for instance, remembered sitting what appeared to be a simple dictation when he applied to a seminary in the late 1900s. Candidates who merely wrote down the words 'cup, slip, lip' in fact failed, no matter how neat their handwriting and accurate their spelling. It was only candidates who realised that they needed to rearrange the words as the proverb 'There's many a slip 'twixt cup and lip' who in fact gained places at the seminary.[132] Laxer standards obtained only in paying establishments, which in some cases – Viktor Shklovsky's St Petersburg establishment included – appear to have taken pretty well anyone who walked through the doors,[133] though entry to some other private schools (for example, the Tenishev College in St Petersburg) was strictly linked to merit.

A not unjustified belief that tests of this kind placed invidious stress on children sitting them made them anathema to educational reformers, and, with the foundation of the 'Unified School of Labour' in 1918, they were officially abolished. Nevertheless, numerous schools did continue to set tests on an individual basis during the 1920s. The new discipline of 'p[a]edology' held it necessary to tailor education to a child's 'mental age', and hence checks were made on this using such devices as gap-filling exercises, comprehension tests, and what would now be described as 'tick-box' assessments (where the child selected from a number of solutions by underlining the correct one). One test from 1927 went like this:

> The crest of the Soviet Union (*pause*). Is it the Hammer and Sickle, the two-headed eagle, the cross? Which answer is right?[134]

Tests were also favoured by teachers for practical reasons: there was a huge variety of attainment levels evident amongst new entrants. Some had, by the age of eight, been reading independently for several years, while others had not, which made it essential to group children in different streams. But the outlawing of p[a]edology in 1936 put an end to entrance testing. It was silently assumed now that all children would have reached the same level at the age of eight, or seven, when that became the official age for entrance to school in 1943. Tests were resurrected only in the 1960s, when special schools began using them to select for admissions, and then according to local, rather than national, arrangements.[135]

Managing the Classroom

Admission to the school as institution made up only part of the process of arrival in the new environment. The child also had to be allocated to a new class and to make his or her way into this new group (or, in the Soviet term, 'collective'). Before the Revolution, when schools were smaller (400 in the largest institutions, such as *gimnazii*), year groups were normally not subdivided: the main problem here was adjusting to the other children within one particular group of forty or so pupils. 'At school, at first I felt intimidated by the other pupils: they pressed round me and laughed at the various things that were wrong with me,' Spiridon Kozlov recalled of his first day at school in the mid-1890s.[136] Teasing and taunting of this kind was especially likely in secondary school, when children who had been taught at home would be mixed up with children who had already attended the preparatory department of the institution, not to speak of 'repeaters' (*vtorogodniki*), who – in boys' schools particularly – formed cynical, battle-weary cliques that liked nothing better than giving newcomers a hard time.

It is fair to assume that this sort of rough welcome continued into the 1920s and early 1930s, given that social conflict was very evident in other areas of school existence, such as life on the playground, at the time.[137] But the harmonisation of the school start dates put an end to territorial conflicts between different age groups within the same class, at least in cities. (In village schools such conflicts remained possible, since the usual structure at primary level was cross-age groups consisting of two or even three conventional classes.) For pupils in a large 'general education' school in a major city, the stresses of encountering prejudice had been replaced by stresses of other kinds. Schools in larger cities were often very big – around 1,000 pupils was a standard number – with the result that there would be several parallel groups in each year. Whether rightly or wrongly, parents were

105   School classroom, Leningrad, late 1920s.

likely to believe that some teachers taking the groups were better than others, and – if they were preoccupied with educational advantage – to do their best to ensure that their child got placed in the 'best' group.[138]

Being sent to the classroom brought with it a shift from a festival atmosphere to an ordinary day. From the beginning, the children would be treated with insistent, though not always unbending, authority on the part of their teacher:

> At the first lesson we all sat as quiet as mice listening and the lesson … the first piece of homework we got – I can remember as though it were yesterday – was to learn the Soviet national anthem by heart. And I found that very difficult, of course I'd learned poems by heart in the kindergarten, but not such long ones. I remember that I didn't find learning it by heart much fun, but I did manage. […] True, we never got tested on it afterwards, which was a bit of a let-down.[139]

The festive side of the First of September acted as a boundary between school life and the world of home, family, and nursery school; the first lesson introduced children to the daily life of the school itself, to the need for stillness and silence, and for work on learning by heart.

At whatever era they began school, children might well encounter formal naming patterns here for the first time. Standard practice throughout the twentieth century was to refer to pupils by their surnames: 'Ivanov! To the blackboard';[140] a teacher might be the first person whom a child had ever addressed by his or her name and patronymic, as opposed to an affectionate nickname such as 'Aunty Olya' (the style for nursery teachers). While teachers were definitely 'You' in the plural and with a capital letter, pupils were 'thou'. Only in the top classes might particularly liberal pedagogues display a sense of egalitarianism by referring to their charges by the formal variant of the second person.

All of these things – the reinforcement of academic skills through rote-learning, the emphasis on patriotic texts, and intensive discipline – were characteristic of Russian classroom life for most of the century between 1890 and 1991. In pre-revolutionary Russian schools, to be sure, discipline was sometimes maintained rather differently from the ways that prevailed in the classroom just evoked. Primary school teachers who were liberally inclined might treat their pupils with a fair degree of informality, making early contacts with school fascinating, rather than daunting. As Spiridon Kozlov recalled: 'On the day I began studying, the teacher gave me a slate, taught me the letter A, and showed me how to write it; the next day she gave me an alphabet book, which interested me more than anything, because there were lots of pictures in it.'[141] For another boy from the same generation, it was the teacher's behaviour that was the biggest shock: 'Imagine my surprise when the teacher, instead of ordering, "Everyone kneel down!" (as my friends' stories had suggested) came up and gently asked me my name. I shyly answered. He said some more words of encouragement and gave me a place at the back.'[142] Normative sources were starting to underline the need for sympathetic treatment too: one alphabet book published in 1890 suggested to teachers that they should start by teaching the letter 'A' because 'A?' [Eh?] was the answer most people gave in the countryside when anyone said their name.[143]

However, many teachers – if memoirs are anything to go by – enforced discipline harshly. Viktor Kravchenko, who attended primary school in Zaporozh'e during the 1910s, recalled that 'corporal punishment for slackness and inattention was a matter of course, and regarded as an essential ingredient in a boy's education'. The usual method adopted was thrashing on the bare bottom with a rod, with the teacher's pet sometimes drafted in to help out if the numbers of those requiring punishment were large.[144] Or a child's ears might be boxed, sometimes – as in the case of one parish priest in the late 1880s – with shouted threats of 'I'll beat the devil out of you' to add to the effect.[145] More 'humane' teachers stopped short of this, but might well give children a sharp slap with a ruler or make them kneel on the floor.[146]

Especially brutal methods were by all accounts adopted in some religious schools. The writer Vladimir Bill'-Belotserkovsky, who attended a *heder* (traditional Hebrew school) in a southern provincial town, was subjected, along with his classmates, to a whole range of punishments: thrashing with a leather strap, standing in the corner with his trousers down, having soot wiped over his face. And Pavlo Tychina, who spent several years at the Trinity Monastery choir school in Chernigov, remembered that errant boys were not only thrashed for every offence, however minor, but usually deprived of their food, the unwanted scraps from the monks' table, into the bargain.[147] At best, teachers were likely to insist on rote-learning, display indifference to their pupils' welfare, and dole out low marks on every possible occasion.[148] Schools attached to mosques appear to have been much the same.[149]

In such circumstances, children who completed three or four years of primary school could be described as plucky as well as fortunate. But by the late nineteenth century, there were some schools where conditions were better. Corporal punishment was relatively rare in Ministry of Enlightenment schools (after his *heder*, Bill'-Belotserkovsky remembered, the occasional mild slap on the neck administered in his city primary school came as a pleasant surprise).[150] And even Pavlo Tychina's dreadful choir school improved when a young seminarian appointed as the boys' tutor and hostel supervisor replaced beatings and insults by encouraging the boys to clean up their dormitory, organising them into running a friendly society, and treating them to occasional trips to the circus.[151] By 1912, a survey of zemstvo schools in Voronezh district, Voronezh province, was able to assert that no corporal punishment at all was in use: the methods of dealing with disciplinary offences were detention (38 schools), standing a child in the corner (14), a strict talking-to (9), and sending out of the class (7).[152]

Regulation of pupils' lives took incentive forms as well. The primary syllabus placed enormous stress on fidelity to the Tsarist regime and on piety. The texts set for beginning readers in one much-reprinted primer of the late nineteenth and early twentieth centuries included a poem with the title 'The King of Heaven', improving tales about animals, and 'The Sixth of May', which drew children's attention to an important annual holiday:

> On the Sixth of May the whole of Russia celebrates the birthday of His Imperial Majesty Tsar Nikolai Aleksandrovich [Nicholas II]; on this royal day the pupils are permitted not to attend lessons. In all the churches the people pray for the Tsar and His Family. The inhabitants of cities and villages decorate their homes with flags. In the evening of the same day, illuminations take place on the streets of cities.[153]

Among the earliest texts taught were prayers and religious precepts, alongside material relating to ethical standards and patriotic poems and songs.

The trajectory of maintaining discipline ran differently in secondary schools. Corporal punishment was officially forbidden from 1874, but Russian secondary schools had a formidable array of other disciplinary weapons to be used against the insubordinate. Pupils might be sentenced to detention after school, their names might be recorded in the conduct book, or *konduit*, or they might be given a low mark for conduct. Anything less than the top marks of 4 and 5 already looked questionable: a 1 meant that the pupil would be placed under police surveillance and have problems with university entrance. A truly recalcitrant pupil could be deprived of normal identity papers and issued an outlaw's docket, the so-called 'wolf's passport' (though in practice this could misfire, as a pupil holding such a passport had no incentive at all to behave well).[154]

Behaviour regulation in secondary schools was incentive and preventive, as well as punitive. Each day began with a formal assembly, including prayers and moral guidance; concerned that this was not enough, the school authorities passed a measure introducing more frequent prayers in 1911.[155] Both at the *gimnaziya* and at the *real'noe uchilishche*, pupils had to attend church twice a week (on Sunday and for Saturday evening vespers), and their deportment in church would be severely scrutinised.[156] There was close supervision of behaviour in secular contexts as well, both in and outside the school. A formidable set of school rules, first promulgated in 1874 but remaining in place till the Revolution, dictated punctuality in all respects, 'unquestioning' obedience to teachers, who had to be formally greeted on the street as well as in the classroom, politeness to schoolmates, and the avoidance of *outré* dress such as canes, whiskers, beards, and moustaches; a whole list of public venues, such as 'masquerades, clubs, tea-houses, coffee-houses, confectioners' shops, billiard rooms and other such places' had to be eschewed. Errant pupils were subjected to a range of punishments, including reprimands in private or public, being made to sit in isolation during class, detention, detention during the holidays, a formal reprimand from the school inspector, a formal reprimand from the school director, a formal reprimand from the pedagogical council, and incarceration in the school punishment cell.[157]

In girls' schools, the *klassnaya dama* (a Russian translation of the French, *dame de classe*) was responsible for overseeing deportment as well as discipline. Pupils were exhorted not to raise their voices, to respond with full sentences rather than mere phrases, to dress appropriately, and to behave in a 'ladylike' manner at all times.[158] In boys' schools, the *klassnyi nastavnik*, or 'class overseer', had a similar function. Teachers at city *gimnazii* maintained elaborate rotas in parks, stations, and other places of public resort in order to place under 'citizen's arrest' any schoolboys found misbehaving.[159] They also hectored their pupils on morals and manners. Paustovsky remembered such a teacher setting little etiquette problems in class: what would a 'polite man' do if he saw a woman come into a room with her eyes red from weeping?[160] The moral-education side of *gimnaziya* education was entertainingly satirised in Sasha Chernyi's serial *Micky the Fox-Terrier's Diary* (written when Chernyi was an *émigré* in Paris), where the dog hero suffered an appalling dream: 'Help, what's this! I've turned into the headmaster of a *gimnaziya* for dogs. The pups all sit round the classroom studying "the lives of famous dogs", "the rules of good canine behaviour", "how to eat marrowbones" and other suitable materials.'[161]

As Chernyi's story illustrates, the academic syllabus of the secondary school was pervaded with the goals of moral education. Pupils were supposed to learn not only about trigonometry and Latin verbs, but also to absorb acceptance of their place in a world subordinated to the authority of God and Tsar. Religious knowledge was a compulsory part of the state secondary school programme (though children who were not of the Orthodox faith were permitted to attend classes held by a minister of religion of their own). All subjects had to be addressed in a politically unexceptionable way, as V. N. Shubkin, a *gimnaziya* teacher working in the Siberian town of Barnaul, recorded in his diary in the early 1910s:

I have to mark the essays not only in terms of factual accuracy and spelling, but of political orthodoxy, and not just orthodoxy from the point of view of the police (that would be fine), but from the point of view of official perceptions of what school teaching should be doing. I keep coming across phrases like 'the cruel suppression of the Decembrist Rebellion', 'the social thought of the 1840s, subject as it was to severe censorship', or 'then the reaction set in, and Nicholas I kept the whole of society subject to strict repression'. It's all perfectly correct in a scholarly sense, and unobjectionable even from a police point of view, but as a teacher I have to remember that it might fall into the hands of the administration and be held against me, so I have to write fierce objections in the margins and cross out all phrases of this kind, as though I didn't agree with them myself.[162]

The syllabus, indeed, sought where possible to avoid tempting pupils into comments of this kind. Inflammatory modern texts such as the novels of Tolstoy and Dostoevsky were left off the literature programme, and the literature of classical Greece and Rome, which could have presented readers with dangerously libertarian ideas, was treated essentially as the material for grammatical analysis. A mechanical approach to material was also encouraged by the standard method of conducting a class. A teacher would begin with examination of the material set for homework, calling on the pupils individually by surname to stand and regurgitate information ('Ivanov! Write on the blackboard the aorist, third person singular, of the verb *prothein!*'). Once this initial part of the class was concluded, he or she would then proceed to exposure of new material (once again, in a formal and regimented style), and finally set further homework to be regurgitated in the next class.

Liberal teachers were stymied not just by the ideological expectations of the Tsarist school, but also by the marks system. Performance, both oral and written, had to be assessed according to a scale ranging from 1 to 5, where 1 was seldom awarded, 2 was considered disgraceful, and, though 3 ostensibly equated with 'satisfactory', the minimum respectable mark was 4. (Some women's secondary schools used a more elaborate system ranging from 1 to 12, but the 1 to 5 ranking prevailed, and was the system recognised in pupil folklore and in society at large.) At end of year assessments, pupils needed to get marks of 'satisfactory' or above in all subjects if they were not to repeat the year. It was in practice a good deal easier to assign grades for strictly factual answers (the names of the tributaries of the Volga) or for regurgitations of a textbook (Evgeny Onegin as a 'superfluous man', as in Ovsyaniko-Kulikovsky's history of Russian literature) than it was to grade a contentious topic – say, a discussion of why Pushkin's poetry should have been so bare of metaphors or whether *Oblomov* was a good novel.

The examination system also worked to enforce conformity. True, essays allowed a little more room for self-expression, but a significant proportion of marks was attached to grammar and syntax, rather than to content.[163] There was a heavy dependence on oral examinations that were conducted in a way similar to 'oral testing' in the classroom, only more daunting because the pupil would be lined up to face an entire tribunal. Candidates would draw a 'ticket' setting out questions to be answered, and would be given a small amount of time to collect their thoughts before reciting all that they knew. Whether assessment was oral or written, the expectation was that answers would be accurate, informative, and neatly presented, and not that they should display original thinking. The presence of external inspectors not only made candidates more nervous, but contributed to the drive in the direction of homogeneity. Dmitry Kuznetsov, born in 1888, recalled in a 1907 memoir the terror inspired by the final examinations at his village primary school, and his humiliation at the hands of the Elabuga visiting inspector, Prince Vyazemsky, for misjudging the content of a regulation essay:

> Suddenly I heard the same deep bass as at the beginning [of the examination] say, 'Kuznetsov!' My heart seemed to turn over at the word. I got up and staggering like a drunk, walked up to the table. When they began asking the questions, I began calming down bit by bit. Then, after they had finished with me, they started questioning the other pupils. When they had finished, I was, to my great astonishment, called to the table again. I walked up, shaking with fear, and came to a stop some distance away. The examiner addressed these words to me: 'My boy, your essay has turned out the best, but it is most iniquitous that its subject should be a fight.' And he began reprimanding me. His voice rose higher and higher until he was almost shouting. Everyone froze at the sound of it: the pupils sat hardly daring to breathe. And what had caused this outburst was my essay, the description of a not very serious fight. I stood pale as a ghost, not daring to move a muscle. He put the essay in his pocket, and made me write another.[164]

Occasions like this put pressure on teachers as well as pupils, and, not surprisingly, there were many who chose to stick to a narrowly official definition of their duties. The critic Dmitry Svyatopolk-Mirsky remembered with despair 'our own inept exercises [in psychological commentaries on *Evgeny Onegin*] written for philistine and obtuse schoolmasters'.[165] For one master at Konstantin Paustovsky's *gimnaziya*, the only measure of writers' merit was whether they were 'reliable', politically speaking, or not.[166] Others taught language in an equally mechanical way: Ardalion Peredonov in Sologub's *A Low-Grade Demon* (1902) thinks of his pupils as 'machines for dragging pen-and-ink across paper and for the rephrasing in filing-cabinet language of what had once been written in ordinary human words'.[167] Though the paranoid Peredonov, who tried at one point to glue to the hall floor the hairy beast that appeared to him in his delirium tremens, was an exaggerated emanation of his creator's satirical genius, his view of the conformist bureaucrat as the ideal product, as well as his poisonous dislike for his pupils, were matched in real-life cases.[168]

Yet, as Shubkin's diary illustrates, there were also, by the late Imperial era, many teachers and educationalists who took a much broader view of teaching and who did all they could to make their subject appeal to the children in their classes. Innovative methods adopted by Shubkin and like-minded colleagues included organising festivals celebrating the work of recent writers (such as Tolstoy and Dostoevsky) to act as a counterweight to the official jubilees for Gogol', Pushkin, and other figures whom the educational establishment saw as belonging to the safely distant past. Literature lessons were turned into real discussion sessions: a class on *Anna Karenina*, for instance, consisted of an oral presentation by one pupil, followed by lively debates, with contributions from the floor.[169] Efforts of this kind were by no means unique. Russian literature classes are recorded by many memoirists, no matter what type of school they attended, as among the highlights of school existence.[170] Pedagogical luminaries of the period included Innokenty Annensky, who was not only a university-trained classicist and specialist in literary history, but also a published poet and essayist, and among whose pupils were several poets, most notably Nikolai Gumilev, one of the founders of the Acmeist movement.

Teachers' capacity for 'personal' input was something of which educational officials were aware, and to which they were not necessarily opposed. When a wide-ranging reworking of the literature syllabus was being prepared in 1905, the officials responsible for organising it openly canvassed teachers, through local 'pedagogical councils', for their opinions on which texts should and should not be included in the new specification. They received widespread opinions in favour of reducing pre-1800 material and allowing more recent writing, with many citing Tolstoy and Dostoevsky as glaring omissions.[171] The officials did not, in the end, satisfy all the demands from the grass roots, but the act of soliciting their views was in itself important. Significant, too, was the amount of leeway left in the final programme for individual interpretation – a point that struck at least one contemporary commentator, V. M. Istrin, as regrettable. The syllabus co-ordinators had recognised that rank-and-file literature teachers might not be ideally prepared, he noted: why, in that case, had they not provided detailed guidance for the sort of provincial bumpkin who might otherwise be assuring his pupils that Raskol'nikov really *was* a superman whom only mischance had cheated of his destiny?[172] In the event, the fact that guidance remained in short supply at least allowed gifted literature teachers to operate without what one might term 'preventive censorship' (though disciplinary intervention might follow if a glaringly 'subversive' interpretation of a text were conveyed to the authorities). In the Soviet era, especially from the mid-1930s, when methodological guidance was provided in profusion, taking personal initiative would become much more difficult.

Read, Write, Count!

It took time for central control to re-establish itself under Soviet power. At first, the new system appeared to represent a total break with the past, both in terms of the material on the syllabus and the ways in which it was supposed to be learned. In the earliest days, the mood was one of iconoclastic euphoria combined with democratic utopianism. Children had been regimented and dragooned; now they were to be free to learn for the joy of it. Pupil organisations had been banned; now every school was to have its pupil organisation.

Liberal and left-leaning Russian teachers were delighted to be able to give full voice to the civic enthusiasms they had been compelled to mute when the Tsarist Inspectorate still acted as an effective force of control. Even school directors sometimes took on the tone of the times. The head of one *gimnaziya* in Yaroslavl' 'congratulated us [the pupils] on being liberated from the yoke of the Tsarist regime, and said that we were citizens now ourselves'.[173] At Ol'ga Berggol'ts's school, pupils commemorated the twelfth anniversary of the 1905 Revolution with mass theatricals and mass declamations, and with the singing of political songs such as 'Hostile Whirlwinds'.[174] From the first days of the February Revolution, disciplinary procedures in many schools were relaxed. In some places, the old five-tier grading system fell out of use (though traces of it remained in the use of one-word evaluations, 'Excellent', 'Good', 'Satisfactory', and 'Unsatisfactory', which teachers tended to use in the same way as they had previously used fives, fours, threes, and twos, awarding pupils 'good plus', 'satisfactory minus', or even 'very bad with two minuses'). There was tolerance of new grassroots organisations, and the old style of school assembly was abolished in many places, being replaced by at most a short prayer recited in individual classes.[175]

After October 1917, the official policy towards political activity shifted from passive tolerance to active encouragement. Participation in demonstrations was a regular part of the school day. Thirty thousand schoolchildren took part in the celebrations for the First of May 1919 held in Petrograd, carrying flags decorated with flowers and garlands to the main building of the People's Commissariat of Enlightenment on Chernyshev Street, and singing the Internationale so loudly that Lunacharsky, who was meant to address the procession, could not make himself heard above the din. For the same occasion, 10,000 children marched through Gomel' carrying banners emblazoned with slogans such as LET US CREATE: OUR LIVES ARE STILL YOUNG and WE ARE THE SWALLOWS OF A FRESH, GREEN SPRING.[176] And in May 1923, schoolchildren processed through Petrograd as part of a demonstration against Lord Curzon, shouting slogans ('We're Bored! With You, Lord!') and singing the Internationale, at that time the unofficial national anthem of the new state.[177]

Political activity was not reserved for special occasions: it was brought directly into the everyday life of schools. Where the Tsarist authorities had waxed timid about even the blandest pupil associations, the Bolshevik regime not only encouraged, but required, the formation of pupil associations. (Even pupils of nursery schools were supposed to have their own assemblies.)[178] Representatives were elected to put forward the views of the pupils at the school council, a body mediating between teachers, educational administrators, and children. And primers relentlessly emphasised the revolutionary nature of the new society, and the part played by schoolchildren in creating it.

To be sure, for the first few years after the Revolution, children generally learned from established reading-books, where the material might not reflect the new order at all. V. Anan'in's *Living Stream*, originally published in 1910 but still in print as late as 1922, even included a story by Dostoevsky about how little children who died would be taken by Jesus to a Christmas tree party in heaven. Sentiments about the village included 'Old-time customs and rituals are firmly preserved in the [Great Russian] people'.[179] It is hard to imagine a less 'Bolshevik' publication. Another kind of reading guide of the day did without study materials at all, advocating that children should be taught their letters by creative methods such as collective story-telling.[180] Local education departments might publish their own materials – for instance *The Unified School of Labour*, which came out in Dmitrievo in 1921, and whose exemplary sentences included 'Honest labour is a sacred thing, making one's life path stretch out wide.'[181] But pupils beyond the reach of these initiatives had to take their chances with less 'politically correct' materials, including left-over reading books from before 1917.

As the infrastructure improved and control tightened, however, the materials for early reading became more obviously politicised. P. O. Afanas'ev's *Read, Write, Count*, first published in 1925, which went through twenty-four editions and reached 650,000 copies by 1930, included a biography that was exemplary in every way:

> I live in a town. My name is Yasha, and my surname is Yarkin [the first name has proletarian overtones, while the surname means 'Bright']. My mother works in a factory. I live in the Red Star Children's Home. My two-year-old sister Zoya lives in a crèche called 'Dawn'.

Naturally, there was also a section, 'What Children Know About Lenin', and among the songs at the back were 'The Song of Labour' and the Internationale.[182] A comparable book for the village school was M. K. Porshneva's *Your Letters*, which ran to thirteen editions between 1924 and 1930, and which had sections on 'The Crèche', 'Octobrists', and on Soviet festivals, as well as the inevitable Vladimir Il'ich Lenin.[183]

Alternatively, rural pupils might cut their teeth on *New Path*, a solidly ideological production with sections on 'How I Saw Lenin on the First of May', 'Seeing Fedya Off to the Pioneer Rally', 'The Agricultural Exhibition', and so on, though some material on seasonal work and rural life generally was included.[184] Maths problems also took on the tenor of the times: *Numbers on the Construction Site* (1931) asked pupils to solve equations that pressed home the importance of the 'struggle to transform daily life':

> A housewife spends the following amounts of time on various activities.
>
> | Cleaning the room | 2 hours |
> | Cooking | 2 hours |
> | Washing up | 2 hours |
> | Sewing | 3 hours |
> | Child care | 3 hours |
>
> How many hours' work a day does that make?

How much time would she be able to spare for socially useful work if there were a canteen and a crèche in the apartment block where she lives?[185]

Political writing was, likewise, an essential part of the activities in many schools. Indeed, in the early days of Soviet power it probably played a greater role than reading, given that there was not the same problem with finding materials. A teacher who introduced a school magazine issued in 1919 with the stirring words, 'I cannot treat this [journal] as a children's whim, I see something deep and serious in it, which must grant us a manifestation of the individuality of the future citizens who will be a support for Russian society as a whole', was articulating the spirit of the times.[186]

Alongside syllabus content, models of how to teach were also changing. Manuals for teachers placed a great deal more emphasis upon personal discovery, hands-on work with materials, and co-operation with one's classmates in teams, than on academic achievement in a traditional sense. A text by V. N. Shulgin published in 1925, for example, suggested that village schools might organise their pupils into surveying local roads and putting up signposts, which would fulfil the double function of keeping the pupils interested because they were doing practical work, and arranging a service to the local community and travellers. Among other tasks that he recommended as both educational and useful to society at large were taking minutes at village meetings, performing fire watches, and carrying out weather forecasts.[187] Teachers were exhorted to bear children's likely background in mind when teaching: there must not be 'too sharp a break from their former way of life (which might oppress them)'.[188] One recommended route to non-oppression was the avoidance of dictatorial behaviour: 'One should not punish, but educate violators of discipline as required,' one pedagogue remarked in 1927.[189] The pupils themselves were supposed to be involved in keeping order: they might vote, for example, on responses to unacceptable acts.[190] Another route to non-oppression was emphasis on children's creativity: a good deal of weight was given to 'free composition', music, and art. And the school programmes of the time lay bare a genuine sense of fresh thinking about traditional subjects. Literature teachers in the primary school were encouraged to inspire enthusiasm by using methods such as 'expressive reading', and getting pupils to write stories and poems themselves; they were informed that it was essential to teach the principles of formal analysis as well as the sociological analysis of content; and they were told that learning about literature should be a way of finding out how to respond emotionally to the world around.[191]

Yet from the first, the Bolshevik regime's policies for education had a repressive edge. Even in the early 1920s, the system struck a visiting Westerner as rigid: 'As is always the case with dogmatic education, there can be no free play of thought.'[192] In the Soviet primary school, indoctrination was just as pervasive as in the Tsarist primary school, though now the political values had changed. Children were supposed to be taught that the Soviet regime 'wanted factories, mines, forests and farmland to be in common ownership', and that it 'wanted peasants and workers to love each other like brothers'.[193] Equally, traditional discipline had not so much disappeared as been devolved: the central controlling force was now the will of 'the collective', as expressed by the teacher and study group (the word 'class' was avoided in this era because of the possibilities of confusion with the political category so named).[194]

The explicitly ideological character of teaching materials persisted through the successive decades of Soviet power. To be sure, later generations of alphabet books were different in terms of the scenes included and in terms of the style of illustrations. P. O. Afanas'ev and N. A. Kostin's *Alphabet Book*, published in 1933 and in print till 1936, concentrated on children with two parents rather than the offspring of a single mother living in an orphanage. Early sentences included 'Papa is at home. Mama is at home': the accompanying picture showed the two decorously seated and listening to the radio. The family home abounded in doilies and lampshades, as well as metal-framed beds of the latest 'hygienic' variety. But politics also loomed large. In one vignette, Masha and Pasha wrote their first words on a blackboard: Lenin and Stalin respectively; later sections dealt with the Red Army, and, once again, Lenin and Stalin.[195] The balance was similar in later generations of schoolbooks, as published in 1938–44 and 1938–52, though the content modulated slightly: more personality cult, and less revolution; a heftier proportion of 'happy childhood' alongside Pioneer work; the introduction of new 'Soviet saints' such as Pushkin alongside the revolutionary activists of the past.[196] In the post-Stalin era, reading manuals also carried ideological education alongside happy families and joyful childhoods, with topical heroes such as Yury Gagarin joining war heroes as role models.[197]

The nature of the 'patriotic education' imparted in set texts developed in similar ways. In the 1920s there was a predictable emphasis on 'revolutionary' motifs, with children learning to sing, for example, 'Forward Go the Pioneers' or 'The Young Marseillaise' alongside the inevitable Internationale and songs about the death of Lenin. From 1932, Russian nationalism played a larger role, with tales such as Lev Tolstoy's *The Prisoner of the Caucasus* or Dem'yan Bednyi's 'The Soviet Sentry' specifically named as required reading.[198] From the second half of the 1930s, the 'cult of personality' was reflected. Throughout the remainder of the Stalin era, texts such as 'Comrade Stalin Gave the Order' were staples of singing classes, and material about the leader figured in readers for Russian classes as well.[199] In the post-Stalin era, Lenin replaced Stalin as the key cult figure.[200]

But study texts at all periods of Soviet history also included a hefty dollop of material that was of an apolitical or even sentimental kind, inculcating love of animals and nature. Children in the 1920s learned Glinka's 'The Lark' alongside the Internationale. Essay topics might include not only 'The World in Fifty Years' Time', or tales about poor little orphan Petya, but cosy autobiographies with much emphasis on the traditional companions of a secure childhood existence, cats and kittens:

> In the summer our cat had two kituns. [...] At night pussy goes to sleep with his mummy. When everyone has fallen asleep, he gets up and walks over all the tables and laps milk. Once little Vas'ka even knocked over the milk jug.[201]

In some schools, weeks would go by with no mention of Lenin, or indeed of any political events and phenomena.[202] Similarly, in the 1930s and 1940s, reading material included animal *skazki*, children's animal classics such as Chekhov's 'Kashtanka', the fables of Ivan Krylov, animal stories by Bianki, and nature pieces by Tolstoy and Nekrasov alongside tales of derring-do by partisans and hymns of praise to the all-knowing, all-seeing leader.[203] Post-Stalinist readers had an opening section on Soviet patriotism to put everything else in context:

> Children have a lovely homeland,
> The stars of the Kremlin
> shine over us,
> their light reaches everywhere.
> Children have a lovely homeland,
> There is no better![204]

But because political subjects were introduced on a calendar-driven basis (copy about Lenin for Lenin's birthday, material about the war for Victory Day, and so on), much of school education was taken up with more general material – the seasons, organising one's day, birds and animals.[205]

Traditional academic skills were extremely important. At primary level, reading aloud, comprehension, tidy and accurate writing, and basic mathematical processes were still the core of teaching, which also emphasised broadly based 'civilising' motifs such as hygiene or accurate reckoning of time (from hours and minutes to days and years, taught as part of mathematics). Reforms carried out to the programme simply tinkered with the amount of material that children were supposed to learn at different points in the course; for example, modifications in 1968 compressed into two years what had formerly been absorbed over four years, and brought forward material once taught at secondary level into the primary programme.[206] At the same time, the primary syllabus always retained at least some sense that 'children will be children'. Throughout the Soviet era, arts education and physical education played a much more prominent part at this level than at secondary level.

On balance, Soviet primary education represented a compromise between the values of 'free education' and those of the official Tsarist classroom. Fidelity to the Soviet state had now replaced fidelity to the autocratic Russian state as a goal, and beliefs about 'brotherly love' between nations replaced beliefs about God's love for man. Indeed, the entire history of primary education from the late nineteenth to the late twentieth century was, when compared with the upheavals and policy reversals evident in the world of secondary schooling, relatively static. Certainly, after 1932 there was a move away from practical subjects, and prescription of material to be covered became much more detailed, with elaborate lists now given of the syllabus for elementary reading as well as for music.[207] But the essential formula remained key skills plus patriotic education, with 'arts education' and physical culture alongside.

Educating Older Schoolchildren

The situation with secondary education was more complicated, with considerably more change evident over time. In this area, early Soviet policy diverged fundamentally from Tsarist policy, not only because there was now one single integrated type of school, but because of the nature of the syllabus. 'Education for labour' and arts education had a toe-hold in the pre-revolutionary primary school, but the secondary system distinguished firmly between vocationally oriented courses (for the lower orders) and academic courses, intended for the socially privileged. Now all pupils were supposed to follow a syllabus that was oriented towards their future working existence and towards society in general (as manifested in the provision of compulsory professional training for all, and in the organisation of excursions to, and work placements in, factories), but at the same time intellectually demanding. The 'free school' orientation was the preferred trend in this period. A competition for outstanding teachers held by *Pravda* in 1923 rewarded not only those who were in tune with the new ideology (for example a teacher who had managed to stop his or her pupils using the phrase 'honest to God'), but what in other circumstances might have been termed liberal values: a director who achieved everything by consultation and reliance on staff initiative, or pedagogues who had organised self-sufficient 'communes' in their schools.[208]

A sense of the contradictoriness and impracticality of official policy, if also of its encouragement of flexible and imaginative teaching, is given by the core syllabus for the higher classes of the seven-year school introduced in 1925–6. Both in conceptual terms and in terms of the amount of material that was supposed to be covered, the syllabus was hopelessly ambitious. The 'Dalton Plan' of subject-based project work hardly impacted on the design of the primary syllabus (where it would have been much easier to introduce it);[209] at secondary level, it reigned supreme. Year 5 (made up of 13-year olds) was assigned a set of key themes that might well have taxed first-year students at university. In literature, the sub-themes were 'Peasant Labour and its Effects on the Daily Life and Ideology of the Countryside', 'Peasants and Landowners', 'Class Contradictions in the City', and 'The Russian Village'.[210] The syllabus made it painfully clear that squeezing some traditional subjects, particularly natural sciences, into a thematic framework was likely to lead to grotesque contortions. Study of weather and meteorology, as well as factory processes, soil and atmospheric conditions passed as physics; the use of energy in industry and hygiene was supposedly chemistry; and 'mathematics' stopped at surveying and the study of a mysterious topic called 'the forms of industry'. In the humanities, on the other hand, the material was a bizarre mish-mash of the old and the new. History (in the sense of a specific subject so named, as opposed to the principles of Marxist-Leninist historical analysis, which shaped the syllabus from start to finish) had totally disappeared, but literature had survived, along with a list of set texts that included some thoroughly conventional choices of works by classic writers (for instance Gogol's *Old-World Landowners* and Pushkin's *Dubrovsky* and *The Bronze Horseman*). Clearly, teachers were likely to have problems in perceiving the appropriate orientation.

To be fair, the educational policies of the early 1920s allowed some truly impressive establishments to flourish. One was the Model Experimental School organised by Vsevolod Lubentsov in Tashkent in the first years after the Revolution. The school was run on co-operative principles: it had no cleaners and janitors, and no conduct supervisors. The pupils and teachers saw to the practicalities of life, and liaised with each other, on a basis of complete equality, a method that, according to eyewitnesses, was risky at the outset, but in the event succeeded in engendering a high level of social responsibility (the school was pulled back from anarchy when the pupils themselves recognised that petty theft and apathy were on the point of destroying the institution). Despite the low emphasis on formal educational targets – the thoroughly Tolstoyan syllabus included physical work such as carpentry, cobbling, sewing and basket-weaving, and even work in the fields – or, conversely, because of this, the teaching stimulated a desire to learn that was as least as great as that generated by education that purveyed a corpus of rote-learned facts. Graduates of the school valued the intellectual curiosity that had been inspired in them by their teachers, and some went on to make a success of their studies at university.[211]

The majority of Soviet schools, though, were not utopian establishments led by pioneering enthusiasts, to be proudly paraded before admiring foreign visitors. They were humbler establishments run by teachers who were, until the end of the 1920s, often survivors of the Tsarist system. Such individuals – whatever their points of dissatisfaction with Ministry of Enlightenment norms – had grown used to different values and different ways of doing things:

> For the last few years I have been living contrary to the dictates of my own conscience, denying myself step by step. I've been teaching according to the 'brigade method', although the entire history of pedagogy has never known such mumbo-jumbo, or at least not since the Middle Ages. I cite the wretched so-called ideas of those half-educated seminarians [i.e. Stalin]. I have to denounce Dostoevsky, to say that Pushkin is not a national poet, but the mouthpiece of the gentry and aristocracy, to go through the farce of school elections …. Everyone has his limit. I've reached mine and I've just had enough.[212]

So wrote V. N. Shubkin in the early 1930s. As a liberal, and a conscientious teacher who had done his best to employ participatory teaching methods before 1917, he was in a tragic position. But even those who were sympathetic to the new methods often had great difficulty in achieving what the handbooks proposed that they should do. To be successful, collaborative forms of teaching such as the 'brigade method' required not only large, light, modern classrooms equipped with tables and chairs rather than old-style desks, but also an abundance of hands-on materials and visual aids. Most Russian schools, especially in the countryside, were totally without such things.

Teachers in many parts of the provinces had their work cut out achieving the minimum standards of basic literacy, and their concern for methodological reform was necessarily small or non-existent.[213] In the assessment of a Western historian of Russian education in the 1920s, 'in primary and secondary schools throughout the Republic, teachers continued to teach, and students continued to learn, by means of the familiar cycle of dictation, memorization, and drill'.[214] A standard strategy was to agree readily to every new ministerial directive that arrived, and then quietly ignore it when one got into the classroom.[215] It is fair to suppose that a conventional teacher employing the 'brigade method' was likely simply to listen to homework regurgitations in the time-honoured way, though now assigning marks to groups rather than to individuals.

Teachers' sense of malaise was exacerbated by the loss of the disciplinary mechanisms upon which they had formerly been able to rely. The conduct mark and other kinds of institutional sanction against pupils had vanished. Formal examinations had been suspended: the 1923 Code of the Unified School of Labour stipulated that the arrangements for moving from class to class should be at the discretion of individual 'school soviets'.[216] The very existence of such soviets, with their pupil participation, had also brought the end of the automatic professional authority upon which teachers could rely before 1917. When a formerly tyrannical *gimnaziya* headmaster had been reduced to working as school janitor, it was hard for his former subordinates to retain any respect for him. If his replacement was a semi-illiterate former worker with no teaching experience, then the new order would not carry much weight either.[217] Disciplinary problems were now a major source of anxiety in the profession, and were widely reported in the specialist press.[218] Soviet humorists had fun with them too. Mikhail Zoshchenko's 1922 story 'The Teacher' had a put-upon protagonist who was forced to address his pupils as 'comrade', and whose pleas to his classes to devote some attention to lessons were met with malevolent mockery.[219]

From Re-Education to Control

In 1932 academic values were restored to pride of place in the schoolroom, and the syllabus, the tutelary and disciplinary practices current in the Soviet secondary school changed quite fundamentally. The subjects affected to the greatest extent were those that formed the core of the traditional humanities: Russian literature and history. The 25 August 1932 Decree of the Central Committee of the Communist Party spoke in alternate breaths of 'significantly strengthening historicism in the social studies, native language and literature, and geography programmes', and of the need to disseminate 'the most important knowledge relating to the national cultures of the peoples of the USSR'.[220] Recreated as an independent school subject in 1931, history was now identified as a key part of the school programme. In 1933, M. N. Pokrovsky's *Russian History* was introduced as a landmark 'stable textbook' for schools across the country.[221] History's importance underwent a further quantum leap in 1934, when the content of the syllabus was made the subject of discussions at the very highest level of the Soviet administration. After Stalin himself had criticised the substitution of 'sociology' for history at a Politburo meeting in March, the education commissar, Bubnov, held discussions with Narkompros officials in which he suggested that Tsarist textbooks, whatever the unsuitability of their 'viewpoint' in some ways, provided a useful model in terms of their structure (i.e. their emphasis on the role of major figures, and the importance of events, rather than underlying causes, in historical development). The composition and vetting of suitable textbooks took several years, but in 1937 A. V. Shestakov's 's *Brief History of the Soviet Union* was established as the key textbook for historical teaching.[222] By the late 1930s, pedagogical guides were underlining the need to teach history in triumphalist style. For example, a teacher telling a class about Alexander Nevsky's battle on the ice with the knights of the Teutonic Order was supposed to include 'not only the usual deductive statements about the material', but to 'underline the greatness of the Russian people, who in such difficult conditions of feudal enslavement and subordination to the Tatar yoke were able to defend their independence and to drive from their native land the foreign invaders'.[223]

The shift towards history and away from social sciences had crucial effects on the teaching of literature, which until 1932 had been understood as the source material for sociological studies of class conflict, industrialisation, the 'fusion of the city and the countryside', and so on. Now, especially from 1936, a direct association began to be drawn between literary analysis and the expression of national pride (in the same way that it had been before 1917, though this comparison was naturally never made). In an article published in *Pravda* in 1936, Kornei Chukovsky called for what he described as more thorough study of literary subjects in schools. The study of Pushkin, Turgenev, Nekrasov, Saltykov-Shchedrin, Lev Tolstoy, and Gorky was vital to the cultural future of the USSR, he insisted.[224] While Chukovsky's article placed stress on the importance of literary appreciation, this part of his text was less in tune with official thinking than his argument about the centrality of works by the great writers of the past.

The superficial effect of the abolition of the 'complex system' was to place a distance between school-teaching and political ideology. On 10 March 1935, a hapless local educational official from Vereshchagin district, Sverdlovsk province, received a stinging rebuke from S. A. Bubnov, then Commissar of Education, for an insufficient grasp of the tone of the times. The official had himself chided local teachers for having unaccountably left out of a class on climatic zones the Soviet Union's role in the international movement, and for teaching the formation of snowflakes without reference to atheist education.[225] The message of the rebuke was clear: teachers should stick to hard information and keep politics in its place. But in fact, one kind of ideological control had been replaced by another. Scientific subjects might now be less 'political', but in the humanities the view that Soviet power was 'the end of history' had triumphed.

In turn, the association between history and literature and inculcation of 'love of the motherland' meant that teachers who exercised initiative in teaching a subject would be seen as 'unpatriotic' as well as unprofessional. Even in the early 1930s, Beatrice King, a shrewd, Russian-speaking Western observer of the educational scene, had remarked that the Soviet system might be 'democratic' in that teachers were allowed a certain consultative role (by means of meetings to discuss educational measures, etc.), but that it '[did] not allow the individual teacher much authority'.[226] Up to the mid-1930s, though, a reasonable amount of variation was still possible. King observed a striking contrast between two lessons in the same school, one on Roman history, which was 'very tame and called forth no activity on the part of the children', and one on maths, where 'the class was very alert and interested'.[227] There could also be wide variation in teaching approaches within the same subject. An article published in *Pioneer Pravda* in 1933 hymned the innovative methods of literature teaching used by a teacher at School No. 27 in Moscow. He would play his pupils music while they were working on Pushkin, get them to write 'Tolstoy Day' essays, and ask them to write imaginary biographies of characters from Neverov's *Tashkent the Abundant* after the novel ended. The pupils made models, wrote reviews, and held debates.[228] But, a year later, a piece on the model schools which appeared in a pedagogical journal commended the use of traditional methods for Russian language and literature teaching: dictation and grammar tests, rather than free composition, and character studies and plot synopsis (rather than sociological or formal analysis).[229]

In the end, the pressures were towards conservatism. Just as before 1917, teachers who called pupils to the blackboard to make them rehearse what they had learned at home tended to grade answers on the basis of the amount of detail correctly

106 Music lesson in the open air, Leningrad, 1936. An illustration of 'teacher led' instruction (though the class is being conducted in a relaxed atmosphere, with the pupils clearly enjoying themselves).

recalled rather than the analytical approach adopted. An exemplary lesson plan in a pedagogical textbook covering a session devoted to the Christianisation of Russia in 988 anticipated precisely such a regurgitation of facts:

1. Repetition of material covered in previous classes and for homework (12–15 minutes). The teacher asks pupils the following questions:
   a) Who ascended to the princedom after Svyatoslav?
   b) With which tribes did Vladimir go to war? (When answering this question, the pupils use a wall-map to illustrate the location of the Bulgarian tribes along the Volga and of the Polovtsian territories conquered by Vladimir.)
   c) With which empire did Vladimir open relations? (The map is used here too.)
   d) Which faith did Vladimir introduce, and why?

The class then proceeded in similar vein with the new material. First of all, the teacher delivered a mini-lecture (illustrated by reference to a map and a reproduction of the painting *The Christianisation of Rus'*), and the pupils then answered a series of factual questions: Who christened the Kievans, and when? How were they christened? How did the Russian people respond to the new faith, and why? What good effects did the introduction of Christianity to Russia have? The teacher's role in all this was to 'correct such inaccurate perceptions as the pupils may have about the life of this era', and to point out (perhaps in collaboration with some of the pupils) any factual errors that occurred when answers were being given to the questions.[230]

This particular model class was supposed to be aimed at pupils in the top year of the primary division (i.e. those of 12 years old or so), but in practice classes at secondary level proceeded in much the same way. Here, too, what was now officially known as 'knowledge-testing' dominated the sessions, though the material regurgitated was of course more complex. Manuals for teachers institutionalised the old tripartite structure of (1) repetition through homework questions or test, followed by the teacher's assessment of how well the questions had been answered; (2) discussion of new material; and (3) the communication of the assignment for the following class. The only anticipated variation in the format was the alternation between spontaneous volunteering of information by pupils in response to a general question, and requests for recapitulation directed by the teacher to an individual pupil.[231]

Marks were supposed to be accorded on the basis of factual command above all else. A mark of 'excellent' was to be given if the pupil 'knew the whole volume of the material in the programme that has been covered and cited many diverse examples', 'brought out what was central and significant', 'made no mistakes of fact and formulated accurately', and 'expounded (whether orally or in writing) all the material required in a systematic and independent-minded manner'. Independence of mind and complete accuracy were not required for a mark of 'satisfactory', but otherwise the guidelines were much the same.[232]

The reintroduction of a compulsory, government-administered, centrally organised examination system in 1935 reinforced this emphasis on regurgitation. A Narkompros order of March 1935 stipulated that teachers should devote the second half of the year to revision in preparation for the examinations, and that 'pupils preparing for examinations should be guided by the textbooks'.[233] The majority of subjects were tested orally, according to the traditional system whereby a pupil was presented with a 'ticket' by an examination panel and then spouted extempore until deemed to have answered the question satisfactorily. Examiners were specifically precluded from prompting the pupil, though some manuals discouraged them from undue strictness and urged them to try and intervene kindly if a child's nerves turned out not to be equal to the occasion.[234] There was every reason to be nervous – from June 1936, pupils who got poor marks in even one subject could be made to repeat the entire year.[235]

Educational procedures, then, concentrated on the 'what', 'who', and 'how' rather than the 'why'. Evaluation was reduced to a minimum, and, where it occurred, was strictly regulated. It would have been quite improper to respond to the question, 'What good effects did the introduction of Christianity to Russia have?' by answering 'None'. What was required was a little speech explaining that Christianity was a more progressive religion than paganism, bringing more sophisticated forms of social organisation, and other benefits such as literacy.[236] Similarly, literature teaching concentrated on easily digestible material from the Russian classics: the biographies of Pushkin, Gogol', Krylov, Nekrasov, Turgenev; the plots and themes of selected artistic works by them; and, above all, the traits of the characters. 'The basic, most essential thing in school-work is analysing characters,' stated the official school programme of 1938. Suggested topics included 'The Prostakov Family' (Class 8), 'The Fathers and Sons in Turgenev's Novel and the Author's Attitude to Them' (Class 9), and '[Gorky's] Davydov as a Case Study of the Bolshevik Activist and Moral Educator' (Class 10). In case the teacher should be in any doubt about the main drift, it was stipulated that literature was to be taught 'with emphasis on the role [of writers] in the formation of great national Russian culture and in the struggle for freedom of the Russian people'.[237]

There was really little leeway, then, for 'independence of mind', if by that is meant the search for alternative causes or for new interpretations. Striving to go beyond the textbook explanations brought few benefits ('independence of mind' was recognised as a praiseworthy quality only in the most able) and many risks, given that school inspectors attended examinations, so that an unorthodox answer from a pupil who was evidently not merely incompetent would reflect badly both on the pupil and on his or her teacher. More insidiously, a teacher who demanded serious thought took the risk that a pupil who got a bad grade despite having given an answer straight out of the textbook might well complain to the school authorities, which might lead to disciplinary proceedings or worse.

Certainly, instruction from the textbook carried certain risks of its own: a teacher who innocently continued to teach from a book that had been rendered unacceptable by some shift in ideological fashion was treated at least as severely as a teacher who deliberately bent the rules of the syllabus.[238] Still, sticking to the letter of the textbook was the safest means of proceeding. The dependence of teachers on textbooks was not simply a formal requirement.[239] It was a real-life feature of the classroom. Indeed, this was one of the main differences between Russian and German education noticed by Wolfgang Leonhard, a German who studied at a Russian school in the late 1930s.[240] And formality was compounded by the severe manner of large numbers of teachers, who resorted to traditional pedagogical weapons – sarcasm and spite – to keep control.[241] While corporal punishment as such was strictly forbidden, and a teacher who hit a pupil was likely to get into serious trouble, it was not unknown for teachers to lash out physically, laying about themselves with rulers and so on.[242]

That said, there still were many teachers who treated their pupils courteously, and some who were prepared to swim against the tide. One woman who was at school in Ivanovo remembers being educated by political exiles from Moscow who did everything they could to tone down the ideological elements in education. Even teachers who had less pressing reasons for distancing themselves from the models set out in the textbooks might do so because they had observed the work of older colleagues who had taught in the more liberal atmosphere of the pre-1917 or 1920s Russian classroom.[243] As time went on, the penalties for non-conformity became greater and the pressures to go through routines higher, but some gifted teachers still did what they could to enthuse their pupils. And, at the worst of times, the style of teaching was effective in conveying the facts: the ablest pupils would leave school able to recite large quantities of poetry, alongside mathematical rules and the capitals of Europe and Asia. Once again, one should remember the historical context: in British and continental European classrooms, many pupils of this period were having a very similar education. At Eric Hobsbawm's Gymnasium in Vienna, for example, history also consisted of learning lists of names and dates unleavened by commentary or analysis.[244] In all such schools internationally, pupils maintained a balance between disliking school and recognising its value. High marks were important to parents, and important to society generally; they were also important within the school. An *otlichnik*, or prize pupil, enjoyed all sorts of little privileges, as Ella Bobrova's poetic memoir, *Irina Istomina*, recalls. For example, Irina was allowed to sit with her friend, which most pupils were not, even after she had taken part in a fight.[245]

Conservatism took a further step forward with the reintroduction of the pre-revolutionary five-tier mark scale in 1944. It was reinforced by manuals for teachers, which not only provided highly formulaic model lessons, but presented as striking innovations very minor variations of the standard pupil–teacher connection, such as getting pupils to chip in with questions from the floor.[246] Yet even in the post-war era, more than a decade after 'paedological perversions' were condemned, some space was left for initiative. Recognising (as liberal teachers had in the 1910s) that the global mark was a very poor way of recording children's varying levels of performance in individual tasks, one contributor to a pedagogical magazine in 1951 recommended his own method of notation, which allowed precise transcription of exactly how well each child had done in answer to a given question, so that under-performers could be asked to repeat an exercise until they had it off pat.[247] Similarly, evocations of 'model teachers' sometimes pointed to genuinely imaginative efforts. An article published in *Koster* in 1947 contrasted the old-fashioned rote-driven approach that had prevailed before 1917, when pupils learning about the Caucasus were required to grind the names of rivers and mountains into their heads, and the much livelier technique of a woman teacher at a boys' school in Leningrad, who had showed her pupils a film about the Georgian Military Highway before asking them to imagine a journey along the road and narrate what they had 'seen'. Other exercises set by this teacher had included drawing sketch-maps of the area round the school, marking the houses where famous people had lived, and organising excursions round the centre of Leningrad.[248]

In real life, too, it was possible to adapt both content and methodology to different effect from that intended in syllabuses and guides. A man who began teaching in the early 1950s remembered how learning poems by heart became an expression of exuberance among his pupils.

> We learned the authors mentioned in the programme in a special way. I used to set a strophe or two for pupils to memorise. But the atmosphere meant that some pupils learned a lot more. They were competing with each other. For instance, Valya Limonchenko once recited the whole of Lomonosov's 1747 'Ode on the Accession of Empress Elisaveta Petrovna'. The pupils in Class 8 learned the whole of Evgeny Onegin by heart. I split the novel up into seven- or ten-stanza segments, and my pupils chose which sections they wanted to analyse. Anyone who didn't feel like it didn't do it. And I never allowed myself to give anyone a mark or two for Pushkin.[249]

Adventurous teaching, though, was more likely in schools where material and cultural provision were above average. A teacher with 35 pupils in his or her class was a good deal more likely to keep careful notes and to try and maintain pupil interest than a teacher who had 50 pupils, or who was working two shifts. The film show and the local tour were options open only to well-equipped schools in the centre of a historic city; it was in turn schools of this kind that tended to attract the best-qualified and most enthusiastic staff.[250]

In any case, ideological rectitude remained the core of the syllabus, whatever the ambitions of the school or of individual teachers. During the war, children were told to write stories on subjects such as 'She Captured a Fascist', and in German they learned the language by parroting phrases useful in wartime situations: '*Waffen nieder! Hände hoch!*'[251] Patriotic education was placed in the foreground after the war too. Inspectors from the Academy of Pedagogical Sciences visiting Moscow schools in 1947 commended a model lesson in School No. 175 as 'suffused with Bolshevik patriotism, and inculcating in the pupils love for, and devotion to the Party and its leaders, a feeling of pride in our Motherland'. Other schools attracted approbation for organising extra-curricular sessions on the biography of Joseph Stalin and for reading Polevoi's *Story of a Real Person* alongside novels by Jack London and Richard Hillary, and hence revealing 'the superiority of the traits of the Soviet person'.[252]

Non-academic subjects also harped on the national and patriotic theme. Physical education classes, for example, were used as preparation for the 'Fit for Work and Defence' programme, which provided schoolchildren with elementary training in orienteering and weapons-handling, as well as in types of physical skill useful on the battlefield (running, weight-carrying, etc.). Pupils were also put through training in how to use gas masks and in other forms of civil defence (or, as Soviet terminology preferred, 'war preparation'), an activity which made concrete the propaganda about the dangers to the motherland carried in the children's press. Education of this kind began in the early 1930s and reached its peacetime peak in 1939, when the Law on Universal Conscription of 1 September 1939 was accompanied by the introduction of military training for middle schools – drilling and weapon use for boys, auxiliary nursing for girls. During the war, emphasis on these activities was naturally stepped up: already by 1941, children were being trained to throw dummy grenades, and by 1942 a wide set of martial skills was on the curriculum, where it remained throughout the post-war decades. (In practice, there were sometimes difficulties in finding sufficient equipment and qualified instructors, but by *design* children, particularly boys, were all supposed to undergo this training.)[253]

Surveillance and Control

Military training was important not only because of the practical benefits, to a bellicose state, of having a pool of young people who had acquired basic battle skills before they were drafted. The unquestioning obedience of the soldier to the command structure was supposed to be a model for Soviet citizenship in the broadest sense. Equally, the emphasis on heroism in literature and history teaching brought into the classroom the stress on leadership that was essential to the Stalinist system, and signalled a shift back to a coercive view of the school's responsibility for moral or character education. The second half of the 1930s and the 1940s saw an increasing focus on the subordination of pupils to teachers, on vertical rather than horizontal methods of discipline. Certainly, horizontal surveillance continued. At 'class meetings', it was standard practice for teachers to call on pupils to criticise the behaviour of their fellow pupils, and pupils holding positions such as 'class elder', 'sanitary monitor', 'day orderly' and so on were able to exercise authority over their fellows. But activities at this level by pupils were carefully guided from above, with 'elections' taking place on the standard Stalinist system, where the vote was used to affirm a single selected candidate rather than to distinguish between alternatives. From the early 1930s, teachers began acquiring a disciplinary arsenal very like that available to their predecessors in the Tsarist school. Once introduced in 1935, personal files became a weapon in the punitive system as well as a means of record-keeping: the worst violations of discipline could be logged in a special section on child's termly reports and stored for future reference.[254] The restoration of individual marks brought with it the return of the conduct mark; once more, anything less than 'excellent' (or, after number marks came back in 1944, 5) could jeopardise further study, or even a child's presence in the school. The most recalcitrant pupils risked doing harm to their prospects of further education by provoking the school into providing a negative testimonial; in the short term, the school could also act against them by a temporary suspension, or indeed by permanent exclusion, which started to be permitted in 1932.

Conduct control worked by prescription, as well as by regulation: for example through the Disciplinary Code for schoolchildren promulgated by the Komsomol in 1935. A direct reversion to the codes of conduct issued by pre-revolutionary Russian schools, this consisted of a long, elaborate, and wide-ranging set of regulations relating to behaviour in the classroom and outside. Children were to return to school after their vacations at the appointed time. They were to be punctual for lessons, and attend them neatly dressed and with their books and writing materials to hand, and their homework done. They were to manifest respect to teachers (they had to stand up when one entered the room, and raise their hand before speaking). Swearing, the use of nicknames, fighting, and squabbling were prohibited. Pupils were expected to help maintain harmony in the school, and to 'refrain from all actions that might disrupt the orderly execution of schoolwork and disrupt the participation in it of others'. They were supposed to behave well outside the school as well as in it: to dress tidily; to refrain from vandalising furniture, flowers, trees, posters; to avoid spitting on floors and picking fights. It was strictly forbidden to sell cigarettes or theatre tickets, to gamble, to carry a weapon of any kind, or to loiter in the vicinity of cinemas and theatres. Free time was to be spent 'in a cultured manner' – that is, in peaceful and civilised pastimes – and children were to keep their dwelling-place and the courtyard outside clean and tidy.[255]

These rules were not the last regulatory measure of the Stalin era. By the summer of 1943, anxiety about acts of 'hooliganism' by children and young people in the Soviet streets (robberies, assault)[256] had become severe enough to prompt further action at the top. A decree of 14 July 1943 attempted to grapple with truancy by forcing offices concerned with the monitoring of residence regulations to produce lists of all the children of school age (8–15) in their administrative district. A pro forma now had to be filled in giving reasons why a child was not attending school. Three weeks later, on 2 August 1943, the Central Committee agreed that Narkompros should be allowed to issue all schoolchildren with identity cards (*uchenicheskie bilety*), which pupils had to carry with them at all times and to present for inspection upon demand. An updated version of the rules for schoolchildren was to be pasted into each card.

Apart from admonitions about general good behaviour (care of school property, kindness to old people and younger children as well as to the sick, obedience to parents, punctuality, keeping one's room and clothes tidy), the new rules contained elaborate instructions on appropriate conduct in the classroom. Pupils were not only to stand up when a teacher came into the room, but were to maintain an upright posture at their desks, and they were to pay attention in class generally, and to take careful notes of homework assignments.[257] Once the old five-tier mark system was made compulsory for all schools in 1944, this was also applied to the grading of conduct: in practice, anything less than a perfect 5 represented an insuperable obstacle to a school-leaver's academic progress.[258] All of these were top-level measures: at lower levels, the social upheaval caused by evacuation and haphazard school provision sometimes provoked administrators into military-style authoritarianism. There were even cases of schools that introduced a lock-up system, *kartser*, on the lines of those operating in pre-revolutionary cadet colleges and in the newly introduced Suvorov colleges.[259]

With anxieties about indiscipline continuing after the war, more measures inevitably followed. In 1947, the post of 'class supervisor' (form teacher) for Classes 5–10 was converted into a post similar to that of the old *dame de classe* or 'class regulator' (though, unlike that post, it was held by an ordinary teacher, who was also responsible for teaching a specialist subject). According to the text of the ministerial decree setting up this position, 'The primary task of the class supervisor is to weld together the pupils in his or her class into a friendly, purposive, hard-working educational collective.[260] The concrete duties by which the class supervisors were supposed to achieve this 'welding' process included close surveillance of the pupils under their care at all times, both by scrutiny of the written records held in their personal files and by direct observation. They also presided over 'class hours', sessions of political, social, and moral indoctrination (covering topics from the Korean War to Communist morality to good manners in a more ordinary sense), and liaised with the Pioneer and Komsomol associations. Class supervisors were, *ex officio*, members of the Pioneer bureau at the school, and of the Komsomol organisation. They were thus empowered in two directions: both as members of the disciplinary structures of the school proper, and as instruments of the quasi-autonomous political associations ensconced in the school.

Class supervisors reported directly to the head of the school, and had regulatory powers over other teachers (they could, for instance, visit their classes and make suggestions). In other words, they had considerable authority within the school. They were also the central facilitators of the school's outreach work, since it was their responsibility to organise meetings of parents and to set up the 'parent task force' (*roditel'skii aktiv*) that singled out 'failing parents'. In addition, class supervisors paid visits to the homes of pupils who were considered problematic in order either to alert parents to their offspring's misdemeanours (if the parents were considered responsible), or to provide guidance on better management of the young (if the fault was considered to lie with the parents themselves).[261] The central method adopted was a thorough talking-to; if this failed, then the problem essentially moved outside the competence of the school. In really recalcitrant cases, the case would be handed over to the 'responsible authorities' (i.e. the police or the criminal justice system) so that action could be taken.[262]

The aim was, though, not to let things get to that stage. Instead, everything was done to emphasise the school's role as a total community, a place where collective and national values prevailed at every point. Certainly, there was no equivalent of the daily prayers held in Tsarist schools. But, beginning in the late 1930s, special occasions were marked by an updated Soviet version of the traditional school assembly, the *lineika*, consisting of patriotic speeches and readings, military-style reports on school activities, and moral pep-talks.[263] 'Class hours' consisted of sessions not only of 'self-criticism', but also of affirmatory discourse: the celebration of Soviet heroes and festivals, the laudatory citation of record-breaking industrial and agricultural statistics, tributes to Party leaders, and so on.[264] As well as exhorting pupils to behave in certain ways, class supervisors (and other teachers) could 'bring them to book' in the most literal sense. A Council of Ministers decree of December 1951 reintroduced the 'conduct book' by another name (now it was termed 'the register': *zhurnal*). A critical article in *Family and School* the following year suggested that some teachers used this resource with the heedless alacrity of their pre-revolutionary predecessors, setting down disciplinary notes when pupils had, for instance, forgotten to bring their gym kit.[265]

Essentially the same pedagogical and disciplinary methods continued in force in the post-Stalin era, partly because of the sheer size of classes (which might be around forty or more).[266] 'Testing of knowledge' remained the standard method of opening a class, and much rote-learning was set for homework. Especially in literature and history, paraphrase was preferred to interpretation, with the latter carried out according to ideologically directed models ('Character X is a typical representative of ...').[267] Marks still tended to be used to discipline pupils rather than to reward initiative.[268] Class supervisors went on being responsible for their charges' moral education, as well as welfare, and were still expected to hold class meetings or 'class hours' – at which they addressed various moral topics, such as 'good and bad friendship', and praised and criticised the performance and behaviour of individuals – and to co-ordinate sessions of 'political information'.

The year 1960 saw the promulgation of yet another set of school rules, on very similar lines to those formulated in 1935 and 1943. Pupils were still instructed to behave well in public, to greet teachers politely and make way for their elders, to eschew bad conduct and to discourage others from this, and to be honest and fair. The only significant difference from previous sets of rules was that the same hortatory material was separately phrased for the various age groups. For instance, younger children were addressed thus: '9. Behave well in public places. Dress tidily, and be attentive to good order. Make sure you keep the highway code.' By contrast, not only pupils of Komsomol age (16 and over), but 12- to 15-year-olds (i.e. older Pioneers) were addressed in the more pompous third person ('Every pupil must ...'), and the manner of address was more formal in other respects too: 'Every pupil must [...] be modest, polite, thoughtful and tidily dressed at school, at home and in public places, and be attentive to good order. He or she must strictly observe the highway code.'[269] Thus, an emphasis on discipline was retained. Only at the very end of the Soviet era did a thoroughgoing criticism of educational norms begin, which was to result in a once-and-for-all transformation of the system after 1991, with the emergence of private schools, often modelled on those of the pre-revolutionary era, and the tolerance of increasing diversity of practice within the state system as well.[270]

In the course of the Stalin era, emphasis on loyalty to the national ideal became increasingly coercive; surveillance in schools became closer and more punitive in character. These innovations were retained – despite criticism of harsh discipline – in the post-Stalin era. Older staff continued to lash out when crossed, or to bombard uppity pupils with chalk.[271] Traditional verbal weapons, such as sarcasm, were not neglected.[272] And teacher control, class monitors, pupil committees, and 'general meetings' were only part of the disciplinary network. The 1930s also saw a full-scale integration of the Pioneer movement into the disciplinary structure of schools. The institution was a central part of the childhood of every Soviet Russian born between about 1925 and about 1980: even before then, it had made considerable impact on the lives of those children who came into contact with it. It therefore deserves exploration separately, and in depth. First it is worth pausing to consider the small, but influential, children's organisations that existed in the Tsarist era.

Scouts and Falcons

Pre-revolutionary Russian schools (some liberal private schools, such as the Tenishev College in St Petersburg apart) generally did not offer the range of extra-curricular activities to be found in Anglophone ones of the same date.[273] The sole physical education offered at some girls' *gimnazii* was croquet and training in deportment.[274] But by the late 1900s, attitudes at the very centre of the Russian establishment were changing. Smolny Institute started to introduce gym in the 1860s; the 1910s saw a much wider range of sports, including outdoor sports, phased in, and the school timetable reworked so that each day began with a compulsory stint of exercises.[275] In 1908, Nicholas II – without bothering to consult his education minister in advance – pushed forward the introduction of drill and calisthenics to schools. The inspiration for the move was the foundation by a school inspector in Odessa, A. A. Lutskevich, of a boys' military society called the Poteshnye, 'Play Regiment', a term derived from the army detachments for boys and young men founded by Peter the Great. Once underwritten by the Emperor, 'Play Regiments' began to spring up in schools, churches, and military units across Russia. Their activities were extensively publicised in a special magazine, *Poteshnyi*, founded in 1910, in newspapers, and even in newsreels.

Contemporary writers connected the Poteshnye with the Boy Scouts of Robert Baden-Powell, but the characters of the two movements were very different. The Scout organisation was totally autonomous in terms of its relationship with the state and the Crown; it was also internationalist (albeit in a strongly imperial way); and it was less militaristic.[276] In fact, the Poteshnye were more like a sort of Ruritanian version of the Officer Training Corps ensconced in British public schools during the early twentieth century, to which the Scouts were later to become a civic and socially conscious alternative.[277] In the same way, the Scout organisation seems to have emerged in Russia as a 'civilian' alternative to the outright militarisation of the Poteshnyi movement, as is demonstrated, for instance, by the proposal, in the liberal Ignatiev education reform plan of 1915, to introduce the movement, on a strictly voluntary basis, into secondary schools. The movement was described here as a 'weapon against hooliganism'. It was a means of disseminating physical education, and of propounding moral education 'under conditions that are attractive to boys and girls – close contact with the world of nature'. The emphasis was on general civic education rather than recruitment to the army. Scout uniforms were to carry a sign identifying the school, and to be worn exclusively during drills and at camps. Though under no compulsion to join the movement, pupils were granted the right to do so: the school authorities were not entitled to prevent anyone becoming a Scout who chose to and who had the permission of their parents to join the organisation. Moreover, membership was supposed to be free of charge, with the school covering the costs of the organisation so that dues did not have to be levelled.[278]

All of this, given the well-established hostility on the part of Russian educational administrators towards pupil organisations, represented a major shift in ministerial policy, perhaps prompted by the part that Scouts had been playing in patriotic activities after the onset of the First World War.[279] In the next two years, quite a number of Russian schools were to make use of the opportunity to found troops: at the time the First Congress of Russian Scouts was held in late December 1915, only 24 Russian cities had Scout troops (and only 4 of them sent representatives to the Congress); a year later, there were said to be 50,000 Scouts and Guides in 143 cities.[280] As well as detachments of *skauty* proper, there were also troops of Girl Guides (known in Russian as *gerly-skauty*) and of Wolf Cubs (*volchata*); special literature had started to be disseminated. A Russian translation of Baden-Powell's *Scouting for Boys* was followed by the publication of various Russian reference materials, including a *Handbook and Notebook for the Russian Scout* in 1916.[281] Books of this kind made familiar to the Russian public the distinctive Scout ethos of social commitment, moral uprightness, and stoicism. In the words of a guide put out by the Petrograd Scout movement in 1916, Scouts were 'children of the Motherland, future citizens of Russia, brothers to Scouts all over the world, young knights who have given a solemn promise to serve others every day, friends, defenders, and patrons of animals'. The Scout was clean, well scrubbed around the neck and ears, straight-backed, energetic, 'pure in thought, word, and deed', and indifferent to misfortune: 'He smiles when it hurts, and whistles when he feels bad.'[282] The Russian Scout imitated the English model so far as he was able, though some concessions were made – for example, 'bare knees may be covered by trousers in bad weather'. By 1916, Scouts in Russia were organising camping trips, just like their counterparts abroad, and they had their own repertoire of Scout songs, mostly of a moralising kind – 'Be Prepared, O Scout, for the Deed of Honour/You must walk the hard and stony track ...', but also including 'Baked Potatoes', a campfire song whose genuine popularity with children can be gauged from the fact that it was later poached for use in the Pioneer movement, where it survived until the 1990s.[283]

The final years of the Russian Empire saw children's associations beginning to put down roots, for the first time in the history of the country. While numbers were still fairly small, the support of the establishment and the growing presence of such associations inside schools (nearly two thirds of the scout troops established by early 1916 were attached to a *gimnaziya* or *realnoe uchilishche*) clearly gave the promise of full-scale institutionalisation later on. In the event, however, it was only in the Russian diaspora that these groups survived long term; the children's organisations that sprang up after 1917 were of a radically different character.

Young Leninists

In its early years, the Pioneer movement was not intended only, or even mainly, as a school organisation. Set up as a junior equivalent of the Komsomol at a comparatively late stage of Soviet power (it was founded only in 1922, four years after the establishment of the Komsomol),[284] the movement went through a considerable number of manifestations over the seven decades of its existence as a state-sponsored, centralised political movement for children. The symbolic trappings of the organisation, its rituals (such as the 'solemn promise' made by new recruits), its laws, and its uniform were all subject to more or less subtle alterations. Even the age limits were not fixed once and for all. From 1922 to 1936, members might be between 10 and 14, while in 1936 the lower age limit became 11, and the upper age limit 16; in 1939, boundaries were altered again, to 10 and 15 respectively, before further changes imposed the age span 9–14 in 1954, and then 10–14 in 1957 (this time for good). But, above all, the social location and political functions of the movement were adapted.

For the first ten years of the Pioneers' existence, *forposty* (Pioneer agitational sections) might be attached to culture clubs, to factories and other places of work, and to apartment blocks, as well as to educational establishments and orphanages. In this period, the primary aim was to enrol children from the proletariat and peasantry; orphans were considered especially fertile territory for enrolment. Political agitation and 'socially useful work' were taken extremely seriously. Pioneers regularly made speeches at meetings; they were called upon to do volunteer work; they participated in campaigns, such as the 'struggle for cultured life' of 1928–32 or the 'Sow More Beet' initiative of 1932–3.[285] Pioneers were the quintessential empowered children, called upon to harangue their parents into mending their ways, and also to agitate among adults generally, disseminating new agricultural methodologies in the countryside or distributing leaflets before elections. They were encouraged to make their needs evident to local Party bureaucrats too. In 1929, for instance, groups in the Zamoskvorech'e district of Moscow, urged to invent political slogans of particular relevance to children, came up with a list including the following:

PIONEERS AND SCHOOLCHILDREN! BOYCOTT DRUNKEN FATHERS!
ALL WAIFS AND STRAYS INTO THE PIONEER MOVEMENT!
TELL YOUR LOCAL SOVIET ABOUT CHILDREN'S NEEDS.[286]

Even the most powerful adults were subject to being buttonholed in this way. A note of challenge occasionally crept into the letters which troops wrote to prominent politicians appointing them as their sponsors. 'We want you to send us your portrait and money for Pioneer suits. You can certainly manage it. There are twenty-three of us in the troop, and we're waiting,' a troop in Tula province wrote to Stalin in January 1925.[287] The First All-Soviet Pioneer Rally, held in 1929, was an important national and international event, attended not just by delegations of Pioneers from all over the Soviet Union and abroad, but by a wide variety of prominent political figures in the Soviet Communist Party and the Communist International, led by Maxim Gorky, the organisation's patron in the world of cultural politics. The Pioneer organisation had borrowed much from the Scouts – its oath and laws, its slogan of 'Be Prepared', its militaristic symbolism, its structure (with 'patrols' renamed as 'troops', *otryady*, and 'sixes' as 'links', *zven'ya*). But the word *skautizm* was a term of contempt, denoting fatuous leisure-oriented activity: Pioneers, unlike Scouts, were serious in their social and political commitment.

Where politics were primary, it followed that other activities seemed unsuitably frivolous. In 1926, a Pioneer newspaper got into trouble for publishing the following unintentionally humorous political rhyme (*chastushka*) sent in by a 'child correspondent':

> If you want to feed a pig
> Go and buy some fodder.
> The Pioneers are meant to help
> Their *komsomol'tsy* brothers.

This innocent, if inept, little piece was pounced on by the Secretariat of the Central Committee of the Komsomol as representing 'an extremely dangerous and excessive swing in the direction of creativity by children'.[288] Yet a lighter touch was sometimes advocated. As in the other areas of work with children, age had a lot to do with approach. The 'Octobrist' organisation for young children, the equivalent of the Cub Scouts and Brownies (though, like the Pioneers, Octobrist groups were coed), was, even in the 1920s, much more strongly associated with leisure than the Pioneers as such. In later decades, it worked like a faintly politicised playgroup for the six to tens.[289] But even the main organisation paid some attention to the likely demands of child psychology. In 1927, an 'exemplary plan' for village Pioneer groups, in Moscow province, underlined that political discussions should not occupy too much time at meetings. It was important that some lighter activities, such as the singing of political songs, should be included.[290] And children's political work was always regulated by adults, and often demarcated from it. Processions followed different routes, and, at ceremonial occasions, Pioneers generally participated in meetings held in the morning, not those held in the evening. It was simply not on to have Pioneer troops marching down Tverskaya Street at midnight, one local Party organiser in Moscow province protested in 1924.[291]

Pioneer camps had a similarly mixed nature. They were intended to be a means of bringing culture to rural populations (in the words of a decree of the Bureau of the Central Committee of the Komsomol dating from 2 September 1924, 'In the country, Pioneer troops should be the disseminators of literacy, hygiene, and physical health and fitness among peasant children').[292] However, the camps were also health and leisure facilities. A timetable of 1924 places 'political education' and 'socially useful work' right in the centre of activities. But time for sport and for 'independent games' was also allocated:

7.00	Roll call, raising the flag
7.30	Gymnastics and swimming
8.00	Tea
9.00	Work assignments, e.g. gardening
12.00	Swimming
13.30	Dinner, followed by rest
15.00	Social work with peasant children, or labour education (factory studies)
18.00	Tea
18.30	Independent games, meetings of the camp soviet, etc.
20.00	Supper, preparation for bed
21.00	'Conversations round the bonfire', selection of night orderlies, lowering of the flag, bed.

At the same time, the topics suggested for 'conversations round the bonfire' were heavyweight ones, such as a discussion of the political pamphlet *Christ Hasn't Risen*;[293] children were primarily on holiday to learn to be good Pioneers.

The changes that overtook the Pioneer organisation in the early 1930s were fundamental and wide-ranging. To begin with, the groups were now firmly located in the educational world. In April 1932, the Central Committee of the Communist Party redefined the Pioneer movement's functions as 'the strengthening of conscious discipline among children and especially in schools'.[294] From now on, the Pioneer and Komsomol organisations began replacing representative bodies, such as the pupil soviets, their disciplinary structures working in parallel with those of the school itself. Enrolment became ever wider: in the 1920s, membership had been considered an honour; by the mid-1930s, it was customary for entire classes to be enrolled, though usually in order of merit (the best pupils first) in order to preserve some sense that membership had to be earned. Recalcitrant pupils could be punished by being signed up late, by not being signed up at all (an extreme measure), or, of course, by being expelled from the organisation once they had become members.

Like schools, the Pioneer movement became more regimented in other ways too. In the past, recruitment had often been very informal. A school-teacher or Komsomol leader might set up a children's group, which would only afterwards be registered with the authorities – a point that explains what administrators termed 'elemental growth' and 'turnover' in the organisation (in other words, wildly fluctuating membership statistics).[295] Leaders also varied a great deal in the kind of work they did with children. A boy from a village in Tver' province who joined the Pioneers in the late 1920s remembered that one leader had made his group do 'nothing but drill', another had taken them on endless expeditions to collect healing herbs, while a third had used meetings for a non-stop narration of funny stories.[296] By the mid-1930s, on the other hand, enrolment had become (as with enrolment in schools) both better organised and more ritualistic. In 1936 entry into the Pioneers was transformed into a solemn, quasi-religious ritual, at which the new entrant swore fealty to his or her country and to the Communist Party:

> I, a Young Pioneer of the USSR, do solemnly swear, in the presence of my comrades, that I will staunchly support the cause of the working class in its battle for the liberation of labouring people all over the world, and for the construction of socialist society, that I will honourably and unwaveringly follow the commands of Il'ich and the laws of the Young Pioneers.[297]

The text of this promise substantially elaborated on the original Pioneer oath, introduced in 1922:

> I give my word of honour that I will be true to the working class, that I will help my comrades and brothers every day, that I know the laws of the Young Pioneer and will obey them.

It also expanded the adapted version of the oath from 1924, which substituted the phrase 'the cause of the working class in its struggle for the liberation of the workers and peasants of the entire world' for 'working class'.[298] The promise was to go through further changes in the course of time – in 1937, 'the cause of the working class' was rephrased as 'the cause of Lenin and Stalin', and 'the

107 Ceremonial rally in drill formation (*lineika*), Pioneer camp, Sverdlovsk province, late 1940s.

liberation of labouring people' became 'the victory of Communism', while from 1942 Pioneers made their promise not only 'in the presence of my comrades', but 'to Great Stalin, the Bol'shevik Party, and the Leninist Komsomol'.[299] However, the solemnity of tone, and the emphasis on patriotism alongside comradeship, were retained throughout the remaining history of the Pioneer movement.

From the mid-1930s, too, emblems asserted themselves ever more insistently. In 1936, Pioneers began to be taught that the three points of their tie symbolised the three generations of Bolsheviks (a development that may have formed the background to the mass hysteria that broke out a year later, when hundreds of Pioneers destroyed their ties in the belief that they had been imprinted with a subliminal image of Trotsky).[300] A command of symbolism was now as important as ideological awareness, or as a grasp of the principles of 'cultured behaviour' (though these still formed part of the 'laws and customs' of the Pioneer).[301]

Equally importantly, the Pioneer movement's character as a leisure organisation started to be boosted. In 1934 a ceremonial appearance was made at the First Congress of Soviet Writers, not by a group of miniature political leaders, but by a delegation of Pioneers from the 'Snub-Nose Centre' – a children's writing group who had published their own anthology.[302] By 1936, in keeping with the new theme of 'happy childhood', hobby-related material had become one of the most dominant strands in Pioneer publishing. The front page of New Year number of *Pioneer Pravda*, under the banner headline DREAMS OF HAPPY CHILDREN, featured one girl whose dream (becoming a pilot) would have been seen as laudable in the 1920s, and two other children whose desires were a mirror of the 'cult of personality' (drawing Stalin; becoming like the record-breaking Tadzhik schoolgirl Mamlakat Nakhangova). The others had desires of a kind that would have been considered thoroughly bourgeois only a few years earlier. They wanted to learn the violin, to skate, and to ride, to learn about philosophy, and to see a production of the opera *The Snow-Maiden*.[303] Certainly, hobby circle work was not supposed to be the *only* form of activity engaged in by Pioneers; group leaders who were considered to have given insufficient emphasis to ideological work were censured.[304] But it was taken for granted that absorption in hobbies was a central aspect of 'happy childhood', and one that should be encouraged by the Communist youth movement.

For a good many Pioneers, such dreams of cultured leisure remained precisely that: dreams. Even in larger cities, *kruzhok* work involved only a fraction of the target population: for instance, in Stalinsk (Novokuznetsk) – site of an enormous steelworks that was one of the showpieces of Stalinist industrialisation, and a town with a population well into six figures, the total number of children involved in *kruzhki* during 1938 was just over 1,200, while the children's library had about 1,000 registered readers.[305] But if the Soviet state did little to improve the private living conditions of its subjects, much effort was put into improving the public spaces of Soviet cities. At this level, children benefited not only from the facilities open to other Soviet citizens, such as culture parks, and from children's stadiums and playgrounds, but also from the Pioneer palaces, which began to be set up in the mid-1930s.

Though every Soviet town of a reasonable size was meant to have its own Pioneer palace,[306] the most impressive was undoubtedly the facility in Leningrad. Here, the conversion of former aristocratic haunts into spaces for children reached its apogee with the selection of the Anichkov Palace, birthplace of Nicholas II, as a location for the Pioneer facility. During 1935–6, an elaborate set of assembly rooms for parties, dances, and concerts, a café and a library, cloakrooms and marble-lined lobby, were set up within the Anichkov. At the centre of the building were two 'rooms for rest and relaxation' decorated with motifs from fairy tales and from works by Gorky; another room had wall-paintings of children with animals, and a third was decorated as a fantasy grotto, complete with aquarium and vivarium. The first-floor salons of the original palace were retained as spaces for ballroom dancing and concerts, and the building also contained a 300-seat cinema and a toy cabinet (*igroteka*) with games, models, and opulent toys. Full facilities were provided for a vast range of hobby circles, right up to a purpose-built theatre, laboratories, and workrooms (though a planned swimming pool was never in fact built). In the instruction provided, ideological concerns were muted: the general pattern was for recognised 'bourgeois experts' to teach their own specialisation to the best of their ability.[307]

Interestingly, no 'Pioneer Palace' as such existed in Moscow till 1962. The central Pioneer meeting place was known more humbly as 'the House of Pioneers and Octobrists'. However, the decoration inside was just as grandiose as it was in any of the palaces as such. The central hall contained a marble fountain and was decorated with favourite characters from Krylov's fables and Chukovsky's poems, and there was a palm court where string orchestras could play, as well as special rooms for the usual range of activities, including a chess room, an art room, a technology room, and a theatre. The building perfectly expressed the new status of childhood as at once beyond and outside politics: if there was nothing inside the building, or indeed in the entertainments provided there, that was particularly 'Soviet' in ideological terms, its outside emphasised the status of the building as 'a visible proof of the vast love felt towards children of our country by the Party and by Comrade Stalin'. By the entrance to this 'house of happy childhood' stood a statue of Stalin, his 'majestic form' towering on an enormous pedestal.[308]

The central ceremony of the year in Pioneer palaces (or houses of Pioneers) was the New Year Tree, or *elka*, party. Every aspect of the occasion was the subject of huge effort and thought, beginning with the specially designed tickets, which might show, for instance, a pop-up fir tree weighed down with baubles and tinsel, and with Grandfather Frost alongside. The tree itself would be set up in the largest and grandest room in the building; adults and children would pack in, dressed in their best, to watch a programme of variety entertainments – comic numbers, magic transformation scenes under coloured lights, folk dancing, demonstration ballroom dancing. Then came the lighting of the Christmas tree, with adults dressed up as Grandfather Frost and the Snow Maiden, and gifts to children. The evening was rounded off by a children's ball, with dancing in costume.[309]

The 'New Year tree' parties were emphatically not intended as an opportunity for children to let off steam, or an occasion for noisy fun. Attended by adult

108　New Year tree party, Leningrad Pioneer Palace, late 1940s.

dignitaries, they were, rather, meant as an elaborate demonstration of well-behaved children enjoying the benefits granted to them by the state, and as an enactment of children's subordination to adult authority. This went with the general restoration of adult governance, including the governance of parents. The new rules for Pioneers promulgated in 1937, for instance, made it incumbent upon members to show not only respect to their elders, but also 'love to parents'.[310]

During the Second World War, the character of the Pioneers in part shifted back again. Children were encouraged to contribute to the war effort. A propaganda article by Arkady Gaidar, 'Children and the War', published in late 1941, insisted that young people's contribution was vital. Apart from learning to shoot and joining the Partisans, there were humbler things that children could do to help the Soviet cause. They could, for example, learn German, so that they could eavesdrop more effectively on what the invaders were saying.[311] Practices in schools underlined these bellicose connections. The Pioneer 'base' in schools was renamed a *druzhina* (cohort), and its 'soviet' now became a *shtab*, or 'staff headquarters'. All pretence at 'elected' representation was dropped and members were openly selected by the Pioneer leader ('elections' were reintroduced only in 1947). Children were encouraged to name their school Pioneer 'cohort' after a famous military hero or general, and received training in 'military spirit': 'discipline, stoicism, endurance, daring, deftness and fearlessness'.[312] But most children were involved at a humbler level. Gaidar's own novel, *Timur and his Team*, about an informal children's association started by a boy living in a dacha settlement to help the families of Red Army soldiers serving at the Front, was written as a response to the Finno-Soviet War, but the 'Timurites' served as a model for children during the Great Patriotic War as well, as they collected scrap metal, picked medicinal herbs, checked the efficiency of blackout curtains, escorted small children and old people to air-raid shelters, organised hospital visits to the wounded, and generally made themselves useful in patriotic ways.[313]

Once the war was over, the Pioneers, like the rest of Soviet society, began demilitarising in an explicit manner. In the first years after the conflict finished, there was little retrospective coverage relating to it in the Pioneer press: instead, propaganda focused on the rebuilding of the cities devastated by occupation and bombardment. National triumphalism mounted, with the celebrations for the 850th anniversary of the founding of Moscow in 1947; the 110th anniversary of Pushkin's death was commemorated as piously in the Pioneer press as anywhere else. Indeed, notable, at any rate in the newspaper *Pioneer Pravda*, was an increasing assimilation of Pioneer journalism to journalism for adults. In its New Year issue for 1939, the paper had begun with a spread about New Year tree parties and winter sports, reserving 'hard news' (an item on the Spanish Civil War) for an inside page. In the New Year issue for 1947, by contrast, the New Year tree celebrations were consigned to a page 3 slot, and the paper led with coverage of Party news, just as *Pravda* of the day would have done.[314]

The sober mood was intensified by a concentration on the need for hard work and personal discipline. Pioneer magazines carried material on 'Pioneer honour', meant for discussion at troop meetings as well as individual absorption; they emphasised the need for absolute commitment to the cause. Fictional texts representing Pioneers followed this general line. Sergei Mikhalkov's play *The Red Tie* (1947), for instance, was a hortatory representation of a 'bad' Pioneer. Valery Vishnyakov, its egotistical anti-hero, was a reasonably assiduous and successful school pupil but lax about voluntary work (refusing to help with the wall newspaper even though he was the only person in the class who could draw). Following the conventions of children's fiction generally, Valery's sister was represented as a preferable alternative – principled and conscientious, though not such a high achiever academically. The gender conflict was offset here by the presence of a model boy, Shura, an orphan taken in by the Vishnyakovs after the death of both his parents (his father at the Front, his mother, of an illness after the war). Valery's recalcitrance led to his expulsion from the Pioneer organisation. At the meeting where the question of Valery's membership was raised once more, Shura was asked to speak about Valery's character and did so frankly. At first branding Shura a 'traitor', Valery eventually learned to see that he had displayed true friendship, and to accept his stricture that 'real Bolsheviks always tell the truth'.[315]

All in all, the 1940s saw a further dilution of the commitment to political activism that had originally sustained the Pioneer movement, and at the same time a rising emphasis on the need for Pioneers to acquire a passive knowledge of politics. Like other Soviet children, Pioneers were now supposed to be curators of the present, rather than fighters for a 'new way of life'. Gaidar's Timur, the boy subordinate to patriarchal authority and well aware of his place in the larger social order, retained his hold over official children's culture.[316] Even the celebrations for the twenty-fifth anniversary of the Pioneer movement's founding in 1947 played down the fiery activism of the early years. Anatoly Rybakov's short novel *Kortik* (1948) turned the tale of an early Moscow troop into a jolly adventure story of Scout-style scrapes and japes. To be sure, some political and social activities remained on the agenda, for example anti-religious work. Children going to church in the post-war era could expect to have their names recorded by members of their own Pioneer troop standing outside the church with notebooks and pencils.[317] But discipline was more important. On 17 January 1951, for instance, the Bureau of the Central Committee of the Komsomol highlighted the appalling case of the Ivanovo Palace of Pioneers, whose organisers had been lax in imposing discipline (Pioneers had been turning up to events late, untidily dressed, and even without their regulation red ties).[318] In 1952, attempts were made to tighten up the recruitment process in order to convey to children that the process of joining the Pioneers was not simply automatic. A child's conduct record and school performance was to be taken into account when an application was made to join the organisation, and school directors and staff, including class supervisors, should co-operate in the administration of the organisation.[319] Thus the disciplinary networks of school and Komsomol organisation were drawn still more tightly together; and practice often outstripped theory in this respect, since it was common, though by no means universal, for a group's 'class supervisor' to act as their Pioneer leader as well.

De-Stalinising the Classroom

From 1953, elusive changes in tone made themselves felt within the Pioneer organisation. Outwardly, however, this was a time of growing homogeneity. More and more children were absorbed by the movement: in 1960 there were 15.4 million members, from a target age group of 16.6 million; in 1970, 23.3 million members, from a target age group of 24.9 million.[320] Oral history suggests that it was in the 1960s and 1970s that the first real Pioneers (as opposed to on-paper Pioneers) appeared in many rural outposts.[321] Increasingly, non-Pioneers were made up of the socially marginal: those languishing in prisons and in youth custody; those excluded from the Pioneer groups in ordinary schools on grounds of bad behaviour or poor educational progress; those living in very remote areas, beyond the reach of Party work in the broadest sense.

If the institutional location of the Pioneers did not change, there were changes to certain aspects of symbolism and ritual, and, more covertly, to the movement's aims and objectives. Even before Khrushchev's denunciation of the 'cult of personality' in 1956, the 1942 reference to 'Great Stalin' was dropped from the Pioneer oath. From 1954, Pioneers began promising 'in the presence of their comrades' to 'be true to the testaments of Lenin'.[322] And the aims of the organisation, as officially stated, were slightly tweaked. In 1954, fostering the love of physical labour was added to support of school-work as a primary purpose of the Pioneer organisation, and the specified duties of the Pioneer were said to include 'socially useful work'.[323] The year 1962 also saw the holding, for the first time since 1929, of an All-Soviet Pioneer Rally, this time to mark the fortieth anniversary of the founding of the association. A much shorter gap was to intervene between this rally and the next in the series: the Third All-Soviet Rally followed in 1967, and further rallies were held in 1970, 1972, and then every two years thereafter. While rallies no longer included the kind of controlled, but live, debate that had characterised the Pioneer movement in the late 1920s, they did address officially approved political topics, such as the peace movement or children's welfare across the world; they were also, in a limited sense, internationalist, with the participation of Pioneer representatives and visiting children from all over the world, including the capitalist countries.

All of this constituted a partial rehabilitation of political activism by children, in step with the revival of 'activist' models for children's behaviour. Yet, while the Pioneer movement's revolutionary heritage was stressed, its function as a leisure organisation was also strengthened. A Party decree of November 1957, 'On Measures to Improve the Character of the Pioneer Organisation', called for more emphasis on honour to the Red Flag, the Solemn Oath, the motto, and other such ritual trappings of the organisation, and for greater attention to discipline and 'moral education'. But it also stipulated better provision of non-political activities for children. There were now to be not only more 'bonfires', but also more competitions, quizzes, festivals, congresses, and conferences for different specialist sections.[324] Similarly, a decree by the Central Committee of the Komsomol on 17 March 1967 underlined the new emphasis on leisure by specifying the aims of the Pioneer organisation as fostering artistic activity alongside education, and bringing into the lives of Pioneers 'romanticism, interest, and play'.[325]

Representations of Pioneer heroes reflected the tension between political commitment and 'play'. The 1960s witnessed the emergence of explicitly de-ideologised, even ironic, representations of Pioneers. A striking example was Elem Klimov's extremely funny and subversive satire on Pioneer camp life, *Welcome and Keep Out!* (1964). The film showed a group of children running rings round the dictatorial and narrow-minded staff of the camp, outwitting the intrusive surveillance of the camp sneak, and reducing to farce a pageant staged on 'Parents' Day', when an important official's daughter was supposed to take a starring role as 'Queen of the Maize'. In fact the child who popped out of the papier-mâché simulacrum of a corn-cob on a ceremonial wagon was the tousle-headed runaway who had been a thorn in the adults' side all along.

Viktor Golyavkin's story, 'Come and Visit!', though less confrontational, was in sum equally subversive. It showed a small boy who got bored and lonely on his dacha holiday, and began visiting the neighbouring Pioneer camp. He was soon (despite the disapproval of the adult organisers) joining in all the activities. While this plot motif (better collective than solitary life) would have been easy to find in early Soviet literature, the nature of the collective activities – a camping expedition, a concert, and a football match, rather than a political rally or even a propagandistic singsong – had changed. An uninformed reader might not have realised that the Pioneers were a political movement at all.[326]

The new emphasis on pastimes was evident also in the handling of Pioneer palaces. To begin with, the numbers of these expanded significantly. By 1977, there were seven Pioneer palaces in Moscow and thirty-two Pioneer houses, running a total of over 4,300 circles and catering to nearly 75,000 children.[327] The nature of the new buildings was markedly leisure oriented rather than politics oriented. Typical was the superb new Central Pioneer Palace in south-west Moscow, near to the university, opened in 1962 and incorporating a cinema, theatre, sweeping lobby with access to cafés and galleries, and extensive exterior landscaping.[328] The Pioneer Palace in Leningrad also opened an extensive leisure and sports complex, in 1972. While most major cities already had palaces dating from the 1930s (Sverdlovsk, Novosibirsk, and Novokuznetsk among them), at this stage some smaller places, such as Berezniki in Perm' province, also acquired palaces of their own.

Interesting, too, is the spirit in which the facilities were run. In 2004, Ol'ga Grekova, the director of the Central Pioneer Palace in Moscow during the 1970s and early 1980s, recalled her time there with much enthusiasm. She saw the palace's function primarily in terms of keeping children interested and developing their intellectual and creative potential in a general sense. The palace staff did not engage directly in moral and character education – this was left to Pioneer groups in schools. Instead, they concentrated their efforts on building up a wide range of hobby circles and perfecting the work of these. They took especial pride in the activities of the song and dance group, successful in many international competitions, but also in their work with 'difficult children', and with the many 'normal' children who travelled from all over Moscow and from the Moscow region to attend the palace. After leaving in 1984 to become editor of *Pioneer Pravda*, Grekova transferred this enthusiasm for work in the arts to the newspaper itself. She revived the 'child correspondent' role, but this now had rather a different function: instead of submitting copy about topics of current interest to the paper from outside, children would visit the editorial offices and contribute to its day-to-day work.[329] Though Grekova was perhaps inclined to play down in retrospect the presence of ideological elements in the Pioneer movement and the extent of the continuity in youth work before and after 1991, there is no doubt that the 'rational leisure' side of the Pioneers became increasingly dominant after 1956, overshadowing more and more the movement's political educational side.

The post-Stalin era also saw extensive development of the Pioneer camp as a leisure facility.[330] Available space was considerably expanded. In Sverdlovsk, for example, 5,500 extra places were added between 1964 and 1968, and the number of city camps more than doubled between 1960 and 1968.[331] According to an official

109 Propaganda photograph of Artek Pioneer camp, early 1950s.

guide to Moscow published in 1977, the number of camps in the Moscow area rose from 708 in 1965 to 724 in 1970. Thereafter, numbers dropped back once more, to 715 in 1975 and 659 in 1976. But camps in towns, rather than in the countryside, increased steadily: from 185 in 1965 to 231 in 1970, 270 in 1975, and 314 in 1976. Over half a million Moscow children now had the chance to spend at least part of their summer holidays in a camp, it was claimed.[332] Enormous effort was put into creating high-specification facilities. The Leningrad Pioneer Palace's camp, Zerkal'nyi, opened in 1969, for example, was an opulent leisure and sports centre covering a considerable acreage in a prestige resort area not far from Russia's 'second capital'.[333] Orlenok, or Eaglet, in Tuapse, Krasnodar region, a prime resort area of the south, was another prestigious camp, established in 1961; it was even the subject of a special song, 'The Eaglets Learn to Fly', by N. Dobronravov and A. Pakhmutova.[334]

Expansion did not guarantee all Soviet children a holiday in an out-of-town Pioneer camp, or even access to 'camp-style' summer playgrounds in a city. According to figures from Sverdlovsk, in-town camps there had catered in 1960 for less than a third of the target population (i.e. children who did not have a place in a Pioneer camp outside the city): even more than doubling the number of city camps by 1968 is unlikely to have provided sufficient accommodation.[335] But the fact was that, with extra places in out-of-town camps, extra places in town camps and playgrounds, as well as space in new types of facility – Komsomol youth work camps (accommodating 5,770 people in 1964), tourist camps (with 5,179 children in 1964), and municipal dachas on the Black Sea (9,537 children in

1964) – a town like Sverdlovsk could now guarantee the majority of its juvenile population – 87 per cent, it was claimed in 1965 – some kind of urban or exurban 'health break'.[336] This represented a very significant change compared with the past. Though the Soviet press had carried regular items about joyful children revelling in their summer break from the 1920s right through to the early 1950s, the sparse figures quoted suggest that only a small proportion of children were reached by the system.[337] Criticism in the press indicated that space in 'city summer camps' was decidedly limited as well.[338]

The 1950s and 1960s also saw an attempt to provide rather more ambitious facilities for those holidaying outside the city. Both before and after the war, accommodation at the live-in camps was rudimentary other than at Artek, the showpiece resort in the Crimea, where the children of the political elite rubbed shoulders with the sons and daughters of prominent foreign Communists and with hand-picked Pioneers who had achieved outstanding marks at school or distinguished themselves in some other way. Unlike Scouts, Pioneers did not necessarily sleep out in tents: expeditions (*pokhody*) of this kind were a relatively minor part of the children's Communist movement.[339] But if Pioneer camps usually had fixed sites, they generally did not have purpose-built accommodation. A peasant hut or two might be rented in a village, or bourgeois dachas requisitioned to serve as living space. By the 1960s, it was common for camps to offer permanent dormitories and washing facilities (usually, to be sure, outdoor, and consisting of no more than a few showers and taps) alongside canteens, with a tarmacked sports and parade ground alongside.

First-hand testimony indicates that the ethos of 'socially useful work' had entirely disappeared, and that the part played by politics in Pioneer camp life was now very limited. The timetable of city camps, according to the recollections of a former visitor, included no political work at all, simply meals and excursions interrupted by the usual compulsory rest.[340] In all camps, ideology surfaced more or less only in 'discussions round the bonfire', the singing of patriotic songs, and in organised games – which, in the post-Stalin era, meant above all Zarnitsa, an elaborate kind of reconnaissance game first introduced in January 1967, which had children adopting military roles (soldiers, radio officers, doctors, nurses), forming into platoons, and carrying out manoeuvres against the opposing side.[341]

The 'mixed messages' in propaganda and organisational activity were reflected in an anthology published in 1962 to mark the fortieth anniversary of the founding of the Pioneers, *LISTEN EVERYONE!* The statements by 517 Pioneers, most aged around 13 and 14, from Gorlovka, a mining town in the Donbass region, paid some service to conventional pieties. Some listed their wishes for the future as hoping people in their school would get only good marks from now on, or that their Pioneer *druzhina* would win the 'Friend of the Seven-Year Plan' prize; all expressed excitement at the lead-up to the Twenty-Second Congress of the Communist Party in 1961. But, at the same time, there were a good many thoroughly unpolitical aspirations. One girl wanted to see a fountain with real goldfish placed in her school playground; another hoped in time to become a pianist 'like Van Clyburn'; one boy's dearest wish was to drive a train himself.[342]

110   Octobrists, 1975, Leningrad.

The political aspirations of these early 1960s Pioneers should perhaps not be interpreted too cynically. In Soviet society generally, this was an era of genuine hopes for democratic participation: in universities, for example, there was a blossoming of societies of all kinds, while the wall newspaper, moribund for three decades, suddenly became a real vehicle for creative expression. But once liberalisation of Soviet organisations was slowed down, the routinisation of the Pioneer movement at a political level, temporarily arrested by the upheavals of 1956–64, began to take hold again. Increasingly, members were expected to go through the motions. They had to memorise the biographies of Pioneer heroes so that they could recite these when required as a test of fitness to join the movement, but afterwards could happily expunge the information from their minds.

'Internationalism' was more than merely a slogan of the day; the Pioneer movement was also becoming increasingly 'international' in the sense that its concerns were converging with those of children's organisations in the West. This in turn made the movement vulnerable when state support started to dry up in the late 1980s: already by the summer of 1991, many camps were almost at a standstill, threatened not just by collapsing finances but by alterations in the attitudes of the public to the annual holiday, and by the growing tendency to see this as an all-family occasion.[343] With commitment on political and moral grounds now unimportant to many members, the Pioneer organisation simply had nothing left beyond its camps, palaces, and hobby circles; once these were privatised, the *de facto* as well as formal demise of the organisation was inevitable.

Outside the Classroom

Official rituals, lessons, and organised extra-curricular activities never comprised the whole gamut of children's experience in the Russian school. Even during the Soviet era, some free time was built into the timetable, in the form of the so-called *peremena* ('break', or 'recess'). Before the Revolution, even younger schoolchildren might have only two breaks in four or five hours of classes, but the standard pattern in Soviet schools was a break of 10 minutes after every class, and a *bol'shaya peremena*, or half-hour refreshment break, in the middle of the day.

This time was, for most of the century in question, not organised in any way. Indeed, some schools did not even have an outside playground where pupils could take exercise.[344] Given the many other demands on teaching staff, they could not consistently supervise break-time activities. The main way that 'rational leisure' was ensured was simply by not allowing schoolchildren to use the playground, or to leave the school buildings, between the start of lessons in the morning and the end of lessons in the afternoon.[345] Otherwise, teachers took little interest in break time, limiting their activities to barking occasional commands at children whom they happened to catch misbehaving as they went from place to place.[346] To be sure, the Cultural Revolution of 1928–32 saw a short-lived campaign to introduce 'rational leisure' to the playground, in parallel to the campaigns going on in city streets and courtyards. Agitational articles portrayed the transformation of playgrounds from places where insulting graffiti were scrawled, spitting contests indulged in, and monotonous songs droned out, to areas where children spent their time out of class in purposeful ways, learning songs from the radio and working on the wall newspaper, or playing 'mass games' outside when weather permitted.[347] But, as with children's play more generally, these campaigns do not seem to have been very successful, though certainly teachers could impose their authority directly to stop what were seen as unacceptable games.[348]

Whether outside in the school yard or in the corridor, children often indulged in the very activities that had most shocked those pressing for reform. Teasing and insult contests abounded. A constant stream of abuse was directed at anyone who stood out in any way, whether tall, small, fat, or thin. Thin children, for instance, would be routinely addressed as 'skellington' (*shkilet*).[349] Children also traded disrespectful nicknames, many of which were passed on from generation to generation (every Shura without fail being referred to as *dura*, idiot). They were repressive, condemning taboo activities, such as whispering, with annihilating crudity: 'Whisper, whisper, up your arse with a clyster.' And the exchange of taunts could develop into formalised exchanges of traditional rhymes, taking the form, for instance, of a trick question that allowed an insult to be delivered as the punch-line:

'Someone I know sent you her best wishes.'
'Who's that?'
'Mary.'

'Who's Mary?'
'Big fat and hairy!!'[350]

Such insult contests could continue almost indefinitely until one or other participant, or an onlooker, shouted a closing formula such as 'Out and no more shout!'[351] – or until the opponents ran out of things to say or lapsed into a fit of the sulks.

All of this was ritualised, predictable, and more to do with containing rather than provoking tension. There were cases, though, where insults led to physical fights – as with an incident in 1940s Leningrad where one boy bent the corner of his jacket into a 'pig's ear' in order to taunt his neighbour, a Bashkir: 'So I lammed into him. Bloodied his nose. And that was it.' Yet even fights did not necessarily lead to permanent rifts. There was, indeed, a common pattern of male ice-breaking, or initiation into the group, by use of physical violence. The case of the 'pig's ear' insult ended like this, for instance: 'And then, so to speak, we started to be friends. More than that: we were in the same class, and I'd do his maths problems for him, for money – well, not for money, actually, for bits of bread and that.'[352] Similarly, in boys' schools before 1917, new boys had to go through a ritual known as 'baptism', where they were set upon by others in order to see how well they could defend themselves.[353]

Often, though, playground hatreds were more to do with exclusion than inclusion. At one late nineteenth-century school where pupils were divided into 'feasters' (*kuteiniki*) and 'cat-skinners' (*koshkodery*) the minute they arrived, little association took place between the two groups throughout their school careers.[354] In those pre-revolutionary schools where pupils helped out with corporal punishment, the teachers' amanuenses naturally came in for reciprocal brutality in the playground. 'After school, of course, we regularly waylaid Kuzya and gave him better than we received – that, too, was part of the ritual,' Victor Kravchenko cheerfully remembered.[355] Top pupils also enjoyed considerable unpopularity. A teacher who wrote, in 1964, 'The teacher's favourite, you'll notice, is invariably the favourite of the group as a whole', had either been lucky with her class, or suffered from impaired powers of observation.[356] Much more often, favourites were strongly disliked. 'People did nasty things to them all the time, were rough and that. Nobody gave them any peace. They'd pinch them, say, hit them over the head with a book,' one working-class woman recalled of her stint at school in the 1970s and 1980s. The key revenge of *otlichniki* was to refuse to let others copy their work, which sometimes held aggression in check. Those regularly getting low marks, on the other hand, were the object of, at worst, affectionate contempt.[357]

Roughing-up 'teacher's pet' sometimes ended in tragedy, as in a 1935 case where an *otlichnik* was stabbed by his classmates.[358] In the best of circumstances, playground teasing and violence often came uncomfortably close to bullying: a big strong pupil who could respond to initiation with violence might well win acceptance and admiration from his classmates, but a small or timid one was likely to be cast in the role of perpetual victim.[359] Nabokov's novel *The Defense* (1930) gives an unforgettable picture of the horrors of a playground for a timid, unathletic, withdrawn child permanently condemned to not 'fitting in'. It goes without saying that children who were in any way different from others – thinner, fatter, taller, smaller, from an ethnic minority, with a strange accent, or simply recent arrivals – would be picked upon in short order.[360] Often, teachers did not need to work *à la* Makarenko for bullying techniques, such as ostracism, to emerge: a pupil who cut against the standards of the dominant group was likely to find him- or herself an outcast in any case.[361]

Bullying was, by all accounts, particularly common immediately after the Revolution, when the practice of throwing together schools of totally different type and status exacerbated social fissures rather than producing cross-class harmony; the need to get used to coeducation was also a cause of upset to many. A pupil at a former *pension* for upper-class girls recalled that the working-class boys who appeared at the school in 1918 'insulted and tormented [*obizhali*] us girls and there was no one you could complain to'.[362] Conflicts of this kind replaced the more traditional activity of faction-fighting between boys from different districts, which now got transformed into scuffles between 'monarchists' and 'revolutionaries', 'Kadets' and 'Bolsheviks', or 'Reds' and 'Whites'.[363] Some of the fights were quite dangerous, with boys using skates and coshes [*svinchatki*] as well as satchels to lash out, along with more traditional weapons such as knives.[364]

Despite repeated exhortations in pedagogical literature, and an explicit prohibition on 'abusive language, the use of nicknames, and fighting' in the school rules of 1935,[365] playground violence of this kind continued to be an endemic problem. In 1938, an article in *Soviet Justice* reported with horror that some pupils attending a school in Gorky had spent one break having a knife-fight, 'while the Pioneer leader stood in a group of other Pioneers coolly watching the spectacle'. The article suggested that events of this kind were common.[366] In this case, the boys involved were all armed, and hence at some level on equal terms: but often it was the vulnerable who were picked on – boys wearing glasses, boys the bullies considered mollycoddled or excessively proper. For the future Academician M. L. Gasparov, a shy and studious only child who began attending school in 1943, the lessons at his primary school were less memorable than were the dreadful class recesses. 'Worn jackets, patched elbows, lowered heads and piercing eyes: they're all different, but they all look the same. They dart about, you can't understand a word, and you don't know the rules. I keep giving the wrong answer, and they fight me for it. They always know the rules of fighting better than I do.' Gasparov remembered once being made to sit down on the pavement when he met a group of class bullies on the way home (though, as 'they were in quite a good mood', they let him get away with using his briefcase as a cushion).[367] Girls did not go in so much for physical fights, though there are recorded cases of girls who got involved in bouts of fisticuffs with boys.[368] But bullying of a mental kind – such as a group of girls deciding to 'gang up' on some perhaps wholly inoffensive individual and torment her – is quite widely recorded from the late nineteenth century to the late twentieth.[369]

Not all activities were so aggressive. In wet weather, girls in particular might find an empty classroom and indulge in a round or two of a paper game such as

Alphabet, where players composed lists of words beginning with a certain letter in a range of categories (trees, books, countries, rivers …), or Balda, where players took it in turns to write down a letter at a time, placing it to one side of a letter or letters already written, until a word was completed (the person who entered the final letter won the game).[370] But, on the whole, children who had been spending time forcibly sitting still preferred games involving more mobility: chase, catch, *slon* (a piggyback battle between two children sitting on the shoulders of others), hopscotch, skipping, or simply running about. Children also smoked, talked desultorily, and worked their way through food and drink.[371] In other words, they engaged in much the same activities that they might have done in streets, courtyards, or indeed at home.

Some features of interaction in the playground or corridor were specific to the world of school. For instance, groups of mixed age were significantly less likely to form here than in corridors or streets, since pupils generally associated with their class or year group. And older children – who played a dominant role in courtyards and streets in any case – were formally empowered in the school, since they were usually assigned the duty of keeping order in the absence of teachers. When provoked, such individuals might take drastic measures to subdue their juniors. Such summary justice was possible because the official school hierarchy was in abeyance, yet pupils themselves, in at least a distant way, replicated the authoritarian structures that prevailed in the school more widely. Explosive behaviour of this kind characterised some teachers when provoked as well, while the singling out for torment of certain individuals recalled the practices of the official schoolroom, though the status hierarchy was reversed, with teachers' pets vilified, while *otpetye dvoechniki* ('hopeless dunces') held sway.[372]

The essential feature of school leisure was not really the restoration to life of the impermissible – though scatological ditties were as widespread here as in the city courtyard, and time during breaks might well also be spent on more innocent activities that were not permitted during lessons: visiting the lavatory, catching up with missed homework.[373] The point was that school folklore, by and large, lived parasitically on official school culture. An idiosyncratic example was the children from the Leningrad Choreographical School who made themselves a subversive version of the official school stamp for documents.[374] But there were also more widespread forms of protest. For instance, special genres of anecdote popular with children undercut the constant schoolroom reminders of the need to behave in a sensible, practical way. One of the most popular heroes was Vovochka, a dimwit boy who, when instructed to paint the windows in the classroom during a stint as class monitor (*dezhurnyi*), returned in puzzlement to say that the glass was all freshly painted, but he wasn't sure what to do with the frames.[375] Other joke figures who violated propriety included Cornet Rzhevsky, Pushkin's contemporary and hopeless boor, the Soviet agent in disguise Shtirlitz, and Cheburashka, the protagonist of stories by the children's writer Eduard Uspensky.[376] Equally popular were scabrous parodies of texts set for compulsory reading and learning by heart in literature classes: the opening lines of Pushkin's *Ruslan and Lyudmila*, or the stanzas on winter from *Evgeny Onegin* ('Winter: the peasant, celebrating ...'), or a rewritten stanza from Mayakovsky's 'Verses on My Soviet Passport', in which the poet extracted from his 'wide trousers' something quite different from the document attesting Soviet nationality of which he had boasted in the original poem. A whole vein of folklore and playground lexis harped upon the official scale of marks. A 2 awarded for whispering the right answer to another pupil, for example, was known as 'woe from wit' (after the title of Griboedov's famous comedy, ground through by generations of schoolchildren in literature classes). Schoolchildren might also pun on their knowledge of foreign languages to describe a pedagogue as *tycha*, which bore a phonetic resemblance to the English word but also worked as a Russian neologism from the verb *tychat'*, 'to jab'.[377] Sometimes, more elaborate cases of 'knowledge inversion' were found: in the early 1980s, for example, a group of pupils at a Moscow school organised 'The Funeral of Pythagoras', at which a pupil posing as the deceased mathematician was carried ceremonially along the school corridor, preceded by mourners holding up copies of his formulae written in exercise books – until the fun was spoiled by the arrival of a strict teacher at the bottom of the stairs.[378]

If influences from the official parts of school life reached into areas of pupils' imaginative lives, there were also sections of their emotional existence which showed the traces of school socialisation: the culture of friendship, for instance. Friendship, as was abundantly documented in propaganda for children, was understood in official discourse to be a phenomenon fraught with danger. Friendship in the sense of absence of hostility was one thing: children were constantly reminded of the importance of maintaining a 'friendly class'. In some discussions, this type of friendship was named 'comradeliness', to distinguish it from emotional relations on a more individual basis, such as might lead children to become involved in subversive activities, or foster an undue dominance, in the class collective, of individual groups threatening atomisation.[379] But it was the individual kind of friendship that predominated in the schoolroom, rather than a disinterested collective spirit. The existence of such a spirit was – by the later stages of Soviet history – in most respects a fiction in any case. Divisions by ethnicity and, more particularly, by social status were becoming extremely evident in Soviet schools, especially in the major cities. By the late 1960s, children's sense of differentiation at the second level was sharpened by the broadening possibilities for the acquisition of consumer goods, including those produced outside the Soviet Union. The compulsory uniform concealed some of this, but, as the strict neighbourhood catchment system meant that schools recruited children who generally lived alongside each other, pupils would see each other in ordinary clothes as well and acquire a very good idea of who owned what.[380]

In any case, as in other circumstances and cultures, the essential basis for friendship tended to be shared interest rather than high moral principles (just as, conversely, juvenile enmity was not usually based on issues of principle, as it supposedly should have been, but on arbitrary factors). A class group was unlikely to consist entirely of people who had an interest exclusively in sport, or in the ballet, or in music, or in particular kinds of books, yet it was precisely on the basis of such exclusive interests that friendships were cemented.[381] Equally, the practices of friendship were less likely to involve high-minded chastisement of companions who were falling below one's own moral standards than everyday rituals of bonding. Among boys in the late nineteenth century, for instance, it was customary to ask friends to sign one's school-book: underneath 'This book belongs to', they would inscribe, 'Witnessed by ...'[382] Among young girls, albums were used on the same lines: a stereotyped text was the 'questionnaire' asking, 'Do you like the person who wrote this questionnaire?' and 'What is friendship?' alongside questions about personal tastes ('Who's your favourite foreign pop star?' 'What cartoon films do you like?').[383]

At the same time, there were elements in children's relationships as lived that bore some relation to the behaviour patterns in books and articles. It was, for example, quite common for children to do homework together, less for frivolous reasons (cutting down effort by copying from each other) than for pedagogical ones – the child who was stronger in a certain subject might help the one who was weaker get to grips with the material.[384] And friendships were sometimes initiated on the grounds of exactly the sort of high-minded feelings that were depicted in ideal representations of schoolchild behaviour. One Leningrad girl made a durable and much-valued friendship with a newcomer to the school whom she had upbraided for taking part in a poison-pen letter campaign against another girl. Rather than taking umbrage at the scolding, the friend was so impressed by her 'noble act' that their relationship immediately entered another phase.[385] Another piquant indication of how emotional relationships developed in the interstices of the school world was the 'mark book', where children kept lists of people they associated with, and awarded marks – on the official school scale – for niceness and friendliness. The 'mark book' was passed around quite widely, so that everyone got to know where they stood in the hierarchy.[386]

The 'mark book' brings out once more the paradoxical conventionality of school pupils. As in schools everywhere, the attitudes of children and teachers were not so much antagonistic as complementary, or indeed collusive. The constant espousal on paper of tough disciplinary measures was accompanied by a fairly persistent ethos of compromise and fudging, if not disorder, in the classroom itself. For instance, throughout the 'long twentieth century' (excepting the 1920s, when pupils' homework was tested on a brigade-by-brigade basis, so that only the most enthusiastic workers answered), the strict process of grading was adjusted by self-help practices. Pupils would 'prompt' their fellows who were under interrogation, copy work from their neighbours during tests, and make use of improvised crib-sheets (*shpargalki*) during tests. Teachers often colluded in such practices because poor performance on the part of pupils rebounded on them; conversely, pupils who were 'cheating' to achieve good marks were acknowledging the value of such marks.[387]

Pupils absorbed the tuition that they were given idiosyncratically. Age was a factor (the dreaded classes for any teachers were those in which 14- and 15-year-olds were present), but so, too, were temperament and background. Journalism tended to highlight cases where children had openly rebelled – from boys and girls going on strike in 1905 to stories of suicides as a result of overwork in the same period, and on to the tales of revolutionary struggle in 1917, *buzina* (prank-playing) in the 1920s, and sensational reports of shoot-outs in the late 1930s. In the Soviet period, archival reports emphasise this side of school life too, with accounts of swastikas drawn in textbooks and of secret societies with anti-Soviet agendas.[388] But such overt rebellion was rare. More common were lower-level, unpolitical gestures of subversion: giving teachers nicknames, deliberately mispronouncing their surnames, pretending that homework had not been set, 'going on strike' when it was considered too hard. As for the intellectual and moral content of the syllabus, that was absorbed according to the child. Academically inclined children often enjoyed the tuition offered in *gimnazii* and Soviet ten-year schools; other children sometimes found it stultifying. Patriotic and religious education, and participation in organisations such as the Scouts and Pioneers, inspired some, while others found it pointless or indeed disgusting. There was also a historical dynamic: members of the intelligentsia brought up in the 1930s and 1940s regarded school much more warmly than their counterparts of the 1900s or 1910s, or than their successors in the 1950s, 1960s, and 1970s. In periods when parents were often absent, and home conditions tough, the school could be a means of social and practical survival.

In whatever generation, the relationship between children and the school authorities was generally chacterised less by open enmity and embittered confrontation than by a degree of understanding and indeed collusion, with both sides recognising that their relationships might be in some respects uncongenial, but had to be endured and survived.[389] And there was a considerable cult of the individual teacher among Russian pupils – fostered, in the Soviet period, by sentimental songs with titles like 'My First Teacher' and by films such as Frez's *The Girl in Class One*, but also existing in its own right, and fostered by the selfless work of many teachers, who provided much extra help to their charges without pay, and sometimes acted as general mentors, indeed friends, as well.[390]

For the entire twentieth century, the school was the primary institution, outside the family, to impact on children's lives. Whether its institutional characteristics were relished or detested, it provided a very different kind of socialisation from that offered in the family – kinder, from the perspective of some, harsher, from the perspective of others; possibly more, possibly less, rational, but at all times distinctive. The same distinctness from family values applies to the socialisation offered in the children's organisations, such as the Pioneers and the Scouts, which were united by their emphasis on self-reliance as a virtue and by their efforts to foster early maturity, though both had a strong commitment to the organisation of enjoyable activities as well.

But if the social location of the school and its ancillary youth organisations was in many respects stable, the nuances of education changed, and with them the details of children's experience and of the impact of education. Education seems to have been most successful in influencing attitudes when it provided children with a sense of security in eras when this sense was otherwise not available. This applies to the *émigré* schools of the 1920s and 1930s in particular, but also – as far as large numbers of children were concerned – to the Stalinist schools of the 1930s and 1940s. In the post-Stalin era, on the other hand, the increasing dislocation between school education and the ethos of 'children first' combined with loss of ideological momentum (so that political indoctrination was understood to be a 'going through the motions') to produce a much greater sense of cynicism about the values propounded in the schoolroom.

The Russian school also suffered, throughout the 'long twentieth century', from the vexed relationship between what was propounded in the schoolroom and the enduring traditions of the playground. On the one hand, the authoritarian character of the classroom reinforced the tendency among children themselves to lay down the law to their fellows, sharpening the potential for conflict between different factions beyond the classroom door. On the other hand, indoctrination in virtue – though it did have some impact upon pupils' attitudes, particularly in the areas of friendship and love relationships – did not always work on the audience in the way that was intended. For instance, insistence on the benefits of civic denunciation, as propounded in the myth of Pavlik Morozov, jarred with the view, current over generations, that 'sneaking' was a disgusting, unworthy activity. The effect of the clash was less to break down the traditional view of informing than to raise doubts in at least some pupils' minds about the value of a system which could so celebrate this activity. And at times the day-to-day practices of the school themselves were likely to prompt scepticism. Activities such as *podskazka* (prompting), and the use of *shpargalki* (crib-sheets) might be 'illegal', but they were also tolerated; the situation drew attention to the prevalence of double standards in school life more generally. Much the same could also be said about the imposition upon children of moral codes of a kind few Soviet adults were able or prepared to live up to. Yet at the same time, in generation after generation, the school did provide an introduction to the rules of public life whether these were (as in the 1920s) the need to state as vehemently as possible one's own, ideologically engaged, point of view, or (before 1917 and through most of Soviet power) the need to keep one's head down and say only what was expected – unless one happened to be an individual who was politically empowered in some way.[391]

For many pupils – the majority from the early 1960s – formal education was not completed at the point where this chapter ends. But even if it did not mean starting a job, or transferring from a mainstream school into a vocational school such as a *tekhnikum* or a 'factory school', the age of 14 or 15 marked a real break. Studying beyond this age in an academic school was a privilege, and most pupils acquired a more dedicated and serious attitude; educational pressure intensified, which might mean more pressure to conformity, but could also lead to a greater sense of camaraderie with teachers and a deeper interest in the work. Equally, for Soviet children, the move from Pioneers to Komsomol in the Soviet era meant transition to a far more serious political environment. For many historical subjects, therefore, there was a real sense of the 'end of childhood' at 14 or 15.

In the words of a Leningrader born in the 1960s: 'I felt that [childhood was finished] at the end of Class 7, because we had the school exams in Class 8, and some of our group had to leave school after that, go to factory schools and so on. And I realised that in a year's time a bit of my life would be finished, that it already practically was finished.'[392] If the child left school, he or she moved into a different world; if not, study continued in a different class group, and in a more serious atmosphere. This formal division was of less significance before 1917, when work was likely to start earlier (from 12) for some, and school to continue longer (up to the age of 18 or 19) for others. In this era, too, there was nothing resembling the Komsomol as an official youth organisation with more or less universal membership among the target age group and its rite of entry as an official marker of progress towards maturity. However, various other changes – altering clothes, perhaps, for upper- and middle-class males in this generation, first sexual experiences – provided a sense that a boundary had been crossed: what ensued was no longer childhood, but youth.

Conclusion:
'The End of Childhood'?

Little children are little worries, but they'll be big ones when they grow up.

(Russian proverb)

'Is it Easy to be Young?'

The history of childhood experience in Russia over the twentieth century is a narrative of infinite variations, of difference according to generation, but also according to social status, to gender, and to age. Yet some underlying generalities can be identified. Childhood was shaped by a central tension between a view of childhood as joyful and sacrosanct, of the child's world as a psychological domain of innocence and wonder, to be preserved intact as long as possible; and a view of childhood as the material of future adulthood, to be disciplined and shaped as early as might be practicable. Few observers adhered wholeheartedly to either view: differences related to the weight given to each alternative perception, and to the age thresholds at which disciplinary procedures, the regimentation of the child's bodily desires and mental processes, were supposed to begin.

The general tradition in Russia throughout the period was to regard the child as relatively 'adult' by as early as seven or eight. At this age by the latest, a child in traditional peasant or working-class households would start being expected to contribute to the household economy by doing simple work tasks, and probably by minding younger sisters and brothers as well.[1] This was also the start date for school education throughout the twentieth century. Within the Communist youth movement, on the other hand, the Octobrist movement spanned both older children of nursery school age, and younger children at school. Therefore, the age of 10 or 11, bringing with it entry to the Pioneers, marked a more significant boundary than the age of seven. A still more important threshold came with entry to the Komsomol at 14 or 15. At this point, much more detailed knowledge of political dogma was required, and the admission process was considerably stricter – those who fluffed their lines, or who appeared to manifest insufficient social and political commitment, would be summarily rebuffed. Sometimes even those who were word-perfect and dedicated to the point of supererogation would find themselves refused, whether because their home background was considered suspect, or simply in order to prove a point. In the words of an official who turned down a teenager for no particular reason in the 1940s, 'Lenin's Komsomol is not a beer-bar, where anyone can enter whenever they wish.'[2]

Learning Komsomol dogma more thoroughly than they had learned Pioneer dogma was not children's only possible response, however. Sometimes they began questioning for the first time whether they wanted to belong to the 'rational collective' for which they were being prepared. In the words of a man born in 1928:

I was never in the Komsomol. [...] I just didn't want to be of my own accord. [I joined the Pioneers] because I was too silly to know any better .... Well, I think so. Because it was, 'O-ho, children, you're going to join the Pioneers tomorrow!' That's what they said in class two, about [joining] the Pioneers .... [And so I go]: 'O-o! O! Mama! Tomorrow they're going to let us join the Pioneers!' and she goes, 'Well, join away then, God help you, join the Pioneers then, God help you.'[3]

As well as a time of increased responsibility and the beginning of a serious attitude to life, adolescence could be regarded as a time of moral striving, of

111 Komsomol literacy campaign, early 1930s.

the search for one's inward identity. Interestingly, this seems to have been the primary meaning of the age for many Russian adolescents themselves, at any rate those with the time and leisure to do more than survive from day to day. In 1911, for example, a 16-year-old *gimnaziya* schoolgirl from Moscow wrote in her diary:

> Every person has inward weaknesses along with his good qualities. Those two principles struggle all his life, and often the former are victorious. [...] People usually say: well, so and so's still young, that's why he's 'going crazy'! It'll all come out in the wash, then he'll settle down and start behaving sensibly. What's meant by sense here is frightful to imagine. And that happens to everyone, everyone. Will it really happen to me as well?[4]

A sense of melancholy could be present in texts whose fundamental drive was to represent youth as a time of optimism and hope: Boris Balter's *Goodbye, Boys!* (1962), a nostalgia-soaked novel about life in a pre-war southern Russian seaside resort, ended with the group of young men at the centre of the novel saying goodbye to their parents and girlfriends. 'For the first time, there were no caring eyes at our backs, and from now on we would be responsible only to ourselves for our actions.'[5]

112   Senior pupils, Elizavetinskaya gimnaziya, late 1910s.

Intellectual and emotional development was, of course, not the only point at issue here. During much of the twentieth century, as in the nineteenth (exemplary texts from that century being Turgenev's *First Love* and Tolstoy's *The Kreutzer Sonata*), adolescence was perceived by Russian intellectual culture as a tragic loss of innocence, a painful process of change for the worse. The best that could be hoped for was rapid disillusion, followed by sublimation of the energies in study or some dignified form of employment, preferably a 'free profession'.[6] Otherwise a rapid descent of the slippery slope would ensue. The biological process of sexual maturation was seen as a major threat. Leonid Andreev's melodramatic story *In the Fog* shows a 17-year-old boy who graduates from masturbation and lewd drawings to furtive and squalid couplings with low tarts, and eventually to self-disgusted suicide once in the grip of venereal disease, all set in an equally hackneyed St Petersburg ('the white pillars looked like the yellow candles by a coffin').[7] In Nadezhda Teffi's terrifying story 'The Book of June', a shy orphan city girl on the verge of puberty is sent to stay with her cousins in the country, only to find herself tormented by everyone around her. She escapes being raped by the whiskery, half-witted maid only because she is rescued by her eldest boy cousin, but she then falls into a paroxysm of guilt and repudiates him hysterically as well. The story finishes with her gripped by paranoia, convinced that everyone else 'knows' what is going on, and that only she is conscious, the sole thinking human in this hell of sexual violence and desire.[8] The belief in a necessarily *sudden* end to childhood innocence, and the fact that this was certain to make transition into adulthood traumatic and confusing, lasted into the late twentieth century: in Anatoly Aleksin's stories from the 1960s, for instance, the sense of adolescence is conveyed in sentences such as 'That old feeling of happy unconcern had left my life'.[9]

'The Facts of Life'

Where sexual activity was associated with sin and with the Fall (even adults who might not have used such terms directly often manifested attitudes allied to Christian puritanism), embarrassment over communicating the so-called 'facts of life' to children was certain to follow. 'At the time of the sexual maturity of young people and of the great psychological upheavals that accompanied it, parents simply paid no attention,' one man brought up in the 1890s recalled.[10] To be sure, by the 1910s, the question of systematic discussion of sexual matters with children was beginning to be addressed by the 'free education' movement and by professional psychologists, such as Bekhterev in his *Sexual Healing* (1910). But the perspective adopted was ascetic if not puritanical: children should be taught about sex in a 'rational' way in order to avoid their becoming ensnared by undesirable activities, such as masturbation.[11]

Even among advocates of liberal upbringing, attitudes tended to be reactive rather than anticipatory. 'A Mother', writing in the journal *Free Education* in 1910, revealed that her husband had no interest whatever in providing her children (all boys) with any information about sexual contact, so that imparting this had been left to an uncle (who thought it was a good thing for young men to 'sow their wild oats'), and to her. The strategy that she had adopted was to counter any attempts at 'cynical' conversation with imprecations about the likelihood of contracting sexual diseases.[12]

Of course, this case involved a parent speaking to children of the opposite sex: however, father-to-son conversations, if more matter-of-fact, tended to be just as terse, as Nabokov recalled in *Speak, Memory*:

> I soon noticed that *any* evocation of the female form would be accompanied by the puzzling discomfort already familiar to me. I asked my parents about it ['naively', the Russian version of his memoirs adds] [...] and my father ruffled the German newspaper he had just opened and replied in English. [...] 'That, my boy, is just another of nature's absurd combinations, like shame and blushes, or grief and red eyes.'[13]

Sometimes fathers attempted, in a bumbling sort of way, to socialise boys into appropriate forms of erotic response. Anatoly Mariengof's father took him, when he was in his late teens, to a *café-chantant* – which had the unexpected effect of boring him so much that he opted for an early night.[14]

With girls, preparation was still more approximate. Concern to maintain girls' purity often meant that they were kept in the dark about physiological matters of all kinds. It was not uncommon for parents' reluctance to address anything sexual to extend to total silence about the existence of menstruation, let alone sexual activity. Instruction to middle-class and upper-class girls took the form of prohibitions above all else: boarding-schools forbade even correspondence with young men, let alone visits from them, and the discovery of an illicit romantic connection, however innocent, was likely to lead to a catastrophic family row.[15]

In polite circles before the Revolution, discussion of reproduction of any kind (even among animals) was discouraged. Ol'ga Forsh was severely punished as a child of about seven for boasting, to the assembled company at a dinner given by her father, the military commander of the city, about how her father's batman had taught her to 'tell girl dogs from boy dogs'.[16] This extreme genteelism would not have been found in a peasant or working-class household (as is indicated by the batman's assumption that it was all right to impart information about sex differences in dogs to a small girl). But candour in discussing human reproduction was rare in low-status social groups as well. Peasant parents traditionally regaled their children with stories of babies delivered by storks or discovered in cabbage patches, and responded with brusque embarrassment to insistent questioning about 'why' and 'how'.[17] Though middle-class observers assumed that premature sexual awakening was inevitable when parents and children slept in the same room,[18] parents from the lower classes usually did their best to keep all intimations of sexual contact from children. A point sometimes mentioned by peasant women petitioning for separation from violent husbands was the fact that they had been forced into sex in front of their children, which indicates that this was not the norm, and there are records of parents who retired to an outbuilding during the daytime in order to engage in conjugal relations (a thoroughly practical way of ensuring privacy when it was customary for each parent to share sleeping accommodation with one or more children of the same sex).[19] Sexual puritanism was widespread, especially with regard to 'maidenly honour', which was guarded much more fiercely than male chastity. Girls who indulged in permissive behaviour with young men were held in general contempt, and parents were ruthless in punishing daughters they felt were in danger of going astray. In the 1910s, for example, Anna Kuznetsova-Budanova's sister, a lively girl who enjoyed going to parties, was first ordered not to go to any more by her mother, and then repeatedly beaten when she disobeyed. Eventually, the quite unfounded suspicion that something untoward might be going on led the parents to force her into an unwanted marriage with a 'suitable' young man.[20]

Some impact of changing attitudes to adult sexuality upon attitudes to juvenile sexuality might have been expected in the first two decades of the twentieth century.[21] Certainly, in this period the influence of liberal schools of child psychology such as paedology did promote frankness about some bodily functions in intelligentsia parents. A mother involved with the paedological movement was neither disturbed nor embarrassed when her five-year-old son asked when he saw her washing her breast which part of it he had sucked as an infant. She simply showed him her nipples, for which he then invented his own term, 'little bells'.[22] She was equally unfazed by discussions of urination and defecation, though she – like other Russian adults – did expect the use of baby-talk euphemisms such as *psi-psi*, and of the French terms *petit* and *gros*.[23]

Frankness about physical matters generally did not always equate with frankness about sex, however. Far more attention was given to preventing masturbation in children than to the question of how to explain 'the facts of life'. Where provided, answers were kept general and vague. Elena Krichevskaya's daughter Marusya, for instance, learned that she had once lived in her mother's 'little tummy', growing from a 'little, little ball', and was happy with this answer. Krichevskaya, who had anticipated, before her daughter was born, that she would find questions about human reproduction deeply embarrassing, was relieved to be able to satisfy her daughter's innocent curiosity so easily.[24] Discomfort could be avoided only if the sexual act itself were passed over in silence. Even the sexual reformer Vasily Rozanov, who so fervently believed in adolescents' need for sexual contact that he argued marriage should be compulsory for all males of sixteen and over and all females of fourteen and a half and over, had a firm belief in the need to curb erotic activity in younger children. One of his central arguments against the non-interventionist child-raising theories in Herbert Spencer's *Intellectual and Moral Education* was that excessive tolerance might lead masturbation to go unchecked. 'Suppose an eight-year-old boy takes to onanism, having discovered by chance, by squeezing himself or something, how pleasant it feels, is his "dear mama" supposed to wait till he gets fed up with the practice round about the age of twenty-one?'[25] All of this was, of course, in tune with contemporary ideas in Western Europe, where onanism was also frowned on, and where emphasis was on safeguarding children from exploitation by adults, rather than on giving them access to sexual self-expression.[26]

The general tone was not permissive, but rather the reverse. 'It is evident what an enormous battlefield opens up before parents and pedagogues who do not wish to remain indifferent observers of the vast changes that are taking place in the nature of children,' the author of one early 1920s pamphlet observed.[27] Preventive measures suggested by him included keeping a watchful eye on nannies (who might use masturbation as a way of soothing their charges to sleep), checking for threadworms (itching might well prove a stimulus to self-abuse), and providing hard beds, well-aired rooms, and plenty of sporting activities, as well as access to coeducation. Comparable was a book on rational dress for children, published in 1929, and advising readers that nightdresses must be ankle length, not only so the child did not get cold, but also to 'stop the bad habit of touching the sexual organs, which leads in its turn to onanism, a fault that is difficult to cure'. The sleeves were to be long as well, or the child would put its hands under the blankets, 'which also fosters onanism'. Boys were not to have frontal openings in their underpants, as this would mean that they needed to touch their sexual organs when urinating: they should be sat on pots in the same way as girls.[28]

The primary audience for twentieth-century publications of this kind was quite possibly teachers and other professionals, and their primary objective, the prevention of masturbation in children's institutions. Child behaviour books aimed solely at parents were generally less obsessed with policing children's sexual behaviour. But such formal anatomical instruction as children got during the early twentieth century was often provided by adults outside the family – teachers, or leaders in youth organisations.[29] Russian parents themselves seem often to have been less relaxed about discussing sex with their children than they were about discussing excretion. Despite being perfectly happy when her son talked of '*psi-psi*', Pavlova was extremely distressed when he described a girl at nursery school as 'a little tart' (*blyadka*), and only just stopped herself from throwing something at him.[30]

Embarrassment about sexual matters was encouraged by the pedagogical establishment. Among nursery teachers at the First Experimental Station in the 1920s, worry about shameless behaviour on the part of working-class and peasant parents persisted. It was not just dirty if children slept with their parents, but also morally disgusting: 'There is a danger that children may witness their parents' sex life. [...] They may not understand, but they'll try to do the same. We see that from the things children say, from their games and so on.'[31] The best that parents could do for their children was to maintain discretion in thought, word, and deed. Makarenko, for instance, argued that there was no need to teach children the 'facts of life': sexual education was no different from any other kind:

> When we instil in the child such qualities as honesty, industriousness, sincerity, directness, the habit of keeping clean, the habit of telling the truth, respect for others, and for his emotional experiences and interests, love for the motherland, and fidelity to socialist ideas, we will also have given him an education in sexual matters.[32]

The central weapons in parents' imposition of this moral code were repression and silence: 'A cultured attitude to love experiences is impossible without a braking system laid down in childhood.' Sex education, then, was not only unnecessary but positively harmful: it was vulgar, it excited curiosity, and provoked irresponsibility rather than sensible behaviour.[33]

As we have seen, because of larger social pressures, Makarenko's advice against spoiling children failed to curb practices that he saw as undesirable. But his advice against frank speaking was perfectly in tune with existing attitudes among much of the Soviet population. In villages, myths about 'cabbage patches' remained in circulation, and children were conceived and born well out of sight of their older siblings.[34] Preparation of girls went no further than dire warnings about the likely harmfulness of, say, kissing, with any manifestations of erotic activity punished severely. Even at this date, arranged marriages were not unknown, and it was simply assumed that young couples would find out all they needed to know when the consummation of the marriage took place.[35]

Traditional attitudes persisted among some educated Russians as well. Beatrice King, a British supporter of liberal, 'progressive' education, noted on the basis of a visit to Russia in the early 1930s that 'Communists of long standing' sometimes held views on sex education 'no more advanced than those of the suburban parents living in other countries'. King was shocked by a friend of hers who had told his 11-year-old son absolutely nothing about reproduction, and who was wondering what he should tell the boy now that he had started picking up information from friends out in the courtyard.[36] In her view, preparation should have begun many years earlier.

To be sure (as King's story shows), Soviet parents in the groups she mixed with did have some concern about inducting sons into the mysteries of sexual intercourse. But their ways of doing it were not usually what she, or some Russian child-care experts of the 1920s, would have called 'modern'. At the end of the 1930s, the father of a male friend of Elena Bonner's invited two 'working girls' round to the family apartment so that the boy and a schoolmate of the same age could have a tutorial in copulation skills.[37] It was rare for Soviet parents to be so interventionist: more often children were simply left to themselves.

Schools did not help a great deal with the dissemination of information about the physical side of sexuality. Even in the 1920s, school biology lessons steered clear of human reproduction: while the hygiene pamphlets then published in large numbers by state presses in part made up for the deficiency, the information given here dwelt on psychopathology and said a good deal more about male anatomy than female anatomy. A boy might reassure himself, by reading a book with the title *Man and Woman*, that his first nocturnal emission was not, say, the side-effect of a bout of scarlet fever he was suffering at the time, but a normal phenomenon of adolescence.[38] However, health guidance of this kind was rather less reassuring about menstruation, which was treated purely as a hygienic problem, a question of appropriate diet and dress.[39]

In the post-Stalin era also, parents (who had, of course, often themselves grown up during the Stalin era) were not necessarily keen to enlighten their children before they positively had to. One woman born into a family only one generation away from the peasantry, and brought up in a country town outside Moscow, recalled that, when she found out the facts of life from a friend and gleefully reported them to her mother, the latter was appalled. 'I can't have taken proper care of you!'[40]

Normative materials in the 1960s also took the attitude, 'Least said, soonest mended'. An article published in 1965, for example, attributed the high divorce rate in Denmark to the fact that children were told everything at a tender age, and (while apologising for the Freudian note of the term) advocated 'sublimation' as a superior alternative.[41] Discussions of reproduction in the classroom tended not to get beyond pollen and stamens: there are records of people born as late as the 1960s who learned about the mechanics of human reproduction only well after they left school.[42] Menstruation was the subject of meticulous circumlocution. Suffering from the condition was an acceptable excuse for missing sport sessions, and hence readily admitted to by pupils who found these a bore, but the accepted technique for putting in a claim to indulgence was to speak of oneself as 'sick' in the abstract, rather than to specify the condition concretely.[43] All behaviour deemed to be sexual in nature was the subject of acute disapproval. It goes without saying that any girl unfortunate enough to get pregnant was likely to be treated extremely badly; she would probably, just for a start, be debarred from taking her school examinations.[44] But even far less physiological matters than this sent the moral regulators into a lather. For example, in the late 1950s, the spectacle of 'the rock-'n'-roll dance' (sic) and 'ultra-tight skirts' were worrying mentors in the Komsomol, while in the late 1970s it was considered indecent for girls to wear trousers (which were viewed as a product of the evil influence of the West; the miniskirt, also the subject of earlier disapproval, had by this time become respectable).[45]

True, by the 1960s even some official manuals were suggesting that parents should tell children about the basic mechanics of reproduction: 'By the time sexual maturity begins (13 to 16 in boys, 11 to 15 in girls) [...] a mother should give her daughter the basic hygienic information about the onset of the monthly cycle, and a father prepare his son for the onset of nocturnal involuntary omissions of semen.'[46] A pioneering example of a genre that had vanished in the late 1920s was an article printed in the popular weekly *Nedelya* in 1966, which pointed out that, if parents did not deal with the 'accursed question' of sexual education, children would end up getting all their information from graffiti on fences and the more knowing among their peers.[47] In 1973, the same weekly ran the translation of a piece on adolescents by Dr Benjamin Spock, emphasising that sexual development was a crucial part of this phase of life. The piece was followed by various articles – not many, to be sure – by local Soviet authors, mostly preoccupied with the issue of teaching about sex in the schoolroom.[48]

By the late 1970s, at least some schools provided pupils with elementary instruction in human sexual biology, with girls and boys divided into separate groups for the session.[49] Some teachers might take the initiative to push discussion slightly beyond what was anticipated by the school programme, telling girls about menstruation, for instance, so they would not have to experience it unprepared.[50] Alternatively, a school doctor or nurse might convey the rudimentary 'facts of life', debunking adolescent myths in the process.[51] In the late Soviet era, too, it became more likely that parents or other 'responsible adults' within the family would enlighten children themselves, perhaps using Western or Eastern European 'child-friendly' brochures and booklets, which became more accessible as print taboos were lifted. The years 1989–91 saw a tide of 'sexual enlightenment' materials, mostly translated, pour off the presses in the Soviet Union.[52] As the social atmosphere became less repressive, children themselves might start to wonder why adults in the family circle were so tight-lipped about discussing sexual activity and reproduction, a reaction recalled by one woman from Nizhni-Novgorod born in 1979.[53]

Yet throughout the post-Stalin era parents remained reticent. The number of informants taking part in our interviewing project who can remember being told anything by their parents is small; on the other hand, typical are recollections such as those of a woman born in 1958 whose doctor parents removed specialist literature on gynaecology from the house before she reached adolescence, or a woman born in 1971 and brought up in an orphanage who was told absolutely nothing about reproduction.[54] A disincentive to explicit commentary was the survival into the 1980s of communal apartments: here, the task parents set themselves was how to *hide* sexual activity, rather than how to broach the subject. Elaborate precautions were taken by parents sharing rooms in communal flats with their children to ensure that sexual relations were concealed, even if the child's bed was not screened off with a partition and a curtain (as became an increasingly common practice in the 1960s). 'They must have waited until we were really soundly asleep,' recalled a lorry driver's daughter from Leningrad, born in 1969, and both of whose brothers, five and fifteen years younger than her, had been conceived in the single room shared by the family until 1984.[55]

A culture of embarrassment also obtained in Soviet kindergartens. Staff might be matter-of-fact about potties (though potty training was considered unmentionable in manuals), but any manifestation of erotic behaviour provoked horror. In the 1960s, a typical reaction by a kindergarten supervisor to an incident when a little boy offered to show his '*piska*' (willy, weenie) to a small girl during afternoon rest was to say that if he ever did that again, she would cut his *piska* off.[56] As late as the mid-1980s, an incident when children at a Moscow kindergarten were found comparing sex organs (also during afternoon rest) led to a major rumpus.[57]

Learning about Romance

Children from the cultural elite were unlikely to learn the so-called 'facts of life' from their parents or indeed from most adults. From a young age children would also be exposed – within their own families – to conversations about sexual relationships at another level: according to the high ideals of romantic love. In Anatoly Mariengof's family, for instance, a sentimental and doting aunt had begun talking of his future marriage from when he was about 12.[58] This was typical not just of the generation brought up around the turn of the century, but of later generations as well. To be sure, the 1920s and early 1930s constituted an exception. Pioneer journals regularly felt compelled to denounce *al'bomy*, the home-made collections of keepsakes and doggerel that were a popular genre among schoolgirls.[59] But schoolchildren did not, of course, live 'by school alone': there was also a full-scale commercial film culture where Love with a capital L flourished luxuriantly, providing them with an alternative set of orientation points, and, of course, 'trash' authors such as Charskaya and Verbitskaya continued to circulate underground.[60]

With the rehabilitation of the family in the 1930s, love – provided it ended at the door of the registry office – started to be a positively welcome emotion. Eager to prevent unseemly behaviour by young people though it might be, the Soviet moral establishment was equally committed to preparing them for 'normal' family relations, which were understood to be based on close emotional ties between man and woman aimed at the conception, gestation, and upbringing of further generations. In other words, sexual activity was essential to the Soviet ideal of marriage, just as it was to the Christian ideal from which this derived. The need to produce individuals suited to a life of progenitive monogamy was a major spur to educational policy, as well as to ideological utterances throughout the Stalin era. The move to single-sex education was accompanied by a good deal of anxiety that single-sex schools should not produce characters whose relationship with the opposite sex was uneasy.[61] An elite Moscow girls' school where boys were not allowed in the building, ever, at any time,[62] was very much an exception; on the whole, contact between the opposite sexes was encouraged at least on certain ritual occasions, such as the 'school-leavers' ball'.

In literature for children, a friendship that became a love relationship culminating in marriage was a widespread theme, being represented, for instance, in Veniamin Kaverin's hugely popular novel *The Two Captains* (awarded a Stalin Prize in 1943 and 1944), as well as, of course, Fadeev's *The Young Guard*. In youth theatre, too, such 'unstable' relationships were a feature of the time. One might mention Vladimir Shcheglov's piece *The Noise of the Pines*, licensed for performance in the Leningrad TYuZ in 1951, which hinged on a conflict in an Estonian lumber camp inhabited by a mixed population of Russians and Estonians. Two of the young lumber workers, Anti Vaklou and Andrei Bezborodov, are in love with Anna Sauko, a young *komsomolka*, and are also rivals at work. Gradually they learn to respect each other, while Andrei develops the courage to make his feelings clear to Anna. The play ends with the wedding of Andrei and Anna, accompanied by toasts to 'the innovators of the forest', and the development of a *tendresse* between Anti and Katerina Varnu.[63] Alongside the usual point that sentimental love is tolerable where it leads to marriage went the intertwining of love and 'friendship of nations' – the central relationship cemented the alliance of the Estonian and Russian peoples. A supremely official kind of affective relationship was allegorically linked to a personal relationship – but one publicly sanctioned as the foundation of society.

In these respects, love could in fact seem (despite the moral threat that it presented if unsuitably indulged) more permissible, more to be encouraged, than friendship. Soviet writing for children provided no negative models of love. Instead, there was a single form of virtuously sentimental close relationship, ending in marriage, very much of the kind to be found in traditional fairy tales, and usually – as there – a relationship that had to endure entirely external obstacles of an insubstantial or chimerical kind.

All the same, careful control was kept over material that was specifically directed at children. Love in the sexual sense – along with death, where not in the form of heroic martyrdom – was one of the subjects considered *per se* unsuitable for children's literature.[64] Nursery versions of the classics carefully excluded anything erotically suggestive. For example, the relationship between Kay and the Snow Queen in Hans Christian Andersen's story was transformed in Evgeny Shvarts's adaptation, which represented Kay as a small boy delighted by the sleigh ride, rather than a pre-adolescent excited and disturbed by the Queen's seductive powers.[65] But classic literature centring on love relationships (*Eugene Onegin*, *Fathers and Sons*) continued to be at the centre of the school programme. In children's literature, too, though neutral 'comradeliness' might be counselled in abstract pieces on affective relationships, representations of boy–girl friendships often had a hint of romanticism. An example was a school story that appeared in *Koster* in 1938. Lida, its heroine, had to endure teasing by her schoolfellows for becoming friendly with Yura, a boy of the same age ('A girl and a boy can't possibly be real friends'). However, she interpreted this as a challenge, rather than as a deterrent, encouraged by another boy who insisted that mixed-gender friendships were possible if one regarded girls as 'comrades of a different order'. At first the relationship between Lida and Yura, therefore, negotiated gender difference by essentially ignoring it: in a somewhat surreal touch (and one that would hardly have reassured any boy readers worried that friendship with girls might be sissy), Lida was shown referring affectionately to her friend as 'Matil'da'. Later, though, Lida became trapped in the stereotypicality of her own expectations: when Yura refused to respond to provocation and to become involved in a fight, she rejected him as 'a coward'. In the end, though, all was resolved joyfully when Yura rescued her after a skiing accident, at the risk of frostbite to himself. After receiving a devoted letter from him as her 'faithful friend', she decided that she was the happiest girl in the world.[66]

The relationship between a girl and a boy that bordered on, while not quite spilling over into, 'love' was seen as a specially elevated form of permissible friendship, one requiring suspension of prejudice in favour of higher ideals on both sides. Boys had to discard their view that 'girls only ever think about clothes and gossip',[67] while girls had to encourage a type of masculine behaviour that did not include such 'backward' activities as fighting. In the pursuit of such friendships, teachers might tolerate flirtation between pupils, provided the classroom behaviour of such pupils remained decorous and marks respectable.[68] In addition, teachers sometimes themselves participated directly in romantic relationships: it was common for girls to develop crushes on, and perhaps also flirt with, male teachers (and supervisors in orphanages), and some male teachers exploited this tradition in order to pay court to girls of 15 and upwards, a practice that was not always welcome.[69] Even school plays produced by a teacher might include lines such as 'My lips are swollen with kissing.'[70] School-teachers thus played a part not just in tolerating, but in encouraging, teenage attachments.

The cult of love continued in force during post-Stalin era, unimpeded by the short-lived return to '1920s values' under Khrushchev. The official Pioneer literature of the day still propounded 'comradeliness' between boys and girls as the ideal, but, just as in previous eras, there was also plenty of encouragement to romance. An encyclopaedia on upbringing published in the late 1960s, for instance, suggested that parents need not worry about first love: it was always very elevated and about pure feelings. Equally, a book on children's cinema published in 1974 argued strongly that sex should be seen as joyful rather than as shameful and dirty, and pointed to Franco Zeffirelli's *Romeo and Juliet* as a positive example: here the aftermath of physical love (Romeo's naked back at the side of the bed) was shown as 'pure and beautiful'.[71] Children would often have access to representations of love – in books, at the cinema, and, increasingly, on television – that might have been branded unsuitably 'adult' in the more emotionally puritanical Anglo-American culture.[72] Even books for quite young children, while eschewing 'physiological' detail, might suggest that parents had their own romantic life – as in a story by Viktor Dragunsky where father, driven into a corner by mother's lengthy sermons about good manners, began wondering aloud to his son about whether politeness really demanded that the hostess should not only show a departing guest out, but spend at least twenty minutes talking to him on the doorstep.[73]

All of this was associated with great emphasis on the distinctions between men and women. The 'strong sex' was meant to exercise 'chivalry' towards the 'weaker' one, which meant not only holding open doors, carrying bags, and helping with coats, but also regarding girls and women with sentimental awe. As Sukhomlinsky put it: 'Respect girls, cherish their honour, dignity, and pride. A girl you take a liking to could become the mother of your children.'[74] In many schools, 23 February (Soviet Army Day) and 8 March (International Women's Day) were celebrated as gender-specific festivals, and girls and boys were directed to honour the opposite sex by organising cards and presents.[75] Some teachers went to the length of formalising these arrangements, allocating every girl a boy on 23 February, and every boy a girl on 8 March. The celebrants were supposed to present their 'consort' with cards, flowers, and gifts, and generally wait on him or her throughout the day.[76] Of course, these 'arranged marriages' would not necessarily overlap with spontaneous friendships (indeed, a Soviet teacher's sense of civic duty would probably have encouraged him or her precisely to work against these by pairing off different pupils). But the shows of sentiment and gallantry created stereotypes that were intended to shape informal relationships as well. Equally, the tension between silence about physical relationships and loquacious celebration of 'love' (an emotion that did not rule out physical contact in the right circumstances) made erotic relationships seem at once permitted and forbidden, and hence powerfully attractive to young people.

'All That Started right from in Class 1'

Given the silence that hung over sexuality among most adults,[77] children were likely, in all generations, to learn about reproduction from other children their own age, or sometimes from older children. Among young children, physical exploration of a limited kind took place in role-playing games, such as 'doctors and nurses', or indeed 'mummies and daddies', which involved 'inspections' of private parts and conversations about excretory processes.[78] Among older children, smutty talk provided information about anatomical detail and sexual techniques; obscene drawings and stories would be passed round, and lewd gossip circulated.[79] A move into voyeurism was possible, with groups of boys spying on women in the local bath-house, or visiting a haunt of low entertainment, such as a cabaret.[80]

Eventually, curiosity was likely to be expressed in a directly physical way. Before the Revolution, it was not uncommon for boys from moneyed families to visit prostitutes (a famous example was the future poet Aleksandr Blok). After 1917, a first sexual contact with friends or acquaintances was more likely. Adolescents would retreat to places such as cellars and lavatories in courtyards, or to deserted staircases indoors, for sessions of 'snogging' (*obzhimanie*) and possibly, in time, full intercourse. At least the preliminaries to this might also take place at teenagers' parties, especially if parents happened to be away.[81]

Experimentation was equally widespread in villages. From their teens, boys and girls first started going to parties and festivals (*gulyan'ya*) at which match-making and pair bonding took place. As late as the 1930s, a girl might be given her first set of underwear when she reached the age for taking part in such events.[82] Some traditional games were explicitly sexual: in one village in Novgorod, there was a Christmas mumming act called Winding the Silk, in which a girl would be led, protesting and wriggling, up to a young man who had wound a length of silk thread round his penis; his friends, gasping with mirth, would ask, 'How long do you want it?'[83] In Smolensk province during the 1940s, the boys would wait until the girls began a round of fortune-telling in the *banya* according to a traditional method, and then pounce:

> A girl takes off her knickers and puts her bum through the [*banya*] window. And if she feels a smooth hand stroke her, then she won't get married that year. But if the hand is hairy, she will. Right? And it sometimes turned out ... happen, the boys'd be listening out, watching for where the girls had gone, and then they'd hide and then someone would put his hand there and someone would put his foot, and someone else who knows what ... [*Laughs*]. If someone was cross with a girl, they'd ... They say a girl got whacked with a spade, once. On the bum.[84]

Courting behaviour as such was also direct: in some places, it was perfectly acceptable for a young man to put his hand into the bodice of a young woman whom he found attractive, even if she were sitting in company.[85] No wonder that girls had problems steering a line between being condemned for excessively free behaviour and accusations of prudishness.[86]

Curiosity about sex did not equate with sexual freedom, or with a relaxed attitude to physical activity. Children's own attitudes shared some of the squeamishness of official culture. Reports of conspicuous sexual activity among children of school age tend to date from periods of extreme social upheaval – the 1932–3 famine, for example.[87] More often, even exchanging a kiss could seem transgressive; to get pregnant seemed no less than monstrous.[88] Girls who seemed too interested in boys were likely to be the object of condescension from their fellows: in one 1930s Moscow school, for example, they were known as 'swamp-dwellers' and 'young ladies'.[89] Like their elders, children drew a firm line between 'innocent' and reprehensible relationships, condemning the latter, but energetically cultivating the former.

Most boys and girls who had reached the age of 12 or so spent a good deal of time mooning over members of the opposite sex. 'I only understand all this dimly, or rather, not at all. All of it (♥) can be described as an illusion, but then most people find it hard, impossible, even, to part with it, the whole human race has got so used to taking all this as read,' wrote a 16-year-old Moscow girl in 1911.[90] Despite disapproval of romances as petit-bourgeois, flirtation persisted after 1917 as well. Lev Kopelev remembered that Pioneer meetings in the second half of the 1920s became an excuse for flirtation, and that, in private, supposedly serious discussions of questions such as, 'Are Pioneers permitted to kiss?' usually turned into Pioneer kissing sessions.[91] One Petrograd school could only exorcise the boiling emotions of its adolescent males, six of whom were in love with the same teenage *femme fatale*, when their class supervisor encouraged them to act out their hurt feelings as a play in the style of the *commedia dell'arte*.[92] Girls continued to keep sentimental albums (as the need to denounce the genre in the Pioneer press made clear). And diaries still waxed enthusiastic about love objects: in the words of 15-year-old David Samoilov: 'I'm in love, I'm in love, thoroughly and tormentedly. That often happens and it doesn't last, but this time I feel it will. [...] She has wonderful black eyes and a dark plait and an oval round pure face ... she's so hard to describe. She's clever and attractive. The first day I got back to school, I decided, "That's her!".'[93] By their teens, girls were likely to find themselves the object of assiduous attention from males of all ages at every public occasion. Nina Kosterina's fifteenth birthday party, held in April 1936, was marked by a lot of dancing with boys and also some clandestine embracing, despite the fact that she moved in a fairly puritanical set where preoccupation with romance and the use of make-up was regarded as trite and vulgar.[94]

After single-sex education was introduced in 1943, conducting romances became more complicated. Girls and boys tended to meet only at social events such as school dances.[95] These occasions could be deeply embarrassing. 'When boys visited the girls school they ... well, they were afraid to lay a finger. Even taking a girl's hand seemed awkward, shameful,' recalled one Leningrad woman of this era.[96] An official inspectors' report from the late 1940s confirmed this, giving a squirm-making depiction of a failed social evening at a Moscow school:

> School No. 19 [for girls] decided to hold evening events in collaboration with the boys' school next door. But it didn't work out: the boys could only dance the foxtrot, and they were afraid to ask the girls to dance. As they left, one group of boys scrawled obscene slogans on the school walls. So then the girls wrote a letter of protest to the boys' school, sending it via the district committee of the Komsomol. They demanded an apology, or else, so they said, they'd never let the boys come in again. A delegation of twelve young men was sent over by the boys' school to apologise for the coarse behaviour of their colleagues.[97]

Perhaps it was incidents like this that provoked some schools to ban boys altogether, even from the leavers' ball.[98] Where the sexes did mix, there might

113 Ballroom
dancing, Leningrad
Pioneer Palace, late
1940s.

be prohibitions on direct contact: for instance, at ballroom dancing lessons given
in Leningrad during the 1940s, boys and girls were forbidden to speak.[99] And
there were boys and girls who absorbed such attitudes. A woman born in 1936,
for example, described her adolescent self as 'very upright, honest, and straight-
down-the line. I only ever had comrades [as opposed to boyfriends].'[100] A slightly
older male contemporary recalled that his attitude to the opposite sex was distant
and entirely idealistic until well into his twenties.[101]

But flirtation still continued among some. At ballroom-dancing classes, for
instance, participants maintained the law of silence, but surreptitiously passed
little *billets-doux* to their partners.[102] And if partners of a comparable age were
not accessible, recourse could be had to older ones. At the age of 14, the future
poet Larissa Miller acquired an older boyfriend (he was aged 21). Her mother
was far from delighted and warned the young man on the telephone that Larissa
ought to concentrate on her school-work, but added resignedly when the telephone
interview was finished, 'He'll be back.'[103]

All of this relates to urban young people. The situation in Russian villages was
different. On the one hand, boys and girls continued to be educated alongside
each other, so that the levels of coyness displayed by some members of the urban

population would have been impossible. But on the other hand, the boundary between the sexes, in this area as in others, remained firmly drawn. Boys and girls tended to sit according to gender in the classroom, and sentimental friendships between the two sides drew the traditional taunt, 'Bridegroom and bride!' Interest was displayed in bouts of teasing and in would-be humorous assaults. At parties, girls and boys would exchange *chastushki* – four-line rhymed ditties – in which they evoked one another's cross eyes, bulging noses, fat cheeks, or other aberrant physical features.[104] Essentially, village life was too tough to admit of much in the way of tender feelings; yet the physicality of agricultural life, and the inevitability of close human contact, could foster self-protective distance as well as intimacy. This was especially the case in an era when 'modernisation' was so strongly associated with physical self-restraint.

Once urban schools went back to being mixed, in 1955, contact between the sexes became much simpler, especially since the general spirit of the era had now become significantly less puritanical with regard to private relationships. Disinterested 'comradeliness' was by all accounts rare between boys and girls in this period, and close friendships generally tended to involve individuals of the same sex. Girls who had a presence in groups of boys usually had an entrée to the group because of a blood relationship (for instance, a brother in the gang).[105] Cases are reported of boys attaching themselves to groups of girls (without there necessarily being a blood relationship), but this seems not to have been the norm.[106] A more characteristic pattern of opposite-sex friendship was the 'school romance', a genre of attachment that tended to flourish from, at the latest, about the age of 15 or so.[107] According to some recollections, indeed, all this began considerably younger: In the words of one woman born in the late 1950s:

> Yes, all that started right from Class 1, definitely, the children's love-making, everyone was doing it all the time … and as a matter of fact there were lots of quite serious, genuine feelings involved, for as long as I can remember there was someone sighing over someone else, and everyone was writing little notes, and the notes would be passed round during break [...] and in class as well, though of course the teacher might always notice![108]

At the same time, it is not clear that, if the teacher had noticed, it would have made a lot of difference, since precisely this sort of relationship was likely to express the 'chivalry' from male to female that was the expected norm. Not for nothing were epistolary novels, or novels with epistolary motifs (*The Sorrows of Young Werther, Evgeny Onegin*) both the staples of the school programme and the favourite reading of many literary young people.

It was not just the explicit precepts absorbed in the classroom, the playground, and the courtyard, and from private reading, that contributed to ideas about sexual relationships. Much was learned, here as elsewhere, from 'eavesdropping', or direct observation of adult behaviour – which might well act as a disincentive. Anatoly Aleksin's stories for young teenagers plausibly suggested that children moving into adolescence were likely to feel a high degree of insecurity about parental relationships on a sexual level. Again and again, the plots of Aleksin's stories turn on a boy's anxieties about his mother's, or his father's, attachments before they were married. In 'Call Up and Drop By!' the protagonist goes to farcical lengths to prevent either parent from hearing or seeing anything connected with the pianist Stepan Potapov, his mother's admirer when she was about 12 years old. 'The Home Front, Oh Yes, the Home Front' also harps on the displaced Oedipal motif: a boy, his mother, and her devoted admirer are evacuated during the Second World War, and a potentially explosive situation that develops when the boy's father is reported killed in battle is melodramatically averted by the death of both the mother and the admirer. In 'Meanwhile Somewhere or Other' the triangle motif is differently configured: this time, the young hero becomes entangled with a mysterious woman who has been writing to his father and turns out to be his father's first wife. When she is also abandoned by the son she adopted during the war, the boy finds himself drawn, half willingly, into her life as a substitute, resolving: 'I cannot become the third person she has lost.'[109] Though Aleksin's narratives tended to have sentimentally reassuring conclusions, the basic situations revealed the capacity for emotional disruption and sexual claustrophobia in small, intense families that were turned in upon themselves, and where despite knowing allusions to relationships clearly at least *potentially* sexual, open discussion of the implications of sexual relationships was taboo.[110] Even normative sources sometimes acknowledged that adolescent difficulties might be exacerbated by relationships with parents, who often, as an unusually frank article of 1967 pointed out, hit their mid-life crisis just at the moment when their children reached puberty.[111]

Living with Love

The emphasis on romantic love in pre-revolutionary and Soviet Russia was striking, but it was not exceptional. Parallel cases can be found in other European cultures; indeed, in most of the Western world (understood broadly) up to the 1960s. And it is misleading to see all this in the classic Freudian terms of repression and sublimation, which suggest impoverishment. The passionate friendships of the Russian schoolroom could be rich and rewarding. The divorce rate in the Soviet Union was no higher than in some Western countries where attitudes to the free expression of sexuality were more approving, suggesting that there was no direct correlation between liberalism in this area and the construction of successful relationships. As in other cultures, sex education, where offered, had to compete with playground folklore: an entertaining example is the Leningrad mother who had dutifully bought her eight-year-old daughter an impeccably tasteful pamphlet about sexual relations some time at the start of the 1990s, and was appalled to find, when she got out the book to show it to her own mother, that the girl had scrawled in a childish hand by one of the explanatory diagrams, *Ebutsya* (They're fucking).[112]

But sometimes puritanical attitudes did cause human misery. A good many adolescent girls learned about menstruation by discovering blood on their underwear and panicking because they supposed themselves to be dying or even pregnant. Once the phenomenon was explained, it was not necessarily any easier to cope with. It was only in the 1990s that disposable sanitary protection started to be widely available; before that even cotton wool was scarce and most women made do with traditional materials such as linen cloths that had to be boil-washed or scraps of wadding or old rag.[113]

There could be emotional costs as well behind the separation of 'love' (an elevated emotion) and 'sex' (a low and animal activity). A survey of Soviet married couples carried out in the 1960s revealed quite a high level of dissatisfaction among respondents, with some heartfelt complaints about having reached married life in an unprepared condition. 'The so-called knowledge you pick up on the street, from dirty jokes and your contemporaries, when you don't learn anything from clever, tactful and experienced people, makes the start of married life full of puzzles and questions,' two respondents in their twenties observed. Another wondered why the only commentary came in the form of 'sickly debates on "Love and Friendship"', and why sexual relations were still considered shameful: was it the (by implication redundant) religious concept of sin?[114] While the survey also turned up many other causes of stress in the Soviet family – lack of time to spend together, crowded accommodation, interference from family members, the burden placed by family relations on women – there were clearly some couples for whom ignorance was a problem.

Lack of free information about sexual matters carried the danger that those who did embark on extra-marital relationships might do so in a dangerously unprepared state, as in the case of one woman, sexually active in the late 1940s, who believed that she was safe from pregnancy if she made love during a menstrual period or if she slept with a much older man, because a combination of an older man and younger woman was 'physiologically incapable' of producing children.[115] Teenage pregnancies might have been taboo, but they were, according to oral history, far from unknown.[116] The cult of innocence ensured that most girls were unlikely to risk sexual relations in the first place, but it also meant that those who did engage in them ran a high risk of coming to grief.

As for the sexual exploitation of children by adults, this was totally unmentionable in the Soviet era, and – with the exception of approaches to adolescent girls by older men – beyond the purview of non-Soviet Russian literature and journalism too. In the late 1980s however, abuse – like many other issues to do with the possible ill-treatment of children in what was no longer supposed to be a paradise for the young – began to attract some publicity. A pioneering item was an article published in *Nedelya* in 1991, which praised the American practice of running informational sessions, with puppet plays and other entertainments, about inappropriate touching, and suggested to parents that, in the absence of such things, they might give children some warnings and guidance themselves.[117]

Oral history indicates that adult–child relations were not always dewily innocent. Sometimes, to be sure, teachers seemed more approachable sources of information about sexual relations than parents, and could supply a mature view that would otherwise have been lacking.[118] But abuse in the real sense of the word

– sexual advances that had violent overtones and were resented or feared by the person being targeted – was probably as widespread in Soviet cities as in major towns abroad at the same period.[119] It was not just girls who were at risk: in Leningrad during the 1970s, boys at one school were pestered by groups of older men who would come and spy on them while they were in the bath-house.[120] Such encounters must have been particularly distressing if those involved were uncertain what the aggressors had in mind but had a strong sense that it was something 'dirty' which should on no account be reported or discussed.

All the same, the agonising nature of adolescence should not be exaggerated. There were many individuals for whom sex, being more or less unmentionable, was either completely unimportant or of very little importance. By and large, it seems, young people were more preoccupied with the vicissitudes of love in the sense of crushes on schoolmates, without any feeling that physical consummation was in view.[121] Romances were often inseparable from antagonism: not only did boys sometimes fight playground duels over who had the right to which girl, but their ways of showing affection to love objects were often decidedly rough: bra-straps might be twanged or hair given a sharp tug.[122] Many relationships were silent, because of concern that emotions were not returned. Fear of disapproval and repudiation was particularly common amongst homosexual young people, who rarely dared to admit their feelings to the objects of those feelings.[123] But unrequited passion was not limited to them.[124] Throughout the Soviet era, it was rare for sexual relationships, or even serious emotional relationships, to begin in the schoolroom.[125]

By the 1980s, it was common for teenage children to feel they knew more about sex than their parents. As comically overstated by one Moscow woman born in 1971, 'We'd all swapped partners all over the place, and our parents were still virgins.'[126] The compartmentalisation of juvenile consciousness could, as in earlier generations, allow ideas to circulate that parents and teachers would scarcely have endorsed. A woman born in 1977, for example, concluded in her early teens that there was no point in having friendly relations with boys when it was better to sleep with them. By 16, her career ambition was to be a prostitute, from which she was fortunately dissuaded by a commonsense explanation from her father about precisely what she might be expected to provide in the way of sexual services.[127] Clearly, this particular case was influenced by the relaxation of censorship and glamorisation of prostitution that took place during the glasnost era and after the collapse of Soviet power, but it was common for weird myths to circulate in the two previous decades as well.

Puberty, then, was less a time of sexual 'enlightenment' than a time when children's established interest in scatology shifted in a different direction, and when talk about 'love' jostled mysterious and sometimes worrying information about physiological functions. Indeed, generally, adolescence, seen from inside, did not necessarily represent the sort of clear-cut divide that was anticipated in referral to 'the later school years', 'youth', or 'the half-grown age' (*podrostkovyi vozrast*). It was a porous boundary, encountered by children at different phases of existence, and meaning different things in different times and contexts. And other milestones of the life-path – the entry to school in the first place, particularly – were at least as important in delineating psychological phases. Yet adolescence did coincide, for many Russian children, especially those born before the 1960s, with a period when greater responsibility was expected, and when tolerance on adults' part diminished. It might not be a period of 'romantic agony', as traditionally expected in literature, or a time of intense self-scrutiny, but none the less it was certainly a time of change: in some senses indeed 'the end of childhood'.

'Where Are the Cynics Coming From?'

The perception of adolescence as an important boundary depends, of course, on the assumption that the lives of children and those of adults are distinct. In the last decades of the twentieth century, some observers, inspired by Philippe Ariès's theory that the late seventeenth century had seen the emergence of a radically new perception of childhood, began to question whether this perception might itself be in the process of being overtaken by history. The prevalence of 'adult' themes in children's literature and broadcasting, the marketing to children of clothes and consumer goods that mimicked adult goods in miniaturised form, and the alleged disappearance of traditional games and pastimes, all seemed to herald major social change. According to a sensational thesis advanced by the journalist Neil Postman, childhood had now simply 'disappeared'.[128] In similar vein, a humorous piece by a British journalist from late 2003 suggested that Enid Blyton's Famous Five, had they lived in the twenty-first century, would never have left the house to have an adventure. Instead, they would have spent their holidays in a basement room with the curtains drawn, playing computer games while mother heated up takeaway pizza for them in the microwave.[129]

Unease of this kind also became pressing in late Soviet and post-Soviet society. Already by the mid-1980s, articles had started to appear suggesting that modern children were more 'cynical' and self-interested than their predecessors. This theme was almost always linked with the wider availability of consumer goods. Now, commentators lamented, children were demanding all sorts of fashionable things, and idealism had vanished.[130] As marketisation took hold, so the laments grew louder. In 2002, a disillusioned teacher contrasted the pupils of the post-Soviet era – not interested in out-of-class reading, obsessed with status symbols, and indifferent to the authority of the teacher – with those he had been used to in the past. In 1964, he had read through 1,139 university entrance essays, all of which had displayed profound respect for truth and justice. Now, such values had gone for good.[131] Other commentators also lamented the disappearance of moral qualities and of concern for others. In the words of a doctor speaking in 2004, 'I remember how when I was a child ... how I wept when I read *Children of the Underground*. [...] And I never thought I'd see anything like that in my entire life. But now I have seen it – malnutrition like you wouldn't believe!'[132] With the real life of Russia coming to resemble the propaganda images of the West that they had been brought up with, observers were naturally inclined to identify a case of 'Western influence', and to blame the outside world for social decline.

Certainly, this understanding was not universal. There were also voices among experts presenting the modern West as a model to be aspired to, in terms of how children were treated there.[133] Sometimes, the positive side of the move to market economics was emphasised: for example, one nursery teacher pointed out that the removal of state funding had led to a surge of parent activism, and that declining attendance had meant that group sizes could be kept smaller, so that the 'truncheon discipline' of the past was at an end.[134] Non-specialists too sometimes voiced such views. In 1989, one commentator suggested that the spread of tolerance of commercial values was having beneficial effects on young people, who could now set up their own co-operatives, and so acquire more useful knowledge and life-skills than had been attainable by contact with the Pavlik Morozov and Timur role models of the past. Equally, the Soviet myth of 'golden childhood' was the subject of some acerbic commentaries, and it was not uncommon to argue that the entire Soviet era had seen 'mass infantilisation', brusquely brought to an end by the collapse of the system.[135]

Representations of childhood, in the literary world as elsewhere, became much more varied. The 'child's eye view' was more widely espoused than at any time since the 1920s, while the range of childhood experience evoked in memoirs broadened considerably.[136] One important drift in the late Soviet and post-Soviet artistic world was the representation of childhoods truncated or torn apart by social anomie, as in Valery Ogorodnikov's *The Burglar* (1986), in which a devoted younger brother took to theft in order to help his elder brother out of a crisis. Other writers and artists were more concerned to question the aims of Soviet regulation of the young. Leonid Gabyshev's novel *Odlyan, or the Air of Freedom* (written in the early 1980s, but not published till 1989), based on personal experience, was an excoriating portrait of a penal colony for juveniles, where bullying was rife (the novel opens with a scene in which a new inmate is viciously beaten by his dormitory companions), and where club activities were intended simply to persuade the children's parents that everything is in order when they visited. Aleksandr Zvyagintsev's 2003 film *The Return* revisited, from a highly critical point of view, the 'Makarenko model' of upbringing. Here, a father's ability to communicate with his sons only by dictatorial behaviour provoked tragedy, rather than fostering self-reliance. The film worked like a satirical remake of *Road into Life*: the bearded patriarch was now fragile and neurotic rather than calmly benevolent, and the obsequies in the final scene, rather than being a public celebration of a child's heroism, had become a furtive, frantic committal to earth of an adult tyrant.

But if some texts questioned the whole Soviet approach to childhood, the myth of 'happy childhood' did acquire a nostalgia-soaked apparent authenticity that it had not radiated before the system it supported vanished. Sometimes this was expressed merely in individual images – as in a photograph published in *Ogonek* in 2002 which showed a school uniform from the 1970s hanging in front of a Soviet-era veneered shelf unit. But there were also texts that set out the idea of 'lost childhood' more analytically, arguing that there had been a fundamental change in the character of juvenile experience as a result of Westernisation, and especially of the onset of commercial culture.[137] Among Russian commentators themselves, such writing often had a nationalist flavour – the changes were seen as the result of the Western obsession with money above all.[138]

As well as increased materialism, another change for the worse was believed to be loss of social control and hence of social cohesion. Such views were widely held by ordinary members of the Russian public:

> You see, people back then used to take an interest. It wasn't like now. You see? Now, you could pretty well get murdered before anyone would take an interest, they seem to take it for granted. But before, they could get on to you for anything: 'Why are you shouting so loudly?' 'What d'you mean, playing right there by the windows, you could break something!' Things like that. 'Stop riding that bike so fast, can't you see there are little children here, you might knock someone off their bike!' Concerned grannies that was, of course.[139]

In the past, according to this perspective, childhood had been part of a settled, harmonious social system, with children knowing their place in an age hierarchy that stretched all the way up to 'concerned grannies', with the middle-aged, parents and teachers, also regarded as authorities.

It was not just the older generation who believed that life had changed irrevocably. A St Petersburg man in his thirties described in 2003 the changes that had overtaken courtyard life in recent years, and how these had adversely impacted on children's play space:

> There used to be just ordinary private cars in the courtyard, just a few of them, so there was plenty of space. Now, that same courtyard ... well, I don't know, if you let in us kids that used to play there twenty years ago, we'd thwack the ball into all the cars, probably. Because now the courtyard is dead posh, and the block is too, there's even a guard. A guard, you have to show your pass, there's a guard and a crash-barrier. Right. And the simplest kind of car will be some Mercedes no more than three or four years old. Right. So if you crash a ball into a car like that, you'll never hear the end of it. There's nowhere left for kids to play.[140]

Such doom-laden comments had some foundation. The post-Soviet period did indeed see a widespread 'privatisation' of life in the larger cities, and sometimes in ways directly impacting on children's lives. Anxiety about safety made parents more wary about sending their offspring to play outside alone, so that more time was spent indoors; far more consumer goods had become available to the prosperous, so the divide between the rich and the poor widened significantly. Psychological as well as material changes made themselves felt. There was without doubt a rise of 'cynicism' (or, to use a less loaded term, scepticism) among children and young people with regard to the values propounded by Soviet propaganda. The liberalisation of the school programme – which meant that teachers could use far more initiative in what they taught – and the revelations about the extent of political repression in the decades of Soviet power, above all in the Stalin era, worked to undermine confidence in the dogmas of former years.[141] The move to market-driven economics brought new pressures: by their mid-teens, children might well have taken up a job, and developed a range of practical skills (for instance sewing, with domestic science lessons now not a waste of time, but a way of learning how to make clothes that could not be afforded any other way).[142] Participation in drug use and sexual activity during the teen years also became more likely; one Moscow girl born in 1986 recalled that from the age of 16 or 17, many of the girls in her school were regularly making use of the 'morning after' pill or 'mini-abortions' in very early pregnancy in order to regulate fertility.[143] With schools playing down or abandoning the moral righteousness of the past, little was done to challenge adolescent status-consciousness: clothes and personal possessions started to count for much more, and children who were economically marginal were 'pointedly ignored'.[144] The ethos of 'everything for the children' stretched parents severely in conditions where coveted goods, such as designer clothes or top-of-the-range mobile telephones, were readily on sale but beyond the budget of most households. Children were the best-dressed and best-equipped members of some families, regardless of what they actually contributed to the family. But providing what they needed, or appeared to need, was now formidably expensive. Placing a child in a hobby circle or summer camp, which in the past had cost very little, now ate up significant amounts of money. For example, 2006 rates for a month's trip to Orlenok stood at 20,000 roubles (£400, or about $700) – which amounted to an entire month's salary for a relatively well paid employee.[145]

Yet, at the same time, views that childhood was no longer childhood dramatically oversimplified the conditions in which children lived after the collapse of the Soviet Union, emanating more from painful personal experience among the elderly or middle-aged than from objective observation of life as lived by their juniors. Children often enjoyed their education more than in the past (the teaching of humanities subjects benefited particularly from the new pedagogical freedom of manoeuvre); leisure activities (among the better-off) became more interesting than they had been in the past; and the increased possibilities for acquiring consumer goods did not necessarily warp personalities. A teenager who was immediately able to walk into a city store and buy a coveted new pair of jeans might be less, rather than more, obsessed with material goods than a teenager who (as in the Brezhnev years) had to spend months wondering how to 'get hold of' (*dostat'*, in the colloquial Soviet term) the coveted item.[146] Drug use and early sexual activity were commonly taken as indicators of moral decline under 'savage capitalism', but these practices had existed under Soviet power too, though less publicly. As a woman born in 1971 put it, 'You'll hear people say that today's youth have come into contact with drugs and there's been a sexual revolution, but all that was going on earlier too, it just wasn't talked about, that is, you couldn't get on the Internet and read about it.'[147] And it is not clear that the solution to social malaise in government circles from the year 2000 proposed by some – a greater emphasis on military education and on disciplinary drilling, as highlighted in the revival of formal children's organisations such as the Scouts[148] – would have particularly marked effects.

The picture in the post-Soviet era was mixed with regard to children's institutions as well. In many respects, the situation became markedly worse. Market reforms brought economic instability, starving children's institutions of money and precipitating a resurgence of child abandonment. Between 1985 and 1990, the number of missing children rose by more than 50 per cent (from 20,200 to 33,700).[149] By the mid-1990s, the number of children abandoned was running at over 100,000 per year (28,000 in Moscow alone), and the state also had to make itself responsible for runaways, of which there were around 30,000 per year.[150] Child inspectors – particularly in the centres of large cities – were overwhelmed. The staff of schools and clinics, suffering heightened levels of stress because of the need to deal with budget deficits, could no longer provide the same level of support in monitoring the children in their care. Referrals of 'at risk' children dropped just at the time when such referrals had become critical.[151] Rising prices mean that fostering and adoption became a less realistic option for Russian families. Throughout the early 1990s there was a downward spiral of rising abandonment, declining institutional provision, and declining numbers of prospective adoptive families. Nursery staff became more and more apathetic.[152] In such conditions, the philosophical rationale behind the care offered became a matter of less interest; no type of home could do a decent job when starved of cash. Overcrowded, under-equipped, and poorly run, 'family type' children's homes were no more of a success than the ramshackle institutions they had replaced.[153]

By the second half of the 1990s, though, there were signs of some changes for the better. There was now a genuine possibility of collaboration with Western colleagues, and Russian specialists were able not only to read about, but also to work practically with, the literature, from Bowlby onwards, dealing with the psychological damage that could be caused by regime-driven care of the traditional variety. 'Family-style' care (according to the principles of 'early intervention') was beginning to be introduced on an experimental basis not only in homes for older children, but also in Ministry of Health baby homes, with groups of children now organised across age groups, rather than by age group, and each group allocated its own unit, which was made to look, as much as possible, like a family apartment. Carers, rather than being drafted in on shifts, would be assigned 'their' group, with which they worked as closely as possible; they were actively encouraged to treat the children affectionately, smiling at them, picking them up, and talking to them with interest and attention.[154] To be sure, experiments of this kind were treated with reserve by some working in state care, with comments along the lines, 'You'll just spoil them, and then when they get to an orphanage, and no one bothers about them, what then?' But the main aim of those working with the new methods was in fact to try and arrange fostering for as many children as possible, so that they did not have to go into the state orphanage system; the belief was that those who did have to be placed in homes would be well prepared by the early socialisation they had received, since this would make them likely to engage actively with carers, rather than sink back into gloomy passivity and torpor.[155] Similar changes were put through in nursery education: a project in Novgorod brought in expertise from British specialists in early learning, leading to a move from very formal organisation of the classrooms (children sitting in rows to listen to teacher) to the use of furniture and teaching techniques that encouraged freedom of movement and modulation between different activities in the same session.[156]

Change affected more than methodology. Though funding from central government continued to be inadequate, other sources of finance were starting to have a greater impact. The old *shefstvo* system had gone, in the wake of the demise of many of the large industrial enterprises that had exercised such 'patronage'. But many orphanages and baby homes got by on a combination of donations from foreign partners or sponsors, support from the local administration, and contributions from local businesses – which might come in the form of materials as well as cash.[157] By the start of the twenty-first century, at least

114 Group of children, Home No. 13, St Petersburg, May 2004

some individuals working in the state care network felt cautious optimism: there was now a good deal more freedom to provide the children in care with the facilities and treatment that they needed, while the penury of a decade earlier – when everything bar staff costs had had to be raised from day to day – had been to a significant degree alleviated.

However, society still had to deal with the effects of institutionalisation of the traditional kind. In 1999, Human Rights Watch reported that children in some Ministry of Health baby homes received so little attention from staff that they spent their days lying torpid on their beds; inevitably, when assessed for mental capabilities at the age of four, many were misdiagnosed as 'oligophrenic' (mentally deficient). Children in invalid homes often received no education, and might be tied to furniture, placed in straitjackets, or dosed on tranquillisers to restrain them; the most helpless were 'to all intents and purposes left to die'.[158] But, with greater sensitivity to the problems of 'hospitalisation', there was now greater likelihood that, in the best homes at least, children would get more considerate treatment, now that the expression of affection had become not just the personal objective of some exceptional staff, but an institutional requirement.

In the area of cultural production for children, the decline in state subsidies hit hard. In the past, this sector had never been driven by a profit imperative: funding (particularly for flagship institutions such as major state film studios or the Central Children's Theatres in Moscow and the most famous puppet theatres) had been generous. Now, contracting funding brought a decline in output. In children's television, a ban on advertising during programmes for a young audience made the TV channel operators, who were dependent on commercial revenue to survive, reluctant to screen such programmes: by 2005, most were providing less than half the legally obligatory proportion of children's material in the schedules (set at two hours a day).[159] However, here too the picture was mixed. The children's theatres that survived, such as Through the Looking Glass in St Petersburg, were often doing more interesting work than in the past, and had a more secure reputation among adult audiences too. And those working for and with children began, in the early twenty-first century, to adopt a more proactive attitude, with television specialists, for instance, beginning to campaign for a new channel with programmes exclusively aimed at children, which would show documentaries and other information programmes as well as the ubiquitous cartoons.[160]

Oversimplifying the present, the view that marketisation had 'put paid' to childhood also oversimplified the past, putting too rosy a glow on what was achieved for children under Soviet power. Certainly, conditions for the large majority of children who did not belong to the educated, moneyed elite did improve dramatically between 1917 and the mid-1980s. Infant mortality dropped; the infectious diseases that had killed so many small children were brought under control; the educational network expanded, so that by mid-century almost all children had access to at least basic education; large numbers of institutions were set up to cater for abandoned children and for children whose parents could not provide them with adequate care and material support. The Soviet system also had remarkable achievements to its credit in more sophisticated areas of child support – the provision of facilities allowing children access to the arts and to sports, both as spectators and as participants; the organisation of hobby circles across a huge range of areas; the construction of an extensive network of children's libraries. Yet, at the same time, there were serious failures: not only the grossly inadequate provision of consumer goods, but the persistence of inequalities in children's experience depending on their social status, and the often dismal provision made for children in institutions once considered the flagships of the new society. In time, as expectations rose, these factors were to produce, at least among more articulate sectors of the adult population, a sense of dissatisfaction, leading to the covert demise of the sustaining myth that children led a uniquely happy life in 'our country' – and hence to the removal of a crucial plank in the Soviet system's political legitimacy.

But the causes behind the collapse of the Soviet system lay not just in failure to deliver, materially speaking. They also, it is clear, stemmed from the very relentlessness of political indoctrination – which in time generated indifference to dogma among many, and a critical attitude among a minority. Indeed, the greatest juvenile success stories of the Soviet regime – the prize-winning schoolboys and schoolgirls – were sometimes the readiest to attack authority, questioning why it did not live up to the standards that were trumpeted in propaganda. A case in point was that of the Moscow girls from a model school who assailed their class supervisor for 'walking out with' a man when she herself was forever giving them lectures on 'maidenly honour'. When a meeting was organised by the headmistress so they could voice their grievances, some made loud complaints about favouritism and other faults in the teacher. 'We were just putting into practice what we were taught in the classes, in history and so on', a former pupil remembered.[161] Equally, some of the sons and daughters of the Party leaders born in the 1930s and 1940s, the products of elite education all, turned into some of the fiercest critics of the regime once political control was relaxed in the 1960s.[162]

In fact, within a system where the idea of revolution – radical self-transformation, both at a general social and at a personal level – was fundamental, the very idea of social conformity from childhood was problematic. In early Soviet society, the classic model of self-presentation was the 'conversion narrative', where a person showed solidarity with the regime by overcoming and eventually purging his or her human faults. Thus, the 'good children' of the Soviet regime could threaten the long-term viability of the system both by intention (because they were fluent in its rhetoric and imbued in its mentality, and ready to assault deviations from what they believed they knew was the appropriate line of development), and passively – because, by simply *remaining what they were*, they enacted the demise of the myth of radical self-transformation upon which Soviet legitimacy was founded.

Yet, at the same time, the *difference* of Soviet childhood, whether this acted as a force for social solidarity or a factor behind collapse, should not be over-emphasised. Much that was claimed as specific to that system could be traced back before 1917 (internationalism, concern with child welfare, the roots of 'child-centred' education, on the one hand, or the propagation of academic values for some, and skills training for the many, 'patriotic education', and concern with discipline and conformity, on the other). And in international context, much in the history of twentieth-century Russian childhood is familiar – from the dire straits of the inmates in the institutions that were laughably misnamed 'homes', to the progressively greater intervention of the state in education, leisure, and family life, to the reinscription of family relationships in the wake of urbanisation and the expectation that children would remain 'children', in the sense of non-productive members of society, for ever longer stretches of their lives.[163]

Of course, there were some specific effects of Soviet childhood. Many children grew up genuinely believing what they were told about living in the best country in the world, though this might in the long run act as a force for disappointment (if things started going badly) rather than loyalty. Asked what they still value from the Soviet era, informants to this day often speak in the moral vocabulary of their schooling, referring to qualities such as 'honesty' or 'diligence', while at the same time asserting that emphasis on these qualities was in many ways a bad preparation for life in the post-Soviet world. Generational changes in upbringing produced different character types: people brought up in the 1920s, 1930s, or 1940s tell their life stories quite differently from people brought up in the 1950s and 1960s, with a far greater stress on privation stoically survived, and much less on personal possessions. The first memories of many informants from the 'everything for the children' generation often involved a trip to the dacha or to a toy shop; in the 1920s, 1930s, or 1940s, it was more often a political event (Stalin's death, Kirov's murder) that proved memorable. Taboos were different – questions about politics produced an embarrassed silence, perplexity, or derision in many of those who had been children in the post-Soviet era, while the key topic to stimulate similar responses from many members of earlier generations was sex. Thus, a correlation can undoubtedly be traced between upbringing and psychological make-up. What is problematic, precisely because of the constantly shifting priorities and values concerning the raising of children, is generalising about the huge variety of practices and making grand statements about 'Russian' or 'Soviet' upbringing.

In the end, when searching for what *was* specific in 'Russian' childhood in this era, one comes back to the kind of customary detail recorded by Vikram Seth in his sketch of Chinese childhood: the incidentals of dress and behaviour that go with climate (Russian children may not have learned closer contact with the earth from the national tradition of standing up to go down ice slides, rather than sitting,[164] but they certainly learned how to stay upright when skidding on ice); the niceties of children's language, saturated with diminutives and affectionate intonations (as revived in the tender baby-talk of the Russian *roman*); and, of course, also the sense of difference (whether as a citizen of the Soviet Union or of the Russian Empire) that was imparted by growing up in a culture where separateness from other nation-states was always emphasised – not just as a result of the difficulties of travel beyond the state borders, but also as a result of the insistent use of 'there' and 'here' oppositions in the literature, art, and propaganda that a child encountered from the nursery onwards.

Notes

Introduction

1 Vikram Seth, *From Heaven Lake: Travels through Sinkiang and Tibet* (London, 1984), p. 85.
2 Oxf/Lev V–04 PF12A, p. 5.
3 See e.g. Oxf/Lev V–05 PF7A, p. 2.
4 Zh. Tkachenko and I. Bratchenko, 'Budet dlya shkoly', *N* 49 (1967), 22.
3 Though there is *some* evidence for this in Russian culture: for example, texts written during periods of food shortage bordering on starvation evoke childhood as a time of constant plenty. On this, see Pamela Chester, 'Strawberries and Chocolate: Tsvetaeva, Mandelstam, and the Plight of the Hungry Poet', in M. Glants and J. Toomre (eds), *Food in Russian History and Culture* (Bloomington, IN, 1997), pp. 147–8.
6 On the stereotype of the idyllic gentry childhood in nineteenth-century Russian literature, see Wachtel. The canonical accounts that Wachtel considers, such as Tolstoy's *Childhood* and Sergei Aksakov's *Family Chronicle*, were republished in editions for Soviet children and were required reading in Soviet schools. (See for example S. T. Aksakov, *Semeinaya khronika* (M., 1981), published in the 'School Library' series.) Yuri Slezkine has asserted (*The Jewish Century*, Princeton, 2004, p. 257) that 'happy childhood' in the Soviet period was particularly likely in Jewish families: 'More of Hodl's children than just about anybody else's had the proverbial Soviet "happy childhoods".' But this is a moot point; while literary sources might suggest this was correct, oral history gives a rather more ambiguous picture.
7 See Part II of the digital version of this book.
8 Part II of the digital version of the book includes a detailed discussion of children's experience of events, based on diaries, memoirs, and oral history.
9 For more details of the oral history project, including basic biographical details of informants, see the digital version of this book.
10 *Svod zakonov grazhdanskikh. Izdanie 1900 goda*, SZRI vol. X.1, article 213.
11 The digital version of this book, II, contains a detailed discussion of these points. See also Yuri Slezkine, *The Jewish Century* (Princeton and Oxford, 2004).
12 K. D. Ushinsky, *Rodnoe slovo dlya detei mladshego vozrasta. God pervyi. Pervaya posle azbuki kniga dlya chteniya* (4th edn; SPb., 1912).
13 V. Anan'in et al., *Zhivoi rodnik: pervaya kniga dlya chteniya v shkole i doma* (M., 1922), vol. 3, p. 283.
14 See 'Some Aspects of the Psychology of the People of Great Russia', *American Slavic and East European Review* 8:2 (1949), 155–66. For a brisk and convincing rebuttal of this argument, see David L. Ransel, *Village Mothers* (Bloomington, IN, 2007), p. 205: Ransel points out that the situation should be seen the other way round, as pointing to the long history of disapproval of swaddling on the part of those seeking to reform child-care practices, and of contempt for it as a hallmark of liberal beliefs: 'Swaddling does not fit in the cluster of modern, liberal values – indeed, is directly rejected as unnatural and unhealthy – and its retreat can be seen as a victory for that set of ideas and for a new way of thinking about what children are.' Nevertheless, 'psychohistory' continues to resurface at intervals with regard to Russia: for a recent example, see J. Iharius, *Swaddling, Shame and Society: On Psychohistory and Russia* (Helsinki, 2001).
15 See e.g. R. N. Coe's 1984 essay 'Reminiscences of Childhood', *Proceedings of the Leeds Philosophical and Literary Society: Literature and History Section*, 19: 6 (1984), pp. 221–321.
16 Eglantyne Jebb, *Save the Child!* (London, 1929), pp. 25–6.
17 And in fact at least some Russian activists might have reacted to this situation more practically – by attempting to bulk out the children's diet with tree bark, or by requisitioning further supplies from the locality: on the significant tradition of improvisation under Soviet power, see chapters 6–9 below.

Chapter 1: Free Spirits and Prodigies, 1890–1917

1 Marina Tsvetaeva, letter to Anna Tesková, 22 April 1935, *Sobranie sochinenii v 7 tomakh* vol. 6 (M., 1994), p. 423.
2 *Vystavka "Detskii trud" (Kievskoe obshchestvo Narodnykh detskikh sadov)* (Kiev, 1911), p. 8.
3 V. Voronov, 'K psikhologii detskogo risunka', *VV* 5

(1910), 112.

4 See e.g. O. A. Shestakova, 'O nemetskikh
zverstvakh nad det'mi v Bel'gii', *OMM* 4 (1917),
341–4.

5 See e.g. P. Alston, S. Parker, and J. Seymour (eds),
Children, Rights, and the Law (Oxford, 1992).

6 As for instance in *Vopros ob okhrane detstva po
materialam predstavlennym Sankt-Peterburgskomu
S"ezdu kriminalistov* (SPb., 1903); P. N. Obninsky,
'O pravovoi zashchite detei', *Zhurnal Ministerstva
yustitsii* 1 (1900), 296–309.

7 E.g. Obninsky, 'O pravovoi'. See also
V. N. Gerard, 'O zhelatel'nykh dopolneniyakh
v zakonakh, kasayushchikhsya okhrany
interesov maloletnikh', *Zhurnal Ministerstva
Yustitsii* 1 (1900), 309–23; I. M. Tyutrunov, 'O
zashchite detei', ibid., 323–39; A. I. Zagorovsky,
'Otnosheniya mezhdu roditelyami i det'mi', ibid. 1
(1902), 45–84, 2 (1902), 1–30.

8 N. A. Okunev, *Angliiskii zakon o detyakh 1908 goda*
(SPb., 1909), is a complete translation of the Act
with a prefatory commentary.

9 'League of Nations Declaration of the Rights
of the Child' (1924), in G. Van Bueren (ed.),
International Documents on Children (The Hague,
1998), p. 3. Even Kate Douglas Wiggin's relatively
imaginative treatment, *Children's Rights: A Book of
Nursery Logic* (Boston, 1892), contained material
on the 'training of the child's social nature'
(pp. 186–7) and the need to protect children from
'fierce or horrible' fairy tales (p. 95), alongside the
child's 'right to his childhood', i.e. to get dirty, to
be disciplined justly, to have things his own size,
and so on.

10 See e.g. the useful discussion in Alston, Parker,
and Seymour (eds), *Children, Rights, and the Law*.

11 See e.g. N. Ndekle, 'Recovering Childhood:
Children in South African National
Reconstruction', in S. Stephens (ed.), *Children and
the Politics of Culture* (Princeton, NJ, 1995), p. 331;
and contrast e.g. the essays collected in A. James
and A. Prout (eds), *Contemporary Issues in the
Sociological Study of Childhood* (London, 1997), esp.
those by J. Kitzinger and by M.Woodward.

12 As E. K. Wirtschafter has summed up (*Social
Identity in Imperial Russia* (DeKalb, IL), 1997,
p. 10), 'tsarist politics accommodated women and
children without according them a clear-cut civic
identity'. For an illuminating specialist treatment
of family law, see W. Wagner, *Marriage, Property
and Law in Late Imperial Russia* (Oxford, 1994).

13 *Svod zakonov grazhdanskikh. Izdanie 1900 goda*,
article 164, *SZRI* vol. X.1, p. 18.

14 On desertion, see *Ulozhenie o nakazaniyakh*,
articles 1513–16, *SZRI* vol. XV, p. 167: depending
on the age of the child, the sentence ran from
two and a half to five years. For the prohibition
on murder (which went back to the 1649 Code),
see *Svod zakonov grazhdanskikh*, article 170, *SZRI*
vol. X.1, p. 18; for the provision of food etc.,
articles 172–3, ibid. On religious upbringing, see
Ugolovnoe ulozhenie, article 88, article 89, *SZRI*
vol. XV, pp. 248–9, which sentenced parents or
guardians who failed to raise children from an
Orthodox background as Orthodox believers to
up to three years' imprisonment (if they brought

up such children in a non-Christian faith) or up
to one year's imprisonment (if they brought up
such children as believers in another Christian
tradition).

15 *Svod zakonov grazhdanskikh*, article 177, *SZRI* vol.
X.1, p. 19.

16 *Svod zakonov grazhdanskikh*, article 165, *SZRI* vol.
X.1, p. 18.

17 *Svod zakonov grazhdanskikh*, article 653, *SZRI* vol.
X.1, p. 70; *Polozhenie o sel'skom sostoyanii* (1902),
1906 supplement, article 164, section 12, *SZRI*
vol. IX, p. 77; 'Ulozhenie o nakazaniyakh', articles
136–45, *SZRI* vol. XV, pp. 14–15.

18 See e.g. *Svod zakonov grazhdanskikh*, article
1257, *SZRI* vol. X.1, p. 112, prohibiting children
from accepting a legacy (a step that also required
acceptance of the associated debts) without the
consent of their parent or guardian. This is a clear
instance of a case where a dishonest adult could
have made use of a child's naïvety to further his or
her own ends.

19 On non-denunciation, see *Svod zakonov
grazhdanskikh*, article 168, *SZRI* vol. X.1, p. 18;
on non-control over finances, ibid., article 217–19
(*SZRI* vol. X.1, p. 21); on criminal responsibility,
'Ulozhenie o nakazaniyakh', article 137, *SZRI* vol.
XV, p. 15.

20 For example, the entry under the headword *Deti*
in *NES* vol. 17, pp. 68–9, drew attention to the
shortcomings of current legislation and provided
a bibliography of works. See also P. Berlin, 'O
pravakh rebenka. (Iz Shveitsarii)', in *VV* 8 (1910),
163–73. On attempts to liberalise family law, see
esp. Wagner, *Marriage, Property and Law*.

21 These children were still referred to in legal
texts as 'illegitimate' (*nezakonorozhdennye*), but
in discussions by jurists the term 'extra-marital'
(*vnebrachnye*) was now preferred. See e.g. 'Deti' in
NES.

22 See *PSZ* 21566 (3 June 1902), articles 131[1] et
seqq., 132[2] et seq.; (3rd series, vol. 22, pp. 492–5);
PSZ 7525 (12 March 1891), articles 131, 132, 144[1]
(3rd series, vol. 11, pp. 111–13); and contrast *Svod
zakonov Rossiiskoi Imperii* (1887 edition), vol. X.1,
article 132. The post-1902 situation is tabulated in
Svod zakonov grazhdanskikh, articles 131[1] et seq.,
132[1] et seq., *SZRI* vol. X.1, pp. 13–15.

23 The central piece of labour legislation was the law
of 1 June 1882 forbidding work by under–12s.
See *PSZ* 931, 3rd series, vol. 2, pp. 265–7. The
legislation on philanthropic institutions and
schools etc. is codified under 'Ustavy uchebnykh
zavedenii MNP' and 'Ustavy uchebnykh zavedenii
drugikh ministerstv' in *SZRI* vol. XI.1.

24 See *PSZ* 931, vol. 1, p. 266: later modifications,
requiring proprietors to allow time off for school
attendance elsewhere if there was no school on the
premises, indicate the toothlessness of the original
law. See 'Ustav promyshlennyi', articles 114 et
seq., *SZRI* vol. XI.2, p. 1206.

25 *Ugolovnoe Ulozhenie: proekt Vysochaishe
uchrezhdennoi Redaktsionnoi Kommisii po
sostavleniyu Ugolovnoe Ulozheniya* (SPb.: Tip.
Pravitel'stvuyushchego Senata, 1895), article 361.

26 *Grazhdanskoe Ulozhenie*, articles 308–9.

27 See the report in *PB* 5–6 (1912), 5; on

philanthropy generally, see Chapter 4 below. In Britain, on the other hand, the National Society for the Prevention of Cruelty to Children had been set up as early as 1884: on the society and the background to its institution, see Louise A. Jackson, *Child Sexual Abuse in Victorian England* (London, 2000), pp. 52–68.

28 'Pervoe zasedanie Obshchestva pravovoi okhrany maloletnikh', *PB* 1 (1914), 111–22.

29 On the 'cooks' children' circular, see P. A. Zaionchkovsky, *Rossiiskoe samoderzhavie v kontse XIX stoletiya (politicheskaya reaktsiya 80-kh-nachala 90-kh godov)* (M., 1970). The circular was preceded by a measure of 11 April 1887 forbidding entry to the children of prostitutes, brothel-keepers, tavern-owners, and so on; it also imposed the infamous quota of 10 per cent of Jews at secondary level. See *Shornik postanovlenii po MNP* vol. 10 (SPb., 1894), col. 803, col. 882.

30 Legislation of 1871, still enshrined in the 'Codex of Statutes on Learned Institutions and Educational Establishments' of 1893, stated that the *gimnaziya* was open to children of 'all estates, callings, and creeds' to attend (article 1487), and that grants were available to children from poor backgrounds to attend this type of school and the *real'noe uchilishche* (articles 1496, 1717). (See *SZRI* vol. XI.1, p. 138, pp. 139–40, p. 162).

31 A useful digest of dates and facts is given in 'Nachal'noe narodnoe obrazovanie', *ES* vol. 20, pp. 728–50. Attendance rates in the developed European nations had reached 80–90 per cent by this era (e.g. over 80 per cent in England, p. 732; 90 per cent in the Netherlands: ibid., p. 737).

32 Ben Eklof, *Russian Peasant Schools* (Berkeley, CA, 1986), pp. 111–16. The article in *ES* has a clear political force, contrasting as it does the situation in Germany, which is clearly an ideal, with the situation in Denmark, where the 'complicated system' of primary education and the 'power of the clergy' were said to be the focus of criticism. Even in Denmark, though, primary education was compulsory (p. 737). The point that the Denmark situation was closely parallel to the Russian one, but that even there compulsory education had been introduced, was certainly meant to be remarked by the article's readers.

33 *NES* vol. 28, col. 147.

34 Eklof, *Russian Peasant Schools*, p. 165.

35 See ibid.; Jeffrey Brooks, *When Russia Learned to Read: Literacy and Popular Literature in Russia, 1861–1917* (Princeton, NJ, 1984); 'Nachal'noe obrazovanie', *NES* vol. 28, cols 123–49.

36 See e.g. V. I. Farmakovsky, 'K voprosu o edinoi shkole', *ZMNP* 4 (1905), section IV, pp. 172–94 (here the 'estate-led' character of the educational system is traced back to a statute of 1828, which had decreed that parish schools were for the lower orders, district schools for the children of craftsmen and merchants, and *gimnazii* for 'those of respectable social estate').

37 A. I. Afanasiev, 'Novaya nachal'naya shkola', *ZMNP* 2 (1907), section IV, 137, 166.

38 Farmakovsky, 'K voprosu', pp. 191–3.

39 According to the timetable for classical *gimnazii* in 1914, for example, pupils in Forms 6–8 did six hours of Latin, two hours of religious knowledge, four hours of Russian, three to four hours of history, two to three hours of general science, two to three hours of physics, two to four hours of maths, four hours of a foreign language, no art, and two hours a week PE – a total of 30 hours per week of instruction. (See *NES*, headword *Gimnaziya*, col. 533.)

40 Farmakovsky, 'K voprosu', p. 180.

41 See S. Rozhdestvensky, *Istoricheskii obzor deyatel'nosti MNP 1802–1902* (SPb., 1903), p. 633; G. Zorgenfrei, 'Obshchestvo klassicheskoi filologii i pedagogiki v 1905 i 1906 godakh', *ZMNP* 8 (1908), section IV, pp. 35–44.

42 Yu. Aikhenval'd, 'Nravstvennaya i umstvennaya individual'nost' uchenika', *VV* 2 (1900), 29–42 (quotations p. 29, p. 34, p. 38). Cf. 'Iz zhizni srednei shkoly', *VV* 5 (1910), 96.

43 L. Prozorov, 'Samoubiistva uchashchikhsya v Moskve', *Obshchestvennyi vrach* 9 (1914), 1086–94, see esp. 1093–4.

44 See e.g. Aikhenval'd, 'Nravstvennaya', p. 31, p. 34 (on Tolstoy); Lidiya Rebinder, 'Uchebno-vospitatel'noe zavedenie d-ra Litsa', *VV* 6 (1905), 136–64.

45 On Tolstoy's views, see above. The fusion of Tolstoy's ideas with those of Western theorists would probably not have struck the master himself as especially to be welcomed. In 'O narodnom obrazovanii' (1874), he had specifically stated: 'Our [Russian] school must not be a model school in the sense of our introducing all kinds of building bricks and pictures and rubbish of that kind invented by Germans, but in the sense of applying the simplest methods to the teaching of those very same peasant children who are also the pupils in ordinary schools.' (*Polnoe sobranie sochinenii v 90 tomakh* (M. and L.: Khudozhestvennaya literatura, 1928–64), vol. 17, p. 127). But it was precisely the combination of Froebelian 'bricks and pictures' and populist, commonsense methodology that was particularly characteristic of nursery and primary teaching in Russia during the early twentieth century.

46 M. Gorbunov-Posadov, 'Neskol'ko vstupitel'nykh slov', *SvoV* 1 (1907), p. 6, p. 8, p. 14.

47 A. D'yachkov-Tarasov, 'O znachenii i organizatsii dal'nikh ucheicheskikh ekskursii po Rossii', *VV* 3 (1910), 139–54.

48 B. Eklof, 'Worlds in Conflict: Patriarchal Authority, Discipline, and the Russian School, 1861–1914', in idem (ed.), *School and Society in Tsarist and Soviet Russia* (Basingstoke, 1993), pp. 98–9 (emphasis original).

49 M. V. Gorbunova and E. E. Kistyakovskaya, *Pervyi opyt svobodnoi trudovoi shkoly: Dom svobodnogo rebenka* (M., 1924).

50 I. Sulina, 'Sel'skaya zhizn'' *SvoV* 7 (1912), 67–73. See also the reminiscences by Gertrud Striedter of the Sablino school (a co-operatively run, coeducational school where pupils sat on the governing body), 'Erinnerungen', extract 2, pp. 1–5 (personal archive of Jurij Striedter, Cambridge, MA); and 'Obshchestvo detskogo vospitaniya', *SvoV* 2 (1911), 38 (on a school run by a parents' group).

51 As happened with the pupils at the 'House of the Free Child': see Gorbunova and Kistaykovskaya, *Pervyi opyt*.

52 N. Teffi, 'Pereotsenka tsennostei', *Sobranie sochinenii* vol. 1 (M., 1997), pp. 51–4. In a similar vein is 'Politika i nauka', ibid., pp. 59–63. On this theme generally, see Laura Engelstein, *The Keys to Happiness* (Ithaca, 1992), pp. 232–6, 240–3.

53 S. Zolotarev, 'Deti revolyutsii', *Russkaya shkola* 3 (1907), 20.

54 See the MNP circulars to this effect printed in *ZMNP* 2 (1906), section I, 86 (ban on pupil organisations of 1 January 1906), and cf. *ZMNP* 2 (1907), section I, 85, quoting a repeat ban of 15 November 1906.

55 Zolotarev, 'Deti revolyutsii', 2, quoting *Russkie vedomosti* and *Stavropol'skii vestnik*.

56 *ZMNP* 2 (1907), section I, pp. 87–9 (school uniform, library books, parent commissions), and cf. *ZMNP* 4 (1906), section I, 28, which revokes a circular of 29 July 1902 decreeing that excerpts from pupils' conduct records for the top three classes of school should be forwarded to the university authorities when they were applying for places.

57 See *Materialy po reforme srednei shkoly* (Petrograd, 1915), pp. 5–9 (timetables), pp. 24–54 (literature programme), pp. pp. 492–8 (aesthetic education). On aesthetic values in the literary programme, see e.g. the section on 'immanent reading', pp. 458–64. For a brief outline of the programme (without much context), see M. V. Boguslavsky, *Razvitie obshchego srednego obrazovaniya: problemy i resheniya* (M., 1994), p. 27. For the 1905 proposals, see *ZMNP* 8 (1905), section I, 40–79 (the rationale), 114–44 (the lists of recommended reading). These proposals had specifically stated that getting pupils to read 'ethically demanding works' was not a good idea (see p. 41). For attacks on the 1905 proposals, see e.g. A. Arkhangel'sky, 'Zametki na programme po istorii russkoi literatury i teorii', *ZMNP* 4 (1906), section IV, 67–97; 5 (1906), section IV, 1–36; 6 (1906), section IV, 45–66; V. M. Istrin, 'Novaya programma kursa russkoi slovesnosti v sredneuchebnykh zavedeniyakh', *ZMNP* 6 (1906), section IV, 67–96; 12 (1906), section IV, 111–41; 1 (1907), section 4, 1–33.

58 See *Materialy po reforme*, pp. 123–4.

59 *ZMNP* 8 (1905), section I, 138: 'Vybor stikhot-vorenii predostavlyaetsya g. prepodavatelyu, ucheniki dolzhny ikh prochest'.'

60 O. D., 'Shkol'noe vospitanie angliiskogo dzhentel'mena', *ZMNP* 10 (1906), section IV, 196–203.

61 *Materialy po reforme*, p. 426; on the procedures for introducing Scouting, see pp. 429–30.

62 For example, the teachers pioneering 'remedial education' for 'backward' children: see Chapter 4.

63 See 'Yubilei detskogo sada', *RS* 5–6 (1898), 383; N. V. Chekhov, 'Podgotovka rukovoditel'nits doshkol'nym vospitaniem detei', *VV* 3 (1905), 84; N. Vinogradov, *Ocherki po istorii idei doshkol'nogo vospitaniya* (n.p.; izd. Puchina, 1925), pp. 148–55.

64 See e.g. 'NP', 'O detskikh sadakh v Rossii', *VV* 2 (1916), 59; Mariya Chekhova, 'Obshchestvo sodeistviya doshkol'nomu vospitaniyu detei', *RS* 4 (1908), 52–7; N. Koshkina, 'Osnovnye zadachi Detskikh Sadov i elementarnykh shkol', *VO* 6 (1902), 193–212.

65 See e.g. 'NP', 'O detskikh sadakh', p. 62.

66 A. Simonovich, 'O detskikh sadakh', *VV* 8 (1896), 184, 186. This kind of argument continued later as well, see e.g. 'NP', 'O detskikh sadakh', p. 59; Nikolai Karintsev, 'Po detskim sadam zagranitsei', *DoshV* 1 (1913), 11–26 (on England and France, with particularly positive views of the latter). The broad picture is also given in P. Kapterev, 'Istoricheskii ocherk uchrezhdenii dlya vospitaniya detei do-shkol'nogo vozrasta', *RS* 2 (1896), 12–23; 2 (1896), 12–23; 3 (1896), 7–29; 4 (1896), 14–28.

67 On the perniciousness of drilling, see e.g. Koshkina, 'Osnovnye zadachi', 202–3; on kindergartens as a place for neglected children, see E. Garshin, 'O besprizornykh detyakh i detskikh sadakh dlya nikh', *RS* 3 (1892), 70–7. A later article voicing the same views is 'Detskii sad', *VO* 3 (1911), 65–74. On cognitive benefits, see Yuliya Markova, 'Detskii sad (iz nablyudenii materi)', *VO* 1 (1895), 14–17; Kapterev, 'Istoricheskii ocherk uchrezhdenii dlya vospitaniya detei do-shkol'nogo vozrasta', *RS* 4 (1896), 14–28.

68 On the legislation, see E. Kovalevsky, 'Uchebno-vospitatel'nye uchrezhdeniya dlya detei doshkol'nogo vozrasta', *ZMNP* 8 (1908), section III, pp. 201–10. See further, Chapter 9 below.

69 See e.g. the series *Obshchedostupnye kursy po doshkol'nomu vospitaniyu* (15 vols; M., 1915).

70 Rebuttal of the arguments against nursery education: N. Lubenets, 'Obshchestvo i semeinye nachala v doshkol'nom vospitanii', *DoshV* 2 (1911), 55–70; 3 (1911), 140–56. Scary visions of conventionally brought up children: M. Bezobrazova, '"Zachem vy ikh baluete?"', *DoshV* 5 (1911), 387–90; O. Bystrova, 'Detskii vopros', *DoshV* 8–9 (1916), 495–514 (with a pen-portrait of a five-year-old 'fashion victim' who lives for the thought of new bootees, p. 503). Nursery education essential to modern mothers: Lubenets, 'Obshchestvo'; see also the report in *DoshV* 8 (1913), 519, which has a working mother calling for factory kindergartens (taken from her speech to the Rodina club in Kiev).

71 *Detskii sad i Elementarnaya shkola E. P. Zalesskoi (Motivirovannye uchebnyi plan i primernye programmy detskogo uchilishcha E. P. Zalesskoi [...]* (M., 1907), p. 5, p. 29. On the programmes, see also S. M. Petersen, 'Plan zanyatii v detskom sadu', *DoshV* 6 (1911), 475–88 etc.

72 *See Detskii sad i Elementarnaya shkola*, pp. 9–19.

73 P. Lesgaft, *Semeinoe vospitanie i ego znachenie* (reprint: SPb., 1906), pp. 139–43.

74 See e.g. E. A. Pokrovsky, *Fiziologicheskoe vospitanie detei u raznykh narodov, preimushchestvenno Rossii* (M., 1884); idem, *Detskie igry, preimushchestvenno russkie* (M., 1884).

75 A. Bine [=Binet] and T. Simon, *Nenormal'nye deti* (M., 1911). An important propagandiser of such tests in Russia at this stage was Anna M. Shubert: see e.g. her *Kratkoe opisanie i kharakteristika metodov opredeleniya umstvennoi otstalosti detei* (M., 1913), and cf. G. I. Chelpanov, *Sbornik statei. Psikhologiya i shkola* (M., 1912), p. 182. See also

A. A. Nikol'skaya, *Vozrastnaya i pedagogicheskaya psikhologiya v dorevolyutsionnoi Rossii* (Dubna, 1995).

76 On the child study movement generally, see Adrian Wooldridge, *Measuring the Mind* (Cambridge, 1993), pp. 36–48.

77 J. Sully, *Studies of Childhood* (London, 1895), p. 4.

78 Ibid., p. 121, p. 129.

79 Ibid., p. 147, p. 158.

80 C. Darwin, 'A Biographical Sketch of an Infant', *Mind* 2: 7 (1877), 285–94; H. Taine, 'On the Acquisition of Language by Children', *Mind* 2: 6 (1877), 252–9. The latter essay had originally been published in *La Revue philosophique* in January 1876.

81 I. A. Sikorsky, *Dusha rebenka* (Kiev, 1909), p. 85 (emphasis original).

82 Ibid., p. 104.

83 G. I. Rossolimo, *Plan issledovaniya detskoi dushi (v zdorovom i boleznennom sostoyanii)* (2nd edn; M., 1909).

84 See e.g. the 1915 diary of Z. I. Stanchinskaya, *Dnevnik materi* (M., 1924), p. 26 etc.

85 A. Levonevsky, *Moi rebenok* (SPb., 1914).

86 Yu. Ladunskaya, 'K voprosu o razvitii ponyatiya o kolichestve', *SemV* 9 (1913), 65–70.

87 Sikorsky, *Dusha rebenka*, p. 140.

88 Caryl Emerson, *The Life of Musorgsky* (Cambridge, 1999), p. 73, p. 75.

89 On the Izdebsky Salon, see A. Parton, *Mikhail Larionov and the Russian Avant-Garde* (London, 1993), pp. 93–4 (though Parton's account has some mistakes, e.g. the inclusion of articles by Kul'bin and Bakst which in fact do *not* discuss children's art). On Tugendkhol'd's article, see p. 41 below. On children's art in Western Europe, see Jonathan Fineberg, *The Innocent Eye: Children's Art and the Modern Artist* (Princeton, NJ, 1997), pp. 9–14. In France, interest developed later than in the German-speaking world, England, and indeed Russia, though the Nabis and Matisse were enthusiasts, and Apollinaire reviewed an exhibition of 'Desseins d'enfants' in 1914 (see Fineberg, *The Innocent Eye*, p. 14).

90 On Benois, see Yu. Molok (ed.), *Staraya detskaya kniga 1900–1930e gody iz sobraniya Professora Marka Ratsa. Opisanie sobraniya [...]* (M., 1996), p. viii; Ya. Tugendkhol'd, 'O detskikh risunkakh i ikh vzaimodeistvii so vzroslym iskusstvom', *Severnye zapiski* 4–5 (1916), 124–33 (this quote p. 124).

91 Tugendkhol'd, 'O detskikh risunkakh', p. 127.

92 See Fineberg, *The Innocent Eye*, pp. 33–4.

93 One of these panels, *Spring*, is reproduced in colour in Parton, *Mikhail Larionov*, plate 11. Parton discusses another panel from the series, *Autumn*, on p. 94: 'There is nothing in this simple schema that a child of [seven or eight] could not attempt.' For a discussion of *Dog on a Chain*, see Fineberg, *The Innocent Eye*, p. 36.

94 A. Kruchenykh, *Sobstvennye rasskazy i risunki detei* (SPb., 1914).

95 *Skazki starukhi-govorukhi o zhivotnykh (iz narodnykh skazok)* (SPb., n.d.: *c.* 1910). A wonderful guide to such materials is Molok (ed.), *Staraya detskaya kniga*. Molok observes that 'the

very concept of "children's book" as an artistic phenomenon only really began forming in Russia during the early twentieth century' (p. iv).

96 See e.g. Putilova, *Russkaya poeziya detyam* (2 vols; SPb., 1997), vol. 1, for an excellent selection of material from the late eighteenth to the early twentieth centuries.

97 V. Voronov, 'K psikhologii detskogo risunka', *VV* 5 (1910), 95–112 (quotation p. 106).

98 See *Katalog magazina "Detskii mir"* (SPb., 1886). The shop was at no. 33 Liteinyi Prospekt.

99 *Katalog magazina 'Detskoe vospitanie'* (M., 1899), p. 7. At this period 10–15 roubles was a standard wage for a live-in servant.

100 See e.g. *Doctor Zhivago* for a description of a Christmas tree party, divided into a decorous afternoon event for younger children and a more relaxed late evening party for older children and adults. For an instance of a revolutionary family with trees, see N. Baranskaya, 'Avtobiografiya bez umolchanii', *Grani* 146 (1990), p. 125. On charity *elki*, see e.g. 'Letopis' Petrogradskikh gorodskikh i prigorodnykh popechitel'sv', *PB* 1 (1917), 26.

101 Baranskaya, 'Avtobiografiya', p. 125.

102 'Anketa o elke', *SemV* 10 (1913), 57–68.

103 E. N. Trubetskoi, *Iz proshlogo* (Newtonville, TN, 1976), p. 8, p. 37.

104 Mariya Redelin, *Dom i khozyaistvo* (2 vols; 3rd edn, SPb., 1900), vol. 1, pp. 50–1.

105 See lot 95, *The Russian Sale, London Thursday 29 April 1999* (London: Sothebys, 1999).

106 See e.g. K. L'dov, *Myau, myaushki, myau* (SPb., 1900), and *Sobachkiny shalosti* (SPb., 1901); I. I. Kosyakov, 'Vse ona' (1889), K. M. Fofanov, 'Naryadili elku v prazdnichnoe plat'e' (1887), D. Merezhkovsky, 'Detyam' (1883), in Putilova (ed.), *Russkaya poeziya detyam*, vol. 1, p. 370, p. 340, pp. 317–20.

107 Putilova, *Russkaya poeziya detyam*, vol. 1, pp. 395–6.

108 See especially *Opavshie list'ya* (St Petersburg: n.p., 1913) – and the illustration reproduced here.

109 'Utomlen'e' (originally published as poem 33 in 'Tol'ko teni', the central cycle of *Vechernii al'bom*), *Sobranie sochinenii v 7 tomakh*, vol. 1 (M., 1994), p. 46. The quotation earlier is from 'Akvarell', ('Detstvo' no. 20 in *Vechernii al'bom*), ibid., p. 40.

110 The ascetic anti-physicality traditional in the Russian intelligentsia – as extensively expounded in cultural histories of Russia, e.g. S. Boym, *Common Places* (Cambridge, MA, 1994); J. Bowlt and O. Matich (eds), *Laboratory of Dreams* (Stanford, 1996), Irina Paperno, *Chernyshevsky and the Age of Realism* (Stanford, 1988) – was no doubt another feature here, given the inextricable link between babies and small children and the 'lower bodily stratum'.

111 Lidiya Zinov'eva-Annibal, 'Bich', *Tragicheskii zverinets* (SPb., 1907), pp. 211–33.

112 For the juridical background, see Laura Engelstein, *The Keys to Happiness* (Ithaca, NY, 1992), pp. 79–80 (the quotation here is from p. 80, citing the procurator of the Samara circuit court).

113 For example Zinov'eva-Annibal, *Tragicheskii zverinets*, a cycle of short stories with a first-person narrator whose biography closely resembles

Annibal's own; or (for a far more explicit and anatomically detailed account of burgeoning sexuality), *The Confessions of Victor X*, ed. D. Rayfield (London, 1984).

114 'Detvora', A. P. Chekhov, *PSS* (M., 1974–83), vol. 4, pp. 315–20.

115 N. Teffi, *Zemnaya raduga* (NY, 1952), p. 54.

116 Kornei Chukovsky, *Krokodil, Stikhi i skazki, Ot dvukh do pyati* (M.: Detskaya literatura, 1981), pp. 92–3. The poem was first published as *Vanya i Krokodil* in 1917; later editions were known simply as *Krokodil*. It was Chukovsky's first work for children, and he began composing it to distract his own son when the latter had a high temperature: see *Stikhi i skazki*, pp. 600–2.

117 Chekhov, 'Sbornik dlya detei', *PSS* vol. 1, pp. 280–1.

118 Chekhov, 'Mal'chiki', *PSS* vol. 6, pp. 424–9.

119 Teffi, 'Prestupnik', *Zemnaya raduga*, pp. 8–15.

120 *Azbuka v kartinakh Aleksandra Benua* (SPb., 1904). My thanks to Mariya Osorina for drawing my attention to this book and discussing some of the images with me, though the ideas set out below are my own. See also M. V. Osorina, 'Ideologicheskoe litso knigi: piskhologicheskii analiz oblozhek sovetskogo "Bukvarya" i "Azbuki" A. Benua', *Detskii sbornik*, ed. E. Kuleshov and I. Antipova (M., 2003), pp. 155–68.

121 'Komitety popechitel'stva ob okhrane materinstva i mladenchestva', *PB* 8–9–10 (1914), 1160.

122 Kruchenykh, *Sobstvennye rasskazy*, p. 40.

123 Influential British writers included Kate Greenaway (whose books, such as *A Child's Day*, seem to have influenced Benois), Beatrix Potter, Edward Lear and, of course, Lewis Carroll.

124 See e.g. M. Gyuio [Guyau], *Vospitanie i nasledst-vennost'* (SPb., 1891), p. xvi. Cf. Tolstoy, *The Kreutzer Sonata*.

125 M. P——n, 'Geograficheskoe predstavlenie v svobodnom geograficheskom sadu', *SvoV* 2 (1911–12), 96.

126 E. Fraser, *The House on the Dvina* (London, 1984), p. 197.

127 See *Deti i voina* (Kiev, 1915), p. 116, p. 115 (letters to soldiers), plate V.1 (wheel), plate VII.1 (Christmas). See pp. 69–78 of the book also for a résumé of war-related literature that could be used in teaching.

128 The phrase comes from Blok's essay 'An Evening in Siena' (1906).

129 Data in this and the previous paragraph are taken from G.-H. Stevens, *Das Wunderkind in der Musikgeschichte* (Münster, 1982): see esp. pp. 158–9, 193–6. See also M. Moiseiwitsch, *Moiseiwitsch* (London, 1965); A. Rubinstein, *My Young Years* (London, 1973); H. R. Axelrod and T. M. Axelrod, *Heifetz* (3rd edn; Neptune City, NJ, 1987).

130 The conservatoire was the only branch of higher education where there was no upper limit on the numbers of Jews who might be admitted (see Chapter 3 below). In her memoir, '… I zori rodiny dalekoi', Alie Akimova records that her parents, Crimean Tatars deported to the Crimea, ambitiously nurtured her musical abilities in exactly the same way, with her mother 'striving to give me the best possible education and thereby snatch me from the hopeless caste of the socially abject' (*Druzhba narodov* 3 (2002), p. 169).

131 See *Rachmaninoff's Recollections, told to Oskar von Riesemann* (London, 1934), pp. 43–4, p. 54.

132 See Moiseiwitsch, *Moiseiwitsch*, p. 27; Rubinstein, *My Young Years*, pp. 5–9. Rubinstein was already fixated on the piano at three, and was taken to see Joachim, who advised that he should have no lessons till the age of six, advice his parents duly decided to follow. For the Prokofiev material, see S. S. Prokofiev, *Avtobiografiya* (2nd edn; M., 1982), p. 43. Prokofiev admitted that this treatment turned him into a rather sloppy performer, but it had the advantage of giving him wide musical experience and a capacity for independent judgement at an early stage.

133 For a case in point, see Natal'ya Sats's account of her education at the E. N. Vizler music school in Moscow, *Novelly moei zhizni* (2 vols; M., 1984), vol. 1, pp. 32–5. The administration of the school allowed themselves to be bullied by Sats herself (aged about five) into taking her on earlier than usual, and, after bad experiences with a teacher who patronised her horribly and with a dragonish old woman who threw her out of the room for 'impudence', she found an excellent and thoroughly competent pedagogue at the third attempt.

134 Equally, the number of Russian child prodigies of the early twentieth century (and later) who managed to make their way forward into successful adult careers is notable – even if some of them (as Axelrod and Axelrod's sensationalist account of Heifetz suggests) turned into rather obnoxious individuals.

135 See D. Sarab'yanov, *Valentin Serov* (L., 1987), pp. 5–7.

136 An accessible English edition of Bashkirtseva's memoirs, originally published in *Severnyi vestnik*, is *The Journal of Marie Bashkirtseff*, trans. M. Blind (London, 1985).

137 T. Shchepkina-Kupernik, 'Literaturnyi put', in *Razroznennye stranitsy* (M., 1966), pp. 3–36.

138 See S. Marshak, *Sobranie sochinenii v 8 tomakh*, vol. 8 (M., 1972), p. 17 n. 6.

139 See Wachtel, esp. ch. 1.

140 For a fuller discussion of pedagogical literature in late eighteenth- and early nineteenth-century Russia, see ch. 1 of my *Refining Russia: Advice Literature, Polite Culture, and Gender from 1760* (Oxford, 2001).

141 By the late nineteenth century, too, the time-lag in translation of Western pedagogical literature was much less considerable than in the late eighteenth and early nineteenth centuries. The first Russian translation of Montessori's *Il metodo della pedagogia scientifica applicato all'educazione infantile nelle case dei bambini* (1913), for example, came out in the same year as the first Italian edition.

142 See Dzh. A. Kolotstsa [Giovanni Amonio Colozza], *Detskie igry: ikh psikhologicheskoe i pedagogicheskoe znachenie* (M., 1909), p. 139.

143 Aleksandr Bogdanov, '"Dom detei"', *Krasnaya zvezda: Roman-utopiya* (M., 1929), pp. 82–91.

144 See further in Chapter 5 below.

145 V. D. Nabokov, 'Plotskie prestupleniya, po proektu ugolovnogo ulozheniya', in *Sbornik statei po ugolovnomu pravu* (SPb., 1904), p. 129, asserts melodramatically, 'Nowhere, it seems, other than in Russia has at least one form of incest attained the character almost of a normal everyday phenomenon, acquiring a corresponding technical term of its own – *snokhachestvo*.' In fact other peasant cultures (e.g. Spain) did have comparable practices, and *snokhachestvo* was also the subject of smutty jokes and snide comments in villages, which suggests its 'abnormal' character there: see A. Ostrovsky, 'Snokhachestvo', *Muzhiki i baby* (SPb., 2005), pp. 615–19. N. Foinitsky, 'Zhenshchina-prestupnitsa', *Severnyi vestnik* 2 (1893), 123–44; 3 (1893), 111–40, draws a causal link between early marriage and murder rates. On child prostitution, see the detailed discussion in Engelstein, *The Keys to Happiness*, pp. 274–84.

146 For a discussion of *Detstvo* in historical context, see Wachtel, ch. 4; Marina Balina, 'Troubled Lives: The Legacy of Childhood in Soviet Literature', *Slavic and East European Journal* 49:2, 249–50.

147 See *NES*, vol. 17, col. 81, headword 'Detskii sad'. The point is not that this represents the two systems accurately (the Froebel one was more liberal than suggested here), but that it conveys the perceived split between 'rational' and 'free' methods. The split is not unique to Russia, of course. Karin Lesnik-Oberstein, *Children's Literature: Criticism and the Fictional Child* (Oxford, 1987) tabulates different Western attitudes to children's literature: those of writers such as Astrid Lindgren or Alison Lurie, who see children's literature as 'liberating the imaginative, questioning, rebellious child within

all of us' (pp. 75–6), or others who place a greater emphasis on efficacy (e.g. on claims that literature contributes to the different stages of psychological development (following Piaget), pp. 107–9). A didactic strand is common even in the first line of argument – so, when people think it's all right for children to read trash, they think that's because it might get them reading better material in due course (p. 123). Whichever way, commentators on children's literature share a conviction that 'we do not make meaning; we are given meaning by the "real child"' (p. 14).

148 See e.g. Ekaterina Yanzhul', 'Detskie sady po sisteme Montessori', *DoshV* 4 (1912), 195–202. It was Froebel, though, who was cited as the journal's founding father in the first issue: 'Zadachi zhurnala', *DoshV* 1 (1911), 1–6.

149 E. I. Tikheeva, *Doma rebenka Montessori v Rime* (Petrograd, 1915), p. 41.

150 See ibid., p. 7, p. 20, p. 34, p. 60.

151 See Jessica Tovrov, *The Family in Imperial Russia* (NY, 1987).

152 Anne Higonnet, *Pictures of Innocence* (London, 1998), pp. 23–4, argues that classlessness is a characteristic of the 'Romantic child' in general.

153 See further in Chapter 5 below.

154 See the unofficial trial transcript (no official court record was kept), *Delo Beilisa* (3 vols; Kiev, 1913), vol. 1, pp. 17–19. For a basic outline of the Yushchinsky murder and the Beilis trial, see *Delo Mendelya Beilis*, ed. R. Sh. Ganelin, V. E. Kel'ner and I. V. Lukyanov (SPb., 1999), pp. 3–23.

155 *Delo Mendelya Beilisa*, p. 6.

156 *Delo Beilisa*, vol. 3, p. 5.

157 Ibid., vol. 3, p. 215.

158 Ibid., vol. 3, p. 271.

159 Ibid., vol. 3, p. 292.

Chapter 2: Pioneers and Pet-Keepers, 1917–1935

1 L. M. Vasilevsky, *Detskaya prestupnost' i detskii sad* (Tver', 1923), p. 4.

2 Ya. A. Perel' and A. A. Lyubimova (eds), *Prestupleniya protiv nesovershennoletnikh*, 'Okhrana detstva i detskoe pravo' series, issue 9 (M.–L., 1932), p. 43.

3 On International Children's Week, see p. 77 below. On foreign visitors, and children's issues as an element in Soviet cultural diplomacy and the conduct of international relations, see Catriona Kelly, 'Young Actors on the World Stage: Children and Soviet Cultural Diplomacy', forthcoming.

4 See e.g. *DD* 3 (1932), 13–17.

5 See further in Chapter 6 in the online version.

6 *Grazhdanskii kodeks RSFSR, kommentarii A. G. Goikhbarg, I. G. Koblents* (2nd edn; M., 1925), articles 418, 420. Otherwise, minors figure in the commentary to article 182 (pp. 237–8), which pointed out that the prohibition on owning more than one 'unmunicipalised' dwelling per family did not apply to minors, who might acquire a dwelling of their own even if their parents already had one. It can have been few minors who were in a position to avail themselves of this

loophole. *Ugolovnyi kodeks sovetskikh respublik*, ed. S. Kanarsky (Khar'kov, 1928), article 151 sexual intercourse with a person below the age of sexual maturity, combined with seduction (*rastlenie*, or perversion), article 152, 'corruption of minors' (*rastlenie maloletnikh*); article 156, desertion of a minor or other helpless person. Striking also is the absence of clear policy in the regulatory practice of the new government. The official legal bulletin *Sbornik uzakonenii i rasporyazhenii rabochego i krest'yanskogo pravitel'stva* is a mess of minor regulations relating to e.g. the internal structure and management of the Commission for the Improvement of Children's Lives, the principles of support for working-class and peasant pupils at schools, and so on.

7 *DSV*, vol. 1, no. 171.

8 See E. Vekker, *Deti i sovetskoe pravo* (Khar'kov, 1925), p. 7.

9 See *Kodeks zakonov o brake, sem'e i opeke, s postateinym kommentariem*, ed. P. A. Krasikova (L., 1927), p. 95, p. 102, p. 111.

10 See A. Goikhbarg, *Sravnitel'noe semeinoe pravo* (M., 1925), p. 219, quoted in *Kodeks zakonov o brake* (1927), p. 95.

11 For more details of this legislation and its limitations in practice, see Chapter 10 below.

12 Lynn Mally, *Culture of the Future* (Berkeley, 1990), pp. 180–1.

13 F. M. Orlov-Skomorovsky, *Golgofa rebenka* (M., 1921), p. 143, pp. 144–5, p. 138, p. 136.

14 *Pervyi vserossiiskii s"ezd deyatelei po okhrane detstva (2–8 febralya 1919 goda v Moskve)* (M., 1920), p. 19, p. 8.

15 See e.g. *Pervyi vserossiiskii s"ezd*, pp. 32–45.

16 See the speech by Comrade Grin'ko of the Central Executive Committee's Agitation and Propaganda section, 'Sotsial'noe vospitanie detei' (27 December 1920), RGASPI f. 17 op. 60 d. 60, l. 28.

17 Il'ina in *Pervyi vserossiiskii s"ezd*, p. 49.

18 See 'Grazhdanstvo detei', commentary to article 36, *Kodeks zakonov o brake* (1927), pp. 97–8.

19 J. Bullard and M. Bullard (eds), *The Diaries of Reader Bullard, 1930–1934* (Charlbury, Oxon., 2000), p. 75.

20 V. Dyushen (ed.), *Pyat' let detskogo gorodka im. III Internationatsionala* (M., 1924).

21 See *ZMNP* 7–8 (1917), section I, p. 10, and *ZMNP* 9 (1917), section I, p. 8.

22 For the quotation, see 'O novom pravopisanii' in *ZMNP* 9 (1917), section I, p. 41 (emphasis original).

23 As announced in *ZMNP* 3–4 (1917), section 1, p. viii.

24 'Ot narodnogo komissara po prosveshcheniyu', ZMNP 11–12 (1917), section I, pp. 3–4 (emphasis original).

25 See *DSV* vol. 3, no. 214. On the studiedly egalitarian nature of Soviet pedagogy, see also W. Bérelowich, 'De l'Enfant à l'homme nouveau: le "futurisme pédagogique" des années 1920', *Revue des Études slaves* 56: 1 (1984), 116.

26 These included above all Nadezhda Krupskaya, who had been an occasional contributor to *Svobodnoe vospitanie*, but also Stanislav Shatsky, the co-ordinator of drop-in centres for 'difficult children' in early twentieth-century Moscow. See William Partlett, 'Breaching Cultural Worlds with the Village School: Educational Visions, Local Initiative, and Rural Experience at S. T. Shatsky's Kaluga School System, 1919–1931', *Slavonic and East European Review* 82: 4 (2004), 847–85.

27 *DSV* vol. 3, no. 214.

28 *Instruktsiya po vedeniyu detskogo sada: Obshchie printsipy vospitaniya detei doshkol'nogo vozrasta* (M., 1921), p. 4.

29 See Holmes, *The Kremlin and the Schoolhouse*.

30 Dr M. V. Vul'f, *Fantaziya i real'nost' v psikhike rebenka* (Odessa, 1926), p. 24 (emphasis original).

31 I. Smirnov, 'Distsiplina v shkole', *Prosveshchenie na transporte* 2 (1927), 3–9: quotes p. 4, p. 8.

32 The process is described in detail by Partlett, 'Breaching Cultural Worlds'. Cf. the comments of Detlef Glowka, *Schulreform und Gesellschaft in der Sowjetunion, 1958–1968* (Stuttgart, 1970), p. 109.

33 See Bérelowitch, 'De l'Enfant à l'homme nouveau', 120.

34 See e.g. P. P. Blonsky, *Pedologiya* (M., 1925), which is a complex and technical discussion of child physiology in its relationship to intellectual development, from the foetus to 'the childhood of permanent teeth', complete with anthropometric tables, and accompanied by instructions in how to apply Binet-Simon tests and how to record biographical data. More practical guides include A. M. Shubert, *Kak izuchat' shkol'nika* (M., 1924); and her ethnically directed guide aimed at encouraging research on divergence with regard to cognitive skills etc., *Izobrazitel'nye sposobnosti u detei evenkov (tungusov)* (L., 1935). On IQ testing in the West, see the discussion in A. Wooldridge, *Measuring the Mind: Education and Psychology in England, c.1860–c.1990* (Cambridge, 1994), ch. 3. There is a good discussion of the practicalities of paedology in *Obrazovanie v Moskve* (M., 2000), ch. 6.

35 See further the discussion in Chapter 10 below.

36 The boundary between *pedagogika* and *pedologiya* was in any case porous. Professional directories such as *Nauchnye rabotniki Moskvy* (L., 1930) and *Nauchnye rabotniki Leningrada* (L., 1934) reveal that numerous individuals, including, for example, Blonsky, described their specialism both as 'paedology' and as 'pedagogy'. Those using the latter self-description significantly outnumbered the former in Moscow (141 versus 59), while in Leningrad the number of specialists in both disciplines was identical (72).

37 On this, see also M. V. Boguslavsky, *Razvitie obshchego srednego obrazovaniya: problemy i resheniya. Iz istorii otechestvennoi pedagogiki 20-kh godov XX veka* (M., 1994), p. 4, p. 60. Compare studies of other areas of early Soviet cultural policy, such as the theatre: Lynn Mally, *Revolutionary Acts* (Ithaca, NY, 2000).

38 *Programmy dlya pervogo kontsentra shkol vtoroi stupeni (5, 6 i 7 gody obucheniya)* (M.–L., 1925), p. 143, p. 17. See also *Programma dlya vtorogo kontsentra shkoly semiletki (V, VI i VII gody obucheniya)* (M., 1927).

39 *Programmy i metodicheskie zapiski dlya edinoi trudovoi shkoly* issue 3 (M.–L., 1927), p. 5, pp. 25–6.

40 *Programmy fabrichno-zavodskoi semiletki*, issues 1–8 (M.–L., 1930), issue 1, p. 4, p. 13 ff. On the 1929 reform, see Holmes, *Stalin's School*, p. 10.

41 S. Fitzpatrick, *Education and Social Mobility in the Soviet Union* (Cambridge, 1979), pp. 223–5.

42 *Pervyi Vserossiiskii S"ezd po doshkol'nomu vospitaniyu: doklady, protokoly, rezolyutsii* (M., 1921), p. 195.

43 The term 'cultural growth' is taken from Kornei Chukovsky, *Ot dvukh do pyati* (4th edn; L., 1934), p. 79.

44 N. Al'medingen-Tumim and G. Tumim (eds), *V pomoshch' doshkol'nomu rabotniku: Sbornik stat'ei* (L., 1925), p. 15.

45 See *Dokumenty TsK KPSS i TsK VLKSM o rabote Vsesoyuznoi pionerskoi organizatsii imeni V. I. Lenina* (comp. V. S. Khanchin) (M., 1970), p. 71.

46 *Rezolyutsii Tret'ego Vserossiiskogo S"ezda po doshkol'nomu vospitaniyu* (M.–L., 1924), p. 22.

47 *Spravochnik po doshkol'nomu vospitaniyu* (M., 1919).

48 M. Ya. Morozova and E. I. Tikheeva, *Doshkol'noe vospitanie i detskie sady* (Kazan': Gosizdat, 1920), p. 9, p. 18.

49 E. Tikheeva, 'Obstanovka v zhizni malen'kikh detei', in N. Evergetov, 'K psikhologii detei doshkol'nogo vozrasta', in N. Al'medingen-Tumim, E. Tikheeva and Yu. Frausek (eds), *Doshkol'noe delo: sbornik statei po voprosam doshkol'nogo vospitaniya* (Petrograd, 1922). For her part, ibid. p. 128.

50 'Po kakoi sisteme dolzhen stroit'sya detskii sad', ibid. p. 77, 'Sistema Montessori', ibid., pp. 95–117.

51 *Rezolyutsii Tret'ego Rossiiskogo S"ezda po doshkol'nomu vospitaniyu*, refer, for example, to the need to foster links with the Pioneer organisation, the importance of inculating labour and organisational skills (*trudovye i organizatsionnye navyki*), and to the fact that collectivism, dialectical materialism, and organisational abilities should be the central points in nursery education (p. 7, p. 12, pp. 21–2). 'Play is not an autonomous biological process', the volume intones (pp. 21–2). See also *Rezolyutsii po dokladam Tret'ego Vserossiiskogo S"ezda po doshkol'nomu vospitaniyu, 15–21 oktyabrya 1924* (M., 1924).

52 *MPDV 6: O gigiene vospitaniya v doshkol'nom uchrezhdenii* (M.–L., 1926), pp. 18–19.

53 *MPDV 14: Igrushka v doshkol'nom vozraste* (M.–L., 1930), p. 24.

54 *MPDV 7: O rabote po prirodovedeniyu* (M.–L.: Gosizdat, 1927), p. 7.

55 *Rezolyutsii po dokladam Vtorogo Vserossiiskogo S"ezda po doshkol'nomu vospitaniyu (25 noyabrya po 2 dekabrya 1921 g.)* (M., 1921), pp. 1–2.

56 *Rezolyutsii Tret'ego Vserossiiskogo S"ezda*, pp. 21–2, p. 7. On the second point, see also *MPDV 3: O svyazi s pionerami v doshkol'nom uchrezhdenii* (M.–L., 1927), pp. 10–11.

57 See e.g. E. G. Bibanova and N. A. Rybnikov (eds), *Kak izuchat' rebenka* (Orel 1923); *Instruktsiya dlya zapolneniya "Pedologicheskoi kartochki"* (L.: Izdanie Detskogo obsledovatel'skogo instituta im. professora A. S. Griboedova, n.d. (*c*. 1928). This type of study goes back through Rossolimo to the writings of Hippolyte Taine and of Darwin (see p. 38 above).

58 See B. King, *Changing Man* (London, 1936), pp. 260–2.

59 For the earlier attitude, see Krupskaya's article 'Samoubiistva sredi uchashchikhsya i svobodnaya trudovaya shkola', *SvoV* 10 (1910–11), republished in *Izbrannye pedagogicheskie proizvedeniya* (M., 1955), pp. 32–9 (*skazki* ref. p. 38); for the later attitude, cf. *MPDV*.

60 See L. Zhmudsky, 'Otzyv: Ershov, *Konek-gorbunok*', *Istoriya sovetskoi tsenzury: dokumenty i kommentarii* (M., 1997), p. 419. (English phrasing reflects the semi-literate Russian of the original.) A. V. Blyum, *Za kulisami 'Ministerstva pravdy'* (SPb., 1994), p. 248, points out that in 1855 a Tsarist censor had complained that Ershov's tale was not Orthodox *enough*.

61 Blyum, *Za kulisami*, pp. 244–6.

62 See 'Pionerskie zhurnaly' (1925), RGASPI–TsKhDMO f. 1 op. 23 d. 388, l. 62. For an example of the new kind of material in *Novyi Robinzon*, see N. Oleinikov, 'Mladshie svideteli Oktyabrya', *Novyi Robinzon* 18 (1925), 1–6 (not in fact fiction, but a selection of memoirs).

63 See e.g. S. Grigor'ev, 'Parovoz "Et 5324"', *Pioner* 3 (1924), 6–7; M. Mikhailov, 'Apchkhi', ibid., pp. 15–17 (continued in no. 4, pp. 12–13; no. 5, 25–7).

64 See e.g. Chapter 6 below.

65 TsAODM f. 69 op. 1 d. 172, l. 46.

66 On *traurnye zasedaniya*, see e.g. the record of such an occasion, in the presence of 43 children and young people, organised by the Anninskaya cell of the Komsomol in Serebryano-Prudskii district in January 1926, TsAODM f. 1884 op. 1 d. 50, l. 4.

67 *Kopii postanovlenii Sekretariata TsK VLKSM po shkol'noi i pionerskoi rabote za 1919–1925 gody* (typescript in TsKhDMO reading room), l. 52.

68 See especially N. Sats (ed.), *Deti o Lenine* (M., 1924).

69 *MPDV 11: O svyazi so shkoloi i o planirovanii raboty* (M.–L., 1928), p. 56.

70 S. Zak, *Kak Pasha provel 1-oe maya* (M.–L.: Gosizdat, 1926), p. 15. *Akh, nadoelo mne byt' rebenkom/Skoro, skoro stanu ya oktyabrenkom*.

71 *MPDV 10: Po zhivomu slovu i knizhke v doshkol'nom uchrezhdenii* (M.–L., 1928), p. 13.

72 See V. Bianki, *Lesnaya gazeta na kazhdyi god* (M.–L., 1928).

73 Dm. Tsenzor, 'Kotenkiny imeniny', *Vorobei* 2 (1923), 37.

74 Samuil Marshak [and Elizaveta Vasil'eva], *Koshkin dom*, originally published in *Teatr dlya detei* (Krasnodar, 1922). The play, rewritten by Marshak in 1945, and thenceforth issued without credit to Vasil'eva, was republished several times: see e.g. *Sobranie sochinenii v 8 tomakh*, vol. 2 (M., 1968), pp. 274–303.

75 N. K. Krupskaya, undated letter fragment (1929?), RGASPI f. 12 op. 1 d. 833, l. 1.

76 T. Karpinskaya, 'Kak oboshlis' bez elki', *DD* 2 (1930), 8. The article praises Pioneers who denounced their parents for the decorated potplant solution. Children were also encouraged to take part in atheist Easter festivals: see e.g. the recommendation, in *Zor'ka* 8 (1932), 20–1, of a celebration involving a pop-up priest in a cardboard egg, and a plywood Easter loaf decorated with a 'shirker' (*progul'shichik*).

77 CKQ M-04 PF5A, p. 11. The informant recalled singing this at the agitprop gathering that replaced the *elka* party in January 1929.

78 Or, to put it differently, the child activist was a miniature version of the ideal of 'youth as enthusiastic vanguard' cultivated in official Soviet propaganda of the day (on this see Gorsuch, *Youth in Revolutionary Russia*, pp. 15–18).

79 See Matthew Cullerne Bown, *Socialist Realist Painting* (New Haven, CT, 1998), plate 198.

80 *Aleksandr Rodchenko* (NY, 1998), plates 277–9.

81 See further in Chapter 12 on the Pioneer movement.

82 *9-ya Mezhdunarodnaya detskaya nedelya* (M., 1929), p. 20.

83 *Detskoe kommunisticheskoe dvizhenie*, Ya. A. Perel' and A. A. Lyubimova (eds) (M.–L., 1932), pp. 65–7.

84 For coverage of international matters, see e.g. *LI* 3 October 1932 (on International Children's Day); *Vskhody kommuny* (the Sverdlovsk Pioneer paper)

29 August 1931 (on International Youth Day), etc.; Kelly, 'Young Actors on the World Stage'.

85 In its early years, *Druzhnye rebyata* published large amounts of writing, especially poetry and documentary sketches, by children: from 1933, when the magazine was renamed *Kolkhoznye rebyata*, contributions by adult, professional writers began to predominate.

86 On 'Drug detei', see the society's own magazine, *DD*; on the *kul'tpokhody*, see *PP* 1928 and 1929, *passim*; on the 'intelligence agents of industry', see *Druzhnye rebyata* 12 (1932), 12; on the 'Dogonim amerikantskuyu kuritsu' drive, see *Detskoe kommunisticheskoe dvizhenie*, p. 123.

87 V. N. Shul'gin, *Obshchestvennaya rabota shkoly i programmy GUS'a* (M., 1925). On comparable efforts in the Pioneer movement, see Chapter 6 below.

88 TsKhDMO f. 1 op. 23 d. 458, l. 15.

89 D. Bednyi, *SPA* vol. 1, p. 129.

90 V. Kin, *SPA* vol. 3, p. 347. On the 'nightmare childhood' paradigm, see also Marina Balina, 'Troubled Lives: The Legacy of Childhood in Soviet Literature', *SEEJ* 49:2 (2005), 250–62.

91 See especially E. Wood, *The Baba and the Comrade: Gender and Politics in Revolutionary Russia* (Bloomington, IN, 1997).

92 For the Rodchenko images, see *Aleksandr Rodchenko* (NY, 1998), plates 277–9. Sats in *Pervyi s"ezd sovetskikh pisatelei: stenograficheskii otchet* (M., 1934), p. 472.

93 *PP* 15 October 1932, p. 2. On Pavlik's story, see also Catriona Kelly, *Comrade Pavlik: The Rise and Fall of a Soviet Boy Hero* (London, 2005), and Yu. Druzhnikov, *Donoschik 001: Voznesenie Pavlika Morozova* (M., 1991).

94 P. Solomein, *V kulatskom gnezde* (Sverdlovsk, 1933).

95 See Kelly, *Comrade Pavlik*, ch. 5.

96 See ibid., ch. 8; for a rather different version (but one equally distinct from the Soviet legends), see Druzhnikov, *Donoschik 001*.

97 See Zamiatin, 'Sovetskie deti' (1932), *Sochineniya*, vol. 4 (Munich, 1988), 565.

98 See Chapter 5 for a full discussion of this point.

99 Mikhail Zoshchenko, 'Schastlivoe detstvo', *Sobranie sochinenii v trekh tomakh* (L., 1986), vol. 1, pp. 296–8.

100 'Zapis' razgovorov detei v detskoi chital'ne Moskvy v 1924', RAO NA f. 5 op. 1 d. 59, l. 280. My thanks to Steve Smith for passing on this reference.

101 There is an interesting discussion of this play in Christina Kiaer, 'Delivered from Capitalism: Nostalgia, Alienation, and the Future of Reproduction in Tret'iakov's *I Want a Child!*', in Christina Kiaer and Eric Naiman (eds), *Everyday Life in Soviet Russia: Taking the Revolution Inside* (Bloomington, IN, 2006), pp. 183–216.

102 See e.g. *LI* 21 November 1932, p. 1.

103 *Mukhina svad'ba* (L. and M., 1924: the text is better-known under its post-1926 title, *Mukha-tsokotukha*.

104 V. Inber, *Kroshki-sorokonozhki* (M.–L., 1925), p. 4.

105 See Chapter 15 below.

106 E. Shabad, *Zhivoe detskoe slovo* (M., 1925), p. 15,

p. 16, p. 19, p. 50.

107 G. Vinogradov, *Detskie tainye yazyki* (Irkutsk, 1926); idem, *Detskaya satiricheskaya lirika* (Irkutsk, 1925).

108 On this, see Shabad, *Zhivoe detskoe slovo*, p. 4; V. Kiterman, 'Detskii yazyk', in *NES*, vol. 17, col. 86, mentions that a Commission for the Study of Children's Language was set up in St Petersburg in 1911, but the scholarly works listed on the subject are largely translations from German and English.

109 A. Kruchenykh, *Sobstvennye rasskazy, stikhi i pesni detei* (M., 1923), p. 1. The second poem is by 4-year-old Elena P, the first by 2-year-old Elena M. The English of the first poem attempts to reproduce the phonetic and grammatical peculiarities of the original: in adultspeak the poem would read, 'Black night she comes/Moon she comes out/Clock goes ding-ding/Time to sleep, sleep./Day comes: time to rise.'

110 There is a vast bibliography on this book, from all sorts of different points of view. On the particular issue of representing childhood, see esp. A. Wachtel, pp. 155–76.

111 Viktor Shklovsky, *Tret'ya fabrika* (M., 1926), pp. 13–14.

112 Boris Pasternak, *Stikhotvoreniya i poemy* (M.–L., 1965), p. 179. The poem comes from the cycle 'I could have forgotten these' (Ya ikh mog pozabyt').

113 Equally, Ariadna Efron's later remembrance of herself as 'a small girl at first hidden in the depths of her own pupils, and then suddenly fully realised one day when, in the mirror, she first associated her living "I" with the conventionality of the representation' was probably independent of the classic Lacanian theory of the 'mirror phase': Ariadna Efron, 'Iz samogo rannego', *O Marine Tsvetaevoi: vosponnisaniya docheri* (M., 1989), p. 52.

114 In editions of Eisenstein's memoirs published after the end of Soviet censorship – for example, *Vospominaniya* vol. 1 (M., 1997) – erotic themes (such as the sight of a neighbour's kimono that 'kept flying apart') and the sense of art as compensation for a repressed childhood (in Eisenstein's depiction of himself as the child who saved his sadism and 'grubbing about in watches' for adult lie) come through much more forcefully than in the extracts published previously.

115 Cf. Ol'ga Berggol'ts's rumination, in *Dnevnye zvezdy* (L.,1971), pp. 6–10, on why the Uglich stage of her life, which as a *conscious* memory was associated with fear and loneliness, should have begun to seem 'a place of the purest, most triumphant, final happiness' in the 1930s. On the other hand, the Tolstoyan tradition persisted, not only in the writings of many Soviet writers (e.g. Stavsky or Konstantin Paustovsky), but also in the work of many *émigré* writers, most notably, of course, Vladimir Nabokov in *Speak, Memory* (Harmondsworth, 1969) (Wachtel, p. 205). However, one should note also contrasting memoirs, e.g. S. E. Trubetskoi, *Minuvshee* (Paris, 1989), pp. 11–14, with its insistence that children are less childlike than adults suppose, and do endure real grief, for instance. And there are some

instances of pre-revolutionary ambivalence towards childhood, for example in memoirs by women (on which see Mary Zirin, 'Butterflies with Broken Wings: Early Autobiographical Depictions of Girlhood', in M. Liljeström, E. Mäntysaari, and A. Rosenholm (eds), *Gender Restructuring in Russian Studies, Slavica Tamperensia* 2 (1992), 255–66). Cf. also Vasily Rozanov's question, 'Why do I so love my childhood? My Tormented and Despised Childhood?' (*Opavshie list'ya* (SPb., 1913), p. 106) – the answer being that, evidently, it was a state he surged back into when involved in the kind of small sensual transaction he most valued: here, he was reminded of childhood while shaking tobacco out of the bottom of a cigarette.

116 Anna Akhmatova, 'Severnye elegii' no. 2, *Sochineniya*, 2 vols (M., 1987), vol. 2, pp. 254–5; Osip Mandelstam, *Shum vremeni, Sobranie sochinenii* vol. 2 (Washington: Inter-Language Literary Associates, 1971), pp. 45–108; Anna Prismanova, 'Pesok', *Sobranie sochinenii* (The Hague, 1990), pp. 66–76.

117 Mariengof, pp. 25–7.

118 Aleksandr Pasternak, *Vospominaniya* (Munich, 1983), pp. 18–86.

119 Quoted from the partial report of the Congress at f. 2306 op. 13 d. 11, l. 6. My source is Wendy Goldman, *Women, the State and Revolution: Soviet Family Policy and Social Life* (Cambridge, 1996), p. 62.

120 N. Starosel'tseva, *Revolyutsiya, iskusstvo, deti* (M.: Prosveshchenie, 1966–67); on the museum, see Yu. Molok, *Staraya detskaya kniga 1900–1930kh godov iz sobraniya Professora Marka Rata* (M., 1996), p. xi: he argues that it was 'oriented to collective consciousness and the education of the "new human being"', but gives no evidence to support this. *Detskoe iskusstvo, BSE*, vol. 21 (1931), 651–61. The article was accompanied by many line illustrations, all in the primitivist manner.

121 See Bown, *Socialist Realist Painting*, plate 130. Bown comments, p. 124: 'It is unclear to what degree this childish quality [in paintings of the day] is self-conscious, or, alternatively, unfeigned.' The standing of children's art of the day means that 'self-conscious' attempts to imitate it are a far more likely explanation.

122 F. D. Zabugin, 'K voprosu o muzykal'nykh vunderkindakh', in *Nevrologiya, nevropatologiya, psikhologiya, psikhiatriya: Sbornik, posvyashchennyi 40-letiyu nauchnoi, vrachebnoi i pedagogicheskoi deyatel'nosti prof. G. I. Rossolimo 1884–1924* (M., 1925), pp. 670–80.

123 Isaak Babel', 'Probuzhdenie', *Detstvo i drugie rasskazy* (Jerusalem, 1979), p. 74, p. 68, p. 69, p. 74.

124 RAO NA f. 1 op. 1 d. 145, l. 177. This sort of attitude also led to the publication of children's creations that were in no way remarkable: see e.g. *Detskoe tvorchestvo: Detskaya Rabochaya Koloniya Soyuza Sakharnikov* (Voronezh, 1923).

125 See Z. I. Stanchinskaya, *Dnevnik materi* (M., 1924), p. 43, p. 44, p. 62.

126 See e.g. the refs. to Pavlova's diary in Chukovsky, *Ot dvukh do pyati*, p. 43, p. 192, and to Rybnikova-Shilova's, ibid., p. 188.

127 There are exceptions, for example V. Sinaiskaya-Finkel'shtein's publication of poems by her 13-year-old daughter, who had recently died of TB, with an enthusiastic introduction by Maksimilian Voloshin (*Nerastvetshaya: istoriya yunoi dushi* (M.–L., 1924]). This publication goes back to an earlier Romantic tradition of admiration for individual talent, especially if its possessor died at an early age. But 'Verusya' had far less impact than the children in Kornei Chukovsky's *Ot dvukh do pyati*, though, interestingly, the book was edited by Chukovsky's son Nikolai.

128 See Zak, *Kak Pasha provel*. Evgeny Steiner, *Stories for Little Comrades: Revolutionary Artists and the Making of Early Soviet Children's Books*, trans. J. A. Miller (Seattle, 1999), is a wide-ranging, beautifully illustrated, if also rather over-polemical, survey of outstanding work by avant-garde illustrators, beginning with the Segodnya (Today) artists' co-operative, set up in Petrograd in 1918, whose participants included Yury Annenkov and Natan Al'tman, and continuing through the textbook illustrations of El' Lissitsky to the work of Marshak and Lebedev.

129 A. Boretsky, *Dogonim amerikanskuyu kuritsu* (M.–L., 1930). See also Steiner, *Stories for Little Comrades*, p. 91, p. 93. It should be understood, however, that this was a brochure rather than a work of fiction.

130 This is one of many reasons why L. Lifschutz-Losev is right to argue that 'it is impossible to differentiate neatly between an "official" and an "independent" writer'. 'Children's Literature, Russian', *Modern Encyclopedia of Russian and Soviet Literatures*, vol. 4 (Gulf Breeze, FL, 1981), p. 83. Steiner, *Stories for Little Comrades*, on the other hand, not only emphasises the political content of early Soviet children's literature to the exclusion of anything else, but also ignores any comparative dimension: cf. the review by Jacqueline M. Olich in H-Net Book Review, H-Russia@h-net.msu. edu (accessed September 2000); and Yu. Ya. Gerchukh's appraisal in *Iskusstvoznanie* 2 (2002), 617–21.

131 Ben Hellmann argues, in *Barn- och ungdomsboken i Sovjetryssland. Från oktoberrevolutionen 1917 till perestrojkan 1986* (Stockholm, 1991), p. 321, 'Fantasy, humour, and a respect for the distinctive characteristics of children were dominant traits in these writers [i.e. Marshak and his cohort], while Vladimir Mayakovsky represented the opposite pole, that is a didactic and ideologically oriented poetry.' I would, rather, follow Karen Lesnik-Oberstein, *Children's Literary Criticism and the Fictional Child* (Oxford, 1987), in emphasising the didactic character of all children's writing: texts such as Marshak's simply have a different objective in mind, that of developing the imagination.

132 See S. Zak, *Borya v ambulatorii* (M.–L., 1928), quote p. 2 (*Razve mozhno/Est' na ulitse morozhenoe?*).

133 V. Bianki, *Boloto* (M.–L., 1931).

134 S. Rozanov, *Priklyucheniya Travki* (M.–L.:

Gosizdat, 1928). Poetry about household items can also be put in this category: e.g. the primus poems discussed by E. Putilova in *Russkaya poeziya detyam* (2 vols; SPb., 1997), vol. 2, p. 36.

135 Cited from S. Marshak, *Skazki, pesni, zagadki; Stikhotvoreniya; V nachale zhizni* (M., 1981), p. 40.

136 A. Neverov, *Tashkent – gorod khlebnyi*, in his *Izbrannoe* (Minsk, 1985), p. 264. On the scatological side of the story, note that this was widely dispersed in 1920s texts for children: cf. L. Kassil', *Konduit i Shvambraniya* (1930), quoted from *Dorogie moi mal'chishki. Konduit i Shvambraniya* (M., 1987), p. 239: the director visits *skotskii vrach* (large animal vet) to ask for help, and cat in its litter tray looks on, aware that it's observing 'historic events'.

137 V. Bianki, *Karabash* (M.–L., 1929). Alison Lurie, see her *Don't Tell the Grownups: Subversive Children's Literature* (London, 1990): on p. xiii she notes that Richard Hughes's *A High Wind in Jamaica* 'never appears on lists of recommended juvenile fiction, not so much because of the elaborations of its diction (which is no more complex than that of, say, *Treasure Island*, but because in it children are irretrievably damaged and corrupted'. She points also to the fact that deaths were generally rare in children's fiction in the first half of the twentieth century, and that even thereafter the protagonist and his or her

friends tended to be spared.

138 More questionably, L. Lifschutz-Losev, 'Children's Literature, Russian', *Modern Encyclopedia of Russian and Soviet Literatures*, vol. 4, p. 81, links Zhitkov's with the Left Front of Arts (Lef) cult of 'the literature of fact' (given that Zhitkov's work is not at all documentary in feel, this seems to be stretching a point).

139 On which see e.g. F. A. O'Dell, *Socialisation through Children's Literature: The Soviet Example* (Cambridge, 1978), ch. 1.

140 N. Evergetov, 'K psikhologii detei doshkol'nogo vozrasta' in Al'medingen-Tumim, Tikheeva and Frausek (eds), *Doshkol'noe delo: sbornik statei po voprosam doshkol'nogo vospitaniya*, pp. 30–41.

141 M. V. Vul'f, *Fantaziya i real'nost' v psikhike rebenka* (Odessa: Voprosy teorii i praktiki psikhoanaliza, 1926), p. 42. M. V. Vul'f was a Russian associate of Freud's whose study of a boy with a dog phobia was praised by the master in *Totem and Taboo*.

142 G. Vinogradov, *Narodnaya pedagogika* (Irkutsk, 1926), p. 24.

143 *Ape, Primitive Man, and Child: Essays in the History of Behavior*, trans. E. Rossiter (New York: Harvester Wheatsheaf, 1992), p. 106, p. 141. Lisa Kirschenbaum's attempt to periodise pedagogical attitudes to the *skazka* as broadly 'pro' before 1925 and 'anti' thereafter (see *Small Comrades* p. 69, pp. 117–18) is somewhat too neat.

Chapter 3: 'Thank You, Dear Comrade Stalin, for a Happy Childhood!', 1935–1953

1 Andrei Grishin, *Prazdnik schast'ya*, ed. E. A. Bogolyubov (Perm', 1939), p. 14.

2 Though Stalin himself disliked *Cradle Song*, which was shelved after 5 days' viewing (see K. Bogdanov, 'Pravo na son i uslovnye refleksy' (publication forthcoming), the text works like a sampler of 'child cult' motifs from High Stanlinism.

3 An excellent overview of the Stalinist childhood is also given in the permanent exhibition mounted in the apartment museum of Sergei Kirov in St Petersburg.

4 See the discussion of *schast'e* in Anna A. Zaliznyak, I. B. Levontina, and A. D. Shmelev, *Klyuchevye idei russkoi yazykovoi kartiny mira* (M., 2005).

5 See e.g. F. Khrapchenkov, 'Organizatsiya domashnei raboty uchashcheisya', *Za politekhnicheskuyu shkolu* 6 (1934), 31–6.

6 *ENKP* 1 November 1936, p. 26. On provision of PE, see Chapter 8.

7 See e.g. the feature on Sh. Slutskaya in *PP* 27 August 1932. On the *udarnik ucheby* generally, see e.g. the spread of features in *PP* 29 August 1932.

8 See e.g. P. Kiselev, 'Isklyuchenie iz shkoly', *Za politekhnicheskuyu shkolu* 3 (1934), 27–31.

9 'Ob organizatsii uchebnoi rabote i vnutrennem rasporyadke v nachal'noi, nepolnoi srednei, i srednei shkole: Postanovlenie SNK i TsK VKP(b) 3 sentyabrya 1935', in *Spravochnik partiinogo rabotnika: dlya predsedatelei, sekretarei i drugikh rabotnikov sovetov i ispol'nitel'nykh komitetov* (M., 1937), pp. 789–91.

10 See further in Chapter 16 below.

11 Anna Bek, *The Life of a Russian Woman Doctor*, trans. and ed. A. D. Rassweiler (Bloomington IN, 2004), pp. 116–21, recounts this process at first hand. Bek found herself increasingly beleaguered while working at Tomsk in 1933–4, and, once the 1936 decree came out, she retired from academic life because she was not prepared to renounce paedology in print, the necessary qualification for continuing to work in her specialism.

12 See L. D. Filonenko (ed.), *Spravochnik o sostave i soderzhanii fondov nauchnogo arkhiva Akademii Pedagogicheskikh Nauk SSSR* (M., 1989), which provides the information in headnotes to archival holdings from the different institutes. For the text of the decree denouncing 'paedological perversions', see 'O pedologicheskikh izvrashcheniyakh v sisteme NKP', *ENKP* 1 August 1936, p. 2; for a signal anti-paedological discussion, see 'Protiv pedologicheskikh izvrashchenii', *SP* 1 (1937), 14–75; on its effects, see Holmes, *Stalin's School*; A. V. Petrovsky, 'Zapret na kompleksnoe issledovanie detstva', in M. G. Yaroshevsky (ed.), *Repressirovannaya nauka* (L., 1991), pp. 126–35.

13 A. Makarenko, *Izbrannye pedagogicheskie sochineniya* (4 vols; M., 1944), vol. 4, p. 109, p. 116, p. 110.

14 'O likvidatsii detskoi besprizornosti i beznadzornosti. Postanovlenie SNK i TsK VKP (b) 31 maya 1935', *Spravochnik partiinogo rabotnika*, p. 814. See also the detailed discussion in Chapter 9 below.

15 D. Paperno, *Zapiski moskovskogo pianista* (Tenafly, NJ, 1983), p. 18. The group became the nucleus of

a special musical school not long afterwards.

16 For a first-hand recollection of the contest, see Lev Druskin, *Spasennaya kniga* (London, 1984), p. 41 (Novyi Petergof), pp. 55–6 (tours). L. Ostrov's painting, *Smotr yunykh darovanii*, is reproduced in *Yunyi khudozhnik* 11–12 (1939), 10. On the Stalin concert, see *Deti o Staline* (M., 1939). There were also *smotry yunykh darovanii* at the local level, e.g. in Kiev (see *Pravda* 7 January 1936).

17 See D. Paperno, *Zapiski moskovskoga pianista* (Ann Arbor, 1983), p. 125.

18 Kabalevsky, also the author of work for adults, including full-scale works evoking children such as *Rekviem* (1962), a contribution to the Soviet official peace movement in the vein of Prokofiev's *On Guard for Peace*, is the single internationally famous member of a whole pleiad of Soviet composers best known for their work for children, including Aleksandr Gedike (1877–1957), Isak Berkovich (1902–72), Ivar Arseev (b. 1937), Georgy Struve (1933–2004), and Aleksandr Karasev (b. 1962).

19 For cases of anxiety about nervous strain, see A. Gol'denveizer, 'O muzykal'nom obrazovanii detei', *Pravda* 16 December 1936, p. 4 (the writer also expressed concern about 'the poisonous effects of success'); and M. Barskaya and B. Shumitsky, 'Proizvodstvo detskikh kinokartin', *Pravda* 2 April 1935, 3, which insists that child actors must be limited to four hours' work per day maximum.

20 On the celebrations for *otlichniki* in Khar'kov, see *PP* 85 (24 June 1936), p. 3. On *otlichniki* and Stalin, see several of the personal histories in *Deti o Staline*.

21 See RGASPI f. 12 op. 1 d. 750, l. 31.

22 V. Lyadov, 'O geroyakh v detskoi literature', *Pravda* 25 February 1934, p. 4.

23 See *O partiinoi i sovetskoi pechati: sbornik dokumentov* (M., 1954), p. 378.

24 D. A. Berman, *Kornei Chukovsky: bibliograficheskii ukazatel'* (L.: Publichnaya biblioteka, 1984), pp. 18–19 (*Moidodyr*), p. 20 (*Mukhina svad'ba*), pp. 19–20 (*Tarakanishche*).

25 *O partiinoi i sovetskoi pechati*, p. 427.

26 See A. B. Ustinov, 'Delo detskogo sektora 1932 g.', in G. A. Morev, *Mikhail Kuzmin i russkaya kul'tura XX veka: tezisy i materialy konferentsii 15–17 maya 1990 goda* (L., 1990), pp. 125–36; I. Mal'sky, 'Razgrom OBERIU', *Oktyabr'* 11 (1992), 166–91.

27 In the 1920s, Narkompros had huge influence over the censorship of children's books (see Chapter 2 above); in later periods of Soviet history, the education ministry appears to have had weight only when selecting material for dissemination within the school system. (Cf. the comments from a former editor at Leningrad Detgiz (from 1963 to 1994) to me in a letter of May 2002: 'As far as I know, neither the Ministry of Education nor its local offices had anything to do with the "Detskaya literatura" publishing house, though probably the Ministry's views were taken into account when the selection of books for extra-curricular reading in literature was put together.').

28 See KPBTsK 1936–42, ll. 87–8: the results of this 'wreckerdom' were said to be non-fulfilment of the publishing plan and a schism between the house and the writers working for it.

29 See Em. Mindlin, 'Lyudi semidesyatykh godov', *Nashi dostizheniya* 5 (1936), pp. 5–6. On the 'organicist' aesthetics of the Stalin era, see Vladimir Papernyi, 'Nezhivoe – zhivoe', in *Kul'tura 'Dva'* (2nd edn; M., 1996), ch. 6 (pp. 160–82). While Papernyi does not discuss the *skazka* as such, sections 12 and 13 of his book, 'Realizm – pravda' and 'Delo – chudo', are clearly relevant to the topic (see pp. 281–307).

30 N. S. Khrushchev, 'Kak my organizovali Dom pionerov i detskie parki', *Vozhatyi* 8 (1936), 11–12.

31 Gorky's 'O skazkakh', *Pravda* 30 January 1935 (*SS* vol. 27, pp. 392–401) is focused explicitly on the importance of the genre to children.

32 This did not, however, mean that writers who made the move into children's literature were necessarily delighted with their lot. Daniil Kharms, for example, loathed and feared children, and was naturally not best suited to his role as favourite nonsense poet. In the words of Marina Durnovo, his wife: 'He couldn't stand children. He just couldn't bear them. For him they were – yuk, rubbish of some kind, really' (*Moi muzh Daniil Kharms*, comp. V. Glotser (M.: B.S.G. Press, 2001): quoted here from A. Klement'ev's review in *Russkaya mysl'* 10–16 May 2001, 11). Even without neurotic qualms of this kind, there were reasons for disaffection. Whatever literary bureaucrats' assurances to the contrary, the move into children's literature was associated with loss of prestige and influence – hence the need for constant rebukes to well-known writers, such as Mikhail Sholokhov, who paid lip service to the importance of children's writing by promising to produce books for this audience, and then failed to come up with the goods. (See e.g. 'O tete s pal'chikom, o detochkakh-konfetochkakh i o prochem', *Krokodil* 4 (1952), 2.)

33 See *Pravda* 22 September 1936, p. 4. The article on department stores (*universal'nye magaziny*) in the first edition of *BSE*, vol. 56 (1936), col. 82, drew particular attention to the 'Children's World' section of Soviet department stores, which, it claimed, sold everything from 'presents for newborns up to children's clothes, games and furniture. In these sections pedagogues and doctors take an active part in the work.' Readers of *Rabotnitsa* were treated to a special article about another shop in Moscow, the Children's Studio (Detskoe atel'e, no. 5 Arbat), with a publicity photograph of little Masha being bought a coat (see E. Yanub, 'Moi magazin', *Rabotuitsa* 33 (1935), p. 15).

34 As even the 22 September 1936 article in *Pravda* admitted.

35 *Leningradskaya pravda* 27 August 1936, p. 4.

36 Both these characters, certainly Ded Moroz, were traditional figures on Christmas trees in any case – see e.g. Elenevskaya in Fitzpatrick and Slezkine, p. 124. But, from 1936, they were turned from ornaments into live participants in the festival. On the rehabilitation of the *elka*, see E. V. Dushechkina, *Russkaya elka* (SPb., 1995).

37 See K. Petrone, *Life Has Become More Joyous*,

Comrades: Celebrations in the Time of Stalin (Bloomington, IN, 2000), p. 91 (on decorations and costumes: ibid., pp. 85–100 offers a general discussion of representations of the New Year tree in official Soviet writing during the second half of the 1930s); Dushechkina, *Russkaya elka*.

38 'Likvidirovat' prestupleniya nesovershennoletnikh', *SYu* 14 (1935), 1.

39 Mary Leder recalls that the film, which she found 'silly, simplistic and sentimental', was 'loved' by her Russian friends. See *My Life in Stalinist Russia: An American Woman Looks Back* (Bloomington, IN, 2001).

40 *Pervyi vsesoyuznyi s"ezd*, Marshak p. 32 (science and construction), p. 35 (history), p. 27 (Soviet *skazka*). Cf. an article by V. Lyadov, 'O detskoi literature', *Pravda* 31 March 1933, p. 3, speaking of the need to apply 'the dialectical method' to the *skazka*: industrialisation should be given due weight, but so should children's capacity for fantasy.

41 Cf. O'Dell, pp. 124–6, using the example of editions of *Murzilka* from 1928 and from 1938.

42 A late survey of the network is *Detskie zheleznye dorogi* (M., 1957). By this time there were networks in 29 Soviet cities and towns, including Moscow, Leningrad, Gor'ky [Nizhni-Novgorod], Yaroslavl', Stalingrad, Khar'kov, Rostov, Ufa, Chelabinsk, and Krasnoyarsk.

43 See Peter H. Solomon Jr., *Soviet Criminal Justice under Stalin* (Cambridge, 1996), pp. 197–9, pp. 204–10; Peter Juviler and Zh. Rossi (eds), *Spravochnik po GULagu* (London, 1987), p. 199. A fuller account of these measures appears in Chapter 9 below.

44 For exemplary parents, see e.g. I. Aisberg, 'Malen'kie khozyaeva bol'shogo doma', *NZ* 10 (1934), esp. 114–15; Anon., 'Kul'turno vospitat' detei', *Rabotnitsa* 4 (1935), 21; and the pep-talks on upbringing by various model parents in *Pravda* 6 March 1935, p. 3; for a signal failure, see B. Shvartsshtein, 'Kak kommunist Tumanov vospityvaet svoikh detei', *Pravda* 4 March 1935, p. 3 (quote taken from here).

45 V. Utevsky, 'O likvidatsii prestupnosti …', *SYu* 7 (1937), 21.

46 See Catriona Kelly, *Comrade Pavlik: The Rise and Fall of a Soviet Boy Hero* (London, 2005).

47 N. Shklyar, 'Novelly o pedagoge i shkol'nike', *NZ* 2 (1936), 100.

48 See *SYu* 23 (1935) 1 (child abandonment), *SYu* 22 (1935), 24 (infanticide).

49 Unless the partner failed to respond to a summons. See *Kodeks zakonov o brake, sem'e i opeke. S izmeneniyami na 1 iyunya 1938 g.* (M., 1938), article 138, p. 36. The sententia about ensuring a right attitude to the family appears on pp. 47–8.

50 On alimony, see e.g. *SYu* 6 (1933), 23; *SYu* 9 (1935), 12–13; *SYu* 24 (1935), 8.

51 Livshits, 'Rebenok v tsentre vnimatel'nosti sovetskogo obshchestva', *SYu* 24 (1935), 8.

52 *SYu* 9 (1937), 50–1.

53 Quoted in *Obshchestvennitsa* 4–5 (1940), 31–2. The words *chestnost'* (honesty) and *pravdivost'* (truthfulness) occurred with monotonous regularity in the advice for parents (or, more

accurately, mothers) printed in Soviet magazines. See, for example, I. F. Svadkovsky, 'Vospitanie pravdivosti u detei', *Rabotnitsa* 3 (1952), 14. For other clichéd virtues, such as 'cleanliness', 'orderliness', and 'attention to others', see 'Priuchaite rebenka k chistote i poryadku', *Rabotnitsa* 20 (1940), p. 19.

54 *BSE* (2nd edn), vol. 14, p. 134.

55 See *Pravda* 2 April 1935, p. 3; 3 April 1935, p. 3; 9 April 1935, p. 1. For a personal reminiscence of the drive to design sweet-boxes in order to make them attractive to children, see the memoirs of Natal'ya Sats, *Novelly moei zhizni* (2 vols; M., 1984), vol. 1, p. 350. The brands Sats was involved with included Tales of Pushkin, New Year Tree, Uncle Krylov's Little House, Theatre, and About the Metro.

56 See e.g. *PP* 1 January 1932, 1.

57 'Kak rabotat' nad dokladom tovarishcha Stalina v nachal'noi i srednei shkole', *Za politekhnicheskuyu shkolu* 2 (1934), 6.

58 *Pravda* 1 July 1935, p. 2; 3 August 1935, p. 3.

59 *Pravda* 29 June 1936, p. 1.

60 A picture of the celebrations for the anniversary of the October Revolution in *Pravda*, 10 November 1936, shows workers carrying a banner with the Stalin-Gelya image.

61 Kuznetsov's painting is reproduced in A. A. Sidorov, 'Lenin v iskusstve', *Sovetskoe iskusstvo* 1 (1926), 22. For the criticism and the history of the painting, see P. Stupples, *Pavel Kuznetsov* (Cambridge, 1989), pp. 244–6. In any case, this painting (like a drawing by a child in N. Sats (ed.), *Deti o Lenine* (M., 1924), p. 7) shows Lenin as a *model* for children rather than as a cheery avuncular figure: they cluster respectfully round him as though he were a statue (which the child's drawing indeed suggests he is).

62 *Schastlivoe detstvo: Literaturno-estradnyi sbornik* (M.–L., 1939), p. 27. About a quarter of the texts anthologised here evoke Stalin in one way or another.

63 Ibid., p. 69 (See Z. Aleksandrova, 'Artek'), p. 91 (L. Kvitko, 'Pis'mo Voroshilovu').

64 See e.g. the photograph of the Trekhgorka factory's summer dacha in E. I. Papkovskaya (ed.), *Knizhka o malen'kikh trekhgortsakh* (M., 1948), p. 37, or the cover of *Druzhnye rebyata* for October 1936.

65 *Deti o Staline*, pp. 22–3. For an earlier example, see *Pravda* 6 January 1934, p. 3 (letter from the Pioneers and schoolchildren of Novaya Uda in Eastern Siberia to Stalin); 28 June 1934, p. 3 (the same group of Pioneers and schoolchildren thanking him for the gift of a gramophone to their school).

66 A. Podvoisky, 'Ya videl Il'icha', *PP* 19 April 1925, 2.

67 See e.g. 12-year-old Misha Kuleshov in *Deti o Staline*, p. 24. The leader was not always shown to be so considerate to juvenile susceptibilities: in Nina Zdrogova's account, for instance, he straightforwardly addressed her as 'ty' (*Pravda* 1 July 1935, p. 2).

68 Though an intermediate form, 'Uncle Stalin', occurs in a letter from two Young Pioneers to

Kalinin in 1933: see RGASPI f. 78 op. 1 d. 456, l. 4 (Siegelbaum and Sokolov, p. 375).

69 *Yunyi khudozhnik* 11–12 (1939). On the latter point, an informant of mine who attended a music school in Tashkent in the late 1940s recalled that the 'delegations of Pioneers' who took part in ceremonial concerts to mark Soviet festivals there in fact consisted of hand-picked pupils from her school.

70 See e.g. the account in J. Bullard and M. Bullard (eds), *Inside Stalin's Russia: The Diaries of Reader Bullard, 1930–1934* (Charlbury, Oxon., 2000), p. 45, of seeing test-tubes containing substances supposed to smell like poison gases at a Pioneer camp in 1931. A picture of a child on the front cover of *Murzilka* 2 (1932) shows a soldier helping a small child don his gas mask.

71 *Pravda* 27 April 1936, p. 6 (border-infiltrators), 26 September 1936, p. 6 (law-breakers). It is striking, though, that both these items were published in a modest position on the newspaper's back page, an indication of the marginality of child activists.

72 A. Barto, *Na zastave* (M.–L., 1937).

73 S. Mikhalkov, 'Vrag' (also published as 'Shpion', *Izbrannoe* (M., 1947), p. 17.

74 See *Detskii karnaval* (M., 1939), pp. 15–16 ('Nas ne trogai/My ne tronem/A zatronesh'/Spusku ne dadim'). The singing of this number was part of a grandiose finale which included a reading from Stalin's 'war preparedness' speech at the Eighteenth Congress, and a march by children dressed as 'Voroshilov marksmen' and Red Army soldiers round a real live tank.

75 On military preparedness, see e.g. V. Gubarev, 'Strelyaite spokoino i metko!', *PP* 8 April 1939, 1; on PE (work for the 'Bud' gotov k trudu i oborone!' badge), see 'Bud' gotov k trudu i oborone!', *Pioner* 7 (1939), 94–6. Supposedly real-life spy-catching stories (all with a strong flavour of adventure literature) published in the children's press show children co-operating with adults: see e.g. 'Lena Petsenko – bditel'naya pionerka', *PP* 18 July 1937, 1 (about a girl catching a suspicious foreigner on a train). Contrast a supposed memoir by an adult border guard, A. Zuev, 'Vysota zaozernaya', *Pioner* 6 (1939), 24–9.

76 On guard dogs, see *PP* 14 June 1937, 4; *PP* 20 July 1937, 1. For a 'secret agent' game (in which children tried to identify coins and fabrics blindfold, and to pick out various types of plane from their silhouettes), see *PP* 14 November 1939, 4.

77 See *Detskii karnaval*, p. 16.

78 See the excellent account of this in J. Brooks, *Thank You, Comrade Stalin!* (Princeton, 2000), esp. ch. 4.

79 See Karen Petrone, *Life has Become More Joyous, Comrades: Celebrations in the Time of Stalin* (Bloomington, IN, 2000).

80 This might also help explain why the collapse of state control since 1991 has been accompanied by a very significant erosion of community spirit; this process was, of course, well under way before the Soviet Union disappeared.

81 According to a note in Kornei Chukovsky's diary (*Dnevnik 1901–1929* (M., 1991, p. 336), Sologub

thought that everything about the Pioneers that was good was new, and everything that was bad was a hangover from the Russian past.

82 Siegelbaum and Sokolov, p. 65.

83 See e.g. an article about American juvenile courts in *Pravda* 25 February 1935, p. 5.

84 Cf. Naum Korzhavin's recollection that the only child he knew who attended an *elka* party, at the House of Scholars in Kiev, was the daughter of a political *émigré*. 'V soblaznakh krovavoi epokhi', *NM* 8 (1992), 135–6.

85 On this see A. Federol'f, 'Ryadom s Alei', in A. Efron and A. Federol'f, *Miroedikha: Ryadom s Alei* (M., 1996), pp. 268–9. This account dates from the 1940s. The slightly clandestine flavour that private New Year parties had even then is indicated by Federol'f's unpleasant bout of anxiety when the child for whom she acted Ded Moroz boasted at school that 'Father Frost isn't a fairy tale. A real live one came to our house and gave me everything on my presents list!'. 'I fearfully awaited the arrival of his teacher and a reprimand for disrupting ideological work' (p. 269).

86 On children's parties as a way of 'enabl[ing] Party bureaucrats and political officials to replicate themselves', see Petrone, *Life Has Become More Joyous, Comrades*, p. 97. Petrone rightly describes telephones as 'important tools', but their function was more than simply utilitarian: they were attributes as well as instruments of power.

87 See e.g. Miller, pp. 18–19.

88 See M. N. Gernet in *Deti-prestupniki* (M.: Knigoizdatel'stvo M. N. Znamenskoi, 1912), p. 6.

89 N. Zabolotsky, 'Kak myshi s kotom voevali', *Chizh* 10 (1933): reprinted in *Sobranie sochinenii v 3 tomakh* (M., 1983), vol. 1, pp. 483–5. This places rather heavy interpretative weight on a piece whose ending proclaims it was written to amuse Zabolotsky's young son (the mice are told that they have been punished for waking him up at night); but it is notable that a 'Chukovskian' piece by Zabolotsky, in which a young boy alone defies terrifying Mr Cook Barla-Barla (1935), a bogey who frightens everyone else, is explicitly set in America (*Chizh* 1 (1935): reprinted in *SS v 3 tt.*, vol. 1, p. 486).

90 See Sheila Fitzpatrick, *Everyday Stalinism: Ordinary Life in Extraordinary Times: Soviet Russia in the 1930s* (NY, 1999), p. 172, p. 258 n. 26. For numerous comparable examples, see the digital version of the present book.

91 'kak odin iz starykh, upolnomochennykh chlenov kollektiva', A. Makarenko, *Kniga dlya roditelei*, (M., 1937), p. 194, pp. 201–2. For an earlier condemnation, see A. Epshtein, 'Ne bit', a razumno vospitvyvat'', *DD* 2 (1930), 2–5.

92 *Pravda* 20 July 1936, p. 3.

93 See e.g. 'Beseda s roditelyami detskikh sadov bratskikh respublik (26 dekabrya 1937)', *Izbrannye pedagogicheskie proizvedeniya*, pp. 695–8.

94 See N. N. Golosnitskaya, 'Vospitanie u detei samostoyatel'nosti i interesa k trudu' (paper presented at the second 'scholarly and practical' (*nauchno-prakticheskaya*) conference of Soviet nursery teachers in Moscow, 1941), reprinted in E. I. Volkova (ed.), *Vospitateli detskikh sadov o*

svoei rabote (M., 1948) (this quotation p. 121). (In terms of consistency of opinion among nursery teachers, it is worth noting also that the date of the Volkova reprint was 1948, a time by which the pre-revolutionary *gimnaziya* had become the ideal of Soviet secondary education.)

95 *Programmy nachal'noi shkoly – gorodskoi i sel'skoi* (M., 1932), pp. 7–8.

96 A. Gaidar, *Sochineniya* (M., 1946), p. 359, p. 357. Cf. the contents of *Murzilka*, explicitly targeted at the 'younger schoolchild' age group. While including some obviously ideologised material – e.g. pieces on Lenin and Stalin, or adventure stories about guarding crops (no. 10 (1934), 4–6) – it also had plenty of texts that any children's journal in an urbanised society could have mustered (e.g. a 'what to do if you get lost – ask a policeman' piece in no. 3 (1932), 24–5); it also had plenty of narratives about childish mischief, cuddly animals, and the like. The illustrations were far more colourful and lively than those in journals for older children, and the magazine included pull-out games (e.g. a shadow theatre in no. 6 (1933), 18–19).

97 Quoted in S. Marshak, 'Gor'kii i deti', *Pravda* 13 July 1936, p. 4.

98 A. Efremov, St Petersburg, Sept. 2001 (personal information)

99 M. Bown, *Socialist Realist Painting* (New Haven and London, 1998), plate 218.

100 *Uchitel'skaya gazeta*, 10 May 1945: quoted in Dunstan, p. 195.

101 Bown, *Socialist Realist Painting*, plate 262.

102 Pavel Antokol'sky, 'Ballada o mal'chike, ostavshemsya neizvestnom', *Izbrannoe 1936–1944* (M., 1946), p. 61. The poem was also set to music by Prokofiev, whose cantata under the same title (written 1942–3) was first performed on 21 February 1944 in Moscow. See *S. S. Prokof'ev: Stat'i i materialy* (M., 1965), p. 594.

103 On war children generally, see Lisa A. Kirschenbaum, 'Innocent Victims and Heroic Defenders: Children and the Siege of Leningrad', in J. Master (ed.), *Children and War: A Historical Anthology* (NY, 2002), pp. 280–3.

104 A. Barto, *Podrostki* (M.: Sovetskii pisatel', 1943), p. 4.

105 Aleksei Pakhomov's much-praised works were awarded a Stalin prize: see Bown, *Socialist Realist Painting*, p. 209. News photographs of the time include 'Zapomnite! Otomstite!', *O* 6 (1943), showing slaughtered children, or 'Deti obvinyayut', *O* 12–13 (1945), 8–9, which shows children rescued from a concentration camp. For a selection of Blockade news photographs with tragic images, see V. Nikitin, *Neizvestnaya blokada: Leningrad 1941–1944; fotoal'bom*, e.g. p. 149 (a child's funeral), p. 167 (child in open coffin being transported by another child); p. 169 (dystrophic girl in hospital).

106 Barto, *Podrostki*, p. 8.

107 A. Surkov, *Stikhotvoreniya* (M., 1950), p. 155.

108 Pavel Antokol'sky, 'Katya Kozlova' in *Syn: poema, stikhi* (M, 1943), pp. 57–62.

109 See Dunstan; G. V. Andreevsky, 'V sovetskoi shkole', in his *Povsednevnaya zhizn' Moskvy v*

Stalinskuyu epokhu (2 vols; M., 2003), vol. 2, pp. 367–9.

110 See Dunstan, pp. 171–4. The move to coeducation had been planned already in 1941, on the grounds that teaching military skills was easier if the sexes were kept separate. Village schools were excluded because of the fear that dividing establishments at this level would lead to a proliferation of 'dwarf schools' (*karlikovye shkoly*). RGASPI f. 17 op. 126 d. 2, ll. 85–96. The reform was delayed by the war, but went through in 1943.

111 On embroidery in Pioneer groups, see CKQ E-03 PF3A, p. 6.

112 For the image, see Bown, *Socialist Realist Painting*, plate 321; for the critical history, ibid., p. 289.

113 B. Polevoi, *Povest' o nastoyashchem cheloveke*, in his *Sobranie sochinenii v 9 tomakh* (M.: Khudozhestvennaya literatura, 1981), vol. 1, pp. 235–516; P. Zhurba, *Geroi Sovetskogo Soyuza Aleksandr Matrosov* (M., 1949); A. Fadeev, *Molodaya gvardiya*, in his *Sobranie sochinenii v 7 tomakh* (M., 1970), vol. 1, pp. 7–658. (This collection reprints the 1951 redaction of Fadeev's text.) Both Polevoi's text and Fadeev's were compulsory reading in Soviet schools; they were also publicised to children via magazines and newspapers. (For example, *Pioner* 4 (1947), 33, carried a piece on the Polevoi novel, and *Pioner* 12 (1948), 22–33 a spread about the film adaptation of the text, with contributions from the actors playing the different roles about their weighty responsibilities.)

114 S. Mikhalkov, 'Karta', *SS* (M., 1963), vol. 1, p. 288.

115 On the general monument, the museum, and the street, see L. Kassil' and M. Polyanovsky, *Ulitsa mladshego syna* (M., 1951), pp. 505–11.

116 A. Krushinsky, 'Ser'eznye nedostatki detskikh zhurnalov', *Pravda* 29 August 1946, p. 3.

117 Ibid.

118 A. Barto, 'Mashen'ka rastet', *O* 27 (1949), p. 23.

119 S. Marshak, 'Kolybel'naya', (*Stikhi*, M., 1952), p. 14. This poem does not appear in editions of Marshak's work published after the death of Stalin.

120 *Nachal'naya shkola: Nastol'naya kniga uchitelya*, ed. M. A. Mel'nikov. (M., 1950), p. 107.

121 Ibid., p. 170.

122 Dunstan, p. 201.

123 'RAO NA f. 32 op. 1 d. 160, ll. 5–6.

124 On the cadet schools, see the decree of 21 August 1943 in *KPSS v rezolyutsiyakh i resheniyakh s"ezdov, konferentsii, i plenumov TsK* (8th edn; 15 vols; M., 'Politicheskaya literatura', 1970–84), vol. 6, pp. 98–104. Nine schools, each with 500 pupils, administering a seven-year programme, were founded: the decree explicitly stated that they were modern equivalents of 'the old cadet corps'. See also Dunstan, p. 202. For a propaganda image of a Suvorov cadet, see Fedor Reshetnikov, 'Home from the Holidays' (1949), where the boy salutes his elderly and delighted, if bemused, grandfather, while his small sister beams from her homework at the spotless dinner table (reproduced in Bown, *Socialist Realist Painting*, plate 270).

125 The *Metodicheskie pis'mo po doshkol'nomu vospitaniyu*

no. 14 (1930), for example, does not list toy soldiers in its model inventory, though it does suggest that, while girls generally prefer playing with baby dolls, boys are more likely to play with 'Red Army Soldiers' (p. 24); it also warns against 'stimulating aggressive play' (as in a case where children first squealed at a snake and then killed it, p. 21). N. Bartram, 'Igrushka', *Pechat' i revolyutsiya* 5 (1926), only mentions patriotic toys in the context of negative phenomena of the past, for example, the figures of brave Cossacks pummelling the Japanese, or caricatures of Kaiser Wilhelm, manufactured by 'vulgar patriots' (*kvasnye patrioty*) during the Russo-Japanese and First World Wars (p. 55).

126 B. E. Vladimirsky, mislabelled 'Young Pioneers at Play' (Pioneers were always represented wearing red scarves, and in any case, at eight and above, were considered too old for 'babyish' items such as ducks and teddies), Sotheby's, The Russian Sale, Wednesday 10 May 2000, lot 201. For other militaristic images of children, see e.g. Fedor Reshetnikov, 'Home for the Holidays' (1949), which shows a Suvorov cadet.

127 *Krokodil* 4 (1952), 8. Note also the cartoon, p. 13, satirising publishers' broken promises to print plenty of *skazki*.

128 See Catriona Kelly, 'Riding the Magic Carpet: The Stalin Cult for Little Children', *Slavic and East European Journal* 49: 2 (2005). The mediation of meetings was in part a reflection of Stalin's growing inaccessibility to the public in the post-war years, though there was a notable tour in 1948 to southern Russia, during which he stopped at Sochi and treated a group of children to ice-cream and sweets in a local café. See Simon Sebag Montefiore, *Stalin: The Court of the Red Tsar* (London: Phoenix, 2004), pp. 578-9.

129 *Pravda* 4 May 1952, p. 1.

130 *Pravda* 22 June 1946, p. 5.

131 Bown, *Socialist Realist Painting*, plate 244.

132 The school uniform introduced in 1943 was directly modelled on that current before 1917, and in the post-war years class teachers (*klassnye rukovoditeli*) were given a role not far distinct from that of the pre-revolutionary *klassnye damy* and *klassnye nastavniki* who had been responsible for policing the values of their charges. See further in Chapter 8.

133 See A. Vitman in *NM* 7 (1947), 275-9. On the *internaty*, see Chapter 3 below.

134 See A. B. Geraskina, *Attestat zrelosti*, P'esy (M., 1962), 7-88. The original title of the play contains an untranslatable chime on the literal meaning of the Russian word for 'matriculation certificate', 'Proof of Maturity'. On the Soviet school story in the 1930s and 1940s generally, a good source is Evgeny Dobrenko, '"The Entire Real World of Childhood": The School Tale and "Our Happy Childhood"', *SEEJ* 49: 2 (2005), 225-48.

135 K. D. Ushinsky, *Izbrannye pedagogicheskie sochineniya*, ed. V. Ya. Struminsky (M., 1945), p. 4.

136 Ushinsky, *Izbrannye*, p. 135 (Slav family), pp. 136-7 (patriotic education), p. 79 (corporal punishment).

137 For example, *Pedagogicheskaya poema* stayed in print throughout the 1940s and beyond (it had reached its seventieth edition by the glasnost era), as did *Kniga dlya roditelei*, which went through 13 editions between 1953 and 1987 (see the Russian National Library catalogue); *Lektsii o vospitanie detei* (1940) continued to be reprinted until 1988 as well (ibid.). Makarenko's works were also translated into all the languages of the Warsaw Pact countries, where they went through repeated editions (see the catalogue of RGB OR), and exercised some influence here: for instance, in Hungary the phrase 'the Makarenko slap' was used to encapsulate humane but effective discipline (personal information from a participant at the 'Globalization in Eastern Europe' conference, Budapest, February 2003).

138 *Pravda* 9 July 1944, 1-2. See also the claims of enthusiastic reports from working mothers: 'Stalinskaya zabota sovetskogo gosudarstva o materyakh i detyakh', *Pravda* 12 July 1944, 3, and 'Sovetskie lyudi goryacho privetstvuyut zabotu gosudarstva o detyakh i materyakh', *Pravda* 13 July 1944, 2.

139 'O peredache na vospitanie detei razvedennykh suprugov', *SZ* 7-8 (1946), 30.

140 B. A. Arkhangel'sky and B. N. Speransky, *Mat' i ditya* (M.-L., 1948), 5. Cf. L. A. Zalkind, *Zdorovyi brak i zdorovaya sem'ya* (M., 1951), p. 3: 'It is often considered that questions of family life are the private affair [*lichnoe delo*] of each person. That is quite incorrect.' F. Vigdorova, *Diary of a Russian Schoolteacher* (trans. R. Prokofieva; NY, 1960), emphasises above all consideration for others and not standing out: e.g. 'Dima Kirsanov', 162-77 describes the conversion to collective values of an intelligent, aloof boy, who at first despised his unintellectual class pen-pal, but after a stay in hospital realised the latter's human worth.

141 Homework: L. N. Skatkin, 'Kak rukovodit' det'mi pri samostoyatel'nom reshenii arifmeticheskikh zadach', *SemSh* 1 (1952), 13-15; leisure time: O. Chkalova, 'Sem'ya - druzhnyi kollektiv', *SemSh* 2 (1953), 12; regime: G. Belousov, 'Kak my vospityvaem vnuchku', *SemSh* 6 (1952), 30.

142 N. Nosov, *Vitya Mamleev v shkole i doma*, in *Sobranie sochinenii v 3 tomakh*, vol. 1 (M.: Detskaya literatura, 1968), pp. 489-661: the will-training cake episode occurs on pp. 538-9.

143 See e.g. the unsigned editorial 'Sovetskoe izobrazitel'noe iskusstvo v 1952 godu', *Sovetskii khudozhnik* 1 (1953), 6, which describes the painting as 'a little novella about the Soviet family, about children, about school'.

144 Ibid., 6.

145 Bown, *Socialist Realist Painting*, plate 334.

146 Ibid., plate 280.

147 Where mischief did occur, this tended to be of an innocent kind: see e.g. M. I. Sizova's *Istoriya odnoi devochki* (M.-L.: Gos. izd. Detskoi literatury, 1959), which included material on pranks at the Mariinsky ballet school in the 1920s, but emphasised the wisdom of the teachers and their authority - in a pedagogical context - over the pupils. (The book was originally published in 1946, but later editions expanded the 'school japes' material.)

148 Similarly, in Nosov's *Vitya Mamleev*, the hero's sister was happy to sit down to her homework straight from school right from the beginning of the novel, and needed no retraining. On the other hand, Nosov was more collusive with disruptive behaviour by boys than many of his contemporaries. There is even an interesting undertow of impatience with discipline full stop: the story 'The Policeman', for example, shows a child reduced to neurotic terror by parents who have used policemen as bogey figures, so that he becomes utterly incoherent when he is lost and a policeman tries to help. Any 'message' here is self-evidently directed at adults rather than children. (See *SS* vol. 1, pp. 237–9). This restiveness about correct behaviour probably explains why girls have an extremely marginal place in his pre-1953 work, with 'Ya pomogayu', about little Nina who helps the Pioneers with their scrap collection, the only piece with a female protagonist at all (*SS* vol. 1, pp. 240–52).

149 V. Oseeva, *Rasskazy* (M.–L.: Detgiz, 1952).

150 A. A. Mayakovskaya, *Detstvo i yunost' Vladimira Mayakovskogo: Iz vospominanii avtora* (M.–L., 1953), p. 10 (New Year), pp. 12–13 ('birthday'), p. 7 (reading), p. 8 (love of animals), p. 30 (tidy), p. 26 (school marks), p. 15 (lack of children's organisations in Tsarist times), p. 37 (goes to political meetings), p. 54 (grown up at 13).

Chapter 4: 'Let There Always Be Sunshine', 1953–1991

1 A. D. Sergeeva, 'Deti v dni narodnoi skorbi', *SemSh* 4 (1953), 6–9.

2 Oxf/Lev T-05 PF9A, p. 5.

3 'PPBTsK 1948–1954', typescript held on open access in the reading room of TsKhDMO, l. 186.

4 See Reid, *passim*.

5 'LO izdatel'stva "Detskaya literatura". Otchet ob izdatel'skoi i finansovoi deyatel'nosti za 1962', TsGALI-SPb. f. 64 op. 1 d. 166, l. 11.

6 Sergei Mikhalkov, 'Bud' gotov', *Sobranie sochinenii v 4 tomakh* (M.: Khudozhestvennaya literatura, 1963), vol. 1, p. 323; full text of poem, pp. 320–9.

7 See e.g. *N* 33 (1962), front page, p. 3; *N* 1 (1960), 4 (Khrushchev with children during his visits to Indonesia and India).

8 As, for instance, in a piece by Slava Shutov, who was one of a Pioneer delegation at the Twenty-Fifth Congress of the Communist Party in 1976, and who described how flustered he was on having to present a bouquet to one of the delegates: *N* 9 (1976), 19.

9 See e.g. L. I. Brezhnev, 'Vospominaniya. Zhizn' po zavodskomu gudku', *N* 45 (1981), 3–5.

10 As discussed by M. Tumarkin, *Lenin Lives!* (Cambridge, MA, 1983), p. 260.

11 R. P. Corsini, *Caviar for Breakfast* (London, 1965), p. 143. Much material about Lenin was also contained in reading primers (see the digital version of this chapter for references).

12 I recall seeing this image, for instance, on a visit to a Pioneer camp in the Gulf of Finland in summer 1979.

13 Pioneer initation in Moscow: see e.g. Oxf/Lev M-04 PF36B, p. 15; Local Lenin statue: Oxf/Lev T-04 PF2B, p. 11; Lenin monuments (in this case the *shalash*, or grass hut, where Lenin camped out in the Gulf of Finland during the 1910s): CKQ SPb.-03 PF2B, p. 15. Initiation ceremonies of this kind were also favourite propaganda moments: see e.g. *N* 18 (1968), front page (Pioneers from Podol'sk being initiated next to the Lenin mausoleum).

14 See e.g. A. Nikolaev and P. Popov's letter to their 'dear little friends' (*dorogie mal'enkie druz'ya*), thanking them for their greetings and telling them to think about being astronauts when they grow up: *Murzilka* 12 (1962), 16–17.

15 See A. Gusev, *God za godom: iz pionerskoi letopisi* (M., 1961), pp. 77–118. Cf. later items on the war, e.g. *N* 12 (1975), which has a woman's reminiscences of a boy Partisan she had seen fighting in Latvia.

16 *Vozhatyi* 5 (1961), 8.

17 Gusev, *God za godom*, p. 102, p. 82, pp. 108–9.

18 Kirschenbaum, 'Innocent Victims and Heroic Defenders', 283–5. The Soviet press also carried a large number of items about war children, especially during the Blockade, at this period. See e.g. L. Ivanova, 'Pust' vsegda budet mama, pust' vsegda budu ya', *N* 10 (1965), 12.

19 More than 140 works devoted to Makarenko's pedagogy were published in the Soviet Union between 1953 and 1987 (see the catalogue of the Russian National Library, St Petersburg).

20 See e.g. V. A. Sukhomlinsky, *Kak vospitat' nastoyashchego cheloveka. Sovety vospitatelyam.* (Izhevsk, 1980).

21 On manners for children, see e.g. O. Chkalova, 'O kul'ture povedeniya detei', *SemSh* 3 (1956), 11–13; Irina Babich, 'A mne tak udobnee…', *N* 19 (1965), 20; 'Shkola izyashchnykh maner', *N* 37 (1969), 21–2, and numerous following issues. There was also a spate of brochures on these topics from the late 1950s onwards: see C. Kelly, *Refining Russia* (Oxford, 2001), ch. 5.

22 See e.g. N. I. Boldyrev, *Vospitanie kommunisticheskoi morali u shkol'nikov* (2nd edn; M., 1956).

23 See 'Pust' vsegda budet solntse!', *Literatura i zhizn'* 14 December 1960. The poem was later set to music as a song for peace by L. Oshanin and A. Ostrovsky.

24 K. K. Paramonova, *Kino – detyam* (M., 1970), p. 3.

25 Bamm et al. (eds), *Semeinoe vospitanie: Slovar' dlya roditelei* (M., 1967), p. 247.

26 See e.g. L. Luk'yanova, 'U skazki v gostyakh', *O* 1 (1975), 32–3, on special costumed animal shows at the Kaliningrad Zoo. For more on this theme, see Chapter 11 below.

27 D. A. Berman, *Kornei Ivanovich Chukovsky: Biobibliograficheskii ukazatel'* (M., 1999), pp. 27–46.

28 For example, V. I. Leibson, *Chemu uchat stikhi?* (M., 1964), takes its examples almost exclusively from Chukovsky, Marshak, and Pushkin, the 'founding father' of Russian adult literature.

29 V. Shklovsky, '*Zolotoi klyuchik* i *Povest' o fonare*',

Pravda 25 June 1936, p. 3.

30 V. Shklovsky, *Staroe i novoe: Kniga statei o detskoi literature* (M., 1966).

31 B. Hellmann, *Barn- och ungdomsboken i Sovjetryssland* (Stockholm, 1991), pp. 324–5 (author's own English-language summary).

32 T. Marakova, *Skazka o murav'eve, po imeni Muravei* (M., 1973).

33 This is based on personal information from several well-known children's writers in 1989–91. Interestingly, both editors I interviewed were more positive, especially the more senior of the two.

34 An exception to the general trend was the reprint of L. Panteleev and G. Belykh's novel of orphanage life *Respublika Shkid* (see ch. 6) in 1960 (L: Detgiz).

35 S. Baruzdin, *Skazhi, chelovek!* (M., 1962).

36 V. Golyavkin, *Udivitel'nye deti* (3rd edn; M., 1979), pp. 178–82.

37 N. Nosov, *Priklyucheniya Neznaiki* (1954): reprinted in *Sobranie sochinenii v 3 tomakh* vol. 2 (M., 1969), pp. 7–192. See also the discussion 'Neznaika – pro i contra', *NLO* 75 (2005).

38 Catriona Kelly, interview with former editor at Leningrad Detgiz, September 2001.

39 E. Bogopol'skaya, '... pochemu v zhurnale tak malo geroev-pionerov, a vse kakie-to zaichiki da loshadki', *RM* 4254 (21–27 January 1999), 10. On Statsinsky, see also V. Pribylovsky, 'Zavetnye risunki Vitaliya Statsinskogo', *RM* 23–29 November 2000, 18.

40 These artists and others are reproduced in V. Glotser, *Khudozhniki detskoi knigi o sebe i svoem iskusstve: stat'i, rasskazy, zapiski, vystupleniya* (M., 1987). The anthology also makes it clear that remarkably interesting and vital work was done in the post-Stalin era by some artists of the older generation, such as Natal'ya Basmanova (b. 1906) or Tat'yana Mavrina (b. 1902).

41 Gavril Zapolyansky, 'Evreyu – ot Sovetskogo Soyuza', *Znamya* 9 (2001), 155.

42 An example of the first category was Vasily Belov in his *skazki*: see e.g. 'Mishuk (Skazka dlya Anyuty),' in *Izbrannye proizvedeniya v 3 tomakh* (M., 1983), vol. 2, pp. 422–9.

43 Yu. Koval', *Priklyucheniya Vasi Kurolesova* (M., 1971).

44 E. Uspensky, *Dyadya Fedor, pes i kot* (M., 1974), pp. 93–5.

45 E. Uspensky, *Akademik Ivanov* (M., 1974), p. 7.

46 See R. I. Zhukovskaya, 'Igra kak sredstvo vospitaniya detei', *SP* 5 (1956), 21–37.

47 L. Chaga and A. Mikhailov, *Risunki nashikh detei* (M., 1962). The comments by V. V. Favorsky and A. M. Mikhailov are on p. 3 and p. 7.

48 See *O* 10 (1958), 24–5.

49 V. Glotser, *Deti pishut stikhi* (M., 1962), pp. 200–1 (war stories), p. 242 (outer space poem).

50 Bamm et al., *Semeinoe vospitanie*, p. 343 (recommendation of Glotser).

51 A. Mazurova, 'Zametki k zasedaniyu Soveta Vsesoyuznoi Pionerskoi Organizatsii po imeni V. I. Lenina po voprosu "O dal'neishem razvitii initsiativy i samodeyatel'nosti vo vsesoyuznoi pionerskoi organizatsii imeni V. I. Lenina"', RGASPI-KhDMO f. 2 op. 1 d. 148, l. 41;

untitled report on Yaroslavl's School No. 21, ibid., l. 121.

52 As, for example, in a comic scene where Chik confers on himself the duty of acting as referee during a football match, but agrees that he ought to stay on as a player too because otherwise his team would be one short. F. Iskander, *Sobranie sochinenii v 6 tomakh* vol. 1 (Khar'kov, 1997), pp. 393–401.

53 'Programma KPSS', section V part 1, *KP* 2 August 1961, 2. See also the discussion in Kelly, *Refining Russia*, ch. 5.

54 *KPSS v rezolyutsiyakh i resheniyakh s"ezdov, konferentsii, i plenumov TsK* (8th edn; 15 vols; M., 1970–84), vol. 9, pp. 139–47.

55 See Kelly, *Refining Russia*, ch. 5.

56 *O*, inside front cover of 8 (1958); back cover of 10 (1958). *Nedelya* items included M. Gorskaya, 'Karetu mne, karetu!', *N* 8 (1966), 18 (on prams); 'My proverili – vypolneno', *N* 9 (1960), 22 (on soft toys); 'Magaziny, v kotorye my pridem zavtra', *N* 24 (1960), 2 (which includes a picture of a new children's department store on Leninsky Prospekt, Moscow); A. Semynina, 'Krasivo i prosto', *N* 24 (1966), 20 (on children's fashion). Among books on goods for children were *Detyam – khoroshuyu odezhdu* (M., 1959); *Detskaya mebel' iz gnuto-vykleinykh elementov* (M., 1959); *Detyam khoroshuyu igrushku. Sbornik 1960* (M., 1960). See further in Chapters 3 and 8 below.

57 On transforming books into commodities, see Stephen Lovell, *The Russian Reading Revolution* (Basingstoke, 2000).

58 Information based on interview with Andrei Efremov, September 2001.

59 Interview with Andrei Efremov, September 2001; the Beryozka ref. is from my own recollection.

60 Mikhalkov, *Sobranie sochenii*, pp. 83–93.

61 See e.g. Samvel Gasparov's popular film of 1980, *Khleb, zoloto, i nagan.*

62 For more on this, including the group called Young Friends of the Soviet Police, see Chapter 12 below.

63 L. Razumovskaya, *Dorogaya Elena Sergeevna, Sad bez zemli: P'esy* (L. 1989), pp. 53–93. Quotations on p. 56, p. 64. The play was banned in 1983, but not because of the way in which insubordination was interpreted; rather, it was felt that the representation of teenage disaffection in it was unduly pessimistic.

64 As in Yury Miloslavsky's story 'Syn Lyudmily Ivanovny', *Ot shuma vsadnikov i strelkov* (Ann Arbor, 1984), pp. 7–18, about a 14-year-old youth imprisoned for his part in a gang rape (see also Chapter 12 below).

65 J. Brodsky, 'The Bust of Tiberius', trans. A. Myers with the author, *Collected Poems in English* (Manchester, 2001), p. 282. The original Russian reads, 'sonmy chmokayushchikh tvoi shershavyi/ mladentsev: 'swarms of slobbering on your ugly thing/infants': *Sochineniya Iosifa Brodskogo* vol. 3 (SPb., 1997), p. 274.

66 Compare *Pravda* 16 November 1958, pp. 1–3 and *Pravda* 25 December 1958, pp. 1–2. The discussions appeared at frequent intervals between these two dates.

67 See e.g. *Pravda*, 19 November 1958, 3.
68 There was extensive discussion of this in the Soviet press in 1956–58. See, for example, 'Vsenarodnoe obsuzhdenie voprosa ob ukreplenii svyazi shkoly s zhizn'yu i o dal'neishem razvitii sistemy narodnogo obrazovaniya v strane', *Pravda* 21 December 1958, p. 3.
69 See e.g. A. Petrov, 'Bol'shie perspektivy shkol-internatov', *Pravda* 21 December 1958, p. 3; and also Chapter 4 below.
70 For a full discussion of the reforms from this angle, and of the reactions to them, see Detlef Glowka, *Schulreform und Gesellschaft in der Sowjetunion, 1958–1968* (Stuttgart, 1970), pp. 55–6.
71 Ibid., p. 57: though note that the Jewish quota remained in force.
72 M. S. Bernshtein, 'Obuchenie i vospitanie odarennykh detei v SShA', *SP* 6 (1961), 118–26: after a prudently guarded introduction, this article gave a fairly detached and factual account of special schools, and of special groups within mainstream schools.
73 John Dunstan, *Paths to Excellence and the Soviet School* (Windsor, 1978), p. 61 (art and music schools). On the sports schools, see ch. 4.
74 Ibid., ch. 6, esp. p. 129.
75 On 'profile schools', see ibid., ch. 7; on optional courses, ibid., ch. 9.
76 See the editorial, 'Osnovatel'no izuchat' inostrannye yazyki', *SP* 2 (1961), 10–16.
77 See *KPSS v rezolyutsiyakh*, vol. 9, p. 29.
78 Glowka, *Schulreform*, p. 76.
79 See Dunstan, *Paths to Excellence*, ch. 7 and ch. 8 on these, and also on the use of special coaching.
80 *KPSS v rezolyutsiyakh*, vol. 9, pp. 139–56.
81 See the discussion by J. Dunstan, 'Soviet Education beyond 1984: A Commentary on the Reform Guidelines', *Compare* 15:2 (1985), 161–87; B. B. Szczely, 'The New Soviet Educational Reform', *Comparative Education Review* 30:3 (1986), 321–43.
82 Dunstan, *Paths to Excellence*, pp. 41–2. This is confirmed by our own oral history work with teachers, which turned up not one case of a pro-streaming advocate.
83 Aleksandr Sharov, 'Vzroslye i strana detstva', *NM* 10 (1965), 130–51.
84 Ibid., p. 151.
85 K. Chukovsky, *Zhivoi kak zhizn'* (M., 1963), 156 (emphasis original).
86 *SP* 9 (1956), 3–18, see esp. p. 9.
87 See Glowka, *Schulreform*, pp. 135–44.
88 O'Dell quotes surveys indicating dissatisfaction with stodgy school-teaching (e.g. p. 216).
89 'Ukreplenie distsipliny i poryadka v shkole – nasushchnaya zadacha', *SP* 11 (1955), 9–17.
90 See e.g. the attack on slavish repetition of political material in 'Preodolet' posledstviya kul'ta lichnosti v pedagogike', *SP* 9 (1956), 3–18, or G. I. Gober, 'Samostoyatel'nyi analiz proizvedenii zhivopisi shkol'nikami' *SP* 6 (1961), 93–8, on the work of an art history group in Class 9.
91 See e.g. O. A. Apraksina and N. A. Vetlugina, 'Sostoyanie i zadachi muzykal'nogo vospitaniya v shkole', *SP* 9 (1956), 46–58.

92 Cf. e.g. the republication of P. N. Shimbirev [and E. I. Shimbireva], *Pedagogika* (M., 1940) as in 1954, or V. P. Esipov, *Pedagogika* (M., 1946) in 1967.
93 See e.g. V. A. Sukhomlinsky, *Serdtse otdayu detyam* (Kiev, 1980); idem, *Pavlyshevskaya srednyaya shkola* (M., 1969), reprinted in his *Izbrannye pedagogicheskie sochineniya* (M., 1979–81), vol. 1, vol. 2, respectively.
94 I. S. Vygotsky, *Sobranie sochinenii v 6 tomakh* (M., 1982–4).
95 If evidence came through that pupils were alienated by this, then the assumption was that they were wrong – the school must 'correct' the bad influences that had brought about alienation. See e.g. I. Ovchinnikova, 'Vechnaya tsennost' klassiki', *N* 41 (1975), 10–11.
96 See 'Ustav srednei obshcheobrazovatel'noi shkoly', *Spravochnik direktora shkoly* 1971, p. 15 (homework), pp. 79–81 (exams). These norms are similar to those established in 1951 (see Boldyrev (ed.), *Klassnyi rukovoditel'*, p. 101).
97 See 'O merakh dal'neishego uluchsheniya raboty srednei obshcheobrazovatel'noi shkoly' (Decree of the Central Committee and the Council of Ministers, 10 November 1966), and 'Ustav srednei obshcheobrazovatel'noi shkoly' (approved by the Council of Ministers on 8 September 1970): *Spravochnik direktora shkoly* (1971), p. 6, p. 13.
98 See E. G. Tuneva, '"Skazka o Voennoi Taine" A. Gaidara kak sredstvo patrioticheskogo vospitaniya uchashchikhsya IV klassa', in L. A. Khinkova, N. I. Rybakov and A. A. Frolov (eds), *Tvorchestvo A. P. Gaidara* (Gor'kii, 1975), p. 200.
99 F. Kuznetsov, *Besedy o literature* (M., 1977), p. 78, commenting on A. Moshkovsky.
100 On which see Chapter 8 below.
101 S. Knizhnik, 'Sumerki pedagogiki. Pod svodami khrama vospitaniya', *N* 39 (1989), 8–9.
102 M. Zhvanetsky, 'Detskii sad', *God za godom* (L., 1991), p. 437.
103 B. Slutsky, *Stikhotvoreniya* (M., 1989), p. 302.
104 See e.g. 'Demografiya i sem'ya', *N* 52 (1978), 15–17; 'Sluzhba sem'i i demografiya', *N* 3 (1981), 2–3, 10–11; 'Krepka sem'ya, krepka derzhava', *N* 15 (1987), 15–19; 'Pis'mo iz GDR', *N* 11 (1987), 18 (favourably contrasting the GDR with the USSR). On the demographic crisis generally, see L. Attwood, *The New Soviet Man and Woman* (Basingstoke, 1990).
105 See e.g. 'Otkuda berutsya tsiniki?', *N* 13 (1989), 8; T. Kolomina, 'Deti v ocheredi', *N* 8 (1991), 2.
106 For reassessments of the Soviet regime, see e.g. N. Kolesikova, 'Ya tebya porodil', *N* 11 (1991), 22–3, which argues that the ethos of *schastlivoe detstvo* (happy childhood) stopped people from seeing child abuse even when it was right in front of their eyes. The UFO story, 'Sensatsiya', appeared in *N* 25 (1990), 4.
107 E. Kamusnik, 'I zachem ya rodila?', *N* 35 (1991), 6.
108 On the collapse of the 'happy childhood' myth, see further Chapters 8, 9, 10 and Conclusion.

Chapter 5: The Kindness of Strangers, 1890–1917

1 Vl. Simyakov, *Sbornik derevenskikh chastushek* (Yaroslavl': self-published, 1913), p. 418.

2 B. M. Firsov and I. G. Kiseleva (eds), *Byt velikorusskikh krest'yan-zemlepashtsev:* (SPb., 1993), p. 199.

3 See e.g. the account by Konstantin Trenev, *SPA* vol. 2, p. 456.

4 See *BVR*, vol. 2:2, p. 6, pp. 28–30, pp. 36–7, pp. 63–5.

5 See *BVR*, vol. 1, pp. 49–50, 63–5.

6 Firsov and Kiseleva (eds), *Byt velikorusskikh krest'yan*, p. 199.

7 *BVR*, vol. 1, p. 65.

8 ' 'Pervoe zasedanie Obshchestva pravovoi okhrany maloletnikh', *PB* 1–2 (1914), 113. Risk appears, going by anecdotal evidence, to have persisted after the Revolution as well: for instance, Oxf/Lev V–04 PF24B, p. 3, reports the informant's resentment at having to mind her mother's 'lust child' (*prigulyannyi*).

9 K. Chukovsky, *Dnevnik 1901–1929* (M., 1991), pp. 322–3. The word 'bastard' is in English in the original.

10 For the figures, see e.g. *Vsepoddaneishii otchet po Vedomstvu uchrezhdenii Imperatritsy Marii za 1904* (SPb., 1907), p. 110; *Vsepoddaneishii otchet po Vedomstvu uchrezhdenii Imperatritsy Marii za 1909* (SPb., 1914), p. 58. The most authoritative study of the homes is Ransel, *Mothers of Misery*.

11 *BVR* vol. 1, p. 10.

12 *PB* 9 (1916) 927.

13 Six hundred girls go to the bad: E. Chichagova, speaking at the Pervyi Vserossiiskii S"ezd po semeinomu vospitaniyu, quoted in *SemV* 9 (1913), 76.

14 On the life of the street children generally, see A. I. Zak, 'Kharakteristika detskoi prestupnosti', in M. N. Gernet (ed.), *Deti-prestupniki* (M., 1912), pp. 109–10, and [A. G.] Emel'yanov, 'Prestupnost' nesovershennoletnikh po mirovym uchastkam Moskvy', ibid., pp. 159–62; and the interesting individual biographies in N. A. Okunev, *Osobyi sud po delam o maloletnikh* (SPb., 1911), pp. 55–100.

15 See Zak in Gernet (ed.), *Deti-prestupniki*, pp. 109–10 (on Khitrov Market); Emel'yanov, ibid., pp. 158–62 (also on Khitrov Market), p. 153 (on Smolenskaya Square).

16 On newspaper-selling, see V. M. Levitsky, 'Besprizornye deti i voina', *Deti i voina* (Kiev, 1915), p. 10. On theft, S. A. Sokolinskaya, ibid., p. 271.

17 A. A. Bakhtiarov, *Bryukho Peterburga: ocherki stolichnoi zhizni* (1888): this sketch is printed on pp. 190–3 of the abridged edn (SPb., 1994).

18 Emel'yanov in Gernet (ed.), *Deti-prestupniki*, p. 126, states that a full 89.5 per cent of cases coming before the Moscow magistrates involved boys.

19 E. I. Chichagova, 'Bytovye usloviya zhizni devochek', in Okunev, *Osobyi sud*, p. 92. The biographies that follow deal with two or three cases of girls who had got sucked into selling themselves in a haphazard way, rather than ending up in brothels (pp. 97–8), as well as a case of a girl who had lived with two different men after reaching the age of 14 (p. 96).

20 See V. Gal'perin in Gernet (ed.), *Deti-prestupniki*, p. 369 (age of entry, quoting *Statistika Rossiiskoi Imperii*), p. 377 (rates).

21 Gal'perin in Gernet (ed.), *Deti-prestupniki*, p. 374. Accounts of such cases must of course be treated with caution, since they were coloured by commentators' assumptions that juvenile sexual expression of any kind was 'abnormal', and best handled by a cleansing spell in a reformatory. On this set of attitudes, see Laura Engelstein, *The Keys to Happiness* (Ithaca, NY, 1992), p. 292, p. 298.

22 The anonymous *Deti naberezhnoi: Iz zhizni Odesskogo porta*, held in the University of Helsinki Slavonic Library, depicts an exploitative boy–girl relationship where the boy, Sen'ka Gorokh, aged 12 or 13, trades vodka for services on the part of the girl, his *barokha* (roughly, 'moll').

23 Song from M. Oshanin, 'Semeinye usloviya v svyazi s detskoi prestupnost'yu', *PB* 9 (1916), 923. This article (full page-run 915–38) also contains some general information on the life of street children, e.g. on drinking. For other accounts of the life of pre-revolutionary street children, see 'Besprizornye deti v Moskve', *PB* 3–4 (1915), 242–6; V. Ogronovich, 'Polozhenie besprizornykh detei v Petrograde v svyazi s voinoi', *PB* 1–2 (1916), 61–82, etc.

24 V. M. Levitsky, 'Besprizornye deti i voina', *Deti i voina*, cites 'Nich'i deti' as a figure of popular speech; Levitsky himself uses the more official term *besprizornye*. The word is not listed in Dal's dictionary, not even in the fourth edition (see *Tolkovyi slovar' zhivogo velikorusskogo yazyka* vol. 1 (SPb.–M., 1912). The *Slovar' sovremennogo russkogo yazyka* vol. 1 (M.–L., 1950), col. 420, cites 1891 as the earliest dictionary reference. Bakhtiarov, *Bryukho Peterburga*, used the term *peterburgskii gamen* (a *gamin* of St Petersburg) for his sketch of a street child.

25 D. A. Dril', *O merakh bor'by s prestupnost'yu nesoveshennoletnikh* (M., 1908). (Also published in *Zhurnal Ministerstva Yustitsii* 12 (1908), p. 9)

26 For the image, see M. Oshanin, 'Semeinye usloviya v svyazi s detskoi prestupnost'yu', *PB* 9 (1916), 931.

27 For the cross-empire figure, see 'Romanovskii komitet i Obshchestvo pravovoi okhrany maloletnikh v dele pomoshchi besprizornym detyam', *PB* 1 (1917), 55; for the Petrograd figure (1,640 through the juvenile court in 1913 and 2,096 in 1915: here different figures are given for the Russian Empire, of 20,724 crimes by juveniles reaching magistrates' courts in 1913 and 26,137 in 1915), see Ogronovich, 'Polozhenie besprizornykh detei', *PB* 1–2 (1916), 62–3; for the Moscow figure (1,514 cases at the juvenile court in 1913, 1,649 in 1914, and 2,009 in 1915), see S. Bakhrushin, 'Bor'ba s detskoi prestupnost'yu v svyazi s voinoyu', *PB* 4 (1916), 384.

28 Yakovlenko, 'O polozhenii pokinutykh detei v zemskikh guberniyakh', *Zhurnal obshchestva*

russkikh v pamyat', N. I. Pirogova 5 (1901), p. 321.

29 *Vsepoddaneishii otchet [...] za 1909*, pp. 13–14, pp. 22–4. Valuable information about the operation of the Empress Maria institutions is available not only from these *otchety*, but also from the series *Sostoyashchee po Vysochaishim Ikh Imperatorskikh Velichestv pokrovitel'stvom Vedomstvo Detskikh Priyutov* ... (SPb., 1900), comprising brochures about different aspects of the Department's work with children in orphanages.

30 *BURI*, vol. 1, table 1.

31 A. Kaizer, 'S"ezd 11–16 maya 1914 g. o prizrenii detei', *PB* 8–9–10 [i.e. one number for three months] (1914), 1071–2. On the early history of the homes' endowments, see Ransel, *Mothers of Misery*, pp. 42–4.

32 *BVR*, vol. 1, p. 135.

33 Lindenmeyr, pp. 152–3.

34 P. M. Erogin in *Otchety ob osmotre detskikh priyutov* (SPb., 1903), p. 19 (Chistopol'), p. 65 (Ufa), p. 53 (Ekaterinburg), p. 55 (Irbit), p. 11 (the opulent orphanage at Selo Novoe).

35 See N. P. Malinovsky, 'Goryachie zavtraki dlya shkol'nikov', *PB* 2 (1913), 10.

36 See Map 1, after p. lxxx, in *BVR*, vol. 1.

37 *Sbornik statisticheskikh svedenii o zavedeniyakh zakrytogo prizreniya detei, v tom chisle sirot sel'skogo naseleniya* (Petrograd, 1916), p. ix.

38 *BURI*, vol. 1, p. 9.

39 *BURI*, vol. 1, p. 24, p. 33.

40 See the account of the society's activities given at a meeting of the City Duma (which supported it to the tune of 1,000 roubles a year), TsGIA-SPb f. 792 p. 1 d. 8001, ll. 2–2 ob.

41 See *Komitet Kazanskogo Obshchestva popechitel'stva o bednykh: Otchet za 1891 god* (Kazan', 1892), ... *za 1895 god* (Kazan', 1896); ... *za 1900 god* (Kazan', 1901); *Otchet komiteta Obshchestva popechitel'stva o bednykh i bol'nykh detyakh v g. Kazani: 1910 god* (Kazan', 1911) (the statistics on the shelter are on p. 37, and on the hospital, pp. 52–6).

42 For the cruelty initiative, see *Detskaya pomoshch'* 14 (1885), 763–4; for support to needy schoolchildren, ibid., 17 (1885), 843–7; for work with the blind, ibid., 7 (1885), 397–403; a representative set of sentimental poems is Leonid Trefolev, 'Pesni o spasennykh detyakh', ibid. 1 (1885), 25–6, which evokes e.g. some children left orphans alongside the body of their mother, dead from cold and hunger.

43 TsGIA-SPb f. 792 p. 1 d. 8001, l. 6.

44 *SPb-Pv-1903*; *Kul'tovye zdaniya Peterburga: ukazatel' russkoi literatury 1717–1917* (2 issues; St PPb.: RNB, 1998–99). The activities of such societies are traceable in their own publications (see e.g. *Detskii priyut trudolyubiya v Vyazemskom dome (Fontanka 95/20)* (SPb., 1898). Information on late nineteenth- and early twentieth-century child-oriented philanthropy is available also in Lindenmeyr, esp. pp. 62–3, 145–62, 182–91; V. I. Kapusta (comp.), 'Istoriya Peterburgskoi blagotvoritel'nosti', *Nevskii arkhiv* 1 (1993), 429–59.

45 On the first, see *Deti – rabotniki budushchego* (M., 1908), p. 17; on the second, Lindenmeyr, p. 182 (dealing with the specific case of anxiety about the fate of children cooped up with alcoholic and indigent adults in the *doma trudolyubiya*, city workhouses).

46 The society had one hostel for 160 children, at Ozerki, on the northern outskirts of St Petersburg: see TsGIA-SPb f. 254 p. 1 d. 10180, l. 4.

47 *BVR*, vol. 1, p. 73, p. 77.

48 See Chapter 5.

49 See e.g. 'Pervoe zasedanie obshchestva pravovoi okhrany maloletnikh (30 yanvarya 1914 goda)', *PB* 1–2 (1914), 111–22.

50 On the former, see 'Popechite'stvo o maloletnikh, zhivushchikh lichnym trudom v Sankt-Peterburge', *PB* 4 (1913), 11–21; on the latter, see N.S. Nelyubov, *Obzor deyatel'nosti obshchestva Detskii gorodok Petrogradskoi chasti, 1910–1915* (Petrograd, 1916).

51 See 'Sinii krest', *PB* 8–9–10 (1914), 1095–104, for general information about the Popechitel'stvo; 'Deyatel'nost' Moskovskogo Otdela Obshchestva Popecheniya o bednykh i bol'nykh detyakh v Sankt-Peterburge', *PB* 10 (1913), 33–41, for information about one of the local sections and its activities.

52 See *Ustav obshchestva 'Detskii mir'* (SPb., 1912). No annual records relating to this charity could be found, and it was not covered in the periodical press relating to charities.

53 *PB* 7 (1912), 3. 'Detskaya pomoshch'', on the other hand, could only raise 4,544 in 1898: *BURI*, vol. 2 (SPb., 1900), p. 645. On the other charities, see the *guberniya*-by-*guberniya* breakdowns in *BURI*, vols 2 and 3; *BVR*, vols 2.1 and 2.2; and the occasional reports published in *PB*.

54 See Lindenmeyr, p. 162.

55 On the founding of the society and the congress, see Lindenmeyr, pp. 162–3.

56 *BVR*, vol. 1, p. 1 (emphasis original).

57 P. Gatrell, *A Whole Empire Walking* (Bloomington, IN, 1999), pp. 75–6 (on the Tatiana Committee), p. 144 (on schools).

58 On the latter two categories, see *BVR*, vol. 1, pp. 93–109, 'Soslovnoe prizrenie'.

59 *Sel'skie detskie priyuty Vedomstva uchrezhdenii Imperatritsy Marii Fedorovny*, issue 1 (Petrograd, 1915).

60 *Sbornik statisticheskikh svedenii*, p. vii.

61 See *PSZ* 7337, 31 December 1890, (3rd series, vol. 10.1, p. 835; emphasis added). For boys, progression to an academic curriculum required successful completion of Class 1; otherwise mechanical skills formed the core of the course. The difference was no doubt due to the fact that girls were expected to become teachers or governesses, boys craftsmen or engineers.

62 For the variety, consult *Sbornik statisticheskikh svedenii*; the figure of 28,197 children of peasant origins out of an overall orphanage population of 39,666 on 1 January 1914 comes from here, p. vii.

63 *K voprosu ob organizatsii zemledel'cheskikh priyutov dlya sel'skikh sirot* (Petrograd, 1915), p. 9, pp. 11–12.

64 'Proekt normal'nogo ustava sel'skikh detskikh priyutov dlya sirot, Vedomstva uchrezhdenii Imperatritsy Marii', in *Sel'skie detskie priyuty*,

issue 1, pp. 29–49, p. 39 (*smotritel'*), p. 41 (*zakonouchitel'*, hygiene inspection).

65 *Detskaya pomoshch'* 1 (1885), 14.

66 *Komitet Kazanskogo Obshchestva popechitel'stva o bednykh i bol'nykh detyakh … Otchet za 1900*, pp. 19–20.

67 *Detskii priyut trudolyubiya*, p. 3.

68 'Svedeniya o sostoyanii priyutov [v SPbskoi gubernii] so svedeniyami ob uchenikakh i uchenitsakh', TsGIA-SPb f. 218 p. 1 d. 1232, l. 2, l. 4, l. 6, l. 8, l. 10, l. 12, etc. (There are records of nineteen orphanages in this file, running ll. 1–38 inclusive.)

69 As e.g. in *Detskii priyut trudolyubiya*.

70 See e.g. the photographs of the Tsesarevich Aleksei Charitable Society (Alekseevskoe obshchestvo del miloserdiya) on Uspensky Island in St Petersburg: TsGAKFD SPb. box 174, nos A6977–10332 etc., or the Society for the Protection of Homeless Children, also in St Petersburg, ibid., E15646 etc.

71 *BURI*, vol. 1, table 1; Sbornik statisticheskikh svedenii o zavedeniyakh zakrytogo prizreniya detei, p. xv.

72 See N. Tulinov, *Spisok blagotvoritel'nykh uchrezhdenii g. Peterburga i okrestnostei, imeyushchikh tsel'yu okazyvat' prizrenie bedstvuyushchim detyam* (SPb., 1907).

73 See e.g. on Scotland, Lynn Abrams, *The Orphan Country: Children of Scotland's Broken Homes from 1845 to the Present Day* (Edinburgh, 1998).

74 The reports on the financial activities of parish societies in St Petersburg in the mid-1880s published in *Detskaya pomoshch'* 16 (1885), 793–800, 17 (1885), 834–43, 18 (1885), 860–7, 19 (1885), 914–20, and 20 (1885), 946–53, indicate that these engaged in a huge range of welfare activities, including old people's homes, cheap accommodation for the poor, soup kitchens, Sunday schools, and shelters for children; and that the financial circumstances of such societies in the richer parts of the city were very comfortable indeed (overall income in 1875, the second year of their operation, had reached 134,668 roubles, of which 31,872 roubles was spent on children's needs). In the ten-year period 1896–1905, by contrast, private donations to the Empress Maria Institutions totalled 224,481 roubles: see *Otchet o dvizhenii summ Kantselyarii po upravleniyu vsemi detskimi priyutami VUIM za 1895–1905* (SPb., 1906), pp. 333–7.

75 See Lindenmeyr on these two kinds: p. 150 and p. 165 on suspicion of charity; p. 82 on a clerical supporter of 'scientific charity', Father G. P. Smirnov-Platonov, editor of the journal *Detskaya pomoshch'*.

76 *Deti – rabotniki budushchego. Pervaya kniga Moskovskogo obshchestva 'Setlement'* (M., 1908), p. 19, p. 22, p. 140. See also V. Ogronovich, 'Detskii dom o-va "Detskii trud i otdykh" v Moskve', *PB* 5 (1916), 213–18, which praises the architecture, the self-help ethos, and the emphasis on self-reliance: 'Morally ruined children dissolve in this joyful, friendly family'.

77 *Deti – rabotniki*, p. 28.

78 Ibid., pp. 34–7, 42–4.

79 Ibid., pp. 54–61.

80 Ibid., p. 17, p. 16.

81 Ibid., p. 3.

82 M. I. Berlinberger, *Fizicheskoe razvitie detei v sirotskom priyute Moskovskogo gubernskogo zemstva za 1901–1905 gg.* (M., 1908), p. 5. 'Pravila i instruktsii dlya vnutrennego rasporyadka v priyutakh i shkolakh Obshchestva popechitel'stva o bespriyutnykh detyakh', *PB* 2–3 (1917), 183 (I have schematised from a running narrative).

83 See *Sel'skie detskie priyuty Vedomstva Imperatritsy Marii*, issue 2 (Petrograd, 1915), p. 94, p. 97, p. 80.

84 Berlinberger, *Fizicheskoe razvitie*, p. 6. A bucket contained just over 12 litres.

85 W. Barnes Steveni, *Through Famine-Stricken Russia* (London, 1892), p. 27.

86 See P. Stasova, *Obzor deyatel'nosti obshchestva 'Detskaya pomoshch'' za 10 let ego sushchestvovaniya* (SPb., 1904).

87 *Obzor deyatel'nosti obshchestva 'Detskaya pomoshch'' za 1902 god* (SPb., 1903).

88 *Otchet o deyatel'nosti obshchestva 'Detskaya pomoshch'' za 1908 god* (SPb., 1909).

89 *Otchet obshchestva 'Detskaya pomoshch'' za 1915* (Petrograd, 1916).

90 *BURI*, vol. 1, table 1.

91 *SPb-Pv-1903*.

92 On the general population of Smolensk, see P. V. Tsezarsky, *Zemskaya meditsina v Smolenskoi gubernii* (M., 1904), p. 2; on provision for abandoned children, see table in digital version of this chapter.

93 See Ransel, *Mothers of Misery*, p. 257. Later admissions once record-keeping was introduced, meaning that mothers had paperwork to complete before they could lodge their children, improved the situation somewhat (see ibid., p. 113). In 1904, 60 per cent of St Petersburg inmates (and 40 per cent of Moscow inmates) were two weeks or more old when deposited (*Vsepoddaneishii otchet […] za 1904*, p. 112). However, even at this stage the death rate remained high.

94 *BM*, p. 62.

95 *Zhurnal obshchestva russkikh vrachei v pamyat' N. M. Pirogova*, 5 (1901), pp. 321–36.

96 A. A. Romanov, 'O prizrenii pokinutykh detei', *Trudy VIII Soveshchaniya gg. Zemskikh Vrachei i Predstavitelei Zemskikh Uprav Voronezhskoi Gubernii, 25-go avg.–3-go sentyabrya 1903* (Voronezh, 1903), vol. 2, part 2, p. 286.

97 *Zhurnal obshchestva russkikh vrachei v pamyat' N. M. Pirogova* 1 (1901), p. 30.

98 For a report of this kind, see A. A. Romanov, 'Otchet po prizreniyu pokinutykh detei v Voronezhskom Gubernskom Zemstve 27 aprelya 1904–6 maya 1912', *Trudy X Ocherednogo Soveshchaniya gg. Vrachei i Predstavitelei Upravy Voronezhskoi Gubernii, 27 aprelya–6 maya 1912* (Voronezh, 1912), vol. 1, p. 266.

99 Romanov, 'O prizrenii', *Trudy VIII Soveshchaniya*, vol. 2, part 2, p. 266. Cf. figures from Smolensk for 1911 and 1915: death rates among 'foundlings' (i.e. those placed anonymously) stood at 33.82 and 56 per cent respectively, and rates among the 'illegitimate' (i.e. those placed by their mothers)

at 13.46 and 20 per cent: *Otchet Smolenskoi Gubernskoi Zemskoi Bol'nitsy za 1911 god*, comp. S. A. Alexandrov (Smolensk, 1912), p. 38; *Otchet o deyatel'nosti Smolenskoi Gubernskoi Zemskoi Bol'nitsy za 1915 god*, p. 77.

100 Romanov, 'O prizrenii', *Trudy VIII Soveshchaniya*, vol. 2, part 2, p. 272 (the home); A. A. Romanov, 'Otchet po prizreniyu pokinutykh detei v Voronezhskom Gubernskom Zemstve za 5 let s 1902–1906 gg.' *Trudy IX Soveshchaniya gg. Vrachei i predstavitelei zemskikh uprav Voronezhskoi Gubernii* vol. 1 (Voronezh, 1908), p. 22. By 1906, however, overcrowding had forced the percentage up to 15.2 per cent (ibid.)

101 V. P. Gerasimovich, 'Gospitalizm grudnykh detei, staryi i novyi', *Trudy Pervogo Vserossiiskogo S"ezda Detskikh Vrachei v Sankt-Peterburge s 27–31 Dekabrya 1912 goda* (St Petersburg, 1913), pp. 99–2.

102 *Otchet o Smolenskoi Gubernskoi Zemskoi Bol'nitse za 1905*, comp. S. A. Alexandrov (Smolensk, 1906), p. 37.

103 Romanov, 'O prizrenii', *Trudy VIII Soveshchaniya*, vol. 2, part 2, p. 267.

104 Romanov, 'Otchet po prizreniyu', *Trudy X Ocherednogo Soveshchaniya*, vol. 1, p. 265.

105 *Otchet Smolenskoi Gubernskoi Zemskoi Bol'nitsy za 1911 god*, p. 64.

106 On the general opinion, see Chapter 5 in online version. For an opinion from a doctor involved in orphanage work, see Romanov, 'Otchet po prizreniyu', *Trudy X Ocherednogo Soveshchaniya*, vol. 1, p. 258 – attributing the increased level of death to the increase in artificial feeding, so that babies were weaker when they left the nurseries to go out to the countryside.

107 Romanov, 'O prizrenii', *Trudy VIII Soveshchaniya*, vol. 2, part 2, p. 275.

108 TsGIA-SPb f. 254 p. 1 d. 10180, l. 4.

109 Romanov, 'O prizrenii', *Trudy VIII Soveshchaniya*, vol. 2, part 2, p. 273.

110 See Levitsky in *Deti i voina*, p. 17; Yaroshevich in *Deti i voina* pp. 94–6 (on lack of organisation and waste of goodwill), pp. 90–1 (on bad premises and food in the shelters).

111 As in the case of the Chistopol' home inspected in the 1900s (*Otchety ob osmotre detskikh priyutov* (SPb., 1903), p. 19): see below, p. 176.

112 *Detskii priyut trudolyubiya*, pp. 11–12.

113 Okunev, *Osobyi sud*, pp. 64–5; p. 60 describes a similar case, the intelligent, articulate 'Aeroplane', who simply disappeared the second time he was let out 'on his honour'. Contrast, though, the case of the former child prostitute who settled down and became communicative and successful in the orphanage (p. 99). The success rate with girls, judging by the cases cited here, seems to have been better.

114 *Detskii priyut trudolyubiya*, p. 11.

115 See e.g. Okunev, *Osobyi sud*, pp. 62–3 (on a tough-nut 16-year-old boy), pp. 96–7 (on a girl who ran away from the orphanage at 14, and who rapidly developed a track record of thefts and sexual partnerships).

116 Levitsky, 'Iz kamery sud'i' [part 3], *PB* 10 (1916), 984.

117 R. E. Zelnik, 'On the Eve: Life Histories and Identities of Russian Workers, 1870–1905', in L. H. Siegelbaum and R. G. Suny (eds), *Making Workers Soviet* (Ithaca, NY, 1994), pp. 62–3.

118 *Otchety ob osmotre*, p. 50 (Perm'), p. 65 (Ufa), p. 19 (Chistopol'), pp. 22–3 (Vyatka), p. 21 (staff ratios – from an orphanage in Perm').

119 For example, a short report in *PB* 2 (1912), 2–3, argued that the 9 roubles per month paid to needy families in St Petersburg would be quite beyond the resources of most places.

120 See Lindenmeyr, pp. 147–56.

121 On fosterage by the Imperial Foundling Homes, see Ransel, *Mothers of Misery*; on the zemstva, see Yakovlenko, 'O polozhenii pokinutykh detei', p. 321.

122 On the VUIM scheme, see *Ob organizatsii prizreniya besprizornykh detei v krest'yanskikh sem'yakh* (SPb., 1900).

123 *SPb-Pv-1903*.

124 See Khr. Shranebakh, 'K voprosu o registratsii mladentsev, otdannykh v derevni na chastnyi patronazh', *PB* 3–4 (1915), 344–6.

125 As in Kaizer, 'S"ezd 11–16 maya', *PB* 8–9–10 (1914), 1883–4: mentioning particularly adoption here.

126 On lack of regulation in the Imperial Foundling Homes, see Ransel, *Mothers of Misery*, pp. 276–7; on the zemstva, see e.g. the report in *PB* 2 (1912), 2–3.

127 For instance, in the Moscow Imperial Foundling Home in 1904, the death rate among farmed-out infants under the age of one was 74 per cent, and in the St Petersburg Home, 61.6 per cent: *Vsepoddaneishii otchet [...] po 1904*, p. 124. See also table 1 in the digitised version of Chapter 9 on the zemstvo homes.

128 *Ob organizatsii prizreniya detei*, pp. 1–5.

129 Romanov, 'O prizrenii', *Trudy VIII Soveshchaniya*, vol. 2, part 2, pp. 290–1, p. 292.

130 Kvyatkovskaya, 'Delo prizreniya', *Trudy VII Soveshchaniya*, vol. 2, pp. 283–4 (adoption), p. 277 (neglect), pp. 282–3 (boy and foster mother).

131 Romanov, 'O prizrenii', *Trudy VIII Soveshchaniya*, vol. 2, part 2, pp. 276–7.

132 A. Balashova in Chaadaeva, pp. 103–6.

133 V. Dement'eva in Chaadaeva, p. 80.

134 See Zelnik, 'On the Eve', pp. 35–7.

135 Cf. e.g. the introduction of account books and report forms for the Empress Maria orphanages in 1900: *Sbornik tsirkulyarov [...] s 1891 po 1905 g.* (SPb., 1906), pp. 90–107, pp. 126–7; or the call for a dedicated full-time inspectorate in *Otchety ob osmotre*, p. 137.

136 See e.g. I. Betskoi, *Kratkoe nastavlenie, sobrannoe iz luchshikh avtorov s nekotorymi fizicheskimi predstavleniyami o vospitanii detei ot rozhdeniya ikh do yunoshestva* (SPb., 1766). Seven edns of this publication were produced in all.

137 *K voprosu ob organizatsii zemledel'cheskikh priyutov dlya sel'skikh sirot* (Petrograd, 1915), p. 9, p. 40.

138 Ibid., *passim*: and see also the illustrations to this publication.

139 *Otchet obshchestva Detskaya pomoshch' za 1915* (Petrograd, 1916) p. 10; the 'big family' quotation is ibid., p. 13.

140 TsGIA-SPb f. 254 p. 1 d. 10180, l. 4.
141 See N. V. Nesmeyanov, 'O formakh prizreniya detei', *PB* 4 (1916), 270.
142 *BVR*, vol. 1, p. 12.
143 See A. F. Selivanov, 'Ob ustroistve remeslennykh otdelenii pri priyutakh i drugikh blagotvoritel'nykh obshchestvakh', *PB* 6 (1913), 31–4.
144 D. A. Dril', *Maloletnie prestupniki* (2 issues; M., 1884–88), issue 1. For the case histories, see issue 1, pp. 76–82.
145 See Dril', *O merakh bor'by s prestupnost'yu nesovershennoletnikh*; for the general background, P. Lebedinsky in his review of Rubashova and Tarasova, *Yundichesleü Vestusk* 2 (1913), 287; compare the remarks of V. Ogronovich, 'S"ezd deyatelei suda po delam maloletnikh', *PB* 1–2 (1914), 98.
146 E. Ginzburg, 'Istoriya popechitel'skoi raboty', *PB* 6–7 (1917), 540. I have not been able to trace any information about the Washington congress Ginzburg mentions.
147 See P. Lebedinsky's review of A. M. Rubashova, *Osobye sudy dlya maloletnikh* (M., 1912), and E. P. Tarasova, *Detskii sud zagranitsei i v Rossii* (M., 1912), in *Yuridicheskii vestnik* 2 (1913), 289.
148 Russian jurists took part, for instance, in the various World Prison Congresses held from 1872, and the fifth such congress, held in 1890, was convened in St Petersburg. See Kh. Chernykov in Gernet (ed.), *Deti-prestupniki*, p. 37. Gernet's volume also contains a piece by E. Tarasova on juvenile courts outside Russia (pp. 439–82), which approvingly cites the opinion of Reicher in *Der Erziehungsnotstand des Volkes* that punishment of young offenders amounts to cruelty (p. 518), and points out that the introduction of educational methods in Western European countries had led to a drop, rather than rise, in child crime (p. 523).
149 'Ob izmenenii form i obryadov sudoproizvodstva po delam o prestupnykh deyaniyakh maloletnikh i nesovershennoletnikh, a takzhe zakonopolozhenii o ikh nakazuemosti', 2 June 1897, *PSZ*, 3rd edn, vol. 17, No. 14233.
150 Cf. the comments of Gurevich in Gernet (ed.), *Deti-prestupniki*, p. 13.
151 Charykov ibid., p. 43 ff.
152 See e.g. the comments of Gurevich ibid., p. 17 (on supervision orders), and Emel'yanov, ibid., p. 222, on suspended sentences. M. K. Zamengof ibid., pp. 386–7, gives figures totalling 41.65 per cent for those receiving non-custodial sentences from the Moscow district courts (17.64 placed under 'public supervision' and 4.3 per cent under police supervision, 16 per cent bound over, 2.81 per cent confined to the Moscow city limits, 0.82 per cent required to pay caution money (*zalog*), 0.08 per cent required to surrender domestic passport).
153 Bocharov in Gernet (ed.), *Deti-prestupniki*, p. 527.
154 Levitsky in *Deti i voina*, p. 6.
155 'Ob ispravitel'nykh priyutakh', 5 December 1866, *PSZ* 2nd series, vol. 41, no. 43949. For earlier legislation determining special conditions for minors within the ordinary prison system, see e.g. *Ustav o Soderzhashchikhsya pod strazhei* art. 1035, note 2, *Prodolzhenie Svoda Zakonov Rossiiskoi*

Imperii, izdannogo v 1857 godu (SPb., 1863), p. 81, which specified that such individuals were to be given skills training in workshops, rather than made to labour there.
156 The 5 December 1866 statute stated that the organisers of 'corrective shelters' were allowed to run annual lotteries to help with funding, to petition the Ministry of State Property for land allocations, if they ran an agricultural commune, and to charge parents up to 3 roubles a month towards expenses. But no precise thresholds for budget input were set.
157 A. A. Fidler, 'Ocherk deyatel'nosti predydushchikh s"ezdov predstavitelei russkikh vospitatel'no-ispravitel'nykh zavedenii (1881–1911 gg.)', *T 8S PVIP*, p. 25.
158 See the archivist's note 'Istoricheskaya spravka Moskovskogo gorodskogo Rukavishnikova priyuta dlya nesovershennoletnikh (dlya maloletnikh prestupnikov)', in the catalogue to RAO NA f. 115 (op. 1, ll. 2–8).
159 *T 7S PVIP*, pp. 70–1.
160 'Povedenie vospitannikov [Rukavishnikova] priyuta 1906', RAO NA f. 115 op. 1 d. 21, l. 1 ob., l. 2 (bread and water, no dinner), l. 1 (no mattress), l. 2 ob. (solitary confinement), l. 2 ob. (reprimand).
161 'Dnevnikovye zapisi vospitatelei o povedenii vospitannikov' (1908), RAO NA f. 115 op. 1 d. 40 l. 1 (knife attack on director, 5 April), l. 6 (knife-fight, 2 August).
162 'Dnevnikovye zapisi', l. 21.
163 Vl. Anofriev, 'Russkie ispravitel'nye zavedeniya dlya maloletnikh', *VV* 7 (1900), 158.
164 S. V. Bakhrushin, 'K voprosu o postanovke dela ispravitel'nogo vospitaniya maloletnikh', part 1, *PB* 4 (1917), 264.
165 *T 7S PVIP*, p. 79 (the questioner was V. P. Kashchenko, on whom see the digital version).
166 Anofriev, 'Russkie ispravitel'nye zavedeniya', 158–60.
167 *T 7S PVIP*, p. 80.
168 Use of older mentors as regulators: *T 8S PVIP*, p. 56, pp. 233–6 (Vladimir), p. 66 (Kursk); responsibilities, p. 46 (Yakovlevsky); rewards/incentives: *T 8S PVIP*, p. 59 (Vyatsk), p. 90 (Poltava); reprimands, treat deprivations, *T 8S PVIP*, p. 52 (Vladikavkaz), p. 62 (Ekaterinodar). Employment: *T 8S PVIP*, p. 47 (Yakovlevsky). Family regime, *T 8S PVIP*, p. 52.
169 Anofriev, 'Russkie ispravitel'nye zavedeniya', 160–2; *VV* 8 (1900) 145–59.
170 Fidler, 'Ocherk deyatel'nosti predydushchikh s"ezdov", *T 8S PVIP*, pp. 33–4.
171 *T 8S PVIP*, p. 60, though contrast the Poltava regime (ibid., p. 90), which required four hours' school work, about four hours in the workshops, and three hours' work in the garden and market garden, and allowed only an hour and a half off.
172 'Polozhenie o vospitatel'no-ispravitel'nykh zavedeniyakh dlya nesovershennoletnikh', 19 April 1909, *PSZ*, 3rd series, vol. 29, no. 51727; *SZRI* vol. XIV, pp. 263–7.
173 *Ustav Smolenskoi Gubernskoi Zemskoi vospitatel'no-ispravitel'nogo kolonii-priyuta dlya nesovershennoletnikh* (n.p., n.d.: Smolensk?, 1915?

– year given in the ministerial imprimatur of A. Khvostov at the top of p. 1), p. 10.

174 Charykov in Gernet (ed.), *Deti-prestupniki*, p. 63.

175 Emel'yanov, ibid., p. 221, argued that, in Moscow, the *mirovye sudy* themselves were reasonably consistent, but noted a wide variety of practice with regard to whether children were detained in police custody, pp. 212–13.

176 *Deti i voina* (Kiev, 1915), p. 10.

177 'Iz deyatel'nosti Obshchestva pravovoi okhrany maloletnikh v Sankt-Peterburge', *PB* 3–4 (1914), 337. Even in its first year of operation, the five guardians at the St Petersburg court had to deal with 5,437 cases: see Okunev, *Osobyi sud*, p. 25.

178 See E. Ginzburg, 'Usloviya popechitel'skoi raboty', *PB* 6–7 (1917), 526–8. On brutality by the police, see also S. V. Bakhrushin, 'K voprosu o postanovke dela ispravitel'nogo vospitaniya maloletnikh', part 2, *PB* 5 (1917), 402, which refers to beatings, starvation, and even torture by burning with cigarette-ends.

179 P. Bel'sky, 'K pyatidesyatiletiyu russkikh vospitatel'no-trudovykh zavedenii', *PB* 10 (1916), 1016. And this despite the fact that the Tsar had been the official patron of the reformatories and shelters for prisoners' children since 1895: see 'Polozhenie o vospitatel'no-ispravitel'nykh priyutakh dlya nesovershennoletnikh' (1909), article 1, *SZRI* vol. XIV, p. 263.

180 On the responsibility of the zemstva, see 'Ustav o zemskikh povinnostyakh' (1899), article 159, *SZRI* vol. IV, p. 156; for the 1900 figures, *BVR*, vol. 1, p. 62.

181 V. Ogronovich, 'S"ezd deyatelei suda po delam maloletnikh', *PB* 1–2 (1914), 102. Though some interest was taken by the voluntary sector: see e.g. *SemV* 7 (1913), 76–7, on a 'forget-me-not day' for the Varshavsky corrective shelter in Moscow (though the money raised consisted mostly of one large private donation of 1,000 roubles and a subsidy of 20,000 roubles from the city authorities).

182 For the 1881 and 1914 figures, see 'Iz deyatel'nosti Obshchestva pravovoi okhrany maloletnikh v Sankt-Peterburge', p. 348. For the 1900 figures, see Anofriev, 'Russkie ispravitel'nye zavedeniya', 151. On the early history of the colonies (the earliest reformatories were in the Baltic States, set up in the 1840s and 1850s), see Bel'sky, 'K pyatidesyatiletiyu', 1010–18.

183 *T 7S PVIP*, p. 62, *T 8S PVIP*, p. 89.

184 M. Bekleshov, 'Russkie vospitatel'no-ispravitel'no zavedeniya dlya nesovershennoletnikh', *TV* 2 (1910), 139.

185 'Ob assignovanii 1000 r. v posobie ot goroda Tsentral'no-vospitatel'nomu priyutu dlya devochek pri SPb. damskom blagotvoritel'nom Komitete' (9 Avgusta 1897 goda – 16 yanvarya 1898 goda). TsGIA-SPb f. 792 p. 1 d. 6821, l. 1.

186 *T 8S PVIP*, p. 46, p. 74.

187 Cf. the claim by the director of the Rukavishnikov shelter that only one director participating in the 1908 Congress of reformatory staff had been 'spared' such events: *T 7S PVIP*, p. 68.

188 *T 8S PVIP*, p. 84. See also, on the later upheavals, *Pravo* 1912, p. 1372, p. 1426.

189 *Pravo* 1912, p. 1372.

190 *T 8S PVIP*, p. 86.

191 S. Gogel', 'Detskaya prestupnost' v Sankt-Peterburge v 1910 godu, po dannym popechitelei detskogo suda', *Pravo* 1911, p. 1171 (quoting E. N. Tarnovsky in *Zhurnal Ministerstva Yustitsii*, 1899). For the composition of the shelters, see the constitution of the Smolensk Provincial Zemstvo Educational-Corrective Shelter in 1915: those with criminal convictions or on remand, those who had been found begging or 'lack shelter or supervision in the eyes of the Provincial Zemstvo Administration', and those referred by their parents or guardians for correction. *Ustav Smolenskoi Gubernskoi*, p. 6.

192 *Otchet S-Petersburgskogo Obshchestva Vospitatel'no-Ispravitel'nykh Priyutov za 1913 god* (SPb.: Parovaya tip. L. V. Gutmana, 1914), p. 19.

193 *T 8S PVIP*, p. 99, p. 105.

194 *Otchet S-Petersburgskogo Obshchestva Vospitatel'no-Ispravitel'nykh Priyutov za 1911 god* (SPb., 1912), p. 22. In 1913, the rates in fact dropped (to around 2.5 per cent), though there was no policy change: see *Otchet S-Petersburgskogo Obshchestva Vospitatel'no-Ispravitel'nykh Priyutov za 1913 god*, p. 35.

195 Ogronovich, 'Polozhenie besprizornykh detei', *PB* 1–2 (1916), 65–6.

196 Ginzburg, 'Usloviya popechitel'skoi raboty', 494–552.

197 On alternatives to prison, see Ogronovich, 'S"ezd deyatelei suda po delam maloletnikh', 105–6; on diversifying institutions, see Bakhrushin, 'K voprosu o postanovke', part 1, *PB* 4 (1917), part 2, *PB* 5 (1917), *passim*.

198 See 'Sankt-Peterburgskii vospitatel'no-ispravitel'nyi priyut', *PB* 6 (1913), 37–8. For the total number of cases (1,640), see Ogronovich, 'Polozhenie besprizornykh detei', p. 62. This number includes girls, but, as these invariably constituted a fairly small minority of those undergoing arrest and trial, a figure of, say, 1,300 boys would be a safe estimate.

199 'Istoricheskii ocherk vozniknoveniya Tambovskogo zemskogo vospitatel'no-ispravitel'nogo priyuta', *TV* 11 (1911), 1334.

200 *Otchet S-Petersburgskogo Obshchestva Vospitatel'no-Ispravitel'nykh Priyutov za 1913 god*, p. 27.

201 Between 1890 and 1895, the prison and provincial zemstva authorities dealt with more than fifty cases of children who had ended up in adult prisons: see the case file in TsGIA-SPb f. 254 op. 1 d. 12284. The quotation (l. 1 ob.) is from the Novaya Ladoga Predstavitel' dvoryanstva, Naryshkin (no first name given) to the Governor of St Petersburg province, 18 July 1890; he had been shocked to find a 14-year-old boy locked up for two months after he and his brother committed a theft. In 1896, the head of the Directorate of Prisons (Tyuremnoe upravlenie) wrote to the Governor of St Petersburg province to urge him to have all minors currently in adult prisons and serving sentences of more than six months transferred to the reformatory system (ibid., l. 209).

202 Emel'yanov in Gernet, *Deti-prestupniki*, p. 223.

203 M. K. Zamengof, ibid., pp. 386–7.
204 V. I. Kufaev, *Yunye pravonarushiteli* (M., 1924), p. 36.
205 *Sbornik uzakonenii i rasporyazhenii po tyuremnoi chasti.*(Perm', 1903), p. 245 (§ 58).
206 P. V. Vsesvyatsky in Gernet, *Deti-prestupniki*, pp. 423–5.
207 *T 8S PVIP*, p. 299.
208 Vsesvyatsky in Gernet, *Deti-prestupniki*, pp. 413–27. On the catamite terms, see p. 420. *Margaritki* is also listed (though as a general term for a 'passive pederast') in V. F. Trakhtenberg, *Blatnaya*

muzyka ("Zhargon" t'yurmy), ed. I. A. Boduen-de-Kurtene (SPb., 1908), p. 37.
290 Vsesvyatsky in Gernet, *Deti-prestupniki*, p. 421.
210 S. K. Gogel', 'Ob udalenii nevinnykh detei iz tyurem', in *O prizrenii bespriyutnykh arestantskikh detei* (SPb., 1901), pp. 4–31. Offical concern for such children in earlier periods had been limited to allocating them a budget for food rations (*kormovye den'gi*): see *Ustav o Soderzhashchikhsya pod strazhei*, article 138, *Svod Zakonov Rossiiskoi Imperii*, *izdannyi v 1857 god* (SPb., 1857), vol. XIV, p. 30.
211 *Detskii priyut na katorge*, (SPb., 1894), pp. 10–12.

Chapter 6: Orphan Heroes, 1917–1935

1 Goldman, pp. 69–70.
2 Ibid. On the famine, see also L. A. and L. M. Vasilievsky. *Kniga o golode* (3rd edn; Petrograd, 1922).
3 F. A. Mackenzie, *Russia before Dawn* (London, 1923), pp. 128–41.
4 L. M. Vasilevsky, *Detskaya prestupnost' i detskii sud* (Tver', 1923), p. 128.
5 RGASPI f. 2554 op. 1 d. 17, l. 224.
6 Goldman, p. 65.
7 N. Deyanova, 'Ob uteryannykh detyakh', *Detskii dom* 3 (1928), 25.
8 Ball, pp. 22–3.
9 The 35,000 figure is given in S. Kopelyanskaya, 'Podkidyvanie detei', *SYu* 13 (1932), 23: she also gives the figures of 15,000 for 1927, and 6,000 for 1929 (across the Soviet Union as a whole). The figure of 300,000 comes from Goldman, p. 93. In Leningrad in 1924, there were still 6,835 children in institutions: *Otchet o deyatel'nosti rabochego patronata Tsentral'nogo raiona za vremya s 1 maya po 1 dekabrya 1924 g.* (L., 1924).
10 On the overall figures, see A. Berelowitch and V. Danilov, *Sovetskaya derevnya glazami VChK-OGPU-NKVD*, vol. 3.1 (M., 2003); Viola, 34–5, 39 (47 child and 11 adult deaths on 189 echelons sent in February 1930).
11 On cannibalism, see V. Bazarov, *Durelom* (2 vols; Kurgan, 1997), vol. 2, p. 63; for a case of a child temporarily consigned to an orphanage, see that of Mariya Belkina, p. 217 below.
12 *DG* doc. 73, p. 119.
13 On the founding of the Ministerstvo gosudarst-vennogo prizreniya, see S. Gogel', 'Ministerstvo Gosudarstvennogo Prizreniya', *PB* 6–7 (1917), 480; on the committee work, see 'Soveshchanie po voprosam sotsial'noi pomoshchi detyam pri Ministerstve Gosudarstvennogo Prizreniya', *PB* 6–7 (1917), 564–9.
14 On the Provisional Government, see Gogel', 'Ministerstvo Gosudarstvennogo Prizreniya', *PB* 6–7 (1917), pp. 491–4, which anticipated that the Ministry would act to co-ordinate and supervise charitable initiatives and the raising of funds from state and other sources.
15 On this and its effects, see esp. Caroli.
16 Zenzinov, pp. 10–14.
17 *BSE*, 1st edn, vol. 23, cols 509–10; see also Ball, pp. 143–4; Caroli, pp. 63–75.
18 On the American Relief Association, see *DG* p. 47; on the Save the Children Fund, Eglantyne

Jebb, *Save the Child!* (London, 1929), pp. 25–6; Kathleen Freeman, *If Any Man Build* (London, 1965), pp. 30–2.
19 Zenzinov, p. 14.
20 See *DD* 9 (1932), 10–11; *DD* 1 (1933), 1. On attacks, see also Ball, p. 144.
21 Caroli, p. 75.
22 *DSV* vol. 4, no. 254: Decree of 27 March 1919. See also Stevens, pp. 248–50.
23 *DSV* vol. 12 no. 102. For information on the activities of the Detkomissiya, see Ball, p. 91; Caroli, pp. 56–61.
24 B. S. Utevsky, *Bor'ba s detskoi besprizornost'yu* (M.–L., 1932), pp. 61–4.
25 Of course, this fracturing of responsibility with regard to children's issues was characteristic of other modern states as well. It was only in the early twenty-first century that Britain acquired a minister for children. A notable exception was the Third Reich, where the official youth organisations (Hitlerjugend, Bund deutscher Mädel) gradually came to preside over almost all matters affecting children in the 10–18 age group, including the juvenile court system, and not just leisure and political indoctrination, as in Russia. By the time the final piece of legislation had been put in place in March 1939, only education was beyond their purview. (See Arno Klönne, *Jugend im Dritten Reich*, Munich, 1990, p. 29, p. 35.)
26 *BNKZ* 4 (1922), pp. 4–5, item 27.
27 *BNKZ* 15 (1922), p. 4.
28 *BNKZ* 13 (1923), pp. 5–6.
29 *BNKZ* 5–6 (1922), p. 6, item 41.
30 TsGA f. 2554 op. 1 d. 16, ll. 17–18.
31 *ENKP* 31 May 1925, p. 7.
32 See Chapters 11–12 below.
33 See A. A. Makarenko, *Pedagogicheskaya poema* (M., 1944), p. 220.
34 Gertrud Striedter, 'Erinnerungen', extract 3, pp. 9–10. Typescript in the personal archive of Jurij Striedter, Cambridge, MA.
35 *ENKP* 30 December 1922, pp. 7–9; see also *Okhrana detstva* (Khar'kov, 1922), pp. 30–4; TsGA f. 2552 op. 1 d. 2918, l. 49.
36 See *ENKP* 13 August 1926, pp. 2–6; 'Ob organizatsii postov okhrany detstva v zhaktakh', *Sbornik po voprosam okhrany detstva Komissii po uluchsheniyu zhizni detei* 12 (1932), 25; 'Obshchestvennaya inspektsiya po okhrane detei', *SYu* 6 (1933), 23.
37 Vasilevsky, *Detskaya prestupnost'*, p. 190. The

course ran for 300 hours over the four months (ibid.)

38 *ENKP* 13 August 1926, pp. 2–6.

39 Cf. a report by A. P——yaev (aged 13), in T. E. Segalov, 'Deti-brodyagi', *Pravo i zhizn'* 9–10 (1925), 91. See also Voinov's account of an encounter in Vladikavkaz in 1931, after he and a friend were caught thieving in the marketplace: the police knew that the use of whips and sticks was 'bourgeois barbarism', but that did not deter them from giving the two boys a thorough beating with their fists, despite the young age (8 or 9) of the pair: p. 41. Caroli, p. 102, p. 107, also cites such cases.

40 See e.g. Starzhinsky, pp. 43–4. For the details of their experiences (they were better treated by their fellow prisoners than by the system itself), see Chapter 2 above.

41 For example, in April 1919, Petrograd had eight district reception points run by Narkomsotsbes: see TsGA f. 2554 op. 1 d. 27, l. 80.

42 TsGA f. 2554 op. 1 d. 27, ll. 1–1 ob.

43 *Okhrana detstva*, p. 50.

44 For a description of earlier programmes, and of the change, see A. M. Batuev, *Po zovu serdtsa* (L., 1986).

45 TsGA f. 2554 op. 1 d. 16, ll. 35–36 ob. describes such a holding centre run by Narkomsotsbes.

46 *Okhrana detstva*, p. 42.

47 For the quotation, see *Pervyi vserossiiskii s"ezd deyatelei po okhrane detstva (2–8 febralya 1919 goda v Moskve)* (M., 1920), p. 5; compare also K. N. Venttsel', *Detskii dom* (2nd edn; M., 1917). This of course fitted the general ideal of childhood in the 1920s; see Chapter 2 of the present book.

48 K. Studitsky, 'K rabote s besprizornikami v detskikh domakh', *Detskii dom* 3 (1928), 43.

49 See G. Belykh and L. Panteleev, *Respublika Shkid* (L., 1968), p. 52.

50 For the box office figures, see M. Turovskaia, 'The Tastes of Soviet Moviegoers during the 1930s', in T. Lahusen with G. Kuperman (eds), *Late Soviet Culture* (Durham, NC, 1993), p. 99. At the time when the film was released, Ekk underwent fierce criticism for representing street children in an insufficiently class-aware manner: see Peter Kenez, *Cinema and Soviet Society, 1917–1953* (Cambridge, 1992), pp. 120–1.

51 A direct source on the lives of the *besprizornye* is the autobiographies collected by Ol'ga Kaidanova, *Besprizornye deti: Praktika raboty opytnoi stantsii* (M., 1926); and T. E. Segalov, 'Deti-brodyagi: Opyt kharakteristiki', *Pravo i zhizn'* 7–8 (1925), 84–9; 9–10 (1925), 89–95. See also V. I. Kufaev, *Yunye pravonarushiteli* (M., 1924); Ball; Vasilevsky, *Detskaya prestupnost'*, pp. 65–6.

52 *BNKZ* 18–19 (1922), 18 (Kiev); *BNKZ* 11 (1923), 14 (Kursk). For improved figures from Orel in 1924, see *BNKZ* 7–8 (1924), 47.

53 On the Dom materi i rebenka generally, see *BNKZ* 21 (1925), 8–9; on comparative mortality rates, *BNKZ* 1 (1926), p. 20.

54 E. M. Konyus, *Puti razvitiya sovetskoi okhrany materinstva i mladenchestva (1917–1940)*, ed. V. P. Lebedeva and G. N. Speransky (M., 1954), p. 185.

55 *BNKZ* 17 (1922), 15–16: the comparative figures given are two towns similar in location and population profile, Vladimir, with good nursery support and abandonment rates of 5–6 per month, and Ivanovo-Voznesensk, with poor nursery support and abandonment rates of 28–32 per day. Figures for 1923 and 1925 point to a rise in crèches from 447 to 534, and a concomitant drop in mother and child homes from 110 to 94 and in infant homes from 491 to 287. *BNKZ* 1 (1926), 20.

56 *Pervyi vserossiiskii s"ezd*, p. 7.

57 *Okhrana detstva*, p. 53. For a statement on self-government, see e.g. 'Polozhenie o trudovykh kommunakh podrostkov' (24 December 1925), *ENKP* 5 March 1926, p. 20, No. 154.

58 *Pervyi vserossiiskii s"ezd*, pp. 58–60.

59 *BNKZ* no. 13 (1923), pp. 5–6, 'Instruktsiya vracham po OZD'.

60 Where external reports are almost uniformly negative, internal reports seem absurdly defensive: for example, a report from the shelter for backward children at Udel'naya from 1919 claimed that the children, so far from being underfed, were being given sturgeon, pike-perch, catfish, eggs, meat, and butter in generous quantities – a claim that is hard to credit at this period of severe food shortages: TsGA f. 2554 op. 1 d. 16, ll. 38–38 rev.

61 E. Tikheeva, 'Obstanovka v zhizni malen'kikh detei', in N. Al'medingen-Tumim, E. Tikheeva, and Yu. Fausek (eds), *Doshkol'noe delo: sbornik statei po voprosam doshkol'nogo vospitaniya* (Petrograd, 1922), p. 127. Cf. the reports on Petrograd and Leningrad orphanages held in TsGA, e.g. 'Doklad o rezul'tatakh osmotra detskogo priyuta v Kadnikove' (1919), f. 2554 op. 1 d. 17, l. 205.

62 'Protokoly delegatskikh sobranii rabotnits: protokol zasedaniya 27-go marta 1923', TsAODM f. 69 op. 1 d. 172, l. 13.

63 As is proved by the amount of space given to this issue in, say, the meetings of the Party women's section in Krasnaya Presnya in 1923: see TsAODM f. 69 op.1 d. 172, l. 4, l. 5, l. 9, l. 12, l. 13. etc.

64 Shefner, p. 409.

65 'Protokol No. 33 Zasedaniya Pedagogicheskogo Soveta pri Petrogradskom Gorodskom Otdele sotsial'nogo obespecheniya, sostoyavshegosya 27 avgusta 1919 goda', TsGA f. 2554 op. 1 d. 14, ll. 48–53.

66 See Agrippina Korevanova, *Moya zhizn'* (M., 1938): quoted from S. Fitzpatrick and Yu. Slezkine, *In the Shadow of Revolution* (Princeton, NJ, 2000), p. 184.

67 Striedter, 'Erinnerungen', extract 5, p. 1.

68 See Kaidanova (ed.), *Besprizornye deti, passim*.

69 Ibid., pp. 33–4 (woman teacher's recollections), pp. 27–8 (*skazki*), p. 43 (heroes), pp. 37–8 (nature and countryside), pp. 22–4 (personality types).

70 A. Polevaya, 'Dom rebenka (Iz praktiki detskogo sada-internata g. Odessy)', *Vestnik prosveshcheniya* 7–8 (1923), 116–27.

71 See Oxf/Lev SPb.–02 PF5A–B.

72 *Otchet o deyatel'nosti rabochego patronata*. The exact figures were 5,531 school-age inmates, and 399 pre-school (p. 11).

73 TsGA f. 2552 op. 1 d. 2866, l. 1.
74 On the 1921–2 decrees, see Goldman, p. 74; for the 1924 decree, *ENKP* 22 February 1924, pp. 7–8.
75 Osichek in Kaidanova (ed.), *Besprizornye deti*, pp. 56–7.
76 On staff's inability to keep track of inmates, see TsGA f. 2554 op. 1 d. 14, l. 51 ob.; for a sample regime from 1919, TsGA f. 2554 op. 1 d. 16, ll. 35–36 ob.); on poor conditions, see e.g. the abundant material on Narkomsotsbes institutions in TsGA f. 2554 op. 1 d. 17, e.g. l. 33, l. 35, l. 55.
77 Goldman, p. 96 (no exact date is given: the sum was a regular allocation from Narkompros in the mid-1920s).
78 *Pervyi Vserossiiskii s"ezd*, p. 61.
79 Polevaya, 'Dom rebenka', 125–6.
80 'Iz dnevnika vos'pitatel'nitsy malyshei-negramotnykh', in Kaidanova (ed.), *Besprizornye deti*, p. 27. Cf. the records of psychological problems of children in Petrograd orphanages, 1918: TsGA f. 2554 op. 1 d. 16, l. 5.
81 For a first-hand account of this, see Voinov; for general surveys of drug use, crime, and prostitution among *besprizornye*, see Anne E. Gorsuch, *Youth in Revolutionary Russia: Enthusiasts, Bohemians, Delinquents* (Bloomington, IN, 2000), p. 145, pp. 155–8; Ball, pp. 37–57.
82 Theft represented up to 80 per cent of juvenile cases processed by the legal authorities both in the 1920s and the 1930s. Kufaev's figures for 1921–2 (*Yunye pravonarushiteli*, p. 114) indicate that actual bodily harm (*telesnye povrezhdeniya*) and 'fights, violence against the person, assault' made up anything between 60 and 85 per cent of crimes against the person, with 'insulting behaviour' (*oskorblenie slovom i zhestom*) contributing a further 10–20 per cent. But in 1922, murder amounted to 21.49 per cent of crimes against the person across the RSFSR (the figures for Moscow and Petrograd in the same year are significantly lower, at 3.6 and 10.7 per cent) (ibid). On prostitution in girls, see Gorsuch, *Youth in Revolutionary Russia*, p. 152; Ball, pp. 57–9; in boys, see Ball, ibid.; Daniel Healey, 'Masculine Purity and "A Gentleman's Mischief": Sexual Exchange and Prostitution between Russian Men, 1861–1941', *Slavic Review* 60: 2 (2001), 256. (For more details, see digital version of the present chapter.)
83 Yu. Sokolov, *Russkii fol'klor* (M.: Gos. Uchpedgiz, 1932), part 4, p. 66.
84 *V nashu gavan' zakhodili korabli ...: pesni gorodskikh dvorov i okrain* (Perm', 1995), p. 45.
85 Ninety per cent of the 145,032 cases involving minors brought before the Commissions on Affairs of Minors in 1922–24 involved boys (Goldman, p. 81). This profile continued to be valid in the early 1930s as well. Only 13 of 400 children apprehended for misdemeanours in Orekhovo-Zuevo in 1932 were girls, and only 12 of 488 in 1933 ('O detskoi prestupnosti', *SYu* 21 (1934), p. 18). The Moscow-wide figure for 1934 was 5 per cent girls, 95 per cent boys ('O merakh bor'by s prestupnost'yu sredi nesovershennoletnikh', *SYu* 13 (1935), 11). For the lower involvement of younger children (those under 12), see 'O merakh bor'by',

p. 12 (though the contribution of the 8–12 age group to crime statistics rose significantly between 1924 and 1934, from 26 per cent of cases to 37 per cent of cases).
86 On escapes, see e.g. 'O pobegakh detei iz uchrezhdenii i ob otpuskakh iz nikh' (mentions escapes as a critically worsening problem, though gives no figures) (1919): TsGA f. 2552 op. 1 d. 2918, l. 16–21; on inmate violence, see e.g. Ball, p. 41 (rape of small boys by older ones at the Moscow Labour Home); p. 110 (influence of most hardened children on others). A report from a Petrograd orphanage in 1919 which attributes the bullying to 'class war' (the older children, former cadets, and inmates of shelters for noble orphans had been bullying the younger proletarian ones) smacks of wishful thinking: TsGA f. 2554 op. 1 d. 12, l. 80.
87 Shefner, pp. 453–5, p. 409, p. 408, p. 417, p. 413, p. 417, p. 448, p. 440, p. 426.
88 Utevsky, *Bor'ba s detskoi besprizornost'yu*, pp. 17–21.
89 Stevens, p. 261; Goldman, p. 306.
90 On the rise of concern with discipline in 1927–9, see Stevens, p. 261.
91 N. Shvar and V. Narvsky, 'O podrostkakh, vypuskaemykh iz detskikh domov v zhizn', *Detskii dom* 2 (1928), 29–40.
92 *ENKP* 12 October 1928, p. 24, no. 903; ibid., 1 March 1929, p. 31 no. 249; ibid., 15 January 1933, pp. 5–6, no. 5. The 'sanitary minimum' referred to is cited in *Vestuik zdravokhraneniy* 13 (1932), pp. 5–7, which refers to kindergartens rather than to orphanages or schools, as is implied in *ENKP*, but the point is no doubt that these model regulations were to be imposed on all institutions.
93 Officially, it was claimed that the numbers of homeless children had dropped to 10,000 by October 1928, having earlier stood at 125,000; though unpublished materials from the Children's Commission suggest that the overall figure was significantly inflated, they also suggest a sizable drop: Goldman, p. 306.
94 For the point about unsupervised schoolchildren, see Goldman, pp. 316–18.
95 See 'O merakh bor'by s prestupnost'yu sredi nesovershennoletnikh', *SYu* 13 (1935), 12; V. Tadevosyan, 'Prestupnaya sreda i pravona-rusheniya nesovershennoletnikh', *SYu* 31 (1935), 9.
96 Bazarov, *Durelom*, vol. 1, p. 364: 4,065 and 6,274 are the raw figures.
97 'Obshchestvennaya inspektsiya', 23.
98 For critical remarks on this practice, see e.g. 'Bor'ba s detskoi prestupnost'yu', *SYu* 30 (1935).
99 Figures from *DG*, doc. no. 105, p. 176. Orphanage numbers were 1,475 versus 2,045.
100 See *DG*, doc. 87 (p. 146: Ukraine), doc. 92 (p. 151: Moscow).
101 A. Saranin, *Child of the Kulaks* (St Lucia, 1997), pp. 126–31.
102 B. Sokolov, 'O material'noi kul'ture v detskom dome', *Detskii dom* 3 (1928), 59.
103 Vydrin (no first name given), 'Kakim dolzhen byt' detskii dom', *DD* 1 (1932), 19–21.
104 On Home No. 3, see see *DD* 5 (1930), 10–11; for the opposite case, Z. Tyumina in *Detskii dom: uroki proshlogo*, pp. 20–53.

105 'Shubin priemnik', *DD* 1 (1928), 17.
106 Drs N. Shvar and V. Narvsky, 'O podrostkakh, vypuskaemykh iz detskikh domov v zhizn'', *Detskii dom* 2 (1928), 30 (diseases), 33 (hunger).
107 D. Futer, 'K voprosu o tipologii trudno-vospituemykh detei', *Detskii dom* 1 (1928), 29.
108 As recalled by Z. Tyumina in *Detskii dom: uroki proshlogo* (M., 1990), pp. 20–53.
109 See Voinov for an account of doing this.
110 S. Murzin, 'O rabotnike detskogo doma', *Detskii dom* 1 (1928), 78–9.
111 K. Savchenko, 'V Prezidiume Detkomissii VTsIK: O rabote zdravorganov po obsluzhivaniyu detuchrezhdenii', *Sbornik po voprosam okhrany detstva* ... 1 (1932), 4.
112 Voinov, p. 19.
113 Cf. the discussion of fostering at a meeting of the Krasnaya Presnya Communist Party Women's Section, 27 June 1923, TsAODM f. 69 op. 1 d. 172, l. 33. On the general subject of adoption and fostering, see L. Bernstein, 'The Evolution of Soviet Adoption Law', *Journal of Family History* 22:2 (1997), 204–26.
114 Goldman, p. 92.
115 See Stevens, p. 244. A slightly different figure is given by Goldman, p. 91 n. 94: 79 per cent peasants and working-class, but the proportion of 15 per cent white-collar workers tallies in both cases.
116 V. Pavlovsky, 'O patronate detei rannego detskogo vozrasta v Moskve i Moskovskoi gubernii', *BNKZ* 13 (1928), 60–4.
117 See *ENKP* 8 May 1926, p. 5; Utevsky, *Bor'ba s detskoi besprizornost'yu*, p. 18; Goldman, p. 97.
118 Goldman, pp. 97–100.
119 A. T., 'Protiv patronata', *DD* 9 (1930), 21.
120 'Nashi udarniki', *DD* 4 (1932), 29.
121 *DG*. doc. 105, p. 176.
122 A. T., 'Protiv patronata', 21, asserted that foster children were generally overworked and denied a chance to continue their schooling, basing her case on two individual negative experiences (Zhenya T., aged 15, Nina L., aged 15). On 25 November 1935, the use of *opeka* for selfish reasons, e.g. the acquisition of extra living space, was outlawed, and a sentence of three years imposed (*Ugolovnyi kodeks RSFSR* (M., 1953), article 158¹.
123 See S. S. Tikhanov and M. S. Epshtein, *Gosudarstvo i obshchestvennost' v bor'be s detskoi besprizornost'yu* (M., 1927), pp. 17–18.
124 See *ENKP* 28 May 1926, p. 2, pp. 3–6; 6 April 1928, pp. 18–19; 1 February 1930; 15 February 1937, pp. 7–8.
125 *ENKP* 6 April 1928, pp. 18–19.
126 Pavlovsky, 'O patronate', 62, 64. On eagerness to foster (here in Novgorod province), see Striedter 'Erinnerungen', extract 6, p. 2.
127 Oxf/Lev P–05 PF28A, pp. 5–7. On being driven out, see p. 2. This woman was eventually collected by her father, after she wrote him a letter, and lived at home till 1937, when her father was arrested for the second time, and she altered the date on her passport so as to be able to find work, pretending she was 14 (p. 9). For similar recollections – the orphanage as infinitely preferable to a life of begging on the family's

behalf as a 4-year old, and as generally offering reasonable living conditions, with decent food (except during the war), reasonable clothes, and good treatment; apart from one sadistic supervisor (though all had to work hard on the orphanage allotment) – see Oxf/Lev P–05 PF17A–B.
128 Kufaev, *Yunye pravonarushiteli*, p. 76.
129 TsGA f. 2552 op. 1 d. 2918, l. 5. Such attitudes were often coupled with a pious belief that, in time, children's institutions would simply wither away: see e.g. *Informatsionnyi byulleten' Leningradskogo gubernskogo otdela narodnogo obrazovaniya* 17 (1925), 4.
130 *DSV*, vol. 1, no. 223.
131 TsGA f. 2554 op. 2 d. 27, ll. 28–9, sets out these rules.
132 Kufaev, *Yunye pravonarushiteli*, pp. 43–5 (arrangements for assessment by the Commission), p. 46 (exceptional cases sent to courts), p. 48 (crimes committed by children not 'crimes'), pp. 71–2 (Tatar boy).
133 See e.g. ibid., pp. 21–2. There were some commentators who even thought the term 'moral defectiveness' was 'ideologically unsound' as it pathologised proletarian children, and preferred to see the situation in terms of pure environmentalism: see e.g. *Bor'ba s besprizornost'yu: Materialy Pervoi moskovskoi konferentsii po bor'be s besprizornost'yu 16–17 marta 1924 g.* (M., 1924), esp. the speech by P. I. Blonsky, pp. 11–18.
134 *DSV*, vol. 7, no. 167, pp. 300–4.
135 See D. Caroli, 'L'Assistance sociale à la déliquance juvénile dans la Russie soviétique des années 20', *Cahiers du monde russe* 40/3 (1999), 398–400.
136 Caroli, 'L'Enfance abandonée', p. 121.
137 Ibid., p. 140. This book contains useful archive material on the history of the commissions generally: see also pp. 119–21, 132–3.
138 See report of 29 March 1920, TsGA f. 254 op. 1 d. 31, l. 142.
139 Figures from Goldman, p. 82, table 2.
140 See Potalak (no first name given), 'Novaya zhizn', *Detskii dom* 3 (1932), 54–8. This type of 'conversion myth' remained in force throughout the Stalin era too. A 1949 official life of the war hero Aleksandr Matrosov repeated the patterns of the 'conversion narrative', representing the young 'Sashka's' deprived childhood and time spent in a penal colony as 'character education'. At first Sashka had been rude and rough, but the colony had taught him to be 'steadfast in achieving his ends, tidy and clean in daily life and sensitive towards his comrades'. Irked to begin with by the demands made on him by the supervisors, he had come to recognise them as beneficial, and his devotion to the motherland had been such that he had enlisted the moment war began. P. Zhurba, *Geroi Sovetskogo Soyuza Aleksandr Matrosov* (M., 1949), pp. 8–21 (quotation p. 14).
141 *DG*, doc. 13.
142 *DG*, doc. 28.
143 *DG*, doc. 29.
144 *DG*, docs 56, 61, 76.
145 Lev Razgon, *Plen v svoem otechestve* (M., 1999), p. 255.
146 'Imennoi spisok vospitannikov, vospitannits

"Doma dlya nravstvenno-defektivnykh detei No. 1'", 16 July 1918, TsGA f. 2554 op. 1 d. 33, l. 6.

147 Segalov, 'Deti-brodyagi', 88.

148 Ozerov in Kaidanova (ed.), *Besprizornye deti*, p. 60.

149 Anon. ibid., p. 71.

150 Mariya Belkina, 'Arina's Children', in Fitzpatrick and Slezkine, p. 232.

151 Natal'ya Noskova (b. 1928), remembering her orphanage in Bogoslovsk in February 1933. Bazarov, *Durelom*, vol. 1, pp. 322–3.

152 Kaidanova (ed.), *Besprizornye deti*, p. 60, p. 67.

153 *ENKP* 10 April 1925, pp. 6–9.

154 See *BME*, vol. 8, col. 72, 'Detskii dom'.

155 V. Kufaer, 'I togi vypuska vospitateki iz detskikhdanov', *Detsküdom* 2 (1928), 93.

156 Oxf/Lev SPb.–02, PF6–A, 17 November 2002, p. 19.

157 Voinov, p. 104 on food; p. 106 on Stalin. For an account from a later generation of giving orphanage food to schoolmates, see Oxf/Lev P–05 PF29A, p. 8. Cf. Oxf/Lev V–05 PF8B, p. 8: '[The orphanage children] did stand out among the locals [in a Novgorod province village]. They were much better dressed, their clothes were really good. And as for us ... others, well our father was in work, and he had the money so Mam could buy us some material and so on, herself ... earlier you got this "devil's skin" [*chertova kozha*], she'd make a suit herself, with her own hands. But they had bought stuff, stuff that had been made at the factory – dresses for the girls and suits for the boys. So they probably were better dressed, and as for food – they were fed much better, always. They had meat in their rations, it was all strict,

everything was for them [...] they were just better off than us.'

158 See M. N. Gernet in Kufaev, *Yunye pravona-rushiteli*, p. 7.

159 The most sensational example is Germany under the Third Reich, on which see Nicholas Stargardt, *Witnesses of War* (London, 2005), ch. 3. On abuse in British children's homes, see L. Abrams, *The Orphan Country* (Edinburgh, 1998), p. 103, p. 110, p. 202. Corporal punishment was not formally regulated in Scottish orphanages until 1918 (ibid., p. 103), and even then only a limited number of strikes to the hand or 'posterior' was permitted. Several informants on 'A Pocket Full of Posies', BBC2 Television, 13 July 2001, a historical documentary about childhood in the early twentieth century, gave appalling accounts of life in workhouses and orphanages during the first decades of the twentieth century. One woman remembered being placed in a geriatric ward of the workhouse; another, committed to an orphanage in the early 1920s, remembered that the staff were obsessed with physical and emotional hygiene. She and her twin sister, then aged six or seven, were split up and placed in different dormitories, and when the informant requested permission to visit the lavatory she was denied this; on further requests, she was thrashed by a nurse, and then, when she lost control of her bowels during the thrashing, had her face rubbed in her own faeces.

160 On these points see Abrams, *The Orphan Country*, pp. 96–8.

Chapter 7: Children of the State, 1935–1953

1 *ENKP* 10 July 1935 p. 1, item 349.

2 *ENKP* 8 (1940), pp. 13–14, decree of 14 April 1940.

3 On such a 'log-jam' in 1938, see *ENKP* 15 October 1938, p. 10, item 300.

4 On transfers, see *ENKP* 8 (1940), pp. 13–14. For a critique of inflexibility at a later period, see Zoya Svetova, 'Gosudarstvennye deti', *Russkaya mysl'* 4262 (18–24 March 1999), 11. A. Solzhenitsyn, 'Maloletki', *Arkhipelag GULag*, vol. 2 (Paris, 1974), p. 453, records the case of Zoya Leshcheva, who was transferred from an ordinary orphanage to a home for 'defective' children after being branded as a 'trouble-maker'.

5 *EKNP* 1 January 1936, p. 15. For movement 'downwards' into invalid homes, cf. the criticism of 'dustbinning' of the more difficult cases of mental handicap in Ministry of Social Welfare homes in E. Ustinova and G. Bagaeva, 'Za oshibkoi – sud'ba rebenka', *SO* 1 (1989), 27–8, which estimates that 10 per cent of the population of the invalid homes, or 3,500 children, came into this category.

6 See 'Polozhenie o detskikh priemnikakh raspredelitelyakh NKVD' (1945), *Deti GuLaga*, pp. 436–42.

7 Oxf/Lev SPb.–03 PF10A, p. 9, recalls a new director 'who was connected with the NKVD somehow. To be honest, I didn't like her. The kind

of lady she was ... she enjoyed bawling out the nannies [auxiliary supervisors]. She left us alone, she knew we were from the RONO, and so ... Well, teachers were supposed to know everything. But she liked bawling in this dictatorial way ... everyone came in for it.' The main work this informant records was *sanobrabotka* (p. 10). Better experiences were remembered by Zinaida Tyumina, who worked at the Saratov station in Moscow in 1930–31, and who was lucky enough to have an intelligent and humane director, but Tyumina also remembered that his predecessor, and the other staff, had been rough and much disliked by the children under their care (see the account of her experiences by her daughter Sof'ya Tyumina in *Detskii dom: uroki proshlogo* (M., 1990), p. 20).

8 One notes also the adoption of charity-style activities by state institutions: for example, Dzerzhinsky's Children's Commission raised funds through the sales of cigarettes, tobacco, and matches: Caroli, p. 58. A due on stamps was also payable for the support of *besprizornye*: see *SURRKhP* 70 (1926), 553.

9 Unlike Obshchestvennitsa, the women's soviets have not been the subject of much scholarly attention. Genia Browning, 'The Zhensovety Revisited', in M. Buckley (ed.), *Perestroika and Soviet Women* (Cambridge, 1992), pp. 97–117,

contains some brief remarks on the history of these organisations.

10 Documents in RGASPI f. 74 op. 1 d. 425 contain details of meetings, reports about the orphanage's work, etc.

11 *ENKP* 10 November 1934, p. 9, no. 571. On *Road Into Life* as the last *besprizornyi* movie, see M. Turovskaia, 'The Tastes of Soviet Moviegoers during the 1930s', in T. Lahusen with G. Kuperman (eds), *Late Soviet Culture* (Durham, 1993), p. 99.

12 A. Makarenko, *Pedagogicheskaya poema* (M., 1944), p. 564.

13 Ibid., p. 41, p. 612.

14 Ibid., p. 409 (*nakhal*), pp. 181–2 (highway robbery), p. 309 (pigsty), p. 206 (village girls).

15 *Pravda*, 1 June 1935, p. 1. The standard translation of the decree's title oversimplifies somewhat: the Russian in fact reads, 'O likvidatsii besprizornosti i beznadzornosti', i.e. child homelessness and lack of parental supervision: for more on this distinction, see Chapter 6.

16 See above, pp. 197–8.

17 See A. Kopylenko, 'Komnata pionerskogo forposta', *Pravda* 31 March 1935, p. 3. The precise phrasing of the original is 'Nado delat' tak, chtoby ulitsa stala tol'ko bol'shevitskoi'.

18 *SYu* 20 (1935), 21.

19 *ENKP* 10 August 1934, p. 3 (order of 10 May 1934).

20 *SYu* 20 (1934), 22.

21 'Poryadok peredachi detei na vospitanie (patronat) v sem'i trudyashchikhsya', *SYu* 23 (1936), 18. L. Prozorov, 'Kak patronirovat' detei-sirot', *Voprosy sotsial'nogo obespecheniya* 9 (1940), 9, celebrates some model foster families (one where a woman's foster children had ended up in the Red Army), and suggests that, in the best circumstances, families could still rely on material support: a mother in Voronezh with several foster children was receiving 17 kg. of flour, 3 kg. of coarse semolina (*krupa*), 1 kg. of oil and butter, and 16 kg. of potatoes along with her cash subsidy. The food was probably more useful than the cash, which amounted to no more than a tenth of even the lowest monthly wage packet of the day (say £60 in today's money).

22 A. Bazarov, *Durelom* (Kurgan, 1997), vol. 1, p. 391.

23 For the figure of 19,000, see p. 212 above: Goldman, p. 93, states that less than half the total *besprizornye* population of 300,000 in 1926 was housed in orphanages, giving an estimate of say 140,000.

24 On supportive care in Scotland, see L. Abrams, *The Orphan Country* (Edinburgh, 1998), pp. 168–9.

25 For one of the occasional voices questioning institutionalisation, see S. Kopelyanskaya, 'Sud i okhrana detei', *SYu* 2 (1936), 10, which suggests it might be better to place abandoned children with a living relative, e.g. a grandmother, and make an alimony order.

26 *Sanitarnye pravila dlya detskikh uchrezhdenii* (2nd, corrected edn; L., 1940), pp. 21–6.

27 TsGA RSFSR [GARF] f. 1575 op. 6 d. 4, l. 86, cited here from Ball, p. 94.

28 By 1932, the 'culture of blame' was well ensconced. Vilification was sometimes excited by inertia rather than by stepping out of line (see e.g. the report on the trial of six orphanage workers in Ivanovo province publicised in *Sbornik po voprosam okhrany detstva* 7–8 (1932), 46–7, but cases of excess initiative, such as the use of capital punishment, were also lambasted (see ibid., 5–6 (1932), p. 47).

29 *ENKP* 8 (1940), pp. 3–4. No figures are given by this source for earlier periods, but the frequent calls for more staff training (e.g. 20 January 1931, p. 8, no. 52), are some indication of the size of the problem.

30 *Spravochnik sovetskogo rabotnika* (M., 1937), p. 816.

31 KPSTsK 1935–40, l. 60.

32 Igor' Zolotussky in *Rossiya molodaya: XX vek* (M., 1998), p. 412. NB this reminiscence is not first hand: Zolotussky joined Home No. 3 only in 1941.

33 Misha Nikolaev, *Detdom* (NY, 1985).

34 Anon, 'Na bor'bu s beznadzornost'yu detei', *SYu* 19 (1935), 15. Conversely, Viola, p. 58, describes an orphanage for kulak children, inspected in 1934, where mange was widespread and diet poor, but where there does not appear to have been actual brutality. Archival documents from Stalinsk (Novokuznetsk) paint a similar picture: 1926: 'filth, disorder, windows and doors wide open, the supervisors sometimes drunk'; 1933: 300 children in home with space for 100, 275 children without footwear, no sheets, food shortages, practically no supervision, and more and more children arriving; 1937: children two to a bed, verbal abuse from supervisors. (See V. Bedin, M. Kushnikova and V. Togulev, *Kemerovo i Stalinsk*, Kemerovo, 1999, p. 384, p. 389, p. 440.) For similar stories, see Siegelbaum and Sokolov, pp. 389–93.

35 Makarenko, *Pedagogicheskaya poema*, p. 39.

36 Vsevolod Sablin, 'Detskii dom No. 32', *Vozhatyi* 12 (1949), 25–9.

37 See V. Leongard [W. Leonhard], *Revolyutsiya otvergaet svoikh detei* (London, 1984), pp. 57–8. Before entering this home, Leonhard had spent several years in a special orphanage for the children of Austrian *Schutzbündler* (members of the Social Democratic Defence Organisation), where conditions were totally different: inmates' clothing was made in special workshops, they had an Austrian cook and a clinic, music lessons and a theatre club, as well as a wonderful library (though even here books were subject to censorship – foreign publications had suspect material blacked out to make it unreadable).

38 Voinov, pp. 100–2.

39 See 'U khoroshego zava – khoroshii detskii dom', *DD* 1 (1933), 14–16. The item is purely anecdotal, but the tone here is instructively different from a review of *Putevka v zhizn'* published only a year earlier, *DD* 7 (1931), 27, which criticises the film for placing too much emphasis on the orphanage director's individual achievements. For the official line, see *ENKP* 1 September 1935, pp. 15–16.

40 See O. N. Lyubchenko, 'Arbat 30, kvartira 58', *Istochnik* 5–6 (1993), 30, 32. Cf. the story in Oxf/Lev SPb.–04 PF58B, p. 89, about taking a

child from the Dom rebenka to the orphanage: as the child prattled brightly about being 'off to the orphanage', 'everyone in the tram carriage was in tears' (*ves' vagon plakal*).

41 See e.g. V. Tadevosyan, writing in *SYu* 31 (1935), 44.

42 *Pravda* 8 April 1935, p. 1.

43 Voinov was able to keep in touch with his old gang even at the end of the 1930s: pp. 182–5, pp. 195–7. Minor offences against public order, such as busking, also persisted into the 1930s: see e.g. D. Granin, *Leningradskii dnevnik* (L., 1986), p. 33.

44 On the February 1940 report, see *DG*, doc. 186, pp. 327–8.

45 'Vtoraya godovshchina zakona 7 aprelya 1935', *SYu* 7 (1937), 19.

46 S. Potravnov, 'Imushchestvennye prestupleniya nesovershennoletnikh', *SYu* 8 (1938), 12.

47 On this measure, see V. Tadevos'yan, 'Bor'ba za likvidatsiyu detskoi prestupnosti v SSSR', *SZ* 5 (1945), 8.

48 Goldman, p. 327. It is certainly true that expansion of the dedicated reformatory system was under severe budgetary constraints: for example, the 15 July 1943 order 'On the Intensification of the Struggle with Child Homelessness' ('Ob usilenii mer bor'by s detskoi besprizornost'yu') stipulated that the money for expanding the colony network was to be found in the budget already allocated to the NKVD (*DG*, doc. 225, p. 384).

49 On reluctance to adopt, see Ball, p. 147; to employ, ibid., pp. 186–7.

50 On the latter, see Makarenko, *Pedagogicheskaya poema*, p. 43. Villagers' hostility was partly the result of aggressive behaviour by orphanage and colony inmates. Cf. Shefner's accounts of fights with the local village boys (insults of 'Orphanage rats' – *priyutskie krysy* – and 'Free toads' – *vol'nye zhaby* – would be exchanged) (*Imya dlya ptitsy*, in his *Lachuga dolzhnika* (SPb., 1995), p. 413), and Makarenko's accounts of the same (pp. 116–17).

51 For criticisms of hasty and slow processing, see 'Kak v Tomske sumeli izvratit' postanovlenie pravitel'stva 7.iv.1935', *SYu* 29 (1935), p. 40; on grim premises, see I Budovnits, 'V narodnom sude po delam o nesovershennoletnikh prestupnikakh', *SYu* 8 (1938), 18–19; on tactful interrogation, see 'Taktika doprosa', *SYu* 20 (1936), p. 18; on special chambers, see 'Vo Vsesoyuznom Institute yuridicheskikh nauk', *SYu* 1 (1937), pp. 34–6.

52 P. Solomon, *Soviet Criminal Justice under Stalin* (Cambridge, 1996), pp. 204–5.

53 'Vo Vsesoyuznom Institute yuridicheskikh nauk', 35. See also Solomon, *Soviet Criminal Justice*, p. 206.

54 On the vicissitudes of the chambers – which in any case only ever operated in certain major cities, such as Moscow, Leningrad, and Khar'kov – see Solomon, *Soviet Criminal Justice*, p. 208.

55 Ibid., p. 197.

56 *DG*, doc. 56, p. 96.

57 *DG*, doc. 187, p. 331.

58 *DG*, does not include any number breakdowns for the 1930s, but the figure of 50 colonies,

1,200 staff, and 25,000 inmates per year allows the composition of this average (see doc. 187, pp. 331–2).

59 *DG*, doc. 142, pp. 240–1.

60 *DG*, doc. 173, p. 311.

61 *DG*, doc. 115, pp. 195–7 (quotation here p. 195).

62 *DG*, doc. 167, p. 301 (purpose), p. 302 (work norms), pp. 303–4 (committees), p. 305 (camp property, forbidden activities).

63 *DG*, doc. 175, pp. 313–15.

64 'Polozhenie o trudovoi kolonii NKVD dlya nesovershennoletnikh', 1 March 1940, *DG*, doc. 188, pp. 332–8.

65 See e.g. ibid., p. 337.

66 Our evidence for the existence of an order to this effect comes from a late period of camp history (informant in Oxf/Lev P-05 PF1A, p. 2, who worked in a colony during the late 1980s and early 1990s), but the statistics from earlier eras confirm that such an order must have been in existence during the 1930s and 1940s: rates of escape could not have been so high if guards had been able to shoot those trying to get away. In the 1980s, camps responded to the problem with strict regulations about how to handle an escape – local transport nodes would be cut off and a guard set up at the young offender's home address (Oxf/Lev P-05 PF1A, p. 6). It is reasonable to suppose that these measures also operated in earlier decades, though it was no doubt easier to escape completely in wartime or at other times of social crisis.

67 See e.g. the criticism of the Ul'yanovsk labour colony in an NKVD order of 29 December 1937: 'kul'turno-massovaya i politiko-vospitatel'naya rabota sredi vospitannikov pochti otsutstvuet', *DG*, doc. 142, p. 240.

68 *DG*, doc. 16, p. 16 (16 April 1921).

69 *DG*, doc. 114, p. 194. Moscow was the only city with a special remand prison for juveniles, on Shabolovka.

70 *DG*, doc. 288, p. 363.

71 See the petition to E. P. Peshkova, 19 December 1929, *DG*, doc. 38, pp. 74–5. The anthology does not record whether this appeal was successful.

72 See the case records at doc. 160, *DG* pp. 283–93.

73 Zh. Rossi, *Spravochnik po Gulagu* (London, 1987), p. 200. Solomon, *Soviet Criminal Justice*, p. 206, argues that the convictions of children under 12 were usually cancelled on appeal; but that required their getting to appeal in the first place. As Rossi points out, 'often, a little thief of 8–10 will conceal his or her address and the name of his or her parents, and the police won't make a fuss: they'll just write down "age about twelve" in the records, and that allows a judge to send a child to the camps quite "legally"' (p. 199). Criticisms of this type of practice in the legal press provide confirmation of Rossi's allegations.

74 See e.g. Rossi, *Spravochnik*, p. 199. This is borne out by official Soviet sources too, e.g. an article in *SYu* 7 (1937), 19, castigating the courts for sloppiness on this point.

75 See Rossi, *Spravochnik*, Supplement 1, pp. 472–3.

76 L. Razgon, *Plen v svoem otechestve* (M., 1999), p. 256.

77 *DG*, doc. 258, p. 428.

78 See the memoir of I. A. Dubova, *DG*, doc. 143, p. 252.

79 On the terms ChSVN [Chlen sem'i vraga naroda], ChSIR [Chlen sem'i izmennika rodiny], and ChSR [Chlen sem'i repressirovannogo], see Rossi, *Spravochnik*, p. 42. Conviction as a ChSVN carried a sentence of 5–8 years in 1936–9, and 10 years in 1939–40; as a ChSIR, 10 years in 'ordinary' (*obshchie*) camps in 1942–3, 15–20 years in hard labour camps (*katorga*) in 1943–46, and 10–25 years in *spetslageri*, or prison, in 1947–53. On the use of article 7 of the 1926 Criminal Code, see Veselaya in S. Vilensky, *Till My Tale is Told* (Bloomington, IN, 1999), p. 302, describing how she was arrested under this article. On the importance of 'milieu' rather than blood relationship in applying the legislation, see Rossi, *Spravochnik*, p. 246.

80 For the decree, see see *KhSZUP*, vol. 2 (M., 1959), p. 332: 1934 decree on the need to take into care. On the need to provide for young dependants of suspects in custody and convicts, see 'O poryadke ustroistva detei lits, nakhodyashchikhsya pod strazhei', *SYu* 2 (1935), 24, and 'Ob obyazatel'nom rassmotrenii sudami i prokurorami voprosa o polozhenii detei, ostavayushchikhsya posle aresta ili osuzhdenii roditelei', *SYu* 29 (1936), 24.

81 'Operativnyi prikaz Narodnogo Komissara Vnutrennikh Del SSSR No. 00485', 15 August 1937, *DG*, doc. 139, pp. 234–9.

82 Cf. the account of G. M. Rykova, *DG*, doc. 144, pp. 256–7, about how the NKVD took her and her sister away from their grandmother by trickery (a car that was supposed to take them to school dropped them off at the Danilov Reception Centre in Moscow).

83 As in the case of Boris Trapezontsev, the 14-year-old author of a pathetic petition pleading for the return of his mother from exile: see GARF f. 7523 op. 23 d. 200, ll. 1–2, quoted in Siegelbaum and Sokolov, p. 415. No information is given as to whether this petition was successful, but the fact that it survives in a handwritten copy (documents passed higher up the hierarchical chain were retyped) suggests that no action was taken.

84 One such case is reported in *SZ* 4 (1950), 61. It is notable, though, that this involved a legal minor whose mother had been imprisoned under section 162 of the Criminal Code (theft). It is extremely doubtful whether the son or daughter of a person imprisoned under article 58 (political subversion etc.) would have dared to mount such a challenge, let alone won the case. In 1940, the response to a suit brought by E. N. Zhukova against S. N. Zakharova established that orphanage inmates were not entitled to a claim on their family's living space if this had been removed from the family in any case – which, obviously, indicated in reverse that they *were* entitled to such living space in other circumstances (e.g. if it had been sealed up, but not reassigned). (*SYu* 15 (1941), 29.)

85 On 'family members of enemies of the people' as waifs, see e.g. *DG*, doc. 145, p. 262.

86 See the survivor memoirs in *DG*, doc. 143, pp. 241–51, esp. N. N. Smirnova (p. 245:

orphanage in camp zone, children forage on rubbish tips for food, beaten and made to kneel in corner for hours); S. N. Kogteva (p. 247, beaten, ordered to forget parents – this in a reception centre); E. A. Grabovskaya (p. 250, Pioneer leader keeps saying 'apples never fall far from the tree'). N. S. Cherushev, *Dorogoi nash tovarishch Stalin! ... i drugie tovarishchi* (M., 2001), includes some comparable material.

87 As happened to Aleksei Petrovsky, son of the Comintern official Max Petrovsky and the British Communist Rosa Cohen, both purged in 1937. Petrovsky later vehemently assured his British cousin that his parents had definitely not been Trotskyists, which she, no doubt rightly, saw as evidence that Soviet ideology had made an impact (the belief that the term 'Trotskyist' was meaningful had taken hold) (Francis Beckett, *Stalin's British Victims*, Stroud, 2004, pp. 137–8).

88 For instance, when L. M. Konstenko and her brother ran away from their orphanage, they were accused of having made an attempt to join the 'spy ring' with which they and their mother were supposed to be associated. *DG*, doc. 143, p. 251.

89 See *DG*, doc. 171 (pp. 308–9), a report by Nikolai Semashko (in his capacity as the head of Detkom) from 29 September 1938 about an orphanage in Buisk, where the inmates had set up a society. Eating sand and drinking manure water were required as an initiation ritual, and the society's alleged activities included tearing down portraits of the leaders. Semashko's recommendation was that orphanages should no longer be comprised purely of family members of enemies of the people.

90 As e.g. in the case of M. K. Sandratskaya's son, who went deaf in one ear after a beating from fellow inmates because he refused to participate in stealing. *DG*, doc. 148, p. 264. For an analysis of the fate of children of 'enemies of the people', based on the cases of Vladimir Moroz and Galina Rykova, see C. Kuhr, 'Kinder von "Volksfeinden" als Opfer des stalinistischen Terrors', in S. Plaggenborg (ed.), *Stalinismus* (Berlin, 1998), pp. 391–418.

91 See the memoir of A. Semenova, *DG*, doc. 153, pp. 273–5.

92 As in the case of L. M. Kostenko and her brother, who did all they could to be troublesome (*navredit'*) in order to avenge the arrest of their mother. *DG*, doc. 143, p. 251.

93 *DG*, doc. 163, pp. 296–7.

94 *DG*, doc. 19, p. 41 (Ratner letter); *DG*, doc. 4, p. 22 (numbers of children), p. 19 (order to release minors).

95 Vilensky (ed.), *Till My Tale is Told*, photographs, p. 39, suppression of letters, p. 205. However, women *were* allowed to receive letters from their families: cf. A. Federol'f, 'Ryadom s Alei', in A. Efron and A. Federol'f, *Ryadom s Alei. Miroedikha* (M., 1996), p. 219, about mothers crying over these and reducing the whole cell to weeping when they read them out.

96 Vilensky (ed.), *Till My Tale is Told*, p. 99.

97 See the extract from M. K. Sandratskaya, 'Deti na etape', *DG*, doc. 148, p. 262. Sandratskaya's

particular group was fortunate because they were advised by a doctor of the need to keep infants at the breast all the time to ensure adequate nutrition, and because desperation fostered camaraderie: 'Misery brought us together. We were like one big orphaned, condemned family ...' (ibid.)

98 On the amnesties, see *DG*, doc. 250, p. 426, *DG*, doc. 279, p. 477 (this latter amnesty contains a longer and more complex list of excluded categories, running through counter-revolutionary offences, banditry, premeditated murder and violent crime (*razboi*), theft of socialist property, if a repeat offence, committed in participation with a group, or involving property to a significant value).

99 *Sbornik uzakonenii RSFSR*, articles 46, 57: quoted by Rossi, *Spravochnik*, p. 100.

100 Rules of 1938 specified a nine-month access period, but this was reduced to six months the following year. For information about this, and access regulations, based on confidential documents of April 1938 and November 1939 held in GARF, see Emma Mason, 'Women in the Gulag in the 1930s', in M. Ilic (ed.), *Women in the Stalin Era* (Basingstoke, 2001), pp. 141–4. Rossi, *Spravochnik*, p. 201, gives the time allowed for nursing as 12 months, so there was presumably a change in the rules after the war.

101 See Mason, 'Women in the Gulag', p. 141, for this point.

102 See 'Prikaz NKVD SSSR No. 0457: S ob"yavleniem instruktsii po sanitarnoi sluzhbe tyurem NKVD SSSR', *DG*, doc. 194, pp. 343–5.

103 Hava Volovich in Vilensky, *Till My Tale is Told*, pp. 262–3. Some of this was of course matched in crèches in the 'free' world – see Chapter 9 below – but it seems reasonable to assume that nurses in camp crèches would have been more likely to treat their supervisees with outright contempt.

104 See N. A. Ioffe, *Vremya nazad* (an extract appears in *DG*, doc. 151, p. 270).

105 *DG*, doc. 174, pp. 312–13.

106 See F. Treivas in *Zhenskaya sud'ba v Rossii* (M., 1994), pp. 93–6.

107 See *DG*, doc. 148, p. 263.

108 See e.g. the memoir of A. L. Voitolovskaya, *DG*, doc. 180, pp. 319–20.

109 *DG*, doc. 148, p. 264.

110 Vilensky (ed.), *Till My Tale is Told*, p. 263.

111 For a particularly vivid description of the activities of the *maloletki* (under-age prisoners), see Solzhenitsyn, *Arkhipelag GULaga*, vol. 2, pp. 334–54. See also Rossi, *Spravochnik*, pp. 198–200; Razgon, *Plen*, pp. 255–7, laconically presents the polarisation between victimisation and exploitation.

112 Work by orphanage inspectors to round up blockade children: S. Kotov, *Detskie doma blokadnago Leningrada* (SPB., 2002), p. 27; Oxf/Lev SPb.–03 PF10A, p. 7.

113 RGASPI f. 17 op. 126 d. 39, l. 46. For a detailed breakdown of these figures, see digital version of this book, Chapter 7.

114 M. Zoshchenko, *Izbrannoe* (L., 1981), pp. 239–42.

115 Of course, the British billeting situation had its

negative side too, widely reported in literature and memoirs. See *The Children's War*, comp. J. Gardiner in association with the Imperial War Museum (London, 2005); S. Goodman, *Children of War* (London, 2005). In Germany, on the other hand, children tended to be evacuated to camps, if at all: see N. Stargardt, *Witnesses of War* (London, 2005), pp. 50–1, p. 294.

116 See *KhSZUP*, vol. 3, p. 328. Fostering was also one of the official nominated destinations of 'graduates' from Ministry of Health baby homes: see *Ukazanie po obsluzhivaniyu detei v domakh rebenka*, ed. L. V. Grechishnikova (M., 1949), pp. 98–110.

117 Harwin, p. 22.

118 See e.g. 'Sovetskaya sem'ya', *O* 45 (1942), 6–7.

119 On the regulations in the later period, see e.g. G. M. Sverdlov, *Sovetskoe semeinoe pravo* (M., 1958), pp. 239–47, pp. 258–64. Information about how well the schemes worked is hard to come by, but material about administrative regulations already suggests that fostering, in particular, was rather badly thought out in some respects. In the Russian Federation (as opposed to Ukraine), foster parents took charge of a child only until it was 14 years old, after which an independent existence was required; and, though the 1936 decree lost its force in the post-war era, it was not replaced by any overall measures clarifying the status of foster parents (whether these were officially 'guardians' or not). (See Sverdlov, *Sovetskoe semeinoe pravo*, p. 260, p. 262.)

120 *DG*, doc. 218, pp. 376–7.

121 'Postanovlenie SNK SSSR: Ob uluchshenii raboty detskikh domov', 1 September 1943, *DG*, doc. 228, pp. 390–1; 'Instruktsiya Narkomprosa', 29 August 1944, *DG*, doc. 245, pp. 413–14.

122 *KPSS v rezolyutsiyakh i resheniyakh s"ezdov, konferentsii, i plenumov TsK* (8th edn; 15 vols; M., 1970–84), vol. 6, pp. 98–104.

123 'Postanovlenie SM SSSR: Ob uluchshenii raboty po ustroistvu detei i podrostkov, ostavshikhsya bez roditelei', 25 April 1947, *DG*, no. 270, pp. 466–7.

124 Quoted (without a source citation) in E. V. Taranov, 'Synov'ya neba', *MPV*, p. 628. The rest of Taranov's piece, pp. 627–9, gives a brief anecdotal history of the school and its inmates.

125 Though Bertha Mannick, *Everyday Life in Russia* (London, 1938), pp. 124–5, cites a Tatar *besprizornyi* who was now a successful young musician. However, the emphasis during the 1920s was on the transformation of 'social defectives' into useful workers. See e.g. Gorky's statement that the penal colonies in the USSR had turned hardened young criminals into 'thousands' of skilled workers and 'hundreds' of agronomists, doctors, and technicians: 'O vospitanii pravdoi', *Pravda* 5 August 1933 (*SS* vol. 27, p. 61).

126 'Rasporyazhenie Narodnogo komissariata stankos- troeniya SSSR sekretaryu Partbyuro zavoda "Krasnyi proletarii" t. Elkinu ob organizatsii pri zavode detskogo doma', TsAODM f. 412 op. 1 d. 182, l. 5, *MPV*, p. 608. Oxf/Lev T–04 PF22–3 is an account of life at an orphanage run by the combine harvest factory in Taganrog in the early 1950s.

127 GARF f. 8009 op. 21 d.73, l. 16 (the individual figures were 15 in Krasnodar, 16 in Rostov, 9 in Stavropol). Another privileged category of children, the offspring of soldiers and officers in the Red Army and of partisans, were also admitted to these institutions.

128 See N. Vostokova, 'Return Them Their Childhood', *Anglo-Soviet Journal* 7: 3 (1946), 38–43. No Russian source is given.

129 *Rukovodstvo dlya meditsinskogo personala detskikh domov* (M., 1953), pp. 294–312.

130 See Ol'ga Grechina's fascinating and stark memoir of life as an orphanage supervisor during the Blockade, 'Spasayus' spasaya', part 2, 'Skazki o gorokhovom dereve (1942–1944 gg.)' (L., 1978–81). (Maria Osorina, personal archive.)

131 Kotov, *Detskie doma*, p. 16.

132 Both are described in Grechina's 'Spasayus' spasaya', part 2, p. 6 (bureaucratic director), p. 8 (freeloading dignitaries).

133 For the figures, see V. Snegov, Zam. ministra prosveshcheniya RSFSR, 'O sostoyanii raboty po preduprezhdenii detskoi besprizornosti, vospitaniyu detei, ostavshikhsya bez roditelei, i o meropriyatiyakh po dal'neishemu uluchsheniyu etoi raboty', 25 December 1947, RGASPI f. 17 op. 125 d. 559, ll. 145–6.

134 See *BME* (2nd edn), vol. 9, cols 731–2.

135 See *Ukazanie po obsluzhivaniyu detei v domakh rebenka* (M., 1949), p. 5.

136 Snegov, 'O sostoyanii raboty', ll. 145–6.

137 See the very moving description of the anguish of such children in Oxf/Lev SPb.–04 PF57A, pp. 5–6.

138 *DG*, doc. 235, p. 401.

139 GARF f. 8009 op. 21 d. 71, l. 64 (TB), l. 59, l. 61 (soap and bed shortages), ll. 74–80 (bed-sharing, furniture shortages, sometimes no water).

140 GARF f. 8009 op. 21 d. 207, l. 1.

141 Ibid., ll. 1–2.

142 Ibid., l. 12 (the full report, including information about overcrowding, shortages of equipment and bedlinen, inadequate diet, syphilis infection etc., is in ll. 8–17).

143 Ibid., l. 2.

144 RGASPI f. 17 op. 126 d. 39, ll. 48–50. The overall figures were 24,925 places and 15,655 inmates (ibid., l. 50); Leningrad had 1,264 inmates and space for 975 (ibid., l. 49), Pskov 377 and 300 (ibid.), and the Tatar Republic 344 and 335 (l. 48).

145 V. Snegov, l. 147. Zima, *Golod v SSSR 1946–1947 godov* (M., 1996), p. 82, gives a figure of 1–2 abandonments per day in some places (52 in a month in the Crimea, 49 a month in Latvia).

146 M. Zakharov, 'Spravka o sostoyanii detskikh domov, domov rebenka i priemnikov-raspredelitelei v Stalingradskoi oblasti', 17 March 1947', RGASPI f. 17 op. 125 d. 559, l. 22.

147 GARF f. 8009 op. 21 d. 207, l. 87, l. 88.

148 Zakharov,) 'Spravka o sostoyanii detskikh domov, RGASPI f. 17 op. 125 d. 559, ll. 20–8.

149 S. Zinov'ev, 'Dokladnaya zapiska o detskom dome imeni tov. Budennogo, Maslyanskogo raiona, Tyumenskoi oblasti', RGASPI f. 17 op. 125 d. 559, ll. 142–3.

150 *Ukazanie po obsluzhivaniyu*, pp. 13–14.

151 See e.g. the report on the baby home in Stalingrad: Zakharov, 'Spravka o sostoyanii', RGASPI f. 17 op. 125 d. 559, l. 27 (milk), and V. Kinzikeev, 'Otchet o prodelannoi rabote po proverke i okazaniyu pomoshchi detskim domam, domam mladentsev i priemnikam-raspredelitelyam v Bashkirskoi ASSR', ibid., l. 55.

152 See Zima, *Golod*, p. 83.

153 *BME*, vol. 9, col. 732.

154 Oxf/Lev SPb.–04 PF58A, p. 34 (salary), 58B p. 44 (partner pressure).

155 Oxf/Lev SPb.–04 PF57A, p. 12 (contrasts food handling in past and current regulations), 57B p. 17 (regime should work without yelling and regimentation), 57B, p. 13 (*elka* and puppet theatre), p. 18 (give inoculations at doll's tea party), 58B, p. 32 (need for individual treatment).

156 Oxf/Lev SPb.–04 PF57B, p. 21 (ban on 'mama'), p. 36 (no 'spoiling'), p. 37 (scary tests).

157 GARF f. 8009 op. 21 d. 71, l. 54 (better conditions vs. crowding), l. 69 (market garden), ll. 74–80 (problems, including the Omsk situation).

158 Oxf/Lev V–04 PF15A, p. 3.

159 Cf. a statement sent by the director of the Moscow Gorkom Schools' Department in April 1945, which recorded that there had been no proper planning of supply of consumer goods to orphanage workers: some were without footwear other than galoshes. *MPV*, pp. 603–4.

160 Here and below, quotations from Oxf/Lev SPb.–02, PF1A–PF5A.

161 NGPU–04 PF2, p. 1. Cf. also Oxf/Lev T–04 PF16A, 1–3, in which the informant recalls 'the director [...] was like a second mother'. This type of recollection is a topos in interviews from this generation.

162 NGPU–04 PF1, p. 1 (hunger, hobby circles), NGPU–04 PF3, p. 1 (being ground down).

163 Oxf/Lev P–05 PF29A, pp. 2–3, PF29B, p. 17.

164 Oxf/Lev P–05 PF30B, p. 12, p. 19.

165 Oxf/Lev SPb.–02, PF3B, p. 76 (teasing), PF1A, p. 6 (loss of ability to speak).

166 Oxf/Lev SPb.–02, PF8A, p. 16. The informant's sister is said to have witnessed this scene.

167 Oxf/Lev SPb.–02, PF4A, p. 94.

168 As happened to the informant in Oxf/Lev P–05 PF30A, p. 9.

169 For the official line, see e.g. Agniya Barto, *Naiti cheloveka* (M., 1970), taken from the writer's popular series of programmes on Soviet radio in the 1960s, which attempted to reunite people separated from relations during the war with their lost family members. Many cases cited were of children who had ended up with adopted or foster parents. For a less rosy picture, see Oxf/Lev P–05 PF30A, p. 4 (rubbish tips), p. 7 (accusations of theft).

170 Oxf/Lev T–04 PF16A, p. 7. Interestingly, too, this reminiscence was introduced when the informant was happily discussing the New Year tree as the high point of the year, rather than as testimony of how tough orphanage life could be.

171 Oxf/Lev SPb.–02 PF1A, p. 4 (change of staff; leverage of war orphans); PF1B, pp. 27–8; PF4B, p. 111 (Palkin).

172 D. Filtzer, *Soviet Workers and Late Stalinism* (Cambridge, 2002), p. 150. On the other hand, this wasn't necessarily interpreted as an 'advantage' by inmates themselves. Cf. L's reference to protests on the part of her and her contemporaries: 'Are we to blame that we lost everything in the war? Are we to blame that Kalinin passed this [decree]?' However, she also records that a typical 'boy who was bad at lessons' would have been glad to leave and go off to the factory school, because 'you could live more freely there than in the home.' Oxf/Lev SPb.–02 PF3B, p. 74.

173 Oxf/Lev T–04 PF1A, p. 7. This former inmate, b. 1941, was himself sent on to a military band college once he finished with the orphanage. His recollections – of a clean, well-run, welcoming orphanage, with clean bedding and even tooth powder, three edible meals a day, and good support services when you left – are comparable to L's. Not surprisingly, he also felt that he owed the orphanage a lot: it had taught him the principles of honesty and decency, and helped him make his own family life a success. 'I was raised purely by our state' (PF1B, pp. 11–12).

174 For Zolotussky's full story – his father was arrested in 1937, and his mother in 1941, and he went through the Danilov monastery, then used as a reception centre by the NKVD, and then through Orphanage No. 3 in Moscow – see *Rossiya molodaya: XX vek* (M., 1998), pp. 411–12.

175 Oxf/Lev SPb.–02 PF3B, p. 73.

176 Ibid. (work destinations); PF1A, p. 7.

177 Report of 12 February 1945, *MPV*, p. 597.

178 *MPV* p. 477: the precise figures were 4,217 from the last quarter of 1946 and 4,525 for the first quarter of 1947.

179 *DG*, doc. 217, p. 376.

180 *DG*, doc. 255, pp. 383–4; *DG*, doc. 242, pp. 408–9. The text of this decree specifically stated its relationship with the decree of June 1943 (ibid., p. 408).

181 Ibid., and *MPV*, p. 597.

182 'Spravka o nalichii detskikh trudovykh vospitatel'nykh kolonii MVD SSSR po sostoyaniyu na 1 yanvarya 1946', RGASPI f. 17 op. 126 d. 39, ll. 51–2; 'Spravka o nalichii detskikh trudovykh kolonii MVD SSSR po sostoyaniyu na 1 yanvarya 1946', RGASPI f. 17 op. 126 d. 39, ll. 53–4; 'Spravka o nalichii detskikh priemnikov-raspredelitei, trudovykh i trudovo-vospitatel'nykh kolonii MVD SSSR, detei i podrostkov v nikh po sostoyaniyu na 1-e yanvarya 1947 goda', RGASPI f. 17 op. 125 d. 559, l. 139.

183 *DG*, doc. 270, p. 466.

184 Solomon, *Soviet Criminal Justice*, p. 208: though, once again, only in major cities.

185 V. Tadevosyan, 'Bor'ba za likvidatsiyu detskoi prestupnosti v SSSR', *SZ* 5 (1945), p. 11.

186 *Sbornik deistvuyushchikh postanovlenii plenuma Verkhovnogo Suda SSSR, 1924–1957* (M., 1958), no. 8, pp. 17–18, 17 February 1948.

187 K. Yankov, 'Otvetstvennost' roditelei za prichinennyi det'mi vred', *SZ* 6 (1950), 32–45. Yankov's own answer was that the responsibility of parents was 'subsidiary' in nature, and limited to cases where they had either participated in a crime, or conspicuously failed to provide their children with moral instruction (pp. 42–3, p. 39).

188 On the Ukrainian boy, see M. I. Kireevsky, *DG*, doc. 292, p. 504; on the children, E. A. Kersonovskaya, *DG*, doc. 258, p. 428. See also Solzhenitsyn, 'Maloletki'. Part of the background to this was continuing shortage of space in the colonies: ukases from above were not always enacted on the ground, and sometimes the colonies that had been ordered in Moscow were simply not built. For a case of this in Chelyabinsk province, see 'O vypolnenii postanovleniya TsK VKP(b) i SNK SSSR ob usilenii bor'by s detskoi besprizornost'yu i beznadzornost'yu' (12 August 1944), RGASPI f. 17 op. 126 d. 39, l. 21. In addition, there were 'demand bulges' from region to region, so that, at the start of 1946, when the colony system generally was riding at well under capacity (13,991 inmates and 16,850 places), there was slight overcrowding in Novosibirsk (323 versus 300) and Bryansk (312 versus 300), and more serious overcrowding in Saratov (379 versus 300).

189 F. Berger, *DG*, doc. 276, p. 474.

190 See *DG*, doc. 220, p. 379; doc. 224, p. 382; doc. 256 p. 444.

191 As in the Sarov labour ASZ in early 1944: see the report in *DG*, doc. 237, pp. 402–3.

192 For other problems, see e.g. the Sarov report, *DG*, doc. 237, pp. 402–3; for the escapes, *DG*, doc. 289, pp. 406–7 (445 inmates from the 47 colonies). This report cites poor living conditions and under-employment, as well as lack of leisure facilities, as the main reasons for the problems. Oxf/Lev SPb.–03 PF10B, p. 29, recalls how a group of boys who had run away from a colony turned up at the orphanage she was running in the Urals: 'there was iron discipline. Work, eat – that was it. And the rule was: if you didn't do something, your bosses would sort you out – the other kids, that is.'

193 *DG*, doc. 258, p. 452.

194 See Filtzer, *Soviet Workers and Late Stalinism*, pp. 152–3.

Chapter 8: Freedom and Punishment, 1953–1991

1 R. D. G. Gal'ego, *Beloe na chernom* (SPb., 2004), p. 94.

2 'Postanovlenie SM SSSR: O merakh likvidatsii besprizornosti', 8 April 1952, *DG* doc. 290, pp. 495–501. The law also raised the age at which children were eligible for institutional care, placing those up to 17 in the catchment of the reception centres.

3 See *KhSZUP*, vol. 4, p. 576. The expression used is *ushchemlenie prav*.

4 Cf. the account by a graduate from such a school in the Urals in Oxf/Lev P–04 PF14 – despite the fact that several of the ex–inmates went on to have good careers and were clearly of normal intelligence.

5 This point is made very forcefully in a report of 18

February 1956 by the director of Orphanage No. 44 in Leningrad: TsGA f. 5039 op. 6 d. 6, l. 4.

6 Oxf/Lev SPb.–04 PF53A, p. 10 (records dealing with up to 80–90 people a day in reception sessions).

7 See V. Vinogradov, 'Poslednii porog', *N* 44 (1976), 16.

8 I. Ratushinskaya, *Seryi- tsvet nadezhdy* (London, 1989), p. 92, records that a camp guard with whom she and other women prisoners had been in serious conflict was transferred to 'children's room' work. As Ratushinskaya observes, 'Poor kids!'

9 Yu. Miloslavsky, 'Syn Lyudmily Ivanovny', *Ot shuma vsadnikov i strelkov* (Ann Arbor, 1984), p. 10.

10 Oxf/Lev P–05 PF24A, p. 11.

11 Oxf/Lev SPb.–04 PF53A, p. 14.

12 As pointed out by a teacher who began work in the early 1980s: see Oxf/Lev M–04 PF30B, p. 12. Cf. a comparable account by a doctor, Oxf/Lev SPb.–05 PF73A, p. 6 (a family of alcoholics kept producing new children, but nothing could be done till the youngest daughter was hospitalised after her mother died; she was then sent from there to an orphanage). On the other hand, in less extreme cases, such intervention could achieve results: for example, Oxf/Lev M–04 PF35B, p. 16, recalls that getting access to problem parents was much easier in the Soviet era because one could get into the apartment concerned (there were no entryphones); Oxf/Lev M–04 PF29B, p. 12, remembers that parents were grateful for the help.

13 'Postanovlenie SM SSSR: O meropriyatiyakh po uluchsheniyu raboty detskikh domov', 30 January 1954, *DG*, doc. 295, pp. 507–8.

14 *Spravochnik direktora shkoly* (1971), p. 177.

15 'O merakh uluchsheniya vospitanya detei v detskikh domakh', Postanovlenie SM, 15 September 1956. The amounts specified were 300g wheat bread, 300g rye bread, 20g flour and 35g *krupa* (semolina), 35g macaroni, 100g meat, 90g fish, 300g potatoes, 340g veg., 15g dried fruit, 50g butter, 17g oil, 250g milk, 33g *tvorog* (curd cheese), 17g *smetana* (sour cream), 10g cheese, 60g sugar, 16g biscuits, 16g sweets, 0.3g tea, 0.3g eggs, and 15g salt (*KhSZUP*, vol. 5, pp. 599–600). Though there was no fresh fruit, the diet was reasonably nutritious; compared with the rations for children in prison camps, these children were supposed to be offered nearly twice as much of most things.

16 *Spravochnik direktora shkoly* (1971), p. 177.

17 F. Beckett, *Stalin's British Victims* (Stroud, 2004), based on an interview with Rosa Rust. Even this school, though, left its former inmates with some classic after-effects of institutionalised life: when she met her parents again as a young adult, Rust could feel no affection for them at all (ibid., p. 116). And, by the late 1930s, facilities for foreigners were closer to the Soviet norm: see e.g. the secret report of 1 February 1941 on a home for Spanish children in Evpatoriya, written by the director of the Red Army sanatorium in the town, and the report on the follow-up (the director of the home and deputy director had been sacked),

RGASPI f. 17 op. 126 d. 2, l. 1, ll. 2–3. On one notable boarding-school of this type, Interdom in Ivanovo, see the institution's website, http://www. interdom.info/history.php (accessed 15 February 2006).

18 On the national minorities *internaty*, see E. Lyarskaya's dissertation abstract, *Severnye internaty i transformatsiya traditsionnoi kul'tury (na primere nentsev Yamala)* (SPb., 2003). Archival data, e.g. a 1947 report held in RGASPI f. 17 op. 125 d. 557, l. 7, indicate that conditions in these were as grim as in other institutions of the day – dirt, poor washing facilities, dietary problems, and so on.

19 Oxf/Lev SPb.–04 PF45B, p. 31. See also the material on Dobroe *internat*, run by the Ministry of External Trade (MVT): http://dobroe.kochini. com/history/scheblanov_ii_hist.html (accessed 15 February 2006). There were cases also where members of the Party elite placed their children in the best supplied boarding-schools, such as those for war orphans: my thanks to Vitaly Bezrogov for this information.

20 A small number of schools continued to provide 'gifted' children with a highly specialised education. See e.g. V. Akhlomov and V. Yankulin, 'Shkola Nyutnov v Davydovke', *N* 9 (1964), 7, on a physics and maths school affiliated to Moscow State University. See also the sites, http://www. tutornet.ru/news/channel_show.asp?cPath=/ science/&nbFlags2=33&ntBSize=10 and also http://www.prosv.ru/forum/post.php?action=edit &fid=9&tid=341&pid=336 (accessed 15 February 2006). Another example of this was a school offering intensive Chinese outside Leningrad, operating until the mid-1960s (see Oxf/Lev SPb.–04 PF65–6).

21 N. Kaz'min, *Vsesoyuznoe soveshchanie po shkolam-internatam, 19–23 aprelya 1957 g. Stenograficheskii otchet* (M., 1958), p. 3. Cf. the comments by O. Nekrasova, a supervisor from a Kiev *internat*, 'A mama ne dovol'na', *N* 8 (1961), 19, who states that, although boarding-schools are a material help to parents, the main point is to provide children with a better upbringing than they would get at home.

22 Cf. the comments of a school director from Arkhangel'sk province at the 1957 conference, that 170 of the 260 pupils at his school came from families that could be described as 'in need': single mothers, families with a disabled parent, many-child families, or families under surveillance by the authorities (*podopechnye*); there were also eight orphans. Kaz'min, *Vsesoyuznoe soveshchanie*, p. 73. In the early 1960s, there were plans to make the network free of charge by 1980: 'Vse vo imya cheloveka, dlya blaga cheloveka', *N* 45 (1961), 4–5.

23 TsDOO SO f. 161 op. 27 d. 59, ll. 4–10.

24 See the handlist (*opis'*) no. 6 to GASO f. 233, ll. 5–8a.

25 See Harwin, pp. 27–8.

26 See the handlist (*opis'*) no. 6 to GASO f. 233, ll. 5–8a.

27 See Harwin, p. 28.

28 TsDOO SO f. 161 op. 31 d. 45, ll. 40–60.

29 Kaz'min, *Vsesoyuznoe soveshchanie*, p. 24. It was

mainly by holiday visits and writing letters that contact was maintained.

30 Harwin, p. 60.

31 For an example of the system at its best, see R. Izmailova, 'Na kachelyakh dushevnykh', *N* 16 (1963), 22–3, describing how Trekhgorka workers would call in at their *podshefnyi* orphanage on Saturdays and Sundays to entertain children who had no parents to go home to.

32 Oxf/Lev SPb.–03 PF19 A, pp. 7–9.

33 Oxf/Lev SPb.–04 PF46A, p. 5.

34 Oxf/Lev SPb.–03 PF39B, pp. 6–7.

35 Ibid, p. 7.

36 See e.g. Oxf/Lev SPb.–05 PF69B, p. 18.

37 See Oxf/Lev SPb.–04 PF48A, p. 33–4 (coats, tights), PF48B, p. 51 (bras). On clothes, see also Oxf/Lev SPb.–04 PF45B, p. 29.

38 Oxf/Lev SPb.–04 PF47A, p. 10.

39 Oxf/Lev SPb.–04 PF45A, p. 6.

40 See e.g. Oxf/Lev T–04 PF5A, p. 1 (informant, b. 1972, comments on the good conditions in the home and the warmth of the staff).

41 See e.g. Oxf/Lev T–04 PF22B, p. 24: the informant proved to have an encyclopaedic knowledge of Pioneer songs, despite having an impaired memory after a stroke.

42 Oxf/Lev SPb.–03 PF39B, p. 20.

43 Oxf/Lev SPb.–05 PF69B, p. 21 (attempted suicide – and the inmate later gave birth to the child fathered on her by her rapist); p. 9 (intimidation); p. 8 (bars on windows).

44 Oxf/Lev SPb.–05 PF67A, pp. 15–17; quotation p. 15.

45 As witnessed by a former worker in the baby home system: Oxf/Lev SPb.–04 PF57B, p. 19. On abandonment, see ibid., 57A, p. 10.

46 Oxf/Lev SPb.–04, PF57A, p. 16.

47 This disapproval is evident in the observations of the informant in Oxf/Lev SPb.–04 PF57B, p. 20.

48 V. Mukhina, *Bliznetsy* (M., 1969), p. 190, p. 346. The records date from 1966 (when the children had just turned five) and 1967 (when they were nearly six).

49 See e.g. GASO f. 1427 op. 2 d. 24, ll. 8–16 (1955).

50 CKQ SPb.–04 PF4B.

51 TsDOO SO f. 166 op. 32 d. 50, l. 22.

52 *N* 3 (1981), 2–3, 10–11, mentions such facilities in the context of a general discussion about the family to mark the fifth anniversary of the paper's 'Social Council on the Family' ('Obshchestvennyi sovet po sem'e'). See also Harwin, pp. 42–3.

53 'Bylo by zhelanie', *N* 39 (1975), 22.

54 'Srazu shestero detei', *N* 8 (1990), 4. Note the change here from the model of the USSR that obtained in earlier generations – the non-family collective: see Yuri Slezkine, 'The USSR as Communal Apartment', *SR* 53:2 (1994), 414–52. The metaphor is borrowed from I. Vareikis, writing in 1924 (p. 415). Svetlana Boym, 'The Architecture of Banality', *Public Culture* 6:2 (1994), 263–92, deals with the other side of the story – the communal flat as a model of the Soviet Union.

55 GASO f. 1427 op. 2 d. 24, l. 12.

56 An offbeat example of this was a woman who, having placed her baby in a state home when she gave birth to him while unmarried, then returned to pick up the child once she was married – without informing her new husband of the real situation. Oxf/Lev SPb.–04 PF58B, p. 43.

57 Irina Ovchinnikova, 'Eti nerodnye rodnye deti', *N* 20 (1982), 7. The 'new family' rationale was understood here to require total secrecy about the child's origins as an adoptee. Readers' letters were not all in favour of this (*N* 38 (1982), 12), but not telling children that they were adopted remained quite widespread: cf. the cautious comments by the psychiatrist Anna Spivakovskaya, interviewed in 1988, concluding that, on the whole, such silence was not a good idea (*N* 32 (1988), 12).

58 Oxf/Lev SPb.–04 PF57B, p. 23.

59 Harwin, p. 42.

60 Ibid., p. 96.

61 *SO* 9 (1987), 52–4, cites the measure of 12 August 1970 and the rate of payment at 20 roubles per month. See *SO* 7 (1985), 53–5, on temporary relief for those with problems in securing alimony.

62 N. Kolesnikova, 'Chetvertushka gor'kogo yabloka', *N* 47 (1988), 16, presents typical stories: a girl living with her mother forced to give up the child to save the 'family honour', and women migrants living in big-city hostels 'persuaded' by the authorities that 'renouncing the child' was the best solution, since it was the simplest solution in bureaucratic terms. Cf. I. Ovchinnikova, 'Devochki-mamy', *N* 27 (1989), 22–3.

63 Cf. the criticism in Ovchinnikova, 'Devochki-mamy', who also cites the maintenance figures. In addition, financial support for single mothers did not necessarily reach the neediest cases: cf. the report in Oxf/Lev SPb.–04 PF56B, p. 17 that women who were actually living with a male partner (but who had remained unmarried) would claim single-mother status in order to access these benefits. With the continuing disapproval of unmarried mothers in the Soviet system, it was indeed likely that such a woman, in a relationship that appeared to neighbours etc. to be a formal marriage, would be more inclined to keep the child, and then claim benefits, than would a woman whose single status made her the subject of scorn; yet the financial need of the person in the second case was of course significantly greater.

64 Harwin, p. 73.

65 'Otkrytyi konkurs: Detskii dom novogo tipa', *N* 1 (1988), 6; ibid., 2 (1988), 4; ibid., 24 (1988), 12; ibid., 41 (1988), 4–5.

66 On the activities of charities, see *N* 48 (1987), 5; *N* 28 (1989), 5; *N* 17 (1991), 11 (foreign charities); *N* 4 (1991), 7; *N* 31 (1991), 8, *N* 50 (1991), 6. See also Harwin, pp. 74–8.

67 Though such provision was usually at a rudimentary level. For instance, NGPU NN–2004 PF3 p. 2: a woman who left the orphanage in 1956 recalls getting an autumn coat, though at the time she left the orphanage it was winter; NGPU NN–04 PF2, p. 3, where a woman recalls being provided with a set of men's underwear.

68 NGPU NN–04 PF3, pp. 2–3.

69 NGPU NN–04 PF1, p. 3: 'I don't talk to anyone in the yard. I'm the kind of person that doesn't want to see or talk to anyone.' The only

person with whom this woman had succeeded in establishing contact who was not a former inmate of the home was a doctor at the psychiatric hospital where she worked, who had helped her sort out her difficult relations with neighbours in the communal flat (ibid.)

70 Ovchinnikova, 'Devochki-mamy', 22–3.
71 See Chapter 8 of the digital version of this book.
72 N. Kolesnikova, 'Bez mamy i papy. Kak zhivetsya detyam v internate?', *N* 36 (1990), 14.
73 See Conclusion below.
74 *Kommentarii k Ugolovnomu kodeksu RSFSR 1960 g.*, ed. M. D. Shergorodsky and N. A. Belyaev (L., 1962), pp. 33–6. See also 'Ugolovnaya otvetst-vennost' nesovershennoletnikh i primenenie k nim sudom prinuditel'nykh mer vospitatel'nogo kharaktera', *SYu* 6 (1961), 12–13.
75 *Kommentarii*, pp. 34–5.
76 'O sudebnoi praktike po delam o prestupleniyakh nesovershennoletnikh', 3 July 1963: *SPPVS 1924–1963*, no. 74, pp. 305–16. See also R. Bamm and 17 others, *Semeinoe vospitanie: Slovar' dlya roditelei* (M., 1967), p. 207.
77 G. Vittenberg, 'Strogo soblyudat' zakonnost' v deyatel'nosti kommissii po delam nesovershenno-letnikh', *SYu* 15 (1965), 12–14.
78 See the recollections of a long-term supervisor at such an institution, Oxf/Lev SPb.–04 PF62A, p. 2.
79 A. Bessmertnyi, 'Trudnyi mal'chik (zametki pedagoga)', *N* 1 (1960), 19. Cf. A. Grinina-Zemskova, 'Detstvo bez lyubvi', *N* 33 (1966), 20, about an unloved boy going to the bad.
80 'O sudebnoi praktike po delam o prestupleniyakh nesovershennoletnikh' [revised and expanded version of the 3 July 1963 law], *SPPVS 1924–1973*, p. 317, pp. 320–1, pp. 322–3.
81 For the text of the law, see *SYu* 3 (1968), 24; for a discussion of the system, D. Ryabov, 'Sud i vospitanie nesovershennoletnikh pravonaru-shitelei', *SYu* 10 (1968), 18.
82 V. Kudryavtsev, 'Sudy dlya nesovershennoletnikh v Anglii', *SYu* 2 (1967), 27–8.
83 Ryabov, 'Sud i vospitanie', 18; cf. Z. Pospelova, 'Sud i podrostok', *SYu* 18 (1969), 5–7, which also emphasises the need to take into account children's special psychology when taking evidence – their tendency to shift their story, etc. – and to bear in mind mitigating circumstances (two-thirds of juvenile criminals, she claimed, were educational dropouts).
84 *SPPVS 1924–1973*, no. 64, pp. 329–35; *SPPVS 1924–1977*, no. 111, pp. 273–85.
85 As in Vittenberg, 'Strogo soblyudat' zakonnost'', for instance. See also the Supreme Court measure of 4 December 1969 stating that minors who did not get a prison sentence were not to be left with the feeling of 'going unpunished' (*chuvstvo beznakazannosti*): *SPPVS 1924–1973*, p. 324.
86 TsDOO SO f. 161 op. 27 d. 60, l. 29 (1956).
87 GASO f. 2259 op. 1 d. 678, ll. 32–3.
88 TsDOO SO f. 161 op. 35 d. 50, ll. 44–5 (gang-rape, 1962); TsDOO SO f. 4 op. 67 d. 156, l. 147 (stabbing, 1965); GASO f. 2259 op. 1 d. 678, ll. 32–3 (crime levels).
89 TsDOO SO f. 4 op. 67 d. 156, ll. 23–3.

90 TsDOO SO f. 61 op. 16 d. 178, l. 7.
91 TsDOO SO f. 161 op. 27 d. 60, l. 8.
92 TsDOO SO f. 61 op. 16 d. 176, l. 23.
93 See TsDOO SO f. 166 op. 32 d. 50, l. 22.
94 TsDOO SO f. 166 op. 27 d. 64, l. 38.
95 TsDOO SO f. 161 op. 32 d. 50, l. 58 (figures for 1958), TsDOO SO f. 61 op. 16 d. 117, l. 51 (figures for 1959).
96 GASO f. 1159 op. 1 d. 800, l. 25, l. 30–33, l. 22.
97 GASO f. 2259 op. 1 d. 800, l. 102.
98 TsDOO f. 166 op. 32 d. 50, l. 24.
99 See e.g. GASO f. 2259 op. 1 d. 800, l. 104 (two persistent thieves of 11 and 12 were to be dispatched to No. 1 Orphanage, Nizhnii Tagil').
100 GASO f. 2259 op. 1 d. 800, l. 170.
101 *DG*, doc. 301, p. 514 gives a figure of 36,950 inmates in 62 colonies overall, with 19,700 in the labour colonies and 17,250 in the labour-education colonies.
102 See A. Sakharov, 'Alkogol' i prestupnost' nesover-shennoletnikh', *SYu* 16 (1965), 22–4. This seems all the more belated as reports of alcohol abuse by children had been published regularly since the 1920s. For example, A. Katanskaya, 'Alkogolizm detei shkol'nogo vozrasta i metody bor'by s nim', *Na putyakh k novoi shkole* 1–2 (1925), 147–9, reported the results of an impromptu survey of a group of schoolchildren in her class by Katanskaya, a village teacher: 50 per cent of the group had begun drinking by the time they were 6–8 years old and the rest even earlier; 50 per cent of the group thought drinking was good for one's health, and 50 per cent were afraid not to drink in case they got beaten.
103 S. Mikhalkov, 'Dyadya Styopa – militsioner', *Sobranie sochinenii* (M., 1963), vol. 1, p. 92.
104 On the 'Yunye druz'ya militsii', see K. Speransky, 'Preduprezhdenie beznadzornosti – neobkhodimoe uslovie likvidatsii prestupnosti sredi nesovershen-noletnikh', *SYu* 19 (1965), 16–17.
105 See Sakharov, 'Alkogol' i prestupnost' nesoversh-ennoletnikh', which reported that 60 per cent of young offenders who underwent arrest were found to have been drinking.
106 See T. Plesser, 'Rebenok vozle pivnoi', *N* 13 (1984), 7; 'Mal'chiki nachinayut s piva', *N* 30 (1985), 7; G. Blinov, 'Rokovaya kaplya', *N* 33 (1985), 7.
107 It was, however, claimed in 1976 that the work of the 'Friends' was useful to the police in some places: see e.g. Vinogradov, 'Poslednii porog'.
108 Vittenberg, 'Strogo soblyudat'', 13.
109 Anna Mogilat, 'Gde vash syn?' *N* 5 (1984), 6; 'Nedelya poluchila otvet', *N* 13 (1984), 7.
110 'Derzkie, neponyatnye mal'chishki', interview with I. I. Karpets, *N* 7 (1985), 9. Cf. 'Skazhi, kto tvoi otets …', *N* 15 (1986), 14–15 (an interview with a deputy minister of internal affairs).
111 *N* 12 (1988), 6–7; ibid., 21 (1988), 16.
112 V. Pavlov, '"Kriminal'nyi" malysh', *N* 49 (1989), 5.
113 I. Ovchinnikova, 'Kto bez grekha?', *N* 44 (1989), 20–1; A. Vasinsky 'Pedagogicheskii reportazh', *N* 25 (1987), 19. The latter article backed up the portrait with statistics: 31 per cent of young offenders lacked one or both parents, 25 per cent had parents that were divorced, and 40 per cent

had smoked and drunk alcohol before arriving in the colony.

114 N. Dar'yalova, '"Zdes' vam ne lager'!"', *N* 27 (1989), 15.

115 S. P. Val'eva and P. I. Shpital'nik (eds), *Detskii gorodok v Nizhnem Tagile* (M., 1963) (for citation of Makarenko, see p. 7, on self-monitoring, see p. 95, for inmate and ex–inmate testimony, pp. 125–38).

116 Oxf/Lev SPb.–04 PF62–63; PF64; PF65–6. For full references, see digital version.

117 Ibid.

118 *DG*, doc. 305, pp. 522–3: 37,345 places in 112 colonies.

119 *DG*, doc. 310, pp. 536–44.

120 See e.g. V. Eremin, 'Tainy retsidiva', *N* 13 (1989), 18–19.

121 Vasinsky, 'Pedagogicheskii reportazh', 19.

122 GASO f. 2259 op. 1 d. 676, l. 3–4 (inmate numbers 1959); l. 8 (runaways, accidents); l. 38 (inmate numbers 1960); l. 42 (behaviour of adults and children).

123 Based on the forward projection in *DG*, doc. 305, pp. 522–3, which gives 37,345 places in 112 colonies.

124 Oxf/Lev P–05 PF1A, p. 4.

125 Details here and below from Oxf/Lev P–05 PF1A.

126 'Forum Fimy Zhigantsa: Vse o zhizni v t'yurme', http://forum.tyurem.net/read. php?3,756,756,quote+1, accessed 26 January 2006.

127 Ekaterina Efimova, *Sovremennaya tyur'ma: byt, traditsii i fol'klor* (M., 2004). Other studies include V. F. Pirozhkov, *Zakony prestupnogo mira molodezhi (kriminal'naya subkul'tura)* (Tver', 1994); and the collection *Fol'klor i kul'turnaya sreda GULAGa* (SPb., 1994).

128 Efimova, *Sovremennaya t'yurma*, p. 41, p. 262, p. 266, pp. 300–1, pp. 309–10. On girls' traditions, see p. 113, pp. 119–21, p. 192. On self-harm in a girls' colony, see Dar'yalova, 'Zdes' vam ne lager'!', 14.

129 Cf. the similarity of the material on adult prisons in Efimova, *Sovremennaya t'yurma* and Rossi, *Spravochnik po Gulagu* (London, 1987), and the stability of prison slang and criminal cant over the generations, as reflected in e.g. *Slovar' zhargona*

prestupnikov (M., 1927), *Zhargon prestupnikov* (M., 1952), and indeed back to Trakhtenberg, *Blatnaya muzyka*. Songs remaining in the repertoire for generations include 'Murka', a famous ballad about the gangster's moll who turns into a gang leader (for a reference to performance in the 1990s, see Efimova, *Sovremennaya t'yurma*, p. 285), and 'The Young Offender's Hymn', also going back to the post-revolutionary era (ibid., p. 142).

130 Cf. the criticism of the transferral of inmates in V. Marchenko, 'Izmenit' sistemu perevoda iz trudovykh kolonii dlya nesovershennoletnikh', *SYu* 19 (1967), 27–9. If they 'graduated' into ordinary life, inmates were likely to suffer from the relative absence of back-up (in contrast to what was offered to orphanage inmates). For instance, it was only in the post-Soviet era that those serving sentences of more than three years retained a right to the accommodation that they had previously inhabited. (Oxf/Lev P–05 PF1A, p. 9.)

131 Oxf/Lev SPb.–04 PF61B, pp. 39–41. The informant seems 'in denial' about exactly what using her particular favourite to manage the group meant, though she records having seen him hit another boy, p. 41. She also records some horrendous cases of violence (e.g. the murder of two girls because one of them had been a witness to another murder by the youths concerned, PF61A, p. 29), and the continuing record of dumping by social services (PF60A, p. 4).

132 Rossi, *Spravochnik*, p. 201.

133 Ibid., p. 201.

134 Dar'yalova, '"Zdes' vam ne lager"!', 14 (on girls in adult prisons), 15 (statistics for repeated offences).

135 Autobiography of Marina N., Ryazan' Youth Colony, December 2000. V. Abramkin (ed.), *Deti v tyur'me* (M., 2001), p. 4. The instances of broken homes etc. come from other autobiographies in the selection. For the figure of 40,000 juveniles, see ibid., p. 1.

136 Figures from Marina Polivanova, '"Tyur'ma delaet cheloveka khuzhe": Zametki psikhologa', *RM* 30 November–6 December 2000, 11.

137 M. Rakhmanova, 'My sami ikh kalechim', *N* 43 (1989), 8.

138 Oxf/Lev SPb.–05 PF70A, p. 2.

Chapter 9: Babyhood

1 Russian proverb: quoted here from M. Leder, *My Life in Stalinist Russia* (Bloomington, IN, 2001), p. 171.

2 I. Paderin, *SPA*, vol. 5, p. 349.

3 Cited, from conversations with Bely, Mariengof, p. 73.

4 Pokrovsky, E. A. Pokrovsky, *Fiziologicheskoe vospitanie detei u raznykh narodov, preimush-chestvenno Rossii* (M., 1884), part 1, pp. 41–3; N. Petersen, 'Dirty Women', in H. Goscilo and B. Holmgren (eds), *Russia: Women: Culture* (Bloomington, IN, 1996), pp. 189–90. Other places besides the *banya* were also considered to offer protection from the evil eye, for instance a closet, barn, or Russian stove; see Z. O. Michnik, *Besedy po okhrane materinstva i mladenchestva v*

derevne (M., 1928), p. 69.

5 On behaviour before conception and during intercourse, see D. A. Baranov, 'Obraz rebenka v narodnoi embriologii', *Materialy po etnografii* vol. 1 (SPb., 2002), pp. 12–22. On behaviour during pregnancy and birthing, see Pokrovsky, *Fizicheskoe vospitanie*, pp. 41–3; Michnik, *Besedy po okhrane*, p. 69; I. Shangina, *Russkie deti i ikh igry* (SPb., 2000), pp. 15–19.

6 See A. K. Baiburin, *Ritual v traditsionnoi kul'ture* (SPb., 1993), pp. 40–5; Shangina, *Russkie deti i ikh igry*, pp. 15–19.

7 Shangina, *Russkie deti i ikh igry*, pp. 27–8; A. K. Baiburin, 'Polyarnosti v rituale (tverdoe i myagkoe)', in *Polyarnost' v kul'ture: Al'manakh "Kanun"* 2 (1996), 157–65.

8 Pokrovsky, *Fizicheskre vosjitanic*, p. 41.
9 Ransel, *Village Mothers*, pp. 125–45, esp. pp. 127–8.
10 See ibid., p. 26.
11 Shangina, *Russkie deti i ikh igry*, pp. 30–1.
12 E. Shestakova, *Detskaya smertnost'* (SPb., 1913), pp. 7–8; E. A. Pokrovsky, *Ob ukhode za malymi det'mi* (M., 1889), p. 41.
13 See Baiburin, *Ritual*, pp. 40–7; idem, 'Rodinnyi obryad u slavyan i ego mesto v zhiznennom tsikle', *Zhivaya starina* 2 (1997), 7–9.
14 D. K. Zelenin, 'Umershie neestestvennoyu smert'yu v pover'yakh russkogo naroda', *Izbrannye trudy* (M., 1995), 70–3; Baranov, 'Obraz rebenka', p. 37. Oxf/Lev V–05 PF6A, p. 26, records this tradition in Novgorod province during the 1930s and 1940s, though the survival was due in part to the fact that the nearest official cemetery was some distance away, and transporting the remains was difficult.
15 Baranov, 'Obraz rebenka', pp. 35–6.
16 Baiburin, *Ritual*, p. 45; Zh. V. Kormina, 'Institut krestnykh roditelei v traditsionnoi kul'ture', in A. K. Baiburin et al. (eds), *Problemy sotsial'nogo i gumanitarnogo znaniya* (SPb., 1999–2000), vol. 1, pp. 222–3. For the timing of the christening, see e.g. Dmitry Nabokov, 'Detskie gody v Suprunovke', *NM* 11 (1967), 110, recalling that the *Sunday* after the birth was customary in his family, which would have given a maximum age of 8–10 days (a christening could scarcely have been arranged in less than 2–3 days, so a child born on Friday or Saturday would presumably have waited till the following Sunday for baptism).
17 Baiburin, *Ritual*, p. 49.
18 Shangina, *Russkie deti i ikh igry*, p. 23.
19 For this practice, see Alekseev, p. 78: in Alekseev's own family of eight children born in the 1920s, there were two Mariyas and two Evdokiyas. And cf. D. Nabokov, 'Detskie gody', p. 110, on the birth of his brother 'Mitroshka' (i.e. a second Dmitry); Nabokov himself does not even remark on the coincidence, an indication of the fact that nothing was considered odd in it.
20 Baiburin, *Ritual*, pp. 47–51; Kormina, 'Institut', pp. 225–6.
21 Shangina, *Russkie deti i ikh igry*, 32–3; D. A. Baranov et al. (comps), *Russkaya izba: illustrirovannaya entsiklopediya* (SPb., 2004), pp. 81–4. The photo-spread between pp. 96 and 97 of this book includes a fine photograph of a cradle, dating from 1914.
22 S. M. Loiter, *Russkii detskii fol'klor Karelii* (Petrozavodsk, 1991), p. 53: recording from 1987.
23 For a lengthy discussion of all this, see Valentin Golovin, *Russkaya kolybel'naya pesnya v fol'klore i literature* (Åbo, 2000), e.g. pp. 207–19, pp. 231–2, pp. 254–9, pp. 135–47.
24 *DPF*, no. 261.
25 Ransel, *VM*, p. 211 (unwashed nappies), p. 210 (powder), p. 207 (cradles with excreta).
26 On *ne zhilets*, see Ransel, *VM*, p. 187 (though the translation 'goner' here is misleadingly crude – *dokhodyaga* would be the Russian equivalent of this). The expression *ne zhilets* (fem., *ne zhilitsa*)

was used of adults as well: see V. Dal', *Tolkovyi slovar' zhivogo velikorusskogo yazyka* (4 vols; M., 1880–82), vol. 1, p. 542.
27 Ransel, *VM*, p. 126.
28 Michnik, *Besedy po okhrane*, p. 15.
29 V. P. Ivanov, *Metkoe moskovskoe slovo* (M., 1985), p. 176, records a pre-revolutionary street sign: 'Midwife withshelter [*sic*] for secret [children]'. In Smolensk in 1911, 234 of the 909 admissions were illegitimate births (*Otchet Smolenskoi Gubernskoi Zemskoi Bol'nitsy za 1911 god* (Smolensk, 1912), p. 88).
30 See N. Pushkareva (comp.), '*A se grekhi zlye, smertnye*' (M., 1999), pp. 109–11. Of course, it is important to remember that 20 years was still a severe penalty: crimes such as bestiality (3–16 years) or failing to have a child christened (one year) provide some sort of broader context.
31 M. N. Gernet, *Detoubiistvo* (M., 1911), p. 281.
32 A. S. Saburova, 'Ot chego umirayut v derevne malen'kie deti', *OMM* 1 (1916), 129.
33 W. Barnes Steveni, *Things Seen in Russia* (London, 1913), p. 33.
34 See Ransel, *VM*, p. 198 (pacifier), p. 210 (cradle).
35 M. A. Novosil'tseva, 'Ob organizatsii pomoshchi materi i rebenku v derevne', *OMM* 1 (1916), 100–1.
36 See Ransel, *VM*, p. 205. For an early attack in Russia, see e.g. I. Sharlovsky, *Vospitanie i nachal'noe obuchenie* (Warsaw, 1870), p. 48.
37 Novosil'tseva, 'Ob organizatsii', 99.
38 For this kind of argument, see e.g. A. V. Popova, 'Okhrana materinstva', *OMM* 5 (1917), 397.
39 See Shestakova, *Detskaya smertnost' v Rossii* (this book also contains extended comparisons with Western countries; for a comparable approach, see N. A. Russkikh's introductory note to the first issue of *OMM* 1 (1916), 17; L. I. Bezlichenko, 'Rodovspomozhenie v Petrograde i ego rol' v okhrane materinstva i mladenchestva', *OMM* 1 (1916), 72). For the 1905–9 infant mortality figures, see 'Staticheskaya khronika', *OMM* 1 (1916), 188. These figures are confirmed in *Zhenshchiny i deti v SSSR* (M., 1961), p. 61.
40 See S. Gaupt-Kerner, 'Deyatel'nost' Komissii detskoi gigieny Saratovskogo seminarnogo obshchestva: Otchet dvukh punktov "Kapli moloka" za 1915 god', *OMM* 2 (1916), 193.
41 Informant from Vologda province, recorded in 1898: from the records of the Tenishevskoe Byuro, Russian Ethnographical Museum, St Petersburg, f. 7 op. 1 d. 348, l. 21, quoted here from Golovin, *Russkaya kolybel'naya pesnya*, p. 125.
42 For instance, Mikhail Lyn'kov, whose parents could not even afford their own house, remembered being taken to a *znakhar'* in the early 1900s (*SPA*, vol. 4, p. 367). Cf. the comments of G. Vinogradov, *Narodnaya pedagogika* (Irkutsk, 1926), p. 16. (Ransel, *VM*, p. 189, also has instances of this.)
43 K. Trenev, *SPA*, vol. 2, p. 456.
44 For the laying-out, cf. Afanasy Salynsky, *SPA*, vol. 5, p. 395 (Salynsky himself was taken for dead, but revealed himself to be alive when he blew out the candle).
45 Proverbs: see V. Dal', *Tolkovyi slovar' zhivogo*

velikorusskogo yazyka (4 vols; M., 1880–82), vol. 1, pp. 437–8.

46 For the rate in England between 1540 and 1599, see N. Orme, *Medieval Children* (New Haven, CT, 2001), p. 113.

47 Z. I. Klibanskaya, 'Prizrenie grudnykh detei v derevnyakh, kak odin iz faktorov bor'by s detskoi smertnost'yu', *Pediatriya* 4 (1914), 283.

48 Dubova is in Engel and Posadskaya-Vanderbeck, p. 21; O. Vishnya, *SPA*, vol. 1, p. 253; M. Isakovsky, *SPA*, vol. 1, p. 488.

49 A. Dovzhenko, *SPA*, vol. 3, pp. 205–6.

50 D. L. Ransel, 'Infant-Care Cultures in the Russian Empire', in B. E. Clements, B. A. Engel, and C. D. Worobec (eds), *Russia's Women* (Berkeley, CA, 1991), 116–17. See also 'Detskie ponosy', *OMM* 1 (1917), 93–4. Gastro-enteritic complaints remained the major killer of small children later in the twentieth century as well: see e.g. Yu. A. Polyakov and V. B. Zhiromskaya (eds), *Naselenie Rossii v XX veke: Istoricheskie ocherki* (2 vols; Moscow, 2000–1), vol. 2, p. 123, who indicate that in 1942 these carried off 27.1 per cent of infants dying before the age of one, or around a third, if one counts dysentery and haemocolitis.

51 D. Ransel, 'Mothering, Medicine, and Infant Mortality in Russia: Some Comparisons', *Occasional Paper, Kennan Institute for Advanced Studies* 236 (1990); V. Varshavsky, 'K voprosu o detskoi smertnosti i merakh bor'by s neyu', *Pediatriya* 4 (1913), 311. N. Vigdorchuk, 'Detskaya smertnost' sredi Peterburgskikh rabochikh (po dannym ankety)', *OV* 2 (1914), p. 238, quotes mortality rates of 47.6 for the 0–5 age group among Orthodox believers, 39.5 among Muslims, and 23.9 per cent among Jews (the figures date from 1900–4). Similar arguments for a later period are advanced by V. A. Tushnov, 'K kharakteristike byta grudnogo rebenka v tatarskoi sem'e', *Zhurnal po izucheniyu rannego detstva* 6: 2 (1927), 160–5.

52 See e.g. E. A. Bakhmutsky, 'Iz proshlogo i nastoyashchego voprosa ob okhrane materinstva i mladenchestva', *OMM* 3: 1 (1917), 24.

53 For the fantasies, see e.g. Saburova, 'Ot chego umirayut deti', 130.

54 V. Gilyarovsky, 'Bani', *Moskva i moskvichi* (1926), *Sochineniya v 4 tomakh* vol. 4 (M., 1967), p. 309.

55 Figures from E. Waters, 'Teaching Mothercraft in Post-Revolutionary Russia', *Australian Slavonic Studies* 1: 2 (1987), 48. On St Petersburg/Petrograd, see also A I. Bublichenko, 'Rodovspomozhenie v Petrograde i ego rol' v okhrane materinstva i mladenchestva', *OMM* 1 (1916), graph after p. 80; 83; on Moscow, S. Grauerman, 'Opyt okhrany grudnogo rebenka v Gorodskikh Uchrezhdeniyakh imeni S. V. Lepekhina i L. I. Timistera', *Trudy pervogo vserossiiskogo s"ezda detskikh vrachei* (SPb., 1913), p. 39; on provincial towns, N. M. Kaluzhskii, 'Novye puti v dele rodovspomozheniya v gorode Saratove', *OMM* 2 (1917), 154. *Adres-ukazatel' vol'no-praktikuyushchikh vrachei-spetsialistov g. Kazani*, (Kazan', 1910) lists 16 doctors with a specialism in obstetrics and gynaecology, 18 midwives, a free lying-in facility in the zemstvo hospital, and an expensive private maternity home. *Ves' Ekaterinburg* (Ekaterinburg, 1910), lists 18 midwives and a lying-in hospital. For an individual example of a high-status St Petersburg mother using a hospital, see Shefner, 346–7: though the author's mother did not in fact quite make it from her home in Kronstadt to the Chernyshev pereulok Maternity hospital in central St Petersburg, and the young Shefner was born in the hansom cab on the way over, the intention was that he should have arrived in hospital.

56 On this facility, see *PZK* 7 (1905), p. 92; E. E. Gart'e, 'Iz deyatel'nosti gorodskogo priyuta dlya nedonoskov v Petrograde', *OMM* 1 (1917), 47–86.

57 See A. Popova's note on the conference, *PB* 3 (1913), 17–19.

58 *Lechebnitsa dlya detei grudnogo vozrasta v Moskve, uchrezhdennaya G. N. Speranskim* (M., 1911). This pamphlet is not very informative about the infirmary's work, but does include some handsome illustrations of model cots, nurses dandling infants, etc.

59 See *PB* 1 (1914), 88.

60 See e.g. A. A. Redlikh, 'Strakhovanie materinstva, kak mera okhrany ego', *OMM* 3 (1917), 129–46.

61 On the Congress, see *PB* 8/9/10 (1914), 1077; on maternity supplements, see Aleksandra Kollontai, 'Zhenshchina-rabotnitsa v sovremennom obshchestve' (1909), in *Marksistskii feminizm* (Tver', 2003); 'Krest materinstva', *Sovremennyi mir* 11 (1914), 42–54 (here the argument is that support is essential to a healthy population); for analogies with the West, see e.g. A. Popova, in *PB* 3 (1913), 17–19; K. Moroshkin, 'Novyi frantsuzskii zakon ob okhrane materinstva', *OV* 4 (1914), 566–74.

62 On Russkikh, see S. A. Ostrogorsky, 'Deyatel'nost' K. A. Raukhfusa po okhrane materinstra i mledenuchestrom', *OMM* 1 (1916), 28; 'N. A. Russkikh: nekrolog', *OMM* 2 (1916), 9–14. On the Union, see also S. M. Yampol'sky, 'Kaplya moloka Khar'kovskogo otdela Soyuza bor'by s detskoi smertnost'yu', *Trudy Pervogo Vserossiiskogo s"ezda detskikh vrachei*, p. 115.

63 S. Gaupt-Kerner, 'Deyatel'nost' Komissii detskoi gigieny Saratovskogo sanitarnogo obshchestva: Otchet 2-kh punktov "Kapli moloka" za 1915 god', *OMM* 2 (1917), 187–202.

64 See e.g. A. A., 'Ob uchrezhdeniyakh po okhrane materinstva', *PB* 1 (1913), 17–25 (on Soyuz bor'by, Kaplya moloka); or Z. O. Michnik, 'Pomoshch' materyam', *PB* 5 (1914), 529–51. Varshavsky, 'K voprosu', cites Dufour's 'Goutte de lait' in Fécamp as a precedent, p. 314.

65 See e.g. the news item in *SemV* 8 (1913), 89–90.

66 'Kratkii obzor deyatel'nosti Soveta Popechitel'stva do 1917 goda', *OMM* 1 (1917), 1–6.

67 *Otchet blagotvoritel'nogo obshchestva "Okhrana Materinstva" pri besplatnykh rodil'nykh priyutakh g. Moskvy za pervyi (1908) god* (M., 1909) (for budget figure, see p. 13); *Otchet o deyatel'nosti Blagotvoritel'nogo Obshchestva "Okhrana Materinstva" s 22 aprelya 1914 g. po 24 aprelya 1916 g. [...]* (M., 1916): for budget figures, see pp. 22–3.

68 'K deyatel'nosti Obshchestva okhrany materei i

grudnykh detei v Tsarskom Sele', *PB* 3–4 (1914), 317–22.

69 On district nurses, see Z. O. Michnik, 'Individual'noe prizrenie grudnykh detei i patronazh', *OMM* 3 (1916), 27–55; on leaflets, cf. the series produced by the Pirogov Society through its Dissemination of Popular Hygienic Knowledge Commission, which included *How to Feed Infants* (Kak nado vskarmlivat' grudnykh detei) (SPb.; n.p., n.d.), reprinted several times in the early twentieth century.

70 See M. Ratynskaya, 'Postanovka okhrany materinstva i mladenchestva v Liverpule', *OMM* 1 (1917), 89–96.

71 On the Tsarskoe Selo society, see 'K deyatel'nosti', 147; on the Moscow 'Protection of Motherhood', *Otchet o deyatel'nosti Blagotvoritel'nogo Obshchestva OMM*, p. 24.

72 A.A., 'Ob uchrezhdeniyakh', 17–25.

73 Z. O. Michnik, *Okhrana materinstva i mladenchestva na Vasil'evskom Ostrove v tsifrakh 1915–1925* (L., 1925), p. 10.

74 Cf. the comments of Dr G. L. Grauerman in *Otchet o deyatel'nosti Blagotvoritel'nogo Obshchestva OMM*, p. 27. The Pirogov Society's *Kak nuzhno vskarmlivat' grudnykh detei* begins with the assertion, 'Every mother, if she is healthy, must feed her child herself', before going on to stipulate regular feeds, scrupulous cleanliness, and avoidance of alcoholic drink and of chewed-bread dummies.

75 V. Zhuk, 'Novyi metod iskusstvennogo vskarmlivaniya detei', *Akusherka* 3–4 (1905), 34.

76 Z. O. Michnik, 'Ob estestvennom i iskusstvennom vskarmlivanii grudnykh detei', *OMM* 2 (1916), 46.

77 See e.g. V. P. Gerasimovich, 'Kormilichnyi promysl i mery zakonodatel'noi ego regulirovki', *OMM* 6 (1917), 469–86.

78 On the dangers, see e.g. E. Terrien, 'Sifilis detei i kormilichnoe vskarmlivanie', *Akusherka* 11/12 (1905), 172–7; V. Zh-k, 'P'yanstvo kormilitsy', *Akusherka* 15/16 (1905), 225–35; on vetting, see e.g. A. P. Popova, 'Ukhod za novorozhdennym', *PZK* 8 (1906), p. 266.

79 On the IPS, see *Blagotvoritel'naya Rossiya* (SPb., 1901), p. 215. On the Sankt-Peterburgskii chastnyi rodil'nyi dom, see *SPb.–Pv-1903*, p. 94); on the Priyut dlya kormilits, also in St Petersburg, see ibid., no. 6 (1904), p. 88. The introduction fee charged by the latter institution was 10 roubles (twice the cost of subscribing to an upmarket children's magazine for a year, or roughly half a cook's wages for a month).

80 V. N. Zhuk, *Mat' i ditya* (9th edition; SPb., 1911), p. 668. In the first year of its operation, the Bureau passed 75 per cent of the women who came through it (ibid.)

81 *PZK*, vol. 13 (1911).

82 Zhuk, *Mat' i ditya* (1911), p. 638 (breast-feeding), p. 668 (vetting a wet-nurse), p. 687 (types of teat).

83 L. Kassil', *SPA*, vol. 1, p. 526.

84 E. Hill, *In the Mind's Eye* (Lewes, 1999), pp. 10–12. Hill (b. 1900) and her siblings were the children of a British businessman and a Russian gentlewoman, and had a largely Russian

upbringing, though they attended a German school.

85 Ibid., p. 10.

86 Grauerman, 'Opyt okhrany grudnogo rebenka v Gorodskikh Uchrezhdeniyakh', pp. 41–5.

87 See e.g. Iv. G., 'Psikhologiya rebenka (po povodu knigi Kompeire)' (a digest of G. Compayré, *L'Évolution intellectuelle et morale de l'enfant*, Paris, 1893), *VV* 5 (1894), 187–202, esp. 191–2).

88 Pokrovsky, *Ob ukhode*, pp. 45–6 (*soska*), p. 29 (breast-feeding), p. 100 (crèches). See also *Sovety materyam po ukhodu i vkarmlivaniyu grudnykh detei* (M., 1914).

89 See e.g. Zhuk, *Mat' i ditya*, ch. 2 section V; on walking frames (which attracted his disapproval), p. 898. Another innovation that was more positively received was paper nappies, as introduced at the Moscow exhibition of 1882 by the Moscow firm of Nurenberg (p 502).

90 See especially the section on smallpox vaccination (a subject on which Zhuk had independent publications), *Mat' i ditya* (1911), pp. 917–37.

91 Ibid., pp. 507–22 (anti-swaddling; Zhuk's preferred alternative was a sort of portable sleeping bag known in French as a *porte-bébé* and by him as a *konvertik* (envelope): pp. 507–11). On teething and chills, see p. 845;   on wet-nurses and morals, p. 671.

92 Ibid., p. 553 (room). On clothes, see pp. 498–9; weight, p. 307 (with chart); furnishings p. 547. The central points in discussion emerge more clearly from the abridged version of the book, *Rebenok: Obshchedostupnaya gigiena* (Odessa, 1897).

93 G. N. Speransky, *Fiziologiya rebenka i ego bolezni* (M. 1909), pp. 84–5 (nursery), p. 86 (baths), p. 77 (weighing), p. 90 (dummy, rocking, mouth-rinsing), pp. 57–8 (feeding regimen).

94 See e.g. Eric Pritchard, *Infant Education* (London, 1907). There is a useful general discussion of this text and many similar ones in Christina Hardyment, *Perfect Parents* (Oxford, 1995): see esp. pp. 125–40.

95 V. N. Zhuk, *Ditya: dnevnik materi* (SPb., 1892).

96 Zhuk, *Mat' i ditya*, p. 498.

97 S. F. Svetlov, *Peterburgskaya zhizn' v kontse XIX stoletiya (v 1892 godu)*, ed. A. M. Konechnyi (SPb., 1998), p. 62. One notes also Zhuk's own view that the idea of keeping the best room for the nursery was 'contrary to established beliefs' (see p. 304 above).

98 On the figures for apartment sizes, see editor's note to Svetlov, *Peterburgskaya zhizn'*, p. 119, n. 3 (relating to 1890); L. I Bublichenko, 'Rodovspomozhenie v Petrograde i ego rol' v okhrane materinstva i mladenchestva', *OMM* 1 (1916), 74 (relating to 1900).

99 *Detskoe vospitanie* (SPb., 1899) (the store's catalogue for September 1899), pp. 6–8.

100 M. P. Stakhorskaya, 'Dnevnik materi', in N. I. Gavrilova and M. P. Stakhorskaya, *Dnevnik materi* (M.: Prakticheskie znaniya, 1916), p. 95.

101 E. Krichevskaya, *Moya Marusya (Zapiski materi)* (Petrograd, 1916), p. 18.

102 Gavrilova, 'Dnevnik materi', in Gavrilova and Stakhorskaya, *Dnevnik materi*, p. 5, p. 12, p. 27, p. 15. On *ladushka* (still very popular in the late

twentieth century), see Aleksandra Piir, 'Detskie igry', typescript inventory, SPb., 2003, p. 1.

103 Bublichenko, 'Rodovspomozhenie', 74.

104 On working-class birthing experiences generally, see Anne L. Bobroff, 'Working Women, Bonding Patterns, and the Politics of Daily Life. Russia at the End of the Old Regime', PhD, University of Michigan, 1982, vol. 1, p. 117; on St Petersburg, see N. Vigdorchik, 'Detskaya smertnost' sredi Peterburgskikh rabochikh', OV 2 (1914), p. 219.

105 On farming out, see e.g. Evgeniya Nikadorova (b. 1880, Moscow province), Tat'yana Dontsova (b. 1886, Moscow province), and Iraida Komissarova, in Chaadaeva, p. 97, p. 116, p. 127; on survival rates, see Bobroff, 'Working Women', p. 112 ff, p. 121, p. 123.

106 Vigdorchik, 'Detskaya smertnost'', p. 222.

107 See Bobroff, 'Working Women', pp. 143–75.

108 See Vigdorchik, 'Detskaya smertnost'', p. 217. By contrast, in families with an income of more than 50 roubles a month, only 6.6 per cent of mothers worked.

109 Vigdorchik, 'Detskaya smertnost'', p. 221.

110 A. O. Gershenzon, '"Kaplya moloka" i Konsult'atsiya dlya grudnykh detei v Odesse', Trudy Pervogo Vserossiiskogo S"ezda detskikh vrachei, p. 53, 57, p. 52, p. 54.

111 K. Svetozarskaya, Zhizn' v svete, doma i pri dvore (SPb., 1890), p. 96; Shangina, Russkie deti i ikh igry, p. 21.

112 E. O. Kabo, Ocherki rabochego byta (M., 1928), p. 200, estimates on the basis of her sample that 100 per cent of Moscow working-class families had their children christened before 1917.

113 Svetozarskaya, Zhizn' v svete, p. 96.

114 Stakhorskaya, Dnevnik materi, p. 130.

115 Svetozarskaya, Zhizn' v svete, p. 97.

116 See Shefner, p. 346.

117 On inviting priests to the home, see A. Balov, 'O predchuvstvii smerti. Opeka. Skazka o barine i muzhike. Promysly. Svershenie religioznykh obryadov. O brake. Ekonomicheskoe polozhenie krest'yanskoi sem'i' (1899). Archive of the Russian Ethnographical Museum, f. 7, op. 1, d. 1826, ll. 14–15. On christening, see also S. Pridol'sky, 'Krest'yanskii mir i prikhodskoi pricht', Severnyi vestnik 1 (1885), 42–64. (My thanks to Veronika Makarova for these references.)

118 E. Fen, A Girl Grew Up in Russia (London, 1970), p. 30.

119 The poet Konstantin Bal'mont's daughter was named 'Mirra', after the poet Mirra (real name Mariya) Lokhvitskaya, with whom he was in love at the time of the girl's birth, and Tsvetaeva's elder daughter was named 'Ariadna'. Some of Tsvetaeva's friends, though, found the name pretentious (salonno): see her memoir, 'Alya', Sobranie sochinenii v 7 tomakh, vol. 4 (M., 1994), p. 556.

120 Cf. Anna Kuznetsova-Budanova's account of how her classmates at the gimnaziya called her 'Anya' and not 'Nyura' – I u menya byl krai rodnoi (Munich: self-published, 1979), p. 156.

121 Ben-Ami, 'Gody gimnazii: vospominaniya', VV 3 (1910), 154.

122 This continued to be the trend right through

the twentieth century. Cf. Naum Korzhavin's joking observation that any bisyllable ending in -a was accepted as a legitimate name by Russian Jews – even, he alleges, 'Grina' (as a feminine equivalent of 'Grigory'). ('V soblaznakh krovavoi epokhi', NM 7 (1992), 168.)

123 Ransel, VM, pp. 109–10.

124 R. K. Urazmanova and S. V. Cheshko, Tatary (M., 2001), p. 357 (naming rite), p. 337 (choice of names).

125 Ibid., p. 358.

126 Ben-Ami, 'Gody gimnazii', 154.

127 Pokrovsky, FV, part 2, pp. 136–8.

128 Ibid., part 2, p. 187 (cradles); part 1, p. 49 (clothes).

129 Pokrovsky, FV, part 2, p. 195 (tchoch); part 1, pp. 120–1 (clothes).

130 Pokrovsky, FV, part 3, p. 276.

131 Urazmanova and Cheshko, Tatary, p. 358.

132 Pokrovsky, FV, part 1, p. 89. Examples of Russian Jews active in the child protection movement included Z. O. Michnik, M. F. Levi, and E. M. Konyus.

133 See e.g. E. B., 'Iz dnevnika materi', SemV 1 (1914), 31.

134 For instructions, see e.g. A. Dernova-Yarmolenko, 'Kak pisat' dnevniki', SemV 1 (1914), 41–6, which emphasises that diaries must be accurate, detailed, regular, objective, and true. For examples of such diaries, see – besides those already cited – A. Rumyantseva, 'Opyt kharakteristiki mal'chika 4½ let', SemV 3 (1913), 1–24; Yul. Ladunskaya, 'K voprosu o razvitii ponyatiya o kolichestve', SemV 9 (1913), 65–70; A. Levonevsky, Moi rebenok (SPb., 1914).

135 Zhuk, Mat' i ditya, pp. 845–53 (teething), p. 880 (finger).

136 Pokrovsky, FV, part 1, p. 41.

137 K. G. Khrushchov, 'Akusherskaya pomosch' v Voronezhskoi gubernii i zhelatel'nye v nei uluchsheniya', Trudy VII Soveshchaniya gg. zemskikh vrachei i predsedatelei zemskikh uprav Voronezhskoi gubernii, 25–31 avgusta 1900 (Voronezh, 1900), vol. 2, p. 187, p. 184.

138 Ibid., p. 173.

139 I. I. Godytsky-Tsvirko, 'Kratkii statisticheskii otchet zemsko-meditsinskoi organizatsii v Voronezhskoi gubernii za 1902 god', Trudy VIII Soveshchaniya gg. vrachei i predsedatelei zemskikh uprav Voronezhskoi gubernii 25 avg.-3-go sent. 1903 (Voronezh, 1903), vol. 1, p. 1.

140 A. M. Kholodkovsky, 'Akusherstvo i ginekologiya v zemskoi meditsine', Trudy VIII Soveshchaniya, vol. 1, p. 399.

141 For the populations of the two districts, see Trudy IX-go Soveshchaniya gg. vrachei i predstavitelei zemskikh uprav Voronezhskoi gubernii 21 aprelya–1 maya 1908 (Voronezh., 1908), vol. 2, p. 11, p. 21; figures for attended births in Bobrovsky district, 1903–06 (473, 460, 513, 369), and Bogucharsky district, 1906 (438) appear ibid., p. 16, p. 31. For the 1910 figures, see Trudy X Ocherednogo Soveshchaniya gg. zemskikh vrachei i predstavitelei uprav Voronezhskoi gubernii 27 aprelya–6 maya 1912 (Voronezh, 1912), vol. 1, p. 498, p. 261.

142 See table 1 in digital version of this chapter.

143 For the population of Krasninsky district, see *XII S"ezd zemskikh vrachei Smolenskoi gubernii (s 8-go po 15-oe avgusta 1901 goda)* (Smolensk, 1902), p. 73; for live births in 1900, see *Prilozheniya k Trudam XII S"ezda zemskikh vrachei Smolenskoi gubernii* (Smolensk, 1902), p. 25; for medical attendance, *XIII S"ezd vrachei Smolenskoi gubernii* (Smolensk, 1905), p. 150.

144 *Sanitarnyi obzor Permskoi gubernii za 1895 god* (Perm', 1896), p. 1 (population in mid-1890s); *Sanitarnyi obzor Permskoi gubernii za 1910 god* (Perm', 1913), p. 1 (population in 1911); *Sanitarnyi obzor Permskoi gubernii za 1900 god* [Perm' 1902], pp. 13–14. Again, the figures do not include provision in the cities, which was certainly better (in Ekaterinburg district, not including the city, there were five maternity homes in 1900, which accommodated a full 1,735 births: see *Sanitarnyi obzor … 1900*, p. 14).

145 *Trudy VIII Soveshchaniya*, vol. 1, part 2, p. 192.

146 *Trudy IX Soveshchaniya*, vol. 1, p. 34.

147 As recorded from first-hand experience by the woman doctor S. Grin, 'Voina s batsillami', *Vestnik Evropy* 10 (1900), 601.

148 See e.g. Saburova, 'Ot chego umirayut', p. 130 (Saburova refers to 'kindergartens', but the age group she has in mind is clearly the crèche one).

149 Bobroff, 'Working Women'.

150 See e.g. 'O deyatel'nosti Kievskogo Obshchestva Narodnykh Detskikh Sadov po otchetu Obshchestva za 1908', *SemV* 1 (1911), 75–80.

151 See P. F. Kapterev (ed.), *Entsiklopediya semeinogo vospitaniya i obucheniya* (3 vols; SPb., 1898–1902), vol. 2, no. 29, pp. 21–4.

152 Vigdorchik, 'Detskaya smertnost'', p. 221.

153 N. A. Russkikh, 'Popechenie o detyakh grudnogo vozrasta', *Trudy Pervogo Vserrssiistergo s"ezda derskileh vrachei v Sankt-Peterburge* (SPb., 1913), p. 34. Costs in the country could vary widely, however: in Cherdynsk district, the figures ran from just over a kopeck to the best part of 30 kopecks per child per day. The crucial factor was the size of the nursery (i.e. staff costs – since there was no worry about keeping supervisor–child ratios high, larger nurseries were cheaper to run). (For the Cherdynsk figures, see *Otchety o deyatel'nosti sanitarnykh vrachei Permskogo Gubernskogo Zemstva za 1913 god* (Perm', 1915), p. 80.)

154 See e.g. A. Pomeryantseva in *Sel'skie priyuty-yasli* (SPb.1902), p. 2.

155 *Trudy VIII Soveshchaniya*, vol. 1, part 2, p. 199.

156 See *Sel'skie detskie priyuty: Priyuty-yasli* (SPb., 1900), p. 15.

157 Alina Gibsh, 'O postoyannykh yaslyakh, v svyazi s narodnymi detskimi sadami', *SemV* 8 (1913), 35.

158 *Trudy IX-go Soveshchaniya*, vol. 1, p. 35.

159 An example of such a philanthropist was Anna Pomeryantseva, who contributed a clarion call on the importance of the *yasli* network to *Sel'skie priyuty-yasli*, pp. 1–19.

160 *PB* 1 (1912), 3.

161 V. I. Binshtok, 'Deti v yaslakh Popechitel'tsvo letom 1916 goda', *OMM* 3 (1917), 277–84.

162 *Otchety o deyatel'nosti*, p. 80.

163 *Sel'skie priyuty-yasli*, p. 12. Similar attitudes obtained among Old Believers. An article published in an Old Believer journal in 1908 recorded that getting parents to agree to smallpox vaccination was extremely difficult: it was felt to be a sin to interfere with 'God's will'. The author of the article had been able to combat this attitude only by asking whether the villagers would really fail to step in if they saw a neighbour's house burning down – which brought in 20 recruits. 'The peasant women were prepared to believe people from their own religion'. Porfiry Shmakov, 'Staroobryadtsy i ospoprivivanie', *Staroobryadtsy* 6 (1908), 396–7.

164 Binshtok, 'Deti v yaslakh', 277–84.

165 I. M. Polyakov, 'Letnie yasli v techenie 1915 goda v Penzenskoi gubernii', *OMM* 2 (1916), 69–74.

166 *Sel'skie priyuty-yasli*, p. 12.

167 *Sel'skie detskie priyuty*, p. 13.

168 Gibsh, 'O postoyannykh yaslyakh', p. 38. Cf. M. Ya. Bezbokaya, 'Organizatsiya popecheniya o detyakh grudnogo vozrasta v selakh zemskoi Rossii', *Trudy pervogo vserossiiskogo s"ezda detskikh vrachei* (SPb., 1913), p. 48.

169 A. I. Shingarev, *Yasli-priyuty dlya detei v derevnyakh vo vremya letnei rabochei pory* (M., 1902), p. 20, p. 21, p. 24 .

170 Z. I. Klibanskaya, 'Prizrenie grudnykh detei v derevnyakh, kak odin iz faktorov bor'by s detskoi smertnost'yu', *Pediatriya* 4 (1914), 289–91.

171 Ibid., p. 286.

172 *Otchet o deyatel'nosti pravleniya obshchestva Detskaya Pomoshch' za 1896* (SPb., 1897), pp. 22–3.

173 P. Medovikov, 'Otchet o Vserossiiskom Soveshchanii po prizreniyu detei (10–14 avgusta 1917)', *OMM* 5 (1917), 429.

174 Z. O. Michnik, 'Okhrana mladenchestva', *OMM* 5 (1917), 405–18. Cf. M. M. Raits, 'Kak postavit' dela prizreniya detei v Rossii', *OMM* 6 (1917), 497–508.

175 Discussions include Michnik, *Besedy po okhrane*; E. M. Konyus, *Puti razvitiya sovetskoi okhrany materinstva i mladenchestva (1917–1940)* (M., 1954); Waters, 'Teaching Mothercraft'; Waters, 'The Modernization of Motherhood in Soviet Russia', *Soviet Studies* 1 (1992), 123–35; David Hoffmann, *Stalinist Values: The Cultural Norms of Soviet Modernity, 1917–1941* (Ithaca, NY, 2003), ch. 3; I. V. Il'in (ed.), *Organizatsiya rodovspo-mozheniya i ginekologicheskoi pomoschi v SSSR* (M., 1980), pp. 4–22.

176 Waters, 'The Modernization of Motherhood', p. 125; for a first-hand account, see A. W. Field, *The Protection of Women and Children in Soviet Russia* (NY, 1932), p. 30, pp. 102–6.

177 M. F. Levi, 'Dvadtsat' let deyatel'nosti organov okhrany materinstva i mladenchestva', *Akusherstvo i ginekologiya* 11 (1937), pp. 5–18.

178 M. F. Levi, *Istoriya rodovspomozheniya v SSSR* (M., 1950), p. 138.

179 *BNKZ* 11 (1923), 13.

180 *BNKZ* 14 (1924), 12.

181 For instance, in Ivanovo-Voznesensk, 1926, 55 per cent of costs were paid by the local administration, 35 per cent by enterprises, and 10 per cent by FUB (*BNKZ* 5 (1928), 67).

182 Konyus, *Puti razvitiya*, p. 185, p. 304.

183 Levi, *Istoriya*, p. 138. On the background to the expansion in services, see C. Davis, 'Economics of Soviet Public Health 1928: Development Strategy, Resource Constraints', and 'Health Plans', in S. G. Solomon and J. F. Hutchinson (eds), *Health and Society in Revolutionary Russia* (Bloomington, IN, 1989), pp. 146–72.

184 Michnik, *Okhrana materinstva i mladenchestva na Vasilievskom Ostrove*, p. 5 (mother and infant clinic), p. 9 (district nurses); pp. 2–3 (sections). Therapies such as quartz crystal, ultrasound, short-wave electricity, galvanic baths, ultraviolet light etc. remained popular up to the 1980s for use in paediatrics. (My thanks to Evgeny Dobrenko for this information.)

185 *BNKZ* 16 (1924), 13.

186 *BNKZ* 20–21 (1924), 23.

187 On the activities of these women, see Michnik, *Besedy po okhrane*, esp. pp. 76–84.

188 See Samuel C. Ramer, 'Feldshers and Rural Health Care in the Early Soviet Period', in Solomon and Hutchinson (eds), *Health and Society in Revolutionary Russia*, p. 134.

189 Levi, 'Dvadtsat' let deyatel'nosti', p. 13. In *Istoriya*, Levi gives the figure at slightly *over* 50 per cent – 17,851 of 33,387 beds.

190 For the 27 June 1936 *Pravda* decree, see Chapter 1 above; for the figures, Levi, 'Dvadtsat' let deyatel'nosti', p. 15.

191 Author interviews with woman born *c.* 1924 in Tavda district and woman born 1930 in Tavda district, Gerasimovka, 19 September 2003. Larger-scale interviewing work confirms this picture. Older informants in our village project in Leningrad province had usually done without much in the way of perinatal care (see e.g. Oxf/Lev V–04 PF4A, p. 33, Oxf/Lev V–04 PF14A, p. 45), while those born from the late 1920s onwards were more likely to have given birth in hospital (e.g. Oxf/Lev V–04 PF3A, p. 24, Oxf/Lev V–4 PF16B, p. 34). See also Ransel, *VM*.

192 In cities, women were more likely to be given their entitlement, but it was not necessarily sufficient. Leningrad records of 1951 reveal that women in the shipbuilding yards would try to leave work as soon as possible, because conditions were gruelling and dangerous. They would complain of weakness at 32 and 33 weeks, not wishing to work till 39 weeks. Some are described as 'creating scenes' and 'employing emotional blackmail' (*vymogatel'stvo*): the report-writer recommends extending maternity leave in this industry (TsGA–SPb., f. 9156 d. 136, l. 131).

193 Oxf/Lev V–05 PF18B, p. 18.

194 Ransel, *VM*, p. 73: grotty conditions in 1937, 1940; p. 75, poor personnel; p. 128, callous doctor.

195 Cf. Praskov'ya Krivolapova, from Tambov province, quoted by Ransel in *VM*, p. 128: 'My fourth child [in 1939] was born in the hospital. We had to get there because by then you couldn't find babki anymore. They were being persecuted.'

196 Oxf/Lev V–05 PF18B, p. 17.

197 Waters, 'Teaching Mothercraft', pp. 48–9. See also Waters, 'The Modernization of Motherhood'.

198 *Moskva v tsifrakh 1917–1977* (M., 1977), p. 127.

199 Waters, 'Teaching Mothercraft', p. 55.

200 Inna Shikhaeva-Gaister, *Semeinaya khronika vremen kul'ta lichnosti, 1925–1953* (M., 1998), p. 19.

201 'Maternity Hospital Interview, 1988' (tape recording, author's personal archive).

202 Larisa Vasil'eva, *Deti Kremlya* (M., 1997), p. 170. Vasil'eva – the daughter of a famous Soviet engineer and inventor – was very much at the bottom end of the clinic's catchment, which included the wives of top Party officials. Indeed, Nadezhda Allilueva had been scheduled to give birth to Vasily Stalin there, but had in the event jinked off to suburban Moscow after quarrelling with her husband: see Vasil'eva, *Deti Kremlya*, p. 112.

203 Yet accidents did happen, even here. Svetlana Stalina, for example, went down with toxicosis when giving birth to her daughter, Katya Zhdanova, in 1950. This incident was later to form one of the accusations of 'medical sabotage' underpinning the so-called 'Doctors' Plot', the charge that Jewish doctors had tried to poison members of Stalin's inner circle and the dictator himself (S. S. Montefiore, *Stalin: The Court of the Red Tsar*, London, 2004, p. 636). The problem with medical treatment at this level could stem from the doctors' terror of doing anything that might lead to an accusation of malpractice, which naturally encouraged pusillanimity and indecision.

204 The status of the Krupskaya hospital can be gauged from the fact that foreign visitors were taken there, always a sign that the authorities were confident about the quality of an institution. Herschel and Edith Alt, who visited in the Khrushchev era, noted that the hospital was clean and well-run, though they also reacted with informed scepticism to a claim by a member of the medical staff that there were 'no infections' in the hospital, and observed that another, more ordinary, hospital had obvious sanitation problems (*Russia's Children: A First Report on Child Welfare in the Soviet Union*, Westport, CT, 1959, pp. 144–8, p. 156).

205 Cf. Kuznetsova-Budanova's record of having problems with getting a job in a crèche, but none when she decided to transfer into a maternity hospital. *I u menya*, p. 282.

206 Ibid., p. 282.

207 Donald Filtzer, *Soviet Workers and Late Stalinism* (Cambridge, 2002), pp. 112–13 (from an official report on the hospital at Perovo, a major junction on the route between Moscow and Gor'ky [Nizhny-Novgorod], dating from the early 1950s).

208 'Analiz mertvorozhdaemosti za 1951 god', TsGA–SPb., f. 9156 op. 7 d. 69, ll. 1–10.

209 After suffering a spontaneous abortion, Freda Utley, the British wife of a Russian official, had to attend an abortion centre for D & C: the only soap was the sliver she had brought with her, and, when she needed to be cleaned up, the nurse picked some filthy cotton wool off the floor. Because of incompetence by the referring doctor (not medically qualified at all), she was operated on twice. *Lost Illusion* (London, 1949), pp. 87–8.

210 On practical problems, see 'Godovye otchety rodil'nykh domov za 1946 god', tt. 1–3. TsGA–SPb., f. 9516 op. 4 d. 702, d. 703, d. 704, *passim*:

e.g. d. 703, l. 18 (heating problems), l. 61, l. 65 (crowding), d. 704 l. 5 ob. (potty shortage), l. 55 (staff shortages).

211 Oxf/Lev SPb.–02 PF6A, p. 25. In 1946, an official report on one Leningrad maternity hospital recorded that nearly two thirds of women, or around 680, had got there by themselves, and a further 10 had given birth on the street: TsGA–SPb., f. 9156 op. 4 d. 703, ll. 4–5.

212 Freda Utley, for instance, got herself into 'one of the best maternity hospitals in Russia', the Roddom im. Klary Tsetkin, 'by a combination of wangling and money': *Lost Illusion*, p. 145.

213 Author, personal information, Moscow, 1985.

214 Oxf/Lev SPb.–02 PF6A, p. 25.

215 Leder, *My Life in Stalinist Russia*, p. 188. This birth, of course, took place in the middle of the panic that accompanied the German invasion of the Soviet Union, but conditions were not much better at more normal times.

216 See G. Bucher, '"Free, and Worth Every Kopeck": Soviet Medicine and Women in Postwar Russia', in W. B. Husband (ed.), *The Human Tradition in Modern Russia* (Wilmington, DE, 2000), pp. 180–5 (on the late 1940s and early 1950s). For the early 1980s, cf. also the remarks of the informant in R. Lourie, *Russia Speaks: An Oral History from the Revolution to the Present* (NY, 1991), pp. 352–6: filthy, rough treatment by nurses and doctors, half the children on the ward died.

217 E. A. Belousova, 'Prima materia: sotsializatsiya zhenshchiny v rodil'nom dome', in A. K. Baiburin (ed.), *Trudy fakul'teta etnologii* (SPb., 2001), p. 80.

218 In Leningrad during 1946, painkiller use, where mentioned, tended to run between 20 and 35 per cent, with other hospitals either naming smaller proportions (down to 2 out of 2,516 at the Moskovsky district maternity hospital), or not mentioning painkillers at all. TsGA–SPb., f. 9156 op. 4 d. 703, ll. 4–5.

219 See 'Maternity Hospital Interview, 1988'.

220 See e.g. Irina Krasnopol'skaya, 'Poltapochki na god', *N* 39 (1989), 10–11, who mentions lack of hospital wear for the women (only one slipper each, etc), newborns dressed in rags, dreadful sanitary facilities, but above all shortages of staff.

221 CKQ Ox–03 PF4A, p. 12.

222 Utley, *Lost Illusion*, p. 145.

223 On medical procedures, see Belousova, 'Prima materia'; on removal of personal items, 'Maternity Hospital Interview, 1988'.

224 Belousova, 'Prima materia', esp. p. 83.

225 Oxf/Lev SPb.–03 PF16A p. 81.

226 CKQ M–04 PF7, p. 23.

227 Vasil'eva in *Deti Kremlya* remembers that she needed to send a female visitor with a small bribe for the nursery-room staff in order to get news of her infant son (p. 170). The only unusual part of this story is that the visitor turned out to be Svetlana Stalina.

228 Tat'yana Kardinalovskaya, *Zhizn' tomu nazad* (SPb., 1996), p. 120, recalled writing her own name on her daughter's back when the latter was born in 1925 to avoid such confusion.

229 Waters, 'Teaching Mothercraft', p. 38, makes this argument with reference to the specific issue of

pain during labour, but it is applicable to other areas of obstetrics and paediatrics as well. It is interesting to note that a number of midwives working before 1917 also offered massage: see *Adres-ukazatel' vol'no-praktikuyushchikh vrachei-spetsialistov g. Kazani* (Kazan', 1910), pp. 25–6 (5 out of 18). This sensible combination seems to have disappeared after 1917.

230 Waters, 'Teaching Mothercraft', p. 54.

231 Oxf/Lev M–04 PF37A, p. 23.

232 See e.g. CKQ Ox–03 PF4A, p. 12; CKQ E–03 PF1B, p. 4.

233 Oxf/Lev P–05 PF12B, p. 13.

234 On maternal mortality in the 1920s, see A. N. Antonov, 'O materinskoi smertnosti', *Zhurnal po izucheniyu rannego detskogo vozrasta* 7 (1929), 546–53. Figures from Leningrad in 1940–51 give the following rates: 1940 0.20; 1943 0.30; 1944 0.18; 1945 0.18; 1946 0.14; 1947 0.09; 1948 0.09; 1949 0.05; 1951 0.09. See TsGA–SPb., f. 9516 op. 4 d. 702, d. 703, d. 704; f. 9516 op. 7 d. 68, d. 69.

235 On perinatal deaths, see 'Godovye otchety rodil'nykh domov za 1946 g.', tt. 1–3, TsGA–SPb., f. 9156 op. 4 d. 702, d. 703 d. 704, *passim*.

236 'Statisticheskie otchety roddomov i zhenskikh konsul'tatsii za 1951', TsGA–SPb., f. 9156 op. 7 d. 135, d. 136. See also table 2 in digital version of this chapter.

237 GARF f. 8009 op. 21 d. 276 l. 51.

238 Waters, 'Teaching Mothercraft', p. 52. The 1926 figure for the Soviet Union totalled 5,500,267 live births and 954,836 deaths of children under 12 months, giving a death rate of approximately 16.5 per cent, as compared with the 1905 death rate of 27.2 per cent. Figure for Moscow: ibid.

239 A. I. Mordovtsev and Tomilin [sic], 'Detskaya smertnost' sredi tekstil'shchikov g. Serpukhova', *BNKZ* 5 (1934), 31–5.

240 V. F. Zima, *Golod v SSSR, 1946–1947 godov* (M., 1996), pp. 160–1, p. 162.

241 *Zhenshchina v SSSR: kratkii statisticheskii spravochnik* (M., 1960), p. 61 (figures for 1957, 1960); GASO f. 1428 op. 1 d. 809, l. 94, l. 95 (figures for 1962, Moscow 1957: this latter is given as being in the range 2.2–2.6 per cent).

242 GARF f. 482 op. 50 d. 6566, l. 57, gives figures of 4.6 per cent for Vladimir in 1960, and 3.1 per cent for the same province in 1962. For the 1970 and 1985 figures, see *Zhenshchina v SSSR*, p. 61.

243 For first-hand descriptions of this, see the memoir by T. Kardinalovskaya (whose infant son died aged three months in 1928, of combined flu and meningitis), *Zhizn' tomu nazad* (SPb., 1996), p. 122; and the poetry of Ol'ga Berggol'ts, both of whose daughters died of infectious diseases in the late 1930s (see Chapter 1 above).

244 For instance, *Itogi vsesoyuznoi perepisi naseleniya 1959 goda. SSSR. Svodnyi tom* (M., 1962), p. 260, indicates that life expectancy at birth was 70 in England and France, but 68.59 in the Soviet Union.

245 TsGA f. 9516 op. 7 d. 68, d. 69.

246 Stephen White, *Russia Goes Dry: Alcohol, State, and Society* (Cambridge, 1996), p. 40.

247 'My sami ikh kalechim', *N* 43 (1989), 8. For

earlier shock reports on infant mortality, see e.g. 'Malen'kie deti – bol'shie zaboty', *N* 7 (1987), 16–17; Yu. Rakhval'sky, 'Otvechat' za svoe zdorov'e' and 'Lozh' ne vo spasenie', *N* 15 (1987), 18; 'O malyshe i professional'nom urovne vracha', *N* 33 (1987), 33; V. N. Mudrak 'Dlya zdorov'ya malyshei' *N* 2 (1988), 2; and especially 'Okno v mir statistiki', *N* 44 (1988), 12–13, and 'Puteshestvie za initsiativoi', ibid., p. 18.

248 Konyus, *Puti razvitiya sovetskoi okhrany materinstva i mladenchestva*, p. 304.

249 Waters, 'Teaching Mothercraft', p. 50.

250 On the legal side of the clinics, see Z. O. Michnik and M. Ya. Slutsky, 'Ob organizatsii konsul'tatsionnogo obsluzhivaniya detei rannego vozrasta', *Voprosy pediatrii i okhrany materinstva i mladenchestva* 1 (1940), 43–6. Many clinics had offered support of this kind long before it became mandatory: on a Leningrad pioneer, see the obituary of Pavel Isaevich Lyublinsky in *Voprosy pediatrii i okhrany materinstva i mladenchestva* 1 (1940), 47–9.

251 On post-natal care in the 1920s, see e.g. Michnik, *Okhrana materinstva i mladenchestva na Vasilievskom Ostrove*, pp. 9–10; for later eras, see e.g. *Pediatriya* 12 (1940), 115–16. These norms were not necessarily always fulfilled: in Leningrad after the war, for example, a shortage of trained staff meant that infants might be seen at most twice a month rather than once a *dekada* (every ten days): *Voprosy pediatrii i okhrany materinstva i detstva* 1 (1946), 41–6.

252 Waters, 'Teaching Mothercraft', pp. 31–7.

253 A. N. Antonov and Z. O. Michnik, *Mat' i ditya* (M.–L., 1937), p. 224. A photograph of such a 'corner' is also reproduced. See also Z. O. Michnik, *Kak ustroit' ugolok rebenka v krest'yanskoi izbe* (L., 1928).

254 On the hygiene ethos, see G. N. Speransky, *Azbuka materi* (M., 1924); Field, *Protection of Women and Children*, pp. 219–24.

255 On air, see e.g. G. Speransky, *Ukhod za rebenkom rannego vozrasta* (4th edn, M., 1929).

256 See Z. O. Michnik and A. N. Antonov, *Mat' i rebenok* (L., 1925), esp. pp. 67–74; A. N. Antonov, *Pamyatka materi* (L., 1925), p. 11.

257 Michnik, *Kak ustroit'* [p. 3] [pages unnumbered].

258 A. N. Antonov and Z. O. Michnik, *Mat' i ditya* (M.–L., 1937), p. 145.

259 Sitting up: ibid., p. 255; eating tidily: ibid., p. 195.

260 G. Speransky, *Ukhod za rebenkom rannego vozrasta* (4th edn; M., 1929), p. 125. Before the Revolution, this procedure had been coming into fashion among older children (see Chapter 14 below), but it appears to have been only after 1917 that 'tempering' was advocated for infants.

261 My thanks to Nicholas Stargardt for this information.

262 Mary Truby King, *Mothercraft* (London, 1934), p. 4. On Truby King's biography, see pp. 1–4, and Hardyment, *Perfect Parents*, pp. 178–81.

263 Truby King, *The Expectant Mother and Baby's First Month* (London, 1924), pp. 117–18, p. 35.

264 See M. Crubellier, *L'Enfance et la jeunesse dans la société française 1800–1950* (Paris, 1979), 210 (original emphasis).

265 Speransky, *Ukhod za rebenkom*.

266 On such contests, see Christina Kiaer, 'Delivered from Capitalism: Nostalgia, Alienation, and the Future of Reproduction in Tret'iakov's *I Want a Child!*', in Christina Kiaer and Eric Naiman (eds), *Everyday Life in Soviet Russia* (Bloomington, IN, 2006), p. 207.

267 Michnik and Antonov, *Mat' i rebenok*, p. 20 (nature), p. 27 (vomiting and diarrhoea), p. 33 (TB), p. 44 (artificial feeding).

268 Speransky, *Ukhod za rebenkom*, p. 49.

269 Antonov, *Pamyatka materi*, p. 9.

270 A. Makarenko, *Kniga dlya roditelei* (M., 1937), p. 320.

271 Truby King, *Feeding and Care of Baby* (Christchurch [NZ], [1940]) (quotation p. 96); Crubellier, *L'Enfance*, p. 216.

272 Leder, *My Life in Stalinist Russia*, p. 189.

273 See the article in *N* 8 (1962), 13, stating that production had been pioneered in Kiev in 1955.

274 Conversely, Michnik and Antonov, *Mat' i rebenok*, described high-quality milk substitute for babies as 'an ideal that we should strive towards', p. 49, making clear that their opposition to artificial feeding was not only dogmatic; Antonov, *Pamyatka materi*, p. 10, countenanced 'supplementary' feeds of cow's milk if necessary.

275 E. Piccard, *Lettres de Moscou, 1928–1933* (Neuchâtel, n.d.), p. 106 (16 June 1930).

276 In later decades, milk continued to be paid for, but mothers were expected to donate it.

277 Cf. Tsvetaeva's fruitless attempts to find such a nurse for her daughter Irina, born in 1916, in May 1917, before she made efforts to sign the child up for a supplementary feeding programme, 'Detskoe pitanie': *Marina Tsvetaeva: Neizdannoe: Sem'ya, istoriya v pis'makh*, ed. E. V. Korkina (M., 1999), p. 240.

278 Indeed, Tsvetaeva herself had breast-fed Irina before deciding she did not have enough milk (ibid.).

279 Ransel, *VM*, pp. 109–15. For the boiling water method, see p. 110.

280 Ibid., pp. 200–1. On disapproval, see e.g. Michnik and Antonov, *Mat' i rebenok* (any dummy is bad), pp. 73–4.

281 As recorded in Oxf/Lev P–05 PF28A, p. 7 (referring to the mid-1920s: it is not clear how widespread this practice was in later eras).

282 Speransky, *Ukhod za rebenkom*, p. 118, bans *svival'niki*. See also Michnik and Antonov, *Mat' i rebenok*, p. 65; Michnik and Antonov, *Mat' i ditya*, p. 212; Waters, 'Teaching Mothercraft', pp. 41–2.

283 See e.g. the line drawings in G. Speransky, *Azbuka dlya materei* (M.–L., 1924); B. A. Arkhangel'sky and B. N. Speransky, *Mat' i ditya: shkola molodoi materi* (M., 1948), pp. 98–101; Yu. F. Dombrovskaya, *Pamyatka molodoi materi* (M., 1954), p. 14.

284 Herschel Alt and Edith Alt, *Russia's Children*, pp. 114–15. The Alts' conclusion was that people knew the practice was considered old-fashioned by Westerners and so denied that it was going on, which is possible, but just as likely is a terminological confusion: the practice looked like 'swaddling' to the Alts, but was not what

Russians would have described as *svivanie*.

285 Oxf/Lev SPb.–02 PF6A, pp. 13–14: this informant describes how it was done in her family in the mid-1930s, 'so that the legs didn't end up crooked', and how she did not realise that medical opinion was against the practice until she entered medical school in the 1950s. Cf. H. K. Geiger, *The Family in Soviet Russia* (Cambridge, MA, 1968), p. 273: informants relate that swaddling continued in 1950s. Note also Michnik and Antonov, *Mat' i ditya*, p. 212, describing the practice as 'very common'.

286 Ransel, *VM*, pp. 206–8: the shift varied – in terms of the areas studied by Ransel – from the mid-1940s, in Moscow region, to the mid-1950s, in Smolensk, with the Urals and the Volga region somewhere in between. The interview material cited by Ransel also makes clear that binding cloths were almost uniformly made from used material, such as old shirts, rather than made specially, which is attributed here to economic deprivation, but may also have had a ritual resonance (putting the child into used clothes was one of the methods employed to underline its resemblance to the rest of the family, and thus make it human: see discussion at pp. 288–9 above).

287 Oxf/Lev T–04 PF20A, p. 37; cf. Oxf/Lev T–04 PF7B, p. 24.

288 For a reference to the chaw (here from the 1930s or 1940s), see Oxf/Lev V–05 PF17B, p. 6: the informant's wife recalled 'they'd chew some bread for the little 'un in a cloth and he'd suck it'.

289 See V. A. Rybnikova-Shilova, *Dnevnik materi* (Orel, 1923), p. 54.

290 I. R. Klyuchareva, *Iz dnevnika materi* (M., 1951), p. 5. (The account refers to the mid-1930s.)

291 Michnik, *Okhrana materinstva i mladenchstva na Vasilievskom Ostrove*, p. 11: 82 per cent of women trusted the advice given in 1922, and 92 per cent in 1924. Care graded as 'satisfactory' by health visitors rose from 56 per cent in 1917 to 87 per cent in 1924 (ibid.)

292 This statement is based on our village interview project; cf. Ransel, *VM*, and Waters, 'Teaching Mothercraft', p. 55.

293 Michnik, *Okhrana materinstva i mladenchestva na Vasilievskom Ostrove*, p. 23. Low-quality care was found in 21 per cent of illiterate mothers, as opposed to 6 per cent of literate ones, but in 1 per cent only of mothers from higher socio-economic groups, as opposed to 20 per cent of those from lower ones.

294 Ransel, *VM*, pp. 210–11.

295 For a reproduction of these paintings, see Matthew Cullerne Bown, *Socialist Realist Painting* (New Haven, CT, 1998), plates 186 and 185.

296 As described in Nina Mikhal'skaya, [Vospominaniya] (b. 1925), untitled typescript, p. 13.

297 Field, *The Protection of Women and Children*, p. 222. Prohibition on kissing children: ibid., p. 225: 'do not kiss children' on a poster.

298 Leder, *My Life in Stalinist Russia*, p. 191.

299 Michnik and Antonov, *Mat' i rebenok*, p. 29.

300 Speransky, *Ukhod za rebenkom*, p. 129.

301 *PP* 15 March 1925, 3.

302 See Agrippina Korevanova's account in Fitzpatrick and Slezkine, p. 189.

303 Bown, *Socialist Realist Painting*, plate 191.

304 On the former case, see Oxf/Lev V–05 PF19A, p. 2. On the latter case, cf. the instance of an official who refused to register a woman born in the late 1940s as Polina because he alleged this was not a name (personal information, 2005).

305 See Kabo, *Ocherki rabochego byta*, p. 200: the sample of families is very small though, and the figure of 70 per cent is still high by the standards of some late twentieth-century Western countries: contrast 25 per cent in Britain in 2000: *Sunday Independent*, 30 July 2000, p. 1.

306 On the use of a layperson, see Oxf/Lev V–05 PF5B, p. 13 (this in the late 1940s); on delays, Ransel, *VM*, pp. 168–9.

307 'Ob otvetstvennosti za sovershenie religioznogo obryada nad det'mi bez soglasiya roditelei', *SYu* 13 (1935), 29.

308 Kormina, 'Institut', p. 236. 'Close friends' translates 'witnesses', the modern equivalent of the traditional *druzhki* of the bride and groom.

309 Mikhail Zoshchenko, 'Roza-Mariya', *Krokodil* 14 (1938): *Sobranie sochinenii v 3 tomakh* (L., 1986), vol. 2, pp. 329–32. The baby ends up with the double name of 'Roza' (for the purposes of the registry office), and 'Mariya' (for the purposes of the Church).

310 The 'Leonard' example comes from an informant with family roots in Vologda province personal information, May 2001). Obviously, more detailed comment on naming patterns would require extensive work in birth registration archives, a neglected topic of research so far. For an exceptional case of a girl (b. 1960) who was named after a saint, see Oxf/Lev P–05 PF12B, p. 10.

311 This development was partly encouraged by advice literature, which started to take a more permissive attitude to offbeat monickers: see e.g. 'Dobroe imya', *N* 21 (1960), 18–19.

312 See e.g. Oxf/Lev V–05 PF19A, p. 2, where the names the informant wanted to give her daughters, after two aunts, were the absolutely standard Natal'ya and Ol'ga. Another case of naming after relatives (this time Nina and Tolya) is mentioned in Oxf/Lev V–05 PF13A, p. 26.

313 As is pointed out by Naum Korzhavin, 'V soblaznakh krovavoi epokhi', *NM* 7 (1992), 169.

314 Urazmanova and Cheshko, *Tatary*, pp. 359–60.

315 Ibid., p. 337.

316 CKI SPb.–4. Sometimes this assimilation was welcome, from the children's own point of view: on the trials of having an unusual name, see Alie Akimova, '… I zori rodiny dalekoi', *Druzhba narodov* 3 (2002), 165.

317 For big-city figures (in this case, from Sverdlovsk), see TsDOO SO f. 161 op. 27 d. 67, l. 10. By 1951, Leningrad already had 58 'women's consultancies' (gynaecological and pre-natal): see 'Statisticheskie otchety roddomov i zhenskikh konsul'tatsii za 1951', TsGA–SPb., f. 9156 op. 7 d. 135, d. 136. The information about illegal residents comes from first-hand observation of a friend, from

a non-Russian Soviet republic but settled in Leningrad, who had her child in a maternity home (where she counted as an 'emergency' case), but did not have pre-natal treatment (which she 'should' have received in her official place of residence).

318 RAO NA f. 126 op. 1 d. 259, l. 2, l. 7.

319 As recorded in 1951 in Leningrad at the Karl Marx Factory Women's Consultancy: see TsGA–SPb., f. 9156 op. 7 d. 135, l. 69.

320 See Geiger, *The Family in Soviet Russia*, p. 273.

321 Cf. Terry Bushell, *Marriage of Inconvenience* (London, 1985), p. 109, which has an account of his wife's punctilious washing and cleaning.

322 As reported e.g. by Oxf/Lev V–04 PF4B, p. 33.

323 Ransel, *VM*, p. 7 – on maternity pay; pp. 137–8, on attitudes to traditional birth, quoting a woman from Smolensk province.

324 Ibid., p. 201, p. 207, p. 211.

325 Oxf/Lev V–04 PF7A, p. 69.

326 Oxf/Lev V–04 PF3A, p. 28: the informant laments the discomfort of that great lump of cotton wool between a child's legs.

327 The legal press did report such cases in the early 1930s: see e.g. A. Kismis, 'Delo o detoubiistvakh trebuet bolee chetkogo podkhoda so storony narodnykh sudov', *SYu* 13 (1930), 22–4, which reports 33 cases over three months in the Urals (after the start of forced collectivisation, though the article does not mention this background). It concluded that 'false shame' and a desire to be rid of the children were the main promptings, with material want playing little role. This interpretation pointed to a harder line on infanticide than before 1917, which was also reflected in the penalties meted out, ranging up to a custodial sentence of three years.

328 TsGA–SPb., f. 9156 op. 7 d. 1055, l. 23.

329 TsDOO SO f. 161 op. 27 d. 67, l. 2.

330 Ransel, *VM*, p. 201. Oxf/Lev V–04 PF7A, p. 69, suggests increasing use of bought-in baby food from the late 1960s.

331 TsDOO SO f. 161 op. 27 d. 67, l. 2.

332 Across the RSFSR, numbers of milk kitchens rose from 2,898 to 3,490 between 1963 and 1964 (see GARF f. 8009 op. 21 d. 276, l. 50). But this rise – just over 20 per cent – was not necessarily equal to the problem. For instance, demand was outstripping supply by more than 66 per cent in Sverdlovsk in 1956. (TsDOO SO f. 161 op. 27 d. 67, l. 2.) On problems with the facilities (elderly equipment, insanitary conditions, insufficient mechanisation), see the 1964 report at GARF f. 8009 op. 21 d. 284, l. 6.

333 See e.g. Oxf/Lev P–05 P12A, p. 7: 'I was hardly ever ill. I think it's because I was breast-fed for ages, till I was two and a half. Because Mum was at home and I was with her all the time. She'd be sewing and I'd come and say, "Mum, put that down, take Galya, give us your tit." So it must have been that milk that helped me not get ill, and I had no colds either, because I was at home the first two and a half years.'

334 Comment from informants suggests that in the early 1960s acquiring goods for infants was rather easier. See e.g. CKQ M–04 PF7A, p. 24.

335 Bushell, *Marriage of Inconvenience*, p. 108, p. 109, p. 116.

336 See e.g. CKQ Ox PF4A p. 12.

337 For a reproduction of the painting, see Bown, *Socialist Realist Painting*, plate 353.

338 See e.g. Oxf/Lev T–04 PF3B, p. 20: 'My husband did everything: he bathed the baby, I was even afraid to pick it up … I remember even being scared to pick up the older one, but he bathed it and put the nappies on at first […] you could say he brought our older child up, really.' Normative sources include e.g. L. Rubashkin, 'Otets v sem'e', *N* 4 (1968), 20; *N* 3 (1968), 21 (a splash on a machine for heating baby food, which is said to be aimed especially at 'papas').

339 See Bown, *Socialist Realist Painting*, plate 340.

340 R. Bamm et al. (eds), *Semeinoe vospitanie: slovar' dlya roditelei* (M., 1967), p. 131.

341 V. A. Rybnikova-Shilova, *Moi dnevnik* (Orel, 1923), p. 32 (enemas), p. 40 (anxiety that a child could be 'spoilt' when ill by being cuddled too much); R. Orlova, *Vospominaniya o neproshedshem vremeni* (Ann Arbor, 1983), p. 126. Soviet baby books recognised the greater likelihood of co-operation on the part of these mothers: works specifically addressed to working-class and peasant women, such as Speransky's *Azbuka* (originally published as *Azbuka materi-krest'yanki*) and A. W. Antonov's *Rabotnitsa-mat'* (M.–L., 1030), or the later collection, *Mat' i ditya: sbornik stat'ei dlya materei* (M., 1945), adopted a much more patronising and dogmatic tone than Speransky's *Ukhod za rebenkom* or Arkhangel'sky and Speransky's *Mat' i ditya*, both of which were also more opulently produced than the former modest pamphlets.

342 As recorded directly by Z. I. Stanchinskaya, *Dnevnik materi* (M., 1924), p. 100.

343 Communal flat life is discussed in much more detail in the digital version of this book, Chapter 6. An excellent introduction to the material substance of communal flat living is the 'virtual museum' set up by Ekaterina Gerasimova and Il'ya Utekhin on http://www.kommunalka.spb.ru.

344 See especially Rybnikova-Shilova, *Moi dnevnik*, p. 31 (omelette), p. 8 (stools).

345 A. L. Pavlova, *Dnevnik materi. Zapiski o razvitii rebenka ot rozhdeniya do 6½ let* (M., 1925), p. 17.

346 Field, *The Protection of Women and Children*, p. 225.

347 Bushell, *Marriage of Inconvenience*, p. 108, p. 143.

348 V. Dyushen (ed.), *Pyat' let detskogo goroda imeni III Internatsionala* (M., [1924]). See also the discussion in Chapter 2 above.

349 See e.g. *Mat' i ditya* (L., 1933); M. Ilin, *The Little Citizen of a Big Country* (M., 1939).

350 B. Pares, *Moscow Admits a Critic* (London, 1936), p. 49, was deeply impressed by these mother and baby rooms at stations.

351 GASO f. 1428 op. 1 d. 1601, l. 205 (population of under-ones); GARF f. 8009 op. 21 d. 274, l. 43 (population in creches). (The latter figure is the average for crèches in cities across the USSR, so it is possible that the figure for the general crèche population in Sverdlovsk was higher. In that case, however, the very small proportion of under-ones would be still more revealing.) For the Leningrad

figure (1947 was the peak), see TsGA SPb. f. 9156 op. 11 d. 4, l. 11. The proportion of the target age group in crèches in 1949 was 13.2 per cent (see p. 344 below), and it was probably smaller in 1947, as around 500 new places were being created a year.

352 For the change in structure, see 'Itogovyi material obsledovaniya ob"edinennykh doshkol'nykh uchrezhdenii goroda Moskvy', RAO NA f. 126 op. 1 ed. khr. 34, l. 2.

353 For a criticism of this vedomstvennost', see GARF f. 8009 op. 50 d. 806, l. 6.

354 GARF f. 8009 op. 21 d. 276, l. 13.

355 See the comments in 'Itogovyi material', RAO NA f. 126 op. 1 ed. khr. 34, l. 14; ibid., ed. khr. 35, l. 216.

356 E.g. (examples from Sverdlovsk), GASO f. 1428 op. 1 d. 809, l. 110.

357 BNKZ 1 (1926), p. 20. Konyus, Puti razvitiya, p. 185, gives the 1925 figure as 584.

358 BNKZ 1 (1935), 45–9.

359 TsAODM f. 69 op. 1 d. 686, l. 13 verso: from 1929 report to members of the Krasnaya Presnya District Committee agitprop dept. In 1926, the overall population in Moscow province minus the city itself was 2,554,937 (see Vsesoyuznaya perepis' naseleniya 1926 goda, vol. 1, section 1 (M., 1928), table 4, p. 88), i.e. c. 250,000 0–3-year olds.

360 BNKZ 5 (1928), 67–8.

361 Z. O. Michnik and M. Ya. Slutsky, 'Chislennost' yasel'nykh kontingentov i okhvat yasel'nym obsluzhivaniem detei Leningradskikh rabotnits', Voprosy pediatrii i okhrany materinstva i mladenchestva 2 (1935), 146–53.

362 Pravda 24 July 1936, p. 4; Pravda 3 October 1936, p. 6, 'Dlya samykh malen'kikh'.

363 See e.g. BNKZ 13 (1931), 21, 23, 25 on the need to increase places for workers by 50 per cent, keep nurseries open longer hours, and give priority to 'shock workers'.

364 See V. Buchli, Materializing Culture (Oxford, 1999), pp. 75–6.

365 On parental organisation in villages, see TsAODM f. 3 op. 11 d. 385, l. 5 verso (from the minutes of a 16–17 February 1926 meeting of the regional soviet of Moscow volost peasant women's organisations); on co-operatives, see BNKZ 6 (1924), 12–13; BNKZ 22 (1928), 90–1; BNKZ 1 (1929), 28–30.

366 Zhenshchina v SSSR (M., 1936), quoted in Goldman, p. 314.

367 See the design for a mobile field crèche in DD 5 (1932), 8–9. Some of these temporary crèches/playgroups also operated in towns: see Instruktivnoe pis'mo po rabote na letnei gorodskoi ploshchadke (2nd edn; M.–L., 1929). Comparison with the RSFSR figures above, which are evidently for permanent nurseries, suggests that perhaps 90 per cent of available places were in such facilities.

368 BNKZ 20–21 (1924), 23.

369 Ransel, VM, p. 77.

370 Figures ibid., 76–7: Ransel himself thinks that the decline in places in the country may have been something to do with the purges; however, the gain of 4,009 full-time town places is close enough to the loss of 3,490 country places to suggest that a direct transfer of staff may have taken place. The loss of over 14,000 summer play-group places was probably at least partly attributable to the new emphasis in the Pioneer movement upon socially directed leisure for children rather than 'socially useful work' by children (see Chapter 16 below).

371 GARF f. 8009 op. 21 d. 73, l. 7.

372 Ibid., ll. 5–6.

373 Ocherki istorii shkoly i pedagogicheskoi mysli narodov SSSR, 1941–1961 (M., 1988), p. 14. This source also reports (ibid.) that factory nurseries were commandeered to offer any unfilled places to the children of mothers not working there.

374 TsGA SPb. f. 9156 op. 11 d. 7, l. 1 (1945 and 1946 figures), TsGA SPb. f. 9156 op. 11 d. 4, l. 1 (1949 figures), l. 3 (supply of places as percentage), l. 4 (queues), TsGA SPb. f. 9156 op. 11 d. 91, l. 1 (1951 figures, with information also about place losses offsetting place gains), l. 4 (queue size), l. 3 (overcrowding). On the other hand, Ocherki istorii shkoly reveals that conditions were not as bad here, or anywhere in the Russian Federation, as in some other republics, above all Belorussia, where 1945 capacity was around 45 per cent of the 1940 figure (p. 16). For the rising birth rate, cf. figures from Leningrad mother-and-child clinics indicating that attendance among the under-ones had risen by 7.3 per cent in the first quarter of 1946 as compared with the first quarter of 1945, and, among children under one month old, by 23.3 per cent (M. M. Katsenelenbogen, 'Sostoyanie patronata detei pervogo goda zhizni v Leningrade (po dannym detskikh konsul'tatsii i ob"edinennykh detskikh poliklinik)', Voprosy pediatrii i okhrany materinstva i detstva 4 (1946), 41.

375 TsGA SPb. f. 9156 op. 7 d. 1055, l. 8.

376 Narodnoe obrazovanie v SSSR, 1917–1967 (M., 1967), table 2, p. 39.

377 For further details, see Chapter 10.

378 GARF f. 8009 op. 21 d. 276 l. 2 (1959 and 1962 percentages), l. 43 (1965 percentage); GARF f. 482 op. 50 d. 8520, l. 45 (waiting list, 1963); GARF f. 8009 op. 50 d. 805, l. 23 (waiting list, per cent demand satisfied, 1969). On the other hand, these figures should be put in perspective: in 2004, the number of children under three attending a day nursery for the whole of the United Kingdom was only 200,000, also around a third of the age group (and the majority of these places were in the private system). See Madeleine Bunting, 'Nursery Tales', Guardian G2 section, 8 August 2004, pp. 4–7.

379 Moskva v tsifrakh, pp. 129–30.

380 See the article 'Ei blagodarny materi i deti', SYu 11 (1963) 22–3, about an official in charge of such a commission, who understandably looked forward to the time when there would be places for all.

381 Rezolyutsii Tret'ego Vserossiiskogo S"ezda po doshkol'nomu vospitaniyu, 15–21 okt. 1924 (M.–L., 1924), p. 4.

382 For the fees, see KhSZUP, vol. 4, p. 199.

383 Michnik and Slutsky, 'Chislennost' yaslennykh kontingentov', p. 152.

384 A literal translation of the Russian, *sidet' s rebenkom*, i.e. 'to baby-sit'.

385 Leder, *My Life in Stalinist Russia*, describes *domrabotnitsy* as easy to find, p. 158. On the official procedure for registering etc., see Valentina Bogdan in Fitzpatrick and Slezkine, p. 395. In practice, arrangements were often much more informal: Utley, *Lost Illusion*, pp. 80–1, gives a vivid account of the long hours worked by the women and the instability of tenure. Duties included not only child-minding, but also housekeeping and, most important of all, shopping (ibid.)

386 On *nyan'ki*, see e.g. Anna Dubova in Engel and Posadskaya-Vanderbeck, p. 24; Kabo, *Ocherki rabochego byta*, p. 89.

387 M. Vitukhovskaya and E. Gerasimova (eds), *Na korme vremeni* (SPb., 2000), pp. 108–9. See also Oxf/Lev M–04 PF19A, p. 4, for an account by a woman who almost killed her baby brother by putting a coin in his mouth to quiet him when she was left alone with him as a small child (this in *c.* 1940); and Oxf/Lev V–04 PF3B, p. 2, by an informant who would, as a girl, simply dump her smaller siblings and go off and play (this in the late 1930s); or Oxf/Lev V–05 PF6B, p. 14, which records how the informant was held up shopping and returned to find that a fire had started, but that fortunately her eldest daughter, still a child at the time, had been able to put it out.

388 Oxf/Lev V–05 PF5B, p. 4.

389 Gertrud Striedter gives a vivid account of encountering such feelings from fathers as well as mothers in the early 1920s: 'Erinnerungen' extract 4, pp. 1–2; typescript (archive of Jurig Striedter, Cambridge, MA).

390 Michnik and Slutsky, 'Chislennost' yaslennykh kontingentov', p. 152.

391 See Anna Dubova (b. 1916) in Engel and Posadskaya-Vanderbeck, p. 39.

392 There are stories like this in the magazines of the 1920s, and see also Ransel, *VM*, p. 62.

393 See Sarah Davies, *Popular Opinion in Stalin's Russia* (Cambridge, 1997), p. 68 – referring to the specific case of late 1939/1940, after the Law on Mobilisation of 1 September 1939 forced women to take over the factory jobs left by men press-ganged into the Soviet armed forces.

394 Galina Shtange in Garros, Korenevskaya, and Lahusen, p. 180.

395 Kuzetsova-Budanova, *I u menya*, pp. 272–81.

396 TsGA SPb. f. 9156 op. 7 d. 91, l. 10.

397 For example, in 1949, Leningrad had a 3.3 per cent shortage of sisters, a 10.5 per cent shortage of pedagogues, a 3.1 per cent shortage of nannies, and a 4.1 per cent shortage of technical personnel. TsGA SPb. f. 9156 op. 11 d. 4, l. 9.

398 See the protocol for a July 1921 meeting of the Women Workers' Section of the Krasnaya Presnya District Committee of the Communist Party, TsAODM f. 69 op. 1 d. 89, l. 50 rev. Mary Leder, *My Life in Stalinist Russia*, p. 23, reports how systematic theft of food at a commune in Birobidzhan during 1931–32 had created problems with feeding the children.

399 *Pravda* 25 August 1935, p. 1, 'Sovetskim detyam – obraztsovye yasli'.

400 GARF f. 8009 op. 21 d. 44, l. 16, l. 30 rev., l. 34, l. 71, ll. 81–2.

401 GARF f. 8009 op. 21 d. 376, l. 18 (crowding, lack of verandas, diet norms still those of 1949 [1965]), GARF f. 8009 op. 50 d. 806, l. 5, l. 7 (hygiene problems, crowding [1969]), GASO f. 1428 op. 1 d. 809, l. 1, l. 13, l. 54 (lack of outdoor facilities, no 'tempering', *zakal [1961]*).

402 'Analiz deyatel'nosti yaslei goroda Leningrada za 1951 god po dannym godovykh statisticheskikh otchetov p. F. No. 22 i ob"yasnitel'nykh zapisok', TsGA SPb. f. 9156 op. 7 ed. khr. 91, l. 1 (overall yasli figures), l. 4 (waiting list; premises), ll. 6–8 (problems with buildings and equipment), l. 10 (staff training), l. 9 (staff turnover), l. 29 (dysentery), l. 30 (mortality rate). A first-hand account of losing a child to what was termed 'dyspepsia', but was probably in reality dysentery or gastro-enteritis, is given in Oxf/Lev V–04 PF4B, p. 33 (this in the mid-1950s).

403 'Analiz deyatel'nosti', p. 35.

404 'Sistematicheskie otchety yaslei za 1955 god', TsGA SPb. f. 9156 op. 7 ed. khr. 1053, p. 85 (Kuibyshev district), p. 65 (Kirov district), p. 38 (Kalinin district).

405 Field, *The Protection of Women and Children*, p. 150.

406 Ethel Mannin, 'Playtime of the Child in Modern Russia', in H. Griffith (ed.), *Playtime in Russia* (London, 1935), pp. 171–2.

407 GARF f. 8009 op. 21 d. 73, l. 7.

408 The only categories of working mothers who were exempted from night work were those who were pregnant or nursing, and in practice the rules prohibiting work by these were often violated, not infrequently with the connivance of the women workers themselves, since claiming special treatment tended to impact negatively on wage levels and to create friction in the work group. On this situation in the 1920s, see Melanie Ilic, 'Biding Their Time: Women Workers and the Regulation of Hours of Employment in the 1920s', in L. Edmondson (ed.), *Women in Russian History and Culture* (Basingstoke, 2001), pp. 149–50.

409 GARF f. 8009 op. 50 d. 807, l. 15.

410 Alt and Alt, *Russia's Children*, pp. 113–14.

411 TsGA SPb f. 9156 op. 7 d. 1053, *passim*, TsGA SPb. f. 9156 op. 7 d. 1054, *passim*, TsGA SPb. f. 9156 op. 7 d. 1054, *passim*. This report is organised district by district, with no round-up figures, but it was standard for there to be about 2,000 children in a district's nurseries, and for about 700 of these to be taken away (see e.g. TsGA SPb. f. 9156 op. 7 d. 1053, l. 7).

412 TsGA SPb. f. 9156 op. 7 d. 1053, 1054, 1055, *passim*. For instance, 838 vaccinations against measles were performed in Kalinin district in 1955 (TsGA SPb. f. 9156 op. 7 d. 1053, l. 38).

413 Oxf/Lev V–05 PF6B, pp. 31–2.

414 E. Goldschmid, 'Moscow Nurseries', *Anglo-Soviet Journal* 25.2 (Autumn 1964), 24–9.

415 'God raboty po-novomu', *Doshkol'noe vospitanie* 5 (1960), 3–5. See also M. Yu. Kistyakovskaya, 'Vospitanie rebenka rannego vozrasta', *Doshkol'noe*

vospitanie 4 (1960), 29, emphasising not just 'good care' but 'educative actions' from the supervisors.

416 'O merakh po usileniyu gosudarstvennoi pomoshchi sem'yam, imeyushchim detei', Postanovlenie TsK KPSS ot 22 yanvarya 1981, No. 235. http://www.niv.ru/biblio/biblio5.pl?id=006&nt=066, accessed 15 February 2006. For further commentary on this statute, see Chapter 14 below.

417 Susan Jacoby, *Inside Soviet Schools* (NY, 1974), p. 55; *N* 18 (1972), quoted Jacoby, p. 38.

418 See V. Mukhina, *Bliznetsy* (M., 1969), p. 21 (entry for 21–27 September 1961): on physical culture, see also p. 10, entries for 13 March 1961 (when the children were a month old and she began the 'tempering') and 19 March 1961 (when they suffered a first bout of pneumonia, which she at this point decided had been 'cured' by the doctor's regime of tempering).

419 See the very interesting discussion by Alix Holt, based on interviews with a small group of Moscow women, in her 'Domestic Labour and Soviet Society', in J. Brine, M. Perrie, and A. Sutton (eds), *Home, School, and Leisure in the Soviet Union* (London, 1980), p. 37.

420 Oxf/Lev SPb.–04 56A, pp. 8–10.

421 *Pravda* 20 March 1987: see also Jim Riordan,

'Introduction', in idem (ed.), *Soviet Education: The Gifted and the Handicapped* (London, 1988), p. 5.

422 L. Proshina, 'O tete Gale, kotoraya nikogo ne boitsya', *N* 12 (1991), 12.

423 See e.g. M. Buyanov, 'Prigolubit', prilaskat'', *N* 41 (1984), 7; I. Stal'kova, 'O chem plachet malysh?', *N* 7 (1988), 18–19. Similar anxieties proliferated in Britain during the late 1990s and 2000s, as the institutional child-care network expanded: see e.g. Bunting, 'Nursery Tales', pp. 4–7, esp. p. 6. In the 1960s, on the other hand, attitudes to crying were still usually 'disciplinary': cf. E. Arzunyan, 'Rebenok plachet', *N* 28 (1967), 20–1, which warned that a baby attended to when crying would soon be running the house.

424 A. Mikhailovsky, 'Malysh, "Krepysh", i "Burenka"', *N* 29 (1988), 18–19.

425 *N* 47 (1989), 8–9.

426 Figures for birth defects in parts of post-Soviet Russia were still high. For example, in Irkutsk province in the year 1999, 720 of 26,000 newborns had congenital defects of one kind or another – heart, lung, kidney, and intestinal problems. Elena Visens, 'Za predelami Sadovogo kol'tsa', *RM* 23–29 March 2000, 5.

427 Oxf/Lev P–05 PF21A, pp. 6–7.

Chapter 10: Nursery Days

1 Ransel, *Village Mothers*, p. 211. Ransel's discussion refers to the twentieth century, but it is fair to assume a longer history, though the total neglect of 'potty-training' in most contemporary accounts of child-rearing in nineteenth-century Russia (see e.g. Pokrovsky, *FP*) creates an evidential problem.

2 Alex Saranin, *Child of the Kulaks* (St Lucia, 1997), p. 36.

3 A. K. Baiburin, *Ritual v traditsionnoi kul'ture* (SPb., 1993), pp. 55–6. Other rituals included carrying the child round the yard in a sack, or placing it in a new-ploughed furrow so that the growing grain would work by sympathetic magic: D. A. Baranov et al. (comps), *Russkaya izba: illustrirovannaya entsiklopediya* (SPb., 2004), p. 122.

4 A. K. Baiburin, 'Concepts of the Word and Language in Traditional Russian Culture', *Forum for Anthropology and Culture* 2 (2006), 301–7.

5 Pokrovsky, *FP*, vol. 45, part 3, p. 236.

6 E. A. Pokrovsky, *Detskie igry, preimushchestvenno russkie (v svyazi s istoriei, etnografiei, pedagogikoi i gigienoi)* (M.: Tipografiya A. A. Kartseva, 1887), pp. 96–8. This discussion also contains examples similar to the more elaborate games given below.

7 S. M. Loiter, *Russkii detskii fol'klor Karelii* (Petrozavodsk, 1991), p. 55 (recorded in 1987 from a woman born in 1931). The game has an exact equivalent in Britain: 'Leg over leg as the dog goes to Dover/He came to a stile and WHOOPS! he went over'.

8 On coming to terms with the environment, see M. V. Osorina, *Sekretnyi mir detei: v prostranstve mira vzroslykh* (SPb., 1999), ch. 1.

9 M. L. Krotova, *Babykinskii dnevnik* (M., 1998), p. 151, recorded in late 1986, but referring to some forty years earlier (Krotova was born in 1921, and

married just after the war).

10 Loiter, *Russkii detskii fol'klor*, p. 95: this recording 1978, but another similar one dates back to the 1920s.

11 For the translation history of Sully, Preyer, Piaget et al., see Chapter 1. Vygotsky's 'Rannee detstvo' (lecture given at the Herzen Pedagogical Institute in 1933–34) sees young children as 'situation-dependent', emotionally responsive to objects on the same level as people, and with an undeveloped sense of autonomous selfhood. In 'Krizis pervogo goda zhizni', he devotes considerable attention to the development of language as the basis of thought. See *Sobranie sochinenii* vol. 4 (M., 1984), pp. 340–67, pp. 318–39.

12 Both these examples are taken from N. I. Gavrilova 'Dnevnik materi', in N. I. Gavrilova and M. P. Stakhorskaya, *Dnevnik materi* (M., 1916), p. 74, p. 83. See also E. B., 'Iz dnevnika materi', *SemV* 2 (1914), pp. 25–7; A. Rumyantseva, 'Opyt kharakteristiki mal'chika 4½ let', *SemV* 3 (1913), 1–24; 4 (1913), 1–27; and (in this case a father's diary), A. Levonevsky, *Moi rebenok* (SPb., 1914), pp. 176–212.

13 Aleksandra Piir, 'Detskie igry', typescript inventory (SPb., 2003), p. 1.

14 As recalled by Kirill Kobrin in '"Slova" i "veshchi" poslestalinskogo detstva', *Logos* 3 (24) (2000), 46.

15 Levonevsky, *Moi rebenok*, pp. 28–9. See also e.g. Gavrilova, 'Dnevnik materi', p. 25.

16 V. Zhuk, *Mat' i ditya* (SPb., 1909), pp. 898–9.

17 On scalding, see e.g. entry in S. A. Tolstaya, *Dnevniki v dvukh tomakh* (M., 1978), vol. 1, p. 342, entry for 20 January 1898. Such incidents were not unique to working-class and peasant households: Samuil Marshak's daughter died

in November 1915 after being inundated by a samovar: see his letter to E. P. Peshkova of 20 November 1915, *Sobranie sochinenii v 8 tomakh*, vol. 8 (M., 1972), p. 85.

18 A. L. Pavlova, *Dnevnik materi* (M., 1925), p. 59. On the age of potty-training, cf. Alice W. Field, *Protection of Women and Children in Soviet Russia* (NY, 1932), p. 157: in crèches, a child of 18 months was expected to know when it wanted to urinate and be able to go at set times, and alone by two and a half. A normative guide of the late 1920s also suggests an early age (starting as soon as the child can sit): E. G. Bibanova, *Kak gotovit' iz rebenka v vozraste do 3-kh let budushchego stroitelya novoi zhizni* (M.–L., 1927), pp. 52–3.

19 For an example of the first usage, see a letter from Tsvetaeva to her 14-year-old daughter about the monkeys at the zoo peeing everywhere: M. Tsvetaeva, letter to A. S. Efron, 15 March 1926: *Neizdannoe: Sem'ya, istoriya v pis'makh*, ed. E. B. Korkina (M., 1999), p. 322.

20 Specialist work has been done in this area recently by T. O. Gavrilova: see e.g. 'Registr obshcheniya s det'mi (baby talk): nekotorye osobennosti intonatsii', in A. K Baiburin and V. B. Kolosova (eds), *Antropologiya, fol'kloristika, lingvistika* issue 1 (SPb., 2001), pp. 227–38.

21 E. A. Zemskaya, *Russkaya razgovornaya rech'* (M., 1978), p. 239, p. 249. Punctuation and speaker names inserted by me.

22 As recorded in Chukovsky's *Ot dvukh do pyati* (see Chapter 2 above). A later study in the same vein, containing many examples (e.g. the derivation of *armyane* from *armiya* by a child of 5.8, p. 9), is that of V. K. Kharchenko, *Slovar' detskoi rechi* (Belgorod, 1994).

23 Cf. Levonevsky's note that his son had learned, before he was three, the words *nyanechka* (nanny, diminutive), *papochka* (daddy, diminutive) and *mamochka* (mummy, diminutive) (*Moi rebenok*, p. 192). He also records the conversation: 'Dima ubit papu, a ty papa ubish' Dimu?' (2:8): (Dima oves daddy, do you ove Dima, daddy?) In both cases, the child is obviously reproducing adult discourse to him.

24 As possibly in the case of Dima in Levonevsky, *Moi rebenok*: cf. the boy's own use of *nyanechka* about her (see n. 23 above).

25 Cf. the cartoon in *Novyi Satirikon* 34 (1915), 8: 'Motherly feeling': a woman and her smart cavalier see a child and his nanny on the street: 'Look, Sergei, how sweet! I wonder whose little boy that can be?' 'But Madam, you don't mean to say you don't know your own Vasen'ka?' Hiring a nanny is seen here as benign neglect.

26 G. N. Speransky, *O zakalivanii detskogo organizma* (M., 1910). See also the coda to Pokrovsky, *Fizicheskoe vospitanie detei*, pp. 367–75, which refers to Russian traditional upbringing as being like that of the Spartans, producing 'tempered individuals' (*zakalennye natury*) (though with a propensity also to kill small children off).

27 A. Dernova-Yarmolenko, 'Za chto my nakazyvaem nashikh detei', *SemV* 1 (1911), 18.

28 P. Lesgaft, *Semeinoe vospitanie i ego znachenie* (SPb., 1906).

29 Ibid., p. 211.

30 A. N. Filippov, 'O perekarmlivanii detei', *SemV* 1 (1911), 5–12; 2 (1911), 1–15.

31 On toys, see Vl. Ladunsky, 'Detskie igry i igrushki', *SemV* 1 (1914), 24; on cruelty breeding cruelty, Alina Gibsh, 'O rezhime v sem'e', *SemV* 1 (1912), 53–7; on physical damage, G. Gordon, 'Gigiena nakazanii', *SemV* 8–9 (1911), 1–14.

32 Ladunsky, 'Detskie igry', 22.

33 N. E. Rumyantsev, 'Sovmestnoe obuchenie s psikhologicheskoi tochki zreniya', *SemV* 9 (1912), 77–8 (outline of a lecture given on 8 December 1912).

34 See e.g. M. P. Stakhorskaya, 'Dnevnik materi', in N. I. Gavrilova and M. P. Stakhorskaya, *Dnevnik materi* (M., 1916).

35 See illustrations in A. S. Virenius, 'Iskrivlenie pozvonochnika', in P. F. Kapterev (ed.), *Entsiklopediya semeinogo vospitaniya i obucheniya* (3 vols; SPb., 1898–1902), vol. 1, part 15, p. 30.

36 The picture is reproduced in A. Rusakova (as Russakowa), *Michail Nesterow* (L.: Aurora, 1990), plate 76. For further discussion of gender socialisation at this period, see Catriona Kelly, '"Khochu byt' traktoristkoi!" Gender i detstvo v dovoennoi sovetskoi Rossii', *Sotsial'naya istoriya: Ezhegodnik* 2003, 385–410.

37 Fedor Kudryavtsev, *Primechaniya k ankete* (M., 1990), pp. 18–19.

38 M. Ignatieff, *The Russian Album* (London, 1987), p. 61. See also Catriona Kelly, 'The Education of the Will: Masculinity and "Backbone" in Early Twentieth-Century Russia', in B. Clements, R. Friedman, and D. Healey (eds), *Masculinities in Russia* (Basingstoke, 2002), pp. 131–51.

39 Charters Wynn, *Workers, Strikes, and Pogroms* (Princeton NJ, 1992), pp. 73–4, describes factory workers' children hanging round with *besprizornye* in a major provincial industrial region.

40 A. Kuznetsova-Budanova, for instance (*I u menya byl krai rodnoi* (Munich, 1975), pp. 48–51) remembers a perpetually busy mother.

41 F. F. Fidler (ed.), *Pervye literaturnye shagi* (M., 1911), p. 240.

42 Dostoevsky's *Writer's Diary* and *Brothers Karamazov* had begun highlighting this problem back in the 1870s.

43 Mariengof, p. 22.

44 For knickerbockers, see e.g. the photograph of Mariengof, aged about six, reproduced in *Moi vek*, opp. p. 448.

45 See *Preis-kurant bel'ya: Torgovyi dom "Paul' Karlson" (S.-Peterburg, Morskaya no. 18)* (SPb., c. 1900), pp. 51–3.

46 T. Talbot Rice, *Tamara* (London, 1996), plate opposite p. 146.

47 'Portrety detei podpischits, prislannye na konkurs detskoi krasoty', *Zhenshchina* 7 (1914), 32–3; 8 (1914), 32–3.

48 Talbot Rice, *Tamara*, pp. 8–9.

49 T. Karsavina, *Theatre Street* (London, 1930), p. 7. Cf. E. Hill, *In the Mind's Eye: The Memoirs of Dame Elizabeth Hill* (Lewes, 1999), p. 17: 'I feared my mother but I greatly admired her.'

50 L. Panteleev, 'Ya veruyu', *NM* 8 (1991), 139: 'O kakoi blizosti mozhno govorit', esli obrashchayas' k ottsu ya ego nazyval "na Vy"?'.

51 As recalled by Hill, *In the Mind's Eye*, p. 18.
52 Zinaida Manakina remembered a birching as quite a small child, when she was late for dinner (see her memoir in *Zhenskaya sud'ba v Rossii*, ed. B. S. Illiaznor (M., 1994), p. 9). Corporal punishment is a given also in Mikhert Zoshchenko's memoir *Before Sunrise*.
53 O. Forsh, *SPA*, vol. 1, p. 579.
54 E. Fen, *A Russian Childhood* (London, 1961), p. 96. For the 'token slap on the hand', see ibid., p. 33.
55 N. Teffi, 'Vospitanie', *Sobranie sochinenii*, vol. 4 (M., 2000), p. 346.
56 See the illustration, M. Davydoff, *On the Estate* (London, 1986), p. 81, with the family at Christmas dinner and the small girl on her high chair, elbows flailing.
57 Mariengof, p. 70. Cf. the collection of quaint sayings in Elena Krichevskaya, *Moya Marusya (Zapiski materi)* (Petrograd, 1916), pp. 63–78.
58 Talbot Rice, *Tamara*, p. 10. For earlier examples of nanny-worship, see e.g. S. M. Solov'ev, *Zapiski dlya detei moikh, a esli mozhno, i dlya drugikh* (in his *Izbrannye trudy: Zapiski*, ed. A. A. Levandovsky and N. I. Tsimbaev, M., 1983, p. 229).
59 Panteleev, 'Ya veruyu', 139, 143.
60 V. Nabokov, *Speak, Memory* (Harmondsworth, 1969), p. 68. Religious literature of the day also perpetuated the 'suffer little children to come unto Me' image: see e.g. *Detskii sad, ili dukhovnye uroki dlya detei* (SPb., 1911).
61 I. Shmelev, *Leto gospodne* (1934–44) (NY, 1983), pp. 256–7 (on name-day cakes), pp. 12–13 (on Lenten sweetmeats). These reminiscences date from the 1880s (Shmelev was born in 1873), but are relevant to life in traditional families in later decades as well. On almond milk, fish, and potatoes and mushrooms, see Panteleev, 'Ya veruyu', 141.
62 Shmelev, *Leto gospodne*, p. 12.
63 Panteleev, 'Ya veruyu', p. 140.
64 Shmelev, *Leto gospodne*, p. 10.
65 See e.g. Kudryavtsev, *Primechaniya*, pp. 23–4, on being taught even these prayers only when it turned out he could recite exclusively the Latin Catholic versions, having been taught them by a French governess.
66 On the recruitment rites, see Zh. V. Kormina, 'Roditel'skoe blagoslovenie (pri provodakh v armiyu)', *Trudy fakul'teta etnologii* vol. 1 (SPb., 2001), pp. 38–61.
67 *SPA*, vol. 2, p. 456.
68 See the instructions for Old Believers set down in Grigory M. Karabinovich, *Kratkoe khristianskoe uchenie: Uchebnik po Zakonu Bozhiyu dlya Staroobryadtsev* (1916) (reprint: M., 1997), p. 7 (learning prayers), pp. 15–16 (prayers at different times of day), pp. 28–30 (cross and belt), p. 36 (table manners), p. 38 (drinking), p. 47 (fasts).
69 B. M. Firsov and I. G. Kiseleva (eds), *Byt velikorusskikh krest'yan-zemlepashtsev* (SPb., 1993), p. 266 (diet), p. 184 (table manners); cf. Kuznetsova-Budanova, *I u menya*, p. 20 (table manners).
70 Firsov and Kiseleva (eds), *Byt velikorusskikh krest'yan-zemlepashtsev*, p. 185, p. 216.
71 A. Gulyutina in Chaadaeva, p. 67.
72 K. Ukolova, ibid., p. 60.
73 E. Nikadorova, M. Rogacheva, D. Mitina, ibid., p. 98, p. 78, p. 90.
74 Kuznetsova-Budanova, *I u menya*, pp. 103–5 (Christmas), p. 68 (Easter).
75 *SPA*, vol. 1, p. 399.
76 Ol'ga Adamova-Sliozberg, *Put'* (M., 1993), p. 233.
77 R. K. Urazmanova, S. V. Cheshko, *Tatary* (M., 2001), p. 338, pp. 356–7.
78 Vadim Andreev, *Detstvo* (M., 1966), p. 86.
79 N. Teffi, 'Nyan'kina skazka pro kobyl'yu golovu', *Yumoristicheskie rasskazy* (M., 1990), pp. 75–9.
80 Talbot Rice, *Tamara*, pp. 11–13.
81 *Detskii sad i Elementarnaya shkola E. P. Zalesskoi* (M., 1907), p. 5; cf. 'The worst punishment for a child is excluding him from communal work' (p. 29).
82 *SPb-Pv-1903*, p. 107, p. 115. A free kindergarten had been opened in 1893 or 1894 ('Detskii sad', *NSE*, vol. 17, cols 80–1; N. Vinogradov, *Ocherki po istorii idei doshkol'nogo vospitaniya* (n.p., 1925), p. 148, gives discrepant dates), but had evidently closed before this guide was published.
83 Mariya Chekhova, 'Obshchestvo sodeistviya doshkol'nomu vospitaniyu detei', *RS* 4 (1908), 52–7.
84 *Vystavka "Detskii trud" (Kievskoe obshchestvo Narodnykh detskikh sadov)* (Kiev, 1911), p. 5, p. 17.
85 See *PZK* 13 (1911), p. 183, p. 186.
86 L. Tezavrovskaya, 'Narodnyi detskii sad', *SvoV* 7 (1913–14), 91–116; Vinogradov, *Ocherk po istorii idei doshkol'nogo vospitaniya*, p. 149.
87 For the Moscow figure, and for a sketch of the early history of the kindergarten movement in Russia, see Kirschenbaum, *Small Comrades*, ch. 1 (this figure at p. 29).
88 *PZK* 8 (1906), p. 65.
89 *DoshV* 6 (1911), 507–10.
90 *DoshV* 2 (1913), 66. See also *Vystavka "Detskii trud"*, esp. pp. 24–55 (describing the work of individual institutions, some run by the society and others private).
91 A. Simonovich, 'O detskikh sadakh', *VV* 8 (1896), 187 (Odessa, Tiflis); M. Stalinovskaya, 'Iz deyatel'nosti Chelyabinskogo Obshchestva doshkol'nogo vospitaniya', *SvoV* 10 (1911–12), 71–100.
92 On Saratov, see *DoshV* 3 (1912), 181; on Tomsk, *DoshV* 1 (1913), 59.
93 On St Petersburg, see 'Obshchestvo doshkol''nogo vospitaniya', *SemV* 2 (1911), 35–48; on the Kiev society, see 'O deyatel'nosti Kievskogo Obshchestva Narodnykh Detskikh Sadov po otchetu obshchestva za 1908', *SemV* 1 (1911), 75–80; on Astrakhan, 'V obshchestve sodeistviya doshkol'nomu vospitaniyu', *SemV* 2 (1911), 101; on Yeisk, 'Doshkol'noe vospitanie detei', *SemV* 4 (1911), 117; on Poltava, *SemV* 11 (1911), 120–1.
94 *SemV* 11 (1911), 120–1.
95 *Vystavka 'Detskii trud'*. For the relative underdevelopment of this sector before the 1910s, note e.g. the fact that only one facility specifically describing itself as being for working-class children appears in the list of kindergartens published in *PZK* 13 (1911), 183.
96 On the Poltava kindergarten, see *DoshV* 4

(1915), 313–16; Astrakhan', *DoshV* 9 (1913), 607; Taganrog, *DoshV* 8–9 (1915), 592–4; for examples of religious bodies, cf. the St Vladimir Society kindergarten in Penza (*DoshV* 5 (1913), 311), or the Borisglebskoe *bratstvo* in Kiev, *DoshV* 2 (1913), 66.

97 *DoshV* 2 (1911), 114 (M.); 5 (1912), 114 (SPb.)

98 E. I. Papkovskaya, *Kniga o malen'kikh trekhgortsakh* (M., 1948), pp. 4–8.

99 On the Khar'kovskii parovozostroitel'nyi zavod kindergarten, see *DoshV* 3 (1912), 179.

100 See 'Obshchestvo doshkol'nogo vospitaniya', p. 35: 16 of the kindergartens in St Petersburg in 1911 were of this type.

101 *DoshV* 6 (1912), 360–1. The article states that the change had been made by a ministerial circular dated 17 June 1909.

102 *DoshV* 5 (1915), 376.

103 *DoshV* 1 (1915), 47.

104 *DoshV* 8–9 (1916), 615–18.

105 *DoshV* 4 (1915), 313–16.

106 *Nakaz litsam, neposredstvenno zavedyvayushchim detskimi priyutami* (SPb., 1900) (quotation p. 3).

107 *Detskii sad i Elementarnaya shkola*, pp. 9–19. Cf. M. Kh. Sventitskaya, *Nash detskii sad* (M., 1913).

108 *Material dlya besed s malen'kimi det'mi* (M., 1914), p. 18, pp. 22–4.

109 *Sbornik igr dlya detei* (2 issues; SPb., 1871, 1874) lists, besides the games just mentioned, musical games, *kolodka*, *gorodok*, *lapta*, *kamchatka*. On the team-picking rituals, see issue 1, p. 81.

110 'M. P——n', 'Geograficheskoe predstavlenie v svobodnom detskom sadu', *SvoV* 2 (1911–12), 89–108 (quotations p. 96, p. 95). Such representations were, of course, rather stereotypical: see discussions in Chapter 1, above.

111 O. Volosistova in Chaadaeva, p. 76.

112 See V. Ogronovich 'Osnovnye nachala pravil'noi postanovki dnevnykh priyutov-yaslei dlya besprizornykh detei', *PB* 8–9–10 (1914), pp. 117–46.

113 See *Detskii sad i elementarnaya shkola*, p. 39; *Vystavka "Detskii trud"*, p. 26.

114 See *KhSZU*, vol. 2, p. 33.

115 See N. P. Eiges, *Vospitanie rebenka do 4 let* (M., 1948), p. 12; and cf. A. N. Antonov and Z. O. Michnik, *Mat' i ditya* (L.–M., 1937), p. 244.

116 E.g. A. S. Griboedov, *Vospityvaem zdorovykh detei: Pamyatka* (L., 1935), p. 4.

117 On the theme of Soviet collectivism generally (with some reference to issues of socialisation), see Oleg Kharkhordin, *The Collective and the Individual in Soviet Culture* (Berkeley, CA, 1999).

118 'Rodnaya mat' – luchshaya vospitatel'nitsa dlya rebenka pervykh let zhizni i domashnyaya obstanovka – nailuchshchaya obstanovka dlya ego fizicheskogo i psikhicheskogo razvitiya': A. N. Antonov, *Pamyatka materi* (L., 1925), p. 12.

119 A. Babina, *Kak organizovat' dosug detei* (M., 1929), p. 7.

120 N. F. Al'tgauzen, A. Yu. Lur'e, and E. P. Melent'eva, *Besedy s devushkami o materinstve i mladenchestve* (M.–L., 1929).

121 A. A. Makarenko, *Besedy s roditelyami* (1937): page references from edition published in Stalingrad, 1941: pp. 9–10 ('battle with idleness'), pp. 19–21

(punishments), pp. 52–6 (good and bad parenting).

122 A. A. Makarenko, *Kniga dlya roditelei* (M., 1937): for the phrase 'senior executive member of a collective', see p. 202; for the factory analogy, see p. 4, 'We must have no child catastrophes, no non-successes, no percentage of waste and damaged goods, even fractions of percentages!'

123 Ibid., p. 142.

124 See ibid., pp. 244–84, pp. 90–6.

125 For post-war examples, see e.g. Yu. Uzvyakov, 'O malen'kikh dlya bol'shikh', which shows desperate parents weaning a fat 6-year old off cigarettes by stuffing him on chocolate, and a beribboned small girl demanding to know why her father's official car has failed to turn up and made her late for school. (*Krokodil* 20 (1952), 5); L. Soifertis, 'Vospitanie ottsov', 1 (1948), 11; E. Shcheglov, 'Plody vospitaniya', 6 (1948), 14.

126 Makarenko, *Kniga*, p. 100. This particular phrase makes it sound as though spoiled boys were more of a worry, but in fact Makarenko sketched some spoiled girls as well, e.g. the librarian's daughter above. There was also a medical literature on the problems of the single child: see e.g. P. F. Frantsov, 'Nervnye deti i edinstvennyi rebenok', *Pediatriya* 5 (1930), 381–92.

127 Makarenko, *Kniga*, p. 17.

128 N. F. Al'tgauzen, *Otets i rebenok* (M., 1929), p. 14 (contraception), p. 24 (maternity hospital), p. 27 (boy versus girl), pp. 29–30 (help with child care), p. 33 (person and citizen, comradeliness).

129 For example, Lidiya Seifullina's story *The Young Lawbreakers* (Pravonarushiteli) concludes with the orphanage supervisor chivvying girls out of their 'girlish' ways. On fears, see Chapter 8.

130 CKQ Ox–03 PF5B, p. 6.

131 CKQ Ox–03 PF1A, p. 2.

132 A. N. Rybnikova-Shilova, *Moi dnevnik* (Orel, 1923), p. 98, p. 137. Contrast A——skaya, 'Iz zapisok materi', *Svobodnoe vospitanie* 10 (1907–8), 57–90, which juxtaposes the amoral attitudes prevalent among *gimnaziya* schoolboys with the principled uprightness of her own 12-year-old son, who had got into trouble with his fellows for reporting them when they were using *shpargalki* (cribs) and whispering correct answers to one another during tests on prepared work.

133 Z. Stanchinskaya, *Dnevnik materi* (M., 1924), p. 54, p. 128, p. 84.

134 T. V. Mikhal'tseva, 'Dacha – liricheskoe sochinenie na zadannuyu temu', unpublished memoir, 1999, pp. 6–7.

135 See D. Obolensky, *Bread of Exile: A Russian Family* (London, 1999), p. 42.

136 This assertion is based on e.g. CKQ M–04 PF4, CKQ M–04 PF5–6, CKQ Ox–03 PF1, CKQ Ox–03 PF5–6, etc. A rare exception (RAO M–03 PF1A, p. 5) concerns a woman who was slapped once in an extreme situation – she had not looked properly after her younger sister when the two were left alone, and her mother hit her on the leg with a rubber slipper as a punishment.

137 On locking children up, see Elena Rzhevskaya, *Znaki prepinaniya* (M., 1989), p. 16.

138 CKQ Ox–03 PF14A, p. 3, p. 5.

139 See e.g. the memoirs of Nina Mikhal'skaya,

[Vospominaniya], p. 98, who recalls being christened, but this not having much impact.

140 Oxf/Lev V–05 PF13A, p. 10.

141 CKQ Ox–03 PF14A, p. 3.

142 CKQ Ox–03 PF14A, pp. 7–8. How accurate this claim might be is difficult to say. It is presumably based on the informant's own sense of the size of the believing Jewish population in Leningrad. Given the concentration of Soviet Russian Jews in Moscow and Leningrad (see ch. 6, digital version), his estimate may have some validity.

143 A case in point is Oxf/Lev V–05 PF12A, p. 14.

144 L. Kopelev, *The Education of a True Believer*, trans. G. Kern (London, 1981), pp. 39–46, pp. 78–9 (bar mitzvah). Anatoly Rybakov had a less steadfast attitude, consenting to accompany his observant grandfather to the synagogue, but recalls never having felt any belief even as a small boy (*Roman-vospominanie* (M., 1997), p. 9).

145 G. Bashirov, *SPA*, vol. 4, p. 49. For a small-scale survey where participants recall religious grandparents (but recall having felt respectful distance themselves), see Gyuzel' Sabirova, 'Kak stat' i ostat'sya musul'mankoi: opyt raznykh pokolenii', in E. Yu. Meshcherkina, *Ustnaya istoriya i biografiya: zhenskii vzglyad* (M., 2004), pp. 191–220.

146 CKQ Ox–03 PF2A, p. 2.

147 Cf. CKI M–2, for the Jewish case, and Oxf/Lev V–04 PF7B, p. 6, for the non-believer case.

148 Kh. Zain, 'Shkoly otrezvlyayut narod', *OND* 11–12 (1929), 41. For an account of icon-burning, see Petr Kruzhin in Novak-Deker, pp. 187–8; of speech-making, Andrei Gromyko (b. 1909), *Memories*, trans. H. Shukman (London, 1989), p. 9.

149 See e.g. CKQ Ox–03 PF5, 6, PF2, 3, PF8, 9, 10.

150 V. S. Mukhina, *Bliznetsy* (M., 1969), p. 342.

151 Pavlova, *Dnevnik materi*, p. 107.

152 Rybnikova-Shilova, *Moi dnevnik*, p. 64.

153 I. R. Klyuchareva, *Iz dnevnika materi* (M., 1951), p. 4, pp. 26–7, p. 9.

154 Pavlova, *Dnevnik materi*, p. 107.

155 *SPA*, vol. 5, p. 174.

156 A. Shastov, 'Opyt analiza detskogo truda v shkole 1 stupeni (Ot 8 do 12 let)', *Na putyakh k novoi shkole* 5–6 (1926), 35, 39. On adventurous play by girls in the 1920s and early 1930s, see Kelly, '"Khochu byt' traktoristkoi!"'.

157 See e.g. the picture of the small girl with her teddy in Chapter 15 below.

158 Cf. Oxf/Lev SPb.–02 PF3A, p. 59: informant, b. 1937, recalls that the girls at her school favoured not only ribbons but also top-knots (*puchki*), though the latter got them into trouble with the Komsomol secretary.

159 See Donskaya, unpublished memoir, 1996 (excerpted in Bim-Bad and Kosheleva, *Priroda rebenka v zerkale avtobiografii*, p. 111).

160 Several women informants from these backgrounds, and brought up in the 1920s and 1930s, proudly refer to themselves as *shkody*, or 'pranksters': see e.g. Oxf/Lev V–04 PF1A, p. 13; Oxf/Lev V–04 PF19B, p. 25 (where the informant's husband jokingly refers to her 'sliding off roofs on her arse'), ibid., p. 17 (informant

recollects having stabbed a boy in her class with her pen-nib when he tried copying her work). Cf. CKQ E–03 PF1A, p. 4: 'I'd fight with the boys, I'd give them grief, and I got punished for that, sometimes sent out of class.'

161 See e.g. Oxf/Lev V–04 PF25A, p. 18 (girls not friendly with boys), though e.g. Oxf/Lev V–04 PF1A, p. 7 does record boys and girls playing together. This seems to have depended partly on the game being played (see Chapter 11 for further details).

162 On *patsanka* and *atamanka*, see e.g. Oxf/Lev V–05 PF15B, p. 13 (this in the 1940s).

163 As is clear from e.g. Yu. A. Polenov and V. B. Zhiromskaya (eds), *Naselenie Rossii v XX veke* (2 vols; M., 2000–1), not only did the overall birth rate fall in the course of the twentieth century (see Introduction above), but the number of children per family was also in decline. See digital version of this chapter for further details.

164 See E. Shvarts, *Obyknovennoe chudo* (Kishinev, 1988), p. 524.

165 Cf. I. Paperno, 'Personal Accounts of the Soviet Experience', *Kritika* 3: 4 (Winter 2002), 596–7; C. Hooper, 'Terror of Intimacy: Family Politics in the 1930s Soviet Union', in C. Kiaer and E. Naiman (eds), *Everyday Life in Early Soviet Russia* (Bloomington, IN, 2006), esp. pp. 65–6.

166 I. R. Klyuchareva, *O povedenii detei* (M., 1954), p. 12.

167 Rosa Rust, daughter of two British Communists living in Moscow during the late 1920s and early 1930s, was so lonely that she took to the streets, joined a gang and 'became a little hooligan, stealing things in shops for the excitement. It was better than sitting at home, alone.' (Quoted from a 1990s interview with Rust by F. Beckett, *Stalin's British Victims*, Stroud, 2004, p. 8).

168 Miller, *Dim and Distant Days*, pp. 71–2.

169 See Klyuchareva, *O povedenii detei*, pp. 47–8, p. 31; A. S. Griboedov, *Vospityvaem zdorovykh detei* (L., 1935), p. 12 (no spoiling), p. 11 (cheerful atmosphere, no crushing – *nasilie* – of will).

170 'Father always said: "My child's a genius!"' CKQ Ox–03 PF5B, p. 8.

171 For instance, Larissa Miller: parents' friends, who listened to her read stories as a small girl, received her efforts with blissful astonishment: Aunt Liza wept with emotion, while Uncle Alyosha, in terser manly style, encouraged her to 'keep it up!' (*Dim and Distant Days*, p. 77).

172 This phrase is used in Makarenko, *Kniga*, p. 272.

173 See e.g. Oxf/Lev SPb.–02 PF1B, p. 14.

174 Almost all our interviews, irrespective of place and generation, refer to such family celebrations.

175 For a description of such a birthday party, see CKQ Ox–03 PF5A, p. 4 (in this case, one toast was to Stalin, and the informant, the best friend of the child having the birthday party, refused to drink it, causing uproar).

176 Ransel, *Village Mothers*, p. 210: reminiscences from the 1920s and 1930s.

177 Oxf/Lev V–04 PF6B, p. 54. These memories are confirmed by contemporary evidence, such as the questionnaires circulated by the First Experimental Station to teachers working in

its kindergartens in Kaluga province during 1929–30. Children had no special 'corner', they ate the general family diet, vessels were shared, clothes were not looked after with care (though changed weekly), not all children had underwear, and washing (apart from the hands before meals) took place weekly. RAO NA f. 1 op. 1 d. 294, ll. 181–182 rev.

178 See e.g. the description of the diet in Voronezh province and Volokolamsk district in N. A. Rybnikov, *Krest'yanskii rebenok* (M., 1930), pp. 41–3.

179 Description from M. Alekseev, referring to the Povol'zhe in the early 1930s) (*Karyukha. Drachuny*, M., 1988, p. 219).

180 RAO NA f. 1 op. 1 d. 145, l. 59. (Meeting of 19 March 1924.) According to I. Shangina, *Russkie deti i ikh igry* (SPb., 2000), p. 27, in Russian villages blankets were scarce items, to be found only in wealthy households.

181 V. Zenzinov, *Vstrecha s Rossiei* (New York, 1944), p. 389.

182 See Firsov and Kiseleva, *Byt velikorusskikh krest'yan-zemlepashtsev*, p. 216.

183 See Alekseev, *Drachuny*, pp. 219–20.

184 Author interviews in Gerasimovka, 19 September 2003.

185 See e.g. Oxf/Lev V–04 PF1A, p. 13 (clothes), Oxf/Lev V–04 PF24B, p. 7 (child-minding), Oxf/Lev V–04 PF3A, p. 26 (domestic work on top of work in fields). In Oxf/Lev V–04 PF6B, p. 62, an informant born in 1938 recalls that the only woman in the village to wear trousers – the tractor driver, whose job meant that wearing a skirt would have been indecent – was known locally as *patsanka* (ladette) and *razmuzhichka* (an untranslatable term referring to a person who has crossed the boundary between femininity and masculinity).

186 According to the recollections of a working-class Leningrader, born in 1931, boys and girls were not treated differently at all in the 1930s and 1940s, when he was growing up: (Oxf/Lev SPb.–02, PF9A, p. 47, p. 49); however, his description of concrete activities indicates that, while he helped with cooking and with minding smaller siblings (PF8A, p. 13), it was exclusively his mother and sister who did the cleaning (PF8B, p. 33). The ingrained distinctiveness on gender grounds in this milieu was also noted by external observers: see e.g. V. Shul'gin, 'K voprosu o polovom vospitanii', *Na putyakh k novoi shkole* 12 (1928), 37–46, who also points out (p. 43) that teachers could reinforce such attitudes by making boys and girls sit together as a punishment.

187 On the former, see Oxf/Lev V–05 PF2B, p. 2.

188 Oxf/Lev V–05 P5A, p. 17.

189 A. Koptyaeva, *SPA*, vol. 5, p. 298.

190 Oxf/Lev V–04 PF19A, p. 3; Oxf/Lev V–04 PF24B, p. 6.

191 Oxf/Lev P–05 PF3A, pp. 5–6.

192 CKQ E–03 PF1A, p. 2.

193 See e.g. Oxf/Lev SPb.–02, PF8B, p. 18, or Oxf/Lev V–04 PF10B, p. 6.

194 On incentives, see e.g. the account, by a working-class Leningrader, of being given a bicycle as a

form of 'encouragement' (*pooshchrenie*) in the late 1930s: Oxf/Lev SPb.–02 PF8B, p. 18.

195 E. Kabo, *Ocherki rabochego byta* (M., 1928).

196 RAO NA f. 1 op. 1 d. 140, l. 12 verso, l. 13.

197 S. N. Tsendrovskaya, 'Krestovskii ostrov ot nepa [sic.] do snyatiya blokady', *Nevskii arkhiv* 2 (1995), 81, 84–5.

198 A. Tseitlin, 'Voprosy distsipliny v detuchrezhdenii v svyazi s pedologicheskimii osobennostyami rebenka', *Prosveshchenie na transporte* 2 (1927), 17–22.

199 The state prosecutor's concluding oration was published in *SYu* 23 (1935), 2–6. For a full discussion of the case, see S. Fitzpatrick, *Everyday Stalinism* (New York, 1999), pp. 147–50.

200 How well this measure worked is a different matter. A year later, S. Kopelyanskaya, 'Sud i okhrana detei', *SYu* 2 (1936), 10, was still calling for the enforcement of parental responsibility, and, two years after the law was passed, an article in *SYu* 7 (1937), 55–6, had to draw legal personnel's attention to its existence.

201 Goldman, pp. 106–8, p. 297.

202 For cases of this in the 1920s, see ibid., p. 242.

203 Miller, p. 44.

204 *Demograficheskii ezhegodnik SSSR 1990* (M., 1990), pp. 220–1, gives the ratio of divorces to marriages as 4.3: 11.1 in 1979, and 3.9: 9.4 in 1989. In 1989, there were over 0.5 million divorces in the RSFSR, over 200,000 of which terminated marriages that had lasted four years or less (ibid., pp. 306–7).

205 For example, only occasional articles were carried in *DV* about the impact of divorce on children: e.g. N. Naberezhnova, 'Kogda razrushaetsya sem'ya', *DV* 11 (1960), 52–4. On the role of the father, see e.g. D. Ya. Vol'finzonz, 'Khochu govorit' ob otsakh', *DV* 1 (1963), 71; I. Vorob'ev, 'Otsy ne imeyut prava byt' na storone', *DV* 4 (1963), 62.

206 See e. g. the 'true life story' by M. L. K., 'Kak ya ostalas' odna', *N* 27 (1987), 19–20, which represents a woman's guilt when she realises that her marriage broke down because she was too demanding.

207 See e.g. I. Ovchinnikova, 'U menya dva papy', *N* 20 (1985), 14–15; 'Voskresnyi papa', *N* 39 (1985), 18; I. Kon, 'V sem'e posle razvoda', *N* 50 (1987), 14; T. Snegireva, 'Posle razvoda', *N* 26 (1986), 10.

208 E. Vorob'eva and I. Samyshkina, 'Naryadnaya odezhda detei', *DV* 9 (1963), 11.

209 I. Samonina, 'V poiskakh luchshego', *DV* 10 (1963), 18. See also G. Lyamina, 'Odezhda dlya malyshei', *DV* 4 (1964), 33–4.

210 See e.g. Samonina, 'V poiskakh luchshego'; E. Vorob'eva and I. Samonina, 'Krasivo odevat' detei', *DV* 6 (1964), 33–4; 'Odezhda i obuv' detei', *DV* 6 (1963), 14–15; E. Rusakova, 'O detskoi odezhde i obuvi', *DV* 7 (1963), 18–21.

211 R. Bamm et al., *Semeinoe vospitanie: Slovar' dlya roditelei* (M., 1967), p. 61.

212 Ibid., p. 174.

213 See S. Mikhalkov, *Sobranie sochinenii v 4 tomakh* (M., 1963), vol. 2, p. 214, p. 199.

214 For the original article, see S. Soloveichik, 'Balovannye deti', *N* 9 (1970), 14; for reader

reactions and the defence by a member of the paper's staff, I. Ovchinnikova, 'My i nashi deti', *N* 13 (1970), 13; for critical reaction from professionals, see *N* 20 (1970), 13.

215 See e.g. S. Soloveichik, 'Shchedrye deti?', *N* 46 (1980), 5; idem, 'Ne uchite menya zhit'', *N* 44 (1982), 20–1. Between 1971 and 1986, Soloveichik was the most widely published author on child care in the paper.

216 See e.g. 'Mudraya pedagogika Batyrovykh', *N* 15 (1973), 16–17. For a general 'non-interventionist' line, see S. Soloveichik, 'Zabotlivye deti', *N* 37 (1974), 4. For an emphasis on reward, see also a book by another writer, B. I. Naumov, *Pooshchrenie i nakazanie v sem'e* (M., 1962).

217 'Patsient – sem'ya', *N* 15 (1972), 11.

218 On the publication history of Spock, see C. Kelly, *Refining Russia* (Oxford, 2001), ch. 5. An article in *N* 18 (1974), 10–11, emphasised his radical credentials; a year earlier, the newspaper published two pieces on adolescence: *N* 24 (1973), 14–15, and ibid., 25 (1973), 16.

219 V. A. Sukhomlinsky, *Kak vospitat' nastoyashchego cheloveka* (Kiev, 1975); see also idem, 'Ob uvazhenii detskikh chuvstv', *N* 2 (1963), 16 (on allowing children to be self-reliant); 'O vospitanii', *N* 34 (1972), 12, *N* 35 (1972), 21; 'Net vospitaniya vne truda', *N* 36 (1972), 13. Cf. also the satirical representation of 'smothering' behaviour by parents in the form of a story about a little boy embarrassed by his over-solicitous granny: *N* 31 (1971), 14.

220 *N* 26 (1971), 17; cf. *N* 51 (1973), 18–19; *N* 5 (1972), 18–19.

221 See e.g. G. N. Speransky, 'Rezhim dlya doshkol'nikov', *N* 30 (1960), 16–17; 'Ot trekh do shesti' (exercises for pre-schoolers), *N* 7 (1965), 21; V. Kolbanovsky, 'V chem nuzhdaetsya Vash rebenok?', *N* 15 (1963), 18–19, which emphasises 'education for labour' and reverentially cites Makarenko; A. Tyrnavskaya, 'Ne speshite prizemlyat' mechtu', *N* 7 (1965), 21 (on 'education of the will').

222 See e.g. *N* 18 (1963), 20–1; 'Chto mozhet rebenok?' *N* 18 (1978), 8–9. Material was also published at this period which dealt more specifically than before with children's health: see e.g. A. Akhmedov, 'Beregite zuby rebenka', *N* 1 (1961), 11; E. Belostotskaya, 'Rebenok plokho vidit', *N* 19 (1968), p. 19 (on avoiding myopia).

223 See *N* 43 1967), 22; *N* 31 (1970), 19–20; *N* 47 (1970), 21–2; *N* 1 (1973), 19; *N* 44 (1972), 19–20, etc.

224 For 'boys will be boys' items, see e.g. 'Mal'chishkoi do sedykh volos', *N* 17 (1967), 3; the 'Kogda ya byl mal'chishkhkoi' series running in *N* during 1973: no. 1, pp. 19–20, no. 21, pp. 19–20, etc., and also the sympathetic account of a young boy stowaway on a Soviet ship: *N* 11 (1971), 21. For items on physical exercise, see e.g. *N* 27 (1972), 19–20.

225 For the 'tomboy' ethos, see e.g. A. Lavrov and O. Lavrova, 'Vospitanie lyubvi', *N* 43 (1967), 22, which suggests that telling young girls that they should do the washing up because it's a 'woman's job' is likely to backfire, given that this age

group is extremely conscious of women's rights. But, conversely, see *N* 15 (1982), 11, arguing in favour of housekeeping classes for girls: a family where the man peels the potatoes and washes up is 'an impossibility' (*nel'zya*). For an analysis of the revival of role complementarity, see Lynne Attwood, *The New Soviet Man and Woman* (Basingstoke, 1990).

226 For a case of parents committed to reasoning, see CKQ Ox–03 PF10A, p. 4. 'My father had a principle [*politika*], that children shouldn't ever be beaten or scolded, they should have everything explained to them. And so I was hardly ever punished.' But contrast e.g. Oxf/Lev P–05 PF12A, p. 4 (child punished for repeating drunken father's swearing). For an example of equable distribution of labour between parents, see Oxf/Lev P–05 PF8B, p. 19; for an example of a father who, when not absent, glued himself to the television, Oxf/Lev P–05 PF13A, p. 15.

227 The preservation of elements of religious belief seems to have been commoner in the provinces, but these comments about the limitations of this preservation are also based on our interviews from there: see e.g. Oxf/Lev P–05 PF24A, pp. 1–2.

228 E.g. Oxf/Lev WQ1 KM, p. 4, questionnaire completed by woman b. 1979, Nizhni Novgorod. Sometimes children from families with non-Christian roots were caught up in this mood too: in about 1990, a friend from a completely secularised Jewish background in Leningrad told me with horrified amusement that her daughter had asked permission to wear a cross; to the girl's disappointment, she had told her this was totally inappropriate, given the family's confessional past.

229 See e.g. Oxf/Lev WQ1 GM, p. 3.

230 Ibid. Questionnaire work from the post-Stalin era pointed to very low levels of belief among schoolchildren: 3 per cent of a group of 1,619 Class 10 pupils in Leningrad (questioned anonymously in 1966–67). But on the other hand levels of contact with religious belief (having a relation or acquaintance who believed) were still high enough, at around 60 per cent of the sample group, to cause anxiety to 'scientific atheism' campaigners (N. N. Ogryzko, *Deti i religiya* (2nd edn; L., 1970), p. 8, p. 21). Questionnaire work in Pskov province twenty years later gave a similar picture, and also indicated that significant proportions of young people (over 50 per cent in some social groups) felt that religious belief 'did no harm' or was 'a personal matter' (TsKhDMO f. 1 op. 95 d. 371, ll. 29–36). In sum, the 'normalisation' of atheism had in fact fostered tolerance and even curiosity.

231 For the case of an indulgent father who meted out punishment with a special white belt, see CKQ Ox–03 PF2A, p. 3.

232 E. Arzunyan, 'Udar remnya', *N* 40 (1968), 18, reported that an informal study carried out by him at a *tekhnikum* (a standard destination for working-class young people) had turned up 62 cases of children who had been beaten by their parents. The size of the sample is not given, but is unlikely to have been larger than 100. Our work with interviewees born into urban and rural non-

intelligentsia families at this date confirms the picture. It is rare for informants from these groups to recall that they were definitely *not* beaten.

233 On interrupting, see CKQ Ox–03 PF9A, p. 17. On the other hand, Oxf/Lev SPb.–03 PF15A, p. 33, remembers a 'free regime' at table – children turned up and ate when they felt like it. The same informant (15B, p. 64) recalls that it was at school that she was taught how to lay the table, etc.

234 L. Panteleev, *Nasha Masha: Kniga dlya roditelei* (L., 1966), p. 257 (entry of late November 1960). Masha was 4.3 years old at the time. Eliko Panteleeva, the child's mother, heartily approved of this punishment technique: 'I myself urged her to be firm, "not to give way"' (ibid.)

235 *Domovodstvo* (M.: Kolos, 1965), p. 63.

236 Zemskaya, *Russkaya razgovornaya rech'*, p. 238. Cf. the increasing interest in creative language-learning in post-Stalinist normative literature: see e.g. 'V sem'e rastet malysh', *N* 37 (1985), 14–15.

237 Quotation from Oxf/Lev SPb.–03 PF17A, p. 9.

238 Oxf/Lev SPb.–03 PF17A, p. 2 (note also the interviewer's agreement with the informant on this point, ibid.). Cf. (from a slightly earlier generation) CKQ Ox–03 PF1A, p. 2, recording how the informant would stand mutinously in the corner refusing to apologise, until her grandmother took pity on her and let her off. On smacking, see also CKQ Ox–03 PF9A, p. 19: this informant recounts how she was taken to task by British witnesses after smacking her daughter in the street in Oxford.

239 CKQ E–03 PF3B, pp. 6–7.

240 CKQ Ox–03 PF9A, p. 18.

241 A case of self-conscious strictness in a late-onset father (in this case, the mother was also middle-aged) was the writer L. Panteleev, whose diary, *Nasha Masha*, records his efforts to avoid indulgence and foster 'character' in his small daughter.

242 This is based partly on personal observation of child socialisation by friends and acquaintances in the 1980s, and partly on interview material. For example, Oxf/Lev WQ1 GM, p. 4, recalls lectures on not being clumsy; Oxf/Lev P–05 PF24A, p. 5, remembers getting told off for playing with boys.

243 'ya budu vse za tebya delat"': personal information, March 2001.

244 Cf. an informant's surprise at a story from a friend that Norwegian boys are brought up to be tough and manly: 'they get very soft treatment in Russia' (*v Rossii ochen' baluyut*) – (personal information, March 2001).

245 RAO M–03 PF4A, p. 2 (in this case, the informant observes that she wore her brother's cast-offs and 'acted like a boy' (*predstavlyalyas' mal'chishkoi*).

246 I. I. Lunin and G. V. Starovoitova, 'Issledovanie roditel'skikh porolevykh ustanovok v raznykh etnokul'turnykh sredakh', in A. K. Baiburin and I. S. Kon (eds), *Etnicheskie stereotipy muzhskogo i zhenskogo povedeniya* (L., 1991), p. 15 – though the authors also point out (ibid.) that the finding is problematised by the fact that the Leningrad families studied had one child, and the comparative groups of Canadians and Abhazians had

several. Possibly expectations of a single child are stricter.

247 Oxf/Lev WQ1 GM, p. 2, contains a first-hand account of the contrast between neighbour relations in middle-rise Brezhnev-style blocks (distant), and the closer relations in low-rise blocks built in earlier decades. On 'forcing in' through the isolation of the individual family, cf. the dreadful account of childhood in CKQ M–03 PF1A, p. 3–1, B, p. 5.

248 Cf. complaints from an informant from Moscow province, born 1922, recorded in the late 1990s: 'We reared the children in work. [...] But nowadays upbringing scarcely occurs' (Ransel, *Village Mothers*, p. 152: similar observations from other sources, p. 213). I myself heard this kind of view widely expressed when doing interviews in the village of Gerasimovka, on the Urals–Siberian borders, in 2003. See author interviews, Gerasimovka, 2003.

249 E.g. (on clothes), *N* 48 (1962), 21; *N* 10 (1963), 23; *N* 6 (1965), 20–1; *N* 33 (1966), 20; *N* 50 (1968), 19; *N* 2 (1971), 15; *N* 31 (1971), 14; *N* 34 (1976) 14–15; *N* 32 (1979), 24; *N* 42 (1980), 16; *N.* 1 (1982), 12; *N* 21 (1982), 18–19; *N* 32 (1983), 14–15, and so on.

250 *N* 26 (1973) 22–3; cf. *N* 5 (1977), 16 (Italian furniture); *N* 29 (1980), 5 (Soviet made cutting-edge children's bicycles).

251 *N* 29 (1980), 9.

252 *N* 32 (1983), 14–15.

253 *N* 44 (1979), 18–19 (lace jabot for a baby); *N* 13 (1977), 19–20, *N* 38 (1978), 14 (hairdos).

254 On parties, see *N* 52 (1971), 19, *N* 30 (1970), 13; on trees and other New Year decorations, *N* 51 (1970), 16–17.

255 As recalled by many of our informants: see e.g. CKQ E–03 PF3B, p. 8.

256 P. Kushner (ed.), *The Village of Viriatino*, trans. S. Benet (NY, 1970), p. 263 (children's interests), p. 239 (children's clothes), p. 263 (children's books), pp. 263–5 (upbringing).

257 On 'everything for the children', see e.g. CKQ Ox–03 PF7A, p. 6, 'Rebenku vsegda davali samoe luchshee.'; CKQ Ox–03 PF2B, p. 6.

258 See e.g. *N* (1988), 18–19 (on a children's clothing store in Berlin).

259 See e.g. 'Kak pereshit' veshchi', *N* 48 (1967), 21; 'Plat'e podrostka', *N* 42 (1969), 18 (how to adjust and remake clothes for growing children); *N* 24 (1965), 20–1; *N* 16 (1968), 18 (making clothes); 'Poliklinika kukol', *N* 2 (1962), 12–13; 'Byuro detskikh uslug', *N* 7 (1968), 3 (places to get toys mended).

260 CKQ Ox–03 PF4A, p. 12.

261 *N* 13 (1991), 2.

262 V. I. Gur'ev, 'Skol'ko nas, kakie my, kak my zhivem?', *N* 44 (1988), 13 shows a quite dramatic drop in the birth rate in the early part of the post-Stalin era: from 25.7 per thousand in 1951–60 to 19.2 per thousand in 1961–70. Thereafter, the rate stabilised, declining to 18.1 per thousand in 1971–80 and 19.2 in 1981–85. However, in the post-Soviet era, it fell steeply again (see p. 152 below).

263 *Zhenshchina v SSSR* (M., 1960), p. 88; *Deti v*

SSR (M., 1979), p. 9; *Itogi Vsesoyuznoi perepisi naseleniya 1979 goda* (M., 1989–90), table 4; Polenov and Zhiromskaya (eds), *Naselenie Rossii v XX veke*, vol. 2, p. 265, p. 271; *Demograficheskie perspektivy Rossii* (M., 1993), p. 16. For a full discussion, see digital version.

264 Bown, *Socialist Realism*, plate 519; plate 503.

265 GARF f. 482 op. 50 d. 8520 l. 45, l. 48.

266 On maternity leave in the 1980s, see 'O merakh po usileniyu gosudarstvennoi pomoshchi sem'yam, imeyushchim detei', Postanovlenie TsK KPSS ot 22 yanvarya 1981, No. 235. http://www.niv.ru/biblio/biblio5.pl?id=006&nt=066, accessed 15 February 2006. A ministerial decree of 23 February 1984 allowed 56 days before and after the birth, and fixed the one-off payments. *SO* 7 (1986), 60–2. On 22 August 1990, another decree increased the period of part-paid maternity leave to 18 months at 50 roubles per month (*SO* 11 (1990), 48–51). However, in this period, this was less than one-third of the officially declared average wage.

267 As described by Irina Stal'kova in *N* 33 (1989), 19. Stal'kova, something of a Soviet superwoman, evidently, was eventually to achieve an academic career, plus a profitable sideline as a journalist, plus no fewer than five offspring.

268 Figures compiled by me from the list of informants in E. Belousova, 'Prima materia: sotsializatsiya zhenshchiny v rodil'nom dome', *Trudy fakul'teta etnologii*, vol. 1 (SPb., 2001), pp. 89–93.

269 Data from our village interviews suggest closer spacing, in the range 2–4 years apart (see e.g. Oxf/Lev V–04 PF7B, p. 2: this is a particularly interesting case as the family concerned came from the 'village elite' – the father was an agronomist).

270 Distance: see e.g. CKQ Ox–03 PF2A, p. 3, and contrast Oxf/Lev SPb.–03 PF14A p. 3, where informant records fighting with slightly younger brother. Child-minding: for this see CKQ Ox–03 PF2A, p. 3, Oxf/Lev SPb.–03 PF14A, p. 11. Surrogate parent: CKQ Ox–03 PF2A, p. 3.

271 Cf. the comments of a St Petersburg man with daughters born 1974 and 1985: 'Oni kak by iz raznykh pokolenii' (personal information, 2005). Asked to expand, this person said that drug-taking and so on had been simply unheard of when his elder daughter was at school, while it was all over the place when the younger one was educated.

272 CKQ Ox–03 PF10A, p. 3.

273 For this, see CKQ Ox–03 PF2A, p. 3, Oxf/Lev SPb.–03 PF14A, p. 11.

274 *Spravochnik po doshkol'nomu vospitaniyu* (M., 1919), p. 50.

275 For the health check-up, see ibid., pp. 59–60; for a later sanitary regimen, see *MPDV* no. 6 (*O gigiene vospitaniya*) (M., 1926). A later manual, *Rukovodstvo dlya vospitatelya detskogo sada* (M., 1954), underlines hygiene as a central requirement of kindergarten management (p. 3), but advice offered is mostly about fresh air and exercise rather than simply cleanliness (see esp. p. 4, p. 15); and cf. V. P. Usova (ed.), *Voprosy obucheniya v detskom sadu* (M., 1952), pp. 9–71, which

contains much material on *zakal* as well as on the inculcation of 'cultured habits'.

276 'Sanitarno-gigienicheskii minimum dlya doshkol'nykh uchrezhdenii', *Sbornik po voprosam okhrany detstva Komissii po uluchsheniyu zhizni detei* 7–8 (1932), 58–9.

277 On manners, see e.g. Usova (ed.), *Voprosy obucheniya*, pp. 93–8, pp. 109–15; on nature study, see E. I. Volkova (ed.), *Vospitateli detskikh sadov o svoei rabote* (M., 1948), pp. 305–84; ibid., on the arts, pp. 385–420.

278 V. Voinovich, 'Vospitanie komunyan', in his *Moskva 2042* (Ann Arbor, 1987), p. 190.

279 M. Markovich, 'Dramatizatsiya v doshkol'nom vozraste', in N. S. Sher (ed.), *Deti i teatr* (L., 'Mysl'', 1925), quoted from V. Loisha, '"Esli vy budete krichat', Lenin nasovsem umret', *Rodina* 4 (1999), 69. On political games, see also Chapter 11 below.

280 Papkovskaya, *Kniga o malen'kikh trekhgortsakh*, p. 139.

281 For geography lessons and school preparatory sessions, see Usova, *Voprosy obucheniya*, p. 102, p. 94; for the statue example, see K. N. Grekova, 'Nash rodnoi gorod Magnitogorsk', in Volkova (ed.), *Vospitateli*, p. 190.

282 For trips to the forest, see N. S. Khramilova, 'Vospitanie lyubvi k Rodine', in Volkova (ed.), *Vospitateli*, pp. 109–15; for proverbs and folklore, see L. M. Chudimova, 'Russkie narodnye zagadki, poslovitsy, pogovorki', ibid., pp. 282–94. Cf. A. I. Sorokina, *Doshkol'naya pedagogika. Uchebnoe posobie dlya doshkol'nykh pedagogicheskikh uchilishch* (M., 1951), on the provision of dolls from different Soviet nationalities to foster the 'friendship of nations', or the use of Russian literary classics and folklore to encourage patriotic ideas (p. 128, p. 180, p. 253).

283 Sorokina, *Doshkol'naya pedagogika*, pp. 133–6 (physical exercise), pp. 202–33 (will and character), p. 191 (friendships). Papkovskaya, *Kniga o malen'kikh trekhgortsakh*, p. 115 (nature and pets); on values circulating outside, see 'Sel'skie detskie sady Pervoi Opytnoi Stantsii Narkomprosa (1919–1935)', RAO NA f. 1 op. 1 d. 294, l. 10; *MPDV*, no. 1: *O doshkol'noi rabote v derevne* (M.–L., 1926), p. 21.

284 Cf. *Programmy i metodicheskie zapiski edinoi trudovoi shkoly: vypusk shestoi* (M.–L., 1927), p. 90 (meetings); Babina, *Kak organizovat' dosug detei*, p. 18, on meetings, and p. 20, reading brochures; N. Krupskaya, 'Beseda s roditelyami detskikh sadov bratskikh respublik, 26 dekabrya 1937', in her *Izbrannye pedagogicheskie proizvedeniya* (M.: Akademiya pedagogicheskikh nauk SSSR, 1955), pp. 699–703. On this side of the Soviet kindergarten, see also the helpful account in Kirschenbaum, pp. 46–8, p. 101.

285 As can be seen from the advice on child management cited above in the section on early Soviet 'rational upbringing' (p. 371 ff).

286 *Programmy i metodicheskie zapiski edinoi trudovoi shkoly: vypusk shestoi* (M.–L., 1927), p. 88 ('up to 24 hours' for the *fabrichnyi ochag*); *MPDV* no. 1: *O doshkol'noi rabote v derevne* (M., 1926), p. 19 (programme runs 6–7 a.m. to 7 p.m.).

287 *MPDV* no. 1: *O doshkol'noi rabote v derevne*, p. 19. The outline timetable remained much the same throughout the Soviet era: compare e.g. *Rukovodstvo dlya vospitatelya detskigo sada* (M., 1954), p. 15.

288 *MPDV* no. 11: *O svyazi so shkoloi i o planirovanii raboty* (M.–L., 1928), pp. 42–51.

289 *MPDV* no. 9: *Uchet raboty v doshkol'nom uchrezhdenii* (M.–L., 1927).

290 RAO NA f. 1 op. 1 d. 294, ll. 14 recto and verso, 15 verso, 37 recto, 38 recto and verso. And cf. Al. Selensky, 'K voprosu ob internatakh', *Prosveshchenie na transporte* 1 (1927), 83–4, which talks of the usefulness of boarding-schools in inculcating cultured habits in children from poor homes: 'how to move about in a cultured way, how to stand, to sit, to speak, to drink, to eat, to dress, to wash, to treat one another, other members of the collective, and the supervisors, and the objects in the boarding-school, in a cultured way'.

291 *Instruktsiya po vedeniyu detskogo sada* (M., 1921), p. 5. Instructions of this kind problematise the generally valid emphasis in cultural histories of the 1920s upon the collectivism of the era: see e.g. V. Papernyi, 'Kollektivnoe – individual'noe', in *Kul'tura "dva"* (2nd edn; M., 1996), pp. 146–59.

292 *Kak organizovat' detskii sad* (L., 1929) p. 9.

293 S. Zak, *Pro rebyat, pro detskii sad* (M.–L., 1930).

294 See e.g. the photograph of children from the kindergarten at Voroshilov Collective Farm, Novoukrainsky district, published in *Pravda* 16 May 1936, p. 4, or the photograph and article about Kindergarten No. 1 in Pyatigorsk, *Pravda* 7 June 1936, p. 3.

295 M. Ilin, *The Little Citizen of a Big Country* (M., 1939), p. 26, p. 28.

296 This was true in the Stalin era as well: see e.g. A. M. Levshina, A. I. Sorokina, and A. P. Usova, *Doshkol'naya pedagogika* (M.–L., 1946); T. S Babadzhan, *Organizovannye podvizhnye igry detei rannego vozrasta* (M., 1950); and cf. the 1954 *Rukovodstvo dlya vospitatelya*, with a syllabus including fairy tales and riddles as well as a poem about Stalin (pp. 33–4), and where children's books are praised as 'having a good influence on the child's feelings and giving children knowledge' as well as for inculcating 'a correct attitude to Soviet reality and love of the Motherland' (p. 7).

297 N. Al'medingen-Tumim, E. Tikheeva, and Yu. Fausek, *Doshkol'noe delo: po voprosam doshkol'nogo vospitaniya i pedagogiki* (Petrograd, 1922), p. 6, p. 10. The estimate of existing nursery schools in 1919 is based on *Pervyi Vserossiiskii s"ezd po doshkol'nomu vospitaniyu* (M., 1921), p. 38, which cites 259 kindergartens in 192 different *uezdy*. While the survey that gave this figure covered only 20 of 30 *gubernii*, an estimate of 400 for the total 30 regions would seem reasonable.

298 See Kirschenbaum, *Small Comrades*, table 1, p. 39.

299 *Detskoe kommunisticheskoe dvizhenie i doshkol'noe vospitanie* (M., 1926), p. 41; *Spravochnaya kniga po doshkol'nomu vospitaniyu* (M., 1928), p. 7. Kirschenbaum, table 4, p. 91, gives rather different figures (0.6 per cent of the target age group served in 1926–27, and 1.61 by 1930–31): whichever way,

the fact of decline or stasis since 1919 is not in question. The figure for permanent kindergarten places was even lower: *Statisticheskii spravochnik SSSR za 1928 god* (M., 1929), p. 880, gives the number of kindergartens and 'shelters' (*ochagi*) in the RSFSR as 1,376, with 71,826 'clients' (*sic*) (as opposed to 79,602 primary schools with 5,991,475 pupils): in 1926, there were around 20 million children in the 0–7 age group, so this would represent around 0.3 per cent of the target population.

300 For 1928–32, see B. King, *Changing Man* (London, 1936), p. 270: figure for 1932–33 compares with primary school population for that year of 18,179,400: i.e. it was running at roughly 6 per cent of the target population; for 1940, see *Deti v SSSR*, p. 19.

301 See S. Fitzpatrick, *Stalin's Peasants* (New York, 1994), p. 264, for a 'millionaire' sheep-raising kolkhoz of this kind; or the photograph of the Novoukrainsk district collective farm nursery school mentioned above.

302 See Kirschenbaum, *Small Comrades*, p. 93. Temporary nurseries were also widely used during school holidays in cities. See e.g. Tezarovskaya (initial not given), 'Kak organizovat' detskuyu ploshchadku', *Drug detei* 5 (1931), 26–9.

303 Kirschenbaum, *Small Comrades*, p. 137.

304 See *SYu* 7 (1934), 23, for the announcement about the arrangement in the first place; reminders appeared in *SYu* 22 (1935), 22, *SYu* 32 (1935), 21, and *SYu* 8 (1936), 14.

305 For a story from the early 1930s about how the directorate of a residential co-operative frustrated the plans of the women's group to open a kindergarten there, see Agrippina Korevanova, *Moya zhizn'* (M., 1938) (cited from Fitzpatrick and Slezkine, p. 204).

306 *SYu* 16 (1935), 22.

307 *SYu* 1 (1937), 39.

308 Ransel, *Village Mothers*, p. 77: quoting report by Dr Polotskii, GARF f. 482 op. 29 d. 2, l. 15.

309 On this point, see M. Ivanova in *Pravda* 7 June 1936, p. 3.

310 *Deti v SSSR: statisticheskii sbornik*, p. 19. Figures for day schools may usefully be compared: there were 20,229,000 pupils in the RSFSR in 1940–1, and 18,611,000 in 1950–51 (ibid.)

311 *Narodnoe obrazovanie v SSSR, 1917–1967* (M., 1967), pp. 40–1.

312 According to V. S. Gel'fland, *Naselenie SSSR za 50 let (1941–1991)* (Perm', 1992), there were 1.7 million in the 0–4 age group alone across the USSR in 1950, and 2.3 million in 1955, rising to 2.5 million in 1960 (p. 64, table 10, p. 79, table 15, p. 94, table 20).

313 See the official report for 1947 quoted in *MPV*, pp. 626–7.

314 See *Rezolyutsii po dokladam Tret'ego Vserossiiskogo S"ezda po doshkol'nomu vospitaniyu, 15–21 oktyabrya 1924* (M., 1924), p. 4.

315 'Sel'skie detskie sady', l. 28; 'Usloviya priema detei v yasli i na ploshchadke', RAO NA f. 1 op. 1 d. 294, l. 153.

316 On the 1935 fee levels, see *Pravda* 10 July 1935, p. 1, 'Zabota o detyakh nashei strany'. Starzhinsky

alleges that no one in the village where he lived paid for child care: p. 56.

317 See *KhSZUP*, vol. 4, p. 199.

318 Oxf/Lev P–05 PF17B, p. 15.

319 See, for example, the photographs from *Nashi dostizheniya* in the late 1920s/early 1930s.

320 This information is taken from Papkovskaya, *Kniga o malen'kikh trekhgorkakh*, pp. 17–60.

321 E. I. Iordanskaya, 'Sovremennaya praktika Leningradskikh doskhol'nykh uchrezhdenii', in N. Al'medingen and G. Tumim (eds), *V pomoshch' doshkol'nomu rabotniku* (L., 1925), pp. 19–20.

322 J. Bullard and M. Bullard (eds), *Inside Stalin's Russia: The Diaries of Reader Bullard 1930–1934* (Charlbury, Oxon., 2000), p. 97.

323 Ethel Mannin, 'Playtime of the Child in Modern Russia', in H. Griffith (ed.), *Playtime in Russia* (London, 1935), pp. 171–2.

324 For a case of a former 'model' institution gone to seed, see '"Bolezni" detskoi ploshchadki', *DD* 6 (1930), 7–9. For the relative costs of wages versus equipment, see A. Tezavrovskaya, 'Kak organizovat' detskuyu ploshchadku', *DD* 5 (1931), 26–9, and idem, 'Organizatsiya shkol'noi ploshchadki', *DD* 7 (1931), 22.

325 Kushner (ed.), *The Village of Viriatino*, pp. 265–6.

326 See e.g. E. A. Arkin, *Detskii sad v svete sotsial'noi gigieny i biologii* (M., n.d. [1925]), and a variety of articles by A. Ya. Gutkin in *Gigiena i sanitariya* (details in digital version of this chapter).

327 GARF f. 8009 op. 2 d. 73 (problems with age/experience of staff); GARF f. 2306 op. 75 d. 2358, l. 13 (patriotic education going well, 1951). Reports of this kind are found at later stages as well, e.g. the mid-1950s: GARF f. 2306 op. 72 d. 5737 (similar complaints, 1957); GARF f. 2306 op. 72 d. 4806, l. 35 (bad music teaching), GARF f. 2306 op. 72 d. 3947, l. 18 (ungrammatical speech should be given more attention).

328 A decree of the Soviet of People's Commissars of 3 May 1937 stated that exceptions might be made to the usual rules provided that agreement was obtained from the organisation running the kindergarten and from the local representatives of Narkompros (*SYu* 13 (1937), 48). At Larissa Miller's kindergarten in Moscow, her grandmother, the only member of staff who had education beyond secondary level, held the special post of 'teachers' adviser' (*Dim and Distant Days*, p. 57).

329 *Rezolyutsii IV Vserossiiskogo s"ezda po doshkol'nomu vospitaniyu* (M.–L., 1929), p. 33. For the report from Kursk province in 1919, see *Pervyi Vserossiiskii s"ezd*, p. 143.

330 *SYu* 16 (1935), 22.

331 See the report of 14 April 1945 in *MPV* 603–4: nursery staff had only galoshes or shoes tied together with string to wear, inadequate winter clothing, and only one dress of any kind.

332 Oxf/Lev V–04 PF1A, pp. 5–6.

333 GARF f. 2306 op. 75 d. 2358.

334 T. S. Babadzhan, *Organizovannye podvizhnye igry detei rannego vozrasta* (M., 1950), pp. 62–3, p. 53.

335 Oxf/Lev V–04 PF12B, p. 18 (from the late 1930s).

336 Official statistics – see pp. 403–5 above – are borne out by oral history. Few of our informants in the village survey who grew up in the 1920s and 1930s had any experience of kindergartens. One informant who did attend a *detsad* pointed out that it existed because her village was close to a major industrial town (Oxf/Lev V–04 PF12B, pp. 16–17). According to another, children were usually parked with grandparents (Oxf/Lev V–04 PF4B, p. 30).

337 Cf. Inna Shikhaeva-Gaister's memory that the home-worker, Natasha, was closer to her than her mother was: it was Natasha who took the children in when their parents were arrested. *Semeinaya khronika vremen kul'ta lichnosti, 1925–1953* (M., 1998), pp. 35–6. It was common to use the word *nyan'ka* (nanny) in the Soviet period too.

338 For instance, Anatoly Rybakov's nurses were former French maids: see *Roman-vospominanie* (M., 1997), p. 21; cf. the women who taught Svetlana Stalina to draw, to read and write in two languages, and to do musical dictations, *Dvadtsat' pisem k drugu* (London, 1967), p. 32.

339 E. M. Konyus, *Perestroika detskogo byta i zhilishchnaya kooperatsiya* (M., 1935). The figures appear on p. 12, and the material on playgroups is on pp. 21–3. On private nurseries during NEP and up to 1932, see Kirschenbaum, *Small Comrades*, p. 97, p. 138. On the other hand, school managements did not always react well to the products of such groups: Nina Mikhal'skaya, [Vospominaniya], pp. 15–16, recalls having to sit a test when she entered ordinary school for the first time, aged 10, having been educated previously in a private group.

340 On the Narkomfin crèche, see V. Buchli, *Materializing Culture* (Oxford, 1999), p. 169. Svetlana Stalina attended a 'pre-school music group' in the early 1930s (see *Dvadtsat' pisem k drugu*, p. 214).

341 For the survival of such groups, see e.g. M. L. Gasparov, *Zapisi i vypiski* (M., 2000), p. 75.

342 As in the case of Andrei Sergeev, whose mother and grandmother feared a nanny would foist a religious upbringing on him, and who did not send him to nursery school. See *Al'bom dlya marok*, in *Omnibus* (M., 1997), p. 13.

343 Fitzpatrick and Slezkine, p. 415.

344 'God raboty po-novomu', *DV* 5 (1960), 6.

345 GARF f. 8009 op. 21 d. 276, l. 3.

346 *Deti v SSSR: statisticheskii sbornik* (M., 1979), p. 19. One might compare the figures for day schools – 18,736,000 in 1960–61; 23,235,000 in 1970–71; 20,176,000 in 1976 (ibid.). In 1960, the total under-16 population in the RSRSR was 35,094,000 (i.e. the potential kg enrolment would have been *c.* 17 million, meaning under one-third was in kgs).

347 Compare *Zhenshchina v SSSR* [1960], p. 85 (1958, 1960), and Gel'fland, *Naselenie*, table 18; and *Deti v SSSR*, p. 19, and Gel'fland, *Naselenie*, tables 20, 26, and 31.

348 GARF f. 2306 op. 72 d. 5737, l. 16.

349 Harwin, p. 93. By the 1990s, the proportion had begun to decline once more, reaching 63.9 per cent in 1991 (ibid.).

350 V. Belov, 'Vospitanie po doktoru Shpoku', *Izbrannye proizvedeniya v 3 tomakh* (M., 1983), p. 305.

351 *Moskva v tsifrakh 1917–1977* (M., 1977), p. 129.

352 Galina Kulikovskaya, 'Semeinaya arifmetika', *O* 6 (1970), 16.

353 GARF f. 2306 op. 72 d. 5737, l. 1.

354 'Shirokoe razvitic doshkol'nykh uchrezhdenii v derevne – pervoocherednaya zadacha', *DV* 3 (1961), 4–5.

355 See Ransel, *Village Mothers*, p. 214.

356 Kulikovskaya, 'Semeinaya arifmetika', pp. 16–17.

357 GARF f. 2306 op. 72 d. 3944, ll. 16–17 (Rostov); GARF f. 2306 op. 72 d. 4828, ll. 6–14 (Rostov); GARF f. 2306 op. 72 d. 3943, ll. 2–5 (Leningrad); GARF f. 2306 op. 72 d. 3947, l. 22–9 (Irkustsk: this file also contains material on Pskov (ll. 1–5) and on the Buryat-Mongolian Republic); GARF 2306 op. 72 d. 5737, l. 3 (collective farms).

358 RAO NA f. 126 op. 1 d. 34, l. 130 (Ryazan'), l. 132 (Oryol), l. 136 (Orenburg), l. 118–19 (Moscow); RAO NA f. 126 op. 1 d. 35, l. 69 (overcrowding, high infection rate); l. 8 (dirt spattered on walls), l. 266 (dialogue).

359 S. G. Zmeul and L. T. Vikhrova, *Detskie sady i yasli: voprosy proektirovaniya* (M., 1957).

360 See e.g. Yu. Maksimov et al., 'Kompleksnyi proekt detskogo sada v zhizni', *DV* 7 (1964), 34–40; 9 (1964), 22–31.

361 For the former, see e.g. L. Russkova, 'Inspektora znakomyatsya s yaslyami-sadami', *DV* 7 (1964), 27–9; for the latter, see e.g. K. N. Chernukhina, 'Vospitanie kul'tury povedeniya', *DV* 7 (1960), 25–9.

362 A. I. Sorokina (ed.), *Doshkol'naya pedagogika* (3rd edn; M., 1961).

363 See e.g. 'Eto dolg kazhdogo vospitatelya', *DV* 7 (1961), 3–5.

364 See e.g. S. G. Kovaliya, 'O lyubvi k Rodine', *DV* 10 (1961), 65–6, which contains the wonderful *non sequitur*, 'As the father of five children, I understood that our parental duty is to instil the elements of patriotism into a person' (p. 65); K. V. Dmitrieva, 'Pionery v detskom sadu', *DV* 4 (1961), 14–16.

365 See photograph in Maksimov et al., 'Kompleksnyi proekt', part 1, pp. 34–5.

366 Jacoby, p. 50.

367 Oxf/Lev SPb.–03 PF14A, p. 13.

368 Jacoby, p. 58 (difficulties with staff), p. 64 (slaps administered to children by elderly supervisor), p. 50 (bright room), p. 52 (warm relationships).

369 See e.g. 'Zadachi detskogo sada i sem'i ediny', *DV* 8 (1960), 50–3.

370 RAO NA f. 126 op. 1 d. 35, ll. 73–4.

371 I owe the information about the Western radio broadcasts to Nadezhda Azhgikhina (personal information, Moscow, Aug. 2003). For non-official literature, cf. e.g. Voinovich's *Moskva 2042* (see p. 398 above).

372 Harwin, p. 93.

373 See 'Vnimanie – deti v bede', *N* 26 (1988), 12; 'Detskii sad 2000 goda', *N* 23 (1988), 18–19. At the same time, even new Soviet designs tended to assume over 20 children to a group: see ibid.,

p. 19, which shows a new school with 660 children divided into 28 groups.

374 A. V. Fedulova, 'Kakim byt' detskomu sadu', *N* 40 (1988), 2. The wish-list here includes better qualified staff, better supplies, and placements for all children outside town in summer.

375 On 'family atmosphere', see e.g. 'Detskii sad 2000 goda', 19; M. Matvinenko, 'V sadu khorosho, no doma luchshe', *N* 49 (1988), 20–1; idem, '"Malopopulyarnyi" rebenok?', *N* 44 (1988), 18–19.

376 Harwin, p. 93.

377 As early as 1988, the size of fees was mentioned as an increasing source of dissatisfaction: see Fedulova, 'Kakim byt'', 2.

378 V. Mukhina, *Bliznetsy*, p. 327 (entry for 4 November 1966).

379 Ibid., pp. 334–5 (21 November 1966).

380 Oxf/Lev M–04 PF38A, p. 5.

381 Oxf/Lev T–04 PF4 refers frequently to the thieving that took place in a kindergarten in Taganrog during the mid-late 1980s, and to the scams operated by the director, who used, e.g., to sign staff up for double-time and then pocket the difference herself, and who expected to be given presents by the parents and staff: see esp. 4A, p. 4, 4B, p. 13.

382 See e.g. Oxf/Lev M–04 PF38A, pp. 2–3 (this woman, b. 1962, worked in a specially designed modern kindergarten; the only material problems were that children living in the locality sometimes came in off the street and damaged the equipment in the playground). On the regime, see ibid., pp. 6–7: games, hygienic procedures, naps, preparation for festivals, etc. Interesting in this context, too, is the persistence of regimes of this kind into the post-Soviet period: see e.g. CKQ_SPb.–04 PF6B, p. 7, p. 14, though, as this informant points out, the content of the programme, as opposed to its structure, has now changed: for instance, children play riverboat excursions and McDonalds Fast Food alongside *dochki-materi* (Happy Families, on which see Chapter 11).

383 Except when they learned a drinking song from one of the other children, which Mukhina *did* note in her diary: see *Bliznetsy*, p. 322 (entry for 10 October 1966).

384 On Lenin corners, see Oxf/Lev M–04 PF33A, p. 6; p. 7 recalls that Pioneer heroes were more for school (this informant began work in 1972); cf. Oxf/Lev PF38A, p. 9 (revolutionary festivals celebrated); PF38B, pp. 10–11 (Pavlik Morozov, however, not mentioned). (This informant started work in 1981.) A similar emphasis on politics is suggested by Oxf/Lev T–04 PF4A, pp. 6–7 – but this informant worked for quite a lot of her career in a Russian kindergarten in Uzbekistan, another rather specific environment.

385 Oxf/Lev M–04 PF35A, pp. 4–5. This supervisor (who began work in 1958) herself expresses doubt about the dacha system.

386 A 1968 study concluded, from data showing that the levels of over-sixties living in two-person family units was around 50 per cent of the levels of 35–59-year-olds living in two-person units, that an extended family set-up remained the norm (Yu.

Rakhmanov, 'Kak zhivesh' mama?', *N* 8 (1968), 18). Obviously, not all co-resident grandparents necessarily helped with child care, but it is reasonable to conclude that the majority did. On 'playgroups', see e.g. CKI-M2 (the informant's daughter, born in the late 1950s, attended one of these regularly as a small child. The venue was frequently changed to avoid detection by the authorities).

387 See e.g. E. Mushkina, 'V ocheredi deti', *N* 9 (1962), 18–19; 'A my rastem bystree!', *N* 50 (1962), 3 (on shortages); *N* 21 (1962), 20, *N* 26 (1962), 20 (on the *sluzhba nyan'*); L. Yunina, 'Srochno nuzhna nyanya', *N* 3 (1966), 20, 28 (on good job for pensioners); O. Vasil'eva, 'Segodnya – ya vospitatel'nitsa', *N* 32 (1962), 11 (on parents and grandparents helping out). I. Krasnopol'skaya, 'U dobrogo dela mnogo druzei', *N* 15 (1962), 4–5, is a laudatory article on a kindergarten set up on the initiative of a local pensioner, its premises set in order by pensioners working for nothing, and staffed by students at the Moscow Pedagogical Institute.

388 For reader comment, see e.g. 'Vidy na babushek', *N* 34 (1975), 4–5; for adverse comment by experts, see e.g. A. Petrovsky of the APN SSSR, 'Babushki, vnuki, i klimat sem'i', *N* 9 (1981), 18–19. Leonid M., 'Za chto ya ne lyublyu svoyu babushku', is criticism from a grandson: see *N* 39 (1975), 22.

389 E. Bonner, *Dochki-materi* (M., 1994), p. 58.

390 As Evgeny Dobrenko has pointed out to me (personal information).

391 Compare the kindergarten dinner menu of 'potato soup with meat and baked semolina with cranberry sauce' and the sample dinner menu for a family with an income of 650 roubles of 'chopped herring, bortsch, fried fillet of steak, buckwheat, string beans and carrots, and chocolate cream', both dating from 1935–7, given by Bertha Malnick in *Everyday Life in Russia* (London, 1938), p. 40, p. 211.

392 See e.g. Oxf/Lev M–04 PF24B, p. 14.

393 CKQ SPb.–03 PF1A, p. 2.

394 As in CKQ M–04 PF6A, p. 4.

395 Shefner, p. 351.

396 See Kirschenbaum, *Small Comrades*, p. 79, on the clearing up. Girls also (one imagines) dominated the sewing sessions, while boys no doubt dominated sessions of carpentry and building.

397 V. A. Aulik, 'Trudnosti v rabote molodogo vospitatelya', *DV* 6 (1961), 41, for a vignette of these complementary activities.

398 As Naum Korzhavin recollected (referring to the early 1930s) in 'V soblaznakh krovavoi epokhi', *NM* 7 (1992), 179.

399 Oxf/Lev SPb.–03 PF24A, pp. 1–2.

400 Miller, p. 58.

401 Ibid., p. 57.

402 Ol'ga Grechina, 'Spasayus' spasaya', part 2, 'Skazki o gorokhovom dereve (1942–1944 gg.)', pp. 21–2, Archive of Mariya Osorina, SPb. This, it should be noted, was the work of the nannies rather than of the supervisors themselves.

403 CKQ Ox–03 PF2B, pp. 6–7.

404 Oxf/Lev SPb.–02 PF8A, p. 17.

405 CKQ E03 PF1A, p. 3.

406 CKQ Ox–03 PF7B, p. 8; on pets, see Oxf/Lev SPb.–03 PF24A, pp. 1–2.

407 Cf. Oxf/Lev M–04 PF24B, p. 13 (here the role-playing game was based on the popular film, *Seventeen Moments of Spring*, about Shtirlitz, a Soviet double agent in Hitler's Germany).

408 V. Bogdan, quoted in Fitzpatrick and Slezkine, p. 415.

409 D. Shturman, *Moya shkola* (London, 1990), p. 120.

410 On left-handedness, see e.g. Oxf/Lev SPb.–02 PF2 A, p. 14.

411 Sergeev, *Al'bom dlya marok* in *Al'bom dlya marok* in *Omnibus* (M., 1997), p. 9.

412 On 'correction' of left-handedness in schools (which continued right into the post-Soviet era), see M. M. Bezrukikh, *Problemnye deti* (M., 2000), pp. 5–259.

413 Sorokina, *Doshkol'naya pedagogika* (1961), pp. 308–9.

414 As in e.g. 'Deti idut v shkolu', *DV* 8 (1960), 3–5; M. N. Skei, 'Detskii sad i shkola', *DV* 11 (1960), 15–19; 'Vsestoronne gotovit' svoikh pitomtsev k shkole', *DV* 9 (1961), 12–14.

415 N. Rybnikov, *Derevenskii shkol'nik i ego idealy* (M., 1916), p. 23.

416 D. Bednyi, *SPA*, vol. 1, pp. 127–8.

417 D. Nabokov, 'Detskie gody v Suprunovke', *NM* 11 (1967), 81.

418 Oxf/Lev P–05 PF12A, p. 4.

419 On female and juvenile alcoholics, see S. White, *Russia Goes Dry* (Cambridge, 1996), p. 40; for a first-hand account of an alcoholic female neighbour in the early 1980s who often neglected even to feed her children, see Messana, *Kommunalka*, p. 156.

420 CKI SPb.–5.

421 CKQ Ox–03 PF5A, p. 15. The reaction of the teacher in her class was to express horror at such a 'vulgar' wish and to assign the girl a fail.

422 Oxf/Lev SPb.–03 PF24B, p. 25.

423 Iraida Komissarova in Chaadaeva, p. 138.

424 Rybnikov, *Derevenskii shkol'nik*, p. 21.

425 This is particularly vividly described in Oxf/Lev WQ1 GM, p. 3.

426 On the former, cf Mariengof's systematic efforts to annoy his mother, e.g. by responding to her sentimental dreams of how he will be a famous pianist by saying he wants to be a famous hurdy-gurdy player, with a parrot, *Moi vek*, p. 27; on the latter, Arbuzov's description of life with his parents, a haphazardly and overwhelmingly attentive mother, and a father who let the boy smoke from the age of eight. Neither was any good at providing Arbuzov with what he needed, a sense of stability (*SPA* vol. 5, p. 45).

427 As in CKQ Ox–03 PF12, p. 6.

428 On the child as mediator, see e.g. CKQ Ox–03 PF12A, pp. 5–6.

429 'Fridge full of Snickers bars': Oxf/Lev WQ1 KM, p. 5; helping on the vegetable patch, ibid., p. 13.

430 On this, see Miller, p. 45 (Pioneer camp), p. 88 (missing one's father), pp. 31–2 (typewriter, new partner).

431 Rzhevskaya, *Znaki prepinaniya*, pp. 6–7. Cf. Gasparov, *Zapisi i vypiski*, p. 73: his mother's

visitor was regularly referred to as 'your father' by women in the yard, but 'he was her friend, not ours', and 'I grew up feeling that I had no father'.

432 Miller, pp. 87–8.

433 See e.g. Panferov in *SPA*, vol. 2, p. 171.

434 See e.g. Esenin, *SPA*, vol. 1, p. 397, p. 399; Paustovsky, *SPA*, vol. 2, p. 209.

435 *SPA*, vol. 1, p. 396. Roughness to younger children seems to have been common: cf. Vladimir Dubovka's story about how his brother and some friends, all aged about five, announced to his mother that they proposed to drown Vladimir because they had had enough of his crying. (*SPA*, vol. 3, p. 229.)

436 Though on the whole, if memoirs are to be believed, it was servants who, in high-status Russian families, were often the source of warmth: see, for example, the memoirs of Ol'ga Forsh (*SPA*, vol. 1). One might compare the recollections of some British memoirists brought up in the late nineteenth and early twentieth centuries: see, for example, Brian Fairfax-Lucy and Philippa Pearce,

The Children of the House (London, 1968), a grim recollection of four children growing up isolated in a large English country house.

437 Oxf/Lev WQ1 GM, p. 9.

438 CKQ E–03 PF1B, p. 5. The phrase is illustrated by a story about how the informant messed around while supposed to be working out in the fields, then took fright at the thought of punishment and hid, which made things a lot worse because a search party was sent out. Her mother was, however, so relieved that she did not actually punish her daughter.

439 'Diary of Vladimir Petrovich Stavsky', in V. Garros, N. Korenevskaya, and T. Lahusen (eds), *Intimacy and Terror*, trans. C. A. Flath (NY, 1995), p. 221. (Punctuation follows this translation.) The phrase 'distant, irretrievable, and eternally beloved childhood' is patterned on a famous passage in Tolstoy's *Detstvo*. On the continuing influence of this text, see Wachtel.

440 N. Ries, *Russian Talk* (Ithaca, NY, 1997), p. 5.

Chapter 11: In Their Own Time

1 A. R. Hochschild, *The Commercialization of Everyday Life* (Berkeley, CA, 2003), pp. 172–81.

2 Oxf/Lev M–05 PF43B, p. 49.

3 See S. F. Svetlov, *Peterburgskaya zhizn' v kontse XIX stoletiya (v 1892 godu)*, ed. A. M. Konechnyi (SPb., 1998), pp. 44–5. On walks in the park from personal memories, see e.g. V. Shklovsky, *Tret'ya fabrika* (M., 1926), p. 19.

4 M. Tsvetaeva: 'Moi Pushkin', *Sobranie sochinenii v 7 tomakh* vol. 5 (M., 1994), pp. 57–61.

5 M. Dobuzhinsky, *Vospominaniya* (M., 1987), p. 20, recalled his slow progress round the St Petersburg zoo, with his father patiently waiting as he spent ages staring into every cage.

6 See e.g. CKQ M–04 PF6A, p. 4.

7 On the early Soviet era, see A. Yu. Gutkin, 'Osnovnye gigienicheskie ustanovki i normativnye pokazateli po planirovaniyu detskogo gorodka parka kul'tury', *OMM* 5–6 (1933), 1–11. On the later period, personal observation

8 On neighbourly intervention, see e.g. the comment by the Sverdlovsk working-class informant in CKQ E–03 PF2A, p. 4, 'Yes, in our time things were very strict, you were scared of adults, sort of, well, even if a neighbour said, she did this or that, didn't say hello when I met her, or something … you used to run into people a lot then.'

9 For a discussion of the normative literature advocating intervention, see Catriona Kelly, *Refining Russia* (Oxford, 2001), chs 4 and 5.

10 For a description of such behaviour, and an interesting analysis of its impact on children, see M. V. Osorina, *Sekretnyi mir detei* (SPb., 1999), ch. 14, esp. pp. 252–9.

11 CKI SPb.–5; on drinking, see also Chapter 10 above.

12 On tram-buffer riding, see e.g. V. Ya. Gutkin and E. S. Gefter, *Detskii ulichnyi travmatizm* (M.–L., 1939), pp. 19–35. A British Slavist recalls hearing a stirring warning against this activity as recently as the early 1970s, when an announcement was

made in a Moscow cinema that a child had just been killed when attempting to ride in this way (my thanks to Robert Russell for this information).

13 On photography and reading, see p. 489 below; on sewing, see CKQ E–03 PF3A, p. 2.

14 Osorina, *Sekretynyi mir detei*, pp. 63–4.

15 Village informants regularly relate how they were thrashed for letting animals stray and so on when they had got distracted: see e.g. Oxf/Lev V–04 PF15A, p. 6.

16 Time to play only on holidays: see V. Kozlov and E. Semenova, 'Obydennyi NEP: sochineniya i pis'ma shkol'nikov 20-kh godov', *Neizvestnaya Rossiya: XX vek* 3 (1993), 281 (this reminiscence comes from the mid-1920s, but the situation certainly obtained before 1917 and in later decades as well).

17 Yakov Kozlovsky remembered playing in cornflower fields outside Istra (then Voskresensk), near Moscow, in the late 1920s and early 1930s (*SPA*, vol. 5, p. 282) – also riding bareback and gathering berries and mushrooms.

18 See e.g. A. Federol'f, 'Ryadom s Alei', in A. Efron and A. Federol'f, *Miroedikha; Ryadom s Alei* (M., 1996), p. 247 (dogs); K. Smirnova, 'Moi kot Vas'ka', *Sami pisali* (M., 1931), pp. 16–18: the child author doted on this Methuselan animal, who was so old he had lost all his teeth, and fiercely resisted her father's suggestions it was time to kill the creature and skin it.

19 On collecting 'treasures' (or *tsatski*, as the children called them), see Dmitry Nabokov (b. 1889), 'Detskie gody v Suprunovke', *NM* 11 (1967), p. 71; on the other occupations, see Alekseev, *passim*. (Alekseev was brought up in the 1920s and early 1930s in the Volga region.)

20 *Sbornik igr dlya detei* (SPb.: no publ., 1871–4), issue 1, pp. 23–4; RAO NA f. 1 op. 1 d. 49, l. 3 (recorded in October 1916). On animal games (mostly from a 'totemistic' point of view), see

N. E. Mazalova, 'Detskie igry v zhivotnykh u vostochnykh slavyan', in G. N. Simakov (ed.), *Narodnye igry i igrushki* (SPb., 2000), pp. 79–93.

21 RAO NA f. 1 op. 1 d. 49, l. 13.

22 *Sbornik igr dlya detei*, issue 1, pp. 23–4.

23 RAO NA f. 1 op. 1 d. 49, l. 16 (recorded in October 1916).

24 Ibid., l. 44.

25 For a 'fortress' game, see the account of Stone Walls (*Kamennye steny*), played in Kursk province in the early twentieth century: ibid.

26 See e.g. I. Shangina, *Russkie deti i ikh igry* (SPb., 2000), pp. 193–4. This game was also known as *ryukhi* (see e.g. Oxf/Lev V–04 PF15A, p. 7: the informant was brought up in Pskov province).

27 On *gorodki*, see V. Dal', *Tolkovyi slovar' velikorusskogo yazyka* (2nd edn; M., 1880–82), vol. 1, p. 381; Shangina, *Russkie deti*, pp. 195–7; on *lapta*, Dal', *Tolkovyi slovar'*, vol. 2, p. 237; Shangina, *Russkie deti*, pp. 203–6. For a particularly full and detailed list of games played in the 1900s, see A. Kuznetsova-Budanova, *I u menya byl krai rodnoi* (Munich, 1975), pp. 69–73. The description of *lapta* is taken from Oxf/Lev SPb.–02, PF8A, p. 10.

28 On these games, see Shangina, *Russkie deti i*, p. 177, p. 178. On gendering, though, contrast Oxf/Lev SPb.–02 PF8A, p. 10: Informant b. 1931, who recalls that girls *did* play *lapta* in his part of Leningrad (Vasilievsky Island) in the 1930s.

29 Oxf/Lev SPb.–02 PF8A, p. 10; note also the interviewer's comment (ibid., n. 2), from her own researches on courtyard culture, that playing *mayalka* was generally considered 'improper' for girls. Archive of the European University, St Petersburg, recording EU Pb–00 PF1B p. 10, also remembers *mayalka*.

30 Oxf/Lev SPb.–02 PF8A, p. 10.

31 On girls' games, see Shangina, *Russkie deti*, p. 8 (*dochki-materi*), pp. 81–2 (skipping and mime), pp. 169–71 (flax game); on *chekharda*, ibid., p. 178; on *klassy*, ibid. p. 183 (this is also mentioned in Kassil', *Konduit i Shvambraniya* (1930), quoted from *Dorogie moi mal'chishki. Konduit i Shvambraniya* (M., 1987).

32 Oxf/Lev SPb.–02 PF8A, p. 9; EU Pb.–00 PF1A, p. 1. See also Aleksandra Piir, 'Detskie igry' (typescript inventory, SPb., 2003), p. 4.

33 Piir, 'Detskie igry', p. 4. An exception was the game called 'Ring' (*kolechko*), where a girl pressed a coin acting as the 'ring' into the hand of one other girl in a line, and this second girl then had to break free of the others and would become the 'leader' if she managed. Here, being 'leader' was regarded as an honour rather than a disgrace (ibid.)

34 On counting games, see Shangina, *Russkie deti*, p. 121. The fact that it was young children above all who enjoyed counting games is clear in the transcription of one quoted in ibid., p. 117: 'Raz, dva – kruzheva; tri, chetyre – pritsepili …' It is only with the weak r characteristic of under-sevens that *chetyre* and *pritsepili* can be made to rhyme. On games with sand (*pesochnik*), see Z. K. Manskina (b. 1899), in *Zhenskaya sud'ba v Rossii* (M., 1994), p. 9.

35 Shangina, *Russkie deti*, p. 81. Cf. Kuznetsova-Budanova, *I u menya*, p. 70: *salki* in the settlement where she lived was played with a hard rubber ball thrown full-speed by the 'it' at the quarry. Dmitry Nabokov recalls that 'snivellers' would be banned from playing games such as ball and *babki* for at least two weeks. 'Detskie gody', p. 72.

36 Piir, 'Detskie igry', p. 1 (*ladushki*, or 'clap-clap handies', was considered babyish by most once they reached the age of seven); p. 5 (*kolechko* not played after Class 1), etc.

37 RAO NA f. 1 op. 1 d. 49, ll. 72–3 (recollection of the 1900s or 1910s); Salynsky in *SPA*, vol. 5, p. 395 (from the 1930s); 'Dvor stal pionerskim', *PP* 23, July 1933, 4–5 (from the 1930s). Oxf/Lev SPb.–02 PF8A, p. 11. CKQ_Ox–06 PF15A, p. 7, remembers playing this in Paris after her family emigrated.

38 After school hours: see Oxf/Lev V–05 PF4B, p. 6: 'After we'd finished school and we was supposed to go home … We'd sort out the people who'd done us down. The girls would bring us some stones, and we'd go for them.' On holidays, Oxf/Lev V–05 PF7B, p. 13 (1930s and 1940s); Oxf/Lev P–05 PF26A, pp. 4–5 (1960s and 1970s; the holiday mentioned here is 'Russian Winter', a Soviet update of the traditional Shrovetide festival).

39 On playgrounds, see Chapter 12 below.

40 All these examples are from J. Bushnell, *Moscow Graffiti* (London, 1990), p. 19. The literal translation of the second scrawl is 'Vanya's an escapee from the insane asylum.'

41 Almost all our village informants, in particular, remembered such names being common: one informant was called Gagara (from the northern diver or loon) (Oxf/Lev V–05 PF7B, p. 18), another remembers her sisters being called Stanusha (from Tanya) and Tynta (Oxf/Lev V–05 PF12B, p. 7). See also Oxf/Lev V–05 PF14A, p. 7.

42 See V. Kataev, *Beleet parus odinokii* (M.–L., 1951), pp. 217–18, pp. 228–35, pp. 250–6.

43 E. Pokrovsky, 'Ploshchadki dlya igr i fizicheskikh uprazhnenii', *VV* 3 (1894), 50–76.

44 'Otkrytie ploshchadki dlya detskikh igr i fizicheskikh uprazhnenii v Orenburge', *VV* 5 (1894), 221–4.

45 See N. Polyakhin, 'Detskaya ploshchadka, kek vazhnyi faktor bor'by s berpinzomost'yu' *PB* 9 (1916), 987.

46 For further details, see N. S. Nelyubov, *Obzor deyatel'nosti obshchestva Detskii gorodok Petrogradskoi chasti, 1910–1915 gg.* (Petrograd, 1916); *PB* 9 (1916), 987–96; *PB* 10 (1916), 1005; and the digital version of the present chapter.

47 *Detskii proletkul't. Organ Tul'skoi Detskoi Kommunisticheskoi Partii (bol'shevikov)*, 7 November 1919, 1.

48 Vl. Rogov, 'Rabota RKSM sredi detei za 5 let', RGASPI-TsKhDMO f. 1 op. 23 d. 98, ll. 4–5; KPBTsK 1919–28, l. 3. All of this is, of course, related to broader anxieties about the subversive potential of youth: for a good discussion of this issue, see Gorsuch, ch. 7.

49 Z. Lilina, *Roditeli, uchites' vospityvat' svoikh detei*

(M., 1929), 5–9. Cf. Belev [first name not given], 'Zabytyi uchastok', *SYu* 13 (1932), 25–6, which describes children drinking and playing cards with adults in hostels in the Smolensk area.

50 'Stalinskaya konstitutsiya i okhrana prav nesover-shennoletnikh', *SYu* 12 (1938), 12–13. Cf. several articles in *Pravda* during 1935: e.g. 'Kogda konchayutsya uroki', *Pravda* 26 April 1935, on children in Stalingrad playing heads or tails and knucklebones and battles based on the Civil War hero Chapaev, dancing to the accordion, and calling for supervised games.

51 TsKhDMO f. 1 op. 23 d. 458, l. 17.

52 G. T. Rittersporn, 'Formy obshchestvennogo obikhoda molodezhi i ustanovki sovetskogo rezhima v predvoennom desyatiletii', in T. Vikhovainen (ed.), *Normy i tsennosti povsednevnoi zhizni* (SPB., 2000), pp. 51–3 (on 'Reds and Whites' and 'show trials'); on the former, see also V. Tadevosyan, 'O merakh bor'by s prestupnost'yu nesovershennoletnikh', *SYu* 13 (1935), 12, and the 1936 Komsomol Central Committee blacklist, KPBTsK 1936–42, l. 8, which cites a 'counter-revolutionary game' known as 'Voting' (Golosovanie).

53 *Pioner* 4 (1924), 15: on the term 'American Fascists', see *Pioner* 7 (1924), 17.

54 *Devyataya Mezhdunarodnaya detskaya nedelya* (M.: Molodaya gvardiya, 1929), p. 20, p. 22.

55 N. Aristova, 'Nashi igry', *Druzhnye rebyata* 1 (1932), 20–1.

56 RAO NA f. 1 op. 1 d. 49, l. 55.

57 Salynsky in *SPA*, vol. 5, p. 395 (referring to the 1930s: Salynsky and his friends made hobby-horses out of sticks as well). On icicles, see Alekseev, p. 105.

58 Oxf/Lev V–05 PF19B, p. 12.

59 RAO NA f. 1 op. 1 d. 191, l. 211 verso – 212 verso.

60 S. Tomarchenko, 'Misha Kuz'min ushel iz pionerotryada', *Pravda* 13 April 1935, p. 3. On *chizhiki*, see Dal', *Tolkovyi slovar'*, vol. 4, p. 603.

61 KPBTsK 1936–42, l. 8.

62 S. M. Loiter, *Russkii detskii fol'klor Karelii* (Petrozavodsk, 1991), p. 230 (recorded in 1956).

63 Oxf/Lev SPb.–02 PF8A, p. 11.

64 Oxf/Lev SPb.–02 PF8A, p. 15 (the informant and two friends made cigarettes of moss while living in Yaroslavl' in 1943, during evacuation from Leningrad; as a result, they were expelled from the Pioneers); Oxf/Lev V–05 PF18A, p. 26: moss cigarettes in a Novgorod province village, late 1930s. Cf. CKI SPb.–5: 'We used leaves to make cigarettes. It was hard to find moss in the South. [...] Ten? No, at ten we already smoked like real professionals. No, it was earlier than that, of course.' Cf. Oxf/Lev V–05 PF7A, p. 6 (smoking empty 'cigarettes', as there was no tobacco).

65 As described in Fazil' Iskander's autobiographical cycle of stories *Detstvo Chika* (1988): see *Sobranie sochinenii v 6 tomakh*, vol. 1 (Khar'kov, 1997), pp. 385–404, pp. 63–5, pp. 233–4; cf. Oxf/Lev SPb.–02 PF9A, p. 10.

66 For a particularly detailed account of the way the courtyard was used by older children, see Oxf/Lev SPb.–03 PF24B, pp. 17–19 (territorial disputes,

fights with weapons, leadership criteria), p. 23 (glue-sniffing), PF25B, p. 50 (criminal records). I have been helped here also by Aleksandra Piir's note, 'Detskie igry'.

67 On the 'layers' in the countryside, see especially Oxf/Lev V–05 PF5B, p. 9; general material on games in the countryside is offered in all our village interviews, see e.g. Oxf/Lev V–05 PF8B, p. 5; on courting games, my Conclusion below.

68 RAO NA f. 1 op. 1 d. 49, l. 44.

69 Ibid., l. 313. Cf. I. F. Petrovskaya, *V kontse puti* (SPb.: no publ., 1999), p. 10.

70 For Border Guards, see Anfisa Dudina in Novak-Deker, p. 238 (referring to the late 1930s). The other 1930s games are listed in 'Gazety kolkhoznykh rebyat', *Pravda* 2 July 1934, p. 3. Adaptations of 'mothers and daughters', at least, undoubtedly persisted: see e.g. Oxf/Lev V–04 PF5A, p. 5.

71 Petr Kruzhin in Novak-Deker, p. 185.

72 'War games' were played in at least two different ways: face-to-face confrontations on the pattern of Cossacks and Robbers, a game in which two lines of players were drawn up and a person, once his or her name was called, had to break through the opposing line; and a more complicated, long-drawn-out, type of game in which each side had its 'headquarters' (*shtab*), used for plotting against the other: Piir, 'Detskie igry', pp. 2–3 (*kazaki-razboiniki*), p. 8 (*voinushka*).

73 On Reds and Whites, see Salynsky, *SPA*, vol. 5, p. 395; on 'Red Cavalry', Daniil Granin, *Leningradskii katalog* (L., 1986), pp. 54–5; on the anti-capitalist games, see Shefner, p. 546. On Soviets and Fascists, see e.g. Oxf/Lev SPb.–02 PF8A.

74 A. Pasternak, *Vospominaniya* (Munich, 1983), pp. 25–7.

75 Libedinskaya in Fitzpatrick and Slezkine, p. 287. Cf. an account of a similar game from the late 1930s: Heroes' Wives, in which girls at a Moscow school would pretend to be married to the Chelyuskin pilots, Chkalov, and so on (Oxf/Lev M–05 PF45A, p. 7).

76 On shops and doctors and nurses, see N. A. Rybnikov, 'Iz roda v rod: Istoriya sem'i Rybnikovykh (za dvukhsotletnii period ee sushchestvovanie)', part III, OR RGB f. 367 Rybnikovy, karton 8, ed. khr. 2, l. 17; Piir, 'Detskie igry', p. 10.

77 See e.g. Oxf/Lev V–04 PF25A, p. 17. In cities, on the other hand, this tended to be a game for very small children: Piir, 'Detskie igry', p. 1.

78 Oxf/Lev V–05 PF5B, p. 10.

79 'A my proso seyali, seyali' (Oxf/Lev V–04 PF25A, p. 17; other informants also mention this game); houses, Oxf/Lev V–04 PF2A, p. 10, V–04 PF13A, pp. 20–1; don't play shops in them, Oxf/Lev V–04 PF19A, p. 6; do play dairy farms, V–04 PF24B, pp. 3–4.

80 Oxf/Lev SPb.–02 PF8A, p. 11 (skating and basketball); for Giants' Footsteps, see e.g. Oxf/Lev P–05 PF24A, p. 4.

81 RAO NA f. 1 op. 1 d. 140, l. 9 verso.

82 In the 1950s, boys in Baskov pereulok, at the back of Nevsky Prospekt, would amuse themselves by

playing a climbing game which required them to edge perilously along the cornices and window-ledges of the girls' school (a neo-classical building dating from the mid-nineteenth century) at the end of the street. (My thanks to Mariya Osorina for this information.)

83 On boys' play after the Second World War, see Luzhkov in *MPV*, p. 630; N. Dubrovin in Novak-Deker, p. 243; Oxf/Lev M–04 PF24A, p. 4.

84 Shefner, p. 542, remembered that *lapta* was still played in his courtyard in Leningrad in the late 1920s, but that *kikan'e* (kicking round, from the English) of a rag ball was just as popular. See ibid., p. 555 on *gorelki*. On football, see e.g. Evgeny Evtushenko, *Volchii pasport* (M., 1998), pp. 66–7, and the discussion pp. 487–8 below.

85 On *lodyzhki*, see Aseev in *SPA*, vol. 1, p. 90; on *shashki* (in the sense of Aunt Sally, rather than the more usual meaning of the term, draughts), see RAO NA f. 1 op. 1 d. 49, ll. 74–5.

86 Loiter, *Russkii detskii fol'klor Karelii*, p. 236. I remember playing a British version of this for hours when I was about 11 or 12 (i.e. in the early 1970s).

87 Anon., 'Sirotka', in A. Kruchenykh, *Sobstvennye rasskazy i risunki detei* (SPb., 1914), p. 40.

88 Shefner, p. 543.

89 See e.g. A. Kondratovich (b. 1920s), 'Nas voloklo vremya', *Znamya* 3 (2001), 162; N. Rybnikov (b. 1880) OR RGB f. 367 Rybnikovy, karton 8, ed. khr. 2, l. 13; on village-to-village fighting: Oxf/Lev V–04 PF19A, p. 7; on courtyard-to-courtyard fighting in big cities, e.g. EU Pb–00 PF1A, p. 3; in small towns, *Pravda* 4 April 1935, p. 3, 'Khuliganstvo shkol'nikov v Luganske'.

90 On the theft of fruit and vegetables, see e.g. Dmitry Kuznetsov's autobiography, RGIA f. 803 op. 16 d. 2372, l. 7; in the Soviet period, e.g. Oxf/Lev V–05 PF18A, p. 26. If caught, the children were treated to a traditional punishment – being thrashed with nettles (ibid.)

91 See Starzhinsky, e.g. p. 90.

92 S. M. Loiter, 'Kraeved I. M. Durov i ego kollektsiya detskikh igr' (these from the 1920s and 1930s), *Zhivaya starina* 1 (45) (2005), 33–43. Cf. also Oxf/Lev V–04, V–05 *passim*.

93 For the 'Indian' costume, see E. Rzhevskaya, *Znaki prepinaniya* (M., 1989), p. 74.

94 E.g. L. Kopelev, *The Education of a True Believer*, trans. G. Kern (London, 1981), p. 24.

95 See also the sections on the communal flat in Chapters 6, 8 of the full digital version of this book.

96 V. Nabokov, *Speak, Memory* (Harmondsworth, 1969), p. 20.

97 See Osorina, *Sekretnyi mir detei*, p. 169.

98 RAO f. 1 op. 1 d. 49, l. 213.

99 Z. I. Stanchinskaya, *Dnevnik materi* (M., 1924), p. 128.

100 On toys for 'early learning', see e.g. N. I. Gavrilova and M. P. Stakhorskaya, *Dnevnik materi* (M., 1916), p. 101 (on Froebelian balls and bricks); Nabokov, *Speak, Memory*, p. 24 (on building bricks). On the Trinity (Troitskaya) Workshop, see Svetlov, *Peterburskaya zhizn'*, p. 55, note 13 p. 107.

101 Elisaveta Fen, *A Russian Childhood* (London, 1961), p. 89.

102 Dobuzhinsky, *Vospominaniya*, p. 15.

103 RAO NA f. 1 op. 1 d. 49, l. 308.

104 Gavrilova and Stakhorskaya, *Dnevnik materi*, p. 138.

105 Toys were widely imported into Russia from Germany, so one may assume that bears were as well. An early home-made imitation, dated by its owner to 1909, is held in the collection of El'vira Smirnova in St Petersburg, which includes over 100 teddy bears made in, or imported to, Russia. See the news item on http://news.ntv.ru/spb/74468/ (accessed 5 November 2005).

106 Interestingly, this pacifist attitude to toys sometimes resurfaced in the Soviet period: see e.g. *N* 2 (1961), 9 (an attack on war toys by Gianni Rodari).

107 On playing soldiers, see N. Teffi, 'Gde-to v tylu', *Zemnaya raduga* (NY, 1952), pp. 47–53 (here a girl tries to join in); S. Eisenstein, *Memuary* (M., 1987), vol. 1, section 2.

108 Konstantin Paustovsky, for instance, invented names for his fleet, e.g. Walter Scott, Sirius, Polar Star, and 'the most startling itineraries' (*Sobranie sochinenii* (8 vols; M., 1967–70), vol. 4, p. 67).

109 Prokofiev, for instance, bought an engine in 1903 (aged 12), haggling the price down from 13 roubles 70 kopecks to 12 (*Avtobiografiya* (2nd edn; M., 1982), p. 127).

110 T. Karsavina, *Theatre Street* (2nd edn; London, 1936), p. 17.

111 S. Solov'ev, *Moi zapiski dlya detei moikh, a esli mozhno, i dlya drugikh*, in his *Izbrannye trudy: Zapiski* (M., 1983), 231.

112 S. Prokofiev, *Avtobiografiya*, p. 42.

113 As remembered by the informant, b. 1914, in Oxf/Lev V–05 PF5A, p. 11.

114 See W. Barnes Steveni, *Things Seen in Russia* (London, 1913).

115 See N. Oleshchuk, 'Detstvo v tsarskom dome', *RM* 21 March 2001, 12. The swan-shaped pram is pictured. For another case of a well-off child buying bazaar toys, see Prokofiev, *Avtobiografiya*, p. 128.

116 On 'Chinese shells', see e.g. Lidiya Zinov'eva-Annibal, *Tragicheskii zverinets* (SPb., 1907), p. 223.

117 E. M. Almedingen, *I Remember St Petersburg* (London, 1969), p. 159.

118 On 'American devils', see Nabokov, *Speak, Memory*. On 'uidi-uidi' dolls, N. Sats, *Novelly moei zhizni* (2 vols; M., 1982), vol. 1, p. 23.

119 See G. L. Dain, *Russkaya narodnaya igrushka* (M., 1981). A log doll (*kukla-poleno*) is pictured on p. 23. Cf. Shangina, *Russkie deti*, pp. 49–50: rattles, pottery toys, ceramic and tin whistles, tops; Federol'f, 'Ryadom s Alei', in Efron and Federol'f, *Miroedikha*, on the wood chips.

120 Kuznetsova-Budanova, *I u menya*, p. 46.

121 See N. Bartram, 'Igrushka', *Pechat' i revolyutsiya* 5 (1926), 39–62, for an indication of prevailing pedagogical attitudes to toys.

122 See Libedinskaya in Fitzpatrick and Slezkine, pp. 289–90.

123 Daniil Granin (b. 1919) describes many

traditional toys in *Leningradskii katalog*, pp. 53–4; Andrei Sergeev (*Omnibus*, M.: NLO, 1997, p. 14) remembers that pedlars still sold such traditional toys in late 1930s Moscow, but that he was not allowed to have any because mothers of the day (i.e. educated mothers) considered them dangerous and unhygienic.

124 *ENKP* 20 July 1931, 26. Cf. E. Drozdov, 'Deti trebuyut revolyutsionnuyu igrushku', *DD* 2 (1932) 12–13.

125 See e.g. KPBTsK 1929–35, l. 107 (decree, 14 August 1932, mandating a commission to look into the state of toy manufacture); KPBTsK 1936–42 l. 24 (decree, 10 July 1936, ordering further investigation of the topic).

126 *Pravda* 3 February 1936, p. 4, 22 February 1936 p. 4, 25 March 1936, p. 4, 5 April 1936, p. 4, 22 September 1936, p. 4; and cf. M. Gorky, [Zametki o detskikh knigakh i igrakh], *SS* vol. 27, pp. 518–20.

127 See *Pravda* 22 February 1936, p. 4.

128 On the bonus, see Vlasovskaya in Fitzpatrick and Slezkine, p. 361. On wages generally, see S. Davies, *Popular Opinion in Stalin's Russia* (Cambridge, 1997), p. 24.

129 Andrei Sergeev, *Al'bom dlya marok* in *Omnibus*, p. 23 (the cars); M. L. Gasparov, 'Moe detstvo', in his *Zapisi i vypiski* (M.: NLO, 2000), p. 75 (the horse on rockers and alphabet blocks).

130 Oxf/Lev SPb.–02 PF7A, p. 39.

131 See e.g. CKQ M–04 PF6A, p. 3.

132 Pavel Starzhinsky, *Vzrosloe detstvo* (M., 1991), p. 120. On toy manufacture in towns, see Oxf/Lev SPb.–02 PF9 A, p. 48; on toys for the tree, Oxf/Lev SPb.–02 PF7A, p. 37.

133 Oxf/Lev V–05 PF5B, p. 14.

134 Oxf/Lev V–04 PF1A, p. 12, Oxf/Lev V–04 PF3B, p. 8, Oxf/Lev V–04 PF10B, p. 5, Oxf/Lev V–04 PF2B, p. 19, Oxf/Lev V–04 PF15A, p. 7, Oxf/Lev V–05 PF15B, p. 13.

135 A. Mass, 'Raznotsvetnye cherepki', in his *Raznotsvetnye cherepki* (M., 1970).

136 Based on CKI SPb.–1, on personal information from the informant in CKQ SPb.–03 PF1–2, and on our formal interviews (e.g. Oxf/Lev V–05 PF13B, p. 4; Oxf/Lev V–04 PF3B, p. 8).

137 CKI M–1.

138 Oxf/Lev SPb.–02 PF4A, p. 87.

139 'Demonstrationnyi zal Krokodila', *Krokodil* 4 (1952), 6. For average incomes etc., see Chapter 3 above.

140 On chess, see p. 483 below. On other board games, see e.g. Oxf/Lev SPb.–03 PF36B, p. 26 and Piir, 'Detskie igry'. On paper games, an intriguing source is the memoir of Stalin's daughter Svetlana Allilueva, *Dvadtsat' pisem k drugu* (London, 1967), pp. 147–9, which recalls the comic letters that Svetlana used to exchange with her father, parodying official documents (he would pose as her subordinate First Secretary, she as the supreme 'She-Boss', *khozyayushka*).

141 Karsavina, *Theatre Street*, p. 17.

142 Sergeev, *Al'bom dlya marok*, p. 15.

143 Oxf/Lev V–05 PF2B, p. 6.

144 As remembered in Oxf/Lev V–05 PF16A, p. 8.

145 CKQ Ox–03 PF1A, p. 2.

146 'My proverili – vypolneno', *N* 9 (1960), 22. See also *N* 22 (1961), 24; *N* 9 (1962), 17; *N* 37 (1963), 4–5; *N* 4 (1968), 2; *N* 4 (1972), 6; *N* 29 (1972), 19; *N* 7 (1974), 10–11; *N* 14 (1974), 12; *N* 44 (1980), 4; *N* 13 (1983), 3; *N* 46 (1983), 8–9; *N* 49 (1987), 3; *N* 8 (1966), 8.

147 R. Bamm and 17 others, *Semeinoe vospitanie: Slovar' dlya roditelei* (M.: Prosveshchenie, 1967), pp. 99–101, p. 200. See also *N* 6 (1961), 21; *N* 7 (1961), 21; *N* 16 (1961), 20–1; *N* 28 (1965), 18; *N* 17 (1967), 20–1; *N* 3 (1969), 19; *N* 5 (1969), 21; *N* 24 (1977), 12; *N* 33 (1980), 15, etc.

148 'Chelovek poshel v shkolu', *N* 39 (1966), 20.

149 V. Mukhina, *Bliznetsy* (M.: Prosveshchenie, 1969), pp. 23–4, p. 29, p. 93, p. 31, p. 35, p. 45, p. 59, p. 59, p. 60, p. 63, p. 65, p. 94, p. 170, p. 407. Also note their visits on several occasions to Detskii mir – and not only as a leisure facility (they bought a toy wheelbarrow there in May 1965, see p. 173).

150 CKQ Ox–03 PF10B, p. 7. On a toy elephant from East Germany, see CKQ Ox–03 PF2A, p. 4.

151 Oxf/Lev SPb.–03 PF14A p. 1.

152 Oxf/Lev M–04 PF24A, p. 6, p. 10.

153 On toys in the village, see Oxf/Lev P–05 PF26A, p. 2 (this in the late 1960s); on the doll and bear, Oxf/Lev P–05 PF23A, p. 2 (also in the 1960s).

154 On the 1940s, see CKQ Ox–03 PF1A, p. 5; on the 1960s, CKQ Ox–03 PF2A, p. 4; Oxf/Lev M–04 PF36A, p. 11.

155 See e.g. Oxf/Lev P–05 PF24B, p. 22.

156 See e.g. *N* 5 (1990), 22–3; *N* 45 (1990), 14–15. A 1960s item on the attractiveness of Japanese toys (*N* 13 (1989), 19) included no brand names. Alongside these articles on foreign toys, there was also a rash of items about defects in Soviet-made items – see e.g. *N* 11 (1989), 6 (poisonous dye used for a red animal); *N* 18 (1989), 5 (follow-up report).

157 See e.g. P. I. Lebedev-Polyansky (speech of March 1927), in D. L. Babichenko (ed.), *'Schast'e literatury': gosudarstvo i pisateli 1925–1938. Dokumenty* (M., 1997), p. 34.

158 *SPA*, vol. 2, p. 314.

159 N. Rybnikov, *Derevenskii shkol'nik i ego idealy* (M., 1916), p. 13.

160 *SPA*, vol. 2, p. 143.

161 *SPA*, vol. 2, p. 304.

162 Vladimir Sosyura, *SPA*, vol. 2, p. 380.

163 Dmitry Furmanov *SPA*, vol. 2, p. 586; Vladimir Bakhmet'ev; Vladimir Bill-Belotserkovsky (*SPA*, vol. 1, p. 155.

164 See e.g. A. B. Zaks, 'Krug chteniya v detstve i yunosti', *Chtenie v dorevolyutsionnoi Rossii* (M., 1995), p. 162.

165 See e.g. Agniya Barto in *SPA*, vol. 4, p. 38; Margarita Aliger in *SPA*, vol. 4, p. 18; Blok in F. F. Fidler (ed.), *Pervye literaturnye shagi* (M., 1911), p. 85. See also Zaks, 'Krug chteniya'.

166 Dobuzhinsky, *Vospominaniya*, p. 25.

167 Ibid., p. 25, is a case in point.

168 See I. Vladislavlev, *Chto chitat'? Ukazatel' sistemat- icheskogo domashnego chteniya dlya uchashchikhsya* (2nd edn; M., 1914), issue 1, pp. 5–6, pp. 21–84.

169 See the Introduction to N. A. Rubakin, *Kak zanimat'sya samoobrazovaniem* (M., 1962), p. 14.

170 References to these writers are ubiquitous in memoirs by children from the cultural elite. See e.g. Nabokov, *Speak, Memory*, p. 152, p. 153, pp. 156–8 (on Mayne Reid). A relatively rare reference from girlhood is Sofiya Pregel', *Moe detstvo* (3 vols; Paris, 1973), vol. 1, p. 104 (Cooper, Reid, Verne).

171 *SPA*, vol. 3, p. 409.

172 See Vygodskaya in B. Bim-Bad and O. Kosheleva (eds), *Priroda rebenka v zerkale avtobiografii* (M., 1998), p. 229 (here, on *The Children of Captain Grant*).

173 A recent selection of material by L. A. Charskaya is *Volshebnaya skazka: povesti* (M., 1994).

174 K. I. Chukovsky, 'Lidiya Charskaya', *Rech'* 9 September 1912: reprinted in his *Sobranie sochinenii v 6 tomakh*, vol. 6 (M., 1969), pp. 150–62.

175 S. Larsen, 'Girl Talk: Lydia Charskaia and Her Readers', in L. Engelstein and S. Sandler (eds), *Self and Story in Russian History* (Ithaca, NY, 2000), pp. 149–50.

176 Larsen, 'Girl Talk', p. 149, n. 20. Some fan mail was also sent to other writers: for instance, Boris Lazarevsky recalls getting it after publishing his *Uchenitsa* (1905), whose portrait of a girl in love appealed to schoolgirls (see F. F. Fidler (ed.), *Pervye literaturnye shagi*, p. 7).

177 Yury Tynyanov, *SPA*, vol. 2, p. 483.

178 Fen, *A Russian Childhood*, pp. 275–9.

179 Fidler, *Pervye literaturnye shagi*, p. 91.

180 See Vygodskaya in Bim-Bad and Kosheleva (eds), *Priroda rebenka v zerkale avtobiografii*, pp. 228–9, on Grimm and Alcott; Dobuzhinsky, *Vospominaniya*, p. 24, on Andersen. Frances Hodgson-Burnett's books were published repeatedly during the early twentieth century: see catalogues of the Russian National Library and Russian State Library.

181 See *Katalog magazina "Detskii mir"* (SPb., 1886); *Katalog magazina "Detskoe vospitanie* (SPb., 1899). For the text of Styopka-Rastyopka, see *Stepka-rastrepka: Pokhozhdeniya odnogo neispravimogo shaluna. Rasskazal I. K——ev* (M.: Tip. T-va I. D. Sytina, 1912); on reading it in childhood, see e.g. Dobuzhinsky, *Vospominaniya*, p. 14.

182 Zaks, 'Krug chteniya v detstve i yunosti', pp. 163–4.

183 O. Kaidanova, 'Iz zhizni odnoi shkoly', *SvoV* 1 (1911–12), 43–4.

184 *SPA*, vol. 5, p. 423.

185 See E. Dobrenko, *The Making of the State Reader*, trans. Jessie M. Savage (Stanford, CA, 1997), pp. 190–1 (which gives detailed lists taken from the *Instruktsiya*). H. Ermolaev, *Censorship in Soviet Literature, 1917–1991* (Lanham, MD, 1997), p. 7, describes the removal of Charskaya in 1923. Cf. Gorky's assertion in 1933 that far less of pre-revolutionary children's literature than of pre-revolutionary adult literature was recuperable for Soviet readers ('Literatura – detyam', *Pravda* 11 June 1933, *SS*, vol. 27, p. 32).

186 On P. Blyakhin, *Krasnye d'yavolyata* and L. Ostroumov, *Makar-sledopyt*; see E. O. Putilova in *Russkaya poeziya detyam*, vol. 2 (SPb., 1997), pp. 8–9.

187 See the extract from A. Tolstov, *Trudovaya shkola*, in N. N. Iordansky (ed.), *Svobodnye sochineniya i detskoe tvorchestvo v programmakh Gus'a* (M.–L., 1926), p. 67.

188 Dobrenko, *The Making of the State Reader*, p. 192.

189 See A. V. Blyum, *Za kulisami 'Ministerstva pravdy': Tainaya istoriya sovetskoi tsenzury, 1917–1929* (SPb., 1994), p. 256; *O partiinoi i sovetskoi pechati: shonik dokumentor*, p. 377.

190 On Tarzan, see Siegelbaum and Sokolov, p. 79; on Verne, *O partiinoi i sovetskoi pechati*, p. 428.

191 For instance, a 1936 film adaptation of Verne's *The Children of Captain Grant* attracted an ambiguous review of this kind: it was a pity that the directors had not chosen a Soviet story, and also that they had not been clear-cut enough about distinguishing positive from negative characters in the narrative when adapting it for film. See *Pravda* 27 August 1936, p. 6.

192 L. Kassil', *Delo vkusa: Zametki pisatelya* (2nd edn; M., 1964), 115. On myths of the Soviet reader, see particularly S. Lovell, *The Russian Reading Revolution* (Basingstoke, 2000), esp. ch. 2.

193 'Detskoi knige – pochetnoe mesto v sem'e', *SemSh* 7 (1953), 4.

194 For a detailed discussion of this, see Kelly.

195 'Khronika tsentra', *Prosveshchenie na transporte* 1 (1926), 163–4.

196 On this, see particularly Evgeny Dobrenko, *The Making of the State Reader*, pp. 190–1.

197 E. Uvarova, 'Novye puti bor'by s detskoi besprizornost'yu i beznadzornost'yu', *Detskii dom* 3 (1928), 12.

198 Ella Bobrova, *Irina Istomina: povest' v stikhakh* (Toronto, 1967), p. 8.

199 *Programmy i metodicheskie zapiski edinoi trudovoi shkoly*, issue 3 (M.–L.: Gosizdat, 1927), p. 36. There were 22 texts on the 'optional' list, including Pushkin's *skazki*.

200 *Programmy fabrichno-zavodskoi semiletki*, issue 4 (M.–L., 1930), pp. 70–2.

201 Raisa Orlova, for instance, remembered being told to condemn Charskaya at school, aged 14. See *Vospominaniya o neproshedshem vremeni* (Ann Arbor, 1983), p. 131.

202 See N. I. Boldyrev (ed.), *Klassnyi rukovoditel'* (M., 1955), pp. 195–200, Appendix 18, pp. 344–8. For a class discussion of such reading, cf. ibid., Appendix 13, p. 325, which stipulates that the class supervisor should hold group sessions on 'How to Handle a Book', and on 'Gorky's Story "How I Studied"'.

203 See e.g. the rubric in *Rabotnitsa* in 1930s, 'Knigi dlya malen'kikh detei' (P. Dymshits in *Rabotnitsa* 22 (1939), p. 19; cf. no. 25 (1939) p. 2; 13 (1940) p. 2). *Sem'ya i shkola* ran such items too: see e.g. 'Detskoi knige – pochetnoe mesto v sem'e', *SemSh* 7 (1953), 1–4, recommending Mayakovsky, Gaidar, books about Lenin and Stalin by A. Kononov, M. Bol'shnitser and M. Chiaureli, Yu. German, 'Rasskazy o Dzerzhinskom', L. Kassil', *Ulitsa mladshego syna*, etc. For guidance for parents, see e.g. V. Osipov, *Kniga v vashem dome* (M., 1967).

204 See (on the 1950s and early 1960s), L. G. Soboleva, 'Uchim detei vybirat' sebe

knigu', in A. A. Khrenkova, *Detskie biblioteki – v pomoshch' kommunisticheskomu vospitaniyu. Iz opyta raboty* (M., 1959), pp. 169–72; (on the 1970s) E. C. Miller, *Reading Guidance in Soviet Children's Libraries* (Birmingham, 1978), esp. pp. 1–5.

205 See e.g. an article published in 1983 arguing that children should be encouraged to read adventure stories because these developed their emotional and imaginative capacities: I. A. Svirskaya, E. L. Ogurtsova and L. N. Asinovskaya, 'Priklyuchencheskaya literatura v sovremennoi detskoi biblioteke', in *Differentsial'noe rukovodstvo chteniem detei: Sbornik nauchnykh trudov* (L., 1983) [no ed. given], pp. 37–50.

206 See L. A. Anishchenko, 'Pionerskaya gazeta i ee yunyi chitatel'', in *Differentsial'noe rukovodstvo*, pp. 121–33.

207 Mikhail Kolesnikov (b. 1918), (*SPA*, vol. 5, p. 292).

208 Cf. Oxf/Lev SPb.–02 PF9A, p. 51 (Barto, Mikhalkov, Marshak). The informant also recalls how cheap such books were.

209 A. Salynsky on Neverov: *SPA*, vol. 5, p. 39.

210 See Marina Dubrovskaya, 'We Have Read Different Tales', in A. M. Fasick (ed.), *Young People and Reading: International Perspectives* (The Hague, 1994), pp. 1–9.

211 Granin, *Leningradskii katalog*, p. 73.

212 *Krokodil* 4 (1952), 8, 16.

213 Oxf/Lev SPb.–03 PF14B, p. 29.

214 Anna Balashova, b. 1904, in Fitzpatrick and Slezkine, p. 244.

215 See e.g. Oxf/Lev SPb.–03 PF25B, pp. 36–7.

216 Cf. the survey p. 457 above; and e.g. CKQ M–04 PF7A, p. 14; Oxf/Lev P–05 PF8B, p. 20; Oxf/Lev P–05 PF23A, p. 7.

217 *SPA*, vol. 5, p. 212.

218 On orphanage inmates' reading of Charskaya, see Oxf/Lev SPb.–02 PF3A, p. 67; female informant, b. 1937. For reading by girls in families, see e.g. Elena Bonner, *Dochki-materi* (M., 1994), p. 188; Drunina, *SPA*, vol. 5, p. 175. As before, the odd boy consumed Charskaya in secret too: see e.g. Granin, *Leningradskii katalog*, p. 64.

219 Fitzpatrick and Slezkine, p. 370.

220 Omry [as Omri] Ronen, 'Oborvysh', *Zvezda* 11 (2001), 233.

221 On Greek and Latin literature, see e.g. Drunina, b. 1924, *SPA*, vol. 5, p. 175; Ronen, 'Oborvysh', 231. On Cicero: CKI SPb.–6.

222 Said of Barto by a man b. 1950. CKI SPb.–7.

223 See Kelly.

224 On the reading preferences of these generations, see e.g. the responses of Leonid Kostyukov (b. 1959), Stanislav L'vovsky (b. 1972), Denis Osokin (b. 1976), and Yana Tokareva (b. 1976) to a questionnaire about childhood reading: Il'ya Kukulin, 'Sovsem vneklassnoe chtenie: otkrytiya i vospominaniya', *Novoe literaturnoe obozrenie* 60 (2003), 273–7; see also Oxf/Lev WQ1 KM, p. 6. Translated material of this kind was given wide publicity when it first appeared – cf. the items in *N* 13 (1969), 20, advertising Boris Zakhoder's version of *Mary Poppins*, or the excerpt of *Pippi Longstocking* in *N* 32 (1969), 21–2.

225 See Chapter 2.

226 On the expansion of private book-collecting, see Lovell, *The Russian Reading Revolution*, pp. 66–7.

227 *Jane Eyre*, for instance, was popular among Russian children in the 11–14 age group because it was rare for a Russian classic to have such a gripping plot. (My thanks to L. N. Kiseleva for this information.)

228 Oxf/Lev SPb.–03 PF17B, p. 18.

229 Osipov, *Kniga v vashem dome*, p. 102. By contrast, Osipov recommends that parents read guides to children's books such as the brochures published by I. N. Timofeeva, *What Should My Children Read?* and study the school programmes before deciding which works by classic writers to give their children (ibid., p. 102, p. 105).

230 *SPA*, vol. 5, p. 212.

231 K. Chukovsky, *Ot dvukh do pyati* (4th edn; b., 1934), p. 139.

232 See F. Kuznetsov, *Besedy o literature* (M., 1977), p. 14.

233 See e.g. L. Kassil', 'O Gaidare', in A. Gaidar, *Sochineniya* (M., 1946), pp. 6–12; R. I. and V. S. Fraerman, *Zhizn' i tvorchestvo A. P. Gaidara* (M., 1954).

234 E. G. Tuneva, '"Skazka o Voennoi Taine" A. Gaidara kak sredstvo patrioticheskogo vospitaniya uchashchikhsya IV klassa', in L. A. Khinkova, N. I. Rybakov and A. A. Frolov (eds), *Tvorchestvo A. P. Gaidara* (Gor'kii, 1975), p. 201, p. 206.

235 For this phrase, see Tuneva, '"Skazka o Voennoi Taine"', p. 207.

236 Osorina, *Sekretnyi mir detei*, p. 157. Reminiscence from the 1980s. For another reminiscence of Timur games, this time in the countryside, see Oxf/Lev V–04 PF6B, p. 60.

237 See V. K. Kuznetsova, 'Detskii chitatel' v kontekste vremeni', *Mir bibliotek segodnya* vyp. 1 (M., 1995), 68–73. Alongside Soviet classics, translated fiction was also extremely popular, especially in the fantasy genre.

238 A. P. Chekhov, *Polnoe sobranie sochinenii i pisem v 30 tomakh* (M., 1974–83), vol. 6, pp. 430–49. Other lost and found stories include Sergei Rozanov's *The Adventures of Travka* (1928) (see Chapter 2 above).

239 Fidler, *Pervye literaturnye shagi*, p. 85.

240 Ibid., p. 92.

241 Ibid., p. 241.

242 *Moi vek*, p. 57. Cf. Vadim Andreev's recollection of his own lyric *Meisterwerke*, composed under the name Prince Beelzebub (Knyaz' Vel'zevul), to his writer father Leonid's great amusement: *Detstvo* (M., 1966), p. 122.

243 Kassil', *Konduit*, pp. 137–40.

244 *SPA*, vol. 2, p. 304.

245 *SPA*, vol. 5, p. 176.

246 On albums in the late nineteenth and early twentieth centuries, see Zaks, 'Krug chteniya v detstve i yunosti', *Chtenie v dorevolyutsionnoi Rossii*, p. 165. On the Soviet period, see the well-illustrated discussion in V. V. Golovin and V. F. Lur'e, 'Devichii al'bom XX veka', in A. F. Belousov (ed.), *Russkii shkol'nyi fol'klor: ot 'vyzyvanii' Pikovoi Damy do semeinykh rasskazov* (M., 1998), pp. 269–98. Oxf/Lev WQ1 KM, p. 5

describes this type of activity in the late Soviet era. On the sentimental function of albums, see my Conclusion below.

247 On albums in reformatories, see Chapter 12. School magazines were strictly regulated by the school authorities before 1917: where licit in the first place, they would be organised under the supervision of a teacher, and might be closed down if they were deemed to be 'subversive'. The files of the First *Gimnaziya* in St Petersburg contain an example of the genre, *The Inexperienced Pen* (*Neopytnoe pero*), a mimeographed collection of stories and essays: RGIA f. 139 op. 1 d. 12664, ll. 12–27 (l. 3 is a letter from the director of the school to the school inspector forwarding a copy of the journal). On the 'wall newspaper', see Chapter 8 above. The informal school magazine was to a large extent replaced by the 'wall newspaper' in the Soviet period, but there are records of the former in some schools: see e.g. Oxf/Lev P–05 PF3B, p. 17.

248 This point is made with a certain didactic overemphasis in Kassil', *Konduit i Shambraniya*, in *Dorogie moi mal'chishki*, p. 283, where Faniya Kaplan's assassination attempt on Lenin marked the first day that the boys did not play Shvambraniya.

249 Miller, *Reading Guidance*, p. 23. She also points out that 25 per cent was the proportion recommended by the Ministry of Education.

250 See e.g. Oxf/Lev M–04 PF25A, p. 28: an informant b. 1968 and brought up in a 'settlement' (small town) near Moscow recalls that exposure to the theatre came in the form of amateur performances, and occasional visits by touring groups, often invited by the local authorities themselves. CKQ M–04 PF5A, p. 10: the informant, brought up in Tula province in the 1920s, recalls taking part in amateur theatricals as his main experience of drama.

251 See p. 482 below. Radio drama had considerable impact on intellectual audiences in the cities, but is clearly a different and more cerebral genre compared to television drama.

252 E. Anthony Swift, *Popular Theater and Society in Tsarist Russia* (Berkeley, CA, 2002). On the villages, see *Narodnyi teatr: sbornik* (M., 1896); Ivan L. Shcheglov, *Narodnyi teatr v ocherkakh i kartinakh* (SPb., 1898).

253 On the fairs and on amateur dramatics, see A. Benois, *Reminiscences of the Russian Ballet* (London, 1941), ch. 3; Dobuzhinsky, *Vospominaniya* (p. 23); Paustovsky (*Sobranie sochinenii*, vol. 4, p. 63); Sosyura (*SPA*, vol. 2, p. 381); Korneichuk (*SPA*, vol. 3, p. 368).

254 On mumming shows (which persisted until recent times), see e.g. Oxf/Lev V–04 PF2B, p. 16; V–04 PF19A, p. 11 (this informant recalled that they stopped during the war).

255 Benois, *Reminiscences of the Russian Ballet*, pp. 48–9; Arbuzov, *SPA*, vol. 5, p. 45; Fedin, *SPA*, vol. 2, p. 565.

256 V. S. Glagolin, *Neskol'ko slov o detskom teatre* (2nd edn; Saratov, 1905).

257 V. F. Stel'skaya, *Nedotroga* (2nd edn; Petrograd-M., n.d. [c. 1915]).

258 A. Chumachenko *Lyulli-muzykant* (M., 1913). A performance copy, with censorship cuts (mostly removing religious references such as 'the Virgin Mary') is held at the Theatre Library, St Petersburg, on TV33610.

259 See e.g. *Petrushka: Ulichnyi teatr* (M., 1912: reprinted 1914, 1915, 1916); *Petrushka: lyubimyi narodnyi ulichnyi teatr* (M., 1910; reprinted 1913, 1915, 1917); for a general discussion of the text, with some material on these adaptations, see Catriona Kelly, *Petrushka, the Russian Carnival Puppet Theatre* (Cambridge, 1990).

260 See *Pervyi vsesoyuznyi s"ezd sovetskikh pisatelei: stenograficheskii otchet* (M., 1934), p. 471.

261 N. N. Bakhtin, *Obzor p'es dlya detskogo i shkol'nogo teatra* (SPb., 1912).

262 Irina Shikhaeva-Gaister remembered seeing *The Little Hunchback Horse* at the Bol'shoi in early 1930s: Fitzpatrick and Slezkine, p. 371. Cf. Sats on the Bol'shoi's total uninterest in expanding this repertoire: *Novelly moei zhizni*, vol. 1, p. 127.

263 For example, the Irkutsk TRAM (Young Worker Theatre), founded in 1928: *T* 11 (1978), 32. This was converted into a TYuZ in 1937.

264 *T* 11 (1978), 32 (on Irkutsk). See also Lynne Mally, *Revolutionary Acts* (Ithaca, NY: Cornell University Press, 2000).

265 *Teatral'naya Moskva*, pp. 195–6.

266 Ibid., pp. 193–5.

267 Ibid., pp. 197–8. Cf. the material on the Children's Book Puppet Theatre (founded in 1932 by Gosizdat) (ibid., p. 199).

268 Ibid., p. 201.

269 Cf. data from our village interviews, e.g. Oxf/Lev V–04 PF8A, p. 10, where the informant recalls having acted 'Tanya' in a play about the Partisans (this was quite possibly a staging of the life of Zoya Kosmodem'yanskaya, since the informant's first name was the same, though she casts doubt on this identification herself in PF8A, p. 16).

270 *Nash drug – teatr*, comp. N. P. Kuraptseva and L. G. Surina (L., 1962), p. 29. This book is generally a useful guide to the activities of the 'delegates' at different periods.

271 See e.g. *Teatral'nyi Leningrad* (M.–L., 1937), pp. 76–8.

272 Vladimir Urin, 'O "spetsifike" TYuZov i o mnogom drugom', *T* 2 (1987), 107–10.

273 For an account of the theatre's history by Sats herself, see her *Novelly moei zhizni*, vol. 1, pp. 110–54.

274 *Pervyi vsesoyuznyi s"ezd*, p. 472.

275 *The Moscow Theatre of Children* (M., 1934); for the comment on *The Pearl of Adalmina*, see p. 16.

276 *Pervyi vsesoyuznyi s"ezd*, p. 473.

277 Sats, *Novelly moei zhizni*, pp. 316–18.

278 On *skazki*, see B. Leman in E. Vasilieva and S. Marshak, *Teatr dlya detei* (Krasnodar: Izd. Kubano-Chernomorskogo Otdela Narodnogo Obrazovaniya, 1922), p. 7; on theatrics, see Vasilieva and Marshak's own introduction, p. 12, and the sample prologues on pp. 19–40.

279 S. Lunacharskaya, *Teatr dlya detei kak orudie kommunistichestergo vospitaniya* (M., 1931), p. 10.

280 Sergei Obraztsov, *Po stupen'kam pamyati* (M.: Iskusstvo, 1987), p. 169.

281 'Perechen' rabot, osushchestvlennykh zasluzhennym artistom SSSR Evg. Demmeni [za period s 1924 po 1936 gg.]', TsGALI-SPb. f. 86 op. 1 d. 60, ll. 2–3.

282 On being taken to the theatre, see e.g. Oxf/Lev M–04 PF26B, p. 20.

283 See e.g. Nina Mikhal'skaya [Vospominaniya] (unpublished typescript, author's archive), p. 25.

284 Sats, *Novelly moei zhizni*, vol. 2, pp. 6–69.

285 Some details of the history of the theatre are available on http://www.teatr-sats.ru/theatre/.

286 For complaints about limitations in the repertoire, see e.g. 'Ne zabyvaite o shkol'nikakh', *T* 1 (1950), 85–6. Contemporary reviews such as *T* 7 (1951), 47–9 (on yet another *skazka* adaptation) or *T* 4 (1953), 91–102 (on a Soviet morality play for the older child audience) are optimistic in tone, but their descriptions of plots and staging devices suggest a lacklustre reality. For an attack on Demmeni (his book on the theatre hammered as *ideino-nepolnotsennaya*), see *T* 4 (1950), 83.

287 *T* 2 (1950), 91–3.

288 *T* 3 (1954), 160. The basis for the calculation was ticket sales.

289 See e.g. Sergei Mikhalkov in *T* 3 (1954), 161; *T* 3 (1954), 165–9; *T* 6 (1954), 169–72; *T* 8 (1955), 174, 177–8.

290 On the congresses, see *T* 6 (1954), 157, *T* 6 (1957), 145. On theatre numbers, see *T* 6 (1958), 154.

291 For material on participation in festivals, see e.g. *T* 3 (1958), 163–8.

292 On the Andersen (a revival of Vera Smirnova's adaptation, originally performed in the late 1930s), see *T* 5 (1955), 160; on *Emil*, see *T* 5 (1958), 48, 50.

293 See e.g. *T* 2 (1958), 154.

294 On international festivals, see e.g. *T* 7 (1980), 37–42; for reports from abroad, see e.g. *T* 1 (1979), 121–5 (Berlin), *T* 12 (1979), 78–80 (Yugoslavia), *T* 7 (1973), 126–35 (USA and Canada).

295 On Bambi, see I. Segedi, 'Dolgii put' k detstvu', *T* 7 (1978), 13; on *Mary Poppins*, *T* 7 (1979), 26–9; on Harper Lee, *T* 10 (1966), 69; on *Peter Pan*, *T* 12 (1967), 24–5.

296 *N* 19 (1962), 9.

297 See e.g. *T* 6 (1961), 49 (on Rozov).

298 On Efros, see e.g. *T* 4 (1960), 116 and *T* 7 (1961), 122. On Dodin, see e.g. *T* 5 (1972), 77.

299 On new buildings, see e.g. the description of the Leningrad TYuZ, *T* 2 (1955), 155; for recommendations about sightlines and staff training, see the comments by A. A. Bryantsev (long-term director of the Leningrad TYuZ), *T* 10 (1966), 28.

300 *T* 7 (1972), 28.

301 On Ryazan', see *T* 7 (1979), 12–14; on Chelyabinsk, see *T* 1 (1979), 15–17; on Tallinn and Magnitogorsk, see *T* 6 (1978), 53–62; on the Moscow Province Puppet Theatre, see *T* 1 (1969), 46–51. Leningrad and Riga were the subject of a great deal of laudatory review coverage in *T* in the 1960s and 1970s.

302 *N* 29 (1982), 7.

303 For the figure, see *T* 7 (1972), 31; for the dominance of the *skazka*, see e.g. 'Skazki-byli', *N* 7 (1962), 20.

304 'Gazety pishut o tyuzakh', *T* 10 (1966), 86–91.

305 For material on 'teen drama', see e.g. *T* 2 (1970), 53; Yu. I. Rubina, *Teatr i podrostok* (M.: Prosveshchenie, 1970); *T* 9 (1970), 111–12. A striking and much-remarked-upon example of the genre was Feliks Knorre's *Otets*, which showed a mother throwing out her children's father and embarking on a live-in relationship with a stranger: *T* 12 (1965), 41. On school plays, see e.g. *T* 7 (1978), 32–43.

306 *T* 11 (1978), 32.

307 Cf. the favourable comments on her recent work by reviewers: *T* 2 (1976), 88–90; *T* 7 (1981), 28–39.

308 For a tactful assault on the *travesti* custom, see the comments by P. Khomsky, director of the Moscow TYuZ, *T* 10 (1966), 18–20.

309 See e.g. *T* 6 (1961), 71–6; *T* 10 (1966), 3–5, 80–5; *T* 12 (1971), 80–9; *T* 7 (1974), 18, etc. These general reports are confirmed by individual reviews, e.g. of a frightful *skazka* adaptation at the Pushkin Theatre, Moscow (*T* 3 (1962), 46–7), or a crudely staged harlequinade at the Saratov Theatre of the Young Viewer, *T* 11 (1963), 54–62.

310 N. Dolinina, 'Shkol'niki etikh let', *T* 10 (1966), 42–6; cf. *T* 7 (1974), 11.

311 V. Dmitrievsky, 'Teatr i deti', *T* 2 (1987), 95 (12 *tyuzy* out of 33 is the exact figure).

312 *Moskva v tsifrakh: statisticheskii sbornik* (M., 1977), p. 155.

313 *T* 5 (1970), 111 (figures for 1970); *T* 7 (1975), 3 (TYuZ figures for 1941). For the 1986 TYuZ figures and the 1958 puppet theatre figures, see p. 000 above.

314 *T* 8 (1983), 16. On the overall decline in audiences for the theatre (around 15 per cent between 1955 and 1970), see E. P. Mickiewicz, *Media and the Russian Public* (NY, 1981), p. 89.

315 Dmitrievsky, 'Teatr i deti', *T* 2 (1987), 98–9.

316 On such sessions, see *T* 7 (180), 43–8 (in Chelyabinsk).

317 For rising proportions of children's drama in 'adult' houses, see N. Zhegin, 'Vzroslyi teatr i deti-sponsory', *T* 5 (1991), 102–3; on new troupes, and 'new blood' in leading houses, cf. the comments by directors in *T* 11 (1990), 130–42; on amateur/studio activities involving children, see e.g. *T* 12 (1988), 176–7.

318 Yu. A. Dmitriev, *Sovetskii tsirk v samom kratkom ocherke* (M., 1980), p. 47. See p. 43 for the wartime figures, and p. 23 for the 1939 figures.

319 Dmitriev, *Sovetskii tsirk*, p. 18 (liberty horses), p. 32 (elephant), p. 34 (bear taming).

320 On clown acts in the post-Stalin era, see *N* 34 (1974), 12; *N* 5 (1981), 21.

321 See e.g. CKQ Ox–02 PF1A, p. 6.

322 A rubric running in *Nedelya* during the 1960s, 'The Club of Dyed-in-the-Wool Theatre Enthusiasts' (*Klub zavzyatykh teatralov*), sums up with uncomfortable accuracy the status of professional drama with the Soviet public.

323 *SPA*, vol. 2, p. 483.

324 N. Zabolotsky, 'Rannie gody', *Izbrannye proizvedeniya v 217*, vol. 2 (M., 1902), p. 212.

325 Zaks, 'Krug chteniya v detstve i yunosti', p. 165.

326 *Teatral'naya Moskva*, p. 244. The range was 80 kopecks to 1 rouble 75 kopecks.

327 A. Salynsky, *SPA*, vol. 5, p. 398.

328 See *Detskoe kino* (M., 1930), pp. 75–6: based on V. A. Pravdolyubov, *Kino i nasha molodezh' na osnove dannykh pedologii* (M.–L., 1929).

329 See *Detskoe kino*, pp. 49–52. Cf. E. Y., 'K voprosu o detskom kino i detskom teatre', *Detskii dom* 3 (1928), 18: of 2,000 Moscow schoolchildren surveyed in 1928, 88 per cent visited 3–4 times per month or more, and 64 per cent at least once a week.

330 Salynsky, *SPA*, vol. 5, p. 398, remembers seeing the original film.

331 Eugenie Fraser, *The House by the Dvina* (London, 1984), p. 312.

332 E. Y., 'K voprosu o detskom kino', 19. B. Leman, 'Shkola zhizni', in S. Marshak and E. Vasilieva, *Teatr dlya detei* (Krasnodar, 1922), p. 4, contrasts the children's theatre and its positive effects with the effects of watching 'all the vices of large cities' on screen.

333 Cf. *Detskoe kino* p. 52, commenting with disapproval on the fact that 92.8 per cent of parents didn't monitor their children's viewing.

334 G. O. Gordon, *Chto takoe kommunisticheskoe vospitanie?* (M., 1929), p. 20.

335 As e.g. in [no initials given] Virkins, *Budushchie kino-zvezdy* (M., 1929).

336 It was claimed at the Seventh Congress of the Komsomol that 30 per cent of young criminals had chosen their path because of bad influence from the cinema: *Sed'moi s''ezd Vsesoyuznogo leninskogo kommunisticheskogo soyuza molodezhi* (M.–L., 1926), p. 459.

337 *SYu* 6 (1933), 23; KPBTsK, 1929–35, l. 204, no. B–180 p. 4.

338 B. Gotlib, 'Nado li rebyatam poseshchat' kino?', *Rabotnitsa* 9 (1930) p. 16. Cf. A. Volkova, 'Ob organizatsii dosuga detei', *Rabotnitsa* 11 (1939), p. 19.

339 See e.g. Oxf/Lev V–04 PF8A, p. 9.

340 Oleg Krasovsky in Novak-Deker, p. 140; Inna Shikhaeva-Gaister in Fitzpatrick and Slezkine, p. 371.

341 See e.g. Oxf/Lev SPb.–02, PF8B, p. 19. (Informant b. 1931.)

342 For example, M. Barskaya and B. Shumatsky, 'Proizvodstvo detskikh kinokartin', *Pravda*, 2 April 1935, 3, claimed that 15–18 films were planned for 1935, but also pointed to the need for special studios and specialist scriptwriters. In March 1935, a children's film festival was held (see *Pravda* 20 March 1935, p. 3).

343 A. Kal'varskaya, 'O detskom fil'me', *SK* 3 (1935), 46–9.

344 N. Stepanov, 'O geroicheskom, fantasticheskom i komicheskom v detskom kino', *SK* 3 (1935), 59–62.

345 N. Popov, 'O detskom fil'me', *SK* 10 (1935), 32–9.

346 Peter Kenez, *Cinema and Soviet Society, 1917–1953* (Cambridge, 1992), p. 160. Maiya Turovskaya, 'Mosfil'm – 1937', in Marina Balina, Evgeny Dobrenko, and Yury Murashov (eds), *Sovetskoe bogatstvo* (SPb., 2000), p. 283, records that one of the only two scenarios agreed by GUK, the state censorship body, in 1937 was for a cartoon version of the *Wolf and Seven Kids* (a story whose Freudian

347 interpretation, one must assume, struck no chords with the guardians of Soviet propriety).

347 See S. Hutchings, *Russian Literary Culture in the Camera Age* (London, 2004), pp. 97–102, pp. 102–9.

348 See A. Ptushko's own commentary in "Kak sozdavalsya "Novyi Gulliver"', *SK* 3 (1935), 50–8, Kh. Khersonskii '"Novyi Gulliver"', *SK* 5 (1935), 63–8, and V. Volchek, 'Vysokoe masterstvo', *SK* 5 (1935), 69–72.

349 N. Khodataev, 'Puti mul'tfil'ma', *SK* 4 (1935), 46–8.

350 For example, G. Zel'dovich, 'Tri detskikh fil'ma', *IK* 10 (1936), 6–11, is quite critical about the technical features of *The Children of Captain Grant* and L. Maslyukov's *Karl Brunner*, both of which are remembered by informants as films they enjoyed, and is far more complimentary about N. Shpikovsky's *Three Kids from One Street* (*Troe s odnoi ulitsy*), which does not come up in oral history. On *Deti kapitana Granta*, see e.g. CKQ Ox–03 PF7A, p. 7; on *Timur i ego komanda*, CKI SPb.–1.

351 Kenez, *Cinema and Soviet Society*, p. 160, p. 210.

352 M. Turovskaia, 'The Tastes of Soviet Moviegoers during the 1930s', in T. Lahusen with G. Kuperman (eds), *Late Soviet Culture* (Durham, NC, 1993), p. 104.

353 *Chuk i Gek* is particularly frequently mentioned in interviews: see e.g. Oxf/Lev SPb.–03 PF14B, p. 29, CKQ Ox–03 PF7A, p. 7.

354 For a fuller discussion of *Dobro pozhalovat'*, see Chapter 12 below.

355 For the 1957 figure, see *XIII S''ezd Vsesoyuznogo Leninskogo Kommunisticheskogo Soyuza Molodezhi, 15–18 aprelya 1958. Stenograficheskii otchet* (M., 1959), p. 35. For output in the early 1960s, see K. K. Paramonova, 'Detskoe kino', in *Kino: Entsiklopedicheskii slovar'* (M.: Sovetskaya entsiklopediya, 1986), pp. 119–20.

356 A. Golembievskaya, 'Kto lyubit mul'tfil'my?' *N* 27 (1968), 10–11. Cf. the item on *Zamarashka*, *N* 5 (1962), 19; on *Belaya shkurka*, *N* 13 (1969), 19–20. For general introductions to animation, see D. MacFadyen; B. Beumers, *Pop Culture Russia!* (Santa Barbara, 2005), pp. 99–104.

357 Oxf/Lev P–05 PF21A, p. 8.

358 Cuban cartoons: *N* 22 (1969), 8, 'Zhizn' bratskikh stran'.

359 A. S. Stroeva, *Deti, kino, televidenie* (M., 1962), p. 3.

360 As attested in interviews: see e.g. Oxf/Lev M–04 PF21, p. 7 (informant b. 1951): 'We used to try and get to the evening showings, but they kept a strict eye on those: if it said no under–16s, then they didn't let us in, of course.'

361 Bamm et al., *Semeinoe vospitanie*, p. 70.

362 Yu. Babushkin, 'Shkol'nik idet v kino', *N* 15 (1969), 18–19.

363 L. A. Anishchenko, 'Pionerskaya gazeta i ee yunyi chitatel'', in *Differentsial'noe rukovodstvo*, p. 124.

364 The magazine has a useful website, http://www.eralash.ru, which carries selections of material going back to 1974 as well as an archive of more recent issues.

365 Oxf/Lev M–04 PF25A, p. 28 (informant born

1968). In working-class areas of large cities, cinema also remained a collective pursuit: see e.g. the description in Oxf/Lev P–05 PF24A, p. 11, of how the 'entire courtyard' would turn out to watch e.g. *Sinbad* at 10 kopecks a time.

366 Oxf/Lev SPb.–03 PF14B, p. 29. Oxf/Lev P–05 PF26B, p. 19, recalls 'a Japanese film about a dinosaur' (evidently one of the Godzilla series).

367 See *N* 35 (1970), 16.

368 E. Uspensky, *Krokodil Gena (fil'm-skazka)* (M.: Soyuz kinematografov, 1970). For newspaper items, see e.g. *N* 51 (1973), 24. On the merchandise, see an account from the early 1980s: 'We all had Cheburashkas. They'd sent a load to the shops [*vykidyvali*, lit. were chucking them out in the shops], and everyone was buying in bulk' (Oxf/Lev P–05 PF10A, p. 5).

369 Cf. Lev Kopelev, *The Education of a True Believer*, trans. G. Kern (London, 1981), p. vii (saw radio set in the mid-1920s for first time – at a schoolmate's house, son of wealthy physicist). Cf. CKQ M–04 PF5B, p. 12, 'We had all the latest technology for one simple reason: my father made it all' (he was chief engineer at an important provincial factory).

370 1931, the *Children's Friend* reported that School No. 3 in Moscow now had a receiver in every classroom; this was evidently meant to be seen as a model. *DD* 3 (1931), 31.

371 See e.g. Oxf/Lev V–04 PF22A, p. 57 (informant b. 1937, Pskov province).

372 A. Men'shikova, *Radio – detyam* (M., 1966), p. 27.

373 R. Kovaleva, 'Children's Broadcasts in the USSR', *Anglo-Soviet Journal* 9: 2 (Summer 1948), 23.

374 CKQ M–04 PF5A, p. 10; CKQ M–04 PF6A, p. 12; CKI SPb.–1; CKQ Ox–03 PF13B, p. 7; G. A. Kazakov, 'Programmy dlya detei', in *Ocherki istorii sovetskogo radioveshchaniya*, vol. 1 (M.: Mysl', 1972), pp. 241–3.

375 *PP* 11 February 1947, 3: 'Vnimanie! Govorit shkol'nyi radiouzel'.

376 Kovaleva, 'Children's Broadcasts', 23.

377 My thanks to Evgeny Dobrenko for this description.

378 For the schedules, see Kovaleva, 'Children's Broadcasts', 23–5, and cf. *PP* for 1947 and 1948. For *Ugadai-ka!*, see the cartoon 'Children's Encyclopedia', in *Krokodil* 4 (1952), 9, where the programme is said to be better than many programmes for adults.

379 *PP* 4 March 1947, p. 4.

380 CKQ Oxf–03 PF1, 3 (radio always on, *Ugadai-ka!*, reading aloud, dramatisations). Oxf/Lev SPb.–02 PF4A, p. 95 (Maria Petrova readings); Nina Mikhal'skaya, [Vospominaniya], p. 92 ('Teatr u mikrofona').

381 Men'shikova, *Radio-detyam*, p. 21 (*Ugadai-ka*), pp. 28–59 (post-Stalin repertoire more generally). See also the schedules printed in *Vechernyaya Moskva* 1962.

382 Men'shikova, *Radio-detyam*, p. 4.

383 Oxf/Lev T–04 PF19B, p. 18; Oxf/Lev T–04 PF7A, p. 9. Cf. Oxf/Lev M–04 PF22A, pp. 6–7.

384 Oxf/Lev SPb.–03 PF14B, p. 31.

385 *Demograficheskie problemy sem'i*, ed. T. V. Ryabushkin et al. (M., 1978), p. 18.

386 Ibid., p. 18.

387 See e.g. Oxf/Lev SPb.–03 PF14A, p. 3 – colour in 1984, CKQ Ox–03 PF2A, p. 2; CKQ Ox–03 PF7A, p. 7 (TV by end of 1950s).

388 Mickiewicz, *Media and the Russian Public*, p. 85.

389 *Krokodil* 4 (1952), 9.

390 'Ostorozhno – televizor', *N* 23 (1966), 20.

391 *Bukvar'* (M.: Gos. uch.-ped. izd., 1963), p. 80.

392 See the daily programmes in *Vechernyaya Moskva* and *Vechernii Leningrad* for 1962.

393 See the daily programmes in *Vechernyaya Moskva* and *Vechernii Leningrad* for 1972, 1975, 1978.

394 Limited information about the history of 'Spokoinoi nochi, malyshi!', still running at the time of writing, can be found on the programme's website, http://www.rutv.ru/prog?rubric_ud=606&brand_id=360 (accessed 22 August 2005).

395 See e.g. Oxf/Lev T–04 PF7A, p. 9 (the two programmes the informant recalls best are *Spokoinoi nochi* and *Vremya*).

396 As e.g. in Oxf/Lev M–04 PF24A, p. 2: in this case, a 1970s TEMP brand with a large screen, in black and white.

397 Oxf/Lev SPb.–03 PF14B, p. 19, TV in brother's room once family in three-room flat from 1984.

398 Watching at a neighbour's: see P. Messana, *Kommunalka* (Paris, 1995), watching at a friend's: CKQ Ox–03 PF0A, p. 2, this from the late 1940s.

399 V. Irov, unpublished memoir of 1996, excerpted in Bim-Bad and Kosheleva, *Priroda rebenka*, pp. 133–4.

400 *Vechernii Leningrad*, 11 September 1962. Interestingly, *Vechernyaya Moskva* did not carry the same warning to viewers.

401 The choice here is hypothetical; however, 'Zanimaites' proizvodstvennoi gimnastikoi!' and 'Raspredelenie natsional'nogo dokhoda v devyatoi pyatiletke' were both showing in 1962: see *Vechernii Leningrad* for the year.

402 See *Vechernii Leningrad*, 19 May 1972, 3 September 1972. It is not clear whether *The Merry Roundabout* was an adaptation of the BBC's *The Magic Roundabout*, showing at the time in Britain, or indeed the original programme.

403 On *mul'tiki*, see Oxf/Lev M–04 PF36A, p. 8; Beumers, *Pop Culture Russia!*, pp. 99–104.

404 See the show's website, http://amik. ru/?page=history&id=8 (accessed 22 August 2005).

405 V. Mukhina, *Bliznetsy* (M., 1969), p. 301, 20 May 1966. For an instance of them enjoying more conventional material (a film of *Kashchei Bessmertnyi* (at four and a half: this in July 1966) – see ibid., p. 199. On *skazki* (in this case, the programme *V gostyakh u skazki*), see also Oxf/Lev T–04 PF7A, p. 9.

406 Oxf/Lev M–04 PF36A, p. 2.

407 J. Riordan, *Sport in Soviet Society* (Cambridge, 1977), pp. 145–6 (early Soviet period), p. 179 (introduction of two hours' sport per week to programme). From 1967, the number of hours per year was reduced to 70 (p. 327).

408 Ibid., p. 178.

409 John Dunstan, *Paths to Excellence and the Soviet School* (Windsor, 1978), ch. 4; idem, 'Gifted

Youngsters and Special Schools', in J. Riordan (ed.), *Soviet Education: The Gifted and the Handicapped* (London, 1988), p. 42; see also Riordan ibid., pp. 95–121.

410 For the official programme, see *Tipovoe polozhenie o detsko-yunosheskoi shkole (kompleksnoi)* (M., 1970). An enthusiastic account of studying at a sports school is given in CKQ M–03 PF3A, p. 3.

411 See e.g. S. Kanevskaya and E. Rubin, 'Deti i sport', *N* 19 (1963), 22–3; 'Segodnya den' fizkul'turnika', *N* 33 (1966), 2; V. Barkanova, 'Privedite syna v sportszal', *N* 47 (1966), 22; 'Zolotye nashi mal'chishki', *N* 14 (1967), 18; 'Sport – delo semeinoe', *N* 47 (1969), 22–3.

412 An official history, M. Kondratyeva and V. Taborko, *Children and Sport in the USSR* (M., 1979), points e.g. to the 1975 statute, 'On Measures to Improve Sports and P.E. Work among Children and Adults', leading to a large-scale founding of sports clubs. But activity had started up more than a decade earlier: see e.g. *N* 2 (1965), front cover, p. 2 (on the 'Olimpiiskaya snezhinka' programme).

413 Bamm and 17 others, *Semeinoe vospitanie*, p. 228, entry 'Roditels'kii komitet pri domoupravlenii'.

414 E.g. *N* 8 (1971), 14 – on the need for more ice-hockey sticks.

415 Riordan, *Sport in Soviet Society*, p. 330.

416 *SPA*, vol. 2, pp. 368–9.

417 *SPA*, vol. 5, p. 328.

418 As described in Fazil' Iskander's autobiographical cycle of stories *Detstvo Chika* (1988), pp. 385–404 (football).

419 See e.g. Oxf/Lev T–05 PF13A, p. 18; Oxf/Lev M–04 PF25A, p. 24; Oxf/Lev P–05 PF6A, p. 6; Oxf/Lev P–05 PF8A, p. 11, etc.

420 Oxf/Lev T–04 PF21A, p. 9 (home-made skates); Oxf/Lev T–04 PF24A, p. 7 (training sessions). Cf. Oxf/Lev T–05 PF17B, p. 12 (making the sports trunks and T-shirts needed for school).

421 On private collecting, see e.g. Nikolai Aseev (who collected labels off beer bottles, cigarettes, etc.: see *SPA*, vol. 1, p. 90); on stamp-collecting in the Soviet era, see e.g. Oxf/Lev T–04 PF7A, p. 1; Oxf/Lev T–05 PF24A, p. 7.

422 Cf. Oxf/Lev SPb.–03 PF25B, pp. 42–3: this working-class Leningrad man loved photography, as did many of his mates from school and the local courtyard, and a major remembered happiness was saving up for a coveted Smena-8 camera. Camera ownership, like TV and radio ownership, increased in the post-Stalin era, if official figures are to be believed: *Demograficheskie problemy* claimed rates of 18 per 100 families in 1960, 24 in 1965, and 27 in 1970 (at this point, ownership reached a plateau and had increased no further by 1976).

423 A particularly large amount of material was published about this kind of activity in the 1960s. See e.g. 'Masterite sami', *N* 10 (1960), 16; *N* 16 (1961), 20–1; *N* 28 (1965), 18; *N* 17 (1967), 20–1. The supplements to *Nedelya*, *Nedelya rebyatam* and *Nedel'ka* also published much material of this kind: see e.g. 'Sdelai sam', 9 (1960), 20–1; *N* 9 (1961), 24; *N* 32 (1961), 20–1; *N* 14 (1966), 24, etc.

424 Boris Polevoi, *SPA* vol. 2, p. 230).

425 Oxf/Lev T–04 PF20A, p. 25.

426 As remembered in Oxf/Lev V–05 PF16B, p. 16.

427 Oxf/Lev WQ1 GM, p. 7, describes a craze on photography (half the children in her school class were obsessed for a few months, the interest mainly extending to taking pictures of each other); Oxf/Lev WQ1 KM, p. 7, discusses how everyone in her class took up playing the guitar.

428 Nabokov, *Speak, Memory*, pp. 67–8. As Eric Naiman has pointed out to me, this passage has literary antecedents (in Proust's *A la recherche du temps perdu*, vol. 1). Nevertheless, whether exclusively based on Nabokov's actual experience or not, it is a witty and plausible evocation of a child's capacity to, in adult language, 'fiddle' and 'dawdle'.

429 Almost without exception, the informants in our oral history study recall that their parents owned *khodiki* (pendulum clocks), and this in homes without electricity, ornaments, pictures, interior decoration other than whitewash, and so on.

430 Mukhina, *Bliznetsy*, p. 160. With my own niece and nephew, then aged twelve and eight, I tried an experiment in 2004: getting them to narrate a story in which absolutely nothing interesting happened. They could keep the banality up for a few sentences, but sooner or later catastrophe broke in. A typical story went, 'Peter got out of his bed. The weather was not very nice. Slowly he went down the stairs. He opened the cupboard to get out the cereal. Then there was a HUGE BANG as the kitchen blew up …'

431 cf. Dobuzhinsky, *Vospominaniya*, p. 17, on illuminations for Alexander III's coronation in 1883. T. Kolliander, 'Peterburgskii dnevnik: glavy iz vospominaniya', *Nevskii arkhiv* 2 (1995), 36, remembers the joy of revolutionary demonstrations and of being swayed by any orator; Granin, *Leningradskii katalog*, p. 90, recalls the fun of early Soviet demonstrations.

432 CKQ M–04 PF5B, pp. 18–19.

433 Watching river traffic: Kassil', *Konduit, Dorogie moi mal'chishki*, p. 144. The boys also made marine traffic a central part of their invented country, Shambraniya, and imagined their parents' house as a ship: pp. 145–6.

434 Visitors: Tynyanov, early childhood in Rezhitsa, Vitebsk province: *SPA*, vol. 2, pp. 480–2; traffic, Shklovsky, *SPA*, vol. 4, p. 686. Tractors: Egor Isaev remembered going to school in the mid-1930s, and the appeal of tractors on the road (*SPA*, vol. 5, p. 230).

435 A. Mariengof, *Moi vek, moi druz'ya i podrugi* (M., 1990), p. 23.

436 CKQ Ox–03 PF6B, pp. 4–5 (woman b. 1949).

437 See Catriona Kelly, *Comrade Pavlik* (London, 2005), esp. ch. 5.

438 Oxf/Lev P–05 PF5B, pp. 22–3.

439 CKQ Ox–03 PF10B, p. 5 (woman b. 1975).

440 A. N. Martynova, *Detskii poeticheskii fol'klor* (SPb., 1997) no. 9. This was a particularly popular rhyme in later generations too: cf. the recollections of a woman born in 1938, and brought up in a rural area of Leningrad province: Oxf/Lev V–04 PF6B, p. 63; Svetlana Boym (b. 1959) has informed me

that she remembers it from her own childhood in 1960s Leningrad.

441 Belousov (ed.), *Russkii shkol'nyi fol'klor*, p. 68.

442 Reminiscences of Dimitrii Kuznetsov, b. 1888. Written 1909. RGIA f. 803 op. 16 d. 2372,

l. 57 rev.; M. Kh. Sventitskaya in V. Dyushen (ed.), *Pyat' let detskogo gorodka imeni III Internationatsionala* (M., [1924]), p. 108.

443 Belousov (ed.), *Russkii shkol'nyi fol'klor*, p. 562.

Chapter 12: Years of School

1 Marina Boroditskaya, 'Vstan'te, kto pomnit chernil'nitsu-neprolivaiku', in her *Okazyvaetsya, mozhno* (M., 2005), p. 41.

2 CKQ E–03 PF1B, p. 3; on how birthdays were celebrated in this person's home only after the war (i.e. 4–5 years after she began attending school), see ibid, PF1A, p. 3.

3 On interference by inspectors before 1917, see V. N. Shubkin's 1911–15 diary, *Povsednevnaya zhizn' russkoi gimnazii* (SPb., 1988), e.g. p. 354; in the Soviet era, see e.g. Oxf/Lev M–04 PF35B, pp. 14–15.

4 For the official exhortations, see N. I. Boldyrev (ed.), *Klassnyi rukovoditel'* (1954) (2nd edn; M., 1955), pp. 95–6.

5 For comments on this, see e.g. Oxf/Lev M–04 PF30A, p. 2.

6 A major study of teachers in the early part of the period is E. Thomas Ewing, *The Teachers of Stalinism: Policy, Practice, and Power in Soviet Schools of the 1930s* (History of Schools and Schooling, no. 18). (NY: Peter Lang, 2002).

7 CKQ M–03 PF1A, p. 4.

8 Evgeny Dobrenko, personal communication, 12 February 2005. This development was even recognised in official sources: I. Ovchinnikova, 'Luchshie minuty', complains that she brought up her daughter valuing honesty and effort, only to find her bounced from an expedition to Artek because the daughter of a top Party official had been sent instead: *N* (1969), 16.

9 The imposition of a public examination system on the pattern of those obtaining in the US and Western Europe – where papers were set and assessed by officially appointed examining boards – came about only in 2004. Up to this point, the local education office (RONO or GorONO, or local office of the MNP before 1917) would send along an inspector, but this person only presided at the examinations themselves, and could not prevent abuses such as tipping the pupils off what the questions were going to be, etc. For cases of teachers offered bribes, see p. 498 above.

10 *SPA*, vol. 1, pp. 490–1. To be sure, there were also charitable institutions that specialised in helping children like this, and most secondary schools had funds to help out pupils in need. See e.g. *Otchet o deyatel'nosti Obshchestva vspomoshchestvovaniya nuzhdayushchimsya uchenikam Imperatorskoi Nikolaevskoi Tsarskosel'skoi Gimnazii* (Tsarskoe Selo, Tsarskosel'skaya Tsentral'naya tipografiya, 1908).

11 Elena Bonner had to take a job as a cleaner to pay her way through school after her parents were arrested, and, since that provided her with less than a third of the amount needed (400 roubles), she survived at school only because the headmistress paid the rest out of her own

pocket (*Dochki-materi* (M.: Izd. gruppa 'Progress', 'Litera', 1994), p. 241).

12 Alex Saranin, *Child of the Kulaks* (St Lucia, 1997), p. 42, p. 57; the scholarship application was, however, refused on class grounds at a higher level (p. 58).

13 RAO NN01 PF12A, p. 41.

14 CKQ Ox–03 PF3A, p. 9.

15 CKQ Ox–03 PF1A, p. 4.

16 See ch. 16 (digital version)

17 See Boldyrev (ed.), *Klassnyi rukovoditel'*. The duties dwelt on here included (alongside all the political consciousness-raising) fixing up work trips to collective farms, organising sports sessions and excursions to the theatre, and checking up that pupils were doing their extra-curricular reading.

18 See Aleksandr Neverov in *SPA*, vol. 2, p. 114.

19 D. A. Zasosov and V. I. Pyzin, *Iz zhizni Peterburga 1890–1910-kh godov* (L., 1991), p. 134.

20 SPb-PV–1903, 130–1.

21 See Charles E. Timberlake, 'N. A. Korf (1834–83): Designer of the Russian Elementary School Classroom', in B. Eklof (ed.), *School and Society in Tsarist and Soviet Russia* (Basingstoke, 1993), pp. 12–35.

22 *SPb-PV–1903*, pp. 130–2, indicates under 20 in 1903.

23 Prokofiev, *SPA*, vol. 2, p. 266.

24 V. V. Smirnov, *Peterburgskie shkoly i shkol'nye zdaniya* (SPb., 2003), p. 64.

25 Many of these schools survive in their original use today. An excellent example is School No. 330, 9 Bol'shoi Kazennyi pereulok, Moscow, which was founded as a 'House of Education' for fatherless girls in 1884, and named the Elizavetinskaya Gimnaziya in 1887. The school's main building was designed by I. I. Rerberg (1869–1932), the architect of the Kiev station and other important public buildings in Moscow, and it has a handsome interior with a fine *aktovyi zal*, canteen, and other facilities, and spacious classrooms. (See illustrations to this chapter.) In 1930, the school was turned into a FZU (factory school), and in 1943 it became a boys' *gimnaziya*; mixed once more from 1955, it became a school with maths specialisation in the higher classes in 1962.

26 O. Kaidanova, 'Iz zhizni odnoi shkoly', *Svobodnoe vospitanie* 1 (1911), 6–60. Pictures of the school appear at pp. 53–4. Régis Ladous, *Un Bonheur russe* (Lausanne, 1997), is a study of another private 'free education' initiative, set up by the millionaire Nikolai Neplyuev in Chernigov.

27 Mariengof, p. 43.

28 E. Fen, *A Girl Grew Up in Russia* (London, 1970), p. 10.

29 'Svod ustavov uchenykh uchrezhdenii i uchebnykh zavedenii Vedomstva Ministerstva Narodnogo

Prosveshcheniya. Izdanie 1893 goda'. *SZRI* vol. XI:1, p. 138.

30 *Shkol'naya gigiena* (SPb., 1900) (Offprint from *Spravochnaya kniga po Voprosam Obrazovaniya Evreev v Rossii*). See also M. D. Mitr——n, *Shkol'naya gigiena* (Petrozavodsk, 1905) (mainly on ventilation).

31 *Otchety o deyatel'nosti sanitarnykh vrachei Permskogo Gubernskogo Zemstva za 1913 god* (Perm', 1915), p. 15.

32 For examples of energetic activity, see e.g. ibid., pp. 57–9, and the materials from Voronezh province, *Instruktsiya dlya nachal'nykh uchilishch Bobrovskogo uezda po khozyaistvennoi chasti* (Bobrov, 1913); N. Tezyakov, *Beseda o gigiene v primenenii ee k narodnoi shkole* (Voronezh, 1899). Slacker practices are recorded in e.g. *Trudy XIV S"ezda zemskikh vrachei i chlenov zemskikh vrachebno-sanitarnykh uchrezhdenii* vol. 1 (Smolensk, 1912), p. 166 (Bel'sky district: no medical control over school planning, though inspections of pupils carried out), p. 193 (Krazhinsky district: doctors only inspect school sites).

33 V. I. Radkevich, *Opisanie sanitarnogo sostoyaniya zemskikh shkol Voronezhskogo uezda po dannym ankety 1912 g.* (Voronezh, 1913), p. 5. The book also records that 63 local schools were of brick, and 43 of wood.

34 See e.g. 'Nauchnyi otchet o komandirovke v gorod Sverdlovsk i sverdlovskoi oblasti [*sic!*] po voprosu izucheniya opyta shkol, rabotayushchikh po novomu uchebnomu planu', RAO NA f. 32 op. 1 ed. khr. 655, l. 23.

35 Oxf/Lev SPb.–03 PF30A, p. 4. See also Gertrud Striedter, 'Erinnerungen', extract 8, p. 3 (archive of Jurij Striedter, Cambridge, MA), which describes a railway school in Leningrad during the late 1920s which was 'brand new, with countless classrooms, workshops, gyms, showers and "special subject rooms" [*kabinety*]. The roof had an observatory with its own telescope and a wonderful view. [...] The classes ran along a corridor; there were about twelve, huge, bright and with modern school furniture – no old-fashioned desks – and this was 1929!'

36 Smirnov, *Peterburgskie shkoly i shkol'nye zdaniya*, p. 109, p. 119.

37 'Nauchnyi otchet o komandirovke v gorod Sverdlovsk', l. 19, l. 39.

38 See e.g. G. A. Gradov, *Gorod i byt* (M.: Izdanie literatury po stroitel'stvu, 1968), pp. 96–104.

39 *BNKP* 15 February 1929, pp. 30–1.

40 *BNKP* 1 February 1931, p. 17.

41 Smirnov, *Peterburgskie shkoly i shkol'nye zdaniya*, pp. 126–7. For the general 1969 figures (e.g. 50 per cent schools in Moscow province *tipovye proekty*, 66 per cent in Ulyanovsk), see GARF f. 8009 op. 50 d. 70, l. 39. The basic regulations for *tipovye proekty* were concerned simply with square footage per rouble: see e.g. the list of plans, *Perechen' deistvitel'nykh tipovykh proektov ob"ektov prosveshcheniya po sostoyaniyu na 1 sentyabrya 1968 g.* (M., 1968).

42 As even with Internat no. 72 in Leninskie gorki, despite its close relationship with the Academy of Pedagogical Sciences as an 'experimental school'.

43 Bella Ulanovskaya, 'Journey to Kashgar', in C. Kelly (ed.), *A History of Russian Women's Writing, 1777–1992* (Oxford, 1994), p. 370. The Russian original, 'Puteshestvie v Kashgar', appeared in *Neva* 2 (1991), 69–81.

44 See e.g. D. D. Bekaryukov (ed.), *Okhrana detei v shkolakh* (M.–L., 1926). Pages 97–130 here are on the hygiene of school premises, as opposed to children's illnesses, etc.

45 See 'O sanitarno-tekhnicheskom pasporte shkoly', *Gigiena i sanitariya* 1 (1936), 58–9.

46 *ENKP* 12 (1941), pp. 8–13.

47 *ENKP* 5 September 1931, p. 9 (desks), ibid. 5 September 1932, p. 2 (slates).

48 *ENKP* 1 August 1934, p. 24.

49 A three-shift system was formally introduced in 1941 in the centres of evacuation, with a special slimmed-down school programme, which also stepped up the patriotic content (e.g. the attention given to the Napoleonic invasion). RGASPI f. 17 op. 126 d. 2, ll. 164–9.

50 *Nachal'naya shkola: Nastol'naya kniga uchitelya*, ed. M. A. Mel'nikov. (M., 1950), p. 837.

51 *Spravochnik direktora shkoly: Sbornik zakonodatel'nykh, rukovodyashchikh i instruktivnykh materialov* (M., 1971), p. 335.

52 'Do shkoly – tri nedeli', *N* 32 (1964), 18–19; 'Shkola zhdet', *N* 34 (1964), 5.

53 On the craze for technology, see e.g. the many items on gizmos of various kinds published in *Nedelya*: *N* 33 (1965), 20–1; *N* 19 (1970), 21; *N* 10 (1971), 8–9; *N* 49 (1972), 18–19; *N* 8 (1984), 5; *N* 12 (1987), 9; etc. Oxf/Lev SPb.–03 PF28A, p. 9 is a recollection of a school in the early 1980s that actually had some technology of this kind: an illuminated buzzer-board for question sessions.

54 See e.g. V. Veselovsky, 'Shkol'naya tetrad', *N* 2 (1965), 2–3.

55 'Nauchnyi otchet o komandirovke v g. Sverdlovsk i Sverdlovskoi oblasti [*sic*] po voprosu izucheniya opyta shkol, rabotayushchikh po novomu uchebnomu planu', RAO NA f. 32 op. 1 ed. khr. 655, ll. 15–67. On war damage, see also Chapter 7 above.

56 See the Russian edn of Nabokov's memoirs, *Drugie berega*, ch. 10, section 3 (*Speak, Memory*, Harmondsworth, 1969, p. 144, just has 'soap'). Cf. Mariengof, p. 43: 'And the lavatory! No sooner had I walked in than I bolted out.'

57 Evgeny Dobrenko, personal information.

58 Oxf/Lev SPb.–03 PF24B, p. 19. For a nineteenth-century description, see Anna Bek, *The Life of a Russian Woman Doctor: A Siberian Memoir, 1869–1954*, trans. and ed. A. D. Rassweiler (Bloomington, IN, 2004), p. 29.

59 For memories of taking your own food, see e.g. Oxf/Lev V–04 PF24B, p. 15.

60 See e.g. CKQ Ox–03 PF6B, p. 14 (on how Leningrad schools operated as canteens during the Blockade). Even in the less desperate conditions of Moscow during the war and post-war years, school food was a godsend: Rita Frumkina recalls classmates taking morsels back home to younger brothers and sisters: *O nas naiskosok* (M., 1997), p. 48.

61 CKI SPb.–5.

62 Evgeny Dobrenko, personal information.

63 CKQ Ox–03 PF13 B, p. 12.

64 CKQ Ox–03 PF2A, p. 3.

65 In 1936, a portrait of Ezhov (the NKVD chief) in a school in Mordovia was pelted with bread, and one of Krupskaya ornamented with a moustache; in 1935, pupils at Moscow's Secondary School No. 4 attacked a picture of Kaganovich with a catapult (Siegelbaum and Sokolov, p. 368. Original sources not given). On this type of incident, see also G. Rittersporn, 'Formy obshchest-vennogo obikhoda molodezhi i ustanovki sovetskogo rezhima v predvoennom desyatiletii', in T. Vikhavainen (ed.), *Normy i tsennosti povsednevnoi zhizni* (SPb., 2000), pp. 347–67.

66 This is mentioned in the detailed memoir of daily life at School No. 232 in Leningrad/St Petersburg written by Alexander Rogachevsky, St Petersburg (to whom I am grateful for allowing me to see a preliminary outline of the book).

67 Shubkin, *Povsednevnaya zhizn' russkoi gimnazii*, pp. 158–9, p. 165. By contrast, Yury Olesha records, *Ni dnya bez strochki* (M., 1965), p. 273, that only the richer boys at his school wore uniform jackets.

68 On getting one's uniform made, see F. M. Orlov-Skomorovsky, *Golgofa rebenka* (M., 1921), p. 45; on the 'pencils', see A. Vertinsky, *Dorogoi dlinnoyu* (M., 1991), p. 19.

69 K. Paustovsky, 'Avtobiografiya', *Sobranie sochinenii* vol. 4 (M., 1982), p. 80.

70 M. Tsvetaeva, 'Natal'ya Goncharova', *Sobranie sochinenii v 7 tomakh*, vol. 4 (M., 1994), p. 78; cf. Pavlova in Engel and Posadskaya-Vanderbeck, p. 54. Sofiya Pregel' recalled being thrown out of her school canteen for wearing scent: *Moe detstvo*, vol. 2 (Paris, 1973), p. 89.

71 On hoods (*balyki*), see M. A. Osorgin, *Vremena* (M., 1989), p. 39; E. Fen, *A Russian Childhood* (London, 1961), p. 36.

72 See T. P. Glavatskaya in A. Alieva-Myasnikova (ed.), *Deti XX veka* (Ekaterinburg, 2000).

73 This is confirmed by Oxf/Lev V–04 PF21B, p. 14, recording that only the 'comfortably off' had uniform; CKQ M–04 PF7, p. 17.

74 Frumkina, *O nas – naiskosok*, p. 48.

75 Oxf/Lev SPb.–03 PF20A, p. 34.

76 Ibid.

77 This is based on extensive personal observation: see also Oxf/Lev T–04 PF6B, p. 25.

78 Z. S. Lapshina, 'Gigienicheskaya otsenka formennoi odezhdy', *Gigiena i sanitariya* 12 (1959), 30.

79 Interviewer's note to Oxf/Lev SPb.–03 PF20A, p. 34.

80 CKQ Ox–03 PF13A, p. 9, p. 11.

81 On uniform in the *prodlenka*, see E. Kostyashkin, 'V shkole polnogo dnya', *N* 4 (1977), 7; for the discussion leading up to abolition, see e.g. *N* 42 (1988), 6–7.

82 Oxf/Lev M–04 PF24A, p. 3. This informant got his watch when in Class 8 (i.e. 15 years old).

83 RGIA f. 803 op. 16 d. 2370, l. 63 rev.

84 Oxf/Lev SPb.–02 PF8B, p. 23.

85 CKQ M–03 PF1B, p. 6.

86 On dentists, see esp. CKQ Ox–03 PF2B, p. 5.

87 See especially Aleksandr Liarsky, '"School Superstitions" at the Turn of the Twentieth Century: The Adult Perspective', *Forum for Anthropology and Culture* 2 (2006), 252–65.

88 Oxf/Lev M–05 PF48B, p. 150.

89 On the school sanitary commissions, see E. P. Radin, *Chto delaet sovetskaya vlast' dlya okhrany zdorov'ya detei* (3rd edn; Vyatka, 1921), pp. 42–3.

90 CKQ SPb.–03 PF2A, p. 10. Cf. Oxf/Lev T–04 PF2A, p. 6. Boys used to try and avoid taking flowers once they were in the higher classes, seeing this as sissy: see e.g. Oxf/Lev P–05 PF26A, p. 7.

91 *Spravochnik sovetskogo rabotnika* (M., 1937), p. 789.

92 *Nachal'naya shkola*, p. 819.

93 'Pervyi urok', *Pravda* 2 September 1935, p. 5.

94 *Pravda* 2 September 1936, p. 3.

95 E.g. in 1947, *Pravda* carried a report on 1 September (p. 1) that preparations were well in hand, and on 2 September, p. 2, described how things had gone. For the suspension of the festival during the war years, see e.g. Oxf/Lev M–04 PF20A, p. 22 (this informant started school in 1943).

96 S. Marshak, *Stikhi* (L., 1952), pp. 3–4. *Stanitsa*, *aul*, and *kishlak* are local names for village-type settlements.

97 The continuing appropriation of schools by non-educational organisations was a bone of contention for several years after the war: cf. the item in *SZ* 1 (1947), 29, 'O vozvrashchenii vsekh shkol'nykh zdanii …'

98 Holmes, *Stalin's School*, p. 39; School No. 175, Frumkina, *O nas naiskosok*, p. 47.

99 Official figures from 1969 indicate that, by then, only 0.8 per cent of Soviet schools were operating a three-shift system, and 4.1 per cent a two-shift system: GARF f. 8009 op. 50 d. 70 l. 38. However, B. Finansov, 'Ekzamen dlya vsekh', *N* 33 (1965), 20–1, mentions this as a significant problem in 1965. Oral history work confirms the latter picture – e.g. a record of a two-shift system in Odessa from the 1960s: CKQ Ox–03 PF3B, p. 9. Small towns: see e.g. CKI SPb.–5.

100 On the 1930s, see Holmes, *Stalin's School*, p. 39 (80 per cent of schools across Russia generally still operated at least a second shift in 1937); Dunstan, p. 88, states that there were even four- or five-shifts systems operating in some places during the war; for the late 1940s, see a report in *Pravda* 14 December 1946, p. 3, giving no figures, but admitting the prevalence of a three-shift system in 'some places', including Moscow.

101 Oxf/Lev SPb.–03 PF24B, p. 20.

102 V. Bedin, M. Kushnikova, and V. Togulev (eds), *Kemerovo i Stalinsk* (Kemerovo, 1999), pp. 465–6.

103 For the promotion of the 'First Bell' from the early 1960s, see e.g. E. I. Klimov, *Prazdnik prishel v tvoi dom* (Perm', 1965).

104 See e.g. the description in *Kratkii otchet ob Imperatorskoi Nikolaevskoi Tsarskosel'skoi Gimnazii za poslednie 15 let ee sushchestvovaniya* (SPb., 1912), pp. 67–79.

105 RGIA f. 803 op. 16 d. 2370, l. 149.

106 On prayers to start the year (here in a small town primary school on 16 August), see A. Kuznetsova-

Budanova, *I u menya byl krai rodnoi* (Munich, 1979), p. 110; on wearing one's best clothes, ibid.

107 RGIA f. 803 op. 16 d. 2370, l. 124.

108 CKQ M–04 PF5A, p. 3. Cf. CKQ M–04 PF7A, p. 11 (this informant entered school in 1935).

109 See Saranin, *Child of the Kulaks*, pp. 29–30; Anatoly Ul'yanov, 'Vospominaniya o periode 1921–1928 gg.' (1932–33), RGB OR f. 442 kart. 1 ed. khr. 3, ll. 3–3 rev., l. 5 rev., for the 1920s; later accounts in the same vein include Oxf/Lev V–04 PF24B, p. 15; Oxf/Lev V–04 PF25B, p. 39.

110 'Svod ustavov uchenykh uchredenii i uchebnykh zavedenii ...', article 1484, *SZRI* vol. XI: 1, pp. 137–8. In practice, this ceremony seems sometimes to have been held at the beginning of the school year: this happened at the Tsarskoe Selo Tsar Nicholas *Gimnaziya* from 1905 onwards, probably as a result of the unrest during that revolutionary year. The ceremonies were also significantly scaled down, being attended only by educational officials, and no longer, as sometimes formerly, by royal personages. See *Kratkii otchet ob Imperatorskoi Nikolaevskoi Tsarskosel'skoi Gimnazii*, p. 72 (and contrast e.g. p. 69).

111 RGIA f. 803 op. 16 d. 2372, l. 66.

112 Anna Grigorova, *Zapiski uchenitsy* (M., 1928), pp. 48–50.

113 *ENKP* 20 May 1935, p. 9. Not coincidentally, the order was issued a month and a half after the order restoring formal examinations, on the classic 'discipline plus festivity' pattern of the age. For continuation of this into the late Soviet period, see e.g. Oxf/Lev T–04 PF2A, p. 6, which mentions speeches and the presentation of certificates.

114 G. V. Andreevsky, 'V sovetskoi shkole', in his *Povsednevnaya zhizn' Moskvy v Stalinskuyu epokhu* (2 vols; M., 2003), vol. 2, pp. 333–8, gives a detailed description of this.

115 My thanks to Al'bert Baiburin for this reminiscence. Sometimes the 'First Bell' was struck on 1 September in an equally ritualistic way.

116 *Pionerskaya pravda* 85 (24 June 1936), p. 3.

117 Nina Mikhal'skaya, [Vospominaniya], author's archive, typescript, p. 148, remembers having only a 'humble' leavers' party when she left school in 1943.

118 See e.g. *N* 18 (1965), 21–2.

119 RAO-M–03 PF1A, p. 12.

120 My thanks to Evgeny Dobrenko for pointing this out to me.

121 Cf. the ballad, 'The school ball ended/And you called me with a seductive gaze/We left the school ball together/And I walked alongside you//Your parents are not at home/They're off on an official trip/The light in your window went out/And I spent the night with you.' Ekaterina Efimova, *Sovremennaya t'yurma: byt, traditsii i fol'klor* (M., 2004), p. 266.

122 Aurn, 'Vospominaniya o shkol'noi zhizni' (typescript, SPb., 2003, author's archive), p. 6.

123 'Ob organizatsii uchebnoi raboty i vnutrennem rasporyadke v nachal'noi, nepolnoi srednei i srednei shkole'. Postanovlenie SNK SSSR i TsK VKP(b) 3 iyulya 1935', *Sbornik zakonov i rasporyazhenii* 47 (1935), 391, quoted in

V. Papernyi, *Kul'tura "dva"* (Ann Arbor: Ardis, 1984), p. 334. Examples of personal files may be inspected in the archive of Boarding School No. 72, Moscow: 'Lichnye dela uchashchikhsya', RAO NA f. 81 op. 3 ed. khr. 9, 10.

124 RGIA f. 803 op. 16 d. 2370, l. 138 rev.

125 *ENKP* 1 September 1923, pp. 11–16, including the format of the *dnevnik*.

126 *ENKP* 1 June 1933, p. 4.

127 *Leninskie iskry* 28 August 1929, p. 7.

128 Though even so, standard documents seem to be missing from, e.g., some of the personal files in the School No. 72 archive: e.g. RAO NA f. 81 op. 3 ed. khr. 9, ll. 40–53 has general background information on the boy concerned, and two character references (*kharakteristiki*), but no end-of-year reports; l. 209 contains a medical card for one pupil, but this information is missing for most pupils; and so on.

129 Oxf/Lev V–05 PF7A, p. 1.

130 'Uchilishchnyi sovet pri Sinode. Statisticheskii otdel. Avtobiograficheskie ocherki uchenikov tserkovno-prikhodskikh shkol raznykh eparkhii 1909 g.', RGIA f. 803 op. 16 d. 2370, l. 124.

131 Mariengof, p. 29. Cf. Yu. Olesha, *Ni dnya bez strochki: iz zapisnykh knizhek* (M., 1965). p. 271.

132 *SPA*, vol. 2, p. 179.

133 V. Shklovsky, *Tret'ya fabrika* (M., 1926), p. 24.

134 Large numbers of intelligence tests were published for use by teachers in the late 1920s. See e.g. *Shkol'nye testy Pedagogicheskogo otdela Instituta metodov shkol'noi raboty*, ed. A. M. Shubert with M. S. Bernshein and N. A Bukhgol'ts (M., 1927). They included comprehension passages and gap-filling exercises.

135 See Chapter 3.

136 'Uchilishchnyi sovet', RGIA f. 803 op. 16 d. 2370, l. 116.

137 See p. 561 below.

138 CKQ Ox–03 PF10A, p. 2. On the other hand, allocation to a new class sometimes took place at registration, so before the child actually arrived (my thanks to Evgeny Dobrenko for pointing this out); however, even in this case, a child would not encounter its new classmates till the moment it reached the school.

139 CKQ Ox–03 PF10A, p. 2.

140 On this practice in the *gimnaziya*, see Eugenie Fraser, *The House on the Dvina* (London, 1984), p. 176.

141 RGIA f. 803 op. 16 d. 2370, l. 116 rev.

142 RGIA f. 803 op. 16 d. 2372, l. 32.

143 *Bukvar' dlya narodnykh shkol s ob"yasneniem luchshikh sposobov prepodavaniya, s"oobshcha [sic.] sostavlennyi neskol'kimi uchitelyami* (5th edn; SPb., 1890).

144 V. Kravchenko, *I Chose Freedom* (London, 1947), p. 13.

145 Aleksei Novikov-Priboi, *SPA*, vol. 2, p. 182.

146 See e.g. Aleksei Chapygin, *SPA*, vol. 2, p. 616: children got their not very satisfactory revenge by calling teacher *skokukha*, 'the frog'.

147 *SPA*, vol. 2, pp. 501–2.

148 As described in the very detailed memoir of education in religious schools by N. A. Rybnikov, 'Iz roda v rod: Istoriya sem'i Rybnikovykh (za

dvukhsotletnii period ee sushchestvovanie)', part III, OR RGB f. 367 Rybnikovy, karton 8, ed. khr. 2, ll. 37–65.

149 Cf. Alie Akimova's anecdote about her father storming out of such a school (it is not clear whether it was a madrasah or a ministry Tatar school) at some point in the 1910s: Alie Akimova, '… I zori rodiny dalekoi', *Druzhba narodov* 3 (2002), 165.

150 *SPA*, vol. 1, p. 154.

151 See *SPA*, vol. 2, pp. 503–5.

152 Radkevich, *Opisanie sanitarnogo sostoyaniya*, p. 23. One might note also the positive accounts of schooling given in 'Uchilishchnyi sovet', RGIA f. 803 op. 16 d. 2370.

153 M. Vol'per, *Russkaya rech': Uchebnik rukovodstvo, primenennoe k obucheniyu russkomu yazyku tekh detei, kotorye pri postuplenii v shkolu ne umeyut govorit' po-russki* (SPb., 1912).

154 A. Davydoff, *Russian Sketches* (Tenafly, NJ: Ermitazh, 1984), pp. 130–1.

155 Shubkin, *Povsednevnaya zhizn'*, p. 60. Shubkin also records that the management of his school immediately started wondering how to get round the new rule.

156 Zabolotsky, *SPA*, vol. 3, p. 251. A church scene of this kind also plays a key role in Sologub's novel *Melkii bes*.

157 *Pravila dlya uchenikov gimnazii i progimnazii vedomstva Ministerstva Narodnogo Prosveshcheniya. Utverzhdeny g. Ministrom Narodnogo Prosveshcheniya 4-go maya 1874 g.* (M.: V Universitetskoi tip., [1874]).

158 For a description of this extremely unpopular member of staff, see Aleksandra Brushtein, *Doroga ukhodit v dal'* (M.: Sovetskii pisatel', 1985), pp. 196–8. The description refers to the mid-1890s, but *dames de classe* remained in position, both in institutes for daughters of the nobility such as Brushtein's school in Vilna, and in state *gimnazii*, up to the Revolution. According to Shubkin, *Povsednevnaya zhizn'*, they were very little use, in fact, for imposing discipline.

159 Examples of such rotas in St Petersburg are available in the file for the Eighth *Gimnaziya* on Vasilievsky Island: RGIA f.17 op. 2 d. 142, l. 168. It would appear that serious misdemeanours seldom occurred: these files contain only one instance (a pupil who was found in the company of a woman of ill repute, and who defended himself by stating that she had been pestering him); but the elaborate rituals were still maintained, despite considerable costs to the school (*nastavniki* and their deputies were paid extra for supervisory duty).

160 Paustovsky, *Sobranie sochinenii*, vol. 4, p. 222. (The answer was: give up his chair, but make sure it was placed so she was facing away from the light.)

161 S. Chernyi, *Sobranie sochinenii v pyati tomakh*, vol. 5 (M., 1996), p. 134.

162 Shubkin, *Povsednevnaya zhizn'*, p. 196.

163 The collection of marked work at TsGIA f. 139 op. 1 d. 12664, ll. 98–206 gives a good idea of the principles of assessment.

164 RGIA f. 803 op. 16 d. 2372.

165 D. S. Mirsky, *Pushkin* (paperback reprint; NY, 1963).

166 Paustovsky, *Sobranie sochinenii*, vol. 4, p. 220.

167 F. Sologub, *Melkii bes* (SPb., 1908: reprinted Letchworth, 1966). p. 177.

168 A devastating account of schoolmasterly incompetence and inhumanity is given in Rybnikov, 'Iz roda v rod', ll. 41–53, 57–64. Sologub himself had worked as a schoolmaster in St Petersburg province and in his prefaces to *Melkii bes* repeatedly insisted on the book's closeness to life.

169 Shubkin, *Povsednevnaya zhizn'*, p. 316, p. 315.

170 Rybnikov, however, was an exception to this: for him the Latin teacher was the only intelligent and interesting person around ('Iz roda v rod', ll. 54–6).

171 *ZMNP* 8 (1905), section I, 48–51.

172 V. M. Istrin, 'Novaya programma kursa russkoi slovesnosti v sredneuchebnykh zavedeniyakh', *ZMNP* 6 (1906), section IV, 77.

173 *DRE*, p. 250.

174 Ol'ga Berggol'ts, *Dnevnye zvezdy* (L., 1971), p. 151. Cf. the memoirs of children celebrating 7 November 1918 (the first anniversary of the Bolshevik Revolution) published in *N* 46 (1968), 6–7.

175 L. Kassil', *Konduit i Shvambraniya*, in *Dorogie moi mal'chishki. Konduit i Shvambraniya* (M., 1987), pp. 236–7.

176 Anon, 'Kak prazdnovali deti 1-e maya', *Krasnye zori* 2 (1919), 40–9.

177 Berggol'ts, *Dnevnye zvezdy*, pp. 152–3.

178 See *Kak organizovat' detskii sad* (2nd edn; L., 1929).

179 V. Anan'in et al., *Zhivoi rodnik: pervaya kniga dlya chteniya v shkole i doma* (M., 1922), vol. 3, pp. 54–7 (Christmas tree), p. 161 (the 'Great Russian' people).

180 I. I. Shaposhnikov, *Zhivye zvuki: Rukovodstvo dlya obucheniya detei pis'mu i chteniyu bez bukvarya (Po obrazo-motornomu metodu)* (M.–L., 1923). (This book went through seven editions to 1930.)

181 *Edinaya Trudovaya Shkola: Azbuka* (Dmitriev, 1921).

182 P. O. Afanas'ev, *Chitai, pishi, schitai: bukvar'* (M.–L., n.d. [1925]).

183 M. K. Porshneva, *Gramota: Bukvar' dlya sel'skoi shkoly* (M.–L., 1930). This did, however, also include some more 'childish' material, e.g. pictures of a cat lapping milk and people collecting mushrooms.

184 M. A. Mel'nikov with A. G. Kalashnikov, *Novyi put': pervaya kniga dlya chteniya i raboty v sel'skoi shkole I stupeni* (9th edn; M.–L., 1930); *Novyi put': Vtoraya kniga dlya chteniya i raboty v sel'skoi shkole I stupeni* (7th edn; M.–L., 1930); *Novyi put': Kniga tret'ya dlya sel'skoi shkoly* (3rd edn; M.–L., 1930).

185 I. N. Kavuna and N. S. Popova, *Chislo na stroike. Pervyi god matematiki v gorodskoi shkole* (M., 1931), p. 29.

186 S. K., 'Sud idet', *Novaya shkola: Uchenicheskii zhurnal shkol II stupeni Ostrova No. 2 i No. 3 (Pskovskaya guberniya)* 1 (May–June 1919), 2.

187 V. N. Shul'gin, *Obshchestvennaya rabota shkoly i programmy GUSa* (M., 1925), p. 11, p. 12, p. 15.

188 *Programmy i metodicheskie zapiski edinoi trudovoi shkoly vypusk I: Gorodskie i sel'skie shkoly 1-i stupeni: Programmy* (M.–L., 1927), p. 23.

189 I. Smirnov, 'Distsiplina v shkole', *Prosveshchenie na transporte* 2 (1927), 8 (emphasis original).

190 Z. Firsova, 'O distsipline v shkole', *Prosveshchenie na transporte* 2 (1927), 64–8.

191 *Programmy dlya pervogo kontsentra shkol vtoroi stepeni* (M.–L., 1925), pp. 142–3, p. 157.

192 F. A. Mackenzie, *The Russian Crucifixion* (London, *c.* 1930), p. 38, quoting Susan Lawrence, Under-Secretary of the Minister of Health, 1929–31.

193 *Programmy i metodicheskie zapiski edinoi trudovoi shkoly vypusk I: Gorodskie i sel'skie shkoly 1-i stupeni*, p. 64 (political tenets); for the maths syllabus see pp. 112–14, for the reading and writing syllabus, pp. 115–21.

194 See e.g. Smirnov, 'Distsiplina v shkole', p. 4.

195 P. O. Afanas'ev and N. A. Kostin, *Bukvar'* (M.: Gos. uch.-ped. izd., 1936).

196 N. M. Golovin, *Bukvar'* (M.: Uchpedgiz, 1938) (and eight further edns to 1944); S. P. Redozubov and A. V. Yankovskaya, *Bukvar'* (M., 1948) (first published 1938, 7th and final edn. 1952).

197 See e.g. *Rodnoe slovo: Kniga dlya chteniya v I klasse*, comp. E. I. Nikitina (2nd edn; Moscow: Prosveshchenie, 1969), pp. 3–4, p. 168, p. 179; *Rodnoe slovo: Kniga dlya chteniya v II klasse*, comp. E. I. Nikitina (M.: Prosveshchenie, 1969), pp. 73–8 (the October Revolution), pp. 218–50, p. 341; *Rodnoe slovo: Kniga dlya chteniya v III klasse*, comp. E. I. Nikitina (M.: Prosveshchenie, 1970), pp. 21–2.

198 *Programmy nachal'noi shkoly: gorodskoi i sel'skoi* (M.: Narkompros/Uchpedgiz, 1932), pp. 56–7.

199 *Programmy nachal'noi shkoly* (M.: Uchpedgiz, 1945), p. 72, for the song, and *Rodnaya rech': Kniga dlya chteniya v III klasse nachal'noi shkoly* (M., 1946), pp. 367–9, p. 379, etc., for the texts.

200 See e.g. *Bukvar'* (M.: Gos. Uch.-ped. izd., 1963), pp. 82–3; *Rodnoe slovo: Kniga dlya chteniya v I klasse*, pp. 153–9; *Rodnoe slovo: Kniga dlya chteniya v II klasse*, pp. 79–82; *Rodnoe slovo: Kniga dlya chteniya v III klasse*, pp. 118–20.

201 Quoted by Vyatkin (first name not given) in N. N. Iordansky (ed.), *Svobodnye sochineniya i detskoe tvorchestvo v programmakh Gus'a* (M.–L., 1926), p. 16 (the article was first published in *Na tret'em fronte* 2–3 (1923)). 'Kituns' is an attempt to convey a grammar mistake in the original, the plural 'dvukh kotenkov' (for 'dvukh kotyat').

202 As recounted by Oleg Krasovsky (b. 1919) in Novak-Deker, p. 128. This particular school was in Kiev; Krasovsky recalled that in Moscow, where he moved in the early 1930s, politics had a far more important place in lessons (p. 132).

203 See *Programmy nachal'noi shkoly* (1932), pp. 56–7, *Programmy nachal'noi shkoly* (1945), pp. 19–20, pp. 22–3, p. 72, and *Rodnaya rech'*, *passim*.

204 Sergei Mikhalkov, 'Khoroshaya Rodina', *Rodnoe slovo: Kniga dlya chteniya v 1 klasse*, comp. E. N. Nikitina (2nd edn; M., 1969), p. 3.

205 See e.g. *Rodnoe slovo: Kniga dlya chteniya v I klasse*, p. 20 (poem on the stork), pp. 38–72 (*skazki*, many about animals), pp. 73–84 (the seasons); *Rodnoe slovo: Kniga dlya chteniya v II klasse*,

pp. 9–72; *Rodnoe slovo: Kniga dlya chteniya v III klasse*, pp. 151–77. In the third reader, there was an increase in the amount of politicised material, with a good deal of space given to 'The Pioneers', etc.

206 'Na poroge zhizni', *N* 35 (1969), 2.

207 *Programmy nachal'noi shkoly* (1932), and *Programmy nachal'noi shkoly* (1945).

208 'Konkurs "Pravdy" na luchshego uchitelya', *ENKP* 30 June 1923, 4–7.

209 The 1927 *Programmy i metodicheskie zapiski* for the first years of the Soviet school specified 'socio-political topics' and nature study as a mandatory minimum to be covered, rather than suggesting that, say, reading and writing lessons should be combined with work on the life-cycle of the cow or essays on Lenin's tomb.

210 *Programmy dlya pervogo kontsentra shkol vtoroi stepeni (5, 6 i 7 gody obucheniya)* (M.–L., 1925), p. 5.

211 The account here is based on the memoirs of former pupils in *Detskii dom: uroki proshlogo* (M.: Moskovskii rabochii, 1990), pp. 56–69; see also N. I. Popova, *Shkola zhizni* (M., 1922), Natal'ya Sats and S. G. Rozanov's Experimental Arts Education School, founded in 1922 (see *Vestnik prosveshcheniya MONO*, 7–8 (1923), and Shatsky's 'Bodraya zhizn'' (on which see W. Partlett, 'Breaching Cultural Worlds with the Village School', *Slavonic and East European Review* 82:4 (2004)). Anatoly Rybakov, in *Roman-vospominanie* (M., 1997), pp. 43–5, describes attending, for the last two years of his secondary education, a similar establishment in Moscow, the Narkompros Model Experimental School-Commune, that was run on similar lines, with the pupils doling out food at meals, and working independently in the mornings before taking part in seminars during the afternoons.

212 Shubkin (ed.), *Povsednevnaya zhizn' russkoi gimnazii*, p. 417.

213 See e.g. the report from the Kemerovo area in 1923–24 cited in Bedin et al. (eds), *Kemerovo i Stalinsk*, p. 12.

214 Holmes, *The Kremlin and the Schoolhouse*, p. 37.

215 As described by 'N. N.', 'Iz pis'ma Petrogradskogo pedagoga', *Russkaya shkola za rubezhom* 2 (1924), 125.

216 'Ustav Edinoi trudovoi shkoly' (signed O. Bem, Yakovleva, Tolstov), *ENKP* 16 July 1923, p. 7.

217 Cases of this kind are reported by several of the memoirists in *DRE*.

218 See e.g. Firsova, 'O distsipline v shkole', pp. 65–6.

219 M. Zoshchenko, 'Uchitel'', *Sobranie sochinenii v trekh tomakh* (L., 1986), vol. 1, pp. 122–3.

220 See the Decree of the Central Committee of the Communist Party of 25 August 1932, *Izvestiya* 29 August 1932, p. 2, which speaks in alternate breaths of 'significantly strengthening historicism in the social studies, native language and literature, and geography programmes', and of the need to disseminate 'the most important knowledge relating to the national cultures of the peoples of the USSR'.

221 'Kazhdomu shkol'niku – stabil'nyi uchebnik!', *Pravda* 25 February 1933, p. 2.

222 On the background to the syllabus changes, see D. L. Brandenberger and A. M. Dubrovsky, '"The People Need a Tsar": The Emergence of National Bolshevism as Stalinist Ideology', *Europe-Asia Studies* 50: 5 (1998), 873–92; David L. Brandenberger, *National Bolshevism* (Cambridge, MA, 2002), ch. 5.

223 P. N. Shimbirev [and E. I. Shimbireva], *Pedagogika* (M., 1940), p. 275.

224 K. Chukovsky, 'Literatura i shkola', *Pravda* 18 January 1936; reprinted in *Sobranie sochinenii*, vol. 6 (M., 1969), pp. 580–606.

225 *ENKP* 1 April 1935, p. 12.

226 Beatrice King, *Changing Man* (London, 1936), p. 110.

227 Ibid., p. 170.

228 'Uroki pedagoga Gurevicha', *PP* 11 May 1933, 8.

229 N. Pozdnyakov, 'Russkii yazyk i literatura v obraztsovykh shkolakh', *Za politekhnicheskuyu shkolu* 5 (1934), 15–21.

230 Shimbirev [and Shimbireva], *Pedagogika*, pp. 254–5.

231 See the instructions in I. V. Popov, 'K metodike provedeniya urokov, imeyushchikh tsel'yu proverku znanii uchashchikhsya', *Sovetskaya pedagogika* 3 (1952), 43–9. See also E. I. Perovsky, *Ustnaya proverka znanii uchashchikhsya* (M., 1955), esp. pp. 112–19 and pp. 132–50.

232 Shimbirev [and Shimbireva], *Pedagogika*, pp. 306–7. Citations have been altered from the present to the past tense.

233 *ENKP* 1 April 1935, p. 2, p. 4.

234 The description of the examination system is based on E. I. Perovsky, *Ekzameny v sovetskoi shkole* (M., 1948), pp. 120–49. For a later source describing an essentially identical process, see *Spravochnik direktora shkoly* (1971), pp. 82–3.

235 *ENKP* 1 June 1936, p. 2. For a case where this happened (much resented by the victim sixty years after the fact), see CKQ E–03 PF3A, p. 7.

236 As set out in *Istoriya SSSR: Kratkii kurs. Uchebnik dlya 3-go i 4-go klassov*, ed. A. V. Shestakov (M., 1938), p. 18: 'In its time Christianity constituted a step forward in Russia's development compared with paganism. Along with Christianity, Greek culture and learning was spread among the Slavs. [...] Learned Greek monks invented an alphabet for the Slavonic languages. This alphabet then started to be used in the Kievan state.'

237 *Programmy srednei shkoly: Russkii yazyk i literaturnoe chtenie (V–VII klassy). Literatura (VIII–X klassy). Dopolnitel'noe, ispravlennoe izdanie* (M., 1938), p. 27, p. 31, p. 26.

238 As in a case from the Siberian town of Staro-Kuznetsk in 1938, where a teacher was arrested for using Kiorin's history textbook after this had been officially banned from schools: see Bedin, Kushnikova, and Toguleva (eds), *Kemerovo i Stalinsk*, p. 478. Andreevsky, 'V sovetskoi shkole', p. 317, cites a case where a teacher was denounced by parents for assigning homework from a textbook that had pictures of Trotsky, Zinoviev, and other 'enemies of the people'.

239 As stipulated by e.g. the February 1933 decree of the Central Committee calling for the 'stable textbook' (*stabil'nyi uchebnik*) to be made the core

of education (cited in Shimbirev and Shimbireva, *Pedagogika*, p. 226).

240 V. Leongard (W. Leonhard), *Revolyutsiya otvergaet svoikh detei* (London, 1984), p. 15.

241 Cf. the criticism of such methods in A. P. Trofimov, 'Kogda narushaetsya pedagogicheskii takt', *SemSh* 7 (1952), 14–16.

242 For a case of a teacher getting into trouble (here, for physically ejecting a pupil), see Alekseev, p. 185. For reports of low-level violence, see e.g. Oxf/Lev SPb.–02 PF7A, p. 43: here the teacher, irritated by a greedy boy who would not give up eating in class, 'grabbed him by the scruff and hauled him over the top of his own desk and her desk and stuck him in front of the whole class'.

243 For the Ivanovo case, see CKQ M–04 PF7A, p. 15. For affectionate and enthusiastic memories of schooldays in the late 1930s and early 1940s, see Boris Firsov, 'Sovetskoe detstvo (ne po Kelli)', *Antropologicheskii forum* 4 (2006); V. Baevsky, ibid.

244 Eric Hobsbawm, *Interesting Times* (London, 2002).

245 Ella Bobrova, *Irina Istomina: povest' v stikhakh* (Toronto, 1967), p. 8.

246 Perovsky, *Ustnaya proverka*, pp. 132–7.

247 P. I. Gorbunov in *Sovetskaya pedagogika* 7 (1951), 21–7.

248 E. Vereiskaya, 'Pro nashu shkolu', *Koster* 4 (1947), 24–6. The school in question was No. 210.

249 See V. Baevsky's contribution to Forum 4, *Antropologicheskii forum* 4 (2006), pp. 5–11.

250 Though not always: Baevsky's school was in the Donbass. In the Stalin era, the compulsory posting (*raspredelenie*) of graduates was by all accounts taken more seriously than in the 1960s or 1970s, so there was some chance of ending up with a bright teacher even in the countryside.

251 Dunstan, pp. 127–31.

252 RAO NA f. 32 op. 1 d. 160, ll. 5–6, l. 17, l. 25.

253 Dunstan, pp. 119–23. See also Andreevsky, 'V sovetskoi shkole', pp. 367–9.

254 *Sbornik zakonov i rasporyazhenii* 47 (1935), 391 (quoted in Papernyi, *"Kul'tura dva"*, p. 334).

255 See KPBTsK 1929–1935, ll. 203–5.

256 See Dunstan, p. 153, and also my own discussion in Chapter 4 above.

257 On these two decrees, see *Khronologicheskoe sobranie zakonov, ukazov Prezidiuma Verkhovnogo Soveta i postanovlenii pravitel'stva RSFSR*, vol. 3 (1940–47) (M., 1958), pp. 340–5 (monitoring by residence authorities), pp. 346–9 (*bilety*). According to Holmes, *Stalin's School*, p. 68, the point of the 1943 measure was that many schools had failed to comply with the original requirement to introduce the rules and identity cards in 1935.

258 For the Council of Ministers' decree reintroducing marks (10 January 1944), see *Khronologicheskoe sobranie zakonov*, vol. 3, p. 383. See Boris Yeltsin's memoirs, *Against the Grain*, trans. M. Glenny (London, 1990), p. 20, on the effects of a less than perfect 5.

259 See [A. A.] Yakovlev, 'Dokladnaya zapiska o stat'e zaveduyushchego Mosgorono tov. Orlova "O distsipline i povedenii nashikh detei"', RGASPI f. 17 op. 126, d. 13, ll. 23–4. .

260 Boldyrev (ed.), *Klassnyi rukovoditel'*, p. 291.

Interestingly, some former *gimnazii* retained a post analogous to the old *klassnyi nastavnik* (though with more emphasis on support and guidance than on surveillance) into the 1920s: for a reference to such a person, see B. Plaksin, 'Improvizirovannyi teatr, kak sredstvo pedagog-icheskogo vozdeistviya', *Russkaya shkola za rubezhom* 18 (1926), 597.

261 The details of this are given in Boldyrev (ed.), *Klassnyi rukovoditel'*, a very thorough manual for the class supervisor: on the Pioneer and Komsomol organisations, see pp. 149–80; on work with parents, see pp. 242–55. On the class supervisor's relationship with the director, see section 9 of the original decree (*Klassnyi rukovoditel'*, p. 293; on surveillance of other teachers, see ibid., p. 99).

262 Oxf/Lev SPb.–03 PF20B, pp. 45–7.

263 The *lineika* began as a Pioneer event in the early Soviet era, and it had a patchy existence till the post-war years: for instance, in April 1941, *lineiki* and political information sessions (*raporty*) at the beginning of lessons were banned by Narkompros after stories that some schools in Moscow, and in Irkutsk, Orel, Kursk, Vologda, and Ryazan' provinces, had started holding these regularly: RGASPI f. 17 op. 126 d. 2, ll. 64–7.

264 For normative statements on the meetings, see Boldyrev, *Klassnyi rukoviditel'*: on class meetings, see pp. 71–80; on moral and political pep-talks, see pp. 191–210.

265 T. Panfilova, 'O zhurnale povedeniya uchashchikhsya', *SemSh* 1 (1953), 13–15.

266 Oxf/Lev T–04 PF10A, p. 2, on the early 1970s: 'You arrive and there's 45 in every class, just you imagine [...] and if you don't get at least 35 in your class, it's a major tragedy, that's it, panic stations. You run round hunting for children, picking some more, or they won't let you in the classroom.'

267 Cf. the criticisms of N. Mart'yanova, 'Ya – repetitor', *N* 13 (1984), 6; and the comments of the female informant (b. 1966) in RAO M–04 PF4A, p. 7: 'I hated Russian language, Russian literature. I had the feeling they were forcing other people's opinions of who was a positive and negative character down your throat the whole time.'

268 See e.g. I. Stal'kova, 'Dvoika dvoike rozn'', *N* 2 (1988), 5.

269 *Spravochnik direktora shkoly* (1971), pp. 106–7.

270 For the criticism, see e.g. the spread for 1 September, *N* 35 (1988), 2, and the thoroughgoing assault on educational standards in *N* 49 (1988), 1–3. On the post-Soviet system, see Ben Eklof, Larry Holmes, and Vera Kaplan (eds), *Educational Reform in Post-Soviet Russia: Legacies and Prospects* (London: Frank Cass/Routledge, 2005).

271 See e.g. Oxf/Lev T–04 PF1A, p. 9.

272 See e.g. Oxf/Lev M–04 PF17A, p. 16: this teacher would turn difficult pupils into figures of fun, something that ensured they conformed.

273 Nabokov, *Speak, Memory*, pp. 144–5: football and debating society at the Tenishev School in 1910s.

274 Shaginyan, *SPA*, vol. 2, p. 642.

275 N. P. Cherepnin, *Imperatorskoe Vospitatel'noe obshchestvo blagorodnykh devits* (3 vols; SPb., 1914–15), vol. 3, p. 471, p. 483.

276 For details of the *Poteshnye* and a persuasive contrast of the organisation with the Scout movement, see Richard Wortman, *Scenarios of Power* (2 vols; Princeton, NJ, 1995–2000), vol. 2, pp. 417–20.

277 At my husband's school in a British provincial town in the 1960s, for example, boys were offered a choice between the OTC and the Scouts (abstention from both organisations was not a possibility). The more liberally minded boys naturally chose the Scouts. For a discussion of this shift in the Scouts at an institutional level, see Robert H. MacDonald, *Sons of Empire* (Toronto, 1993), p. 8.

278 See 'Zapiska ob organizatsii molodykh razvedchikov (Russkii skaut)', *Materialy po reforme srednei shkoly: Primernye programmy i ob''yasuilel'nye zametki, izdannye po rasporyazheniyu Ministra Narodnogo Prosveshcheniya* (Petrograd, 1915), pp. 426–30.

279 http://www.scoutmaster.ru/ru/main.htm. *Listok obshchestva sodeistviya mal'chikam-razvedchikam 'Russkii Skaut'* 2 (1915), 1, confirms the patriotism story: about half of the Scouts in Petrograd had now obtained permission to enlist in the army. Two had already been wounded, one seriously.

280 O. D. Petrov, *Spravochnaya i zapisnaya kniga RUSSKOGO SKAUTA* (Petrograd, n.d.), pp. 100–3 lists, 74 Scout troops across the Russian Empire. *Listok obshchestva sodeistviya mal'chikam-razvedchikam 'Russkii Skaut'* gives little information about membership, but does state (no. 4 p. 6) that there were now up to 130 *gerl-skauty* in Petrograd.

281 R. Baden-Poel' [=Baden-Powell], *Boi-skauty: rukovodstvo samovospitaniya molodezhi po sisteme 'skauting' sera Roberta Baden Poelya primenitel'no k usloviyam russkoi zhizni i prirody. V pererabotke V. A. Popova i V. S. Preobrazhenskogo* (M., 1917); O. D. Petrov, *Spravochnaya i zapisnaya knizhka RUSSKOGO SKAUTA* (Petrograd, [1916]). See also *Ustav Obshchestva sodeistviya mal'chikam-razvedchikam ('Russkii skaut')* (Petrograd, 1916).

282 *Obshchestvo sodeistviya yunym razvedchikam Russkii skaut* (Petrograd, [1916]), p. 8, p. 13.

283 On camping trips, see e.g. 'Patrul' "Volkov" na prazdnichnoi progulke', *Petrogradskii skaut* 1 (1916), 1; for 'Be Prepared, o Scout', see 'Pesnya skauta', ibid. Several other such songs are quoted in this number of *Petrogradskii skaut* and in the short-lived journal's second number. On modifications to Scout uniform, see *Listok obshchestva sodeistviya mal'chikam-razvedchikam 'Russkii Skaut'* 1 (1915), 2. According to the same source (no. 2 p. 4), uniform might be purchased from the English Shop at no. 15, Nevskii Prospekt.

284 This reflects the priority given in the Komsomol itself to work with the oldest section of the target group. Over-17s made up 90 per cent of the membership of the organisation in 1922, 14–16-year-olds only 10 per cent. See Gorsuch, p. 15.

285 *Na fronte svekly* (Voronezh, 1933).

286 TsKhDMO f. 1 op. 23 d. 942, l. 32 (my emphasis).

287 TsKhDMO f. 1 op. 23 d. 458, l. 27.

288 KPSTsK 1926–27, l. 129.

289 For a fuller account of the Octobrists, see digital version of this chapter.

290 TsAODM f. 1884 op. 1 d. 52, l. 68g. [68].

291 On the routing of demonstrations, cf. the ruling by the Party authorities in Moscow (25 April 1923) that children marching on 1 May were not to come into contact with adult marchers at any point (TsAODM f. 3 op. 11 d. 131, l. 21; on the Tverskaya street incident, see TsAODM f. 634 op. 1 d. 35, l. 82).

292 KPBTsK 1919–28, l. 71.

293 *Pioner* 3 (1924), 23, 3.

294 *Dokumenty TsK KPSS i TsK VLKSM o rabote Vsesoyuznoi pionerskoi organizatsii imeni V. I. Lenina* (comp. V. S. Khanchin) (M., 1970), p. 33. Fisher, p. 201, says that *forposty* transferred to schools in 1931.

295 For a detailed discussion of this situation, see the digital version of this book, Chapter 16.

296 Petr Kruzhin in Novak-Deker, p. 188. The youth of many *vozhatye* was no doubt a factor here: Anastasyan Vairoch recalled becoming a Pioneer leader at 16, while Kruzhin himself was to take over a troop at just under 15, and to have had understandable trouble disciplining the elder Pioneers (Novak-Deker, p. 63, p. 201).

297 *PP* 18 March 1936, 1, 'Kak prinimayut v pionery?'.

298 *DTsK*, p. 76; *Komsomol i detskoe dvizhenie* (M., 1924), p. 14.

299 KPBTsK 1936–42, l. 55, l. 214.

300 On the meaning of the ties, see ibid., l. 55. On the rumours about Trotsky's image, see S. V. Zhuravlev and A. K. Sokolov, '"Schastlivoe detstvo"', *Sotsial'naya istoriya: Ezhegodnik 1997* (1998), 170. Previously, Pioneer symbolism had been less personal: in 1935, Wolfgang Leonhard (see *Revolyutsiya otvergaet*, p. 17) was told that the five logs on the Pioneer tie-clip represented the five continents of the world, and three tongues of flame the three Communist Internationals.

301 Cf. the fact that wearing a tie is one of the main things recalled by informants about belonging to the Pioneer movement in the 1930s: see e.g. Oxf/Lev V–04 PF25A, p. 17.

302 *Pervyi vsesoyuznyi s"ezd sovetskikh pisatelei* (M., 1934), p. 38. See also *Baza kurnosykh* (Irkutsk, 1962).

303 *PP* 1 January 1936, p. 1.

304 As in the case of a woman teacher mentioned by Petr Kruzhin: Novak-Deker, pp. 223–4.

305 See Bedin et al. (eds), *Kemerovo i Stalinsk*, p. 466: the circles offered included radio, theatre, ballet, brass and jazz bands, art, violin, piano, folk music, handicraft, model-building, photography, and 'entertaining chemistry'.

306 Cf. reports on founding of these in Dnepropetrovsk, *Pravda* 4 February 1936, p. 6, Stalingrad, *Pravda* 30 May 1936, p. 5, Odessa, *Pravda* 31 December 1936.

307 This description is based partly on L. P. Bulankova, *Stranitsy zhizni Anichkova dvortsa: dokumenty, memuary, byli, legendy* (SPb., 1996), pp. 36–8, and partly on my visit to the Anichkov palace, including the Pioneer palace museum, in May 2000.

308 See S. Bograd, 'Dom pionerov i oktyabryat', *Pravda* 23 June 1936, p. 6. See *Pravda* 29 June 1936, p. 6, for an account of the official opening, by Nikita Khrushchev, in the presence of, among others, André Gide. On the entertainment programme, see 'Teatr detskogo tvorchestva', *Pravda* 6 October 1936, p. 6: the first shows staged were *Happy Childhood* and *Childhood in Our Country*.

309 Miller, pp. 68–71.

310 KPBTsK 1936–42, l. 54.

311 A. Gaidar, *Sochineniya* (M., 1946), p. 377.

312 *Istoriya VLKSM i Vsesoyuznoi pionerskoi organizatsii im V. I. Lenina*, ed. V. A. Sulemov (M., 1978), p. 197.

313 See e.g. *Druzhnye rebyata* 2 (1943), 21 (on money-collecting and hospital concerts in Arkhangel'sk); *Druzhnye rebyata* 7 (1943) (on collecting money); *Pioner* 4 (1942), 25 (on collecting bottles to make Molotov cocktails), *Pioner* 10 (1942), 28–33 (on running crèches, air-raid warden activities, growing vegetables, visits to hospitals, etc.). These groups are also recalled affectionately in oral history: see e.g. Oxf/Lev V–05 PF1B, p. 22. On plant-collecting, see KPBTsK 1936–42, ll. 175–8 (describing a leaflet for Pioneers on how to collect such plants).

314 *PP* 2 January 1939 versus *PP* 3 January 1947.

315 This scene occurs on p. 59: page span generally is 5–60 in *Sob. soch v 4 tomakh* (M. 1963), vol. 1. *The Red Tie* is one of several plays by Mikhalkov recommended in the 'Children's Encyclopedia' feature published by *Krokodil* 4 (1952), 9. It was serialised in *PP* in 1947.

316 See e.g. a spread about Gaidar in *Pioner* 10–11 (1946), 22, where Gaidar describes his motive in writing the book as being to get children to 'igrat' v khoroshikh lyudei' (play at being good people) and not 'v razboiniki' (at robbers).

317 See Miller, p. 29.

318 KPBTsK 1948–54, ll. 110–16.

319 'Konkretnaya programma dal'neishego uluchsheniya pionerskoi raboty v shkole', *SP* 1 (1952), 13–20.

320 For Pioneer membership, see *Deti v SSSR* (M., 1979), p. 30; for the target age group figures, see Boris Lewytzkyj, *The Soviet Union: Facts, Figures, Data* (Munich, 1979), table 2.10, pp. 40–1.

321 See e.g. Ransel, *Village Mothers*, p. 180.

322 KPBTsK 1948–54, l. 186.

323 Ibid., l. 186, l. 187.

324 *Sbornik dokumentov TsK VLKSM o rabote Vsesoyuznoi Pionerskoi organizatsii imeni V. I. Lenina* (aprel' 1954–iyun' 1958) (M., 1958), p. 82.

325 *Spravochnik direktora shkoly*, 1971, p. 160.

326 V. Golyavkin, 'Ty prikhodi k nam, prikhodi', in his *Udivitel'nye deti* (3rd edn; L.: Detskaya literatura, 1979), pp. 7–80.

327 *Moskva v tsifrakh* (M., 1977), p. 130.

328 See the excellent account in Reid.

329 Author interview with Olga Grekova, 9 February 2004.

330 Note that reports in the Soviet press stressed this aspect of the Pioneer camp too: see e.g. *N* 28

(1970), front page; *N* 25 (1976), 4 (Pioneer items headed 'Holidays!' (*Kanikuly*)); *N* 29 (1978), 3; *N* 28 (1984), front page; *N* 22 (1986), 4.

331 TsDOO SO f. 161 op. 32 d. 50, l. 16 (1960); GASO f. 1428 op. 1 d. 192, l. 1 (1964); GASO f. 1428 op. 1 d. 1583, l. 13 (1968).

332 *Moskva v tsifrakh*, p. 130.

333 See brief comments and description in Bulankova, *Stranitsy zhizni Anichkova dvortsa*, p. 53.

334 G. Reingol'd, 'Mladshii brat Arteka – Orlenok', *N* 42 (1961), 20–1. On the camp and its history, see also http://www.orlenok.ru.

335 The figure of 1,400 places as against a target population of 6,669 children comes from TsDOO SO f. 61 op. 16 d. 117, l. 224.

336 TsDOO SO f. 1428 op. 1 d. 1192, l. 1 (1964 figures); TsDOO SO f. 1428 op. 1 d. 1287, l. 8 (1965 figures).

337 See e.g. *Pravda* 17 June 1946: 100,000 children from Kazan' going to camps, and 100 *otlichniki* to Artek; the stenographic record of a meeting of the Moscow Schools Komsomol activist committee (*aktiv*), 30 March 1945, anticipates the departure from Moscow of only 300 children in 1945: *MPV*, p. 598.

338 See e.g. V. Tomikhina, 'Net raboty s det'mi', *Leninskie iskry*, 9 July 1935, p. 7. (Despite the title, this includes material on summer playgrounds, though it is quite critical of how they are run).

339 Though some attempt to encourage 'tracking' (*sledopytstvo*) and expeditions was made during the 1930s, junior excursions into *turizm* (exploration of wild areas) often went no further than reading about such activities or listening to talks about them.

340 Oxf/Lev M–04 PF24B, pp. 28–9.

341 On the introduction of *Zarnitsa*, see *Istoriya VLKSM*, p. 279. See also the manual *Zarnitsa* (M.: Molodaya gvardiya, 1974). According to one former Pioneer, 'We were given military-style uniforms and it … was just like in the Pioneer camps, really, sort of orienteering, only more military. See, we'd be pilots, every troop would have its own uniform, and really …' (Oxf/Lev V–04 PF3B, p. 22). On the non-political character of Pioneer camps at this date, cf. e.g. CKI SPb–3.

342 *Slushaite vse!* (M., 1962), comp. Anatolii Markusha, p. 11 (fountain), p. 16 (Van Clyburn), p. 14 (wall newspaper).

343 See O. Lesenko, 'Pionerskoe leto, proshchai?', *N* 37 (1991), 13, for a discussion of this.

344 Fraser, *The House on the Dvina*, p. 175, recalls this about her school, the girls' *gimnaziya* in Arkhangel'sk. School No. 330 in Moscow, formerly the Elizavetinskaya *Gimnaziya*, lost its playground in the 1960s, when an indoor gymnasium was built. This could also be used as a recreational facility, but pupils had to use (and still have to use) a nearby park for fresh air. (Personal observation from visit in June 2005.)

345 On not allowing children to leave the buildings, see CKQ Ox–03 PF6B, p. 12. On lack of access to the playground (in an elite Moscow city-centre girls' school during the late 1940s), see CKQ Ox–03 PF2B, p. 8.

346 Email communication from interviewee in

CKQ Ox–03 PF12-PF13, 17 July 2003.

347 See e.g. Elena Shvarts, 'Peremena peremene!', *Zor'ka* 23–4 (1932), 10–11, and A. Vishnevsky, 'Shkol'nye peremeny', *Zateinik* 19–20 (1932), 57–60.

348 For example, a game called *nozhichki* in which players attempted to flick, using a finger or even their tongues, a knife at the soil so that it would land standing upright. For a description of the game, and the comment that 'if you played that in the playground they'd see and chuck you out', see Oxf/Lev SPb.–02 PF9A, p. 46.

349 On *shkilet*, see Viktor Rozov in *SPA*, vol. 5, p. 384 (referring to the early 1930s). On the teasing of fat children, see Inna Shikheeva-Gaister, *Semeinaya khronika vremen kul'ta lichnosti 1925–1953* (M., 1998), p. 11 (on the 1930s); cf. CKQ Ox–03 PF13B, pp. 12–13 (the 1970s).

350 'Fedya-Medya, s''el medvedya.' 'Shop-shop, pas zhopu v gorshok.' 'Tebe poklon poslali.' 'Kto?' 'Masha.' 'Kakaya Masha?' 'Svin'ya nasha.' G. Vinogradov, *Detskaya satiricheskaya lirika* (Irkutsk: Izd. Vostochno-Sibirskogo otdeleniya Russkogo geograficheskogo obshchestva, 1925), p. 37, p. 40.

351 *Pechat' i bol'she ne krichat'!*: ibid., p. 25.

352 Oxf/Lev SPb.–03 PF8B, p. 20.

353 Davydoff, *Russian Sketches*, pp. 124–5.

354 Rybnikov, 'Iz roda v rod', ll. 39–40.

355 Kravchenko, *I Chose Freedom*, p. 13.

356 A. K. Mal'tseva, 'Lyubimchik ili lyubimets?', *PP* 24 November 1964, 1.

357 Oxf/Lev SPb.–03 PF15B, p. 55, p. 74.

358 *SYu* 19 (1935), 11, 'Aktual'nost' zakona …'

359 As remarked by Davydov, *Russian Sketches*, 124–5: Davydoff was one of the lucky boys big enough not to have trouble.

360 For an account of being bullied because of having a Ukrainian accent in Moscow, see Grigory Chukhrai, 'Moskovskaya shkola', *Druzhba narodov* 8 (2001), 126–9. See also the material on Jewish and Tatar children in Chapter 8 of the full digital version. On the hostile treatment of new pupils (here, girls by other girls during the 1980s and early 1990s), see Oxf/Lev WQ1 GM, p. 4; Oxf/Lev WQ1 KM, p. 11.

361 A case of this kind is narrated in Oxf/Lev WQ1 GM, p. 6: the informant, who forgot to bring the jam-pot lid necessary for making compote in her domestic science lesson, was ostracised by the rest of her group (the compote-making was a collective activity).

362 *DRE* p. 49.

363 On faction-fighting before 1917, see e.g. Yury Tynyanov, *SPA*, vol. 2, pp. 383–4; 'monarchists' and 'revolutionaries': Kassil', *Konduit i Shvambraniya*, quoted from *Dorogie moi mal'chishki*, p. 229; Kadets and Bolsheviks, Reds and Whites, *DRE*, p. 178.

364 Kassil', *Konduit i Shvambraniya*, quoted from *Dorogie moi mal'chishki*, p. 175, p. 211.

365 KPBTsK 1929–35, l. 204.

366 V. Tadevosyan, 'Zakon 7 aprelya 1935', *SYu* 10–11 (1938), 50.

367 M. L. Gasparov, *Vypisi i zapisi* (M.: NLO, 2000), pp. 77–8.

368 CKQ E–03 PF1A, p. 4.
369 See e.g. Elenevskaya in Fitzpatrick and Slezkine, p. 129 (the 1910s); CKQ Ox–03 PF12B, p. 12; RAO M–03 PF4A, p. 8 (on how the informant was almost 'done over' (*dazhe devchonki khoteli ustroit' temnuyu*) when she first arrived back in Moscow after spending a few years in the provinces).
370 A. M. Piir, 'Detskie igry v Sankt-Peterburge/ Leningrade', unpublished typescript inventory, October 2003, p. 7. At Eugenie Fraser's pre-revolutionary school, the most popular game was Pebbles (*Kamushki*), a game like knucklebones where the player tossed a stone and attempted to gather up several more small stones before catching the first stone (*The House on the Dvina*, p. 175).
371 CKQ SPb.–03 PF3A, p. 18; CKQ Ox–03 PF4A, p. 11; CKQ Ox–03 PF8B, p. 12.
372 See above, and also Oxf/Lev SPb.–03 PF24B, pp. 14–15 (a *zavuch*, director of studies, who was given to burning pupils on the cheek with a cigarette end when enraged, and a geography teacher who lammed about herself with the blackboard pointer).
373 For examples of scatological ditties, see Sergeev, *Al'bom dlya marok* in *Al'bom dlya marok: Omnibus* (M., 1989), p. 196 ('Pushkin, enough of farting in your hat …'); Sergeev also remembered the joke, *luchshe geroiski pernut', chem truslivo bzdnut'* ('better a brave loud fart than a coward's silent stinker', p. 54). On visiting the lavatory, see CKQ Ox–03 PF4A, p. 11; on homework, CKQ Ox–03 PF12B, p. 12.
374 M. I. Sizova, *Ulanova: Her Childhood and Schooldays*, trans. M. Rambert (London, 1962), p. 115.
375 CKQ Ox–03 PF11A, p. 10.
376 For examples of narrative jokes of this kind, see V. F. Lur'e, 'Materialy po sovremennomu leningradskomu fol'kloru', in A. F. Belousov (ed.), *Uchebnyi material po teorii literatury: Zhanry slovesnogo teksta: Anekdot* (Tallinn, 1989), pp. 118–43; idem (ed.) *Russkii shkol'nyi fol'klor* (M., 1998); idem (ed.), *Shkolnyi byt i folklor* (2 vols; Tallinn, 1990).
377 Belousov, *Russkii shkol'nyi fol'klor*, p. 404; ibid., p. 417.
378 Oxf/Lev M–04 PF24A, p. 9.
379 On the *druzhba/tovarishchestvo*, or 'false/true friendship' divide, see e.g. M. Balan, 'Takaya nuzhna druzhba!', *Koster* 10 (1938), 73; 'Razve v etom druzhba?' *Koster* 10 (1938) 72; D. Brodskaya, 'Dnevnik Lidy Karasevoi', *Koster* 6 (1938), 33–44 [part 1]; 7, 38–48 [part 2]; E. Aleksandrova, 'V druzhbe s uchitelyami', *Vozhatyi* 10 (1950), 10–11. The most relevant source for the period under consideration is probably Valentina Oseeva's

classic children's novel *Vasek Trubachev i ego tovarishchi* (1947), regularly reprinted during the post-Stalin era: see Chapter 3 above.
380 See especially CKQ SPb.–03 PF2B, p. 16: 'I can't say that school was the cementing factor, it was more our family's social position.' In particular, the children of successful engineers working abroad stood out because their clothes were smarter than everyone else's (ibid.) On the other hand, an informant from a small town asserted that social distinctions were not that obvious in her school, even at this period: CKQ Ox–03 PF11B, p. 12.
381 See e.g. CKQ SPb.–03 PF2B, p. 16 (friendships through participation in *pokhody*).
382 Rybnikov, 'Iz roda v rod', l. 62.
383 V. V. Golovin and V. F. Lur'e, 'Devichii al'bom XX veka', in Belousov (ed.), *Russkii shkol'nyi fol'klor*, p. 296.
384 Oxf/Lev SPb.–03 PF15 A, p. 42 (boy and girl doing lessons together); CKQ Ox–03 PF10B, p. 10.
385 CKQ Ox–03 PF13A, p. 12.
386 Rybnikov, 'Iz roda v rod', l. 61.
387 Here and below, comments are based on the discussion in the full digital version of this chapter.
388 See e.g. Rittersporn, 'Formy obshchestvennogo obikhoda'.
389 For more information about this, see the full digital version of this chapter. An excellent introduction to teacher–pupil relations in the late Soviet era is Yury Polyakov's story 'Rabota nad oshibkami' (1984), recently republished in his *Sto dnei do prikaza* (M., 2004), pp. 95–176.
390 On unpaid work, see e.g. Oxf/Lev T–04 PF2A, p. 5, p. 12; Oxf/Lev T–04 PF10A, p. 4. Teachers were also paid only trifling sums for their work as class supervisors (i.e. form teachers, but with an additional disciplinary and regulatory brief: see p. 543 above), and for organising hobby circles in schools.
391 An entertaining inverted portrait of what Soviet schools taught their pupils is offered in Tatiana Esenina's story, 'Zhenya – chudo XX veka', in which a Soviet homunculus who has not been through the educational system (he was created instantly as an adult) makes use of a *shpargalka* when doing the examination for entrance to higher education (fair enough), but (here is the zany part) considers it 'dishonourable' (*nechestno*) to conceal what he is doing. Inevitably, he gets caught, and is about to be expelled from the admissions list in disgrace when it emerges that he is a local celebrity, at which point his mark is hastily increased from a 2 to a 5 (*NM* 1 (1962), 135–6).
392 See e.g. CKQ SPb.–03 PF3A, p. 20.

Conclusion: 'The End of Childhood'?

1 On work tasks, see Part II of digital version; on child-minding, Chapters 9 and 10 above.
2 K. S. Karol, *Solik: Life in the Soviet Union* (London, 1983), p. 30. Translation slightly adapted: the original has 'public house' (which

could also be a mistranslation of 'brothel'). On the seriousness of the exercise, see e.g. (referring to the late 1960s), Oxf/Lev T–04 PF3B, p. 16: 'you had to prepare yourself, read lots, learn it all by heart, if they were going to accept you'.

3 Oxf/Lev V–04 PF14A, p. 39.

4 A. Semenova, *Dnevnik gimnazistki* (M., 2002), p. 8.

5 B. Balter, *Do svidaniya, mal'chiki!* (M., 1991), p. 253.

6 For the sublimation model, see e.g. 'Porechanka', *Dnevnik gimnazistki* (SPb., 1907): here the heroine has a passionate fling (though going no further than kissing) with a 35-year-old army officer, but then decides that the women's courses rather than marriage are for her.

7 L. Andreev, 'V tumane', *Sobranie sochinenii*, vol. 2 (SPb., n.d. [*c.* 1897]), pp. 3–63.

8 N. Teffi, 'Kniga Iyun'', in *Sob. soch.*, vol. 4 (M., 2000), pp. 14–21. This view of adolescence as a painful time of life is of course a topos of Western discussions too. See, for example, Sue Lees, *Losing Out: Sexuality and Adolescent Girls* (London, 1986).

9 A. Aleksin, 'Tem vremenem gde-to', *Zvonite i priezzhaite!* (M., 1982), p. 404.

10 Alexander Davydoff (b. 1881), *Russian Sketches* (Tenafly, NJ, 1984), p. 100.

11 See e.g. Laura Engelstein, *The Keys to Happiness* (Ithaca, NY, 1992), pp. 243–6.

12 See Anon. [as 'Mat''], 'K voprosu o polovom vospitanii detei', *SvoV* 1 (1910), 51–62.

13 V. Nabokov, *Speak, Memory* (Harmondsworth, 1979), pp. 161–2. The passage also appears in Nabokov's *Drugie berega*. But it was only in the English-language version of his memoirs that Nabokov was to refer more directly to his own experience of juvenile tumescence: 'it was there [in the toilet] that, later, I used to compose my youthful verse, and morosely survey, in a dimly illuminated mirror, the immediate erection of a strange castle in an unknown Spain' (*Speak, Memory*, p. 67).

14 Mariengof, pp. 66–9.

15 On the 'no correspondence' rule, see Z. K. Manaskina in *Zhenskaya sud'ba v Rossii* (M., 1994), p. 12 – which also reveals that girls subverted it by using third-party addresses; for a case of a family row, see Sofka Skipwith, *Sofka* (London, 1968), pp. 72–3.

16 Ol'ga Forsh, *SPA*, vol. 1, p. 579.

17 See e.g. Ostap Vishnya, *SPA*, vol. 1, p. 252. A case of more understanding reactions is cited in S. E. Trubetskoi, *Minuvshee* (Paris, 1989), p. 22. The author recalls how, when he innocently asked how you could tell the difference between a horse and a mare, the coachman tactfully said 'everything tells you', though the groom sniggered.

18 See the discussion by Engelstein in *The Keys to Happiness*, pp. 286–7.

19 For a petition of this kind, see Ya. Ludmer, 'Bab'i stony', *Yuridicheskii vestnik* 11 (1884), 464. The husband's invitation to his wife to join him above the stove 'for a certain process between men and women' is described as 'an extremely shameless act'. On sexual relations in sheds, see Anna Dubova in Engel and Posadskaya-Vanderbeck (eds), p. 40; here the informant also states that her parents never shared the same bed.

20 A. Kuznetsova-Budanova, *I u menya byl krai rodnoi* (Munich, 1979), pp. 32–7. The account of *zolotse*

(along with a kissing game called 'I've got flowers in my hand …') also comes from here, p. 72.

21 See especially Eric Naiman, *Sex in Public: The Incarnation of Early Soviet Ideology* (Princeton, NJ, 1997).

22 A. L. Pavlova, *Dnevnik materi: Zapiski o razvitii rebenka ot rozhdeniya do 6 1/2 let* (M., 1925), p. 138.

23 See the discussion in Chapter 6 above.

24 E. Krichevskaya, *Moya Marusya (Zapiski materi)* (Petrograd, 1916), p. 121.

25 V. Rozanov, *Opavshie list'ya* (SPb., 1913), p. 131. On compulsory marriage, see pp. 497–502.

26 See especially Louise A. Jackson, *Child Sexual Abuse in Victorian England* (London, 2000).

27 V. Ya. Kanel', *Polovaya zhizn' detei* (2nd edn; M., 1921), p. 11. For the preventive measures, see p. 27, p. 35 (nannies), p. 11 (worms), p. 33 (avoiding luxury), p. 49 (sport and coeducation).

28 *Odezhda rebenka-doshkol'nika: instruktivnoe pis'mo* (M.–L., 1929), p. 19, p. 22.

29 For instance, Lev Kopelev, *The Education of a True Believer*, trans. G. Kern (London, 1981), p. 53, remembered hearing about 'where children came from' when in the Scouts.

30 Pavlova, *Dnevnik materi*, p. 140.

31 RAO NA f. 1 op. 1 d. 145, l. 59 (meeting of 19 March 1924).

32 A. A. Makarenko, *Besedy s roditelyami* (1937): page refs from edn published (Stalingrad: Oblastnoe knizhnoe izd., 1941), pp. 25–6. For the phrase 'moral reprobate' (*razvratnik*), see A. A. Makarenko, *Kniga dlya roditelei* (M., 1937), p. 235; for the 'since the world was created', ibid., p. 210.

33 Makarenko, *Kniga dlya roditelei*, pp. 233–4.

34 Oxf/Lev V–04 PF4B, p. 31 (mother gives birth at home, but behind curtain); Oxf/Lev V–04 PF12A, p. 4 (parents' room sacrosanct); on cabbage patches, see e.g. Oxf/Lev V–04 PF19B, p. 17 (this person had some rudimentary instruction in human biology at school, however).

35 For an account of someone who only found out the facts of life when she was pregnant, see Oxf/Lev V–04 PF3A, p. 24. Oxf/Lev V–04 PF2A, p. 9, recalls not only being punished for hanging round with a boy, but getting a thrashing when her father saw her rolling round on the grass with some other girls. For a harrowing account of a forced marriage at 16 (this in 1936!), see Oxf/Lev V–04 PF4A, p. 18, pp. 20–1, p. 25. This informant also recalled believing that kissing got you pregnant (PF4B, p. 32). People of this generation (born in the 1920s and early 1930s) passed on similar attitudes when socialising their children. According to David Ransel, *VM*, p. 17, 'some informants told us that they had never, and could not possibly, talk to their children and grandchildren about sexual intercourse, contraception, abortion, and the like, even to offer advice'.

36 Beatrice King, *Changing Man* (London, 1936), p. 102.

37 E. Bonner, *Dochki-materi* (M., 1994), p. 252.

38 As Lev Kopelev did: see *The Education of a True Believer*, p. 89.

39 For example, A. D. Savel'eva, 'Gigiena devochki', *SemSh* 1 (1953), 31–2. This article also fails to address the practicalities of obtaining the sanitary protection it recommends – cotton-wool pads wrapped in gauze (shortages of cotton wool were endemic throughout the Soviet era). Most women no doubt had to fall back on the alternative: cotton cloths that were boiled between wearings (a method commonly used in Western Europe before the Second World War as well). Protection of this kind, alongside newspaper, torn sheets of exercise books, etc., was still widely used in Russia as late as the early 1980s (personal observation).

40 CKQ Oxf–03 PF8B, pp. 12–13.

41 A. Markushevich, 'A nuzhna li skazka ob aistakh?', *N* 5 (1965), 20. Cf. Nikolai Borisov, 'U vas rastut syn i doch'', *N* (1963), 20, which lauds Makarenko's emphasis on chastity as the best route.

42 E.g. Oxf/Lev SPb.–03 PF16B: informant's husband didn't know where babies came from till he got to university.

43 CKQ Ox–03 PF3B, p. 11.

44 Oxf/Lev SPb 03 PF25A, p. 34.

45 *XIII S"ezd Vsesoyuznogo Leninskogo Kommunisticheskogo Soyuza Molodezhi, 15–18 aprelya 1958: Stenograficheskii otchet* (M., 1959), p. 36, p. 37. CKQ Ox–03 PF13A, p. 11.

46 R. Bamm and 17 others, *Semeinoe vospitanie: Slovar' dlya roditelei* (M., 1967), p. 199. Note, too, that this book is less worried about childhood onanism than were earlier normative guides. While being described as not a good idea, it was also said not to be harmful: p. 167.

47 'Proklyatyi vopros', *N* 37 (1966), 20. Interestingly, a Leningrad survey of 1957 and 1964 conducted by S. I. Golod suggested that increase in sexual activity, or increase of reporting of such activity, among young people *preceded* the liberalisation of public discourse relating to sexual matters. In 1957, only 4.3 per cent of respondents (7 per cent male, 1.6 per cent female) said they had had their first sexual contact at under 16. In 1964, this figure had shifted to 6 per cent (10.3 per cent male, 1.7 female). Of course, the survey begs the question of what the respondents understood as 'sexual contact' (kissing? what was known in Britain during the same decade as 'heavy petting'? or actual intercourse?) See Yu. A. Polyakov and V. B. Zhiromskaya (eds), *Naselenie Rossii v XX veke* (2 vols; M., 2000–1), vol. 2, p. 229.

48 B. Spok [=Spock], 'Molodezhi – o zhizni i lyubvi', *N* 24 (1973), 14–15. For Soviet articles of this period, see e.g. G. Aseev, 'Uroki podgotovki k zhizni', *N* 3 (1978), 11; 'Ob aiste i polovom vospitanii', *N* 52 (1978), 15–17 'Vmesto skazki ob aiste', *N* 23 (1982), 18–19.

49 CKQ Oxf–03 PF11B, p. 11.

50 Oxf/Lev SPb.–03 PF16B, p. 77. For an example of this from as early as 1950, see Oxf/Lev V–04 PF6B, p. 54.

51 Cf. the recollection of such a talk in Oxf/Lev M–04 PF36B, p. 15, and of a girl in the class asking whether kissing could get you pregnant.

52 CKQ Oxf–03 PF13A, p. 11, remembered buying such a book, which she recalled had been published in Estonia (see below, p. 587 on its unexpected effects). According to a Leningrad informant, b. 1969 (Oxf/Lev SPb.–03 PF16B, p. 75), her aunt, not her mother, filled her in. Oxf/Lev WQ1 GM, p. 7, recalls learning the 'facts of life' from the translation of an American 'survival guide' for teenagers published in the magazine *Rovesnik* during the late 1980s.

53 Oxf/Lev WQ1 KM, p. 11.

54 See Oxf/Lev P–05 PF21B, p. 14; Oxf/Lev P–05 PF9A, p. 9. In the former case, the parents did not 'purge' the medical literature in question till the girl reached her teens, by which time she had read it all in any case. But she also emphasises how unusual the situation of access to information was.

55 Oxf/Lev SPb.–03 PF15A, p. 38.

56 Personal information, St Petersburg, 1998.

57 Oxf/Lev M–04 PF38B, p. 13 (cited from paraphrase, as the informant did not want to talk about the incident on tape).

58 Mariengof, p. 46.

59 Al. Shif, 'Dnevniki i al'bomy', *Vozhatyi* 17–18 (1933), 65–8. Cf. 'Doloi al'bomy!', a piece in a comparable vein from four years earlier: *Pioner* 5 (1929), 12.

60 See Chapter 7.

61 See e.g. A. Orlov (then Director of the Moscow City Education Dept., Gorono), 'O razdel'nom obuchenii v shkolakh', *Izvestiya*, August 10 1943, (quoted here from R. Schlesinger (ed.), *Changing Attitudes in Soviet Russia: The Family in the USSR: Documents and Readings* (London, 1949), p. 345: 'It is not our objective to erect some "Chinese wall" between boys and girls – boys and girls walking on different pavements – what we aim at is only the separate *education* of boys and girls. That is the main thing. We must not imagine that once separate education has been introduced, there will be no association between boys and girls. They will come together in the "pioneer houses", in institutions outside the school, in the theatres, at "school evenings" [i.e. parties] and so on.'

62 The school concerned was No. 175. See CKQ Ox–03 PF1A-B (female informant, b. 1936) for a description of the curriculum and atmosphere.

63 Typescript in Theatre Library, St Petersburg: C1 5–4–302.

64 Author interview with former children's book editor for Detizdat, Leningrad, 2002.

65 E. Shvarts, *Obyknovennoe chudo* (Kishinev, 1988), pp. 128–75.

66 D. Brodskaya, 'Dnevnik Lidy Karasevoi', *Koster* 6 (1938), 33–44 [part 1]; 7, 38–48 [part 2].

67 Brodskaya, 'Dnevnik Lidy Karasevoi', [part 1], 41.

68 Beatrice King: 'A Kiev School', *Anglo-Soviet Journal* 10: 6 (1937), 11, though she also reports a case where a teacher deliberately humiliated a not very studious boy in a question session in order to break up a relationship between him and a girl who was a star pupil (ibid.).

69 On crushes, see e.g. Oxf/Lev SPb.–02 PF4B, p. 111; on flirtatious teachers, see e.g. Kosterina, pp. 33–4. A teacher had asked Kosterina out, and she disliked this attention rather a lot, commenting, 'Even now I sit at his classes as though on needles, as though something [had] hit

me.' Cf. Miller, p. 123 on how the physics teacher paid court on the day of the school-leaving ball (though this did not evoke the same kind of disgust).

70 Oxf/Lev M–04 PF26B, p. 26.

71 L. R. Kabo, *Kino i deti* (M., 1974), p. 76.

72 Bamm et al., *Semeinoe vospitanie*, p. 199. On reading, see e.g. CKQ Oxf–03 PF3B, p. 11, CKQ Oxf–03 PF8B, p. 12; on TV, Oxf/Lev SPb.–03 PF15A, p. 38 (adult programmes on when children are supposed to be asleep, but the latter in fact watch them).

73 Viktor Dragunsky, 'Gusinoe gorlo', *Deniskiny rasskazy: Dvadtsat' let pod krovat'yu* (M., 1999), p. 79.

74 V. A. Sukhomlinsky, *Kak vospitat' nastoyashchego cheloveka: Sovety vospitatelyam* (Izhevsk: Udmurtiya, 1980), p. 255. For a general study of such socialisation, see Lynne Attwoood, *The New Soviet Man and Woman* (Basingstoke, 1990). For a first-hand reminiscence of this kind of indoctrination about the 'weak sex' and the 'strong sex', see CKQ Ox–03 PF8B, p. 14.

75 CKQ Ox–03 PF8B, p. 15.

76 CKQ Ox–03 PF11B, p. 10. The arrangements were made at a *klassnyi chas* (from teacher's pep-talk hour).

77 Before 1917, servants seem to have been exceptions: there are even some sensational accounts of full-scale sexual initiation by them: see e.g. *The Confessions of Victor X*, ed. Donald Rayfield (London, 1984).

78 Aleksandra Piir, 'Detskie igry', typescript inventory, SPb., 2003, p. 10.

79 On pornographic manuscripts, see Oxf/Lev SPb.–03 PF25B, p. 46; on playground smut, ibid., and also CKQ Ox–03 PF13A, p. 11; CKQ SPb.–03 PF3A, pp. 18–19; for pre-1917, F. M. Orlov-Skomorovsky, *Golgofa rebenka* (M., 1921), p. 46 (told by a boy, 'That hole is where your mother had the baby out of'), p. 61 (smutty rhymes and backchat among schoolgirls).

80 On Peeping Tom activities, see e.g. Anatoly Ul'yanov, 'Vospominaniya o periode 1921–1928 gg.' (1932–33), RGB OR f. 442 kart. 1 ed. khr. 3, l. 20 rev; Oxf/Lev SPb.–02 PF8B, pp. 23–4. On visiting low entertainments, see K. Chukovsky, *Dnevnik 1930–1969* (M., 1994), p. 80, which complains about children from a playground lingering so as to watch shows in the *café-chantant* next door after darkness fell.

81 On 'snogging' see Aleksandra Piir, 'Generations in the Leningrad Courtyard', forthcoming in *Forum for Anthropology and Culture* 4 (2007); the 'staircases' comment is based on my personal observations during the early 1980s; on parties, Evgeny Dobrenko, personal information.

82 See Oxf/Lev V–04 PF4A, p. 23.

83 Oxf/Lev V–05 PF20B, p. 19. This reminiscence dates from the late 1930s, but the game is clearly significantly older, going back to the days of visiting pedlars.

84 Oxf/Lev V–04 PF21B, p. 42. Cf. the Winding the Silk game described above.

85 See V. Kholodnaya, 'Ukhazhivanie', in *Muzhiki i baby: Muzhskoe i zhenskoe v russkoi traditsionnoi*

kul'ture: *Illyustrirovannaya entsiklopediya* (SPb., 2005), pp. 658–64.

86 Cf. the interesting discussion by T. A. Bernshtam, 'Sovershennoletie devushki v metaforakh igrovogo fol'klora (traditsionnyi aspekt russkoi kul'tury', in A. K. Baiburin and I. S. Kon (eds), *Etnicheskie stereotipy muzhskogo i zhenskogo povedeniya* (SPb., 1991), p. 254.

87 The British diplomat Reader Bullard and his circle were appalled by what they saw as precocious sexual behaviour by young teenagers in this period, which they were inclined to attribute to school education. However, what they reported they had seen – e.g. girls apparently as young as 12 selling themselves to sailors in Leningrad (p. 193) – could be explained equally well as a survival strategy during a period of famine and social anomie.

88 CKQ Ox–03 PF8B, p. 12 (the kiss); Oxf/Lev SPb.–03 PF25A, p. 34 (pregnancy. The disapproval of this informant is particularly striking, given that he was involved in a gang, drank, and smoked from his early teens, and also sniffed glue: see ibid. 24B p. 23).

89 Kosterina, pp. 99–100 (entry for 25 October 1937).

90 Semenova, *Dnevnik gimnazistki*, p. 103, 3 March 1911.

91 Kopelev, *The Education of a True Believer*, p. 74 (flirtation at Pioneer meetings), p. 94 ('are Pioneers permitted to kiss').

92 B. Plaksin, 'Improvizirovannyi teatr, kak sredstvo pedagogicheskogo vozdeistviya', *Russkaya shkola za rubezhom* 18 (1926), 594–600.

93 D. Samoilov, 'Dnevnik schastlivogo mal'chika', *Znamya* 8 (1999), 151.

94 Kosterina, pp. 11–12 (the party), pp. 99–100 (contempt for frivolity and make-up). Not much later, a middle-aged writer called Fishberg, a family friend, was making up to Nina (p. 61).

95 See e.g. Oxf/Lev SPb.–02 PF4B, p. 113.

96 Oxf/Lev SPb.–02 PF4B, p. 115. And compare the similar comments (from a male point of view) in Oxf/Lev SPb.–02 PF8B, p. 29, who additionally attributes later marital difficulties (failure of classmates to marry, high rate of marital breakdown) to this sexual puritanism.

97 'Spravki o sostoyanii ideino-politicheskogo vospitaniya v shkolakh goroda Moskvy, sostavlennye po rezul'tatam obsledovaniya shkol v period s 20–30.04.48', RAO NA f. 32 op. 1 d. 160, l. 41.

98 CKQ Oxf–03 PF1B, p. 3.

99 See e.g. CKQ Oxf–03 PF6B, p. 10, informant 3, b. 1931.

100 Oxf/Lev M–04 PF20B, p. 44.

101 Oxf/Lev M–04 PF26B, pp. 23–6 (and this despite the fact that the informant recalled first feeling physically excited by a member of the opposite sex – a small girl – at the age of five, and that he had masturbated regularly from 14: see p. 24, p. 25).

102 See e.g. CKQ Oxf–03 PF6B, p. 10, informant 3, b. 1931: this informant also had an intense (though totally innocent) romance with a boy that she did music with (ibid.)

103 Miller, p. 121.

104 See e.g. the selection in A. F. Belousov, *Uchebnyi material po teorii literatury: Zhanry slovesnogo teksta: anekdot* (Tallinn, 1989); and the discussion in S. Adonyeva, 'The Pragmatics of the Chastushka: A Socio-Linguistic Analysis', in *Forum for Anthropology and Culture* 1 (2004), 159–82.

105 Cf. the account of a *patsanka* (ladette) of this kind in Oxf/Lev SPb.–03 PF18A, p. 41. For the official view of *tovarishchestvo* between boys and girls, see e.g. V. Oseeva, *Vasek Trubachev i ego tovarishchi* (1947), vol. 1, p. 94 (L., 1978), 'Ya stoyu za druzhbu devochek s mal'chikami, ne nado nikogo obizhat' i peresmeivat' (a contribution to the class *stengazeta*); and the 'Boys and Girls' discussions running in *Leninskie iskry* for 1961: e.g. 'Vopros o devchonkakh i mal'chishkakh', *Leninskie iskry* 9 December 1961, 3.

106 CKQ PF11A, pp. 9–10.

107 CKQ SPb.–03 PF3A, p. 18; cf. Oxf/Lev SPb.–03 PF16A, p. 75.

108 CKQ Oxf–03 PF3B, p. 10.

109 Aleksin, 'Zvonite i priezzhaite', 'V tylu kak v tylu', and 'Tem vremenem gde-to', in *Zvonite i priezzhaite! Povesti*: quote at p. 415.

110 Not surprisingly, this approach created controversy: cf. the discussion between Anatoly Aleksin and Nataliya Sats, *N* 59 (1969), 4–5, where the latter criticises plays about 'whether papa has the right to be unfaithful to mama'. Aleksin's response was that treatment was everything and that, in any case, 'divorce is part of life' (*razvod – eto zhizn'*).

111 A. Lavrov and O. Lavrova, 'Vospitanie lyubvi', *N* 43 (1967), 22. It was standard for Soviet parents to produce a first child in their late twenties at latest, but its younger sibling, if the widely favoured spacing of eight to ten years was observed, would then arrive in its parents' late thirties, which made the situation considered here highly possible.

112 CKQ Oxf–03 PF13A, p. 11. The verb *ebat'sya* (to fuck), it should be understood, was a good deal more taboo than its English equivalent then was.

113 On finding out about menstruation traumatically, see e.g. Bonner, *Dochki-materi*, pp. 202–4; Malakhova (b. 1919) in Engel and Posadskaya-Vanderbeck, p. 185. Oxf/Lev P–05 PF23A, p. 10, reports that she actually fainted when she found out; only then did her mother explain what was going on.

On the practicalities of sanitary protection, see e.g. Oxf/Lev SPb.–03 PF8B, pp. 12–13. As vividly described in Oxf/Lev V–04 PF6B, p. 55, it was not uncommon for this rudimentary domestic protection to fall out during dances in the local hall, leading to mortification on the part of the girl concerned. Girls in orphanages were particularly badly off: see e.g. Oxf/Lev SPb.–02 PF2A, p. 40, which describes how inmates removed the stuffing of mattresses to use.

114 'Problemy sovetskoi sem'i' (December 1961–February 1962), B. A. Grushin (ed.), *Chetyre zhizni Rossii v zerkale oprosov obshchestvennogo mneniya*, vol. 1 (M., 2001), p. 287, p. 285.

115 Karol, *Solik*, p. 133.

116 For instance, Oxf/Lev M–04 PF36B, p. 16: this informant, b. 1950, records that several girls in her school became pregnant soon after leaving, and one in Class 9 (i.e. aged 16). In justice, it should be mentioned that this informant went on to say (p. 17) that she had done everything 'right' according to modern ideas (i.e. told her daughter the facts of life herself), only for this daughter then to become pregnant at 18.

117 N. Gaidarenko, 'Rebenok protiv nasiliya', *N* 28 (1991), 12.

118 Oxf/Lev M–05 PF50A, p. 178, recalls a physics teacher (female) who was prepared to talk to her male pupils about how much she enjoyed sex with her husband and show them erotic pictures. In this particular case, the term 'abuse' seems inappropriate because no one was offended by the behaviour concerned.

119 Bonner, *Dochki-materi*, p. 39, recalls an exhibitionist in a communal flat (in the 1940s). In one courtyard in late 1950s–early 1960s Leningrad, the big hazard was an older boy who used to grab hold of young girls and assault them, so that even crossing the space was frightening (CKI SPb.–2). Cf. Oxf/Lev SPb.–03 PF14A: in the early 1980s, aged 13 or 14, this Leningrad girl was confronted by a flasher in the entrance to the apartment block where she lived; he undid his trousers and she started screaming, he covered her mouth to shut her up, but fortunately someone came out of a flat at that point and he was disturbed. Oxf/Lev M–04 PF35B, p. 16: the informant (who worked as a teacher from 1958 to 1998) recollects a sinister person gaining entry to an apartment where a small girl was on her own: 'he didn't do anything, but it gave her a psychological trauma'. Occasionally, abuse cases reached the legal press. In 1938, *SYu* reported that a teacher had been tried under article 152 of the Criminal Code for the corruption (*razvrashchenie*) of three pupils, aged 9, 10, and 11. However, the burden of the report was that the accusations had been absurd: the abuse was supposed to have happened during lessons for 18 months, yet no one had found out. The case was cited as an example of children's liability to become confused when repeatedly interrogated – i.e. the unlikeliness that they would give reliable evidence about cases such as this. 'Otmena prigovora', *SYu* 15 (1938), 34. On the taboo nature of abuse cases, see also my Introduction above.

120 Oxf/Lev SPb.–03 PF24B, p. 26.

121 See e.g. Oxf/Lev M–04 PF26B, p. 19. This informant reveals that he engaged in masturbation as an adolescent, but it does not appear that the activity was of any great significance to him; certainly, it does not seem to have provoked a particular sense of guilt.

122 Playground duels: CKQ Ox–03 PF3B, p. 10; CKQ Ox–03 PF11B, p. 10; brusque ways of showing affection: CKQ Ox–03 PF11B, p. 10; Oxf/Lev SPb.–03 PF16A, p. 73.

123 See CKQ M–03 PF1–2, PF3–4.

124 On unrequited love, see CKQ Ox–03 PF11B, p. 11.

125 CKQ Ox–03 PF13A, 13B, p. 10: this informant records that 'it all depended what group you

were in', and recalls that the sons and daughters of Leningrad theatre professionals, for instance, often led quite an energetic sex life, making use of the All-Soviet Theatre Society's 'house of rest' in Komarovo for their assignations. But this reminiscence is exceptional.

126 Oxf/Lev M–05 PF48B, p. 144 (the original reads, 'My tut uzhe vse perezhenilis', a papa s mamoi u nas devstvenniki'). This informant also related a horrific story that one of her classmates, fed up with lectures from her parents on the beauties of virginity, ruptured her own hymen with a bottle to put an end to the nagging (PF48B, p. 146).

127 Oxf/Lev P–05 PF10B, p. 17, PF10A, p. 6.

128 Neil Postman, *The Disappearance of Childhood* (London, 1985).

129 John O'Farrell, 'Aah, hasn't he grown!' *Guardian* 12 December 2003, p. 27.

130 See e.g. *N* 12 (1985), 7; *N* 13 (1989), 8; I. Medvedev and T. Shishova, '"Novye modeli povedeniya"?', *Vospitanie shkol'nika* 5 (1998), 26–8.

131 Lev Aizeman, 'Pokhmel'e – iz zapisok uchitelya', *Znamya* 2 (2002), 166–82.

132 Oxf/Lev SPb.–04 PF56A, p. 14.

133 Interview with baby-home specialists.

134 Oxf/Lev M–04 PF27A, pp. 1–2.

135 See S. V. Zhuravlyov and A. K. Sokolov, '"Schastlivoe detstvo"', *Sotsial'naya istoriya: Ezhegodnik 1997* (1998), pp. xxx–xxxi for the former, and E. Dobrenko, 'Vse lushchee–detyam (totalitarnaya kul'tura i mir detstva)', *Wiener Slawistischer Almanach* 29 (1992), 159–74 for the latter.

136 For an exemplary 'child's eye view' narrative, see Svetlana Bychenko, 'Vozvrashchenie' *NM* 7 (1999). Among interesting memoirs published in this period are those by Samoilov, Kremer, Korzhavin, Dm. Nabokov, and others included in the Bibliography. The change in memoir practices was beginning to come through in the late 1980s as well: there is, for instance, a very marked difference between the fifth volume of *SPA* and the first four volumes of the series.

137 E.g. E. K. Zelensky, 'Popular Children's Culture in Post-Perestroika Russia: Songs of Innocence and Experience Revisited', in A. Barker (ed.), *Consuming Russia* (Durham, NC: Duke University Press, 1999), pp. 138–60.

138 See especially I. Medvedeva and T. Shishova, 'Novoe vremya – novye deti?', *Oktyabr'* 2 (1997), 132.

139 Oxf/Lev SPb.–03 PF15A, p. 43.

140 Oxf/Lev SPb.–03 PF28A, p. 8.

141 Oxf/Lev WQ1 KM, p. 11.

142 On this pattern, see Oxf/Lev WQ1 GM, p. 6 (sewing), p. 9 (job).

143 On sexual activity, see e.g. CKQ M–03 PF4A, pp. 6–7; on drug use, H. Pilkington, '"The More Discussion There Is of It, the More You Feel Like Doing It": Reflections on the Discursive Production of Generational Experiences', *Forum for Anthropology and Culture* 1 (2007), though this also emphasises a range of drug-related attitudes among young people, from enthusiasm to suspicion or outright condemnation.

144 On the role of *kompanii* and their values in adolescent consciousness, see Oxf/Lev WQ1 KM, p. 10 (this on the mid-1990s); on ignoring the socially marginal (here, a girl from a many-children family with an alcoholic mother), see Oxf/Lev WQ1 GM, p. 7.

145 http://www.orlyonok.ru, accessed 17 February 2006.

146 Cf. the comments of Aleksei Pankin in 'Materialism at Spiritualism's Expense', *Russia Profile* 11: 10 (2005), 31, recalling chewing gum in his school: 'One of the kids managed to get hold of a few packets […]. But there were other kids ready to scrape it up immediately from the ground and start chewing it in their turn while some of the flavor still remained. What were cheap and everyday mass consumer goods in other countries became objects of desire and forbidden fruit in our socialist society.' Similar points are made by A. Yurchak in *Everything Was Forever, Until It Was No More: The Last Soviet Generation* (Princeton, NJ, 2006), e.g. pp. 170–5.

147 Oxf/Lev M–05 PF47A, p. 114.

148 For the revival of military education, see N. Marlevich, 'Zdravyi smysl i voennoe delo v shkole', *RM* 17–23 February 2000, 11 (taking a critical standpoint on the phenomenon); for the Scouts, see e.g. the report on the international rally of summer 2000, M. Visens, 'Za predelami Sadovogo kol'tsa', *RM* 3–9 August 2000, 6.

149 Harwin, p. 89.

150 Ibid. For the Moscow figures, see E. Visens, 'Za predelami Sadovogo kol'tsa', *RM* 27 April–3 May 2000, 4. Computations of the numbers of abandoned children, once state control had broken down, started to vary widely. A. L. Aref'ev, 'Besprizornye deti Rossii', http://socis.isras. ru/SocIsArticles/2003_09/Arefyevldoc (accessed 5 November 2005), gives a variety of different indicators: 900,000 children outside the school system in 1998; between 1.1 million and 4 million neglected children in 2002; and over 650,000 abandoned in 1998, rising to 700,000 in 2002. The article also, drawing on small-scale surveys of street children, reconstructs their everyday life, making clear that little has changed since the early twentieth century. Though in the absence of tar boilers children now sleep on central-heating outlets, they still frequent cellars, entrance halls, and attics, boys still predominate over girls (66 per cent), and means of support still include odd jobs, begging, and theft, with a minority involved in prostitution and drug-dealing.

151 Harwin, pp. 90–1.

152 Clementine Creuziger, a commentator with a fair command of Russian who observed conditions in late Soviet Russia over some months, noted of an orphanage that she visited in Leningrad in 1990–1 that staff 'ignored the children much of the time, and, in effect, were glad to "allow" the children to engage in "free play", since they found their job demeaning and did not care much about the children's well-being' (p. xxi).

153 Harwin, p. 101.

154 CKQ SPb.–04 PF4A, PF4B, 5A.

155 Ibid. Cf. Irina Aleksovskaya, 'Deti Dmitrovskogo

detdoma: Zapiski detskogo vracha', *RM* 18–24 May 2000, p. 8.

156 My thanks to Rosemary Peacocke, a participant in the project, for this information.

157 CKQ SPb.–04 PF4A, PF5A. Cf. Zoya Svetova, 'Est' li v Rossii blagotvoritel'nost", *RM* 5–11 October 2000, 1, 19.

158 Zoya Svetova, 'Gosudarstvennye deti', *RM* 18–24 March 1999, 11.

159 See Igor' Potapov, '"Detskoe televidenie doveli do unizitel'nogo polozheniya"' (interview with Boris Grachevsky, the editor of *Eralash*), *Izvestiya* 22 December 2005 (http://izvestiya.ru/media/304197, accessed 24 January 2006).

160 Potapov, '"Detskoe televidenie"'. The mid-2000s also saw the initiation of a 'Children's Television Day' (Den' detskogo televideniya), held in December.

161 CKQ Ox–02 PF1A, p. 4.

162 A striking example is Pavel Litvinov. The poet Natal'ya Gorbanevskaya, another outspoken and brave dissident, was a pillar of the Komsomol in her high-school and student years (personal information from a former classmate of hers). Donald Raleigh has argued along similar lines in his introduction to *The Sputnik Generation* (Bloomington, IN, 2006).

163 This applies to sexual socialisation as well, as is pointed out by Anna Rotkirch, '"What Kind of Sex Can You Talk About?" Acquiring Sexual Knowledge in Three Soviet Generations', in Bertaux, P. Thompson, and A. Rotkirch, *On Living Through Soviet Russia* (London, 2004), pp. 99–119.

164 For the argument about learning 'closeness to the earth' from sliding standing up, see Mariya Osorina, *Sekretnyi mir detei* (SPb., 1999), p. 241.

List of Further Reading

Only substantial works in English and French are included. The Bibliography in the full digital version of this book (available in 2008 at www.yalebooks.com) is a multilingual, international collection of relevant material: please see this for a wider choice of discussions.

Ball, Alan, *And Now My Soul Is Hardened: Abandoned Children in Soviet Russia, 1918–1930* (Berkeley, CA, 1994)

Caroli, Dorena, *L'Enfance abandonée et délinquante dans la Russie soviétique (1917–1937)* (Paris, 2004)

Creuziger, Clementine, *Childhood in Russia: Representation and Reality* (Lanham, MD, 1996)

Dunstan, John, *Soviet Schooling in the Second World War* (Basingstoke, 1997)

Fisher, R., *Pattern for Soviet Youth: A Study of the Congresses of the Komsomol, 1918–1954* (New York, 1959)

Goldman, Wendy, *Women, the State and Revolution: Soviet Family Policy and Social Life* (Cambridge, 1996)

Gorsuch, Anne, *Youth in Revolutionary Russia: Enthusiasts, Bohemians, Delinquents* (Bloomington, IN, 2000)

Harwin, Judith, *Children of the Russian State, 1917–95* (Aldershot, 1996)

Holmes, Larry E., *The Kremlin and the Schoolhouse: Reforming Education in Soviet Russia* (Bloomington, IN, 1991)

——, *Stalin's School: Moscow's Model School No. 25, 1931–1937* (Pittsburgh, 1999)

Jacoby, Susan, *Inside Soviet Schools* (NY, 1974)

Kelly, Catriona, '"Thank You for the Wonderful Book": Soviet Child Readers and the Management of Children's Reading, 1950–1975', *Kritika* 6:4 (2005), 717–51

Kirschenbaum, Lisa A., *Small Comrades: Revolutionizing Childhood in Soviet Russia, 1917–1932* (London, 2001)

——, 'Innocent Victims and Heroic Defenders: Children and the Siege of Leningrad', in J. Master (ed.), *Children and War: A Historical Anthology* (NY, 2002)

Kosterina, Nina, *The Diary of Nina Kosterina*, trans. M. Ginsburg (London, 1968)

Lindenmeyr, Adele, *Poverty is Not a Vice: Charity, Society, and the State in Imperial Russia* (Princeton, NJ, 1996)

MacFadyen, David, *Yellow Crocodiles and Blue Oranges: Russian Animated Film Since World War II* (Montreal, 2005)

Miller, Larissa, *Dim and Distant Days*, trans. K. Cook and N. Roy (M., 2000)

Novak-Deker, N. K. (ed.), *Soviet Youth: Twelve Komsomol Histories* (Munich, 1959)

O'Dell, Felicity, *Socialisation through Children's Literature: The Soviet Example* (Cambridge, 1978)

Reid, Susan, *Khrushchev in Wonderland: The Pioneer Palace in Moscow's Lenin Hills, 1962* (Carl Beck Papers in Russian and East European Studies, no. 1606: Pittsburgh, 2002)

Stevens, Jennie, 'Children of the Revolution: Soviet Russia's Homeless Children (*Besprizorniki*) in the 1920s', *Russian History* 9: 2–3 (1982)

Viola, Lynn, '"Tear the Evil from the Root": The Children of the *Spetspereselentsy* of the North', in N. Baschmakoff and P. Freyer (eds), *Modernisation in the Russian Provinces*:

Studia Slavica Finlandensia 17 (Helsinki, 2000)

Voinov, Nicholas, *Outlaw* (London, 1955)

Wachtel, Andrew, *The Battle for Childhood: The Creation of a Russian Myth* (Stanford, CA, 1990)

Zenzinov, Vladimir, *Deserted: The Story of the Children Abandoned in Soviet Russia* (London, 1931)

Index

Page numbers in italics refer to an illustration.